BROTHERS AGAINST THE RAJ

LEONARD A. GORDON
BROTHERS AGAINST THE RAJ

A Biography of Indian Nationalists
Sarat and Subhas Chandra Bose

COLUMBIA UNIVERSITY PRESS
NEW YORK

Columbia University Press
New York   Oxford
Copyright © 1990 Leonard A. Gordon
All rights reserved

Library of Congress Cataloging-in-Publication Data

Gordon, Leonard A.
Brothers against the Raj : a biography of Indian nationalist leaders
Sarat and Subhas Chandra Bose / Leonard A. Gordon.
p.   cm.
Includes bibliographical references.
ISBN 0-231-07442-5 (alk. paper). — ISBN 0-231-07443-3 (pbk.: alk. paper)
1. Bose, Subhas Chandra, 1897–1945.
2. Bose, Sarat Chandra, 1889–1950.
3. Revolutionists—India—Biography.
4. Nationalists—India—Biography.
I. Title.
DS481.A1G67   1990
954.03′5′0922—dc20 [B]
90–1607
CIP

*Casebound editions of Columbia University Press books are Smyth-sewn
and printed on permanent and durable acid-free paper*

Printed in the United States of America

c 10 9 8 7 6 5 4 3 2 1

*This book about two devoted brothers
is dedicated to two loving and beloved sisters,
my mother and my Aunt Regina*

Contents

Acknowledgments

First, last, always, I would like to thank the family of Subhas and Sarat Chandra Bose for all the help they have given me for many long years. Foremost are Sisir K. Bose and Krishna Bose who have assisted me in uncountable ways and shown me continuing kindnesses and hospitality over the years. They have shown me many documents, worked on their translation, directed me to people and places to see, and made me feel at home in India. I also must thank their children, Sugata, Sarmila, and Sumantra, who have gone out of the way innumerable times for me, and also become my friends. Several of them have now written their own versions of the Boses' lives, but they have never told me how to write mine. We have shared our love of animals (their dog, Basco, and our cats, Prince, Fatty, Azi, and Tux) who have occasionally trampled across our manuscript pages and brought good cheer.

Many other Bose family members have been most helpful and I would especially like to thank Asoke Nath Bose, Gita (Bose) Biswas, Roma (Bose) Roy, Meera (Bose)Roy, Pradip Bose, Ranajit Bose, the late Aurobindo Bose, and the late Sailesh Bose. The late Charu C. Chowdhuri sat for many hours with Krishna Bose and me, trying to help me understand the early letters and views of Sarat Bose. Emilie Schenkl and her daughter Anita (Bose) Pfaff have shown much kindness on my visits to Vienna and Mrs Schenkl spent long hours answering my questions.

My former teachers, friends and colleagues in South Asian and related studies have been supportive as well as critical of my endeavors and I would like to mention particularly Ronald B. Inden, Edward C. Dimock, Jr., Daniel H.H. Ingalls, Michael Brecher, Frank E. Manuel, Bernard S. Cohn, Milton Singer, Edward Shils, W.H. Morris-Jones, Clark Blaise, Marcus Franda, Philip Calkins, Ralph B. Nicholas, A.K. Ramanujan, Peter Bertocci, Wendy Doniger O'Flaherty, Maureen L.P. Patterson, Kali Bahl, Alan Roland, David Lelyveld, Selig Harrison, William Fisher, Harpreet Mahajan, McKim Marriott, Razi Wasti, William Roff, Thomas Rusch,

Geraldine Forbes, Judith Walsh, Phillips Talbot, Philip Oldenburg, Tapan Raychaudhuri, Hugh Tinker, Diya Bhattacharya, Peter Fay, Christoph Kimmich, Margaret L. King, Paula Fichtner, John Dower, Carol Gluck, Arthur Tiedemann, and Paul Varley. Myron Weiner graciously lent me political pamphlets of the 1930s and 1940s from his collection. Ainslie T. Embree let me impose this work on him, year after year, chapter by chapter, and his comments have always been astute and insightful. Bharati Mukherjee helped with the critical reading of some sections, translating, and choosing of chapter titles. Dennis Dalton also read all the chapters and gave searching, detailed comments and encouragement which always buoyed me up. Johannes Voigt, Milan Hauner, Joyce Lebra, K.K. Ghosh, and Hugh Toye, all of whom have written fine accounts of Subhas Bose during the Second World War, generously helped me to write mine and my debts to them are evident in these pages. In Calcutta, Tridib Ghose, Shipra Chatterjee, Suman Chattopadhyay, Kasturi Dutta, Piyali Guha Thakurta, Bani Nath Bose, and Bandana Mukhopadhyay helped with the collecting of material and making translations from Bengali to English. Robert Cessna of the Southern Asian Institute at Columbia gave assistance and encouragement as I pressed on to the finish line. Lila Greewald also urged me for some years to get to the end of this project. My friends who read the text have advised me, but final responsibility is, of course, my own.

Since the research for this project has taken me to so many foreign parts, I have had to ask the help of many people in those countries. My friends and colleagues in India, Bangladesh, and Pakistan have been gracious and forthcoming and among them I would like to mention: P. Lal and Shyamasree Lal, Jyotirmoy and Meenakshi Datta, B.R. Nanda, D.N. Panigrahi, Amales Tripathi, Rajat Ray, Hiren Chakravarti, Gautam Chattopadhyay, Barun De, Nikhil Chakravartti, Shila Sen, S.R. Mehrotra, Anisuzzaman, Rounaq Jahan, Mushirul Hasan, P.K. and Lakshmi Sahgal, G.S. Dhillon, Gopal Halder, Satyajit Ray, Sunil Das, M.K. and Sue Haldar, Bipan Chandra, Ashin and Uma Das Gupta, Ramesh Jain, Tasneem Zakaria, Nina Rao, and Suneet Chopra.

Friends who have helped me to do research in other countries, particularly ones completely new and strange to me, and who have shown gracious hospitality include: John and Maria Tagliabue in West Germany, Nomi Rowe and Paula Reif in London, Nirad C. and Amiya Chaudhuri in Oxford, the late Fujiwara Iwaichi in Japan, Americk Singh in Malaysia, Sharif al Mujahid and Khalid Shamsul Hasan in Karachi, the late Lothar Frank in Wiesbaden, Wilhelm Lutz in Stuttgart, Vera Eisenberger in Vienna and Clarita von Trott zu Solz in Berlin. Akashi Yoji and Masayuki Usuda in Japan, Hideko Wayman and Akiko Matsunobu in New York have assisted with translations of Japanese sources.

The staffs of the India Office Library and Records, London; the British Library, London; the Nehru Memorial Museum and Library, New Delhi; the National Archives of India, New Delhi; the National Library of India, Calcutta; the West Bengal State Archives, Calcutta; the Netaji Research Bureau, Calcutta; the Imperial War Archives and Foreign Office Archives, Tokyo; the Foreign Office Archives, Bonn, West Germany; New York Public Library; Columbia University Library; Library of Congress, Washington, D.C.; and, the University of Chicago Library have all been helpful. Martin Moir and Richard Bingle at the India Office Library and D.N. Panigrahi, V.C. Joshi, B.R. Nanda, and Ravinder Kumar at the Nehru Library have gone many miles to help me find what I needed.

Over the many years I have worked on this project I have received support from the American Institute of Indian Studies, the Indo-American Sub-Commission on Education and Culture, the Social Science Research Council, the Research Foundation of the City University of New York, the Committee on Research in the Social Sciences, Columbia University, the American Council of Learned Societies, the American Philosophical Society, and the National Endowment for the Humanities. Pradeep R. Mehendiratta and Tarun Mitra of the American Institute of Indian Studies, in particular, were helpful at every turn.

David Davidar of Penguin India has been enthusiastic about this book since he first learned of it and he has helped me to carry through this project to completion with the help of the staff of Penguin India. Judith Aronson has spent innumerable hours trying to improve this manuscript and to shorten it since she knew readers would not want a book that went on forever.

Several dear friends who encouraged me to carry out this project have not lived to see its completion. They are Jamini Roy, David McCutchion, Susobhan Sarkar, Kumar Goshal, Chinmohan Sehanavis, Romesh and Raj Thapar, Samar Sen, Hugh Owen, Ratna Ray, Bishnu Dey, Fujiwara Iwaichi, Niranjan Majumdar, Lindsay Emmerson, Abu Sayeed Ayyub, A.R. Mukherjee and B.N. Pandey.

My wife, Marie, and my stepdaughter, April, have borne with the imposition of this book onto their lives with unfailing patience, cheerfulness, and support. I have appreciated the support of Mike and Helen Sansone, and Barbara and Tom Dalton. My brother Jim has helped me in many practical ways and shared in the creation of the Netaji Slide Collection and in preparing photographs for this book. Neither my late father, who launched me on the study of imperialism, nor my mother, who proof-read an earlier book for me, are here now, but they remain with me in my heart.

In Search of an Indian Hero

Do you love Netaji?

Mrs Sen, an elderly Bengali
woman, 1976 [to the author]

Netaji passed my way (just the other day).

Major Satya Gupta, Bengal
Volunteers, 1964 [to the author]

. . . and Rumour walked blazing among them. . .

Homer, *The Iliad* [1]

I

The crowd gathered in downtown Calcutta, January 23, 1964, as they they
did every year on that day to celebrate the life and triumphs of Bengal's
foremost nationalist leader, Subhas Chandra Bose. Immense representations of Bose were paraded through the streets en route to the Calcutta
maidan (park). 'Netaji ki jai. . . Netaji zindabad. . .' (Victory to the revered
leader Subhas Bose. . . Long live the revered leader) they shouted. It was
my first winter in Calcutta where I had come to do research on Indian
nationalism.

Subhas Bose, born in 1897, had died in a plane crash on Taiwan in
August 1945. Or had he? During the following months I saw pictures of a
sadhu (holy man) on Calcutta lampposts and billboards throughout the
city. His head was shaved and he stood beside the dead body of Jawaharlal
Nehru, India's recently deceased prime minister. The sadhu wore glasses
(as did Bose), he was a little older, a little plumper, but he did resemble
Bose, or 'Netaji' as he is commonly called. Beneath the picture in Bengali
it said: 'Who is this sadhu?' Many ordinary Hindus in the middle and lower
classes of the metropolis and the outlying districts believed that it was
Bose. He was biding his time, waiting for a time of crisis when he would

return, take the helm of the ship of state, and guide it through the troubled seas of independence.

Small cult groups told of his imminent coming to this or that public meeting, but he did not appear. Major Satya Gupta, once an 'officer' in the Bengal Volunteers, sent me an invitation to an exhibition which he said Netaji would attend. Gupta said, 'Netaji passed my way,' suggesting that he had seen him recently. I went to the exhibition of a small, scale-model of a religious community at Shaulmari in north Bengal where Bose was said to be resident. I was nervous, unsure of myself; I waited, but no Bose. With the help of a young Bengali businessman, I gathered weekly publications which told of Bose's activities since 1945, his present powers, and prospective deeds. I also read a popular Bengali book about the secret of the Shaulmari ashram. Gupta and his associates insisted that Bose was there now, alive and well, although the sadhu denied being Bose. A few years later, I learned from a senior and respected Bengali Congressman, leader of the Congress Party in the Rajya Sabha, that he had traveled to the ashram in the hope of finding Bose whom he had known well. 'I could tell right away,' he said, 'it was not Bose.'[2]

II

Having gathered material for a doctoral dissertation on aspects of the nationalist movement in Bengal, I went home and finished my thesis, revised it, published it, and began teaching. In 1975, in connection with research on the partition, I secured an interview with Lord Mountbatten. Within the brief hour-and-a-half I spent in his company, I not only heard him explain his approach to the question of a united Bengal in 1947, but witnessed how he could alternate fierce expressions of authority with an outgoing charm. Since he was busy advising on the running of the Royal War College when I arrived, and did not want an unknown interviewer poking around, he locked me in his bedroom. Twenty minutes later, when I thought he had forgotten me and already left for Germany, he unlocked the door and said, 'Now I am all yours.' I saw how eager he was to have his version of the past and his view of his own role in history accepted by the general public and posterity. He also explained that his aversion to the Indian National Army (INA) meant that he would not see Sarat Bose during the crucial months in 1947 when the question of partition was being decided.

I returned to India and continued my research on nationalism and the partition and heard some, but fewer tales of Bose. When I returned during the Emergency in 1976, I learned at the Netaji birthday gathering from the then chief minister of West Bengal, Siddhartha Shankar Ray that, 'Bose is undying and will live forever.' Furthermore, he said, Bose was against fissiparous tendencies and taught obedience to authority, authority such as that wielded by the present central government of Ray's ally, Mrs Gandhi. Then the governor, A. Dias, told the assembled throng, 'Netaji highlighted the salient points of the twenty-point program.' That is, Bose, long dead, was a founder and backer of Mrs Gandhi's program.

On this and later visits, I heard from politicians of every persuasion that Bose was wise, prescient, and their ally, if not when he was alive, then in the present when they needed support. Communists, Congressmen, independents, left, right, center, Bose would always be available for their contemporary needs. They had conveniently forgotten how many of them had vilified Bose when he was alive. A dead hero is often a more convenient prop than a live one. Some liked to rewrite history. Acharya J.B. Kripalani insisted that Bose and he had gotten along beautifully when Bose had been Congress president. Well, I had just been reading a letter that Kripalani had written in 1938 to Jawaharlal Nehru in which he explained that he wished to resign his post as general secretary of the Congress because he could not stand Bose. When I waved my notes on this letter before him, he brushed them aside imperiously. He was going to have the past his way.

In 1979 I went to Calcutta University to talk to the history faculty and students about 'Myths of a Hero,' exploring the tales of Bose and the uses to which he had been put since 1945. I was met with a wall of silence. I was assured that Indians did not believe in myths any longer. My mentor, a senior Calcutta historian, told me to bring just 'cold, hard facts' the next time I came to talk. I was disappointed that they did not see—as I thought I did—that Bose was being assimilated into the Great Tradition of India. He was being linked to India's mythology, to her heroes, sadhus, and saints of bygone days. Myths are important constituents of the beliefs of millions of ordinary Indians. But more than this, people's hopes for the return of Bose also had to do with their discontent in the present and their disillusionment with politicians on the scene.

In the same year, on January 23, 1979, Bose's birthday, I was startled to open my daily newspapers and see a picture purporting to be that of Subhas Bose, alive. Keener eyes than mine in the Bose family immediately saw that the hands and body of the figure in the so-called 'photograph' belonged to Sarat Bose, whereas the head was that of Subhas Bose. Indeed, it was admitted a few days later by Mr Samar Guha, who had presented the item to the press, that he had gotten it 'somewhere' and it was a forgery. He said that he had not spotted the forgery himself and was simply a middleman. He was not responsible for the hoax that had been perpetrated on the Indian public.

III

Somewhere along the line of my investigations, I saw that Subhas Bose was extraordinarily close to his brother Sarat Bose and Sarat made important contributions to his brother's activities, to the Bose family, and to Calcutta, Bengal, and India. It made sense, therefore, to include him in a dual biography. Some biographies of Subhas hardly mentioned Sarat and there was no biography of Sarat—a few memoirs, but no significant historical writing. This decision drew me further into the Bose family which I learned was—like many large and famous families in India and elsewhere—replete with conflicts and rivalries, even hatreds, as well as love and kindred feeling. For a long time I was, and still am, identified with one unit of the extended Bose family, Dr Sisir Bose (Sarat Bose's third son) and his immediate family. I had no axe to grind, but I was beholden to Dr Bose and his immediate family for their help and direction, and even more for their support and warm friendship over many years. I learned, too, that there were a number of family members who did not want to go through Sisir, but who wanted to speak to me. I might be a major or a minor chronicler of the Boses—who could tell?—but they wanted to give me their version of the past.

A scurrilous pamphlet, 'Granada Television and Dr Sisir Bose,' was produced accusing Dr Bose, his immediate family, and their American contact, myself, of having and distributing monies from abroad for special purposes. This absurd Bengali pamphlet—a tapestry of lies—seemed to be the work of a few harboring special grievances for reasons I never learned. I was described as the notorious 'Dr Leonard Gordon, alias Lenny'. However, we all took this as comic relief after the nasty machinations of the Granada television producer whose efforts culminated in a distorted film on Bose and the INA which was shown throughout the West.

Some within the family who had helped me remained suspicious of an outsider and when the *Statesman* published a wildly inaccurate account of a speech which I gave in New Delhi, they came to condemn Sisir Bose for having helped the dreadful wretch who had said such things. After the *Statesman* agreed to publish my version of what I had said (and it seemed rather mundane and even accurate), these voices quieted. One family member, though, was still not satisfied and said he would sue me for what the *Statesman* had invented. I invited him to do so.

IV

As I made the rounds of the Bose family, of Indian politicians of an earlier generation, and then ventured to Europe, Southeast Asia, and Japan to interview others who had known the Boses, I gradually learned that many of these people had their special agendas, and wanted their versions of their lives and that of the Boses to be injected into my biography. The truth or complete falsehood of some of the stories I was told was often hard to sort out. They usually exaggerated their own importance and closeness to the Boses. Old grievances and desires and present purposes often combined to shape tales. I tried to compare these tales to relevant documents of the period as a check, but in some cases there was no way to do this.

One of the areas of conflicting tales had to do with the marriage and family of Subhas Bose. He had certainly lived with Emilie Schenkl and she had raised a daughter, Anita, and Bose had informed his brother Sarat that this was his wife and daughter. Some Indians refused to believe that Bose had married or produced a child while India was in bondage. Others wondered whether they had in fact been married. Mrs Schenkl had her version. Others close to the couple were usually vague about details or gave very different dates and stories about the marriage ceremony. Some of these details are presented at the appropriate place in this account.

For this project, I made my first trip to Germany to find some of those who had worked with Bose during the Second World War and to consult the German Foreign Office records. In Stuttgart, I was greatly helped by Captain Wilhelm Lutz who told me among other things that Hitler's only fault was that he had lost. My Jewish identity had never entered directly into the research process before, but at Captain Lutz's home his wife asked me, 'Is Gordon a Scottish name?' Since I wanted further frankness in my talks with Lutz, I simply replied, 'Yes.' I did not go on to say that it was a name assigned to my Jewish grandfather when he got off the boat from Russia in New York late in the nineteenth century. A few days later, as Lutz and I enjoyed a beer before I left for Munich, I asked about the slaughter of the Jews. He used the old metaphor of having to break some eggs to make an omelet. I decided that I would just listen.

In the summer of 1979, I went to Japan to pick up the thread of Bose's foreign connections. It happened that Anita (Bose) Pfaff was in Tokyo at the same time and a luncheon was held for us by an Indo-Japanese friendship society whose members were mainly retired military officers. The warmth of the feelings that they had for Bose thirty-four years after they had last dealt with him and the respect they accorded him struck me. This led me to contrast the way he had related to the Germans and the

Japanese. I came to the conclusion that he had little rapport with the Germans and particularly the Nazi drive behind German aggression, whereas in the minds of some of his Japanese contacts, he was 'an Indian samurai', and in tune with fundamental beliefs of theirs.

V

The inability of some to come to terms with his death and the efforts by others to exploit his mysterious death instructed me about the present as well as the past in Bengal. Now living through unhappy days, and finding no political man of his stature since Indian independence, some Bengalis were trying to resurrect a long-lost hero. And, clearly, there was something about the way that Bose had lived that continues to tap powerful emotions in India.

A much criticized as well as beloved leader during his life, Bose is becoming an unassailable hero and perhaps will in time become a deity. Indeed, to some, his story has already begun to resemble that of an Indian deity. Students of Indian culture remember that the Buddha and Rama and probably Krishna all began as warriors and later became accepted as avatars (incarnations). According to popular Hindu belief, the tenth and final avatar of the god Vishnu, called Kalki—a messiah figure—will come on his white horse to save the world from destruction.[3] In pictures sold for a few paise on the street, Bose is shown on a white horse in an emperor's uniform. If he does not come as a sadhu, he may then arrive as Kalki, the ruler of a revived, powerful Indian empire. We cannot yet know the ultimate versions of the story of Netaji, but even now it is clear that his very real contributions to Indian nationalism have been overlaid with myths.

As a foreign researcher on Bose's life, I have been assigned a title, 'Netajiwallah,' (the one who does Netaji) and given a variety of ceremonial roles to help remember him. I have also frequently been abused and misunderstood when I did not present the Bose that a particular audience wanted to hear about. These experiences have taught me that Bose—like Gandhi and perhaps others—lives on in the memories and in the fantasies of many Indians. Amidst all the tales, projections, and special agendas of so many, it has been difficult to sort through the rich, but enormous veins of material to find the humanity and historicity of Subhas Bose and of Sarat Bose. Using my own materials and the work of others, particularly on the Second World War period on which excellent studies have been done, I have done my best to present the Boses as I have found them in the following pages. Although I have tried to be fair-minded and objective, I have my own values and point of view which are built into what follows.

CHAPTER ONE

The Boses of Kodalia, Cuttack and Calcutta

Contact with the West led to our discovery of our heritage and history. It started a dialogue with others and within the self.

A.K. Ramanujan[1]

I

The Bose family of Kodalia village in 24-Parganas, West Bengal, Cuttack in Orissa, and 38/2 Elgin Road, Calcutta,. is renowned in modern Indian history because of the political activities of Subhas Chandra Bose. In India it is common for the parents of a prominent leader—if they appear at all— to be slotted into familiar stereotypes: noble father and pious mother. The other relatives slip away. The parents stand quietly off-stage or rear-stage, the eminent offspring appears full-blown as Pallas Athena from the head of Zeus. These families of notable men are often lost in the mist of history.

Subhas Bose needed a base from which to move out into the world of action and to which to repair for respite from conflicts. His family provided the base. First, the parental household was the ground for shaping and supporting Subhas and, in adulthood, Subhas needed the home of Sarat Bose and his wife, since Subhas was not a householder himself. Moreover, Sarat Bose was more than a supporting householder: he was a partner in politics.[2]

Janaki Nath Bose, born in 1860, and Prabhabati Bose (nee Dutt), born in 1869, were formed by the living traditions of Bengal and touched by the rapid changes of the nineteenth century under the British Raj.[3] The Bengal of 1880—the year Janaki Nath and Prabhabati were married—covered about one-third of British India. It included Bengal proper, Bihar, Orissa, and Chota Nagpur and was predominantly rural with one great city, Calcutta. Nearly sixty-seven million people inhabited the domain of the lieutenant-governor of Bengal of whom some thirty-five million were in Bengal proper, an area approximately 84,000 square miles. In comparison, the state of Minnesota has about the same area and in 1987 had 4.25 million people. Great Britain has 89,000 square miles and has a population of about 56.65 million. Today West Bengal plus Bangladesh have an area of 89,000 square miles and a population of more than 165 million.[4]

Janaki Nath was born in Kodalia, a village on the southern outskirts of Calcutta. He was descended from a junior family in the Boses of Mahinagar, a Dakshin Rarhi Kayastha clan. The elaborate Indian caste-ranking system varied a good deal from region to region. Although 'clean' Sudras in the four-varna (Brahmin, Kshatriya, Vaishya, Sudra) model of ancient India, the Bengal Kayasthas ranked next to the Brahmins in caste status, the regional ranking lacking Kshatriyas and Vaishyas. Among Kayasthas, the *kulins* (Bose, Ghose, Mitra) were the highest ranking clans. So, though Sudras, the Boses were near the top of the complicated regional caste hierarchy. The family had once lived in the village of Mahinagar when the Hoogly, a major tributary of the Ganges, flowed by it to the sea. Although the Boses were said to have numbered prominent public figures among them in earlier centuries, by the early nineteenth century, Janaki's recent ancestors, including his father, were poor landholders living in Kodalia. His father Haranath married twice and Janaki was born of his second wife, Kamini. Haranath probably knew no English. Kamini died when her son Janaki was sixteen; Haranath continued to live in the village until his death in 1985.[5]

The family by tradition was Shakta, devotees of the consort of the god Siva, usually in the form of Durga. An image of Durga sits almost inconspicuously in one room of the family house in Kodalia today and Bose family members occasionally visit during the puja (religious festival) season. Haranath is said to have been a Vaishnava, devotee of one of the forms of Vishnu, the principal deity and progenitor of the other main form of Hinduism in Bengal. In family lore, Haranath is said to have stopped a goat sacrifice during Durga Puja one year. Little else is directly known of him.[6]

All four of Haranath's sons moved out of the village in search of education, employment, and higher socio-economic status. Although their status in the caste hierarchy was relatively high, they were much lower on the economic ladder. Devendranath, Haranath's son by his first wife, joined the government education service, served ·as principal of Krishnagar College and also worked in Cuttack, Orissa, and is responsible for the connection of the Boses to Cuttack. Jadunath worked in the Imperial Secretariat and Kedarnath also moved to Calcutta. So all of Harnath's sons were educated in English and at least three flourished in positions associated with the Raj.[7]

Kodalia is in deltaic Bengal. Through the centuries the main course of the Ganges had been shifting eastward, and Kodalia in the time we are speaking of lay in the drier old delta studded with swamps and marshes. Disease was frequent, life expectancy—by contemporary standards—short. The district of 24-Parganas was hit by a cyclone in 1864 and a famine two years later in the years of Janaki's childhood. For many of his social and cultural background, this was a period of rising expectations as it was of rising prices. Western education was essential to participate in the upward mobility of high-caste Hindus. Janaki passed his matriculation examination from the Albert School, Calcutta, in 1877, and then joined St Xavier's College. Six months later he switched to the General Assembly's Institution. In August 1879, he made yet another change, moving to Cuttack, where his half-brother Devendranath resided, and joined Ravenshaw College. He passed his First Arts examination in the first division and won a government scholarship of Rs. 20. He was a bright, poor boy from a village and on his way up.[8]

While still an undergraduate student in Cuttack, his marriage was arranged and consummated in 1880 to Prabhabati Dutt of the well-known Hatkhola Dutts of north Calcutta. In traditional Bengali status terms, Janaki was from a higher-ranking *kulin* Kayastha family, his in-laws from a lower-ranking *mullik* (or *maulik*) Kayastha family. But the Hatkhola Dutts were an old Calcutta family, renowned for their fair skins and eloquent tongues, and were called 'aristocrats' by the family chroniclers of the day. The family lived in Baranagar, formerly a favorite pleasure resort for Calcutta Europeans, but by 1909 a busy industrial suburb which had two large jute mills and produced castor oil for export to Europe. Janaki was twenty, his bride eleven, typical marriage ages for the time. Prabhabati's grandfather, Kasi Nath Dutt, had broken from the Hatkhola residence (in north Calcutta) and moved to Baranagar. He was well educated and worked for the British firm, Messrs Jardin, Skinner and Company. His son, Ganganarayan Dutt, like all the other Hatkhola Dutts, sought marriage links to *kulin* families. Janaki brought his high traditional status and his promise of achievement under the Raj, and Prabhabati brought her family name, fair skin, and higher economic status to the match.[9]

In 1882 Janaki passed his B.A. examination in the second division from Ravenshaw College and in 1884 was for nine months the headmaster of Jaynagore Institution, a school outside Calcutta. He had undertaken legal studies after his B.A. and in 1884 passed his B.L. examination from the Metropolitan Institution, Calcutta, founded by the famous scholar and social reformer Vidyasagar. The same year the first child of Janaki and

Prabhabati, a girl, Pramila, was born in May at Baranagar. After the puja vacation, Janaki and Prabhabati moved to Cuttack, where Janaki joined the Cuttack bar on January 15, 1885. Although his roots were in Kodalia and he had gained much of his education in the metropolis of Calcutta, he was to make his mark in life and raise his family in Cuttack, one of the satellite cities of greater Bengal.[10]

Of Cuttack, about 300 miles southwest of Calcutta, W.W. Hunter wrote in 1877 that it was '... situated on a tongue of land formed by the Mahanadi and Katjuri rivers at their point of bifurcation' and '... owes its creation, its wealth, and its disasters to the Mahanadi, "the Great River," which bursts abruptly upon the plains a little above Cuttack city from a picturesque gorge.'[11] It was situated between the thickly wooded hills and the coastal marshes of Orissa. Tigers, bears, leopards, wild buffaloes, deer, foxes, and wild hogs abounded in the region. The deltaic area between Cuttack and the sea was cut by innumerable creeks and small rivers still abounding in fish-eating and man-eating crocodiles. The district of Cuttack was poor, predominantly rural, and only 7.7 per cent literate in 1901. By this date the divisional town was connected by rail and road to Calcutta and its Bengali settlers and British officers looked to Calcutta as the center of their universe.[12]

Cuttack town had been the center of Mughal and then Maratha administration in the area before the British supplanted the Marathas in Orissa at the beginning of the nineteenth century. Utilizing Cuttack for administrative purposes, the British gave it new life. Although the population grew slowly from about 43,000 in 1872 to 51,000 in 1921, the town was a center of commerce, seat of the principal civil court, and headquarters of the divisional commissioner. The greater part of the population were Oriyas, but immigrant Bengalis entered and virtually monopolized the high executive and clerical positions in the government. Telugus entered the region from the south and the indigenous Oriyas resented the invaders from both north and south. Some of the Bengalis were only temporarily in Orissa for professional reasons and continued to identify with Calcutta and Bengal. These were 'birds of passage'; others merged more with the local population.[13]

Janaki Nath Bose had an intermediate position: he spent most of his adult life in Cuttack and became a leader of the native community, but he never broke his connections to Kodalia and Calcutta. He continued to identify as a Bengali but without the usual snobbery of high-caste Bengalis who called the Oriyas 'Orey,' and thought them good only as cooks. By the 1890s, he had become the most prominent Bengali resident and president of the Bengali Settlers' Association. He was very successful as a lawyer, excelling as a cross-examining counsel. In time he was appointed to the prestigious position of government pleader. His business demanded contact with the top strata of British officials in Cuttack and he was proud of these connections. Janaki Nath was one of the curious, but familiar mixtures of Indian and European culture.[14]

Though he was Anglicized—he often wore European clothes, read the *Statesman* (then a leading newspaper of the British in India), had a dining room table (unlike most Indians) and was devoted to English literature and British liberalism—he was also a Hindu, a Bengali, and a proud Indian. He was called 'Janaki Nath Sahib'. Usually only Europeans in India were sahibs, but the term was also used to refer to persons of high rank, Westernized in their ways. Janaki Nath Sahib he might be, but he was able to mix with people of all kinds. Almost six feet tall, solidly built, with a mustache and squarish face, he was an imposing, grave, smiling man. More than for his words, he was remembered for his deeds. A granddaughter recalled a friendly, soft-spoken man, who really listened to you, even though you were just a small girl. Fitting the traditional Indian model of a man of high standing, Janaki Nath was generous with the money he earned and secretly paid the expenses of a number of poor students. As a self-made man, he appreciated and helped the efforts of indigent village boys. He returned to Kodalia for the pujas, not forgetting his roots. He retained a living interest in his ancestral village and provided a library and dispensary for it.[15]

An avocation, a private passion, was the reading of English literature. He read John Milton, William Cowper, Matthew Arnold, Rudyard Kipling, and loved Shakespeare, particularly *Hamlet*. This devotion to literature bonded him to a neighbor, Professor Gopal C. Ganguli, who taught English at Ravenshaw College, the foremost government institution in Cuttack. Prof Ganguli was not only Janaki Nath's friend, but the teacher of his sons, several of whom, in time, became equally passionate about English literature. Janaki Nath was very concerned about education and sent his sons first to an English-medium school where Bengali was not taught. He wanted his sons to speak perfect English for he believed this important in gaining access to English society; proper intonation in speaking was as vital as grammatical correctness. English to Janaki Nath was essential if one was to get on; Bengali was optional. To many of the Western-educated of those days, as one of Ganguli's sons put it, 'English literature was so tempting and Bengali literature was backward.'[16]

In agreement with the great majority of the Western-educated middle class Bengalis of the late nineteenth century, Janaki Nath believed that British rule was benevolent. He felt a sense of gratitude to the British for their gifts to India: law and order; reforms such as the creation of legislative councils with Indian members; and, of course, their language, literature, and science. He was rewarded by the Raj for his loyalty. First, government pleader, then an appointment to the Bengal Legislative Council in 1912, and finally the title of 'Rai Bahadur'.[17]

Janaki Nath served in the Bengal Legislative Council for only three brief months, January to March 1912. These were the last meetings held in the Durbar Hall of the large and elegant government mansion, Belvedere, Alipore, Calcutta, and the last ones which included representatives from Bihar and Orissa, shortly to be separated from Bengal. Although the debates included sharp disagreements among the members on the views of the 'people' and on points of fact and law, they sound as if the turmoil of the Swadeshi period, 1905 to 1908, and acts of revolutionary terrorism which dotted the following years, had never taken place. The debaters were British officials, European business representatives, and Indian loyalists. No questioner of the authority of the Raj was present as discussions unfolded on the Orissa Tenancy Bill of 1911. The government wanted to regularize the agrarian code in Orissa and take the particular conditions of that region into account, differentiating it from Bengal proper.[18]

Although some ultra-conservative Orissa landlords wished no changes in the land law, the government needed someone who would make a coherent case for their reformist bill and speak for public opinion in Orissa. They found a stalwart in Janaki Nath Bose, who, speaking against an indefinite delay in considering the bill, said,

> I crave your Honour's permission to oppose this motion. I oppose this motion, Sir, on several grounds. One of these is this: there is a general feeling amongst the intelligent people of Orissa that this Bill should be dealt with by this Council. I have consulted several gentlemen who take a lively interest in this measure, in fact, members of public Associations in Cuttack and other gentlemen connected with the administration of the law in that province, and most of them, I think, were of the opinion that this Council should deal with the Bill, not only in Select Committee, but should pass the Bill after proper deliberation. . . . I can say, very safely, that the ordinary public does not take much interest in the work of legislation. It is the intelligent, educated portion of the community that really takes any interest in the measures which are before the Legislative Council. Now the Orissa Association of Cuttack is of long standing and is composed of many educated, intelligent and respectable people of that district, and I can very safely and emphatically assure the Council that the Orissa Association as a body does want to have this Bill passed by this Council.[19]

Janaki Nath took his stand with the government and also with the landholders and maintained that discussing the bill immediately would give the Council the benefit of the '. . . views of important Bengal landholders, who have the interest and welfare of Orissa at heart.'[20] Janaki Nath's view of representation was in accord with the outlook of loyalist and moderate Indian political spokesmen of the second half of the nineteenth century and early decades of the twentieth century, a self-selected elite which had risen to the top by birth, education, and wealth and was accepted by the Raj as the leaders of the native population. It was assumed, naively or cynically, that they would consider the welfare of the whole community as their goal.[21]

Later, in the debate over this measure, Janaki Nath stood to oppose an Orissa landholder critical of the Government of Bengal. He said, in part,

> I am really sorry, Sir, that a remark which was unfortunately made by the Raja of Kanika at the meeting on the 9th January has been repeated. He said that the Government of Bengal was guilty of injustice to the people of Orissa. Of course, my friend the Raja of Kanika is a young man, and I did not think it worth my while to answer his accusation, but I do not think that I shall allow this opportunity to pass without entering my solemn protest against an accusation like this.
>
> On the other hand, I have been in the province for about a quarter of a century, and I have seen that Orissa has all along been treated like a pet child. The return that child now gives is to accuse this Government of gross injustice.[22]

Apart from his general defenses of the Indian elite of Orissa, the Government of Bengal, and the work of the Select Committee on the bill (of which he was a member), Janaki Nath participated actively in the shaping of the bill, concerning himself with precise language and possible legal difficulties in implementation.

He was also concerned with the wording of the clauses about properties contributed to religious endowments. He showed himself an expert on Oriya usage and on the historical development of tenancy law and tenancy conflicts in Orissa. He had, obviously, been nominated by the government to the Council for the express purpose of helping them put through this legislation and also because of his expert knowledge of his adopted region. A picture emerges from the proceedings of a man strictly loyal to the government, a member of the educated and wealthy elite of his own society, scrupulous in his attention to linguistic and legal matters, and concerned in general with the good of his society as he understood it. He was a keen debater and showed skill in drafting legal documents. The government, for its part, must have been delighted with the champion of their cause whom they had appointed to Council.[23]

While Janaki Nath held forth in the august chambers of the Bengal

Legislative Council in Calcutta, his wife Prabhabati quietly and efficiently ran his large household in Cuttack. Janaki Nath, like many other busy men of affairs then, had little time to devote to household management, so this fell into the hands of Prabhabati, or *Ma-janani* as she was called. She became pregnant at fourteen and had her first child, Pramila, in 1884. She had fourteen children, thirteen of whom lived into adulthood: Sarala, a daughter in 1885; then five sons, Satish in 1887, Sarat in 1889, Suresh in 1891, Sudhir in 1892, Sunil in 1894; next a daughter Tara Bala in 1895; then Subhas in 1897; followed by three daughters, Molina in 1898, Protiva in 1900, Kanaklata in 1902; and then two sons, Sailesh in 1904, and Santosh in 1905, the one child who died young. So Prabhabati had her fourth child in her twentieth year and had had nine children by her twenty-eighth birthday. The first two were born at her paternal home in Baranagar; the next twelve in Cuttack. She must have been healthy and resilient to bear all these sprightly and surviving offspring.[24]

Prabhabati had no formal education, but had private lessons and could read Bengali. Though she later had lessons in English (and knitting), she never learned to speak English, though she could understand a little. According to several of her grandchildren, she was a strong-willed woman with sharp likes and dislikes, intelligent, logical, and a perfectionist. Sarat Bose used to tell his friends that his father gave him ambition and his mother discipline. Prabhabati did not have birthday parties for her children because she thought such special attention would give them inflated ideas of themselves. She was very fair in skin color—one who knew her said she could pass for an Italian or even an Englishwoman—and favored the lighter-colored among her children and grandchildren. When choosing a prospective bride for one of her sons, she would lay her arm side by side with that of the girl and compare the skin color on the inside of their forearms. In most cases, the girl had to be fairer than Prabhabati to be selected. The belief that the fairer were superior had an ancient lineage in India dating at least to the Aryan invasions and was reinforced by the British conquest. Though some benefited from this ranking by color, many others, including some in the Bose family, suffered a lifelong stigma.[25]

Janaki Nath Bose's house in Cuttack was a large L-shaped, two-storey dwelling in the center of town. It had several small quarters (for the servants) attached to the main building, which surrounded a large court-yard. Prabhabati supervised the household but required the assistance of servants since she rose late, spent about two hours in her bath, and took a long nap in the afternoon. The school-going children did not see that much of her on a usual day. This pattern was a familiar one in the aristocratic households of Bengal.[26]

Prabhabati was an orthodox Hindu and traditional Bengali Hindu customs and pujas were observed. All the children had to attend these pujas without excuses. Although there was no special room (called a *Thakur-ghor*) for religious observances, Prabhabati followed the lead of the family priest and of her chosen guru, Anukul Thakur. She was a Shakta like most high-caste Bengalis and worshipped forms of the Mother Goddess. Her children, in turn, became similarly devoted to the Mother Goddess, particularly Durga. Fond of Bengali hymns, she joined in the singing of religious songs. Religious observance was mainly her province. In the 1880s, Janaki Nath, who preached 'plain living and high thinking' and never had contempt for things Indian or for the traditional customs of his society, had been attracted to the Brahmo Samaj as led by Keshub Sen. Janaki Nath was also an admirer of the disciple of Ramakrishna, Swami Vivekananda, founder of the Ramakrishna Mission, a different kind of Hindu reform movement of the nineteenth century. Both the orthodoxy of Prabhabati and the more eclectic Hindu beliefs of Janaki Nath had an impact on their sons.[27]

II

Sarat Bose, the fourth child, and second son of Janaki Nath and Prabhabati, was marked by his father for special favor. In many ways, he resembled his father, and was closest to being his successor among the fourteen children. Most studies of the birth order factor have been based on Western experience and on analyses of much smaller families. Alfred Adler and subsequent psychologists have suggested that the eldest child or elder children tend to be more like the parents, more conservative, more responsible, and are given more power in the family. As there are more children in the family, the older ones are treated more like the eldest. The elder children show seriousness, a strong conscience, and high need for achievement. One psychologist writes, 'They (*the oldest*) may be moralistic, disciplinarian, and perfectionist in the requirements they place upon their children.'[28] Such suggestions may be taken as general guidelines rather than specific findings. What is important, as Forer argues, is how birth order is experienced. Each child in the same family grows up in a slightly different environment at a slightly different time, and each youngest child is, in turn, 'dethroned', as Adler puts it, by the next born, until the last child in the family is born.[29]

In India, male children are considered more important than female children since most of India is organized patrilineally and the eldest son performs the *shraddha* or funeral rites for his parents. In most parts of India, a dowry is given by the wife-giving family and in this exchange, the wife-taking family is thought to be superior. So sons are thought to be more blessed and a man is thought lucky to have many sons and few daughters. The eldest son is normally the successor and has a position of honor, respect and power after his father.[30]

The first son in this family was Satish, born in 1887, two years before Sarat, *Mej-da* to his younger siblings. But Sarat showed more ability, drive, and intelligence, and was favored over his elder brother, in non-formal ways. Sarat had a strong competitive spirit and his first goal was to catch up with his *Dada*, his elder brother, and later to surpass him. Satish Bose, who was a warm and pleasant person, attended the same elite college as all but one of his brothers and much later was called to the bar in London. But Sarat caught Satish when they embarked on their college education and then passed him in educational, professional, and political achievement.[31]

There is little record left of the youth and coming of age of any of the Bose children other than Subhas. But fragments can be pieced together to give a brief sketch of Sarat's early years, education, and young manhood. Sarat became and remained a devout Hindu throughout his life. According to his children, he accepted the orthodox Shakta Hinduism of Bengal in all its particulars. He did his puja to the Mother Goddess every morning and was most respectful to his parents and wanted to carry out his duty to them in every way. He was also affected by the religious revivalism of the late nineteenth century as preached by Swami Vivekananda.[32]

These traditional Hindu elements were already in place by the time he entered the Protestant European School in Cuttack. All the Bose sons from Satish to the youngest, Sailesh, attended this school in their father's quest to have them read, understand, and speak perfect English—the English of a sahib. Sarat Bose later said that his English—spoken and written—was better than his Bengali. When he was older, he became known as a superb orator in English, particularly in the chambers of the Bengal Legislative Council and the Calcutta High Court. He was extremely proud of his deep resonant voice. As boys, Satish and Sarat and other English-speaking Cuttack youth often went down to the banks of the Mahanadi and recited Shakespeare and famous speeches of British leaders, projecting their voices across the wide river.[33]

After several years at the English-medium school, Sarat and his brothers were switched to the Ravenshaw Collegiate School in which Bengali, Sanskrit, and other Indian subjects were taught in addition to Western ones. Though Sarat and all his brothers learned to speak and read Bengali and were certainly bi-lingual, their English was better. Satish was several years ahead of Sarat, but they took their matriculation, or school-leaving examination at nearly the same time and both entered Presidency College, Calcutta, in 1905. Sarat is reported to have said, 'My *Dada* has taken the exam, I will also take the exam.'[34]

With the entry of two sons into Presidency College in 1905, the locus of the Bose family shifted from Cuttack to Calcutta, the capital of British India and the second city of the British Empire. A British resident of those days wrote, 'But Calcutta is withal a Queen of two faces: a city of startling contrasts, of palaces and hovels, of progress and reaction, of royal grandeur and of squalor that beggars description.'[35] In the later part of the twentieth century, the notion of Calcutta with 'royal grandeur' has disappeared from the minds of outsiders and only the idea of 'squalor that beggars description' remains. In order to understand the main environment in which the Boses grew and thrived, it is necessary to know the earlier Calcutta.[36]

Calcutta, chosen by the agents of the East India Company as a site for a factory or trading post at the end of the seventeenth century, developed in a most inhospitable spot. Rhoads Murphey has called it 'the city in the swamp,' for Calcutta was built on alluvial deltaic land, once marsh, and only slightly above sea level.[37] Though cool and pleasant enough in the winter (October through February), it is hot, humid, and sticky from March to September and its wider roads as well as its numerous, narrow, twisting lanes are subject to severe flooding in the summer monsoon months. It is situated at 22° 33' North Latitude and 88° 23' East Longitude, near the Tropic of Cancer. It has grown along the left bank of one main channel of the Ganges, the Hooghly, about 120 miles upstream from the Bay of Bengal. It extends more than four-and-a-half miles along the river and at least one-and-a-half miles inland. It has always had its spiteful critics and strong defenders from the eighteenth century to the present. One nineteenth century wag wrote, 'its situation is so bad by nature that there is little that man could do to make it worse, but that little has been faithfully and assiduously done.'[38]

From 1773 to 1912, it served as capital of British India and was long a leading port (along with Bombay) as well as the commercial, industrial, financial, political, and cultural center of eastern India. The geographer O.H.K. Spate has written of it,

> In the orientation imposed on the economic geography of 19th century India by its gearing to British needs, the advantages of the Calcutta neighbourhood were many: the sea-entry to the areas of greatest population and (at least until the rise of Punjab and Deccan cotton) of highest agricultural productivity—including that of the great early staple exports, opium, téa, indigo; a monopoly of world jute supply at its doors; the only well-

developed network of internal navigation in India; the region where British
territorial power on any large scale was oldest; the seat of Government and
above all of a forceful, not to say ruthless, dominant minority of British
businessmen.[39]

Across the river from Calcutta, a large industrial area developed running
several miles from Hooghly to Howrah. Calcutta proper remained more
commercial and administrative. During the pre-independence period
much of the industrial and commercial activity was run by Europeans
though from the late nineteenth century, Indian businessmen, largely non-
Bengali, increasingly entered the field. The Calcutta metropolitan area
was a huge magnet attracting those with capital to invest, as well as poor
laborers from all over eastern India and beyond. Gradually, much of the
manual labor and factory work came to be done by non-Bengalis from
Bihar and Uttar Pradesh, while educated Bengalis took the clerical and
lower administrative positions inside and outside the government. The
professional groups were largely Bengali and the native culture thrived.
Calcutta became and remains one of the liveliest cultural centers in India.
Though Kipling mocked the city and its babus in 'The City of Dreadful
Night,' both its permanent European residents and its Indian citizens took
pride in its positive charms which for them far outweighed its crowding,
filth, and dangers.[40]

At first the Boses did not have their own base in Calcutta. So Satish and
Sarat resided at the Government Eden Hindu Hostel for undergraduates
from Presidency College. They lived with their peers, away from home for
the first extended stay.

The Calcutta of those days was growing and well-to-do Indians were
buying property and settling in the southern part of the city. One of the
favored areas was Bhowanipore, to the east and west of the southward
extension of Chowringhee, the main thoroughfare of central Calcutta. This
region contained headquarters of the Church Missionary Society, a lunatic
asylum, and the main Hindu shrine Kalighat.[41] Sir P.C. Mitter arranged for
a plot of land on which a substantial three-storey house was completed in
1909, 38/2 Elgin Road. This became, in time, the main Calcutta base of the
family. Two decades later Sarat Bose built his own house just across the
road. The extension of Chowringhee, now Sir Ashutosh Mukherjee Road,
was already inhabited in the eighteenth century by bell-metal traders who
were followed by goldsmiths and silversmiths and later jewelers. Pradip
Sinha, a leading historian of Calcutta writes,

> Historically, Bhowanipur was dominated by a professional middle class,
> which, from about the late nineteenth century to the early decades of this
> century, was the most dynamic element in Bengali society. In Bhowanipur

this class consisted primarily of people connected with the legal profession and secondarily, of doctors. Roy Choudhury produces as evidence of this dominance the fact that in the annual report of a local philanthropic society for 1891 all the members on the list were barristers, advocates, *vakils,* district judges and attorneys, with Sir Ashutosh Mukherjee, the High Court Judge, as President, and Sir B.C. Mitter, Member of the Privy Council, as one of the members.[42]

Sinha proposes that this period saw the rise of intermediaries between the old Calcutta families (like the Tagores, or Prabhabati's family) and the Indian masses most of whom lived in north Calcutta. The Boses were *kulins* and by now a top family in Cuttack, but they were parvenus to the Bengali elite of Calcutta. It was the accomplishments first of Janaki Nath and then of his sons that made the Boses a leading family of Calcutta. They had roots in a nearby village, ties to Cuttack, and later a link to Kurseong, near Darjeeling, where they vacationed, but in the generation of Janaki Nath's sons, they became Calcutta men. First their educational life, then their professional, social, and political life, with some exceptions among the sons, was in Calcutta. They were shaped in the city and, in adulthood, they contributed to its vital activities.

Among the institutions of Calcutta founded and long dominated by Western-educated high-caste Hindus was the Hindu College which became Presidency College in 1855. Started by private Hindu initiative in 1817, the Hindu College was a center of Western learning supported by private funds and some government assistance. It was decided by government officials in 1854 to transform this Hindu institution into a non-sectarian institution and bring it under the aegis of the government's Council of Education. In the second half of the nineteenth century, Presidency College as an integral part of the newly (1858) established Calcutta University became the premier college of northern India. The law and civil engineering departments were eventually separated out and concentration was upon instruction in the arts and sciences through the M.A. level. Gradually more Indian faculty members were appointed, but many of the staff were Europeans into the 1920s. In 1905 there were thirty-six members of the teaching staff and 923 students, but a decade later there were fifty-nine teachers for the same number of students. Although the student body was drawn from the different strata of the society, most were high-caste Hindus. One critic said that institutions like Presidency College displayed 'a despotism of caste, tempered by matriculation.'[43] There is no doubt that the upper strata of Bengali society dominated. Janaki Nath Bose contributed six of his sons to the rolls of this elite institution. The Register of the college published in 1927 includes:

Basu, Saratchandra (1905-1908); B.A. 1907 (Honours in English); M.A.–
1908 (2nd class in English); B.L. 1910.

Basu, Satishchandra (1905–1907 and 1908–1910); M.A. 1910 (in
English); B.L. 1911.

Basu, Sureshchandra (1907––1913); B.Sc. 1913 (Honours in Physics).

Basu, Sunilchandra (1909–1911); I.Sc. 1911; joined Calcutta Medical
College, 1911.

Basu, Sudhirchandra (1909–1915); B.Sc. 1915.

Basu, Subhaschandra (1913–1916); I.A. 1915 (1st division); Secretary,
Presidency College Union, 1913-1914.[44]

After his father's death in 1934, Subhas Bose wrote a brief account of
his father's life in the course of which he said that his father had not been
authoritarian, had tried to foster independence in his children, and that
each son was free to choose his own career. The daughters were all slated
for early, arranged marriages, preferably to *kulins*, but the sons did have
to make some choices and chart their own directions with parental
guidance. The eldest two sons both elected to study English literature, then
law, and, when opportunity allowed, were called to the bar in Great Britain.
The younger sons displayed much more variety in their choices and picked
career paths unlike their father.[45]

Sarat Bose entered Presidency College at sixteen; brother Satish also
entered, but at eighteen, both in the momentous year 1905, the year Bengal
was partitioned and the Swadeshi movement erupted. Sarat Bose later
mentioned singing Swadeshi songs in the street and said he was connected
to the Congress from that time, but, except for this brief comment, there is
no record of any political activity until the 1920s. He likely had his
patriotic sympathies aroused and marched with thousands of other young
Bengalis through the streets of Calcutta—sometimes led by the poet
Rabindranath Tagore—but he was not seriously involved in politics until
much later.[46]

A few of Sarat's books of those days remain, marked 'Sarat Chandra
Bose, 5th year class, Presidency College'. Among these are Dickens' *Old
Curiosity Shop*; James Russell Lowell's *My Study Windows*; the French
positivist H.A. Taine's *History of English Literature*; and Walter Skeat's
edition of Chaucer's *Canterbury Tales*, with incredibly detailed notations
throughout the book and on the covers. Sarat Bose was an avid buyer and
reader of literature, history, religion, and politics. Reading gave him
immense pleasure and provided an opportunity to understand the traditions and accomplishments of the British rulers of India. He loved English
poetry, had a photographic memory, and continued to read and recite
poetry throughout his life. Familiarity with the great traditions of the

English helped him to perfect his linguistic and oratorical skills. The literature taught in Presidency College included Chaucer, Milton, Shakespeare, the Romantic poets, and the Victorians, Tennyson, Arnold, and Hardy. These were the staples of the Western-educated Indian's literary diet. Although Sarat Bose continued to read widely, he did not seem to explore the new and important poets of the period from the First World War forward.[47]

Sarat Bose had some difficulty with examinations. He failed his First Arts examination and then passed. One suggestion is offered in the following comments by his 1946 biographer. I will offer another in dealing with his student years in England below.

> Somehow neither at school nor at college did Sarat Chandra shine as a student. He got a second class in B.A. while his brilliant friend Rajendra Prasad topped the list. But there was always something striking about him. His teachers never had any doubt that Sarat would be 'somebody' some day. As a school boy at the Ravenshaw Collegiate School and later as a student of the Ravenshaw College he impressed everybody by his unusual gravity, his perfect manners and his remarkable proficiency in English. Even at that early age he showed himself to be a fluent and skilful debater. When he joined the Presidency College for his B.A. he continued to neglect his books but maintained his reputation as an invincible debater. In due course he took his Master's degree in English and the Law degree, but, as usual, failed to distinguish himself.[48]

While Satish and Sarat Bose were still students, the former finishing his work in English, the latter already ahead of his elder brother and studying for a law degree, Janaki Nath and Prabhabati arranged their marriages. The bride chosen for Sarat was Bivabati Dey, daughter of Akshoy Kumar Dey, of the well-known College Street Dey family. Sarat and his prospective bride had accidentally seen each other on the beach at Puri in 1908. It was unusual, in those days, for the couple to see each other before the wedding ceremony. Biva had already been chosen for Sarat, but there was a delay in finding an appropriate *kulin* match for Satish.

The Deys were fidgety because no *asirbad*, or engagement ceremony had been held. It is said that Akshoy Dey encountered Janaki Nath and asked, '*pukka-dekha*?' (shouldn't we have an engagement ceremony?), to which Janaki Nath replied, '*amar kothae dekha.*' (my word is enough, or my word is the engagement ceremony). No *asirbad* ceremony was held for any of Janaki Nath's children. The usual exchange of gifts and visits took place, but no meeting between the couple and no engagement ceremony was performed.[49]

Once a proper *kulin* bride was found for Janaki Nath's eldest son, the wedding took place on December 9, 1909. Bivabati, born in 1896, was thirteen, Sarat was twenty. Like Sarat's mother, Biva, as she was usually called, had had no formal education, but could read and write Bengali. She later studied English, sometimes with Sarat, and understood a good deal, but did not use it actively because she was afraid of making mistakes. Some people found her reserved, but she was not shy. In time she had eight children and she was a hard task-master with a temper that occasionally flared. But the children were closer to her than to their busy father. By every report, this was a remarkably close and happy marriage and Sarat's parents were proved to have chosen wisely for their favored son.[50]

The Elgin Road house was finished for occupancy just before the double wedding ceremony. Both the new husbands still had to complete their educations. Sarat received his B.L. degree from Calcutta University in 1910 and enrolled as a vakil in Cuttack where he started his legal apprenticeship in 1911–12. Satish received his B.L. in 1911, enrolled as a vakil at the Calcutta High Court, from 1911 to 1915, and then shifted to the Patna High Court, from 1915 to 1919.

Sarat had chosen to work in Cuttack where his father was one of the most prominent legal practitioners at the local district court. There are different stories about the following events. One account has it that he argued a will case against his father and the English judge was so impressed with Sarat that he encouraged the young man to go to England to be called to the bar. Sarat asked his mother, who put it to his father, who finally agreed. Whatever the precise details were, the family did decide that Sarat, though he was the second son, would become the first to go across the seas to Europe for higher education. In December 1911, Biva gave birth to their first child, a son, Asoke. In 1912 Sarat left for London and spent the better part of the next two years there. Sarat regretted having to leave his first-born so soon, but the opportunity to study and be called to the bar in London was too glorious to postpone or turn down.[51]

Although there were Indian visitors to England in the first half of the nineteenth century, Indian students did not seek higher education there until the 1860s. Many had to face family, caste, and religious proscriptions. When Romesh C. Dutt, Surendranath Banerjea, and a third friend left Calcutta for England in 1868, they had to steal out at night to avoid the opposition of family and friends. Mahatma Gandhi had to brave excommunication when he went to sit for the bar in 1888.[52] As the years passed and the pattern became more common, the resistance dissolved.

When the secretary of state for India's Committee on Indian Students in the United Kingdom reported in 1907, they estimated that there were about 700 Indian students, 380 in London, 150 in Edinburgh, 85 in Cambridge, 32 in Oxford, 16 in Manchester, 11 in Birmingham, and 74 elsewhere. 320 of the London students were sitting for the bar. Figures for the number of Indians admitted to three of the Inns of Court in Sarat's period are:

	Lincoln's Inn	MiddleTemple	Gray's Inn
1909	76	60	19
1910	186	116	56
1911	27	25	13
1912	29	25	15
1913	45	15	16
1914	7	10	16
1915	4	16	17

By 1920, when Subhas Bose and Satish Bose were both studying in the United Kingdom, after the First World War lapse, there were about 1,450 Indian students enrolled.[53]

For many young Indians the European experience was both exhilarating and trying. It was the opening of a new world of experience, but also a yanking from the familiar familial womb. Noting the extensive liberty of the Indian students in the United Kingdom, the authors of the 1907 report worried,

> ... we feel strongly that for the young Asiatic, a stranger from a distant land, and for the most part unattuned to his new surroundings, the entire absence of guidance and control in a large European city may be fraught with serious consequences.[54]

For Sarat Bose, who had hardly moved out of his Bengali and family circle, there were dangers and temptations as well as opportunities that had to be tried gingerly. However, Sarat at twenty-three felt prepared because he knew English very well, had a previous law degree, and had already practised as a vakil in India. His time and education in London were structured by the goal of his trip to be called to the bar, and by the institution, Lincoln's Inn, to which he was affiliated.[55]

The four Inns of Court were already well-organized by the fourteenth century and Lincoln's Inn had been settled on the same site in east-central London since about 1350. The aged and elegant buildings of Lincoln's Inn dated variously from the fifteenth, seventeenth, and nineteenth centuries. Students had generally been drawn from the upper strata of society and by the mid-nineteenth century, the educational level was low. Then in 1852, the Council of Legal Education was founded which set the examinations and requirements and, in the course of the nineteenth century, set stiffer and stiffer requirements.

Indians began to sit for the bar in England after the establishment of the High Courts in Calcutta, Bombay, and Madras in 1862. In order to practise on the original side of the High Court, it was necessary to be called to the bar in England, and this gave an Indian lawyer greater scope and prestige. To be called to the bar, it was necessary to pass the examinations, and to be in residence for twelve terms, or the better part of three years. The terms were Michaelmas in the fall, Hilary in the winter, Easter and Trinity in the spring. An Indian vakil, if he had been enrolled in a high court in India (Sarat had been enrolled in Calcutta) and if he read for a year in a barrister's chambers in London, was granted a dispensation of four terms. Lectures were optional as was working in the chambers of an established barrister. If the candidate was able to pass the final examination with honors, he could get an additional dispensation of two terms.[56] Sarat attended the lectures quite studiously, worked in a barrister's chambers, and put in long hours of careful preparation for his examinations, but did not pass with honors and had to stay in England almost two years, from 1912 to 1914.

Sarat Bose's first home in London was in Bayswater, on the north side of beautiful Hyde Park, an area then and now heavily populated by foreign residents and visitors. Later he rented rooms with a friend, Anil Basu, at 86 South Hill Park, Hampstead, near the large, picturesque park overlooking London called Hampstead Heath. They provided for their own meals and also took their required dinners at Lincoln's Inn. Sarat loved to eat, liked the European way of serving and eating food, and relished his dinners at the Inn, though with some limitations. He kept to his promise to his mother never to drink alcohol or to eat beef or pork. It is likely that he adhered to this vow throughout his life. He became a skillful critic of Western food, priding himself on his taste in soups and puddings. He regularly wore Western dress, ordinary suits and a black morning coat when required. His taste ran to Saville Row suits. In those spheres of life where he adopted European customs, he wanted the best that he could find and afford. He shaved his mustache because the sahibs did, and gradually, after much hesitation, took up smoking.[57] He wrote to his wife on February 12, 1914:

> I know smoking is not good. Why should I say it is good? Many pressed me to smoke. But I at first did not. Now when offered, I take it. . . . I should like to ask you, if I take cheroot (cigars), will you mind?[58]

He tested some other European customs and attended the theater. It was not common for members of his family to go to the theater in those days—it might be thought fast or frivolos—but Sarat found that he enjoyed it immensely:

> Maybe you will think I am just after merriment. I went because the others went, but I am glad I went. What scenes! What acting! In our country, no one will dream that such things can take place. I think that people who come here should go to the theatre. One can learn many things. But don't think I will go too much. If you go too much, then it gets to be a habit and I won't do that. I have been only 4 times, while others have gone 40 times.[59]

Sarat felt that he had to report on his relaxations and the threats of European corruption. He said that some of his fellow Indians gave in easily to wine, women, beef, and the theater, but he was selective in cautiously testing European ways. He met European women upon occasion and a Mrs Webb, a Theosophist, mothered him, fed him, and even wrote charming notes to his wife. At one of these teas, he met a Miss Bigelow with whom he had great satisfaction in speaking, especially when she complimented him on his perfect English. He thought this the grandest praise he received during his European visit.[60]

These visits to English women and his London days stimulated him to a brief reflection on love in Western society and in Bengal. He wrote to Biva, August 15, 1913,

> For a Bengali woman, she must love her husband. It is her duty. So the value of that love is less. But here, if a woman loves a man and marries a man that love is more valuable. Love of a woman of good character is more praiseworthy than love of a woman of good character in our country because she has liberty here and must have strength of character. The men here live correct lives, but when our boys come here they become libertines, so don't you think they are more praiseworthy?[61]

Sarat Bose did not become a libertine and in time he came to earn and treasure his wife's love. But like many young Indians who came to Europe—the poet Rabindranath Tagore is another example—he was impressed with the strength and positive qualities of Western women.[62] This, however, did not make him less appreciative and attached to those two women at home who meant most to him, his wife and his mother.

As the first member of his family to cross the *kalapani*, the great black waters between India and Europe, Sarat frequently expressed his ties to loved ones at home in his letters. He wrote to his wife that he thought that his mother must be suffering all the time he was away. In one letter he told of a dream in which he had his head in his mother's lap. He yearned for this maternal tenderness and also remembered that his mother had been the family disciplinarian.[63] His studies for the bar demanded much of him and the self-control and ordering of his life had to come from within; his parents were no longer on hand to provide it.

His letters also express his strong attachment to his young wife and baby

son. He demanded that his wife write to him from time to time in English
and corrected each of her mistakes in usage. He saw himself as the guide
and teacher of his wife, particularly in the great world of Western culture.
A very happy moment for him came when his mother wrote him a letter
praising his wife.[64] But a conflict involving his wife was the event back
home that aroused his greatest anger during these years. Sarat wanted his
wife constantly in Bhowanipore taking care of his parents whenever they
were there. Her parents wanted her to stay with them at times in College
Street. He reminded her of an aphorism that a Bengali son says to his
mother at the time of marriage: 'I am bringing a *dasi* (slave) for you.'[65] He
said that in his family the daughter-in-law was expected to remain almost
all the time with her in-laws. But, he wrote,

> Your family has the habit of sending the daughter and then calling her back
> a few days later. I don't like that. You don't stay in Bhowanipore at all. I felt
> hurt by that. Tears came to my eyes. Now I have frankly told you
> everything.[66]

This tempest was eventually resolved. One consolation for him in all
matters was his religious view of the world. At the top of each letter home,
he wrote, *Sri Sri Iswar sehai* (God is my help). He told his wife that he
was in God's hands in each step he took through life. God had taken him
across to Europe and God would get him through the examination. Even
when he failed the final exam the first time he took it, he thought this also
God's will, though he said it hurt deeply and kept him separated from his
family for an additional four months. Hard work was necessary, but God's
help was vital in successful action.[67]

Sarat Bose tried to study hard most of the time, apprenticed in the
chambers of a barrister, heard cases in the courts and debates in the House
of Commons and House of Lords, but he was apprehensive of the results
of his efforts; he also had a typical student problem, difficulty in concentrating. He wrote to Biva: 'After all, I am human.'[68] A high point in his
studies was writing an excellent optional paper on criminal law, winning
a small prize, and getting a compliment from Professor Odgers, one of his
lecturers: 'You have written the criminal law paper very well.'[69] The low
point was his failure in the final examination which required him to take
the examination again.[70]

Part One of the examinations set by the Council of Legal Education
consisted of four sections: Roman Law; Constitutional Law (English and
Colonial) and Legal History; Criminal Law and Procedure; and a choice
between Hindu and Mahomedan Law or Roman-Dutch Law or Real
Property and Conveyancing. Sarat chose Hindu and Mahomedan Law in
Section Four in which there were questions on marriage and inheritance

and gifts. In Roman Law students might be asked to explain the characteristic features of Roman civil procedure at different periods of Roman history. Two of the questions from his constitutional law exam were : 1. Give an account of the works of Glanville and Bracton, and of their importance in English legal history, and 2. Give an account of the varieties of Second Chambers to be found in the Self-Governing Dominions. Sarat passed this examination early on in his studies.[71]

Part Two, the final examination, consisted of four sections: Common Law; Equity; the Law of Evidence and Civil Procedure; and a general paper on the subjects of the first three parts. He took this exam first in the Hilary term, December 15–18, 1913. There were questions on contracts for the sale of goods, leases, compensation for damages, legacies and trusts, building covenants, mortgages, on admissible evidence, and on the problem of a wife giving evidence against her husband. Sarat was very eager to pass this exam, but this intense desire may have contributed to his overstudying and his growing anxiety.[72]

Up to this point he had resisted a device used by many other students at the Inns, employing a crammer, a barrister who would coach one for the examination. Now, in the winter and spring of 1914, he decided that he could use the help. This decision was a good one. He took the exam again in the Trinity term, May 1914, and came out tied for second in Class II. Out of 109 called to the bar that term from the four Inns of Court, he was tied for the twelfth position. Of his Indian contemporaries, K.P. Khaitan, Ranjit Pandit, and Bisheshwari Prasad finished in Class I. Khaitan, a Marwari, was the first of his community to go to England to sit for the bar and after establishing a good practice in Calcutta, became standing counsel to the Government of India in the 1940s. Ranjit Pandit also practised in Calcutta for some time, then married Vijayalakshmi Nehru, and moved to Lucknow.[73]

After taking the final examination the second time, Sarat visited Oxford in early June 1914. He wrote to Biva,

> Maybe instead of being a barrister, I should have stayed 3 or 4 years—that would have been better. Instead of studying properly, I have just memorized a few law books and am going home. It is a waste of time. I did not realize this when I came. . . . In this life I could not really go in for learning. Let us see if I can do it in the next life.[74]

But he had been channeled into the barrister course and he was, as time was to amply demonstrate, well-suited to this profession. He was following the model of his father by moving into the legal profession and going beyond him in studying in England and being successfully called to the bar. Among the thoughts about his future life which he expressed to Biva at that time were these:

I don't know if I can earn as much as I would like to spend. If I earn a lot, well and good; if not, I don't care. I would prefer peace of mind to a lot of money. Whatever little I earn, I would like to spend for all. That is my wish. My father is helping the poor. I want to keep up that work, but I know we will not be able to do that. I don't want to be like the people of Calcutta. They are very selfish, especially the barristers.[75]

He was soon to join the ranks of the Calcutta barristers and make his mark, but first he did a little more touring. He had been to the famous places of London including the British Museum, the Houses of Parliament, and Westminster Abbey. Between terms he had visited Bournemouth, Windsor Castle, Eton and finally, Oxford. He was an enthusiastic tourist when he had the opportunity. En route home he stayed four or five days in Paris and met the famous Irishwoman Maud Gonne MacBride. Both Boses, like many Indians, had intense sympathies with the Irish struggle for independence from the British Empire. Then Sarat went to Lucerne, Milan, and finally to Trieste where he boarded a ship for home.[76]

It had been an eventful and testing two years for him. He had overcome his anxieties and done well enough. But more than merely memorizing a few books to pass an examination, Sarat had been shaped into a true believer in English liberties. The justice and fairness of the British system of law, liberty, and politics as it existed in theory and should work in practice, not only in Great Britain, but in India under British rule, was a theme of his later life. In the Bengal Legislative Council, and Assembly, in the Calcutta Corporation, in politics, and in private correspondence, Sarat argued that the British must live up to their ideals and that full legal rights (e.g., *habeas corpus*) of citizens must not be abridged. He shared the idea of one of his favorite authors of this period, Walter Bagehot, whose *The English Constitution* had been published at the height of the Victorian period, that the British system of law and individual liberty was something very special among the creations of the people of the world. It was to be understood, treasured, and utilized for the benefit of all the citizens of the British Empire, regardless of color or nationality.[77]

Although Sarat does not seem to have been a political man in these years, he must have seen that Indians could understand and work a just legal system and a political system as well as their rulers. He had been to the capital of British democracy and had a living experience of it and through the remainder of his life he was to work at the law and at politics, having the lessons of English law and English democracy always with him.

Few of Sarat's books of this period survive—only Bagehot's *English Constitution* and Francis Wellman's *Art of Cross-Examination*. In a marginal note next to a passage on the House of Commons in the former book, he wrote, 'The House of Commons makes the English people hear, what otherwise they would not.'[78] His interest in the value of legislative bodies—in several of which he later served with distinction—dates from this period. The year he went abroad, 1912, also happened to be the year in which his father served in the Bengal Legislative Council. It is also likely that he began reading the writings of Bernard Shaw and H.G. Wells in these years. The prospective of the Fabian Left seemed congenial to Sarat as the outlook of the Gladstonian Liberals was to his father.[79]

Sarat returned to Calcutta in the summer of 1914 and did not go abroad again until the very last years of his life. Britain became for him a country of the mind. He continued to hold to British ideals, to enjoy British literature, and, eventually, to oppose the representatives of the British Raj who ruled India.

Upon his return, he enrolled at the Calcutta High Court Bar and joined the chambers of Sir Nripendra Nath Sircar, a distinguished barrister, who became his mentor and friend. This connection helped him to rise without the great struggle that some other young lawyers had.[80]

Sarat Bose worked very hard at perfecting his legal skills and followed his father in renown for his mastery of cross-examination. Though he had often complained while in England of his inability to concentrate, as an adult, his great powers of concentration, discipline, intelligence, and remarkable memory were conspicuous assets in building his practice and reputation. One of his juniors later wrote of him that '. . . even work to him was an expression of life itself and not merely the means of earning subsistence.'[81] He was never a slave to financial success and did not turn away poor litigants. He worked in both the civil and criminal fields and soon—by the 1920s—was in great demand. He was ambitious, a perfectionist, and combative. But he was not greedy and he knew how to work within the rules and customs of the bar. He had, in time, many European as well as Indian friends at the bar. P.B. Mukherjee, the junior of Sarat's mentioned above, described him as self-assertive and yet unselfish, cheerful and a devoted friend, but with a power of satire and ridicule that did not endear him to every opponent. From the unsure young man sitting for the bar in London, he became known as 'Bose-Sahib', one of the proud and able leaders among the Indians at the Calcutta High Court Bar. 'Bose-Sahib' indicated a certain formality in personal style as well as Westernization. As his income increased, he did contribute handsomely to charities and to helping poor students.[82]

A more Indian world for him was his own family. With many of his siblings living at 38/2 Elgin Road and the birth of many children, more space was required. For a time a house next door at 38/1 Elgin Road was rented. When the house at 38/2 was in full use there were perhaps thirty or more Boses and eighteen servants, including three cooks, several drivers, and other servants and maid-servants. At lunch they sat on the floor and had Bengali food. At dinner they had Western food and sat at a dining table. Sarat taught many, including his children, to eat in the Western way, i.e., sitting at the table and using silverware.

The years following Sarat's return to India saw the birth of his and Biva's other seven children: Amiyanath, 1915; Meera, 1917; Sisir Kumar, 1920; Gita, 1922; Roma, 1928; Chitra, 1930; and Subrata, 1932. Biva also became close to one of Sarat's younger siblings of whom he had been especially fond and to whom he formed a special tie from an early age. This was Subhas.[83]

CHAPTER TWO

Subhas Bose: Good Boy and Mischief-Maker[1]

The prospect of the young is forward and unbounded, mingling the future with the present.

Henry David Thoreau, *A Week on the Concord and Merrimack Rivers* [2]

When Subhas sat down at about the age of forty to write an account of his earlier years, he decided to call it *An Indian Pilgrim.* He did not explain why he chose to describe himself as a pilgrim, but he was connecting his own life course with the ancient Indian traditions of searching or questing for truth and fulfillment.[3] The pilgrim may lead a lonely life, but he may also serve as path-breaker for others in reaching for the far shore of freedom. He may be someone who connects the human and divine, a person with a special mission given to him—to lead, to teach, to raise, to show the way.[4] Many years earlier, at eighteen, Subhas had written to his closest friend from Darjeeling:

> If one wants to lead an extremely individualistic life, there is nothing more satisfying than the life of a wandering pilgrim. I feel like crossing the mountains to Sikkim and Nepal. There is a road to Tibet also . . . But, in the current age the life of a wandering pilgrim is not for the youth of Bengal. He has very onerous duties to shoulder.[5]

How did Subhas come to take certain duties upon himself and, yet, become a pilgrim too, a pilgrim who worked at the politics of freedom within his society?

In *An Indian Pilgrim*, Subhas mentioned repeatedly that as a child he felt small and insignificant.[6] Western students of birth order (though they have not studied non-Western families) suggest that 'later middles' in large families use the older siblings as models and constantly strive to catch up. Whereas the older children are more conformist and conservative and more like the parents, the younger ones demonstrate more freedom and variety and conform less to authority. The younger ones are more human-oriented as contrasted to the task-oriented older siblings. The older children have more power in the family. As time passes, the younger siblings gain more power outside the family.[7]

These investigators agree: what is important is how one experiences one's place in the family.[8] Subhas, the sixth son and ninth child, felt insignificant, he said, for a lengthy period in childhood, especially distant from his father, who was reserved and had many outside responsibilities. He felt somewhat closer to his mother and did try to confide in her.[9] His experience in his first school, the Protestant European School run by the Baptist Mission in Cuttack, also contributed to his early feelings that he was not special. This school, populated by European children and some Indians, was an English-medium school in which Indian languages were not taught. To the children in this school, the family of Janaki Nath Bose could not be of the highest status because such ranks were reserved for Europeans.[10]

Subhas entered school at five eagerly since he had hated being left behind when all his elder male siblings were out busy at school. For six years he attended the school headed by Reverend Young and staffed by Anglo-Indian (as Europeans in India were known in those days) teachers. Good manners, discipline, and correct English were demanded. The English stress on games was present, but Subhas often begged off this part of school life. Sometimes at home, however, he and some of his young siblings and other relatives who crowded the Bose house did play their own games. Subhas' ideal of those days was (according to a schoolmate), Sir B.C. Mitter, the Anglicized advocate general of Bengal. There is no denying that Subhas learned English very well, could be a disciplined and excellent student when he wanted to, and internalized some of the values of the ideal Englishman. He also became better acquainted with the history and geography of the British Isles than of India.[11]

But, as he wrote in his autobiography, he lived in two worlds. At home Bengali was spoken—his mother only spoke Bengali and she was in charge of the household—and Subhas was initiated into the religion, literature, myths, and folklore of his own Indian society. He heard stories from the Indian epics, the *Mahabharata* and the *Ramayana,* as well as Bengali songs, mainly religious. Like the other Boses, he liked music and singing. Although both his parents were religious, his father was more influenced by the currents of religious reformation, mainly the Brahmo Samaj teachings of Keshub Sen, while his mother was devoted to Durga and Kali in the more traditional fashion. Sarat followed his mother more exactly. Although Subhas learned from his mother and took her as a kind of religious counsellor and general guide, he began searching for himself.[12]

From his early years Subhas displayed a nurturing side to his personality. He took a great interest in raising plants and working in the garden when other boys were at play. As he entered his teens, he began to find situations in which he had to nurse others, often poor people who were generally neglected in their distress. He wanted to be his mother's son and fill any special role or calling she set for him, and he also developed a mothering, nurturing part of himself.[13]

In 1909 the twelve-year-old Subhas shifted—as his brothers before him had—to the Ravenshaw Collegiate School where he spent the next four years and completed his secondary education. This was a much more Indian school in which Bengali and Sanskrit were taught and it was shaped anew during his first year by a soul-stirring headmaster, Beni Madhab Das. The new school, new peers, and the new schoolmaster had a powerful impact on Subhas. Although his fine English and his high family status counted for more, he was ridiculed for his mediocre knowledge of Bengali. He vowed to learn it well and, in time, came to the top of his class.[14]

But even more important were the cultural, religious, and political currents of the late nineteenth century and early twentieth century with which Beni Madhab Das brought him in touch. In his own household, Subhas wrote, politics was a tabooed subject.[15] To his new mentor at the Ravenshaw School, however, the forces of cultural revivalism and nationalism which were beginning to percolate through wider and wider circles in India were a vital and necessary part of life for the teenagers under his wing. He taught them even more about the religious traditions of India, the Vedas, epics, and Upanishads, than they had learned at home. Subhas was particularly receptive. He changed to Bengali dress and felt more in touch with his own society, less torn between two worlds. He continued his European education throughout his life, but became less attracted to Anglicized ways than his father or brother Sarat and began to make his own synthesis of the cultures of the West and India.[16] This became fully articulated when he reached adulthood.

The modern formulations of Hinduism by Sri Ramakrishna and his disciple Swami Vivekananda were central to Subhas' synthesis. Ramakrishna (1836–1886), a Brahmin priest of a temple up the Hooghly River from Calcutta at Dakshineswar, asserted that all the world religions offered viable paths to Oneness with the Divine. Since all routes 'worked', it was best to choose the closest and most familiar path, one's native religion. Persuading through the use of earthy parables (many of which were written down for the illiterate Ramakrishna by a disciple, 'M') and the spiritual example of his own life, Ramakrishna won many Hindus back to their own religion from flirtations with Christianity and 'Westernized' Hinduism.[17] After his death, his disciple Narendranath Dutt (1863–1902), known to the world as Swami Vivekananda, put the teachings of his Master in terms even more appealing to Westernized Indians and preached his gospel from Colombo to Almora and in the West as well. Vivekananda said that the West was spiritually backward and that the whole world needed India's religious message. At the same time, India lagged in material culture and needed some of the West's vitality, skill in coordination, self-confidence, and strength. He demanded that his listeners utilize the powers within themselves (their *shakti*) to build their country.[18]

Many of Subhas' early letters to his mother and to friends echo the vision and teachings of Vivekananda who decried the fallen state of India, praised her essential religiosity, and propounded the need for selfless service to the Motherland. Subhas wrote in 1913 to his mother,

> What was India and what is she now? . . . . Where are those saints, those sages, those philosophers—our forefathers who had explored the farthest limits of the realm of knowledge? Where is their fiery personality? What is their strict Brahmacharya? . . . . All is gone! . . . . But there is hope yet—I think there is hope yet—the angel of hope has appeared in our midst to put fire in our souls and to shake off our dull sloth. It is the saintly Vivekananda. There stands he, with his angelic appearance, his large and piercing eyes and his sacred dress to preach to the whole world, the sacred truths lying embedded in Hinduism![19]

Through his mid-teens, Subhas Bose was engrossed in a search for a goal or goals in life and for the best path for himself, and his mother served as one of his sounding boards while Swami Vivekananda was one of the main guides. Letters remain to document his search and his reaching out to his mother. In one, undated, but in the 1912–13 period he wrote to her:

> Will the condition of our country continue to go from bad to worse—will not any son of Mother India in distress, in total disregard of his selfish interests, dedicate his whole life to the cause of the Mother? . . . A life in the service of others is the only one worth living. Mother, do you know why I am writing all this to you? To whom else can I talk? Who will listen to me? Who else will take all this seriously? Those whose lives are motivated only by selfish considerations, cannot afford to think on such lines—will not think on such lines—lest their self-interest be impaired. But, a mother's life is not motivated by selfish considerations. Her life is dedicated to her children—to the country. If you read the history of India, you will see that so many mothers have lived for the sake of Mother India and have, when the need arose, sacrificed their lives for her. Think of Ahalya Bai, Meera Bai, Durga Bati—there are so many—I cannot remember all their names. We are reared on mother's milk—there, nothing can be more educative and elevating than

what instruction and guidance we get from the mother. . . . I pray I may
continue all my life in the service of others.[20]

In these reflective, rambling letters, Subhas runs together the Motherland
and his own mother and expresses his own powerful attachments to both.
Bound in here, too, is his religious devotion to his favored divinity, the
Mother Goddess in the form of Durga or Kali. Subhas is picking up the
themes in the implicit teachings of the Bengali novelist Bankim Chandra
Chatterjee (1838–1894) in his novel, *Ananda Math*—read by all young
Bengalis of those days—where Indian sons rally to their fallen Motherland's cause and devote themselves to her service. Though he still had
many twists and turns to make, Subhas had found what he was looking for:
the goal was to be his Motherland's freedom and revival; his activity was
to be selfless action for this end. Sometimes the actions were for the poor
and distressed as in famine relief or medical aid, but in time, his major
effort was in political work to free India at the soonest possible time—by
any means necessary—from British rule. The emphasis in the early letters
is on Indians' responsibility for their own fallen condition. These were still
pre-political days and his vision was a cultural and religious one, but the
sense of a mission of life was awakening.[21]

From about the age of fourteen, Subhas was troubled by strong sexual
desires and concerned to suppress them. Writing in his autobiography—
when he was well-acquainted with the writings of Freud (he read *The
Interpretation of Dreams* twice in the 1930s)—he described the struggle:

> The burden of Ramakrishna's precepts was—renounce lust and gold. This
> two-fold renunciation was for him the test of a man's fitness for spiritual life.
> The complete conquest of lust involved the sublimation of the sex-instinct,
> whereby to a man every woman would appear as mother. . . . Ramakrishna's
> example of renunciation and purity entailed a battle royal with all the forces
> of the lower self. And Vivekananda's ideal brought me into conflict with the
> existing family and social order. I was weak, the fight was a long-drawn one
> in which success was not easy to obtain, hence tension and unhappiness with
> occasional fits of depression.[22]

For Subhas, sexual desires were to be transformed and transcended and the
energies were to be used elsewhere; woman was not to be the object of
sexual desire. He assumes—in a pre-Freudian manner—that a child's
attachment to his mother is asexual. Subhas does not appear unconcerned
with sexual desire nor above it; indeed, it appears he was often in danger
of succumbing. Consciously, he did try to become a brahmacharya.

At the same time he asked his mother to tell him what she wanted him
to be, he informed her of his search and its fulfillment. He now also began
to look outside his family. Writing in retrospect, he described this period
of his life:

I was soon able to get together a group of friends who became interested in Ramakrishna and Vivekananda. At school and outside, whenever we had a chance, we would talk of nothing else but this topic. Gradually we took to long walks and excursions. . . . At home and abroad we began to attract attention. . . . My parents noticed before long that I was going out frequently in the company·of other boys. I was questioned, warned in a friendly manner, and ultimately rebuked. But all to no purpose. I was rapidly changing and was no longer the goody-goody boy afraid of displeasing his parents. I had a new ideal before me now which had inflamed my soul— to effect my own salvation and to serve humanity by abandoning all worldly desires and breaking away from all undue restraints. I no longer recited Sanskrit verses inculcating obedience to one's parents; on the contrary, I took to verses which preached defiance. . . . The more my parents endeavoured to restrain me, the more rebellious I became. When all other attempts failed, my mother took to tears. But even that had no effect on me. I was becoming callous, perhaps eccentric, and more determined to go my own way, though all the time I was feeling inwardly unhappy. To defy my parents in this way was contrary to my nature and to cause them pain was disagreeable, but I was swept onwards as by an irresistible current. There was very little appreciation or understanding at home of what I was dreaming at the time, and that added to my misery. The only solace was to be found in the company of friends and I began to feel more at home when away from home.[23]

In this and all subsequent rebellions, Subhas stated that there was a larger goal, whether a transcendent religious aim, a cultural ideal, or a political objective. In the revolt of the fifteen to sixteen-year-old Subhas, he challenged the restraints placed· upon him by his parents. He felt powerful guilt when he went against their wishes, but said he was driven by an 'irresistible current'.[24] He wanted their love and understanding and the lengthy letters to his mother and the rebellions themselves may be seen as a reaching out to them. His feeling of smallness and insignificance with respect to his parents was mentioned earlier. The rebellion brought attention, tears, efforts at understanding and reconciliation. These early episodes seem to have pulled Subhas further from his parents, made him as he said, 'the despair of his parents', but also made him more important to them, shown them the need to give him more attention, and effected a partial reconciliation.[25]

Along with his school chums in Cuttack, a new young man, perhaps a year older than Subhas, now entered his life and became his closest friend and favorite confidant from 1912 to 1919. This was Hemanta Kumar Sarkar. Up to this time, Subhas' group was in the Cuttack area, but Hemanta was a member of a Calcutta group '. . . which had as its ideal—

spiritual uplift and national service along constructive lines.' It was headed by a medical student, Suresh Banerjee, later active in the national movement.[26]

At this time, Subhas was just finishing at the Ravenshaw School in 1912 and took the matriculation examination under the umbrella of Calcutta University. Of all the students taking the exam, Subhas finished second, a remarkable result for a young man caught up in spiritual distractions which 'had inflamed (his) soul.'[27] Subhas showed on this occasion and at later examinations that he was a superb student and exam-taker. He was a competitive person and usually studied more than he allowed others to know. He was not afraid of competition and it gave him—one of the smaller boys in his large family—an opportunity to shine, to show that he was somebody to be reckoned with. Sarat also was a competitive person and formidable in verbal debate, but Subhas was the superior test-taker, more adept under the stressful conditions of this situation.[28]

After school, Subhas was ready for Calcutta. His family had its establishment at Elgin Road, he had already made contact with the Suresh Banerjee group through Hemanta, and his high standing in the matriculation exam had given him something of a name among the students entering college.[29] Like his brothers before him, he entered Presidency College beginning the arts course in 1913. Calcutta was the center of the Bengalis' world and in the generation of Subhas and his brothers, the Bose family was at the hub of Bengali activity, no longer occasional participants from the periphery. Subhas wrote of his association to the city:

> This was not my first visit to Calcutta. I had been there several times since my infancy, but every time this great city had intrigued me, bewildered me beyond measure. I had loved to roam about its wide streets and among its gardens and museums and I had felt that one could not see enough of it. It was like a leviathan which one could look at from outside and go on admiring unceasingly. But this time I came to settle down there and to mix with its inner life.[30]

Subhas chose philosophy as his major subject of study and applied himself to its questions, on and off, through the following seven years at different institutions. He wanted to solve, he said, 'the fundamental problems of life', and his readings of systematic philosophy included Kant, Hegel, Bergson, and other Western thinkers. Some reading in Indian philosophy began here.[31]

Janaki Nath Bose's sons moved to Calcutta in the decade starting in 1905, the very years in which the Swadeshi movement grew and then sputtered to a halt (1905–1908) and the time in which revolutionary terrorism began in Bengal. This political activity impinged on the lives of many, especially the urban youth, but Subhas was much more sensitive to these influences than his siblings.[32]

The Swadeshi movement was the result of long-term cultural, political, and economic forces, and of the short-term actions of the British Raj under the viceroyalty of Lord Curzon (1899–1905). The long-term trends were pressures for increased Indian participation in the life and running of their own society, polity, and economy. These pressures had been gathering slowly during the last quarter of the nineteenth century and one manifestation was the formation of the Indian National Congress as a national and enduring forum for the expression of Indian opinion.

The Congress was a moderate and loyalist body during its first twenty years and was dominated by lawyers, other professionals, and some businessmen and landholders from the three most modern urban centers under the Raj: Bombay, Calcutta, and Madras. Although it had a national executive body which did some light lobbying throughout the year, its main activity was an annual three-day gathering passing resolutions demanding greater Indian participation in the public life of British India. The small elite of Indian leaders running the Congress were generally in tune with British liberal ideas, but wanted them applied to India, and some envisioned eventual Indian self-rule within the British Empire. They were willing to move slowly to persuade their rulers by constitutional methods and gentlemanly lobbying that Indians should be accorded a greater share in ruling their own country. They felt that gains in national unification and Western education had been made by India under British rule, but they wanted a much larger role for men like themselves, the enlightened, Western-educated elite.[33]

During the last quarter of the nineteenth century, other voices began to be raised, usually in the background, often individual, critical of the British Raj and of the Moderate leaders. These voices, among them those of B.G. Tilak in Maharashtra and Aurobindo Ghose, called for a rapid end to British rule, and suggested directly or indirectly that unconstitutional means, non-violent and perhaps even violent, might have to be used to achieve this goal. Tilak was imprisoned in the 1890s for allegedly encouraging violent acts against British officials, several of whom were murdered by the Chapekar brothers in Tilak's home city of Poona.[34]

Tilak became a national leader of the minority Extremist group within the Congress and one of his supporters was young Aurobindo Ghose who became one of the ablest Swadeshi publicists, a secret plotter of revolutionary violence, and the political hero of Subhas Bose's teenage years.

Aurobindo, born in 1872, was taken when only a boy of seven with his brothers from Bengal to Britain by his parents. For the next fourteen years he grew, studied, and suffered in loneliness and poverty away from his parents who had decided upon a European education for their sons. Aurobindo proved to be a brilliant classical scholar at St Paul's School and then at Cambridge. He passed the written section of the Indian Civil Service (ICS) examination, but failed to appear for the riding test and returned to India. He joined the service of the Gaekwar of Baroda and began his political writing with two series of articles in 1893, one, 'New Lamps for Old,' on the failures of the Congress Moderates, the other on the Bengali novelist Bankim Chandra Chatterjee, whom he hailed as an immense cultural figure and a prophet of the New India. From western India, with the help of his younger brother Barindra Kumar Ghose, Aurobindo began to make connections with potential revolutionaries in Bengal in the early 1900s. At the same time he was working in Baroda and forging contacts, he was also studying Indian philosophy and religion and beginning to practise yoga.[35]

The political and administrative decision by the Government of India under Lord Curzon to realign provincial boundaries in eastern India and to divide the Bengali-speaking region into two new provinces was the spark that set off the powder keg of anti-government sentiment in Bengal. The protests against this administrative fiat welled into a popular movement (the Swadeshi, or 'own' country movement). A boycott of British goods showed some effectiveness for a few months and protest meetings and plans for Indian educational, cultural, economic, and political activities to circumvent the Raj spread to some rural areas of Bengal and to some other parts of India.[36]

Aurobindo chose this moment to return to Calcutta and threw himself into the political maelstrom for the next five years. He worked in the national education movement trying to develop an alternative higher education system to the government-backed one, joined the Congress in an effort to wrest control from the Moderates, wrote elegant and passionate political articles in the English-language, Indian-owned press, and, secretly, helped to plot acts of violence against British officials. He was careful to distance himself from actual violent deeds and though Barin Ghose, his younger brother, was arrested and convicted for revolutionary activity, Aurobindo spent only one year in prison awaiting trial.[37]

Aurobindo's most coherent political statement was a series of articles entitled 'The Doctrine of Passive Resistance'. He argued that the immediate need was for political independence and that this had to precede the reconstruction of battered and exploited India. In part, he wrote:

> We recognize no political object except the divinity in our Motherland, no present object of political endeavour except liberty, and no method of action

as political good or evil except as it truly helps or hinders our progress towards national emancipation.... The circumstances of the country and the nature of the despotism from which it seeks to escape must determine what form of resistance is best justified and most likely to be effective at the time or finally successful. . . . The present circumstances in India seem to point to passive resistance as our most natural and suitable weapon. We would not for a moment be understood to base this conclusion upon any condemnation of other methods as in all circumstances criminal and unjustifiable. . . . Under certain circumstances a civil struggle becomes in reality a battle and the morality of war is different from the morality of peace. To shrink from bloodshed and violence under such circumstances is a weakness deserving as severe a rebuke as Sri Krishna addressed to Arjuna when he shrank from the colossal civil slaughter on the field of Kurukshetra.[38]

Aurobindo mentioned three kinds of resistance to oppression: armed revolt, aggressive resistance short of armed revolt, and defensive resistance, whether passive or active. Though publicly he argued for passive resistance, privately he planned and encouraged acts of violence which were pointed, in the long term, towards armed revolt to take place when Indians were fully prepared. In the present he wanted total boycott of British institutions and the withdrawal of Indian cooperation in any sphere of life with the British Raj.[39]

Unlike the conciliatory Moderates, Aurobindo and others in the Extremist party within the Congress (and outside) openly expressed aggressive instincts and feelings of hatred towards their rulers. They were often younger and less established than those of the Moderate party and less ready to admit to any positive British achievement in India. They denied that Indians needed any additional tutelage from their rulers before they would be ready for self-rule.

The Extremists also mingled the religious and the secular. Aurobindo saw the awakening of India as part of a divine plan and said that God was calling him to help liberate his country. He believed also, as had some of the cultural revivalists of the nineteenth century, that India had a special spiritual mission to fulfill in the world. Aurobindo acted upon the political stage of Bengal until 1910 when he said that God had sent him a new message to retreat from active politics and work for the spiritual upliftment of India and of mankind. So he journeyed to Pondicherry in French India, and established a religious community or ashram from which he did not emerge during the remaining forty years of his life. He wrote extensively on religion and even touched upon political matters, but his main concerns had shifted from day-to-day nationalist ones to more eternal and spiritual ones.[40]

By 1913 the Extremist group had left the scene—to prison, to voluntary exile, or to other political views. The Congress was left to the Moderates and during the First World War, they maintained their loyalty to the Raj. Sporadic acts of violence and larger plots were undertaken by small bands of revolutionary terrorists, but these were shortly crushed—for the moment at least—by strong repressive measures of the Raj.[41]

Writing in his autobiography, Subhas commented,

> In my undergraduate days Aurobindo Ghose was easily the most popular leader in Bengal, despite his voluntary exile and absence since 1909. . . . He had sacrificed a lucrative career in order to devote himself to politics. On the Congress platform he had stood up as a champion of left-wing thought and a fearless advocate of independence. . . . His close association with Lokamanya B.G. Tilak had given him an All-India popularity, while rumour and official allegation had given him an added prestige in the eyes of the younger generation by connecting him with his younger brother, Barindra Kumar Ghose, admittedly the pioneer of the terrorist movement. Last but not least, a mixture of spirituality and politics had given him a halo of mysticism and made his personality more fascinating to those who were religiously inclined. . . . In those days it was freely rumoured that Aurobindo had retired to Pondicherry for twelve years' meditation. At the end of that period he would return to active life as an 'enlightened' man, like Gautama Buddha of old, to effect the political salvation of his country. . . . We felt convinced that spiritual enlightenment was necessary for effective national service. . . . I was impressed by his deeper philosophy. . . . He worked out a reconciliation between Spirit and Matter, between God and Creation, on the metaphysical side and supplemented it with a synthesis of the methods of attaining the truth—a synthesis of Yoga, as he called it. . . . Vivekananda had no doubt spoken of the need of Jnana (knowledge), Bhakti (devotion and love) and Karma (selfless action) in developing an all-around character, but there was something original and unique in Aurobindo's conception of a synthesis of Yoga. He tried to show how by a proper use of the different Yogas one could rise step by step to the highest truth. . . . All that was needed in my eyes to make Aurobindo an ideal guru for mankind was his return to active life.[42]

Even before the influence, Subhas had begun meditating and experimenting with different forms of yoga in Cuttack. It was clear he wanted an Indian religious philosophy that would shape, channel, and support action in the world. He found this in the teachings of Vivekananda and Aurobindo. But unlike the two—Vivekananda encouraged activism under divine inspiration but was cautious to deal with political life directly and Aurobindo retreated to an ashram after a few years in politics—Subhas became an activist with a religious side.[43]

However, at the period we speak of, Subhas was still at a stage where the idea of social service appealed more than direct political activity. Through contact with Hemanta Sarkar, he had joined Suresh Banerjee's group upon moving to Calcutta. Although there were political groups among the youth and the revolutionaries used the college campuses and hostels and messes as recruiting grounds for new members, Subhas was not enticed. He had developed a powerful identification with his Indian homeland—especially seen as an impoverished and wretched Mother India—but his commitment was to be fulfilled through social service. When he found the opportunity, he helped to nurse the poor. Upon returning from his first year in college, he wrote (later):

> Once, when my parents were out of town, I was invited to join a party of friends who were going into the interior on a nursing expedition in a locality which was stricken with cholera. There was no medical man in the party. We had only a half-doctor. . . . We were to be the nurses in the party. I readily agreed and took leave of my uncle, who was then doing duty for my father . . . . He did not object, not knowing at the time that I was going out to nurse cholera patients. . . . In those days cholera was regarded as a fatal disease and it was not easy to get people to attend cholera patients. Our party was absolutely fearless in that respect . . . a week's experience opened a new world before my eyes and unfolded a picture of real India, the India of the villages—where poverty stalks over the land, men die like flies, and illiteracy is the prevailing order.[44]

Subhas was beginning his discovery of India. This exploration of one's own country and awakening of concern and conscience was the theme of Rabindranath Tagore's famous novel *Gora* published just a few years earlier and is a common experience recounted in the memoirs of many of India's twentieth century leaders.

Subhas and his Calcutta friends also made a trip to Plassey and Murshidabad, scenes of crucial events in Bengal's past at the time of the British conquest. Again, they were touching upon a theme of Tagore's writings: Indians must stop accepting the European version of the Indian past. They must search through the documents and artifacts of the past and construct their own ideas about Indian culture, traditions, and society, as a step in the reconstruction of India.[45]

During college vacations and even term-time, Subhas regularly made brief forays away from his homes in Calcutta or Cuttack. But in the long vacation period of 1914, Hemanta and Subhas disappeared for several months into the religious heartland of northern India in search of spiritual truth and a guru. The trip was carefully charted in advance and Hemanta went off first. If he had promising contacts, he was to summon Subhas to join him. Subhas' letters to Hemanta of that period and also Hemanta's later account of their relationship survive and vividly portray the close and passionate friendship between two sensitive young men.[46] Their feelings for each other mingled with their religious yearnings. In one letter, Subhas blended Hemanta with the god Krishna, put himself in the role of Radha, and declared his undying love for his godly friend. In extravagant rhetoric, Subhas said that he would love Hemanta forever, whatever others thought of his friend.[47] In this world of teenage males, the strongest emotional ties are among themselves: women are distant, abstract, idealized, perhaps dangerous.[48] Mother became the mother of all Indians, not a close, cherishing maternal figure, and young women, if present at all, could only be sisters, never lovers or potential lovers. Subhas had transferred some of his affection from his family to his special friend (and his peer group) and his innermost thoughts and desires and designs for his life were communicated to Hemanta rather than to any other person.[49]

Subhas later described their tour:

> ... the desire to find a guru grew stronger and stronger within me and, in the summer vacation of 1914, I quietly left on a pilgrimage ... Of course, I did not inform anybody at home.... We visited some of the well-known places of pilgrimage in Upper India—Lachman-Jhola, Hrishikesh, Hardwar, Muttra, Brindaban, Benares, Gaya.... At all these places we looked up as many Sadhus as we could and visited several 'Ashrama' as well as educational institutions like Gurukul and Rishikul.... This tour which lasted nearly two months brought us in touch not only with a number of holy men, but also with some of the patent shortcomings of Hindu society, and I returned home a wiser man, having lost much of my admiration for ascetics and anchorites.[50]

Among the lessons Subhas learned was that other Indians, holy men or not, thought Bengalis unclean fish-eaters and young men particularly were suspect as possible revolutionaries. Subhas received a lot of advice— including that he return home and abjure the company of women, even though he was not ready to become a sannyasin—but he did not find the guru he sought. He also contracted typhoid fever and incurred the heartache and ire of his family.[51]

Subhas described his return in a long letter to Hemanta:

> Mother was informed. Half way up I met her. I made *pronams* to her—she could not help weeping on seeing me. Later, she only said, 'It seems you have come into this world to kill me. I would not have waited so long before drowning myself in the Ganges; only for the sake of my daughters have I not done so.' I smiled within myself. Then I met father. After I had made my *pronams*, he embraced me and led me to his room. On the way he broke down and in the room he wept for quite some time holding on to me.... Then he lay down and I massaged his feet—it appeared as if he was feeling some heavenly pleasure. Thereafter both of them went on enquiring at length

where I had been. I told them everything frankly. . .[52]

This was one of the fullest outpourings of pent-up feelings by Subhas'
parents mentioned in any of the documents of his youth. But Subhas
through this period said that he felt quite detached from them and unfeeling
whatever they said or did. He had long discussions with his father about his
ideals for life. Subhas summarized these talks with his usually distant and
busy father who suddenly found time for his would-be-sannyasin son:

> What he wanted to drive at during the discussion was: (1) whether it was
> possible to practise *Dharma* while leading a worldly life, (2) that renuncia-
> tion needs preparation, (3) whether it was right to shirk one's duty. I said in
> reply—(1) Everybody cannot have the same medicine because everybody
> has not got the same disease and the same capacity—(2) Whether or not re-
> nunciation is possible depends on how much cleansing one needs—all may
> not require much in the way of polishing up—(3) Duty is relative—higher
> call may completely supersede lower calls—when Knowledge comes,
> action becomes redundant. . . . He said at the end, 'When your higher call
> comes, we shall see.' I have so far not opposed father actively—passively
> I have won the victory. Now he is unable to force anything upon me. And,
> when I go away next time, he will probably give up the idea and the effort
> to get me back.[53]

Although the reunion brought Subhas closer to his parents, the familial
bonds were strained and continued so for some time. He had gone in search
of a guru, of a wise, male figure (of whom he had some idealized notion)
who would supplant his parents and give him the guidance he sought.
Paradoxically he wanted to win a victory over his parents, but he also
wanted them there when he needed them.[54]

Things gradually quieted down at the Bose's Cuttack house, but not
before many angry words with Subhas and against Hemanta were
exchanged. Subhas was down with typhoid for some time and he and
Hemanta constantly exchanged letters and Hemanta came to visit. Subhas
became particularly enraged with Satish, his *Dada*, who spoke up for the
parental side. Sarat Bose, Subhas' favorite sibling and Janaki's favorite
child, had not yet returned from London and was not available to conciliate
father and son as he was able to do on other occasions. Subhas even
threatened to go off and become a sannyasin, but eventually returned to
Presidency College to resume his studies and his Calcutta life.[55]

With Sarat Bose now his resident guardian, Subhas returned to Calcutta
and threw himself into a range of college and non-college activities. He
became secretary of the debating union, secretary of a famine relief
committee for East Bengal, a member of the staff of the newly started
Presidency College Magazine, and, the following year, the representative
of the third-year Arts' students on the Students' Consultative Committee.[56]

In the course of recruiting prospective debaters, he met a classmate—Dilip Kumar Roy—who became one of his favorite and lifelong friends. Dilip was the son of the famous poet, playwright, and song-writer, Dwijendralal Roy. In a touching and acute memoir, Dilip charmingly recounted how Subhas came to him and insisted that he join the debaters—India needed debaters. Feeling that this was not his line, Dilip said he would listen, but not speak.[57] Dilip knew that his calling was for music, art, literature, and friendship bordering on hero-worship. Through his sense of fun and by the beautiful purity of his singing voice, he could bring forth laughter, tears, and a range of emotions in others. He was also a religious seeker who could tap the mystical strain in others. On and off through the next thirty-five years, Dilip made Subhas laugh with the great heartiness of which he was capable, increased his appreciation of music and literature, and helped him to plumb his spiritual capacities and test his faith in the course of life he chose. Of all the friends of his teenage years, Dilip, strongly devoted to Subhas, was the one who was always there through all the hardships and the delights, the self-doubts and achievements, as well as the fumblings of life.[58]

In the course of trying to persuade Dilip to become a debater, Subhas said,

> What I want is that we all should learn the art of thinking on our feet. Besides, the practice of debating, arguing one's case like an advocate, does initiate one somewhat into the art of self-discipline and self-reliance which must be reckoned a splendid gain. Don't you see how we, Indians, are utterly dependent on others—for action, views, drive—in fact, everything?[59]

Dilip then follows this up in his book with a comment on the Subhas of those days as he saw him:

> ... I have quoted him only to emphasise what a forceful personality he was even in those days, and how precocious, besides. For it must be borne in mind that we were hardly seventeen yet. ... But whenever we, undergraduates, talked with Subhash, we somehow all looked up to him as our senior if not our mentor. He had a native power to lead, and he knew it.[60]

What Dilip also found remarkable in Subhas was that he was never condescending and that he showed an 'aristocratic generosity' that matched his fine features, fair skin, and proud bearing.[61]

While Subhas was recruiting debaters—to be advocates like his father and elder brothers—and spending energies on famine relief collecting, he did not have much time for his studies. He finished in the second class in his intermediate Arts examination—not bad, but not nearly at the level of which he was capable—and entered into the honors course in philosophy. He wrote in a letter to Hemanta at that time,

What is the good of studying philosophy? It is this—that you come to know your own questions, your own doubts. . . . You come to know how so many others have thought about them. You may then organize and properly direct your line of thinking.[62]

The study of philosophy fitted with his religious concerns, and his questioning mood was heightened during trips to the Himalayas.

The mountain spot which drew the Boses as it did many well-to-do Bengalis was Darjeeling. Now renowned for its tea, Darjeeling—'the place of the dorje,' or mystic thunderbolt in Tibetan Buddhism according to one writer—was a hill station favored by officials and wealthy babus in the hot season. It was 7,000 feet above sea level in an area ceded to the British by the Raja of Sikkim in 1835. Darjeeling was constituted as a municipality in 1850 and grew rapidly in the nineteenth century into a summer capital of Bengal and a resort second to none in eastern India.[63] A gazetteer writer in the early twentieth century described the setting:

The spectator in Darjeeling town stands on the stage of a vast amphitheatre of mountains, which in the spring form a continuous snowy barrier extending over 150 degrees of the horizon. . . . In front of him, at a distance of only 45 miles, the great twin peaks of Kanchenjunga tower above the titanic group of snowy mountains . . . (and) completely dominate the landscape. The rising sun sheds a golden radiance on the eastern slopes, which turns to dazzling whiteness as the day wears on. At evening the western flanks catch all the rosy glow of sunset, and as the sun sinks behind the hills the crimson hues fade away only to reappear in a delicate afterglow. At last even this disappears; but if the moon be near the full, its light streams down upon the snows, outlining their contours with an awful purity.[64]

Subhas first accompanied his father to Darjeeling in 1907 and in 1915 came again to Kurseong, a town twenty miles from Darjeeling on the main rail line. Although the Boses visited Darjeeling frequently, Kurseong became their special place in the mountains and Sarat Bose finally bought a house there in 1923 with a commanding view of the hills and plains below. Subhas, Sarat, and other family members returned again and again for respite from what Subhas described as the 'ceaseless and frantic activity and movement, which you see in Calcutta.' It was a place for relaxation, reflection, and brisk walks in the cool mountain air.[65]

More at peace with his family and himself, Subhas wrote to Hemanta in October 1915:

Since coming here I have been well from all points of view. . . . The mountains are most wonderful; I think these slopes are the most fitting abode of the heroic Aryans. One should not live in the degenerate plains . . . . There is no better way of reviving our Aryan blood than to consume meat and scale mountains.

That pure Aryan blood no longer flows in our veins. Slavery of ages—so much of adulteration. . . .

As I wander about the hills, I think of this very often. The sense of power must permeate our entire being. We again have to leap across mountains—it was only when the Aryans did such things that they were able to produce the *Vedas*.

The Hindu race no longer has that pristine freshness—that youthful vigour and those unmatched human qualities. If we want to get them back we must begin from the land of our birth—the sacred Himalayas. If India has something priceless, something noble—something to be proud of—the memory of all that is linked up with the Himalayas. That is why when you are face to face with the Himalayas, such memories come back to your mind . . . . [66]

This recovery was to become a central theme of Subhas' life. A few weeks after the letter on Aryan power and creativity, he wrote to Hemanta in a more off-hand way,

I was sorry to receive your letter as you have showed me up as a mischievous person. You know very well that I have always been a 'good-boy'—am I capable of any naughtiness? So, what is the meaning of this accusation of yours? Can one who has always been a 'good boy' be up to any mischief at any time? So, I cannot be a 'naughty boy' and any mischief on my part is impossible.[67]

However, a severe trial was just around the corner for the 'good boy' who was also a mischief-maker when he returned to Presidency College as an unsuspecting third-year student.

Though a slow trickle of Indians had begun to enter the services of the Raj—Indian Civil Service, Indian Educational Service, *et al.*—the great majority of those in the elite services were still Europeans. So the Indian students of Bengal's premier colleges were taught by men of another and dominant culture. These were the days of the First World War and the pages of the Presidency College Magazine were filled with exclamations of British patriotism, some even written by Indians. M. Ghosh contributed 'A Song of Britannia' to the September 1916 issue singing of 'Britannia . . . the fair . . . the strong . . . the free . . . the sage . . . the good . . . the sublime.' There was an awareness—ripe with hate—of the evil Huns and their wicked (and rival) nationalism, but scarcely a word about the nationalism of the subject Indians.[68]

But Indian nationalism did exist quite strongly. Even the spokesmen of the Education Department of the Government of India felt this force of Indian nationalism at work, though they described it in their own way:

. . . we hold it undeniable that during the last 10 years there has been a ferment amongst students in general, due mainly to what may be called

causes of a political character. . . . This has led in many instances to a
manifest spirit of insubordination and a reluctance to render unquestioning
obedience to rules and orders promulgated by lawful authority.[69]

The writer was correct: the 'manifest spirit of insubordination . . . due
. . . to causes of a political character' dated from the Swadeshi period a
decade earlier and continued its life, no matter what loyalist claims their
elders might make to the Raj, amongst the students of Calcutta.

The sparks that now lighted the short fuse of student nationalist
sensitivities were struck by Mr E.F. Oaten, Professor of History at
Presidency College. In an address to students at the Eden Hindu Hostel in
late 1915, Mr Oaten said, 'As the Greeks had hellenised the barbarian
people with whom they came in contact, so the mission of the English is
to civilise the Indians.'[70] Although the students felt highly insulted at these
remarks, it was not until another run-in between Professor Oaten and some
noisy students in a hallway of the college in early January 1916, that the
students decided to act. He allegedly grabbed one of the boys by the neck
and pushed others. A protest to the principal, Mr James, brought no
satisfaction, so the students called a strike at the college which lasted from
January 10 to 13, 1916. The protest ended with nothing resolved and
tempers continued to simmer. When another run-in between Professor
Oaten and some students took place on February 15, a group of students
including Subhas Bose, as a member of the Students' Consultative
Committee, decided '. . . to take the law in their own hands.' The result was
that Mr Oaten was subjected to the argument of force and in the process
was beaten black and blue. 'From the newspaper office to Government
House. . . there was wild commotion.'[71]

Coming down the broad staircase from the second floor, Oaten was
surrounded by a group of students who beat him with their sandals—and
fled. Although Oaten himself was not able to identify any of the attackers,
a bearer said he saw Subhas Bose and Ananga Dam among those fleeing.
Rumors in student circles also placed Subhas among the group. An
investigation was carried out by the college authorities, and these two were
expelled from the college and rusticated from the university while several
other students were less severely punished. More than a decade later,
Subhas wrote,

> I can still clearly recall the day my Principal had summoned me to his
> presence and told me that I was suspended from the college. His words still
> ring in my ears—'You are the most wicked boy in this college.'[72]

Subhas appealed the sentence and hoped for reinstatement in Presidency
College, or, at least, permission to transfer to another college. He wrote to
Hemanta at that time,

... I have much in my favour. I am well-known as a 'good-student', I am known at least by name in high circles, the vast majority of the public feel that I am innocent, Ashu Babu knows of me personally and the evidence of the orderly against me is much too weak. So, there is every possibility of my being found innocent and let off. At least, I should get a transfer.[73]

From his correspondence at the time, it is clear that Subhas wanted to avoid punishment for the incident in which he was involved. In his own statement to the investigators, he said he was not there, but would not condemn the attack. A few years later, he wrote to Sarat that he should have declared his responsibility and taken the punishment which he received anyway.[74] More than two decades later he reviewed these events and put them in a more heroic light.

Lying on the bunk in the train at night I reviewed the events of the last few months. My educational career was at an end, and my future was dark and uncertain. But I was not sorry—there was not a trace of regret in my mind for what I had done. I had rather a feeling of supreme satisfaction, of joy that I had done the right thing, that I had stood up for our honour and self-respect and had sacrificed myself for a noble cause....

Little did I then realise the inner significance of the tragic events of 1916. My Principal had expelled me, but he had made my future career. I had established a precedent for myself from which I could not easily depart in future. I had stood up with courage and composure in a crisis and fulfilled my duty .... I had a foretaste of leadership—though in a very restricted sphere—and of the martyrdom that it involves. In short, I had acquired character and could face the future with equanimity.[75]

From contemporary sources, it seems that Subhas was less composed and more concerned with his darkened future than he later wrote. All the family connections were utilized to influence Sir Ashutosh Mookerjee, vice-chancellor of Calcutta University, a barrister colleague of Sarat Bose and acquaintance of Janaki Nath Bose, to allow Subhas to attend another college. It took some time before this pressure worked.[76]

For the college and the educational system, there were also changes. Principal James was suspended and then forced into retirement, the Students' Consultative Committee was abolished, and officials vowed to take a stronger hand against any signs of student indiscipline. A Department of Education report on these incidents gives an idea of the official mentality of those days:

The evidence proves conclusively the presence in the college and the collegiate hostel of a number of turbulent youths whose capacity for mischief is by no means of a restricted character and who are evidently able to make their presence felt whenever there is an occasion calculated to excite the students to an outbreak against authority.... If a student has a grievance, he can make his submission to his principal, but he must distinctly realise that the principal's decision is final and has to be accepted loyally and cheerfully. The position becomes intolerable when a student, who fails to obtain from the authorities of his college what he deems to be just redress. considers that he may take the law into his own hands and even call on his fellow-students to go on strike. Even a tacit acquiescence in so pernicious a doctrine must inevitably lead to defiance of law and order and speedily end in the annihilation not only of all academic but of all civilised communal life.[77]

The Students' Consultative Committee had to go because it had attracted '. . . what may be called the demagogue type who are not necessarily the most desirable members from an intellectual and moral standpoint.'[78] To the government, the students were unruly children and had to be brought into line and only 'constitutional' means of questioning the actions of the rulers were permissible. In a microcosmic form this event and other similar events during the Swadeshi agitation were rehearsals for the bigger and more directly political events of the coming years.

One of the most sensitive commentators on these events was the poet Rabindranath Tagore, himself an educator. He said in his essay, 'Indian Students and Western Teachers,' that Indian students needed sympathy and inspiration, but that, 'the least insult pierces to the quick.' The university, he argued, could be the arena for the beneficial meeting and sharing of cultures, but it could never be such as long as the British stereotyped the Bengali, made men into adjectives rather than nouns, and demanded a relationship based on fear and hate. In his own Indian-run school, Tagore said that there were both good and bad European teachers, but only in an atmosphere of free intercourse between men, could the desirable relationship exist.[79]

Subhas was taken back into the fold of his family and given the vital support which he needed at the time. He was not criticized for blackening their name or ruining his prospective career. To the government he was a mischief-maker and a demagogue, to some of his fellow students he was a hero and a martyr, to others a fool, but to his family, he was a young son in need of their care.

Subhas' youngest brother Sailesh, was still at home in Cuttack when his *Chot-da* (youngest of his older brothers) returned and has described some of his activities:

A restless mind like my Chotda's could not rest in peace. Young students of the Ravenshaw College of Cuttack approached him with the problem of having no place to stay though they received admission in the college. Subhash approached my father and obtained his consent to giving away one of my father's two-storeyed houses which was converted into a hostel for the Ravenshaw College students.

A young scheduled caste student by the name of Arjun Mahji was unable to get any admission at the Government hostel. . . and wanted my Chotda to help him. . . . A meeting of the inmates of Ravenshaw was called and the students who were all caste Hindus were requested to admit Arjun Mahji.

The boys, 20 in number, all agreed. . . . Arjun Mahji got an attack of typhoid . . . there was no one to nurse him during the day. Subhash asked our mother who readily agreed to nurse the untouchable.[80]

In Subhas' own account, he said that he did most of the nursing and was overjoyed when his mother agreed to help him. He mentioned also that at this time, '. . . my relations with my family did not suffer a set-back, but rather improved.'[81] As he moved back again towards his family, he distanced himself a little from Suresh Banerjee's Calcutta group. Though he continued to correspond with Hemanta Sarkar until 1921, the friendship was not nearly as close and exclusive as it had been a few years earlier.

To pass the time in Cuttack—and Subhas did not know whether he would ever be a student again—Subhas organized social service activities working with student friends to nurse cholera and smallpox victims. They also went on excursions

. . . to different places of religious or historical interest. Life in the open with plenty of walking was good for the health and it gave opportunities for that intimate communion with other souls which is never possible within the four walls of a room. Moreover, it helped me to keep away from home where I had nothing particular to do, because individualistic Yoga had no longer any attraction for me and the study of text-books did not interest me. I now tried an experiment in using our religious festivals for developing our group life.[82]

Subhas also described efforts to organize community festivals and claimed that there was a good deal of success on the 'social side' of these activities. He went through periods when quiet meditation was very important to him. He was increasingly beset by disturbing dreams at this time, some directly sexual and others in which he was surrounded by poisonous snakes or wild animals. He claimed that by conducting experiments with facing his fears just before going to sleep he was able to conquer these threats and also others about being arrested and failing examinations.[83] As Sailesh Bose noted, he was a restless young man and threw himself into activity to use his energies and overcome his anxieties.[84] He visited his father's house on the beach at Puri, a nearby religious center and resort area where he made the acquaintance of Khitish Chattopadhyay and Nirmal Kumar Bose, both of whom became distinguished anthropologists. They used to run on the beach together and Khitish recalled in a brief memoir of Subhas that he had heard that Subhas was 'orthodox' and so was surprised to see Subhas

eating with people of different castes. Subhas laughed at this characterization and, in time, Khitish understood that Subhas' orthodoxy meant his
great love of Indian traditions, but not his uncritical acceptance of them.[85]

After about a year in Cuttack, Subhas returned to Calcutta trying to get
permission to continue his education. Before the matter was decided
Subhas volunteered for military service in the 49th Bengalees. He passed
all the tests except the one for vision and was rejected. He was upset, but
this was just the first of his efforts in this line and later ones were more
fruitful.[86] Meanwhile, Sarat Bose, his Calcutta guardian, met the new
principal of Presidency College, Mr Wordsworth, who was amenable to
allowing Subhas to join another college. First, though, he wanted an
interview. He asked Subhas many questions about the events of the
previous year and finally agreed to drop objections to Subhas' entering
another college. On July 20, 1917, the Syndicate of Calcutta University
granted him permission to resume his studies and, with the assistance of
Dr Urquhart, principal of Scottish Churches College (now called Scottish
Church College) in north Calcutta, Subhas was able to join this college and
take up the honors course in philosophy.[87]

Back in the mainstream of college life, Subhas threw himself with
renewed vigor into two activities: philosophical studies and military
training.[88] Subhas began to read modern philosophy again and, with an eye
on popularizing the investigation of philosophical questions; he became
secretary of the students' Philosophical Society at a college already known
for the excellence of its studies in philosophy. Willing to test himself in the
battleground of argument, Subhas spoke twice during 1918 to meetings of
the Society. On February 1, with Dr Urquhart in the chair, and thirty-four
attending, he presented 'A Defence of Materialism' maintaining that,

> Materialism can satisfy common sense for the following reasons:
>
> (i)   The external world appears to be a tangible material world and
>   not an ideal one.
> (ii)   Knowledge of matter is direct and primary—that of life and
>   mind indirect and derivative.
> (iii) Materialism throws a very optimistic outlook before man.
> (iv)   Materialistic nations attain national power and glory. From
>   the philosophical standpoint too materialism is a justifiable
>   position. . . . Materialism is not anti-moral.[89]

The paper was most mercilessly criticized and it seemed that,

> the Essayist by condemning spiritualism had wounded the feelings of many
> philosophers in the room.
>
> The President then in his beautiful short speech said 'India wants more
> Idealism and not Materialism. No ethics is ever possible with a materialistic
> metaphysics.'[90]

It is not known what response Subhas made to this fusillade of criticism. But it appears that he himself was only taking a position opposed to his own true views.

Later the same year, on September 6, again with Dr Urquhart presiding, Subhas read a paper on 'A Defence of Idealism.' The minutes record that,

> The Essayist supported Idealistic Monism of the Hegelian type but differed from Hegel and Schopenhauer in conceiving of the absolute not as Pure Reason or Pure Will but as Spirit in all his fulness, striving through all the processes of the world to rise into the bliss of Self-consciousness in the life of man. He held that such a view could reconcile both Science and Religion and supplement the popular and scientific conception of things with (the) metaphysical.[91]

The audience was much more appreciative of the speaker's efforts this time and in his positive closing speech, Dr Urquhart '. . . referred to two difficulties in a Hegelian type of philosophy—(1)The relation between eternity and time, and (2) the freedom of the human will.'[92] Subhas' presentation of idealism in this forum came close to the mature statement of his philosophical views in the final chapter of his autobiography written years later. It is also worthy of notice that he saw Spirit as '. . . striving through all the processes of the world to rise into the bliss of Self-consciousness in the life of man.'[93] This is a blending of Hegel and Vivekananda and Aurobindo. He continued to read philosophy during the next two years and felt that the essence of Spirit was love.

In the waning days of the First World War, the Government of India started a university unit of the Indian Defence Force. Subhas and other students eagerly joined. Among the Bengalis—whom the British considered one of the non-martial Indian races and unsuitable material for the military—there seemed to be much latent interest in things military.[94] A reporter for the Scottish Churches College Magazine noted underneath a list of thirty-one students' names in the University Volunteer Corps in 1917, that,

> We believe that the military enthusiasm of one of the Hostels has risen to such a pitch that military titles have been distributed. One of the residents has risen to the rank of 'Colonel,' but we have not yet heard of a 'Field-Marshall.'[95]

Subhas was one of the most zealous recruits and described in an article for the college magazine and then in his autobiography how a rabble of students was transformed into a well-trained and smartly turned-out company by its British officers. They spent four months at a summer camp which Subhas enjoyed immensely. He had defied his professors at Presidency College, but he soon fell into line under Captain Gray. This is how he described his experience:

> Our O.C., Captain Gray was a character. . . . It would be difficult to find a
> better instructor than he. A rough Scotsman with a gruff voice. . . he always
> wore a scowl. . . . But he had a heart of gold. . . . When he joined our
> Company, the staff officers in Fort William were of the opinion that we
> would be utter failures as soldiers. Captain showed that their estimate was
> wrong. . . . What ordinary soldiers would take months to learn we would
> master in so many weeks. After three weeks' musketry training there was
> a shooting competition between our men and our instructors, and the latter
> were beaten hollow . . . on parade we were quite smart . . . the military
> secretary to the Governor complimented us on our parade, the day we
> furnished the guard-of-honour to His Excellency at the Calcutta University
> Convocation. . . . This training gave me something which I needed or which
> I lacked. The feeling of strength and of self-confidence grew still further. As
> soldiers we had certain rights which as Indians we did not possess . . . the
> first day we marched into Fort William . . . we experienced a queer feeling
> of satisfaction, as if we were taking possession of something to which we
> had an inherent right but of which we had been unjustly deprived.[96]

One of the themes of Subhas' life was the gaining of strength and
confidence. The strength was mental, spiritual, and physical. Although
Indians such as Vivekananda and Aurobindo preached confidence in the
spiritual power of India and its message for the world, this was not
sufficient. Vivekananda encouraged young men to build their biceps and
play football; Aurobindo as revolutionary theoretician told young men to
practise with lathis and with pistols when they could get them. Subhas
sought out military training because of some-elemental pleasure he found
in it, but also for its national value. At this point he probably was not sure
what its uses would be, but it is clear that he wanted to be equal to
Europeans and overcome his sense of inferiority and lack of confidence in
the physical-military prowess of himself and all Indians.

In his autobiography written about twenty years after his Scottish
Churches College days, he devoted three pages to the Indian Defence
Forces and one sentence to his studies in philosophy. But there is no doubt
that he applied himself to his studies with all of his mental energy and in
the final college examinations he placed second in the First Class, that is
second among all philosophy students in Calcutta University, and was
awarded the Pratap Chandra Majumdar Medal and the Philip Samuel
Smith and William Smith prizes. As a kind of valedictory, he drew up a
'Scheme for the Improvement of the Philosophical Society' to be carried
out by younger students.[97]

He himself decided to shift his studies to experimental psychology for
his M.A., since he believed that philosophy developed the critical

faculties, but did not lead to the solving of fundamental problems. However, a few months later, after consulting with Sarat, Janaki Nath Bose offered his prize-winning son, Subhas, the option of going to England to continue his studies and to sit for the ICS examination. He gave Subhas twenty-four hours to make up his mind. To Sarat and Janaki Nath, the ICS might have seemed an eminently suitable career for a brilliant young Indian student. But for Subhas, trying to chart out his own mission of life and more fiercely nationalistic and anti-British than his elders, the choice created inner turmoil. The provincial adviser for studies in England, a Presidency College professor who remembered the troublesome Subhas, tried to dissuade him by insisting that he had no chance whatsoever in the ICS examination against the 'tip-toppers' from Oxford and Cambridge. Asked why his father wanted to send him, Subhas replied, 'My father wants me to throw away (the) ten thousand rupees.'[98] To Hemanta, he wrote expressing his confusion and decision:

> It is my considered view that there is no hope of my passing the Civil Service examination. . . . My primary desire is to obtain a university degree in England; otherwise I cannot make headway in the educational line. If I now refuse to study for the Civil Service, the offer to send me to England will be put into cold storage for the time being (and for all time). . . . Under the circumstances, should I miss this opportunity? On the other hand, a great danger will arise if I manage to pass the Civil Service examination. That will mean giving up my goal in life. Father had been to Calcutta. He made the offer yesterday. . . . And I have agreed to sail for England.[99]

Overcoming his doubts, perhaps harboring a secret plan to resign even if he did manage to pass, bent on an English university degree, he left for Europe on September 15, 1919 and reached London on October 20.[100]

Subhas' Civil Service application demonstrates his family's connectedness to the small, interrelated elite of Bengal. For references, he gave the names of the two highest-ranking Indians in the councils of the British-Indian establishment, Lord Sinha of Raipur, Under Secretary of State for India and the first Indian to serve as governor of a province under the Raj, and Mr Bhupendranath Basu, a wealthy Calcutta solicitor and a member of the Council of India in London. There appeared to be a lack of seriousness in his listing (in order) of the provinces in which he might like to serve. He listed Bombay, Upper Bengal, Madras, Bihar and Orissa, and then Bengal and Assam in fifth position. The rationale for each choice was far-fetched. He claimed that he had served in the army in the Calcutta University Infantry unit of the Indian Defence Force and wrote, 'We were liable to service anywhere within India.'[101]

In London, Subhas stayed with his brother Satish (who was sitting for the bar) in Belsize Park, not too far from where Sarat had lived. His attention, however, was on obtaining admission to some Cambridge college, though it was past the deadline. With the help of other Indian students including Dilip Roy, and the approval of the censor of Fitzwilliam Hall, Mr Reddaway, he was admitted and began to study and attend classes.[102]

He plunged into preparations for the Mental and Moral Sciences Tripos (his Cambridge course) and for the Civil Service examination. For the latter he had to prepare in nine subjects: English Composition, Sanskrit, Philosophy, English Law, Political Science, Modern European History, English History, Economics, and Geography (including cartography). Philosophy was the most familiar subject and appeared in the two exams. He had to spend the most time on unfamiliar subjects since the ICS exam was the following August. He attended evening lectures on Sanskrit and English Law and noted about his new studies:

> ... the study of Political Science, Economics, English History, and Modern European History proved to be beneficial. This was specially the case with Modern European History. Before I studied this subject, I did not have a clear idea of the politics of Continental Europe. We Indians are taught to regard Europe as a magnified edition of Great Britain. Consequently we have a tendency to look at the Continent through the eyes of England. This is, of course, a gross mistake, but not having been to the Continent, I did not realise it till I studied Modern European History and some of its original sources like Bismarck's Autobiography, Metternich's Memoirs, Cavour's Letters, etc. These original sources, more than anything else I studied at Cambridge, helped to rouse my political sense and to foster my understanding of the inner currents of international politics.[103]

Many of Subhas' Cambridge books—he mentions how delightedly he bought books there—survive in the family library. Among the most carefully marked of these books are: A.F. Pollard, *Factors in Modern History*; Arthur D. Innes, *A History of England and the British Empire*, 4 volumes; Samuel R. Gardiner, ed., *The Constitutional Documents of the Puritan Revolution 1625–1660;* E.W. Ridges, *Constitutional Law of England*; A.H. Johnson, *The Age of the Enlightened Despot 1660–1789;* and, John Maynard Keynes, *Indian Currency and Finance*. From his many detailed marginal notes, it is evident that he saw many contemporary links to historical developments, viewing history as a real drama in which he could identify powerfully with some (usually noble and self-sacrificing) actors, and that he made connections between the British struggle for liberty and the Indian one.[104]

For Subhas Bose this was a much broader experience than simply reading books and taking exams. It was his first time out of his Indian nest, away from much that was familiar, and in the homeland of the rulers of his native land. He—like many of his countrymen—had a complicated relationship to Great Britain and British people that spanned love, hate, admiration, disgust, anger, and envy.[105] One passage in a letter written to Hemanta after Subhas had been in England a few weeks expressed some of these mixed feelings:

> Whether one wills it or not, the climate of this country makes people energetic. The activity you see here is most heartening. Every man is conscious of the value of time and there is a method in all that goes on. Nothing makes me happier than to be served by the whites and to watch them clean my shoes. Students here have a status—and the way the professors treat them is different. One can see here how man should treat his fellow man. They have many faults—but in many matters you have to respect them for their virtues.[106]

In his general experience of Englishmen he was wounded by any tinge of racism or sign that Indians were an inferior people. But he was also able to separate out individuals and to appreciate them as human beings. The rage about the Amritsar massacre of earlier the same year stayed with him, but a friendly and sympathetic human being could be accepted on his or her own terms.[107]

Subhas pressed his fellow Indian students to live up to a high standard of duty and moral conduct. Dilip Roy was one of those under Subhas' thumb and, in retrospect, he thought Subhas had an inferiority complex:

> . . . I gulped down my resentment and prepared to 'follow the leader.' For he *was* our leader. And didn't he say: 'Let your one ambition be to leave behind an impression here of flawless spruceness, for these insular people lack imagination and can never separate the chaff from the kernel of culture.'
>
> 'Why then try to make an impression on such muddle-headed philistines?' I riposted, half-angry, half-amused by his inferiority complex.
>
> But he never suspected this: he called it superiority. 'We must prove it home to them that we can more than hold our own against them. We must beard the lion in his own den.'[108]

Dilip was right. Subhas pushed himself and others because he felt inferior. Although he was sharply critical of British limitations, he wanted to learn from them. Following Joseph Levenson's analysis of China and the West, we can say that Subhas was expressing the need for non-Westerners in the age of imperialism to find cultural equivalency, equality of native and European traditions. So what is involved here is not personal pathology, but rather a societal dilemma for the most modern Indian culture-bearers.[109]

Since Subhas was a leader, his personal view of the important issues at stake was writ large. One of his edicts was, ' "And, above all, never court the company of women—no playing with fire if you please!" . . . And we obeyed him in spite of ourselves whenever he commanded!'[110] For this demand, some of his compatriots dubbed Subhas a prig. With hindsight and Subhas' autobiography in hand, we can see that he was tormented by sexual desires and a powerful voice within commanded him to control and destroy these impulses.

An arena in which Subhas became a spokesman for other Indian students was in the effort to join the University Officers' Training Corps. Subhas had found personal enjoyment and social benefits in his earlier military training at Calcutta University and when a similar training was opened at Cambridge, Subhas and others attempted to join. They were refused. Subhas was delegated to speak to officials at the War Office and the India Office to try to have the ban removed. Each ministry blamed the other: the War Office maintained that they did not object, but the India Office did not want trained Indian military officers returning to India; the India Office said it did not object, but that the War Office did not want commissioned Indian officers in the British Army perhaps commanding British troops. Subhas had felt from his teenage years that India was deficient in military skills and organization. This was an arena in which to get Western training of long-term value to the Indian nation. He did not give up easily, but the ban was not removed.[111]

He had gone to London to see Lord Lytton in connection with this matter as a representative of the Indian Majlis at Cambridge. This organization had existed, at least since the late nineteenth century, as a forum and meeting ground for Indians at Cambridge, to which prominent Englishmen and Indians were invited to speak and to debate. Subhas also joined the Union Society. He recalled later that Hugh Dalton, Oswald Mosely, John Simon, and others enlivened that forum and he heard pro-Irish speeches there at the time of the Irish troubles and civil war. [112] Like Sarat Bose before him, Subhas learned many lessons in British justice and British injustice during his two-year stay.

The Indian Majlis also chose him as one of their representatives to speak before the Committee on Indian Students set up by the India Office to examine the facilities, education, and life of young Indians in the United Kingdom. Subhas, in his testimony, argued that many Indians came to Britain because this was the only way they believed they could effectively compete for the ICS. He wanted simultaneous examinations to be given in India. A fellow Muslim student, M. Rahim, and Subhas also suggested that students on government scholarships should not be allowed to compete for the ICS and protested that preparation for the ICS precluded the study in depth of any one subject. The burden of much testimony was that the ICS exam should be held in Great Britain and India at the same time, and educational facilities in legal studies and accounting and other areas should be improved in India, so that the enormous expense of foreign study could be avoided.[113]

By the time Subhas testified on May 26, 1921, however, he had been studying hard for almost two years, had already taken the ICS exam, was about to receive his Cambridge degree, and had more than spent his father's Rs. 10,000. Subhas took the open competitive examination for appointments in the Indian Civil Service in August 1920 which was to fill six places in the Service. Having but nine months to prepare and failing to follow instructions in the Sanskrit section of the exam and thereby losing points, Subhas was convinced he had no chance. But he had already proved himself an excellent test-taker, much better than Sarat, and again he distinguished himself. Of all the candidates, he finished fourth and tied with another Indian for highest marks in English Composition. Indians finished first, third, fourth, fifth, sixth, and seventh. The candidates who finished first and second scored many of their points in Greek, Latin, and Greek and Latin history. Those who placed third and fifth gained many of their points in mathematics. Subhas did well in English Composition, history, psychology and logic, moral and metaphysical philosophy, and political economy and economic history. Since he was preparing for the Tripos in mental and moral sciences, and had concentrated in philosophy as an undergraduate in India, his showing in these areas could have been expected. However, the study of history and economics was much less familiar and he did well to even score in these areas.[114]

When he learned how well he had done, Subhas was flabbergasted, but proud. Although he may not have wanted to join the ICS, he certainly made every effort to perform well on the examination. Fitting with the advice he gave to Dilip Roy, he wanted to show the British that he was their equal, and what better place to demonstrate this than in the ICS competition.

The open competitive examination was the first, but vital step in the process of selection. Subhas had passed the medical exam. The final exam was to be held in 1921 and this included many more Indian subjects with questions on the Indian Penal Code, Evidence Act, Indian history, and Indian language, and one optional Indian subject plus the riding test. And Subhas could ride. Aurobindo Ghose many years before could not ride and failed several times to appear for the riding test, but this and the examination subjects held no fear for Subhas. Now he knew he could join the ICS if he wanted to.[115]

From the fall of 1920 to the spring of 1921, he wrestled with the decision. His proud father wanted him to join and on the surface, it appeared that his mother and brothers, Sarat and Satish, also wanted him to accept. In a letter to Sarat Bose written in late September 1920 from Leigh-on-Sea, Subhas put forth his dilemma:

> I have sent father a copy of the mark-sheet. . . . I have been getting heaps of congratulations on my standing fourth in the competitive exam. But I cannot say that I am delighted at the prospects of entering the ranks of the ICS . . . . A nice fat income with a good pension in after-life—I shall surely get . . . . The Civil Service can bring one all kinds of worldly comfort but are not these acquisitions made at the expense of one's soul?
>
> . . . But for a man of my temperament who has been feeding on ideas which might be called eccentric—the line of least resistance is not the best line to follow. Life loses half its interest if there is no struggle—if there are no risks to be taken. The uncertainties of life are not appalling to one who has not, at heart, worldly ambitions. Moreover it is not possible to serve one's country in the best and fullest manner if one is chained on to the civil service. In short, national and spiritual aspirations are not compatible with obedience to Civil Service conditions.[116]

Subhas was concerned with his responsibilities to his family and the possible familial obligations of a householder. In the same letter to Sarat, he wrote,

> Though I am sure that the Civil Service has no glamour for you, father is sure to be hostile to the idea of my not joining the Civil Service. He would like to see me settled down in life as soon as possible. Moreover if I have to qualify for another career it will add considerably to the financial burden which is already on your shoulders. . . . But I may say without hesitation that if I were given the option—I would be the last man to join the Indian Civil Service. . . . I am not going to marry—hence considerations of worldly prudence will not defer me from taking a particular line of action if I believe that to be intrinsically right.[117]

Subhas returned to Cambridge and to his studies for the Mental and Moral Sciences Tripos, reflected, and wrote many more letters to Sarat and to his parents and to friends like Hemanta and Charu Chandra Ganguly. His peers in Calcutta, particularly Hemanta and the Suresh Banerjee group, were with him in opposition to the ICS—it was seen to be incompatible with a higher and nobler and freer service to the nation.[118] For some young men, the mystique of the Raj, the loyalty to the British Government in India and the British Empire was gone. Government measures in the early 1900s, the Swadeshi agitation, and the post-war massacre at Jallianwala Bagh in April 1919 had destroyed the legitimacy of the Raj forever. And, the cultural revivalism of the late nineteenth century and early twentieth century was still reverberating in the minds of many younger Indians.

Subhas was torn by his duty to his parents, especially his father, and his duty to himself. In this situation, Sarat served as a mediator. The month he made his final decision on the ICS, April 1921, he wrote at length to Sarat, and his thoughts show how closely personal and national concerns were woven together in his mind and how important it was for him—before all other commitments—to be true to himself.

> Since the 15th of August last, one thought has taken possession of me—viz. how to effect a reconciliation between my duty to father (and mother) and my duty to myself. I could see from the very outset that father would be against my proposal—in fact, my idea would seem to him preposterous. It was not without a shudder therefore—shudder at the thought of causing him pain—that I asked you to communicate my intention to father. In fact, I did not then have the heart to write to him direct. . . .
>
> Since then the struggle has been going on in my mind—a struggle intensely painful and bitter in view of the issues involved. I have failed to arrive at a reconciliation. We, who have grown up under the influence of Swami Vivekananda on the one side and Arabindo Ghosh on the other have, fortunately or unfortunately, developed a mentality which does not accept a compromise between points of view so diametrically opposed. It is quite possible that I have been nurtured on a wrong philosophy. But it is the characteristic of youthful minds to have more faith in themselves than in others. . . .
>
> You know very well that in the past I had occasion to cause great pain not only to father and mother but to many others including yourself. I have never excused myself for that and I shall never do so. Nevertheless, conditioned as I was by temperament and circumstances, there was no escape for me out of an intellectual and moral revolt. My only desire then was to secure that amount of freedom which was necessary for developing a character after my own ideals and for shaping my destiny after my own inclination.[119]

He said in this letter (and others) that he felt responsible to his parents and Sarat. They constituted the parental generation in his family and had been economically and legally responsible for him. He also explained that his parents' health was declining and such factors did weigh on him. He said,

> I realise that all along I alone have been instrumental in introducing so much discord into our otherwise quiet family. The reason is that certain ideas have taken possession of me and these ideas have unfortunately been unacceptable to others.[120]

Trying to explain, he blamed the ideas at work in him—the ideas of self-strengthening and political independence—and felt that he had a mission that was tied in with India's struggle for independence.

So the forces were arrayed in the battlefield of his mind. There were family pressures for a fine career, economic well-being, and high status, and for accepting the legitimacy, even if only on a trial or temporary basis, of the Raj. Against these forces were his own values and sense of personal mission, tied in with the liberation and development of India. Once, a young man, an Indian young man as well as a British young man, could have seen joining the ICS as one of the significant ways in which he could work for India's best interests and fulfillment. This idea was still alive in Janaki Nath Bose and, to a lesser degree, in Sarat Bose. They suggested that Subhas sign the covenant and try the service for a few years at least. But even the covenant, a vow of loyalty and service within the administrative cadre of the Raj, was impossible for Subhas. He could not sign it, whatever the cost in parental pain.

So, on April 22, 1921, he wrote to the Right Hon. E.S. Montagu, Secretary of State for India, that, 'I desire to have my name removed from the list of probationers in the Indian Civil Service.'[121] As far as service to the Raj, he was finished. Officials in the India Office tried to dissuade him and even dispatched his eldest brother, Satish Bose, then sitting for the bar in London, to Cambridge to persuade him to withdraw his resignation. All these efforts failed.[122] Later Subhas revealed that the censor of Fitzwilliam Hall, Mr Reddaway, who had helped him to gain admission, encouraged him to follow his own inner light and stick to his resignation. Subhas intimated that he wanted to be free of responsibility to the government and said he wanted to be a journalist. But writing to Sarat, he made it much more explicit that he felt he was making a sacrifice for the sake of the nation. He thought that each Indian family should make a sacrifice, that is, should contribute one member to true service for the nation, regardless of economic and personal costs.[123]

This was the third of Subhas' youthful rebellions, the first, running away from home in search of a guru, the second, the attack on Professor Oaten and its consequences. In the first he overthrew the day-to-day authority of his parents and searched for a religious guide which they could not or did not provide. In the second, he attacked the authority of a professor and of the educational hierarchy of the Raj in Bengal. Here he was rejecting a position in the elite service of the Raj, against the best advice and hopes of his father. But there was some ambivalence in all this. He wanted the authorities, including the British officials, to recognize his accomplishments, but he also wanted to put their prizes aside and follow his own inner voice.

By the beginning of 1921 he was looking away from the ICS. He focused his thoughts by writing to Chittaranjan (C.R.) Das, the leader of the Indian nationalist movement in Bengal, about his preparation and achievements and his hopes to do whatever work Das had for him, particularly in national education, in propagating nationalist ideas, and in helping to organize the movement among ordinary people. Das wrote back encouraging Subhas to return to Calcutta.[124] Subhas was now ready for more directly political work in the movement which, under the new hand of Gandhi on the national level and Das in Bengal, was rapidly growing.

Once his course was clear Subhas hoped to have his family with him in the path he had chosen. He had believed all along that Sarat probably sympathized with his view, though could not say so directly. He wrote to Sarat,

> I received a letter from mother saying that in spite of what father and others think she prefers the ideal for which Mahatma Gandhi stands. I cannot tell you how happy I have been to receive such a letter. It will be worth a treasure to me as it has removed something like a burden from my mind.[125]

In the same letter he also mentioned that he had heard positively from Das and so was prepared to sail for home in June 1921 once he had completed his course at Cambridge.

The European diploma which he had long ago told Hemanta that he wanted and which would help him through his life, came as an anti-climax. He worked away reading and studying for the examination. His carefully-marked books included: Edward Caird, *The Evolution of Theology in the Greek Philosophers;* H.W. Joseph, *An Introduction to Logic;* John Stuart Mill, *A System of Logic;* Margaret Floy Washburn, *The Animal Mind;* Boris Sidis, *The Foundations of Normal and Abnormal Psychology;* W.H.R. Rivers, *Instinct and the Unconscious;* James Ward, *Psychological Principles;* P.C.S. Schiller, *Formal Logic;* and W.R. Sorley, *Recent Tendencies in Ethics.* Subhas made extensive marginal notes in the books, and listed questions perhaps from old examinations. In his copy of Joseph, he wrote a long series of questions on 'The Nature of Truth and of Knowledge'. This was one of the periods of hardest and most systematic studying of his life. He read a good deal later in his life, but this was never focused study as the ICS and Cambridge examinations demanded.[126]

Once he had decided to toss aside the ICS and join the national movement, his heart was not in his preparations for his Cambridge examination, and consequently, he did poorly by his previous standards, passing but standing in the Third Class. He did not stay to pick up his own diploma and left it for Khitish Chattopadhyay to collect.[127]

During their stay in England, Subhas, Dilip, and Khitish began to visit a Punjabi doctor, his European wife, and their two young daughters. The three young men became known as 'the trio'. For Subhas, this was the beginning of a lifelong friendship with the Dharmavir family who were then living in Buruley, Lancashire. He became particularly attached to

Mrs Dharmavir whom he came to call '*Didi*', or elder sister. He also liked
her husband a good deal and always referred to him as 'doctor'. Later in
life he acted like an elder brother towards their two daughters, Sita and
Leila. He was at his most relaxed in their household.[128] Dilip recalled,

> We often talked far into the night with a glow of heart that only youth can
> command. Sitting before the crackling fire, we fell to discussing the portents
> of the Labour Party in England and Communism in Russia.[129]

Dilip argued that these new forces embodying the will of the proletariat
would come to India's rescue. But Subhas responded,

> No, Dilip, Sri Aurobindo was perfectly right when he said in the Swadeshi
> days that no outsider would help India. If we ourselves can't win our
> freedom none will come to our rescue.[130]

Dilip wrote that Subhas went on to advocate revolutionary organization by
Indians to combat the Raj. Claiming that the Bengal revolutionaries in the
post-Swadeshi period had not failed, Subhas cited an Irish parallel:

> You might just as well say that the Sinn Fein movement is a failure also since
> it hasn't delivered the goods yet. When De Valera was sentenced the other
> day to death whoever thought that he would be released and then reimpri-
> soned again in 1918 only to escape from Lincoln Jail and visit America
> where he would raise six million dollars for the Irish Republican move-
> ment? A revolutionary movement for national liberation is not like a chance
> detonation which makes the age-long prison-walls topple once and for all.
> It is a slow laborious work of building up brick by brick a citadel of strength
> without which you can't possibly challenge the powers that be. The Bengal
> revolutionary movement at the dawn of this century was the first real
> movement, real in the sense that it gave our supine prostrate people the first
> hint about the reality of their own, unaided strength. It was the first
> movement that created a nucleus of national consciousness. . . .[131]

Although Subhas was in Great Britain during a terrible and difficult time
for Ireland—and later made a trip to Ireland and felt great kinship with
them—this is one of the few references to the similarities he saw between
these two movements—Indian and Irish—against the British Empire.[132]
He saw the need for hard and careful and persistent work in building a
movement. He also saw the need for a mass base, as is clear from a passage
in a letter of this time to his friend Charu Ganguly:

> Swami Vivekananda used to say that India's progress will be achieved only
> by the peasant, the washerman, the cobbler and the sweeper. These words
> are very true. The Western world has demonstrated what the 'power of the
> people' can accomplish. The brightest example of this is—the first socialist
> republic in the world, that is, Russia. If India will ever rise again—that will
> come through that power of the people.[133]

His growing political understanding and interest was, of course, linked to
his rejection of the ICS. As he wrote to Sarat, also in the same period,

My greatest objection to joining the service was based on the fact that I
would have to sign the covenant and thereby own the allegiance of a foreign
bureaucracy which I feel rightly or wrongly has no moral right to be there
.... I have come to believe that compromise is a bad thing—it degrades the
man and injures his cause. Where I was hauled up for assaulting Oaten, I
denied any complicity in the affair. I was then labouring under a delusion
that the end justifies the means. Later on when I joined the I.D.F., I took the
oath of allegiance to the higher authorities—though in my heart of hearts
there was no feeling of allegiance. I have learnt from all this that one
compromise always leads to another. The reason why Surendra Nath
Banerji is going to end his life with a knighthood and a ministership is that
he is a worshipper of the philosophy of expediency which Edmund Burke
preached. We have not come to that stage where we can accept a philosophy
of expediency. We have got to make a nation and a nation can be made only
by the uncompromising idealism of Hampden and Cromwell.[134]

Subhas' European experience and education and his continued reflection upon his own actions and maturation as a young nationalist led him to
admire the passionate true-believers like Cromwell and Danton. The
latter's call for audacity, always audacity, according to Dilip Roy, was
frequently on Subhas' lips.[135] Dilip Roy has mentioned that at this juncture
Subhas was idealistic and cocksure and also had not yet been involved in
politics.[136] And, though he saw the need for slow and careful organization-
building, he was by temperament impatient and impulsive. Only work in
the movement would show whether he had the capacity for organization-
building and the patience to carry it out through long, difficult years.

Subhas—like Sarat and many other Bengalis—was a passionate and
emotional man. Both liked to recite poetry and some moments of the long
evenings with the Dharmavirs were spent in the company of poetry and
song. Dilip was a fine singer and, in time, became a famous one. Sarat Bose
was known for his wonderful, resonant speaking voice. But Subhas, too,
liked to recite and to sing. Dilip has written that a favorite verse of Subhas
was by G.K. Chesterton:

> It is something to have smelt the mystic rose,
> Although it break and leave the thorny rods.
> It is something to have hungered once as those
> Have hungered who have ate the bread of gods.[137]

Subhas was prepared—intellectually, if not emotionally—for the struggles
ahead, but what particular shape the 'thorny rods' would take, he did not
know.

As he was ending his stay in England, he wrote to his chosen *Didi* in
Europe, Mrs Dharmavir,

> Looking back upon my stay in England, I may say that I was never happy

during my residence there. Our political relations with England are such that happiness is impossible. A sensitive Indian is reminded every moment of his stay in England about his position in the world. That reminder is of the most galling sort. I do not think I shall be happy merely by returning to India. The same reminder will be haunting me even in India. But while I am there, I shall have the assurance and the consolation of trying to do my little bit for the creation of a new India. That consolation I could not find when I was in England.

But there is one exception to what I have said about my stay in England and that is my stay at Buruley. I was genuinely happy during my short stay there—why I was so, I do not perhaps know. But I can say this, that both you and Doctor were responsible for it.[138]

The Dharmavirs became briefly a surrogate family for Subhas and he saw them as an Indian family. In the new and trying environment of England, he sought out a nest, like ones that he had at home. Here with friends Dilip and Khitish in a family circle, he was happy. Mrs Dharmavir was more than a sister; she was a substitute mother. He kept in touch with her and her family and hoped she would visit India, writing,

When you come to India—you will find many things you like and many things you do not like. But I can assure you one thing on behalf of the people of India—that whatever their virtues or failings may be, they possess a heart . . . one can more easily make friends with the Oriental people than with the Occidental.

You will find in India a people highly unconventional in many ways— a people for whom civilization does not consist in the accumulation of factories, sky-scrapers and beautiful clothes—but for whom civilization consists in the elevation of the human spirit and in the increasing approximation of the human spirit to the Divine. You will find there a people who respect most—not the politician or the millionaire or the business man—but the penniless ascetic whose only wealth is God.[139]

His characterization of the contrast of East and West fits with the views of the leaders of India's cultural revival of the late nineteenth century and early twentieth century, Keshub Chandra Sen, Swami Vivekananda, Rabindranath Tagore, and Aurobindo Ghose. India's spirituality, her soul and heart, was contrasted with the materialism and superficiality of the West. Subhas had learned many lessons from his European contact, but he was all through a proud Indian man in touch with his Indian roots.

From his sweeping remarks about Oriental and Occidental peoples, he turned back to a few small details of his stay at Buruley which indicate his mood of those days and point to the deep personal needs satisfied during his stay with the Dharmavirs. He mentioned in his letter to Mrs Dharmavir that one or two things,

. . . touched me very deeply. The first was when you said one day in the car—

' a penny for your thought.' It is not always that we find somebody who is eager to know what we think and feel. I believe that some of the loneliest moments come when we are in the midst of many people.[140]

He went on to describe his lonely hours aboard ship amidst the crowded merriment. The second incident he remembered fondly was when Mrs Dharmavir pressed packets of nuts and fruits upon her guests as their train was about to depart. 'There was something characteristically Oriental in the whole incident. My mind at once travelled home and I was reminded of what an Indian mother would do under similar circumstances.'[141] Subhas was able to accept Mrs Dharmavir, a European woman, as *Didi* or substitute mother, but he had to connect her to India and to Indian customs. He could, cautiously, move close to a Westerner—a Mr Bates with whom he stayed on another occasion gained his admiration and respect, if not affection—but it was very hard for Subhas to accept tenderness and compassion as cultural traits of Western people in the whole. There were a few exceptional individuals—and he could accept them as people—but his Indian pride and resentment at foreign rule and racism in India made this process a torturous one.

By the spring of 1921, with his Cambridge exam finished, Subhas was ready for his return home and new challenges. His mentor in this phase was C.R. Das, the leader of Indian nationalists in Bengal. Das had served as Aurobindo Ghose's defense lawyer in the Alipore Bomb Case in the Swadeshi years and by his clever strategy, obtained an acquittal. He was associated with the Extremist group, but he was also a respected member of the bar, and in the mainstream of Congress affairs. So Subhas had a cause and a leader to serve awaiting him and his own family ready to welcome him home. It was up to Subhas to find his own political footing and see whether he could pull others of his family over to the new, revivified nationalism led by Gandhi and C.R. Das. It was also unclear just how Subhas would redefine and shape his earlier view of himself as 'good boy' and 'mischief-maker' as he stepped onto the stage of Indian politics and adulthood. From the last moments of his stay in England, Dilip Roy recalled how Subhas used to recite 'in his warm, bass voice' a stanza of Kipling, that he revised to fit the cause of Indian nationalism:

There is but one task for all—
One life for each to give.
What stands if freedom fall?
Who dies if India live?[142]

CHAPTER THREE

'My country is my own': Into Politics, 1921–22

I have forgotten who is my own and who is not,
I have broken the ties of home,
My country is.my own, it is my home. . . .

As we see the terrible hangman's rope
We laugh a loud laugh of triumph
We are indestructible, we have no fear.

Nazrul Islam, *'Yugantarer Gan'*[1]

I

The course of Indian politics and culture for almost three decades preceding independence in 1947 was influenced by one man above all others: Mahatma Gandhi. Superficially mild and friendly to devotee and foe alike, Gandhi was tough and determined beneath his homely mien. He rejected the use of violence, learning to use what he said was a force born of truth and love, the force of non-violent resistance or satyagraha. He believed this to be a mighty weapon, having perfected its use during his residence in South Africa (1893 to 1915). Gandhi was born in Gujarat, western India, in 1869 and had been called to the bar like Sarat Bose, Jawaharlal Nehru, and many other talented, ambitious Indians. But he had failed as a barrister in India and accepted a law position in South Africa, and gradually became public advocate for the minority Indian community there. He came to the attention of leaders in the Indian National Congress during the early twentieth century and he and they saw to the passing of resolutions supporting his work. In 1915, he returned to India, and within a few years took up his greater work, the revivification and independence of India. Since he combined within himself both moralist and politician, and since he set in motion dramatic confrontation between a powerful empire and an unarmed mass, in a very short time he became a world-historical figure and he influenced numerous men and women in India as well as abroad.[2]

So it was only natural that a young and impatient Subhas Bose should hurry off his boat from Britain and seek out the leader of the national movement which he had joined in lieu of service to the Raj. This meeting was the beginning of a complex and troubled twenty-five-year relationship which spanned sunshine and shadow. Bose described the opening moments in an account written years later:

> I reached Bombay . . . and obtained an interview with Mahatma Gandhi. My object . . . was . . . a clear conception of his plan of action . . . . I began to heap question upon question. . . . There were three points which needed elucidation. . . how were the different activities . . . going to culminate in the last stage of the campaign . . . how could mere non-payment of taxes or civil disobedience force the Government to retire from the field . . . how could the Mahatma promise 'Swaraj' within one year. . . . His reply to the first question satisfied me . . . his reply to the second question was disappointing and his reply to the third was no better . . . though I tried to persuade myself . . . that there must have been a lack of understanding on my part, my reason told me clearly . . . that there was a deplorable lack of clarity in the plan which the Mahatma had formulated and that he himself did not have a clear idea of the successive stages of the campaign which would bring India to her cherished goal of freedom.[3]

During the following years, Bose never approached Gandhi with a reverential attitude. The young Bengali had been nourished by Congress Extremists like Aurobindo Ghose, who believed that all means were permissible in driving an alien power from the Motherland. Neither Bose's religious orientation, nor his political background committed him to non-violence. He was determined to join Gandhi's movement since it was the mainstream of nationalist India, but he never accepted Gandhi's belief about the centrality of non-violence in political life, or Gandhi's conception of the tactics of the struggle. Gandhi, however, sent Bose on to the leader of the Congress and Indian nationalism in Bengal, C.R. Das, and in him Bose found the leader whom he sought.

He had met Das when he was a rusticated student in 1916 and had corresponded with him from Great Britain. From the next visit in summer 1921 and for the succeeding four years of Das' life, Bose had his mentor.[4] Das became for him and for many other Bengalis a political guru. While supporting Gandhi, the Congress, and non-violent resistance at this time, Das was more flexible and pragmatic than Gandhi and understood the idealism of the revolutionaries. He also saw the need for a leader of Bengal to make a rapprochement with the politically-awakening Muslims as well as reach out to the workers and peasants. During the years 1920 to 1925,

Das emerged as the foremost leader of Bengal and one of the most talented and acute leaders of the Indian national movement.

Chittaranjan Das was a high-caste Bengali, a Vaidya, from Vikrampur, near Dacca, in East Bengal. Several in his family had been called to the law as a profession and to the Brahmo Samaj as a reformed branch of Hinduism. Born in 1870, Das, like the Bose brothers, attended Presidency College, Calcutta, and then went to Britain for further education. He failed the ICS examination, but was called to the bar from the Inner Temple, and returned to practise at the Calcutta High Court bar. His father left many debts, and after years of struggle, Das paid them off and became a successful lawyer.[5]

At the same time he was attracted to Vaishnavism. His religious urges and perceptions were expressed through several books of poetry, the most popular of which was *Sagar Sangit* (*Songs of the Sea*). The affinity to emotional Vaishnavism rather than the more intellectual, rational Brahmo creed paralleled the experience of several other prominent Bengalis of the late nineteenth century, among them Rabindranath Tagore, Bipin Chandra Pal, and Bijoy Krishna Goswami. Das had a keen interest in music as well as poetry and his sensual nature, emotional energy, and lack of puritanism made him a different kind of man and model from the more austere Gandhi.[6]

During the Swadeshi period, Bengal was divided and the Extremist group of the Congress flourished for a few years (1906–1909). Das joined this group and gained a national reputation through his shrewd and passionate defenses of Aurobindo Ghose and others charged in political cases. As a lawyer he was practical, pragmatic, resourceful, and, in his political cases, he also found scope for his powerful patriotic emotions. Most of those within the Extremist camp left the scene for prison, exile, or religious endeavors, but Das continued to work at the law and at the more quiet politics of the period from 1910 to 1917. He earned a lot of money and gave a good deal away, gaining a reputation for his charitable works. During this period, his opponent in the Dumraon Case, which dragged on for years, was Motilal Nehru, father of Jawaharlal. It was said that they joined legal battle in the daytime and met convivially in the evening to drink whiskey and to discuss topics of mutual interest. Years later they became political comrades in arms.[7]

At the time the First World War opened—and tens of thousands of Indian troops were called to defend the empire—the Extremist party in the Congress did not exist as a group and the Congress organization was left to the Moderates who preached loyalty to the Raj. Beyond the pale of open and legal nationalist endeavors, small groups of revolutionaries undertook 'actions', political robberies and murders in the name of Indian freedom from British rule. During the war, the Raj successfully combated them using extra-legal measures under the Defence of India Act, the ancient and valuable (i.e., to the rulers) Regulation III of 1818 (which allowed indefinite imprisonment without charges), and excellent intelligence work. By 1916, the battlefields were clear of the revolutionaries.[8] Home Rule Leagues were organized by Annie Besant and B.G. Tilak, an Extremist somewhat tamed by a long term in Mandalay Prison. The Congress, a rump Congress some said, still held meetings, and it was to a session of the Bengal Provincial Congress that the Moderate leader of Bengal, Surendranath Banerjea, invited C.R. Das to give the presidential address in 1917.[9]

In this speech, he reached out to all Bengalis, rural and urban, Hindu and Muslim, rich and poor, Extremist and Moderate. He said,

> We can frankly tell the Anglo-Indian community that there are no Extremists among us, no Moderates. The Hindus and Mahomedans of Bengal are all Nationalists—they are neither Extremists nor Moderates .... we shall accept no Self-Government, no Home Rule unless it recognises and includes within it the teeming millions of India. When I ask for Home Rule, for Self-Government, I am not asking for another bureaucracy, another oligarchy in the place of the bureaucracy that there is at present. In my opinion, bureaucracy is bureaucracy, be that bureaucracy of Englishmen or of Anglo-Indians or of Indians. We want no bureaucracy, we want Home Rule, we want Self-Government by the people and for the people. We want Self-Government in which every individual of this country, be he the poorest ryot or the richest zemindar—will have his legitimate share. Every individual must have some voice. We want Home Rule, broad based on the will of the people of India.[10]

In this same speech, Das unfurled the flag of Bengal patriotism and decried the gap between the Westernized Bengalis and the masses.[11] Developing a theme that Gandhi was working on in his own way at the same time, Das said that the educated and more politicized people must reach out to the mass of their poorest countrymen through the medium of their common culture. Political education and messages must be in Bengali, as Rabindranath Tagore had long been saying.[12] Das spoke as a Bengali populist reaching across class, ethnic, and caste lines. Here and in the following few months as he toured Bengal, he enunciated most of the themes of his blossoming political life. First, he called for the revival and utilization of Bengali culture as the common denominator of the public to whom he was speaking. Second, he wanted a greater awareness of and participation by the lower classes, rural and urban, in politics. Third, he knew that a true (and successful) Bengali leader must have support from both the Hindu and Muslim communities.[13]

Das was no doubt aware of long-term trends in the development of and relationship between the two major communities in Bengal and India. In Bengal proper, the Muslims constituted about 51 per cent of the population in 1901, the Hindus 46 per cent. By 1931 the Muslims had grown to 54 per cent of the Bengal population of approximately 50,000,000, and the Hindus had declined to 43 per cent.

The high-caste Hindus of Bengal had long played paramount roles in positions allotted to Indians in the British Raj, in the professions, and in the cultural life of Bengal. Men from the higher castes had flooded into Calcutta, the sons of Haranath Bose among them; as it grew apace in the nineteenth century. They constituted a disproportionately high percentage of Calcutta's population which went with their preponderate participation in institutions of the British-Indian establishment. They were faster to take to Western education and other paths to success in British India, and were also continuing to fill high status roles that their caste forebears had carried out, albeit with different content, during earlier ages in Bengal. These men of the higher Hindu castes constituted roughly 30 per cent of Calcutta's Hindu population, but only 5 per cent of Bengal's population, while in Bengal as a whole, the Muslims with a slightly higher birthrate, were slowly strengthening their numerical majority.[14]

The nationalism propagated by the Indian National Congress (of which Bengalis served as presidents during twelve of its first thirty-two years) was a territorial creed. Within Indian territory—British India plus the princely states—were a variety of cultural groups who together formed the nation. Ideally, the Congress wanted Muslims, Sikhs, Christians, Parsees, as well as Hindus, to flock together under the Congress banner and work for increased participation by Indians in ruling their own country. The land might have specifically Hindu connotations for many Hindus as in Bankim Chandra Chatterjee's famous novel *Ananda Math*, but the Motherland was to be a home, early Congressmen said, for the children of all communities. Das, and later both Bose brothers, continued to adhere to this idea of territorial and composite nationalism.[15]

For thirty years the Congress was a small elitist organization that made no extensive or sustained efforts to recruit Muslims and low-caste Hindus, or to build a mass organization. Leaders in the Swadeshi period had talked of such objectives, but had not significantly carried them out. The Muslims in Bengal (as classified by the census, at the time) lagged behind the Hindus in education, the professions, and the government services. Most of the Muslims were lower-class cultivators in the eastern districts of Bengal proper and were tenants on Hindu lands. The Hindus, though highly stratified themselves by class and caste, included the dominant Indian minority functioning in collaboration with the British rulers. The Muslims were much slower to gain Western education in Bengal and even those few interested in regional and national politics often stayed clear of the Congress, though there were a few notable exceptions in the Swadeshi years.[16]

There is difficulty, however, in lumping together all the Muslims resident in Bengal as an ethnic category. Many of those in the small Muslim elite were Urdu-speaking Muslims who usually did not speak Bengali and did not identify with the masses of Bengali-speaking Muslims in Bengal. The models followed by the Urdu-speaking Muslims were Arabic and North Indian aristocratic, cultural, and religious ones. Appeal was made to the Great Tradition of Islam and prestige was given to foreign birth, Arabic names, descent from the Prophet, Urdu speech, and membership in the Ashraf, or upper-class Muslim community in India. Members of this group, whether they had lived in Bengal for generations or were recent arrivals, identified themselves as Muslims rather than as Bengalis. They looked down upon all those who spoke Bengali, to them the language of idolatry and cowards. They saw Bengali-speaking Muslims as closer to Hindus than to the world of Islam. The Urdu-Muslims in Bengal tended to be more urban than rural and to live in the western rather than the eastern districts of Bengal, though urban Urdu-Muslims lived in Dacca and the towns of eastern Bengal.[17]

Bengali-speaking Muslims often had an unsure identity and complicated feelings of inferiority relative to the Urdu-speakers, to the Bengali Hindus, and to Europeans. A hint of their problem is given in the very terms used to refer to the population of Bengal by Bengalis: 'Bengalis' and 'Mussulmans'. Bengali Muslims who gave predominance to the Bengali identity element were in an unlabeled residual category because they tended to be rural, illiterate, lower-class peasants. As one prominent Bengali Hindu writer said in an interview shortly before his death, 'I would always go to a Muslim tailor or a Muslim book-binder.'[18] For him and for many others the Bengali Muslim masses were peasants or craftsmen; they were people to whom one did not pay much attention and from whom one did not expect any exceptional achievement.

These Bengali Muslim masses spoke Bengali with some admixture of Urdu or Persian words, but Bengali nevertheless. They read and wrote in a tradition of *dobhasi* literature geared specifically for Muslims; however, those literate in Bengali read the works of Hindu Bengalis as well. They were subjected to ridicule for speaking and writing a language which some of their co-religionists said was a Hindu language, the mere use of which

smacked of idolatry. But as one of Bangladesh's leading literary historians, Anisuzzaman, wrote recently, they knew they were Bengalis and they
knew they were Muslims. Some tried to participate more fully in the Great
Tradition of Islam by learning Urdu, but the great majority did not.[19]

At the beginning of the twentieth century when the Boses were growing
up and coming to political consciousness, three long-term political trends
were at work: the further development of Indian nationalism, the rising
political consciousness of Muslims in Bengal and India, and the slow
retreat of British imperialism. One vital period during which there was a
confluence of the three trends was the years of the first partition of Bengal,
1905 to 1912. The decision to partition Bengal was made by permanent
officials of the Raj and approved by the viceroy, Lord Curzon. The first
partition encouraged the idea of a Muslim-majority East Bengal and a
Hindu-majority West Bengal, or the division of the province on the basis
of community, though the British publicly insisted that the partition was
made for administrative reasons only. This partition helped arouse Muslim
political consciousness, scared the economically-dominant Hindu
minority of East Bengal, and set off a brief flurry of communal riots in a
few rural areas. It also precipitated a temporary revival of Dacca as a place
of protest and aroused the demand for more attention to the long-neglected
districts of East Bengal.[20]

A second action by the British Raj which contributed to communal
cleavage was the legislative councils reforms of 1909 which included the
provision for separate Muslim and General or Hindu electorates. This
stipulation, favored by the viceroy, Lord Minto, and the Urdu-Muslims of
North India, had the long-term effect of encouraging political organization
and electoral appeal on the basis of community affiliation with a given
territorial constituency.[21]

A third development in which the British rulers played a controversial
role was the founding of the Muslim League at a meeting of upper-class
Muslims in Dacca during 1906. It does not seem important for the purposes
of this book to argue about whether the British were at the back of its
formation, but rather to see what the organization represented in terms of
the Bengal and Indian Muslim community. Although the meeting was held
in Dacca, the main body of men were upper-class Urdu-speakers from
northern India. The Dacca host, the nawab of Dacca, and his compatriots
were devoted loyalists, supporters of the Raj, whose aim was the protection of the rights of Muslims. The League claimed to speak for the Muslims
of India and its London lobbyist, the Aga Khan, worked for the acceptance
of communal electorates as a step in this direction.[22]

With the revocation of the Bengal partition in 1912 and the involvement of Britain in a war partly against Turkey, home base of the Muslim Caliphate, some Muslim Leaguers swung towards alliance with the Congress and a number of staunch loyalists left the League. The 1916 Congress-League Lucknow Pact marked the honeymoon period of Hindu-Muslim relations which lasted fitfully until the mid-1920s. The pact provided for a full-scale reform scheme to be considered by the Government of India. Among the points agreed to was an allotment of Muslim and non-Muslim seats in the provincial legislative councils. The pact allotted only 40 per cent of the Bengal seats to the Bengal Muslims, although they constituted slightly more than 50 per cent of the population. Here, as in many future bargains between national political organizations, or between these organizations and the Raj, some regional voices were strong, some were weak. The Bengal Hindus in the Congress argued that in their region they were superior in talent, accomplishment, and political consciousness, so they merited a majority of the seats, though they constituted a minority of the population.[23] All-India Muslim leaders and a few Bengal leaders accepted the pact, but in future years, those who wanted support from the Muslim community in Bengal had to back a demand for seats in the council proportional to the Muslim percentage of the population. During the opening years of this honeymoon period, the first important Bengal Muslim leader emerged. He was A.K. Fazlul Huq, a talented, mercurial lawyer who spoke English in court, but eloquent Bengali in his populist, political speeches. Huq went along with this pact, but like other Bengali Muslim leaders, soon recanted and advocated the larger demand. The rise of Huq was a sign of the slow, but continuing development of a Bengali Muslim middle class and their entry into politics.[24]

While Das knew that he needed Muslim support to become an all-Bengal and all-India leader, he first had to gain some role in the existing Hindu-dominated nationalist organizations. His main thrust in the years 1910 to 1919 was to challenge Surendranath Banerjea's band of Moderates in the Bengal Provincial Congress and also to join hands, if possible, with the remnants of the Extremist party in the national Congress. At the national level, he also had to confront the new political tactics and mobilization skills of Mahatma Gandhi, as well as to respond to post-war steps taken by the Government of India and its superiors in London.

In 1917, before the First World War had ended, the Secretary of State for India, Sir Edwin Montagu, had announced on behalf of the British Government, that India was to move towards responsible self-government.[25] This step was in keeping with Woodrow Wilson's Fourteen Points, which included national self-determination for subject peoples at the war's end. It also coincided with the upsurge of nationalism and demands for self-government in Ireland, Egypt, Turkey, and Eastern Europe that marked the war period. The Russian Revolution which captured the nationalist and populist sentiments of many in imperial Russia also began to resonate in India.[26]

There was a lull in the protest as Montagu came to India during 1917–18 to survey Indian opinion on the measures to be taken. He listened to many voices including that of Das whom he found a 'most sensible fellow' though he had been told that Das was 'the head of the revolutionary movement in Calcutta.' Das told him, '. . . there is no intermediate possible between responsible government and complete irresponsibility.'[27] Of Gandhi, Montagu said, 'He dresses like a coolie, forswears all personal advancement, lives practically on the air, and is a pure visionary.'[28] After this round of interviews, the Montagu-Chelmsford Report was released on July 8, 1918, with its plan for dyarchy.[29]

The deliberation over the reforms was complicated by the stick of repressive legislation—the Rowlatt Bills—which accompanied the carrot of dyarchy.

To the European community, the *Statesman*, and the Government of India, Gandhi stirred up unrest, but there was a more serious foe: the small, but dangerous revolutionary movement, or anarchists and terrorists as the government called them. The Rowlatt Acts gave the Government of India special powers to combat this movement which Justice Rowlatt's Sedition Committee had inflated in importance.[30] The revolutionary movement was a sporadic, small, and regionally-limited one which had been effectively contained by the government by 1916. In asserting that it still existed, the committee was correct, but this was as a potentiality rather than as an active force. This small movement exerted more pressure by the specter it created than the deeds it consummated.

Gandhi declared a national satyagraha the day after the Rowlatt Bills became Acts. Widespread discontent and agitation ensued, Gandhi was arrested, and then one of the blackest actions of British imperialism in India occurred on April 13, 1919. Ignoring a ban on demonstrations, many Indians gathered in an enclosed park, Jallianwala Bagh, in Amritsar.[31] With scarcely a warning, General Dyer ordered his troops to fire on the assembled throng who could not easily exit from the enclosed park. Several hundreds were killed, many more wounded. In the aftermath, Dyer was given the mildest reprimand, the government's Hunter Commission whitewashed the affair, and the House of Lords congratulated Dyer for helping to enforce law and order. This event and the responses to it significantly turned many politically conscious Indians against the Raj and helped prepare the ground for Gandhi once he had set his course on non-cooperation in 1920.

The gap between nationalist and British India is evident from listening to the *Statesman*, the leading English-language voice for the Europeans in India, assessing responsibility for the Punjab affair:

> So much has been said regarding the wisdom or unwisdom of the methods adopted by General Dyer at Jallianwala Bagh that people are apt to forget that the real and final responsibility for the fate of those who lost their lives in the Bagh rests not upon General Dyer but upon those who caused the unlawful assembly. If there had been no assembly there would have been no firing by troops. . . . The Report of the Hunter Committee confirms the opinion that the unrest which culminated in the savage excesses of mob violence arose from the agitation against the Rowlatt Acts and from Mr. Gandhi's Satyagraha movement. . . . Mr. Gandhi's agitation against the Rowlatt Acts took the form of 'civil disobedience to law'. If he had not been inebriated with conceit in his own influence, Mr. Gandhi must have perceived that his process of purification and penance, if adopted by a mob, would infallibly lead to violence.[32]

Throughout the period from non-cooperation to independence, the small revolutionary movements existed in one form or another, haunting the government and the European community and pressing them to deal with Gandhi. He, at least, believed in non-violence, and always said he was ready to work through a compromise.[33]

Furthermore, Gandhi, with the assistance of men like C.R. Das who had influence in their native regions, had been carrying through a transformation of the national movement into something approaching a mass movement. So it was imperative that India's rulers deal with him. Gandhi did not—contrary to Montagu's view—'live on air', nor was he a 'pure visionary'. Fitting with his Vaishya caste heritage and his personal inclinations, he was a keen organizer of men, a superb recruiter of lieutenants, and an excellent fund-raiser. Using these practical skills which he had honed in South Africa for twenty years, he built the Indian National Congress during 1918 to 1921 into a formidable political organization, one capable of mobilizing for specific actions such as the all-India *hartal* against the Rowlatt Acts, yet able to carry out different functions, that would endure at least as long as India was subject to British rule; and able to reach a significant number of the Indian people.[34]

After the Rowlatt satyagraha and the Jallianwala Bagh massacre, the Congress set up a Punjab Enquiry Committee composed of Gandhi, Das, Motilal Nehru, Abbas Tyabi, and M.R. Jayakar (replacing Huq). Here Gandhi, Das, and Nehru gained more intimate acquaintance with each other and more mutual respect.[35] Gandhi was also shifting in 1919–1920 from cooperation to non-cooperation with the government and its

Montagu-Chelmsford reforms package. Once he was sure of his position and had incorporated righting of the Punjab and Khilafat wrongs as short-term goals of the Non-Cooperation Movement, Gandhi set about gathering support. He toured from province to province in 1920 seeking converts and allies. He gradually gained a majority within the All-India Congress Committee (AICC) to support his tactics as well as his plans for reorganization of the Congress itself. In 1920 the Congress adopted a new constitution, dividing British India on the basis of linguistic regions rather than the British-designed provinces, setting up an executive or working committee, laying down model rules for regional, district, and local Congress committees, and setting a very low annual dues charge. From the beginning of what Jawaharlal Nehru called Gandhi's 'super presidency' of the Congress, Gandhi insisted that the working committee should be a homogeneous body, with unanimity of view. The AICC and the annual sessions—to which delegates were now to be elected in a more orderly manner—would be forums for diverse opinions, but the executive was to act as one. Gandhi was able to listen to others and, upon occasion shift his views, but accompanying his strong desire to persuade others of the correctness of his views, was an authoritarian streak.[36]

Through 1920, Gandhi sought both true believers in his methods and outlook and allies. He gained victories at the special Calcutta Congress in September and, even more decisively, at the Nagpur Congress in December. Although such Congress veterans as Bipin Pal and C.R. Das of Bengal, Motilal Nehru from UP, Lajpat Rai from the Punjab, and Tilak's followers from Maharashtra were skeptical, the swing in the Congress towards Gandhi influenced them to join Gandhi and put their doubts in abeyance. At the end of 1920, the Congress adopted Gandhi's program for non-cooperation with its boycott of foreign goods, and of the Raj's judicial and educational systems, as well as his constructive program for India. The number of district committees throughout India was greatly increased, large numbers joined the Congress, and Gandhi's genius for collecting funds from Gujarati and Marwari businessmen from Bombay, Ahmedabad, and Calcutta was to underpin many of his activities for decades to come.[37]

Along with determination and organizing capacity, Gandhi brought with him a number of ideas and concepts which he had put together during his South African years from a mélange of sources, Indian and foreign, Hindu and Christian. For Gandhi, the goal of his and each individual life was moksha, or spiritual fulfillment and liberation. The societal goal for India was swaraj, which seemed to mean self-rule, but was given a broader and vaguer meaning by Gandhi. It meant self-control of every unit in society from village to nation, and the ideal nation was to be a great collection of disciplined, self-controlling village units in which work was shared by all. In so far as possible, each of these units was to be self-sufficient, producing its own goods and services for its inhabitants.[38] Since this was a distant goal that could not be reached overnight, Gandhi had to start with the distribution of wealth and property as it stood when he came on the scene. Not favoring a revolutionary overturning of society, he came up with the idea of trusteeship. Those who already had wealth and property were conceived as trustees of it for the good of the whole society or community. Whether this idea was put forth ingenuously or out of other motivations, it did seem more agreeable to Gandhi's wealthy backers (like the increasingly influential G.D. Birla) than the concept of a more abrupt break with the past and a redistribution of property.[39] The events of the Russian Revolution were often described in the Indian press of these years and the apparition of fanatical, egalitarian Bolsheviks began to haunt propertied Indians and Europeans in India. The *Statesman* called Bolshevism a 'fanatical and insane creed.'[40] Gandhi's gentle idea of trusteeship was much preferable.

For those who were to stand in the front lines of Gandhi's satyagraha campaigns either in some small area, or throughout the nation, there were an elaborate set of rules and instructions to learn. These included chastity, prohibition, and strict discipline within the group. Severe steps like complete non-cooperation were to be used only after other measures had failed.[41]

The coming to power of Mahatma Gandhi in the nationalist movement signaled a shift of regional power. The nationalist movement had been concentrated for decades in the three coastal Presidencies, but now a man from Gujarat with support in the Hindi heartland of North India and in South India as well, had come to the fore. This meant a loss of predominance within the movement for Maharashtra and Bengal particularly. And leaders from these two areas did not quietly step aside to let Gandhi enter. They continued to argue with him through the pre-independence years, not having forgotten that they (or their nationalist forebears) had first brought the movement to life.[42]

Within Bengal, there were significant changes related to those taking place at the all-India level of nationalist organization. When C.R. Das led his challenge to the older Moderates, he charged that they were the leaders of yesterday and that they made backroom deals with India's rulers rather than consulting the public's sentiments. In the period from 1918 to the end of 1920, the Moderates, newly rechristened Liberals, left the Congress to Gandhi and Das.[43] From 1920 to 1925 there were always men more devotedly committed to Gandhi and his ideas who wanted control of the provincial Congress committee, but Das was generally recognized by Gandhi as well as the Government of Bengal as the Congress leader in Bengal. At the same time, he achieved national stature as well within the Congress and was chosen as its president in 1921 and 1922.[44]

During the period when the Congress was expanding and deepening its hold, the number of District Congress Committees in Bengal increased from four in 1918, to sixteen in 1919, to twenty-nine in 1921. Of the members from Bengal in the AICC in 1921, twenty-one of twenty-five were from Calcutta, in 1922, twenty-seven of forty-eight, and in 1923, only twenty-five of forty-eight. So the Bengal Congress Committee had spread from a concentration in the metropolis to a wider web covering the province. Although many based themselves in Calcutta, there was no doubt that there was greater contact with district towns and the mofussil than there had been before.[45]

Das shared some talents with Gandhi, among them the ability to raise money when needed and skill in selecting lieutenants. One of Das' colleagues of those days, M.R. Jayakar, described him in this way,

> To begin with there was C.R. Das, with his large ideas, welling emotion, burning patriotism, and indifference to wealth. . . . He hated British rule, as most of us did, but his ideas about its Indian substitute were sound and practical. . . . His hatred was for their (the British) system of government. In this behalf he resembled Gandhi, though he was not such a friend of the British as Gandhi was. . . . His conceptions of Indian Home Rule were critical and inclusive of a democratic broadening out of popular freedom and liberty. In securing and maintaining power, he was often inclined to be intolerant and autocratic. . . . The Party Machine . . . was, his critics averred, lubricated freely with undue patronage. . . . His followers always evinced a commendable regard and reverence for him, and he trusted them implicitly. . . . He had a great capacity for begging. . . . He was a magnificent talker, well grounded in ancient Hindu history. In his emotion, he was a typical Bengali, and could rise to heights which often reminded me of some . . . of the life of Chaitanya. . . . His cultural conception of India was sound and he looked forward to the creation of an era of blended culture, in which Hindu and Moslem, Brahman and non-Brahman, Aryan and Dravidian, each brought into the common output his quota to enrich the growth of a national culture and refinement.[46]

But more than his views and talents it was Das' renunciation of his substantial legal practice, and of his elegant and sensual lifestyle, in favor of a more severe Gandhian style which seemed to have an impact on wavering potential nationalists. Even Subhas Bose in Cambridge was moved by Das' sacrifice, which helped influence him to give up the ICS for the cause of Indian nationalism.[47]

II

Subhas Bose's return to Calcutta to join the Non-Cooperation Movement also meant a return to home and family. In his letters to Sarat Bose from England, he disclaimed any immediate interest in marrying and having his own nuclear family. But this did not mean that he was committed to living alone or family-less. Upon his return, it was determined that the family house at 38/2 Elgin Road was insufficient and a house next door, 38/1 Elgin Road, was rented for Sarat and Bivabati Bose, their five children, and Subhas. Janaki Nath and Prabhabati Bose were still based in Cuttack and came to Calcutta several times a year. At other times, Sarat Bose remained parent-in-charge, head of the family in Calcutta. The eldest son, Satish Bose, was called to the bar in London, and upon his return to India in 1921, stayed only briefly in Calcutta, and then moved to Patna to practise at the high court there.[48]

Of the other sons, Sunil Bose was abroad from 1920 to 1923 gaining further medical training and doing research, but upon return he took up a position as physician and heart specialist at the Carmichael Medical College Hospitals, Calcutta. Sudhir Bose was also abroad studying for a degree in metallurgy at Sheffield University which he was granted in 1924. Suresh Bose had left the provincial civil service over a matter of principle, and was trying to make his way in business, and Sailesh was still a student. The opening decades of the twentieth century were a period of continuing expansion of higher education and rising aspirations for the sons of high-caste families who, their parents hoped, would get European advanced degrees and take up professional careers. Formal and higher education for women was coming much more slowly. Only in the next generation did young women like the daughters of Sarat Bose begin seeking such education in significant numbers.[49]

While his brothers took to their careers with greater or lesser success, Subhas Bose had decided to become a full-time political worker. From this work he had no regular income. He received some support from his parents, help from Sarat and Biva, and income on those rare occasions when he was elected or appointed to a paying position (chief executive officer of the Calcutta Corporation, 1924; mayor of Calcutta, 1930–31). Later, when he became a prominent figure in politics, a few patrons, men with money who appreciated his work and suffering, made contributions privately to him.[50]

Although he did not become a householder until very late in his life, Subhas Bose, perhaps because he was a single man, was very involved with his family of birth. He and his parents had weathered the storms of his adolescence and ICS resignation, and had emerged with renewed under-

standing. He lived with Sarat, Biva, and their children and grew ever closer
to them. And he made yet a third familial commitment to C.R. Das and his
wife, Basanti Devi. Not only did Das become his political guru, but Das
and his wife became like surrogate parents and Subhas' mother was heard
to wonder aloud whether her son had become closer to Basanti Devi than
to herself. He became a familiar figure at dinner with Mr and Mrs Das. Late
one evening, Subhas received an urgent summons to come to their home.
He was working late and had not had his dinner. Mrs Das told him that a
wealthy Bengali had offered a large donation for the non-cooperation
cause if Subhas would marry his daughter. Subhas became angry at this
method of blackmailing him into marriage, and dismissed the offer,
demanding of his surrogate mother that she serve him his usual *bhatebhat*
(rice and vegetables cooked together—a Bengal villager's favorite) without delay. Mrs Das, who outlived her husband by more than forty years,
and remained a special confidante of Subhas Bose during his lifetime,
insisted that he never said that he would not marry. He simply did not have
time for it. His vocation, the politics of independence, came first. He was
probably also troubled by his lack of a regular income and of a stable life.[51]

In so far as he did have a regular life and a stable home base, Sarat and
Biva were responsible for it. Sarat Bose was in sympathy with the Non-
Cooperation Movement, but was not yet really involved in politics. He was
thriving in his career and raising his family. But he was wary, at the same
time, of coming to worship the idol of wealth. One of his juniors, P.B.
Mukherjee, has told this story:

> Of his distaste for money I will give you one illustration. When professional
> fortunes smiled on me he detected that I was perhaps going the way that
> many successful lawyers had gone and he felt that pursuit of professional
> success will later end only in a mechanical pursuit for money. One evening
> he sent for me and took me out on a drive on the Strand. He said nothing
> while we came out on the drive, he quietly got down and took me to one of
> those quiet spots overlooking the River Hooghly where it beautifully arches
> the City of Calcutta. . . . Then the silence was broken by his soft and
> mellifluous voice. . . . He told me then what he felt and said that nothing
> could be more tragic if the man lost himself, his mind and life in the pursuit
> of mere professional success, money and wealth. He recounted a very
> personal anecdote of his life. He said that he was a victim of that failing also
> when he was rising in his profession and winning its laurels. Then one day
> he remembered that he must rescue himself from that common life. After
> having worked in his chambers late in the evening that day, he came to the
> very same spot on which we were standing then, and started throwing a few
> of the silver rupees which he had brought with him in his pocket while he
> came out from his chambers, one by one into the Ganges that flowed as it

flowed on the day he was talking to me, and with every throw he promised to himself that he would never be a slave to silver or gold. He never was.[52]

But Sarat Bose was ambitious to do well at the bar and to live well. In the 1920s, according to several reports, he was making about Rs. 20,000 per month, a very handsome income. He had moved into the higher strata of Bengali society, though not at the very top with the richest aristocrats or businessmen.

The lifestyle of his family was a mixture of Bengali and Western. As parents, Sarat Bose and his wife Biva were demanding of their children, insisting the sons learn to read, write, and speak English as perfectly as their father and his brothers did. Their food was a combination of Bengali and Western with Sarat the instructor to all in Western ways of eating and the refinements of European cuisine. In this household, Subhas Bose was the embodiment of a more native type—he was called Subhas-Babu, never Bose-Sahib, like his brother. In habits, Subhas Bose seemed to prefer Bengali food, literature, and dress more than his elder brother.[53]

But Sarat Bose never approached the more thoroughgoing Westernization of some of his contemporaries at the bar. His lifestyle was a rather eclectic mixture of the two cultures, but in his religious life, he was a devout Hindu. It was only in the house that he eventually built for his own family that there was a *Thakur-ghor*. He adhered strictly to his faith throughout his life, accepting it entirely, and, yet, at the same time, was an eager reader of works by atheists such as Bertrand Russell, Leon Trotsky, and Bernard Shaw. He did not appear to be an intensely conflicted man and could manage within himself traditional Hindu views as well as those of some of the advanced thinkers of the West.[54]

About 1922, Sarat Bose purchased a vacation house set on a mountain side near Kurseong, some miles down the road from Darjeeling. He liked what the Bengali writer Sudhin Datta has called 'the cathartic mountains' and this was his favorite place of respite from the hectic life of Calcutta. He appreciated the cool mountain air, the chance to ride and walk and to take in the spectacular panorama of the plains from Giddapahar ('bird's peak'), his Kurseong home. Subhas Bose also enjoyed this vacation spot and was equally devoted to the mountains.[55] But most of their time and energies were spent in the plains, in Calcutta, and it is to the political movement and the life in the Calcutta of 1921 that we must now turn.

III

Subhas Bose entered the nationalist movement in 1921 at an exciting time, a moment at which many men and women felt that India was going through a rebirth or energizing transformation. The poet laureate of the day in

Bengal was a young Muslim writer, Kazi Nazrul Islam. The passionate force of his verse, the quest for greatness, for justice, equality, and freedom that swept through and forth from his words awakened some of his passive countrymen.[56] Nazrul welcomed Gandhi:

> Who is this mad traveller that has rushed into the yard of the prison where the mother is immured in chains?
>
> Thirty crores of my brethren sing the death defying song and march with him.
>
> Who is he that has arrived to sever the shackle of sorrow of the subject country?
>
> Who is he that sounds the conch of liberation on the heart of the altar of the goddess of chains? . . . salvation lies in one's own being, not in beggarly solicitation.
>
> The triumphal drum of eternal truth resounds through the world; untruth dies today of its own poison . . .
>
> Why these tears? Today it is time to make a new augury. Sound the trumpet, fly the flag and come along.[57]

Inflamed by words such as these, young Bose sought his assignments from C.R. Das directly. He did not enter as a lowly and unknown volunteer, but as someone who had already made some sacrifices for his country by his rustication from college and his resignation from the ICS. His academic achievements signified mental prowess. Now his talents were to be offered and used along new lines.

Subhas Bose, then twenty-four, looked even younger, and had many of the Bose family features: black hair, dark brown eyes, broad forehead, straight nose, oval face, and fair complexion. He exchanged his British three-piece suit and bow tie for white, Indian-made native garb, pajama and punjabi or the more Bengali dhoti, occasionally topped by a Gandhi cap. Henceforward, Subhas wore only Indian dress in India, though when he returned to Europe, he again adopted European clothes.

As a favored son, a young man of gifts, connections, and commitment, Bose was assigned by Das to work as the principal of the Bengal National College, as a captain or organizer in the National Volunteer Corps, and with a nationalist Bengali weekly, *Banglar Katha*. At the same time he joined the Indian National Congress, and shortly was doing the publicity work for the Bengal Provincial Congress Committee, as well as constructive work through the Bhowanipore Sevak Samity. He began to meet Bengal's Congressmen and had his first contacts with leaders from other parts of India who assembled for a Calcutta meeting. Soon the Bose family house in Bhowanipore became an *adda* (center), an informal meeting place for those involved in the nationalist cause. Subhas' mother commented that when he was there, it became like a marriage house, a hub of friendly interchanges. Sunday gatherings were held and Dilip Roy, Subhas' close friend, often sang at them.[58]

But on other days, Subhas was hard at work elsewhere. A colleague in the movement, Upendra Nath Banerjee, has described Subhas as the principal of the National College:

> Subhas's dutifulness, his devotion to work was unique, unusual. When the National College was established, Subhas became its principal. He did everything with equal zeal, from arranging the benches, chairs, tables in the classrooms to teaching the boys. With meticulous care he used to do the book-keeping for the college, taking care of every single farthing earned or spent by the college. This work of accountancy often kept him busy late in the night and Subhas never cared—the job must be done thoroughly and well. . . . Gradually when the students began to lose their enthusiasm and the attendance became thinner and thinner, Subhas remained steadfast in his duties. Once I went to the National College to find out whether Subhas was there, I saw my friend Kiron Sankar Roy sitting in a room downstairs reading the newspapers. I asked him, 'Where is Subhas?' Laughingly Kiran Babu said, 'Subhas, he is in the classroom teaching the benches.' I went upstairs and found the classroom empty, Subhas sitting on a chair engaged in writing. Well, the students might be absent, but he must be present in the classroom—that was his duty and he must do it.[59]

The empty benches indicated the problems of implementing the call of Mahatma Gandhi and C.R. Das for national education and boycott of the government-regulated educational system. When the call was issued, first in Nagpur in December 1920, and then throughout the country in 1921, it was not clear just how the national schools would differ from the government-related ones and, even more importantly, whether such new educational institutions could be created overnight. Also unknown was whether Indian parents and educators would fight or support the call for withdrawal from established institutions.[60]

There had been a similar call with slight but enduring results at the time of the Swadeshi agitation, 1905 to 1908. This new summons by the Mahatma of a new age was presented and broadcast on a much larger scale. There was a drop in attendance of about 25 per cent in many schools and colleges for a few months in 1921, but then with the evident failure of the new institutions, most returned to the old ones. However, even government officials responsible for education saw that the new plans for an alternative educational system had powerful appeal on political, economic, and educational grounds.

> A large number of students who responded to the appeal did so under the impression that they were thereby in some obscure way serving their country. The power of the appeal was strengthened by a very genuine

discontent with a course of education which appeared to lead to nothing but the acquisition of the degree, an honour no longer worth the money spent in obtaining it. . . . All classes of students have been affected; and among those who responded to pressure are those whom colleges could least afford to lose as well as those whose departure caused no regret. . . . The call to 'national' service and self-sacrifice found a quick response among the best. . . . Imagination has been fired and a spiritual 'uplift' initiated. Something that had long been wanting in our college life had been supplied.[61]

Students and volunteers picketed outside colleges and a few of these were temporarily closed. Some students left never to return and joined the nationalist movement. But, most did return to the government-related schools and colleges because the nationalists never set up an attractive alternative. Then, too, several powerful and influential stars in the educational firmament, Sir Ashutosh Mookerjee and Rabindranath Tagore, opposed the boycott. Thousands of parents and educators also resisted and eventually their weight told in the actions of their charges.[62] So dutiful Subhas sat before empty benches in 1921.

Subhas retained a lifelong interest in education and the young. One of his most powerful identity elements was as a young man in the dawn of a new day for his country. The program for the National College is not readily available, but from the later writings of Subhas, it is evident that his concept of national education included the more thorough dissemination of Bengali literature which would link the people of Bengal together. He also thought, following Swami Vivekananda and other national revivalists, that physical fitness was a necessary element of a complete education.[63]

As he sat in the classroom, he may well have been writing an article or editorial for *Banglar Katha*, one of the nationalist papers started by C.R. Das during his leadership years. Das, like Gandhi, Jawaharlal Nehru, and other nationalist leaders, had a strong belief in the need for nationalist voices to spread the word of his party. *Banglar Katha*, which began in 1921 and continued for some years was one such voice. It is very difficult to tell just what Subhas' contribution was to this paper and to the more ambitious English-language daily, *Forward*, started in 1923, or to the Bengali *Atma Sakti*, started in March 1922. From testimony of his contemporaries, we know that he did write and help to manage these papers. Although it is always hard to measure the impact of one or several nationalist papers, the Government of Bengal, Home Department, certainly felt that these papers played a major role in directing the minds of the young to the nationalist cause.[64]

A third string to Subhas' bow in 1921 was his work as an organizer of non-cooperation activities and demonstrations, such as boycotting European goods and British-controlled and regulated institutions, spinning with the charkha and generally, building Indian institutions to replace the boycotted ones. There were also political objectives such as the righting of the Punjab and Khilafat grievances and social ones, such as the furthering of communal harmony between Hindus and Muslims. And beyond all these specifics stood the goal of swaraj.[65]

Following his triumphs of 1921 at the special Calcutta Congress and at Nagpur, Gandhi, with wider support than ever before, pressed forward with non-cooperation activities and with plans for civil disobedience. His promise of 'Swaraj in one year'—whatever it meant to his listeners and to him—was a stimulus to organizing volunteers to spread the boycotts, to the collection of funds, and to the new sense of freedom and pride which Jawaharlal Nehru has described so graphically in his autobiography.[66]

Among the workers were many recently released revolutionaries in Bengal who had agreed at a secret December 1920 meeting with Das to give Gandhi his one year to work his magic. They agreed to eschew violent actions for the year, and to work devotedly for the movement. They soon became influential in the Bengal Congress.[67] Many Muslims were also active because the Khilafat cause was tied to the Congress campaign more closely and directly than at any time in the history of Indian nationalism.[68] Gandhi was in Calcutta at the beginning of the year full of confidence:

> I am not ashamed to repeat before you that this is an attempt to revolutionise the political outlook—that this is an attempt to spiritualise our politics . . . my faith has never burnt as brightly as it burns to-night, as I am talking to you young men of Bengal. You have given me greater hope, you have given me greater courage, you have given me greater strength. . . . I know, if I know Bengal at all that you will not shirk it (*non-cooperation's special demands*) and you will respond.[69]

Many young men joined the national volunteers and before the summer of 1921 was out, Subhas Bose had enlisted and risen overnight to captain. Shops selling foreign cloth were picketed, schools and colleges were picketed, and legal practitioners were asked to boycott the law courts. Like the boycott of the schools and colleges, the boycotts of foreign cloth and the courts were briefly successful, the former more than the latter.[70]

As in 1905 and 1919, the streets of Calcutta were worn down a little more by the frequent marches of demonstrators. The leaders of the movement were learning, as one journalist-observer put it, that a great city can serve as a political weapon. Although no longer the capital of British India, Calcutta was still one of the largest and most important administrative and economic centers of India and the seat of the Bengal government.

So demonstrations in Calcutta had high visibility. On the fringes of the movement were the poor and also some of the criminal elements of the city who might seize the opportunities provided by the demonstrations to further their own ends. In time, political leaders had their own squads of *goondas* or hoodlums to use as the need arose. But even the more genteel middle-class demonstrators, usually from the younger set, found Calcutta trams a most inviting target. Government chroniclers of the events insisted that coercion and intimidation were used to enforce the boycott. The leaders of the movement, of course, maintained that only peaceful means of persuasion were employed.[71]

Later in the year, Mrs C.R. Das joined the volunteers in picketing and was arrested. The outcry was so great that Mrs Das and several other women were released in the middle of the night, but the publicity was a boon to the movement.[72]

On November 17, the Prince of Wales arrived in Bombay for a long-planned visit and the non-cooperators shut down Calcutta. This closing up shop throughout the city for a day, a *hartal*, was, by every account, almost completely successful, and Subhas Bose was one of the key organizers. Around India some 25,000 Congress workers were arrested, but Das wanted Subhas on the outside, not in a prison cell.[73] Upendra Nath Banerjee has portrayed the Subhas of those days:

> Never in my life did I see such a tireless worker. Laxity is almost an universal trait of the Bengalis. We are rather fond of taking our time in doing anything, we procrastinate. Subhas was entirely different. He had, what in English is called 'Bulldog tenacity.' He never gave up something in the middle and once a job was started by him, it was to be finished. A must for him. And hardship was no problem for him; he was ready to go without food, rest, sleep to finish the job. So he was also not ready to tolerate the laxity of others working with him and any sign of it in others made him mad, though he often did not express his anger outwardly; rather he used to suffer inwardly from suppressed anger and disappointment. Sometimes he even wept like a child. When everybody was ready to go to jail, Subhas was not permitted by Deshbandhu to go to jail. Subhas felt so 'piqued' that he burst into tears. Seeing this Deshbandhu laughingly named him 'our crying captain.'[74]

In November the Congress appointed 'dictators' to direct the movement in the different provinces and Das became Bengal's dictator. Das had been touring, speaking, directing throughout the year. One fervent speech was entitled, 'The Call of the Motherland,' in which Das told the students of Bengal that the strength within them was not their own, but rather 'the divine will of the country and the God of our being.'[75] Like his former legal client Aurobindo Ghose, Das found manifestations of the divine within nationalism. The power, or *sakti* within, was to be used in selfless service to the Motherland. The idea of the fallen Motherland, the fusing of the political and the religious imagery was passed down from Bankim Chandra Chatterjee and Aurobindo Ghose to Das and certainly found resonance within Subhas Bose.

Shortly after the November *hartal*, the Government of Bengal and other provincial governments began to move against the Non-Cooperation Movement. The nationalist press claimed that this showed both the success of the movement and the fears of the British Raj. Congress and Khilafat volunteers were declared unlawful associations under the Criminal Law Amendment Act of 1908. The nationalists ignored these strictures and many thousands were soon imprisoned. Subhas Bose had his desire fulfilled and both he and Das with other Bengal organizers were arrested on December 10 and sentenced to six months in jail.[76]

On December 12, 1921, Janaki Nath Bose wrote to Sarat Bose:

> We are proud of Subhas and proud of you all. I am not at all sorry as I believe in the doctrine of sacrifice, in fact I was expecting it almost daily.
>
> Your mother has taken the incident in a bold spirit and thinks that such sacrifices will ultimately lead to Swaraj. Please convey to dear Subhas our heartfelt blessings.[77]

The one-time loyalist of the 1912 Bengal Legislative Council, Janaki Nath Bose now moved in the direction of his son. Once Subhas had dived into the waters of political action and found them invigorating, he brought his father and brother along with him. Janaki was old and unwell, so he sat on the shore and praised Subhas' feats. Before long, Sarat stepped in, gingerly at first, then he too was whole-heartedly in the swim of things. It was not at all unusual in those days for the younger members of a family to rush ahead of their elders, find their sense of place and mission, and then recruit their older family members to the cause.

A few years later—while imprisoned in Mandalay—Subhas had occasion to describe his first incarceration side-by-side with C.R. Das:

> I had the privilege to be in the same jail with him for eight months in 1921–22. For a couple of months, we were in the Presidency Jail occupying two adjacent cells, and the remaining six months we were in one big hall along with several other friends in the Alipore Central Jail. During those few months I used to look after his personal comforts. We did the cooking too for him in Alipore Jail. I consider it a rare privilege to have had the opportunity of serving him for those eight months. Prior to my arrest in December 1921, I had worked under him only for three or four months. During that brief period, I had not had the opportunity of knowing him very intimately. But during the eight months I spent with him in jail I came to know him really well. There is a saying in English, 'familiarity breeds contempt,' but of the Deshabandhu, at least, I can safely say that having known

> him most intimately my love and admiration for him increased a
> hundred-fold. . . .
>
> The Deshabandhu had an endless fund of humour and fun in him. . . .
> It flowed out as spontaneous as a mountain torrent. . . . The Deshabandhu's
> humour was of such simple and innocent type that it never made us feel ill
> at ease in spite of our difference in age and status.[78]

Subhas went on to recall Das' wide knowledge of English and Bengali
literature:

> His ordinary talk and even his jokes were interspersed with literary quota-
> tion so that sometimes I missed the point unless he explained things for me.
> He was forgetful about many things, but in matters literary his memory was
> prodigious. By introducing a literary flavour in his daily life he made
> literature an object of perennial interest—a thing to be enjoyed and appre-
> ciated by all.[79]

During this first jail period, Subhas not only had an opportunity to draw
closer to his chosen leader, but also to exercise the tender, caring nurturant
side of his personality. His respect and love for the older man is expressed
throughout the several letters and essays he wrote about Das in 1925.[80]

The first month, Pandit Malaviya was meeting with top officials of the
Raj and serving as a go-between to the Congress leadership, some of whom
imprisoned, some outside. Das was eager that some results be accomplished by the end of 1921, for, after all, Gandhi had promised 'Swaraj in
one year . But it was Gandhi who rejected a government proposal for a
round-table meeting which, at the least, would have marked a step forward
for the Congress as a recognized spokesman for the Indian people in the
eyes of the rulers. Das was angry with Gandhi as he said to Gandhi and his
countrymen in a statement some time later:

> I myself led people to prison. I started the movement in Bengal. I sent my
> son first to jail. My son was followed by my wife, and then I went to prison,
> because I knew there was electricity there. I knew that the spirit of resistance
> that manifested itself was mighty and the proudest Government did bend to
> it. You bungled it, and mismanaged it. Now you turn round and ask people
> to spin and do the work of the Charka alone. The proudest Government did
> bend to you. The terms came to me and I forwarded them to the Headquar-
> ters, because at that time I was in jail. If I had not been in jail, I would have
> forced the country to accept them. After they had been accepted, you would
> have seen a different state of things.[81]

But Das was in jail, Gandhi was in command, and the negotiations failed.
Non-cooperation continued and planning went ahead for civil disobedience during the year 1922. At the annual Congress session in Ahmedabad
in late December, Gandhi read out Das' presidential address and acted to
defeat a complete independence resolution put forward by Hazrat
Mohani.[82]

By the end of 1921, Gandhi, for his part, was angry at the Bengalis because Bengal was far short in its production of khadi. Although several Gandhian-type ashrams had been established by his more fervent followers in Bengal, there was not as enthusiastic support of the Gandhian constructive program in Bengal as in some other provinces. Even the *Statesman*, antipathetic to Gandhi and Das, was moved to comment on Gandhi's suggestion that, 'If, then, there are not enough volunteers in Bengal, I should think she should be swept into the Bay of Bengal and make room for better men and women.'[83] The leader writer for the *Statesman* said,

> There are distressing signs that Mr. Gandhi is losing his temper. . . .
> Intellectual Bengal has rejected the charka and has virtually given Mr.
> Gandhi to understand that what counts is mind. Hence all that interferes with
> the freedom of the intellect is mischievous and reactionary. Mr. Gandhi is
> apparently unable to understand this answer. He has no conception how men
> and women can fill up their leisure unless they are spinning and weaving.
> It is time that he should realize that in Bengal professional men are often so
> much occupied that they are unable to give themselves the pleasure of
> reading a book of the hour.
> Mr. Gandhi flatters himself that 'Bengal will not lag behind when once she
> is fully awakened.' He has yet to realize that Bengal is lagging behind, as
> he puts it, simply because she is too wide awake.[84]

There had been incidents of violence throughout the subcontinent in 1921, particularly in Bombay at the time of Prince of Wales' visit, and the Moplah disturbances in South India. None of these, however, brought forth such a powerful reaction from Gandhi as the Chauri Chaura incident of February 5, 1922. According to a government report,

> On the 5th February 1922 at Chauri Chaura in the Gorakhpur district of the
> United Provinces, a mob of 2,000 villagers led by volunteers attacked a
> police station, killing and burning the entire police staff, consisting of two
> Sub-Inspectors, 18 constables and one chowkidar. This gave Gandhi the
> requisite excuse and, on the ground that India was clearly not yet sufficiently
> non-violent to indulge in civil disobedience, he called a meeting of the
> Working Committee of the Congress at Bardoli. . .[85]

When the Working Committee met, it passed resolutions suspending the planned civil disobedience and stopping all Congress activities 'designed to court arrest and imprisonment'. All picketing was ended, except by designated Congressmen in front of liquor shops. It also instructed peasants not to withhold rent payments from landlords and informed the latter that the Congress 'in no way intended to attack their legal rights.'[86]

Many senior and junior Congress leaders were extremely upset by Gandhi's move, but the Mahatma had the votes to pass these resolutions in the Working Committee and later in the All-India Congress Committee. Motilal Nehru and C.R. Das, among many others who had gone to prison to push the movement forward, sharply criticized Gandhi for calling off the movement because of this one incident. It left the Congress with only one focus: Gandhi's constructive program centered around the spinning wheel. Neither of these senior lawyers and experienced politicians had been entranced by the charkha and now they were left to either spin or find a new course for the movement without the active assistance of Gandhi.[87]

Shortly thereafter the quiescent movement was deprived of its leader when Gandhi was convicted of publishing seditious articles in *Young India* in 1921 and 1922. He made no defense and on March 18, 1922 was sentenced to six years imprisonment. The government had long waited for an appropriate moment and thought the waning days of non-cooperation when even many of his co-workers and allies had deserted him was the time.[88]

Das, in the Alipore Jail, was reassessing and evaluating Gandhi's movement of the last fifteen months. As Subhas Bose later reported, Das did appreciate the progress of the movement under Gandhi, but,

> ... what has to be regretted is that he did not show sufficient diplomacy and prudence when the crucial hour arrived. In this connection I am reminded of what the Deshabandhu used frequently to say about the virtues and failings of Mahatma Gandhi's leadership. According to him, the Mahatma opens a campaign in a brilliant fashion; he works it up with unerring skill; he moves from success to success till he reaches the zenith of his campaign—but after that he loses his nerve and begins to falter.[89]

Das had shifted to support Gandhi in 1920 because Gandhi had showed that his non-cooperation program had the backing of the majority within the Congress. With the termination of this campaign and the vacuum of program and leadership created by Gandhi's imprisonment, Das and sympathetic allies moved toward a new strategy during 1922.

During this period, others recalled the dissident and confused voices of the time. For example, a government report on the press of the period said:

> There appeared to be a good deal of uncertainty even among the Extremist papers as to the ultimate object of the non-cooperation agitation. The *Amrita Bazar Patrika* thought that 'those who advocate non-cooperation, believe that long before the last stage (of complete paralysis of the present administration) is reached, Government will realise the coming doom and offer some compromise which will lead to the establishment of a national state without any violent revolution.' The *Servant*, on the other hand, thought that 'the primary object of non-cooperation was not paralysis of Government. The primary object is self purification. Its direct result may be a paralysis of a government which lives on our vices and weaknesses.' Similarly, the

Liberty held that 'the main object of the campaign is not so much to paralyse the administration just at present as to rouse the sleeping demons of India and make them stand on their own legs.'[90]

The range of objectives stated demonstrates that even among the foremost nationalist spokesmen there was either confusion or a good deal of difference in emphasis as to where they were headed under Gandhi's direction. The *Patrika*, one of the longest lasting of the nationalist papers, stressed the political goal, while the *Servant*, a Gandhian paper, presented the inner, moral development of Indians as the goal of the movement. The *Liberty* picked out the objective of political mobilization, focusing on a process rather than a clear-cut goal. None of these objectives were incompatible with each other or with Gandhi's most frequently stated specific aims or with his vaguer notion of swaraj.

Fundamental criticism of the movement and its aims was left to political opponents, officials, or to unattached intellectuals, like the foremost Indian writer of modern times, Rabindranath Tagore. Many of the criticisms enunciated during non-cooperation were simply ignored by Gandhi and the Congress. But Tagore's was a voice too well-known and respected by friend and foe to be disregarded.

Tagore had commented on the plight of Indian students when Subhas Bose was rusticated from Presidency College. Subhas joined a delegation of students to see the poet at Santiniketan a few years before that and then met him again on his return voyage from Europe in 1921.[91] Tagore had worked and lived for more than thirty years, sometimes on the fringe, sometimes in the center of the nationalist movement. His most biting verbal darts against Western imperialism were thrown during the 1890s and his period of vital action in the center of nationalism was the Swadeshi era of 1905 to about 1908. The songs and poems of Tagore were on the lips of Subhas as a young man and he remained an admirer of Tagore throughout his life.

Tagore was never in full agreement with any of the political leaders, though in the last decade of his life he was sympathetic to the approach of Jawaharlal Nehru. Tagore never entered politics quite so directly after his disillusionment with Swadeshi. He remained, however, a frequent and penetrating commentator on the development of the movement and his relinquishment of his knighthood after the Jallianwala Bagh incident in 1919 was widely applauded in India. Certainly from the year of his Nobel Prize, 1913, Tagore stressed his international concerns and shrewdly denounced the excesses of nationalism not only in India, but in Japan, China, and the West.[92]

In October 1921 Tagore published his first major essay on Gandhi and non-cooperation, 'The Call of Truth', which argued that truth was of both the head and the heart; while Gandhi stressed inner truth and love, he was fostering blind, unquestioning obedience to his message of charkha by one and all. Tagore wanted Indian economists and leaders to fully investigate whether this made any economic sense. Tagore had his doubts and he resented that all were told to simply 'spin and weave.'[93]

Tagore also objected to the burning of foreign cloth because it was foreign. Gandhi stressed the need for Indian self-sufficiency in every sphere of life, while Tagore saw the need for international cooperation and sharing. In the modern age, the poet insisted, India must learn from abroad, for example, in science, as well as look inward. Tagore believed that India had a message for the world, but he thought India must also incorporate others' messages into her own cultural repertoire. Like Gandhi, Tagore believed that inner swaraj and cultivation of the self was vital, and some aspects of Gandhi's constructive program were not foreign to the oft-repeated teachings of village reconstruction and paths to Indian revitalization which Tagore had put forward.[94]

Gandhi answered Tagore with his essay, 'The Great Sentinel,' published in *Young India,* October 1921. Gandhi said that the spinning wheel had been chosen as the centerpiece of his program after due reflection and he wanted all to spin because, 'When a house is on fire, *all* the inmates go out, and each takes up a bucket to quench the fire.' Ignoring Tagore's suggestion of research and evaluation by economists, Gandhi insisted that the constructive program including the charkha would be the economic salvation of India. He also implied that Tagore did not have the welfare of India's masses at heart and preferred, along with other non-spinning aesthetes, the soft life.[95] Neither really spoke directly to the other's concerns.

Where Subhas Bose stood is not clear, but neither he nor his mentor C.R. Das were known as enthusiastic spinners. They were political men and when Gandhi offered what seemed to them an effective program pointing to independence, or at least dominion status, they would work concertedly with him. When Gandhi seemed to offer little in the way of platform or leadership, then they would look for other avenues. In the non-cooperation period from December 1920 to February 1922, Das and then Bose (July 1921 to February 1922) were certainly closer to the Gandhian pole of organized action against the Raj than to the Tagorean practice of questioning the efficacy of each move for its negativism or its shortcomings from an international perspective.

In looking back at non-cooperation, it is clear from both Congress and government assessments that while some thousands of students left their schools and some lawyers briefly abandoned their work in the official court system, these boycotts were not successful. No alternative systems of schools, courts, or administrative bodies were established. Appeals to the army for defections also went unheeded. The boycott of foreign-made cloth had some impact, but it too was not widely and sharply effective, though it gave a boost to Indian textile production. Since the Gandhi-directed movement was helpful to Indian producers, some Indian capitalists began to support the movement. One of the most famous of those who entered was G.D. Birla, then based in Calcutta, who became a confidant of Gandhi and a significant financial backer of the Mahatma.[96]

Non-cooperation also tied in to the industrial unrest and economic downturn which followed the end of the First World War boom. One recent student of the industrial activity and union organizing of the period has argued that the peak period of strikes began in mid-1920 and was already fading when non-cooperation was seriously launched. These strikes were over limited economic issues and not closely linked to the political activity of the non-cooperators. The All-India Trade Union Conference met in 1920 and it can be suggested that the beginnings of the complicated history of all-India trade union activity are here, although roots go back to the nineteenth century.[97]

C.R. Das supported a strike by tea coolies in eastern Bengal and Assam in early 1921 that also attracted the support of Gandhi's friend and co-worker, C.F. Andrews. Das' interest in labor organization grew once he became Bengal's foremost Congressman, but his concern was to link such organizing to the national movement rather than to organize unions *per se*. Another recent student of non-cooperation in Bengal has pointed out that there was some peasant involvement particularly in the districts of Midnapore, Rangpur, Chittagong, and Tippera, led by peasants from the dominant castes. The Congress, as noted above, when ending many non-cooperation activities and calling off the planned civil disobedience action, opposed rent strikes by peasants against their landlords. The Congress wanted and needed the support of the wealthier strata in society and was not willing to challenge economic vested interests.[98]

The Congress Civil Disobedience Inquiry Committee, which included Hakim Ajmal Khan, Motilal Nehru, C. Rajagopalachari, and Vithalbhai Patel among its members, was critical of the failures of the school and legal boycotts, but split on the issue of continuing non-cooperation from *within* rather than from *outside* the reformed councils.[99] After Gandhi called off the movement, left for prison, and told those on the outside to continue the constructive program, many Congress workers and supporters were left disenchanted. Recriminations flew this way and that and many of the survivors were not at all satisfied to ply the charkha rather than engage in some more direct form of political activity.

CHAPTER FOUR

Swarajists in Calcutta and Mandalay, 1923-27

What's this I hear at this red dawn of night:
I hear the roar of liberation in the resounding chains of prisoners:
Who are they that smile the smile of liberation in jail?
The bounds of fear have dissolved in their free hearts.

Nazrul Islam, 'Ovation to the Prisoner'[1]

I

For more than a year after the end of non-cooperation, the plains of political action were relatively quiet. As the *Banglar Katha* of January 26, 1923 stated:

> Non-Cooperation has lost its terror. Inertness has taken the place of courage in people's hearts. The clarion call of the Mahatma is heard no more, and the workers have become worn out with the struggle. . . swaraj will neither fall from heaven nor will it come from beyond the seas as a reward from pleasing Parliament. It will have to be forced from the British Government, the necessary requisites being self-reliance and self-confidence.[2]

However, the temporary lapse of action vis-à-vis the Raj did not mean that Indian nationalists had gone into a long winter's sleep. First, they continued a range of humanitarian and constructive activities. Second, they were arguing with each other about what new ways they could devise to topple the Raj. Subhas Bose, released from prison in August 1922, was shortly involved in work on both of these fronts.

The month after his release, Subhas served as the chairman of the reception committee of the All Bengal Youngmen's Conference, with Dr Meghnad Saha, the famed scientist, as the president. According to the report of a contemporary,

> . . . Subhas pleaded for sincere work and patient suffering. He stressed on all important topics—spread of mass education, Swadeshi, unity amongst different communities, removal of untouchability, prevention of early

marriages, abolition of dowry, social service, discipline, upholding truth and justice everywhere. . .[3]

Subhas was soon called to action. News of serious flooding in Bogra, Rajshahi, Pabna, Dinajpur, and Rangpur reached Calcutta on September 28, 1922. Subhas was sent by the Bengal Provincial Congress Committee to tour the area. He made Santapur his center and shortly afterwards Sir P.C. Ray formed the Bengal Relief Committee with Subhas responsible for distributing aid. With the assistance of local workers and Congressmen from throughout Bengal, he put together a force of 1,000 workers. For six weeks he directed them, and according to all reports, did an admirable job of carrying out the relief efforts. Janaki Nath Bose visited Subhas en route to the family's Durga Puja. Subhas would not leave his work and told his father, 'No father, no, you all go to worship Durga at home and I go to worship my real mother Durga with the helpless.'[4]

After this tour of duty, Subhas returned to Calcutta. C.R. Das had spent this period in the Punjab trying to recover his health and was now ready for a new campaign. When Gandhi had conquered the Congress in 1920 with his non-cooperation program, he temporarily silenced the advocates of alternative strategies. Das' idea was for non-cooperation to be extended to the legislative councils. Congressmen would run and win the seats and then bring these bodies to 'a halt by their negative actions within the chambers. Now that the Gandhi program was without what many nationalists would call a 'political' aspect, Das' plan appealed to a significant number of Congressmen. During the next several years, those who joined Das to work at non-cooperation from within the legislative councils were called the Pro-Changers, while the more orthodox Gandhians were known as the No-Changers. Congress meetings, henceforward, became a battleground for their unceasing arguments.[5]

As Das explained his program, it was a logical extension of Gandhi's non-cooperation. But Gandhi and his No-Changers maintained throughout that the temptations of ministerial office would prove too much for Congressmen elected to a majority in the councils. Once Congressmen were offered such posts, all pretence of non-cooperating would be dropped and they would work with officials of the British Raj and give noble and selfless reasons for doing so. Although the No-Changers were wrong with respect to C.R. Das and his compatriot, Motilal Nehru, they were not completely wrong about the eventual line of one group within the Pro-Changers or Swarajists, as they came to be called.[6]

The serious struggle within the Congress began at the end of the Congress' Gaya session held in December 1922, of which Das served, for the second successive year, as president. He delivered a lengthy and powerful address to the Congress putting forward his case for non-cooperation from within the councils as well as the continuation of other swadeshi activities more in line with Gandhi's program. Das drew upon his knowledge of British history and of the struggles of the British people for freedom. He also stipulated that any swaraj worth its name must involve freedom for the masses of ordinary Indian workers and peasants as well as for a well-fed bourgeoisie. He later formulated this as 'Swaraj for the 98 per cent,' and he called for close cooperation between Hindus and Muslims in India and between all Asiatic peoples.[7]

On the last day of the Congress session, a vote was held on the council entry proposal and the Gandhians prevailed by 1,748 votes to 890. Once the results were in, Das resigned as president and Motilal Nehru resigned as general secretary of the Congress, although they retained their memberships. The next day, January 1, 1923, they formed the Swarajya Party with Das as its president. Elections for the legislative councils in the provinces and at the center were to be held in the year ahead and the Swarajists intended to fly their own banner.[8]

Over the next several years, C.R. Das and his party were able to mount an effective challenge to the Raj in the legislative councils and to the Gandhians in the Congress in large part because of Das' skills as a leader. He was a peer of Gandhi in age, professional achievement, experience, and intelligence, and they shared other talents: they were both shrewd judges of men, astute recruiters of lieutenants, and excellent fund-raisers.

It had cost Das no effort to bring Subhas Bose into politics: Subhas came, sat on his doorstep, and requested his assignments. Others, often with distinguished professional records, came along, but had to be persuaded that their talents and energies would be of use. Das, an East Bengal man from Vikrampur, brought in more men from East Bengal, who were invidiously called *bangals* by West Bengal and Calcutta men. Among these were J.M. Sen Gupta, an able lawyer from Chittagong, and Nalini Ranjan Sarker, a self-made businessman from Mymensingh. From West Bengal, Das recruited B.N. Sasmal, a lawyer from Midnapore, Nirmal Chandra Chunder, a wealthy Calcutta barrister, Tulsi Goswami, a talented speaker and scion of the family of the Raja of Serampore and an M.A. from Oxford, as well as Sarat Chandra Bose. In the 1923 election to the Bengal Legislative Council, the Swarajya Party supported an independent candidate, Dr B.C. Roy, who defeated the most famous Bengal Moderate, Surendranath Banerjea, in the 24-Parganas Municipal North constituency. Sarker, Goswami, Chunder, Sarat Bose, and Dr Roy were later dubbed 'The Big Five' by a Calcutta journalist. Others who entered into Das' party included Kiran Sankar Roy, Anil Baran Roy,

Pratap Chandra Guha Roy, Maulana Akram Khan, and Satya Ranjan Bakshi. Of all these men (besides his beloved brother) Subhas Bose grew closest to Bakshi who assisted him in every political endeavor throughout his life. Bakshi never sought the limelight; he found his fulfillment in getting things done.[9]

Das not only recruited a cadre of men, but he tried to give each one the roles and responsibilities suited to him. He tried to minimize conflicts between young and ambitious men and to settle party strife. He was not always successful, but he was more adept than those who came before and after him in Bengal politics. Subhas Bose was one of those to whom Das began to give more responsibility. In the period from late 1922 through October 1924, Subhas was closely associated with weekly and daily papers giving the Swarajist point of view as well as coverage of the news. He worked with Das and Upendra Banerjee on *Banglar Katha*, a Bengali weekly, and then with Bakshi and others on *Forward*, an ambitious, first-rate English-language daily begun in 1923. Sarat Bose served along with Das, Motilal Nehru, B.N. Sasmal, and P.D. Himatsingka on the Board of Directors of *Forward*. Sarat Bose was being gradually drawn into politics by Das and Subhas in this period.[10]

Banglar Katha supported the Swarajist position on council entry and also amplified Das' point about freedom for the masses. It recommended the organizing of workers and peasants as part of the nationalist mobilization of all Indians. From 1922 some other papers, notably *Atma Sakti* and *Bijali*, spoke a more radical line of organizing the working class and became, in time, critical of the more careful line of the Swarajya Party and its papers. Subhas Bose, who took Das as his leader and worked whole-heartedly for him, was also associated with the more radical, critical, and independent voice of *Atma Sakti*. A 1925 Home Department report on 'Revolutionary Press Propaganda in Bengal' describes him as the 'Managing Director of *Atma Sakti* in 1923–24.'[11] Whether he was responsible for the day-to-day leaders and articles of the paper is not altogether clear, but it can be suggested that he had sympathy with these more radical views and they helped him to shape his own perspective.

In a leader of February 7, 1923, the writer for *Banglar Katha* came closest to the position of *Atma Sakti* and *Bijali*, when he wrote:

> The swaraj which the Congress had so long knowingly or unknowingly wished to have, is the swaraj of the rich and the middle classes. We do not always properly realise the fact that the masses of the country are still lying outside the Congress arena. We often assume that the interests of the middle classes and those of the masses are identical, which they are actually not. Their interests in most cases conflict with one another, and it well nigh

impossible for the parties to work in cooperation where this conflict or interest exists. But without co-operation swaraj can never be attained. The masses too want freedom, and with the removal of their social and economical disadvantages. We must first of all try to bring about a reconciliation between the interests of the masses and those of the rich and the middle classes, if we seriously desire to emancipate ourselves from the grip of the bureaucracy. But every attempt to bring about this reconciliation will meet with failure until and unless the peasants and labourers of our country form well organized associations of their own.[12]

Although we do not know that Subhas Bose wrote this leader, it is likely that it came close to his views of this period and later. We may call this the class-conciliation nationalist position. It did not call for expropriation of the property of the rich and middle classes. The *Banglar Katha* supported this view and Das' council entry strategy for immediate political action.

In a brief article in 1925, *Forward* congratulated *Atma Sakti* on entering its fourth year and commented:

Founded and edited originally by the veteran journalist Srijut Upendra Nath Banerjee, the paper was taken charge of by Srijut Subhas Chandra Bose after its editor was thrown into prison in 1923, under Regulation III. Srijut Subhas Chandra Bose with his wonderful power of organization conducted the weekly with credit, maintaining the traditions set up by its worthy founder, until some time last year when he was deprived of his own liberty. Young Bengal has been watching the progress of the paper all these years with considerable interest and have no doubt that it has all along given a proper lead to the thinking section of our young men whose organ it claims to be.[13]

What was the lead that *Atma Sakti* was giving to young Bengal during 1923 and 1924? First, that the masses had to be organized and that their interests were not necessarily reconcilable with those of the upper classes; second, that the use of violence in the pursuit of freedom or swaraj was not unthinkable.[14]

The success of the Bolsheviks in overthrowing the Kerensky Government and the elimination of the Romanovs from the rule of Russia had a great impact on the minds of young Asians in the 1920s. With that victory and the formation of the Third Communist International in 1919, socialist and communist ideas began to spread rapidly among the politically interested throughout the colonial world. A Bengal revolutionary, M.N. Roy, was now working for the Comintern and messages and agents were beginning to seep into India.[15] But these few men and their pamphlets were only one link between Indian nationalists and these ideas. Books and articles appeared in the press and before a decade was out, important Indian leaders including Jawaharlal and Motilal Nehru and Rabindranath Tagore had traveled to the Soviet Union and written positive accounts of what they had seen. Efforts were made to read the smuggled pamphlets and books of M.N. Roy and also the works of Marx and Lenin. Bertrand Russell's sympathetic account of socialism, anarchism, and syndicalism, *Roads to Freedom* (first published in 1918) was read by the Bose brothers and others. Although the British Raj banned the writings of M.N. Roy and some other communist writers, they could not effectively insulate India from works on socialism and communism published in Great Britain, particularly at a time when the British Labour Party was rapidly becoming a major party in the homeland of empire. So by the early 1920s, Subhas and Sarat Bose had certainly begun their socialist education.[16]

In a typical *Atma Sakti* editorial of the 1923–24 period, the writer described the full meaning of swaraj:

> The majority of the people of this country are composed of peasants and labourers, but so long the question of their hopes and fears has been avoided in all our so-called national agitations. But the tables have now been turned and there is no room in swaraj for those who want to make a cat's paw of others and live in luxury on other's money. In most cases those who raise crops, by tilling the soil in Bengal have no proprietory rights over the land. Those who enjoy profits, varying from 200 to 300 per cent, by establishing mills and factories, and whose mill-hands pass their lives with their little ones in tattered clothes and in dark rooms, never think that most of the money they earn ought morally to go to those labourers and that money which they spend on luxury is really stolen money. We often hear them speak of swaraj. To them swaraj means monopoly of committing this theft. It is high time to make it clear to them that swaraj and theft cannot go hand in hand. We must gird up our loins against those who, by refusing to identify their interests with those of the people, have become impediments in the way of swaraj, no matter whether they be our own countrymen or foreigners. We must build up the ideal of making the interests of the masses the foundation of the movement and every attempt must be made to curb influences which are hostile to every just means for the establishment of that swaraj.[17]

Many of the most sharply worded articles in *Atma Sakti* were written by Subhas Bose's youthful companion, Hemanta Sarkar. As Sarkar grew ever more critical of the bourgeois Swarajya Party, he and Subhas parted. Sarkar went his way with asperity still flowing from his pen; Subhas left with sadness and disappointment in his heart.[18]

In the same period, writers for *Atma Sakti* also seemed to propose armed rebellion as an alternative in case non-cooperation were to fail to bring the Raj to its knees. These words from the February 10, 1923 issue resonate with Aurobindo Ghose's very similar ones in his Swadeshi articles, 'The

Doctrine of Passive Resistance':

> Call it swaraj or what you will, there are only two ways for a subject nation
> to be free from the bondage of slavery. The one is true non-cooperation and
> the other an armed rebellion. There is besides these, no other course. It is the
> inherent cowardice of the nation that has prevented the non-cooperation
> movement from assuming a terrible form and from destroying the bureauc-
> racy. So, first of all, attempts should be made to remove by all means
> timidity from the country. The object of the nation has now become clear
> and bright. What the nation now wants is full self-government and inde-
> pendence free from association with foreigners. . . . This cowardice has
> prevented us from carrying on the bright torchlights of awakening to the
> centre of our strength, which is the united popular force of this vast India
> . . . it is quite incomprehensible that one should remain non-violent at all
> times and under all circumstances. No sane man will ever brand it as an act
> of bare impiety if we have to resort to brute force to combat brute force, with
> a view to secure freedom for our mother-land.[19]

It was articles such as this which landed Upendra Nath Banerjee in prison,
for the Government of Bengal would not allow such advice to stream out
uncensored. Although this article was published before Subhas Bose came
closer to the operation of the paper, it is a view which he shared.

When Subhas Bose was a college student, he joined a group of young
men devoted to social service. Around them at that time during the First
World War there were numerous other groups organizing for revolutionary violence. By 1916, by dint of severe repressive measures and good
intelligence work, the Raj was able to gain control over this movement and
jail many of the revolutionaries. With the end of the Great War, the post-
war reforms, and a hope that these men would turn to peaceful activity,
most of them were freed. Many of them joined the Congress and the Non-
Cooperation Movement after secretly meeting with Das in 1920. Das knew
they had skills he could use and he preferred to have them working with
him on peaceful mass mobilization, rather than committing political
dacoities and assassinating officials. The main groupings of
revolutionaries, Jugantar and the Anushilan Samity, refrained from violent acts as long as Gandhi's campaign held the center of the stage.
However, once, Gandhi was imprisoned and Das was set on council entry,
they began to move toward renewed activity outside the Congress'
strategies and framework.

The connection of Subhas Bose and later Sarat Bose with the revolutionaries is not a simple matter. Subhas Bose knew and sympathized with
them and wanted them to continue to work with him in the Congress and
support the Swarajya Party. Even though he may have believed that
eventually the British would have to be driven from India by force of arms,

he did not think the time was ripe. Some of the revolutionaries were now Congressmen and did not think of returning to a life of hiding, secrecy, and violence. Others were beginning to turn to socialism, though the major conversions took place in the later 1920s and the 1930s. But some others began again to prepare for revolutionary actions.[20]

They had behind them their history of violent actions from 1908 to 1916. They were also spurred on by the violent path and results of Irish nationalism. The Sinn Fein Movement, the Easter Rebellion, and the struggle of Irishmen against the Blacks-and-Tans from 1919 to 1921 were well known to the educated young men of Bengal. There were frequent reports of Irish developments in the nationalist press and books were beginning to appear in Bengali on the Irish struggle for freedom. Shortly, Dan Breen's *My Fight for Irish Freedom* appeared and became, according to one participant, 'one of our bibles.'[21] To the young revolutionaries, it seemed that the violent actions of Irish nationalists had culminated in the establishment of the Irish free state.

Subhas Bose was not ready for direct involvement with those who thought that non-cooperation was dead and armed rebellion was the only way. But the Government of Bengal was already beginning to take the view that he was, indeed, one of the revolutionaries. Since his return to Calcutta and his entry into politics, Subhas Bose was under the close scrutiny of the Intelligence Bureau, Home Department. His contacts with revolutionaries were known to them. They were also investigating whether Das and Subhas Bose had made any positive response to communications from the Cominterns. These overtures, they learned, had been rejected, but the revolutionary contacts went on and the agents of the Raj watched, filled their log books, and waited.[22]

The swarajist and leftist press of the early 1920s is filled with calls for organization and mobilization of the masses. Das, Subhas Bose, and many of the Swarajist leaders were urban men who focused on city problems and concerns. So, though they talked of the peasantry, their first efforts to organize the masses were among workers in urban centers although they did not do much day-to-day, down-to-earth organizational work.[23] C.R. Das served as president of the All-India Trade Union Congress(AITUC) in 1922 and worked to settle a railway workers' strike at Kharagpur and steel workers' grievances at Jamshedpur in 1924 as head of a Conciliation Board. At that time all management positions at Tata Iron and Steel Company (TISCO) were held by foreigners. Moni Singh, an organizer at Jamshedpur, has recounted how Das challenged the workers at a joint meeting with management to aspire to Indianization of all these jobs.[24]

Subhas Bose also showed his first interest in the labor field at this time, working in the South Calcutta Congress Committee's efforts at organizing a workers' association there. Several years later, he was to follow Das in presiding over the AITUC and in acting for the workers' interests at Jamshedpur. Das and later Subhas Bose wanted unions to extend the field and consciousness of nationalism and not simply work for the settlement of economic grievances.[25]

After release from prison in mid-1922, Subhas Bose gradually began to take on greater responsibility within the Bengal Congress organization. In 1923 he became the secretary of the Bengal Provincial Congress Committee and often spoke at political meetings and youth conferences throughout Bengal. He started to attend All-India Congress Committee meetings in other parts of India. He was beginning to emerge as a young nationalist politician on his way up. He was, perforce, intimately involved with the on-going factional struggle in the Congress between the Swarajists and the Gandhian No-Changers. Though Subhas Bose continued to refer to the Gandhians as the majority party—which they were on the national scene—they were not the majority in Bengal. The sniping by the No-Changer faction in Bengal went on unabated, and Subhas Bose, who had learned his debating skills in Presidency College, in the Philosophical Society in Scottish Churches College, and at the Indian Majlis in Cambridge, needed all his training and experience to defend his party's views and actions.[26]

For example, Subhas had to write endless letters to the press correcting their reports of meetings and proposals in order to keep the clearest and most accurate presentation of the swarajist position before the public. He wrote to the *Amrita Bazar Patrika* on June 4, 1923, commenting on reports of his statement before the AICC meeting in late May in Bombay:

> My attention has been drawn to certain inaccurate reports that have appeared in some of the Calcutta papers.... I stated at that meeting that the boycott of the Bengal Legislative Council along the old lines would be a failure. The last bye-election in Calcutta at which 40 per cent of the voters voted in spite of the complete inactivity of the Swarajya Party and the vigorous anti-council propaganda of the Majority Party, bore testimony to what I said. I added that there were two bills, dealing with university matters and tenancy rights, which might come up before the next council. These two bills were of such vital interest to the intelligentsia, the middle classes and the masses that whatever might be the attitude of the Congress with regard to the Council the great mass of voters in Bengal were in my opinion sure to send their representatives to the Council at the next election. I concluded that under such circumstances, anti-council propaganda in Bengal appeared to me to be utterly futile.[27]

Although he vigorously opposed the Gandhian view on council entry, this did not stop Bose from playing a key role in organizing a Gandhian-type institution, the Dakshin Kalikata Sevak Samity, started in 1921 under another name, to produce khadi, and reorganized in May 1923 to foster industrial production, social service work, and a library. He worked as secretary and treasurer of this institution and also as secretary of the South Calcutta Sevasram, an orphanage. He also spoke frequently at youth conferences in different districts encouraging young men to work in the nationalist movement, do constructive work, and also collect information systematically about villages in their areas.[28]

The intra-Congress battle between the Swarajists and the No-Changers was fought over more than just council entry. Two issues vital to Swarajist support in Bengal came before the AICC in late 1923 and 1924. The first concerned the Bengal Pact and the second, the Gopinath Saha Resolution. Bengal's No-Changers had opposed these resolutions when they were brought before meetings of the Bengal Provincial Congress, but both had passed. They met a different fate in the all-India arena.

As indicated above, Das had long thought that Muslim support was crucial. The Muslims were a majority of the population in Bengal, and about 20 per cent of India's population, and the nationalists could not ignore such a substantial segment of the Indian community. Gandhi, too, had made an effort to reach out to the Muslims by including the Khilafat issue as one of the goals of the Non-Cooperation Movement. But this was a distant, international issue.

Disturbed by communal riots in Bengal and other places in India, and seeing the practical necessity for Muslim backing if the Swarajists were to succeed in blocking governmental actions, Das forged the Bengal Pact in 1923 with Muslim leaders in Bengal. He agreed that Muslims—who lagged in government employment—would get 60 per cent of all new appointments in political arenas where the Swarajists were elected to power. This would continue until they had positions commensurate with their share of the population. He promised an even greater share of appointments in the Calcutta Corporation if the Swarajists were successful there. This appeared as a bread-and-butter issue to both communities and many Hindus in Bengal led by the Gandhian spokesman, Shyam Shunder Chakravarty, opposed the pact when it came before the Bengal Provincial Congress. An analysis of the Bengal Provincial Congress Committee during 1924 shows that only 13 per cent of the membership were Muslims. But Das' influence was sufficient for the pact to secure passage. Many politically active Muslims thought it was a sign of Das' good faith and non-communal spirit and during his lifetime, rendered him their support.[29]

Surviving attacks in the Calcutta press by the *Amrita Bazar Patrika,*

Basumati, and the *Servant,* Das raised the proposal for a nationwide pact along the same lines at the Cocananda session of the Congress in December 1923. He felt that there was great resistance to his proposal, and asked, 'Why is (there) this resentment against Bengal? . . . Bengal demands the right of having her suggestion considered. . . . You cannot delete Bengal.'[30] His pleas for the plan were not answered by the national representatives and it was defeated. However, it remained in effect in Bengal, in so far as the Swarajists could fulfill it.

Just as Das wanted Muslim support and reached for it, he also wanted the continued help of those men. and shortly women, who were involved in revolutionary organizations but still willing to work non-violently in the Congress. So he supported a resolution about Gopinath Saha, a revolutionary who had murdered a Mr Day while trying to assassinate Sir Charles Tegart, Calcutta police commissioner, and the revolutionaries' Enemy Number One. The resolution passed at the Bengal Provincial Conference at Serajgunge in 1924, read:

> This conference, whilst denouncing (or dissociating itself from) violence and adhering to the principle of non-violence, appreciates Gopinath Saha's ideal of self-sacrifice, misguided though that is in respect of the country's best interest, and expresses its respect for his great self-sacrifice.[31]

Saha had been captured, tried, and executed, and entered the revolutionaries' pantheon of martyrs. Though Das was committed to open and non-violent activity, he would not condemn violent actions out-of-hand as a Gandhian would. Subhas Bose, who did not attend the Serajgunge meeting, was, however, involved in a small incident related to Saha's death:

> Gopinath was cremated in the Jail compound by his brother Madan Mohan Saha and three others. Hearing that a permit would be given to enter the Jail to perform the funeral rites, Subhas and Sj. Purna Das accompanied by many college students went to the Presidency Jail early in the morning but failing to get permits could not enter, but when the last relics of Gopinath—the clothes given by Jail authorities to his brother—were touched by Subhas, he was very much moved. This does not mean Subhas entertained sympathy for terrorism, but the spirit of sacrifice filled him with admiration. . . .[32]

Shortly thereafter, Subhas was addressing a meeting in Harish Park and said,

> Our duty is to see that the pockets of Britishers are touched. There are two ways to teach them a lesson—either by force or by doing things which touch their pockets. As the first is unsuited to India constitutionally, we must have recourse to the second.[33]

Although neither the touching of Saha's clothes, nor the speech which referred to the use of force involved any commitment to the use or support of violent acts, Subhas was probably unaware how closely he and other Swarajists were being watched by the Home Department intelligence agents.

A few months later in June the Saha Resolution was brought by Bengal Congressmen before the AICC meeting at Ahmedabad. It lost by only seventy to seventy-eight. Gandhi was shocked that so many Congressmen could vote for it, and in an article entitled 'Defeated and Humbled,' which he published in *Young India* after the meeting, Gandhi called the amendment a breach of the Congress creed or the policy of non-violence.[34] Again, a Bengal point of view did not prevail in the National Congress, and it showed the difference in values and political perspective between the majority in the Bengal Congress and the dominant Gandhian standpoint. Since the Boses adhered to the Das-Bengal view throughout their lives, it is necessary to emphasize the gap that remained even when Gandhi and Das came closer together, at least according to Gandhi, in the following year.

Gandhi failed to expel the Swarajists from all executive positions in the Congress and the majority and minority factions, Pro-Changers and No-Changers, continued their hostile truce. For their part, the Swarajists spent 1923 and part of 1924 working energetically in election campaigns, first for the Bengal Legislative Council, then for the Calcutta Corporation. To run in such elections was new to the Congress, but they proved equal to these first challenges.[35]

Under the 1919 Government of India Act (Montagu-Chelmsford reforms) a system of dyarchy together with expanded legislative councils was instituted. In Bengal, the new council was to have 140 members, 114 elected and twenty-six nominated. Of the elected seats, thirty-nine were for Muslims, while fifty-seven were general or Hindu constituencies. There were also elected seats for Europeans, Anglo-Indians, commercial bodies, and nominated seats in a variety of categories. There were not to be more than twenty nominated officials in the house. Dyarchy meant that certain transferred departments, particularly having to do with 'nation-building' areas, were to have Indian ministers in charge of them. Matters considered vital, finance and security, were still under official control. The idea of the formulators of the scheme was that Indians were to gradually learn the art of self-government, slowly taking some responsibility for limited areas of government.

The 1919 Act also provided for the expansion of the electorate which numbered about 1,000,000 in 1920, slightly more for the 1923 election, and more than 1,100,000 in 1926. Only a fraction actually voted, but this number was higher in 1923 and 1926 when Swarajist candidates ran than in 1920 when the Congress boycotted the elections.[36]

Although the Congress remained on the sidelines, Moderate nationalists, now called Liberals, a variety of Muslim candidates, and a wide range of independents, mostly loyal to the Raj, did run. The Bengal Legislative Council operated from 1920 to 1923 with members drawn from these sources. Three Indian ministers served the government, the most prominent of whom was Surendranath Banerjea. He served as minister in charge of local self-government. After a long and distinguished career as a nationalist leader (which dated back to the 1870s), Banerjea had decided that to work the reforms was in India's best interest. Hampered though he and the other ministers were by legal restrictions and lack of funds, they did try to put through some constructive legislation. Banerjea successfully steered the Calcutta Municipal Bill through the rocks and shoals of the Council, though it provided for separate Muslim electorates, over his strenuous objections. In 1899 he had resigned from the Calcutta Corporation when it had been 'officialized'—had its percentage of official members increased and elected members decreased—and now he was proud to preside over the passage of a bill which would give more widely elected members control of the affairs of the Calcutta city government.[37]

For the most part, the Council operated in an air of unreality trying to ignore the tumultuous happenings outside as the Non-Cooperation Movement swept past their door. Many members did object to the repressive laws that the government pushed through to deal with the movement. Although the Moderates and Loyalists saw Gandhi as the harbinger of anarchy and revolution, they were willing to argue against the harsh measures instituted by the government and also to try to work in their small sphere for India's gradual advancement. But for all the talents and concern of the 1920–23 councillors, they had no real party organization or program for their country. Once they had to face more formidable and organized opposition for their seats, many of them fell by the wayside including Surendranath Banerjea.[38]

In the 1923 elections for the Bengal Council, the Swarajists won forty-seven seats and many others were won by independents sympathetic to their strategy and positions. According to the official Government of Bengal report on the reforms:

> By 1923, the Swarajist party had arisen with improved organisation, a defi-
> nite political programme, substantial party funds and a declared policy of
> contesting on behalf of the party in as many seats in the council as possible.
> The party discipline was also good, and not more than one Swarajist
> candidate was put forward in any constituency. Consequently in 1923 and

1926 the Swarajists gained a large number of seats and were able to form a powerful party in the Council.[39]

C.R. Das led the Swarajists into the council chambers determined to block the government when possible. He declined the governor of Bengal's (Lord Lytton) offer of a ministership and tried to prevent any ministers from serving. He also planned on blocking repressive laws and increased funding for the police.[40]

To gain his objectives, Das needed wider support than his party members and he needed a significant number of Muslim members on his side. One Muslim Swarajist, Abdur Rashid Khan, served as secretary of the Swarajya Council Party, and a rising Muslim politician, H.S. Suhrawardy, though not a Swarajist Party man, worked with them. Muslims with nationalist sympathies and even some of the Moderates cooperated upon occasion with the Swarajists. During the first council session in 1924, the Swarajists moved that ministers' salaries be reduced to one rupee per annum. This was passed by sixty-three to sixty-two, to the cheers of the Swarajists. Again ministers were appointed and in August 1924, a second vote to reduce their salaries to one rupee was passed by sixty-eight to sixty-six. The Swarajists effectively prevented any ministers from serving from 1924 through 1926. They also scrutinized the budget and, in some cases, blocked grants for departments and activities which the government thought essential.[41] Led by Motilal Nehru in the Central Legislative Assembly, with the help of independent members, the Swarajists were able to defeat the government on some important divisions of the house during 1924 and 1925.[42] So, on the destructive side, the Swarajists had some early triumphs in their efforts to resist the Raj from within the councils.

On the government side in the Bengal Council, an effort was made to split the Muslim backers and members away from Das' Swarajya Party by bringing the issue of the immediate implementation of the Bengal Pact before the house. The effort failed because the Muslim backers of the Swarajists, including H.S. Suhrawardy, stood firmly with Das. The Hindu-Muslim alliance in the Bengal Council lasted through 1924 and 1925, and marks one of the effective efforts at communal cooperation that dotted the decade after the Lucknow Pact between the Congress and Muslim League in 1916.[43]

Though he considered himself an enemy of the new nationalists—Gandhians and Swarajists—Surendranath Banerjea prepared the ground for the return of the nationalists to the Calcutta Corporation. In early 1924, the Calcutta Municipal Act of 1923 was implemented and elections were held for councillors and aldermen. The councillors then chose the mayor

and the mayor selected the chief executive officer to be responsible for the
day-to-day running of the Corporation. Das was elected mayor and Sarat
Bose an alderman. Das then considered several candidates for the
executive position, including B.N. Sasmal, and over some objections,
picked Subhas Bose for the post. Bose asked Das, 'Have I given up the ICS
to be Chief Executive Officer of the Calcutta Corporation?' Das replied,
'You must serve.'[44] Bose had to secure approval from the Government of
Bengal. Regardless of their private·reservations, they approved his appointment and he took up office on April 14, 1924. In line with nationalist
reservations about benefiting from the fruits of office, he took only half the
monthly salary of Rs. 3,000 and contributed most of what he did take to
charity.[45]

In the Calcutta Corporation, the Swarajists, for the first time, could act
in a practical and responsible way and try to demonstrate to the public, to
their rulers, and to themselves, that they were entirely capable of self-
government. C.R. Das set forth the aspirations of his party in his opening
speech to the Corporation:

> . . . the great work which I have undertaken for the last 10 or 15 years is the
> building up of a Pan-Indian people consisting of diverse communities with
> diverse interests, but united and federated as a nation. In this Corporation I
> find plenty of work possible in that direction. So far as it lies in me you will
> find that no communal interest will be sacrificed unless that interest goes
> against the well-being of the whole community, by which I mean the Indian
> people or the citizens of Calcutta in this particular respect. . . . It is the great
> ideal of the Indian people that they regard the poor as *Daridra Narayan*. To
> them, God comes in the shape of the poor and the service of the poor is the
> service of God to the Indian mind. I shall, therefore, try to direct your
> activities to the service of the poor and you will have seen that in the program
> which I have drawn up (for) most of the items deal with the poor; housing
> of the poor, free primary education, and free medical relief—these are all
> blessings for the poor, and if the Corporation succeeds even to a very limited
> extent, it will have justified itself.[46]

In addition to these goals for the poor, Das also said that he wanted to
achieve: (1) a purer and cheaper food and milk supply, (2) a better supply
of filtered and unfiltered water, (3) better sanitation in the bustees and
congested areas of the city, (4) development of suburban areas, (5)
improved transport facilities, and (6) greater efficiency of administration
at a lower cost. This list must have made a great impression on Subhas
Bose, for he put forth the same list as his goals when he became the mayor
six years later.[47] Would·not such a list still be appropriate for the Calcutta
of today?

Das now had gained the 'Triple Crown'—he was leader of the Swarajists in the Bengal Legislative Council, president of the Bengal Provincial Congress Committee, and mayor of Calcutta, as well as leader of the all-India Swarajya Party. With this multiplicity of roles to fulfill, he was delighted to turn over the day-to-day operations of the Corporation to Subhas Bose.[48]

Subhas moved to nationalize some practices of the Corporation, to fulfill the spirit of the Bengal Pact, and to start on Das' long list of goals for improving municipal life. The Corporation began to provide cotton uniforms for its different categories of employees made only of khadi, although this did not please the powers-that-were in Writers' Building. With the aid of several councillors, Bose encouraged Indian production of other items required by the Corporation. Binoy Jiban Ghosh, secretary of the Corporation, wrote in a 1954 memoir of the swarajist period:

> The distinguished old revolutionary Sri Amarendra Nath Chatterjee and another old revolutionary Sri Satish Chandra De founded the Bengal Belting Co. for manufacture of hose pipes in this country and the Corporation resolved that henceforward hose pipes of Indian-make alone would be purchased by the Corporation. For lighting of approximately 10,000 electric lights, the Corporation has to purchase bulbs worth many thousands of rupees. The Bengal Lamp Co. started by Sri Satish Chandra De mentioned above, began the supply of bulbs made in this country to the Corporation, which reiterated the principle that articles of indigenous-make should have preference. Similarly for supplying mantles for about 20,000 gas lamps in the city, Sri G.C. Laha was, at the personal insistence of Netaji, persuaded to take up the manufacture of gas lamp mantles here in the city.[49]

Starting with improvements for the Corporation's employees, Bose organized the Corporation Workers Cooperative Stores to give them advantages in purchasing goods for themselves; he made beneficial changes in their tiffin room (for which henceforward, once every year, the employees offered him joint thanks); he suggested that the Corporation Provident Fund be established; and he played a part in the organization of the Corporation Employees Association.[50]

According to his contemporary, Hemendranath Das Gupta, Subhas brought both his nationalist ardor and his ICS seriousness and sense of decorum to play on the workings of the Corporation. The most difficult officer for him to deal with was Mr Coates, the chief engineer, a European with equal pay and long years in his post. Coates did not hesitate to smoke before his new superior, as he had done before previous Bengali chairmen. Bose did not think this proper. Das Gupta recounts,

> ... one day Subhas in his usual serious manner with the smile of an ICS man just reminded the Chief Engineer—
>   'Is it proper, Mr. Coates, to smoke before a Superior Officer?' Mr.

Coates—'Sorry.' (and he left it in the trash).

'Since then Mr. Coates did not smoke a second time unless Subhas gave him permission.'[51]

In this incident, as in others which were to follow throughout his career, Subhas had a sense of office and status and what was due to him. Informal and warm among his friends and colleagues, he demanded proper respect in more formal situations, and particularly vis-à-vis Europeans and other non-Indians.[52]

For the citizens of Calcutta, Bose worked on a proposal for ward health associations and suggested changes to the city's engineers on improving the water supply. A special interest of his had always been education and he was fortunate to secure the assistance of his long-time friend and compatriot in England, Khitish Chattopadhyay. Chattopadhyay, an anthropologist by training, had to be persuaded to enter the more practical and political business of the Corporation as education officer. He threw himself into it and did research on the history of public education in Calcutta and in conjunction with a sub-committee of the Corporation made a survey of schools presently operating in Calcutta and of the level of literacy of the city's population. He found 53 per cent literacy for males and 27 per cent for females in Calcutta, and a relatively small number of Corporation schools, and set to work arranging for the rapid expansion of free primary education. The goal of Das, Bose, and Chattopadhyay was to have free and compulsory education for all Calcutta's children. Although there were some rancoros debates, particularly on what education was appropriate for Muslim children, the number of Corporation primary schools grew quickly in this period.[53]

Das and Subhas Bose and their colleagues in the Corporation also had the idea for a weekly Corporation paper. Out of this proposal, speedily implemented, grew the *Calcutta Municipal Gazette*, skillfully edited by Amal Home, and published weekly from November 15, 1924 to the present. It remains an excellent and enduring record of the affairs of Calcutta.[54] Another of Bose's plans was for a Calcutta Corporation Commercial Museum which was to emphasize home industries' products. This too was established.

The Calcutta Corporation was a large employer. Following the spirit of the Bengal Pact, Bose moved immediately to give a very high percentage of new and replacement positions to Muslims where qualified workers from this community were available. Bose was challenged by Hindu members of the Corporation, and in answer to the probing of Lt Bijoy Prasad Singh Roy, in mid-July 1924, Bose replied,

There are 96 vacancies in various departments of the Corporation. This figure however includes all classes of appointments, such as Bailiffs who are appointed on the nomination of Heads of Departments concerned. . . 33 have been filled up in the course of the last fortnight. 25 have been given to Muhammadans. . . . There were more than 1,000 applications of various kinds. . . . There were some B.A.'s and M.A.'s among the candidates whose claims were considered. I am however of opinion that academic qualifications alone do not prove the real worth of a candidate. . . . I entirely repudiate the suggestion that the appointments have been made in utter disregard of the best interests of the Corporation. I am fully conscious of the responsibility that rests on me. I have no Hindu-Muslim pact before me but I have certainly taken cognisance of what I consider to be the just claims of the Muhammadans, and in future propose to do so.[55]

Bose also presented an amplification of his views. He said, in part:

In filling up the vacancies I have used my own discretion and the responsibility is therefore mine. . . . Not only academic qualifications, but character, energy, devotion and honesty as well, have to be taken into account in judging the fitness of a particular candidatee . . . whatever may be the claims of the intellectually advanced classes in the matter of appointments to the higher offices, so far as ordinary posts are concerned there is hardly anything to fear, even if all the posts go to Muhammadans, Christians and members of the depressed classes. . . . If the persons who have been appointed are not up to the mark, it will be my duty to get rid of them and I shall not shrink from that unpleasant task. . . . Appointments to the higher offices are everywhere made by direct recruitment and that is because it is felt that the introduction of fresh blood into the administration system gives healthy tone to the whole organism. I am further of opinion that claims of the different sections of the people have got to be considered in making appointments. I do not think I shall be wrong if I say that in the past Hindus have enjoyed what may be regarded as a sort of monopoly in the matters of appointments . . . the new Corporation standing . . . for a new epoch—has got to respond to the spirit of the times . . . though it is sure to give rise to a certain amount of heart burning in the ranks of the Hindu candidates.[56]

Subhas went on to discuss the plight of the educated unemployed and said they must have proper technical education to help alleviate this problem. For his efforts at communal rapprochement, he was abused in a variety of nationalist newspapers. Das, of course, defended him, and even Gandhi came to his defense in *Young India*, July 31, 1924:

I note that the chief executive officer of the Calcutta Corporation has come in for a good deal of hostile criticism because of his having given 25 out of 33 appointments to Mussalmans . . . . I have read the statement made by the chief executive officer . . . it is a creditable performance. I have no doubt that appointments have not till now been made with impartiality, whether by Europeans or Indians. There is no doubt, too, that in many cases Hindus have influenced decisions in their favour. It ill becomes them to quarrel against many posts having now gone to Mussalmans. . . . Personally, I would like appointments to go to the best men irrespective of parties, and should, therefore, be made by a permanent non-party board. But if Hindus wish to see India free, they must be ready and willing to sacrifice in favour of their Mussalman and other brethren.[57]

Subhas Bose realized that the Congress (including the Swarajists) had to reach out to ever wider groups and cross communal lines sympathetically and generously if it was to uphold its claim to be *the* spokesman for all Indians. Bose attended a September meeting in Harish Park presided over by Pandit Gopabandhu Das who was forming an Oriya labor organization. Oriya workers from all over Calcutta thronged to the park, and *Forward* reported that,

> Babu Subhas Chandra Bose spoke in Oriya amidst loud cheers and clappings. He expressed his appreciation of the activities of Pandit Gopabandhu who as he said might be called the uncrowned king of Orissa. The Oriya Labour Union in his opinion was a necessity as it would prove beneficial to the labourers themselves and to their masters. He assured the audience of his full sympathy and support to the institution which he said was a movement of mainly social character. If the movement proceeded steadily, he would try to secure help for it from the Calcutta Corporation to establish night schools and to provide medical aid.[58]

Bose endured the abuse of some of his fellow Hindus over allotment of Corporation jobs and was bringing in new recruits—including several who had been detained in prison for revolutionary beliefs and actions. He was thriving in his new position.

Then, on October 25, 1924, everything suddenly changed. As Subhas Bose remembered the moment a few years later,

> In the early hours of the morning of October 25, 1924, I was roused from my sleep as I was wanted by some police officers. The Deputy-Commissioner of Police, Calcutta, on meeting me said: 'Mr. Bose, I have a very unpleasant duty to perform. I have a warrant for your arrest under Regulation III of 1818.' He then produced another warrant authorising him to search my house for arms, explosives, ammunition, etc. Since no arms, etc. were forthcoming, he had to content himself with taking a pile of papers and correspondence.[59]

No specific charges were ever made public and Bose—along with seventeen others in this particular round-up—was jailed for an indefinite term. No charges, no hearing, no right of *habeas corpus*, no judge, no jury. This was the Raj's special method of dealing with those suspected of revolutionary involvement. Taken within one brisk October day from his home, family, and the highest seat of executive power in the second city of the British Empire, Bose became simply another political detainee in the

New Alipore Central Jail.

There was little recourse except angry words. The government ignored challenges to make the charges public and hold a trial. The Swarajists, of course, were in an uproar since several of their leading members were held. A meeting of the Corporation a few days later focused on these arrests. Many referred to the 'violence of the Government' and to their 'lawless laws'. Das, obviously upset, said,

> All that I say is that Mr. Subhas Chandra Bose is no more a revolutionary than I am. Why have they not arrested me? I should like to know, why? If love of country is a crime, I am a criminal. If Mr. Subhas Chandra Bose is a criminal, I am a criminal. Not only the Chief Executive Officer of this Corporation, but the Mayor of this Corporation is equally guilty.[60]

There was one rumor that Das had inadvertently sent a police agent on to Bose, but whether true or not, Das insisted that the arrest of Bose and several other Swarajists was part of a deliberate plot by the government to make nationalist government of the metropolis impossible. Das is reported to have conversed with the Conservative governor of Bengal, Lord Lytton, and said, 'You are taking my healthiest shoots.' To this Lytton replied, 'You are not my gardener. . . . I must protect my police and officials.'[61] Several attempts had been made on the life of Police Commissioner Tegart and other officials.

But was Bose involved in these actions and, as the *Catholic Herald* wrote, the brain behind the revolutionary conspiracy, and a young man whose own father lamented his revolutionary associations? From interviews with former revolutionaries and close Bose associates as well as from published memoirs and Hemendranath Das Gupta's excellent contemporary biography of Bose, it appears that Bose met with active revolutionaries and knew in a general way what they planned to do, but was not himself directly involved in planning or directing their actions. His interest at this point in his career was with open, mass organizational work and with the administration of the Calcutta Corporation, the Swarajya Party, and the Bengal Provincial Congress Committee. What is important in the life of Subhas Bose is what the Government of Bengal's Home Department *believed* was his connection to the revitalization of the revolutionary movement which had been relatively quiescent since the middle of the Great War, the better part of a decade earlier.

According to a 'Brief Note on the Alliance of Congress with Terrorism in Bengal,' prepared in the Home Department:

> Mr C.R. Das was supported by the terrorists without whose help he could never have won victory for Council entry over the no-changers. It is known that the leader of the Swarajya Party was aware that his terrorist allies were

engaged in criminal conspiracy. It is also known that his connivance at it was the price that the terrorists demanded for their support which was essential to his success in elections. Government attacked this conspiracy by arresting ring leaders under Regulation III. Most of them were members of both the terrorist party, known as Jugantar Party and of the Swarajya Party . . . in 1923 it was noticed that the headquarters of both parties in Calcutta were at one and the same place. . . . In 1924 the terrorist members of the Swarajya Party supported the candidature of Mr. Subhas Chandra Bose as Chief Executive Officer of the Corporation and it was noteworthy that after his appointment to that post many jobs in the Corporation were given to terrorists . . . 28 ex-detenus or political ex-convicts were office-bearers of the Bengal Provincial Congress Committee and 21 revolutionaries or sympathisers were elected to the All India Congress Committee.[62]

In an earlier report on the 'Revolutionary Press Propaganda in Bengal', it was stated in a note about Subhas Bose, who was listed as managing director of *Atma Sakti*:

While in England he closely identified himself with the revolutionaries there and in Berlin. He was a staunch follower of C.R. Das and an important Congress organiser. He was convicted and sentenced to six months' rigorous imprisonment under section 17 (1), Criminal Law Amendment Act, in February 1922. In 1923 he was Secretary of the Bengal Provincial Congress Committee. He became the leading organiser of the revolutionary movement in Bengal and was in close communication with others abroad and with Bolshevik propagandists. He was deeply concerned in the conspiracies to assassinate police officers and to smuggle arms into India.[63]

In other files, it was noted that Bose was a 'prominent Congress Communist agitator' who expressed seditious and blood-thirsty feelings which were unbalancing the mental equilibrium of his young hearers. It was asserted that he had agreed to the assassination of Police Commissioner Tegart, met with Bolshevik agents, and was using Corporation funds to buy and smuggle arms into India.[64]

Many angry protests were made in response to the imprisonment of Bose and several score of political workers, some held indefinitely under Regulation III of 1818, others held for a specified period under the Bengal Criminal Law Amendment Act Ordinance of 1924. The ordinance was put before the Bengal Legislative Council as a bill in early 1925 and the Swarajists managed to defeat it much to the chagrin of the Government of Bengal. But under his reserve powers, the governor of Bengal certified the act and prisoners were to be held for up to five years until the expiration of the act.[65] While imprisoned, Subhas Bose was moved from the Regulation III category to the Bengal Criminal Law Amendment Act category. No charges were ever made public, no trial was held.[66] Even

Sarat Bose's legal acumen could find no workable lever to spring his brother free.

II

For the first six weeks of imprisonment Subhas Bose was held in a Calcutta jail. Furthermore, he was allowed to continue his Corporation work. Files flowed to his prison cell; officers of the Calcutta municipal government including Europeans came to see him at his cell-cum-office. But the Government of Bengal shortly decided that this pattern would not do. In the first week of December 1924, Subhas Bose was severed from the business of the Corporation and with other detenus transferred to Berhampore Jail, more than a hundred miles from Calcutta.[67]

Jogesh Chandra Chatterji, then a member of the Anushilan group of revolutionaries and a fellow prisoner in Berhampore has described jail life there. During the month-and-a-half he was held there–and was one step further removed from his Calcutta life–Subhas entered into the prisoners' activities. He was a participant in the big badminton match between the state prisoners and the detenus. Still a state prisoner, Bose and his fellow Swarajist Anil Baran Roy represented this group, while Jogesh Chatterji and another detenu played for the other team. The state prisoners lost. But Bose, who had not previously thought much of badminton came to understand the necessity for physical exercise and took to it with zest in Berhampore and later jails.[68]

Chatterji also says that he was in direct contact with his party men outside the jail and that their leader, Naren Sen, stayed in a house visible from the jail. The prisoners put together a secret hand-written monthly 'magazine' for which Bose produced an article on the independence of Poland, and Chatterji wrote about Ireland. Saraswati Puja was soon to be celebrated and Chatterji asked Bose what the prisoners should do if they were not allowed to celebrate it properly. Bose did not like protests against the jail officials for trivial matters, but for the sake of a proper *puja*, he said they might have to carry through a hunger strike.[69]

Less than two months later, Bose and seven others were packed up for another journey:

> On January 25th, 1925, I suddenly received orders of transfer to Calcutta. On my way I learnt to my great surprise that my real destination was Mandalay Prison in Upper Burma. At midnight I reached Calcutta and was taken to the Lalbazar police-station to spend the night there. The room in the police-station was a dirty hole and thanks to mosquitoes and bugs, it was impossible to have a wink of sleep . . . if there is a hell on earth, it is the Lalbazar police-station.[70]

Since the group was considered one of highly dangerous political prisoners, transfers were made quietly and often at night. On the long trip by van, boat, and rail to Mandalay, they were accompanied by Mr Lowman, assistant inspector-general of police for Bengal. Surprisingly,

> Our four days' voyage was rather interesting. Mr Lowman was jovial and communicative and we discussed all possible subjects. . . I even raised the question of the torture of political prisoners by the police. . . . On the whole, though I began with a strong prejudice against him, I came to hold a favourable opinion of him.[71]

Burma was to be his 'home' for the foreseeable future. He had no idea how long he would be there and even the authorities had not settled on a precise term. One of the most prominent nationalist leaders of the preceding generation, Bal Gangadhar Tilak, had spent six long years there and was never again the same fiery patriot.

Subhas Bose and his batch of seven detenus joined some other political prisoners, as well as ordinary convicts in the jail of wooden palisades at Mandalay. The Burmese had been forced to cede Lower Burma to the British in the 1820s and moved to Upper Burma where King Mindon built the last capital of the Burmese kingdom near a steep hill believed to have the characteristics of a sacred mountain. A Buddha was built part-way up the hill and a small capital was laid out surrounded by walls. While the royal buildings and the jail were within the walls, the homes of the ordinary Burmese and of aliens including Chinese, Indians, and hill tribesmen were outside the walls.[72]

In the 1880s the British moved on Upper Burma, conquering it in 1882. According to one analyst, 'Under British rule, Mandalay was transformed from the center of the universe into a small provincial town. . . . The focus of Burma during the colonial period ceased to be the palace and became instead the port located in Rangoon.'[73] Mandalay is located in a dry zone set back from the more moist coastal region. Subhas Bose described the dry season in the spring in a letter to Sarat:

> Babu Jitendriya Bose once described his favourite Cossipore as 'a kingdom of dust'. I am sure he has not seen the real kingdom of dust–for that is Mandalay. . . in Mandalay the dust is in the air–therefore you must inhale it. It is in your food, therefore you must eat it. It is on your table—your chair and your bed–therefore you must feel its soft touch. It raises storms, obscuring distant trees and hills–therefore you needs must see it in all its beauty.[74]

In time Subhas came to learn that rain-storms as well as dust-storms could howl through the palisades as he experienced the round of the year in Mandalay.

But dust or rain, hot season or cool season, he never felt well or comfortable during almost two years there. Part of this had to do with the construction of the prison, as Subhas sketched it,

> The interior of a Burmese prison is somewhat different from that of an Indian prison . . . the jail-buildings were built not of stone nor of brick, but of wooden palisading. From the outside and especially at night, the inmates of these buildings appeared almost like animals prowling about behind the bars. Within these structures we were at the mercy of the elements. There was nothing to protect us from the biting cold of winter or the intense heat of summer or the tropical rains in Mandalay . . . we had to make the best of a bad situation.[75]

Besides adapting physically as best he could, Bose also had to learn how to adapt psychologically and socially to this new environment. Unlike his previous imprisonment during the Non-Cooperation Movement, Bose had not sought this indefinite term, nor believed that it was deserved. The manifest unfairness of it all added to the difficult conditions in Mandalay. As a political prisoner, locked away in unhealthy conditions by the imperialist rulers of India, he made an indirect contribution to the nationalist cause by being considered so dangerous that he had to be incarcerated. The pressures of physical and psychological distress were softened by a belief which emerged from his understanding of Hindu philosophy that individual suffering would contribute to a long-term social good.

Many thousands of Indians sought or were given terms of imprisonment during the nationalist period, but their experiences have never been systematically studied. Some tried to continue working by participating in secret networks. Some gave themselves over to reflection, writing, research, or meditation. Others became incapacitated and hobbled along until their eventual release.[76]

Subhas Bose was normally an active and hard-working man who had found his calling: nationalist worker striving for the independence of his country. Imprisonment limited his political and administrative work, but did not cut it off entirely. The ties to his former life were maintained by letters and visits. At first he could write only two letters a week, but receive any number. At least one of these letters was usually to Sarat Bose or his wife and the other was shared between a number of other correspondents. A good number of these letters survive, including many written to him and by him, but I do not know how many have disappeared and how many were upheld for censorship reasons and never released. One primary limitation on these letters as a source is that most political discussions were forbidden.[77]

Subhas kept in as close touch as possible with his two main families: Sarat and Biva and his family of birth, and Mr and Mrs C.R. Das, his adopted family. Sarat was his main link for all practical matters, finances, requests for reading matter, food, et al. Sarat was also his primary legal adviser for questions on his detention and some of the strictures he was subject to, and in number of law suits with Calcutta newspapers whom he believed had libeled him. Although Sarat did not go to court in these cases, he chose Subhas' legal representatives and served as link to and from his younger brother. Sarat paid all of Subhas' bills and picked up many of his charitable and social service contributions for the duration. Sarat was also a connection to the affairs of the Calcutta Corporation, *Forward*, and Indian politics, in all of which Sarat was becoming increasingly involved. He was also the first family member to venture out to Mandalay and visit Subhas in his wooden prison in April 1925. This gave him a better sense of Subhas' life there, his needs, and complaints.[78]

Sarat's wife Biva was also a frequent correspondent and to her Subhas recounted the details of the prisoners' domestic arrangements and every-day life. Subhas' picture of the cooking, cleaning, games, animals, etc.— all the minutae of the prisoners' world—was described to Biva as the person in Calcutta most responsible for organizing the mundane family existence in which Subhas participated when he was a free man.

Here is a part of Subhas' description for Biva of the jail household:

> Our household is not of mean size. The family consists of nine members. But, needless to add, they are all men. If we include servants etc., we are no less than twenty. We live in a small jail inside the big jail. The inmates, master or servant, may not mix with the rest of the prisoners. In our household there are all kinds of people, cook, cook's mate, cleaner, sweeper, etc. Apart from living quarters, this small jail also contains a kitchen, a tank, a tennis court, etc. The bathroom has been under construction for the past six months. . . . Here we have a household but no housewife. In the absence of a housewife we have appointed a Manager—needless to say, he is a prisoner without trial like the rest of us. He keeps accounts; he draws up daily marketing lists and he is supreme in household matters; this great family is at his beck and call. We hold him responsible for our food and clothing and do not hesitate to take him to task when food is bad. We have named our household—so and so's hotel.[79]

The servants of the class A and B political prisoners were chosen by the authorities from among the ordinary convicts. Meeting and interacting with them was valuable and instructive to Subhas who wrote,

> I have now ceased to have any bad feelings about convicts. Many of them are compelled by circumstances or distress to commit crime and many get sentenced without any guilt. Many of them are warm-hearted and I have no

doubt whatever that in a healthy environment they may become good citizens.[80]

Most of his time in and out of jail had been and was spent with members of the upper and middle strata of society. In the close confinement of Mandalay Jail, he had to spend time with those from the lower strata and often those from the lowest depths of existence. This led Subhas to reflect upon imprisonment, jail conditions, and the causes of crime. Further, he drew up an outline for a work on prison life and conditions, but never came to write it. Most of the writing he did in prison was of short pieces and fragments, but this activity like participating actively in the jail household, playing badminton, and swimming in the small tank, were all part of coping in as healthy a way as he could with the forced and indefinite confinement. He wrote to several people that, 'men eat molasses when honey is scarce.'[81]

Beyond his immediate jail family, Bose quickly began to learn about the Burmese and Burma. He wrote in the *Indian Struggle*,

> From one of the state prisoners . . . we took our first lessons in the Burmese language. I was not there long before I developed a strong liking for the Burmese people. There is something in them which one cannot help liking. They are exceedingly warm-hearted, frank and jovial in their temperament. They are of course quick-tempered. . . . What struck me greatly was the innate artistic sense which every Burman has. If they have any faults, it is their extreme *naivete* and absence of all feeling against foreigners.[82]

Mandalay had become in the nineteenth century one of the most important handicraft centers in all of Burma and this may have led Bose to stress the artistic sense of all Burmans. It remains today a flourishing handicraft center where local artisans turn out intricate painted designs and beautifully carved Buddhas.[83]

In his letters from this period, Bose expresses some of his other thoughts about the Burmese. He wrote to Dilip Roy during his first year there:

> Burma is in many respects a wonderful country and my study of Burmese life and civilization is furnishing me with many new ideas. Their various short-comings notwithstanding, I consider the Burmese—like the Chinese— to be considerably advanced from a social point of view. What they do lack most of all is initiative—what Bergson would call 'elan vital'—the vital impulse to overcome all obstacles and march along the road to progress. They have developed a perfect social democracy—women . . . are more powerful here than in any European country—but alas! the enervating climate seems to have robbed them of all initiative. . . . You probably know that the percentage of literate people in Burma, both among males and females, is more than in any other part of India. This is due to the indigenous and wonderfully cheap system of primary education through the agency of

the priests. In Burma, even today, every boy is supposed to don the yellow robe for a few months, if not for a few years, and to study at the feet of the priests. This system has not only an educative and moral value but has a levelling effect as well—since rich and poor are thus brought together.[84]

Burma was still a part of British India and as Bose learned more about Burmese politics, he understood the split between those who wanted to be separated from India–as independent Burma had always been—and those who did not. He was also impressed greatly by the egalitarianism and lack of caste in Burma. Although he saw them as deficient by Bergson's measure of the vital creative spark, he thought that socially they had progressed further than India because of the pervasive feeling of equality. He attributed this equality in large measure to the impact of Buddhism on Burmese society. He was a devoted Hindu, but learned more about the day-to-day life of a Buddhist society during his imprisonment in Burma than during any other period of his life.[85]

One of the few things which Bose brought back with him from Burma was a marble, seated Buddha with one hand touching the earth. This is a gesture—the *bhumi* position—of calling the earth to witness his right to attain Buddhahood after having overcome the temptation of the evil Mara. It is a meditative position and during this imprisonment, Bose spent time meditating and reflecting.[86] He also turned to the studies of Bengali religion and literature to make up for what he considered 'my neglected education.'

One fellow prisoner, Surendra Mohan Ghosh, who like Bose had a religious turn of mind, claims that he directed Bose to these studies, but the promptings could as well have come from a combination of his inner desires and the conditions of captivity. Ghosh, along with Bose and some of the other prisoners, certainly participated in these studies. In college and during his Cambridge period, Bose was an avid student of Western philosophy and was awarded Calcutta University prizes and a high placement in the ICS examination because of his proficiency. But now the focus was mainly Indian religion, philosophy, and literature, although his Western interests were not completely neglected. Bose ordered the complete works of Nietzsche in many volumes from Calcutta, made his way through them, and urged Ghosh to join him.[87]

He not only had jail study companions, but he had a precious friend in Dilip Roy with whom he exchanged letters. Dilip was eager to bring out the philosophic Subhas and Subhas knew that in Dilip he had a keen listener to his innermost ruminations. Through their correspondence, Subhas and Dilip enjoyed what the latter called 'the sweets of friendship.'[88]

Deprived of the opportunity to do his nationalist work, Bose was sure—as a believer in a divine power behind the manifest workings of the universe—that God had some important purpose for having him imprisoned and causing him this suffering. The dream faculty and the philosophic side of the personality came to the fore. He wrote to Dilip,

> As long as that idealism is present, I believe a man can brave suffering with equanimity—and even joy. Of course one who is philosophically inclined can turn his suffering to a higher purpose, enriching himself thereby. But then is it not true that we are all philosophers in embryo and it only requires a touch of suffering to awaken the philosophic impulse?[89]

He wrote to another friend in a similar way the following year:

> I have now been in prison for exactly fourteen months. . . . Prison life has taught me a lot; many realities which were vague and distant now appear clear to me; many new experiences have strengthened and enriched my life . . . . I am of course a prisoner—but there is nothing to be unhappy about. To suffer privation for the Mother is a matter of glory. You have to believe me when I say that there joy in suffering. Otherwise, one would go mad, one could not laugh with his heart brimful with joy even in the midst of privation! What to external appearance is suffering, appears to be a source of bliss when you go deep into it. Well, of course, I do not feel this way every day in the year or every hour in the day; after all I can feel the fetters on my body.[90]

His inherited and chosen form to worship the divine was in the form of the Mother Goddess, especially as Durga or Kali. However, in the past two generations the significance of the Mother had been broadened to include Motherland, so that devotion to the divine also meant intense attachment to one's country, i.e., patriotism. Thus political activity or service to the country was at the same time religious action. Political workers were *karmayogins* striving for the liberation of their country as well as for personal salvation or moksha. This was a lesson that Subhas Bose learned from religious texts like the *Bhagavad Gita* and from his nationalist forebears, particularly Bankim Chandra Chatterjee and Aurobindo Ghose.[91]

To a few of his correspondents Subhas Bose served as a teacher-leader, such as with several members of the Bhowanipore Sevak Samity who wrote to him asking advice about their problems. To Hari Charan Bagchi, he recommended work, regular exercise (which Subhas himself had probably never done before his imprisonment) and emphasized the need for study, contemplation, and meditation as part of one's personal *sadhana*. Of meditation, he wrote,

> . . . just as regular exercise improves the physique, similarly regular meditation cultivates the good faculties and destroys the evil ones. Meditation has two aims: (1) Destruction of the evil faculties, principally to

overcome lust, fear and selfishness, and (2) Manifestation of love, devotion, sacrifice, intellect and such other noble attributes.[92]

He suggested,

It is possible for one, through his own efforts, to develop love and devotion and thus reduce selfishness. By gradually enlarging one's love, man can leave all narrowness behind and eventually lose himself in the Infinite. So, one should think of and meditate on objects of love, devotion, and reverence. Man becomes exactly the image of what he contemplates. . . . The way to conquer fear is to worship Power. The images of Durga, Kali, etc. are the expressions of Power. Man can attain power by invoking any of its forms in his mind praying to Her for strength and offering all his weaknesses and faults at Her feet. Infinite strength lies dormant inside us, we must bring it to life. . . . You must contemplate some form of Power every day, seek strength from Her, offering all the five senses and all evil at Her feet.[93]

What Subhas was advocating was what he was trying to practice within the walls of Mandalay prison, utilizing the two predominant religious traditions of Hindu Bengal, Vaishnavism and Saktism. In addition to quiet and solitary meditation, he gathered together and probably sang—to himself or with others—*kirtans* (old devotional songs) and recent devotional songs by his favorites, D.L. Roy (Dilip Roy's father), Rabindranath Tagore, and Nazrul Islam. There are even some songs in his prison notebooks which may have been his own efforts or fragments of songs by others. These songs expressed the growing love of the bonded, earthly believer and his surrender to the divine. They also contain many images of imprisonment and a passion for freedom. The religious predominates but floods its banks to mingle with the patriotic. So there is love of the Mother and the Infinite, but also Golden Bengal.[94]

In several of Subhas Bose's writings from his teenage years, there are references to lust and the search for ways to conquer it. In his letter to Hari Charan Bagchi, Subhas utilizes the Ramakrishna-Vivekananda approach:

The best means of conquering lust are to visualise the mother-image in all women, to invest women with that halo and to worship God in the mother-form, such as Durga or Kali. When man contemplates God or Guru in the form of the Mother, he learns to see divinity in all women; when he reaches this state he has overcome lust.[95]

This seems to be a procedure which he adopted as a teenager and adhered to for many years. In Western terms, we might say that this was his defense against powerful sexual drives which were with him even in the male community of his Burmese prison. This running together of ordinary women and the Mother Goddess brought him to complications which we will see later. This 'solution' appears curious to Westerners. In the psychoanalytic age, many believe that desire for the mother is the first that a young boy feels and to have a healthy sexual life, it is necessary to go beyond this desire and focus upon sexually appropriate and available women. Bose's theory was to make all threatening women into distant and god-like mothers, while in practice, he tried to treat the actual women in his life as sexually unapproachable females to be dealt with as mother or sister figures.[96]

Whether this was a complicated way of dealing with the lack of female company and a mature man-woman relationship in his life is a matter of speculation. More explicitly, Subhas Bose did write to his friends and relations that he missed many things and imprisonment taught him the value of lack he was missing so much. He said that he missed the sights and scents—especially certain flowers—of Bengal. He regretted not having had more training and knowledge of art and music.[97] To Biva, he said,

> I am writing to Mejdada to engage teachers in drawing and music for the children. I do not know how he feels about the matter—but I miss these two things in my own life. So, if children get the proper kind of education I shall feel happy.[98]

What he also missed, of course, were the children he was closest to, the many nieces and nephews whose company he loved, especially the children of Sarat and Biva. The keeping of cats by the prisoners in Mandalay proved a very poor substitute. And he knew that as his life was passing in a distant jail, life and politics were whirling ahead in Calcutta.

When Subhas Bose was arrested in 1924, the *Catholic Herald*, a small Calcutta paper, printed an article claiming that Subhas was the brain behind the revolutionary conspiracy and also fabricated letter from Janaki Nath Bose to Subhas saying how unhappy he was with Subhas' revolutionary connections. Two other much more important papers, the *Englishman* and the *Statesman* printed articles based on the report in the *Catholic Herald*. Under Sarat's direction, Subhas sued all three papers for libel.[99] Through his term of imprisonment, the suits went on to their conclusions although the Government of Bengal refused to let him testify in any of them. Sarat chose those who represented Subhas and helped them to prepare the cases. Subhas was victorious in his suits against the *Catholic Herald* and the *Englishman* and awarded Rs. 4000 damages against the former and Rs. 2000 against the latter as well as costs. Sarat wrote to Subhas on May 5, 1926 after these two cases were decided,

> Justice Gregory's judgement in the suit against the *Catholic Herald* was quite a strong judgement. He held that the words used by the *Catholic Herald* constituted '*very serious libel*' and he awarded Rs. 4000/- damages. The Editor *Catholic Herald*, has fled the country and the paper has also been stopped. There will be considerable difficulty therefore in realising

damages from the Editor, *Catholic Herald*. The Englishman will, in all probability, pay up soon.[100]

The *Stateman's* article was worded more ambiguously and a different judge was trying this suit. Sarat wrote to Subhas,

> In the meantime you might also prepare a note on the libellous statements contained in the *Statesman* article. I suppose you remember that the libel consists in describing you 'as the directing brain of the revolutionary conspiracy.' Of course, the onus of proof is on the *Statesman*. But any facts which would enable us to destroy the defendant's case would be helpful.[101]

The suit against the *Statesman* was lost in late 1926 and Sarat wrote to Subhas,

> The hearing of your libel action against the *Statesman* was over on Tuesday last. Justice Buckland seems to be of the opinion that the *Statesman* has not asserted *any facts* but has merely commented on the Governor's Maldah speech. How any one could possibly come to hold that opinion I fail to see.[102]

The attorneys for the newspapers sought help from the India Office and the Governments of India and Bengal to produce some evidence for Bose-the-revolutionary. The governments refused to assist and it was widely believed that there was no documentary evidence of any kind against Subhas, but simply some verbal statements by one or more police informers. To dangle such trifles before an open court would have embarrassed the governments, so they kept quiet.[103]

Throughout the first seven-and-a-half months of Subhas' imprisonment, from October 1924 to June 1925, the work of the Swarajists in the Calcutta Corporation and the Bengal Legislative Council proceeded under the leadership of C.R. Das, though he was often in poor health and had to leave the city for periods of recuperation. After two defeats at the hands of the Swarajists over the question of ministers' salaries in March and August 1924, the governor of Bengal, Lord Lytton, had prorogued the Bengal Legislative Council in disgust.[104] The Council met again in January 1925 and, *inter alia*, debated the Bengal Criminal Amendment Bill. The government spokesman, Sir Hugh Stephenson, implied that the revolutionaries had new sources of funds—he did not mention the Calcutta Corporation, but it was whispered in the chamber and outside—and invoked what the opposition labeled 'the Bolshevik bogey.'[105] The Swarajists denied any connection to terrorist schemes and, with their allies in the Council defeated the introduction of the bill sixty-six to fifty-six. The governor was forced to enact it under powers given him by the Government of India Act of 1919. In December 1925, the Council voted fifty-five to thirty-five to repeal the Bengal Criminal Amendment Act, but this was simply an act of defiance and did not change the government's position. But the Swarajists continually raised questions in the chamber about the condition of the prisoners held under the act, and, indeed, all political prisoners, and this probing probably led to more frequent checks by the government and better treatment of the prisoners.[106]

Das had been ill, but he came to the Council chamber for a March 1925 meeting to debate again the question of ministers' salaries. On this occasion, he had as an ally Fazlul Huq, who had been a minister for eight months during the previous year and had become disillusioned with the 1919 reforms. Das defended Huq's change of heart and summarized the Swarajist position. Ministers, Das said, without responsibility, power, and funds were a sham. If there were significant changes granting Indian ministers all three of these attributes, then the Swarajists would cooperate.[107] Until then his party would staunchly oppose the government. The Swarajists were again able to defeat the motion for ministers' salaries, this time by sixty-nine to sixty-three. In consequence, from March 26, 1925 until early 1927, the governor took over the transferred departments.[108]

Although Sarat Bose was not yet a member of the Bengal Legislative Council, he had become an alderman of the Calcutta Corporation, the other Swarajist bastion, and was one of the founder directors of the Swarajist daily *Forward*. With the imprisonment of Subhas and the passing from the scene of one important Swarajist after another, Sarat gradually assumed more responsibilities and spent more of his time on this public work. His extensive legal practice continued and he came to reserve part of the day for legal work and the evenings particularly for politics. Sarat was taking on so many different activities, that Subhas was moved to write from prison that he had too many irons in the fire and was driving himself too hard.[109]

Sarat Bose was one of Subhas' conduits to the Calcutta Corporation. The other was Santosh Kumar Basu. Subhas tried to stay in touch with the affairs of the Corporation though an acting chief executice officer had moved into his place. For the duration of his imprisonment, the Corporation councillors insisted that Subhas be listed as CEO unless he was convicted of some offense. Failing this, Subhas continued, without pay, to officially hold the post. His letters to Sarat and Santosh Basu are filled with plans for the extension of drainage, for the municipalization of the gas company, for a cold storage plant in the municipal market, for extending compulsory primary education to all children, for improving Calcutta's roads, and for combating smallpox. A stream of suggestions and plans issued from his pen in Mandalay.[110] As he wrote to Sarat shortly after his transfer to Mandalay. 'The solution of these problems depends on our conception of civil expansion and on our vision of Calcutta as she should be in future.'[111]

Sarat worked on his own behalf in the Corporation as well as on Subhas' plans. In the case of several voluntary social service organizations, the Bhowanipore Sevak Samity and the Dakshin Kalikata Sevasram, Sarat made financial contributions in Subhas' stead, but did not involve himself in their workings. When they floundered, Subhas took the blame for not having properly organized them before he was incarcerated.[112]

To some extent, Subhas fell out of touch—as was inevitable—with important political matters such as secret negotiations which C.R. Das was carrying on the spring of 1925 with the governor of Bengal and other officials. Das believed that he had demonstrated to the government that dyarchy and the Montagu-Chelmsford reforms were dead on the ground. He thought that the Swarajist efforts in the Bengal Legislative Council and at the center had clearly shown that nationalist India was effectively against these reforms because they gave no significant power and equality to India as a member of the British Empire. He talked to officials about some advance toward real power and equality, offering in return a public statement of his opposition to the use of violence. The previous year Lord Oliver had attacked Das in the House of Lords as a believer in the use of violence to drive the British out.[113] This was also implied in the detention of the group of Swarajist leaders in October 1924. In Das' public declaration in the spring of 1925, he said, in part,

> I have made it clear and I do it once again that I am opposed on principle to political assassination and violence in any shape or form. It is absolutely abhorrent to me and to my party. I consider it an obstacle to our political progress. It is also opposed to our religious teachings. As a question of practical politics I feel certain that if violence is to take root in the political life of our country it will be the end of our dream of Swaraj for all time to come. . . .
>
> I have also made it clear and I again make it clear that I am equally opposed to and equally abhor any form of repression by the Government. Repression will never stop political assassination. It will only encourage and give life to it. . . . We are determined to secure Swaraj and the political equality of India on terms of equality and honourable partnership in the Empire.[114]

Contrary to the opinions of some officials of the time and some historians since then, this declaration did not mark a sudden shift in Das' attitudes, but was in keeping with his views of many years standing.[115] For pragmatic political reasons, he worked with those revolutionaries who had joined the Congress, and tried to persuade them to work in his program of mass mobilization, Hindu-Muslim cooperation, and non-cooperation both outside and inside the legislative councils. Seeing these former detenus and revolutionaries in the Congress, Swarajya Party, and the Calcutta Corporation, officials assumed that Das was soft on violence and secretly advocated its use.[116]

Das made another statement in a similar vein at the provincial Congress meeting at Faridpore. However, he had not made any major advance in his quest for constitutional changes for India when his deteriorating health forced him to leave for Darjeeling late in the spring where he was visited by Mahatma Gandhi and Sarat Bose among others. Before leaving Calcutta, Das had put his own large home in trust for the nation and divested himself of many of his worldly goods. But even these steps had not prepared his followers or political India for his sudden death on June 16, 1925.[117] His body was returned to Calcutta by train, and about half a million mourners led by Gandhi accompanied it to the cremation site. Gandhi said at the condolence meeting,

> Deshbandhu was one of the greatest of men . . . when I parted from him only a few days ago at Darjeeling, I said to a friend that the closer I came to him, the more I came to love him. I saw . . . at Darjeeling that no thought but that of the welfare of India occupied him. He dreamed and thought and talked of freedom of India and of nothing else. . . . He was fearless. . . . His love for the young men of Bengal was boundless and even his adversaries admitted there was no other man who could take his place in Bengal. His heart knew no difference between Hindus and Mussalmans and I should like to tell Englishmen, too, that he bore no ill-will to them.[118]

Abruptly, Bengal was deprived of its foremost nationalist, Calcutta of its mayor, the Bengal Provincial Congress Committee of its president, and the All-India Swarajist Party of its president. Das had held together a fragile coalition of forces and in the months and years following his death, these overlapping, but different coalitions disintegrated. His death was a grave blow, for he had earned widespread trust and a significant following shaped by his political acumen.[119]

Communal relations were worsening through India in the mid-1920s, and more than one Muslim leader bitterly regretted the passing of Das for he had earned their trust more than any other Hindu Congress leader. Among the tributes was one by a Muslim alderman of the Calcutta Corporation, Wahed Hosain, who said that Das combined the qualities of sufi and statesman. He thought that the Bengal Pact was the outcome of Das' recognition of the legitimate rights of all parties. Hosain went on,

> He had a firm conviction in the efficiency of the Pact and he fought for it against odds. It is a foul calumny to insinuate that he acknowledged

communal rights to please the Muslim community.[120]

Hosain further said that Das embodied a love of political freedom, determination, great organizing ability, simplicity, sincerity, and a charming manner.

Even the foremost newspaper of the European community, the *Statesman*, provided him with their encomium,

> With dramatic and awful suddenness death has called the tribune of Bengal. To friend and foe alike the news of Mr. Das's premature passing will come as a stunning blow. . . .
>
> Writing within an hour or two of his death it is not possible fully to appraise his policy. To its destructive aspects we have always been firmly opposed; and yet to those who looked below the surface it was evident that Chitta Ranjan Das had the makings of a statesman. . . .
>
> On C.R. Das as a personality all voices are unanimous. He had a remarkable influence upon all those with whom he came into contact, whether friend or foe. Those who expected to find him half ogre and half demagogue fell irresistibly under the sway of a cultured mind, a courteous manner, and a keen and subtle intellect. Upon his followers his influence— compact of eloquence, inspiration and the prestige of his self-denying ordinance—was unbounded. . . . Whatever controversies may have raged round his actions and career, these facts stand out–that he was a leader in a thousand, and a power in the land.[121]

Those who remained tried to continue and enlarge upon his work. Sarat Bose helped to build up the Deshbandhu Fund, to continue his work in the Calcutta Corporation and in the running of *Forward*. Eventually, he would also continue Das' work in the Bengal Legislative Council with considerable skill. He at least could find some outlets for his grief in work. But for Subhas Bose, still a detenu in Mandalay, the news was even more chilling and devastating, for he could only think about it day after day and night after night, uncertain whether he would ever be released to continue the work of his beloved leader, friend and guru.[122]

Shortly after Das' death, Subhas joined with his fellow prisoners in writing a letter to Basanti Devi expressing their sense of loss of one who had been 'a superb combination of father, friend and leader' for the young men of Bengal. They called upon Basanti Devi, whom they referred to as 'the mother of all Bengalees' to give them 'strength, courage and solace in this hour of distress'. They wanted her to come forward and take the vacated leadership position.[123] This was also a theme of Subhas' private letters to her when he was finally able to overcome his paralyzing despair and write to her. For the next few years he wrote to her frequently, often asking her again to consider leading nationalist Bengal and requesting her advice on what work he should do.[124] He also started to write letters and essays in which he tried to come to terms with what Das had meant to the country and to him. Some of his thoughts were shaped in a long letter to the famous Bengali novelist Sarat Chandra Chatterjee. Chatterjee had just published his 'Reminiscences' of Das in the Bengali magazine *Basumati* and Subhas was very moved by them feeling that the author was one of the few to pass beyond cliches in describing Das' character. Subhas wrote, 'The following words in your article appealed to me most—`The gnawing in one's heart that man feels for the most beloved and the most intimate— this is it.`` We, who were around him, have today no words to express our bitter sorrow; neither do we feel like expressing it to others.'[125]

Attempting to understand and correct versions of the recent past and Das' leadership, he wrote to Chatterjee:

> Many people think that we followed him blindly. But he used to fight most of all with his principal lieutenants. As for myself I can say that I fought with him on innumerable questions. But I knew that however much I might fight, my devotion and loyalty would remain unshaken and that I would never be deprived of his love. He also believed that come what may in the shape of trials and tribulations, he would have me at his feet. Our quarrels were settled by mother's (Basanti Devi) mediation. But, alas, 'the refuge for lodging our grievances and recording our discontent has now ceased to exist.'[126]

Bose went on to explain how Das had to overcome the opposition of other Indians by 'gruelling labour' and his spirit of sacrifice led him not only to offer himself, but his whole family 'at the altar of the motherland.' At one point, he mused on Indians' exploitation of their own leaders:

> Sometimes I cannot help feeling that Deshbandhu's countrymen and followers are partly responsible for his premature demise. If they had shared his burden to some extent, it would perhaps not be necessary for him to over-work himself to death. But our ways are such that once we accept somebody as the leader, we burden him so much and expect so much from him that it becomes humanly impossible for him to carry all that burden or fulfil all the expectations. We are content to sit back leaving all political responsibilities in the leader's hands.[127]

Subhas Bose wrote an even longer letter about Das and his legacies to Hemendranath Das Gupta, a fellow political worker and biographer of Das. In this letter, Bose interwove his understanding of Das with his growing awareness of the cultural traditions of Bengal. Since Das had been his one chosen guru and the editor of a leading cultural journal, Deshbandhu had served to bring Bose into closer touch with his cultural roots and with a political direction with which Bose could feel comfortable. He wrote to Das Gupta.

Everyone will wonder to think how a man can at once be a big lawyer, a great lover of men, a devout Vaishnava, a shrewd politician, and a conquering hero. I have tried to get a solution of this problem through anthropological studies. . . . The present-day Bengalee race is an admixture of Aryan, Dravidian and Mongolian blood. . . . Due to this admixture of blood the genius of the Bengalee is so versatile and Bengal's life so colourful. The religiosity and idealism of the Aryans, love of art and devotionalism of the Dravidians, intellectuality and realism of the Mongolians have all very happily blended together in the Bengalee character.[128]

Bose went on to argue that though the Bengali was the product of all these other peoples, he was the developer of a unique synthesis. He wrote,

Bengal's culture has something uncommon and unique about it. On its cultural side three strains are visible–(1) *Tantra*, (2) *Vaishnavism* and (3) *Navanyaya* and Raghunandan's *Smriti*. On the side of *Nyaya* and *Smriti*, Bengal has a close kinship with *Aryavarta*; through *Vaishnavism* she maintains a lifeline with the south, while through the *Tantras* she has a relationship with the races living in the Tibetan, Burmese and Himalayan regions.[129]

Bose spelled out at length how Das embodied 'the finest elements of Bengal's culture and tradition'—how he was a Vaishnava who 'accepted the world and human life in its fullest' how the 'pursuit of *Nyaya* has helped the Bengali to be logical and argumentative' and thus Das became 'a formidable barrister' and how, though not a Tantric worshipper, Das was greatly influenced by 'the Tantric conception of the Mother.'[130]

Bose mentioned the most important lessons that he had learned from Das,

Both his virtues and failings were peculiar to the race he belonged to. The greatest pride in his life was that he was a Bengalee. That was why he was so much loved and adored by the Bengalees. . . . He felt wounded if any one made fun of or satirized the Bengalees as being emotional. It was, he thought, a matter of pride, and not of shame, that we are susceptible to emotions.

That Bengal has a certain distinction, which has expressed itself in her landscape, her literature, her folk-songs and her character I do not think that any one before the Deshbandhu had expressed with such emphasis. . . . I for myself can say that it was from him and his writings that I have learnt about this uniqueness of Bengal.[131]

While fully aware that Das' ideas about Bengal were derived from Bankim Chandra Chatterjee, Rabindranath Tagore, Dwijendralal Roy, and others, Bose still felt that through his journal *Narayana* and personal contact with the young men of Bengal, Das had been the foremost purveyor of the messages of Bengal's distinctive culture.

At the same time that he had great pride in the Bengalis, Das taught that 'culture is both one and many', and India's culture too was both one and many. Bengal shared in the unity and also expressed the diversity. And Das saw beyond the boundaries of India to the culture of Man. A conquered people, however, must first see to the development of *its* culture, and then it can participate fully in humanity's growth.[132] These many teachings of Das were incorporated by Bose into his own extensive reading while imprisoned, shaping his view of Indian history, the culture and role of the Bengalis, and the long-term crisis created for India and the Bengalis by the conquest and rule by the British.

Bose shared many of the ideas of his contemporaries including the labeling of cultural groups as racial ones and a belief that some aspects of culture were inherited by blood. He also accepted the ideas of nationalist historians that the glory that was Indian and Bengali culture had declined before the coming of the European conquerors. This degeneration was, assisted by the British whose subjugation of the Indians was aided in turn through the betrayal of their fellow Indians by tne Bengalis.[133] Bose wrote in one of his prison notebooks,

> A hundred and fifty years ago it was the Bengalees who betrayed the country to their foreign enemies. The Bengalees of the twentieth century certainly owe it to themselves to atone for that great sin. It will be the duty of Bengal's men and women to revive the lost glory of India. How best to accomplish that end is Bengal's greatest problem.[134]

With the British entry, the Bengalis had committed the heinous sin of collaboration and declined into ridiculousness and weakness. Accepting the British stereotype of the effete babu, Bose berated his fellow Bengalis for becoming physically feeble, for lapsing into pettiness, and for tearing at each other rather than uniting and rebuilding. The Bengali language, too, had deteriorated and lost its purity by becoming 'feringi' or Anglicized Bengali.[135] The revival of a purer Bengali literature and its spread to a wider circle of readers was part of the program which Bose laid out.

In his lengthy eulogy for Das, Bose also pointed to Das' intimate connection with many young people in Bengal. Bose wrote,

> . . . he was ever new and youthful—he had an instinctive understanding of the hopes and aspirations of the youth. He could sympathize with them in their joys and sorrows. He liked the company of the young, and they too did not like to part company with him. It is for all this that I have . . . called him the King of the Youth.[136]

This characteristic, too, Bose learned from his master and even though Das had called Subhas a 'young old man' because of a certain gravity in his manner, Subhas continued to identify with the young and their hopes and dreams even as he grew older.[137]

He decried those who were only 'good boys'—those who adhered to a narrow academic course and career and also those who were unadventurous and retreated from life's challenges. In one of his prison writings, he was concerned to illustrate the shortcomings of the good boys who should 'be called misguided, worthless invalids.' He continued,

> Those who are considered good boys in the society are in fact nothing but eunuchs. Neither in this world nor in any other has any great work been achieved or will any great work be done by these people. These boys somehow or other reduced their burden of sin and they follow the track of the most orthodox people like a herd of sheep. Throughout their most prosaic life there is no taste of anything new or novel, there is no outburst of full-hearted laughter, there is no inspired self-sacrifice . . . the Bengalis will never become manly unless the so-called good boys are totally unrooted . . . and unless a new race is born in India. One has to express himself in the free wind and under the open sky by breaking through all the barriers of life and by razing them to the ground.[138]

The influence of Vaishnava songs, of Rabindranath Tagore and the poems of Nazrul Islam is present here and throughout his messages to the young. In contrast to the narrow good boys, he presented the model of the robust, socially concerned, adventurous young men, giving as examples, P.R. De, who had walked alone through the hills from Calcutta to Rangoon on foot, Lord Robert Clive, Sir Francis Drake, Shivaji, and Tennyson's Ulysses. The last-named was also a favorite of Sarat Bose, who often quoted the line, 'To strive, to seek, to find, and not to yield.'[139]

Although he was often in poor health while in prison, Subhas took the time whenever possible for exercise and playing games. He noted that, 'We have altogether given up the practice of lathi play and gymnastics in fear of the police or for the sake of gentility.'[140] In reaction to his own unathletic youth and to the derision by the British of the effeminate Bengalis, Bose stressed the physical and masculine side of human development. Although he had within himself and admired in others the protective, gentle maternal ideal, he emphasized the tough, determined, courageous male ideal in these writings. He was accepting the terms for cultural and individual achievement laid down by the Bengalis' British tormentors. He stressed the activism which Swami Vivekananda and the political Aurobindo Ghose had called for among the youth of Bengal. Subhas, in this incarnation, decried those who ran away, those who fled from the nationalist struggle. Among those who had run away he included himself as a young man, and then remembered Aurobindo and Anil Baran Roy, formerly a Swarajist, who had left Calcutta recently for Aurobindo's ashram. Though he himself was involved in daily yoga and meditation, such activity was not to become more important than one's responsibilities to the revival and freedom of one's country. One could not, in Subhas' view, work out such duties by private and individual yogic practices, and he lamented the loss to the movement of those who had left for the Pondicherry ashram.[141]

Das' death also had the effect of making Subhas seek the support and guidance of his widow, Basanti Devi. He wrote of her,

> If in speaking of the Deshabandhu's life we forget to mention another person—his wife—then little will have been said. That goddess, embodying service and serenity, removed from public gaze, always stood by his side like a shadow. . . The Deshabandhu was King of Youth. His devoted helpmate was their mother. After the Deshabandhu's death she is not merely Chitaranjan's mother, or of the young men only—today she is Bengal's mother. The highest offering of the Bengalee heart is laid at her sacred feet.[142]

Subhas Bose was consciously aware that Bengalis ran together notions of the Mother Goddess, the Motherland, and ordinary mothers. Following Das' demise, he kept writing to Basanti Devi, addressing her as the Mother of the Nation and the Mother Goddess. The death of Das had created a problem of succession. Subhas' first idea was to encourage Basanti Devi to assume the role. She had made some political speeches, had been present at many political meetings, and had even been arrested during non-cooperation. However, in the very same essay on Das quoted at length above, he noted that she always remained, by choice in the background. It took her a long time to convince Subhas that this was what she wanted. He wanted the mother of the youth to emerge as an activist Goddess leading the nation to freedom, but she wanted to remain a private, motherly person who encouraged the nationalist movement from the sidelines.[143]

It may well have been the long months of captivity which brought out the religious beliefs of Subhas Bose and fused them with his political outlook. And it was the annual celebration of the festival of the Mother Goddess in the form of Durga which brought about a crisis during his imprisonment. The Bengali political prisoners in Mandalay learned that there was a financial contribution made by the government for religiously-incurred expenses. So in the fall of 1925 they approached the officials seeking financial assistance for all the expenses involved in properly celebrating Durga Puja.[144] Before the matter was decided, the Puja came and was celebrated. Subhas wrote to Biva at the time,

> I wonder if I ever felt so happy at any other Puja. The reason why we felt so happy was probably because we earned the right to perform the Puja after a lot of fighting. Who knows how long we shall have to be in prison? But, all our suffering will be bearable if we get the chance of worshipping the Mother once in a year. In Durga we see Mother, Motherland and the

Universe all in one. She is at once Mother, Motherland and the Universal Spirit.[145]

In a letter to Sarat Bose, exactly a year later, he gave further elaboration to his thoughts about it,

To one accustomed to an uneventful and monotonous life, an occasion like the Durga Puja has much more than its normal value. It is a source of aesthetic enjoyment, intellectual recreation and religious inspiration and affords abiding solace. Today is Bijoya Dasami and throughout Bengal relations, friends and even enemies—children of the same Mother—will be soon embracing one another in fraternal love.[146]

So Durga Puja was the moment in the round of the year when he and his Bengali prison-mates felt united with the Bengali people from whom they had been arbitrarily separated.[147]

It was, therefore, both a religious-cultural and political issue when they confronted British officials over payment for their prison Durga Puja. An official denial of funds for the Puja and a request for a refund from the prisoners of monies advanced to them precipitated the hunger strike which began on February 18, 1926. Communications were cut off, but three days into the strike word was out and *Forward* was printing bulletins. Not only were the officials chagrined that information about the strikers had slipped out, but also unpublished, evidential parts of an Indian Jail Committee of 1919-21 report suddenly appeared in the hands of the Swarajists. According to secret testimony by a high prison official, Lieut-Col. Mulvany, he had been forced to fabricate optimistic health reports on prisoners which belied their true condition. Motilal Nehru and Tulsi Goswami raised the issue in the Central Legislative Assembly and the Swarajists and the strikers had the Raj officials on the defensive. The strike persisted and Subhas' weight continued to drop. Although he had tried to keep news of his medical problems from his parents, word of his physical condition made the front pages of the nationalist press. As the days passed and the threat of serious health damage hung over the strikers, Sarat and other nationalists began to ask the strikers to give up their fasting. They had, Sarat said, made their point and made it well. Finally, on March 4— about two weeks into their fast—the government made concessions and they gave up the hunger strike.[148] Subhas wrote to a Calcutta friend explaining the gains they had made:

. . . our hunger strike was not altogether meaningless or fruitless. Government have been forced to concede our demands relating to religious matters and henceforward a Bengal State Prisoner will get an annual allowance of thirty rupees on account of Puja expenses . . . our principal gain is that the government have now accepted the principle which they refused to do so long . . . the government has also met many of our other demands.

However, speaking in the Vaishnavic spirit I have to say, 'All this is merely the exterior.' That is to say, the biggest gain of hunger strike is the inner fulfilment and bliss. ... Without suffering man can never realise his oneness with his spiritual ideal and unless he is put to the test, he can never be sure and certain of the limitless power that he possesses inside himself. Thanks to this experience I have come to know myself far better and my self-confidence has increased manifold.[149]

Subhas never mentioned Gandhi in his letters and account of the hunger strike, but the Mahatma was most responsible for using this old Indian cultural technique in a new nationalist context.[150] The hunger strike also reawakened public opinion about the imprisonment itself and the Swarajists again called for the release of men who had never been publicly charged with any crime.

After the death of C.R. Das, a leading Swarajist and barrister from Chittagong, Jatindra Mohan Sen Gupta, was chosen to wear the Triple Crown (mayor of Calcutta, leader of the Swarajists in the BLC and president of the Bengal Provincial Congress). Sen Gupta was from Das' native East Bengal and had been educated at Presidency College, Cambridge University, and Gray's Inn, London. He joined the Calcutta High Court Bar, taught law, and plunged into the Non-Cooperation Movement in 1921. By 1923 he had been elected to the Bengal Legislative Council and been selected as secretary of the Bengal Swarajya Party, the Congress group in the BLC, and of the Congress Municipal Association. He had also helped organize strikes by oil workers and railwaymen as president of the Burma Oil Labour Union (Chittagong) and of the Assam-Bengal Railway Union.[151] Sarat Bose wrote to Subhas,

> There has been great excitement lately over filling up the positions held by Deshbandhu. It has been eventually decided (on the advice of Mahatma Gandhi) that J.M. Sengupta is to occupy all the three positions. Personally I think it is a great mistake to put any other man into all the places filled by Deshbandhu. But the Mahatma's decision was accepted.[152]

There were some objections to Sen Gupta's rapid return to the bar after he had quit it during non-cooperation. During 1926 there were several serious disagreements between a group called the Karmi Sangha (Workers' Society) formed from among released political prisoners in the Calcutta area and the Sen Gupta leadership in the Bengal Provincial Congress. There was also a conflict with B.N. Sasmal, a Swarajist leader from Midnapore, stemming from tactless remarks by Sasmal at a provincial Congress meeting about members of secret societies in the Congress. Sasmal stepped down as the president of the meeting, but shortly the dispute between the Karmi Sangha and Sen Gupta came to a head and the BPCC was dissolved and reformed without the former group.[153]

Sarat Bose was by now much more active in Bengal politics and with Dr B.C. Roy, Tulsi Goswami, Nalini Ranjan Sarker, and Nirmal Chunder, issued a manifesto on the work facing the country. This loose, temporary coalition of five—all with wealth and connections—was labeled the 'Big Five' by Priyanath Gupta in his *Statesman* column.[154] They served on the Board of Directors of *Forward* and as trustees of the Deshbandhu Village Reconstruction Fund. They worked out a compromise with Sen Gupta on the election board for the upcoming BLC elections, with Sen Gupta serving as president and Dr Roy as secretary. Sen Gupta was more able in the mayoral chair and the legislature than in carrying out the organizational work of the Bengal Provincial Congress. But he had a firm tie to Gandhi and the central Congress leadership and this served him in good stead throughout the remainder of his life. He had become Bengal's foremost Gandhian spokesman.[155]

Amongst the activities in which Sarat Bose became most energetic were the running of *Forward* and the operations of the Calcutta Corporation. He took pride in the English-language daily founded by Das and shortly was writing to Subhas that it was the best nationalist paper in India. Satya Ranjan Bakshi, a close co-worker of Subhas, was now, Sarat wrote, the best writer on the paper and a skilled journalist. With Sarat at the helm as managing director, *Forward* took over the running of the Bengali paper, *Atma Sakti,* so the Swarajists had both English and Bengali papers in the field.[156]

Sarat was also much more active in the Calcutta Corporation for the two years following Das' death. He began to participate in several committees, becoming the deputy chairman of the Finance, Estates, and General Purposes Committee, and the secretary of the Committee on Chittaranjan Hospital. His pet resolution was one calling for prohibition within the city limits of Calcutta which he persuaded the Corporation to pass. The Government of Bengal, however, rejected this resolution as impracticable and decried the loss of revenues it involved.[157]

In most of his work Sarat Bose was quite composed and business-like. An exception was a debate in the Corporation in August 1926. A European councillor had described the Swarajists as 'a party which walked in and out of Council in a theatrical way in obedience to the Member for Chittagong.'[158] He called them disloyal to their constituents and prone to vote one way or another because of the on-going election campaign. Sarat Bose answered by quoting Burke's remark that, 'he had not surrendered his conscience to his constituency.' As the fires were stoked by European and Indian loyalists in the Corporation, Sarat charged that the Europeans had surrendered their conscience to an arbitrary executive and that they were not people's representatives at all. He berated them for their support of the Bengal Ordinance and Regulation III of 1818, finally calling them 'tailors of Tooley Street.'[159]

Some months later, Sarat Bose argued in the Corporation for a preference to be shown for Indian tenders when the Corporation asked for bids. He maintained that politics could not be kept out of the affairs of the Corporation and concluded,

> It has been said by ... Sir Ashutosh Chowduri, that a subject-nation had no politics. But my humble opinion is that a subject-nation has nothing but politics. It is nearer to truth that politics is the religion of a subject race. Like the great Italian patriot Mazzini who said 'Rome has been the dream of my young years, regenerating idea of my mental conception, key-stone of my intellectual edifice and religion of my soul,' let young Bengal say 'independence has been the dream of my young years, regenerating idea of mental conception, key-stone of my intellectual edifice and religion of my soul.'[160]

With these remarks in view—and they angered the Europeans and the Indian loyalists greatly—it is no wonder that the *Statesman* wrote in assessing the quality of the Corporation, 'Among the Hindus, Alderman S.C. Bose is, by general consent, the best speaker, but racial bitterness mars his otherwise undoubted gift.'[161]

These exchanges show that Sarat Bose had now come out into the open in Bengal's political life. He was a passionate, emotional nationalist who became one of the chief Swarajist spokesmen in the Corporation, a political arena in which they had some real power. He could, like C.R. Das and his brother Subhas, display flashes of temper in defense of his party's views. In the instances described above, he was even more angry than he might have been because his beloved younger brother had suffered from the 'lawless laws' he was attacking. His quotations from Burke and Mazzini were characteristic of one who had studied the speeches of great Western orators and nationalists and had a photographic memory. The identification with the Italian leaders who unified their country in the nineteenth century is typical of Indian nationalists who grew up in the last quarter of the century. Burke's views on the relationship between a legislator and his constituency were familiar to one trained for the bar in London and who had attended sessions of the House of Commons and studied the British parliamentary system.[162]

The views of the Europeans and the Indian loyalists also ring familiar. Their narrow view was that politics was to have no place in municipal affairs and that parties and nationalism should function, if they had to function at all, somewhere else. The leading Indian Liberal who was responsible for the passage of the Calcutta Municipal Act under which the Swarajists had entered the Corporation, Surendranath Banerjea, said that it had become a den of 'failure and favouritism.'[163] His Liberal colleague, C.C. Biswas, thought Sarat Bose's remarks which brought in nationalist concerns quite irrelevant.

The comment in the *Statesman* that Sarat Bose's gifts were marred by 'racial bitterness' raises a slightly different point. Throughout the period of the Raj and even years later in books by Britishers about Indian nationalists like Subhas Bose, all hostility by Indians against their European rulers is explained as 'racism.'[164] It seems to me that this was a quaint and inappropriate way to deal with grievances which had little to do with racial feeling, but a lot to do with legitimate political views and objectives. Indian nationalists were not racists who thought that the British should be removed because they were white or European. They believed they should have rulers who were chosen by the native inhabitants of India. The Boses, like all Indians, were sensitive to color, but did not harbor racial antagonism to all Europeans. Sarat Bose had many European friends who were his colleagues at the bar. As peers before the bar, as friends in the bar library, they were accepted. But as rulers from a small group of islands thousands of miles away, simply because of their conquest of India in the eighteenth century, they were the enemy. Subhas Bose was less enamored of Western customs than his brother, but he too had Western friends.

In the year after C.R. Das' death, one event more than any other marked the passage to a new, more disquieting time. It did not have to do with the hostilities between Indians and Europeans, but rather between Hindu and Muslim Indians. Although there had been communal riots in many parts of India in the years between 1917 and 1925, there had not been any serious communal violence in Calcutta since 1918. Even the 1918 Calcutta disturbances mainly involved non-Bengalis. But the 1926 Calcutta riots indicated a serious, perhaps dangerous turn in communal relations. For the first time there were attacks on Hindu temples, Muslim mosques, and Sikh gurudwaras, and Bengali Hindus and Muslims were involved. If the riots did not sound the death knell of Das' Bengal Pact between Hindus and Muslims, they certainly hastened its demise.[165]

Beneath the elite level on which the Bengal Pact was made, relations were not so harmonious. Activities of the Arya Samaj and the Hindu Mahasabha, including the Suddhi, Tanzim, and Sangathan movements begun in the 1920s were at work in Calcutta in 1925. Provocative speeches by Hindu communalists touched Calcutta Muslims as well as Hindus, spreading mutual disaffection. Sir Abdur Rahim, a Calcutta Muslim leader, warned Muslims of Hindu domination if ever swaraj came. Although he gave this speech in Aligarh, his views were known to Calcutta Muslims. The Jamiat-ul-Ulema-i-Hind met in Calcutta in March 1926 and featured communal speeches.[166]

The first riots were precipitated by an Arya Samaj procession past a mosque with Hindu drummers starting a confrontation which led to a Muslim attack on the marchers. At the beginning, the rioters were Muslims and up-country Hindus, but as attacks on temples and mosques took place, more Bengalis became involved. The bloodshed was confined mainly to north Calcutta, but troops had to be called out and when this phase was over, the official figures were 44 killed and 600 injured. After a pause of two-and-a-half weeks, the rioters were at it again, from April 22 to 27, and fifty-six were killed and 365 injured according to the Home Department. The government blamed outside agitators, *goondas* who took advantage of the breakdown of law-and-order, and the communal press. There were also accusations against the Swarajist deputy mayor of Calcutta, H.S. Suhrawardy, who was said to have spurred on the riots. A third phase took place from July 11 to 25 and the official figures were twenty-eight killed and 226 injured. Other incidents took place outside Calcutta in Kharagpur, Pabnabalia, and most significantly for future developments, in Dacca, during September 1926. Since the British had disarmed the Indians after the rebellion of 1857, guns were hard to come by.[167] Most of the deaths and injuries occurred through stabbing or beating. This was the case throughout the nationalist period.[168]

The skillful work of C.R. Das was beginning to unravel and one result of the riots was the end of the Bengal Pact. J.M. Sen Gupta tried to preserve it, but Muslim members were slipping away from the Swarajya Party and even Sarat Bose thought the pact was a dead letter. In July 1926 Sarat Bose toured several Bengal districts helping to set up an organization to combat Hindu-Muslim fratricide. He wrote to Subhas,

> After staying at Rajshahi for a couple of days, we went to Puttia, Natore and Naogaon. In spite of the communal conflicts in the adjoining district of Pabna, Rajshahi has kept her head cool. We succeeded in forming a volunteer organisation in the Rajshahi district to combat communal troubles and do relief work in the villages, etc. If all the districts of Bengal work on these lines, I think we shall steadily (though perhaps slowly) solve the communal question. Of course, preachers (specially reliable Mahomedan preachers) and trained instructors are needed to make the volunteer organisation a success. I very much wish I were able to devote more time to this work but unfortunately, that is not to be.[169]

Sarat also attended the discussions of the Calcutta riots in the Corporation and was chosen to be a member of the enquiry committee set up to investigate Deputy Mayor H.S. Suhrawardy's role in them. However, he decided to resign from the committee and stated to the Corporation,

> As one who has been (and still is) in charge of a daily newspaper, information from various sources came to me regarding the alleged acts and conduct of the Deputy Mayor during the last riots. In the circumstances I am not sure that I shall be able to bring an open mind to bear on the question.
>
> Further the Deputy Mayor is a brother-barrister of mine and it is difficult for me to say that fact will not even unconsciously affect my judgment.[170]

This disengagement did not mean unconcern. Indeed, the communal question and efforts to promote harmony between the two major communities of Bengal became a theme in the lives of both Boses. They well understood the lessons of C.R. Das that no Hindu could be a real leader of Bengal without support from the Muslim community. The lives of the two communities were so tightly woven together that every effort to cooperate must be made. Although Sarat Bose thought the particular terms of the Bengal Pact would no longer work, he searched at different moments throughout his career for avenues which would be effective.

In the aftermath of the Suhrawardy investigation, the deputy mayor was forced to resign over the strenuous objections of many of the Muslim councillors who had threatened to resign. In the end, many of them withdrew their resignations, but three, Mr Unsud Dowla, Dr K. Ahmad, and Mr A. Halim, withdrew from the Corporation. From Mandalay, Subhas Bose wrote to Sarat that he was very distressed about the resignation of Suhrawardy and that he had been giving much thought to the communal question. He said that he was firmly against separate electorates.[171] The question of joint or separate electorates was one which had long caused dispute and soul-searching. Many Muslims who had years earlier supported the Congress position of joint electorates, had turned around and now insisted on separate electorates and also began to demand a much larger percentage of reserved seats for Muslims in the Bengal Legislative Council.

The 1926 elections for Council, however, were carried out under the 1919 Government of India Act and this gave the Bengal Muslims only 40 per cent of the seats though they constituted a much larger percentage of the Bengal population. C.R. Das had the support of a solid block of Muslim BLC members who were essential to his successful efforts in defeating the government. But in the 1926 elections, the Swarajists no longer had such Muslim backing and serious cracks began to appear throughout the party edifice. Subhas Bose lamented that Motilal Nehru, effective in the Central Legislative Assembly, did not have the skill of Das as a national party leader.[172]

In 1926, Sarat Bose decided to run for the Legislative Council and chose the Calcutta University seat as the one for which he would stand. Then the question arose as to whether Subhas would run for the Council from prison. At first he decided that it involved too many difficulties and was not sure he wanted to become a member even if he could be elected through the electioneering efforts of others. After many persuasive letters, Sarat won Subhas over to what they called an old Irish strategy employed against the British: 'Vote him in to get him out.' Sarat assured Subhas that J.M. Sen Gupta and Kiron Sankar Roy–the official BPCC leadership–as well as the Karmi Sangha heartily supported his candidacy.[173]

Initially Sarat thought that both he and Subhas might run unopposed, he for the university seat, Subhas for the north Calcutta non-Muhammadan seat. Eventually, however, both were opposed, Subhas by J.N. Basu, a Liberal Party leader who had defeated the Swarajist candidate for the same seat in 1923. Sarat was gradually finding out which aspects of the political game he would most like to play and could play well. Organizing election campaigns was one of these areas in which the direct and open competition for votes called forth his aggressive, argumentative, and emotional traits and in which he came to flourish. With Subhas behind bars, Sarat had to organize both campaigns. Subhas wanted processions and public meetings on his behalf. He wrote of the efforts for him, 'Modern electioneering methods were used by the Party, including the use of rockets for distributing leaflets and posters showing the candidate behind prison bars.'[174] The Government of Bengal refused to release Subhas' election manifesto addressed to the voters of north Calcutta. Sarat wrote to him, 'Your election manifesto has been withheld and the reason assigned by the Deputy Secretary, Political Deptt., for withholding is that political prisoners are not allowed to issue appeals to the public.'[175]

In his own election letter to potential voters, Sarat Bose portrayed himself as a Congressman and 'a humble camp-follower of our late leader Deshabandu Chittaranjan Das.' He said that the larger issue behind the campaign was the freedom of the country. Shrewdly using the words of the late, renowned Vice-Chancellor Sir Ashutosh Mookerjee that the relations between the university and the government should be governed by, 'Freedom first, Freedom second, Freedom always,' Sarat continued,

> My Alma Mater has as its motto—'The Advancement of Learning'. I feel this is not the motto of the University alone, but a national motto, the battle-cry of our struggling militant nationalism seeking ever to express itself and to fulfil itself against the forces of injustice, oppression, squalor, poverty and ignorance. 'Freedom and Advancement'—that is the problem for you

and me; and I can assure you in all humility that to the solution of that problem I shall direct all my thoughts and actions, and bend all the force of my education and understanding in even a larger measure than I have been able to do as Managing Director of 'Forward' and as an Alderman of the Corporation of Calcutta. This is the national problem and to its solution, the University, the lecture hall, the press, the platform and the Council Chamber must all co-ordinate their resources.[176]

Since Subhas could not send out his manifesto, Sarat wrote it for him and, not trusting the possible tricks of the Government of Bengal sent his second youngest brother, Sailesh, to Mandalay to get Subhas' signature on the nomination papers and to consult with him on election strategy. Although Subhas did not feel this was necessary, the twenty-two-year-old Sailesh made the trip and completed his mission.[177] Mrs C. R. Das proclaimed her support for Subhas and a strong campaign was waged for the absent candidate.

The voting took place on November 17, 1926, and Subhas won a large majority. Sarat, too, was handily elected. So both were now members of the new Council. Subhas, however, was not released from prison. He wrote, '. . . the Government of India was less responsive to public opinion than the Government in Ireland. . . .'[178] Amidst the congratulations he received, Subhas had to note in reply, that he was in poor health and his illness involving steadily declining weight created the circumstances for his next confrontation with the Government of Bengal.

After six weeks in Mandalay, in March 1925, Subhas was writing to Sarat of 'the extreme lethargy induced by a disease which I can best describe as dyspepsia-cum"flu".'[179] He never felt physically well in Burma and from these early weeks, he continued to ask for a transfer to a healthier place. The prison superintendent was usually also a doctor and frequent checks were made on the health of the prisoners, though complaints were viewed with a skeptical eye. Subhas' doctor-brother, Sunil, came to examine him in February 1926, and Subhas tried to find the best course for himself after hearing the advice of Sunil, the prison doctor, and also an Ayurvedic doctor in Calcutta with whom he was constantly in touch. In December 1926, the prison officials were seriously concerned enough to send him to Rangoon for a more thorough examination. He had a continual fever and his weight was down from about 161 pounds in early 1925 to 138 pounds. Sarat was quite upset about Subhas' health and could no longer keep the details from their father since articles about it were appearing in the press. Janaki Nath was prepared to make the journey to Burma with Sarat in late 1926, but the trip was put off.[180]

In February 1927, Subhas was brought to the Rangoon Central Jail and permanently removed from Mandalay while officials and doctors tried to decide what to do for and about him. Sunil came to examine him again. He learned that one of the other prisoners in Mandalay had tuberculosis and found that Subhas had some of the symptoms of the disease. Sunil suggested that Subhas be allowed to go to Switzerland for treatment. The government doctors did not agree with this diagnosis, but considered the suggestion about sending him abroad.[181]

While the matter was being debated, Subhas ran into difficulties with the chief jailor and superintendent of the Rangoon Central Jail. Subhas had sent a note to the chief jailor asking for his customary morning newspaper and was notified by the superintendent, Major Flowerdew, that he was not to give orders to the chief jailor. Subhas then wrote to the governor of Burma,

> I am painfully conscious of the fact that whatever my status in society and my position in the public life of India may be—within the four walls of the Rangoon Jail I am to a great extent at the mercy of the Jail officers from the Superintendent downwards. . . I am not so presumptuous as to think that I can 'give orders' to Jail officers. I am making this statement from my experience in dealing with subordinates as the Chief Executive Officer of the Calcutta Corporation. Your Excellency may be aware that as an officer I have European subordinates of high education and international reputation some of whom at least draw salaries almost double that drawn by Major Flowerdew. . . . Under the law of the land I as a detenue am entitled to treatment in keeping with my rank and station in life. I therefore feel that the Superintendent . . . has in an unwarranted manner hurt my feelings as gentleman and humiliated me in the eyes of his staff by writing a note which to all fairminded and reasonable men will appear as discourteous and insulting.[182]

The numerous pinpricks of long months of imprisonment and his poor health added to his anger about this small incident. He may have been overreacting, but he demanded to be transferred. With this wish, the authorities shortly complied, moving him to Insein Jail just outside Rangoon, late in March.

Meanwhile, the Government of Bengal in consultation with the Government of India laid down terms for the release of Subhas Bose, including that he was to go directly from jail to a boat bound for Europe and not come back before the expiration of the Bengal Ordinance in 1930. On the government side, the viceroy explained the view in India in a communication to the secretary of state of April 9, 1927,

> In general we have taken the line in regard to those detained under the Bengal Criminal Law Amendment Act that while we are closely concerned with the policy and general administration of the Act the treatment of

individuals is left to Bengal Government. But this general attitude is obviously subject to exceptions where the individuals have an importance which extends beyond Bengal. We believe that Bengal fully understands this position. . . .

As regards particular action taken in this case we were all agreed on general policy of releasing whenever this was not likely to lead to fresh outrages. . . . With regard to stipulation that he should go to Switzerland we fully recognise your special interest and responsibility in this matter. . . . Our reasons for thinking that Subhas Bose might be permitted to go to Switzerland apart from the fact that on medical grounds there is a good case are first that the Bengal revolutionary movement is essentially localised and though it may be susceptible of some stimulation from outside, real driving force lies within the movement itself and in Bengal. Consequently any of these conspirators when outside India is less dangerous in regard to this conspiracy than he would be in India. Second that in Bengal Subhas Bose is a national hero, while outside India, even if he associated himself with groups of Indians engaged in anti-British activities, it is believed that his capacity for harm would be much less than in India. . . . Bengal have not yet received any communication from Bose regarding his suggested release and we are prosecuting enquiries into possibility of transferring him to a jail in more suitable climate in India.[183]

While the Governments of Bengal and India and the India Office were considering the matter, Subhas was writing to Sarat:

... who can be sure that the Act will run out in 1930 and that it will not be given another lease of life? . . . I shall not be surprised if in 1929, serious attempts are made to put the Bengal Criminal Law Amendment Act of 1925 permanently on the Statute Book. In that case my absence from home will be made permanent and I shall have to thank myself alone for exiling myself from India. . . . Again, I have not been given any assurance as to the extent of freedom I shall be allowed in Europe. Will the Govt. save me from the kind attentions of the numerous spies that swarm in Switzerland. . . . Unfortunately I am now 'bete noire' to the Govt. and the difficulty that I shall have to encounter can be easily imagined.[184]

Subhas went on to explain to Sarat what his brother already knew and what even intelligence officers confirmed: he was not a communist revolutionary. He wrote,

If I had the remotest intention of becoming a Bolshevik agent, I would have jumped at the offer made and taken the first available boat to Europe. If I succeeded in recouping my health, I could then have joined the gay band who trot about from Paris to Leningrad talking of world revolution and emitting blood and thunder in their utterances. But I have no such ambition or desire.[185]

In listing and explaining all the reasons why he could not accept the

Government of Bengal's offer, one of the most powerful had to do with his attachment to his family. He wrote to Sarat (as he also explained to the government in rejecting the offer):

> There is one aspect of the Hon'ble Member's proposal which struck me as particularly callous. Government know that I have been away from home for nearly two-and-a-half years and I have not met most of my relations— including parents—during this period. They nevertheless propose that I should go abroad for a period which will be at least two-and-a-half or three years without having an opportunity of meeting them. This is hard for me— but much more so for those who love me—whose number is I think very large. It is not easy for a Westerner to appreciate the deep attachment which Oriental people have for their kith and kin and I hope that it is this ignorance—rather than wilfulness—which is responsible for what I cannot but regard as a heartless feature of the Government offer. It would be typical only of a Western mind to presume that because I have not married— therefore I have no family (taking the word in its large sense) and no attachment for anyone.[186]

Most of this long letter to Sarat rejecting the government's offer was released by Sarat to the press. Subhas' insistence that Bengal was the only place he desired to live and work, that he did not desire to be a permanent exile, and that he was being callously treated by foreign bureaucrats ruling over India, all fell on the sympathetic ears of the nationalist public. The government could not have been pleased with the widespread and unfavorable publicity they were getting vis-à-vis a very sick political prisoner whom they thought probably had broncho-pneumonia rather than tuberculosis.

In May, Subhas received an order of transfer from Insein to Almora in the United Provinces where prisoners with tuberculosis were often sent for rehabilitation. Subhas writes of the next developments:

> Once again arrangements were made with the utmost secrecy and early one morning in May 1927, I was removed from Insein Jail to a boat sailing from Rangoon. On the fourth day I reached Diamond Harbour at the mouth of the river Hooghly. Before our boat reached Calcutta, she was stopped and I was met by Mr Lowman . . . who wanted me to alight. Thinking that he wanted to smuggle me out of Calcutta, I refused. But I was assured that His Excellency the Governor had placed his launch at our disposal and that I had to appear before a Medical Board. . . . I spent the day in the Governor's launch, and next morning Mr Lowman, with a telegram in his hand, came to inform me that the Governor had ordered my release.[187]

There were some curious details about the release and Subhas was sure that the police tried hard to have him transferred to another prison. He believed that the release had been approved because '. . .the new Governor, Sir Stanley Jackson, had come with an open mind and he was a strong man.'[188]

Whatever the whole story, Subhas Bose was now a free, though seriously ill, man after more than two-and-a-half years' imprisonment.

After a few weeks in Calcutta with his family, Subhas was moved to a rented house in Shillong where he stayed from June to October 1927 slowly regaining his health. Various family members including his mother, a sister, Sarat and Biva and their children, and others were with him for varying lengths of time during these months. He did not have tuberculosis and Dr B.C. Roy and his brother Sunil came to Shillong to examine him and chart his progress towards recovery. His mind turned from almost exclusive concern for his bodily health and personal fate to thoughts about the present state of nationalist politics in Bengal and throughout India.[189]

One theme in his writing after the death of C.R. Das was the growing factionalism, disunity, corruption, and lack of strong leadership in Bengal. He wrote to a Calcutta political worker before he left Mandalay in 1926,

All over Bengal today there are only groupism and internecine quarrels; and where there is less of work, there is more of quarrel. . . . I no longer hear of selflessness and sacrifice anywhere. So noble a life, having spent itself to the very end, merged with the Infinite; it came before us like a ball of fire and the embodiment of sacrifice; with the aid of that divine light the Bengalis had for a moment a glimpse of Heaven; but, as the light went out, Bengalis again took refuge in their narrow selfish world. Throughout Bengal today, a scramble for power is in progress. Those who have power are much too occupied in holding on to it. Those who have none are determined to grab power. Both the sides say: 'If salvation of the country is to be achieved, let the salvation come through me and me alone; otherwise let there be no salvation at all.' Is there no such worker in Bengal today who can offer silent self-immolation in disregard of the quarrels of the power-thirsty politicians?[190]

He reiterated this theme in letters to political colleagues, to relatives, and most often in his pleas to Basanti Devi to come forward and continue the work of her late husband. In July 1927, he wrote from Shillong to her,

The question I put to you in Calcutta has been solved. The answer is that if you do not accept our leadership there is no one else in Bengal whom we can accept from our heart as the leader. If someone is invited to be the chairman of a meeting he does not necessarily become the leader. There are many such leaders in Bengal. But a real leader–to whom one's heart bows down with reverence–is rare in Bengal today. If we do not get you, then this pack of vagabonds will have to fend for themselves. Your blessings will undoubtedly be a priceless thing for us but we want a little more than that.[191]

Subhas was preparing himself to enter the maelstrom of Bengal politics, however unsavory it appeared to him, but he had doubts. In the same letter to Mrs Das, he wrote that, '. . . I am always troubled by the thought of my unworthiness . . . sometimes I am apprehensive lest I may not be able to give to the country what she expects of me.'[192] He wrote to Biva,

> I used to be an utterly inferior being and extremely weak-minded; whatever strength I have been able to muster has been the result of continuous internal struggle during the last sixteen or seventeen years. There is no end to this struggle because there is no limit to one's mental elevation; the more you rise, the more is the desire to rise further. The result is that the struggle goes on and on.[193]

He had learned many lessons in prison, or so he thought. One of these lessons was that though he could aim for the goal of non-attachment—as laid out in the *Bhagavad Gita* and other religious texts—he could never reach that ideal. He wrote to Biva, as he had earlier written to Basanti Devi from Mandalay, that he was too tied to his family and dearest friends to reach the ideal,

> I felt rather uncomfortable after you all left suddenly. The empty house gave a forlorn feeling—the mind became restive—I seemed to have lost for a while the moorings of my daily life—it will be no exaggeration to say that I felt a pang in my heart. I have not had such a feeling for a long time. I used to think that I had risen above worldly attachments. Now therefore, Nature ordained this blow to bring it home to me that I was not yet entirely non-attached. I shall not discuss for the present if this is a matter of joy or sorrow.[194]

In letters to Basanti Devi and to Biva, he kept referring to himself as a 'vagabond'. Writing to Biva, he said that Sarat should be more careful of his diet and his health because, 'His position is such as they say in English—that he cannot afford to be ill. He is not a vagabond like myself, so that it hardly matters whether I live or die.'[195] Sarat was, after all, the main man in his generation of the Bose family, especially for Subhas. Sarat was a householder and the most important person to be consulted about family matters after Janaki Nath Bose. Subhas' work and career were to some extent dependent on the continued support, financial as well as emotional, of Sarat.

The brothers were gradually sorting out the most rewarding forms of work for each of them. It was fortunate that their interests and work were so complementary. Subhas knew that he wanted to devote all his energies to his public work. Sarat was learning to compartmentalize his life so that he could continue to meet his family obligations and do his professional work, and also devote some of his considerable energies to public work. Sarat was learning that the election campaign and the legislative chamber, rather than mass organizing and the leading of street demonstrations, were his political fortes.

Besides his other activities, Sarat was also involved in working for the development of their ancestral village, Kodalia, on the outskirts of Calcutta. While Subhas was in prison, Sarat had gone with his father and other family members to Kodalia to initiate a program of village reorganization work. On this particular occasion, the Bose family was seeing to the opening of a dispensary for the village. It was started in the house in which Janaki Nath grew up and was named after his mother.[196] Subhas, of course, supported such activities, but Sarat was able to make more direct contributions particularly since he could afford more charitable donations. Sarat did not want the political limelight and only came into it when Subhas was not available or when it was a sphere of activity in which Subhas was not very interested. Sarat was and continued to be the firm foundation of the family and Subhas the 'vagabond' who was working night and day to free his country.

Subhas was becoming more widely known in Bengal and India even while he was serving his time in prison. Indeed, the prison term and the suffering he endured there contributed to his reputation. He was becoming known as a hero and martyr for India. Anil Baran Roy told Jogesh Chatterji, 'Subhas Chandra is the rising sun of India.'[197] How far and in exactly what direction he would go, no one yet knew. Subhas himself was probably not sure, but he thought of a favorite poem of Rabindranath Tagore in writing to a friend,

I am building my mind all by myself
and growing worthier for the tasks ahead. . .
Who knows when shall I be able to declare with all my heart:
I have reached my Realisation,
Come all, follow me,
The Master is calling you all,
May my life bring forth new life in you all
And thus may my country awake.[198]

Janaki Nath Bose and family, 1905, Sarat Bose (standing center), Subhas Bose (extreme right)

Sarat Bose as a law student in England, 1914

Group photograph of Indian Defence Force, Calcutta University
(Subhas standing second from right), 1917

Subhas Bose (standing right) with friends in England, 1920

Sarat Bose with wife Bivabati, 1921

Janaki Nath, Bivabati, Subhas and Sarat Bose with family friends at Shillong, 1927

Sarat Bose with family, Kurseong, 1926

Calcutta Congress, 1928: J.M. Sen Gupta, Motilal Nehru and Subhas Bose

Subhas Bose with Congress Volunteers, 1929

Subhas Bose as Mayor of Calcutta demonstrating on Independence
Day, January 26, 1931

Subhas Bose speaking in Berlin, 1933

Subhas Bose with the Mayor of Vienna, 1933

Subhas Bose performing his father's 'Sradh', Calcutta, January 1935

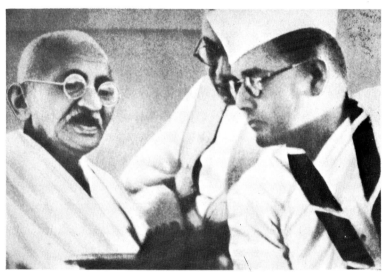

Mahatma Gandhi and Subhas Bose

Sarat and Subhas Bose at their house in Calcutta, 1937

The Bose family: (standing) Suresh, Satish, Sailesh, Subhas, Sunil, Sarat, Sudhir. The Bose brothers' mother sits in front of Subhas Bose and the wives of the other brothers sit in front of their respective husbands, 1939

Subhas Bose with Vallabhbhai Patel, Sarojini Naidu and Jawaharlal
Nehru, 1938

Subhas Bose with Indira and Jawaharlal Nehru, 1938

Congress Working Committee meeting at the Bose house, Calcutta, 1938

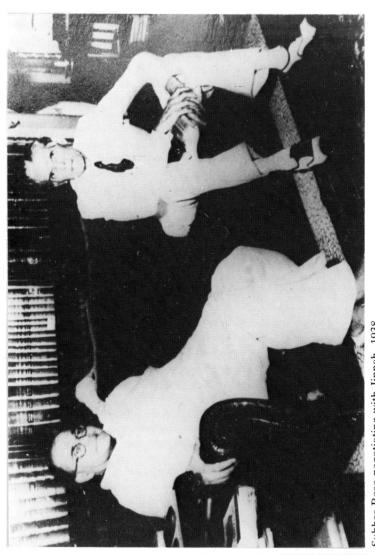

Subhas Bose negotiating with Jinnah, 1938

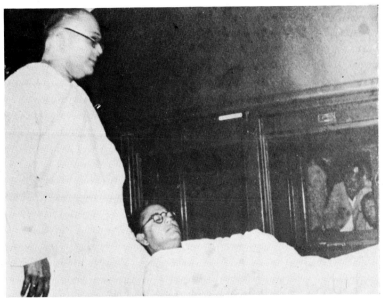

Sarat and Subhas Bose in a rail compartment on the eve of the
Tripuri Congress, 1939

Subhas Bose with the Left Consolidation Committee at his house in
Calcutta, 1939

Subhas Bose after his release from prison with his mother, brother and the Mayor of Calcutta, A.R. Siddiqui, December 1940

CHAPTER FIVE

'Rushing along like a storm': On to the National Stage, 1927–28

I am rushing along like a storm—it is necessary to understand whither I am going—towards good or evil. . . . Mother, I am an absolutely unworthy and useless son. Your love is taking.me towards full manhood.

Subhas Bose to Basanti Devi, 1929[1]

I

The period between Subhas Bose's release in the spring of 1927 and the imprisonment of both Bose brothers for an extended period beginning in 1932 coincided with a period of renewed and expanded activity by the Congress as well as by revolutionaries and communists who worked inside and outside the Congress organization. It was also marked by the widening, though not yet unbridgeable, gulf between the Hindu and Muslim communities and the exit of many Muslim nationalists from the Swarajist and Congress Parties.[2]

Extension of the contacts between India and the world outside, which took place during the First World War, continued with renewed vigor. Comintern agents appeared to help spur efforts at labor organizing and building the Communist Party of India, and India increasingly sent some of its politically and culturally active sons to the West. Some like Motilal and Jawaharlal Nehru went to learn from Western experiments in nation-building and to contribute to the West's understanding of India.[3] Others like the poet Rabindranath Tagore went to see, but also to teach the West spiritual and cultural lessons gleaned from Indian civilization.[4] The connection between India and the world also meant increased economic interdependence, so that India was affected by the world economic depression which began in 1929. This trauma led to efforts to combat it by vigorous state action. Indians kept their eyes on these efforts in Germany, Italy, the United States, Britain, and the Soviet Union, although they did not as yet have the responsibility for managing their own economy. These experiments gradually had an impact on Indian thinking and action.[5]

Just before Subhas Bose returned from his years in Burma and his months of recuperation in Shillong, Sarat Bose entered the Bengal Legislative Council for the first time in January 1927. He was a member of the disciplined Swarajist group which numbered about thirty-nine in a Council of 140. The Swarajists in Bengal and nationally had suffered from defections and splits, but were still a force in the Bengal Council as the single largest party. But they did not have a majority and had lost virtually all their Muslim members from the heady days under Das when they had about twenty Muslim councillors with them.[6]

Sen Gupta, Gandhi's choice to replace C.R. Das and a skillful speaker, headed their party and Dr B.C. Roy was his deputy. Nalini Sarker was their chief spokesman on all issues touching the economy. Sarat Bose, though a novice in the Council, was a worthy addition to this team. His long years of advocacy at the bar and his experience in the Calcutta Corporation were perfect preparation. He was not hesitant to speak and to cross-examine the ministers and executive councillors, quickly expanded his repertoire of issues from detenus and the police to the fate of the dyarchical system, the budget, irrigation, and education, and did his homework on these issues.

Though the Swarajists accepted the label of 'obstructionists,' they participated actively when they were attending. So to see them simply as a group trying to prevent action of the Council is misleading. They were resolutely opposed to any grant for ministers' salaries and to any ministers serving. They believed that all real power remained with the governor and his officials and for Indian ministers to serve was to convey the mistaken message that Indians had gained some real power by the dyarchic arrangement under the Montagu-Chelmsford reforms. But on numerous bills and issues they debated, offered amendments and bills of their own, negotiated compromises, and voted, so that even though Bengal's Swarajists were not considered 'responsivists' in the terminology of the day, they were active participants in the work of the Council during those years and months when they attended.[7]

In the Das years of 1924 and 1925, the Swarajists were able to block and defeat the ministers' salaries and, to the dismay of the government, no ministers served through much of this period. The issue arose again at the opening of the new Council in January 1927. The governor, the Earl of Lytton, urged the Council to give dyarchy a chance, but he instructed the members that if salaries for ministers were not included in the budget, he would operate without them as he had been doing for some time.[8]

The Swarajists took the debate on ministers' salaries as an opportunity to launch an attack on the entire system of dyarchy, and Sarat Bose's maiden speech was made in this debate. He said in part:

> Now, Sir, it is not necessary for me to mention the defects of the present constitution. I have it on high authority, prominent officials and non-officials alike, that the defects of this diarchical system of Government have been pointed out more than once and that Government has been provided with plenty of evidence on that score. If that is so, what is the necessity of attempting to work diarchy, the defects of which are still in existence? What attempts have you made to remove these defects? Without remedying them, what right have you to ask the Members of this House to join with you in working this system?[9]

In answer to the charge that the Swarajist policy of obstructionism was barren, he said,

> Is it news . . . that the policy of obstruction was systematically pursued in the Dominion of Canada year after year, until it succeeded, until that policy was recognised as effective by Lord Durham, and a change in the constitution took place. The new Viceroy, Lord Durham, came to Canada and condemned the policy that had been followed till then in the Dominion Government of setting class against class, creed against creed, race against race—a policy which I say that the present Government is pursuing in this country. . . . The policy of obstruction did succeed in Canada, it did succeed in the United States to this extent that it ultimately led to the independence of America.[10]

Summing up his case for the opposition, Sarat Bose insisted that,

> We, on this side of the House, have made our position clear. We are not going to support any ministry, for we realise that it will mean possibly a team of two or four crouching cringing slaves of the Secretaries. We are not going to support a ministry because in the circumstances in which we stand to-day, these gentlemen, however honourable they may be, have not the right, even if they had the inclination, of opposing the views of their Secretaries. . .We are not going to be a party to this rule which has got in detention without any trial more than 100 of our young men. . .[11]

But, however forcefully and eloquently the Swarajists argued, they did not have the votes to stop salaries for ministers from being included in the budget by a vote of ninety-four to thirty-eight. The governor selected Byomkes Chakravarti and A.K. Ghuznavi to serve as the first pair of ministers for this new Council term. Sarat Bose and his colleagues were accurate in their charge that the Government of India and the officials responsible for India in Great Britain had judged dyarchy to be a failure. The journey to new constitutional advances which led from the Simon Commission through the Round Table Conferences, the Communal Award, and Poona Pact, and to the Government of India Act of 1935 was underway. The Government of India Act of 1919 continued in operation until 1936.[12]

After two ministers were in place, the Swarajists continued their criticisms. They insisted that the Bengal ministers did not have majority support of the elected members. Sarat Bose, in speaking for the move to refuse salaries for the two sitting ministers, said in part,

> At the outset I would like to remind the House of what the Select Committee of the Lords and Commons of Great Britain said regarding the appointment of Ministers. In clause 4 of their report they say that 'they are of opinion that the Ministers selected by the Government to advise him on the transferred subjects should be elected members of the Legislative Council, enjoying its confidence and capable of leading it.' Sir, as we all know, there are 57 Hindu members in this House. May I ask the Hon'ble Minister for Education how many Hindu members of this House he enjoys the confidence of, not to speak of his being capable of leading them? There are 39 Muhammadan members of this House. May I ask the Hon'ble Minister for Local Self-Government as to how many Muhammadans he enjoys the confidence of, not to talk of his capacity for leading them? It really comes to this—that the Ministers who choose to call themselves popular Ministers have to enthrone themselves on the strength of the 44 Government and Government nominated members. People's ministry, no doubt![13]

Sarat Bose continued, 'We, on this side of the House do not lay any great stress on narrow Hindu interests, or narrow Muhammadan interests. We seek to interpret those interests in the light of the higher and noble national interests. . .'[14] Part of the thrust of his work in the Council was to criticize and bait the ministers, to lay bare their lack of knowledge and their lack of commitment to the national welfare. It was almost like a courtroom drama with the added spice of national feeling and several of the most effective Swarajist champions had honed their weapons at the bar. These thrusts did not go unanswered and one of those who struck back at Sarat Bose and Dr B.C. Roy was Sir P.C. Mitter, a relation of Sarat's who called Sarat and the Swarajist leaders 'pseudo-leaders' more interested in their own advancement than the national good. He said that if such men joined him and tried to work the reforms, then there could be united action on significant problems like public health.[15]

There was one issue on which all members of the Bengal Council—Swarajists, Liberals, Muslims, officials and nominated members—could agree, and that was the bad financial deal they believed Bengal was getting from the central government. Before 1927 was out, a motion was passed calling for the Government of Bengal to approach the Government of India to request that the export duty for jute be allocated to Bengal for improvements in agriculture, sanitary conditions, and free primary education. Such a measure could be passed unanimously.[16]

Sarat had criticized Mitter's performance as education minister in previous years and his membership in the Rowlatt Committee. In the course of these remarks, Sarat, as member for Calcutta University, united the Swarajist viewpoint, with the interests of his alma mater and of his constituency:

> ... if co-operation means the introduction of Bills which have the promotion of national good as their object, which will mean a new chapter in our University education, and which will mean the democratisation of the University, which will mean giving right to the graduates of the University to take part in their University affairs, which will give real responsibility to the citizens and replace the dumb-driven, official cattle—if co-operation means the production of a Bill, or Bills, which will promote the healthy growth of the University life and education, then, surely, the late Minister of Education knows that the members belonging to the Congress Party are pledged to support all such measures. (Hear, hear) If we have failed to co-operate, we have failed to co-operate with misdeeds ... we shall never fail to co-operate in matters which will promote national interest, which will promote national unity, which will give higher and better education to both Hindus and Muhammadans and to all other communities inhabiting this country, which will promote the larger interests of the country as opposed to the smaller interests of the official cattle.[17]

Sarat Bose insisted that the Congress sought the national good by pushing for long-term significant national power and responsibility.

The Swarajist efforts were largely negative and they did not put forward an alternative budget or concrete schemes of improvement. They attacked the large expenditures for the police and the European establishment. Sarat Bose fired some salvos at the item for the governor's band, but he was even more intense about examining and cutting monies alloted for the secret service. He said,

> Now, Sir, I have given the House some idea as to the manner in which secret service money is spent—I submit that I am entitled to comment upon it, because though this challenge was thrown out in July, 1924, it has not yet been accepted: though these political detenus asked for the constitution of a fair and impartial tribunal, that tribunal has not yet been constituted. And why not? The reason is not far to seek. Because the agents of the State—these dark powers had not the courage to face the enquiry, because they knew that once this enquiry was held in the presence of these two gentlemen, all their talk about criminal conspiracies, about smuggling of arms and revolvers would vanish into thin air, and it would be discovered that out of the secret service money the agents of the State had been coining—concocting—evidence with a view to putting innocent men into jail.
>
> Now, Sir, the activities of the secret service are not new to this country or any other country. The British secret service played the same trick in other places; and it is now a matter of history ... disclosed by the biographer of

Michael Collins that Burns who used to pass off as 'Jameson' in British Labour circles and posed as a Bolshevik was really a British secret service agent living on British secret service money, fattening on it and trying to concoct false evidence against Michael Collins and his associates.[18]

Sarat Bose continued at length to explore the ways in which the British had practised duplicity in fabricating evidence in Ireland and Bengal and he mentioned the names of several Bengalis who had suffered from false and secret charges. He left it to others to bring up the case of his brother which may have been too painful for him to mention. Mr P.C. Basu said in the course of the same debate that one day the Government of Bengal would matter-of-factly announce that 'flowers of our nation, namely, Srijut Subhas Chandra Bose, Satyendra Chandra Mitra and the rest were all innocent as babes so far as anarchical crimes were concerned.'[19]

The Swarajists continually raised questions about the detenus in the Council. One cannot be certain, but it appears that in some cases, particularly that of Subhas Bose, this pressure from the nationalist side may have affected the government. In replying to P.C. Basu and Sarat Bose in this debate, the executive councillor responsible for the Home Department, A.N. Moberly, admitted that, 'Unfortunately, Government have received unfavourable accounts of Mr Bose's health.'[20] Within two months, Subhas Bose was freed unconditionally.

As an elected member of Council who had never taken his seat, Subhas Bose decided, against doctor's orders, to enter the Council chambers and take 'the oath of allegiance to the Crown' on August 23, 1927, and, amidst cheers, he walked to his place with the Swarajist Party.[21] Although the Legislative Council was not at all a favorite forum for his political activity, Subhas Bose attended, somewhat irregularly, through the next two-and-a-half years and was even re-elected in the spring of 1929. He participated actively in the question periods, demanding information about detenus and jail conditions. He was much slower than Sarat—perhaps because he considered the councils something of a farce—to expand the range of issues on which to speak and debate. Nonetheless, he did attend many sittings through these years and argued often in the Congress organization for the continuation of Congress participation in the councils following the 'non-cooperation from within the chambers' line which his mentor C.R. Das had first formulated at the end of 1922. He was loathe for the Swarajist wing of the Congress to give up this forum to cooperating Liberals, independents, Muslims, landlords, business and labor representatives, and the Europeans.[22] He also had an opportunity to duel, verbally at least, with one of his 'jailers', i.e., the home member, A.N. Moberly, who was at the time preparing reports on the threat to the country posed by Subhas Bose.[23]

The twenty-sixth session of the Bengal Council, attended by both Boses, was marked by a Swarajist triumph, a majority vote of no-confidence in the ministers. Dr B.C. Roy moved the motion and argued that all real power was held by the governor and that the 1919 Act showed a fundamental distrust of Indian capabilities for responsible action. In such a situation, ministers were 'the creatures of the Government,' 'a prop of the bureaucracy,' and should not serve.[24]

There were two major issues in 1927 which brought the Swarajists and many of the elected Muslim members together. The first was a Swarajist motion for the release of all political prisoners which virtually every elected Indian member voted for. The second was this no-confidence motion which the Swarajists and a large group of Muslim members, primarily the followers of Sir Abdur Rahim, backed for different reasons. A large majority of the elected Muslim members were now willing to work the dyarchic system, but, argued Rahim, ministers must have solid support in the Council. Of Ghuznavi, Rahim said, 'The public has no confidence in him. . . . The whole community is opposed to him.'[25] Ghuznavi had some Muslim and Liberal support and said that Rahim's opposition was personal and not political. There were charges pending in the court against Chakravarti about financial swindles and many members were persuaded of his dishonesty even before the cases had been decided.

Ghuznavi insisted that he had been working effectively for the interests of the Muslims and for communal harmony and Chakravarti denied the charges against him. Both had the support of the large official and nominated bloc and also all the European votes. Some of the independents and Liberals, as well as groups which called themselves the 'Responsivists,' and 'The Union Party,' as well as the landholders voted for the ministers. But the opposition was too strong: sixty-six to sixty-two against Ghuznavi, sixty-eight to fifty-five against Chakravarti.[26] Rahim explained that there were issues which brought the Swarajists and the Muslims together just as there were issues which divided them. After these negative votes, the governor, Sir Stanley Jackson, prorogued the Bengal Council. Both Boses had attended the debate and voted against the ministers, although neither had spoken.

When the Council met again on December 13, there were two new ministers, Sir P.C. Mitter, a Bose relation and a minister in previous years, and Musharruf Hosain. The Council met for only two days, but this was sufficient time for the leading Swarajists including Subhas and Sarat Bose to get into heated arguments with the new ministers, executive councillors, and the elected president of the Council, Raja Manmatha Nath Roy Chaudhuri of Santosh. Sarat Bose had made some investigation of

sericulture (silkworm production) and in several sessions of the Council
pressed the ministers (since this was a transferred department) with searching questions about the operation of the Sericulture Department. He,
Subhas, and others but also had a fusillade of questions ready on education, political prisoners, and jail conditions. They were determined to em-
barrass the ministers and executive councillors, especially the former,
whenever they could. At one point the president chastised Sarat Bose and
asked him to desist from his questions, 'It is more or less a criticism that
you are trying to level against the knowledge of the Hon'ble Minister with
regard to the department he is administering.' Sen Gupta defended his stalwart interrogator, 'Is it a *mala fide* procedure to get out information for the
purpose of showing that the Minister is absolutely unfit for office?'[27] Sarat
answered the President by quoting at him the Legislative Council manual
on question procedures, and Subhas asked why the ministers did not bring
their files and were so uninformed on their departments. Subhas continued, 'On a point of order, Sir, would you like us to put questions in Bengali
to the Hon'ble Minister in charge of Education, since we find that he cannot understand the questions put to him in English?'[28] It must have been
with relief that the officials, ministers, and president of the Council learned
that the Swarajists, in their peripatetic manner, had decided to refrain from
attending the twenty-eighth session of the Council in the early 1928.

II

Subhas Bose's return to Bengal also meant rejoining his own family. Just
before Subhas was arrested, he and Sarat's family had been living in 38/
1, Elgin Road, adjacent to the main family house at 38/2. During 1927,
Sarat Bose constructed a new house across the street and just a few paces
down the street cross-cutting Elgin Road, Woodburn Park. At the end of
1927 this house at 1 Woodburn Park was ready and Sarat moved in with
his immediate family. The house was a handsome three-storeyed one with
a patio and lovely garden adjoining the sitting-room on the ground floor.
Subhas stayed first at 38/1 with Sarat, then at 38/2 Elgin Road while his
mother was still in Calcutta, but thereafter moved into the Woodburn Park
house where he lived on the top floor from 1928 to early 1932. This new
house and living arrangement allowed more space for all involved.

Of Sarat and Bivabati Bose's eight children, five were born between
1911 and 1922, with Gita, the second daughter, born in 1922, as the
youngest of this group. There was a gap between the first five and the last
three of more than six years, Roma, born in 1928, Chitra in 1930, and
Subrata in 1932, were known as the 'kiddies'. The older ones spent more
time living with Subhas and came to know him better.[29]

Sarat Bose was an organized person who tried to follow a daily routine which allowed for his professional work, politics, family, and friends. He rose early, at 5.50 a.m. or even earlier, took a stroll, usually in the park next to the Woodburn Park house, then returned to do his daily puja in the *Thakor-ghor* set aside in his new house for this activity. He saw his children briefly, had tea, and was at his desk, filling his morning with legal matters and preparations for court appearances. If he had to attend court, he dressed in a suit. Once his court appearance was finished, he changed from suit to dhoti in his chamber at the court and headed for the Bengal Council (later Assembly) if it was meeting, or to the Corporation. He then returned to his desk at home and worked until the evening when he often attended political meetings. If a very important case came up, he worked on it late into the night. He slept only four or five hours per night. Walking was his only form of exercise in Calcutta and later in life he hired a skilled masseur. He was a methodical man who liked everything in its place and his house immaculate.[30]

The charge of the household was in the hands of Bivabati under whose direction worked a staff of two cooks (one Brahmin; one Muslim who cooked meat and chicken), maidservants, a sweeper, driver, and Sarat's personal bearer. Sarat loved to eat and the Boses ate a typical upper-middle class Bengali diet of fish, meat, rice, fruits, and sweets, which Sarat adored. Subhas liked fried items such as cutlets and these were also part of the fare. At noon they ate in the Bengali style, in the evening in the Western style. The latter cuisine included roast chicken or mutton, soups, and puddings. The rather heavy eating took its toll. Sarat developed diabetes and Biva had chronic gastric problems.[31]

In this household, the parents were so much in tune that their children never saw them quarrel. Though Sarat, during working days, did not have much time for them, the children have said that he was a loving father and they never wanted for affection.[32] This household, though, also had a young uncle, who loved children and found his most important relaxation playing and talking with them. He romped and played with Sarat's children and with the children of his other brothers and sisters. To them Subhas was 'Rangakakababu,' or shortened forms thereof. They teased him, hit him, confided in him, and every one of the children of the new Bose generation has only the tenderest feelings for the uncle they knew when they were young. They spoke nonsense to him and often played hide-and-seek In this game, Subhas hid in dangerous places and took chances. Although the children may have occasionally disturbed his work, he never became annoyed. One niece told me that he talked to her in such a serious, adult, and searching way and listened to her as well, that she felt closer to him than

to her own father. Subhas did not lack for a rich family life and for relationships with children of all ages. They returned the love and affection
he gave. Several became expert masseurs practising on their Rangakaka.[33]

Subhas had a special bond with Sarat, and with Biva, which continued
through life, differences on cultural matters, friends, and even political
strategies notwithstanding. Subhas had a stronger attachment to Bengali
literature than did Sarat, while Sarat appeared to give a higher evaluation
to men who spoke English well and had a European education. Sarat also
felt that, while he demanded first-rate people to work for and with him,
Subhas was much too lax in his standards. Partly in jest, partly seriously,
Sarat would occasionally say that Subhas should keep 'his Tagore', while
Subhas would say that Sarat could keep his 'inriji' (English).[34]

Subhas grew ever closer to his *Mejboudi*, Biva, and she often favored
him and helped him in schemes that Sarat would not countenance. He also
wanted her to play a more active role in politics, but Sarat was against this.
Indirectly, she eventually did play a role. Biva never went against Sarat's
word, though she did upon occasion work out a compromise so that the
wishes of both Subhas and Sarat could be fulfilled. Once Subhas invited
to dinner a woman dancer named Menoka Devi who had provided money
for his political work. To Sarat's conservative and strict view, she was
preceded by a bad reputation. Sarat with some annoyance said to Subhas,
'She's a bad lady. No dinner for her. Tell her the dinner is cancelled.'
Subhas was upset and consulted Biva. She said to Subhas, 'Don't worry,
I will manage it.' She told Sarat he did not have to attend. Sarat said, 'Do
as you think best. But I will not attend.' The dinner was held: Sarat was
absent. Sometimes Sarat would come to Biva and say, 'Did Subhas come
and get money from you?' And Biva would reply, 'I gave him from my
money, so why do you ask?'[35]

On the schooling of the children, particularly the girls, Subhas and
Sarat did not always agree, though Sarat came around more to Subhas'
view. Sarat thought that girls should finish their secondary education and
then be married; Subhas believed that they should have a fuller, richer education, including a college education, and, if they wished and had promise,
a postgraduate education. Meera, the older daughter, did not get a higher
education, and had some regrets, especially after Gita, Roma, and Chitra
all went on to college and Chitra obtained an advanced degree. Subhas said
to the girls, 'Your father is old fashioned.' By the time Gita was ready,
Subhas had won the argument, though she studied English literature as
Sarat wanted and not the philosophy that Subhas suggested.[36] All the girls
went to the Protestant diocesan school. Gita went on to Loretto House and
gained her B.A. in English in 1942. All the children learned excellent

English as had the sons of Janaki Nath Bose.

When Gita was a teenager, Subhas wrote in her autograph book:

> The difference between man and the animals is this, man can live for an ideal and if necessary die for it, but animals live only for living. When I look around, I see many men who live only for living (like) animals. Then I feel their lives as human beings are completely futile. If you want to have a life of fulfilment, it will be desirable to give up stereotyped ways of living and adopt new ways.
>
> The lives of women are no less valuable than the lives of men and the purpose of the lives of women do not merely consist in cooking and having children. Women can also have a life of fulfilment if they can accept an ideal and follow it. If you can do that, then I shall be really happy and there will be full justification of your birth as a human being.[37]

Subhas did not have any regular source of income. Family members have told me that he did get some money from those in his joint family household and also is said to have received Rs. 500 per month from his father in the period between his return from England in 1921 and his father's death in 1934. Subhas also had a number of wealthy patrons and these were said to include Sarat's close friend Debendra Lall Khan of Narajol, Kumar Bishunath Roy, Bimbal Sinha of Paikpara, the Maharaja of Mymensingh, the Goswami family of Serampore, and a few others, all among the wealthy landed class of Bengal, who held nationalist sentiments and were struck with Subhas' talents, intelligence, and appearance.[38]

Sarat and Subhas remained intimately tied to the rest of their large family. Janaki Nath Bose and his wife came to Calcutta two or three times a year and stayed for a lengthy period at Puja time in the fall, when the parents were keen that as many as possible of their children and grand children be with them. In Janaki Nath's time, they made a visit to Kodalia, his ancestral village, the place where he, but not his children, had grown up, and Subhas used to swim in the village pond with the children. Janaki Nath also had property in several places in Orissa and built a house near the seaside at Puri. Sarat and Subhas greatly preferred the mountains to the seaside and took their vacations in Kurseong rather than at Puri.[39]

The sons learned and accepted Janaki Nath's views on the responsibilities of an adult householder to care for those less fortunate economically than himself. Sarat gave to many charities, as his father had and often also preferred to remain anonymous. Subhas, though not a regular earner, was a regular contributor to the welfare of others and paid out about Rs. 200 to 300 per month to poor boys and girls. He also gave some money to those engaged in clandestine activities, though the dates, extent, and precise purpose of this are not clear.[40]

III

Subhas' return to his family in Bengal signaled his entry late in 1927 into the troubled politics of the Bengal Provincial Congress Committee. When he indicated his willingness to serve in the BPCC he was more acceptable to the revolutionaries, both those working in the open and those underground, and J.M. Sen Gupta appeared weary of the conflicts. So Subhas was elected president of the BPCC in November 1927 just after his return from convalescence in Shillong.[41]

For the next twenty years, the Boses, either Subhas or Sarat, or both, headed the most important faction in the Bengal Congress, but were often fighting fiercely with other factions. Upon occasion these conflicts moved from words to blows. It sometimes appeared like a water polo match in which membership in the teams changed from time to time and suddenly a leader or group that had been playing on one side bobbed up sporting just as staunchly for the other team. Through some of these years, the 'other team' opposing the Bose team was likely to be aligned with the Gandhian high command of the national Congress organization. This was true in the 1929 to 1932 period and again from 1939 to 1941, but usually the factions were multiple and the alignments complex and changing. Bengal's 'Gandhians' were not only true believers in Gandhi's method and constructive program, but also included some Bengal politicians who found it worthwhile, for a combination of political and personal motives, to align themselves with the national Gandhian network. J.M. Sen Gupta was the most important of these men in the period from 1925 to his death in 1933. Dr B.C. Roy and Nalini Sarker, an important spokesman for Indian big business in Calcutta, both moved closer to Gandhi.[42] Among the true believers, P.C. Ghosh and Satish Das Gupta were in the front ranks, and long opponents of the Boses. The *Amrita Bazar Patrika* usually presented the Gandhian point of view, while *Forward* (later called *Liberty*), edited by Satya Ranjan Bakshi, presented the Bose perspective. The *Patrika* and some Congressmen also leaned towards the Hindu communalist viewpoint of the Hindu Mahasabha, opposing the Boses who tried to observe the spirit—though the letter was dead—of the Bengal Pact allying Hindus and Muslims.[43]

The differences between the Bose faction and other factions were sometimes over substantive issues and views, e.g., the ends and means of the national movement, the value of legislative council participation, the timing of a civil disobedience campaign, assessment of the actions of the revolutionaries, etc., but sometimes there were simply personality conflicts, naked power struggles, or other less specific reasons for the skirmishes.

On the issue of the unity resolution which was an effort to preserve Das' Bengal Pact with the Muslims, the Boses were in agreement with all political leaders that, although the pact, as it had been made was dead, this should not mean the end of attempts at cooperation with the Muslims. The Boses, like all Hindu politicians felt the pressure of the Hindu nationalist lobby which was already crying 'Hinduism in danger' and 'Beware the foreign allegiance of the Indian Muslims', but continued to try harder for a rapprochement with Bengal's Muslim leaders during the next two decades.[44]

After returning permanently from Shillong, Subhas Bose addressed a large audience in Shraddhananda Park under the auspices of the Bengal Provincial Hindu Sabha. He spoke for Hindu-Muslim unity and attacked the views of the sponsoring organization of the meeting and the Muslim League. He asked the Hindus to bend over backwards to respect the rights of the Muslims and pleaded for concentration on the most important task at hand: the struggle for Indian freedom. Dividing along communal lines would weaken this fight. He said,

> The Moslems are not enemies of cows. In Moslem houses cows are well looked after—sometimes better than in Hindu homes. The Moslem peasants in Bengal love the cow as much as the Hindu peasants—because without that, milk is not available nor cultivation possible.[45]

He asked the meeting not to pass a resolution against cow-killing, because this might lead to polarization of the two communities. He put his own popularity—at a high point just after his release—on the line and insisted that all should look to the Congress for settlement of communal grievances and not leave the Congress to form separate communal organizations.

> I know that by asking you to make a compromise I run the risk of losing the popularity which perhaps I possess. But believe me, I do not give so much value to popularity that I will forsake truth for it. . . . I am prepared to forgo the popularity which threatens to deflect me from my duty. . . . The Congress is the only body which is fit to arbitrate because it is neither Hindu nor a Mahommedan organisation. The duty of Bengal in this crisis is quite clear. Bengal Hindus and Moslems must make up their differences. . . . We have to atone for the sins of Mirjaffar and Umichand by taking a leading part in the fight for freedom. There is a very close connection between the Hindus and Moslems of Bengal. Moslems enriched the Vaisnavic literature of Bengal and Hindus also used to be well versed in Persian, Arabic, and Urdu literatures. Besides they speak the same language. Therefore Hindu-Moslem unity must commence in Bengal.[46]

After he and all the Swarajist Congressmen present left, the meeting chairman and some other speakers proceeded to criticize him. The *Amrita Bazar Patrika's* editorial columns for the next few days were filled with harsh words on the audacity and wrongheadedness of Bengal's young Congress leader.[47] Subhas had many hard lessons to learn about the fate of idealistic words for unity.

The Indian National Congress held its annual meeting in Madras at the end of December 1927. Bose was not able to attend, but sent a message which was read. One returnee to Indian politics who did attend was Jawaharlal Nehru, fresh from one-and-a-half years in Europe, including a trip to the Soviet Union. He and the Madras leader, Srinivasa Iyengar were among those who worked for the passage of a resolution declaring complete independence to be the goal of the Congress. Although the vaguer term 'swaraj', roughly meaning self-rule, had been in vogue for some years, the complete independence resolution put the matter much more baldly.[48] To the surprise of many, it was passed. *Forward* commented on December 29, 1927:

> The die is cast; the Rubicon has been crossed. The goal of India's political aspirations has been unambiguously defined by the Indian National Congress as nothing short of complete independence. Having pledged themselves to the securing of independence they must in the words of Mr Saklatvala, begin by refusing 'contact with the economic interests to the British Capitalists' representatives in India'. . . It is the cheap Indian labour and illimitable raw materials of India which are exploited by the British capitalists. Mr Saklatvala's appeal to the Indian National Congress to take immediate steps 'to awaken our working masses, organise our teeming peasants, take these myriads of India's toiling children right inside our national organisation by direct affiliation (sic), discipline them within their Trade Unions and with All-India Workers' and Peasants' Party for direct economic action', is quite in consonance with Deshabandhu's programme and seems to be the best way in which the Congress resolutions may be immediately given effect to.[49]

Saklatvala, a scion of the Tata family, had emigrated to Great Britain and as a member of the Communist Party of Great Britain, had succeeded in being elected to the House of Commons. During 1927, he toured India and was one of those helping to push Indian nationalists toward a more left and ideological course. He also met with members of the small Communist Party of India and the Workers' and Peasants' parties formed in several provinces between 1925 and 1927. That *Forward* gave such a positive response to his views shows that the Boses, too, were swimming with the leftward current and not against it.[50]

However, it is one thing to recognize the importance of the task of organizing workers and peasants for the national movement; it is another to actually bring them in an active, participatory way into the Congress. The Boses did work in the Bengal Provincial Congress Committee which carried out important demonstrations, participated in the Civil Disobedience Movement, and later ran election campaigns. They also echoed Saklatvala's call. What they do not seem to have done effectively is recruit an able cadre of lieutenants or build a mass organization. One variable at work may simply have been age: Subhas Bose was only thirty in a society in which older men usually hold the powerful positions. When C.R. Das was at his political best, he was between fifty and fifty-five years old. Gandhi came to the forefront of Indian politics in 1918 at the age of forty-nine and flourished into his late seventies. Young men could commit reckless acts, be imprisoned or die, and gain recognition or martyrdom. What was more difficult was to work laboriously at building an organization which would recruit talented people through decades of often discouraging endeavor.

In the spring of 1928, Subhas Bose was defeated by a Liberal, B. K. Basu, for mayor of Calcutta, thirty-seven to forty-six. J.M. Sen Gupta had stepped down and had nominated Subhas, with the backing of the Calcutta Municipal Association. But a combination of Europeans, independents, Liberals, some Muslims, and disgruntled Congressmen voted against him. Sen Gupta had to defend himself against charges that his indifference had caused the defeat of the Swarajist candidate and the forfeiture of Swarajist positions in Corporation committees. As always, he talked himself out of this corner and insisted he had done as much for Subhas as he could.[51] Subhas Bose and J.M. Sen Gupta continued to cooperate at the Bengal Provincial Congress meeting in the spring when Sen Gupta served as president of the meeting and Subhas was president of the Bengal Provincial Congress Committee. Resolutions were passed against the Simon Commission (for the boycott of its work), for independence, against resigning permanently from the legislative councils, and for the cultivators limiting jute production.[52]

With some of his provincial work in hand, Subhas Bose went on a tour in late April and early May to the Bombay Presidency. He was accorded warm receptions in Nagpur, then Bombay, and finally, Poona, where he was elected president of the Maharashtra Provincial Conference. His long speech on this occasion was the fullest statement of his views on a spectrum of issues that he was to give directly to an Indian audience for many years.[53]

In the nationalist tradition of Tilak and Aurobindo, he said that, 'Swaraj is the sovereign remedy for all our ills.' He argued that economic and cultural issues should not be forgotten or neglected, but that real change would occur only after India was completely free of British rule. In contrast, Gandhi and Tagore, in their different ways, wanted social,

economic, and cultural reconstruction to proceed during the struggle for
political freedom. Also in the tradition of Tilak and Aurobindo, Bose felt
called upon to give a defense of nationalism in the new atmosphere of the
1920s. He said,

> Nationalism is sometimes assailed as narrow, selfish and aggressive. It is
> also regarded as a hindrance to the promotion of internationalism. . . . My
> reply . . . is that Indian nationalism . . . is inspired by the highest ideals of
> the human race, viz. *satyam* (the true), *shivam* (the good), *sundaram* (the
> beautiful). Nationalism in India has instilled into us truthfulness, honesty,
> manliness and the spirit of service and sacrifice. What is more, it has roused
> the creative faculties which for centuries had been lying dormant in our
> people and as a result we are experiencing a renaissance in the domain of
> Indian art.[54]

He maintained that only through further developing its own genius could
Indian culture make a distinctive contribution to world culture for 'true
unity can manifest itself only through diversity.'

Nationalism, Bose felt, was also under attack from another angle, that
of international labor or communism. His answer to this attack was,

> This attack is not only ill-advised but unconsciously serves the interests of
> our alien rulers . . . before we can endeavour to reconstruct Indian society
> . . . we should first secure the right to shape our own destiny. . . . When
> political freedom has been attained, it will then be time to consider seriously
> the problem of social and economic reconstruction. As far as I am aware this
> is also the opinion of prominent communists in other lands. To introduce
> fresh cleavage within our ranks by talking openly of class war and working
> for it appears to me at the present moment to be a crime against nationalism.
> To what straits we may be reduced by a mal-assimilation of Karl Marx and
> Bakunin becomes manifest when we come across a certain class of Indian
> labourites (or communists, if you call them so), who openly advocate the use
> of British or foreign cloth on the plea of internationalism.[55]

Bose followed this defense with a plea for a coalition between labor and
nationalism.

For Bose—at this point in his life at least—nationalism in India meant
the Indian National Congress. The Congress was, in theory if not in
practice, to reach out to all groups and all strata of the Indian population.
It was not bound by any cultural, religious, regional, caste, or class barriers.
Its goal was to mobilize the entire Indian people and turn out the foreign
rulers as soon as possible. He pointed to key sectors of the population
which the Congress had not done a good job of reaching. These included
labor, the peasantry, youths, and women. In the Poona speech, he dealt
with each, but gave most of his attention to labor or the masses and at one
point said that this term was to include the peasants as well as urban
workers.

Through local Congress committees, Congressmen were to carry out the building of what Bose envisioned as a national army. He seemed to like the metaphor of such an army and he put it this way:

> We have to remember that programmes like that of boycott of British goods are . . . sorties in a general campaign and these sorties or spurts are possible only when the army itself is fit and efficient. The efficiency of the national army can be maintained only by keeping up a spirit of resistance among our people.[56]

In pointing to failures of the 'national army', he mentioned the let-down of 1922 when the Non-Cooperation Movement was halted. His critique was,

> We are easily upset by failures. We lack the dogged tenacity of John Bull— and unlike him we cannot therefore fight a losing game. We do not realise that during the Great War it was the tenacious nibbling policy of the French's contemptible little army in the midst of the most hopeless situation which made subsequent victory possible. I, therefore, say that opposition to Government is never futile—it is the psychological basis of the nationalist movement. It is only at uniform, consistent and continuous obstruction that we can keep up an atmosphere of resistance to the bureaucracy and develop that moral stamina, lack of which is the one psychological cause of our degradation and slavery.[57]

Besides this analysis of the character shortcomings of the Indian nationalists, Bose tried to assess why the workers, for the most part, still stood outside the nationalist movement. He felt that the Congress had neither spoken to their concrete interests, nor showed them how their economic fate was tied up with the nationalist movement. Here was a dilemma which Bose and many other nationalists never solved: how was the Congress to work directly for the economic interests of the workers without harming the interests of Indian business? Gandhi had come up with the idea of trusteeship. Bose put the hardships of Indian labor even more starkly than Gandhi. However, Bose wanted class harmony among Indian nationalists. What do you do when the interests of significant segments of the Indian population are not the same, whether they are workers and employers, peasants and landlords, or debtors and money-lenders? Bose did not solve this problem and simply appealed for Indians to band together. He did a better job in identifying the predicament of those who wanted an all-class alliance against the Raj than in providing a solution. This conundrum was to bedevil his work with Bengali Muslims and with more avowed leftists who called for class war. From his vantage point, any move or strategy which detracted from Indian unity against the Raj was 'a crime against nationalism'.

In a fervent plea to young men (and women) to join the Congress

movement, Bose called for special attention to 'the spontaneous self-
expression of the national soul' which he thought common in young
people.

> If we want to rouse the divinity in man (we should, sic) awaken the infinite
> power and energy which lie dormant within him—we have to infuse into
> him the desire for freedom . . . the secret spring of all our creative faculties.
> When a man is intoxicated with the desire for freedom his whole aspect
> changes—as does nature under the magic influence of spring, and, he goes
> through a process of complete transformation.[58]

Youths, he believed, were more idealistic and had more of this unrealized
energy within. Therefore, those seeking to free and build the nation, had
to give more attention to their recruitment to the national cause.

His mention of young women—that he would even be concerned with
singling them out—is in keeping with his special interest in bringing
women more fully into the life of the nation. In this speech, he had two
passages devoted to women. In one, he said,

> I venture to think that there is room for country-wide political organizations
> among our women. It should be the primary object of these organizations to
> carry on political propaganda among women and to help the work of the
> . . . Congress. These organizations can incidentally work for the social,
> intellectual and moral uplift of our women.[59]

In his vision of the future India, he said,

> The status of women should also be raised and women should be trained to
> take a large and more intelligent interest in public affairs. I do not want the
> feminist movement of Europe and America to be reproduced in India. I have
> no love for bobbed hair and short skirts. On the other hand, I firmly believe
> that the women's movement in India will be inspired by our national ideals
> and traditions and will follow its own distinctive course. But I would like to
> point out that the present position of women in some sections of our society
> has no sanction either in our scriptures or in our past history and admits of
> great improvement.[60]

He paid some attention to village re-organization and uplift, calling for
more local initiative. He did not have much that was original to say about
this. He did, however, become much more emotional when he talked about
communalism. He made it clear that he wanted the Indian Muslims side-
by-side with other Indians in the national movement and said they had
remained too long behind barriers and had never established what he called
'cultural intimacy'. He offered one solution,

> In order to facilitate cultural rapprochement, a dose of secular and scientific
> training is necessary. Fanaticism is the greatest thorn in the path of cultural
> intimacy and there is no better remedy for fanaticism. . . . Secular and
> scientific education is useful in another way in that it helps to rouse our

'economic' consciousness. The dawn of 'economic' consciousness spells the death of fanaticism. There is much more in common between a Hindu peasant and a Muslim peasant than between a Muslim peasant and a Muslim zemindar. The masses have only got to be educated wherein their economic interests lie and once they understand that, they will no longer consent to be pawns in communal feuds. By working from the cultural, educational and economic side, we can gradually undermine fanaticism and thereby render possible the growth of healthy nationalism. . .[61]

It all seemed so easy to Bose and many Indian nationalists who leaned to the left that a good dose of economic self-interest would knock out the infection of communalism. However, the easy solution did not work—at least not during the nationalist period—and the communal problem, like class conflict, did not go away.

In two other long sections of the Poona speech, Bose talked about the conclusion of the British Raj, the endgame of foreign imperialism in India, and the new India he envisioned. He talked of a total national strike and boycott, complete with parallel institutions pushed with unwavering determination. Although he praised Nagpur nationalists for opposing the arms act, he did not call for a violent war. He believed at this time that such a national strike would lead the British rulers to decide to leave. He mentioned Irish parallels three or four times in this speech and wondered aloud whether the British had learned the lesson of a timely retreat from their experiences in Ireland. He hoped that they had. It would mean a more rapid and less bloody exit from India.[62]

He called for an 'independent federal republic' outside the British Empire, in which,

> If we want to make India really great we must build up a political democracy on the pedestal of a democratic society. Privileges based on birth, caste or creed should go and equal opportunities should be thrown open to all, irrespective of caste, creed or religion.[63]

When it came to economic reconstruction, he took note of the socialist program and talked of how it might be used, but not imitated in India:

> If the Russians were to follow Karl Marx, Russia would not be what she is to-day, because according to the great German thinker, capitalism and industrialization must precede socialism. Blind imitation, therefore, will not do. Further, in India, the main problem is that of land. And we find that in Russia, which is the only example of a successful socialistic state, the land has been nationalized only in name and in practice, peasant proprietorship exists . . . more experience is necessary before we can finally decide what sort of economic reconstruction would suit India best and help her to fulfill her destiny.[64]

Before Bose concluded, he mentioned a number of immediate steps that

Indian nationalists should be taking, particularly with the Simon Commission, on Indian soil. Indians were to draw up their own constitution, including a declaration of elementary rights and joint electorates. During this same year, he was to work with the Nehru Committee to draw up such a constitution.

At the end, Bose said,

> Sisters and brothers of Maharashtra, I thank you once more for the honour you have done me. May Maharashtra and Bengal stand shoulder to shoulder in the fight that is before us. May I with your blessings, prove in some measure to be worthy of the love and esteem you have been pleased to shower on me.[65]

Throughout the nationalist period there was an affinity between Bengal and Maharashtra, the two areas of India in which Indians took most speedily to Western education and which provided the leaders for the first generation of Indian nationalism. Bengalis and Maharashtrians were somewhat displaced by the new leader of Indian nationalism, Mahatma Gandhi, and his lieutenants. Bengal and Maharashtra provided some of those nationalists most resistant to the spell of the Mahatma.[66]

Even as Bose was delivering his speech in Poona, his work was being scrutinized by the editorial writers for the Calcutta nationalist newspaper, the *Amrita Bazar Patrika*. Taking off from a speech by Subhas Bose condemning communist labor organizers, the *Patrika* said,

> The Swarajya Party's programme was . . . evolutionary in character. But the programme was allowed to be on paper only and its activities were gradually narrowed down to the delivery of hot speeches in the legislatures, and to similar vocal and literary feats. If anyone ventures to remark that we have had enough condemnation of British rule and that the time has come to translate our words into action, he is at once marked down as one who has no love for his country . . . whether the President of the BPCC admits it or not it can hardly be denied that there is wide-spread dissatisfaction at the way in which the fight is being conducted. . . . It is the toiling masses alone who when organized can give a short shrift to communalism and it is they who once they are convinced that political freedom for the nation is no mere change of masters for them, would be the most zealous guardians of that freedom . . .[67]

Among labor leaders there were several types: the non-political moderates, e.g., N.M. Joshi, the nationalists like Subhas Bose, and the more radical organizers inspired by and often members of the Communist Party of India or the Workers' and Peasants' Parties. The moderate non-political men dealt with economic issues only. They thought that mixing in politics would harm the workers' quest for a living wage and satisfactory working conditions. The nationalists like Bose wanted to bring the workers into the mainstream of the nationalist movement, but did not want to encourage class conflict. The third group wanted to encourage class conflict and class consciousness and thought that only militant organizing, unity of all workers in a particular industry, and determined action including lengthy strikes would move the working class forward to their share of the economic pie and transformation of society. The more radical organizers did not have Gandhi's or Bose's ambivalence about Indian capitalists. Capitalists were capitalists. Just as Bose believed that the radical organizers were harming the nationalist cause by the way they worked, so the radicals thought that Gandhi and Bose were harming the interests of the workers by the way they operated. There were, of course, some moments of cooperation and some strikes which all supported, but there were also many occasions on which those of different trade union persuasions fought each other as hard as they fought the capitalists or the Raj.[68]

After the post-First World War rise in labor unrest and organizing from 1918 to 1922, the labor movement had been relatively quiescent. At the end of 1927, a revival and expansion was led by members of the small Workers' and Peasants' Parties of Bombay and Bengal. Their experienced men included Philip Spratt, Ben Bradley, and George Allison, 'loaned' by the Communist Party of Great Britain, while K.N. Joglekar, S.V. Ghate, and S.A. Dange in Bombay, Dharanikanta Goswami and Muzaffar Ahmad in Bengal, and Sohan Singh Josh in the Punjab were among the Indian members of these small activist parties. They moved quickly into labor organizing, much more slowly into work with the peasantry. In his sober assessment at the end of 1927, Philip Spratt, credited by all with superior organizational talents and a penetrating mind, wrote,

> The present movement operates in conditions of economic stability and political quiescence. . . . It is mainly a movement of the upper grades of workers for extremely limited aims. The organisation is fairly thorough, but narrow as regards activities, the classes of workers involved, and the areas from which they are drawn. There is little interunion organisation or solidarity, little class-consciousness, and a general avoidance of political activity . . . it is almost certain that the immediate political future of the British empire, and Asia generally, is a stormy one . . . it is even safer to predict that the present political quiescence in the country will not last for more than a year or two.[69]

The relative quiet did not last very long. 1928 saw widespread strikes in Bombay and Bengal, and elsewhere in India. More worker-hours were lost in this year than any year before 1946–47. Militant trade union activity became more common and the 'Red Flag' Girni Kamgar Union of Bombay textile workers was the most effective union the radicals had organized to date. It was a dream in 1927, a reality in 1928.[70]

Subhas Bose had begun to take a small part in labor work before his long imprisonment and years in Mandalay. Once released, he decided to devote some of his energies to trade union activity. Workers were to be the troops—along with others—in the army of Indian nationalism. In order to gain their support, he knew that their economic interests would also have to be accommodated.

Bose became involved during 1928 in three important strikes in Bengal. These were the strike of the railway workshop workers threatened with retrenchment at Lilloaah and other parts of the EI and BN Railways, the first major strike of Bengal jute workers, and the strike of steelworkers at the Tata Iron and Steel Corporation at Jamshedpur.

At Lilloaah in the early part of 1928, the railway authorities tried to retrench 2,600 workers and this led to a strike. Both radical trade unionists (Dharani Goswami, K.N. Joglekar, Philip Spratt), and moderate ones (K.C. Mitra, K.C. Roy Chowdhury) were enlisted to aid the 14,000 locked out. The radicals claimed that there was no central railway workers' union and not sufficient organization to combat the railway authorities. The timid moderates (who had K.C. Mitra as secretary of the East India Railway Workers' Union) led the workers to defeat. Even a police firing at Bamangachi in which two workers were killed and several wounded, did not arouse enough solidarity and public resentment to help the workers.[71]

In this situation, Subhas Bose worked only marginally, giving numerous speeches and raising money for a relief fund. He entered more directly, however, into a dispute between different groups of railway workers attempting to work out their grievances against each other in the Bengal Nagpur Railway Indian Labour Union. The differences of opinion led to the formation of independent unions at Garden Reach, Kidderpore, and Kharagpur. When Bose went to Kharagpur on April 16, he was '. . . given a rousing reception . . . at a meeting attended by over 6,000 men.'[72] After listening to the accusations of each side,

> Mr Bose finally advised them to call a general meeting in which all should take part and reconstitute the union on a sound basis. . . . Mr Bose expressed his gratitude for the cordiality of the reception and was all the more grateful because he said he had not yet been able to render any service to the cause of labour. But, he said, those who were engaged in the sacred task of effecting the political emancipation of the country were also working for labour because in disputes between workers and employers the latter had all the resources of the state behind them, while the Government in its efforts to put down the movement for freedom (was) aided by the employers. . . . labour should be united and should close up its ranks to face the common enemies.[73]

From Kharagpur, Bose returned to Calcutta and continued to appeal to the public:

> We appeal to the public to come forward with help for relief to the distressed workers, to do their bit for the workers in their fight against capital backed up by all the resources of the state.[74]

With this common opponent, the Government of India, he was more radical in his rhetoric and identification with the workers. This was also possible in the case of the jute workers, who carried out their first extensive strikes in 1928, against another common opponent: many of the jute mills were owned by foreign capital. In the case of the Jamshedpur strike, however, matters became more complex for nationalists. At the same time the Tata workers were fighting for union recognition, better wages, and other benefits, the Indian members of the Central Legislative Assembly were working for tariff benefits for Tata Iron and Steel as against foreign steel companies.[75]

The Tata Iron and Steel Company was one of the early, important ventures of Indian capital and their main plant was on a tract of land in the Chota Nagpur area about 125 miles west of Calcutta. Besides its plant, the company constructed housing and facilities for its staff and workers, and dominated the area. Efforts at unionization began after the First World War and the Labour Association was formed after a short, unsuccessful spontaneous, strike. The workers in India often called upon outsiders to help them organize their unions and strikes, and one student has written,

> Reliance on external leadership has a long history in the Indian labor movement. Fears of victimization, feelings of inadequacy in articulation of grievances and lack of skills in negotiations are some of the factors which explain why the Indian workers often sought the assistance of skilled and articulate professionals, especially those who had established a political reputation or a reputation for advocacy in the language of imperial power.[76]

During the first half of the 1920s, C.R. Das and Motilal Nehru worked out an arrangement with Tata to help them in their application for tariff protection in return for recognition of the workers' union.

The Labour Association more successfully recruited Bengali clerks than non-Bengali laborers from the steel plant to its membership. Gandhi came to Jamshedpur in 1925 to address the workers and also sent one of his lieutenants, C.F. Andrews, to play a more active part. Andrews was a British sympathizer with Indian nationalism and a moderate trade unionist. As the 1927–28 strike at TISCO unfolded, a group of more militant workers hired a local pleader and former Tata employee, Maneck Homi. A number of outside trade unionists were brought in to try to unify the workers, including V.V. Giri, N.M. Joshi, and Mukundalal Sarcar.

After none of these experienced hands could settle matters, the Strike Committee asked Subhas Bose to intervene. He finally agreed and came to Jamshedpur in August 1928. Management saw that it was to its advantage to have Bose work out an agreement because it would increase their leverage with the nationalists.[77]

Bose did arrange a settlement, but it was not very advantageous to the workers since the door was left open to retrenchment and did not give clear and enduring recognition to the Labour Association. Homi, who had responsibility for inviting Bose in the first place, denounced the settlement and formed a rival union, the Labour Federation. He roused sentiment against Bose, the many Bengali members of the Labour Association, and the agreement. When Bose came to address the workers,

> News of his arrival brought forth insulting and threatening language as *mari, nakaldeo*, etc., toward him instead of words of welcome. . . . The Deputy Commissioner met and intimated to him that it would be unwise on his part to be there judging from the situation and requested him to leave the place.[78]

Not one to be intimidated by an angry throng, Bose addressed the workers, protected by the police, and placated them to some degree. But the workers' grievances and divisiveness continued through the 1930s and Bose continued to intervene from afar. Management at one point favored the Homi group, at another the Labour Association, and they went back on promises to both groups.[79] Bose could not spend much time at Jamshedpur during the following years. The Labour Association benefited from his popularity when he could come; its support dwindled when he could no longer take an active role. The division between the white-collar Bengali workers and the blue-collar non-Bengalis, and also between more moderate and radical approaches to labor organizing were also factors.[80]

Gradually Bose came to see his role as that of a mediator. He would have liked to unite both groups of workers and also work out a mutually satisfactory agreement between Indian labor and Indian capital. He did not succeed in either endeavor. He was forced to identify with one organization of workers and to argue with management for years for recognition. He came more and more to take the workers' side, though one writer about these events has maintained that he had an elitist view of the uneducated workers and was too eager to work out an agreement beneficial to capital as well as labor.[81] Although he had now wet his feet in labor activity, the result was not a satisfactory one for Bose. He was criticized by all parties involved. However at the end of April, he addressed a meeting of the Bengal Trade Union Federation and denounced capitalists before 5,000 cheering railway strikers. He said that Congressmen had to come forward and stand with the workers in their days of trial.[82]

Before 1928 was out, the Bengal Swarajists were called upon to put forth their views and their votes with respect to the other large, neglected segment of the Indian population, the peasantry. In early 1928, the Swarajists boycotted the Bengal Legislative Council and missed the budget session. Later in the year, however, they returned and became intensely involved in the lively, bitter, and occasionally tumultuous debate on the Bengal Tenancy (Amendment) Bill of 1928 which was carried on during long, hot afternoons and evenings in August and early September. To proponents and opponents of major clauses of this bill, the first important revision of the tenancy laws in more than forty years, it seemed that the basic economic rights of millions of peasants and laborers and the ownership rights of the landlords and rent-receivers were at stake. Emotions became intense, charges and countercharges were hurled through the chamber, and dire promises of either future enslavement of all the cultivators or a Bolshevik revolution were made, if one clause or another were passed or deleted.

Although the greater Calcutta area in 1928 was already one of the main industrial areas of India and the Calcutta port one of the two centers for overseas trade in India, Bengal was still, for most of its people, an agricultural society. By the passage of the Permanent Settlement of 1793, the new, foreign rulers of India, hoped that a class of capitalist landlords would work to improve their land, increase production, and not harm the interests of those who actually tilled the land. The landlords, or zamindars, never fulfilled the expectations of the British rulers as far as increased production, but did prove to be a solid pillar of support for the Raj. With title to the land and a limit on how much they could be taxed, the zamindars became willing loyalists. Some, through bad management or dissolute lives, were, in time, unable to pay even the fixed taxation rates, and so had to sell their lands or default. There was a good deal of turnover in land titles and, over the long haul, a great increase in the number of intermediary rent-receivers between the zamindars and the peasants or ryots.[84]

In time, also, some of these ryots employed laborers or used share-croppers to help them till the land. Moved by the distress of the ryots and the desire to prevent any large-scale social unrest, the Government of Bengal passed tenancy bills in 1859 and 1885, which gave limited protections to the tenants but no protection to the share-croppers or bargadars or to the ordinary laborers. In Bengal's demography, the eastern districts had a great majority of Muslims actually working the land—ryots, bargadars, and day laborers—and the majority of the landlords and moneylenders were Hindus. The western districts had a majority of Hindus on the land, but again, the majority of the landlords were Hindus. Although there were Muslim landlords as well, in gross numbers, Bengal had a predominantly Hindu landlord class and a class of Muslim cultivators. Each group wanted to protect and enhance its rights and interests and the cultivators were not as united or as politicized as the landlords who had a phalanx of representatives in the Bengal Council.[85]

The Government of Bengal spokesman, Sir P.C. Mitter, claimed that the new bill was the fruit of serious compromises by each side—zamindar and cultivator—and was aimed at protecting the rights of all classes on the land.[86] The Swarajists, led by J.M. Sen Gupta, generally supported the government bill and took an active part in the discussion and voting. This was not 'non-cooperation' from within; this was certainly active responsivism. The Swarajists debated, proposed amendments, argued, and finally, voted as a bloc on every important provision of the bill. They were under the whip of their leader and his lieutenants, J.C. Gupta, Dr B.C. Roy, Nalini Sarker, Akhil Datta, and J.C. Chakraburtty. There was only one Swarajist rebel, J.C. Bannerjee. The Boses voted with their party and generally played a very small part in the discussion of the bill. Sarat Bose spoke at some length once; Subhas not at all. They left the debating to others, either because of lack of special knowledge or special interest, or, perhaps because they had decided to vote with their party no matter what. Twice during the debates, a Swarajist spokesman indicated that the Swarajist legislative group had been meeting privately about the bill for weeks and throughout the session. Akhil Datta said,

> . . . we have been meeting day after day and discussing these amendments clause by clause—one after another. We have had, in some instances, more detailed discussions in our party meetings than probably we do here in this open House. And when it is pointed out to any member who has tabled an amendment that his amendment is not for the good of the country as a whole, then, if he is convinced—I shall make no secret of it—if the majority of the party are against his amendment, then it is his duty as a member of the party, as an honest member of an honest party. . . to give way to the opinion of the majority.[87]

The Boses may have said more in these private sessions.

The group in the Council speaking for the rights and interests of the ryots, under-ryots, bargadars, and hired laborers was almost entirely composed of elected Muslim members. The pro-tenant group had about twenty to twenty-five votes in a Council of 140 where attendance was between ninety-five and 120. The Muslim pro-tenant bloc included Sir Abdur Rahim and his followers, Fazlul Huq and his followers, Azizul Huque, Ekramul Huq, Nausher Ali, Tamizuddin Khan, and sometimes Nazimuddin. If they wanted an amendment, they needed either the government bloc (officials and nominated non-officials) or the Swarajists (who numbered around forty) with them. But on most of the key provisions of the bill, the Swarajists voted with the government bloc and the Muslim pro-tenant group was badly outnumbered.[88]

The most bitter debates concerned granting the ryots the right of transferability of their holdings and, since this had been generally agreed to by all, whether the landlords should get a transfer fee when a ryot did sell his holdings. The Muslim members argued that there should be no fee since the landlords had done nothing and what had transpired was only the entrance of a new tenant. The landlord side, which included the government, the Swarajists, the Europeans, and the landlords, maintained that the landlords were granting a new right to the tenants and so should be compensated for it. Once the landlords' right to a transfer fee was passed over the votes of the Muslim bloc, much argument ensued as to what percentage of the sale this fee should be. The landlords wanted thirty-three per cent; the government and Swarajists came up with twenty per cent; while the Europeans, on a number of occasions found to be more pro-tenant than the Swarajists, came up with ten per cent. Before the majority came to the compromise figure of twenty per cent, one member of the Swarajist group defected and took the tenant side, arguing against the transfer fee or *salami*, as it was called, and against the compromise figure.[89] Jitendralal Bannerjee moved on from the specific issue to an attack on the Permanent Settlement itself and upon his old party:

> ... Sir, here I must enter my protest against the superstitious veneration with which some people speak of the Permanent Settlement. . . . Everything else in this mundane world may be fleeting, transitory and evanescent—but not so the Permanent Settlement which stands like the Rock of Ages—firm, durable and inviolable.[90]

After comparing Mr Gladstone's more generous settlement with the Irish farmers to the bill put forward by Sir P.C. Mitter for the Government of Bengal, he said,

> Sir Provash has not the vision of Mr Gladstone, he has not the imagination, nor the wide human sympathies of the great Liberal Chief. If he had these qualities, he would not to-day have taken his stand on that wretched piece of legislation which he keeps flaunting in our face with such parade of generosity and wisdom. . . . Sir, I have been sermonised very often within the last few days. One of my moral censors was Mr J.C. Gupta, leader of the Swaraj Party sub protem. He said the other day that they were out to harmonise the rival and conflicting claims of different classes of society. Well and good! But what if the claims happen to be incurably and fundamentally antagonistic? How could you reconcile them then—by what alchemy, known to my friends, but unknown to the very gods? But Mr Gupta,

overflowing with newly acquired wisdom, told the House that there was *no* conflict of interests between zamindars and tenants, that their interests were one and identical.... Sir, I know that, on this question, I am up against a very stiff proposition. The Swarajists, the Government and the zamindars, what a combination, and what an alliance![91]

Bannerjee's was one of the few Hindu voices raised on the tenant side. For the most part, the fiercest critics of the Swarajists were Muslim champions of the tenants, including Fazlul Huq, who said at one point,

It is time, Sir, that my friends on the left—my Swarajist friends, who always pose to be the defenders of the rights of the people—should be told a plain word as regards the happenings of the last few days in this Council. I do not believe that this opposition of my Swarajist friends comes from a real understanding of the situation. It seems, Sir, they are simply watching the interests of the zamindars, and that is the reason why they are out to curtail the interests of the tenants. . . . If the absentee landlords reside in Chowringhee and attend theatres and cinemas, they cannot know their tenants; and this is the class of landlords which my friends, the Swarajists, are out here to support. The division list will show that they have walked into the same lobby with the zamindars with questionable facility.[92]

The Swarajists sternly maintained that they were looking at the big picture, the interests of all groups in the society. Dr B.C. Roy said, 'I refute the charge that has been levelled against us that we have been mere tools in the hands of the zamindars' party.'[93]

As each issue was debated and voted upon, the Swarajists usually ended up in the division lobby with the government and the landlords. The Muslims and some European members talked of the peasant majority in the Bengal population which would one day vote and shape matters in their interest. Sarat Bose entered the debate to answer three critics of the Swarajists, Fazlul Huq, Nurul Huq Chaudhuri, and Tamizuddin Khan. Supporting the Swarajist line, he said, in part,

Maulvi Nurul Huq Chaudhuri has talked of being a tenants' representative. He is now posing as a tenants' man in this Council. That reminds me of the old familiar story which we learnt in our nurseries of three tailors of Tooley Street talking in the name of the British Parliament! It is easy after you are returned to the Council on one ticket to pretend that you are representatives of somebody else. To my friends here, who are talking in the name of tenants, I say that I wish that they will have the courage when the occasion comes . . . to come back to the Council with the mandate of their constituencies in support of the proposals they are now bringing before the house. . . . Sir, let us not talk of 'posing' and 'posers.' Let us appreciate the view points of both tenants and landlords and let us, casting passions aside, address ourselves to the main question as to how a beneficient system of land laws can be introduced into this country which may be of lasting benefit, both to the tenants and the landlords.[94]

Sarat Bose, like his colleagues, Sen Gupta, Dr Roy, and Nalini Sarker, kept insisting that they had been fair to both sides. J.M. Sen Gupta put it most succinctly,

> The attitude that the Congress Party have taken is in consonance with their election manifesto, namely that so far as the relations between the landlord and tenant were concerned they would see that justice was done, so that neither the one nor the other was in the slightest way injured. They would see that during their fight for freedom, and until this fight for freedom was over, the interests of the tenants and the interests of the zamindars should be so adjusted—so reasonably adjusted—as not to create a civil war in the country before freedom was gained. Sir, I am not here today to lead my party in such a way as to be told or to be charged that the Congress Party was forgetting the interests of the tenants. . . . [95]

The problem for the Swarajists was that they could not satisfy both sides on many provisions of this bill. J.L. Bannerjee was right: there were conflicting interests. The tenants wanted the right of transfer, but no transfer fee. The landlords were willing to concede the right of transfer, but they wanted their *salami*; and they also wanted the right of repurchase, i.e., they wanted to be able to reject a prospective buyer of the tenant's land and purchase it themselves for the quoted price plus ten per cent. The tenants felt this a very unfair restriction and felt that both the transfer fee and the repurchase right would keep down the price the tenant might get. As Nalini Sarker, the businessman Swarajist who leaned to the landlord side even more than most of his party members, said,

> It would be seen that the right of repurchase, which it is proposed should be given to the landlords, is more or less in the nature of (a) necessary complement to the free right of transfer with which the ryots have now been invested.[96]

Sarker said it was a safeguard for the landlord against getting a tenant he did not want on his land. Although the Swarajist spokesmen tried to tell the house they favored neither side and wanted balance, compromise, and civil peace and not civil strife, they did not at all persuade the elected Muslims.

The Muslim pro-tenant group saw the Swarajists support the transfer fee of twenty per cent, vote against any tenancy rights for the bargadars, and then support the landlord and government side on the repurchase or pre-emption issue. Council members were surprised when a leader of the European group rose to argue against the pre-emption clause, again outflanking the Swarajists on their left. Mr F.E. James said,

> I desire to say that we as a party oppose the wholesale right of pre-emption as it is in the Bill . . . there is coming a time when there will be a peasants' party in this House and their demand will be far stronger than the demands which we have put forward and which the Muhammadan tenants' represen-

tatives have put forward today. Is it not therefore wise to realise that these days are coming and to shape your policy accordingly? I ask that question today and if it is not answered I am perfectly sure that those of you who are in the House on that day will find that the answer will be given with no uncertain voice.[97]

Even as Tamizuddin Khan announced that the right of pre-emption would be '. . . the climax of this nefarious process. . . . This will complete the enslavement of the riyat,' the Council immediately voted by seventy-six to twenty-five for this clause. The government, landlords, and Swarajists joined on the majority side; the Muslims and a few Europeans, and three Hindu members formed the minority.

Mr James proved to be more prescient than the Swarajists. In fact, their actions in the Council pushed the Muslims to form their own Praja Party which later became the Krishak Praja Party (KPP) and spoke more clearly for the peasantry, especially the small landed peasants, than the Congress. The Swarajists said they were being even-handed. But even-handedness in a situation in which a rich minority exploits a poor majority favors the status quo, i.e., the continuation of exploitation. To help the 'people', meaning the majority of the population, there needs to be a change in the situation, eventually bringing, as the Marxists would put it, structural change to the society. The Swarajists called for class collaboration to work for freedom from the British Raj. But the pressures for economic and social change and the patterns of exploitation for decades, if not generations, could not be ignored. The communists in the Workers' and Peasants' Parties were not ignoring these ugly facts; even fellow travelers in the Congress were beginning to pay attention to them. And Bengal Muslim leaders were unwilling to ignore them.[98]

At this point, the elected Muslim membership of the Council and the politically-conscious Muslims were not strong or united. But they were on their way to become a formidable force in Bengal. There were *praja samitys* in some districts and just after the new Bengal Council election of June 1929, the twenty-seven Muslim members met in Calcutta and formed the Bengal Muslim Council Association to work for the goals of the Muslim community. At the same time, the Nikhil Banga Praja Samity (All-Bengal Tenants' Party) was formed with Sir Abdur Rahim as president, Akram Khan as secretary, Mujibur Rahman, Abdul Karim, Fazlul Huq, Abdulla Suhrawardy, and Abdul Momen as vice-presidents, and Shamsuddin Ahmad and Tamizuddin Khan as joint secretaries. Although this party was not without its internal conflicts, particularly after Rahim left for Delhi, it became a strong force for Muslim political action and representation. Its genesis in some measure was due to the 'even-handedness' of the Swarajists which left the peasantry of Bengal outside the Congress and in search of other leaders. Unfortunately, for the Congress and its work, the economic and religious cleavages coincided to a large extent. Muslim leaders insisted on separate electorates and a share of the seats in any new Bengal representative body commensurate with their share of Bengal's population, i.e., about 54 per cent, so that they could pass bills aiding their community members (and generally the tenants of Bengal). If they could achieve this, then they would overcome the 'even-handedness' of the Congress and the Government of Bengal as well.[99]

This was an excellent time to be laying out goals, strategies, and ideas of representation, and deciding who one's allies were. In 1927 the British Government had appointed the Simon Commission. The Indian Statutory Commission, headed by Sir John Simon and composed of members of the British parliament, was appointed to investigate the working of dyarchy and to map out new steps towards responsible government suitable for India. From the moment of its appointment, it was anathema to a wide spectrum of Indian political opinion because it was all-British. Even many Moderates including Sir Tej Bahadur Sapru, Mr Chintamani, and Mr Jinnah who were constitutionalists and surely would have cooperated were antagonized. So Liberals, Congressmen, and one part of the Muslim League (that headed by Jinnah) joined in the boycott of the Simon Commission.[100]

When the Simon Commission was appointed, the secretary of state for India, Earl Birkenhead, said it would have been too difficult to find representative Indians to serve on such a commission, and furthermore, he challenged Indian political groups to get together and draw up their own scheme for Indian political advance. With the gauntlet flung down before them, Indian political leaders chose to pick it up, and formed the All Parties Conference which appointed a committee headed by Motilal Nehru.[101]

Subhas Bose, president of the Bengal Provincial Congress Committee, was responsible for organizing the Bengal *hartal*—complete one-day stoppage of activity—against the Statutory Commission. He was also invited to become a member of Motilal Nehru's Committee which was drawing up the 'swaraj constitution' which Srinivasa Iyengar and others had called for in 1927.

When the Simon Commission landed in Bombay on February 3, 1928, a *hartal* was observed throughout India with thousands of Indians waving signs, 'Simon, Go Home!' Most observers adjudged the one-day demonstration by the nationalists a success. A *Forward* leader writer assessed the event,

The freedom of India will not long remain the dream of the visionary. The spell of foreign domination is a spent force. The hypnotism which prevented the people from being conscious of their own power is gone. Indians have deeply realised that their destiny and the future of their Motherland are in their own hands and not in the keeping of British Imperialists or their accredited agents. That is the great significance of the unique hartal spontaneously and cheerfully observed throughout the length and breadth of India by all classes of people on the day on which the members of the Simon Commission set their foot on Indian soil. Friday's hartal marked the beginning of the long and weary struggle through which India will have to pass in order to secure her inalienable right of swaraj. For Indians want to develop their own institutions in accordance with their own national traditions and genius. . . . The moment they (*the people*) would decide to withhold for good (their willing allegiance), the bureaucratic institutions as well as foreign capitalism and all that it means would tumble down like a house of cards.[102]

The success of the *hartal* brought calls for a militant boycott of British goods and institutions and *Banglar Katha*, later in February, demanded renewed Swadeshi activities:

As a result of inhuman oppression and deception practised on us for a long time we have not understood what the condition of the country was and why and . . . how our prosperity has come to an end . . . deluded by Western civilization and education, we have forgotten our country, countrymen and religion . . . and . . . the lure of fine yarn has led us to twist the noose of the English round our necks without casting a glance on the sorry faces of the weavers. . . . A new life is dawning upon us and hence competent workers are needed first of all. But in Subhas Chandra we have found an untiring worker and captain and the next requisite is a band of soldiers, who will give up everything and go about from village to village, holding the banner of freedom initiating the masses into the cult of Swadeshi.[103]

Despite the charges Commissioner Charles Tegart made about Congress intimidation, the *hartal* had been a success. But in Bengal, not always in tune with national politics, there were additional problems for the nationalists: though national Muslim and Liberal leaders supported the boycott, Bengal's Muslim leaders opposed it. The matter came to a head in debates in the Bengal Legislative Council.

First, there was a debate on a Government of Bengal motion for a committee of the Council to cooperate with the Simon Commission; then several weeks later there was a debate on a motion by Sir Abdur Rahim to the effect that India should be a self-governing dominion with full, responsible self-government in its provinces. Trying to sidetrack the government motion, Nalini Sarker, for the Swarajists, moved that consideration of it be postponed *sine die:*

We want freedom in spite of all our shortcomings. . . . The spirit of war is abroad and if you want that this should disappear you should adopt the means of diplomacy based on principles of natural justice not hampered by pettifogging constitutionalism. That is what members on this side of the House have always demanded, and can now point to a definite precedent in the settlement of the Irish question. Such a Round Table Conference in Downing Street with Michael Collins and Lord Birkenhead and other Irish and British leaders finally settled a matter which generations of British statesmen and Irish leaders were not able to settle for ages.[104]

Numerous speakers referred to the Irish precedent for a negotiated settlement which had been applauded by Sir John Simon because the Irish had done it themselves, i.e., drawn up a 'swaraj constitution', which led to the British exit from most of the country. Swarajists also pointed to the precedent of the American Revolution and said that such a complete break was also possible.

When so many others including the foremost Liberals and Muslims like Jinnah were against it, the Bengal Muslim leaders wanted to cooperate with the Simon Commission. They felt that they had suffered in the past by compromises on an all-India level, e.g., the Lucknow Pact of 1916. They were determined that neither all-India Muslim interests nor the goal of rapprochement with the Hindus would prevent them from gaining the best political arrangements for their community in this round of negotiations. Azizul Huque said that the Muslims were against the boycott because when they had boycotted, they had lost out in public life. He said the Muslim Swarajists had been beaten in the last Bengal Council election because the community wanted them to cooperate. Challenged by Subhas Bose's, 'Would you seek an election now?', Huque replied that he was ready to do so at any time and, 'The Simon Commission is a machinery and we want to work it.'[105]

More importantly, the Bengal Muslim leaders no longer had the same trust in the Bengal Hindu leaders that they had had in the time of C.R. Das. The fullest statement of the new mistrust was made by Fazlul Huq:

. . . Whenever the country had made a demand on Moslem patriotism, we have never been behind any community in India. Why is it, then, that to-day we go into the same lobby with the Europeans? It is because of the mischievous activities of the Hindu Mahasabha which have made it impossible for us to place any confidence in Congress leaders . . . it is not from choice but from necessity that the Muhammadan members have to-day voted against the Congress. If my friends want to win back the Moslem members, let them go and control the Hindu Mahasabha. . . . .I give this assurance to the members of the Congress party that as soon as the Muhammadans find that they can place confidence in our respected leaders, the leaders whom we

have always followed, we will go back to the Congress fold, stand side by
side with the Congress and fight battles for the freedom and liberty of India
. . . . Our present attitude is due to the hypocrisy and dishonest influence of
the Hindu Mahasabha. . . . I appeal to them (*the Congress members*) to make
it possible for us to go back once more to the Congress fold. . . . If they can
do that, then the gentlemen who are sitting over there will pack and board
the next ship to take them back to England. Let them not do it by
domineering over the Moslem community, but conceding to them what is
good for the people, good for the country, and good for all communities. We
stand here for equal rights; we are against domination by autocrats; we do
not want autocracy in any shape; we want freedom for all castes, creeds and
communities and equal opportunities for all.[106]

The Congressmen won few Muslim votes on their side and Sarker's
motion for indefinite postponement lost by forty-five to eighty-two.
Several amendments were made to the government resolution trying to
insure a kind of equality when the Bengal Legislative Council Committee
met with the Simon Commission. Once these amendments were worked
out to the satisfaction of the Muslim members, they voted with the majority
by seventy-two to fifty, to set up the cooperating committee. The Boses did
not speak at length in this debate, though both of them interrupted the
debate with points of procedure and showed, along with their Swarajist
colleagues, how much they were involved emotionally and how much of
a setback this motion was to the nationalist cause. It also showed that
though Hindu-Muslim relations were strained and damaged, still as Huq
argued, this was not yet an irreparable break.[107]

The second debate raised the important question of joint versus separate
electorates, an issue which was fundamental in any constitutional scheme
for India that had to have Hindu and Muslim agreement. Sir Abdur
Rahim's motion was to be a self-governing dominion, a federation of
autonomous states, with full responsible government in the provinces,
protection of minorities, and representation of all important groups in the
legislature assured. It did not mention joint or separate electorates and
these were raised by B.K. Basu (joint) and Fazlul Huq (separate). The
Swarajists were ready and willing to approve Rahim's motion to show that
Hindus and Muslims could stand together and were unhappy to go off on
the issue of the kind of electorates the new dominion would have. But once
the train of debate was started in that direction, its momentum carried it
along.

The great majority of the elected Muslim members clearly supported
separate electorates. A few Muslim spokesmen differed and said that joint
electorates should be tried in an effort to bring the two communities
together. Abdul Karim from Burdwan, in an effort at conciliation, said that

neither form of electorate was a panacea. He mentioned that C.R. Das had wanted joint electorates at the time of the Bengal Pact, but had agreed to continue separate electorates as a concession to the Muslims. Karim argued there was not enough trust between the communities for the Muslims to give up reserved seats and separate electorates, and he also said that since the Muslims were backward in education and economic status compared to the Hindus, the former would continue to suffer until there was universal suffrage. In the course of his remarks, he made some prophetic comments and brought in the work which Subhas Bose had been trying to do for communal amity:

> The Mussalmans of Bengal, as people all the world over, are getting self-conscious. They are not likely to take things lying down as they did in the past. . . . If there be no amicable settlement the worst passions will be appealed to and this certainly will not make for peace and order in the country . . . in these days when there is a loud cry for self-determination it would be well to permit the Mussalmans to settle their own affairs without undue interference. If anything is forced upon them against their wishes the result might be disastrous. . . . I hope and trust good sense would prevail. . . . I should not omit to mention in this connection that I have noticed with much satisfaction the earnest efforts that are being made by my young friend Mr. Subhas Chandra Bose and others of his way of thinking, to bring about a relation of amity and cordiality between the two communities. . . . The Hindus and Mussalmans have to live together and die together in this the land of their birth and they cannot afford to constantly quarrel over any matter without seriously damaging their vital interests.[108]

Though Subhas Bose was certainly for communal amity and critical of the Hindu Mahasabha, he was at one with his Swarajist and Congress colleagues throughout India in supporting joint electorates. Dr B.C. Roy pointed out in his speech that the Hindus of East Bengal would lose out if there were joint electorates and yet the Bengal Congress still thought that there should be joint electorates in the interest of the country.[109]

Neither side persuaded the other. In an effort to move away from this increasingly bitter debate, J.M. Sen Gupta rose to say that there was nothing in Rahim's original motion which was incompatible with the ultimate aims of the Congress. He was sorry that the two motions about joint and separate electorates had been raised. He could not refrain from pointing out, however, that in Bengal there were seven Hindu majority districts and nineteen Muslim majority districts, so that the Muslims would likely benefit, in time, from joint electorates. Finally, Fazlul Huq's amendment was defeated by thirty to fifty and the Hindu and Muslim members joined to pass Rahim's original motion. It may have been innocuous and did not mention the Simon Commission, but it at least proved to be a common meeting ground for leaders of the two communities on a general set of goals for the future of their country.[110]

However, the debate showed that there were serious differences on the electorates and other constitutional issues which could not be avoided by the committee of the All Parties Conference headed by Motilal Nehru. Appointed by the conference on May 19, 'to consider and determine the principles of the Constitution for India,' it met in July and issued its report in August. The Nehru Committee included Motilal Nehru, S. Ali Imam, Tej Bahadur Sapru, M.S. Aney, Mangal Singh, Shuaid Qureshi, G.R. Pradhan, and Subhas Bose. Other Indian leaders attended their meetings by invitation. While the Simon Commission was attending to its report on India, some Indians in 1928 recalled Simon's statement of 1921:

> At any rate there is a real element of hope and confidence here in that this constitution is not a constitution which the British Parliament formulates and offers to confer upon Ireland, it is a constitution which the Irishmen themselves have drawn up and which they now apply to the Imperial Parliament to ratify.[111]

The Nehru Committee noted that India was most like Ireland among the dominions of the British Empire and they used the constitution of the Irish Free State as one of their guides.[112]

There was no difficulty in the Committee's agreeing that India should be a self-governing dominion. Those from many communities and regions could easily accept this, although it did not accord with Subhas Bose's belief that India should be free and independent. For the moment at least, he was willing to accept the status of a dominion if the Committee could come to one view on other outstanding points. Some of the same points which were at issue in the Bengal Legislative Council were at stake in the Nehru Committee's deliberations, though now on the larger and more complex national canvas. The communal question loomed large and decisions had to be made about joint versus separate electorates and about the reservation of seats for backward majorities as well as for minorities in the different provinces.

The Nehru Committee, for the most part, followed Congress positions on these matters. It came out for joint electorates, arguing that separate electorates were anti-national and that competition between candidates and across community lines in the electorate was necessary to have a healthy growth of democracy in India. Subhas Bose, like his fellow Congress leaders, was strongly in favor of joint electorates. As the Bengal expert on the Committee, he was asked to supply evidence to support its view that separate electorates and reserved seats were not needed by

Bengal's Muslims. He gathered information about the district board elections and put the evidence together in his letter of July 12, 1928, to Motilal Nehru:

> After my first visit to Allahabad I had sent a circular to all the districts asking for information about the present composition of the district boards. I am sorry I have not yet received replies from many of the districts. I am, therefore, sending you what information is available from an official document. . . . This information is at least two years old. During the last two or three years, owing largely to the communal awakening in the Province, the elections to the district boards have been run on communal lines. The impact of this communal awakening is not so clear in the figures for the year 1925–26 which I am sending herewith. The effect . . . has been amply demonstrated in the recent district board elections in Eastern Bengal. In the election in Mymensing held about a year ago, out of 22 members not a single Hindu has been returned in spite of the existence of joint electorate. This is practically the case in Chittagong, Noakhali, Tippera, Barisal and other districts. In the election at Jessore held a few months ago Muslims have swept the polls and the offices of Chairman and Vice-Chairman hitherto held by Hindus have been captured by Muslims for the first time. As a result of this I am told, Maulvi Nausher Ali, MLC Chairman and Maulvi Abdur Rauf, MLC Vice-Chairman, who were formerly supporters of separate electorate have now changed their views. I am also told that this has also influenced Sir Abdur Rahim who has till very recently been a staunch supporter of separate electorate. . . . I am trying to collect information regarding the recent elections. . .[113]

Information supplied by Bose formed the basis for Appendix C of the Nehru Report and was used to buttress their argument that where the Muslims had a population majority, they would do very well in the elections, and therefore did not need the protection of separate electorates and reserved seats.

Although he attended the important July meeting of the Nehru Committee, Bose was unable to attend its final meeting, so he wired to Motilal Nehru his views on a number of issues just before the report was issued in August. His telegram of August 6 read, in part,

> I oppose reservation for non-Muslim minorities central legislature support Muslim reservation on population basis if demanded by Muslims but oppose demand one-third Muslim reservation . . . urge omission reference to communal councils page fourteen stop am personally satisfied Oriya speaking tracts should be amalgamated also constituted separate province if financially possible. . . Kripan for Sikhs need not be mentioned in declaration of rights stop notwithstanding above remarks your decision binding on me. . .[114]

Although it was easy enough for Subhas Bose to agree with Motilal Nehru on joint electorates, no reservation of seats for the Muslims in Bengal and the Punjab, and seats in the Central Assembly for Muslims on the basis of population, it was something else for this report to be accepted by Indian Muslims. Many Muslims had already expressed displeasure at the direction the Committee was taking in going back on the Congress acceptance of the Muslims' Delhi proposals of 1927.[115]

The report embodied the beliefs of Motilal Nehru, Sapru, and Bose, that if communal electorates were eliminated, and if reservation of seats were minimized at every level of government, then the communal problems of heterogeneous India would gradually disappear. They wanted a secular state, but their views as worked out in the report seemed to show concessions to the communalist Hindus inside and outside the Congress, while they conceded little to the Muslims who were an equally important constituency to whom they had to 'sell' their groundplan for a new India.

Since India was so heterogeneous and the Muslims were a majority in some provinces, a minority in others, Muslims in these different regions responded differently to it. As Bose had said in his letter to Motilal Nehru, some Bengal Muslims, including Sir Abdur Rahim, were changing their views and were willing to accept joint electorates and, if there was universal suffrage, they were willing to forego reserved seats, since they had an absolute population majority. The report also had many Muslim supporters in the Punjab. However, some key Muslim leaders in the United Provinces who stood to lose the most by the adoption of the report, and the Ali brothers who felt that the Congress had betrayed Muslims who had worked with the Congress for years, were fiercely against it.[116] Lobbying went on until the All Parties Convention met in Calcutta on December 28.

The crucial moment at the meeting—attended by 1,200 delegates from a wide range of organizations—came when M.A. Jinnah, long an advocate of Hindu-Muslim cooperation and once a Congressman, rose to introduce his amendments to the report. Of his amendments, three were most important:

> 1. In the Central Legislature Muslims should have 33 1/3 per cent of the seats.
> 2. That the residuary powers should vest in the provinces and not the center (as the Report specified).
> 3. That Muslims in Punjab and Bengal should be represented on the basis of population for ten years subject to subsequent revision of this principle.[117]

Pleading for support of his amendments by the largely Hindu Convention, he said, in part,

> I do ask you once more to consider this question of the security of the

minority before you can expect to carry it with you. Please don't think that I am threatening you, because I am liable to be misunderstood. If we don't settle this question to-day we will settle it to-morrow. We are sons of this land, we have to live together. We have to work together and whatever our differences may be let us not arouse bad blood. If we cannot agree let us agree to differ, but let us part as friends. Nothing will make me more happy than to see Hindus and Muslims united. I believe there is no progress for India until Muslims and Hindus are united. Let not logic, philosophy and squabbles stand in the way of your bringing that about.[118]

The Convention rejected Jinnah's basic amendments. This overwhelming defeat cost the Nehru Report most of its Muslim support. Many Muslims joined at an All-Parties Muslim Conference in January 1929 and the All-India Muslim League passed a full version of the Jinnah amendments and Muslim demands as the Fourteen Points, on March 28, 1929. A great opportunity for compromise between the major communities of India had been lost.[119]

One careful student of these events has argued that the Hindu Mahasabha and Hindu communalist politicians who moved freely back and forth from it to the Congress exerted too much influence on the Congress secularists like the Nehrus, Gandhi, and Bose.[120] The Congress secularists and particularly those moving in a socialist direction believed that the communal question would disappear if it were de-emphasized and economic issues and the political challenge to the Raj were stressed. Through the following decades they continued wishing this were true, sometimes working for cooperation with the Muslims, and more actively organizing the poorer sections of the society. But, somehow, the communal question did not go away, much to the dismay of those—however religious they were in their private lives—who hoped that religion would come to mean less and less in the public life of India.[121]

The All Parties Conference held in Calcutta during late December 1928 was only one of several significant meetings which took place in the second city of the British Empire that month. The Indian National Congress gathered for an important session, the All-India Youth Congress met, the All-India Workers' and Peasants' Party was formed at a session in Calcutta, and, more secretly than these, representatives of revolutionary organizations from several parts of India decided it was an opportune time to exchange views.

Subhas Bose was now a prominent leader of the Indian National Congress, but as the joint secretary of the Independence of India League, he differed with the older leadership about the goal of dominion status. He had agreed to sign the Nehru Report, but wanted complete independence and would not keep quiet about this essential point. He was also the GOC, general-officer-commanding, of the Congress Volunteers and a member of the reception committee for the Congress session which was headed by J.M. Sen Gupta. Bose was the chairman of the reception committee for the Youth Congress (which he addressed) and aware of the meetings of communists and revolutionaries being held. This extraordinary confluence of meetings was a vibrant expression of the great reawakening of Indian political life in 1928.

Although Subhas Bose was greatly responsible for the whole organization of the Calcutta Congress which was a lavish national spectacle as well as an important political occasion, he is most remembered for the energy and care with which he filled the role of GOC. Nirad Chaudhuri recalled that,

> . . . Bose organized a volunteer corps in uniform, its officers being even provided . . . with steel-chain epaulettes . . . his uniform was made by a firm of British tailors in Calcutta, Harman's. A telegram addressed to him as GOC was delivered to the British general in Fort William, and this was the subject of a good deal of malicious comment in the Anglo-Indian press. Mahatma Gandhi, being a sincere pacifist vowed to non-violence, did not like the strutting, clicking of boots, and saluting, and he afterwards described the Calcutta session of the Congress as a Bertram Mills circus, which caused great indignation among the Bengalis.[122]

Bose had devoted much time to gathering and training a volunteer corps numbering about 2,000. Among his announcements to the press about the corps, he said,

> The Committee which has been given the charge of the volunteers' corps is training up the volunteers in a way very similar to military training. Many of those persons from India who joined the First World War have joined the corps as leaders. Volunteers are doing regular parades in different parks of Calcutta. . . . Most of them (the volunteers) are young men and students of local colleges. . . . Various Samitis, Associations, Sanghas, etc. have expressed their desire to join the . . . corps collectively with the members of their organizations. I am submitting to them very humbly that no Samiti . . . etc. will be recruited in a body, collectively . . . their members must come individually to be recruited. . . . Those recruited must have to undergo necessary training. . . . To organise a Womens' wing of the volunteer corps a sub-committee . . . has been formed. . . . These are the different Divisions of the V.C.—(a) Bicycle Division, (b) Motorcycle Division, (c) Cavalry Division, (d) Band Division, (e) Coded Messages Division. . . . We are getting a large number of applications from persons living . . . outside Calcutta . . . I am . . . informing that those who want to join . . . should bear the travelling expenses for coming to Calcutta themselves. In Calcutta they must undergo medical examination and must be declared medically fit . . .

during the period of training, they must meet the expenses for food themselves, but their residence will be arranged by us free of cost. When their training period will be over and they will start working as regular volunteers all expenses . . . will be borne by us.[123]

Subhas Bose took this job seriously. The volunteers were to be well trained and to march in disciplined formation on ceremonial occasions and to look after the delegates during the meeting. He rode—on a brown horse—in front of his unarmed troops, thinking of them, perhaps, as the kernel of a future army of mass struggle. Military analogies abounded in his many speeches of the preceding year-and-a-half. Literally, Bose wanted the Indianization of the Indian army since free India would have to defend itself and military training was better started sooner rather than later.

In line with Bose's thinking about a militant, if not military, volunteer corps, other developments at the time brought up this same theme. The Skeen Committee had recommended the Indianization of the Indian army in 1928, but the government rejected this proposal.[124] In the following year, proposals were put forward in the Central Assembly (by Dr Moonje) and in the Bengal Legislative Council (by B.K. Bose) for military training and systematic physical exercise for all young Indians. The motion in the Central Assembly was disallowed, but, after a lively discussion, it was passed with some modification by the Bengal Council. Officials of the Bengal government, worried about the recrudescence of terrorism, argued that there was no money in the budget for such training.[125] The following year, 1930, saw the publication of Nirad Chaudhuri's lengthy and insightful articles on 'The ''Martial races'' of India,' in the *Modern Review* in which he argued that the British had changed their ideas over the years as to which Indians were suitably martial and which not, often for political reasons. He mentioned the 'Punjabization' and 'barbarization' of the Indian army which he said had taken place since the revolt of 1857. Chaudhuri maintained that the way in which the army was chosen was yet another aspect of the British exploitation of India and the process was eroding the manhood of young men from many sections of the country, including Bengal.[126]

Therefore, it may not be improper to see Subhas Bose's recruitment of a small, unarmed, but disciplined corps as a mark of the new awareness among Indian nationalists that real military training modeled on this small step, but involving weapons, might at some future time be the order of the day. As mentioned above, Bose himself had sought military training as a Calcutta and as a Cambridge student. Now the germ of an idea about an army trained and commanded by him may have begun to sprout.

Besides the volunteers briskly marching through the Calcutta streets,

Bose wanted a show of national pride and celebration for the Congress president, who was potentially the leader of a free India. Motilal Nehru, who had accepted the presidency at the urging of Subhas Bose, among others, rode from Howrah station in a carriage pulled by twenty-eight white horses. Bose also saw to it that Congress guests, from the president and his party down the hierarchy, were well taken care of by their hosts in his home city.

During the meetings, Bose became embroiled in the controversy over dominion status. As president of the Bengal Provincial Congress, which had passed a resolution supporting complete independence at its conference, he was committed to that goal. Pressed by his friends in the revolutionary and leftist movements and by his own inclinations, he went back on a tacit agreement not to bring up the potentially divisive issue of complete independence versus dominion status at the Congress session. He rose and offered an amendment to Gandhi's resolution accepting the Nehru Report. Bose said that Great Britain and India had nothing in common and that India should forsake the empire and become the leader of Asia. Jawaharlal Nehru made a speech supporting Bose.[127] Then Gandhi spoke. He said that Young Bengal was making a serious blunder, for to call for complete independence was merely to chant a hollow phrase. As he had done in 1920, Gandhi said, 'If you will help me and follow the programme honestly and intelligently, I promise that Swaraj will come within one year.'[128] Bose's amendment lost by 973 to 1,350 votes. About two-thirds of the Bengali delegates backed Bose, but Dr Roy, Nalini Sarker, and J.M. Sen Gupta are believed to have voted with the Gandhian majority. The Nehru Report, with its various provisions for joint electorates and some reservation of seats for the Muslim minority and its list of fundamental rights, was passed.

Yet another meeting which was taking place at the same time as the Congress session was the Rashtra Bhasa Sammelan (National Language Meeting) of which Subhas Bose served as chairman of the reception committee. Speaking to the assembled delegates in Hindi, he said,

> There may be a few among us who are under the misapprehension that the Hindi propaganda has been started with the ultimate aim of stamping (out) our mother tongue, Bengali. This fear has no foundation. As far as I know 'Hindi Prachar' has one aim which is to substitute Hindustani in place of English. We can never relinquish our own language, Bengali, which is dearer to us than our mother. For exchange of ideas with people of a different province we ought to learn Hindustani as an interprovincial language. Not only that, I believe that the youth of a free and self-governing India will have to learn one or two European languages, French, German, etc., to keep

themselves abreast in international affairs. I will not raise the question whether we should adopt the Hindi or the Urdu script for our national language. I agree with Mahatmaji that we must learn both the scripts. . .[129] He called on young Bengalis to learn Hindi-Urdu and asked affluent speakers of the language resident in Calcutta to help pay for the necessary teachers and facilities. His concern for the national language problem was one which continued throughout his life and at a later stage, he took some practical steps to implement his ideas.

Bose served as chairman of the reception committee for the All-India Youth Congress meeting and addressed them. As usual in his speeches to the young, he called for them to dedicate themselves to the liberation of their country. They might be called upon to offer their very lives, but they should not hesitate. He also said that they must hold to the ideal of activism in quest of their goal of freedom for India and he decried the passivity he saw embodied in some institutions like the Sabarmati Ashram of Gandhi and the Pondicherry Ashram of Sri Aurobindo. These statements did not go unchallenged by devotees of the Mahatma and the sage of Pondicherry. The Youth Congress adopted the creed that its object was the attainment of independence by 'all possible means' in contradistinction to that of the Indian National Congress which specified 'all peaceful and legitimate means.'[130] Meetings of youths and students were often attended by Bose at this time and in subsequent years. He had a powerful identification with the young which continued even as he himself grew older. They would shape the new India that he might not even see, so what better audience to try to persuade to his particular vision of that future.

Bose was considered a guru by some of the students who insisted on touching his feet at the time of the Calcutta Congress. Bose and his associates in the Bengal Congress became linked in the next few years with the Bengal Presidency Students' Association. He also became involved around this time in a big flap at City College, one of Bengal's famous colleges and a Brahmo institution. The students there wanted to hold a puja ceremony. The authorities of the college were against it. Although he tried to serve as a mediator, Subhas came down in support of the students and found himself opposed by the college officials, the parents of the students, and even the venerable Rabindranath Tagore. For his troubles, Subhas Bose was barred from visiting this college until the students insisted years later that the president of the Indian National Congress could not be *persona non grata*.[131]

Another development of the late 1920s and early 1930s was the entry of young women into all branches of the national movement, including the revolutionaries. Hitherto, for the most part, they had been told by Gandhi to spin and weave and to help with the selling of khadi. Some women of the Das family were arrested at the time of the Non-Cooperation Movement. By the mid-1920s, some revolutionary groups began to allow participation by women and feeder groups for women were formed. One such group was the Deepali Sangha established by Leela Nag in Dacca in 1923. The group also had a wing for Gandhian work called the Mahila Satyagraha Samity and started a journal called *Jayshree*. Branches were set up in several districts and this organization was close to the revolutionary group Sree Sangha which Anil Roy formed in 1924 at the behest of Hem Chandra Ghosh.

Latika Ghosh, at the urging of Subhas Bose, set up the Mahila Rashtriya Sangha with Prabhabati Bose as honorary president and Latika Ghosh as secretary. At the Calcutta Congress, the women's division was arrayed behind Colonel Latika Ghosh. Another group called the Chattri Sangha was formed in Calcutta by Kalyani Das in 1928 and members of this group were active in Gandhian and revolutionary activities in the following years. Geraldine Forbes, who has interviewed many of these women, has written, 'If there were a living figure who encouraged their activities, it was Subhas Chandra Bose, considered by many of the women revolutionaries Bengal's greatest champion of women's rights.'[132] Subhas' encouragement of women to live a full life and devote themselves to an ideal, just like men, went way beyond his concern for his own nieces. He truly believed in equality for women and thought that their participation in the national movement was essential. Subhas Bose's feminism is an important and neglected aspect of his vision and work.[133]

Another part of his work which has not been neglected, but which remains confusing nevertheless, is his connection to the revolutionary movement. Government agents were constantly investigating this connection and compiling their findings and fantasies for the files of the Home Department. Furthermore, many old revolutionaries verbally and in print have told of their work with Subhas Bose. Some undoubtedly worked with him; others seem to have woven elaborate webs of connection on the basis of a scanty thread. He did have an alliance through these years with members of the Jugantar Party, but starting about this time he was much closer to those in a group called the Bengal Volunteers, or BV as they are known. One of the ablest organizers among the BV was Jyotish Joarder.[134]

Joarder himself was born in 1907 in Mymensingh district and, as a student of physics, obtained a MS degree from Dacca University. About 1925 he joined a secret society sometimes referred to as the Mukti Sangha. Members of this group all joined the Congress and were in the Congress Volunteers for the 1928 Calcutta session. The Congress or rather Bengal

Volunteers for this session were shaped into companies and battalions under the GOC and trained in close order drill. Subhas Bose never meant this to be simply a Bengal organization, but Gandhi's opposition to it led to a failure to form a more national volunteer corps. Among the volunteers were members of many secret organizations, but even many of these left. Remaining were one group founded by Hem Chandra Ghosh (to which Joarder belonged) with Satya Ranjan Bakshi, editor of *Forward*, as a key link directly to Bose, and a second group under Surja Sen of Chittagong.

Once the Calcutta Congress was over, it was Bose's plan that the discipline and skills of the volunteers should reach the villages of Bengal. Part of this entailed going out to the countryside and holding drills, cross-country marches, learning about the rural areas, and explaining the cause of national liberation to the people. They worked at crowd control and on numerous occasions tried to quell communal riots. They lived parsimoniously and took some contributions from rural people. They trained in Dacca and had strong local units in Dacca and Mymensingh and a connection to a group in Midnapore district. Headquarters, however, was in Calcutta where it was possible to be in close communication with Bose and Bakshi. The hidden intention of the BV was to prepare for a military campaign and to be ready for violent activity against the Raj. The police kept close watch on them and they were later banned from 1934 to 1938 and again in 1940. Although the BV were the most devoted and unswerving of Subhas Bose's revolutionary supporters, there were others. A member of the Jugantar Party, Nishi Kanta Gangapadhyaya, has told in his memoirs of a visit by Subhas Bose to Sankar Math, Barisal, in 1928 or 1929. This *math* was openly a religious institution, but secretly also the base for Jugantar activities. Subhas Bose communicated to the inmates his desire for complete independence for India without compromise, and they assured him of their support.[135]

Besides the many other meetings taking place at the time of the Calcutta Congress, revolutionaries from different parts of India were gathering and young Bhagat Singh came to join them. Not only was the Gandhi-led Congress gearing up for a new campaign, but those warriors not pledged to non-violence were also trying to decide their future course of action.[136]

The Congress itself was pledged to peaceful means. Gandhi had told the Calcutta throng that if dominion status did not come within 1929, then he would agree on the goal of complete independence that Subhas Bose and Jawaharlal Nehru and many younger men wanted. In the coming year these two became general secretaries of the national Congress organization and Subhas Bose was a member of the Working Committee or executive of the Congress. He was entering the national stage.

CHAPTER SIX

'What is *wrong* with Bengal?' 1929–32

King George V to Sir John Anderson,
Bengal's New Governor, 1932[1]

I

When the great show of the Calcutta Congress and associated meetings was over, the real work of nationalism remained: to organize Indians against the Raj and for the reconstruction of their own society. Although the resolution for complete independence had been defeated, the pressure of the independence advocates had been sufficient to make Gandhi and the careful Congress elders agree that if significant progress towards dominion status was not made in 1929, complete independence would be the goal.

Gandhi understood that Bose's way was not the same as his and that he could not keep Bose under close rein. He wrote to one of his closest 'pure-khadi' associates in Bengal, Satish Das Gupta, on August 24, 1929,

> Subhas Babu will never pardon the loin-cloth. We must bear with him. He cannot help himself. He believes in himself and in his mission. He must work it out as we must ours.[2]

Gandhi held that quiet constructive work on the local level was just as important as mass rallies calling for independence. Answering a reader of *Navajivan* who wanted to know why Gandhi did not allow the young firebrands, Jawaharlal Nehru and Subhas Bose, to organize a crore of volunteers to press for complete independence, Gandhi said, in part,

> It is a gratuitous insult to Pandit Jawaharlal or Subhas Chandra Bose to say that they are awaiting my permission or mandate to organize the youth of the country, and are being kept back for want of it. They are already doing the work of organization to the best of their power and ability. They need no permission from me for doing their part. If they are true soldiers as I believe they are, I could not hold them back if I would. But the plain, painful fact of the matter is that today not to talk of one crore volunteers, there are not ten thousand who are prepared completely to sacrifice themselves for duty's sake. I know that they can get ready in no time if they wish, but 'the will to do' is lacking. You cannot get swaraj by mere speeches, shows, processions, etc. What is needed is solid, steady, constructive work; what the youth craves for and is fed on is only the former.[3]

This was a challenge to Bose to provide more than processions as a junior Congress leader.

Subhas worked energetically at mobilizing a number of Indian groups during 1929, touring and speaking relentlessly, first within Bengal, and then in other regions of India. He served as the president of many youth and student conferences, headed a number of trade unions and then the All-India Trade Union Congress, continued to serve as a member of the Bengal Legislative Council and Calcutta Corporation, and as president of the Bengal Provincial Congress Committee. Of all these positions and roles, that of BPCC president was foremost, for this was *the* nationalist organization, and the one to which he adhered, through dark and happy days throughout his life.

In this work, he understood that youths and workers had their special concerns and issues, but he stressed that every Indian had to look beyond these issues and participate in the national movement, i.e., join in the Congress-led effort to free India from British rule. So while he spent time on the particular issues of concern to these groups, he was constantly recruiting from amongst them for the main national task at hand.

One prong of his message was that all Indians should be equal and that special concern had to be given to the needs of the exploited. At the Rangpur Political Conference in March 1929, he said, '. . . we must abolish the entire caste system, or convert all castes into Sudras or Brahmins.'[4] Equality and unity must be fostered between high and low in the social order and between Hindus and Muslims. In the years from 1928 on, Bose spoke more openly and strongly for socialism, an Indian socialism. He thought that Indian socialism had its roots in ancient Indian ideals and in the Indian renaissance of the nineteenth century:

> In the work of man-making, Swami Vivekananda did not confine his attention to any particular sect but embraced the whole of society. His fiery words—'Let a new India emerge through the workshop and from the huts and bazaars'—are still ringing. . .
>
> This socialism did not derive its birth from the books of Karl Marx. It has its origin in the thought and culture of India. The gospel of democracy that was preached by Swami Vivekananda has manifested itself fully in. . . Deshabandhu Das, who said that Narayan lives amongst those who till the land, prepare our bread by the sweat of their brow. . .and they are revolutionizing the thoughts of many, but the idea of socialism is not a novelty in this country. We regard it as such only because we have lost the thread of our own history. It is not proper to take any school of thought as unmistakable and absolute truth. We must not forget that the Russians, the main disciples of Karl Marx, have not blindly followed his ideas. . . . We have therefore to shape society and politics according to our own ideals and according to our needs.[5]

He declared that the present era was that of non-cooperation and socialism. In this phase of his life, 'freedom' and 'socialism' were the major goals, and part of his endeavors was to state, and state, and state again the ideals that Indians should hold for themselves and their society. India was to be free of foreign rule and was to be, in time, a more egalitarian, industrialized, and vibrant society.

As Bengal Congress president, Bose sent out a detailed memorandum to all BPCC members in March 1929, formulating the Congress program as agreed to at Calcutta and presenting a plan for regularly scheduled events. Boycott of foreign cloth and production of khadi material was, of course, central, but other elements in the Congress constructive program were listed as part of the Sunday programs:

> *On Sunday March 17th* and thereafter on the *first Sunday of every month* special attention should be paid to the propaganda for the boycott of foreign cloth and khadi should be hawked.
>
> *On Sunday March 24th* and thereafter on the *second Sunday of every month* a special effort should be made to carry on propaganda in favour of total prohibition of intoxicating drugs and drinks.
>
> *On Sunday March 31st* and thereafter on the *third Sunday of every month* wrestling matches, drill, lathi play and other national sports should be held in which all classes and communities should be invited and induced to participate.[6]

Alluding to the more extensive and systematic recruitment, he continued,

> In order to give effect to this programme, it is necessary to strengthen and reorganise the Congress organization in this province. Without a well-disciplined extensive Congress organization it is impossible to give effect to any programme. For this reason the Bengal Provincial Congress Committee has decided to adopt the following programme as preparatory measures:
>
> (1) To enlist five lacs of Congress members in this province.
> (2) To raise two lacs of rupees for doing Congress work.
> (3) Enroll at least 1000 volunteers in each district.[7]

Although spinning was mentioned, it was not given the priority that Gandhi wanted. Bose was keen on training volunteers with physical and martial skills and this surely accorded with the kind of activity that the representatives of revolutionary groups in the BPCC wanted. Among the revolutionaries in the BPCC were Arun Guha, Hem Chandra Ghosh (leader of the BV), and Surja Sen.[8]

As Bose toured the Bengal districts, visiting towns and villages throughout the province, he often reviewed the volunteers. For example, *Liberty* reported that on August 20, 1929, Bose, together with S.M. Ghosh (a Jugantar leader) attended the Rajshahi district Students' Conference

where the volunteers, male and female, marched in military style, raised
the national flag, and paraded in to listen to Bose. He spoke on the need for
discipline and physical as well as military training. He maintained that
money spent on their uniforms was not wasted because they helped to build
esprit de corps. The loincloth and the bullock cart, Bose declared, will not
do, for we cannot go back to village ways as Gandhi wants. He told the
assembled youths at a gathering on August 17, that Nietzsche's superman
ideal held the ground in Europe, but that Indians must shape out their own
ideals for the new man and the new society.[9]

Most often, Subhas Bose went to the larger towns for his speeches and
meetings, but Sabitriprasanna Chattopadhyay has given a moving account
of a visit to an East Bengal village which probably took place in this
period.[10] He recounts how Subhas and a few Congress workers arrived
through the muggy summer heat at a Padma ferry crossing. The boatman,
observing the threatening clouds, said to Bose,

'Sir, I think we should wait a while . . .'

Subhas smiling, said : 'My dear fellow, why do you want to wait—are you
afraid?'

'Well, Sir, I am not afraid for myself, as fighting the storm is a challenge.
But you are the passengers, so I must be careful.'[11]

The boatman pushed off into the broad river and Subhas upon further
questioning learned that the boatman had lost a son to the swirling waters
of the Padma. 'Subhas's eyes filled with tears, and in the fading light of that
cloudy day a shadow of sadness fell on his face.'[12] Shortly after that he
asked the boatman to sing, for he said,

'I am very fond of listening to songs.'

Greatly encouraged, the boatman cleared his throat and sang:

'To know the mystery of the river
You must plunge into its depths
And if you are ready to brave the depths
Why should you fear the storm
When the river erodes the banks on both sides
Into the silted channel rushes the flood tide.
If you want to reach a distant destination
Sometimes, you must go against the current.'[13]

Touched by this *bhatiali*, or boatman's song, Subhas asked if anyone
would sing *shyama sangit* (a song dedicated to the goddess Kali). He said,

'Since none of you will sing, I will do so myself.'

To our surprise, he hummed for a while, then he sang this song:

'When will you dance again, oh Mother Shyama
Making the garland of skulls around your neck move.
Through the darkness of the clouds

The scimitar in your hand flashes like a flame.
Oh Mother! By the fire of your three eyes
Reduce to ashes all the impurities of the mind,
And I will never be afraid of the terrible.
Oh Mother Kali! Give me your mantra of the fearless
Oh Mother! Again and again I call thee.
Can you escape being the Mother?
This time I offer at your feet
A garland of blood-red oleanders.'[14]

A big crowd welcomed Subhas at the village. He could have stayed with the richest man in the village, but instead chose to stay with a poorer Muslim Congress worker. The next day he spoke in a field adjoining the village school to a gathering of Hindus and Muslims, men and women, old and young. 'They were intrigued by his good looks, his quiet, steady voice, and his caring words.'[15] He conducted the meeting meticulously for he thought even seemingly insignificant jobs had to be conducted with devotion. When he had to make his own remarks, he spoke of village reorganization, the need to set up panchayats where there were none, the need to improve cottage industries, the necessity for women's education, the importance of physical exercise, the significance of personal hygiene, and, most importantly, how to organize and carry on the ceaseless and uncompromising struggle to attain a free India.[16]

Although Bose made it a practice to search out the Muslim leaders of any locality he visited and to pay special attention to Muslim Congress workers, the communal divide continued to grow dangerously wider in these years. His appeals for communal unity were no doubt in earnest, but he could not see how his stands on a number of issues contributed to the Muslim estrangement from the Congress. The Congress position on the Bengal Tenancy Bill of 1928 bewildered and hurt the nationalist Muslims and those who spoke for the poorer peasantry. Though the Congress said their stand represented even-handedness, such unwillingness to help change agrarian relations in favor of the poorer Muslim peasantry in fact preserved the rights of the wealthy landed interests.[17] Second, Bose's insistence that only joint electorates without reservation of seats would bring national unity may have been true, but his insistence that there was only one position did not foster dialogue with many Muslims.[18] Third, Bose had campaigned vociferously against the Government of Bengal's treatment of Sachin Sen of Barisal during 1929. Sen led the Patuakhali Satyagraha which was based on the demand of Hindus to be allowed to play music before mosques. Bose may well have been right that the government had treated Sen unfairly and was rearresting him in March

1929 for charges that had previously been dropped, but the whole issue had a communal flavor. It appeared to be a narrow Hindu issue and position for which Bose demanded national support.[19]

The one arena in which Subhas Bose had defied Hindu criticism and worked significantly for communal rapprochement was in the Calcutta Corporation under the terms of the Bengal Pact when he had been chief executive officer under Mayor C.R. Das in 1924. But the Bengal Pact was dead now and though Hindus and Muslims sat in the Corporation, they did not usually sit together. The Muslims were in a distinct minority and if the elected Congress members voted or worked together, the Muslims might be cut out of what they felt to be their share of seats on committees, aldermanic positions, appointed positions, and their hold on the deputy mayor's chair. Once Congress unity was gone, then the question of the Muslims' share of these different kinds of positions got twisted into the conflicts between Congress factions.

Although Subhas Bose was a Corporation councillor, elected from Ward XI, in 1929, and Sarat Bose was one of the five elected aldermen, they did not immediately play a role in Corporation affairs. Sarat Bose began to assume a larger role in the Corporation, after he declined to stand for re-election to the Bengal Legislative Council in the spring of 1929. With his brother on the scene to run Bengal Congress affairs, Sarat Bose attended more and more to the nuts and bolts of municipal concerns through 1929 and in following years.[20] One issue over which Sarat Bose became particularly enraged and which involved a conflict between the popularly-elected Indian Corporation, the Government of Bengal, and the European community, was the appointment of Dr B.N. Dey as chief engineer of the Corporation.[21]

The Corporation had voted to hire Dr Dey who had excellent qualifications and had been working as an engineering consultant in Europe, and would be the first Indian chief engineer. The Government of Bengal vetoed the appointment on financial grounds, claiming that the costs of bringing Dr Dey to Calcutta and paying him a salary commensurate with his previously held positions were too great. Then the Corporation voted to give Dey a temporary special appointment. After this had been approved, a European councillor, Mr H.H. Hessling, raised questions about Dey's fitness for the post. Many Indian councillors answered Hessling, but Sarat Bose became the most angry, even calling Hessling dishonest, for which Mayor Sen Gupta, in the chair, cautioned Sarat Bose. The latter said, in part,

> Looking at the conduct of Mr Hessling on the last occasion . . . (I found)
> . . . that Mr Hessling was prompted by malice aforethought in making that

attack upon a person who did not belong to the same race and same
nationality as himself. . . . It was clearly his intention to broadcast these
charges all over the country. . . . The broadcasting of the charges was part
of a vile propaganda (campaign) which was proved by a leading article on
Dr Dey in the *Statesman* which spoke of India producing no engineers of
merit save one or two.[22]

The special appointment was approved and Dey went on to do some
distinguished work for the Corporation.[23] The controversy showed how
quick Sarat Bose was to anger and to find racial slurs in European political
opposition. The slights were there, but no other member of the Corporation
had as much confidence and pride as Sarat Bose in challenging members
of the opposition from amongst the non-official Europeans. In this forum,
the Swarajist Congressmen were in a majority, so that they could gain a
measure of revenge as well as holding to their power and authority.

Though Subhas Bose was not an active councillor, he did have the
confidence of his fellow Corporation members as was evinced by his
election as their representative to the Bengal government's Waterways
Advisory Committee on June 29, which was to consider the Grand Trunk
Canal Project. Even the *Amrita Bazar Patrika*, often critical of Subhas,
praised him as a worthy representative who would fight for the best
interests of Indians in questioning a scheme costly and damaging to Indian
interests.[24] Subhas Bose retained his Corporation seat up to January 1930
and, at the same time, held a seat in the Bengal Legislative Council to
which he was re-elected in the spring of 1929.

During the period both Subhas and Sarat Bose were Bengal Council
members, the two ministers, M. Hosain and the Raja of Nashipur were
challenged by the elected members. Angry words and charges of buying
votes filled the hall before the crucial ratifying vote on February 20, 1929.
The Swarajists joined with many of the Muslim members and the Unionist
group and won their no-confidence motion by sixty-five to fifty-nine.[25]
The governor and his advisers decided to run the government with only
executive councillors and officials. In the spring, the government called
for a new Council election. Feeling that it was important to retain this
forum for a strong nationalist voice, Subhas Bose ran for re-election and
campaigned throughout the province for Swarajist candidates. About the
same number were re-elected, but their Muslim support had completely
fallen away.[26] Pressure   to step down continued from the Gandhi-
dominated Congress but Subhas Bose argued that once a beachhead was
established in any arena, the nationalists should not give it up to the
opposition without a struggle. Resigning meant 'going back' and that is
something he never wanted to do. Forward, ever forward, is what he

wanted. And what 'forward' signified, he had to determine himself and not be told by Gandhi or any other authority.

There were few important issues that the Council could or did decide during the remainder of the year. A majority including the Swarajists voted to send the Bengal (Rural) Primary Education Bill of 1929 to a select committee. Many Muslim members were tired of the delay and frustrated with the arguments that Hindus gave about the costliness of education for the rural masses. But again the Swarajists and the government preferred a select committee and that is what they got.[27] On August 9, an adjournment motion concerning labor was made because striking jute workers had been badly beaten up.[28] This adjournment motion was the occasion for the only real speech that Subhas Bose ever made in the Bengal Council. He began by raising questions about the so-called Pathans who were said to have attacked the strikers, but then quickly moved to the larger issues at stake:

> One of the (European) speakers . . . tried to make out that there was really no cause for the workers to go on strike; that the strike had been engineered by outside interference and that intimidation had been at work. . . . Who is practising this intimidation? . . . I think I can prove . . . that the members of the police had been practising intimidation on the workers. It is no news to this country that whenever unfortunately there is a labour dispute the agents of Government, the police, always side with the capitalists. No wonder. We have it from Lord Curzon that administration and exploitation must go hand in hand and this will go on until we are a free people.[29]

Bose, who had been spending a great deal of his time on labor matters throughout the year, began to list the many grievances and fears of the workers,

> Personally I have had on several occasions to visit in some of the slums and I know the horrible conditions under which the Hindu and Mussalman mill-hands have to work and live. But there is another side of the picture, Sir.
>
>   We find that these mill authorities are making crores and crores of money. Have not the workers a right to ask for a living wage and a decent condition of life? If the hon'ble members sitting opposite admit that right in the case of their own countrymen, why should not they admit the same right in the case of the coloured people? . . . the condition of the slums . . . are all the more horrible when one considers for a single moment the huge profit made by these mills . . . they make crores and crores of rupees, but they will not give a decent living wage to the Indian worker who asks for nothing more at present. I am afraid if this modest and moderate demand is not conceded now in full, the time will come, and that time is not far off, when these workers will no longer be content with this modest demand but will put forward a bigger claim for the ultimate ownership of capital.[30]

After explaining how the government had used its powers to help the mill owners time and again, he asked for government intervention:

... I would demand of Government as an act of bare justice that they should intervene and see to it that the strike is terminated as early as possible. I do not believe in an appeal, I stand on my rights and I demand that Government should intervene as soon as possible in order to bring about a satisfactory and honourable settlement of the dispute. If they do not desire to do that let them throw the Trade Disputes Act into the waste paper basket.[31]

Was Bose simply being naive in appealing to the government or did he think that for the sake of social order they might take a more active role? Perhaps he shared the fast diminishing faith of many Indian nationalists trained in the British system of law and justice as practised in Great Britain—like Gandhi and his brother Sarat—that the government eventually would act evenhandedly. In any case, even though this was his only full speech and his other participation was limited mainly to asking questions about political prisoners, he was loathe to have the Swarajists give up this forum.[32]

In arguing against Gandhi for continued use of the Council as a forum, he said that Congress workers were only giving a small part of their energies to the Council, and if they left it, '... we would practically hand over to the enemy an important field of activity which we had captured after a long struggle.'[33] He also said that he cared nothing for offices, and his political life is speckled with resignations from one office or another. But he liked the power and ceremony which went with office and believed in the weight of symbolism. To confront Mr Moberly of the Political Department, or other officials, or to have the power and patronage which went with the mayor's chair in the Calcutta Corporation meant that Indians were the equals of their rulers and ready to run the Indian government.

The image one gets of Subhas Bose in these years from his party's paper *Liberty* is of a man constantly in motion. Every day he had one, two, three meetings and he was traveling a good deal of the time. Some small glimpses about how he felt about all this activity are given in letters to C.R. Das' widow, his beloved Basanti Devi. He was forced to take a brief rest and wrote to her from Shillong in June, on Das' death anniversary,

After coming here I have had some physical rest. But I have had little time to think. I am rushing along like a storm—it is necessary to understand whither I am going—towards good or evil. Besides, I need self-analysis— it is not possible to carry out self-analysis unless there is time enough for it ...

Mother, I am an absolutely unworthy and useless son. Your love is taking me towards full manhood. Mother, bless me so that in lives to come I may have the good fortune of having a mother like you.

He who was at once my friend, philosopher and guide in my life's mission—is no more. Today I am utterly destitute. You are the only refuge of this helpless person. Even if I lose everything else while going through vicissitudes of fortune, conflict and struggle, may I not lose your affection ever![34]

This was a rare moment of doubt, for he had by now become confident in his mission. It was only when he temporarily stopped his racing-motor life that he wondered what made the engine work and whether it should be in motion all the time. His devotion to the Mother Goddess, his *ishta devata* (chosen deity) and to his adopted and idealized mother continued throughout his life. Basanti Devi, for her part, always supported him and cherished him even when the 'vicissitudes of fortune' brought him low.

One of the many ways in which he continued the work of his mentor C.R. Das was in the labor field. Although he did not have as much experience of Indian village life and the peasantry as some of his Congress colleagues, he did get a thoroughgoing acquaintance with the lives, sufferings, and aspirations of industrial workers. This was a stormy period of labor organization, strikes, arrests of labor leaders, and then in October 1929, the Great Crash, which eventually spread its tentacles to every corner of the globe. With Calcutta as his base, Bose tried to help the railway workers at Lillooah and the iron and steel workers of Jamshedpur in 1928, as has been described earlier. In 1929, he pressed the case of the jute workers, but expended most of his energy helping the tin-plate workers at Golmuri, who formed a union and struck for higher wages for more than ten months beginning in April 1929. The Tinplate Company of India had started as an enterprise allied to Tata Iron and Steel Company and was owned by the Burmah Oil Company (two-thirds of the stock) and Tatas (one-third of the stock). Many outsiders, including V.V. Giri, Jawaharlal Nehru, and Rajendra Prasad, visited Golmuri in efforts to facilitate negotiations and get the government to intervene. The workers' demands for an impartial enquiry committee, no victimization of strike leaders, and the withdrawal of cases pending against strikers arrested for picketing were, on the whole, moderate. In August 1929, oil workers in the Burmah Oil Company's mills in Budge Budge also struck partly for their own grievances, and partly in sympathy with the Golmuri workers.[35]

Subhas Bose called for a boycott of Burmah Oil Company products and wrote to legislators at the center and in Bengal asking that the protective duty which benefited the company be withdrawn. To his fellow members of the Bengal Legislative Council he wrote that the Burmah Oil Company was taking an unreasonable stance with respect to the workers' grievances, and pressure had to be put on the company. He said that this foreign company was being protected at the expense of Indian consumers and workers.[36] Through the second half of 1929, he spoke to workers' rallies at Golmuri, in Jamshedpur, and at Budge Budge almost every week. He told the workers that they must build strong unions to fight for their rights. He could not do the day-to-day union-building that others could do, but he simply tried to raise their awareness.[37]

His second constantly reiterated point was that the 'swaraj and labor movements must unite.'[38] He saw the two movements as aspects of India regaining control of herself and gaining the benefits of her productive capacities. In the pages of *Liberty* during these years the economic critique of the earlier nationalists, Romesh Chunder Dutt and Dadabhai Naoroji was picked up, continued, and made relevant to present circumstances.[39] They thought that the financial drain was evident and the writers set out to show how the British, government and business interests, in collusion, were exploiting India. Occasionally carried away by his dreams of freedom, Bose told 14,000 workers of the EIR Union at Lillooah on August 16 that as soon as swaraj came, all the workers' grievances would disappear. Therefore, they should organize unions in the present and fight in the nationalist-battle as well.[40]

In 1929 Subhas Bose, with the extensive help of Dr Haris Chandra Sinha, compiled a small book entitled, *Boycott of British Goods*, which drew on historical records, official statistics, and some historical analyses to present a picture of the British impact on the Indian economy and charted out a course for Indian nationalists to follow.[41] The first section traced the decline of the Indian cotton industry and the rise of British imports through the eighteenth and nineteenth centuries. Generally following the arguments of the early economic nationalists, Bose found 'lessons of history' to be learned by Indian nationalists of his day:

> Unjust, coercive and uneconomic methods were applied against our indus-
> try in the past. In the future, therefore, we are not entitled to hope that purely
> economic methods will be sufficient to reconstruct our industry, and thus
> taboo politics and sentiment in business. The arm of political power which
> struck our industries in the past is still there and may have to be disabled by
> non-economic weapons. It stands to reason, therefore, that businessmen and
> industrialists should in their own interests join hands with nationalists and
> politicians in the present movement for boycott.[42]

Bose further argued that India should not be surrounded by a high tariff wall, for many economists had argued that this had a 'numbing, enervating influence.' So he maintained that,

> . . . if boycott is successful, it will create a gap, which *Swadeshi* must rush
> in to fill. *Swadeshi* is a great constructive effort, which is to be preferred to
> protection. . . . Its special merit is that it is purely voluntary. Nobody is
> compelled to buy the same thing at a higher price, or a worse thing for the
> same price, unless he feels inclined to make that sacrifice in the cause of the

country. Such conscious acts will help to knit the nation much more closely than if India is surrounded by a high tariff wall.[43]

Trying to answer the arguments of British writers who said that boycott and swadeshi would not make a significant dent in British-Indian trade patterns, Bose devoted the second section of the book to analysis of India's and Britain's international trade with each other and India's trade with all other foreign partners. He said that the swadeshi boycott (ca. 1906–9) had had an impact as had the First World War and that there was an overall decline in India's import of British goods through the last several decades. He showed that India's trade with Japan and also the United States, Italy, China, and the Netherlands was 'biting into the British share.'[44]

Together with the National Congress, the Bengal Congress had declared a complete boycott of British goods in 1928 and Bose outlined many of the necessary steps that nationalists, allied with Indian business interests, would have to take. He concluded,

> The gravity of the task should not daunt Indian nationalists but should only inspire them with hope and courage. Even if nothing spectacular is achieved, there will be some positive gain, for, to the extent that there is a reduction of British imports, there is a corresponding emancipation from the economic bondage of the nation. Even if industries are not started in India now, it will be easier to oust non-British goods at a subsequent date when that is called for in the interests of the country's economic welfare.
>
> If eternal vigilance is the price of political liberty, it is no less true that ceaseless struggle is the price of economic freedom of a nation.[45]

Much of this book was based on the compilation and work of Dr Sinha, but it was also founded on Bose's reading of economic history while he was in Cambridge and subsequently. Bose still believed that history was the source of lessons which, in turn, would guide present and future action. He felt that the record of British spoliation of the Indian economy was manifest, and it was for Indian nationalists to give these economic relations a new turn, this time in India's favor. What is also important to note is that though he said harsh words about foreign capitalists, he saw Indian capitalists as necessary allies of the Congress in its struggle with the British and not simply another set of exploiters to be expropriated forthwith.[46]

For Bose, independence was primary, and unionization secondary, while for some other organizers, including British and Indian communists, the radicalization and organization of the workers was primary. The Government of India decided to arrest and try all of the main radical organizers early in 1929. Preparing for this case, the viceroy telegraphed the secretary of state for India,

The trial would take many months and would be costly, but in comparison
with the advantages of success the time and money would be of little
account. When once a case has been launched, the main activities of the
Communists would, we think, be paralysed, for the number of Communist
leaders in India is not large, and all those of any account would be included
in the case.[47]

After a communist gathering in March, the government moved swiftly,
arresting about thirty labor organizers, many of whom were communists.
The Meerut Conspiracy Case dragged on for years and aimed at crippling
radical labor organizing in India.[48] The chief prosecution counsel, Mr
Langford James, attempted to show in his opening remarks that the
accused advocated were working for international communism and were
opposed to Indian nationalism. He said, *inter alia*,

> The Indian National Congress is stigmatised as a misguided, bourgeois
> body, which has to be captured and converted to the peculiar views of these
> accused, or else destroyed. . . . This revolution that these accused have
> visualised is not a national revolution. It is an anti-national revolution. They
> appear to me to entertain feelings of hatred toward a very large number of
> people, but it is reserved for those gentlemen, who are usually accredited
> with working for the attainment of Swaraj in India, it is reserved for those
> gentlemen to execute the particular odium of those accused. . . . Jawaharlal
> Nehru is dubbed a tepid reformist. Mr Subhas Bose is a bourgeois and a
> somewhat ludicrous careerist.[49]

The government's objective of splitting the radical organizers from the
Congressmen was not successful and Jawaharlal Nehru, in particular,
devoted considerable energies to gathering funds and the best lawyers for
their defense.[50] Subhas Bose also supported them and visited them in
Meerut on several occasions, the first time in late October 1929, just as the
trial officially opened.[51] Although some of the Meerut prisoners had
mocked the left Congressmen, many had done effective work in the labor
field and some shared Nehru's and Bose's approach to labor. The
nationalists would not allow the government to trick them into opposing
the radical labor organizers especially in a political trial.

Although those of a more nationalist orientation like Subhas Bose were
not among those swept into the Meerut fold by the Government of India,
the Home Department of the Bengal government watched Bose scrupu-
lously and debates were carried on within the intelligence branch as to
when it would be helpful to put him away. A.N. Moberly, in charge of
Bengal's Political Department, mentioned in his secret report of August
28, 1929 that the trade union work of Subhas Bose and others in the
Calcutta metropolitan area, '. . . obviously represent a scheme to control
oil and petrol supplies and road transport to Calcutta.'[52] Moberly argued

that a minority of Indians, namely the Congress leadership, was bent on intimidating a majority of Indians and creating unrest. The key members of this minority, he felt, should be put away immediately. Another intelligence report of this year described Subhas Bose as 'the most dangerous of the extremist leaders in Bengal.'[53] But Bose was not jailed in 1929 and his major clash with the law was an arrest for leading an illegal procession and chanting seditious slogans in the streets of Calcutta in August. The trial was put off until late October and Bose was free to ply his nationalist trade through the year.[54]

While some of the radical labor organizers were out of the field after the Meerut arrests, others, well known to Bose, and of a different persuasion, were just getting into gear for a new campaign against the Raj. These were the young men and women that the government called 'anarchists' and 'terrorists' and the nationalists called 'revolutionaries'. Demands for violent action were being argued out among Bengal's revolutionary groups in 1929. As these internal discussions were going on, Bhagat Singh, a leader of the Hindustan Republican Socialist Army in northern India, and his comrades threw a bomb in the Legislative Assembly Hall in Delhi on April 8. No one was injured and the bomb-throwers were captured. They were linked to other violent acts and with other confederates put on trial in the Lahore Conspiracy Case. A young Bengali, Jatin Das, assistant secretary of the South Calcutta Congress Committee, and well known to Subhas Bose for years, was arrested in this case and taken to Lahore to await trial.[55]

Ajoy Ghosh, later general secretary of the Communist Party of India, and then a member of Singh's organization, wrote of those days:

> We were henceforth (from 1928) the Hindustan Socialist Republican Association with a Socialist State in India as our avowed objective.... As for the most important question ... the question in what manner the fight for freedom and Socialism was to be waged, armed action by individuals and groups was to remain our immediate task. Nothing else, we held, could smash constitutionalist illusions, nothing else could free the country from the grip in which fear held it. When the stagnant calm was broken by a series of hammer blows delivered by us at selected points and on suitable occasions, against the most hated officials of the Government, and mass movement unleashed, we would link ourselves with that movement, act as its armed detachment and give it a Socialist direction.... Things seemed to be moving apace....We felt a big fight was ahead.... We were feverishly busy preparing to play our part in it—collecting arms and money, training our cadres in the use of arms. Jatin Das was brought from Calcutta to teach us how to make bombs.[56]

Many members of the group were caught in the police net and several turned approvers after being tortured by the police.

On Political Prisoners' Day in Calcutta on July 6, 1929, Subhas Bose called for the release of all the prisoners held in Bengal, the Punjab, and at Meerut.[57] Although he ostensibly was against isolated and limited acts of violence, he was sympathetic with those who did believe that this was the route to the end of British rule. Jatin Das had worked under him in aiding the victims of the north Bengal floods in 1922, and in the South Calcutta Congress Committee, and had helped found the South Calcutta Tarun Samity, a social service group dedicated to aiding the poor, disabled, and destitute. He was also in charge of the South Calcutta Volunteer Corps and through the volunteer corps had contacts with many groups of revolutionaries. Some reports have it that Bhagat Singh came to the Calcutta Congress to make revolutionary contacts and strategy. He must have seen Jatin Das in Calcutta.[58]

When Jatin Das was taken to the prison in Lahore, Bhagat Singh and B.K. Dutt were already on a hunger strike for removal of certain kinds of discrimination in the treatment of political prisoners. Das took up the hunger strike and resisted forced feeding. On September 13, 1929, Das died, saying at his last that he did not want orthodox Bengali rites, because, 'I am not a Bengali; I am an Indian.' His body was taken by train to Calcutta and arrived on the evening of Sunday, September 15. The *Calcutta Municipal Gazette* reported that, 'Mr Subhas Chandra Bose kept a night-long vigil by the side of the coffin with a band of Congress volunteers.'[59] The next day Subhas Bose, J.M. Sen Gupta and other Congress leaders— bare-headed and bare-footed—headed an enormous procession through the streets of Calcutta. Some said it was the biggest funeral procession to be seen in Calcutta since the death of C.R. Das. Gandhi, however, remained silent, and implied in a later comment that the hunger strike— as well as the HSRA's activities—should never have been taken up.[60]

Just as the presence of Jatin Das as one of the accused in the Lahore Conspiracy Case linked Bengal and the Punjab, so Subhas Bose reaffirmed and strengthened these ties by making his first tour of the Punjab in October and talking repeatedly of the kinship of the two regions. Greeted with enthusiastic shouts of 'Long Live Revolution,' 'Down with Imperialism,' 'Bande Mataram,' and 'Long Live Subhas Babu,' Bose was taken in a huge procession to the opening session of the Punjab Provincial Students' Conference over which he was to preside.[61] He delivered a passionate address to the students.

> Little do you know how much Bengali literature has drawn from the earlier history of the Punjab in order to enrich itself. . . . Tales of your heroes have been composed and sung by our great poets including Rabindranath Tagore

.... Aphorisms of your saints have been translated into elegant Bengali and they afford solace and inspiration to millions in Bengal. This cultural contact has its counterpart in the political sphere and we find your political pilgrims meeting ours not only in the jails of India but also in the jails of distant Burma and in the wilds of the Andamans across the seas.[62]

Praising the 'glorious martial tradition' as well as the 'chained heroes' and the 'undying martyrs' of the Punjab, he called upon the students to join the national movement and do practical work and not limit themselves to a bookish, intellectual education. Bose said they had glorious models before them of heroic self-immolation in the Bengali Jatin Das, and, continuing bravery in Bhagat Singh of the Punjab.[63]

He moved gradually from the specifics of the moment and the Lahore Conspiracy Case to broader themes. He talked of the changing balance between Asia and Europe during past eons.

There is hardly any Asiatic today to whom the spectacle of Asia lying strangled at the feet of Europe does not cause pain and humiliation. But I want you to get rid of the idea, once (and) for all, that Asia has always been in this state. Europe today may be the top-dog but time was when Asia was the top-dog. History tells us how in days of old Asia conquered and held sway over a large portion of Europe and in those days Europe was mightily afraid of Asia. The tables are turned now but the wheel of fortune is still moving and there is no cause for despair. Asia is at the present moment busy throwing off the yoke of thraldom and the time is not far off when rejuvenated Asia will rise resplendent in power and glory out of the darkness of the past and take her legitimate place in the comity of free nations.[64]

In asking them to join the national movement, he said they must have a clear goal and the desideratum he held before them was 'freedom':

By freedom I mean all-round freedom, i.e., freedom for the individual as well as for society; freedom for man as well as for woman; freedom for the rich as well as for the poor; freedom for all individuals and for all classes. This freedom implies not only emancipation from political bondage but also equal distribution of wealth, abolition of caste barriers and social iniquities and destruction of communalism and religious intolerance. This is an ideal which may appear utopian to hard-headed men and women—but this ideal alone can appease the hunger of the soul.[65]

Bose did not explain how all could be free and not impinge on the freedom of anyone else, or how the rich could be free but wealth be distributed equally. Much suffering and pain would have to be endured because India was subjugated, but free India would be pain-free.

To bring about this new day of freedom, Bose called upon the students to play a crucial role in spreading the message of freedom. They were to be self-sacrificing missionaries in the cause of national liberation and regeneration. As president of the Hindustani Seva Dal, the national volunteer movement, he asked them to step forward immediately and follow the example of the Bengal Volunteers of the Calcutta Congress of the previous December. They were to prepare in the short run for the up-coming Lahore Congress session in December 1929, but also for a prolonged national struggle against the British in which they would have to be in the front lines. Even repression and police actions, which he said were unduly harsh in the Punjab, were of benefit in the long run because in fighting against a brutal enemy, they would learn how to better fight and live as free men and women.[66]

After the Students' Conference, Bose gave other speeches in Lahore, Amritsar, Meerut, and Delhi. He formally applied for permission to see the Lahore Conspiracy Case prisoners, but was refused. He was allowed to see the Meerut prisoners and spent several hours with them. He could not dally in North India, however, because the magistrate in his own Calcutta trial (for sedition) summoned him to court and would brook no further delays. So Bose rushed from Meerut to Delhi to Calcutta. From Howrah Station, he went with Kiran Sankar Roy and Nalini Ranjan Sarker to the court and Sarker stood surety for him. The case was called for November.[67]

The Punjab trip had been a kind of respite from Bengal Congress politics and an emotional high for Bose. En route home to Calcutta, he wrote to Kalyani Devi,

> I have been shy by nature since my boyhood—and I continue to be so till today—in spite of the fact that I go about making speeches at public meetings. Whatever I may be—I am not a vain person—because I know that I have nothing to be vain about. Where I surrender, I do so with all my heart .... People of the Punjab have, on this occasion and everywhere, given me love, kindness and honour in an abundant measure. This was all due to Jatin Das's self-immolation. In fact, the atmosphere of the Punjab appears to have changed completely.[68]

The day after his return, he attended a memorial service for Jatin Das and spoke of his long personal relationship to him, and how, when one is on a hunger-strike, one's mind 'undergoes a radical transformation after some time.'[69] The death of Jatin Das had touched him deeply. Das had done in practice what Bose had called for in himself and others, i.e., self-immolation, giving up the self for a glorious cause.

Bose also had to attend to the mundane, painful, and even squalid conflict within the Bengal Congress which, after long, low rumbling, had finally come into the open in the third quarter of 1929. The infighting between the Bose-backers and the J.M. Sen Gupta-backers within the Bengal Congress organization and the BPCC bedeviled the productive working of the Bengal Congress and almost every other political and nationalist service organization in Bengal for the next two years.[70] It lasted until all the main parties were off the scene either for health reasons or due to incarceration. Even though Subhas Bose and J.M. Sen Gupta themselves were each imprisoned for at least half of this two-year period and Sen Gupta was in poor health almost throughout, the quarrels went on in Bengal and spilled the dirty water of Bengal into the national Congress reservoir as well, exacerbating the relations between the Bengal leaders and the Gandhian leadership of the Congress. King George V was referring to revolutionary activity when he asked, 'What is *wrong* with Bengal', but Gandhi or the Nehrus, senior and junior, might have been moved to ask the same question in referring to the Bengal Congress intramural quarrels.[71]

The roots of the division lay in the succession to C.R. Das. When Das died, Gandhi nominated, or rather suggested strongly, that J.M. Sen Gupta, an able barrister and Congressman from Chittagong take up all three positions that Das had held, mayor of Calcutta, president of the BPCC and leader of the Swarajists in the Bengal Legislative Council. From the first, other able and talented men in the Congress wondered why Sen Gupta, who had not had any particular pre-eminence over the others, should have all three positions, particularly since Das had not placed him in front of his other lieutenants and since no one was sure whether he had the skills, talents, and moral fire that brought Das to centerstage in Bengal. But Gandhi prevailed and Sen Gupta served in all three positions until he gave up the presidency of the BPCC to Subhas Bose at the end of 1927.[72] As mayor and as Swarajist leader in the Bengal Council, Sen Gupta did a masterful job, given the circumstances of imperial rule and declining Swarajist fortunes. He spoke and argued well, he acted with dignity, and, until 1929 was able to conciliate the different groups and personalities at work, though there was a nasty fight between B.N. Sasmal and some of the revolutionaries in the BPCC, and he did not always see eye to eye with those called the 'Big Five' (B.C. Roy, Tulsi Goswami, Sarat Bose, Nalini Sarker, Nirmal Chunder).[73] By giving up the BPCC presidency to Subhas Bose, he seemed to have given a post of importance and power to the most charismatic of the other Bengal leaders. Sen Gupta also declined to run for mayor in 1928, but when Subhas Bose ran, he claimed that tepid support from Sen Gupta led to his defeat. In the spring of 1929, Sen Gupta was elected mayor for the fourth time. So, in the Corporation and the Council, the Boses were in his group and beholden to his authority, while in the BPCC, Subhas Bose was president of an organization with quite diverse factions, personalities and interests at work, and had a higher position than Sen Gupta.[74]

By August 1929, communications had reached the Congress president,
Motilal Nehru, and other Working Committee members about the contro-
versies over elections to the BPCC and AICC from several Bengal
districts. Particularly at issue were delegates from Sylhet, Chittagong, and
Darjeeling. An indication of the tone of the disputes can be gleaned from
Sen Gupta's letter to Jawaharlal Nehru, the Congress general secretary, on
August 15, 1929, in which he wrote in part,

> I am sorry to say that there is a determined attempt on behalf of a group of
> men with which the executive is in league, to exclude people from member-
> ship of the Congress in the fear that the group would lose its power and
> would not be able to run the Congress according to their group ideas. This
> is my deliberate conviction having watched the trend of events in Bengal for
> the last two years. Further proof, if it were needed, of this nefarious
> conspiracy to prevent fresh people from coming to the Congress is to be
> found in the difficulties created in the way of Congressmen in enrollment
> of new members. Several District Congress Committee Secretaries have
> created difficulties in the way of Congressmen getting receipt books so
> much so that I had to complain to the BPCC sometimes with very indifferent
> results . . . . I wonder if you, as General Secretary, could mend matters in
> any way . . .[75]

Subhas Bose also wrote to Jawaharlal Nehru explaining why he could not
come to a Working Committee meeting:

> The annual meeting of the Provincial Congress Committee comes off on the
> 16th and 17th inst. . . . As you may be aware Mr Sen Gupta is up in arms
> against me and is at the moment busy organising his party for the purpose
> of hounding me out of the Bengal Provincial Congress Committee. In these
> circumstances, I cannot be absent from Calcutta on the 17th.[76]

Getting many conflicting messages from the two main parties, and seeing
no way to easily resolve the matter, Motilal Nehru sent Pattabhi
Sitaramayya as his representative to Calcutta in late 1929 to hear the
evidence and make a ruling. The issues became even more entangled when
the Bose group strenuously objected to the way Sitaramayya did his work
in Calcutta and sent ever more heated letters and telegrams to Motilal
Nehru protesting against the whole operation and claiming that
Sitaramayya favored Sen Gupta.[77]

An effort was made by representatives of the two factions (Subhas and
Sarat Bose, Kiran S. Roy, Satyendra Chandra Mitra, and Sudhir Roy for
the Bose group; Jyotish Chandra Ghosh, Bipin Ganguly, Suresh Chandra
Mazumdar, Pratul Ganguly, J.C. Gupta, Shyamapada Bhattacharjee,
Pramatha Natha Banerjee, Nishith Nath Kundu, and Prafulla Chandra
Ghosh, on the other side, against the entrenched leadership) to formulate
their own compromise, but this failed.[78] In light of the objections to

Sitaramayya's visit and assessment, and finding that the Bengalis in the BPCC could not make their own agreement, Motilal Nehru decided in mid-December 1929 that the sitting Bengal members of the AICC should continue until after the forthcoming Lahore Congress when he would renew the effort for a settlement. The BPCC as constituted was not to do anything but fill vacancies, and the recent elections were held in abeyance until the Congress president could make a further ruling in 1930. Although this decision pleased neither side, Nehru thought that this was the only way to allow Bengal to be represented at the Lahore session and not have either side stalk away in anger. It was his belief that the two sides had been more fairly represented in the voting for the BPCC and AICC in late 1928, so that the continuation of those elected more than a year ago was fairer than allowing new men to come in when the election procedures were being disputed.[79]

It was evident that members of the Jugantar Party in the BPCC sided with the Boses, while the members of the Anushilan Samity and the Atmonnati group of Bipin Ganguly (another small revolutionary group), stood with Sen Gupta. Those connected to the BV were with Bose, while the more dedicated Gandhians and the *Ananda Bazar* group lined up with Sen Gupta. Nalini Sarker leaned to the Boses and Dr B.C. Roy was also with the Boses, though he was beginning to emerge as an independent force in Bengal Congress politics with his own special relationship to Gandhi and the high command. He was trying to mediate, but was seen as closer to the Bose camp. Another underlying element that some contemporaries have mentioned is that Subhas Bose was more completely identified as a Calcutta man and a West Bengali, whereas Sen Gupta, from Chittagong, was, no matter how long he was active in Calcutta life, still identified as a *bangal*, a term used by those from the West to refer to those from the East of Bengal with somewhat invidious overtones.[80]

While the struggle within the BPCC was on hold, Subhas Bose became involved in a controversy with the Gandhian leadership on another matter. The viceroy, Lord Irwin, upon returning to India issued a statement on October 31, 1929, which said in part,

> I am authorized on behalf of His Majesty's Government to state clearly that, in their judgement, it is implicit in the declaration of 1917 that the natural issue of India's Constitutional progress, as there contemplated, is the attainment of Dominion Status.[81]

Leaders of several parties including the Congress met shortly thereafter in Delhi and expressed appreciation of the sincerity underlying his offer, and offerred cooperation in formulating a dominion constitution for India. The signatories, including Gandhi and Motilal Nehru, expressed their belief that the business of the Round Table Conference would be to draw up a dominion constitution for India.[82] Jawaharlal Nehru at first would not sign the Delhi Manifesto, but Gandhi's wishes prevailed, as they so often did, and the younger Pandit Nehru signed. Several who called themselves left-wingers, including Subhas Bose and Dr Kitchlew of the Punjab, issued a separate statement and opposed the goal of dominion status and participation in the Round Table Conference.[83]

Feeling that he was no longer in accord with the great majority of the Congress Working Committee and that his membership in it would prevent him from voicing his opposition, Bose sent in his letter of resignation from the Working Committee. However, after an exchange of views with Gandhi and Motilal Nehru, Bose withdrew his resignation, feeling that he could still agitate for independence and continue in the Working Committee.[84]

During this time, Bose wrote occasionally, usually on the run, to Basanti Devi. In a letter of November 5, he said, 'I returned from Delhi yesterday. . . . Jawaharlal has now given up Independence at the instance of the Mahatma.'[85] Bose always hoped that the younger Nehru would stand with him and push the Gandhian leadership to a more radical position, but time and again Nehru stuck his neck out but then quickly drew it back. This often left Bose exposed and ally-less, which did not stop Bose from continuing to make his challenges, but frequently meant that these challenges were less successful. And Bose, slowly but increasingly, came to feel more resentment against Jawaharlal than against Gandhi.[86]

As the conflict with Sen Gupta and his followers developed, Bose gave his evaluation to Basanti Devi. On November 5, he wrote, 'Mr Sengupta and his group are making a desperate effort to drive us out of the B.P.C.C. Let us see what happens. Most probably we shall not lose.'[87] About five weeks later, when the Congress president had intervened, Bose wrote,

> Sengupta's party tried repeatedly to outmanoeuvre and destroy us but so far without success. Our dispute is now in Pandit Motilal's hands. Even though we did not do anything unfair in the elections, I somehow apprehend that Panditji will support Sengupta and invalidate the elections to B.P.C.C. and A.I.C.C. from Sylhet. . . . The help that was expected of Dr Roy at this time of our difficulty has not been forthcoming. Nirmal Babu is doing a lot.[88]

Bose was correct in his assessment that Motilal Nehru would invalidate the elections, but did not foresee how sweeping the invalidation would be. Nirmal Chunder, one of the Big Five, continued to side with the Boses and so earned his approbation, while Dr Roy, who was trying to mediate—as was Motilal Nehru—did not.

A showdown, of sorts, was coming at Lahore, for all the disputing parties on national and Bengal issues were gathering together for the annual Congress conclave. En route to Lahore, Bose wrote briefly to Basanti Devi,

> For some time now since you left Calcutta, I have been passing through all sorts of anxiety and struggle. Every day I feel like coming to you and seek your love and blessings. . . . It is so difficult to liberate myself from the trammels of work. Even so, the feeling that your love and blessings are always with me gives me sustenance. When I feel mentally tired out, your love and blessings bring me new life. It is indeed true that in my life there is no other treasure or refuge. I do not know if the course I have taken is the right one—you will please show me the path of truth. . . . I am on the way to Lahore. I hardly know what will happen there.
>
> Time and again my opponents have banded together and tried with all their might to defeat me. By the grace of some Unseen Power I have also been able to foil their attempts. I cannot of course say what the final outcome is going to be. But please remember that the son's victory means a triumph for the mother; the son's defeat is a defeat for the mother.[89]

When he was troubled and anxious, Bose signed his letters to Basanti Devi, 'Your unworthy son,' but when he was surer of his way, he simply signed 'Devotedly yours'. Although he was also a favorite of his own mother, the tie to Basanti Devi was special because she had chosen him as a 'son' and he had chosen her as a 'mother' and her late husband as his true parent and guide in politics and cultural matters. Bose seemed to need her maternal support as he also sought divine sustenance from a female deity.

As the Lahore Congress session was opening, Bose, learning of Motilal Nehru's ruling which barred the newly elected members of the AICC from Bengal, and finding that a majority of the Working Committee supported this, wrote a bitter letter to the elder Nehru offering his resignation from the Working Committee for the second time in two months. It read, in part,

> This decision is arbitrary, unconstitutional and unprecedented. It is clear from the communications received from the President that the decision of the President re: A.I.C.C. election was directly influenced by representations from Mr J.M. Sengupta and his party who have openly opposed the present B.P.C.C. and that the President made no reference to us and did not give the B.P.C.C. a hearing before he arrived at his decision. The Working Committee by arriving at this decision has trampled upon the rights and dignity of the B.P.C.C. and has ratified the fiat issue by Pundit Motilal Nehru from Lucknow. The W.C. which under the Congress Constitution is an executive body has not only usurped the functions of the Election Disputes Committee of the A.I.C.C., but has overridden the constitution of the Indian National Congress in order to uphold the action of an important member of that body.

I beg, therefore, to tender my resignation from the WC as a protest against such illegal and unconstitutional procedure.[90]

Bose sometimes burnt his bridges faster and more thoroughly than they could be rebuilt, but at this moment, Dr B.C. Roy stepped in and persuaded all parties to allow an election disputes panel working with Motilal Nehru to confront this matter after the Congress session. In effect, he made Bose back off from his sweeping charges against the president and Working Committee and rejoin the Congress executive. As his rage cooled, Bose realized that it did no good to his cause and to himself to alienate Motilal Nehru. He offered an apology and said that the Pandit was like a father to him. The obstreperous son had temporarily conciliated one important Congress father, but more confrontations lay just around the corner.[91]

Shortly before the Lahore Congress, a bomb had been thrown at Lord Irwin and Gandhi insisted on a strong resolution condemning this outrage. He said of such acts, '. . . each bomb outrage has cost India dear. . . . Let me tell you that if we oppose this resolution it means we are not true to the creed of non-violence.'[92] Gandhi argued that if the Congress were to be true to its non-violent creed, it must swiftly denounce any breach of this creed. Some Congressmen did not agree with Gandhi's view on this matter and privately felt that non-violence was a tactic and not an absolute value. However, Gandhi got his resolution on this matter in Lahore, but by a relatively close vote of 942 to 794, which disturbed him greatly.[93] Bose's views on this question did not coincide with Gandhi's, but he saved his disagreement in the open session for another issue.

Gandhi, agreeing that progress had not been made for achievement of dominion status within the year, now moved the resolution for complete independence which he had opposed in 1928. He was not happy about this. Subhas wanted to push Gandhi a step further and introduced an amendment to Gandhi's resolution which called for the setting up of a parallel government in India. He said,

> . . . I take this opportunity of conveying my cordial and hearty thanks to Mahatma Gandhi for coming forward to move a resolution which declares Swaraj to mean complete independence. But I move this amendment because I believe that the programme laid down by his resolution is not such as to carry us towards the goal of complete independence. My amendment is consistent with the goal, and in keeping with the spirit of the times. I have no doubt it will find favour with the younger generation in this country.
>
> Mine is a programme of all-round boycott. . . . Let us be for complete boycott or none at all. I am an extremist and my principle is—all or none.[94]

Opposing Subhas' amendment, Gandhi maintained that he had great regard for Bose, but that the old Mahatma was not out of touch with the young as his opponent had suggested. Gandhi said further that,

We are not yet prepared for parallel government. We ought not to bite more
than we can chew. . . . Hence I ask you to reject summarily the resolution
of Mr Subhas Chandra Bose. . . . I know that he is a great worker in Bengal;
he has shone in many a field; he was the commander-in-chief of our forces
in Bengal. . . . I would like to follow him through and through if I considered
a parallel government a present possibility. . . . But I suggest to you that we
have not that ability today.[95]

Bose's amendment was soundly defeated. Bose argued that if the entire
government structure was not to be boycotted, then Congressmen should
not give up their places in the legislative councils. But Gandhi defeated
him on this point as well and Congress members were ordered to resign
their seats.[96]

As the Congress session was concluding, the new Working Committee
for 1930 was named. Most of the old membership was kept, but Bose and
Srinivasa Iyengar, often allied with Bose, were dropped. Sen Gupta
remained a member. Bose was bitter once more at his Congress colleagues.
Some said that there were 'temperamental' differences, others said that
policy disagreements made it too difficult for the Gandhian high command
to keep Bose on the Congress executive.[97] Whatever the reasons, perhaps
including the fact that Gandhi wanted to put Bose in his place, Bose and
some others made a loud public objection. A few years later in his account
of the period, Bose wrote,

There was a strong feeling in the A.I.C.C. that at least the names of Mr
Iyengar and the writer should be retained. But the Mahatma would not listen.
He said openly that he wanted a committee that would be completely of one
mind and he wanted his list to be passed in its entirety . . . the House did not
want to repudiate him. . . . Altogether the Lahore Congress was a great
victory for the Mahatma. Pandit Jawaharlal Nehru, one of the most prominent spokesmen of the Left Wing, was won over by him and the others were
excluded from the Working Committee. The Mahatma could henceforward
proceed with his own plans without fear of opposition . . . within his cabinet,
and whenever any opposition was raised outside his cabinet, he could
always coerce the public by threatening to retire from the Congress or to fast
unto death.[98]

Bose had been given a lesson. Gandhi would brook only so much
contrariness. The good son, the conciliatory leftist of the younger generation, Jawaharlal Nehru, was rewarded with the Congress presidency at
Lahore. The difficult young man who continued to make trouble again and
again was eliminated from the Working Committee. Gandhi had always
said that there should be homogeneous executive bodies and Bose's views
at this moment were too heterodox for the Mahatma. Dropped from the
Working Committee, Bose objected and sulked, but as usual, continued his

mission to drive India to independence.[99]

The Congress difficulties were not the only ones in which Bose became entangled during the last weeks of 1929. The first serious split in the All-India Trade Union Congress also took place in December just as Bose was assuming the presidency of this organization. Since renewed trade union activity got underway in the late 1920s, the communist, socialist, and nationalist left within the AITUC had been growing. At the Nagpur session of the trade unionists at the beginning of December, the politically-left nationalists defeated the right on a number of issues. These included affiliation with the Pan-Pacific Trade Union Secretariat (which the right maintained was a communist organization), boycott of the Whitley Commission on Indian Labour, and membership of the Girni Kamgar Union. With their defeats on all of these issues, the right-wing members of the AITUC executive committee walked out.[100]

In a statement published on December 6, 1929, Bose appealed for them to return. He said, in part,

> . . . there is a fundamental difference of mentality and outlook between the Right Wing and the Left. . . . I should state most emphatically that it is a mistake to regard a Right Winger as an agent of British Imperialism and a Left Winger as an agent of Moscow. . . . I do not know why the Right Wing suddenly developed a defeatist mentality and withdrew from the Congress. Pandit Jawaharlal Nehru has made it perfectly clear . . . that if the Right Wing had rallied all their supporters they could still have commanded a majority . . . . If they (*i.e., the Right Wing*) believe in democracy they cannot object to the growing importance of the Left Wing in the T.U.C., nor can they grudge the recognition granted to the Girni Kamgar Union. Further, they should take the verdict of the Executive Council . . . on the question of the boycott of the Whitley Commission, in a sporting spirit and abide by the decision of the majority.[101]

Bose's appeal went unanswered and the Right Wing of the AITUC moved to form their own organization, the Indian Trade Union Federation, which later became the National Trade Union Federation. In this situation, Bose, who leaned to the left, tried to mediate the dispute, but failed. Nehru, who was in accord with Bose's views, praised his conciliatory efforts, but neither he nor Bose could bring about a compromise.[102]

Even before the end of 1929, Bose anticipated that he might soon have to leave the battlefield of political work for imprisonment. Bose, Kiran S. Roy, J.M. Das Gupta, and about nine others were convicted under the sedition and unlawful procession charges of August 1929. They were prosecuted under section 124-A of the Indian Penal Code and section 120–B read with section 124–A.[103] In preparation for a term of incarceration, Bose resigned from his seat in the Corporation, writing to Mayor J.M. Sen Gupta of his decision. The nationalist members of the Corporation asked that he not resign, but Bose was convinced that he should do so.[104] He wrote back to the mayor,

> I am profoundly grateful to the Corporation for this resolution, which I construe as a vote of confidence in me. . . . I appreciate this resolution all the more because I am on the point of walking into the prison house along with my comrades. I feel that as I have to serve a term of one year's imprisonment, no purpose will be served by withdrawing my resignation. Rather I shall be doing an injustice to my electorate if I retain my seat while I shall be in jail.[105]

The Indian judge said that it was unfortunate that such 'highly cultured people' should come under the purview of the law, but that since they were creating 'bitter feeling of hostility towards (the) government established by law in British India, they deserved the sentence of one year in prison.[106] Upon appeal to the Calcutta High Court, the sentence was cut to nine months because the defendants had 'no deliberate intention to be "aggressive".'[107]

Just as he was entering prison, Bose wrote to Basanti Devi: 'I was today sentenced to one year's imprisonment. We are all well—we shall joyfully begin our victory march to the Royal temple.'[108] To others he explained that they would have to carry on without him and they should do their best for the movement. His messages went to Congressmen in Bengal, to trade unionists, to the Bengal Volunteers, and to the Corporation. In one of his last speeches before entering prison, he drew upon the Irish case,

> The resolution setting forth complete independence as our ideal has been passed but it will have to be probed as to how far the same will prove useful. As regards its ability, the history of Ireland provides a very pertinent example. The Irish Nationalists not only passed a resolution setting forth independence as their goal but also declared complete independence. Some of them who were instrumental in making that declaration have stated in their memoirs that though only a handful of men supported that declaration yet it was essential at that time because the nation could not be roused unless such an ideal was placed before it. After that the whole national outlook of Ireland underwent a complete change.[109]

Bose found the Irish situation instructive at almost every turn of the Indian struggle.[110] He went on to talk of Indian self-help and the kind of parallel institutions—in city and village—that Indians could create. He did not mention the Easter Rising and the violence employed by Irish nationalists, but left it for some well-informed listeners who read the frequent articles on Ireland in the Indian nationalist press to fill in the blanks.

Gandhi sent a message which read:

My congratulations to Sjt. Subhas Bose and his companions on one year's
rigorous imprisonment for having dared to serve the country. Bengal may
be rent into many divisions and parties. But Bengal's bravery and self-
sacrifice can never wane.[111]

While Bose had to endure the privations of the Alipore Central Jail, and
learn to cope with imprisonment once more, Gandhi and the Congress
were moving to implement the Lahore independence resolution and chart
out a means that would lead the country—sooner or later—to complete
freedom.

II

During the early months of 1930, Gandhi was preparing for a new
campaign with the sanction of the Working Committee, shaping out the
organization's program as he saw fit.

> In the opinion of the Working Committee civil disobedience should be
> initiated and controlled by those who believe in non-violence for the
> purpose of achieving Purna Swaraj as an article of faith and as the Congress
> contains in its organisation not merely such men and women but also those
> who accept non-violence as a policy essential in the existing circumstances
> in the country, the Working Committee welcomes the proposal of Mahatma
> Gandhi and authorises him and those working (with) him who believe in
> non-violence as an article of faith of the extent above indicated, to start civil
> disobedience as and when they desire and in the manner and to the extent
> they decide.[112]

Gandhi was wary of rushing into a national civil disobedience campaign
but this was preferable to the violent acts of impatient youths. He wrote in
the 'Duty of Disloyalty,' that,

> There is danger in civil disobedience only because it is still only a partially
> tried remedy and has always to be tried in an atmosphere surcharged with
> violence. For when tyranny is rampant much rage is generated among the
> victims.[113]

He felt he had to plunge ahead with his 'partially tried remedy' because of
the threat of two kinds of violence.

> . . . I find that the Government's organised violence goes on increasing day
> by day and the group wanting to meet violence with violence is becoming
> correspondingly stronger. Hence, if non-violence has the power to check
> violence or if I am truly non-violent, I must be able to find a non-violent way
> to restrain the double violence which I have mentioned.[114]

Gandhi felt that the government would not be more accommodating to
Congress demands without the pressure that a mass campaign might bring.
As Gandhi was preparing his forces for the Salt March and a nation-wide
Civil Disobedience Movement, Subhas Bose was adjusting to life in the
Alipore Jail.

A contemporary in the Congress of those days, has written of this jail term,

> He was again in a serene atmosphere, mixing with friends, doing service to
> workers, thinking, reading and spending time in meditation in a secluded
> corner conveniently partitioned by him in his cell with a sheet, where he
> used often to pray.[115]

Bose started to keep a diary during this jail term and a few fragments
remain, written in Bengali, during the first half of February 1930. Perhaps
because he had a specified term for this offence, Bose seemed to retain his
good spirits during these first weeks in prison. After an initial refusal, the
superintendent said he would allow the political prisoners to participate in
the school program for the younger political and criminal prisoners. Bose
also plied the charkha in true Gandhian fashion while in the Alipore Jail
and tried to make the officials see the benefits of having all prisoners spin
if they wanted to. So along with discussions, reading, and meditating, Bose
added spinning to his daily regimen.[116]

Since the jail was in Calcutta, it was not difficult for family members
to visit him. During these first weeks both of his parents, an elder sister, and
Sarat Bose's wife Biva came to see him.[117] The prisoners formed their own
communities in the walls. Contacts with the outside were severely
restricted, so even the addition of a new prisoner was cause for celebration
as Bose described.

> At last just in front of the jail, there was high-pitched shouting of 'Bande
> Mataram'. Then it did not take us long to understand that Gananjan Babu
> had really come this time. We also in excitement said, '1,2,3...' and started
> shouting. Big or small nobody was excluded. Noticing our enthusiasm and
> joy a prisoner from the European yard behind asked, 'Are you all going out?'
> The answer sent—no, more are coming in—He said hearing this 'Hurrah!'
> Only the prisoners know what a tremendous delight is caused in the hearts
> of the old political prisoners when some new ones come into the jail.... For
> a long time we asked questions of Gananjan Babu about the outside world.
> And after that in due time we went out for the evening walk.[118] ·

While Subhas Bose was dealing with life in his temporary jail home, Sarat
Bose had to take a more active role in Indian politics to compensate for the
loss of his brother and of other important Bengal Congress workers.

Sarat Bose was already beginning to play a much more active part in the
Calcutta Corporation at the end of 1929. With Subhas Bose in jail, Sarat
Bose, along with Dr B.C. Roy, had to shoulder more of the work of the
BPCC as well.

The split in the Bengal Provincial Congress continued, and festered, as
will be discussed later, but the two principals, Subhas Bose and J.M. Sen
Gupta, were out of action for a good deal of the time. Subhas Bose was in
prison from January to September 1930 and from January to March 1931.

Sen Gupta, who was suffering from high blood pressure and constantly in poor health, left Calcutta in late January 1930 for a sea voyage to Rangoon and Singapore and returned in February. Shortly after his return, still in poor health, he was arrested and taken back to Burma, where he was tried and sentenced to ten days for a seditious speech. He came back to Calcutta on April 3, still suffering from his condition, and was arrested again. He served a prison term in the Alipore Jail from April 12 to September 25. After a month out of bondage, he was arrested again on October 25, tried, convicted, and forced to serve another prison term until January 27, 1931. During part of this last imprisonment, Mrs Nellie Sen Gupta, his politically-active, British wife was also jailed in Delhi.[119] In October 1931 Sen Gupta sailed to England, primarily for health reasons, and when he returned to India on January 20, 1932, he was immediately imprisoned and never left captivity alive, dying in Ranchi, still a prisoner, on July 23, 1933.

While Subhas Bose was incarcerated and Sen Gupta in poor health, tens of thousands of Indians led by Mahatma Gandhi began the Civil Disobedience Movement of 1930. Gandhi chose to violate the regulations on making salt. The government salt monopoly touched every Indian, the poor more than the rich. Gandhi led many Congress satyagrahis in the Dandi March to the sea to make salt. This was a signal to the vast army of Congress men and women throughout the country to open the campaign. Congress members made salt wherever they could, more easily on the sea coast.[120] Bengal Gandhian Satish Das Gupta, president of the Bengal Council of Civil Disobedience, tramped six miles from Calcutta to Mahisbathan at the Salt Lakes and made salt in violation of the law.[121]

The name of Das Gupta's organization (BCCD) differentiated it from the Bengal Provincial Congress Committee which was also carrying out a campaign of civil disobedience in response to the Congress mandate and Gandhi's call. With the president of the BPCC in jail, Dr B.C. Roy took a more important role in the BPCC in 1930. The BCCD was the Sen Gupta-backed organization and had the support of Bengal's rural and urban dedicated Gandhians like Das Gupta and P.C. Ghosh. With members of the Anushilan Party of revolutionaries also involved and Congressmen in quite a few districts who supported Sen Gupta, the BCCD was as proficient as the BPCC in leading a campaign. The civil disobedience campaign also involved boycott of foreign goods, particularly British-made cloth, and the production and selling of Indian goods. Efforts were made to put pressure on merchants dealing in foreign piece goods, and to bother, even harass those who used such goods.[122]

Coupled with the effects of the world-wide depression which were spreading in India during 1930, the campaign led by the BPCC and the

BCCD was most effective in the period following April 1930. The most thorough going boycott and production and distribution of Indian salt and cloth in Bengal was carried out in Midnapore district. A bastion of effective Congress work and organization in 1921–22, and again in 1930–34, Midnapore had a somewhat distinctive population with heavy concentrations of Mahisyas, Hindu peasants, which produced many able leaders, foremost of whom was B.N. Sasmal. The Congress organization in Midnapore was committed to non-violent mass activity, but many of the peasant members wanted to utilize the movement to redress local grievances, including some against the upper strata of their society.[123]

The BPCC was able to carry out picketing and valuable boycott propaganda in Calcutta and in many of the district towns of Bengal. Members of the Jugantar Party and the BV did join this activity. The government noted that, 'The Bengal terrorists took an active part in the civil disobedience movement in 1930 and many of them were imprisoned for picketing.'[124] But the in-fighting between the two major Congress factions undoubtedly weakened the overall Congress effort in Bengal and the anger that Sen Gupta fostered at what Subhas Bose called the 'indiscipline and spirit of revolt', is evident in Bose's statement about the year's developments made when he was a free man in November.[125]

As Gandhi's nation-wide campaign continued, more of the Congress leadership was arrested. A few weeks after the Salt March had been triumphantly completed, Gandhi, following most of his lieutenants, was arrested and held for the remainder of the year. Approximately 60,000 were jailed during 1930, leaving many thousands outside to continue with nationalist work.[126] Sarat Bose continued his work in the Bengal Congress and the Calcutta Corporation.

Although he was never the mayor of Calcutta, Sarat Bose was indisputably one of the most active and constructive Congress workers in the Corporation. Under the resolutions of the Lahore Congress, Congressmen had to resign from provincial legislative councils, but resignations from local bodies such as municipalities were optional. A war was going on in the Bengal Congress, but both sides agreed that the Congress should continue to work in the Corporation where it could achieve an elected majority and have considerable power. And opposed though he might be to Sen Gupta for control of the BPCC, Sarat Bose was one of the most eloquent in defending Sén Gupta against charges of sedition leveled against him for a speech Sen Gupta had made in Rangoon.[127] If Sen Gupta is guilty of sedition, then we all are, Bose declared.[128] In opposing the repressive acts of the government, Congressmen stood together.

In April 1930, elections were held for the five aldermen to sit as members of the Corporation. Of the thirty-three candidates, Dr B.C. Roy received fifty-six votes, Sarat Bose fifty-two, Upendra Chandra Das Gupta forty-one, and Bimal Chandra Ghosh and J.M. Sen Gupta thirty-four each. For the first time, all the aldermen were Hindus. With Sarat Bose in the chair, the election for mayor was held and Sen Gupta was re-elected, though he was in prison, and Santosh Kumar Basu, of the Bose-wing of the Congress, was elected deputy mayor.[129] The Congress had a majority without the support of Muslim councillors and considerable bitterness was expressed by some Muslim members at the lack of a Muslim alderman or deputy mayor. Fazlul Huq spoke most passionately against the exclusion of the Muslims. After congratulating Sen Gupta and Santosh Basu, he said,

> ... at the same time I will not withhold from the House my sense of regret that the Congress Party in the Corporation, which happens today to be in the majority, have not had the generosity to recognize the spirit in which the late Mr C.R. Das used to work with the Mahomedan community, both in the Corporation and in other fields of political activities in the country. I will say that the action of the Corporation in this particular matter, in opposing the election of a Mahomedan Deputy Mayor, spells a little of selfishness which I cannot but condemn at a period of political activity in this country.[130]

Huq argued that under Das, it had been agreed that two of the five aldermen and either the mayor or deputy mayor would be a Muslim. He said,

> I fully admit that the late C.R. Das not only made these proposals but, at a time when his influence was supreme in this country, when he could have made his will felt in any form he liked, he kept strictly not only to the spirit but to the letter of the pact in order to bring Mahomedans into the field of political activity from which they had hitherto been absent.[131]

Huq then traced the pacts made during subsequent elections. He said that only when the Congress got an absolute majority in 1930 did they go back on their argument. It appeared that the election of Muslim aldermen or at least one alderman and the deputy mayor from the Muslim community got caught up in the fight between Congress factions. Some Muslim councillors voted for Sen Gupta in the aldermanic race, and some did not, irritating both sides. Then the dominant Congress, with Sen Gupta behind bars, decided that they had to have a Hindu Congressman as deputy mayor to carry out their program in the Corporation, for the deputy mayor would be acting mayor for the foreseeable future.[132]

Huq concluded his speech with a message to the Congress from a Muslim who had once been a Congressman and was generally sympathetic to them,

> It pains us that they are not strictly following the spirit in which the late Mr C.R. Das used to work. . . . We have to work with those who are out to fight for the Motherland. I also want Swaraj. I am a Swarajist. I have been in the

Congress for 20 years. . . . I have occupied all positions of honour in the Congress short of being President. . . . We do not only want to carry on the fight for the Motherland but we also want to be in a position to carry our community with us. . . . I want that our countrymen who claim, as members of the Congress, to be soldiers in the fight for freedom should be free from communalism and from narrow party spirit so that they may all unite in the fight for India's freedom and set an example before those who have the destiny of India in their hands.[133]

Many Congressmen rose to answer Huq, some angrily, some more judiciously. Sarat Bose closed the meeting by pointing out to Huq that the BPCC had selected a Muslim, Mr K. Nooruddin, as an aldermanic candidate, but that he was too late in submitting his nomination paper.[134] When Sarat Bose was re-elected as an alderman, the *Calcutta Municipal Gazette* wrote that,

Mr Sarat Chandra Bose, perhaps the most vivid personality in the Corporation, stands in the forefront by his fearless espousal of the people's cause and eloquent vindication of the people's rights.[135]

In the struggles ahead within the Congress camp, between Hindus and Muslims, and with the Raj, he would not only need his fearless eloquence, but he would also need some tact and ability to work out compromises.

In the following month, members of the various standing committees of the Corporation were chosen and Sarat Bose became deputy chairman of the Estates and General Purposes Standing Committee, the work of which touched many areas of Calcutta life. When the appointments to all these committees were announced, the Muslim councillors found that they had been given fewer places than they felt they deserved. Almost all the Muslim councillors walked out and began holding protest meetings and issuing heated statements to the press. Sarat Bose and former deputy mayor M.A. Razzak played key roles in working out a compromise which allowed the Muslim councillors to return and work together with the Congress.[136] In the debate over this matter, Sarat Bose spoke for the Congress, claiming that the Congress was trying to satisfy all communities in the city and trying to be:

. . . fair and reasonable under the circumstances. . . . I recognize that there are certain other matters . . . which have to be approached in a spirit of entire fairness because the Congress Party more than anybody else recognises the fact that when it is a question of recognising the religious susceptibilities of any party, Hindu, Mahomedan, Christian or Parsi, the utmost courtesy should be observed regarding the religious susceptibilities of any party.[137]

Since he was a devoutly religious person himself, as well as a man of wide vision, Sarat Bose was keen to see that the religious rights of others were protected. Working out a rapprochement with the Muslim leaders on one issue or another became one of the themes of his political career. Huq's speech and the subsequent controversy over the standing committees are small signs of the gap between the predominantly Hindu Congress leadership and the Muslim leaders which had grown in Bengal since the death of Das.

While these controversies were being worked out along peaceful and more-or-less constitutional procedures, some other political workers were moving in a very different direction. Late in the evening of April 18, 1930, not quite on the anniversary of the Easter Rising in Dublin, a large band of revolutionaries led by Surja Sen (called 'Masterda'), with Ananta Singh and Ganesh Ghosh as his main lieutenants, attacked the Chittagong Armoury. Calling themselves the Bengal branch of the Indian Republican Army, they aimed to destroy the British hold on the district and proclaim an independent republic under President Surja Sen. Sen's armed followers numbered more than one hundred. They took the district establishment by surprise, and had some initial successes, seizing many arms and supplies at the armoury, but, unfortunately for them, they overlooked the ammunition for these arms. They did create havoc in the local administration, but a number of mistakes allowed the Bengal administration and military to bring in reinforcements quickly, and confront a large band of the revolutionaries on Jalalabad Hill about two days later. The remaining band was overmatched and the next morning twelve of the raiders were found dead on the hillside. The police and military tracked down the rest, though some were able to hide out in Chittagong district and nearby for almost three years. They were not betrayed to the police by the overwhelmingly Muslim population of the area. Surja Sen was one of the last captured, in February 1933, and he was tried, convicted, and executed a few months later.[138]

An intelligence summary for this period describes the impact of the raid,

> The news of the Chittagong armoury raids was received by revolutionaries all over the province with amazement. Some could not believe that such a daring coup was the work of Bengali terrorists. When the truth was known the effect was electric, and from that moment the outlook of the Bengal terrorists changed. The younger members of all parties, whose heads were already crammed with ideas of driving the British out of India by force of arms, but whose hands had been restrained by their leaders from committing even an isolated murder, clamoured for a chance to emulate the Chittagong terrorists. Their leaders could no longer hope, nor did they wish to keep them back.... Recruits poured into the various groups in a steady stream, and the romantic appeal of the raid attracted into the fold of the terrorist party women and young girls, who from this time onwards are found assisting the terrorists as housekeepers, messengers, custodians of arms and sometimes

as comrades.[139]

Although these intelligence summaries invariably exaggerate the threat and number of the revolutionaries, the Chittagong raid was the signal for a considerable number of violent acts in the following years, particularly aimed at officials of the Raj.

Surja Sen was a member of the Bengal Provincial Congress Committee and had been among the Congress volunteers at the 1928 Calcutta Congress. Many of those in the Chittagong group, the BV, Jugantar, and Anushilan Samity, who were involved in the actions of 1930 and succeeding years were well known to the Boses. Sarat Bose became further implicated with the Chittagong group when he went to court to defend Ananta Singh and several others. Some absconders from Chittagong are said to have contacted Sarat Bose and to have received money, and a hiding place, from him. Writing many years later, Ananta Singh has claimed that Sarat Bose even carried a suitcase with a bomb in it when he came to see him in prison. Singh says that he was given the option of blasting his way out of confinement if he wished. The story of the prison visit with a bomb seems most unlikely. But Sarat Bose did go out of his way to defend some of them and it is likely that he gave them money.[140] Some of this came to the attention of the intelligence branch, and was added to his growing file. Publicly they decried violent acts, but the Boses defended imprisoned revolutionaries. They always opposed their execution and insisted that no one should be held without charges, a trial, and conviction.

To the European community and their publications like the *Statesman* of Calcutta, there was scarcely a difference between the activities of a Gandhi, a Sarat Bose, and a Chittagong raider. The *Statesman* wrote on August 28, 1930,

> Quite bluntly we say that we are unable to make the distinction that we are asked to make between Congress activities and revolutionary crime. Mr Gandhi may preach non-violence with fervour, but he is preaching it to young men of hot blood who believe that they know a shorter cut to that ending of the present authority in India which is Mr Gandhi's avowed intention. When a body like the Congress organizes itself with 'war councils', provides itself with a 'commander-in-chief' and recruits 'volunteers' it demands a faith of which we are incapable to believe that these grandiose titles are concerned solely with the making of salt or the refusal to wear Manchester cloth. Our capacity . . . is further strained when we read in the report of the trial of the Chittagong raiders the following passage: Mr Sarat C. Bose arrived today and informed the Tribunal that he would represent Ananta Singh and Lalmohan Sen.
>
> Not less than two months ago Mr Bose announced his withdrawal from

practice at the Bar in order that he might devote the whole of his energies to Congress activities. Does the defence of those charged with terrorist outrages at Chittagong or elsewhere fall within that category? ... Congress cannot have it both ways. Either it denounces the use of the bomb and the revolver and lends its strength to the pursuit of those who employ them or ... public opinion will lump the terrorists, who find their opportunity in the atmosphere engendered by Congress with the Congressmen.[141]

There is no doubt that Gandhi and the Congress organization in Bengal as well as throughout India used the language and terms of the military. Gandhi also wrote in this period about the need for the spirit of the Kshatriya,

Real freedom is impossible without the spirit of a true Kshatriya. Therefore, the unique quality of a Kshatriya is considered to be his determination never to shrink from a battle. For this reason we too, in everything we do, must never run away from the battlefield.[142]

Gandhi insisted that the *Bhagavad Gita* was about a conflict within the human soul and not about violent actions out in the world. However, this was not a widely accepted view of the *Gita* and his words could be taken in another spirit by the young warriors of India's freedom struggle.[143]

Shortly after the Chittagong rising and Gandhi's Salt March, the prisons became ever more crowded with a variety of prisoners. Non-violent salt-makers and actual and potential revolutionaries, seditious speakers as well as ordinary criminals, were jostled together as the jails bulged beyond stated capacities. Frequently the warders did not have infinite patience with the organized and demanding political prisoners, who were more educated and articulate in demanding their rights. On April 22, feeling there was some provocation, guards in the Alipore Jail began beating accused prisoners in the Mechuabazar Bomb Case with the butt-ends of rifles and lathis. More than a dozen were injured. Some of the special class prisoners including Subhas Bose and J.M. Sen Gupta began shouting 'Bande Mataram' and yelled that the assault must stop. They, in turn, became the object of the armed assaulters,

After dealing summarily with the Mechuabazar prisoners, the Superintendent and the whole force came back to the Special Yard. And at once the same brutalities were repeated on them. Sj. Subhas Chandra Bose protested, Sj. Sen-Gupta also protested. But the Superintendent cried out, 'I care a damn if force is used on you. You have to be dragged to your cells.' Immediately the whole force fell upon them, using fisticuffs, *lathis* and batons. Sj. Sen-Gupta was roughly handled and dragged to his cell. But the force used on Sj. Subhas Bose was much too brutal, he fell down the steps and became unconscious. Several ... prisoners carried him upstairs. ... At about one in the afternoon Sj. Bose recovered consciousness. He has got a

temperature and pain on the head and all over the body.[144]
Satya Bakshi and others who carried Bose to his cell asked that a doctor be
brought, but they were simply locked away in their cells. Outside, rumors
spread that Bose and Sen Gupta had been killed within the prison. A large
crowd gathered and demanded news of their leaders.[145]

The prison officials issued a statement saying that they were trying to
get recalcitrant prisoners to their cells, but there was resistance.

> During the melee Mr Subhas Chandra Bose fell to the ground, while several
> bomb case prisoners received minor injuries. Mr J.M. Sen-Gupta and the
> other special class prisoners were unhurt.[146]

Bose was not seriously hurt and recovered. Protests were voiced in the
Corporation and in the Bengal Legislative Council. But these concerns
were soon drowned in much larger ones about the violence—both
communal and revolutionary—that erupted in different parts of Bengal as
the Civil Disobedience Movement continued.

There was a serious communal riot in Dacca, the second city of Bengal,
in early May. Feeling there was provocation from non-violent satyagrahis,
Muslims in Dacca town and the surrounding mofussil, set upon Hindu
shops and homes. The outbreak was the result of complex social,
economic, and political grievances by the poorer Muslims of the community, but in the end the middle-class citizens of both communities felt
threatened. Finally, after a few days, the police brought order, but the
Hindu People's Association claimed that the police favored the Muslims
and had been very slow to react to the violence. The riots evinced another
kind of quietly growing tension between the two major, and fairly evenly
balanced communities. If the political leaders could not learn to work together, then such riots would build upon the leaders' failures.[147]

After the Chittagong Armoury Raid, members of the BV, the revolutionary group most closely in touch with Subhas Bose, also began a series
of violent actions to assassinate key officials. They wanted to undermine
the willingness of the whole administration corps to remain and rule India.
Members of the group struck in Dacca on August 29, 1930, assassinating
Lowman, the inspector-general of police, and wounding Hodson, the
superintendent of police in Dacca. An even more daring raid was carried
out by kamikaze revolutionaries who invaded the headquarters of Bengal
administration, the Writers' Building in downtown Calcutta on December
8, and murdered Mr Simpson, inspector-general of prisons for Bengal.[148]

Of course, the Government of Bengal did not sit idly by and wait for its
officers to be picked off by revolutionary marksmen. The Bengal Criminal
Law Amendment Act of 1925 had expired in March 1930, but after the
Chittagong raid, the extraordinary powers of arrest and detention were

immediately conferred by ordinance. In July, a five-year Bengal Act VI of 1930 extending these special powers was passed by the Bengal Legislative Council which no longer included the forty or so Swarajist members who had resigned. With the ordinance and then with the act, the police began to act swiftly to round up all the known and important leaders and operatives in the various revolutionary parties. Alongside the clash between the civil disobedience satyagrahis and the police, was another between the revolutionaries and the police, which was to go on for several years.[149]

In commenting on the Chittagong affair, Gandhi said,

> Chittagong seems to be a deliberate planning. . . . I can only appeal to those who believe in violence not to disturb the free flow of the non-violent demonstration. . . . Violence is bound to impede the progress towards independence. . . . Meanwhile satyagrahis must continue their activity with redoubled vigour. We must deal with the double-edged violence ranged against us. For me popular violence is as much an obstruction in our path as the Government violence. . . . Indeed I can combat the Government violence more successfully than the popular . . . in combating the latter, I should not have the same support as in the former.[150]

Gandhi certainly did not know whether such outbreaks of violence had popular support. He believed that they weakened his, the Congress', movement for swaraj. However much Gandhi opposed violence, it can be argued that a Raj threatened day-by-day with murder of its officials and hard put to keep law-and-order would be more willing to come to the conference table with a spokesman for non-violence.[151]

Subhas Bose continued his regimen within the Alipore Jail. An undated manuscript book marked 'Alipore Central Jail' may date from this prison term, though it is hard to specify from internal evidence. It contains the plan for a book, but only a few paragraphs entitled, 'The Meaning of Life' appear in the notebook. He wrote, in part,

> Life means the unfolding of the self. It therefore implies expansion and growth . . . life demands change. . . . Life is dynamic. It is a play of energy. It is a manifestation of that Supreme Power—call it by what name you will—which pervades the universe—Life means activity—ceaseless activity. . . . Life means self-fulfilment—the realisation of that which is latent in us. What is unfolded or achieved is not to be conserved for a selfish purpose—but is to be given up for the benefit of the world and for the service of humanity. By giving, we enrich ourselves and the more we give, the more do we thrive and profit . . . we must give our all and give with a reckless abandon.[152]

In further paragraphs, Bose goes on to link necessary suffering with his ceaseless activity. Bringing in the teachings of Swami Vivekananda and C.R. Das, his chosen gurus, he goes on,

To give oneself completely to the service of others is to the individual a source of joy unspeakable. There is no higher form of worship than unselfish service . . . an idea . . . imparts a meaning to life . . . when one is thoroughly inspired with an idea . . . and has become one with it—then only does life become rich and full.[153]

If these words were written in 1930 or 1931 when he was in the Alipore Jail, they show consistency with his teenage letters to his mother when he discovered Sri Ramakrishna and Swami Vivekananda and with his later studies in philosophy, particularly at Scottish Churches College. He was blending the inspiration for action and the philosophy of Vivekananda with hints of Hegel and Bergson, along with his powerful Bengali emotionalism.

Outside, Sarat Bose had voluntarily given up his practice at the Calcutta High Court bar for three months. He stated, on July 3, 1930:

We are just now passing through a non-violent revolution. Already the hammer of repression has fallen heavy on us. The leaders of the nation and thousands of devoted workers in the cause of the country's freedom have found themselves behind prison bars. . . . It is time (for) our people (to) prepare themselves for the last spurt. I do sincerely and firmly believe that the next few months will very largely determine the political future of India. . . . The next few months will demand from us more vigorous initiative. . . . We enter our last fight. Let the grace of God attend our hosts and give us victory.

During the past few weeks, I have often felt that active professional work in the courts seriously interferes with one's duties as a humble worker in the cause of the country's freedom. I have felt that in times like these, normal occupation ought to be suspended. . . . My conscience and the God of my destiny have dictated to me to suspend my legal practice and place my humble services whole time to the sacred cause of my country and my country's freedom. The call has come. It is irresistible. I bow before it.[154]

Sarat Bose began touring some of the districts and meeting Congress workers and also local legal practitioners, in some cases persuading the latter to suspend their practises.

Sarat Bose became the temporary front man of the Bose group. He frequently exchanged sharp words with the editors of Sen Gupta's paper, *Advance*, which accused him of trying to hound Sen Gupta out of public life in order to replace him himself. Sarat Bose was a strong and accomplished person with solid moorings in his personal, religious, professional, and political life. He did not seek office and was not ambitious to climb up the political ladder. Answering *Advance*, Sarat Bose indicated that he had been a lieutenant of C.R. Das, of Sen Gupta, and remained a lieutenant, not seeking to put himself in Sen Gupta's place. He said that he remained a lieutenant of the president of the BPCC, and of the leader of the Congress in the Corporation, Dr B.C. Roy. Concluding, he said, 'I have begun my political life as a lieutenant and nothing will please me more than to end my life as a lieutenant.'[155] Only when Subhas Bose was in Alipore Jail or otherwise unavailable did Sarat work full-time in nationalist politics.

Subhas Bose also served as a lieutenant to Sen Gupta in the Bengal Legislative Council, 1927 to 1929, but he, in contrast to his elder brother Sarat, did not mind seeking high office. Therefore, when Sen Gupta's fifth term as mayor expired after three months (as he was imprisoned) and a new mayor had to be chosen, even though he remained imprisoned himself, Subhas Bose had his party nominate him. He claimed that Sen Gupta's men and Sen Gupta had gone back on an agreement to have Dr B.C. Roy elected the next mayor and instead were trying to put forth Sen Gupta again. Some months later, Bose insisted that he was not eager for office and that he would have been happier if Dr Roy could serve. But Dr Roy was imprisoned and Bose's group did not feel that they could elect him. They did not have the needed support to elect Subhas Bose. The election process proved to be a nasty battle between the two main Congress factions while the principals remained together in the Alipore Jail. Several of the election meetings of the Corporation members had to be postponed when crowds invaded their chambers, but finally, on August 22, Bose was elected over a Muslim candidate.[156]

On September 23, Subhas Bose was released from the prison and the following day took the oath as mayor of Calcutta. The *Calcutta Municipal Gazette*, always friendly to Bose, wrote, 'The crown of thorns on his brow is replaced by the laurels of loving approbation.' He was garlanded and, 'His table was strewn with floral bouquets.'[157] In his inaugural speech, Bose recalled the objectives that C.R. Das had listed in 1924, of providing better schools, housing, roads, medical care, drainage, lighting, and paying particular attention to the poor. He said that no interests, no section of the population would suffer while the Congress was in power. He insisted he would be fair and impartial and deal with the concerns of the Muslims as he had tried to in 1924 when he had been chief executive officer of the Corporation. He mentioned that Das' program was 'in spiritual garb . . . in essence what Modern Europe would regard as Socialism.'[158]

> . . . I would say that we have here in this policy and programme a synthesis of what Modern Europe calls Socialism and Fascism. We have here the justice, the equality, the love, which is the basis of Socialism, and combined with that we have the efficiency and the discipline of Fascism as it stands in Europe today.[159]

The specifics of the program were familiar. Das had put them forth, so had Sen Gupta, and now Subhas Bose. Bose, perhaps more interested in European experiments, tried to relate the program for the reconstruction of Calcutta and of India to these European experiments. The socialism he referred to was operating in municipalities such as Vienna and in Soviet Russia. Of fascism, he was certainly referring to Mussolini's Italy. While in the Alipore Jail in 1930, Bose read at least two books on European politics: Francesco Nitti's *Bolshevism, Fascism and Democracy,* published in English in 1927, and Ivanoe Bonomi's *From Socialism to Fascism,* published in London in 1924. Both were former prime ministers of Italy and both were critical of fascism. Nitti, who had been Liberal prime minister in 1919, argued that fascism was the 'negation of freedom and democracy' which was making only a temporary appearance in a decadent Europe. He thought it came in by violent means, glorified the state at the expense of every positive civic virtue, and in the long run was doomed.[160] Bonomi was also an opponent of fascism at this time, but he could see why fascism had succeeded in Italy. Bonomi wrote,

> Now order was restored, industrial strife was less acute, and the principles of authority and obedience, which democrats in the years of confusion had vainly insisted were the more necessary the more democracy spread in a nation and the more the community superseded the individual, were honoured again. No one could deny that progress had been made. . . . Patriotic sentiment prevailed once more . . . the sacramental doctrine of the Nation, which Fascism has made a reality, aims at restoring the moral forces of authority, discipline, order and religion. . . .[161]

Although Bonomi, a Social Democrat, also made the case against fascism, he did not do so as passionately as Nitti and it is possible to read Bonomi and come away believing that fascism had a positive side. Bose thought that there was some resonance between the youth movement in several European countries and that just awakening in India.

His mayoral speech is—to my knowledge—the first positive mention of some features of fascism and the new synthesis which India might make of elements of socialism and fascism. Neglecting to mention any negative features, the new Indian synthesis became a familiar part of Bose's program for India in the following years.

When he came to implement his beliefs as the mayor, he was limited by the possibilities of a municipal government under a superior Government of Bengal, by the small and embattled majority that the Congress had in the Corporation, and by the fact that he was also Bengal Congress president and could not focus only on the Corporation's affairs. He himself noted late in 1930, that in 1924 he could work full-time for the Corporation, but now he could not. Nonetheless, he did throw himself into the ceremonial and practical activities of the Calcutta municipality.[162] Sarat Bose had returned to his legal practice, but was spending at least half his time on public endeavors and remained one of the most industrious and best-informed members of the Corporation on the practical details. He made himself knowledgeable about education, hospitals, the transport system, the power supply, and garbage collection. In almost every debate on these matters, he was involved, particularly in trying to see that the Corporation spent its funds wisely and hired appropriate personnel for its requirements.

Both Subhas and Sarat Bose were also determined that they would try to get the best man they could for any Corporation position, even European. In November, Sarat Bose pressed the case to hire Dr Walter Crous, a German, as lighting superintendent of the Corporation because he felt that he was the best available man.[163]

Subhas Bose learned the details of Calcutta's transport system and though he would have preferred that the CTC (Calcutta Transportation Company), a British-owned company, be replaced by an Indian one, he saw that this would not be possible for some years.[164]

In line with his concern for the development of the Indian economy—to go along with Indian self-government—he started, along with some other Calcutta nationalists, the Bengal Swadeshi League in which an effort was made to bring together businessmen, economists, and national workers to maximize swadeshi purchases.[165] Part of the work of the League was the gathering of statistics of the kind that Bose and Harish Sinha had put together in their small publication, *Boycott of British Goods*. Another voice, still with the Boses at this point, was that of the successful businessman and Congressman, Nalini Sarker. He presented plans for a municipal banking corporation that would provide capital for Indian entrepreneurs. He also wanted the Corporation to spend more on education and sanitation. He saw the possibility for many municipal enterprises such as food shops, pharmaceutical works, and transport and lighting systems. Sarker believed—and the Boses were with him in this—that civic consciousness had to be further awakened and the domain of Corporation activity widened to provide more fully for citizens' needs.[166]

While he was mayor, Subhas Bose said he wanted to 'tone up' the administration. Noting that several departments turned in their reports months and even years late, Subhas Bose demanded that they be prepared on time. Following the Congress practice of past years, he continued to bring nationalists, some of them with revolutionary connections, into Corporation jobs. The Government of Bengal and critical Indians have insisted that the Boses were as bad or worse in bringing inappropriate and corrupt people into the Corporation.[167]

In 1930 and early 1931, however, it does appear that Subhas Bose brought an energy and positive spirit to the Corporation. As mayor he was also a ceremonial figure. On October 25, *Liberty* gave a big party for councillors, diplomats, and businessmen at which Sarat Bose, as managing director, was host. A few weeks later, Subhas Bose hosted a large gathering for H.N. Brailsford, British journalist and active member of the Independent Labour Party and sympathizer with India's aspirations.[168]

An even more striking occasion on which the British and Indian establishment came together and Subhas Bose was put into the limelight was the Scottish Churches College Centenary on December 12, 1930. The principal, Dr Urquhart, introduced Bose as, 'One of the most famous students of the College. . . . He had a brilliant career here and was the recipient of the Hawkins Gold Medal.'[169] As Bose rose to read the address from former students, he and the British and Indian officials in the audience were treated to cheers of 'Bande Mataram'. The address, which Bose and others composed and which was signed by many old boys, was an effort to call attention both to India's great heritage and the vital Western education which they had received at the college. He said in part,

> Twenty-two centuries have gone by since Asoka, the greatest missionary-monarch known to History, sent forth to the Western world India's inspiring message of *Dharma*. In the days that followed, the flow of ideas changed channel. Then, when missionaries of an Oriental Religion brought from the West, along with the message of Christ, the message of Intellectual Emancipation, an Era of Renaissance dawned on our ancient land, a spirit of enquiry permeated our intellect and vitalised our minds. . . . Those who assisted in the Awakening deserve our grateful thanks. We are children of that Revolution in the realm of Thought . . . we are enabled now to see, feel and know, with increasing ease and success, not merely the mysteries of Nature but also the deep recesses of our own minds and above all to appreciate more fully our own cultural heritage . . . we all feel . . . the definite impress given to our minds by our education in this College. . . . In congratulating it on such an occasion, we congratulate ourselves; for, we cannot forget that we 'were' this College and the College 'is' us. We pray that the second century of its career be brighter even than the first.[170]

The effort to show thanks and yet pride in 'Oriental' achievements was brewed into a skillful Indian blend.

Subhas Bose was also making efforts to mobilize the publics to whom he had been appealing for some years: students, workers, women, professionals, and businessmen, ordinary Hindus and Muslims of Bengal who were potential recruits to the Congress. The civil disobedience agitation had quieted down in the second half of 1930 and Gandhi was not released from prison until January 1931. Subhas Bose made his tours and tried to keep boycott and Swadeshi work alive in his home province.

Although the goal of independence and the necessity for boycott and Swadeshi were mentioned to every audience, Bose tailored his remarks to fit the different audiences he encountered. The workers had been particularly hard hit by the spreading depression and were confronted by efforts at retrenchment, wage cuts, and all kinds of cost-cutting by employers. It was difficult for them, in such harsh economic circumstances, to rally round the goal of independence when they did not know if they would have a job the following day. Bose, like other important political figures, was the president of several unions including the Budge Budge Oil and Petrol Workers' Union and, during 1930-31, of the AITUC. He continued to tell the workers to build stronger unions, join the Congress, and adjust to its economic policies. Within a few days in November and December, he spoke to a large gathering of oil and petrol workers at Budge Budge who were joined by many jute workers. The day before he had spoken in Oriya to the Calcutta Shramik Mandal in Burrabazar. The president of this organization as well, Bose said that if they were not to be done in by the forces of the deep recession and those of their employers, they must build a powerful union. At both rallies, the workers heartily cheered his words, but Bose did not have the time to help them in this union-building or any sage answers to the dilemmas posed by the depression. A day later he spoke in Hindustani to the members of the Calcutta Corporation Jamadar, Peon and Menial Employees' Association, who presented him with a warm tribute for the aid and sympathy they said he had given them.[171] At the same time, he courted Indian merchants and industrialists for the Congress cause. This was the Congress all-class approach.[172]

In Calcutta and in the outlying districts of Bengal, he also tried to persuade Indian merchants who dealt in foreign piece goods to halt or curtail this trade. He was also concerned with the growing influx of Japanese goods.

When he was touring the districts, he always addressed the women of the towns. For example, in his tour of Nadia district in the second week of December, he addressed several women's audiences, telling one that,

> . . . women had not only duties to their family, but they had also a greater duty to their country. When the gods found their silver almost vanquished in their fight with the demons, they invoked the help of 'sakti' in the form of mother. The country was in a sad plight, therefore the country looked up to the mothers to come forward and inspire the whole nation.[173]

He urged them to boycott foreign cloth and to carry on propaganda among other women. He also said that they should try to form a permanent Mahila Samity for concerted action.

Another favorite audience that he sought out was that of youths and students. In late 1929, the All-Bengal Students' Association (ABSA) split and the Bose-cum-Jugantar forces formed the Bengal Provincial Students' Association (BPSA). The Sen Gupta-cum-Anushilan forces remained in the ABSA, which adhered, sometimes unwillingly, more to the Gandhian line in Congress policy. There were occasional angry, brawling scenes at student conferences when one side or another disrupted the other's meeting. Bose was accused from the time of the split—by the other party— of exploiting the student movement and he vehemently replied that he was the person most responsible for building up the students' movement and he labeled his attackers an ungrateful lot.[174]

Motilal Nehru, in poor health, visited Calcutta first in January and then in September 1930, and a brief patchwork compromise between the feuding factions was worked out in December 1930. But this broke down early in the following year and the debilitating divisiveness continued to bedevil Bengal, much to the chagrin and distaste of Gandhi, Jawaharlal Nehru, and others in the Congress high command. Subhas Bose was outside the inner circle of top Congress leaders and Sen Gupta from late 1929 to 1932 was in the Working Committee and obviously more in tune with Gandhi than was Bose.[175]

Subhas Bose's district tours and mayoral work were interrupted on December 8 when a daring action by three young members of the BV woke up all of Calcutta. Binoy Bose, the assassin of Lowman a few months earlier, together with Dinesh Gupta and Badal Gupta, walked into the Writers' Building in Dalhousie Square, headquarters of the Bengal administration, made their way to the office of Mr Simpson, the inspector-general of prisons, and shot him dead. They soon paid with their own lives for this attack.[176]

At the Corporation meeting a few days later, a resolution was passed condemning the assassination as a 'dastardly outrage'. Subhas Bose gave his perspective, which many other nationalists in Bengal shared. He said, in part,

> I sincerely deplore the tragic incidents of Monday last . . . because I feel that they are a confession of the temporary failure of the Congress programme and also the temporary failure of the Congress leaders to influence cent percent of the younger generation in the country . . . it will not do simply to brand as 'misguided' the youths who are responsible for these incidents. The fact stares us in the face that India today wants freedom very soon. The fact also stares us in the face that there are people in this country, whatever their number may be, who want freedom not merely by following the Congress programme, but if need be they want freedom at any price and by any means.[177]

He then placed the other major share of blame on the repressive actions of the government in restricting meetings, processions, the press, etc., which did not allow the Congress to work in an open non-violent way and drove some nationalists underground and to acts of terror. He said that he and other Congressmen would do their best to reach the younger generation and keep them to the path of non-violence, but this depended on the policies of the government and on the achievement of results. He implied that a lack of progress towards freedom would lead to more violent acts.[178]

Bose's district tours continued into early the following year. Trying to visit Maldah in January, he found that he had been banned. When he pushed ahead with his effort to visit the area, he was arrested, tried, and sentenced to seven days' imprisonment.[179] He had hardly been released, when he learned that the police had banned a Congress procession planned for their 'independence day', January 26, 1931. Bose was determined to lead the procession from the Corporation to the nearby Maidan at the head of hundreds of Congress workers. A game of cat-and-mouse with the police ensued, with the police eager to arrest him before he could bring out the procession.[180] K.P. Chattopadhyay, education officer of the Corporation, described what followed in his statement to the *Calcutta Municipal Gazette*,

> I was with the Mayor, all the time, on his left, until I was struck down. As we crossed Chowringhee, a body of mounted policemen charged into us scattering the people in our rear and isolating the Mayor and a few of us from the main body of the processionists. The mounted men then rode at us, especially the Mayor, hitting us with the short 'lathis' in their hand. The Mayor was attacked on both sides, and I noted him protecting his head with his up-raised right arm, as best as he could. I shouted out to his assailants: 'You have no right to beat Subhas Chandra Bose. You can arrest him, but you have no right to beat him.' I then tried to protect the Mayor's head by holding the pole of the banner in my hand over him. . . . On this one of these men rode at me and struck twice at my unprotected head. As I was then blinded by the blood that poured down my face. . . I was thrown down by the impact of the horse. . . . None of the men who were beating the Mayor and myself were Indians.[181]

After being beaten, at least partly in revenge for having fooled the police in successfully bringing the procession out into the main road, Bose was arrested and taken to Lal Bazar. He was kept incommunicado until the following day and given no food or medical treatment. Bruised and with his arm in a sling, he was produced before Mr T.J. Roxburgh, chief presidency magistrate, Calcutta, the following afternoon, 'on charges of being member of an unlawful assembly, rioting and endangering public safety.'[182] Bose declined to take part in the proceedings, merely condemning the conditions at the Lal Bazar police station as 'a disgrace to a decent Government.' Roxburgh convicted the mayor of the charges and sentenced him to six months' rigorous imprisonment.[183]

Gandhi was released from prison in mid-January, and cabled the *Daily Herald* in London on January 30 about the government's excesses:

> Meetings in Calcutta were prohibited contrary expectation and forcibly dispersed. Mayor Calcutta Subhas Chandra Bose belaboured then arrested and sentenced six months rigorous imprisonment.[184]

While Bose was shut away in the Alipore Jail yet again, Gandhi was moving towards some kind of rapprochement with the government. He asked the viceroy, Lord Irwin, for an interview, and meetings between the two began on February 17, which culminated in the Gandhi-Irwin Pact announced on March 5, 1931. According to this agreement, the Civil Disobedience Movement was called off by the Congress which accepted the government's invitation to participate 'in the future discussions that are to take place on the scheme of constitutional reform.'[185] The government also agreed to compensate some parties for injuries suffered by them during the Civil Disobedience Movement and subsequent repression.

Many Congressmen were extremely unhappy with the terms of the pact which seemed to indicate that the Congress was to join discussions about constitutional advances aiming for a federal system in which the British would continue to control essential matters such as defense, external affairs, finances, and the protection of minorities. Jawaharlal Nehru, still mourning the death of his father Motilal on February 6, was moved to ask, 'Was it for this that our people had behaved so gallantly for a year? Were all our brave words and deeds to end in this? The independence resolution of the Congress, the pledge of January 26, so often repeated?'[186] Finally, he followed Gandhi and worked for its acceptance by the Congress.

Under the terms of the pact, after approval of the pact by the Congress Working Committee, all civil disobedience prisoners, including Subhas Bose, were released, enabling them to attend the forthcoming Congress session in Karachi.

Bose's name had come up in a confusing way in the Gandhi-Irwin talks. During the meeting on February 18, the viceroy reported that Gandhi said he would like to have other Congressmen with him in the discussions including Subhas Bose, who was still in prison. In Gandhi's account of the same meeting, Gandhi reports that when Bose's name came up, he said Bose was not on the Working Committee: 'No, he is not, and he is my opponent and will denounce me; still, if he wants to attend, we must give him a chance to do so.'[187] Given Gandhi's requirement of a homogeneous executive body for the Congress and his disagreements with Bose at the last two Congress sessions, it is unlikely that Gandhi would have been the one to insist that Bose be a party to the discussions.

Gandhi's doubts about Bose must have been fulfilled once again, and when Bose was released from prison, he hurried to Bombay to meet Gandhi. He wanted to persuade the Mahatma that some of the terms of the pact were gravely in error. Bose agreed with Nehru that the Congress had received little in return for all the suffering they had undergone during the past year. He was also unalterably opposed to federation with safeguards. What he wanted was independence. A further stipulation of the pact particularly raised his ire. Not *all* political prisoners were to be released. However, after Bose's talks with Gandhi on March 15 to 17, the Mahatma was still adamant. He felt he could not give an undertaking to the Government that the non-civil disobedience prisoners would not return to acts of violence. The question of political prisoners was one on which most Bengal leaders and Gandhi never saw eye-to-eye. To Bose Bengal still had some 800 political prisoners, including many held and not charged with specific offenses and never brought to trial. For Gandhi, they were not in the same category as his satyagrahis pledged to non-violence.[188]

Among those whom Bose considered political prisoners were the three convicted in the Lahore Conspiracy Case, Bhagat Singh, Sivaram Rajguru, and Sukhdev. Many Congressmen wanted the Government of India to commute their sentence to a term of imprisonment. They thought a show of good faith on the part of the government was necessary after the Congress cessation of civil disobedience. Gandhi had told the viceroy of Bhagat Singh in February during their talks, 'He is undoubtedly a brave man but I would certainly say that he is not in his right mind.'[189]

On March 23, days before the Congress session was to open in Karachi, India awoke to learn that the three Lahore prisoners had been swiftly executed. Many condemned the government for not showing more humanity and political sense. But many, particularly those in the youth movement to whom Bhagat Singh was a hero, blamed Gandhi for not making more effective representations to the government on behalf of the condemned, and for not threatening the Gandhi-Irwin Pact over this issue.

When Gandhi and Sardar Patel arrived a few days later at a Karachi station for the Congress session, some accounts say that 'Subhas youths with black flags' met them; another version is that they '. . . were met with a hostile demonstration and . . . young men offered black flowers and black garlands.'[190] Gandhi insisted that he had asked the viceroy to commute the sentences to life imprisonment on the general grounds of non-violence. He added that Singh might have been brave, but that his actions had not benefited the country. The government's actions, the Mahatma said, show its brute nature.[191]

Bose's view can be glimpsed from an extract from Bose's address to the All-India Naujawan Bharat Sabha on March 27,

> Bhagat Singh was a symbol of the spirit of revolt which has taken possession of the country from one end to the other. That spirit is unconquerable, and the flame which that spirit has lit up will not die. India may have to lose many more sons before she can hope to be free. These recent executions are to me sure indications that there has been no change of heart on the side of the Government and the time for an honourable settlement has not arrived as yet.[192]

Bose went on to criticize the Gandhi-Irwin Pact but, he said for reasons of patriotism, it should not be rejected by the Congress.[193] Bose had recently been traveling with Gandhi and he knew that there was more popular feeling and support for Gandhi than for any other nationalist. So he told the assembled young men in Karachi that they should go beyond the vague program of the Congress and 'do some positive work which will strengthen the nation and the nation's demand.'[194] What was this positive work to be? It was to work for freedom and for 'a socialist republic in India' by organizing workers and peasants, organizing youth 'into Volunteer Corps under strict discipline', organizing women's associations, intensive boycott of British goods, 'abolition of the caste system and the eradication of social and religious superstitions of all kinds', and 'creation of new literature for propagating the new cult and programme.' The new cult was that of a collectivity guided by justice, equality, freedom, discipline, and love.[195]

With his admiration for Bhagat Singh, his reservations about the Gandhi-Irwin Pact, and his idea of a positive program, Bose entered the Congress to the cheers of the young. Unlike his role in the past two Congress sessions, Bose did not oppose Gandhi on any of the three basic resolutions. Nehru proposed a resolution which praised the bravery of Bhagat Singh and his comrades while dissociating the Congress from acts of political violence. It also held that the government lost a chance to conciliate Indians by carrying through the executions. Some tried to have the condemnation of violence removed, but this was not successful.[196] Gandhi supported the resolution and claimed later that the demonstrating 'Subhas youths' and Nehru had not pressured him into backing it.[197]

What Gandhi mainly desired at this juncture was approval of the agreement he had worked out with the viceroy. This he gained by an overwhelming vote, though Jamnadas Mehta and Swami Govindanand made strong speeches opposing it. Another Congressman, Satyamurti, mentioning Subhas' arguments before the Subjects Committee, argued that the

Congress should accept the agreement, not because it was satisfactory, but because Gandhi had made it and the Congress had full confidence in him.[198] Gandhi himself spoke of the necessity to tell the British Cabinet what it was the Congress wanted. He said he might come back empty-handed, but he would never sell out the interests of the country.[199]

With his compromise efforts backed, Gandhi proposed the Fundamental Rights resolution. It included some twenty items, among them freedom of speech, press, association, and no bars to any Indian on account of religion, caste, creed, or sex. It backed the right to bear arms and stipulated religious neutrality on the part of the state. Then it listed a number of measures which were aimed at helping the poorer classes: a living wage for industrial workers, limited hours and healthy conditions of work, no child labor, and protections for women workers. It also called for a progressive income tax, adult suffrage, and free primary education for all. In line with Gandhi's program it mentioned that there was to be no duty on salt and total prohibition. Usury was to be controlled. Then, hinting at socialism, it specified that the state should control key industrial and mineral resources. Although Gandhi moved this resolution, and thus assured its passage, many on the left including Nehru and the secretly-present M.N. Roy have been given credit for formulating this twenty-point program. It was passed by a large majority.[200]

When the Working Committee was announced, Sen Gupta, who had spoken passionately in favor of the Gandhi-Irwin Pact, was on it. Subhas Bose was not. Bose and Gandhi continued on friendly terms, but Bose was still not acceptable in the Congress inner circle. Even Dr B.C. Roy, who had replaced Sen Gupta on the Working Committee when Sen Gupta was imprisoned, was more satisfactory than Bose.[201]

III

Following the Karachi Congress, Bose went on a speaking tour of Sind and the Punjab. In Amritsar on April 8, he substituted for Gandhi in addressing the Sikh League. Bose assured the Sikhs that all Congress leaders including Gandhi and himself would work for justice for small communities like the Sikhs. But then Gandhi's stand-in went beyond what the Mahatma would have said to the assembled throng. He commented,

> ... one young Sikh Sardar Bhagat Singh had inspired the whole country and (the) air was rent with cries of 'Bhagat Singh Zindabad'. If the Sikh community could produce hundreds of Bhagat Singhs, was there any doubt that they would become the most influential community, regardless of their number?

> A few years ago India was in the midst of communal trouble and chaos.

In that dark hour of India's history (the) sacrifices of Jatin Das and Bhagat Singh turned the tide of communal feeling and once again tried to inspire the country with patriotism. Therefore, (I) appeal to the brave Sikhs to produce more patriots having the courage and (spirit of) sacrifice of Bhagat Singh.[202] Bose's call for hundreds of Bhagat Singhs did not go unnoticed. The Home Department in Delhi found it 'thoroughly anti-Government and seditious' and wondered whether it was better, from their point of view, to jail Bose or allow him freedom to go on quarreling with Sen Gupta and thereby weaken the Congress in Bengal. They decided to leave him free.[203]

The *Statesman*, organ of the European community, editorializing on *Liberty*'s report of the speech, said,

We assume the correctness of the report and ask how long the Government of India is to tolerate these verbal incitements to cold and callous murder. Thousands of Bhagat Singhs can mean no more and no less than thousands of men who will shoot down officials in circumstances in which they have not a chance of defending themselves. At the doors of would-be Bhagat Singhs lie the cowardly murder of Mr Peddie, of the shooting of Colonel Simpson, Mr Lowman and half a score other men whose one crime was that they were doing their duty. Mr Bose's speech only differs by a shade more outspokenness from a score of speeches that were delivered at Congress.[204]

Although the *Statesman* continued to lump all Congressmen and perpetrators of violence in the same camp, there were differences. Bose was sympathetic to the revolutionaries. Gandhi saw them as being as much his enemies as the Government of India: both furthered violence and brutality; both severed the Indians and their rulers ever more from each other. Gandhi's aim was to work for India's eventual freedom and reconstruction through non-violent means which would bring the two sides together and convert the opponent. The Mahatma was convinced that these violent acts by young Indians were not bringing freedom closer and were making it more difficult to convert a ruler whose agents and administrators were being shot in the street or even in their own offices. Gandhi had chosen to make a temporary peace, call off civil disobedience, and go to London to talk. This certainly did not satisfy the revolutionaries who continued their campaigns of assassination and terror. Gandhi's British visit scarcely pleased Bose, but he, for the time being, decided to be a good Congress soldier and work within Congress parameters.

En route back to Calcutta, Bose stopped in Delhi and issued a statement calling for an end to squabbling in the Bengal Congress. But he continued to criticize his opponents for daring to suggest in Karachi that the forthcoming elections to the BPCC might be held with less than complete fairness under the auspices of the reigning BPCC officials. Bose wanted

Congress unity, but he could not bring it about. On several occasions, he offered to resign, but did not do so. And the debilitating intra-Congress conflict went on.[205]

During April and May, Subhas Bose made speeches in many of Bengal's districts. In Sylhet and Faridpur, he announced that he had settled the district Congress disputes in these places.[206] He spoke occasionally about his own life, about his rustication from college and how he had taken a 'plunge into the unknown' by rejecting the ICS for the Congress.[207] At a number of meetings he compared Mazzini's dreams for a united and republican Italy to his dreams for India.[208] He held up Mazzini and Russian and Irish heroes before his audiences, but he said that Indians would have to find their own way. Russia has found hers, Italy hers, he told listeners in Noakhali, but India has to find her own version of socialism and equality. Indian freedom, he went on, had to be achieved by karmayoga, by disciplined action, and not through debates and conferences.[209] Besides Congress unity, he stressed communal unity and frequently met the Muslim leaders and citizens of each area he visited. Later in the year, speaking at the Dacca National College, he recognized that there were differences between Hindus and Muslims, but that they had many common interests, foremost among these that they would gain enormously if they could rule their own country.[210]

In late May and early June, elections were held under the auspices of the old BPCC for a new BPCC. The Sen Gupta forces immediately charged fraud and rigging. Bose was in Gujarat and he assured Gandhi that the elections had gone smoothly in twenty-six of thirty-two districts. But the dissident voices were too loud and were recognized by Gandhi and the Working Committee. In June the Working Committee decided to try to put a complete end to the disputes by appointing M.S. Aney 'to be the sole arbitrator to entertain all the matters that might be referred to him by the respective parties and to give his final decisions thereon.'[211] After a few false starts, Aney came to Calcutta and laid down procedures on which the settlement of grievances would be made. Complaints were to be submitted on July 16, and the Sen Gupta side lodged forty-two against the BPCC and the BPCC entered eleven against the opposition. Then each side was given time to reply to the complaints which Aney would then settle. On July 23, Aney had to halt his inquiry and leave Calcutta.[212]

While this matter was delayed, yet another serious dispute came to a head, this one within the AITUC, of which Bose was still president. Although Bose had not been able to persuade the non-political trade unionists of the N.M. Joshi-type to return, he was hopeful that the Congress trade unionists and more radical, predominantly communist trade unionists might continue to cooperate within the AITUC. The Comintern however was going even deeper into its left sectarian phase. Sobhanlal Datta Gupta, in his careful analysis of the Comintern and India, has pointed to a crucial 1930 Draft Platform of Action of the CPI (Communist Party of India). He has summarized it as follows,

> This crucial document virtually set the course of action followed by Indian communists in the years that followed. Reiterating the Comintern's position, the Draft launched a full-scale attack on the Gandhian leadership of the National Congress, but the edge was directed more towards the 'left' elements, i.e., Nehru and Bose, particularly because these sections had a definite influence on the labour movement in the country. The document thus pointed out that under the cloak of revolutionary phraseologies these elements carried on a policy of confusing and disorganizing the revolutionary struggles of the masses, and helped the Congress to come to an understanding with British imperialism. Hence, what was necessary was a 'ruthless war on the "Left" national reformists' in order 'to isolate the latter from the workers and mass of the peasantry and mobilise the latter under the banner of the Communist Party.'[213]

Unfortunately for Bose, he was on the firing line when the AITUC assembled in Calcutta in the second week of July. The Communist group in the AITUC executive was led by the AITUC secretary, S.V. Deshpande, from Bombay. Besides other Bombay communist trade unionists, the group received backing from Bengal communists, Bankim Mukherjee and Bhupen Datta. The Deshpande group, seeing that it was in a minority, disrupted a meeting of the Credentials Committee. After failing to get a censoring motion against President Bose or on the matter of which set of representatives would speak for the Girni Kamgar Union, they walked out of the AITUC Congress entirely and met separately.[214] Shortly thereafter, they formed the Red Trade Union Congress which remained isolated from the mainstream of Indian nationalism and nationalist trade unionists until the 1935 united front line of the Comintern.[215]

Bose insisted that he had desperately tried to keep the communists within the AITUC, for he dreaded splitting the movement again, but that even his rulings in favor of Deshpande's group did not satisfy them. Left to themselves, the nationalist trade unionists continued the meeting. Once it was over, Bose presented his version of the split and its background to the press.[216] Bose first identified the right-wing unionists who had left in 1929. Then he said,

> On the other side there were the Moscow communists led by the Bombay group who followed blindly the dictates of Moscow in the matter of their ideals, methods and tactics. Besides these two parties there were others who could not agree with either group . . . but they were not at the time (*1928-*

29) organised as a party. They wanted to stand definitely for socialism and they also wanted a militant programme. But they refused to hang to the coat-tails of Moscow. . . . At the Nagpur session the Moscow Communists tried to capture the entire secretariat for themselves but owing to the pressure of the third group they had reluctantly to accept me as president. . . . For more than one year they carried on a ceaseless campaign against the Indian National Congress. . . . The Moscow Communists and their Bengal follow-ers have now virtually seceded from the Trade Union Congress, but they did not do so with good grace. They resorted to . . . rowdyism hoping . . . they would drive out the third group. . . . But they had sterner stuff to deal with at Calcutta. The third group, which may be called the socialist group, were determined to remain inside the Congress and to fight every inch of the ground. Since they were in a majority they could not be scared away by the Moscow communists. . . . The Moscow Communists are a serious menace to the growth of healthy trade unionism in India and we cannot possibly leave the field to them.[217]

Bose went on to warn the communists that he would resist their sectarian splitting of the movement and he would fight to bring together the trade unions and the Congress. And, he said, '. . . we shall also fight the domination of Moscow in the affairs of India, for we are convinced that only thereby can we serve the best interests of India.'[218]

Bose remained the president of many unions including the Jamshedpur Labour Association, All-Bengal Railway Indian Employees Association, and Bengal Oil and Petrol Workers' Union. Faced with retrenchments, pressures to cut back wages, and high unemployment, the beleaguered workers and their outside leaders had a most difficult time through these years. Bose tried to do his small part by speaking for the nationalist trade unionists and for the unions of which he was at least the nominal head. This activity continued through 1931. In his presidential address to the AITUC, he said that India needed a 'full-blooded socialism'. The term 'fascism' and its positive features did not enter the picture. He concluded his AITUC address,

> I have no doubt in my own mind that the salvation of India as of the world, depends on socialism. India should learn from and profit by the experience of other nations—but India should be able to evolve her own methods in keeping with her own needs and her own environment. In applying any theory to practice, you can never rule out geography or history. If you attempt it, you are bound to fail. India should therefore evolve her own form of socialism. When the whole world is engaged in socialistic experiments, why should we not do the same? It may be that the form of socialism which India will evolve will have something new and original about it which will be of benefit to the whole world.[219]

Although the Indian communists in 1931 attacked Bose and Nehru as enemies of the people, decades later they reinstated Bose.[220]

While some communist trade unionists were undertrials at Meerut, the revolutionaries were either imprisoned or still at work. Following the murder of Simpson, the district magistrate of Midnapore, Mr Peddie was gunned down on April 7, 1931. The two captured and convicted murderers of Simpson were due for execution. A motion to commute the sentence of these two young Bengalis came before the Calcutta Corporation. Sarat Bose, while agreeing with the condemnation of the assassination which had been previously passed by the Corporation, said that even those convicted of high treason and the present offense deserved a measure of mercy. Taking an example from the case of Sir Roger Casement, who had been convicted of high treason by a British court during the First World War, he said that some of the most eminent British leaders of the day had signed a petition asking that the sentence be commuted to life imprisonment. So why, he continued, would the European councillors and non-Congress members of the body not consider this resolution calling for mercy. The resolution was passed, but failed in its objective. The two young men were executed. In recent years the names of the three revolutionaries who killed Simpson have been immortalized with the changing of the name of the square fronting on the Writers' Building from Dalhousie Square to Binoy-Badal-Dinesh Bag.[221]

In late August—after changing his mind twice—Gandhi embarked for London and the second Round Table Conference. Through the nearly four months that Gandhi spent abroad, Bose continued to hammer at the Congress role. A writer in *Liberty* recounted Bose's remarks at Goila in October during which he stated his position most bluntly,

> He said that a Round Table Conference should be confined only to the belligerent parties and it was a mistake for the Congress to participate in the Conference when other parties who were not fighting the British Government were allowed to participate. The British Government had tried to deceive the Irish people by convening an Irish Convention but the intelligent and farsighted Sinn Feiners did not walk into the trap. They boycotted the Irish Convention and continued to fight for freedom until the time when the British Government decided to negotiate for peace with the Sinn Fein Party alone. Unless the Congress was in a position to speak for India by itself—the Congress could never negotiate successfully with the British Government.[222]

In many of his speeches during 1931, Bose referred to Irish precedents. Both Boses identified strongly with the Sinn Feiners and admired Sir Roger Casement, Michael Collins and Eamon de Valera. Subhas Bose, if not Sarat as well, believed that Indian freedom would have to be won by action as well as negotiation. He certainly did not preclude violent mass action, though he was still committed to mass non-violent action.[223]

During 1931, it was announced that Sir John Anderson would succeed Sir Stanley Jackson as governor of Bengal. Anderson had been under-secretary for Ireland, serving in Dublin Castle during the period of severe repression called the years of the 'Black-and-Tans,' referring to forces used to repress the Irish nationalists.[224] Bose began speaking of 'Black-and-Tan' actions in India. One such action that he referred to in this way had significant consequences for the course of Bengal politics.

A disturbance at the Hijli Prison Camp led to the guards firing on the prisoners, and on September 16 two prisoners, Santosh Mitra and Tarakeswar Sen, were killed. An uproar of protest ensued and there was one further result. M.S. Aney was due back in Calcutta to continue the resolution of the BPCC disputes. Bose decided that the Hijli affair was a sign that the internecine warfare between his party and Sen Gupta's had to halt immediately. So, doing what he had only threatened to do before, Bose resigned as BPCC president and also as an alderman of the Calcutta Corporation on September 18. Further, Bose directed that all complaints filed by the BPCC against the other side were to be withdrawn.[225]

In his statement of resignation, he traced the history of the dissensions in the Bengal Congress back to the late 1920s and said that for ten years there had always been a party opposed to the group in power in the BPCC. He defended his own tenure in office and condemned the insurgents for disobeying Congress rules and disciplinary measures, and splitting every effort at positive work made by the BPCC. Further, he said that there were three possible courses to follow: strictly enforce Congress rules, try to work out a compromise between the two major groups, or, third, leave the field completely. Since he had tried the first two methods and they had failed, he was left with only the third.

> My close associates . . . are aware that for a long time I have been seriously thinking of restoring unity . . . by adopting the third course . . . The conviction has daily strengthened in my mind that no useful purpose can be served by retaining office, if the co-operation of all sections of Congressmen is not secured. . . . Whatever hesitation I felt in resorting to the third course has finally been removed as a result of the terrible shock which the staggering news from the Hijli Detention Camp has given me. The indescribable sufferings of our countrymen in prison and outside are to us a Divine warning that we should close up our ranks and present a united front to our enemies.
>
> I am, therefore, submitting my resignation. . . . I shall be content to work in the capacity of an ordinary humble Congressman and whoever may occupy the Presidential Chair will be able to commandeer my services. If

Bengal can be saved as a result of my self-effacement I shall be happy to pay that price and I shall feel more than amply rewarded if my countrymen will in exchange give me a corner in their hearts.[226]

Sen Gupta and his side responded positively and asked for a meeting with representatives of the Bose group to see if a settlement of the whole conflict could be worked out. Kiran Sankar Roy and Sarat Bose for the Boses, met with Sen Gupta and Nishit Sen for the other side. Tulsi Goswami was involved as a mediator. Aney, in the detailed account he gave as part of his final report, said that a 'spirit of cordiality' grew which made a settlement easier. It was agreed that all complaints would be dropped, that a new election for the BPCC would be held in late January or early February, that Aney, Sen, and Roy would look into all rules of procedure, and that an Election Disputes Board would be set up with three from each side plus Aney as chief arbitrator to see that the election was carried through satisfactorily. It was further worked out that a new twenty-five-member Joint Executive Committee of the BPCC would be formed which would continue until the January BPCC election. Nishit Sen and K.S. Roy were to be joint secretaries, but shortly Aswini Kumar Ganguly replaced Roy. Nirmal Chunder was to become president of the BPCC. In his report of September 25, Aney concluded,

> I desire to congratulate the leading and responsible members of both the parties on the splendid spirit of accommodation, reconciliation and self-effacement displayed by them in sinking their differences and arriving at an honourable settlement at a critical time like this. I hope that the same spirit will soon permeate the rank and file. . .[227]

Many Bengal and Indian papers, including his frequent antagonists at the *Amrita Bazar Patrika,* gave Bose fulsome praise for his act. Some of the Sen Gupta group were less than generous, as Jawaharlal Nehru noted in a letter to Sardar Patel on September 24,

> The *Advance* seems to be continuing to write offensively against Subhas and BPCC. Its comment on Subhas's resignation was in the worst of taste. I am afraid Sen Gupta and his party are putting themselves entirely in the wrong. I wish Aney could do something in the matter.[228]

Aney could do nothing in the matter, but Bose and Sen Gupta shortly made a trip together to the Hijli area to investigate the tragedy. Sarat Bose presented a strongly worded resolution in the Corporation which was passed. The Boses, Sen Gupta and other Congressmen were also concerned with developments in Chittagong where after August 30, 1931, when a Muslim police officer was murdered, riots followed. The police either looked on indifferently or contributed to problems. A government investigation found several police officers at fault and one thereupon committed suicide. He and a number of others were censured for failing in their duty. These officers were said to be working under conditions of great strain, but still derelict in their duty of keeping order and protecting the citizenry.[229]

In his account of these events written a few years later, Subhas Bose argued that most of the terrorist acts were isolated ones and in retaliation for injuries suffered at the hands of a repressive Raj. The Gandhi-Irwin Pact, he maintained, could have been the signal for a more harmonious relationship between the Raj and the people. But,

> ... instead of turning over a new leaf, the authorities decided to copy the Black and Tan methods that had been employed in Ireland. ... At Chittagong an Indian police officer was murdered. The next morning, hooligans were let loose on the town and while the police remained inactive, looting went on in broad daylight. The idea was to teach the people of Chittagong a 'moral' lesson. ... In November a new ordinance was promulgated by the Government which introduced a veiled form of martial law in the District of Chittagong. Under this ordinance, hardship and penalty were imposed on the people as one would expect under martial law.[230]

While Bose was carrying on what he called his 'raging and tearing' campaign against this repression, Gandhi picked up the issue in London where he was attending the Round Table Conference. Sen Gupta, still in poor health, had sailed to London during October and met Gandhi.[231] During his speech to the Federal Structure Committee meeting on November 25, Gandhi said,

> ... Mr Sen Gupta ... has brought me a report signed by members of all the parties in Bengal in connection with Chittagong ... the substance of this report is that there has been an inferior edition of the Black and Tans in Chittagong—and Chittagong is not a place of no importance on the map of India.[232]

Gandhi went on to present his case for complete provincial autonomy under which there would be no troops or martial law or hundreds of detenus in Bengal under Regulation III. Gandhi pressed his case for 'federation with all its responsibility', which was after all why he had come to London. But instead of getting real responsibility, India was getting repression and the Congress was being blamed for every act of terrorism. Gandhi decided to answer this charge as well,

> I have been told so often that it is the Congress that is responsible for this terrorism. I take this opportunity of denying that with all the strength at my command. On the contrary, I have evidence to show that it is the Congress creed of non-violence which up to now has kept the forces of terrorism in check. We have not succeeded to the fullest extent—I am sorry—but as time goes on we hope to succeed. It is not as if this terrorism can bring freedom

to India. . . . I want full freedom for the masses, and I know that terrorism can do no good to the masses. The masses are silent and disarmed. They do not know how to kill. I do not talk of individual instances, but the masses of India have never moved in that direction.[233]

Even though Gandhi brought his protests against government repression in Bengal to the highest circles in London, official and non-official, Bose was not satisfied. He complained that the central Congress organization was ignoring Bengal and not making a powerful enough protest against the repression. In speech after speech in the last months of 1931, he compared India and Ireland under the Black-and-Tans. Both Bose and Gandhi argued that repression did not stop terrorism, that, in fact, it encouraged it. Furthermore, they both indicated that these sporadic acts were harmful to the national cause. Gandhi had always said this. In a speech at Shraddhananda Park in mid-December, Bose is reported to have said,

. . . these outbursts of violent acts did much harm to the national cause. The followers of the cult of violence were no match for the authorities in an armed conflict. But if scattered national forces were organized in a peaceful and non-violent way they could achieve their objective much more expeditiously.[234]

It must be noted, however, that Gandhi's criticisms of terrorist acts and Bose's do read differently. Gandhi is absolutely opposed to terrorism for violence is evil and evil means cannot lead to beneficial ends. Bose, like his mentor Aurobindo Ghose, is against acts of terrorism because they do not work, they do not 'achieve their objective . . . expeditiously'. If he had sufficient force to oppose the Raj on equal terms, would he not then use it? At this point, he did not have to answer that question.

Gandhi did not achieve success abroad in ways that were satisfactory to the Congress. On December 5, he left Britain and en route home through Europe he stopped to see Romain Rolland and also called on Mussolini.[235] On December 28, he landed in Bombay and Subhas Bose was among the Congress leaders there to greet him. In a speech to the Commonwealth of India League immediately after returning, Gandhi again criticized the Bengal Ordinance and the punishment of a large population 'because a few persons ran amuck.'[236] On December 29, he discussed the Bengal and national situation with Bose, who had been saying all fall that the Congress needed a plan of action if no results were forthcoming from Gandhi's London visit.

The Congress Working Committee decided that civil disobedience would have to be resumed if the Government of India did not make any positive conciliatory moves. A small news item in *Liberty* on January 3 indicated the direction in which the Government of India had decided to move:

Mr Subhas Chandra Bose who left for Calcutta this afternoon was arrested on the train at Kalyan, 30 miles from Bombay, under Regulation III of 1818. He was taken by the same train to an unknown destination.[237]

On January 4, with the Congress moving to civil disobedience, the government arrested Gandhi, Patel, Prasad, Nehru, and many other Congressmen in Bombay, Calcutta, and Delhi. Four further ordinances were promulgated to facilitate this repression and all Congress organizations were declared unlawful.[238]

Although civil disobedience was resumed in a few isolated areas such as the eastern parts of Midnapore in Bengal, the government effectively deprived the Congress of many of its leaders for some time to come.[239] On February 6, 1932, another small item appeared in *Liberty* concerning its managing director:

Sjt. Sarat Chandra Bose, Bar-at-Law and Alderman of the Calcutta Corporation, was arrested on Thursday night at Jharia, where he went on a professional call, under Regulation III of 1818, and taken by Bombay Mail to Seoni sub-jail, where Sjt. Subhas Chandra Bose has been kept detained under the same Regulation.[240]

This was the first arrest and detention for Sarat Bose. Why was he taken, and why under a statute usually reserved for those dedicated to acts of violence? A short excerpt from Sarat Bose's 'information sheet' in their file on him and his detention gives their view of his activity,

He has always been careful to keep in the background and to avoid being implicated personally in any 'outrage, but the Bengal Government is satisfied that he has been a direct supporter of the terrorist campaign, which he has assisted with advice and money, both before and after the perpetration of outrage. In particular, he was believed to have instigated and financed the last attempt to murder Sir Charles Tegart, to have afforded support and encouragement to the party which raided the Chittagong Armoury in 1930, and to have been aware of the arrangements made to shelter the absconding members of this party.

Sarat Bose was also a leading member of the section which turned the Calcutta Corporation . . .into a source of revenue for the Congress and Revolutionary parties, and it was through his influence that a large number of terrorists on release from imprisonment, were given appointments as teachers in Calcutta schools.[241]

The file contained more information as to why the Government of Bengal and of India considered him a danger to national security. Two judges reviewed the materials and agreed to this finding, but the prisoner was never allowed to know precisely why he was being held.

The arrests marked the end of an era for the Congress and the Boses. To a great extent, government repression halted the civil disobedience campaign and the British Government moved through the steps to constitutional reform without much input from the major nationalist organization. Though illegal, the Congress, as a long-established organization continued. It worked within greatly reduced bounds during the next few years until the opportunity to struggle on a wider battlefield presented itself again.

For the Bose brothers, temporarily united in prison and 'happy in each other's company', the arrests marked the end of their open Congress work in India for some years to come.[242] Sarat Bose had entered nationalist politics to a much greater extent than ever before in the years after C.R. Das' death and took an especially large role in Bengal when Subhas Bose was off the stage. Sarat Bose had made his contributions to the work of the Calcutta Corporation and not simply in getting revolutionaries employed, as the Government of Bengal suggested. He had also worked to keep *Forward*, then *Liberty*, running as an effective voice for the Bose and Congress point of view. After briefly giving up his practice at the bar to devote himself full-time to the national cause, he could never go back to simply being a barrister. What one of his colleagues called 'comparative disposition' now found fulfillment both in politics and at the bar. He was determined to continue both, as circumstances permitted.[243]

Some have suggested that his legal career had by now become simply a means to an end. It enabled him to support his own and others' work in politics. But this is too simplistic. He became immersed in the law and delighted in its challenges and confrontations. His greatest skill was said to be in cross-examination. The contest for truth, justice, and accomplishment drew him in. He did use his earnings to support activities the British called subversive, but this did not negate his deep involvement with the law. The law and nationalism became the twin goddesses of his life.

If Sarat Bose was a passionate nationalist, what can one say of Subhas Bose? Briefly, Indian independence was the consuming passion, the one major concern of his life. He was by now an important player on the national stage, but his stature in these past few years was diminished by the internecine rivalries in Bengal. His views commanded attention and whenever he went outside Bengal to speak, the eagle eyes and fears of other provincial governments' intelligence men were focused upon him. Why was he so threatening? Because his passion, involvement, and sacrifices had gained him some respect from his nationalist brethren and because of the apprehension that he would encourage mass action and raise mass consciousness in volatile groups like the youths and workers who might not be dedicated to non-violence. So it was not only for these deeds, but also because of the potentialities of their nationalist work that the Boses were now both held under Regulation III of 1818.

CHAPTER SEVEN

Ambassador of India in Bondage, 1932-36

In the nightmare of the dark
All the dogs of Europe bark. . .

W.H. Auden, 'In Memory of W.B. Yeats'[1]

. . . you will have to remember. . . that outside India, every Indian is
India's unofficial ambassador.

Subhas Bose to his nephew Asoke Bose, October 27, 1932 [2]

I

Since the Government of Bengal was particularly insistent in 1932 that
Subhas Bose be jailed outside Bengal, the Government of India arranged
for Bose to be incarcerated in the sub-jail at Seoni in the Central Provinces,
now Madhya Pradesh. Seoni is in hilly country to the south of the Narmada
river and is situated at an altitude of about 2,000 feet in relatively sparsely
populated country. The jail had neither regular doors nor window shutters.
Prisoners were exposed to the heat of the summer and the cold winds of
winter.[3]

Within a few weeks, Subhas was joined in Seoni by his brother Sarat,
also imprisoned under Regulation III. Sarat Bose had just completed a
legal case in Dhanbad, Bihar, when he was arrested in nearby Jharia.[4] This
was Sarat Bose's first term as an unwilling guest of the Raj. Though he
learned to take this experience with some equanimity, he was upset that his
legal mettle could not be used to fight for his freedom because there were
no charges to answer and all his pleas to specify them were disregarded.[5]

Sarat Bose's imprisonment came at a particularly inopportune time for
his family because his father was just recuperating from serious heart
trouble and his eldest son, Asoke Nath, had left the year before for higher
studies in applied chemistry in Munich. During Subhas' previous imprisonments, Sarat had been on the outside earning handsome fees at the High

Court bar and keeping the family running. Now the family's highest paid member, with a considerable establishment to support, was taken away when Janaki Nath Bose was in virtual retirement. An additional burden was placed on Satish Bose, but he could not deal with these obligations. Fortunately, both brothers had staunch friends, some of whom could afford to make substantial contributions to the maintenance of the family. Most notable were Kumar Debendra Lall Khan of Narajole and Sir Nripendra Nath Sircar, law member of the Government of India. The former was a political ally, the latter a political opponent, but a mentor and devoted friend of Sarat Bose. These two and some others made it possible for the Bose family to deal with the financial distress of the next few years.[6]

Just after Sarat's arrest, Satish Bose wrote to his nephew Asoke in Europe,

> Let not those events disturb or worry you. You have gone to Munich on a distinct mission in quest of learning, and may God help you in fulfilling your mission. . . . Father had received the news of your father's incarceration with calmness and fortitude. So, too, mother, who always believes in the will of Providence and sees in every event, His Act and the fulfillment of the Divine will. We all hope and trust that your father's and uncle's incarceration . . . will not be in vain. We are prouder of them today than we ever were before. Thrice blessed are they who by their sufferings hasten the advent of a new and free India. . . . Forget not the words of Srijut Arabindo Ghosh, 'Work that India may prosper. Suffer that she may rejoice.'[7]

So too from his prison cell in Seoni, Sarat Bose continually tried to reassure his son that all financial matters would be taken care of and that Asoke should throw all his energies into study. Shortly physical difficulties began to prey upon the brothers.[8]

Subhas Bose had had serious health problems during his previous long imprisonment in Mandalay and now, again, unsettling symptoms surfaced. He had digestive problems and recurring pains around the waist. He was put on a liquid diet of Horlick's and chicken soup but continued to lose weight. The cause of his symptoms was unclear and gallbladder trouble and tuberculosis were suggested. Sarat Bose was feeling well as long as the weather remained cool, but as the warmer season engulfed them, he began to feel more and more uncomfortable in this prison open to the elements. He already had diabetes, but it became much more severe in prison and before 1932 was out, he was taking regular injections of insulin as well as other medication.[9]

In mid-May, Sarat's wife and several other relations came to visit the brothers in Seoni and this raised their spirits but did not cure their physical infirmities. At the end of May, they were moved to Jubbulpore Central Jail for a more thorough medical examination. Even though there were x-ray facilities in Jubbulpore, Subhas needed more specialized treatment and in mid-July, he was taken to Madras, where both government doctors and two physicians of his own choice, Dr B.C. Roy and Sir Nilratan Sircar, examined him. They agreed that there were signs of tuberculosis and also some abdominal problem. At the suggestion of these physicians, Subhas Bose was next taken to the Bhowali Sanatorium in northern India where it was hoped that his health would improve.[10]

With Subhas' departure, Sarat was left alone in Jubbulpore. As the months passed and he felt more and more alone, his physical ailments and the indeterminate length of his imprisonment preyed upon his mind. Sarat Bose never had the leisure to indulge himself in the pleasures of general reading. Now that the hours were there, he made his way through the major works of the Russian novelists, Tolstoy, Dostoyevsky, and Turgenev. He read some of the novels of H.G. Wells as well as his *Outline of History*, in which he carefully marked passages dealing with the seventeenth century to the present. On European politics, he read R.W. Postgate's *Workers' International*, Harold Laski's *Communism* and *Studies in Law and Politics*, as well as Sir Samuel Hoare's *Fourth Seal*. It also appears that he read Trotsky's *My Life* and John Dewey's *Quest for Certainty* at this time. Through the 1920s and 1930s Sarat Bose read many works of Bertrand Russell and was always an admirer of George Bernard Shaw; he may also have read some of their works in prison.[11]

A nephew has mentioned that he developed more of a taste for Bengali literature in this period. Among the books he surely read concerning Indian affairs at this time were Sir N.N. Sircar's *Bengal under Communal Award and Poona Pact,* and D. Chaman Lall's *Coolie, The Story of Labour and Capital in India*. There were, of course, severe restrictions on what he could read and write about politics—particularly Indian politics—during his imprisonment, and his correspondence with friends and relations is not very revealing in this area.[12]

Some of Sarat's political ideas were expressed, perhaps frankly, perhaps deviously, in his many letters to government officials at the highest level asking for a statement of the charges against him and later for a transfer to house arrest. On July 4, 1932, he wrote at length to the home member of the Government of India and again on August 16.[13] Getting no satisfactory reply, Sarat Bose next tried the new governor of Bengal, Sir John Anderson, to whom he wrote a long letter on September 25. It was structured like a legal brief. He said he had been greatly disappointed with all the official replies to his previous letters and said he remained 'condemned by accusations' that he was not 'given the opportunity to refute, though such accusations may be completely without foundation and capable of being decisively refuted. . .'[14] Then he stated,

> There are two *suppositions* to which I shall address myself. *Firstly*, whether I have taken any part in the prese. it civil disobedience movement, and *secondly*, whether I have taken any part in the revolutionary movement.[15]

In arguing his case for himself at what he suspected were the charges against him, Bose said that from November 1930 on, when he had resumed his High Court practice, he had not engaged in political activity and had resigned from the Bengal Provincial Congress Committee in September 1931. But he added, '. . . it is only the truth to say that I have not ceased to be a Congressman nor have I ceased to subscribe to the Congress ideal, namely the achievement of Purna Swaraj by all peaceful and legitimate means.'[16]

Although he could not know it, Sarat Bose was not a civil disobedience prisoner. So the first part of his brief against the mysterious charges was irrelevant. But the second part—concerning his views of and connections to the revolutionary movement—was apposite. He wrote,

> I have always detested methods of violence to which some young men in Bengal and elsewhere have found themselves driven, to the detriment of the fair name of their country and have said so openly. . . . I can honestly say that I have *never* been approached at any time by any one for giving help or encouragement in any shape or form to revolutionaries or to the revolutionary movement and I have *never* consciously given any sort of help or encouragement to them, pecuniary or otherwise.[17]

Bose explained that many people in need—students and Congress workers most often—approached him for jobs in the Corporation and financial help. He said he helped some and took their requests on trust and could not possibly know if some of them 'secretly entertained revolutionary ideas.'[18]

Then he moved on to the more general question of the revolutionary movement in Bengal and how it was to be handled. In part, he said,

> But while I have always detested methods of violence, I have felt that it will not do to shut one's eyes to the fact that the men who have felt themselves driven to them have clung to their faith with a zeal worthy of a better cause. Tolstoy has said in one of his works that he has been 'unable to doubt the sincerity of the faith that actuated many of them, for they had all to lose and nothing to gain by joining the revolutionary movement.' Similar views have been expressed by the late John Morley . . . . and in recent times by Sir Samuel Hoare. Consideration of the mentality disclosed by revolutionaries, whether Russian or Indian, has led me to express my doubts as to the efficacy of the conventional method of treatment of that serious malady in the body politic, namely, the method of repression and yet more repression. I believe it is there that I and others in public life have been misunderstood. . . .[19]

He went on to discuss his speech in the Corporation supporting Nalini Sarker's resolution asking the government to take Indian leaders into their confidence in helping to fight violence.[20]

From the general issue, Sarat Bose again returned to the particular, this time his role in the defense of the accused in the Chittagong Armoury Raid Case. He said he had been harshly criticized for appearing at a time when he had suspended his practice in order to work for the Civil Disobedience Movement. It was only after some hesitation, he claimed, that he appeared for the defense for a period of six weeks or a month at a time when there was no other prominent lawyer willing or able to defend them. This was, he said, in the finest traditions of the English bar. Further, he said, and here he seems not to be telling the whole truth, that he knew none of the defendants and had only the slightest acquaintance with one, Ambica Chakravarti, whom he had met in connection with Congress affairs.[21]

At the end of his long plea to Anderson, Sarat Bose asked that if the detention orders could not be lifted, then he should at least be allowed some company and be enabled to shift to his own house at Giddapahar, near Kurseong, where he could be better taken care of. This part of his plea did not go unnoticed or unanswered. Although a high official of the government said in response to his many long briefs for himself, '. . . Mr Sarat Bose's record shows that he has for some years been closely identified with terrorist crime and organization in Bengal',[22] Anderson was willing to consider a transfer after receiving this letter. But the matter turned on where and how Sarat's younger brother, the even more dangerous Subhas, would be contained.[23]

Subhas wrote to Santosh Basu on Calcutta Corporation matters from time to time during 1932, but his writing on other political matters was restricted.[24] Like Sarat, he read a great deal, but also, as in Mandalay, turned inward, meditating, reflecting, and formulating some of his spiritual or religious concerns. Now—as throughout his life from his late teens—a most important friend with whom he discussed these matters via letters was Dilip Roy. His companion of Calcutta and England was by now resident in the Sri Aurobindo Ashram.[25]

Dilip usually took Subhas' letters to his guru in the ashram for the latter's comments. By the early 1930s, Aurobindo Ghose, now Sri Aurobindo, no longer talked to anyone but the Mother, Mira Richard, but would receive written communications from his disciples, comment on them and return them.[26] While he was in the Madras penitentiary, Subhas wrote to Dilip to thank him for seeking the spiritual intervention of Sri Aurobindo. To the imprisoned Subhas, the guru applied yogic force, to what end is not clear from the surviving letters. Subhas wrote to Dilip, in part,

I do not know if I am sufficiently 'open' to receive yogic force—probably I am not. Nevertheless, I think that even those who rule out the existence of a supra-mental order have to admit the existence and efficacy of what is popularly styled as 'will-power'. And this force . . . is bound to act, even if the receiver is not 'open' or adequately and consciously receptive. I am grateful to Sri Aurobindo. . . . I know that you will continue to feel for me and I also know that in the long run this cannot prove unavailing. This is a great solace to me—no matter where I may happen to be confined.[27]

In the same letter, he came back to unsettling issues of his life's mission and the search for a guru which had been with him since his early teenage years. He wrote,

I have been studying a bit and thinking more; at times I feel as if I am groping in the dark. But I cannot go wrong as long as I am sincere and earnest—even if my progress towards the truth be more zig-zag than straight. After all life's march is not as straight as a straight-line.

Have not each of a sphere of work allotted to us (taking 'work' in the broadest sense)? And is not this sphere conditioned by our past *Karma*, our present desires etc. and our environment? Nevertheless, how difficult it is to understand or realise our proper sphere of work! This sphere of work is the external aspect of our nature or '*Dharma*'. It is so easy to say—'live in accordance with your *Swadharma*'—but so difficult to *know* what one's *dharma* is. It is there that the help of a 'guru' becomes so necessary—and even indispensable.[28]

From this and other letters to Dilip it is easy to see how Dilip, in writing much later about the life of his friend, found him to be a mystic.

Subhas was unhappy with his recurring and persistent physical ailments. When the shift to the Bhowali Sanatorium did him little good, he was ready to consider other possibilities. In December 1932, he was shifted to Lucknow. In Lucknow, considering his physical problems and the political situation in India which was not propitious for his kind of activism at the present, he seriously considered an offer from the government to go abroad. The Government of India for its part did not want the responsibility for his declining health.

Since they considered him a nationalist revolutionary—and they believed, the leader of the Jugantar Party—rather than an international communist revolutionary, they saw advantages to having him outside of India. At the same time, they did not want him in England inflaming Indian students. Haggling ensued, with Bose requesting that the government pay his expenses abroad and allow him to return to Calcutta before departing to see his elderly parents, particularly his infirm father. However, the Government of Bengal, supported by the Government of India, was adamant: Subhas Bose would under no circumstances be allowed back into

Bengal. He could travel from Lucknow to Bombay and say his farewells there. Also, Bose would have to raise the money for his own expenses in Europe, for the Government of India would release him once he was out of Bombay harbor.[29]

In 1927, Bose had declined a similar offer, but the national and international situation was different in 1932 and, since his physical problems were not being remedied, he decided to go. Biva made a trip to see him and then met officials in Delhi to work out all the details.[30] These were complete in early 1933. It was arranged that he would sail on the S.S. Gange on February 23, 1933 from Bombay, and some friends and relations came to bid him goodbye . There is good evidence that he was tracked and surrounded by police spies on board ship, some of them Indians posing as friends.[31] The release order came as the ship left the harbor. Upon leaving India for his second trip abroad, Bose issued a statement to the press in which he said that he was not allowed to say farewell to his parents and placing the blame for his poor health on the government which had not allowed him to be treated by his own doctors in India and had refused to pay for his treatment abroad. He thanked his friends for their moral and financial support which had enabled him to embark on this trip. Then he added,

> Actually sensitive though I am, I have not hesitated to accept the help offered by my friends and well-wishers, because I have always felt that my family is not confined to my blood relations but is coterminous with my country and when I have once (and) for all dedicated my humble life to the service of my country, my countrymen have as much right to look after my welfare as my nearest relatives have.
>
> I only hope and pray that God. . . may make me worthy, in the same measure of love and affection that has been showered on me by all sections of the Indian community.[32]

Bose ended by saying that the love offered to him would be a potent force in his recovery and was better than any ordinary medicine.

As he neared the shores of Europe in early March, Subhas wrote a long letter about his final months in India and his spiritual concerns to his confidant on these matters, Dilip Roy.[33] He briefly lamented the 'pin-pricks of the Government' which continued until he was aboard ship and prevented proper farewells. He mentioned the continuing abdominal pains and the rough weather as they passed Port Said. But he dwelt at much greater length on his search for the most powerful and beneficial religious symbolism within his own private religious practice. He said, in part,

> . . . I am torn this side and that between my love for Shiva, Kali and Krishna. Though they are fundamentally one—one does prefer one symbolism to

another—I have found that my moods vary—and according to my prevalent mood, I choose one of the three forms—Shiva, Kali and Krishna. Of these three again, the struggle is between Shiva and Shakti. Shiva, the ideal Yogi, has a fascination for me and Kali the Mother also makes an appeal to me. You see, of late (i.e. for the last four or five years) I have become a believer in Mantra-Shakti by which I mean that certain Mantras have an inherent Shakti. Prior to that, I had the ordinary rationalistic view, namely that Mantras are like symbols and they are aids to concentration. But my study of Tantra philosophy gradually convinced me that certain Mantras had an inherent Shakti—and that each mental constitution was fitted for a particular Mantra. Since then I have tried my best to find out what my mental constitution is like and which Mantra I would be suited for. But so far I have failed to find that out because my moods vary and I am sometimes a Shaiva, sometimes a Shakta and sometimes a Vaishnava.[34]

There is nothing particularly original or unusual in Bose's quest as recounted to Dilip Roy. What is important is that the inner religious explorations continued to be a part of his adult life. This set him apart from the slowly growing number of atheistic socialists and communists who dotted the Indian landscape. To an M.N. Roy or even to Jawaharlal Nehru this was an irrelevant and vain quest. Subhas issued no public statements on religion, but his Hinduism was an essential part of his Indianness. Part of his mission to Europe was to tell Europeans about India's contributions to world culture.[35]

With Subhas Bose out of the field, the Government of Bengal was now willing to have the other imprisoned Bose, the less dangerous one, inside Bengal and even in his own house. An official of the Government of India noted in late 1932,

I discussed the case of Sarat Bose with His Excellency the Governor. He has had, in addition to the representation a copy of which came to me, a further letter from Mr Sarat Bose, whom he had invited to define his attitude towards terrorism. Mr Sarat Bose . . . explains that he has never had any sympathy with terrorism and his intention is to use all his influence to attack the movement and dissuade people from joining it. On this His Excellency is disposed to recommend that Mr Sarat Bose should be transferred from jail to domiciliary detention in his own house in Kurseong.[36]

Once the transfer was agreed to by all parties, it remained to work out the restrictions that Sarat Bose would have to abide by in his own home. The Government of India asked him to sign his agreement to a long list of such rules.[37] Although he was eager to move from the lonely and unhealthy situation in Jubbulpore, he refused to sign and explained why in his letter to the home member of the Government of India, dated March 22, 1933:

On Monday last . . . a document entitled 'conditions of release' was handed

over to me . . . for perusal and signature. . . I found that it had not the remotest
connection with any proposal for my 'release' . . . . I feel bound to say that
I consider it derogatory to myself . . . to have to sign an agreement as a
condition precedent to an order for my transfer to my own house. . . . I feel
that I would be untrue to myself, the family in which I was born, to the
education which I have received, to the position which I have held in my
profession as also in public and private life and to the beliefs and sentiments
which I have always held dear if I were to put my signature to any
'conditions' for the purpose of obtaining liberty for myself, either complete
or qualified.[38]

He went on to explain that he did not understand why he had to sign a list
of conditions when he was to remain a state prisoner on grounds of which
he had never been informed. He maintained that he could always be sent
back to jail if the government was not satisfied with his conduct.

After several exchanges passed between officials and Sarat Bose, it was
decided that it would suffice that Sarat Bose had been informed of the
'conditions'. Sarat Bose had made his small legal points, vented some of
his pent-up aggravation, and was now to stay for an indefinite period in his
vacation house near Darjeeling.

Just before his transfer in April 1933, Sarat Bose recorded a few of his
stray thoughts in a notebook. On March 28, he wrote,

The difference between the spirit of Bengal and the spirit of Sabarmati is the
difference between a devout worshipper of 'Shakti' and a devout Christian,
the difference between Vivekananda and Tolstoy. The former includes the
latter; the latter does not include the former. 'Shakti' is the religion of my
soul; it is from her that I seek inspiration.[39]

He added on April 2,

Gandhi is today undoubtedly the greatest Christian in the world. I wish he
had been, at the same time, a great Hindu; for, had he been so, he would not
have committed the blunders he has committed in the fields of religion and
politics.[40]

He did not list or explain what he meant by Gandhi's 'blunders' but a
further entry made in Kurseong gives a hint about his unhappiness with
Gandhian politics,

I see no reason why our ideal should be 'Dominion Status' or the 'Substance
of Independence' (to use a Gandhian phrase). If and when the nationalist
movement is strong enough to win dominion status it will be abundantly
strong enough to win 'complete independence.'[41]

The minds of both brothers—Sarat in Kurseong, Subhas in Europe—were
still on political questions, for important developments had been taking
place in the outside world which were to shape the political field and in
which they would operate once they were again at liberty to do so.

II

During 1932 there had been movement towards a revision of the Government of India Act of 1919. Officially civil disobedience was revived, but this time it was met by severe and systematic repression by the Government of India. The Congress' activity in urban areas was curtailed, although in some rural areas, those with local grievances linked to the Congress program and with their own demands, continued the agitation sporadically through the next two years.[42]

Another important political process at work was the formulation of proposals for the future governance of India. These steps had begun with the work of the Simon Commission in 1927 which had, in turn, stimulated independent efforts by Indians such as the All-Parties' or Nehru Report of 1928. While the Congress had only intermittently participated in the procedures of the imperial government, other Indian leaders including Jinnah, Liberals such as Sir Tej Bahadur Sapru, Hindu nationalists such as M.R. Jayakar, leaders of minority communities, and representatives of the princely states involved themselves at almost every stage at which Indians were consulted. The Congress, though committed to complete independence, was, through Gandhi, still willing to talk about dominion status, the very meaning of which was changing in 1931. Gandhi's pact with Lord Irwin and his trip to the second Round Table Conference in 1931 have been mentioned above. At this meeting, the leaders of groups and organizations within British India attempted to come to some resolution of the communal question. Gandhi himself, eager for such agreement, worked for it, but was foiled, partly by the intercession of the Hindu right. This failure bedeviled the entire work of the conference, and Gandhi had to return empty-handed.[43]

After the Congress was excluded from the process—it had been declared an illegal organization in 1932—the discussions went forward with the remaining actors and parties. The Simon Commission had recommended fuller provincial self-government, no advances at the center, and had not mentioned dominion status, which Lord Irwin, then viceroy, had said was and continued to be the goal. With the Congress outside the process, there was not nearly the same pressure for full self-government and a unitary system. British officials in London and Delhi were more eager to get the agreement of the remaining Indian groups, particularly the Muslims, the Liberals, the princes, and the Scheduled Caste leaders.[44]

Even before the new framework of government was worked out, the National Government of J. Ramsay MacDonald issued the Communal Award on August 17, 1932. Behind the scenes a good deal of haggling had

gone on and the new allotment of seats in the legislative body in Bengal—
the future Bengal Legislative Assembly—was a matter for considerable
disputation even before MacDonald, his secretary of state, the Conservative
Sir Samuel Hoare, and the viceroy Lord Willingdon came to an agreement.
One account of these backstage discussions is given by R.J. Moore, a
foremost historian of the process of devolution:

> In the Bengal case a sharp controversy arose. Hoare's scheme provided for
> 250 seats, of which the Europeans would get 25. . . and the other special
> interests 26. The Muslims would have about 111 seats and the Hindus some
> 88. As the Muslims could not expect to win any of the special interest seats
> they would have only 44.4 per cent of the seats, though they accounted for
> 55 per cent of the population. The Hindus would probably get 42.8 per cent
> of the seats, which almost corresponded to their proportion of the
> population. Hoare's proposal coincided with the recommendations that the
> governor of Bengal (Sir Stanley Jackson) had sent to Willingdon in January.
> Willingdon nevertheless considered it unfair to the Muslims and bound to
> be unpopular. He would give ten of the Hindus' seats (including two of their
> expected labour seats) to the Muslims. Thereby the Muslims would have
> 121 seats (48.4 per cent) and the Hindus 78 (39.2 per cent). Willingdon
> argued that Bengal was an all-India and not a merely local question. . . .
> Anything less than he proposed would 'alienate us from Muslim support not
> merely in Bengal but throughout India'. . .[45]

This is a part of the story. Other voices—obviously not so important to
Willingdon and Hoare—were putting forth a different view and these
included spokesmen of the Hindus of Bengal and the former governor of
Bengal and now a Conservative politician, the Marquess of Zetland.
Zetland maintained that it was an absurd application of the principle of
separate electorates and reserved seats to apply the system to the majority
community and give them a 'permanent statutory majority . . . in the
Legislature.'[46] Willingdon and Hoare were giving away Hindu seats and
ensuring the minuscule European community in Bengal a healthy row of
seats in the Bengal legislature. However, they did not calculate what the
impact would be on the Hindus of Bengal and of India, while they fortified
their position with the Muslims.

Willingdon and the officials of the India Office, who were most
responsible for the Bengal allotment, were not mistaken in their belief that
the Muslims in Bengal, in so far as they were supported by Muslims
elsewhere in India, wanted seats in the Bengal legislature proportionate to
their share of Bengal's population. Although most Bengal Muslim leaders
wanted separate electorates, a small number in the Bengal Nationalist
Muslim Party was willing to accept joint electorates.[47] While the Muslim
leaders were asking for what they saw as their fair share, they did not ask

that the Hindus be so hobbled from their previous strong position in the Bengal legislature. Under the Lucknow Pact and the subsequent Government of India Act of 1919, the Hindus in Bengal had sixty per cent of the elected seats and the Muslims forty per cent. The deterioration of communal relations and the rising political consciousness of middle-class Muslims and the wealthier peasants made it inevitable that the Muslims would fight for a share of the seats closer to their share of the population.[48] Although the caste Hindu leaders were loathe to give up their favored position, they knew there had to be some realignment. But having only seventy-eight seats in a house of 250, with some seats to be gained through the special constituencies, was a catastrophic blow.[49] The protest began from the moment the Communal Award was announced; but then came a second blow from the changes made through the Poona Pact.

Mahatma Gandhi, though imprisoned, was following the fortunes of the political negotiations carefully. He too reacted with alarm to the Communal Award, but for a different reason than his brethren in Bengal. He was upset at the arrangement of separate electorates for members of the Scheduled Castes, who previously had voted with the caste Hindus in the general constituencies. He was, indeed, so concerned that he announced from his Poona prison that he would fast unto death, or at least until the representatives of the Scheduled Castes would agree to rejoin the Hindu fold by accepting joint rather than separate electorates. So the Epic Fast, as it was called, began. Tremendous pressure was exerted upon Dr Ambedkar, the main Scheduled Caste leader, to give up separate electorates. He resisted for some time, but finally capitulated in return for a great share of reserved seats for Scheduled Caste members in the general constituencies.[50] For Bengal this meant that thirty of the seventy-eight general seats had to be held by members of these castes in Bengal, a far greater number than they had ever had and many more than they expected. And to the caste Hindu leaders this seemed another nail in their coffin.[51]

Once Gandhi and Ambedkar had agreed, there was little that Bengal Hindu leaders could do about the Poona Pact, which was accepted by the imperial government and incorporated into the Government of India bill that was being formulated. But about the Communal Award as a whole, those Bengal Congressmen out of prison, Bengal Liberals, independent Hindus, members of the Hindu Mahasabha, and many cultural leaders of the Hindu community, began an agitation which went on almost unceasingly for years and achieved no positive result. In order to make any change in the Communal Award, the agreement of the affected parties was needed. Though the Muslim leaders may have agreed that the caste Hindus had received a setback, the former would not give up any of their 119 seats.

Some informal discussions went on with new formulas suggested, but the Muslims were only willing to have seats taken away from the Europeans and not themselves.[52]

The Communal Award gave encouragement to a Hindu organization, the Hindu Mahasabha, which while never strong in numbers in Bengal, did have some influence upon the thinking and emotions of the caste Hindus in Bengal, particularly in the 1930s and 1940s. In contrast to the composite, territorial Indian nationalism propagated by the Congress, the Mahasabha stressed the association of the Hindus with their sacred territory, Hindustan. In their view, many Christians and Muslims were converts from Hinduism and must, if at all possible, be reconverted by *shuddhi* activities. The Mahasabha's leader, V.D. Savarkar, developed the concept of 'Hindutva' which '. . . embraces all the departments of thought and activity of the whole being of our Hindu race.'[53] Any one who wanted to live in the Hindu nation would have to accept Hindustan 'as his Fatherland as well as his Holy Land, that is, the cradle land of his religion.'[54] So Muslims, *prima facie,* would be excluded from first-class citizenship in such a nation. They would be subjects or perhaps foreigners in the land in which they lived.

The Hindu Mahasabha was never strong as an organization in Bengal, but its leader, Shyama Prasad Mookerjee, became a prominent and articulate spokesman for this point of view during these years. In 1929 he took over Sarat Bose's Calcutta University seat in the Bengal Legislative Council and remained in the Council for many years. He was also a family friend of the Boses, though he differed from them on many political issues. He would fight to get them out of prison and press the government with questions about their health when they were in prison. He, more than any other Hindu leader in Bengal, spurred the fears of high-caste Hindus inside and outside the Bengal Congress. They would, he said, lose their predominance in the economic and educational systems, in the professions and government services, to the numerically superior Muslims.[55] The Mahasabha encouraged inflexibility on a variety of issues touching Hindu-Muslim relations in Bengal: processions playing music outside mosques, tenancy legislation and educational reforms which would assist the predominantly Muslim rural masses, and limitations on the Muslim role in the Calcutta Corporation and Calcutta University.[56]

From 1932 onwards, numerous meetings were held to protest the Communal Award. At one of these a few years later, Sarat Chandra Chatterji, the noted novelist and also a friend of the Boses, expressed some of the fears he had of the prospective disintegration of Bengali culture. The press reported,

Looking at the question as a humble worshipper in the temple of Bengali literature, he would like to say that he had noticed with a feeling of anguish and pain that attempts were already being made aiming a blow at the Bengali language and literature. From his experience as a litterateur he could say that he had always found Bengali language to be rich enough to be a powerful instrument for the expression of any thought that had ever occurred to him. He could not therefore understand the meaning of the demands that were now being made in certain quarters to import certain percentages of words, some from Arabic and some from the Persian languages.

His apprehension was that ten years would not elapse before the Bengali language would take a different shape altogether. The attack had already begun. And perhaps ten years hence Rabindranath would not be there in his field of activities; it might be that the speaker himself might not be also there and he shuddered to think what transformation the Bengali language and literature might undergo in course of these ten years if the dark forces that were already at work were not checked betimes.[57]

It was fear of 'dark forces' and of permanent political subserviency that haunted the minds and threatened the dominance of nationalist Hindus in many areas of Bengali life.

In the political arena, Pandit Malaviya and others who could operate openly and who opposed the Communal Award, formed the Congress Nationalist Party. This small party contested seats for the Central Legislative Assembly in 1934 and it successfully defeated many of the regular Congress candidates in the election. Sarat Chandra Bose, a champion of Hindu-Muslim alliance in Bengal, and still under detention in Kurseong, was elected unopposed from a Calcutta seat with both the Nationalists and the regular Congress claiming his support. With these defeats, the Bengal Congress began to take a stronger and more direct stand against the Communal Award than national Congress policy allowed.[58] Even from far-off Vienna, Subhas Bose wrote to Satyen Mitra in 1934,

I cannot accept—nor can I understand—this attitude of 'don't accept, don't reject' towards the Communal Award. The party of Dr B.C. Roy has done incalculable disservice to Bengal by supporting Mahatma Gandhi on this question. Bengal should have been quite united on this question.[59]

It was clear that the Boses agreed with their brethren in the Bengal Congress.

III

Subhas Bose arrived in Venice on March 6, 1933, and was greeted by a message from the Hindustan Association of Italy, questions from Italian journalists, and his nephew Asoke Bose. After briefly resting in Venice, Subhas Bose and his nephew made their way to Vienna, which was to become his home base in Europe.[60] He had never been to pre-war Vienna, the capital of the earlier Hapsburg Empire.

To Bose, Vienna beckoned as a great medical center, as one of the cultural capitals of the world, and as a great city at the crossroads of Europe, from where he could travel throughout the continent. Bose saw the surface of an elegant city and one which was, as some said, 'red Vienna in a black country.'[61] He soon responded positively to the achievements of the socialist, or red municipal government of Vienna, but he did not seem to have a sense of the political, cultural, and economic changes—some thought catastrophes—which Austria had gone through as a result of the First World War and the sudden collapse of the Austro-Hungarian Empire. To a sensitive German-Austrian the landscape looked much different, as for example, to the noted writer, Stefan Zweig,

> ... that Austria which showed faintly on the map of Europe as the vague, gray and inert shadow of the former Imperial monarchy. The Czechs, Poles, Italians, and Slovenes had snatched away their countries, what remained was a mutilated trunk that bled from every vein. Of the six or seven millions who were forced to call themselves 'German-Austrians,' two starving and freezing millions crowded the capital alone; the industries which had formerly enriched the land were on foreign soil, the railroads had become wrecked stumps, the State Bank received in place of its gold the gigantic burden of the war debt.[62]

To Bose, almost all of continental Europe was new and he was eager to make new contacts with Europeans and with Indians in Europe. During his first months in Vienna and then in Switzerland, one of his confidants and allies was an elderly political leader from India, Vithalbhai Patel, elder brother of the Gandhian, Vallabhbhai Patel. This was an instructive and valuable contact for Bose because the elder Patel was an ally from the Swarajya Party of C.R. Das and had been actually acting on one of Das' plans that was cut short by his early death. Patel had been touring Europe and the United States making positive propaganda and contacts for Indian nationalism. This was the very same task to which Bose had set himself and strengthened him in the belief that it was a vital enterprise. Moreover, Patel had helped found the Indo-Irish League and was able to bring Bose into contact with Mrs M. Woods, an official of this organization, and its president, Maud Gonne McBride.[63] Eventually this organization was able to help arrange Bose's visit to Ireland, the fulfillment of one of his fondest desires.

Not long after Bose reached Vienna, Gandhi called off the Civil Disobedience Movement, much to the dismay of Bose and Patel. They issued 'The Bose-Patel Manifesto' from Vienna in May 1933 which stated that,

We are clearly of opinion that as a political leader Mahatma Gandhi has failed. The time has therefore come for a radical reorganisation of the Congress on a new principle and with a new method. For bringing about this reorganisation a change of leadership is necessary. . . . If the Congress as a whole can undergo this transformation, it would be the best course. Failing that a new party will have to be formed within the Congress, composed of all radical elements. Non-co-operation cannot be given up but the form of Non-co-operation will have to be changed into a more militant one and the fight for freedom to be waged on all fronts.[64]

Although the condemnation was thorough-going, the specification of the new 'radical' leadership and program was certainly imprecise. Patel was severely ill, but he was glad to have met the younger man and to feel that his work would be carried forth. He is reported to have said of Bose at this time,

In him I see a great fighter with an incomparable determination to carry on India's struggle without any kind of compromise. . . . Even at this early age he has all the merits of a great leader, and his statesmanship and diplomacy are something which I have not seen in any other young man in India. . . . Where can you find such a man? It is for this reason that all my hopes are centred on him, and I am leaving all my monies to him to be disposed of for any foreign propaganda that he may decide upon for the uplift of India.[65]

For Bose this was a very positive relationship with one of the father figures of the Swarajists and Congress, by all accounts much less ambiguous, though short-lived, than his relationship to any of the Congress seniors after the death of Das. And for Patel, there is little doubt that he saw Bose as *the* young man or one of the young men who would lead India to freedom as the old men—including Gandhi and himself—stepped aside.

During these first months in Europe, Bose received an invitation to address the third Indian Political Conference in London, to be held on June 10, 1933.[66] He wrote to British authorities for permission to come and speak, but this was not forthcoming. Unbeknownst to Bose, the India Office and other British officials were quite sure that Bose could nòt be kept out of England if he tried to enter because he held a British passport. At this moment and for five years subsequently, Bose did not try to enter for fear of being arrested or being turned away. But it was all bluff. The India Office was behind the effort because they did not want to have Bose in England inflaming Indian students there.[67] So Subhas could not deliver the address in person in June 1933—or believed he could not—therefore he sent it to the conference where it was read out.

It presents a lengthy review of his political outlook at the time, his assessment of Gandhi's blunders, and his view of what was to be done. It was also a preparation for his much longer account to be written the following year. He was very upset with the termination of the Civil Disobedience Movement and wrote,

> We had been engaged in a non-violent war with the British Government— for the attainment of our political freedom. But to-day our condition is analogous to that of an army that has suddenly surrendered unconditionally to the enemy. . . not because the nation demanded it. . . either because the Commander-in-Chief was exhausted as a result of repeated fasting or because his mind and judgement were clouded owing to subjective causes which it is impossible for an outsider to understand.[68]

He then reviewed the history of the Congress movement from 1920 to 1933 and showed how he thought the government had outsmarted Gandhi at each turn, and how he, Bose, had opposed many of Gandhi's moves. He argued that there were no common interests between Britain and India and, therefore, the goal had to be complete independence by the most rapid means. He listed the possible means, including armed force, but ruled this out for the moment because nationalist India was not armed and the Congress was pledged to non-violence.[69]

He called for a 'scientific plan of action and a scientific programme for the future', using terms like objective and subjective factors which rang of Marxist terminology. Then he said,

> Our first task will be to gather together a group of men and women who are prepared to undergo the maximum sacrifice and suffering which will be necessary if we are to attain success in our mission. They must be wholetime workers—'Freedom-intoxicated' missionaries—who will not be discouraged by failure or deterred by difficulty of any kind and who will vow to work and strive in the service of the great cause till the last day of their lives . . . . Let this party be called the SAMYAVADI-SANGHA. It will be a centralised and well-disciplined All-India Party—working amongst every section of the community. . . . The SAMYAVADI-SANGHA will stand for all-round freedom for the Indian people—that is, for social, economic and political freedom. It will wage a relentless war against bondage of every kind till the people can become really free. . . . [70]

The program for free India was not spelled out in more detail. Though some of the speech had resonances in Marxist thought, Bose's call for 'freedom-intoxicated missionaries' surely sounded like the speeches of his boyhood idol, Swami Vivekananda. The India Office, carefully charting Bose's work in Europe, was most unhappy with this speech and with the ways in which Bose talked about war and violence.[71]

With Patel's help, Bose was trying to sort out his proper work for India abroad. Patel had been doing propaganda work for India for some time. 'Propaganda' had not assumed the negative ring that it has today. For Patel and Bose, it meant disseminating positive and accurate information about

India's national struggle against the British Raj and about India's great cultural achievements. The second half of 1933 was darkened for Bose by the serious illness of Patel, who was moved to Switzerland. Bose went there to be near him and to try to improve his own health, which still had not greatly improved. As Patel grew more gravely ill, Bose helped to nurse him. And Bose was by him when Patel breathed his last in late October.[72] Now he lamented that another Congress giant—one of the few along with Das and Motilal Nehru, all of whom he considered peers of Gandhi—had gone and only, or mostly, 'yes-men' were left.

Patel bequeathed to Bose a political and financial legacy and the latter turned into a long and nasty legal dispute with Sardar Patel and other relatives of Vithalbhai. The provision in his will for substantial monies to be left to Bose to be used for propaganda work was challenged in an Indian court which eventually found that Patel's bequest was stated too vaguely. Bose, to his dismay, never got one rupee. He always believed he would have used the funds just as Vithalbhai wanted.[73] This legal battle went on into the late 1930s and did not improve his relations to Sardar Patel, one of the most adept of his Gandhian adversaries in the Congress.

One of Subhas Bose's aims in Europe was to learn about developments there and he was particularly interested in the work of European municipalities. The Vienna municipality for some years had been run by the Social Democrats. This socialist party had made great strides in providing inexpensive municipal housing and in improving services for all citizens of Vienna. Through some of his new friends, particularly Mr and Mrs Vetter, he made contact with officials in Vienna and was shown around. The Vetters became very close friends and when he was on tour, he constantly wrote short letters giving his whereabouts and impressions to Mrs Vetter.[74] Her husband was a high state official, working on opera and music productions and was president of two theaters. As Bose went around in Vienna—and later in many other cities of Europe—he asked ordinary people about the details of their lives and he inquired of officials and politicians about their successes and failures in running city, state, and national governments. At first he was so taken up by the achievements of the Vienna municipality that he wrote to Calcutta's mayor about putting together a book on Vienna for the use of the Calcutta city government, but later dropped this plan. He started to tour Europe, writing short pieces for Indian journals and newspapers about some of the places he visited and people he met.[75]

During 1933, Bose made a trip to Czechoslovakia, Poland, and Germany that lasted about two months. At the end of this trip, he joined Patel for the last period of his life. After the death of Patel, he went to France and then

Rome. From Rome he traveled to Milan and then Geneva, where an Indian information center had been established. In March 1934 he began another lengthy trip, this time to Germany, back to Italy, and then on to Hungary, Rumania, Turkey, Bulgaria, and Yugoslavia. By the end of May, he settled down again in Vienna and worked on a book about Indian politics, the contract for which he had signed with a British publisher. He spent some time in Karlsbad, a famous health resort, where he took the mineral waters, hoping they would alleviate his abdominal problems.[76]

After flying from Vienna to Prague, Bose met Dr Eduard Benes, then foreign minister, who, along with President Masaryk, had led the long struggle for Czechoslovakia's independence. In the smaller nations of Europe which had freed themselves from larger empires, Bose was often able to make contact with the head of state or officials at the highest level, partly through his own resourcefulness, partly with the help of friends like Mr Vetter. In Prague he also made a contribution to the formation of a lasting tie between India and Czechoslovakia by moving to have an Indo-Czech association established. This was carried through the following year by Professor Lesny, the noted Indologist, who had been at Tagore's Santiniketan.[77]

He went on to Warsaw for some days from Prague, saw officials there, and by late July 1933 had reached Berlin. He wrote to Mrs Vetter that, 'I think I strained myself too much at Prague and Warsaw and am now feeling the effect. I am still feeling exhausted and feverish.'[78] He recovered enough to try to see the top officials of the new Nazi regime. Helping him throughout his Berlin visit was Lothar Frank, then a science teacher at a technical high school and a member of the Indo-German Society.[79] Though offered government accommodations, Bose preferred to stay on without official help and lodged at the Grand-Hotel-am-Knie in Charlottenburg. Bose had high hopes for establishing valuable contacts with the German government and for meeting the highest government officials as he had elsewhere in Europe. He undoubtedly knew that Indian revolutionaries had secured limited financial aid, arms, and encouragement from the German government during the First World War and that Berlin had remained after the war one of the centers—outside of India—for Indian activity against the Raj. So he came to Germany in 1933 with high expectations and returned to Germany on future occasions hoping for the best, but often securing only small returns on his investments of time, energy, and optimism.[80]

The Germany that Bose had to deal with in 1933 and later was the Germany of Adolf Hitler and the Nazi Party. Superimposed upon the realpolitik of earlier German regimes was the racist worldview of Hitler and his associates. On Hitler's racial scale, Orientals including Indians were low down, near the Jews, Slavs, Gypsies, and bastard races of the Americas. Moreover, India was ruled by an Anglo-Saxon or Aryan people for whom Hitler had great admiration. In *Mein Kampf*, Hitler referred nastily to Indian freedom fighters as deluded 'Asiatic jugglers'.[81] He went on to argue that these freedom fighters would never be able to drive the British from India and,

> *England will lose India either if her own administrative machinery falls a prey to racial decomposition ... or if she is bested by the sword of a powerful enemy.* Indian agitators, however, will never achieve this. How hard it is to best England, we Germans have sufficiently learned. Quite aside from the fact that I, as a man of Germanic blood, would, in spite of everything, rather see India under English rule than under any other.[82]

So Hitler was not eager in 1933 or later to meet one of these 'Asiatic jugglers' and to offer him encouragement.

There were other signs after Hitler became Reich's Chancellor on January 30, 1933, that times were going to be more difficult for Indians in Germany. On February 28, A.C.N. Nambiar, a journalist and one of the better known Indians in Berlin after nine years' residence there, was suddenly seized by Nazi storm troopers who entered his flat without a warrant and, after threatening to kill him, took him to prison and carried off many of his belongings. He was held without charges until March 25. The British ambassador, no friend of Indian nationalism, had to protest the ill treatment of a British subject. Nambiar was finally released and ordered to leave the country.[83] Coordinate with and following the arrest of Nambiar, only negative articles about India began to appear in the German press and Indian students in Germany began to experience more difficulties.[84]

Though Lothar Frank was a member of the left-wing of the Nazi Party, he could do no more than arrange for Bose to see Dr Pruefer, joint secretary at the Foreign Office, and Mr Dyckhoff and Mr Schmidt-Rolke, other officials in the same ministry. Mr Frank has given an account of these conversations:

> ... (They) did not lead to any practical results. Thus, even those members of the German Foreign Office who were not enthusiastic members of the National Socialist Party, could not do very much. They eventually asked Bose to get into touch with Dr Franz Thierfelder who was at that time Director of the Germany Academy in Munich. Consequently Subhas Bose went down to Munich and met Dr Thierfelder. Through the latter he was able to send a draft programme for Indo-German collaboration, which he himself had prepared, to some members of the German Foreign Office.[85]

Although Bose was well aware of the anti-Indian actions of the German government and press under Hitler, he did not align himself with those Indians in Europe and India who began to call for a boycott of German goods as the racist acts continued. Neither did he try to whitewash these acts as some other Indians in Europe.

Bose protested the anti-Indian actions, criticized Nazi racism directed against Indians whenever he could, *and* worked for positive connections between India and Germany.[86] Privately he may have found their racism abhorrent, but, at the same time, he did not want to alienate as powerful a potential ally against the British Empire as a revived Germany. He was certainly unhappy with the meager accomplishments in Germany, but he was a persistent man and left after some weeks to make contacts elsewhere.

In the fall of 1933, he was preoccupied with the declining health of Vithalbhai Patel and then his death. It was only after Patel's death in late 1933 that Bose began his traveling with renewed energy, now carrying on for himself and for Patel who had seen such activity as immensely important for India's future. In December, Bose went to Rome to attend the Conference of Oriental Students and other meetings concerning Indian students. He believed that Italy under Mussolini was an important world power and that contacts with that fascist regime would be beneficial to India.[87]

Like many other Indian nationalists, Bose had been touched by stories of the Italian Risorgimento of the nineteenth century. He had read of two great patriots and revolutionaries of the period, Mazzini and Garibaldi, who worked outside and inside Italy to bring about a popular government, freedom from foreign powers, and unity to their country. The other Italy was that of the fascists who—to many—seemed to be bringing new energy, life, and awakening to their country.

Whatever the evils and hollowness of fascist Italy, one has to say of Mussolini that he made a considerable effort to court positive foreign opinions. He did this partly by the manipulation of the press, but he also tried to see every important foreigner who came through Italy.[88] This included many important Indian leaders traveling from India to Europe or returning home from Europe. In 1926, for example, Rabindranath Tagore was invited to meet the Duce and Krishna Kripalani has quoted what the poet wrote after the meeting,

> His Excellency Mussolini seems modelled body and soul by the chisel of a Michael Angelo, whose every action showed intelligence and force. ... 'Let me dream that from the fire-bath the immortal soul of Italy will come out clothed in quenchless light.'[89]

Tagore was subsequently angered by the inaccurate press reports issued by the Italian news services which tried to show that he had an even more inflated view of Mussolini, and the poet became critical of Italian fascism.

The next Indian notable whom Mussolini courted and, temporarily at least, impressed was Mahatma Gandhi. On his return from the second Round Table Conference in London, Gandhi was invited to meet Mussolini and see the Sistene Chapel. After meeting the Duce and en route back to India, Gandhi wrote to Romain Rolland,

> Mussolini is a riddle to me. Many of his reforms attract me. He seems to have done much for the peasant class. I admit an iron hand is there. But as violence is the basis of Western society, Mussolini's reforms deserve an impartial study. His care of the poor, his opposition to super-urbanization, his efforts to bring about co-ordination between capital and labour, seem to me to demand special attention. . . . My own fundamental objection is that these reforms are compulsory. But it is the same in all democratic institutions. What strikes me is that behind Mussolini's implacability is a desire to serve his people. Even behind his emphatic speeches there is a nucleus of sincerity and of passionate love for his people. It seems to me that the majority of the Italian people love the iron government of Mussolini.[90]

Of course, Gandhi on other occasions was critical of fascism, particularly because violence and compulsion were employed. But his own first-hand impressions of Italy and Mussolini were certainly positive on balance.

There were other Indian observers who came to Mussolini's Italy. Some of these came away with glowing reports which played down the excesses and brutalities of the regime. Among these visitors was an experienced Bengali revolutionary and nationalist who had spent many years abroad and was an acquaintance of the Boses. This was Taraknath Das, who sent his reports on foreign affairs to the *Modern Review*, one of the best and most cosmopolitan of India's journals, edited by Ramananda Chatterjee in Calcutta. The same year that Gandhi visited Rome, Das wrote in an article entitled 'New Italy and Greater India':

> New Italy, under the leadership of Signor Mussolini, is roused to its very depths of national consciousness. It feels that it has a mission of introducing a higher type of civilization. It had the urge of becoming a great power again . . . Italy must be great through her national power, achieved through the authority of an 'ethical State', supported by national co-operation and solidarity. . . . Every Italian citizen must think first of his duty towards his self-development, welfare of the State and society and make his or her supreme effort to attain the ideal. Class harmony must take the place of the ideal of class-war. So-called democracy must give way to the rule of the aristocracy of intellect. . . . Some superficial and prejudiced observers of new Italy have spoken of 'Fascist tyranny' and condemned the Fascist regime. To me it is clear that the Fascist government or a particular official might have made some mistakes on particular occasions; but Fascism stands for liberty with responsibility and it is opposed to all forms of license. It gives precedence to Duty and Strength, as one finds in the teachings of the *Bhagavad Gita*.[91]

So the reports available to educated Indians in the late 1920s and early 1930s about fascist Italy were mixed.

In early 1934, Bose wrote to Mrs Vetter, giving a summary of what had transpired in Rome. He had attended the opening ceremony of the Oriental Institute of Italy, the Indian Students' Convention, and the Asiatic Students' Congress. The latter event in the Julius Caesar Hall was,

> . . . attended by 600 Asiatic students from different centres in Europe. Travelling was free on the Italian Railways and free board and lodging was given in Rome for one week. Mussolini addressed the Congress on the 22nd December. The speech was a fine one—whatever we might think of the speaker. He said, 'It is nonsense to say that East and West will never meet. Rome has in the past been the connecting link between Europe and Asia and she will be so once again. On this rapprochement depends the salvation of the world. *Rome has in the past colonised Europe—but her relations with Asia have always been of a friendly kind, based on cooperation.*'[92]

Bose noted that he stayed on after the meetings in Rome for a fortnight, 'in order to explore the ground and make some friends if possible for the cause of India':

> There are a few people in Rome genuinely interested in India. . . . People generally do not know anything about India—but there is a desire to know. There is no prejudice against Indians—rather there is sympathy. . . . I think I have been able to create a deeper interest for India in some persons whom I came to know in Rome. . . . The official attitude is extremely favourable now and they want closer contact with the East. If such an official attitude had existed in places like Vienna or even Berlin—I am sure that we could have done much useful work there.[93]

To others of his confidants, Bose revealed details and he wrote to his nephew Asoke, 'I had two meetings with the big boss.' He also toured the municipality of Rome and planned with Professor Tucci to work on an India center in Rome. To his Berlin host Lothar Frank, Bose reportedly gave details of his conversation with Mussolini,

> Mussolini asked Subhas Bose during this conversation: 'Do you really and firmly believe that India will be free soon?' When Bose said 'yes', Mussolini asked him again: 'Are you for reformist or revolutionary methods for achieving Indian independence?' Bose said in reply that he preferred revolutionary to reformist methods. Mussolini said, 'Then indeed you have a chance.' Continuing the discussion, Mussolini asked him again: 'Have you got any plan for such a revolution?' As Bose remained silent, Mussolini told him: 'You must immediately prepare a plan for such a revolution and you must work continuously for its realisation.'[94]

This was the first of Bose's many visits to Italy and the first of his encounters with Mussolini. Throughout the following years, Bose received positive support from Mussolini and no doubt found the attention—from someone whom he believed was among those in world politics who 'really counted'—most flattering.[95] One has to remember that even a recent and most critical biographer of Mussolini has explained that Mussolini had a knack for charming visitors whom he saw infrequently.[96] Then, too, from the few details that have filtered out, it appears that Bose felt that he was treated as an important leader of a significant nation struggling for its freedom, and also that Mussolini—in contrast to the Germans—treated him more as an equal and without racial condescension.

When Bose referred to the accomplishments of fascism, he mentioned the efficiency of the fascist state in transforming a languid society into a dynamic one. The focus was on means, and on the role of the forceful leader. These few positive references to fascism do not specify any particular nation and tend to be vague and general, but it is likely to be with Italy in mind that Bose wrote. Later in 1934, in his lengthy account of Indian politics and the future of India, Bose stated,

> Considering everything, one is inclined to hold that the next phase in world-history will produce a synthesis between Communism and Fascism. And will it be a surprise if that synthesis is produced in India?. . . In spite of the antithesis between Communism and Fascism, there are certain traits common to both. Both Communism and Fascism believe in the supremacy of the State over the Individual. Both denounce parliamentary democracy. Both believe in party rule. Both believe in the dictatorship of the party and in the ruthless suppression of all dissenting minorities. Both believe in a planned industrial reorganisation of the country. These common traits will form the basis of the new synthesis. That synthesis is called by the writer 'Samyavada'— an Indian word, which means literally 'the doctrine of synthesis or equality'. It will be India's task to work out this synthesis.[97]

After a year in Europe, where parliamentary democracy was widely under attack, Bose seemed to be falling captive to a set of ideals for the new India that were not quite the same as he had advocated in the past. He was not unaware or uninformed, so he surely knew of the excesses committed in the name of the progress of the nation in Germany, Italy, the Soviet Union, and elsewhere. Bose and others believed that strong hands at the helm seemed necessary in a time of economic, social, and political crisis, to bring about the positive future they were working towards. But did he intend to close his eyes to the brutalities of these regimes? Did he believe that the positive lesson of these regimes could be separated out from the bestialities and transferred to India?

From Rome, Bose embarked on a second tour which took him to Switzerland, Germany, Czechoslovakia, back to Italy, Hungary, Rumania, Turkey, Bulgaria, and Yugoslavia during the first half of 1934. In his essay

'India Abroad', written during his European stay, Bose had argued that, 'Everywhere there is a colossal ignorance about India—but at the same time there is a general feeling of sympathy for, and interest in, India.'[98] Feeling that 'Indian propaganda abroad was absolutely necessary for our national advancement', his objectives—and those that he felt were necessary for Indian propaganda in general—were:

(1) To counteract false propaganda about India.
(2) To enlighten the world about the true conditions obtaining in India today.
(3) To acquaint the world with the positive achievements of the Indian people in every sphere of human activity.[99]

To reach these goals, Bose wanted Indian representatives at every international congress, positive articles about India in every language of Europe, prominent Indians traveling abroad and speaking about their country, the development of films and slides on India, the invitation of foreign scholars to India, and the creation of mixed societies of Indians and foreigners in every country to foster closer cultural and commercial relations.[100]

Bose realized that he did not have the resources of the British government. But Bose did his best to establish the kind of cultural and commercial associations which might grow, endure, and contribute to long-term links. He also wanted active Indian student associations wherever possible. In Rome in December 1933, he had presided over the meeting of the Federation of Indian Students and he was in constant touch with Indian students wherever he went. This was obviously in line with his role vis-à-vis students in India. He saw students and their training in science, engineering, medicine, and other subjects as the preparation not only for their individual futures, but for the future of India, and Bose talked to European industrialists, businessmen, and officials about internships for Indians with relevant advanced degrees.[101]

In 1933 when he visited Warsaw, Bose made contact with the Oriental Society there and wrote of a Sanskrit scholar he met, Professor Stanislaw Michalski, and hoped that their talks had laid the groundwork for a Polish-Indian Society.[102] In Czechoslovakia, he had met Professor Vincenc and Lesny and Bose returned to Prague in April 1934 for the founding of the Indian Association there.[103] Bose also made contact with A.C.N. Nambiar, the Indian journalist who had been expelled from Nazi Germany and was later to work closely with him. Bose made a number of trips to Switzerland and worked with the India Center in Geneva which brought out a monthly bulletin on India in English, French, and German.[104] After leaving these familiar places, Bose moved on to the Balkan countries and

Turkey. He enjoyed this trip and met leaders in each country, but it was a superficial tour. He did pause long enough in Rumania to meet an Indian doctor, married and settled there, about whom Bose wrote a short and flattering article.[105] Although Turkey was not on his original itinerary, he decided he would include a trip there after Rumania, and then return to Vienna via Bulgaria and Yugoslavia. Turkey—the nation of Kemal Ataturk, whom Bose and many other Indian nationalists held in the highest respect—was a low point. As he wrote to Mrs Vetter,

> I had such glorious expectation about Istanbul that I have been sadly disappointed. It gives one the impression of a state that is collapsing. There is not the romance of the East—nor is there the material prosperity of the West.[106]

From hints in other letters, it appears that he did not improve his opinion of Turkey after touring some of its other cities.

During this long tour from late 1933 to mid-1934, Bose made another visit to Germany. He was happy about the contacts he had established in Austria, Italy, Czechoslovakia, and some of the smaller countries of Europe, but he was hoping for some more positive connections to German officials, organizations, and politicians, because Germany 'mattered' in world politics. As on the first visit in 1933, Bose was held at arm's length by the top leaders of the Third Reich, but he again met lower officials of the Foreign Office and was in frequent communication with Dr Thierfelder of the Deutsche Akademie in Munich.[107]

In a lengthy memorandum to Foreign Office councillor, Dyckhoff, written on April 5, 1934, Bose sharply criticized negative aspects of German-Indian relations since the National Socialists had come to power. He said that he did this in the hope of improving relations. Of particular concern were derogatory articles in the German press and hostile statements by German leaders about India, and Nazi race propaganda as it impinged on Indians in Germany. He wrote,

> The most serious factor threatening friendly relations between Germany and India is the unfortunate effect produced by the present race propaganda in Germany. When I was walking along the streets of München a week ago—I was called 'Neger' by German children. Indian students in München told me they have all been addressed by German children as 'Neger' . . . the general attitude of the people towards Indians is not as friendly . . . as it formerly was . . . in München. . . . Indian students have been even pelted with stones. . . . It has been further noticed by Indians that when German children have misbehaved . . . their parents or guardians instead of rebuking them have encouraged them . . . the draft legislation embodied in the National Sozialistische Strafrecht published by the Ministry of Justice states that legislation against Jews, Negroes, and coloured people is under

consideration. . . . This draft . . . has . . . roused considerable anxiety and resentment among Indians.[108]

Bose insisted that relations between Germany and India would only improve if the negative statements were stopped and the racial legislation shelved. He stopped short of protesting the passage of racial legislation in general, though I believe that he was against it. He did not think it was his task as a visitor in Germany to fight against their racism in general, but only to protest its disastrous effects on the Indian community. Just as Gandhi in South Africa fought against racist legislation as it affected the Indians there, so Bose made his points to German officials on the racist laws as they touched his own countrymen. But this does not mean that Gandhi in South Africa and Bose in Germany were not against racism in general.[109]

There are other signs of Bose's sensitivity to such questions which come out through his friendship to a European couple living in Berlin, Mrs Kitty Kurti and her husband Alex Kurti. They had attended a lecture he gave in Berlin and then chanced to meet him in the street. Struck by the handsome Indian and moved by his message, Mrs Kurti found the courage to ask him to come to lunch. A friendship developed and Bose saw them and wrote to them from time to time.[110] Mrs Kurti asked Bose how he could deal with the Nazis, whom she found loathsome and repugnant. He replied,

> It is dreadful and it must be done. It is our only way out. India must gain her independence, cost what it may. And it may mean the collapse of Europe. But it is a rotten Europe, Mr and Mrs Kurti, and therefore does not concern me. Surely there are excellent people, here and in England, for whom I feel respect and affection; some may perish and die. . . . But let us not be sentimental. I am doing what I have to do; what must be done. Have you an idea . . . of the despair, the misery, the humiliation of India? Can you imagine her suffering and indignation? British imperialism there can be just as intolerable as your Nazism here, I assure you.[111]

Since this was only around 1934, Bose and the world did not yet know how the Nazis would work out their program, particularly the Final Solution to the Jewish question. But it was clear that he was willing to work with the devil to free India.

During ensuing visits, Bose learned that Mrs Kurti had training in psychoanalysis. He asked her to tell him more of Freud and Jung, and Bose said of the former,

> I agree that being a Central European, a Jew, and particularly an Austrian Jew, has been quite an important factor in forming the man and his theories. I myself have lived now for quite some time in Vienna and see clearly that the Austrian mentality is quite peculiar and can become a demanding taskmaster. Particularly at this moment in history, one cannot permit oneself to cherish any illusions. Freud . . . entertains no illusions at all. He is essentially a realist, an analytical mind, and a truly original thinker.[112]

Mrs Kurti agreed with Bose's view of Freud, but she argued that an analyst also had to be a spiritual guide. Jung, in her view, was capable of this; Freud was not since he was anti-religious and too narrowly concerned with sexual life. Partly on the basis of his own limited reading and her description of Jung's approach, Bose answered that India was already teeming with spiritual guides. So what India needed was Freud, the rational analyst, not Jung the analyst-cum-spiritual guide.[113] These conversations and Bose's correspondence with Dilip Roy show Bose's lifelong interest in religious and psychological questions.

On Bose's last visit to the Kurtis, he learned that Mrs Kurti was expecting a baby. Bose said to them,

Conditions are forbidding, the spirit terrible. Why do you stay here? You should leave this country, the sooner the better . . . just don't keep postponing. The very earth is trembling under our feet.[114]

Years later, Mrs Kurti told me that she had never mentioned to Bose that she and her husband were Jewish, but that perhaps he guessed. They had discussed the great achievements and the persecution of the Jews in the course of their talks about psychoanalysis. Writing of Bose's warning to leave Berlin, Mrs Kurti said,

All this was said with great reticence, in the extraordinary way that was his. But beneath it all, I felt his concern and I was grateful for it. I was also glad to note his deep contempt for the Nazis, a feeling which he did not attempt to hide from me.[115]

Bose left a while later and never met the Kurtis again, although he remained in their memories as a cherished friend. He was off on his tour of the Balkans and then he was back in Vienna by June 1934. In Vienna he had built up a circle of friends, foremost of whom were the Vetters and Mrs Hedy Fulop-Müller, the former wife of the noted writer Rene Fulop-Müller, and an acquaintance of Dilip Roy, through whom she met Bose. He was also friendly with Mrs Betty Hargrove, a widowed American from Maine, and with Mrs Helen Ashkanazy, the president of several women's clubs in Vienna, who often arranged speaking engagements for Bose. Like the Kurtis, Mrs Ashkanazy was Jewish and had to leave Austria before the decade was out.[116]

To several of these friends, Bose, for all his intelligence, charm, and friendliness, appeared almost myopic because he had only one interest which consumed him: the liberation of India from British rule. India, as Mrs Vetter reminded me when I visited her in Vienna some years ago, was such a passionate and consuming interest that he collected books on India in French and German which he could not read. And most of what he read was about India and about world politics as it related to India. He did investigate European politics and watched European politicians at work to see what this might teach him vis-à-vis the British. He looked into municipal experiments in European cities, so that he might get ideas about the improvement of Calcutta.[117] Some thought his view was shortsighted, for it led him to care little for the fate of other countries and peoples. He was concerned deeply however for the fate and welfare of his friends.[118]

To help facilitate commercial relations between India and European countries, he worked with a Mr Otto Faltis and, as he wrote to Mrs Vetter,

> . . . together we drew up a practical plan for bringing our two countries together. He was to work at this end and I was to work in India—*on my return*. We were *not* going to do actual business. We would only help business and other relations between our two countries. Later on, if we wanted to do business—that would be a different and a new proposition which we would consider anew.[119]

Bose went on to ask the advice of the Vetters about the reliability of Mr Faltis and the practicability of the scheme. The planned association was established as the Indian Central-European Society, with some funds supplied by Mr Faltis. The society was connected to the Vienna Chamber of Commerce and helped make contact between European and Indian business firms.[120]

In addition to his interest in Austrian business contacts and the working of the socialist municipality of Vienna, Bose did watch the machinations of Austrian politics—in the maelstrom of European power politics—closely. He wrote several articles on Austria, including one entitled 'The Austrian Riddle,' published in the spring of 1934. In this article, he mentioned that he had attended many political and religious-cum-political demonstrations in Vienna during 1933 and 1934, among them a socialist rally, an Austrian Nazi meeting, a celebration of the 250th anniversary of a victory over the Turks at which the para-military Heimwehr marched, and a Catholic Congress for all German-speaking Catholics in September 1933.[121]

From his *Modern Review* article, it seems that Bose was fascinated by skills at political maneuvering and the figure he admired most on the Austrian scene was Herr Engelbert Dollfuss, the head of the Austrian government. He watched with admiration as Dollfuss turned on the Austrian Nazis and then the Socialists, in turn, and contained them, with the help of the Heimwehr. Bose wrote,

> Last year I was of the opinion that the Austrian Government were acting contrary to the laws of political strategy by carrying on the struggle on a double front and that if they wanted to succeed, they should make up with one of the two opposing parties. I must confess that as a student of History,

I never expected that they (the Government) would be so successful in overthrowing both the oppositionist parties. The credit for this belongs largely to the political sagacity displayed by Herr Dollfuss. During the last twelve months he has always acted in the fulness of time. He has never shown any weakness in dealing with his political enemies nor has he been guilty of premature rashness in action.[122]

Bose did not greatly lament the suspension of parliamentary democracy in Austria by Dollfuss. He evaluated the political parties and demonstrations more by his assessment of the virility, enthusiasm, and discipline they showed than in terms of any more enduring human values.[123] He did seem sorry that the Socialists had been pushed from the political scene and that the government had taken over the Vienna municipal government from them, but he blamed the Socialist leaders for not showing more foresight.[124] Bose clearly understood that the Austrian Nazis had infiltrated the government and were still powerful, but he underestimated their potential for violence, for, within a few months of this article, one group in the Austrian Nazi Party assassinated Dollfuss.

When Bose returned to Vienna in June 1934, he had secured a contract from the British publisher Lawrence Wishart to write a book on Indian politics with a deadline later in the year, and he looked for a secretary, a trustworthy person who could help him with the preparation of the book. Through an Indian doctor in Vienna, Dr Mathur, Bose was introduced to Emilie Schenkl, a young Viennese woman. She was born on December 26, 1910, to an Austrian Catholic family. Her paternal grandfather was a shoemaker, her father a veterinarian. Her father was not eager for her to have a formal education, but late in the First World War, he permitted her to attend primary school and then begin secondary school. Displeased that she was not learning grammar well, he sent her to a nunnery for four years to continue her education. She thought briefly of becoming a nun, but dropped the idea. She attended two more schools for a year each and completed her education when she was about twenty.[125]

By then it was the depression and she spent some time without a job. So when the opportunity came to work for Bose, she eagerly accepted it. She knew English well and could take shorthand. She also had the necessary typing skills. Miss Schenkl, a short, attractive, and lively person, was one whom Bose could trust. He was concerned with this because he was under constant surveillance by the British Embassy, not only in Vienna, but wherever he went in Europe.

For about three months, Bose worked daily on this book which was to be published as *The Indian Struggle 1920-1934*. Usually he dictated to Miss Schenkl and she then typed out the text, or, infrequently, he wrote in longhand and she retyped the manuscript. Occasionally, he interrupted his work on the long book to write short articles for newspapers or magazines. He gathered some books and articles in his rooms in Vienna and did not do any extensive library research on this work. She also translated articles from German for him, for, though he was studying German, he was not yet adept.[126]

While he lived in Vienna, Bose never ate beef or smoked or drank. He devoted some of his time to meditation, seeking privacy for this. At first he lived in a hotel, but he shifted to rented rooms and usually had an extra room for Indian acquaintances, students, or his nephew Asoke. Without the usual contingent of servants, Bose had to do more things for himself in Europe. Among other things, he proved to be, according to Asoke, an excellent cook of Indian dishes, particularly chicken preparations and luchis.[127]

The Indian Struggle is Bose's effort to give his version of the recent political history of India. It is concerned especially with the changing strategies of the Congress and the Raj. It does bring in a brief account of the historical background, but does not attempt any searching social or economic analysis of the nationalist movement. It contains sharply etched views of the top leadership of the nationalist movement. It is important not only as Bose's view but also for its impact later on nationalist leaders who were finally able to read it. Interspersed with the political narrative are many vignettes of Bose's personal experiences in the movement, in prison, and interacting with Indian and European figures.

The book contained praise as well as sharp criticism of Gandhi. Bose saw Gandhi as the head of an older, reformist group of nationalists, backed by wealthy capitalists. He saw a dichotomy partly between the haves and the have-nots among Indian nationalists. It was as if he were indirectly borrowing Marxist categories, identifying his political allies and himself with the masses of Indians, and seeing Gandhi, who he admitted was accepted by the masses as their leader, as the head of the oppressive forces. He viewed Gandhi, the Gandhian high command, and the Government of India as restraints on the radical and militant nationalist forces with which he identified. These radical forces had a 'rebel mentality,' rejecting the authority of the government, but also questioning the authority and wisdom of the dominant leadership of the nationalist movement.[128]

One feature of the Congress to which Bose most objected was the lack of criticism of Gandhi, through his various twists and turns. Bose wrote:

> Besides the influence which the first three leaders [*C.R. Das, Motilal Nehru, and Lajpat Rai*] had in their own provinces, their importance was also due to the fact that they were the three outstanding intellectual stalwarts of the

Congress. Many of the blunders committed by the Mahatma as a political
leader could have been avoided if they had been in a position to advise him.
Since the death of these three giants, the leadership of the Congress had
fallen to a low intellectual level. The Congress Working Committee today
is undoubtedly composed of some of the finest men of India—men who
have character and courage, patriotism and sacrifice. But most of them have
been chosen primarily because of their 'blind' loyalty to the Mahatma—and
there are few among them who have the capacity to think for themselves or
the desire to speak out against the Mahatma when he is likely to take a wrong
step.[129]

Although they undoubtedly supported Gandhi through thick and thin, was
it accurate or politically astute to label such as Maulana Azad,
C. Rajagopalachari, and Sardar Patel as operating at a 'low intellectual
level'?

Bose did try to come to terms with Gandhi's hold on the masses, which
none had been able to challenge or break. Bose wrote,

As we have already seen, a large and influential section of the intelligentsia
was against him, but this opposition was gradually worn down through the
enthusiastic support given by the masses. Consciously or unconsciously,
the Mahatma fully exploited the mass psychology of the people, just as
Lenin did the same thing in Russia, Mussolini in Italy and Hitler in
Germany. But in doing so, the Mahatma was using a weapon which was sure
to recoil on his head. He was exploiting many of the weak traits in the
character of his countrymen which had accounted for India's downfall to a
large extent. After all, what has brought about India's downfall in the
material and political sphere? It is her inordinate belief in fate and in the
supernatural—her indifference to modern scientific development—her
backwardness in the science of modern warfare, the peaceful contentment
engendered by her latter-day philosophy and adherence to Ahimsa (Non-
violence) carried to the most absurd length. In 1920, when the Congress
began to preach the political doctrine of non-co-operation, a large number
of Congressmen who had accepted the Mahatma not merely as a political
leader but also as a religious preceptor—began to preach the cult of the new
Messiah.[130]

So Bose saw himself on the side of reason, science, and modern values,
even though he was privately very religious. Later in his book, Bose
condemned numerous blunders of the Mahatma, especially Gandhi's lack
of planning for the second Round Table Conference. At the root of
Gandhi's errors was confusion between the Mahatma's two roles as
political leader and world preacher. Perhaps Bose never thought to
consider that Gandhi's very success may have resulted in part from the
Mahatma's effective fusion of religion and politics, or that his own
popularity in Bengal may have been related to a religious aura that

surrounded him because of his sacrifices and his years of imprisonment. Bose felt that in her struggle against the British, India needed a strong, vigoros, military-type leader—perhaps even himself—not a hesitating, confused, reformist guru. Showing admiration for strong leaders, among whom he listed Hitler, Stalin, Mussolini, and even Sir Stanley Jackson, a former governor of Bengal, Bose claimed that India wanted and needed a strong party, strict discipline, and dictatorial rule.[131] At the end of *The Indian Struggle*, Bose outlined a synthesis of communism and fascism into a new ideology that India might use. He also promised that all his energies would be used for the proper leadership of his country. Whether this new synthesis was at all relevant to India was not clear. But what was to become manifest was that his outspoken criticism of colleagues was not to do him any good in the future.

On the ideological side, Bose seemed to create confusion by running together fascism and communism. He considered himself part of the left or radical tendency of the nationalist movement, but the kind words for fascism were anathema to most of the other members of the Indian left.[132] Jawaharlal Nehru had been, and continued to be, explicit in his criticism of fascism and followed this up with a refusal to meet Mussolini when he traveled through Italy. Nehru is typical of the Indian left in that he condemned fascism, but like Bose, nowhere examined it at any length or with any depth.[133]

The only full studies of fascism done by Indians were the products of men who spent many years in Europe. Besides the works of R. Palme Dutt, who is a special case, for he really should be considered a European by domicile, education, and experience, there is M.N. Roy's *Fascism*.[134] And Roy, though certainly an Indian, spent about fifteen years outside of India from 1915 to 1930. Roy, in keeping with most Marxist critiques of fascism in his time, saw fascism as a reversion to a medieval irrational faith which some leaders fostered to bolster decaying capitalism and divert the masses from socialist revolution. He argued that Gandhism, in its irrational philosophy, as opposed to the scientific rationalism of Marxism, was closer to fascism than many believed. Roy did note that fascism involved the use of violence, a contempt for parliamentary democracy, and faith in a superman or charismatic leader.[135]

For the most part, however, there was not a lot of discussion of fascism in India. Even Bose, who was living through some of the rough days of fascism's rise and spread, was not very concerned with it. What he was looking for was opportunity, opportunity for activities within the context of developing world catastrophe that would help free India. The fate of parliamentary democracy, or of socialist movements did not weigh much with him. He saw the dangers to the established order in Europe and the world as a chance for the overturning of the British Empire, and this, however much chaos was involved, was all to the good.[136]

While he was completing *The Indian Struggle*, Bose was searching for a prominent literary figure to write a preface to his book, for the publisher thought this would help the sales. He wrote to Rabindranath Tagore seeking assistance in contacting Bernard Shaw. He chided Tagore for the perfunctory letter Tagore had written to Romain Rolland on his behalf earlier, and then Bose wrote,

> Apart from Bernard Shaw, it might also be good to get a foreword by H.G. Wells. I had also thought of Mon. Rolland, but he is too much of an admirer of Gandhi. I am not that and I have told him that. So I cannot hope that Mon. Rolland will agree to write the introduction to my book. Bernard Shaw or Wells have a high opinion of Mahatmaji, but they are not his blind admirers, so they might agree. I had also thought of you, but I do not know whether you would be inclined to write something for a book concerning politics. Besides, you yourself have recently become Mahatmaji's blind admirer—at any rate, people may get this impression from your writings. Under the circumstances whether you would be able to tolerate criticism of Mahatmaji, I do not know.[137]

Tagore declined to write to Shaw and he did not comment on the rough-and-ready, blunt manner in which Bose wrote to him. As the skillful historian of the Bose-Tagore relationship, Nepal Majumdar, noted, people usually did not write to Tagore in such a fashion.[138] What Tagore did in his reply was to give Bose a serious lecture on the history of Indian politics. The poet told the politician that before Gandhi the people of India had been dormant. What Gandhi had done was to awaken the Indian people to their strength, and, whatever the Mahatma's deficiencies, Tagore thought that Gandhi had and would have an enduring impact on India. To ignore Gandhi's power, Tagore told Bose, was to blind one's self to the realities of modern India.[139]

Bose completed the manuscript and before long, by the later months of 1934, was reading the proofs of his book. In August he had gone to Karlsbad, a spa, to drink the hot, salty mineral waters to see whether they would cure his abdominal pains. He had hoped to avoid an operation, but now it appeared there was no alternative. One Viennese doctor had come back to an earlier diagnosis that the problem was with the gallbladder and it had to be operated on. He wrote to Mrs Vetter in September from Karlsbad,

> I like the natural surroundings of the place very much because in half an hour ... you can climb a hill and breathe fresh air. ... Sometimes I long to go back home, but am not yet fit from the point of view of my health and besides they

will not spare me when I land. My brother is still in internment, much to the
distress of our family . . . in all probability I shall submit to the knife. I do
not know where I shall spend winter. I wish I could go somewhere south
where I could get the sun. But before I go, I must come to grips with my
surgeon.[140]

Bose would be home sooner than he expected or wished. In the fall
Janaki Nath Bose had a serious heart attack. Asoke Bose, who had just
made a return visit to India and was back in Europe, has described what
followed,

. . . on receipt of the very disturbing news about my grandfather's condition,
he [*Subhas Bose*] postponed the surgical operation pending receipt of
further news from home. On the 26th November, he received a cable from
my grandmother informing him that grandfather's condition was grave and
asking him to come home by air immediately. . . . The time at his disposal
was so short that he had to sit up the whole night without a wink of sleep to
complete reading the final proofs of the book. . . . The planes of all lines
. . . flew only by day stopping over at nights. Uncle took the plane for Rome
in the morning of the 29th from Vienna. . . . Uncle . . . took the Royal Dutch
(KLM) plane thence on the 30th. The plane touched down at Karachi on the
3rd December. At Karachi uncle got the news of grandfather's death which
had taken place earlier on the same day. The plane landed at the Dum-Dum
Airport at about 4 p.m. on the 4th December when an order of home
internment was served on uncle. . . . Father had also come down to Calcutta
on parole and remained there to observe mourning.[141]

So, rapidly and unhappily, Subhas was home. He was able to see his
beloved family, but his father was dead. He had not been able to see his
father since 1931. And he, along with Sarat, was home interned for the
duration of their stay in Calcutta.

IV

The death of Janaki Nath Bose was not unexpected, for he had had serious
heart and kidney troubles. Through 1934, both parents were quite ill.
Prabhabati Bose, like her son Sarat, had diabetes. Still, the family was
hoping that Janaki Nath would pull through. Subhas wrote to Mrs Vetter
after arriving home,

My mother is utterly disconsolate. We, brothers and sisters, are trying our
best to console her but to no purpose. The life of a Hindu wife is so bound
up with that of her husband that life becomes unbearable to her in his
absence. Life in Europe is somewhat different. . . . At present I am staying
at the former address [38/2 Elgin Road] with my mother.[142]

The mourning period was one month and orthodox Hindu customs were
followed under the guidance of Asokanath Bhattacharya and Gauri Nath

Sastri, Brahmin priests from a priestly family long associated with the Bose family. Gauri Nath Sastri went to the Elgin Road house every afternoon to conduct prayers. Subhas was the last of the brothers to shave his head and asked Sastri, 'Do the *sastras* say so?' Sastri replied, 'Yes, they do, but some do not do it today.' Then Subhas had his head shaved like the others.[143] During the mourning period, the sons all slept in one room on the floor resting on straw covered with blankets, for it was the winter season in Calcutta. Sewn garments were not to be worn, so they wore simple short dhotis, wrapped around their bodies. Of course, no shoes were worn, hair was not to be combed, and a thread was tied around the neck from which an iron key was suspended, which was meant to keep evil spirits away. During this period, only boiled vegetarian food was taken, as well as fruits and milk. Cooking was done by the mourners themselves or by near relatives. This was done by the women of the family. The female relatives all slept together in a room apart from the one in which the brothers gathered.[144]

Subhas and the others adhered to these customary rules. But since he had been away so long and wanted to get into touch with current affairs and friends, in and out of politics, Subhas asked Gauri Nath Sastri about the rules. Subhas wondered whether any of his friends, from different communities, could be present at the *shraddha* ceremonies. Sastri allowed that such outsiders could come. So Bose sat, quite piously to all appearances, next to the priest, but at the same time he was exchanging messages with his friends. The ceremony went on for seven hours and the communicating went on throughout.[145]

The death of Janaki Nath Bose meant a change in relationships within the family. Satish was now formally the head of the family, but Sarat, as the most successful in a worldly way and as the favorite of his father, had a strong voice. Properties had to be passed to the next generation and the Elgin Road house was willed to Satish, Sudhir, Subhas, and Sailesh. Sarat and Suresh and Sunil inherited others from among Janaki Nath's rather considerable property holdings in Orissa and in his native village outside Calcutta. Among these Orissa holdings was about five acres along the railway line in Cuttack, the family house in Cuttack and other houses there, a house on the beach at Puri, another large house at Bhubaneswar, properties on the Chilka Lakes, and four or five garden properties in Orissa.[146]

Like Subhas, Sarat was still under internment rules and simply paroled for the duration of the mourning period. But since he had been transferred to his own house in Kurseong in April 1933, the Government of Bengal had not been ungenerous in allowing him to visit his parents, first in Cuttack, and then, near the end of his father's life, in Calcutta. The shift to Kurseong from the lonely prison life of Jubbulpore meant a great change for the better for Sarat. Immediate family members could come and go as they wanted, though they were subject to search. Sarat could read what he wanted, though his mail was still carefully censored. Not only was he much more contented but his health was also better. There was still blood sugar indicating the diabetic condition, but it was not as bad and regulation of diet and exercise helped him to control it.[147]

Throughout Sarat's period of detention—which eventually extended to three-and-a-half years—his eldest son, Asoke Nath, was getting his practical scientific training in Munich, leading to a doctorate, awarded in 1935. Sarat Bose and his wife wrote weekly to their son, and Sarat was concerned with every detail of his son's life, his courses, German tutor, social contacts, and even his religious training. A copy of the *Bhagavad Gita* was sent to Asoke, which he dutifully read. Sarat Bose, in practice, gave his children strong direction, though he wanted his sons to follow their own inclinations. An example when Sarat slackened his directiveness, was when his second son, Amiya Nath, wanted to study arts rather than science. Sarat wrote to Asoke Nath,

> Ami is inclined to take up the arts course for the B.A. degree. It is my desire that he should take up the Science Course. If I find that he is *very keen* on taking up the Arts Course, I shall not press him to give it up. I believe in a man following his own bent.[148]

Amiya Nath took the arts course and was later called to the bar, as his father had been.

Just before and after his father's death, Sarat Bose spent almost two months in Calcutta, but then on January 19, 1935, he returned to Kurseong, since he said that he did not want to take advantage of the parole periods the government had given him. He had resigned the seat to which he had been elected in the Central Legislative Assembly, because he could not attend. Subhas had hoped that Sarat would have an opportunity to join this body, for he thought he would be the equal in parliamentary skills to anyone there. Sarat Bose continued to write to the government asking for a trial or for his release, and calls for the speedy termination of his detention appeared in the press.[149]

Behind the scenes, his wife had gone to see Sir N.N. Sircar, law member of the Government of India, and Sarat's mentor and close friend. Biva said that their financial position was very difficult, their house was mortgaged to the hilt, and they had 'no funds for the marriage of the eldest daughter who has long passed marriageable age.'[150] She asked Sircar to intercede with the home member and with the governor of Bengal, but Sircar at first refused. Then, some time later, he changed his mind. He wrote to the governor, Sir John Anderson, on April 13, 1935,

> I fully realise the inexpediency of relaxation, just at the time when things are getting under control—but I am convinced that there is no risk now in releasing Bose. If any untoward signs are noticed as the result of watching his activities, he can again be dealt with under the Bengal Act.
>
> While Bose, I am sure, will not agree to give any undertakings, as conditions precedent to his release, he must submit, whether he likes it or not, to any directions which may be given under the Bengal Act.
>
> I am sure that if on release he meets me, I can get from him an assurance that he will confine his activities to his profession. I do hope that this time my very earnest request for the release of Mr Sarat Bose, will not have been made in vain.[151]

So the matter now fell to Anderson, who was called 'notorious' by Subhas Bose and many Congressmen. Anderson, however, was a cool and intelligent administrator, whom some have called the ablest British civil servant of the twentieth century.[152] Anderson, who had been brought to Bengal to deal with revolutionary terrorism and serious financial difficulties, decided that the elder Bose brother was not a current threat. He wrote to the new secretary of state for India, and former governor of Bengal, the Marquess of Zetland,

> The decision to release Sarat was not arrived at without much discussion and some heart-searching. I am sure it was right and from all I hear he means to play the game. I have never seen him, but I expect a visit from him next month in Darjeeling.[153]

Once Anderson made his decision in consultation with other Bengal officials, the matter was dealt with expeditiously. In late July 1935, after three-and-a-half years of detention, Sarat Bose was informed of his unconditional release while on a parole visit to Calcutta. He was delighted and went the same afternoon to the Calcutta bar library, where he '. . . was received very cordially by all.'[154]

V

The other Bose, however, was another story. The Governments of Bengal and India were not willing to have Subhas Bose at large in India. He was home interned during every minute he was in Calcutta after his father's death. Bose had been about to schedule gallbladder operation. There were also further European contacts to make. He was probably not enthused by the prospect of agitation in an Indian domestic situation that was still in the post-civil disobedience doldrums. So he decided to return to Europe promptly, but said publicly and privately that he did not intend to be a permanent exile from his beloved native land. He left in January and reached Naples on January 20, 1935.[155]

On his way north, Bose stopped in Rome and had another audience with Mussolini. He presented the Duce with a copy of his recently released book, *The Indian Struggle 1920–1934*.[156] Sir Samuel Hoare announced in the House of Commons that the book had been proscribed by the Government of India 'on the ground that it tended generally to encourage methods of terrorism and of direct action.'[157] The book could not be imported into India and was only circulated in the West. Most of the reviews were positive and the foreign editor of the *Daily Herald* of London, Mr W.N. Ewar, wrote on January 28, 1935:

> Bose, of course, is stamped as an extremist, a wild man, a menace to society. Well, here is his book. It is calm, sane, dispassionate. I think it is the ablest work I have read on current Indian politics. He has his own opinions, vigorously held, yet never unfairly expressed. This is the book of no fanatic but of a singularly able mind, the book of an acute, thoughtful, constructive mind, of a man who, while still under forty, would be an asset and an ornament to the political life of any country. But for the past ten years he has spent most of his life in jail: and is now an exile broken in health. That is one tragedy of the Indian situation.[158]

The work certainly encouraged methods of direct action, but that for a good deal of the Gandhian period from 1919 on, had been the strategy of the dominant part of the Indian nationalist movement. It is certainly dubious that it encouraged terrorism, for Bose did not think that sporadic and isolated acts of violence would bring independence to India. But he did not condemn so-called terrorists out of hand and he did not rule out organized, extensive use of violent means at some future time. This, together with the India Office and Government of India belief that he was *a* or *the* Jugantar leader, was enough to ban the book from the Indian reading public.[159]

While in Rome, he visited the fascist Hall of Martyrs which gave him an idea for a similar project which he wanted to work out one day in Calcutta. Years later the foundation stone was laid, but it was some time before the hall, Mahajati Sadan (The Great Hall of the People) was built. He also had an opportunity to meet Maxim Litvinoff, commissar of foreign affairs of the Soviet Union at the Russian Embassy, and also ex-king Amanullah of Afghanistan, living in exile in Rome.[160] Bose was eager to make contacts with the Soviets, for he hoped to visit the USSR. He may or may not have known that just at this time, the Comintern was reformulating its views on bourgeois nationalists—such as Nehru and himself—in the colonial world.[161] In any case, he believed that a great socialist experiment was going on in the Soviet Union and he anticipated visiting there within the next year. The Soviet Union, with its antagonism to imperialism and capitalism, was, potentially, another ally in the struggle against the British Empire.

From Rome, he went on to Geneva for a memorial service for Vithalbhai Patel held at the La Ligniere Clinique at Gland, Switzerland on March 22, 1935. Although he was in poor health himself, Bose felt that he had to attend this function before going on to Vienna to see to his own health, and in his short speech at Gland he referred to Patel's international work for India which he now resolved to continue.[162]

Once this debt was paid, Bose started for Vienna, but en route was able to carry out another 'pilgrimage' which he had long had in mind, to visit the writer, savant, internationalist, and friend of India, Romain Rolland, in Villeneuve, Switzerland.[163] A decade earlier Dilip Roy had sent to the imprisoned Bose a copy of Stefan Zweig's biography of Rolland inscribed, 'My dear Subhash, This biography of the great soul with whom I had the good fortune of coming into intimate contact will I trust afford you the same inspiration as it has to me.'[164] Later, in 1935, Rolland wrote an appreciation of Bose's *Indian Struggle*, which was published with a subsequent edition of the book. In part, Rolland wrote that, 'It is an indispensable work for the history of the Indian Movement. In it you show the best qualities of the historian: lucidity and high equity of mind. Rarely it happens that a man of action as you are is apt to judge without party spirit.'[165] So the two men were acquainted with each other through their books and reputations. But neither spoke the other's language, which caused some difficulty; they had to use an interpreter.

Bose, in writing an article about the interview, said that he was overjoyed to find that Rolland was not inextricably wedded to the Gandhian view. Rolland, Bose reported, said,

> I am not interested in choosing between two political parties or between two generations. What is of interest and of value to me is a higher question . . . .What really counts is the great cause that transcends them, the cause of the workers of the world . . . if as a result of unfortunate circumstances, Gandhi . . . should be in conflict with the cause of the workers, and with their necessary evolution towards a socialistic organisation . . . for ever will I side with the oppressed workers. . . .[166]

In the version of the interview which was sent to India by Bose in 1935, a number of sections were excised by the censor. And, furthermore, Rolland wrote in his journal that the copy that Bose sent to him had a number of simplifications due to the translation process. It appears that Bose heard some things in the way that he did because he was so eager that Rolland's views coincide with his own.[167] But they certainly did agree on the liberation of India and the colonial world from Western thralldom and on a better future for masses of ordinary men and women everywhere.

Rolland, however, was a dedicated pacifist and thus closer to Gandhi than Bose, and Rolland wrote a book about Gandhi and carried on an extensive correspondence with the Mahatma over many years.[168]

From the hermitage of the European sage, Bose went on to deal with painful and mundane matters in Vienna. Writing to Asoke on April 24 from the Rudolfiner Haus in the Billrothstrasse, Bose said,

> I came here yesterday—for surgical operation. Professor Demel will operate on me this afternoon at 4 p.m. for removal of the gall-bladder. . . .
> Friends here have been and are helping in every way.[169]

There is a report, perhaps apocryphal, that just before the operation, Bose said, 'My love to my countrymen, my debts to my brother.'[170] A few days later, he reported to Asoke Nath,

> I had the operation on Wednesday. Gall-bladder with a big stone inside was removed. Operation performed successfully. Progress steadily maintained . . . . Another week in the Sanatorium thereafter and I shall be out then. No anxiety.[171]

The recuperation, however, was much longer, slower, and more painful than Bose anticipated and he spent a number of months in discomfort, wearing a supportive belt around his abdomen in Vienna, and then in Karlsbad, through mid-1935. Months after the operation, he wrote to Mrs Vetter from yet another health spa, Hofgastein, where he was trying the curative waters,

> I am now taking the cure here and this will continue till the last week of this month. My work is not progressing well at all and at first it made me feel very unhappy. I am now trying to regain my normal health even at the expense of my present work because for my future life, my health is more important.
> After all, I came to Europe for the purpose of regaining my health.[172]

He did take time out from his own recovery to do his small part to help Kamala Nehru, the wife of Jawaharlal. She came to Europe in June to seek the best European medical assistance, but she had advanced pulmonary tuberculosis and hopes were not high.[173] Bose met her in Vienna and later, after Jawaharlal had been released from prison to be with his stricken wife, Bose met them at Badenweiler in the Black Forest of Germany. Nehru, who was just finishing his superb autobiography, *Toward Freedom*, took time to read through Bose's recently published book and pointed out a few factual errors. Bose admitted the mistakes and asked Nehru to list the errors so that they could be corrected in a second edition.[174] They discussed the Indian political scene and Bose treated Nehru in a friendly and respectful manner. Years later Bose wrote to Nehru that he regarded him as an elder brother and, as such, often sought his guidance. The letters between them in this period are restrained and amicable.[175] How different, though, are

Bose's comments in the *Indian Struggle*, where time and again, he portrays Nehru as a timid and willing tool of the more conservative Gandhi.[176]

For example, Bose blamed Nehru for not making more of a protest at the curtailing of civil disobedience, from the time of the Gandhi–Irwin Pact to the present. He wrote,

> With a popularity only second to that of the Mahatma, with unbounded prestige among his countrymen, with a clear brain possessing the finest ideas, with an up-to-date knowledge of modern world movements—that he should be found wanting in the essential quality of leadership, namely the capacity to make decisions and face unpopularity if need be, was a great disappointment. But there was no help for it. What had been expected of him had to be accomplished by lesser men.[177]

In a footnote to the above passage, Bose added that this 'defect' in Pandit J.L. Nehru was manifest in many Congress crises including 1923–24 and 1928–29.[178] For all the agreement on many programs for India and superficial personal closeness, there is also a current of animosity and anger in Bose's view of Nehru. Though Nehru may not have been too bothered by the criticism of Bose, there is now and again a sign that the Pandit was vexed with Bose.[179]

During these long months of convalescence, Bose kept reading and writing, though he had no single project to occupy him and drive him the way the *Indian Struggle* had the previous year. Of all that he read, he seemed most enthusiastic about one book, Robert Briffault's *Breakdown*, published first in 1932, and then in a second edition with a lengthy postscript in 1935. Bose wrote to Amiya Chakravarty from Vienna late in the year,

> . . . I want to convey duly this news to you that I got the book *Breakdown* by Briffault, sent by you. Thank you very much because the book is simply wonderful. I lent the book to a few Austrian friends for their perusal and after going through the book they found it immensely satisfying.[180]

What was this book that Bose found 'wonderful'? Briffault, an English surgeon, anthropologist, philosopher, and novelist, had written a work of popular Marxism, claiming that all hitherto existing societies had been run by and for a small propertied, ruling class. Although idealistic members of these societies could be found, as societies they were all guided by self-interest, and the interests furthered were those of the rulers.[181] Liberal democracy, he said, was a sham, and like fascism, an effort to preserve the status quo or exploitative position of the ruling class.[182] There was only one bright exception: the Soviet Union. Here, though there was one-party rule, it was carried out, he believed, for the good of all.[183]

In a postscript written for the second edition, Briffault said that the four years since the first edition had been marked by the spread of fascism. He added,

> Fascism and capitalist civilisation are today co-extensive terms. [*Some*] European states are ruled by open and avowed fascist terrorism. In those states where the accumulated reserves of capitalist rule are greatest, such as England, France, the United States . . . the open avowal of unprincipled Fascism has as yet been dispensed with. But that nominal pudicity serves mainly as a means the better to disguise the *de facto* fascisation of those countries, the setting aside of democratic principles, the enormous multiplication of police forces . . . the undisguised support of illegal fascist gangs . . . the open favoured treatment of fascist governments . . . the overt substitution of unprincipled foul means for the traditional 'fair' principles of democracy. There no longer exists today a single antifascist government in the capitalist world. There exist only fascist capitalist governments and the Union of Socialist Soviet Republics.[184]

Finally, Briffault claimed that the future belonged to the masses who would not put up with injustice forever and would, in the end, make a socialist world. He prophesied that out of a cataclysmic war, a new, better world would emerge.[185]

Bose probably agreed with Briffault's account of the decline of the Western imperialist countries and with the thesis that the distance between imperialist Britain or France and fascist Italy or Nazi Germany was not so great as some Westerners thought. He also probably agreed that the future belonged to socialism. But it is dubious whether he shared Briffault's belief that every intelligent man in the present day had to be perforce a communist and that the Soviet Union was the only nation where any human progress was taking place.

Also in the convalescent period, Bose wrote on his travels and on politics. Among his articles is 'The Secret of Abyssinia and Its Lesson,' prepared for the *Modern Review* and published in November 1935. Drawing heavily on British journals, he recounted the history of the Italian conquest. He did condemn the Italians—though not with the bluntness that Nehru did in his articles of that time—but he also wanted to get his digs in at British imperialists who denounced the Italians, but did not carry through with any meaningful steps to stop the Italian advance.[186] Speculating on a possible European war in which the Italians would fight the British, Bose—demonstrating that he had been taken in more by Mussolini's words than by his real accomplishments—wrote,

> . . . it is quite certain, that the Italian air-force—one of the most efficient in the world and, by common consent, superior to that of Great Britain today—would have done irreparable damage to the British Navy. Britain would, in consequence, have emerged out of a victorious war, far weaker than she is

today. And with a crippled navy she would have to face the gigantic re-armament of Nazi Germany.[187]

In retrospect, we know that the Italians did not fare very well in direct conflict with the British in North Africa; and even had a hard time putting down the virtually unarmed Ethiopians.[188] As for the Italian air force, it existed in the rhetoric of Mussolini, but not on the ground or in the air.

As for the lessons that Bose was prepared to draw, the first was that,

> . . . in the 20th century a nation can hope to be free only if it is strong, from a physical and military point of view, and is able to acquire all the knowledge which modern science can impart.
>
> The Orient has succumbed bit by bit to the . . . Occident, because it has wrapped itself up in self-complacency and lived in divine (?) contentment . . . and because it has refused to keep abreast of the march of human and scientific progress, especially in the art of warfare. India and Burma . . . have suffered for this reason.[189]

The second lesson had to do with the long-term fate of imperialism, and here Bose may have drawn on Briffault:

> Abyssinia will go down fighting, but she will stir the conscience of the world . . . throughout the world of coloured races there will be a new consciousness. The consciousness will herald the dawn of a new life among the suppressed nations. All imperialists are feeling uneasy about this. . . . There are two ways in which Imperialism may come to an end—either through an overthrow by an anti-imperialist agency or through an internecine struggle among the imperialists themselves. If the second course is furthered by the growth of Italian Imperialism, then Abyssinia will not have suffered in vain.[190]

Bose thought that Europe had come close to war during this crisis. And like Briffault, he believed that war might be the only way that imperialist hegemony might be overthrown and the subject classes and subject peoples liberated to rule themselves. He wanted India, that is Indian nationalists, to be prepared to take advantage of such a conflagration. He had few kind words for fascist Italy or Nazi Germany, but thought that if they fought other imperialist powers, then the subject peoples would benefit from the mutual destruction that these powers wrought on each other.[191]

While he was concerned with European and world politics, Bose's mind was primarily on India. He corresponded with political friends about the Calcutta Corporation.[192] He was returned—albeit through the press and the mails—to a continuing concern, the workers in Jamshedpur at the Tata Iron and Steel Company and associated industries. He wrote at great length in November 1935 to Sir N.B. Saklatvala, chairman of Tata, about the eviction of the Labour Association in Jamshedpur from their company-owned quarters.[193] Bose insisted that the company had gone back on an agreement made with him about this space years earlier and was not interested in a reasonable settlement, but rather with breaking the union. He went through the history of the Labour Association and the way in which the company had dealt with it and with a rival organization. In closing, he said,

> In these circumstances I should be pardoned if I venture to think that the real motive behind this move is that the Company now feels itself able to strike the last blow at the Association. . . . But I would beg you not to forget the past completely nor those who have endeavoured to conduct themselves honourably in their relations with the Company. And, as far as the future is concerned, I do not think that we are out of the picture altogether.[194]

But the Labour Association, with which Bose identified, was in a very weak position and had no leverage on the company to fight for its quarters. Some passages from this letter, in almost the same words, were used in an article which Bose wrote for the *Modern Review* in answering a piece by the general manager of Tata, Mr J.L. Keenan, which appeared in the same periodical in December 1935. In this article, Keenan maintained that Tata had ended the depression for its workers by its fine treatment of them. From 1931, he argued, the workers had become what he called 'labourers of progress,' (able to save, improve their condition) rather than 'labourers of necessity', as all the other steel workers in India. He did note that Indian workers were paid a fraction of what workers in the same industry were paid in Western countries and that conditions in the iron mines were appalling.[195]

Bose's article at once responded to the assertions of Keenan and went on to analyze the major shortcomings of the Tata Iron and Steel Company. The reasons for some economic recovery by the company, Bose answered, were not the skillful management of it, but rather duties placed on continental steel imports and government orders. He charged that the company had lagged on Indianization, was generally wasteful in its practices, and was determined to break any independent union which might organize. It would play off one union faction against another, recognize a company union, or employ *goondas* to break a non-company union.[196] For some of these assertions, Bose supplied data from personal involvement and observation. His economic case was well made and, by contrast, Keenan appeared quite foolish. However, this exchange, even if points are awarded to Bose, could not have helped the cause of the workers in any practical way.

Just as he was recovering his strength enough to undertake a long European tour, he wrote to Santosh Basu, a key contact in the Bengal

Congress and the Corporation,

There is no pleasure in living abroad when one's whole heart is elsewhere. I admit that one can do useful work abroad and I have not been idle either. But doing any effective work requires some money and plenty of moral support from home. I have neither. There is an obvious limit to what one can achieve single-handedly and without financial resources.[197]

This reference most likely refers to the controversy over the Patel legacy. Bose was most unhappy that the last wishes of his friend could not be fulfilled and the very family of the man were—in his view— preventing it.

Bose went on to comment on the wrangling on the Bengal political scene in a way reminiscent of his remarks near the end of his earlier enforced sabbatical from these affairs in 1927. He wrote to Santosh Basu,

Can you tell me what is wrong with Bengal? . . . Are not people tired of quarrelling over such petty details? I could have understood their quarrelling over something substantial—but such trifles! . . . Discipline is completely shattered . . . we shall have to begin again at the very beginning . . . . I don't know when exactly I shall be allowed to resume my public activities in Bengal. But whenever I do, I shall insist on one condition— unanimous support (or virtually unanimous) in Bengal. If this condition is not fulfilled, I shall not touch Bengal politics. I have no desire to appear at the head of one faction. Past experience has taught me one lesson— patience. I can have infinite patience and I shall wait till the forces of evil are played out and exhausted. Meanwhile, I could devote myself to plenty of useful work outside the domain of politics proper.[198]

From afar, Bose could talk of operating without faction in Bengal politics, but from the trenches it was a different story.

Bose was thinking of returning—no matter what the government might do—in the not-too-distant future. But first he wanted to make another swing through Europe. Throughout his stay in Europe, Bose was watched and reported upon, and his name entered a House of Commons debate in December 1935. As he wrote to his friend Amiya Chakravarty, 'I saw the report . . . in the *Times* . . . . Even now they maintain that I am absorbed with secret revolutionary activities and so this makes clear to you the mind of the British authorities ruling over India.'[199] When he applied for a visa for the Soviet Union, however, one of the places he most wished to see, he was refused. He saw the long hand of British diplomacy at work and believed that the Russians wanted to improve relations with Britain and so obliged the British by keeping him out of the homeland of the international communist conspiracy. Bose enlisted the aid of Mr Vetter, but to no avail. To Mrs Vetter, Bose wrote, 'This is rather damning to the reputation of the Soviet Government in India.'[200] Stalin's government may have had its own reasons for not allowing an ardent non-communist nationalist from India to visit at this time.

So Bose put together his program omitting the Soviet Union. He went to Prague and met President Benes and then went on to Berlin in early 1936. Bose passed through before the Indian Students' Association of Berlin celebrated the Congress Jubilee in mid-February. Bose thought that economic conditions in Germany were deteriorating and more criticism of the Nazi government was being made.[201] In addressing the Indian students' organization, he said,

> Since the new regime had come into power in Germany, the position of Indians considerably worsened. The problems were four in number. Firstly, Indian students including those who had graduated from German universities, were finding it difficult to get practical training in German factories. Secondly, anti-Indian propaganda in the press and films had increased, whereas pro-Indian propaganda had been virtually suppressed. Thirdly, the new Race law threatened to discriminate against all Asiatics. Fourthly, Germany was selling much more to India than she was buying from India.[202]

Shortly after Bose visited Berlin, Hitler made a speech which contained some anti-Indian and anti-Asian remarks that aroused protests in India and Europe. Bose, of course, was incensed, and wanted a strong response from the Indian Students' Federation in Europe. Some in the organization did not want to do this for they thought it would further harm the position of Indians in Germany. Bose differed. He thought that such a strong answer would help the Indians rather than harm them, and he now believed that there should be some boycott of German goods in India. He wrote to Amiya Chakravarty,

> Something else should have been said about Hitler. It is not true that the very fact of protest would cause separation from the federation because two years ago a sharp protest was made and its result was not unfavourable. Against Germany we (Indians) have many complaints. The other day (in January), I made known my protest when I was in Berlin. They worship strength as against weakness. I am saying this even prepared for separation from the federation. Against Italy there are complaints from the standpoint of all humanity—not from the standpoint of India's interest or prestige. But against Germany, we have many accusations from India's standpoint.
>
> There is no early possibility of the fall of Hitler's Government. If war breaks out some day and the war weakens Germany, then such a fall is possible, otherwise not. But if as a result of our boycott, Germany's trade suffers, then German businessmen will put pressure on Hitler.[203]

Bose did not appear to have any more success than on previous occasions in meeting high-ranking German officials. But he went forward.

From Berlin, he went briefly to Cologne and to Brussels, and then made a slightly longer stop in Antwerp. The stop in Antwerp was part work, part sight-seeing and relaxation. In 1933, when Bose was caring for Vithalbhai Patel in Gland, he met a Bombay businessman, Nathalal Parikh, who became a devoted friend and associate. Parikh was based in Antwerp and Bombay, and his homes in each city also became homes to Subhas Bose. The latter spent three weeks in Antwerp in early 1936, getting to know the small, wealthy Indian community, talking to Belgians about India, and touring the countryside.[204]

On a tour of the Grotte-de-Han caves, Bose was charmed and said to Parikh, 'What a wonderful thing we have seen. I feel it like a dream.'[205] While visiting a spa, Bose, who dressed in a long Indian coat and cap, was refused entry to the casino when he refused to remove his hat. He said that it was his national dress and he would not bend to the rules. In certain respects, he was still somewhat inflexible in a European environment, feeling that if he adapted too much, it would be damaging to his Indian pride and identity.[206]

After these enjoyable weeks with Parikh, Bose stopped for a few days in Paris. Although his passport was not stamped valid for Great Britain, he had received permission from the Irish government of Eamon de Valera for a visit, and was determined to go. But he did not want to go through Britain and risk trouble with the immigration authorities, so he decided to sail from Le Havre directly to Ireland and return the same way.[207] He did not know that the British were bluffing and were sure they could not keep a British subject like Bose out of Britain. Bose sailed to Cork, where his first act was to pay homage at the grave of Terrence MacSwinney, who died a martyr in a British prison, and was a member of Bose's personal pantheon of heroes.[208]

As early as 1933, Bose had written to Mrs M. Woods, secretary of the Indian–Irish Independence League, which Vithalbhai Patel had taken the initiative in founding, that,

> I have been longing to visit Ireland for years. . . . In part of the country (Bengal), recent Irish history is studied closely by freedom loving men and women and several Irish characters are literally worshipped in many a home. . . . For Madame Gonne MacBride I have a message from my brother whom I met in prison just before I sailed for Europe. My brother met Madame in 1914 in Paris and ever since then, has been one of her admirers.[209]

Sarat Bose had, indeed, met Mrs MacBride two decades before and, like Subhas, was a devoted student of Irish history. The connection to MacBride was revived by Subhas Bose, for she was president of the Indian–Irish

Independence League and one of his gracious hosts in Ireland.[210] Bose was most eager to see President de Valera and to get a sense of the political situation in Ireland. Perhaps because the Irish had been struggling for so many decades, even centuries, with the British, Bose felt a kinship with them that was stronger than he felt for any other foreign people.

For their part, the Irish also felt a connection to the Indian nationalists fighting for complete independence from the British Raj, and so reciprocated Bose's warmth. When Bose mentioned at a reception that he was not presently allowed into Britain, the seconder of a vote of thanks to Bose, Mr. Alex Lynn, asked how many years it would take before Dublin would rise to the dignity of Calcutta and have a mayor who would not be allowed into Britain.[211]

President de Valera interrupted his busy schedule to hold not one but three meetings with Bose. First he greeted him at Government Buildings in his capacity as minister of external affairs, viewing Bose '. . . as something like an ''envoy'' of a friendly nation.' Then he met him at an informal tea held by the Fianna Fail Party, and, finally, invited Bose to a private dinner at his house outside Dublin.[212] Amiya Chakravarty reported in his account of Subhas' version of the visit that de Valera had cautioned him that the British could not be met head-on in battle. And, perhaps as a result of his own experience of leaving Ireland at a crucial moment and going to the United States to seek aid, de Valera told Bose that by staying outside one's country, one got rhetorical support, nothing more.[213] This had a sobering effect on Bose, who knew the British would not leave easily and that there were limits, in the present world situation, in what he could accomplish for India from outside.

In addition to President de Valera and several of his ministers, Bose succeeded in meeting the leaders of other political parties and groupings including Mr Cosgrave, labor leaders, and J.J. O'Kelly of the Sinn Fein Standing Committee. The latter and his group represented extreme republicanism, and had taken to referring to the Irish Free State as 'the Freak State,' for they believed it was still dominated by Britain.[214] Although Bose visited Ireland at the very time when de Valera was reaching the culminating steps of his program to make Ireland an independent republic and break certain bonds of the treaty, the Republicans felt otherwise.[215] As Bose observed in his impressions of the visit, on the conflict between Fianna Fail and the Republicans,

> The Republicans allege that President de Valera is not moving towards a republic which he had promised and that his Government is persecuting the Republicans, 25 of whom have been put in prison. The feeling of the Government is that the Republicans are too impatient and tactless and are

blind to the realities of the situation—namely the existence of a pro-British party in the country and a partitioned Ireland . . . which make it difficult if not impossible to declare a republic at once. . . . On the whole, the existence of a Republican Party independent of the Government Party is in my opinion a blessing. It is a guarantee that Fianna Fail will never forget its republican aims. . . . I would only have liked to see a more cordial relationship between Fianna Fail and the Republicans . . . .[216]

Bose gained some insights by meeting leaders of the political parties as well as cultural and labor spokesmen and women, but he also met with ministers of a functioning government coping with serious post-independence problems. He said of his meetings with the Fianna Fail ministers,

All of them are exceedingly sympathetic, accessible and humane. They had not yet become 'respectable'. Most of them had been on the run when they were fighting for their freedom and would be shot on sight if they had been spotted. They had not yet (become) hardened bureaucratic ministers and there was no official atmosphere about them. With the minister for lands I discussed how they were abolishing landlordism by buying up the big estates and dividing the land among the peasantry. With the minister for agriculture I discussed how they were trying to make the country self-sufficient in the matter of food supply. . . . I also discussed with him the question of restriction of jute cultivation in India. . . . With the minister for industries I discussed the industrial policy of the government. He explained to me that they wanted to make the country self-sufficient . . . also in industry. . . . I found that the work of the Fianna Fail ministers was of interest and value to us in India when we would have to tackle the problems of nation building through the machinery of the state.[217]

Whether his discussions on landholding and tenancy rights made him reflect upon his own involvement in the Bengal Tenancy Bill discussions, Bose did not indicate. He put this question into the post-independence category, for his first priority, as always, was how to free India. Then nation building would follow.

At the reception which the Indian-Irish Independence League held for him in Dublin, Bose talked about the achieving of freedom,

The question of time, he said, was the difficult factor. The winning of their independence would depend on their own exertions and on the world situation.

The essence of leadership should consist in not merely arousing the people to sacrifice, but at the same time utilising the world situation to the fullest extent.[218]

From his reading of Irish history, Bose may well have been familiar with the old Fenian axiom, 'England's difficulty is Ireland's opportunity.'[219] And he was no doubt well acquainted with the mission of Roger Casement and the Easter Rising of 1916. Again clouds of war were gathering over Europe and from his remarks in Ireland, as well as at other stops in Europe, it is clear that he wanted his countrymen to seize the opportunity.

The trip to Ireland was a highlight of Bose's European years. He was treated as an eminent representative of a great country engaged in a struggle with the same empire from which the Irish, or some of them, had fought their way out. Further, he and de Valera, two determined anti-British Empire men, shared a number of perspectives. Both took pride in their national languages and culture; both were connected to political movements for complete independence that had gotten increasingly radical and used ever more extreme means; de Valera was dedicated, as was Bose, to an independent republic and believed that dominion status was not freedom. Both had been in and out of British prisons and de Valera had struggled manfully against the partition of his country, while Bose already recognized the divisive policies of the Raj which he believed had made for the religious cleavage in India.[220] Bose, then about thirty-nine, and a top leader of the Congress below the Mahatma, looked to the fifty-four-year-old de Valera as a guide in his own search for the path to the future of freedom, unity, and a juster society.

Before his ten days in Ireland were up, Bose happened to meet the former officer in charge of the Mandalay Jail, a Col. J.H. Smith, in Dublin. They chatted about their changed circumstances. Bose could see the irony and human interest in meeting his former jailer at another corner of the empire.[221] There was also some recurring physical pain which bothered Bose, but he did not curtail his schedule.[222] Before long, he was off again, to the continent and beyond. He wrote to Mrs Woods some weeks later,

> I often think of the days I spent in Dublin. It is like a dream and those went so quickly. I am grateful most of all to you for making my stay there so interesting and pleasant. . . . [223]

And, in another letter,

> I do not know when we shall meet again. Bhavabhuti, one of our ancient poets, once wrote—'Time is eternal and the earth is a vast expanse,' so maybe we shall meet again—but perhaps not so unexpectedly as when I knocked against my prison superintendent in the Shelbourne Hotel. . . . I shall write to you again as to what I think we should do—or could do—to continue this contact between India and Ireland.[224]

From Ireland, Bose returned to France and spent a few days in Paris meeting political and cultural leaders, including André Gide and André Malraux.[225] He also attended an anti-imperialist conference with members of the League against Imperialism. Speaking to this group, Bose made one of his most internationalist and socialist speeches, linking the cause in

India to the struggle against Western and Japanese imperialism around the world. In part, he said,

> . . . there is a growing feeling in India that the anti-imperialist movement there should be linked up with the anti-imperialist movement in other parts of the world. Modern communications have made it easier to establish this contact . . . it is generally recognised in India that political phenomena like imperialism and fascism affect all humanity. Therefore, we believe that if we lay India's case before the world, we shall get sympathy and support from all over the world. . . . It is necessary for us to think of the means of preventing the growth of Japanese imperialism in Asia. If tomorrow China could be strong and united, if tomorrow India could be free, I am sure it would . . . serve to check the spread of Japanese imperialism.[226]

To this group, he made a more direct condemnation of imperialism and fascism around the world than he usually made. When he spoke of socialism, he did not speak of a higher synthesis of elements of fascism and socialism:

> Our movement aims not only at national liberation, but also at social freedom. It is now felt more than before that our country is faced with the issues of the landlords and the peasants, and capital and labour. The feeling is growing that the Indian National Congress should declare itself more explicitly on the side of the masses. The net result, so far, of this criticism, has been that within the nationalist party, people are beginning to think more on the social question—we are moving in the direction of socialism.[227]

Further, Bose mentioned that Gandhi was still the most important leader of the movement, and that he hoped that Gandhi would advocate social reconstruction. During late 1935 and early 1936, Bose had many occasions to visit with Jawaharlal Nehru, who was caring for Kamala. Since Bose wrote to Nehru on a number of occasions for guidance, for a lead in a radical program of both means and ends, for the nationalist movement, it is possible that he was coming closer to Nehru's views on anti-imperialism and socialism. At least the Paris speech has great similarity with the outlook of Nehru who had often addressed the same group.[228]

Just before the Paris speech, Bose wrote to Nehru,

> Among the front rank leaders of today, you are the only one to whom we can look up to for leading the Congress in a progressive direction. Moreover, your position is unique and I think that even Mahatma Gandhi will be more accommodating towards you than towards anybody else. I earnestly hope you will fully utilise the strength of your public position in making decisions. Please do not consider your position to be weaker than it really is. Gandhiji will never take a stand which will alienate you.
>
> As I was suggesting in our last talk, your immediate task will be a two-fold one—(1) to prevent office-acceptance by all possible means, and (2) to

enlarge and broaden the composition of the cabinet. . . . I was extremely glad to hear that you were desirous of starting a foreign department of the Congress. This falls in with my views completely.[229]

The letter is respectful and also filled with solicitousness about Nehru's own physical exhaustion just after the death of his wife. Bose was also concerned that the Congress was moving in a parliamentary direction *only* and would not be emphasizing the development of a mass anti-British movement. So he took the opportunity to give his priorities to the next Congress president on the eve of the Congress session.

This meeting of the Congress was on Bose's mind as a rendezvous which he wanted to make. He had been telling many friends that he was going to return to India, no matter what the consequences. Writing to Jawaharlal on March 13, 1936, Bose said,

I have just now received an express letter from the British Consul at Vienna which reads as follows:

``I have today received instructions from the Secretary of State for Foreign Affairs to communicate to you a warning that the Government of India have seen in the press statements that you propose to return to India this month and the Government of India desire to make it clear to you that should you do so you cannot expect to remain at liberty.

Then Bose gave his response:

My inclination at the moment as you can very well imagine from your own reactions—is to defy the warning and go home. The only point that one has to consider is which course would be in the public interest. The personal factor does not count at all with me. . . . My only excuse for troubling you on such a matter is that I can think of no one else in whom I could have greater confidence.[230]

Nehru responded as Bose probably expected that he would, for they shared a fierce nationalist pride, which would not allow either to bow to such British strictures. Nehru wrote,

All my personal reaction to such orders and writings is to go against them. And yet I was not quite prepared to advise you to return immediately. . . . Obviously this kind of thing cannot be endured for long—perhaps we have endured it too long already. You cannot submit to indefinite exile.[231]

Bose decided to end his exile, no matter what the consequences. He was not keen to return to jail, but he felt that he had no more to do at the moment outside India, and that there was much to do in India. As he wrote to Romain Rolland, whom he had just visited again,

I feel that it is my duty to return to India at once, regardless of the official frowns. It is, of course, a tragic thing that the best and most creative years of one's life should be spent behind prison walls but that is a price which enslaved peoples always had—and always will have to pay in this world.[232]

Bose sailed from Italy by the Lloyd Triestino boat, S.S. Cante Verde, on March 27, 1936. He had been in Europe for nearly three years, except for the brief visit home at the time of his father's death.[233] He had had a variety of new experiences in a different environment. Although he had had a setback to his health in Ireland, he was generally stronger after the gallbladder operation and it was determined that he did not have tuberculosis as had been earlier suspected.

He had toured most of Europe, west of the Soviet Union and had met leaders and important figures in many countries. Another crucial task to which he had dedicated himself was helping Indian students and assisting the growth of student organizations. He had also played his part in the organization and encouragement of bi-national cultural organizations with several European countries and had discussed economic relations with businessmen, industrialists, and political leaders. He had been as effective a spokesman for Indian nationalism as Tagore, Gandhi, and Nehru had been, each in their own distinctive ways.

Though he had sought moral and political support, he knew that these efforts abroad had their limitations. Eamon de Valera had cautioned him about this out of his own experience; and, despite seeing Mussolini many times, Bose never thought that these European dictators were anything other than selfish.[234] But the support of powerful dictators, or of more democratic leaders like de Valera or Benes could not free India. What could? Bose knew that there was no alternative to building a strong, determined, and widely-based movement within India. But, he also wanted to be ready to take advantage of some weakening of the British Raj, which might occur if there were a new war. Bose had no love for Nazi Germany, as his many protests against their racism and treatment of Indians make clear, but he thought Hitler was reconstructing a potent and aggressive nation which could match the British and perhaps break them. He, like the Irish nationalists whom he admired, and like Indian nationalists before him during a previous war, was poised to take what the world situation had to offer. For the moment, however, he was returning to India to work on the first part of his program: to help build a more vigoros and resourceful nationalist movement inside the country and confront the British rulers.

VI

When the Lloyd Triestino docked in Bombay on April 8, 1936, Subhas Bose was immediately arrested, and faced another indefinite term of imprisonment.[235] The protests had started even before he had returned, for he himself had written to the British and Indian press attacking the caution from the British Consul, and had sent copies of the warning far and wide. Nehru and the Congress, many Indian papers, and British politicians and papers as well, condemned the summary re-arrest and incarceration of Bose.[236]

However, as he had noted in his Paris speech a few weeks earlier, the movement continued, as it had in a variety of ways during the years of his European exile. Further, his brother Sarat was now a free man and since his release in late July 1935, had been actively involving himself in Congress and Corporation work as best he could, while at the same time doing his professional work. Sarat Bose had been on the sidelines for three-and-a-half years and had just re-entered Indian politics and his legal career in August 1935.[237]

Sarat Bose had not been so distant from the scene as Subhas and was quickly learning about the new political groupings and trends at work. He had to take up more responsible positions than he had held previously, partly because of the continuing absence of Subhas from the scene, although Sarat Bose usually preferred to be what his brother called a 'backbencher'. Now Subhas Bose was on the scene, but again imprisoned and held out of the fray for the time being. He was close enough to educate himself about the new configurations of Indian politics and the results which would likely follow the implementation of the Government of India Act of 1935. Sarat Bose had already dived into nationalist work in the new period of struggle and Subhas Bose was awaiting the moment of release so that he too could join the battle.

Subhas Bose meets Adolf Hitler, 1942

Subhas reviewing Indian recruits in Germany, 1942

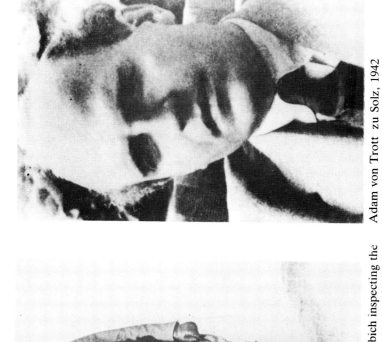

Subhas Bose with Walter Harbich inspecting the
Indian Legion in training in Germany, 1942

Adam von Trott zu Solz, 1942

Subhas Bose with the crew of the Japanese submarine he traveled in

Rash Behari Bose making over the leadership of his organization to Subhas Bose, Singapore, July 1943

Subhas Bose with General Tojo, circa 1943

Subhas Bose inspects the women's regiment of the INA—the Rani of Jhansi Regiment—1943

Subhas Bose visiting the Cellular Jail at Port Blair, Andaman Islands, December 1943

Fujiwara Iwaichi

Subhas Bose at the Assembly of Greater East Asiatic Nations,
Tokyo, November 1943

Subhas Bose's official welcome at Rangoon airport by Burmese ·
leaders led by Ba Maw, 1944

Cartoon showing Subhas Bose driving off Churchill
—from *Manga Mainichi*, a Japanese cartoon daily,
January 1945

Cartoon from an issue of the paper of the
Communist Party of India, 1943

Mahatma Gandhi visits the Bose house in Calcutta, 1945. Sarat
Bose is at the extreme left

Last available photograph of Subhas Bose,
Saigon airport, August 17, 1945

Sarat Bose with Mahatma Gandhi at Noakhali, 1946

Sarat Bose with Aung San, Rangoon, July 1946

The Interim Cabinet, 1946. Sarat Bose is at the extreme left

The Interim Government, 1946. Sarat Bose sits opposite Lord Wavell

Sarat Bose with Eamon de Valera, Calcutta, 1947

Sarat Bose addresses Indians in London together with Fenner Brockway, 1949

Sarat Bose and family with Subhas' wife (standing second from left) and daughter (sitting third from left), Vienna, 1948

Sarat Bose, London, July 1949

ডাক

THE CALL

নেহেরুর শব-পার্শ্বে—

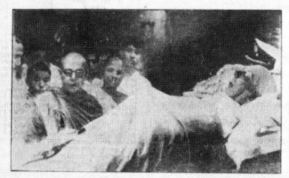

কে এই সন্ন্যাসী?

Sadhu resembling Subhas Bose viewing Jawaharlal Nehru's body 1964. From *Dak*, a Bengali weekly. "Who is this sannyasi?" the editors ask

CITY THROBS

FOR A PERMANENT PEACE
&
PEOPLES' DEMOCRACY

VOL.—1 NO. IV ● CALCUTTA SATURDAY ● JANUARY 23, 1965 ● WEEKLY 8 pages ● 20 paise

NETAJI IS ALIVE
American Sources Confirm

(See page—6)

NETAJI !!
The Nation Pays
Homage To You

Front page of Calcutta weekly, 1965

A garlanded statue of Subhas Bose in Calcutta

CHAPTER EIGHT

Deshanayak [Leader of the Country], 1936–39

As Bengal's poet, I acknowledge you today as the honoured leader of the people of Bengal.

Rabindranath Tagore to Subhas Bose, 1939[1]

I

After his release from detention on July 27, 1935, Sarat Bose had to pick up the pieces of his familial, professional, and political life. He went to the bar library where he was received warmly. He had to immediately begin his professional work, for his family, including Subhas, had been living much more parsimoniously without his handsome income. The marriage of his daughter, Meera, was being arranged at considerable expense, Asoke was continuing his training abroad, and there were expenses for the education of the other children. Subhas, as well, in Vienna and on tour in Europe, was earning little and required financial backing from his political friends and family. Briefs were not wanting for a barrister of Sarat's stature and soon his professional career was thriving again after the three-and-a-half-year lapse.[2]

As a devoted father, Sarat also plunged into the choice of a bridegroom for his eldest daughter. Through personal connections, Dr S.N. Roy, a biochemist with a Ph.D. from Cambridge University, had been proposed as a match for Meera. Sarat Bose met the prospective groom, liked him, and arranged the reciprocal visit for the young man and his family to meet Meera, after which the date of December 10 was selected for the marriage. Sarat wrote to Asoke to make his plans to return from Europe for the wedding. With Sarat back to his various activities, the Bose houses at Woodburn Park and Elgin Road again became centers of Calcutta life.[3]

Sarat had kept himself informed about the course of municipal, regional, national, and international politics, and although he preferred to be a backbencher, with Subhas off the set, the older political Bose had to take a more active frontline position. But what did the new political landscape of 1935 look like?

The Civil Disobedience Movement had been officially ended and Gandhi, though still Congress king, was hidden behind the screen of his constructive program. The Swarajists within the Congress had begun to come to the fore and to demand that Congressmen stand for election under the new Government of India Act. Dr B.C. Roy, by now one of Gandhi's personal physicians, and a leading Congressman of Bengal, was one of the advocates of this strategy which was to seek election, do constructive work within elective bodies if possible, but to paralyze them if positive work for the country was not possible. Sarat Bose's temperament and training suited him more for this kind of Congress work than for mass demonstrations or Gandhi's constructive program. After what some observers said was a tussle with Dr Roy, Sarat Bose became the acting president of the Bengal Provincial Congress Committee and shortly thereafter, the most important selector of Congress candidates for Corporation and Bengal legislative positions.[4]

During his earlier period of Corporation work, Sarat Bose had involved himself closely with the day-to-day affairs of the Calcutta city government, patiently done his homework, and been one of the important members in its running. Now, his role was different. He was concerned and active in the Congress Municipal Association, but not as councillor or alderman.

Just before Sarat Bose's release, Fazlul Huq, a leader of the Muslim community of Bengal and of the Krishak Praja Party, was elected mayor of Calcutta with Congress support. Sarat wrote to Huq from Kurseong,

> ... my love and regard for you prompt me to convey to you once again my sincerest felicitations. Those felicitations proceed from the belief that one who has made the cause of the working population his own, cannot remain content with offering mere lip service to civic ideals, of which we have unfortunately had so much in the recent past. May the Supreme Spirit, who is the Lord of the world, the Beneficent and Merciful Allah of Muhammadans and Brahman of Hindus, inspire and guide you.[5]

And even Subhas Bose, in distant Vienna, recuperating in a sanatorium from his recent operation, wrote to Huq,

> Your election was long overdue—but better late than never. I am sure that a successful tenure of office awaits you and that under your Mayoralty the different communities in Calcutta will be drawn closer together as a result of which, we shall see more of teamwork within the Corporation itself.[6]

However, the high hopes of the Boses were temporarily dashed before the year was out. The minority Muslim councillors proposed a fixed proportion of Corporation positions to be given to Muslims. The Hindu, mostly Congress, members did not agree to this. First the Muslim councillors, and then Mayor Huq resigned. The remaining councillors and aldermen stalled for months during which negotiations to work out a compromise were held. Huq made several conciliatory statements and invited Hindu and Muslim leaders to his house several times early in 1936 to try to find a *via media*. The efforts went on through the spring, with Sarat Bose, along with Dr B.C. Roy, Kiron Sankar Roy, J.C. Gupta, and B.P. Singh Roy, among others, representing the Hindus. With Fazlúl Huq ill during the spring, H.S. Suhrawardy, M.A.H. Ispahani, and the nawab of Dacca spoke for Calcutta's Muslims. No agreement was reached.[7]

In December 1935, Sarat Bose presided over the Ramakrishna Paramhamsa Centenary meeting held in Albert Hall. He spoke of Ramakrishna's teaching of the unity of all religions as providing different paths to the one God. Ramakrishna, he said, had revived India's faith in its spiritual inheritance at a time when the West seemed more glamorous. Ramakrishna, he continued, taught them that they could not have mukti without sadhana.[8] These remarks express Sarat Bose's religious vision and his concern with a universal religious understanding. He was a religious Hindu, but respected by those of other faiths. A tribute to C.R. Das and to Sarat Bose in this regard was offered by an important Muslim contemporary, Abul Mansur Ahmed, who wrote in his memoirs,

> Deshbandhu himself was a devout Hindu, a great Vaisnava devotee. He had unquestionable faith, whole-hearted faith in his own religion. His faith was free from any animosity against any other religious sect; on the contrary his faith was based on universal love. So he had deep respect for the Islamic faith. . . . He was . . . a devout Hindu and at the same time a great devotee of the ideal of Hindu-Muslim unity and harmony. After Deshbandhu I found this quality only in one man among the Bengali Hindu leaders and he was Mr Sarat Chandra Bose, the elder brother of Subhas Chandra Bose. Sarat Babu too was a very devout Hindu. He had faith in pujas and rituals and was ready to make any sacrifice for his faith. Although he was such a devout, confirmed Hindu, Sarat Babu, not for a moment in his life hesitated to accept whole-heartedly the legitimate political demands of the Muslims and did so without any reservation.[9]

Abul Mansur's main point was that the Muslims wanted a linking of the two communities with each side keeping its identity intact. A person of strong religious commitment like Das or Sarat Bose would want his faith to remain intact and have the sensitivity—in their cases, if not in all—to wish others to retain their own faith. During the 1920s and 1930s, Sarat

Bose began to learn more about Islam and read its basic scriptures, so that he might understand his Muslim colleagues. He began to make analogies between the different, yet similar paths which Islam and Hinduism offered to reach the one God. He saw neither religion as inferior to the other and he did not stress the extra-India connections of Islam to Mecca and the Middle East. The understanding that he gained helped him to work with Muslim leaders in Bengal and to gain their trust.

Sarat Bose was frustrated at the failure to work out an agreement with the Muslim representatives in and out of the Corporation during late 1935 and 1936. He felt that in a province with each community having close to fifty per cent of the population, political progress and harmony could only be worked out by compromise. The alternative was disaster.

There was another group to whom, Sarat Bose argued, some positions in the Corporation ought to be given. This group was that of the released political prisoners, almost all of whom were Hindus, and many of whom were linked to the Congress.[10] The early and mid-1930s were a period of shifting outlooks for many of the revolutionaries and their supporters. The combination of determined government repression under Governor Sir John Anderson, and a changing view of the efficacy of individual terrorist acts brought an end to almost all assassinations and political robberies by the mid-1930s.

The revolutionaries inside the various prison camps and their contemporaries outside were educating themselves in a range of ideologies from different versions of communism and socialism to more orthodox Congress views. An example is provided by these extracts from reports on developments inside Deoli Jail.

> So far as the Deoli Jail is concerned, we know that a large number of the detenus there are interested in communism and that an effective organisation if not already in existence is in the process of formation. . . . The difficulty of preventing study of what might be harmless to genuine students but is unwholesome fare for revolutionaries is illustrated by the question papers set by the Calcutta University on such subjects as Comparative Politics and Modern Economic Development. A number of detenus are preparing for Calcutta degrees and their studies comprise literature dealing with the Soviet Union and other extreme or revolutionary movements; in fact the approved textbooks include some which might come within the ban of the general communist notification issued under the Sea Customs Act.[11]

Leonard Pinnell, writing for the governor of Bengal to the secretary of the Home Department, Government of India, listed prescribed texts for the Calcutta University M.A. examination, including Laski's *Grammar of Politics* and *Communism,* Merriam and Barnes' *History of Political Theories,* Le Bon's *Psychology of Revolution,* and Loria's *Karl Marx.*

Much to his disgust, Pinnell concluded that,

> I confess that I can see no remedy for this difficulty. The sample papers
> ... leave the impression that the study is being encouraged by the Calcutta
> University of a range of subjects calculated to promote in the callow and
> unbalanced minds of young Bengalis the very trends of thought which led
> to terrorism and revolutionary activity.[12]

Mr Pinnell, private secretary to several governors of Bengal, and one of Sarat Bose's 'jailers' in Kurseong when he was the ICS officer in charge of Darjeeling district,[13] did not see the difference between communism, socialism, and the forms of revolutionary activity used by small groups of Bengalis for decades. But there had been a change. The new focus for those moving to socialism or communism was on mass organizing. The concern became how to bring about a social transformation as well as how to achieve independence for India.

Other developments were taking place in these years. The Congress Socialist Party was formed in 1934, the Communist International shifted to a United Front line at the Seventh Congress in 1935, affecting the Communist Party of India, and the All-India Kisan Sabha was organized in 1936. Even though the Congress had gone into the doldrums with many of its leaders imprisoned, political life and economic protests continued. The consequences of the worldwide economic depression on India continued. Although the trade union movement was badly fragmented, strikes continued, mainly on economic grounds.[14] The economic issue, what some called 'the problem of India,' haunted the minds of some of those who were looking for new directions. Many of those searchers came to believe that the only answers for India lay with some form of socialism or communism.

After a conference in Poona in 1933 and meetings inside the Nasik Prison in 1932 and 1933, a number of young Congressmen, dissatisfied with the Gandhian and Swarajist approaches of their party, formed the Congress Socialist Party (CSP) in 1934. They included, Jayaprakash Narayan, Minoo Masani, Asoka Mehta, Acharya Narendra Dev, Yusuf Meherally, Kamaladevi Chattopadhyay, Achyut Patwardhan, Purshottam Trikamdas, and R.M. Lohia. Their efforts were encouraged by the imprisoned M.N. Roy and Jawaharlal Nehru, and the exiled Subhas Bose, although these three leftists declined to join the CSP. The CSP called for the AICC to adopt a socialist program, wanted organization of the masses, and advocated a social and economic transformation of Indian society. Though critical of the Gandhian program, they decided to work within the Congress to bring it to their socialist views.[15]

From the late 1920s through the early 1930s, the Third Communist

International or Comintern had been relatively isolated from the Congress and the mainstream of Indian nationalism by their own choice. They bitterly attacked the left of the Congress as social fascists and wanted to shape their own organization, free of Gandhian medievalisms. With the failure of this strategy in several parts of the world and the menacing rise of fascism in Germany and Italy, the Comintern shifted again, this time to the United Front line. R. Palme Dutt in England and some of the Indian communists had been pushing for such a shift even earlier, but sanction and impetus came from the reports and resolutions of the Seventh Congress of the Comintern. In the main report to the Congress in Moscow, Georgi Dimitrov said in part,

> In India the Communists have to support, extend and participate in anti-imperialist mass activities, not excluding those which are under national reformist leadership. While maintaining their political and organisational independence, they must carry on active work inside the organisations which take part in the Indian National Congress, facilitating the process of crystallisation of a national revolutionary wing among them, for the purpose of further developing the national liberation movement of the Indian peoples against British Imperialism.[16]

Following this new orientation, Indian communists joined the CSP and the Congress, some of them becoming able trade union and peasant organizers and valuable builders of the Congress. For the time being, the CSP leadership allowed known communists to enter their ranks. Some visible and some secret communists thus moved into the CSP and Congress organizations to work both for Indian liberation and for international communism.[17]

The movement from a left sectarian position by the communists, and the growth of a socialist group in the Congress, also facilitated the reunification of the trade union movement. Riven by splits in the late 1920s and early 1930s, the All-India Trade Union Congress was consolidated in the second half of the 1930s.[18] Peasant organizing also began to perk up and an umbrella organization, the All-India Kisan Sabha, was formed in 1936. The kisan movement was strongest in Bihar and developed unevenly throughout India.[19] Leftists in the trade union and kisan movements tried to press the National Congress to take a more active, aggressive pro-worker and pro-peasant position. The national leaders, including the Boses, often hedged, saying that they wanted an all-class, national movement against the British Raj.[20]

II

Before leaving Europe, Subhas Bose had issued some statements in strong anti-capitalist language and had taken to calling himself a socialist. Upon his return to India in April 1936, his political voice was stilled, for he was detained by the government. Bose's detention came at a time when most Congressmen had been released, and the Congress president, Jawaharlal Nehru, called for All-India Subhas Day on May 10, 1936. Debates about his continued incarceration were initiated in the Central Legislative Assembly and the Houses of Lords and Commons in London. Although they would not give details, officials of the Raj and government spokesmen in parliament said he was too dangerous to let loose.[21]

At first he was detained in Bombay, then Yeravda Prison, near Poona in Maharashtra. After rumors circulated that he was shortly to be taken to some prison at a hill station, he was moved by the government to Sarat Bose's house in Kurseong in May 1936. Under the same rules, and with Subhas' 'gentlemanly,' but not formal acceptance of them, he was detained there to almost the end of the year. He was allowed family visitors, upon application, and before long, granted permission to take walks within a one-mile radius of the house. At first, he benefitted from the cooler climate and the relatively freer atmosphere. And he was delighted to see Sarat Bose in early June, and then to have the company for some time of his nephews Amiya and Sisir.[22]

During this period, Subhas Bose and Emilie Schenkl began to write regularly to each other. They carried on this correspondence between Vienna and India from August 1936 to October 1937, each solicitous about the welfare of the other. She was concerned about his health and diet and advised him not to stay up late at night reading, as he was wont to do. At the time she was unemployed and often discouraged. But with his encouragement, she agreed that it would be cowardly to give up trying. For a while she cared for a young child, but could find no steady job. She asked him many questions and wondered whether it was proper for a non-Hindu to send *bijaya* greetings to a Hindu. With Miss Schenkl and with his friend Mrs Hedy Fulop-Müller, he occasionally tried his hand at German. Neither party could or did touch on political matters since the correspondence was censored. The regularity and the touching concern with the small and large matters of life suggest that they had established an important relationship which was to go on, regardless of the geographical or political barriers.[23]

III

While Subhas Bose was held in the hills, Sarat Bose was hard at work in the plains, in Calcutta, with his legal briefs and with political affairs. The Government of India Act of 1935 was to take effect in the spring of 1937 and elections were to be held in the cold season of 1936–37. Sarat Bose was placed in charge of the Congress election effort in Bengal. The Congress was committed to contesting the elections under the provincial autonomy provisions of the act, but no decision had been made about whether the Congress would form ministries or simply try to block the implementation of the act after the vote.[24]

One issue which had troubled Bengal's caste Hindus for years also had a bearing on the Bengal Congress electoral effort. This was the Communal Award of 1932 together with the Poona Pact. These specifications for the number of reserved seats for Hindus, Muslims, and other groups, were now provisions of the act. No longer simply labels and numbers on a forgotten piece of paper, these allotments were now to shape Bengal politics. Under the provisions for the Bengal Legislative Assembly, the Muslims were to have about 119 seats with separate electorates and reserved seats in a house of 250; the general non-Muslims were to have seventy-eight seats and some thirty of these were to be reserved for the scheduled castes. The Muslims had complained briefly about not having a statutory majority. But, the caste Hindus of Bengal were angry. From the most sensitive and cultural (e.g., Rabindranath Tagore) to the more communal (e.g., Hindu Mahasabha: Shyama Prasad Mookerjee), to the secular and national (e.g., Congressmen: the Boses), all felt wounded and wronged by the Raj under this award. Bengal caste Hindus were grieved that the National Congress did not make a strong statement in its electoral manifesto in objection to the award. They felt that they had been stung the hardest and been left alone to deal with the consequences by their national organization.[25]

As the acting president of the BPCC, and thus a most important spokesman for the Bengal Hindus, Sarat Bose took up the issue both within the Congress and in the context of the election campaign. He shortly found himself involved in arguments with Jawaharlal Nehru, Congress president, and Sardar Patel, the key figure in the Congress organization and electoral effort. In September 1936, Sarat Bose wrote to Nehru that the Congress' neutral stand on the communal decision was 'responsible for the staggering defeat that Congress suffered at the last Assembly elections in Bengal.' He insisted that the caste Hindu electorate in Bengal would not stand for an equivocal position on the Communal Award.[26]

In response, Nehru wrote to Sarat Bose on September 26 that independence was the vital issue. He said that if the Bengal Congress agitated about the Communal Award, they were distracting the electorate. He and the other members of the high command objected to a resolution passed by the BPCC against the 1935 Act. Nehru said that Bengal did not have its priorities straight.[27]

For his part, Sarat Bose answered, on November 18, 1936: 'Bengal will never subordinate the main issue to the issue raised by the communal decision.'[28] In an earlier letter, he wrote to Nehru, replying to his charge that the Congress Nationalist Party in Bengal had swallowed the Bengal Congress: 'The fact is, that the Nationalist Party in Bengal has become merged into the Congress and not that the Nationalist Party has swallowed the Congress in Bengal.'[29] With their antipathy to the 1935 Act and the Communal Award, the Bengal Congress, as part of the National Congress organization, went to the electorate with the national manifesto and Sarat Bose led their efforts in his home province.

On the Muslim side, there was no dominant party. In 1936, several groups of Muslim leaders had joined to form the United Muslim Party and then the New Muslim Majlis merged with the United Muslim Party to form the revived Muslim League in Bengal. Khwaja Nazimuddin, H.S. Suhrawardy, M.A.H. Ispahani, and many Muslim luminaries from the landed and business communities participated, and Jinnah, now back in India and trying to build one Muslim party, blessed their effort.[30]

The Krishak Praja Party had been founded in 1929 and had considerable support from the Muslim middle-class and peasantry, particularly in the eastern districts. Some members were very socialistically inclined and wanted the abolition of the Permanent Settlement of Bengal and a frontal assault on the landlords and moneylenders of the province, the great majority of whom were Hindus. The party had begun as the Nikhil Banga Praja Samity and aspired to a non-communal role, hoping to gather lower-class support from both major communities. It also sympathized with the Congress but demanded a stronger line against those dominant in the rural areas. Fazlul Huq was the leader of the party, but as a mercurial and ever-shifting leader, some of his party-mates never knew on what side of the bed he might wake up—one day it might be populist and secular and socialist; another day it might be Muslim with a harsh communal antipathy to the Hindus and the Congress as well.[31]

Jinnah encouraged his Muslim League men in Bengal to work out an agreement with the Krishak Praja Party, which he anticipated might give the Muslim League a strong run in many Muslim constituencies. These negotiations broke down in September 1936. At this point Huq issued a statement hostile of Jinnah and the non-Bengali Muslims playing a prominent role in the Muslim League. The League answered back in its papers, *Azad* and the *Star of India*. In its election campaign, the Muslim League stressed the need for Muslim solidarity.[32]

As the Muslims tried to work out their intra-community difficulties, Sarat Bose had his own problems on the Congress side with the long-term factionalism which seemed endemic to Bengal. Also, it had been a considerable period of time since the Congress had mounted a province-

wide election campaign. Sarat Bose wrote privately to Satyendra Chandra
Mitra on October 21, 1936:

> You are right in your surmise that I voted against your selection as the
> Congress candidate from *Noakhali rural*. In answer to your query, I shall tell
> you at once that there can be no question that you are in every respect a most
> fit and proper candidate for the Bengal Assembly. . . . I told Bengal friends
> on numerous occasions that . . . a seat should be found for you. . . . I shall
> now tell why I voted for your rival whom I hardly know, whereas I have
> known you most intimately for about two decades. When I came to Calcutta
> the other day, I found that district recommendations had gone against some
> of my personal friends among whom I count you as one. I had to consider
> whether it would be right to alienate the districts, even though personally I
> might not agree with some of their recommendations. I consider it wise
> . . . to refrain from doing anything which might revive the spirit of hostility
> between the district committees and the Provincial Committee. We have
> suffered a lot in the past on account of this spirit of hostility, and I thought
> we ought to strain every nerve to prevent its revival. That was the *only*
> *reason why* I voted for your rival. I knew I was sacrificing a good and kind
> friend who had stood by me in my hour of need; but I did so only because
> I felt that supporting district recommendations (except in cases where they
> were flagrantly improper or dishonest) was the right thing to do in view of
> the situation facing us.[33]

Even with the reasons he provided for opposing Mitra's candidacy, Sarat
Bose recommended that he persevere with his efforts to secure a
constituency.

Many of the Hindu landlords, lawyers, and businessmen at first
straddled the fence, not joining any party for the elections. Some then came
to the Congress side, some remained independents, and a few joined the
Hindu Mahasabha. Although Subhas Bose wondered whether his brother
was upon occasion too soft on the Hindu Mahasabha and their leader in
Bengal, Shyama Prasad Mookerjee (a personal friend of Sarat's and the
Bose family), when the election came, the Mahasabha was an opposition
party like any other. Nehru wrote in his report on the year that the
disagreement over the Congress position on the Communal Award had
been straightened out during his visit to Calcutta.[34]

The Congress election manifesto read, in part:

> The Congress rejected in its entirety the constitution imposed upon India by
> the New Act and declared that no constitution imposed by outside authority
> and no constitution which curtails the sovereignty of the people of India, and
> does not recognise their right to shape and control fully their political and
> economic future, can be accepted . . . the purpose of sending Congressmen
> to the legislatures under the new Act is not to cooperate in any way with the
> Act but to combat it and seek to end it. . . . The new legislatures, hedged and

circumscribed by safeguards and special powers for the protection of British and other vested interests, cannot yield substantial benefits, and they are totally incapable of solving the vital problems of poverty and unemployment. . . . The Congress representatives will seek to . . . work for the establishment of civil liberty, for the release of political prisoners and detenus, and to repair the wrongs done to the peasantry and to public institutions in the course of the national struggle.[35]

It also contained a strong criticism of the communal decision, declaring it 'wholly unacceptable as being inconsistent with independence and the principles of democracy.'[36]

The Bengal electorate under the 1935 Act was increased to 6,695,000 or about 13.4 per cent of the population, up from an electorate of 1,344,000 in the last election under the Montagu–Chelmsford Act of 1919. In 1937, approximately 40.5 per cent of the eligible voters exercised their franchise, but this percentage was pulled down by the much lower figures for women and scheduled caste voters than in the other constituencies.[37]

The elections in Bengal went off without incident. Although the Congress did exceedingly well among the caste Hindus, it won only seven of the scheduled caste seats, most going to independents, and almost totally avoided contesting the Muslim seats. Since there was some overlap of view with the Krishak Praja Party the Congress gave implicit, if not explicit, support to this party in its contests with the Muslim League and with independent Muslims. The Muslim votes were split three ways: the KPP got 31.5 per cent of the votes, the Muslim League 27.1 per cent, and independents received the remainder. The KPP was definitely stronger in rural areas and in East Bengal, the League more muscular in West Bengal and in urban constituencies.[38] One tabulation of the results of the voting on January 18–20, 1937 gives the following results by party in the Bengal Legislative Assembly:

Congress (including one independent Congress and two women)	43
Labour Congress	5
Scheduled Caste Congress	7
Tippera Krishak Samity	5
	60
Independent Muslims	41
Muslim League (including two women)	41
Praja Party (F. Huq)	35
Europeans	25
Independent Scheduled Caste	23
Independent Caste Hindus	14
Anglo–Indians	4

Hindu Nationalists (caste Hindus)	3
Hindu Sabha (scheduled castes)	2
Indian Christians	2
	250

Once the results were announced, negotiations began between parties, independents, leaders, and communities, with the governor, Sir John Anderson, working quietly to see what kind of ministry could be agreed upon and backed by a majority in the Assembly.[39] India and Bengal were one step closer to parliamentary government, but the framework of the Raj and the 1935 Act still had to be contended with.

IV

While Subhas initially reacted well to the cooler climate of Kurseong, in the fall of 1936, his health began to deteriorate again and his weight began to fall. Since more specialized tests were needed and adequate nursing care required, he was moved to the Calcutta Medical College Hospital on December 17, 1936. Writing to his friend Mrs Vetter, in February of the following year, he described the hospital period:

> I have been undergoing examination and treatment since I came here. They have found some trouble in throat and liver—for which I am receiving treatment. Now my eyes are giving me trouble. . . . I have lost some weight . . . about 10 kilo—but the doctors here say that there is no trouble with the lungs and they tell me that I need not be anxious for the loss of weight. So I tell myself that I have been slimming, as is the fashion in Europe! . . . Mrs Fulop-Müller was in Calcutta recently and she was my brother's guest. . . . Government were good enough to give her special permission to see me. . . . On the whole, I am feeling slightly better since coming here. I am glad to be able to meet my relatives here—who could not go up to Darjeeling—especially my mother. Since my mother is not able to move about, Government have allowed me to visit her twice a week at home. Of course, I have to go and return under police escort.[40]

At the end of his letter, he wrote:

> Lest I forget, may I ask one question? The Indian papers published the news some time ago that Chancellor Schussnigg was secretly married at Mariazell some months ago. The news did not come through the regular news agency—so I do not know if it is only idle gossiping. Nowadays there is so much of idle gossiping going on in Europe about people who are prominent in the public eye.[41]

As another man in the public eye and subject to 'idle gossip' was he just curious, or was there other reason to ask about this particular rumor? At the time he was also reading Freud's *Interpretation of Dreams*, encouraging introspection into his own life.[42]

While talk in Calcutta centered on where Subhas Bose might next be transferred, the Governments of Bengal and India were exchanging notes on the question of releasing him. The Bengal Government sent a note on March 6, 1937 to the center, which said, *inter alia* :

1. The Government of Bengal suggest that the existing situation is one of considerable difficulty for subversive elements in India, who will require time to organize their forces. Their expert adviser in the person of the D.I.G., C.I.D. . . . has been emphasizing the danger resulting from the massing of subversive elements under the slogan of 'The United Front'. I do not think, however, that we have any grounds at the present time to oppose the release of Subhas Bose.

2. The question then arises when should this release take place.

3. There is one consideration of importance which does affect the Government of India and that is the coming Nationalist meetings in Delhi . . . . It seems probably that Subhas Bose, if he were permitted to attend the Delhi meetings, would support the policy favoured by Jawahar Lal Nehru and it is obviously desirable that . . . Nehru should not receive any reinforcements at the National Convention.[43]

Officials at the center accepted Bengal's position and added that they not only did not want him at the meetings in Delhi, but they did not want him to influence the composition of the Bengal ministry. After Governor Anderson put in his view that Bose should be released; finally, after imprisonments, exile, and detention that had lasted from the beginning of 1932, Bose was freed on March 17, 1937.[44] A leading 'subversive' was out, but the subversives and the left were seen as too weak and too disorganized to profit significantly from the release of one more of their number. And the composition of the ministry in Bengal seems to have been agreed upon privately, if not yet announced publicly.

V

Shortly after the January election, Governor Anderson wrote to the viceroy, Lord Linlithgow, on the results and the possibilities for ministry formation. He noted that,

The main lessons that emerge are the great strength of the Congress appeal in the General constituencies and the efficiency of their organization. . . . On the other hand Sir B.P. Singh Roy won easily in a landholders constituency against an opponent set up from behind by Congress. . . . Among the Muslims the defeat of Sir Nazimuddin by Fazlul Huq is a most striking result, and emphasises the powerful appeal to the masses of Huq's emotionalism and his socialistic policy as regards agrarian affairs. It is said, perhaps with truth, that he received substantial aid both from Congress and from Farooqui. . . . Whether the Congress or any of them decide to try for office or whether they decide to follow a policy of remaining in opposition so as both to use the Government for their own purposes when convenient and at the same time bring it into discredit, the key man from their point of view is Fazlul Huq. . . . Opinion in the Congress is divided, roughly as between B.C. Roy's group and Sarat Bose's group on the question of office acceptance, but in either event Fazlul Huq's loyalty either to person or principle is completely unreliable. . . . I am reliably informed, he is expressing himself as anxious to attain Muslim 'unity'. . . . The possibility of a stable combination among the Muslims is clearly the main key to the position. . . .[45]

Anderson went on to say that he would not make any move himself to create a Muslim bloc, because this action in itself would weaken such backing as a possible Huq ministry might get.[46]

Before the election, the Congress left had opposed office acceptance. Nehru and Subhas Bose, and the official Congress were roundly critical of the 1935 Act. So the Congress, even with a majority in many provinces of British India, demanded assurances about containment of the special powers of the governors and the central officials of the Raj before making their choice on office acceptance. The negotiations between the Congress Parliamentary Board and the Government of India went on for some time.

Bengal, however, was not one of the Congress-majority provinces, and matters had to be worked out in the spring of 1937. From the fragments of available evidence, it appears that Sarat Bose was not willing or able to join Fazlul Huq in forming a coalition ministry at this time. Abul Mansur Ahmed reports on negotiations which fell through that even if some sort of concrete proposal had been formulated, it would have had to be approved by the central Congress Parliamentary Board (Patel, Prasad, Azad) and it is unlikely to have gained approval.[47]

Fazlul Huq, as suggested by Anderson, and many other sources, was an able, emotional, and unreliable man. He now swung to the Muslim League, though he had refused to ally with them before the election. He gained the chief ministership for himself, but finally agreed to give the Muslim League four places in a cabinet of eleven, with only Nausher Ali and himself from the Krishak Praja Party. The other places were filled by Hindus from the landlords' group (B.P. Singh Roy and Maharaja Srischandra Nandy of Kassimbazar), the business community (Nalini Ranjan Sarker), and the Scheduled Caste group (Prasanna Deb Raikut and Mukunda Behary Mullick). The Muslim Leaguers were Khwaja Nazimuddin, H.S. Suhrawardy, Nawab Musharruf Hossain, and the nawab of Dacca, Khwaja Habibullah.[48]

Of the five Hindus, the strongest figure was undoubtedly Nalini Sarker, a former Congressman and former mayor of Calcutta, close to G.D. Birla, and a substantial person in the Indian business community. Once a backer of Subhas Bose as a member of the 'Big Five' in the 1920s, he had moved to the right. His acceptance of the important position of finance minister brought upon him exclusion from the Congress. But it did not dim his influence in some Congress circles and with Gandhi.[49]

The dominant force in the cabinet was the Muslim group and particularly the Muslim Leaguers. Huq had either rushed into the arms of the League or been driven there by Congress' reluctance to join him. In any case, he was now dependent upon the League and in a cabinet weighted with landlords, it was hard to see that the agrarian program of the Krishak Praja Party had much chance of fulfillment. Indeed, there were protests from within Huq's party even before the ministry had been announced and, within a few months, Huq split with a large segment of his own party and joined the Muslim League himself. Once on this course, he moved in an ever more communal direction, alienating many in the Krishak Praja Party and some of the Hindus who had once been eager to work with him and defer to his leadership.[50] For his propulsion in that unfortunate direction, the Congress and the Boses bear some responsibility. They had offered him no real alternative in the spring of 1937. This was one turning point for Bengal in the years before partition.

VI

After his release from government custody, Subhas Bose, as happened in 1927, had to gradually recoup his strength and work his way back into Indian politics. He had lost a good deal of weight and all observers said he looked 'emaciated'. One of the first tasks he set for himself was to re-establish his warm relationship with Dilip Kumar Roy. There had been a misunderstanding through the mail over Subhas' criticisms of those who retreated from the world out of blind faith. Dilip and his guru, Aurobindo Ghose, now Sri Aurobindo, objected. On March 17, Dilip was summoned. He wrote,

> I was shocked to see his emaciated frame, though he looked more spiritual than ever. . . . He threw his arms round me and wept like a child. . . . I was struck by a deeper spiritual change that had taken place in him. Years of struggle and disappointment, super-added to frequent incarcerations, had mellowed the exterior austerity of the youthful ascetic.[51]

They discussed the dangers and blessings of *guruwad*—Dilip praising the submission and relation to a wise guide through the course of life, Subhas guru-less and skeptical. Subhas told his friend that he had learned to be more tolerant, especially of his opponents, through his years in prison and exile.

All-Bengal Subhas Day was held on April 6, and a huge crowd gathered at Shraddhananda Park to greet him at his first public meeting in India after more than five years.

> As many as six hundred associations offered garlands and bouquets to Mr Subhas Chandra Bose. The garlands were placed in heaps on a table placed in front of him. The following message of Poet Rabindranath was then read:—'I add my voice to the nation's welcome to Subhas.'[52]

When Subhas rose to speak, he said,

> It is no exaggeration to say that since coming back into your midst after imprisonment, exile and detention, I have been feeling like a political Rip Van Winkle. You must, therefore, give me time to pick up the old threads, to find my bearings and then to look into the future.[53]

He said he would have to discuss plans with Gandhi and Nehru. Then, perhaps as with Dilip Roy, intent on healing old wounds and feeling some guilt for past quarrels, he lamented the passing of his late comrade and rival, J.M. Sen Gupta,

> I am now in the midst of a storm of recollections—both painful and pleasant. . . . Most poignant of all is the thought that some of the greatest and worthiest sons of Mother India—Deshpriya Jatindra Mohan Sen Gupta, President V.J. Patel, Dr M.A. Ansari, Mr Birendra Nath Sasmal . . . are no longer with us. . . . In this part of the country you have undoubtedly felt more than anything else the absence of Deshpriya Sen Gupta. Bengal today is like a benighted province without his leadership and you will have to pull all your strength and all your resources if you are to fill even partially the great void that has been caused by his sudden, unexpected and tragic death.[54]

Subhas wrote to Congress President Nehru about what directions he, as Congress Working Committee member from Bengal and soon president of the BPCC, should take in resolving some of Bengal's outstanding problems. Nehru, replying on April 16, had no magic cures. He hoped that long-standing divisions within the BPCC could be resolved, that proper elections might take place, and he was wary of parties within the Congress and of Congress links with other parties in the Assembly. On the Muslims, particularly the peasantry, he offered his usual formula,

> It seems to me that the best approach to the Muslim masses should be directly through local Congress Committee. Kisan Sabhas may be organised where necessary. But where this is done by semi-Congress people it leads to conflict. Where the same persons function in both organisations it makes little difference. But the real point is that you should have an effective agrarian programme. If this is good enough it will draw the Muslim masses. If the Congress can adopt it, it is desirable that it should do so.[55]

Though Bose surely took note of Nehru's advice, neither the Bengal nor the Indian National Congress prepared 'an effective agrarian programme' and the Muslim masses, and many of the Hindu masses as well, remained outside the Congress. Bose did occasionally call for the Congress to become a party of the peasant masses, but he did not work to make it that.

Some of the warm wishes for him upon his return took a concrete form: the Subhas Congress Fund was started. He wanted the Congress in Bengal to have a house—a place for meeting, research, and honoring its national heroes. It was slow getting off the ground, but a fund was collected and a year later a plot of land was leased from the Calcutta Corporation for a nominal fee. Some time later, the cornerstone of Mahajati Sadan was laid and Rabindranath Tagore, nearing eighty, came to celebrate its founding.[56]

Subhas, however, was too weakened to plunge into his usual round of endless meetings and tours. He had to further regain his health and was told that he needed a cool and dry climate for some time. He had a standing invitation to stay with old friends, the Dharmavirs, whom he had kept in touch with since his student days in England, and who had a house in Dalhousie, a North Indian hill station. Once there in May 1937, he wrote to Mrs Vetter describing his past few months and present prospects. He said, in part,

> I was in Calcutta for more than a month—partly for resting and partly for enjoying the company of relatives and friends. Then I left for Allahabad towards the end of April to meet Mahatma Gandhi and attend a party meeting. After a few days I left for Lahore where I halted for 10 days. Then I reached this place on the 12th May. Dalhousie is a hill station to the north of Lahore and about 2000 metres high on the Himalayan range. . . . This is a small and quiet place nestling in the midst of hills. From the terrace of this house, you can see the plains and rivers in the far-off distance. On the other side of the town you see the Himalayan range—snow-capped at certain places. There are at present no restrictions at all on me—but of course I am secretly watched and my correspondence is secretly opened.[57]

Subhas played a part in the affairs of the Dharmavirs at this time. He felt quite like an older brother or young uncle to Mrs Dharmavir's two daughters, particularly Sita. She had trained to be a doctor and had fallen in love with another young Indian doctor, Santosh Sen, whom Bose had known well in Vienna. In getting her parents' approval of this love match, Subhas played the role of intermediary, and some months later wrote most persuasively to her parents telling them that in his opinion the marriage was 'a wise one and a desirable one.'[58]

He felt most at home with the Dharmavirs and rested, read, wrote, and reflected during these five months. Family members in Calcutta supplied Subhas with Indian newspapers, especially the Bengali ones, and also made sure that he obtained the books and periodicals from India and abroad that he wanted. He regularly received *Foreign Affairs* from the

United States and *International Affairs* and the *New Statesman and Nation* from Britain. He also found time to read and enjoy Robert Briffault's *Europa* and Aldous Huxley's *Eyeless in Gaza*. Noting the erotic passages in both novels, he wrote to Mrs Vetter that 'times and tastes are changing rapidly.'[59]

Part of his regimen in Dalhousie, as probably at other times in his mature life, included what he called 'self-analysis', 'self-assertion', and 'self-surrender'. He described these in detail to a friend in a letter of August 8:

> I believe in God. I also believe in prayer. . . . The mental (or spiritual) exercise that I have been doing is of two kinds—*depending on my mood at the time*. One of these is (the) practice of self-assertion. I sit down peacefully and think hard that I have overcome the *ripu*, viz. the six sensual passions (lust, anger, greed, fear, illusion, jealousy). This practice gives me a lot of strength. . . . I have also received much benefit from . . . self-analysis. Whenever I have time, I sit down calmly and try to look into my mind and find out what weakness, if any, is there. In this way, I have detected many unworthy elements and nipped them in the bud. Detection always means half the victory. . . . Most of the mental trouble that we have is due to the fact that we do not know our own minds. The mind is such a subtle thing that it often deceives itself. Therefore, continual self-analysis is necessary as a daily mental exercise. The study of abnormal psychology—and of psychopathology has helped me to analyse myself. . . . The other practice is self-surrender. I sit down and think of a mighty stream of Divine Energy—something like Bergson's 'élan vital'—and try to merge my existence in it. I try to feel that as a result of this merging the Divine Energy flows through me and that I am but an instrument in the hands of the Divine. I never consciously pray for anything material. It is mean and sordid. . . . I try to repeat to my mind—'Thy will be done'—in a spirit of self-surrender.[60]

At another point in this same introspective letter, Bose said that he did not have time to keep up his interest in philosophy or psychology. As a man of politics, he had to know a little about a lot of subjects, 'I must try to be a *sob janta* (know-all) . . . because a public man must have a general grasp of all problems . . . it cannot be helped because life is short and one's energy is limited.' He wrote:

> The greatest joy I have experienced so far is in living a life of uncertainty and adventure—and a life devoted to a cause. It compensates you for all your suffering and sorrow—and it makes life romantic. The greatest pain I have received is from the behaviour of human beings—sometimes your own friends—from whom you expected better and nobler things.[61]

Some letters were just concerned with 'business'—the Calcutta Corporation or other mundane matters. In other letters from Dalhousie, he mentioned the toll that poor health and inactivity was taking on him.

A long-time friend, Khitish Chattopadhyay, had taken leave of the Corporation educational post which he long held and, apparently, had told Subhas of his 'peace and satisfaction' in his new position of lecturer in anthropology at Calcutta University. Subhas wrote of satisfaction in the life of their mutual friend Dilip Roy, who he regretted had not joined him in Dalhousie, and then talked of peace in his own life:

> ... I must go on. The path is long and dreary. At times I feel weary. Darkness overtakes me—relieved by occasional flashes of lightning. But what of that? There is pleasure in travelling. I am still a homeless wanderer. Peace, Peace!! I have not found peace yet, nor satisfaction. It is not the lightning alone which lures me, but the darkness as well. It is not the bright future alone which calls, but the gloomy uncertainty as well. If I should fall before I reach the light—what of that? There is pleasure in travelling—in groping—also in falling![62]

The theme of groping, of struggle, of moving on to the best of one's ability, is touched on in the titles of his two books, one written before this time, *The Indian Struggle,* the other yet to come, *An Indian Pilgrim*. The theme of the lonely quest, an ancient Indian one, was shortly to be embodied in this second lengthy writing project.

While in Dalhousie, he also occupied himself with trying to understand the monumental clashes and changes in the international scene taking place in the mid-1930s in Europe and Asia. His views were spelled out in two essays he wrote at that time, 'Japan's Role in the Far East,' and 'Europe: Today and Tomorrow,' which eventually appeared in the *Modern Review*. In the essay on Japan, particularly dealing with her invasion of China and the growing East Asia war, Bose showed how the Japanese usually cloaked their intentions, disguised their objectives, and waited for the moment to strike. He pulled no punches in describing their lustful imperialism, which he believed was an outgrowth of their capitalist system. Though his sympathies were with the Chinese, he also had a measure of admiration—that many of his countrymen did not share—for Japanese skill and aggressiveness, as well as for their string of victories without a major defeat during the twentieth century.

At the end of his essay, he wrote,

> Japan has done great things for herself and for Asia. Her re-awakening at the dawn of the present century sent a thrill throughout our Continent. Japan has shattered the white man's prestige in the Far East and has put all the Western imperialist powers on the defensive. . . . She is extremely sensitive—and rightly so—about her self-respect as an Asiatic race. She is determined to drive out the Western powers. . . . But could not all this have been achieved without Imperialism, without dismembering the Chinese Republic, without humiliating another proud, cultured and ancient race? No, with all our

admiration for Japan . . . our whole heart goes to China in her hour of trial.[63]

Then he drew a lesson for India from the clash in East Asia:

> Standing at the threshold of a new era, let India resolve to aspire after national self-fulfilment in every direction—but not at the expense of other nations and not through the bloody path of self-aggrandisement and imperialism.[64]

The sympathies he had for the Chinese were shared by his fellow Congressmen and in the late 1930s, with the guidance of Nehru, Bose, and others, the Congress sponsored a medical mission to China.

In the other, lengthier essay, Bose assessed the intricate shifting of the European powers, as they moved toward a possible conflagration. He sorted out the European nations into the haves and the have-nots, placing Great Britain, France, and even the Soviet Union in the first category, Germany and Italy in the second, though Italy had been among the winners in the First World War. Bose described Italy's triumph in Abyssinia— again overestimating the prowess of her air force and army—and her role in the Spanish Civil War. In the Spanish conflict, he emphasized that Italy had vital strategic reasons for wanting to help the insurgents under General Franco. What he said he could not understand was why there was so much sympathy for the rebels in Britain. He concluded that the rabid anti-communism alive in Britain led them to cloud their minds to what he saw as their self-interest in a loyalist victory. He wrote in a rather detached manner, not showing the passionate concern and involvement with the loyalists that Nehru and the international left demonstrated. What he understood well was that for all his bluster, Mussolini was rather cautious in action and would not move unless he thought he was sure to win. So Mussolini, though he abhorred the British presence in the Mediterranean, would not strike forcefully and directly against the British.

Hitler and Nazi Germany, however, were another story. Hitler was more unpredictable and at the head of a much more powerful nation. But Bose took *Mein Kampf* too literally and believed that the Germans would strike in Central and Eastern Europe and never get into another war with the British. Bose did not grasp the irrationality and ruthlessness of Hitler and he overestimated the diplomatic skills of the French and of Czechoslovak President Benes. Also, like most of his contemporaries, he had no idea of the real military might of Germany and of the grave military weaknesses of the French and the British. He did, though, end on a discerning note: '. . . (the) Russian Colossus has often proved to be an enigma. It baffled Napoleon—the conqueror of Europe. Will it baffle Hitler?'[65]

From the mighty machinations of world powers, Bose turned to the troubles of the Calcutta Corporation. In August he wrote to Santosh Kumar Basu, Congress and Bose-group leader in the Corporation, saying:

> Since my release I have felt worried over the affairs of the Calcutta Corporation. Can you let me have your opinion as to what should be done to cleanse the Aegean Stables?[66]

The same week, a much longer letter from Subhas Bose to a Corporation employee was published in the *Calcutta Municipal Gazette* in which he said, in part:

> Nepotism has been so rampant during the last few years that it makes me hang my head down in shame at the doings of a body in which Congressmen have, or should have, a great deal of influence ... arguments that are usually trotted out for resisting the claims of the poorer employees to an increase in their pay and emoluments would do credit to the most deep-dyed bureaucrat. My sense of fairness as a human being and my conscience as a Congressman revolts at it—but for the time being I am helpless. . . . As a Congressman, I have a certain responsibility for what is happening . . . and I am fully alive to it. . . . The problem will have to be tackled in the near future. . . . I can only tell you this that if I have anything to do with Bengal politics—the Aegean stables of the Calcutta Corporation will have to be swept clean, or, in the alternative, the Congress Party will have to wash its hands of any responsibility . . . what is happening in the Calcutta Corporation is an index of what is going on in the larger sphere of public life in Bengal. A moral inertia has got hold of our men. There is a lack of dynamic idealism. All the idealism we had seems to be locked up in prisons and detention-camps. . . . From this morass, the province can be saved only by a moral resurgence—by a flood of idealism—which will sweep aside everything that is mean, sordid and reactionary and will bring back . . . faith, uprightness and unselfish devotion.[67]

It was not difficult for Bose, at a great distance from the scene and from everyday involvement, to see the evils and call for a moral resurgence. He had done the same after he emerged from prison in 1927. The Corporation councillors elected him an alderman of the Corporation in September, while he was still in Dalhousie, in hopes that the new broom would sweep clean.

VII

For Sarat Bose, there was no sustained respite. In late 1936, he had taken his family to Delhi and then to Simla, hoping that the climate of the summer capital would help Biva's health. En route, he was able to show some of his children the sights of Delhi. There were also brief periods in Kurseong. But for the most part, he was tied to Calcutta. He was leader of the Congress Parliamentary Party, and leader of the entire opposition in the Bengal Legislative Assembly, with larger duties and responsibilities than he had heretofore had; he had in effect picked up part of the mantle of the fallen C.R. Das, who had been leader of the opposition in the Bengal Legislative Council from 1923 to 1925. It is important to note the progression from Das to Sarat Bose in the legislative arena. There were similarities in the work of a skilled barrister and the activities of a legislative opposition leader. Like Das, Sarat Bose filled this role with consummate skill and enjoyed it as well. On most significant issues, he gave the final reply for the opposition before a vote. Years of courtroom practice enabled Sarat Bose to make summation speeches that were artful, logical, and forceful.[68]

Sarat Bose often interrupted during the question period to push harder on the ministers than the advance-notice questions allowed. His main targets were Home Minister Nazimuddin, Finance Minister Nalini Sarker, Labor Minister H.S. Suhrawardy, and Chief-cum-Education Minister Fazlul Huq. As an adroit cross-examiner, Bose almost reveled in the thrust and parry of question and response. His opponents were not unskilled in these arts and so he had to take as well as to give. Through these sessions starting in 1937, the mood of the Assembly shifted from seriousness to humor, from bitterness to conciliation, and back again. Sarat Bose thrived in this setting because, as he himself noted, 'Words flow from me when I am on my feet and get warmed up. . .' He studied the speeches of famous orators of the past and parliamentary procedure in all its intricacies. He was diffident about writing, but not about speaking, and was proud of his resonant voice that could fill the Assembly chamber.[69]

The main protagonists in the duels and discussions in the Assembly were well known to each other. They had often been allies, opponents, colleagues at the bar, and friends, of different degrees of intimacy. As leader of the Congress and the opposition as a whole in the chamber, Sarat Bose, of course, aimed his sharpest thrusts at the governing ministers. Nalini Sarker, the finance minister, was a former ally and now a most bitter enemy, for Sarat Bose believed that Sarker may well have been the person responsible for conveying certain information about him to the Government of Bengal which resulted in his three-and-a-half-year long imprisonment. Sarker had left the Congress fold, by choice, to become a minister and, once in office, steadfastly fought any change in the ministerial alignment. And he had Gandhi's ear.[70]

When Sarker, as finance minister, had to present the budget in the summer of 1937, Sarat Bose set up every roadblock he could find. He objected to Sarker's reading his presentation speech, since, Sarat maintained, parliamentary practice would have him speak, more or less extemporaneously, rather than read out a lengthy document. Once the speaker did allow Sarker to read it, Sarat Bose and his side trained their sights on its contents. In his summation speech for the opposition, he said, in part:

> . . . a budget speech is and ought to be a very different thing altogether . . . . Mr Sarker felt proud to give us an election speech . . . because he had possibly no opportunity to make an election speech before his restricted constituency of 130 souls! . . . it is the same old story of swollen overhead charges, the same old story of swollen police expenditure with no more than mere pitiful doles to the nation-building departments. . . . The expenditure on jails and convict settlements claims a figure of Rs 44,49,000. These are the old and venerable features of the old bureaucratic administration which is supposed to have yielded to a new order of things . . . shall I be wrong in describing it as the old voice—the old master's voice, speaking through the eleven new machines recently installed in this Council Chamber . . . let me point out the pitiful doles to Education, Medical Help and Public Health . . . the budget figures and the budget speech reveal no policy, reveal no plan.[71]

Sarat Bose insisted that the Congress alone provided a solid plan and program. If the Congress had charge—as they did in seven other provinces—they would shift the 'law and order' funds to the nation-building departments.

Sarker answered the opposition in kind and showed that he was particularly stung by Sarat Bose's words. He said,

> I shall take the criticisms even of the Leader of the Opposition, which is nothing but a hymn of hate. . . . One of the honourable members opposite . . . seemed to have thrown a hint that if and when members of his group came to occupy the Treasury Benches, a millenium would be ushered in. . . . I know that . . . criticism is a wonderful weapon when divorced from responsibility. It can conduct a complex and elaborate administration without supplies; it can do away with the Ministers; it can do away with the police force and in fact with all the appurtenances òf Government. The only thing it shirks to do is to replace the existing order by a better one.[72]

Both the coalition ministry and the opposition made efforts to push their agendas. One channel used was to present resolutions during the time allotted for non-official members' business. One of the most sharply debated of these resolutions in 1937 had to do with a subject in which Sarat Bose was intensely involved, namely, the release of political prisoners.

When the Huq ministry took office, 2,304 persons were being detained without trial, and at the beginning of 1938 there were 387 political convicts in Bengal's jails. Not only had both Boses been detained for years, Subhas in the 1920s and 1930s, Sarat from 1932 to 1935, but many of the 'best and the brightest' among the elite of politicized Hindu society, and some few Muslims and also Sikhs, were also detained in Bengal and other provinces.

For the Congress side, it was elementary civil liberties that they should all be released forthwith. All detainees were promptly released in the Congress-ruled provinces, whereas the coalition ministry in Bengal—though release of detainees had been part of the Krishak Praja Party electoral program—began to stall on the matter and act in exactly the same way and with the same rationalizations as the British Raj.[73]

On August 9, Harendra Nath Chaudhuri introduced a resolution on behalf of the opposition which called for the immediate release of all detainees. The ministerial side introduced an amendment that the detainees should be freed as soon as possible consistent with 'public safety'. The opposition argued that in the tradition of English liberty, there should be no imprisonment without charges and trials and convictions. For its part, the ministry, in this case with Home Minister Khwaja Nazimuddin presenting the government's arguments, put forth the view that Bengal was a special and violent province. The minister said that they had released some of the detainees and were committed to freeing others as each case was considered in turn. But a blanket release was not their program. In answering charges that he had gone back on his election pledges, Huq said that though release of detainees was on the KPP program, it was not part of a commitment on the part of the coalition ministry that was actually in office.[74]

Suggesting through actual case histories from Bengal and Ireland that officials of the British in both countries had indeed framed evidence against detainees, Sarat Bose said that the secret procedures and lack of trials opened the door to such abuses. Drawing on his legal and political background, he said, in part,

> ... I say, Sir, that in this matter we should only be guided by the fundamental principles of justice. I heard the Hon'ble Minister talk of the 'rule of law.' I very much doubted ... whether he understood what was meant by the 'rule of law.' ... Under his 'rule of law' persons can be detained without trial! I do not know to which country that 'rule of law' belongs: it does not belong to any civilized country in the world. Sir, we take our stand on the 'rule of law' which has been recognised in all ages and in all civilized countries, and that rule is that no persons can be detained without trial before courts of law .... I would ask members to rely on an opinion ... expressed by the present Lord Chief Justice of England, Lord Hewart ... : 'Evidence not tested by cross-examination is nearly always misleading and practically valueless.' ... if this House accepts the policy laid down by the Hon'ble the Home Minister . . . it would be subordinating this House to the will of the Executive, it would be evading the Courts and it would be rendering the will or the caprice of the Executive unfettered and supreme. I would ask the hon'ble members to whatever race they may belong and from whatever

constituency they may come not to accept the demands of arbitrary power. The exercise of arbitrary power is neither law nor justice. It is a denial of justice.[75]

With both sides drawing on English tradition, one side for liberty, the government side for law and order, the votes were counted. The coalition ministry had the numbers and the resolution as amended—to release detainees as early as possible when consistent with public safety—was passed by 141 to eighty-five. As the amendment was passed, Congress members cried out, 'Shame, shame!' and had to be reprimanded by the speaker.[76]

But for opponents of detention, the Bengal Assembly was only one forum. Other methods of confronting the Government of Bengal and its ministry included public meetings and demonstrations, articles in the press, and also private negotiations. All of these routes were utilized with Sarat Bose, as acting president of the BPCC and president of the Bengal Civil Liberties Union, leading the way. In the interests of getting the detainees and other political prisoners released as soon as possible, Bengal Congress leaders enlisted the aid of Mahatma Gandhi.

As these negotiations were going on intermittently, Bengal political prisoners began a hunger strike in the Andaman Islands. In sympathy, prisoners in other camps began hunger strikes and Sarat Bose presided over a meeting at Town Hall, Calcutta on August 9. He asked the strikers to suspend their efforts while he and other Congress leaders negotiated for their release. Gandhi asked that the Andaman prisoners pledge themselves to non-violence henceforward, so that he could work for their release in good conscience. Eventually most of them made such a commitment to Gandhi. Meanwhile, however, there were fierce demonstrations against the Bengal ministry for failure to act more promptly to release political prisoners. The demonstrations against the coalition government led Chief Minister Fazlul Huq to refer to the 'cult of Congress fascism and party fanaticism which may lead India to a civil war' at a Muslim meeting in Calcutta. A police lathi charge against Congress processionists on All-India Andamans Day did not calm feelings on the other side.[77]

Slowly, due to the popular pressure, the Government of Bengal began to release more of the prisoners. By August 25, 1938, all detainees were freed. The Home Ministry laid down guidelines for considering the cases of convicted prisoners and, in time, many of them were released as well.[78] What did not make the government or more conservative elements happy was that Sarat Bose and other leaders of the BPCC did their best to see that released political prisoners found employment in the Calcutta Corporation. Most of them, though, turned to open political organizing in rural and urban areas of Bengal and to involvement with kisan sabhas, small left groups, and the left-wing of the Congress.

As the Bengal Legislative Assembly continued its sessions through the summer of 1937, some of the extra-legislative issues such as the Andaman prisoners' hunger strike, the jute strike settlement, and an incident at Rajshahi College flooded into the assembly chambers and momentarily caught their attention.

Many issues brought before the Assembly touched a communal nerve and one of these was the discussion—however brief—of an incident at Rajshahi College which led to its temporary closing. Sarat Bose spoke to support a motion to have it reopened at once. He said, in part:

> I am aware that there have been some differences, religious or communal, as between the Hindu students and the Muhammadan students there. Now, I desire to make it clear that orthodoxy—narrow orthodoxy—whether of the Hindus or of the Muslims makes no appeal to me; it has never made, it never will.... I hope the House will agree with me—that these petty differences, should have been solved by the College authorities or by representatives of Government ... with tact and with vision.[79]

Sarat Bose said that he had offered to go with a delegation from the Assembly to try to settle the issue, but had received no reply to their offer. His tone was calm and thoughtful. Fazlul Huq, however, when called upon to reply for the government, said that, '... Mr Sarat Chandra Bose has delivered a speech soaked with communalism from beginning to end.'[80] After abusing Sarat Bose in this way, the ever-irrepressible Huq asked Sarat Bose to get together '... in the name of good-feeling and fellowship to go to Rajshahi and settle the matter in consultation with Muslim leaders, and I shall accept their decision if it is an agreed one and pass orders accordingly.'[81]

Sarat Bose and Fazlul Huq did have a certain regard for each other's position in the Assembly and in Bengal. This relationship, and the capacity of the Bengal Assembly to work together in a constructive way, was tested by the debates over the Bengal Tenancy (Amendment) Bill of 1937, which was introduced in early September. Certain ironies were involved because the bill, which provided some gains for the ryots and under-ryots of Bengal was steered through the Assembly by the revenue minister, a big zamindar himself, and representative of the landholders of the province, Sir Bijay Prasad Singh Roy. Although he objected to some clauses which eliminated fees for landlords when ryot tenants sold their holdings and dropped provisions for the landlords to buy out their tenants, he still presented the consensus of his ministry that these changes from the 1928 Tenancy Act should be made to help the peasantry.[82]

The bill was debated through long September afternoons and evenings and some 500 amendments were dealt with in one way or another, with the Congress playing some role in improving the bill. On a number of issues, the Congress, no longer dominated by the zamindar point-of-view to the extent that it was said to have been in 1928, put forth amendments more beneficial to what they called 'the actual tillers' than the ministry. The Congress, though careful not to alienate their middle-class supporters, was outflanking the ministry on the left.[83]

Though the Congress did not oppose the concessions to the ryots and under-ryots that the bill contained, it opposed the bill at its final reading because they said it did not help the 'actual tillers' enough. Sarat Bose, speaking for his side, said, in part,

> It seems to me, Sir, unaccountable to ordinary and normal human reasoning that a Ministry which commands to-day, through the combination of fortuitous circumstances, a majority in the House, should be so stampeded into hasty and ill-considered legislation. . . . I would . . . like to point out . . . one or two insufficiencies of the Bill. . . . The existing rates of rent are considered by Government to be irksome, if not actually oppressive, in many parts of the province. But the House will look in vain for any provisions in this Bill which are designed to lighten this burden . . . there is no intention in this Bill to give more extensive rights . . . than are at present enjoyed by the under-ryots who are the actual tillers of the soil . . . there is no provision enabling under-ryots to acquire occupancy rights in land by 12 years' possession. The only way in which an under-ryot is left to acquire this right is by proving custom or usage to that effect . . . if Government had the slightest intention to give occupancy rights to the under-ryots, they could have done so in spite of their hurry—which hurry they have put forward as their plea for not being able to deal with the question of occupancy rights for the under ryots.[84]

Sarat Bose insisted that the Congress and many in the opposition were ready to do better for the under-ryots than the government was. He also felt called upon to answer the long-echoed charge that the Congress was the party of the zamindars. He did so in terms not very dissimilar from those he had used a decade earlier, though in these 1930s days he was certainly talking more about helping the 'actual tillers'.

> . . . I desire . . . to say one word about the relations between the Congress and the zamindars . . . the Congress is not in favour—is definitely not in favour of perpetualization of landlordism. We did not look upon, we do not look upon the rights of property as though they were some dread absolute which could not be touched. At the same time we discourage any attempt to describe any class or section of our people as 'blood-suckers. . . . I deprecate the use of such language . . . we believe (in) co-operation among

all classes and sections—(The Hon'ble Mr. H.S. Suhrawardy: Hear, hear)—
Mr. Suhrawardy says, hear, hear; I do not mean co-operation with the
Ministry of the day, but co-operation with the masses of the people—we
believe that by the adoption of the formulae of co-operation, it will be
possible for us to remove once for all distinction between man and man and
between class and class that unfortunately exists at the present moment.[85]

Before closing, Sarat Bose tried to say something about the Congress aims,
which led to bantering between himself and the chief minister:

Sir, the Congress seeks to make its way into the minds of men—(The
Hon'ble Mr. A.K. Fazlul Huq: Stealthily). No, not stealthily. Doing things
stealthily is, I believe the practice of the Hon'ble Chief Minister. Not
stealthily, but openly. Sarat Bose never did anything stealthily in his life and
he challenged the Government more than once to show that he had done
so . . . the Congress seeks to make its way into the minds of men, not merely
by its idealism, but by its realism . . . not merely by its spiritual promise but
by its materialistic prospect. . . . We believe that by persevering in session
and out of session . . . we shall be able to help the masses of the people to
come to their own . . . we shall persevere . . . until the tenants . . . I mean the
actual tillers of the soil—come to their own.[86]

On the final vote on the bill, the Congress group abstained; it passed by 110
to twenty-seven, with some Europeans, landholders, and even Muslim
League stalwart M.A.H. Ispahani, a businessman, voting against it.[87] The
Congress, even though it abstained, had moved to a position much more
sensitive to the needs of the different levels of the peasantry than it had
adhered to a decade earlier.

VIII

After his five months in Dalhousie, Subhas Bose was in better health, but
not fully fit. He came back to Calcutta in early October and went on to
Sarat's house in Kurseong. There Jawaharlal Nehru wrote to him at length
about a variety of issues. Nehru wanted smoother and more systematic
work by the BPCC and an end to the endemic factionalism which had
weakened it since the mid-1920s. He wanted a firm and even hand at the
rudder, and certainly hoped that Subhas Bose could provide this.[88] At this
time he wrote with friendliness, if not closeness.

Among other matters, Nehru was concerned with Muslims' objection
to the song, 'Bande Mataram,' from Bankim Chandra Chatterjee's novel
Ananda Math, and widely used as a nationalist anthem. It was a Bengali,
Hindu song which the Muslim League said the Congress was '. . . foisting
. . . as the national anthem upon the country in callous disregard of the
feelings of Muslims.'[89] Nehru obtained an English translation of the novel
from which the song was drawn and saw how there might be Muslim

hostility to it, if not to the song itself. Following Bose's advice, he arranged to come early to the AICC session that was to be held in Calcutta and discuss the matter with Rabindranath Tagore. Subhas Bose, though nationalist and Bengali, was not dogmatic about the use of the song. Later a song of Tagore's, which was clearly secular and had none of the overtones of '*Bande Mataram*,' was transliterated into Hindi and used as the national anthem.[90]

Even before returning to Calcutta, Subhas Bose had invited the Congress to hold the next AICC and Working Committee meetings in Calcutta. Some Working Committee members were to be offered hospitality at Sarat Bose's house and smaller meetings, such as those of the Working Committee, could also be held there. After exchanges of letters and juggling of dates, it was worked out that the meetings would be held in Calcutta in late October. Within the same few days at the end of that month, perhaps by chance, large kisan sabha and trade union meetings were also scheduled in Calcutta. So Subhas Bose's brief period back in Calcutta was an extraordinarily busy one.

With N.G. Ranga presiding, Subhas spoke to a rally of 10,000 kisans and kisan organizers in Shraddhananda Park on October 27. He told them that the Congress hope was for all classes to flourish and participate in the Indian nationalist movement, yet they also wanted an end to all exploitation. They did not explain how to end exploitation without touching the interests of any other class.[91] Subhas Bose also presided over a meeting of the Bengal Provincial Trade Union Congress held in Calcutta.

After Subhas Bose was released in 1937, at his mother's urging, he lived in his father's room at 38/2 Elgin Road, rather than in Sarat Bose's house across the road at Woodburn Park. He was often helped by his nieces Ila and Shila. Ila in particular was very attentive, working as a secretary, even as a nurse. As his health improved, Subhas regained his hearty appetite, a characteristic which he and Sarat shared.

When Subhas Bose needed to entertain guests, he usually made use of Sarat's newer and more elegant house. Occasionally, with Biva's assistance, Subhas gave dinner parties to encourage Indian cultural ambassadors who were going abroad. Sarat Bose, of course, often entertained guests at Woodburn Park and sometimes at his garden house at Rishra. This house, in the environs of Calcutta, he bought in the late 1930s and often stayed on at weekends. He had more contact with his children there and was inspired to cook, or at least to give precise instructions to whoever was doing the actual cooking.[92]

Also in this period, Sarat Bose hired Nirad C. Chaudhuri as his private secretary. Mr Chaudhuri was a learned Bengali intellectual who had written in English and Bengali for newspapers and periodicals, but had been suffering from poor health and lack of employment. His English was superb and this was a big plus. Mr Chaudhuri came to the Woodburn Park house daily and helped Sarat Bose with his correspondence and the preparation of speeches and reports. For the devoted and industrious private secretary, this job was a way-station. He had already written a series of exceptional articles on 'The "Martial Races" of India', and an extraordinary career as a man of letters in his later life lay ahead of him. For the time being, he was a great help to Sarat Bose, but his excellent English, amazing memory, and pride, also earned him some enemies in the Bose family and outside.[93]

Both Jawaharlal Nehru and Mahatma Gandhi—the latter with his small entourage—stayed at Woodburn Park with Sarat Bose. Nehru and his sister, Mrs Vijayalakshmi Pandit, were no problem for the host family. Nehru, a fastidious eater who watched his weight and health carefully, is reported to have said about the large meals served, 'Sarat Bose's dinners are a nuisance.'[94] The more complicated problems involved the Mahatma. He brought his staff and they occupied one whole floor of the house. Gandhi, too, watched his diet carefully and demanded bread made of the finest flour and the choicest fruits and vegetables of the season. In addition, he took a lot of mashed garlic and had thick plasters made of Ganges mud, both of these presumably to combat his high blood pressure. While Gandhi was at Woodburn Park, large, sometimes unruly, crowds gathered outside. Once Gandhi began his prayer sessions, the obstreperous visitors immediately quieted down.[95]

Another part of Gandhi's work while in Calcutta was to continue the negotiations for the release of the Bengal political prisoners. He met Fazlul Huq, Nalini Sarker, H.S. Suhrawardy, and Khwaja Nazimuddin at Woodburn Park and also at Sarker's house. He met Governor Anderson and also traveled to the Hijli Prison Camp to interview political prisoners there. He was looking for pledges of future non-violent conduct which he could use as bargaining counters with Bengal officials and ministers.[96]

There was yet one more weighty matter which Gandhi and his inner circle were concerned with at this time: who was to be the president of the next Congress session to be held at Haripura in Gujarat. In a note to Sardar Patel written on November 1, 1937, Gandhi said, 'I have observed that Subhas is not at all dependable. However, there is nobody but he who can be the President.'[97] Exactly who was consulted and when their consensus was communicated to Subhas Bose is not clear, but they probably talked to him about it before they left Calcutta a few days into November. The same day that Gandhi wrote the note to Patel, he had a serious attack of high blood pressure.

At the same time his own health was suffering a setback, Gandhi observed that Subhas was still not fully fit, and, perhaps looking forward to the strenuous schedule of a future Congress president, wanted Subhas to take further rest, this time in Europe. Subhas Bose later described this to Mrs Dharmavir:

> It was utterly impossible for me to think of myself in Calcutta when Gandhiji was there—especially after his own 'collapse' on the 1st November—because we had invited him to tackle the case of about 2,000 imprisoned detenus and political prisoners. I must say in fairness to the old man that he pressed me to get away and recoup my health. Without his insistence, it would have been impossible for me to get away.[98]

Before leaving, Subhas Bose took his seat as an alderman on the Calcutta Corporation. He got a hearty ovation and he received an address from the Corporation Employees Association. In reply, Bose called for all Indians to stand together and work for equality and Hindu-Muslim unity.[99] A month earlier when he had heard that the Huq ministry was preparing a bill to change the Corporation, he said to the press, 'Let him not venture where the British Government dared not.'[100] So he both called for the communities to work together, and threatened Huq not to tamper with the present allotment of seats and pattern of electorates. But, like his appearances before the kisan and trade union rallies, his entry into the Corporation was only perfunctory. He was not yet back in the saddle. On November 18, 1937, he left on a KLM plane for Europe.

IX

After landing at the Naples airport, Bose, according to his account, was harassed and thoroughly searched and cross-examined by the Italian police. He complained to a subordinate of Mussolini, Maggiore Rapicavoli, who obtained an apology on behalf of his government. Later Bose corresponded with him about arranging a secret interview with Mussolini during his return trip from Europe to India late in January.[101]

From Naples, Bose made his way by train to Bädgastein, a spa in the mountains with a bracing climate and medicinal bath waters. He wrote of it in the Indian press in December,

> It is this combination of snow, sun, and dry cold which makes Switzerland and the west of Austria such a healthy place in winter. I had found just the weather I needed and the scenery I loved, and I was glad.[102]

The atmosphere of this mountain town and the radioactive, warm, mineral waters had a positive effect on his health.

He asked Emilie Schenkl to join him in Badgastein and help him with a writing project on which he had set his mind, an autobiography, to be called *An Indian Pilgrim*. He had gathered some material in Calcutta, and asked his nephew Asoke to send him additional information from India. During a ten-day period in Badgastein, Bose wrote out a good part of the planned manuscript in long hand. This later amounted to more than one hundred printed pages when it was finally published for the first time by Thacker, Spink in Calcutta in 1948. Beginning with his family back-ground, he wrote about his childhood, education, formative influences on him, his years at college in Calcutta, and his stay in England from 1919 to 1921. At the end of these sections, he included a chapter entitled, 'My Faith (Philosophical)'. The original plan for the book included a treatment of his life up to the time of composition, and a presentation of his economic and political views on 'faith' as well. These other chronological chapters covering 1921 to December 1937 were never written, but in other essays written in the following few years, he did offer his political views to the public.[103]

Why did he write this manuscript at this time? He certainly knew by this time that he was certain to be the Congress president. The 'old man' of the Congress, Gandhi, had written his own kind of autobiography filled with moral tales and inner searching. Jawaharlal Nehru had also written an autobiography which had recently been published in England and gained a wide and appreciative readership throughout the West and India. Bose was also an introspective person with a long interest in psychology. So he was coming to terms with himself when he was becoming a prominent Indian nationalist leader. From his criticism of both Gandhi and Nehru, it is clear that Bose believed that he had his own unique angle of vision and this could be presented through a narrative of his life. *The Indian Struggle* had presented an objective overview of the nationalist movement. The second book, *An Indian Pilgrim,* helped to explain Bose's views and show how he came to them. It was handsomely written and gave insight into his background.

Many of the conceptual terms of his narrative are drawn from psychoanalysis. He talks of the role of self-analysis in his life prior to his acquaintance with psychoanalysis. Drawing on Freud, he talks of the unconscious and the subconscious, of his introverted nature, changing slowly to a more extroverted one, of the significance of dreams, and of the power that the sexual instinct had in him and his efforts to control or sublimate it.[104]

In the course of his account, Bose describes a number of processes by which he—an Indian pilgrim, a man in search of truth, a mission, a cause, himself—came to find them. He mentions several times how he felt insignificant as a boy and that this haunted him. First, he felt inconsequential vis-à-vis his parents, and later with respect to his older siblings, those down the road ahead of him. He also stresses that he was competitive as a student, rebellious, and filled with inner determination, especially after being humiliated.

The theme, or a most important theme of the work, is how he came to 'significance' in his own eyes and in those of others. He explains that gradually he began to have a better opinion of himself and that this was related to real achievements in school and through social service and to his finding his own path, which turned out to be off the beaten track, special and unique. But this special path was also shaped by the teachings of Swami Vivekananda and Sri Ramakrishna, who taught him that self-fulfillment and service to humanity (including to one's country) go together. In order to reach this fulfillment and to help others, renunciation is necessary, in particular the spurning of 'lust and gold'. Though it may seem anomalous, becoming 'significant' and renouncing any worldly gain or sexual satisfaction go together. Becoming a rebel and yet helping others in his own society also go together. In fact, only when he gave up being a 'goody-goody' and became rebellious did he begin to find himself and start to make his contribution to the greater good. He says that he found pleasure in defiance and pleasure in helping others. These often, so he says, went together.[105]

He rebelled against his family, and yet was always closely tied to them. He also learned a great deal from the British in India and in Great Britain, but he also became a rebel against them and their rule in India. So the close ties and the revolt are both there in a number of different relationships and contexts of his life. There is a temporal aspect in the relation to the British as well. In his youth, Indians tended to be loyalists, including his own father. But then they learned that there was no real opportunity for them to fully flourish as long as the British ruled. So they—the leaders of India—had to become rebels against their rulers. For Bose there were lessons to learn about the nature of freedom from the British. There were also lessons about the nature of subjugation and how it must be done away with. From his teenage years, as noted above, he felt an attraction to the military and he mentions how he felt new strength and self-confidence upon learning military skills from the British. Although it was not clear where and when these skills would have to be employed, the very gaining of them gave him—and perhaps other Indians—a feeling of equality that was necessary for them to reconquer their own country and then rule it.

Another lesson he says he slowly learned was that life is a whole, that religion, politics, economics, etc., were all linked. Part of his pilgrim's quest is for an understanding of the whole. He deals with this in part in his chapter, 'My Faith (Philosophical).' He says that truth can be only relative and we gain a fuller grasp of it, step by step. Also, he feels that there is an order to things, an overall meaning of existence, and that 'spirit' is at work, through some kind of evolutionary process, in the world. What is the nature of this 'spirit'? After sorting through a number of possibilities, he decides that the essence of this 'spirit' is love, but only very slowly does love come to work in the world. To do its work in the world, devoted searchers are needed, who are desirous of contributing to the greatest good of the greatest number.[106]

This is an important statement by an Indian leader about himself, his cause, and his culture. But there is yet another reason for wanting to find hints in it of an intimate nature. This reason is that Emilie Schenkl has privately told this writer and at least one other that, during their brief stay in Badgastein in December 1937, she and Subhas Bose were secretly married.[107] In *An Indian Pilgrim*, Bose places the development of love at the center of human life. He also notes that in his earlier days, he expended a lot of energy controlling his sexual passions. But, he says in a note, 'As I have gradually turned from a purely spiritual ideal to a life of social service, my views on sex have undergone transformation.'[108] It seems that through his reading of psychoanalysis and his life experience, particularly in Europe, he had come to see sexual instincts not as an enemy, but as a normal aspect of life that did not have to be completely suppressed. It is also worthwhile noting that in advice to younger friends and relations in 1937 and 1938, he advocated free choice in marriage, rather than arranged marriage by the parents of the prospective couple.[109]

In this same interview, among the stories that Emilie Schenkl told me of her relationship with Subhas Bose, she mentioned a moment in Vienna one day when they were walking in the street, and suddenly, Bose suspected that they were being followed. 'Hand-in-hand,' she said, 'we ran for a tram and escaped.' What is undeniable is that in Europe there was a freer atmosphere for unmarried members of the opposite sex to meet and get to know one another. In Calcutta, Bose would not have been walking in the street with an eligible, unmarried young woman. And, if it ever chanced to happen, they would never have run for a tram, hand-in-hand.

Although we must take Emilie Schenkl at her word, there are a few nagging doubts about an actual marriage ceremony because there is no document that I have seen and there is no testimony by any other person. And there are so many other stories of when and how they married. Krishna Bose, a family member, wrote in the *Illustrated Weekly of India* in 1972,

Emilie Schenkl says that marriage between Germans and foreigners was not at all encouraged in the Nazi regime. It was discreetly suggested to her that she should break off the relationship. When they eventually got married during the war they avoided some of the difficulties by getting married quietly according to Hindu rites.[110]

Other biographers have written that Bose and Miss Schenkl were married in 1942, while Krishna Bose, implying 1941, leaves the date ambiguous. The strangest and most confusing testimony comes from A.C.N. Nambiar, who was with the couple in Badgastein briefly in 1937, and was with them in Berlin during the war as second-in-command to Bose. In answer to my question about the marriage, he wrote to me in 1978:

> I cannot state anything definite of the marriage of Bose referred to by you, since I came to know of it only a good while after the end of the last world war. I am aware of the deep attachment Bose had for Frau Schenkl. He did not keep the idea of marriage out of his mind. Neither did he fail to recognize a responsibility he shared in regard to the daughter. In the extraordinary circumstances in which Bose lived in Europe round the time of the birth of the child he was anxious to see marriage not receiving any marked publicity. As such, I can imagine the marriage having been a very informal one with publicity well avoided.[111]

This is a confusing letter from someone who may have been asked to say nothing, perhaps promising Bose to that effect. It is hard to believe that one so close to both parties on many occasions in the 1930s and 1940s did not have more concrete information.

So what are we left with? We know that Bose had a tie to Emilie Schenkl starting from 1934, and that he last saw her in 1943. We know that they had a close and passionate relationship and that they had a child, Anita, born November 29, 1942, in Vienna. We know they lived together in Berlin from 1941 to 1943, and we have a posthumous letter of Subhas Bose to his brother Sarat stating that Emilie Schenkl was his wife and Anita his daughter. And we have Emilie Schenkl's testimony that they were married secretly in December 1937. Whatever the precise dates, the most important thing is the relationship. A nephew of Bose, Dr Sisir Bose, has said, quite acutely, that it made Subhas Bose a more complete human being.[112] What he and his wife were deprived of was more time together to build a full life and raise their child together.

By December 1937, when Bose was in Badgastein, a war was already underway in East Asia, following the Japanese attack on China. The Germans and Italians had formulated the Anti-Comintern Pact and Hitler was putting great pressure on other Central European countries, particularly those with German-speaking populations. In the face of the Nazi military build-up, Britain was only slowly responding to the threat. Her government, headed by Neville Chamberlain, and with former viceroy

Lord Halifax as its leader in the House of Lords, was bent on appeasement. Civil war, with international participation, was raging in Spain, and Clement Attlee, leader of the Labour Party and of the opposition to the National Government, visited Spain to encourage the loyalists.

In the mid-1930s, British officials, not eager for Bose to visit Britain, had bluffed him out of attempting to do so. They made him believe, incorrectly, that he needed special permission, the equivalent of a visa, to do so. In reality, they knew that as a British subject with a valid passport, he could not be refused entry. In 1937, he asked again for permission, and when explicitly requested, British officials without explanation said that he could enter. So, notifying British and Indian friends, Bose prepared to make his first visit to Great Britain since 1921.[113]

As a student, Bose had come to understand both the freedoms and the limitations for an Indian in Britain. In the 1930s, he felt that he had been unfairly excluded and treated as a dangerous revolutionary who would put the government in jeopardy. But now, as prospective Congress president—that news having leaked out—he had a triumphal week's visit to the heart of the British Empire. There is no doubt that he relished every moment and did his best to speak for Indian freedom. Upon arriving in London,

> He was accorded a reception at the Victoria Station by several Indians representing the Friends of India, the Swaraj League, the Indian Political Group, the Gandhi Society, the Congress League, the Indian Progressive Writers' Association, the Indian Colonial Seamen's Association, the Indian Journalists' Association Abroad, the Oxford, Cambridge and London Majlis, and the Federation of Indian Students Societies. . . . Lord Kinnoull was among those who greeted Mr Bose. . . . The Station Master personally conducted Mr Bose from the train to his car flying the Congress flag. . . . A press reception followed at a west-end hotel where about one hundred journalists . . . gathered to meet him. Mr Bose replied to a barrage of questions fired at him . . . coolly, adroitly, and with the greatest good humour.[114]

Throughout his visit, Bose made his views clear: India, led by the Congress, wanted to frame her own constitution. If the British accepted that, ' . . . there was no reason why India and Britain should not be the best of friends.' But, if the British went on with the folly of the federal scheme, there would undoubtedly be further conflict. He said that he was personally not very optimistic that a negotiated settlement, embodying the Congress demands, would be reached.[115]

The following eight days were a whirl of meetings, receptions, and dinners with leaders of the National Government, leaders of the Labour

Party and the British left, intellectuals, and the Indian community in Britain. On January 11, Bose spoke at a reception in his honor at Saint Pancras Town Hall, presided over by R. Palme Dutt. With many from the Indian community and also the British left in attendance, Bose said,

> India's destiny is bound up with that of the rest of humanity . . . the Congress had begun to realize that India's struggle for freedom, democracy and socialism was part of the world struggle, extending from East to West, through China, Spain and Abyssinia. India could no longer regard herself as isolated.[116]

In a report in the communist *Daily Worker*, Bose is said to have linked India's national struggle with the efforts by peoples all over the world against fascism and reaction, and stressed the Indian support for the Chinese in their war with the Japanese.[117]

During a private interview with Bose, which was later published, Dutt pressed Bose on his kind words about a synthesis of fascism and communism, adapted to Indian conditions. To a large extent, Bose recanted, saying:

> My political ideas have developed further since I wrote my book three years ago. What I really meant was that we in India wanted our national freedom, and having won it, we wanted to move in the direction of Socialism. This is what I meant when I referred to 'a synthesis between Communism and Fascism'. Perhaps the expression I used was not a happy one. But I should like to point out that when I was writing the book, Fascism had not started on its imperialist expedition, and it appeared to me merely an aggressive form of nationalism.
>
> I should point out also that Communism as it appeared to be demonstrated by many of those who were supposed to stand for it in India seemed to me anti-national, and this impression was further strengthened in view of the hostile attitude which several among them exhibited towards the Indian National Congress. It is clear, however, that the position today has fundamentally altered.
>
> I should add that . . . Communism . . . gives full support to the struggle for national independence and recognises this as an integral part of its world outlook.[118]

On this occasion and on many others, Bose advocated some kind of socialist system for free India.

On January 17, 1938, Bose met Lord Zetland, the former governor of Bengal and present secretary of state for India. Zetland, too, wanted to know Bose's view of communism. Suggesting that some Congressmen wanted a social revolution and a communist form of government, Zetland pressed Bose for his opinion. Zetland reported that,

> . . . he brushed the suggestion aside and said that the actual number of

genuine communists was small. He was himself a socialist, but that was a very different thing from being a communist.[119]

Bose had a generally friendly talk with Zetland, who had been governor of Bengal when he was a student. Bose laid out his objections to the federal provisions of the 1935 Government of India Act. He objected to the official control of defense and to the role of the reactionary princes. Bose also outlined Congress suspicions about official controls in back of so-called provincial autonomy and objected to the Communal Award and to the Huq ministry running Bengal.

Throughout this interview, as in all others in Britain, Bose was soft-spoken but forceful in his views. He generally made a good impression, though Zetland referred to his 'fixed ideas.' He saw Lord Halifax, former viceroy, and leader of the Conservatives in the House of Lords. Besides meeting with Conservatives, he met with Clement Attlee, leader of the Labour opposition, and Labour Party members, George Lansbury and Arthur Greenwood. At other meetings he spoke with Harold Laski, of whose works Sarat Bose was an admirer, and with Professor J.B.S. Haldane and Dr Ivor Jennings. At Cambridge he had lunch and tea with several fellows and masters and addressed a large gathering. The following day, January 18, he went to Oxford, where he met G.D.H. Cole and dined with Professor Gilbert Murray. He also met Sir Stafford Cripps.[120]

One other meeting was special and emotional for him: at midnight on January 16, he met Irish President de Valera, 'with whom he discussed the political destinies of India and Eire in detail.'[121] The Irish Free State had now become Eire with a new constitution which detached free Ireland to a greater extent from the Commonwealth and made it a republic under a president and parliament. President de Valera was in London to negotiate the return of the so-called treaty ports to his nation. There is no record of their talks, but Bose was certainly not displeased when the *News Chronicle* called him 'India's de Valera.'[122]

On January 18, Acharya J.B. Kripalani, general secretary of the Indian National Congress, announced in India that Bose had been elected president of the fifty-first session of the Congress, to be held at Haripura in Gujarat. Gandhi sent a telegram to Bose, which read in part, 'God give you strength to bear the weight of Jawaharlal's mantle.'[123] Gandhi's favorite left-wing son had been Congress president for the past two years. Now, perhaps because he thought he had to continue to have a left-wing president, while the rightists controlled the Working Committee and the Congress organization, he had taken a chance on Bose whom he surely thought less 'dependable' and less amenable to his control.

Leaving Croyden by air for India on January 19, Bose stopped in Prague to meet President Benes, who was having his own problems at the time, and flew on to Naples. Although Bose had tried to arrange with Maggiore Rapiacavoli to meet Mussolini secretly in Rome on January 20 or 21, it is not sure whether he did so.[124] Bose wanted to have such a meeting as tensions in Europe grew tighter. Stopping in Karachi, Bose arrived in Calcutta on January 24. It had been an exhilarating two months abroad.

X

Subhas Bose, though he had just concluded ten days of meetings and a trip from London to Calcutta, was in much better health than when he left. The Congress session was just a few weeks away and he had to prepare for his new role. He also met with Dr B.C. Roy, recently abroad and now back in the mainstream of BPCC and Corporation activity, and even with Nalini Sarker and G.D. Birla.[125] Since Gandhi had chosen Bose to be Congress president, Birla and Sarker, whatever their personal preferences, had to have some dealings with him. However, both Boses on one side, and Birla and Sarker on another, continued to take different views on a number of important issues.

On February 11, Bose, together with a Hindi-Urdu tutor, and a large party of family members, entrained for Haripura.[126] Under the general guidance of Sardar Patel, and with a skillful reception committee which had long been preparing for the session, a small city, Vithal-Nagar, named for Patel's brother Vithalbhai, had been built out of a village within just a few months. One report describes this temporary, but elaborate Congress city as follows:

> . . . a huge Nagar over an area 3/4th of a mile in breadth and two miles in length accommodating a residential population of more than 50,000 and a floating population of over two lacs, with all the convenience and comforts of a big city, like waterworks, drainage, electricity, telegraphs, post, telephone, roads, etc., was constructed mainly from rafters, bamboos and the date–mats. An indented parapet wall, of course of bamboo matting, but looking like battlements of a fortified city, was constructed round the whole Nagar.[127]

This construction would not have been possible without extraordinary cooperation from local governments, businesses, and thousands of volunteers. With all these energies and resources brought into harmonious effort, the Congress city was built, operated almost flawlessly for ten days, and then was virtually dismantled.[128]

Subhas Bose arrived at Bardoli in a special train and was received by Sardar Patel. Then he traveled by car to Haripura. Villagers garlanded him as he passed to Haripura. According to reports of his journey:

> He received a most cordial welcome from the rural folk of Gujarat. Seated

in an ancient *rath* driven by 51 lusty bulls of Gujarat he was taken in procession through this new city. . . . The procession took more than two hours to reach Vithal Nagar, a distance of only two miles from the point it started.[129]

The chariot was lent by a local maharaja, and a satyagrahi farmer who had lost all his property during the movement, drove it. The construction of an Indian city with some modern conveniences together with the various ceremonies from the procession through the finale of the meeting, were the Congress' answer to the durbars of the British Raj.[130]

The opening few meetings of the Haripura session were conducted by Jawaharlal Nehru; then Subhas Bose took charge. He was called upon to conduct the main open meeting and also to give one formal and several informal addresses. His presidential address is the lengthiest and most important speech he gave during his career to a truly national audience, including almost all the national leadership of the Congress. Starting from India's imperial context, Bose gave a description of the strengths and weaknesses of the British Empire and its approach to ruling non-European countries. In his analysis, he linked capitalism and imperialism, quoted Lenin favorably, and praised the British Communist Party. Though he advocated socialism and not communism, this speech and many others of the 1930s demonstrated that he had been influenced by the European and Indian left. In the course of his depiction of the British Empire, he said,

> But can the British Empire transform itself into a federation of free nations with one bold sweep?. . . This transformation will be possible only if the British people become free in their own homes—only if Great Britain becomes a socialist state. There is an inseparable connection between the capitalist ruling classes in Great Britain and the colonies abroad. As Lenin pointed out long ago 'reaction in Great Britain is strengthened and fed by the enslavement of a number of nations'. The British aristocracy and bourgeoisie exist primarily because there are colonies and overseas dependencies to exploit. The emancipation of the latter will undoubtedly strike at the very existence of the capitalist ruling classes in Great Britain.[131]

He went on to show how the British used their 'policy of divide and rule' in Ireland, in Palestine, and were trying to extend it even further in India through the Government of India Act of 1935 by dividing the population into increasingly separate compartments, and by giving the reactionary princes a large say in the federal provisions of the act. The federal provisions were to be fiercely opposed and the Communal Award condemned.

He wanted the Congress to keep up the pressure on the British through mass non-violent struggle at home and active propaganda abroad to present its case to the entire world. He spent a good half of the speech, however, not on the past of British rule or the present struggle, but on the reconstruction and problems of India that would follow the British departure. He insisted that,

> ... our chief national problems relating to the eradication of poverty, illiteracy and disease and to scientific production and distribution can be effectively tackled only along socialistic lines. The very first thing which our future national government will have to do would be to set up a commission for drawing up a comprehensive plan of reconstruction. . . . While unifying the country through a strong central government, we shall have to put all the minority communities as well as provinces at their ease, by allowing them a large measure of autonomy in cultural as well as governmental affairs . . . the first problem to tackle is that of our increasing population . . . . It will . . . be desirable to restrict our population . . . our principal problem will be how to eradicate poverty from our country. That will require a radical reform of our land-system, including the abolition of landlordism. . . . To solve the economic problem, agricultural improvement will not be enough. A comprehensive scheme of industrial development under state-ownership and state-control will be indispensable. A new industrial system will have to be built up. . . . The Planning Commission will have to carefully consider and decide which of the home industries could be revived. . . . [132]

These words, welcomed by the entire Indian left, made more conservative Congressmen unhappy. But Bose, like Nehru, put the period of socialist reconstruction in the future. In the present, Bose had certainly given some evidence of wanting to help powerful native economic interests at the expense of foreign interests.

The idea of a planning commission—modeled on that of the Soviet Union and other European nations—was one pet idea that Bose put forward in this speech. Another was the idea that India had to have a common language. He advocated a blend of Hindi and Urdu, written in the Roman script. Although he had originally felt that using a foreign script would be 'anti-national', 'my visit to Turkey in 1934 was responsible for converting me. I then realized for the first time what a great advantage it was to have the same script as the rest of the world.'[133]

Though he indicated that he was not a member of the Congress Socialists, he did agree with them on a number of general principles, including that of collective affiliation, particularly by kisan sabhas and trade unions. His one caveat was that Congressmen should 'in large numbers participate in trade union and peasant organizations.' If they did so, there was less likelihood of a conflict between these organizations of the masses and the Congress.[134]

Before he finished, he again turned to the international context for

Indian nationalism. He said, in part,

> ... we should not be influenced by the internal policies of any country or the form of its state. We shall find in every country, men and women who will sympathise with Indian freedom, no matter what their own political views may be. In this matter we should take a leaf out of Soviet diplomacy. Though Soviet Russia is a communist state, her diplomats have not hesitated to make alliances with non-socialist states and have not declined sympathy or support coming from any quarter.[135]

To implement his ideas in the foreign arenas throughout the globe, he wanted agents of Indian nationalism to fan out to Asia, Europe, Africa, and the Americas and attend every international congress or conference possible.

In his remarks about ignoring the internal policies and forms of government of other states, provided they would assist Indian nationalists, Bose was not completely in tune with the foreign policy resolutions of the Congress itself at Haripura. At this session, the Congress voted to condemn Japanese aggression in China and to call upon the public to boycott Japanese goods, and it criticized fascist aggression in Europe. This resolution concluded,

> India can be no party to such an imperialist war and will not permit her man-power and resources to be exploited in the interests of British imperialism. Nor can India join any war without the express consent of her people. The Congress . . . entirely disapproves of war preparations being made in India. . .[136]

The resolution, however, did not contain the kind of sweeping condemnation of fascism that Jawaharlal Nehru and some others of the Indian left would have wished for. But Bose differed with these same colleagues on utilizing the help of Britain's enemies for the advancement of Indian nationalism, and although not unaware of the abuses of human rights in Germany and Italy, was willing to ignore such oppression if Hitler and Mussolini would help him to defeat the British Raj.

The Haripura session was carried through harmoniously. Sarat Bose got up to support Sardar Patel's resolution on the ministerial crisis in UP and Bihar, and Subhas Bose ran the public session smoothly. When the Working Committee for 1938 was announced, however, it did differ from those in the Nehru years, when the left had more of a presence in the inner circle of the Congress with the Boses and several members of the Congress Socialist Party as members. But now only Nehru and Bose represented the left-wing on its Executive Committee and the more conservative Gandhians held the other places. The Congress Socialists were said to have declined Bose's offer of seats on the Working Committee, for they did not think these places helped them to grow effectively. Harekrishna Mahatab from Orissa was added, but he was part of the Gandhian mainstream, though he later said he was influenced by Bose.[137]

The Congress organizational structure continued as it had been under Nehru. Acharya J.B. Kripalani, a Gandhian who had worked well with Nehru as general secretary of the Congress, was to remain in place and the Secretariat was to stay with him at Allahabad, though Bose preferred a shift to Calcutta. So Bose had a Gandhian framework within which to operate.

Although one historian of the Congress movement in this period has argued that the struggles between the left and the right were essentially faction fights with ideas playing only a small and secondary role, there seems no doubt that the leaders of the CSP, CPI, Royists, and Bose and Nehru, as well as kisan and trade union spokesmen, had different positions on many substantive and organizational issues and in their visions of free India than did the Gandhian high command.[138] The factional fighting severely hampered the left, while the Gandhians, always skillfully guided by the Mahatma, held together, and in the end, came out ahead. Gandhi may have been—as M.N. Roy said at various times—a medieval reactionary, Savanarola in modern garb, a reactionary demagogue, but he knew how to win the non-violent battle for continued domination of the Indian National Congress. At Haripura, Gandhi sent instructions to Sardar Patel,

> I think your speech was too aggressive. The Socialists cannot be won over in this manner. If you feel that you have made a mistake, please get Subhas's special permission and go up to the dais, wipe their tears and make them smile. We ought not to give tit for tat. Forgiveness adorns the strong. Their tongue should not cut like a sword.[139]

While Gandhi's team was guided by him with consummate skill, and had a chief of staff like Patel, one of the most adept nationalists at political in-fighting, the leftists tore at each other. M.N. Roy had emerged from prison in 1936 and his small and able following was still with the CSP. But within a year, Roy led his group out and for the next decade, guided his followers on an independent course. Roy, a man of considerable intellectual gifts, found it hard to take the lead of others. He never followed Gandhi's advice to him to 'Serve in silence.'[140]

With the development of the United Front line by the Third Communist International, the CPI—though officially banned—sent its members into the CSP and through the CSP into the Indian National Congress. Although many of the communists were known as such to their colleagues, they had both an open agenda, to build the anti-imperialist front, and a secret one, to work to gain control of the CSP. If this was successful, they would seek to widen their influence in the Congress itself. Within the CSP, there was a continuing argument as to whether they should allow the communists to work with them in their organization. Jayaprakash Narayan, one of the main CSP leaders, maintained that the communists should not be purged, even when M.R. Masani, a keen and anti-communist socialist, produced a secret memo—never repudiated—about the communist plans to take over the CSP. The struggle within the CSP was heating up in 1938 when Masani published the memo and got hotter through the next two years until the communists were banished. But the CSP was severely weakened.[141]

Since Bose was not a member of any organized socialist group, but was an independent nationalist with socialist views, he did not have to participate in these faction fights. He was also more of a pragmatic nationalist than an ideologue. Since he had seen the unfortunate consequences of his favorable remarks on a synthesis of fascism and communism, he recanted in his interview with R. Palme Dutt. He went further at Haripura by making a favorable comment about the British Communist Party. His speech was greeted positively by Indian communists, and a number of Bengal members of the party, including Somnath Lahiri and Bankim Mukherjee, who worked with him during his presidential year. Another Congressman who leaned to the communists and later became a leading CPI literary figure, Gopal Haldar, was also close to Bose at this time. Of the CSP cadre in Bengal, trade unionist Sibnath Banerjee worked with Bose at this time. Bose also had the cooperation of the national leaders of the CSP and of M.N. Roy. Though the left was relatively small, the backing of the leftists and of the BPCC where the Bose group dominated, gave him something of a base. Though he was extremely popular in Bengal and showed considerable drawing power when he toured other provinces, he never developed a mass following built on a solidly organizational base.[142]

One issue that Bose wanted to pursue was the establishment of a planning committee of the Congress to prepare preliminary proposals for the reconstruction of a free India. Realizing that only someone like Nehru, with his socialist outlook and his ties to the left and the right, could get this committee off the ground, Bose insisted that Nehru head it. Through most of 1938, Nehru was in Europe. Bose tracked him down in loyalist Spain and pressed him to accept. Finally, Nehru agreed. First, a meeting of the industries ministers of the Congress-ruled provinces was held in October with Bose in the chair.[143] Then, after Nehru's return in November, Nehru chaired the first meeting of the Planning Committee which convened in December 1938. As he wrote to Bose the following year,

> The work of the National Planning Committee which you entrusted to me

last year grows bigger and bigger and takes up a great deal of time and energy. It is exhausting business.[144]

Though the official biographer of Nehru has seen fit to ignore Bose's role and gave all the credit to India's first prime minister, at least Nehru himself knew that Bose's initiative and perseverence in the matter had been essential. It is one of Bose's legacies to free India, which has seen fit to persist in shaping a planned economy throughout its existence.[145]

H.V. Kamath, a former civil servant and later a joint secretary of the Planning Committee for some time, has suggested that Bose formulated the following principles for the committee before it actually was formed and met. He wanted,

1. National autonomy in our principal resources.
2. Development of our power supply, metal production, machines and tools manufacture, essential chemicals, transport and communication industries.
3. Technical education and technical research to be furthered.
4. A permanent National Research Council to be established.
5. An economic survey of the present industrial position to be carefully made.[146]

The committee used Bose's suggestions as it went ahead with its work under the chairmanship of Nehru from December 1938. Though the Gandhians were not enthusiastic, Sardar Patel helped to expedite the committee's work, which needed support from the Congress ministries. Indian capitalists, with whom Patel and Gandhi were in touch, no doubt felt that plans formulated with ample room for 'private enterprise' were better than those that did not make such provision. Gandhi was suspicious of planning because he believed that it necessarily implied industrialization and precluded cottage industries. Bose and Nehru both maintained that planning could include both heavy industry and small-scale production. Gandhi had his doubts about planning, and, furthermore, he favored 'trusteeship' rather than any hint of nationalization. Several leading Gandhians, including Patel, had warm ties to wealthy capitalists and were resolutely against socialism. But they wanted to be intimately in touch with developments which touched on the future shaping of the Indian economy, and so went along with Bose's small steps on this score.

During 1938, Bose made a number of speeches on planning and industrialization and one example he used was that of the Soviet Union. Like India, he believed, the Soviets had many resources and for long were chained into a primitive economy open to exploitation by outsiders. The Soviet government had now moved towards an industrial economy under the guidance of a strong party. Their progress had been enormous. He anticipated the same for India once the British exploiters were gone, so he initiated the Congress' Planning Committee.[147]

Besides a future planned economy and the nationalization of key industries, the Congress left and right disagreed on collective affiliation to the Congress, the agrarian program, labor matters, Congress participation in ministries, and the approach to mass mobilization efforts. On some of these issues, Bose hedged during his reign as Congress president, for he was generally more pragmatic than many of his left-wing colleagues in the CSP and CPI. Therefore, Bose and Nehru, while agreeing with the Congress Socialists on collectively affiliating other (particularly peasant and labor) groups, did not fight for it. CSP members simply tried to enroll more members of these labor and peasant groups as individual Congress members.[148]

The kisan sabhas and their umbrella organization, the All-India Kisan Sabha, as well as the CSP, wanted a more radical agrarian reform program than the Gandhian leadership would sanction. Not unexpectedly, once the Congress ministries were in place in most provinces, these radical forces worked for serious reform measures as opposition ginger groups pressuring Congress ministers and legislators for stronger measures than those newly in power would agree to. Fitting with the arguments presented by Sarat Bose in the Bengal Legislative Assembly, the Congress high command stood for an all-class position. They wanted to help poor cultivators and landless laborers, at least rhetorically, but they were not willing to fight for the lowest classes at the risk of estranging the wealthier landed groups. Verbally, Subhas Bose might have spoken of dispossessing the landlords and helping the poor peasants, but before independence he was not going to break ranks with the Gandhian high command on such an issue. Similarly, the Boses wanted to help labor and Subhas Bose had a long history of connection to the trade union movement. Officially the Congress backed the Bombay Industrial Disputes Act, but the Congress Socialists and Bose were critical of it. Nehru asked why Bose did not oppose it when the former returned from Europe in late 1938. Bose informed Nehru that he *had* opposed it and Nehru was simply uninformed on the matter. However, again, Bose was not going to break with the dominant high command on this issue.[149]

During the AICC meeting held in Delhi during the last week of September 1938, the tensions between the left and the right in the Congress briefly burst forth over a so-called 'civil liberties' resolution. The resolution said that some Congressmen were advocating class war, including murder, arson, and looting, in the name of civil liberty. Put forth by the Gandhians, it was meant to be a slap in the face to the Congress radicals taking a strong class position on a variety of issues, such as agrarian and labor reform. It further read that the Congress tradition included support for measures defending life and property and urged Congress governments to pass such measures in the provinces. Bose was presiding over the meeting and, according to Gandhi, allowed all parties to have their full say. When the radicals' amendments were rejected, they walked out of the meeting. Bose and the Congress establishment remained. Later, Gandhi challenged those who had walked out to permanently leave the Congress if they could not agree to its fundamental principles and to measures passed by a majority. Although there was anger on both sides, the radicals declined Gandhi's offer.[150]

Why did Bose not take the radicals' side more forcefully? There seem to be several reasons. First, Bose was not afraid to challenge Gandhi—as he had proved from 1928 on—but he wanted to choose his issues. The issues that Subhas was most concerned with at the time were those relating to the British Raj and how to eliminate it. Matters of social and economic reconstruction were important, but only after independence would they take priority. Second, he liked being Congress president. He was not going to give up this position unless some very vital matter was at stake. As Gandhi had written to Amrit Kaur a few months earlier, 'Subhas is in Wardha. He is looking a picture of health. All he needed was work of the type he loves. He has got it and he is happy.'[151] Bose not only liked the work, but he also appreciated the ceremonial aspects of the position, such as the parade with fifty-one bulls at Haripura and appearing on the cover of the American magazine, *Time,* on March 7, 1938.

Jawaharlal Nehru later related that over the years he learned to work with the Gandhians and discovered that they were fighters. These experiences and shared years in prison with some of them softened his doctrinaire differences with them and earned them considerable respect in his eyes. Bose, too, to a lesser degree, learned to live with the Gandhians during 1938. He worked with them closely in handling the Khare affair and in speaking for the Congress in exchanges with Mohammad Ali Jinnah and the Muslim League.

The 'Khare Affair', or the CP (Central Provinces) ministerial crisis in July 1938, was a conflict between politicians in that province, between Chief Minister Khare and the Congress high command, and a constitutional tussle between the Congress and the Raj. Through its brief but tortured moments, Subhas Bose cooperated so completely with Gandhi, the Working Committee, and its Parliamentary Sub-Committee, that Khare called Bose 'a puppet in the hands of Mahatma Gandhi.'[152]

The Central Provinces included Hindi- and Marathi-speaking areas, and the Congress cabinet was composed of Congressmen from both regions with Khare, a Maharashtrian, as chief minister. Politicians from the province had long struggled for ministerships both under dyarchy and under the 1935 Act. Although Khare had succeeded in gaining the chief ministership, the conflicts did not dissolve and the Congress Parliamentary Sub-Committee (Prasad, Patel, Azad) had had to intervene previously to work out a compromise to stifle the tensions within the ministry. But they continued, with Khare claiming that the Congress high command, led by Gandhi and Patel and his colleagues from the Hindi-speaking regions, were plotting against him. For their part, the Hindi-speaking leaders, particularly D.P. Mishra, maintained that Khare was secretly getting instructions from the governor of the province and plotting against them. Just before a Parliamentary Sub-Committee and Working Committee meeting in late July, Khare resigned along with his two colleagues from Maharashtra, and tried to have the Hindi-speaking ministers do likewise. They refused to do so without sanction from the Congress Parliamentary Sub-Committee, whereupon the governor, using his special powers, dismissed them. Khare then reformed the ministry without them and reclaimed the chief minister's chair.

A few days later Khare was hauled before the Working Committee in a meeting presided over by Bose and was forced to announce that he had resigned again. When he refused to submit a letter apologizing for his actions, he was disciplined by the Working Committee. The Working Committee next summoned the Congress members of the legislature and had them elect a new leader. Bose—along with the Parliamentary Sub-Committee—were the public disciplinarians for the Congress. They worked to force Congress ministers to follow the orders of the central executive. This method of demanding adherence to party orders was labeled 'Congress totalitarianism' by historian and governmental adviser, Sir Reginald Coupland.[153] In his later memoirs, Khare claimed that privately Bose had said he supported him, but there is no independent evidence of this. Khare said that Bose told him that he had to go along with the majority Gandhians because he was just one lone voice. Khare insisted, all those years later, that he warned Bose that 'a similar fate' awaited him from the Gandhi political machine.[154] Bose believed that, in so far as possible, the Congress had to present a united front to the Raj.

Another arena in which he supported his high command brethren was in the relationship to the All-India Muslim League and to Mr Jinnah. Since the breakdown in the 1920s of the 1916 Lucknow Pact, the relations of the Congress and the Muslim League had followed a generally uncooperative and unfortunate course. Bose, like many in the leadership of the Congress, had long opposed separate electorates for Muslims, though this had been part of the bargain at Lucknow during the First World War. As part of the

Congress group under Motilal Nehru which prepared the report for the All-Parties Conference in 1928, Bose had strongly argued for joint electorates as an essential element of a democratic system. He also firmly believed throughout his life that the Congress should and did represent all communities in India and was opposed to political organizations based on religious affiliation. Though he might work with such organizations in a particular situation, his outlook was fundamentally a secular one, linked to a vision of what has earlier been called composite nationalism. According to this view, all communities in India are part of the nation and all Indians are first-class citizens of the nation. If possible, there are not to be separate electorates for religious or ethnic groups, or particular castes or communities.

Bose had to resume the correspondence of the Congress president with the president of the Muslim League that had been carried on with Mr Jinnah since 1935. On August 2, 1938, Jinnah wrote to Bose:

> . . . the Executive Council of the All India Muslim League . . . is fully convinced that the Muslim League is the only authoritative and representative political organisation of the Musalmans of India. This position was accepted when the Congress-League Pact was arrived at in 1916 at Lucknow and ever since, till 1935 when Jinnah-Rajendra Prasad conversation took place . . . so far as the Muslim League is concerned it is not aware that any Muslim political organisation has ever made a claim that it can speak or negotiate on behalf of the Muslims of India. It is therefore, very much to be regretted that you should have referred to 'other Muslim organisations' in this connection.[155]

A number of desultory letters followed between the two, manifesting a fundamental lack of communication.

At the December meeting of the Working Committee, the body's collective opinion was that 'no useful purpose will be served by prolonging the correspondence with (the) League. The President was authorized to write to Mr Jinnah closing the correspondence.'[156] Bose wrote, in part,

> Since the Committee do not find it possible to agree with the Council of the Muslim League as to the basis of the negotiations and since the Council insist that an agreement as to the basis is a *sine qua non* of any negotiations between the Congress and the League, the Working Committee regret that they are not in a position to do anything further in the direction of starting negotiations with the League with a view to arriving at a settlement of the Hindu-Muslim question.[157]

At the national level, the Congress and the Muslim League were at logger-heads and some Leaguers were beginning to protest what they claimed were acts of oppression in the Congress-ruled provinces against the

Muslim community. Bose stood solidly with his colleagues in the Working Committee in their general perspective of Hindu-Muslim relations and approach to the Muslim League. However, Bose hailed from a province in which the Hindus were the minority and in which a Muslim League-dominated ministry ruled. Therefore, his vision, and his concerns, and his political approach perforce had to be different when he confronted Bengal.

XI

As Congress president, Bose had some involvement with all the regions of India and the CP ministerial crisis was an example. He knew of the Andhra movement for separation from Madras, support for which would have been in keeping with the Congress division of the nation into linguistic regions. During the 1930s there was one simmering regional conflict which hit closer to home. This concerned the role of the Bengalis in Bihar and had built up to such heated exchanges that the Congress had appointed Rajendra Prasad to investigate on behalf of the national body and recommend conciliatory steps. However, Prasad's report failed to satisfy anyone and no real changes occurred. The Biharis wanted Bihar jobs for themselves, excluding Bengali residents of the province, while the Bengalis wanted to compete equally.[158]

Since his emergence from prolonged imprisonment and exile in 1937, Subhas Bose had been president of the BPCC, and continued to hold this position while he was president of the National Congress. In addition, he was involved in the workings and reform of the Calcutta Corporation as an alderman and as leader of the Calcutta Municipal Association. Somehow his working hours had to be divided among these multiple concerns.

For much of the time after the death of C.R. Das in 1925, the Boses constituted an important, often dominant faction in the BPCC. When the Boses were working more or less harmoniously with the central organization, they were given a certain amount of leeway to deal with local controversies, unless these became too broad and bitter as during 1929–31 when the Sen Gupta faction and the Bose faction were at each other's throats. Then peace-keepers from outside were necessary and despatched to Bengal. This endemic factionalism continued through the 1930s but was never again so exacerbated that central Congress intervention was called for. Former revolutionaries who had once supported the Boses, shifted away; others who had supported Sen Gupta moved closer to the Boses, including Suresh Mazumdar, a noted newspaper proprietor. His *Hindustan Standard* supported the Boses, while the nationalist *Amrita Bazar Patrika* was often critical.

The 'Big Five' who had worked together after C.R. Das' death were no longer united. Nalini Sarker was now finance minister in Fazlul Huq's government, and some even said he was the dominant personality in the whole ministry. He had become a bitter Bose opponent and though cast out from the Congress, he remained a friend and confidant of Gandhi. Dr B.C. Roy had differences with Sarat Bose and, though they continued to work on the Congress side, they were no longer close; Dr Roy had become one of Gandhi's personal physicians and a Bengal favorite of the Gandhian high command. The so-called 'pure khadi' types, or more ideologically committed Gandhians, included P.C. Ghosh and Satish Das Gupta, and they played their role in the BPCC. Tulsi Goswami and Nirmal Chunder still worked with the Boses, and the former particularly was an ally and friend of Sarat Bose. Another powerful figure in the Bengal Congress was Kiron Sankar Roy, a clever and well-educated Congressman of long-standing on whom the Boses had counted, but who was drifting from them and could no longer be considered a trusted ally.

What Nirad C. Chaudhuri wrote years ago about Bose and his lack of a firm base was true even for this period of pre-eminence in Bengal and National Congress politics:

> Subhas Bose as party leader failed to create a solid party himself. . . . Bose had nothing behind him beyond unorganized popular support. He never acquired any strong or lasting hold on the party bosses of Bengal. . . . The lower ranks of the career nationalists of Bengal gave their loyalty to him according to their estimate of his power to serve or harm their interests . . . . Thus he was never able to knock his party enemies on the head and was paralysed all along by the factious squabbles in which he became enmeshed.[159]

The Boses had some loyal backers and lieutenants, but no extensive party organization or organized mass base, except for the semi-secret BV. Based in Calcutta, they had some allies in the outlying districts of Bengal. Occasional complaints were sent on to the National Congress about the lack of effort at building a rural base. One interesting letter on this theme was written by Amulya Prasad Chandra, secretary, Munshigunj Sub-Division Congress Committee, Dacca district. He maintained in his letter of November 23, 1937, that the Bengal Congress remained dominated by the upper, urban elite, had not reached out to the lower classes, and were distrusted by the lower orders, particularly the Muslims. He advocated that Congressmen live and work among the masses so as to bring them in touch with the Congress.[160]

A foremost concern, perhaps even *the* concern of the Boses, at least as far as Bengal was concerned, was the growing communalization in the

province, spurred on, they believed, by the reactionary Muslim League
ministry running and ruining their beloved Bengal. Early in the Huq
ministry, Sarat Bose was writing to Congress president Nehru about how
to change the direction of affairs in Bengal:

> If we are to break the present reactionary ministry we have to enter into some
> sort of alliance with those groups in the Assembly who will agree to work
> the Congress programme in the legislature. The present ministry is far more
> reactionary than its predecessors under the old Act and unless we are able
> to break it, the future of Bengal is doomed. At the present moment, the left
> wingers in the Proja Party numbering between 20 to 25, are voting with us.
> We shall get further recruits if it is announced that the Working Committee
> will authorise alliances with other groups who will accept the Congress
> policy and programme. The two most mischievous persons in the present
> Cabinet are Sir Khwaja Nazimuddin and Mr Nalini Ranjan Sircar. The latter
> has sedulously spread the report that the Working Committee will, in no
> event, sanction alliances and that has had the effect of isolating the Congress
> party. I have had long discussions on this subject with Srijuts T.C. Goswami
> and Jogesh C. Gupta and the former will place the whole matter before the
> Working Committee. Something has to be done to strengthen the Congress
> party and it should be done immediately.[161]

Though Subhas Bose had been one of those opposed to Congress entering
the ministries, and though Sarat Bose among others has been blamed for
the failure of the Congress to make a coalition with Huq and the KPP in
1937, once the decision of the Congress to accept ministerial office and
make provincial governments had been taken, both worked assiduously to
persuade National Congress leaders and non-Congressmen in Bengal to
allow the Bengal Congress to make a coalition ministry. Otherwise they
feared that the communal divide would become sharper and sharper and,
as Sarat said, 'Bengal is doomed.'

After Fazlul Huq had made his bargain with the Muslim League and
then joined it, he became, however unwillingly, more and more their
captive and spokesman. He did not want to be controlled by extra-Bengal
forces and leaders. However, he did not have a real alternative as yet. All
observers, British and Indian, agree that Huq was a gifted and moving
speaker in Bengali and English, yet he could say quite foolish things in his
extemporaneous performances.[162] His cabinet included several of the most
important Urdu-speaking Muslims of the province, two representatives of
the Hindu landlords, and Sarker, a prominent businessman. Within little
more than a year, the foremost KPP member besides Huq, Syed Nausher
Ali, was squeezed out.[163] He believed that the cabinet would never put
through fundamental planks of the KPP program and that Huq's allegiance
had now shifted to the Muslim League. A large group, at least half, of the

KPP members in the Bengal Assembly left the coalition party and went into the opposition and were now linked to the Congress with Sarat Bose as the leader of the entire opposition. For the Boses, this represented a step towards a Hindu-Muslim coalition ministry, which they firmly believed was essential to the survival of Bengal. What they needed was sanction from the Congress high command and for Fazlul Huq to break with the Muslim League and bring over the remaining KPP members.

The Sarat Bose-led opposition had to speak up on particular issues such as the annual budget debates, challenge the ministry in the question periods, put forward their own bills and adjournment motions, and upon occasion make a no-confidence motion against the ministers and ministry. With the assistance of Gandhi, by mid-1939 all detenus and almost all political prisoners had been released. The Bengal Tenancy (Amendment) Act was passed, though it took almost a year for the governor to give his assent to the act. The KPP platform had included abolition of the Permanent Settlement of Bengal as a prominent plank. After stalling for some time, the ministry appointed the Floud Commission to investigate this and other questions related to landholding. Many KPP members were unhappy that the commission had a Westerner as chairman and many zamindars on it. But they were unable to change it.

The most general debate on the working of the ministry, and its program, or lack of one, came during discussion of a set of no-confidence motions (one directed against each minister) in August 1938. The two sides—ministry and opposition—arrayed their phalanxes for the great battle of words. On one side was the coalition party and its backers, including the Europeans. On the other were all the opposition groups, including the Congress, the KPP section which had deserted Huq, the Hindu Mahasabha, some of the scheduled caste independents, and most of the labor members who were not all in the Congress.

One of the charges was that after sixteen months in office, the ministry had no achievements worth mentioning. Abdul Hakeem, a KPP member, mocked Huq, noting that his main accomplishments were the introduction of dog racing at Behala and an expensive plan for a new building for the Bengal Legislative Council. What had happened, he asked, to the priority for free primary education, a KPP proposal, on the basis of which, along with abolition of the Permanent Settlement, Huq had been elected? Even more severe criticism was offered by KPP leader Tamizuddin Khan who said, in part,

> . . . far from raising their little finger to solve the difficult problem of the province the Ministry have been deliberately pursuing a policy that has already made the communal tension far worse than what it was when they

assumed office. A false and insidious cry of religion in danger has been raised and this has poisoned the very atmosphere of the country. The Ministry, to keep itself in office, is fostering that cry and has all but dragged the country into the mouth of a volcano. Freedom of opinion and speech and other civil liberties of the people have been endangered as never before. Intimidation and assault has taken the place of reason and argument.... How long should Bengal be allowed to groan under the dead weight of a Ministry like this? When will Bengal get rid of this nightmare?[164]

The whole opposition, from S.P. Mookerjee of the Hindu Mahasabha to the KPP leaders, agreed that the ministry was fanning the flames of communalization for its benefit. They appointed men of the 'right' community, but of inferior abilities, as Sir Robert Reid, a senior ICS officer who served as acting governor, noted in his memoirs.[165]

Picking up after Tamizuddin Khan, S.P. Mookerjee added,

... Government ... decided ... that the way to serve the best interests of Bengal was to plan a basis of administration which will be entirely or principally communal in character ... this was done perhaps with the belief of convincing the Muslim members of this House and the Muslim population of Bengal that the Government of the day were really intending to look after the interests of the Muslim themselves. I have no desire here to relate in detail the manner in which the rights and liberties of one particular community have been trampled under foot ... there has spread ... a state of insecurity unparalleled in the history of Bengal. The cry of Islam in danger was shamelessly raised at every time when Government found their policy and action were ruthlessly exposed ... the part played by Mr A.K. Fazlul Huq ... was entirely unworthy of the position which he occupies. Bengal expected better of him.[166]

S.P. Mookerjee was primarily concerned about the consequences for the Hindus of Bengal. Tamizuddin Khan and the KPP opposition—who represented Muslim constituencies—saw that such policies and actions would bring unfortunate results for the entire population of Bengal.

A large bloc of European votes was important to the ministry, though not yet crucial to their continuance in office. Sloughing off criticism that the Europeans should sit on the sidelines without speaking or voting, Sir George Campbell, their leading spokesman, harshly criticized the KPP members who had deserted Huq. Then he called for a realignment of parties so that the Congress could be taken into the ministry. Calling the Congress 'this great Hindu party,' he saw—like the Boses and the opposition KPP—that there had to be some sort of Bengal coalition.[167]

Sarat Bose, who had choreographed the presentation by the opposition, had the opportunity to sum up for his side. After mentioning and putting in perspective many of the points made by his side, he reiterated his concern about the flagrant use of communal appeal to the Muslims of Bengal by several ministers and other Muslim leaders. He said, in part,

> . . . if a Hindu were to raise the cry that Hinduism was in danger because a few appointments were going to a few Muslims and to the members of scheduled castes, I would hang down my head in shame. Hinduism cannot be in danger if 50, 60, or 70 per cent of the appointments were given to the Muslims or to the members of the scheduled castes. Similarly, if a Muslim member were to raise a cry that Islam was in danger—Islam which extended its influence from Western Europe to Eastern Asia—I would also hang down my head in shame. Can there be the least doubt that some members of the present Ministry have not raised their little finger against the writers of poisonous leaflets, such as those which have been placed before the House. . . . If they have not taken any action, can they possibly escape the charge that they are responsible for bringing about an atmosphere of violence in the city?[168]

He maintained that, 'I myself toured throughout Bengal more than once and I have never come across the slightest expression of communal passion in the countryside.'[169] What was happening, he said, was the fanning of communal hatred in Calcutta and the district towns by irresponsible politicians. Answering Sir George Campbell, he said that the Congress was not only a 'great Hindu party,' but also had considerable appeal, again in the countryside, to ordinary Muslims who had not yet been antagonized by communal propaganda and distortions.

In keeping with his belief that there was no unbridgeable Hindu-Muslim divide, he pointed out that about half of the KPP had joined the opposition because Huq had deserted the KPP program. Then he put forward at some length the positive program of the opposition for improving Bengal. The present ministry, he said, was, as usual, starving the nation-building departments. His side would operate differently, given the responsibility of office. In part, he said,

> . . . we are out for communal peace and harmony: we are out for reform of secondary and higher education . . . we are out for the increase of irrigational facilities . . . we stand for ear-marking a substantial portion of the revenue obtained from the jute tax for the improvement of the . . . welfare of the agricultural population and labour. We are out for raising up the prices of produce: we are out for the introduction of free compulsory primary education without taxation on cultivators . . . we stand for recruitment to public services by competitive examinations, subject to this that we shall allow restrictive competition among members of the scheduled castes and Muslim communities: we stand for the levelling up of all the communities which are at present educationally and economically backward by the provision of special educational facilities. . . . We are out for the reduction of high salaries and allowances and the cost of administration of

Government. . . . [170]

From this list of items, Sarat Bose passed on to the politics of coalition-ministry making in Bengal. He said that the Congress would support a Muslim chief minister if such a man backed the program specified in his speech. He also said that, 'We of the Congress Assembly Party are not seekers of office . . . the Congress Assembly Party is not going to accept office, unless this House demands their services.'[171] He was necessarily vague on how the Congress might come to office in a province in which they did not have a majority. He alluded to the behind-the-scenes negotiations with Huq which had continued fitfully since early 1937 and made an appeal to the chief minister at the end of his speech,

> . . . in conclusion, may I appeal from Philip drunk to Philip sober, may I appeal from Mr Fazlul Huq, the Chief Minister, to Mr Fazlul Huq, the man, may I challenge him to say whether in his opinion this is not the best workable programme that can possibly be devised for this province? Sir, I stood by the Hon'ble Fazlul Huq in his days of troubles. . . . I have not had the good fortune of standing by him in his days of glory. . . . I bear towards him personally the same feelings as I did in the past . . . it is because of the want of any policy during the last 16 months, it is because of the atmosphere of violence they have created, it is because of instances of nepotism . . . that . . . I support this motion of no-confidence.·. . .[172]

Although he mentioned the main charges of the opposition against the ministry, Sarat Bose's speech contained no bitterness or rancor, only sorrow and hope.

Answering the opposition, Suhrawardy was pointed and haughty, but Fazlul Huq was more conciliatory. Defending the achievements of his ministry as he had to do, particularly the Bengal Tenancy (Amendment) Act, which the governor finally assented to the following week, Huq reached out to Sarat Bose,

> I would appeal to my friend, Mr Bose, to come and tell me what is it that he wants me to do. He says he is not going to accept office. I should be very glad to sit with him . . . and see what is the programme he wants us to follow. If I fail in my duty after that, then will be the time for them to condemn us. But please give us respite at least for another year and give us an opportunity to do what we are able to do. We have not had peaceful time at all. You do not give us opportunity to work and you then take us to task.[173]

The no-confidence motions were defeated by the ministerial coalition—in most cases by about 130 votes to 111—and the Assembly returned to its normal round of business.[174] However, behind the scenes, maneuvering was going on for a realignment of the ministry. To bolster his position, Huq added two KPP stalwarts, Tamizuddin Khan and Shamsuddin Ahmed, in November 1938. The latter lasted less than a few months in Huq's ministerial company and exited with considerable bitterness against the chief minister and his failure to redeem many of his promises.[175]

For the Boses, who wanted a Congress-KPP-Scheduled Caste coalition, the matter was complicated by National Congress politics and personal ties and animosities. Gandhi had warm relations with G.D. Birla and Nalini Sarker, both non-Congressmen, but nationalist businessmen who worked both sides of the Raj-nationalist divide. When Subhas Bose pressed Gandhi for a Congress coalition in Bengal, Gandhi wrote to him on December 18, 1938:

> I must dictate this letter as I am wilfully blind. Whilst I am dictating this, Maulana Saheb, Nalini Babu and Ghanshamdas are listening [*that is, Maulana Azad, Nalini Sarker, and G.D.Birla*]. We had an exhaustive discussion over the Bengal Ministry. I am more than ever convinced that we should not aim at ousting the Ministry. We shall gain nothing by a reshuffle; and, probably, we shall lose much by including Congressmen in the Ministry. I feel, therefore, that the best way of securing comparative purity of administration and a continuity of a settled programme and policy would be to aim at having all the reforms that we desire, carried out by the present Ministry. Nalini Babu should come out, as he says he would, on a real issue being raised and the decision being taken by the Ministry against the interests of the country.[176]

This was Gandhi at his sweet and manipulative best, opposing the Boses on a matter vital to them—and they believed to the entire population of Bengal—and allowing himself to be guided by non-Congressmen of a certain persuasion. Subhas Bose replied at length in his blunt manner, telling Gandhi, in part,

> The letter which Sjt. G.D. Birla brought from Wardha came as a profound shock to me.... The other day ... it was discussed between us.... My brother Sarat also discussed the matter with you. Both of us have the clear impression that you have always agreed with the idea of a Coalition Ministry for Bengal. I do not know what has happened since I left Wardha.... The position ... is that you attach more value and importance to the views of those three gentlemen [*Azad, Sarker, Birla*] than to the views of those who are responsible for running the Congress organisation in Bengal ... there is a fundamental difference between Moulana Sahib and myself.... [His] view seems to be that in the Muslim-majority provinces like Bengal, communal Muslim Ministries should be allowed to continue in office. . .
>
> I hold ... that it is imperative in the national interest that we should pull down the Huq Ministry as early as possible. The longer this reactionary Ministry remains in office, the more communal will the atmosphere of Bengal become and the weaker will the Congress grow. . .
>
> At long last early in November Sjt. Nalini Sarker had been convinced

that he should resign. . . . He assured me for the last time on the 9th
December . . . that he would resign his office before the next Budget Session.
What made him renege from the position within one week, I do not know.
Your influence is going to be used not to get Nalini Babu to resign but to get
him to stick to office at a time when even his closest friends want him to get
out of the Huq Ministry. It has astonished me that you did not feel it
necessary to even consult me before you arrived at a decision on such a
serious matter.[177]

Bose felt that the Congress right-wing was shortsightedly opposing his
position. He also realized that even though he was Congress and BPCC
president, he was still an outsider to the Gandhi group which controlled the
Congress. Gandhi remained 'wilfully blind' on this issue and it is part of
his contribution to the eventual partition of India.

Besides the link from Bengal to national politics, there was also a close
tie between Bengal and Calcutta Corporation politics where the Boses
were involved. Sarat Bose no longer played the day-to-day role he once
had in the Corporation for he was now committed to his work in the Bengal
Legislative Assembly. Subhas Bose, however, even though he had wide
and heavy commitments as Congress and BPCC president, still devoted
some of his energies to the Corporation. He was elected an alderman in
1937 and returned briefly to a ringing ovation in November of that year.
It was not though until February 1938 that he started on his task of
reforming the Corporation through the Congress Municipal Association.
Many called upon him 'to cleanse', 'to purify' an institution which was
believed to be riddled with corruption and nepotism. His ringing
indictment of the Corporation was met after a few months with the
resignation of many members of the Congress Municipal Association.
Shortly thereafter, Bose himself resigned from the Association and as
alderman, writing, 'I think it is not possible to implement the Congress
programme of work in the Corporation through the Congress Municipal
Association, and I am therefore resigning my Aldermanship of the
Corporation also.'[178] Lively discussions in meetings and the press followed. The *Amrita Bazar Patrika,* no friend to Bose, asked him to push on
with his reform efforts but not to rejoin the Corporation.[179] Bose used his
pending resignation to get himself vested with stronger powers vis-à-vis
the Corporation by the BPCC and the Municipal Association. He said he
wanted strict discipline and an investigation of the Education Department.
Once he gained the stronger powers, Bose withdrew his resignations from
the Municipal Association and the Corporation.[180] It is not at all clear that
Bose made any headway with his reform efforts during 1938, and shortly
other controversies were swirling around the Corporation and the

Congress. Nirad C. Chaudhuri is likely correct that the Corporation remained 'a millstone around his neck.'[181]

The Huq ministry drew up a Calcutta Municipal (Amendement) Bill which would shift from joint to separate electorates for the Muslims, give the Muslims in Calcutta slightly more seats, bring about some reservation of places in Corporation posts for Muslims and the scheduled castes, and give the Bengal government more control over the selection of the chief executive officer, a position once held by Subhas Bose. As with the Communal Award, the Hindu community of Bengal was bitterly opposed to the reform bill introduced in the Bengal Assembly in 1938, debated and passed in 1939.[182] The Corporation, the governing body in a largely Hindu, but cosmopolitan city, was one of the caste Hindu bastions, like Calcutta University, that the leaders of the Hindu community and the Congress did not want changed. There were persuasive arguments on both sides in consideration of the Calcutta Municipal (Amendment) Bill and the Boses tried to marshal as much Muslim support for their side as possible. They, and most of the Hindu political elite of Bengal, looked upon the efforts of the Huq ministry on this bill as yet another manifestation of a communal outlook which would widen the gulf between the communities. Muslim leaders like Huq thought they were simply working appropriately for their place in the sun.

XII

Before 1938 ended, a new, more important conflict began over the presidency of the Indian National Congress for the following year. Not only did the controversy change the position of the Boses in Indian politics, but it had significant consequences for the history of the left and for Hindu-Muslim relations.

Although he well understood the limitations of the Congress presidency, Bose felt, as his term was drawing to a close, that he was one of the few who could represent the Indian left. In feeling his way towards a second candidacy, he said that if a leftist leader like Acharya Narendra Dev stepped forward to contest the post, he would withdraw. None did. Gandhi and the high command happened to meet and checked off Maulana Azad and Pattabhi Sitaramayya as possible candidates. Bose was not on their list. Were there any issues at stake in a possible contest, or was it simply a personality conflict with candidates more or less malleable to the Gandhians' outlook?

During the mid- and late-1930s, Subhas Bose surely was the most prominent Indian spokesman to advocate 'using the international situation to India's advantage'. In March 1938, he wrote to Jawaharlal Nehru,

What has happened in Czechoslovakia recently is but a sequel to the Munich Pact. As a matter of fact, I have been telling Congress friends during the last six months, on the basis of information which I had been getting from Europe, that there would be a crisis in Europe in Spring which would last till Summer. I have, therefore, been pressing for a dynamic move from our side—for an ultimatum to the British Government demanding Purna Swaraj . . . there is no sign of any intention on your part or on the part of the Gandhian group to utilise the international situation for our benefit. . . . I feel that either we should take international politics seriously and utilise the international situation for our benefit—or not talk about it at all.[183]

Differing with Gandhi and his men, Bose wanted to take advantage of the international situation. He advocated issuing an ultimatum to the British, backed with the threat of a renewed non-violent mass movement. Gandhi insisted, and all those amenable to his views agreed, that India, the masses of ordinary Indian nationalists, was not ready. Bose, unlike Gandhi, did not need to make a survey of the public mentality to determine readiness. Bose was ready and thus he thought he could help organize an irrepressible movement against the Raj.[184]

As Bose wrote to Nehru in March 1939, if the latter meant business, he should not simply pass vague resolutions. He should do something. So what did Bose do in late 1938? He started reaching out to foreign powers, particularly to enemies of the British. Among the actual and potential antagonists of the British, he included Germany, Italy, Japan, and the Soviet-directed Comintern. During his visits to Europe from 1933 to 1938, he had made contact, as best he could, with officials of Germany and Italy. He had been denied a visa to the Soviet Union, but now he sent a letter to Comintern officials via his nephew Amiya Bose, who was going to Europe for his advanced studies. On December 22, 1938, Bose met with Nazi official Dr O. Urchs in Bombay, with Dr F. Wulfestieg and Mr N.G. Ganpuley also present.

Bose by this time knew of some of the evils of Nazism. However, in his realpolitik view, Germany was the only power that could stand up to Britain. He wanted to conciliate Germany and India and get a positive statement on Indian nationalist objectives from the Germans. Each of the parties to this discussion listed a number of grievances against the other side. Bose said that Indian students were badly treated in Germany and their number was declining. He said that Nazi leaders continued to make anti-Indian statements and that Indians were concerned with the German approach to 'the race question'. He insisted that he had a friendly attitude to Germany and that only Nehru among Indian leaders was markedly anti-

German. For his part, Urchs mentioned the anti-German attitudes of Indian leaders and the Indian press. It is likely that some word of this meeting slipped out to other Indian leaders and to officials of the Raj. Bose did not seem to take any careful precautions to keep it secret.[185]

Although Bose had expressed sympathies with the Chinese in their war with the invading Japanese, he was also about to reach out to the Japanese, for they were allied with Germany in the Anti-Comintern Pact, and were a powerful potential enemy of the British Empire. An Indian revolutionary of an earlier generation who had fled India just before the First World War and lived his life in Japan had, unbeknownst to Subhas Bose, been reaching out to the new Congress president early in 1938. This was Rash Behari Bose, whose letter to the younger Bose was intercepted by the British. Rash Behari Bose said, in part,

> The fetish of non-violence should be discarded. . . . Let us attain our goal 'through all possible means': violence or non-violence. The non-violence atmosphere is simply making Indians womanly men. . . . The Congress should devote attention to only one point, i.e., military preparedness. Might is still the right. . . .
>
> The Congress should support the Pan-Asia movement. It should not condemn Japan without understanding her motive in the Sino-Japanese conflict. Japan is a friend of India and other Asiatic countries. Her chief motive is to destroy British influence in Asia. She has begun with China. . . . We should make friends with Britain's enemies. . . . It is now the best policy for the Indians to support Japan and utilise this opportunity to increase their influence in world-politics. . . . As in time of war, dictatorship is indispensable, at present in India's struggle for freedom, dictatorship is equally indispensable. . . .
>
> I have faith in you. Go ahead irrespective of criticisms, obstacles and impediments. Lead the nation along the right path. And success will be your's and India's.[186]

Though this letter never reached Subhas Bose, some of the elder revolutionary's views were congenial to him, and he had surely heard of him. But that these two Boses—one in Tokyo and one in Calcutta—might meet was surely far from his mind as yet.

Other Indian views about the course of international events were different from those of Subhas Bose. Jawaharlal Nehru, another Congress leader with considerable foreign exposure and concern, said that, '. . . no enemy of the United Kingdom [*is*] necessarily our friend'.[187] Throughout his adult political life, Rabindranath Tagore had been critical of those using force, man against man, class against class, nation against nation. He had sharp words for the Japanese when he visited Japan at the time of the First World War and in the late 1930s; he was again hostile to their use of force in China.[188] On the political left in India, there were strong anti-fascist sentiments as well as anti-imperialist views. As yet there was no problem of opposing both German and Italian fascism and British imperialism.[189]

There was another point of dispute between the Gandhians and Bose. This was the so-called 'aspersion' with which Bose was charged. The federal parts of the Government of India Act of 1935 had not become operative, while the provincial autonomy parts had. The federal structure that the act called for involved significant participation by the Indian states through their princes. Officially the Congress was dead against it. Bhulabhai Desai, a Congress leader from Bombay, was apparently misquoted by a British politician, Lord Lothian, who announced to the British press that the Congress was ready to compromise on the federal elements of the 1935 Act. G.D. Birla, a conduit from the nationalists to the British, also made such hints. In stories in the British press, Gandhi and Desai were linked and so it was made to appear that the Congress king was behind any remarks of Desai. Rumors were spread that even central ministerial positions had been tentatively parceled out. Jawaharlal Nehru throughout denied that such a possibility was ever in the works.[190] During December 1938 and January 1939, as the election campaign developed, Subhas Bose was quoted in the press as having said on several occasions that there was a possibility of the right-wing compromising on the federation issue and he, as a staunch anti-federationist, would stand against a right-wing candidate.[191]

As early as October 1938, Gandhi wrote to a confidant, 'There is bound to be some difficulty this time in electing the President.'[192] Rabindranath Tagore urged that Bose be re-elected in a letter to Gandhi, but Gandhi said it would be better for Bose not to run.[193] Once the Gandhian group had caucused with the Mahatma in December 1938, Gandhi wrote to Nehru, 'Maulana Saheb does not want the crown of thorns. If you want to try again please do. If you won't or he won't listen, Pattabhi seems to be the only choice.'[194] Nehru would not, and Azad would not listen. That left Pattabhi Sitaramayya from Andhra, a loyal if uninspiring Gandhian, as their candidate. The Gandhi group in the Working Committee with Sardar Patel as their spokesman and including Rajendra Prasad, J.B. Kripalani, Bhulabhai Desai, Jamnalal Bajaj, Shankarrao Deo, and Jairamdas Doulatram, asked Bose to step down and decline to run. Patel and Sarat Bose exchanged telegrams. Patel said that federation was not an issue, insisted there was no necessity for the re-election of Subhas Bose, and asked the latter not to divide Congressmen by running again. Sarat Bose answered that members of the Working Committee should not take sides and that Patel's proposed statement to the press would further accentuate the split in the Congress between right and left. He ended, 'Dr Pattabhi will not inspire country's confidence in come fight. Please do not divide Congress.'[195]

Patel issued his statement on behalf of his majority group in the Working Committee, putting forth Sitaramayya as their candidate and asking Bose to step aside and allow the election to be a unanimous one. Bose declined. He challenged the Gandhians, stating in part,

> . . . the position of the Congress president has been raised to a higher level. . . . The President is like the Prime Minister or the President of the United States of America who nominates his own Cabinet . . . questions of policy and programme are not irrelevant . . . after the Congress of 1934, a leftist has been elected as President every time with the support of both the right and left-wings. The departure from this practice this year and the attempt to set up a rightist candidate for the office of President is not without significance. It is widely believed that there is a prospect of a compromise on the Federal scheme between the right-wing of the Congress and the British Government during the coming year. Consequently the right-wing do not want a leftist President who may be a thorn in the way of a compromise. . . . It is imperative . . . to have a President who will be an anti-federationist to the core of his heart.[196]

Bose then said he preferred not to run and if another leftist would run, he would immediately quit the race. However, he would not step aside for Sitaramayya. The lines were drawn, the contestants ready. On January 29, 1939, Subhas Bose was elected Congress president, besting Sitaramayya by 1,580 votes to 1,375. Subhas Bose had won a victory, but a serious war with the Gandhians was just beginning.[197]

CHAPTER NINE

'We must sail in different boats':[1]
Gandhi vs. Bose, 1939–41

After all Subhas Babu is not an enemy of his country.
Mahatma Gandhi, 1939 statement[2]

Congratulations party contemplating posterior of Jawaharlal Nehru.
Hiren Mukherjee telegram to Jayaprakash Narayan, 1939[3]

The love of my conception, if it is as soft as a rose petal, can also be harder than flint. . . . I had the thought I had gained Subhas Babu for all time as a son. . . . I had the pain of wholly associating myself with the ban pronounced on him.
Mahatma Gandhi, 1940 statement[4]

I

The victory of Subhas Bose in the presidential race came as a surprise to Mahatma Gandhi and his closest colleagues. The leftists throughout India had backed Bose. This was *the* high-watermark of their unity in the twentieth century, perhaps a modest accomplishment. Bose also had considerable backing in some regions of India (e.g., the Punjab) and strong support from his home province, then one of the most populous areas of India. In addition, there was anti-Sitaramayya feeling in Tamilnadu, and some impatience with the Gandhian high command in other areas. So Bose, the much-better known and more charismatic candidate, won through in this round by 1,580 votes to 1,375 and was to be Congress president for 1939.[5]

The victory for a candidate opposing his own choice, however, awakened Gandhi from his somnolence and he issued a hostile and self-accusatory statement from Bardoli two days later. In part, the Mahatma said,

Shri Subhas Bose has achieved a decisive victory. . . . I must confess that from the very beginning I was decidedly against his re-election. . . . I do not subscribe to his facts or the arguments in his manifestos. I think that his references to his colleagues were unjustified and unworthy. Nevertheless, I am glad of his victory. And since I was instrumental in inducing Dr Pattabhi not to withdraw . . . the defeat is more mine than his . . . it is plain to me that the delegates do not approve of the principles and policy for which I stand.

I rejoice in this defeat. . . . Subhas Babu, instead of being President on the sufferance of those whom he calls rightists, is now President elected in a contested election. This enables him to choose a homogeneous cabinet and enforce his programme without let or hindrance. . . . After all Subhas Babu is not an enemy of his country. He has suffered for it. In his opinion his is the most forward and boldest policy and programme. . . . The minority may not obstruct on any account. They must abstain when they cannot cooperate.[6]

Here Gandhi gives hints of what is to come. He says the vote was a defeat for his principles and for the rightist team of Gandhians who had long run the Congress organization. And it was a sign of strength for those Bose called the left and for a program of resolute opposition to the Raj, and issuance of an ultimatum to the rulers by nationalist insurgents. But even more than these suggestions in Gandhi's words, it is a *challenge* to Bose to man the Congress executive and run it according to his principles and program. Gandhi had maintained since he came to the fore in Indian politics after the First World War, that executive bodies had to be *homogeneous.*

Immediately after the election and throughout the next few months, Bose was conciliatory towards Gandhi and the Gandhians. In response to Gandhi's statement, Bose did not express the bitterness he felt about Gandhi's words ('not an enemy of his country'), but rather said,

I do not know what . . . opinion Mahatmaji has of me. But whatever his view may be, it will always be my aim and object to try and win his confidence for the simple reason that it will be a tragic thing for me if I succeed in winning the confidence of other people but fail to win the confidence of India's greatest man.[7]

Gandhi and his men, angry with Bose's description of them in *The Indian Struggle* and elsewhere as has-beens, as tired old reactionaries not prepared for the coming and necessary struggle, were preparing to teach Bose a lesson. On February 22, all the Working Committee members—except the Boses—and seemingly including leftist Jawaharlal Nehru, resigned, leaving the Congress with a president marked for the helm, but without a crew to run the ship.

Bose wanted Gandhi's approbation. He wanted the satisfaction of victory over confining authority, but he wanted approval from the defeated party as well. Bose met with Gandhi on February 15, and thought he would have Gandhi's support, but the resignations were a warning. He had castigated the 'Old Guard' in his book and taunted them as compromisers, and yet he wanted them to continue to run the Congress organization with him. 'He was,' J.B. Kripalani told me, 'living in a fool's paradise.'[8]

M.N. Roy, now leader of the League of Radical Congressmen, suggested a homogeneous leftist Working Committee with himself as the general secretary. Giving his interpretation, Roy wrote to Bose,

> . . . there is absolutely no reason for you not to assert yourself. . . . The significance of the result of this year's presidential election has been correctly. . . characterised by Gandhiji himself; *he has been defeated.* . . . The Congress must be given a new leadership, entirely free from the principles and pre-occupations of Gandhism which until now determined Congress politics. Gandhist principles cannot be reconciled with honest anti-imperialist politics . . . the new leadership of the Congress should have the courage and conviction of acting independently even of the wishes of Gandhiji, when these run counter to the objective revolutionary urge of the movement.[9]

The leftists in the CSP, CPI, Royists, kisan sabhas, and those not in a formal group, had voted solidly for Bose; now the consequences were upon him. The CPI is said to have wanted a group in the executive, while the CSP thought a majority of leftists would do.[10] But Bose had said even before the election that the leftists were disorganized and occasionally irresponsible. They were also a minority in the Congress. Bose did not want a split in the Congress. He wanted to serve as president again, and he wanted all groups with him as he tried to push the Congress towards a confrontation with the Raj. Could he have his *rossogolla* and eat it too?

While the Gandhi group was determining its course of action, Bose was reaching out to the Congress Socialists, to Gandhi himself, to M.N. Roy, and especially to Jawaharlal Nehru. He knew that Nehru was crucial, for the latter was the one person who talked like a socialist but was trusted by all sides. Nehru later wrote about this time, 'I decided to devote my energies towards bridging the gulf between the old leaders and the new socialist group.'[11] However, as Nehru explained to Bose, he did not have the same sharp view of two opposed camps, one left, one right. Nehru wrote,

> . . . there seemed to me no valid reason why there should not be the fullest cooperation between the two in the struggle against imperialism. The old leaders were tried men with prestige and influence among the masses and the experience of having guided the struggle for many years. They were not rightists by any means; politically they were far more left and they were

confirmed anti-imperialists. Gandhiji . . . continued to dominate the Indian scene and it was difficult to conceive of a big struggle without him. The socialists, though a small group and speaking for a minority, represented a vital and growing section. . . . [12]

Nehru told Bose that he had learned to work with the older leaders and that they were real fighters. Nehru did tend to be vague and vacillate upon occasion, but he never questioned the anti-imperialist devotion of the Gandhians and did not think they were ready to compromise on the federation issue. Nehru had warmth and respect for some of the Gandhians like Maulana Azad, and beyond this, Nehru had a relationship of mutual love and trust with Gandhi. Bose did not have such a relationship with the Mahatma. Gandhi did not fully trust him. Gandhi and his 'deputy' for Congress organizational matters, Sardar Patel, were angry, but as past masters of political maneuver they knew that careful planning and calculated moves were preferable to emotional gestures. Gandhi said that the minority—meaning his forces for the moment—must not 'obstruct' and must 'abstain when they could not cooperate.' The resignations from the Working Committee were the first indication to Bose what this was to mean.

The Congress session for 1939 was held in Tripuri in the Central Provinces, opening on March 10. Compared to the previous Congress session in Haripura, where Subhas Bose had made a triumphal entry and a lengthy speech, this was a much more somber occasion. First, there was the dilemma of choosing a new Working Committee. The Working Committee had been scheduled to meet at Wardha on February 22, but since Subhas Bose had fallen seriously ill, he had asked other committee members through Sardar Patel to postpone the meeting until Tripuri. This postponement of ordinary and important Congress business simply because the president was ill angered some Working Committee members. They took it as yet another insult from Bose, i.e., that he could not trust them to conduct any Congress business without his presence. This helped to precipitate their resignations. So for the moment there was no Working Committee. Normally the Congress president would nominate the new committee at the end of the upcoming Congress session.

Second, war clouds were darkening in Central Europe and East Asia. The Germans were in the process of dismembering Czechoslovakia, the Japanese were advancing into China, and Franco's insurgents were triumphant in Spain. Through 1935 to 1938, the British and the French Governments had assiduously followed the policy of appeasement, much to the horror of Winston Churchill and of Nehru, among others. As the Germans seized the Rhineland, pushed their rearmament program rapidly forward, and swallowed Austria and now Czechoslovakia, it was ever clearer that even these steps would not placate Hitler. The Japanese, now allied to the Germans and Italians through the Anti-Comintern Pact, were set on the conquest of China and on access to all the necessary resources for building a mighty empire.

Third, Bose had fallen seriously ill after meeting Gandhi in mid-February. His recovery was slow and irregular. Doctors recommended that he not undertake the long journey and ardors of the meeting where controversy was sure to erupt. He ignored their warnings. He felt that even with a dangerously high fever and incapacitated as he was, he had to attend. So Bose, with a temperature of 104° F, was taken by ambulance, with his niece Ila Bose as nurse, and attended by Dr and Mrs Sunil Bose and his mother, from his Elgin Road house to Howrah Station.[13]

Gandhi, however, decided not to come to Tripuri, insisting that activities in the princely state of Rajkot were a more important claim on him at the moment. The Gandhians, though, were there and were a formidable group. They knew their strengths and they knew Bose's weaknesses. His support was soft and not well organized; theirs was firm and much better marshaled.[14]

The crucial conflict at Tripuri revolved around the Pant Resolution. This was the Gandhians' initiative in round two. In the closed Subjects Committee meeting, Pandit Pant, an able Gandhian leader from UP, resolved that,

> In view of various misunderstandings that have arisen in the Congress and the country on account of the controversies in connection with the Presidential Election and after, it is desirable that the Congress should clarify the position and declare its general policy.
>
> (1) This Congress declares its firm adherence to the fundamental policies which have governed its programme in the past years under the guidance of Mahatma Gandhi and is definitely of opinion that there should be no break in these policies and they should continue to govern the Congress programme in future. This Congress expresses its confidence in the work of the Working Committee which functioned during the last year and regrets any aspersions should have been cast against any of its members.
>
> (2) In view of the critical situation that may develop . . . Gandhi alone can lead the Congress and the country to victory during such a crisis, the Congress regards it as imperative that the Congress executive should command his implicit confidence and requests the president to nominate the Working Committee in accordance with the wishes of Gandhiji.[15]

Bose supporters, principally those from the left, offered amendments and asked that the resolution be postponed because of his ill health. The Gandhians would have none of this. They were set on a test of strength.

As the forces for each side caucused, it soon became clear that the left was now seriously divided. The largest left grouping was the CSP, and they had endeavored to bring as large a delegation to Tripuri as they could. Their foremost leader, Jayaprakash Narayan, was disturbed by Bose's insistence on the issuance of a timed ultimatum to the British. Personally friendly with Gandhi, Narayan now also found himself on the same side of the political fence as the Mahatma on this issue: nationalist India was not ready. Narayan and many other top CSP leaders also felt that Gandhi was *the* essential man in the national movement. They hoped to make him a socialist, but they, like Nehru, could not conceive of a mass movement in the country without Gandhi. After some indecision, Narayan got a majority in the CSP to opt for a national demand to be put before the British without the terminal date which Bose wanted, and neutrality on the Pant Resolution.[16] Since the CSP constituted the largest organized bloc of leftists, their neutrality was a mortal blow to Bose.

Some in the CSP group were unhappy with this decision. Within the CSP bloc were some members of the CPI. Although General Secretary P.C. Joshi was ready to abstain, some Bengal communists would not give way without a further fight. They insisted on a meeting of the CPI Executive Committee. This body decided to vote against the Pant Resolution. Niharendu Dutt-Mazumdar claims that Joshi said, 'Our throat is cut.' Dutt-Mazumdar says he responded to Joshi, 'Your masters in the Communist Party of Great Britain may be annoyed, but this will save India's throat.'[17]

M.N. Roy and Dutt-Mazumdar, among others, offered compromise resolutions in an effort to dilute the Pant Resolution. Dutt-Mazumdar said that the resolution showed 'a spirit of vindictiveness on the part of the members of the Working Committee.' He regarded it as a 'back door method' of attacking the Congress president.[18] All the amendments failed by a margin of about 218 to 135.[19] Though Bose had some leftist support from the Royists, the CPI, and even some CSP members sufficiently disaffected by Narayan's stand to vote against the Pant Resolution, they were outmanned.

Several of the Gandhians spoke effectively for the resolution and C. Rajagopalachari, or Rajaji as he was popularly known, is reported to have said, in part, 'The Nirbada is a very deep river. We can't trust ourselves in a leaky boat.'[20] Pandit Pant also spoke strongly for his resolution. He said that if the delegates wanted Gandhiji back they had to prove it to him. The *Indian Annual Register* reported,

> ... Pandit Pant said that wherever nations had progressed they had done so under the leadership of one man. Germany had relied on Herr Hitler.

Whether they agreed with Herr Hitler's methods or not, there was no
gainsaying the fact that Germany had progressed under Herr Hitler.
Similarly, Italy had risen because of Signor Mussolini and it was Lenin that
raised Russia.[21]

The Pandit reminded the delegates that 'we have Gandhi. . . . Then why
should we not reap the full advantage of that factor?'[22] Pandit Pant denied
the suggestion that the resolution savored of vendetta and he disarmed
some of the opposition by saying, in effect, that the resolution was for
Gandhi, not against Bose. Meanwhile it was reported that, 'When the
discussion on the resolution was going on in the Subjects Committee a
news [report] appeared that through telephonic communication the
approval of Gandhiji had been secured for it.'[23] This event may have been
stage-managed, since Gandhi later said that he had not participated in the
formulation of this resolution. In any case, all amendments failed and the
resolution was passed by the Subjects Committee. Then it was brought
before the open session of the Congress.

In the open session, there was some rowdiness and Nehru was heckled
while speaking. Sarat Bose had to quiet the crowd. However, with most of
the Congress Socialists abstaining, the Pant Resolution was passed. The
Gandhians agreed to pass the national demand resolution in the form
desired by the Congress Socialists.[24] The left, which had united in electing
Bose, was now divided, with some of the left agreeing with Nehru that
national unity took priority and Gandhi was the leader of that unity of
nationalists. In the Marxist terminology of that time: national unity before
class unity. Bose, who like Nehru and the CSP, did not want to split the
Congress, was put in a tenuous position as to choosing the Working
Committee. He now had to select a committee 'in accordance with the
wishes of Gandhiji.'

The European press, represented by the Calcutta *Statesman*, identifying
with the Gandhians, had its own interpretation of the conflict:

> The issue at Tripuri can, we think, be reduced to simple language by saying
> that it is between those who recognize where the menace to India's freedom
> comes from and those who do not. The 'Left' wish to go on believing or
> pretending that Britain is the enemy. The 'Right' know that to throw away
> self-government after it has been won in the Provinces, and undertake a
> struggle with Britain at a moment when the only issue left between Britain
> and India is the regulation of the time programme as regards full status, and
> when free institutions alike in Britain and India are in grave danger, is to
> work for Hitler, Mussolini and the Japanese War Lords. Every vote given
> against Pandit Pant's resolution at Tripuri was a vote for the Axis and the
> defeat of Democracy.[25]

This complacent attitude about the ease of the path to self-government and about how Indians interpreted the world conflict was to be tested and changed by events to come. But it did indicate how much antipathy Bose and some of the left aroused in the hearts of India's European community.

II

Bose went into seclusion with relatives at Jealgora near Dhanbad in Bihar to try to recover his health.[26] He spent more than a month there trying to shake off his 'strange illness.' Some friends and doctors said it was severe influenza. Others had more unusual hypotheses. Family pundit and Sanskrit scholar, Asoke Nath Sastri, along with a few other pundits and astrologers had a meeting, Bose said, to discuss his illness. Their idea was that '. . . somebody in some part of the country had been practising what is known in the Tantra-Shastra as *Marana-Kriya*—that is, attempt to kill by tantric process or will-power.'[27] Bose himself was dubious since he believed that he had a 'rationalistic mind,' but friends pressed amulets on him to help fight the illness. He wrote,

> . . . in a moment of weakness, I yielded. I accepted a couple of rings and four amulets. I accepted only those from friends whom I knew and who were not actuated by any professional motive. . . . I compromised with my innate rationalism—but as soon as the Tripuri Congress was over, I relieved myself of the two rings and four amulets. And now my rationalism is safe and I can trust to nature and my luck![28]

Although Subhas Bose was dubious, he was surrounded by others in whom there still remained some belief in the magical powers of the mind for good and evil. He maintained to the end that the irregular course of the symptoms showed that there was something 'mysterious' or unexplained in it all.

While he remained in Jealgora, he carried on a heavy correspondence with Jawaharlal Nehru, Mahatma Gandhi, and others. Sarat Bose also wrote a number of letters to Gandhi and Nehru, the first of these to Gandhi, filled with bitterness against some of Gandhi's associates for the way they had behaved at Tripuri.[29] The manifest topic was the resolution of the Congress crisis created by the passage of the Pant Resolution. But into this tumbled all kinds of related and unrelated issues, grievances, and feelings.

For his part, Subhas Bose addressed Nehru and Gandhi in very different ways. Gandhi was the movement elder and some believed the main partisan of the opposite point of view, but Bose wrote,

> People who are bitterly opposed for various reasons to Sardar Patel and his group, still have confidence in you and believe that you can take a dispassionate and non-partisan view of things. To them you are a national figure—above parties and groups—and you can therefore restore unity between the warring elements.

If for any reason that confidence is shaken . . . and you are regarded as
a partisan, then God help us and the Congress.[30]

Throughout the extended series of exchanges in March and April 1939,
Bose wrote to Gandhi most respectfully. And he begged, he implored,
Gandhi to compromise. Did Bose really believe that the Mahatma had no
hand in the counterstrike of the old guard against the insurgent Bose and
his supporters? Hadn't Gandhi said that the victory of Bose over
Sitaramayya was his defeat? In light of the Pant Resolution, however, Bose
knew that he had to have some input from Gandhi to form the Working
Committee, and so whatever he might have suspected about Gandhi's role,
he continued to write to Gandhi in a humble and tactful way. He had had
his election victory; now he needed Gandhi's support or at least
acquiescence if he was to serve out his second term in office.

The letters to Nehru were a different matter. They were blunt; they were
bitter; they were often rude and nasty. Bose claimed that he had been
respectful to Nehru in the past,

> . . . ever since I came out of internment in 1937, I have been treating you with
> the utmost regard and consideration, in private life and in public. I have
> looked upon you as politically an elder brother and leader and have often
> sought your advice. When you came back from Europe last year, I went to
> Allahabad to ask you what lead you would give us.[31]

But when the crunch came, when Bose decided to challenge the Gandhians
at the end of 1938, he found that his socialist colleague, his 'political elder
brother', was not with him. Nehru did not view the Congress in quite the
same left versus right terms as Bose, and thought Gandhi was the vital heart
of the movement. Nehru felt that Bose's 'aspersion' against the old guard
was wrong and unwarranted. Even Sarat Bose is reported to have said
privately that Subhas should not have made suggestions which he could
not prove.[32]

Why was Nehru against Bose's re-election? He wrote,

> I was against your standing for election for two major reasons: it meant
> under the circumstances a break with Gandhiji and I did not want this to take
> place. . . . It would mean also, I thought, a set-back for the real Left. The Left
> was not strong enough to shoulder the burden by itself and when a real
> contest came in the Congress, it would lose and then there would be a
> reaction against it. . . . I saw also that you were closely associated with a
> number of odd individuals who were apparently influencing you considera-
> bly. . . . I call them adventurist in the technical political sense. . . . The fact
> that in international affairs you held different views from mine and did not
> wholly approve our condemnation of Nazi Germany or Fascist Italy added
> to my discomfort. . . . I felt all along that you were far too keen on re-
> election.[33]

Nehru also said that he felt that Bose did not stand for any definite program, that Bose's leftism was rather vague. It consisted of loud slogans, not an alternative approach to that of Gandhi. He added that he thought that the Congress organization and secretariat had declined during the Bose regime, that Bose had been a passive executive. In contrast to his experience of learning to work with the Gandhians, Nehru said that Bose had not changed and some of Bose's actions made him realize 'how difficult it was to work together with you.'[34]

Nehru's charges against Bose were blunt, but not spiteful. Nehru was sure enough of himself, of his position. in the Congress, and of his ideological stance that he did not evince the rancor that Bose—who believed that he was the one who had been wronged and maligned—did. Before examining Bose's charges against Nehru and others, it must be made clear that from the time of Bose's re-election, through the Congress session, into the following period, Nehru wanted a compromise between Bose and the Gandhians. As he wrote to Gandhi in April 1939,

> Subhas has numerous failings but he is susceptible to a friendly approach. I am sure that if you made up your mind to do so you could find a way out. . . . I think now, as I thought in Delhi, that you should accept Subhas as president. To try to push him out seems to me to be an exceedingly wrong step. As for the Working Committee, it is for you to decide. But I do think the idea of homogeneity, if narrowly interpreted, will not lead to peace or effective working.[35]

Nehru's concerns were: to prevent a serious split in the Congress, and to keep it working as an effective organization. From his perspective, therefore, it was necessary to have Gandhi and the Gandhians in the leadership, and desirable to have Bose and other socialists. Enforcing a 'narrow' homogeneity might lead to the very cleavage which Nehru wished to avoid. Nehru urged Gandhi to compromise with Bose and to actively help the latter form the Working Committee. But Gandhi had his own perspective on these matters and furthermore, Bose was in a raging mood, especially vis-à-vis Nehru, after Tripuri.

As indicated in the quotation from Bose above about Nehru as his 'elder brother' in politics, Bose expected much from a brother—his real elder brother Sarat was his main supporter in life and politics—and when he felt let down, the bitterness was most profound. In the course of his very long and revealing letter to Nehru of March 28, 1939, Bose said to him,

> . . for some time past you have become completely biased against me. . . since the Presidential election, you have done more to lower me in the estimation of the public than all the twelve ex-members of the Working Committee put together. Of course if I am such a villain, it is not only your right but also your duty to expose me before the public.[36]

In the course of this letter, Bose dissected and attacked Nehru as Congress president, and Nehru's approach to international affairs, Nehru's logic, Nehru's contribution to the Indian left, and tried to show Nehru how cleverly Sardar Patel toyed with the former in Working Committee meetings.

Boxed into a corner as he was by the Pant Resolution, by his lack of allies, and by Gandhi's unwillingness to compromise, Bose struck hard at the person he thought could have and should have helped him the most. In response to Nehru's charge that he had no program, Bose answered that Nehru's contribution to the left had lately become nil and he had become merely a smooth-talking apologist for the dominant right in the Congress. Bose said he was for a 'dynamic move from our side—for an ultimatum to the British Government demanding Purna Swaraj,' and could not understand why Nehru was not with him.[37]

Bose agreed that their approaches to the international context were different. In part, Bose wrote,

> In international affairs, your policy is perhaps even more nebulous. I was astounded when you produced a resolution before the Working Committee some time ago seeking to make India an asylum for the Jews. Foreign policy is a realistic affair to be determined largely from the point of view of a nation's self-interest. Take Soviet Russia, for instance. With all her communism in her internal politics, she never allows sentiment to dominate her foreign policy. . . . Even today, Soviet Russia is anxious to enter into a pact with British Imperialism. Now, what is your foreign policy, pray? Frothy sentiments and pious platitudes do not make foreign policy. It is no use championing lost causes all the time and it is no use condemning countries like Germany and Italy on the one hand and on the other, giving a certificate of good conduct to British and French Imperialism. . . . I have been urging . . . everybody . . . including Mahatma Gandhi and you, that we must utilise the international situation to India's advantage and . . . present the British government with our National Demand in the form of an ultimatum; but I could make no impression on you or on Mahatmaji, though a large section of the Indian public approved of my stand. . . .[38]

Nehru, of course, defended his approach. He said that he wanted to offer asylum to a few well-qualified Jewish refugees and not open the gates of India wide to all Jewish refugees. He did not mention his staunch defense of Republican Spain, but he certainly saw no reason to go back on this because they had lost.[39] Nehru felt a solidarity with certain groups and 'lost causes' in other countries. Bose gave priority to Indian nationalism and to the vanquishing of British imperialism in India that crowded out other concerns. Bose could see the connection of the plight of colonial people throughout Asia and Africa and even comment on it as he did when he was in Europe in 1936 and 1938. But he was an Indian-firster, more narrow and focused in his vision than Nehru. If Bose had some points in common with Nehru, he had fewer points in common with Gandhi.

Gandhi was a political master. Combining native intelligence with legal training and long experience, he was a formidable opponent. Bose tried to persuade Gandhi that the latter was above mere politics, and that Bose accepted him as *the* leader. Gandhi would not bend. He said he bore no ill-will towards anyone, but he had some anger at Bose, hardly even hidden. Seeing the strengths and weaknesses of each side, understanding Bose perhaps better than Bose understood himself, Gandhi offered Bose a challenge in every communication from the election to the end of April. What Gandhi was saying to Bose was: show me your team; show me your program; show me that the country supports your approach rather than mine. If you have no adequate team, if you have no workable program, if you have limited support, get out of the way, and let my men get on with my program. For example, as the correspondence continued, sounding like a broken record, Gandhi wired Bose on April 19,

> Despite many suggestions contained in your letters, I feel helpless, carry out terms of Pant's Resolution in this atmosphere of mutual distrust, suspicions and in face of marked differences between groups. I still maintain you should boldly form committee. It would be unfair to you with the views you hold.[40]

And, in a letter written about the same time to confidante Amrit Kaur, Gandhi said, 'Here is a copy of further correspondence with Subhas Chandra Bose. What is one to do? Resoluteness seems to be the only answer if one has faith in one's judgment.'[41]

Was Bose lacking in 'resoluteness'? Why did he not pick up Gandhi's repeated challenge and name his own homogeneous Working Committee composed of the ablest among the Indian left? Although there was a great outpouring of letters from Bose at this time, it is difficult to answer these questions. However, it does seem that although Bose believed that the Pant Resolution was *ultra vires* and unconstitutional, he felt that when it was brought up, he could not rule it out of order. And once it was passed by the annual Congress session, he had to do his best to abide by its provisions. So he needed Gandhi's approval of whatever Working Committee, he as president, might name. Gandhi would surely not approve a committee of leftists opposed to his program. Bose hoped that Gandhi would eventually shift ground enough to agree to a committee half from the right (named by Patel) and half named by himself.

Second, after the fiasco at Tripuri, Bose had lost faith in many on the left and may even have agreed with Rajaji that such a group could make a sound boat into a leaky one. About the same time that Bose wrote a letter to Gandhi begging him to compromise, he wrote a letter to a relative in which some opinions about stalwarts of the left were expressed. To Amiya Nath Bose, he wrote, in part,

> Our defeat [*at Tripuri*] was due further to the betrayal of the C.S.P. leadership and some bungling in tactics on our side. The C.S.P. is now being shaken to its foundations owing to revolt among the rank and file against the Tripuri policy of the leaders. The Communist Party was also sailing with the C.S.P. but at the last moment, the revolt of the rank and file brought about a reversal of the policy decided by the C.P. leaders. . . . Nobody has done more harm to me personally and to our cause in this crisis than Pandit Nehru. If he had been with us—we would have had a majority. . . . The immediate future is very uncertain. . . It is even possible that ultimately I may have to resign.
>
> The C.S.P. has gone down in public estimation, but that does not mean that M.N. Roy has gained. . . . He is too individualist and cannot go in for team-work. That is a great drawback for him.[42]

So where were the leaders of the left? The CSP had betrayed him, Nehru had done him the greatest damage, and M.N. Roy could not work in a team. By this accounting Bose was left with very few nationally-known and accepted leaders from the socialist tendency of the Congress to pluck for his Working Committee.

Third, Bose was a devoted Congressman. He joined the Congress as a full-time political worker in 1921 and this remained his party. He differed with Gandhi, he wanted to move in different directions at certain times, and he usually wanted to move more rapidly, but he wanted to move with the Congress. He did not want to see it split and he knew that however he had castigated the older 'reactionaries' of the Congress, he needed Gandhi and he needed Patel and his men to run the Congress organization. But they would not serve with Bose. Why were they so adamant? Why was Gandhi unwilling to compromise as even Nehru wanted him to?

Gandhi felt that violence was spreading in India, in the air, and on the ground. He wrote in *Harijan,* in January 1939,

> Strife at Congress elections is becoming a common occurrence. The indiscipline of Congressmen is on the increase everywhere. Many of them make irresponsible, even violent, speeches. . . . Bihar Ministers live in perpetual dread of kisan risings and kisan marches. . . . Rome's decline began long before it fell. The Congress . . . need not fall at all, if the corruption is handled in time. . . . Out of the present condition of the Congress I see nothing but anarchy and red ruin in front of the country. Shall we face the harsh truth at Tripuri?[43]

Subhas Bose as Congress president had not stopped the diffusing corruption and incipient violence. Indeed, one of Gandhi's men, J.B. Kripalani, has said that Gandhi knew a lot more about Bose's connections to men of violence and to plans for potential violence than he ever let on in public.[44] Gandhi may well have known of Bose's meeting with German officials in Bombay in December 1938. The compilers of the *Indian Annual Register* argued at the time that the release in 1938 to the Indian public of Bose's *Indian Struggle* was a crucial factor. Previously, the work had been banned in India. Now all of the old guard could learn for themselves how little Bose thought of them. Although there is no direct testimony to it, it may be that, 'The book stood in the way.'[45] Furthermore, Gandhi likely understood that Bose did believe in trying mass non-violent struggle first, but, if it did not work, if it did not bring freedom for India, Bose was prepared to use other means. As the fuse of the world crisis burnt down to the end, and as he saw increasing violence and corruption around him, Gandhi was less willing to have Bose at the helm in 1939. So Gandhi would not compromise and the matter of the Congress executive was coming to a boil as its leaders came to Calcutta in late April for a meeting of the AICC.

III

Through these weeks of letter and telegram exchanges between the Boses, Gandhi, and Nehru, others also put forth their suggestions. M.N. Roy, following the line he had taken after Bose's election, wanted Bose to go ahead and form a left Working Committee. When Bose hesitated, Roy is reported to have said that a Roman general who won't take advice was not worth fighting for.[46] The CSP was in turmoil and some members, particularly in the small Bengal cadre of the party, resigned. Tridib Chaudhuri and several others eventually formed the Revolutionary Socialist Party.[47] Hiren Mukherjee, a young communist member of the CSP, ill at the time of the Tripuri Congress, says that he sent J.P. Narayan a telegram: 'Congratulations party contemplating posterior of Jawaharlal Nehru.'[48] Sharp criticism of Bose was made by ex-revolutionaries now running the Calcutta newspaper, *Forward*, who said that 'the real revolutionary elements in the country' offered Bose advice on whom he should put on the Working Committee. They continued,

> But Subhas Babu, having revolted for nothing other than the Presidentship, carried a blank mind as far as a plan or a programme was concerned. . . . He had not the courage to accept the plan of action placed before him. . . . When asked why he was not acting in this situation, he replied that his supporters were 'shaking in their shoes.'. . . The fact of the matter . . . is that Subhas Babu is no radical. . . . When it became obvious that he had no lead to give

and no plan of action to put forward, he could no longer keep his supporters together.[49]

Although Bose insisted that ninety per cent of the left was still with him, it was so fragmented that it did not offer him any solid backing. The left forces could carry on some valuable local organizing, write ideological critiques, and contribute to electing Bose Congress president, but they could not gather under Bose's leadership, and run the Congress organization. Nehru was correct in recognizing that the left was too weak for this. Bose learned it as well.

Near the fag end of the negotiations, just before the AICC was to convene in Calcutta on April 29, Bose and Nehru met. Although some nasty charges had been exchanged, Nehru said the meeting was quite amicable.[50] Gandhi was the only one who could resolve the conflict so that Bose and the left and the Gandhians would work together and have representation on the Working Committee. Gandhi also met with Bose just before the AICC conclave, but still, nothing was resolved.

When the AICC met, Bose described his inability to work out a compromise formula with Gandhi and laid a letter to this effect from Gandhi before the assembly. Then he tendered his own resignation, saying, in part,

> Mahatmaji's advice to me is that I should myself form a Working Committee leaving out the members who resigned from the previous Working Committee. . . . If I formed such a committee . . . I would not be able to report to you that the Committee commanded his implicit confidence.
>
> . . . my own conviction is that in view of the critical times that are ahead of us in India and abroad, we should have a composite Cabinet commanding the confidence of the largest number of Congress possible. . . . I could only repeat my request that he should kindly shoulder the responsibility vested in him by the Tripuri Congress. . . .
>
> As a last step, I tried my best to arrive at an informal solution of the above problem. Mahatmaji told me that the prominent members of the previous Working Committee and myself should put our heads together and see if we could arrive at an agreement. . . . Unfortunately . . . we could not arrive at a settlement. . . .
>
> I have been pondering . . . what I could do to help the A.I.C.C. in solving the problem. . . . I feel that my presence as President at this juncture may possibly be a sort of obstacle or handicap in its path. For instance, the A.I.C.C. may feel inclined to appoint a Working Committee in which I shall be a misfit. I feel . . . that it may possibly be easier for the A.I.C.C .to settle the matter, if it can have a new President. After mature deliberation, therefore, and in an entirely helpful spirit I am placing my resignation in your hands.[51]

Bose did not really want to resign and others, particularly, from the left, were not happy with this solution.

Now Nehru, who all along had been arguing privately with Gandhi and others for a compromise arrangement, offered a motion calling for Bose to withdraw his resignation. Nehru said that the Working Committee from the previous year should be renamed and the slots of two members shortly to resign because of ill health should be filled by Bose's choice. In contrast to Gandhi, Nehru maintained that, '. . . there is no difference between Mr Subhas Bose and Mahatma Gandhi on any issue involving principles.' Like Rajaji, Nehru did not want 'to change horses in mid-stream,' but in the group that Nehru wished to retain, Congress-president elect, Bose, was included.[52] Rafi Ahmad Kidwai and Jayaprakash Narayan rose to support Nehru's motion. The meeting was then adjourned for the day.

The following day, Bose said that he was honored that Nehru had asked him not to resign, but wanted greater consideration for his views about a composite Working Committee than he found in Nehru's proposal. He did not withdraw his resignation, but made it clear that he did not want to resign if he could work with a more 'representative' Working Committee. Leaving the matter, he said, in the hands of the AICC, he sat down. The chair of the meeting, Sarojini Naidu, an experienced Congress leader and former president, found Bose's statement too vague. Also feeling that there had not been a clear response to his motion, Nehru withdrew it. Naidu now pushed the gathering to elect a new president. Niharendu Dutt-Mazumdar and K.F. Nariman objected, but she overrode them and the AICC elected Rajendra Prasad to finish the presidential term until the next full Congress session.

Bose was manifestly unhappy and frustrated, and privately bitter at the course of events. The defeat at Tripuri had been followed by an even more ignominious debacle in Calcutta. Local supporters of Bose greeted Nehru, Pant, and Kripalani with a hostile demonstration as they exited the AICC pandal. They had to be protected by Congress volunteers. Nehru was staying with Sarat Bose at Woodburn Park during these meetings. Sarat Bose's daughter, Gita, had to serve the guest tea after her uncle's resignation. Her father instructed her to do it with utmost politeness, for he said that politics should not affect personal relations.[53]

The new president named the Working Committee. As Bose and Nehru declined to serve, he filled their positions with Dr B.C. Roy and Prafulla C. Ghosh, Bengal Congressmen. The latter was a 'pure khadi' Gandhian; the former, once close to the Boses, had now moved closer to Gandhi and had the respect of the Gandhians and of Nehru. The choice of two non-Bose men from Bengal for the Working Committee indicated that the

Gandhians meant to keep Bengal Congress affairs more directly under their control. It was another slap at the Boses.

In a question-and-answer session at the Gandhi Seva Sangh meeting in Brindaban a few days later, Gandhi made it quite clear that he thought there were fundamental differences in principle with Bose. He said,

> I think he still holds the view he had expressed at Jalpaiguri. . . . It includes giving an ultimatum to the Government. He holds that we possess enough resources for a fight. I am totally opposed to his views. Today we possess no resources for a fight. Today the whole atmosphere is so steeped in violence that I cannot think of fighting. . . . This is a great and fundamental difference of opinion. We differ in our ideas of the resources needed for the struggle. My conception of satyagraha is not his. . . . The same is true of the corruption in the Congress . . . sometimes even the difference of degree becomes a fundamental difference.[54]

There are hints here, but not an explicit statement, that Bose was not only willing to act in an atmosphere surcharged with violence (as Gandhi assessed it), but also to use violence. Gandhi also insisted that the socialists did not support Bose and did not want to issue an ultimatum to the government. He went on, 'The differences between me and the socialists are widely known. . . . But even so the socialists are coming nearer to me every day.' And of Nehru: 'There are certainly differences between Jawaharlal and me. But they are not significant. Without him I feel myself a cripple. He also feels more or less the same way. Our hearts are one.'[55]

Gandhi wondered whether anyone or any group supported Bose in his call for an ultimatum. He said that Gandhians, the socialists, and Nehru were not with him. What he said here and what he and his group demonstrated in the machinations of the first half of 1939 was that the Gandhians, those imbued with his views, still controlled the Congress. Bose had challenged them by standing for election and winning the presidential chair. But when the Gandhians concentrated their efforts and made Congressmen see that the choice was Gandhi or Bose, it was not a close contest.

IV

Subhas Bose and those closely associated with him had suffered a major setback. But as Gandhi was later to say of Bose, he was 'irrepressible'. Within a week of his resignation as Congress president, Bose announced in Calcutta on May 3 the formation of a new grouping *within* the Congress to be called the 'Forward Bloc'. He said that the object was to 'rally all radical and anti-Imperialist progressive elements in the country on the basis of a minimum programme, representing the greatest common measure of agreement among radicals of all shades of opinion.'[56] When he moved to form the Forward Bloc, Bose hoped that all 'radicals,' presumably meaning Socialists, Communists, Royists, Kisan Sabhaists, et al., would join in this bloc. However, those in other functioning organizations would not give up their identities. Some of the left elements were agreeable to joint activities and actions, but Bose was not able to gain members for the Forward Bloc except from among his close associates and those who believed that he stood—before all other alternatives—for the right path of action.

Some six weeks later, the first All-India Forward Bloc Conference was held in Bombay. Seeing that most other leftists would not join the bloc itself, the conference approved the formation of a 'Left Consolidation Committee,' which would be a looser grouping. The aim was to swing the Congress program to what Bose conceived of as the left: the ultimatum to the Raj, the exploitation of the international situation as it unfolded, and after independence, steps to make a socialist India.[57] The Left Consolidation Committee was to have an equal number of representatives from the CSP, Royists, CPI, and Forward Bloc. Although there were some preliminary meetings and negotiations, the whole idea was, at this juncture, something of a pipe dream. The CSP and the CPI were at each other's throats for control of regional branches of the CSP, and the CSP purge of all communists was in the works. M.N. Roy was critical of the CSP and these ties were far from harmonious. The weak showing of the leftists at Tripuri and at the AICC meeting in Calcutta at the end of April demonstrated that little could be expected from this Left Consolidation Committee, and little was achieved. By the time Bose called for mass rallies against certain restrictive Congress policies in July, the brief life of the body was over. An organized, concerted challenge to Gandhi and his program was not forthcoming from a unified left within the Congress. Many of the leftists were moving closer to Gandhi just at the time that Bose was calling for them to rebel against Gandhi's program and the Gandhian leadership. Those leftist elements most cooperative to Bose, and his Forward Bloc were in the provincial and All-India Kisan Sabhas led by Swami Sahajananda Saraswati and Professor N.G. Ranga.[58]

In early July, Bose announced the personnel of the Forward Bloc Working Committee. It included: Subhas Bose, president; Sardar Sardul Singh Caveeshar (Punjab), vice-president; Lal Shankarlal (Delhi), general secretary; Pandit Biswambhardayal Tripathi and Mr K.F. Nariman (Bombay), secretaries. Other prominent members included Mr Annapurniah (Andhra), and Senapati Bapat, and H.V. Kamath (Bombay). In the Bengal Provincial Forward Bloc, Satya Ranjan Bakshi, long-time confidant of Bose, was appointed secretary. It was the skeleton of an all-India party with large aspirations, but with hardly any prominent figures in the leadership, in contrast to the Swarajya Party of C.R. Das and Motilal Nehru some sixteen years earlier.[59] By early August 1939, the Forward Bloc had a weekly paper of the same name, for which Bose regularly wrote editorials. A good part of Bose's energy during the fourteen months following his Congress presidential resignation was spent trying to whip up support for his party and views within the Congress. He toured throughout India, drawing large audiences; however, these crowds of listeners did not signify that the Forward Bloc had become a powerful force on the Indian political scene, though Bose himself believed that he was going from strength to strength.[60]

In his writings and speeches of this period, Bose portrayed himself as a courageous rebel, a challenger of the status quo in the country and in the Congress. He contrasted his 'fighting mentality' with the 'constitutional mentality' of the Gandhians.[61] Proudly, he proclaimed himself an adventurer, a darer, a rebel. In retrospect, he said that, 'The decision to offer myself for re-election was an act of dare devilry...'[62] This self-image was quite consistent with that he had used to describe himself and his ideals since the late 1920s and is found in his essays, prison notebooks, *The Indian Struggle,* and *An Indian Pilgrim.* He also continued in this period, though he was in his early forties, to identify with the young. He called the young and manly to join him in his manly fight against all the reactionary forces of imperialism and within the nationalist camp. His bitterness against those in the Congress who had put him down grew, for his opponents did not leave his views unanswered. In Patna, a group shouting 'Long live Gandhism' hurled shoes and stones at him.

Some left voices in the Congress were quite critical of his course, and Nehru went so far as to call the Forward bloc an 'evil'.[63] Jayaprakash Narayan opposed forming factions in the Congress. He called for socialists to march 'shoulder to shoulder in our common fight against Imperialism.'[64] S. Satyamurti, a member of the Central Legislative Assembly, said that the bloc was 'not helping the struggle against British Imperialism. It is only helping the enemies of the Congress and of the country.'[65] When Bose visited his boyhood hometown of Cuttack in August to preside over the All-Orissa Youths' Conference, Hare Krishna Mahatab, a member of the Congress Working Committee, and Biswanath Das, premier of Orissa, asked him to give up his 'rebelling against the Congress,' for they believed it was disruptive to the nationalist movement.[66] These dissident voices did not slow Bose down, for he firmly believed that he was right and other Congress leaders were wrong on the issue of maximum pressure on the Raj at its time of weakness

V

While Subhas Bose was bringing his rallying cry for the Forward Bloc to the far reaches of the subcontinent, his brother Sarat was, for the most part, anchored in Calcutta. He carried on his professional work, continued to lead the Congress group and the opposition in the Bengal Legislative Assembly, and worked in the Congress organization. Whereas Subhas Bose was a full-time political worker and not a householder in the ordinary sense, Sarat Bose was a man of diverse and heavy responsibilities, which he tried as best he could to systematically fit into the limited hours of each day.

A brief glimpse of Sarat Bose, the lawyer and the man, is given in the testimony of Anil Ganguli, one of his juniors in this period. The Ganguli family had been close to the Boses in Cuttack decades earlier. Anil was at the Calcutta High Court from 1933, but he did not approach Sarat for, he said, 'He was too big.'[67] Sarat Bose was feared and respected by other barristers and was a champion of the juniors. He was concerned that these young men be given the opportunity to work, to rise, and to prosper. Mr Ganguli called him 'the natural leader of the juniors.'

In 1940 Mr Ganguli was asked by S.N. Banerjea, a junior to Sarat Bose in a big case of Nabakumar Mahapatra versus Asla Devi, to 'devil' for him. The deviller was not briefed and gained little but experience from the work. But Mr Ganguli needed the work and accepted. Sarat learned that he was 'Gopa-babu's son,' and became by turns 'informal, firm, warm, violent, and cordial' to Mr Ganguli who felt that Sarat Bose had taken him in as a younger brother. The case was fixed for after Easter and preparations began. Mr Ganguli was in Jalpaiguri, Sarat Bose in Kurseong. So the latter invited the former to come to his house at Giddapahar to work together with him.

They worked ten hours every day on the case and Mr Ganguli noted that Sarat Bose often gave references to previous cases and even the page number from memory. Sarat Bose, he observed, was very quick, worked very hard, and concerned himself with only one brief per day. While some senior barristers would move from case to case, leaving a lot of the work to the junior, Sarat Bose would keep on the single case and check the junior's references. He was quite famous for his skill at cross-examination.

One morning in Kurseong, Mr Ganguli noticed that someone had put an extra quilt over him during the night. It had been Sarat. At the same time, Mr Ganguli remembered a severe rainstorm that occurred there which led Sarat to go out and pick up hailstones. A child-like quality complemented the motherliness and the devotion to work that characterized the man. When Sarat saw the brief, he noticed that Mr Ganguli's name was not there.

'I have no brief,' said the latter. Sarat Bose became angry and sullen. Shortly afterwards, Mr Ganguli was 'briefed,' and his name was added. On another occasion, he went to see him at his suburban garden house at Rishra. Sarat had bought a large hilsa fish. As it cooked on the stove, Sarat kept one eye on it, the other on the brief. To his affectionate portrait of Sarat Bose, Mr Ganguli did add caveats about minor flaws in the character of Sarat Bose: the latter liked to be flattered and upon occasion could be bombastic. But these were small matters in the personality of a talented, generous, industrious, and highly intelligent man.

Besides his legal work, Sarat Bose had to second his beloved Subhas. At Tripuri, where Subhas was ill, Sarat had to read his presidential address. The other realm, as noted earlier, where Sarat had primary responsibility was in the Bengal Legislative Assembly. From late 1938 through the first half of 1939, a particular worry was the Calcutta Municipal (Amendment) Bill put forth by the Huq ministry and the deterioration of communal relations to which it added. It called for some crucial changes in the Corporation electorate and seat-distribution pattern. Although it was a Bengal bill and was focused on the Calcutta city government, it had national implications, for it evidenced the downward spiral of Hindu-Muslim relations.

The bill, introduced in February 1939, but in the works for some time, called for separate electorates for Calcutta Muslims and an increase in their reserved seats from nineteen to twenty-two. It also created a labor electorate to which it allotted two seats. It held the number of General (Hindu) seats at forty-six, reserving seven of these seats for the scheduled castes. It also retained the nominated membership at ten, and kept the business seats and councillors' positions as they were. The total number of seats was increased to ninety-nine, but as the mayor and other critics noted, the Hindus, who constituted seventy per cent of Calcutta's population, were to have about forty-six per cent of the seats. An editorial in the *Calcutta Municipal Gazette* said that 'the nation is made to drink ... (from) the poison cup of communalism.'[68] Calling the bill 'the Huq Award,' the editorialist saw it as a defeat for the citizens of Calcutta and a bill that would split them further along communal lines. Through the discussions of the bill, in the first half of 1939, all the Hindus and some Muslims and other minorities rallied against the bill which reinforced the dormant agitation against the Communal Award of 1932 and aroused feelings of 'the Hindu community in danger.'[69]

Once the bill was introduced, the opposition tried to have it circulated, but failed. Then the bill was referred to a select committee that was to report back quite soon. Four Congressmen were on this committee, but their inability to bring about any change in the allotments in the bill led to their resignations.[70] The bill was debated on April 18, when opposition motions were defeated, and then again from May 1 to 11. The coalition ministerialist party agreed to some small changes, including subtracting two seats from the nominated category and adding one of these to the General (Hindu) elected category. They also decided to reserve four of the eight nominated seats for members of the scheduled castes. All opposition efforts to increase the number of elected as against nominated positions failed.

In his final speech for the opposition on the bill, Sarat Bose said that it had three objectionable features: the replacement of joint by separate electorates, the perpetuation of nominated seats, and the reduction of the Hindu majority in a city in which they constituted such a large percentage of the population. Arguing that it was an anti-national and anti-democratic bill, he cited many examples to show that grants to Muslim institutions had been rapidly increasing under the old system. He pointed out that Fazlul Huq had been elected mayor and many other members of the Muslim League had also been elected as councillors. In conclusion, he said,

> The noble edifice that the late Sir Surendranath Banerjee erected on the foundations of mutual love, mutual toleration and mutual cooperation is now sought to be razed to the ground and in its place a miserable structure is sought to be raised, based on foundations of mutual suspicion, mutual jealousy and mutual unhealthy rivalry. We may lose in this House; I know we are faced with that. But I have the hope, the faith,'the confidence and the courage to resist this Bill and to resist this Act, until it is removed from the Statute Book, which it is out to disgrace.[71]

As Sarat Bose well understood, his side did not have the votes to block the bill. Fazlul Huq defended the provision for separate electorates with vigor, insisting that ninety-nine per cent of India's Muslims wanted this procedure. He answered the speeches of Sarat Bose and Shyama Prasad Mookerjee, and was particularly angry with the Mahasabha leader, who he said had challenged and derided the Muslims of India.[72] With Krishak Praja Party members remaining neutral, it passed by 128 to sixty-five.

The following day, Sarat Bose, who continued to hope that he might work more effectively with Fazlul Huq, addressed a letter to Huq which was later made public. He wrote, in part,

> It is only natural that communal passion worked up to such a pitch should seek outlet in legislative and administrative action. . . . I have tried my best to discover a basis in justice and reasoning for the provisions of the [*Calcutta Municipal (Amendment)*] Bill and particularly for the apportionment of seats laid down in it, but I have failed to find any. It is a measure of the most barefaced communalism. . . . All our attempts to . . .

safeguard the legitimate interests of all the communities . . . have failed
. . . . This intransigence will have disastrous consequences for communal
unity. The Bill has given rise to desperation and distrust among the Hindus
. . . . Not less a regrettable part of the matter is the studied avoidance . . . of
all . . . consultation with the Opposition. . . . This has also been seen in the
case of all Bills and proposals of your Government. . . . This attitude is not
only repugnant to all conventions of parliamentary government, but is
doing great disservice to the cause of communal harmony.[73]

Protest meetings were held against the bill and even a *hartal* was
undertaken on April 16, but although there was a delay because of changes
which the Bengal Legislative Council tried to make in the bill, it was
certified in essentially the form passed by the Assembly and came into
effect the following year.[74]

Throughout the debate on the bill, intense pressure was put on the
Hindu members of the Coalition Ministry to speak up for the Hindu
community. Nalini Sarker and Sir B.P. Singh Roy refused to criticize the
provision for separate electorates, but in the Bengal Legislative Council,
Sarker did ask for three more seats for the Hindus, suggesting that this
might decrease their resentment. A writer in the nationalist *Advance* noted
that the Muslim point of view could easily be understood, but,

> . . . the attitude taken up by the Hindu Ministers have really amazed us
> beyond measure. Mr Nalini Ranjan Sarker, who has a peculiar genius for
> reconciling conscience with expediency, put in the other day a very lengthy
> plea in support of the measure. His whole peroration is a wonderful study
> in the art of pliant accommodation to an admittedly difficult situation.[75]

Months later, in another and even more difficult context, Sarker revealed
that he had been very unhappy with the communalistic approach of the
ministry of which he was a key member, but that he was not yet ready to
resign over this bill.[76] Though the Boses were angered, they did not stop
trying to find ways in which to work with Huq and other Muslims. Since
1937, more and more Muslim members in the Bengal Legislative Assembly
had come over to the opposition which now included a large section of the
Krishak Praja Party, the independent Praja group, and in February was
joined by Shamsuddin Ahmed, who had served briefly as a minister.[77]
Sporadic, semi-secret negotiations with Huq himself also went on.

Fazlul Huq, idolized by segments of the Bengal peasantry for his
mellifluous Bengali oratory, could also make wildly exaggerated
statements. He attacked Hindu officers of the government and then had to
back down and ask for their continued loyalty. He also made speeches
about the wicked abuses of the Muslim community carried out in the
Congress-ruled provinces. When Jawaharlal Nehru read of these charges,
he immediately wrote to Huq, challenging Huq to tour with him from

village to village and take testimony about the incidents. Huq at first accepted the Congress leader's challenge. When Nehru tried to pin Huq down on a specific time and place to start the tour and an itinerary for the investigations, Huq always begged off.[78] The Muslim League also published the Pirpur Report in this period, at the end of 1938, and a contemporary historian has recently put together the many documents of the period in which the Muslim League claimed severe repression of the Muslim minority by the Hindu majority in many regions of India.[79] Although the charges by the Muslim League were extensive, the League, like Huq, refused to be pinned down when Congress leaders, or even officials of the Raj, asked them for an evenhanded inquiry with non-Muslim League evidence-takers. There were undoubtedly some instances of insensitivity and discrimination on the part of some Congress politicians in power during 1937 to 1939, but in retrospect, the claims of extensive repression by the League seem very flimsy.

The discussion of the Bengali Moneylenders' Bill was relatively calm. This was a bill that touched on many aspects of the economy and confronted the relations of moneylenders, mostly Hindus and peasants, often Muslims, particularly in East Bengal. The bill was reported out by a select committee in April and then fully discussed by the Assembly during May and June meetings. The government had shifted its position on some matters as pressures were applied to it by European and wealthy Indian interests. At first the bill did not cover banks, then all banks; finally coverage of banks on a scheduled list was excluded. Commercial loans were later excluded.

Many of the changes sought by the Congress and Krishak Praja opposition were defeated. A long discussion of interest rates spurred efforts by the Congress to lower rates for the creditors, by the Krishak Praja Party to lower them still further, by the Indian Chamber of Commerce to raise them, and by the government to hold them as fixed in the Select Committee version. The government prevailed. In his summary speech for the opposition on June 27, Sarat Bose noted that the Congress had done its best to cooperate in considering the bill. He regretted that certain banks had been excluded from coverage. His major concern was, however, that the basic problem of cheap credit for the peasantry was not addressed. After quoting the Congress election manifesto on this issue, he said,

> ... we feel that merely by reducing the rate of interest, merely by enacting retrospective provisions, you cannot give relief to the poor peasants and workers of the land. Simultaneously with these, you have to make provision for cheap credit facilities and that can be effectively made only by the

State.[80]

Responding for the government, H.S. Suhrawardy said,

> . . . another point raised by the Leader of the Opposition was the question
> of the establishment of rural credit for the people of the province. He stated
> that on this point his party differed from Government. Let him not lay this
> flattering unction to his soul that his party is anxious to establish rural credit,
> because . . . not only do we not differ from him, but we are taking steps for
> the purpose of establishing rural credit. . . . We are already overhauling the
> machinery of co-operative banks. . . . [81]

So here, at least, was a issue of economic importance to Bengal on which,
potentially, Hindus and Muslims, the Congress, the Muslim League, and
the Krishak Praja Party might work together.

There were other issues on which tension continued. One of these was
the release of political prisoners. Huq had been elected on a platform which
included their release, but once he was in office heading a ministry in
which more conservative elements predominated and vital interests of the
Raj were at stake, he acquiesced. General responsibility for the matter was
in the hands of Home Minister Khwaja Nazimuddin. Many prisoners were
released, but following strictures from above, he agreed that for the
remaining this should usually be done on a case by case basis. He also
accepted the belief of officials in the Home Ministry in Calcutta and Delhi
that there were still terrorist plots afoot. An advisory committee was set up
in September 1938 on which Sarat Bose and another Congress nominee
sat.

Apparently feeling that the government was stalling and that the
approach of the two sides differed considerably, Sarat Bose and Lalit
Mohan Das, the Congress representatives, resigned in mid-1939,
demanding the release of the remaining prisoners, 'whose only crime had
been that their country's freedom had been the dream of their life.'[82] They
were not, Bose went on, 'murderers,' as a member of the Coalition Party
had interjected. Furthermore, he asked, would anyone call Michael
Collins, Kemal Pasha or de Valera a murderer today? Nazimuddin replied
that he could not release prisoners on the basis of how noble Sarat Bose
thought their motives were.

The discussion had been brought to a head because many of the
remaining political prisoners in Bengal jails had started a hunger strike.
Through the rainy season of 1939, Subhas and Sarat Bose, Gandhi, and
government officials tried to work out a compromise. But their objectives
differed. The Boses wanted all the prisoners released; Gandhi wanted a
pledge of non-violence and the release of all who took it; Nazimuddin and
the Raj wanted to hold those whom they believed would be potential

disrupters of law and order. Although the hunger strike was ended with the Boses playing a large role in bringing this about, the prisoners were not immediately released and the BPCC continued to agitate for their freedom.[83]

Through most of 1939, the Bengal administration was in flux because of the sudden and unexpected death of the widely respected governor of Bengal, Lord Brabourne, on February 23. A former governor of Bombay, and prospective viceroy, a man of charm and intelligence, Brabourne had served barely one-and-a-half years in Bengal following Sir John Anderson. Among the tributes to him in the Assembly was that of Sarat Bose:

> The legacy that had been bequeathed to him was one of political repression, economic depression and intellectual stagnation. He struggled hard and nobly against adverse conditions . . . he throughout acted as a constitutional governor and brought into the administration of this province a large measure of sympathy, good will and hope. Great and valiant as he was in the service of his country, he was even greater as a man and those of us who had opportunities of coming into close contact with him will readily testify to his nobility of character, his appreciation of realities, and his spirit of service.[84]

During 1939, Sir Robert Reid and Sir John Woodhead, senior ICS officers, each acted as governor of Bengal. The British Government chose Sir John Herbert, a forty-four-year-old Conservative MP of Welsh gentry background, as the new governor. He had served briefly as ADC to the viceroy in the 1920s, was assistant whip of the House of Commons in 1939, and was married to Lady Mary Fox-Strangeways, daughter of the Earl of Ilchester. After talks with Lord Halifax, a friend, and the Marquess of Zetland, secretary of state for India, and a former governor of Bengal, Herbert reached India in September 1939. According to several top ICS officers who served under him, including one who was his private secretary, he did not have the talents necessary for the job.[85]

VI

Subhas Bose continued to be in conflict with the powers in his own party, the Congress. The June meeting of the AICC passed two resolutions which Bose and some other leftists fought. One related to 'satyagraha in provinces,' the other to relations between the Congress ministries and the PCCs. Both were resolved by large majorities.

In response to these setbacks, Bose decided to hold large demonstrations around the country on July 9, 1939, against the resolutions, and in effect, against the majority in his own party. As the fated day approached, allies jumped from the good ship Bose, and the Working Committee pressed him to respect the authority and decision-making process of the Congress organization. These cautionary words had no effect; they spurred the rebel on. Insisting that he was simply exercising his democratic rights and not resisting the lawful and necessary authority of his party, Bose held his meetings, backed by a vote of the BPCC. He said he was ready to follow any discipline 'cheerfully'. He was not pleased, however, with the next step.

> The Working Committee considered the situation. . . . It came to the conclusion that in his explanation Shri Subhas Bose had wholly missed the main point which was that as an ex-President of the Congress and as President of the B.P.C.C. he should have realised that after having received instructions from the President it was his clear duty as a servant of the nation to obey them implicitly even though he differed from the ruling of the President. It was open to him to appeal afterwards if he so desired to the A.I.C.C. or open session. If Subhas Babu's contention that every member is free to interpret the Congress Constitution prevails and if every member were to act on that interpretation, contrary to the decision of the President, there will be perfect anarchy in the Congress. . . . The Working Committee . . . decided that for the grave act of indiscipline, Shri Subhas Babu be declared disqualified as President of the Bengal P.C.C. and to be a member of any elective Congress Committee for three years as from August 1939.[86]

This was a harsh step which Bose did not accept 'cheerfully'.

Bose now saw himself as a martyr in the cause of freedom and revolution, sacrificed on the altar of constitutionalism and reformism by the chief priest, Congress President Prasad, and his assistants, the rightist Working Committee. Bose, said, in part,

> I welcome the decision of the Working Committee virtually expelling me from the Congress for three years. This decision is the logical consequence of the process of 'Right-consolidation' which has been going on for the last few years. . . . The action of the W.C. has served to expose the real character of the present majority party in the Congress. . . . By trying to warn the country about the continued drift towards Constitutionalism and Reformism, by protesting against resolutions which seek to kill the revolutionary spirit of the Congress, by working for the cause of Left-consolidation and . . . by consistently appealing to the country to prepare for the coming struggle—I have committed a crime for which I have to pay the penalty. The sentence meted out to me may have come as a shock to the vast majority of our countrymen, but not to me.[87]

He concluded by appealing to the leftists to fight to restore the spirit of struggle and revolution to the Congress.

While Bose had succeeded in calling attention to himself and his actions, he had further isolated himself from the Gandhian center of nationalist power. Though the Congress Socialists and other leftists were unhappy at the rigoros sentence which Bose had received—and did protest—they had not participated in the demonstrations. Maulana Azad had recently warned the left about disrupting the Congress. The Congress Socialists were listening; Bose was not.[88] And other leftists did not see why Bose should waste so much time and energy fighting resolutions of his own party. Was Bose losing sight of the main enemy in his reaction to ejection from the presidential chair?

At the same time that Subhas Bose was disputing with the Working Committee over demonstrations he had called as leader of an all-India bloc within the Congress, he was also intimately involved with the struggle between the Working Committee and the BPCC. Following the placement of Dr B.C. Roy and P.C. Ghosh on the Working Committee, the minority factions in the Bengal Provincial Congress worked together to challenge the Boses with the powerful assistance of the central Gandhian leadership. Bose had been forced to resign as Congress president. He was suspended from holding any elective Congress office and so had lost his post as president of the BPCC. Now he and those close to him were faced with the prospect of fighting for their position of dominance in the provincial Congress.

The Boses, holding a majority in the BPCC, called a requisition meeting. The minority factions of P.C. Ghosh and the pure khadi-wallahs, of K.S. Roy, of the former Jugantar revolutionaries, and Dr Roy, said that proper notice was not given. At the meeting the Executive Committee of the BPCC was dissolved and reformed, giving them an even smaller place. They protested to the Working Committee.

The Working Committee declared the proceedings of the meeting of July 26, 1939 'null and void,' and called for the BPCC to elect a new president.[89] The Bose-dominated BPCC responded by unanimously re-electing Bose as president, deliberately defying the Working Committee. The Working Committee condemned this action and appointed an election tribunal to deal with district matters. The central executive also appointed an auditor to go into financial irregularities. By the end of 1939, the Working Committee, with B.C. Roy and P.C. Ghosh sitting as members, decided that it had had enough of the Bose BPCC. It listed a number of charges and then called upon Subhas Bose, the president of the BPCC, to answer them. Ill again, he could not attend. In his stead Sarat Bose and Satya Ranjan Bakshi went to Wardha to answer. Dissatisfied with the response, the Working Committee dismissed the standing BPCC and appointed a small committee headed by Maulana Azad to be the new, ad hoc BPCC. Sarat Bose prepared an elaborate reply to all the charges, similar to a lawyer's brief, claiming that the central executive was acting undemocratically and unconstitutionally. However, his appeal was made to the same judges who had made the ruling, and who did not intend to overrule their own handiwork.[90] Thus Bengal from late 1939 had two BPCCs, the official or Bose Congress, and the ad hoc BPCC. This split later touched the Bengal Legislative Assembly where Sarat Bose headed the Bose Congress group, and Kiran Sankar Roy the ad hoc Congress group. The *Amrita Bazar Patrika*, with which Sarat Bose had been feuding for some years and which he had accused of collusion with the Government of Bengal, was a loud voice for the ad hoc side. In 1940, the ad hoc BPCC had a new president, Surendra Mohan Ghosh, a long-time member of the Jugantar Party. Once a revolutionary and on the side of the Boses, 'Modhu' Ghosh and his Jugantar colleagues had switched to the other side. They were now linked to Dr B.C. Roy, Kiran Sankar Roy, P.C. Ghosh and the Gandhian high command. Though some Bengal leftists like Gopal Halder and Niharendu Dutt-Mazumdar remained with the Boses, they were seriously weakened at the provincial level. Sarat Bose still insisted that his brother Subhas was 'by far the most prominent person in the public life of Bengal, not to speak of the position he holds in the other Provinces of India.'[91]

Through the series of controversies in which Subhas Bose had been involved from late 1938 through late 1939, one prominent figure, the giant of India's cultural life, Rabindranath Tagore, supported him stoutly. As he explained, Tagore had had his doubts about Subhas, but now, with Subhas besieged, the Poet spoke eloquently for him and to him in an essay entitled, *'Deshanayak'* [The Leader of the Country]. He said, in part,

> As Bengal's poet, I today acknowledge you as the honored leader of the people of Bengal. The Gita tells us that from time to time the eternal principle of the good arises to challenge the reign of the evil. . . . Suffering from the deadening effect of the prolonged punishment inflicted upon her young generation and disintegrated by internal faction, Bengal is passing through a period of dark despair. . . . At such a juncture of nation-wide crisis, we require the service of a forceful personality, the invincible faith of a natural leader, who can defy the adverse fate that threatens our progress . . . . I have . . . witnessed the beginning of your political *sadhana*. In that uncertain twilight there had been misgivings in my heart. . . . Today you are revealed in the pure light of the midday sun which does not admit of apprehensions. . . . Your strength has been sorely taxed by imprisonment, banishment and disease, but rather than impairing these have helped to broaden your sympathies. . . . You did not regard apparent defeat as final: therefore, you have turned your trials into your allies. More than anything else Bengal needs today to emulate the powerful force of your determina-

tion and self-reliant courage. . . . Let Bengal affirm in one united voice that her deliverer's seat is ready, spread for you. . . . Long ago . . . I sent out a call for the leader of Bengal who had yet to come. After a lapse of many years I am addressing . . . one who has come into the full light of recognition. My days have come to their end. I may not join him in the fight that is to come. I can only bless him . . . knowing that he had made his country's burden of sorrow his own, that his final reward is fast coming as his country's freedom.[92]

Privately as well, Tagore had made every effort to help Bose, asking Gandhi and Nehru in late 1938 and early 1939 to accept Bose as Congress president again without a squabble. In December 1939, Tagore asked Gandhi to have the ban on Subhas lifted and his cooperation cordially invited in 'supreme interest of national unity.'[93] They declined his advise throughout. At the end of 1939, after all the arguments with Bose, they had quite a different view of him from that of Tagore. Writing in *Harijan* in early 1940, Gandhi said,

> The love of my conception, if it is as soft as a rose petal, can also be harder than flint. My wife has had to experience the hard variety. My eldest son is experiencing it even now. I had thought I had gained Subhas Babu for all time as a son. I have fallen from grace. I had the pain of wholly associating myself with the ban pronounced on him.[94]

In Gandhi's ever-expanding network of familial relations, Subhas had been taken in like a son. But his rebelliousness led to his rejection. Like Gandhi's own sons, he had to feel the 'flint' side of Gandhi's love. Shortly thereafter, writing to C.F. Andrews, Gandhi mentioned Tagore's wire asking that the ban on Bose be lifted, and told Andrews,

> If you think it proper tell Gurudev that I have never ceased to think of his wire and anxiety about Bengal. I feel that Subhas is behaving like a spoilt child of the family. The only way to make up with him is to open his eyes. And then his politics show sharp differences. They seem to be unbridgeable. I am quite clear the matter is too complicated for Gurudev to handle. Let him trust that no one in the Committee has anything personal against Subhas. For me, he is as my son.[95]

So Subhas remained the son, but he was the spoilt child who had to have his eyes opened by his elders in the Working Committee. However, though Bose had been repeatedly punished and even humiliated, he had not been brought to heel. Gandhi said that he had to see the error of his ways and apologize for his indiscipline. Bose thought that *he* was on the right path. These were two stubborn men. So perhaps the chasm was 'unbridgeable,' and Bose could never be reclaimed by the Gandhians as an honored son of India.

Jawaharlal Nehru, almost always Gandhi's beloved son, and later his chosen successor as leader of India, had been taking from early 1939 an ever more negative view of Bose's actions. Writing to V.K. Krishna Menon in early 1940, Nehru said,

> Subhas Bose is going to pieces and has definitely ranged himself against the Congress. . . . The pity of it is that Bengal is badly affected by all this development. . . . There is a strong feeling, more especially in the districts of Bengal, against the Bose brothers' dictatorship. In Calcutta the youthful elements are largely with Subhas. There is also in Bengal bitter feeling against some members of the Working Committee. I have no doubt that the Working Committee has acted on occasion very wrongly in regard to Bengal, but I have also no doubt that Subhas Bose has made it exceedingly difficult for the Working Committee to act otherwise. He now talks the most arrant nonsense about rival Congress. . . . The Forward Bloc, which represented an anti-programme rather than anything constructive or defi- nite, is fading away in other provinces. Subhas Bose does not seem to have an idea in his head, and except for going on talking about leftists and rightists he says little that is intelligible.[96]

Nehru continued to work with the mainstream Gandhians, tried to bring the Congress Socialists into the fold, but no longer attempted to conciliate Subhas Bose. Nehru had more vital concerns, for the Second World War had started in September 1939, and as chief architect of Congress foreign policy, he was helping to shape out its response to the world crisis.

VII

At 6 a.m. on September 1, 1939, German tanks rolled across the Polish frontier. The air force had already begun its bombardment. Although Hitler and his forces were on their way to a relatively easy military victory, the Germans were surprised at the response of the British and the French. Appeasement was over. War was declared. In Britain, the arch critic of government laxity, Winston Churchill, now joined the cabinet. The British had to mobilize to fight a powerful opponent and for the coming struggle, the resources, military forces, manpower, and strategic position of the British Empire also had to be utilized.

Officials of the Raj, Viceroy Lord Linlithgow in India, and Secretary of State Lord Zetland in Britain, asked that India take her place fighting on the side of democracy against the forces of barbarism. Indian princes and other loyalists pledged their support, and offered financial help and services to the Crown in its hour of need. The Government of India was empowered under the Defence of India Ordinance '. . . to make such rules as appeared to be necessary or expedient for securing the defence of British India, the public safety, the maintenance of public order or the efficient prosecution of war or for maintaining supplies and services essential to the life of the community.'[97]

The sympathies of Mahatma Gandhi, Jawaharlal Nehru, and many other nationalists were with the Allies against the Axis powers. Gandhi told the viceroy that his feelings were with Britain and from the humanitarian point of view, 'It almost seems as if Herr Hitler knows no God but brute force.'[98] Nehru said to the press in Rangoon, 'We have repeatedly stated that we are not out to bargain. We do not approach the problem with a view to taking advantage of Britain's difficulties.'[99] Tagore joined other Bengal luminaries in calling upon India to stand by Britain and '. . . resist the disastrous policy of domination by force. No Indian would desire that England should lose the battle for freedom she is fighting to-day.'[100] Though the sympathies were clear, though the feeling against fascist brutality was powerful, many nationalists were not willing to actively participate in the struggle for Britain's freedom unless India's freedom was also recognized. For many the war period was, as Michael Brecher has described Nehru's experience, a time of 'inner torment'. The viceroy, asking for Indian assistance in mid-September, announced that the federal parts of the Government of India Act of 1935 would remain suspended during the war.[101]

On September 9, the Congress Working Committee met at Wardha. Subhas Bose, along with Jayaprakash Narayan, Narendra Dev, and M.S. Aney, was specially invited. The result after three days was to call upon the British to make clear their war aims. They supported the Polish people against the German invasion, but said they had no quarrel with Germany. It was from their ruler, the British, that they wanted to know how the principle of democracy—which the British said they were fighting to uphold—was to be applied to India. Although Nehru had said earlier that there was to be no bargaining, there was indeed to be. The Congress would not actively support the war effort unless India was to advance toward independence in the process.

On October 17, the viceroy again appealed for assistance and unity in India. He said he was authorized to say that at the end of the war, His Majesty's Government would be willing to enter into consultation with representatives of the several communities, parties, and interests in India, and with the Indian princes, with a view to securing their aid and cooperation in the framing of such constitutional modifications as might seem desirable. A consultative group with representatives of the parties and the princes was formed to encourage Indian public opinion in the right direction on war issues.[102] To the Congress, this statement was most unsatisfactory. Not only was Indian freedom not mentioned, but the Congress, the largest and best organized nationalist body, was given no special recognition.

Angry, disappointed, unhappy, the Congress leadership moved, perhaps short-sightedly, by having its ministries resign in all provinces where they formed the governments. One after another Congress ministries in Madras, UP, Bombay, Bihar, the Central Provinces, etc., stepped down. The Congress now sought some means to pressure the Raj to make a more adequate response to the question of complete self-government in the war situation. Most Congress leaders still sympathized with the Allies, condemned the Axis, and did not want to seriously undermine the war effort. Resisting talk of civil disobedience for the moment, for which Gandhi said the Congress and the country were not prepared, Gandhi and some Congress leaders did begin to use the term 'constituent assembly' as a route to the solution of the communal problem which the British had maintained prevented constitutional advance. The left-wingers wanted more decisive steps by the Congress, and adherence to the anti-imperialist and anti-fascist stance of the Congress in the pre-war period. Nehru—who had rejoined the Working Committee with the outbreak of war—and the Gandhians did not want to take some impulsive, irrepairable action.[103]

Subhas Bose was not only invited to attend the meeting of the Working Committee, but he was also asked to discuss the war situation with the viceroy. He duly met Linlithgow on October 10. All party leaders had similar hearings. Although pleased with the resignation of the Congress ministries, Bose did not proclaim his sympathies for the fate of British and French democracy. In keeping with his views of the 1930s, he wanted to utilize the war situation for India's advantage. The Congress had to act decisively, he believed, and pressure the British by means of a mass movement to quit India. The issue of a constituent assembly, he suggested, was a secondary one. The main issue was swaraj. In addressing a student conference in early 1940, he said that true patriots had to be wary of a Gandhian compromise with imperialism. Continuing, he said,

> ... why are they thus shirking a struggle?... I presume that they are afraid that once a nation-wide campaign is launched, the control and leadership of the nationalist movement will pass out of their hands.... The Rightists are out of touch with the new forces and the new elements that have come into existence during the last few years. What we may ask, are their contacts with the Kisan Movement, the Working-class Movement, the Student Movement, the Youth Movement and similar radical and progressive movements. . . . They have, moreover, lost ground among our Muslim compatriots.[104]

Then, in keeping with his call for a new leadership, a new hero, to come forth and lead India to freedom, Bose said,

The time has come for all of us to dare and act. . . . I am also reminded of the inspiring words . . . by a famous Italian General . . . 'I shall give you hunger, thirst, privation, forced marches and death, if you will follow me.' Let these words ring in our ears now and inspire us to march forward and to dare and act. Only then shall we win victory and Swaraj.[105]

While Subhas Bose was touring India on behalf of the Forward Bloc and criticizing the Congress vacillation, Sarat Bose was called upon to discuss the war in a different arena, the Bengal Assembly. The Muslim League and Muslim politicians generally were also moving cautiously with respect to support for the war effort. Jinnah wanted British recognition of the Muslim League as the sole spokesman for India's Muslims with a veto over constitutional advances. If this was granted, he was willing to back the war effort. Gratified that Congress ministries were no longer in place in most provinces, Jinnah proclaimed a thanksgiving day on December 22. A number of prominent Muslim Leaguers did not understand this almost childish political act by the austere Jinnah.[106]

Some days before this, the Bengal Coalition Ministry put forth a motion in the Assembly backing the British war effort. Fazlul Huq spoke for the government; Sarat Bose was the main speaker for the opposition. In his motion, Huq said that the Assembly was associating itself with the worldwide abhorrence of totalitarianism and had 'complete sympathy with the British Government'. Further, he moved that Britain make it clear that dominion status was to be granted to India immediately after the war, and '. . . the New Constitution formulated should provide sufficient and effective safeguards for the recognised minorities and interests and should be based upon their full consent and approval.'[107] In his speech, Huq defended the actions of the Raj. He said that the powers taken under the Defence of India Ordinance were necessary because the Congress was stalling on supporting the war. Huq's forthright support of the Raj and his motion caused a good deal of controversy within the Muslim League camp. Huq was forced to defend his position for, as M.A.H. Ispahani wrote to Jinnah, 'The Government War Resolution was opposed tooth and nail in the Coalition Party meeting by some of us. . . .'[108] The war issue, particularly the relationship between the ministers and the Raj, was one on which Jinnah and his Muslim League supporters on the one hand, and Huq and some like-minded Muslim politicians in Bengal and the Punjab on the other, diverged.

Sarat Bose offered several amendments, one to indicate that the Assembly opposed imperialistic as well as totalitarian governments, a second to lament the lack of consultation with 'the people of India', and a third that India should forthwith be recognized as an independent nation.

In support of his amendments, Bose gave his lengthiest Assembly speech. Quoting many British authorities on diplomatic history and his favorite writer, George Bernard Shaw, he said,

> Sir, imperialism even more than totalitarianism has darkened the prospects of human freedom in all parts of this world of ours. Imperialism, I confess, is comparatively ancient and seems to have lost some of its virility for the moment. Totalitarianism is comparatively modern. Totalitarians have all the zeal and the energy of new converts. But that is no reason why we should forget the wrong inflicted on the world by Imperialists and Imperialism. Imperialism and totalitarianism are allies and . . . handmaids of Capitalism. Both have wrought havoc so far as India and Indians are concerned, there is for us no choice between the two. If we hate totalitarianism, we hate imperialism more.[109]

He said that cooperation with the Raj could only take place between equals. 'I do not understand co-operation between a master and his bond-slaves. . . .'[110]

He went through a lot of modern history, particularly of the First World War. He urged Britain to grant India independence so that she could take her stand as a free nation in the cauldron of war. He said that the British had made a 'bogey of minorities'—exaggerated the grievances of the Muslims in denying India her freedom. Calling for immediate independence and a constituent assembly, he concluded with an emotional plea,

> Sir, it is unnecessary to review the long list of British promises made only to be broken, the long list of Indian hopes raised only to be dashed to the ground. . . . We refuse to beg with bated breath and whispering humbleness to subsist in our own land. Self-government is our right—a right not to be granted to us by a foreign power. Self-government is our birth-right—the right to feel the Indian sun, the right to smell Indian flowers, the right to think our own thoughts, to sing our own songs, and to love our kind. It is a right which we are not prepared to barter away in exchange for any false promise on the part of Great Britain or any other nation. If to demand our birth-right is to be a rebel in act and deed . . . quoting the words of a great Irishman I shall say, 'I am proud to be a rebel and shall cling to my rebellion with the last drop of my blood.'[111]

All the amendments failed; the War Resolution of the Huq Coalition Ministry was passed by 142 to eighty-two votes. However, it was not an undiluted triumph for the ruling coalition. One member of the cabinet, the most important Hindu and the finance minister, Nalini Ranjan Sarker, spoke against part of the resolution and abstained in the voting.

Sarker supported the British war effort and the first part of the resolution. This was not the problem. He also agreed that dominion status immediately after the war would be appropriate. What he objected to was that a minority community would have a veto over the terms for granting this new dominion, as Huq's resolution specified. He insisted that this was anti-democratic. The opposition cheered this point, the majority coalition shouted 'shame, shame.'[112]

Sarker, still close to G.D. Birla and to Gandhi, resigned on December 19, and said, in part,

> ... During the first year or so, the Cabinet worked harmoniously and was inspired by a desire to bring about a real improvement in the condition of the masses. But since then, and particularly during the last six months or so, a significant change has come over the outlook of the Cabinet as well as in the relations between the Cabinet and the party ... a communal outlook has unfortunately been gathering force in the country at large ... the former feeling of comradeship no longer obtains ... the Cabinet has also gradually lost its leadership to the party ... a Council of ministers have yielded place to the rashness and selfish predilections of a large party, which is predominantly communal in complexion and is still obsessed by the power which the ballot-box has given it.[113]

Sarker said he could do no further constructive work in a situation in which Muslim League interests and a communal orientation dominated. Sarat Bose, once an ally, and for years a bitter opponent of Sarker, now welcomed him to the opposition side.[114] Sarker's resignation considerably weakened the Hindu side of the coalition, and opened the door to new and different alliance possibilities.

VIII

Through 1940, the Boses continued to reach out for allies. Subhas Bose went on touring India and giving addresses. He warned all those who would listen of the potential compromising tendencies of the Gandhian-run Congress. Since the CSP and some other leftists had sided with the Gandhians, he held that these so-called leftists could no longer wear that label. He received some support from Swami Sahajananda Saraswati and Professor Ranga of the All-India Kisan Sabha organization.

At Ramgarh, just adjacent to the annual Congress session chaired by President Maulana Azad, Bose held an Anti-Compromise Conference in March. He protested the treatment of the Forward Bloc by the Government of India, which had begun to arrest some of his prominent followers.[115] Once at the center of Congress affairs during its first two generations, Bose felt that his home province was being shunted aside. As we have noted earlier, during the first thirty-two years of the Congress, about one-third of the presidents had been Bengalis. From 1917 to the present only two more had been added to the illustrious list: C.R. Das and Subhas Bose. Little did Bose realize how prescient he was about the virtual elimination of Bengalis from the center of power in India.[116]

As he spoke about the war situation to audience after audience, Bose thought, like many others in 1940, that the Axis powers would win the war. He did not like their racism, or their totalitarian system, but he had long been fascinated by skill at arms, and the Germans were demonstrating the fruits of such training. For example, he wrote in March 1940,

> It seems that in modern warfare speed and mobility are exceedingly important factors . . . besides detailed planning and adequate preparation, energy and vigour are needed to fulfil a particular programme according to a timetable. All these qualities the Nazis certainly possess. Owing to their speed and mobility they have invariably caught the enemy napping and overpowered him without much difficulty. . . . Germany may be a Fascist or an Imperialist, ruthless or cruel, but one cannot help admiring these qualities of hers. . . . Could not these qualities be utilised for promoting a nobler cause?[117]

At Ramgarh, he did not praise the Nazis, but rather gave examples of leaders who had acted decisively. He chose Lenin and Mussolini, each of whom he said, had changed the course of his country's history. The Congress Working Committee, time and again, had failed to act. Therefore, he charged the Ramgarh Conference collectively with this responsibility. Though proclamations were issued, the kind of action he wanted was still not taken because Gandhi was the only one who could arouse and lead such a movement, and Gandhi said the country was not ready. After the next all-India gathering at which he presided, at Nagpur in June, Bose went to Wardha to exchange views with Gandhi. Both held to their positions.[118] Bose began to use some slightly different phrases: now he called for a 'provisional national government,' and talked of 'all power to the Indian people.'[119]

As some leftists fell away, Bose reached out to others. He had tried for some link on the all-India scene with the Muslim League and the Hindu Mahasabha, meeting with Jinnah and V.D. Savarkar, the leaders of these organizations. But finding each too narrow in his own way, he dropped these efforts.[120] In the context of the operation of the new Calcutta Municipal (Amendment) Act in the spring of 1940, however, he thought that Congressmen would need wider support. A preliminary understanding with the Mahasabha broke down.[121] An agreement was reached between the Bose Bengal Congress and the Muslim League over places for Muslims in the Corporation, over alternation of the mayor's chair between a Hindu and a Muslim, as well as an electoral alliance.[122] The Muslim Leaguers were pleased; the Boses were attacked for allying with a communal organization. Subhas Bose, who had been involved in the Bengal Pact many years before, during C.R. Das' days, and defended his group's efforts said:

> We . . . do not regard the communal organisation as untouchable . . . we
> hold that the Congress should try continuously to woo them over to its side.
> During the last three years, repeated attempts have been made to bring about
> a rapprochement between the Congress and the Muslim League. At a certain
> stage, the writer . . . met Mr Jinnah . . . and several interviews took place.
> At that time, the attempt failed, though the writer had been blessed by the
> Congress Working Committee and by Mahatma Gandhi. Those who had
> not objected to that attempt which failed ultimately, now strongly object to
> the present attempt, because it succeeded. . . . We regard the present
> agreement with the Muslim League as a great achievement not in its
> actuality, but in its potentiality.[123]

A.R. Siddiqi was elected mayor of Calcutta in 1940 with the backing of the
Boses. Just at this time, heated discussions of the communal issue were
underway throughout the subcontinent because of the Lahore Resolution
of the Muslim League (what has later come to be called the 'Pakistan'
Resolution).

The crucial passage in the resolution moved by Fazlul Huq and passed
on March 24, 1940 by the Muslim League session at Lahore, read,

> Resolved that . . . no constitutional plan would be workable in this country
> or acceptable to the Muslims unless it is designed on the following basic
> principle, viz., that geographically contiguous units are demarcated into
> regions which should be so constituted with such territorial adjustments as
> may be necessary that the areas in which the Muslims are numerically in a
> majority, as in the north-western and eastern zones of India, should be
> grouped to constitute 'independent States' in which the constituent units
> shall be autonomous and sovereign: that adequate, effective and mandatory
> safeguards should be specifically provided in the constitutions for
> minorities in the units and in the regions for the protection of their religious,
> cultural, economic, political, administrative and other rights and interests
> in consultation with them. . . .[124]

From a call for separate electorates and protection of their rights as the
largest minority, the Muslim League was now making a bolder and more
far-reaching claim: India divided into separate and *sovereign* regions.
Here was a resolution which, if followed, could mean the division of India.
Once passed, it raised a storm of protest. Organizations from the Congress
to the thoroughly communal Hindu Mahasabha, to the Liberal Federation,
to a number of Muslim groups, objected at once.[125] It was not an issue on
which the Boses differed from Gandhi. To them India was a nation
composed of diverse people, groups, and religions that inhabited a certain
territory. They did not define Indian nationality on the basis of religion.
They would fight against any plan to divide India, unfree or free.

The Boses continued attempting to work and talk with the Muslim

League, the Krishak Praja Party, or Fazlul Huq. The alternative was the division of the nation into separate camps, even separate nations. Among the critics of the Boses, though, were Muslim nationalists who felt betrayed.[126]

In the summer of 1940, while the Germans struck Norway, Denmark, Holland, and France with their blitzkrieg, Subhas Bose started a small satyagraha movement which called for the elimination of the Holwell Monument. This monument to the victims of the so-called Black Hole tragedy in mid-eighteenth century Calcutta, was objected to by many Indians, Hindu and Muslim. Bose wrote on June 29, 1940:

> The campaign against the Holwell Monument, which was the mandate of the Bengal Provincial Conference, has to be taken up at once. The third July 1940, is going to be observed in Bengal as the Sirajuddowla Day—in honour of the last independent King of Bengal. The Holwell Monument is not merely an unwarranted stain on the memory of the Nawab, but has stood in the heart of Calcutta for the last 150 years or more as the symbol of our slavery and humiliation. That monument must now go.
>
> On the 3rd of July next will commence the campaign'. . . the writer has decided to march at the head of the first batch of volunteers on that day.[127]

As he was about to push his satyagraha campaign forward, Subhas Bose was arrested under the Defence of India Act on July 2. In light of the world-pulsing events going on in Europe and East Asia, it seems that Bose picked a small issue on which to court arrest. He is said to have had other, more important, plans which were interrupted by this arrest, but he could not have been surprised to find himself in the Presidency Jail once he precipitated a satyagraha movement with volatile students in a time of war.[128]

Although pressing the Holwell satyagraha forward was the pretext, the Government of India wanted Bose arrested regardless of whether the monument was removed, and the satyagraha suspended. Many visible members of the Forward Bloc had already been arrested.[129] Eventually Bose was charged with violating the Defence of India Act regulations. While these charges were pending, Bose was held in Presidency Jail indefinitely. Bose believed that he was to be detained for the duration of the war.

IX

Throughout the turmoil in the Bengal Congress and Subhas Bose's continuing tours for the Forward Bloc, Sarat Bose went steadily about his business at the bar and in the Bengal Legislative Assembly. Although the position of the Boses and their supporters in the Bengal Congress was under challenge, Sarat Bose went on acting as leader of the Congress

Parliamentary Party in the Bengal Assembly and leader of the whole opposition until late in 1940, when disciplinary action was taken against him by the Congress leadership.

Some familiar subjects came before the Bengal Assembly: the budget, an incident involving police brutality, another Calcutta Municipal (Amendment) Bill, an education bill—this one concerned with secondary education—and, most often, the suppression of fundamental civil liberties through the application of the regulations under the Defence of India Act.

The main method used by the opposition in the Assembly in challenging the restrictions on civil liberties was through the introduction of adjournment motions. Although they could not win the final vote on any of these motions, they could air their views. Arguing that the Government of Bengal, purportedly a popular government, did not have to implement the regulations under the Defence of India Act, Sarat Bose said that the rules had been put in place, '. . . not for the defence of India's freedom but for the perpetuation of India's slavery.'[130] Almost rhythmically through the year, in February, April, and July, the opposition put up adjournment motions related to fundamentals of free speech, freedom of the press, and freedom of association.

Not surprisingly, a number of these motions and debates focused on the public activity of Subhas Bose, for he was the most prominent and noisiest agitator on the Bengal scene, the one most threatening to the forces of law and order. The April debate focused on a government order which prohibited reports in the press about the programs held by the 'suspended Bengal Provincial Congress Committee, or any body affiliated thereto or connected therewith or Mr Subhas Chandra Bose and Swami Sahajananda or either of them.'[131] Sarat Bose tried to show just how ridiculous this order was. Meetings, processions, or assemblies that Subhas Bose and his cohorts organized were not banned, nor were reports about mainstream Congress activities. Why then were reports of Bose's meetings to be banned in the press? Sarat Bose went on,

> This order is no doubt very flattering to Mr Subhas Chandra Bose and Swami Sahajananda and their followers, among whom I have the honour to count myself as one . . . they have been singled out for this mark of favour from the Government. But it is not a case of one individual here or one individual in an adjoining Province—it is a question of the rights of the people, the liberties of the people; and in the name of those rights and liberties, I on behalf of the Opposition do enter again my most emphatic protest.[132]

In his response Nazimuddin—who had the votes on his side but not the best of the argument—maintained that many people supported the order. Sarat Bose dared him to name them and interrupted to tell Nazimuddin that he did not have the courage to name them. Nazimuddin then read the program of the suspended Congress and the establishment Congress. The Bose program, he said, 'comes within the mischief of the Defence of India Act.'[133]

After the arrest of Subhas Bose, adjournment motions were again offered. Muslim members heatedly said that Bose was acting for all Indians, Hindu and Muslim, in demanding that the monument go. In arguing for the release of news about the agitation—which was also banned—Sarat Bose said in the course of yet another adjournment motion debate, that the restrictions in India were more severe than in Britain which was under siege. In part, he stated,

> The war . . . is at the door of England, but still war news is not banned. News of the movements of the German armed forces . . . are not banned. Does the Hon'ble the Home Minister ask us to believe that the war is at our door and therefore all news about this agitation for the removal of the Holwell Monument is to be banned? I would describe this attempt . . . as the British Indian edition of Western Nazism. . . . It is useless, Sir, to indulge in this claptrap in the name of law and order. . . . The law and order which we appeal to is higher, older, nobler. . . . It demands freedom of speech, it demands freedom of thought, it demands freedom of association. . . .[134]

Following his British legal training and experience and adherence to British concepts of legal and civic freedoms, Sarat Bose throughout these many speeches on fundamental freedoms referred to British laws, British customs, and to the freer society which the British had at home than the one they shaped out in India. He called for a liberal and democratic India and he asserted that people such as Fazlul Huq and Nazimuddin were building an India that was more like a prison camp than a free society.[135]

A few weeks later, Fazlul Huq announced that the monument would go. But when Sarat Bose asked why then Subhas Bose had not been released, government spokesmen said that he knew why he was still held.[136] So the monument was on its way out, the agitation was over, many other prisoners were released, but Subhas Bose, more dangerous than the rest, was held.

Two other issues aroused passions in the Assembly during 1940: the Secondary Education Bill and the Calcutta Municipal (Amendment) Bill for 1940. Both touched the communal nerve. In speaking against both of these bills, Sarat Bose made two of the longest Assembly speeches he ever made.[137] He felt that the education bill was vague and did not offer a truly national and comprehensive education program. If such a program were put forward following the recommendations of the Sadler Commission, he said that he would support it. On the further reform of the Calcutta Corporation that the Coalition Ministry sought, Sarat Bose and other experienced Corporation hands maintained that the bill was aimed at close

Bengal Government control of municipal affairs which the nationalists were determined to resist.

Later in the year, however, the cleavage between the Boses' Bengal Congress, now called the suspended Congress, and the ad hoc Congress supported by the central organization, reached the Congress Parliamentary Party when Sarat Bose did not follow a directive from the center. He was expelled from the Congress and later those members of the Assembly who continued to support him were expelled. This split the Congress in the Assembly into a group headed by Sarat Bose and a group headed by Kiran Sankar Roy. During this period, Subhas Bose was elected to the Central Legislative Assembly from a Dacca constituency while still imprisoned. And he challenged those who clung to the Gandhian team to stand for re-election against candidates supported by the suspended Congress. Santosh Basu, a Bose stalwart, asked Maulana Azad to withdraw the disciplinary action taken against Sarat Bose in order to 'save the Congress Party and the entire opposition in the Bengal Assembly from the inevitable doom.'[138]

While debates in the Assembly and disciplinary actions were going on, the Congress-Raj dialogue was also continuing. The concessions offered by the government were so limited that the Congress, albeit reluctantly, moved toward some kind of challenge to the Raj. The pressure had been building up on Gandhi and the high command to act for some time. In the fall, again put in charge of Congress actions, Gandhi agreed to limited, individual satyagraha. This meant that some Congressmen would offer non-violent resistance and court arrest, but only in small numbers. So this was a compromise between the views of those—like Subhas Bose—who wanted mass and widespread civil disobedience, and those who felt so strongly about fascism that they did not want to undercut the war effort in any way.[139] Subhas Bose felt that he was beginning to have some impact on the Congress.[140]

X

Days and months passed by and Subhas Bose was still detained in the Presidency Jail. From fragments of written and oral testimony, it is hard to know just when he determined to flee India and work for her independence from outside. But in the months after war broke out in Europe, the idea was certainly alive in him. As he had been suggesting in many speeches during the pre-war and war period, Indian nationalists had to take advantage of Britain's hour of weakness. This meant getting assistance from her enemies if nationalist resources did not suffice. During the war, Bose wrote an account of Indian politics and of his own perspective at this time. He said in part, that he was convinced of three things,

Firstly, Britain would lose the war and the British Empire would break up. Secondly, in spite of being in a precarious position, the British would not hand over power to the Indian people and the latter would have to fight for their freedom. Thirdly, India would win her independence if she played her part in the war against Britain and collaborated with those powers that were fighting Britain. The conclusion . . . was that India should actively enter the field of international politics.[141]

There were precedents. During the First World War, Indian revolutionaries had sought help from the Central Powers, particularly Germany. After the Great War, the Soviet Union was willing to back the development of a communist movement in India with some of its resources. Bose knew his nationalist and revolutionary history. He imbibed awareness of these plots and plans, hopes and strategems, as he grew up. However, dating to his days in the Scottish Churches College and the officers' training corps, he had a larger aspiration. If he was to work from outside India with foreign help, he wanted to prepare a military force that would challenge the British in India.

His schemes were vague at first. Germany was fighting Britain. The Italians had entered the war on Germany's side in 1940. Japan was allied to Germany, but was fighting China at this time and was not yet at war with Britain. Of these nations, Italy and its dictator had afforded him the warmest welcome, but was the weakest militarily. So he looked to the other three, the USSR, Japan, and Germany. Only the last of these was at war with Britain and the British Empire. Although he had met with German officials in Bombay in December 1938, he had never had an enthusiastic response from them. During 1939 and 1940, he tried to send out feelers to the Soviets and to Japan. His nephew, Amiya Bose, second son of Sarat Bose, was a student in England. Upon returning to Europe in 1939 after a summer in India, he took messages from his uncle, one of them for Comintern officials in Europe.[142]

In 1938, Bose met with Japanese officials in Calcutta, including Mr Ohasi, a high foreign ministry officer, at a house rented by the wealthy communist S.K. Acharya, in Ballygunge. He thought it wise to use a communist's house and Acharya was agreeable. In 1940, Bose sent one of his trusted followers, Lal Shankar Lal, general secretary of the Forward Bloc, to Japan seeking some response there. After all, Japan was talking of Asia for the Asians and had been a haven for nationalists from Vietnam, China, as well as for Rash Behari Bose. Lal, with the help of Dwijen Bose, another nephew, obtained a passport under the name Hiralal Gupta, and went on a Japanese ship from Calcutta to Japan. There he met Rash Behari Bose and Japanese officials in an effort to learn of their plans and how India might fit in. Later Lal was caught by the British and his mission revealed.[143]

Just what Bose learned from sending out this mission is not known. He was fishing; whether he had a nibble or caught anything is unclear.

Bose also wanted to know what the CID knew about him and who was passing information to them. Several Bose associates claim that one night in early 1940, he was given his own police file from Lord Sinha Road headquarters, which he read carefully and returned the same night. He did learn from this file about the trustworthiness or untrustworthiness of some associates and relations. One distant cousin, he learned, was a police informer and gave detailed information on the doings at 38/2 Elgin Road.[144]

Also early in 1940, Bose asked political contacts and allies in the Punjab and the Northwest Frontier province about help in crossing the frontier into Afghanistan. The Kirti Kisan Party, linked to the CPI, had the best underground network of contacts, and though there were differences between Bose and the communists, they were agreeable to helping him.[145] These efforts at working out a practical escape plan from India were interrupted by Bose's imprisonment.

Languishing in his Calcutta cell through July, August, September, and into October, Bose finally decided that he had to get out of prison by any means possible. Legal solutions failed. He turned to desperate means. At the end of October, he wrote to the home minister and to the superintendent of the jail. Of the first, he requested his release; to the second, he said that for two months he had been contemplating a hunger strike to protest his unjust imprisonment. If his detention order was not lifted, he wrote,

> There is no other alternative for me but to register a moral protest against an unjust act and as a proof of that protest, to undertake a voluntary fast. This fast will have no effect on the 'popular' Ministry, because I am neither the Maulvi of Murapura, Dacca nor a Muhammadan by faith. Consequently, the fast will, in my case, become a fast unto death. . . . I was in England when Terence Macswiney, Lord Mayor of Cork, was on hunger strike on a similar issue. The whole country was moved . . . but Lloyd George's Government was adamant . . . life under existing conditions is hardly worth living. . . . I shall not permit forced feeding . . . this letter, written on the sacred day of Kali Puja, should not be treated as a threat or ultimatum. It is merely an affirmation of one's faith. . . .[146]

But it was a threat. At this point Nazimuddin and other officials did not move. They intended to see whether Bose was bluffing. Bose waited. There was no response. He wrote again on November 26, this time a lengthy letter to the governor, chief minister, and Council of Ministers, announcing that his hunger strike would begin on November 29. He said, in part,

> The classic and immortal examples of Terence Macswiney and Jatin Das

are floating before my mind's eye. . . . Life under existing conditions is
intolerable for me. . . . Government are determined to hold me in prison by
brute force. I say in reply: 'Release me or I shall (?) refuse to live—and it
is for me to decide whether I choose to live or to die.'. . . The individual must
die, so that the nation may live. Today I must die, so that India may live and
may win freedom and glory.[147]

Declaring that he would take only water with salt, Bose began his hunger
strike. A few days later, on December 5, 1940, the detention order was
lifted, but the government intended to detain him again when his health
improved. His house was to be watched around the clock, but he was not
under arrest.

He went to his home on Elgin Road, staying in his father's room, where
for the next six weeks, he received relations, colleagues, friends, and
carried on an extensive correspondence. He was also working out all the
practical details of his planned escape from India with as much foresight
and precision as he could.[148] Agents of the Kirti Party were contacted and
several were sent to Afghanistan and two on to the Soviet Union to try to
prepare the way for Bose. One of the two entering the Soviet Union died
in an accident en route.[149] Mian Akbar Shah, a member of the Forward Bloc
Working Committee, came to Calcutta and then went back to the Frontier
Province, to work out the necessary contacts. Bhagat Ram Talwar, a young
Hindu whose family lived in the frontier area and one of whose elder
brothers had been executed by the British a decade earlier, was recruited.
Knowing the necessary languages and the frontier area well, he was
considered to be the perfect companion for Bose as the Indian leader made
his way, by one means or another, across the frontier, and out of British
India.[150] A small circle of political workers and family members had to be
told of the plan, but Bose tried to keep the circle of those who knew as small
as possible. Months before there had been a rumor that he might try to
leave India. He could see the police watch out his window; he knew of the
deceitful cousin and others with loose tongues around him. He had to be
extra careful.

Once out of prison, Subhas started writing letters on political matters.
To Gandhi he wrote about the need for a mass movement. He was in touch
with Jayaprakash Narayan about secret plans to rebuild the left.[151] Bose
wrote to Viceroy Linlithgow, whom he had met some months before, on
December 29, about the coalition government in Bengal and growing
communalism. He said that, 'On communal questions, the Muslims are
given a free hand, while on political issues the will of the governor and the
British mercantile community is allowed to prevail.'[152] The consequences
of this pattern of dominance in Bengal affairs was that, '. . . a wave of

communalism is spreading over Hindu Bengal, as an inevitable reaction to Muslim communalism.'[153] He asked the viceroy to intervene and either help to put in place a new ministry that had significant backing from Hindus and Muslims, or to suspend the constitution.[154] This was surely a cry of desperation. Bose, though his letter was politely acknowledged, knew that the viceroy was unlikely to act unless the law and order situation got out of hand or enemy warriors stood on the doorstep. It marked his frustration with the Congress leadership, for it had prevented the Boses from allying with Fazlul Huq from 1937 to 1939.

Shortly after Gandhi called off his limited and individual satyagraha movement in December 1940, Bose wrote to him encouraging him to carry on with a wider civil disobedience effort. He also criticized Maulana Azad for the steps taken against the Bose-dominated BPCC and against Sarat Bose's group in the Bengal Assembly. Gandhi answered on December 29 from Wardha,

> You are irrepressible whether ill or well. Do get well before going in for fireworks. . . . I read . . . about the decision [*of Azad, expelling Sarat Bose*] I could not help approving of it. I am surprised that you won't distinguish between discipline and indiscipline. . . . I know that in Bengal it is difficult to function effectively without you two . . . the Congress has to manage somehow under the severe handicap. . . . As for your Bloc joining C.D. I think with the fundamental differences between you and me, it is not possible. Till one of us is converted to the other's view, we must sail in different boats, though their destination may appear but only appear to be the same.
>
> Meanwhile let us love one another remaining members of the same family that we are.[155]

Gandhi was certainly unconverted by anything Bose had to say. Bose remained a lost son of the Gandhi family.

Of the nationalist political groups not formally allied with the Forward Bloc, the CSP most closely matched Bose's response to the war. They were less concerned than the CPI with the fate of the Soviet Union, less obsessed with fascism than M.N. Roy, and less ambivalent about the fate of Britain and the Allies than the Gandhi group in the Congress. Late in 1940, Jayaprakash Narayan sent a secret letter to Bose outlining a program for mass struggle, writing, in part,

> . . . our basic task today is to chalk out a line of action that is fundamentally independent of the Congress. . . . The task of destroying what would remain of imperialism and of carrying forward the democratic revolution devolves on the workers, peasants and the lower middle classes. . . . Let us form a new revolutionary party out of the C.S.P., the Anushilan, the Forward Bloc, the Kirti, the Labour Party and other such groups or elements. A party based

squarely on Marxism-Leninism independent of all other political organisations and parties. I think this is eminently possible if you only wish it. . . .
I have not mentioned the C.P. . . . because the C.P. by its very constitution
. . . cannot merge its identity in another socialist party.[156]

What reply Bose made, if any, is not known. Bose may have reflected that
had the CSP been with him at Tripuri, the course of Congress politics might
have been very different. A year-and-a-half later, Narayan was seeking to
link up with Bose and push off from the Congress right and the war-time
hesitations of Gandhi.

XI

Bose's efforts to bring Gandhi and the mainstream of the Congress to his
views had failed—at least for the time being—so, he now prepared to leave
India and seek help abroad. He renewed his contacts with members of the
Kirti Kisan Party and dissident Congressmen from the frontier area
through Punjabis in Calcutta. Seeking practical help from one of his few
intimates from that area, he called a Forward Bloc Working Committee
meeting in Calcutta for which Mian Akbar Shah came down from the
NWFP.

From the surrounding web of Boses, he selected a few family members
to help him with his plot in its preparation, execution, and cover-up. His
niece Ila nursed him and was a trusted assistant. The plan that he chose
involved a long night-time drive to the Bengal-Bihar border area, and he
selected his nephew, Sisir Bose, a young medical student and third son of
Sarat Bose, as the driver and for other chores. In the later stages of his
planning, he brought his nephews, Aurobindo and Dwijen Bose, into the
scheme, for limited but vital help. They had both carried out small missions
for him previously and Aurobindo was active in student politics. They
were to help get Bose out of the house. Once Sarat Bose and his wife
returned from vacations outside Calcutta, they too had to be informed of
the secret activities afoot and Sarat Bose made some changes in the details
of the final arrangements.

Who else knew? Bose had been discussing the possibility of leaving
India for some months with political intimates of the Forward Bloc,
including Sardar Sardul Singh Caveeshar and his long-time associate
Satya Ranjan Bakshi. He had talked over such a step with N.N.
Chakravarty while the two were in prison together. Others have claimed
for knowledge and even credit for the whole idea. In later accounts, some
have said that V.D. Savarkar, leader of the Hindu Mahasabha, and one who
plotted from abroad during the First World War, recommended this course
to Bose.

When Mian Akbar Shah came to Calcutta, he and Sisir Bose purchased the clothes appropriate for an up-country Muslim. A visiting card was printed that read: Mohd. Ziauddin, Travelling Inspector, The Empire of India Life Assurance Co., Address: Civil Lines, Jubbulpore.[157] To complete his Frontier Muslim disguise, Bose began growing a beard. Bose had a mole which was noted on his passport as an identifying mark. It had been removed and his growth of facial hair covered the scar.[158] He had decided, in consultation with his confederates, that in disguise, he would leave in the dead of night, driven by Sisir Bose in the Wanderer automobile registered in the latter's name, when the police watchers on the corner would be asleep. Sisir Bose had practised for the drive to Dhanbad in the Bengal-Bihar border area where his eldest brother Asoke was employed. This try run had been made on Christmas day to Burdwan and Asoke had been told to expect an important visit soon. From there, Bose would board a train at either Gomoh or Asansol for Peshawar. There he would be met by a contact and guide from the Kirti Party and assisted across the frontier into Afghanistan and to Kabul. In Kabul, a beehive of diplomats and spying activity, he would seek contacts with the appropriate diplomatic missions so that he could go to Europe. Besides all his 'rational' planning, Bose consulted astrologers and palmists in 1940.[159] What he needed was good planning and assistance, secrecy, luck, the help of the gods, and proper alignment of the stars.

Bose set late night January 16-early morning January 17, 1941 as the departure time. He was due in court in one of the two cases pending against him; he pleaded ill health and got a doctor's certificate to that effect. Shortly before the chosen day, Bose ostentatiously went into seclusion, seeing hardly anyone and receiving his food on a tray behind a screen in his room. This behavior was to match up with a story of religious withdrawal which was to be the main covering rumor floated about once he 'disappeared'. Aurobindo kept bringing him his meals and the empty trays would reappear from behind the screen. Only those who were involved in the actual plan for escape met with him now.

On the evening of January 16, Dwijen Bose was to keep watch from within the house and notify the others when the police watchers were asleep. After midnight, he gave the signal, and Subhas Bose with Aurobindo and Sisir made their way towards the car parked in the covered driveway at the side of the house. The luggage was in place and Sisir and Subhas Bose entered the car. Only one door slammed loudly. Sisir started the motor, put the car in gear, and drove out from the house, heading south. The police watchers apparently slept through the exit, for Sisir Bose occasionally drove from the house.[160]

After traveling south briefly to fool any watcher on Elgin Road, Sisir Bose turned left and left again, and headed north on Lansdowne Road. He drove through the dark and empty streets of Calcutta to Howrah Bridge, across the bridge, and then onto the Grand Trunk Road. Now began the long drive through the night heading for Asoke Bose's house in Bararee, near Dhanbad, more than 200 miles to the west. At one point, after the driver had to make a sudden stop, the fuel-line clogged and the car stalled. Cool-headed, Sisir Bose, young but an efficient, experienced, and enthusiastic driver, waited briefly and then started his motor. Now the car revved up and they were off again. They drove through the French territory of Chandernagore without being stopped. Early in the morning they neared Asoke Bose's house. Subhas Bose, in his Muslim disguise, left the car a fraction of a mile away, while Sisir Bose drove in to the front of Asoke's house. Asoke had been forewarned by his uncle that a visit was to be expected just after mid-January, but the exact day and other details had not been told to him. He had had to make certain preparations and had already done so.[161] Sisir entered the house. Some moments later an unknown visitor arrived and had his card sent in to the master of the house. It announced an insurance agent, Mohd. Ziauddin.

Asoke Bose was overwhelmed by the effectiveness of the disguise and could hardly identify his uncle. They talked in English and it was arranged that Asoke would meet with the visitor later in the day, after work, and that the latter would stay in the guest room until he returned late in the afternoon. Asoke went to work, and Subhas Bose, having been up all night, calmly fell asleep for a few hours of much needed rest. Asoke returned for lunch but he ate with his wife and Sisir, while the visitor had his meal served in the guest room. None of the servants present in the house had ever seen Subhas Bose.

After work, Asoke returned and met with his uncle. They arranged that Sisir would drive Subhas Bose to Gomoh, some thirty miles distant, in the evening. Since he was not familiar with the road, Asoke would accompany them. Asoke could not leave his wife alone in the house, so it was decided that she too would make the drive and be told the identity of the visitor. Subhas Bose walked out of the gate. Soon Asoke, his wife, and Sisir, in the car, drove out. They picked up Subhas a short distance away and drove to Gomoh. They were early for the Kalka Mail. They stopped and chatted and waited for the train. Asoke remembers that Subhas Bose said he expected to go to Berlin, but nothing was fixed. Darkness deepened. The train was heard in the distance. Subhas Bose alighted from the car. It was a poignant farewell from the last remaining family members he might see for a while. As they parted, Subhas said, 'I am off; you go back.' They waited as he boarded the train. A while later they drove back to Asoke's house. Sisir slept the night there and returned to Calcutta in the morning.

According to plan, Subhas Bose rode the Kalka Mail to a station outside Delhi. Then he descended, waited for the Frontier Mail, and boarded this train for the remaining trip to Peshawar, capital of the Northwest Frontier Province. Mian Akbar Shah boarded the train, checked that Bose was there, and watched him descend at the Peshawar Cantonment Station and take a tonga to the Taj Mahal Hotel. In his Muslim dress, complete with fez, he checked in for the night of January 19. An agent of Mian Akbar Shah met him and told him of further arrangements, but as these were already understood, Bose felt this was an unnecessary step. Bose was moved to a rented house the following day. On January 21, he was introduced to his young guide, Bhagat Ram Talwar, whom he had expected to be bigger and burlier. Bhagat Ram, for the purpose of this mission assigned to him by the Kirti Kisan Party to which he was devoted, took the name Rahmat Khan. He and Bose decided that since the latter did not know the languages of the frontier area,

> ... he would impersonate as a deaf and dumb Muslim gentleman going to Adda Sharif on a pilgrimage. He would continue using Ziauddin as his name. He was dressed like a Pathan wearing Malaysia cloth salwar, kamiz, Pathan leather jacket, khaki kulla and lungi as head gear and Peshawari chappals as footwear. He also carried a Kabuli blanket. By this time he had about an inch long beard. Because of good build, sharp features and fair complexion, he looked like a real Pathan.[162]

Together they planned the steps leading to Kabul.

Bhagat Ram had procured additional supplies and with driver and guide, they departed by car for the border the following morning, January 22. They left the car near a British military camp about eleven miles outside Peshawar and started to walk. After some time, they crossed out of British territory. Upon learning this, Bose became elated, now out of the clutches of his foe. They ate a brief meal, then continued on their way and reached a small village late that night. With traditional Pathan hospitality, they were given food and a place to sleep. However, the community guest room with some twenty-five men resting in it proved too stuffy for Bose and he had to go outside frequently for fresh air. The next morning, they rented mules and rode them into Afghan territory. At one point, Bose, never a very good rider, fell from his mule and had to be picked up by the guide. They reached a village of the Shinwari tribe where they spent the following night.

The next day they again mounted their mules and traveled for some time, reaching the Peshawar–Kabul road. By trekking and mule-riding, they had crossed the border about thirteen miles south of the Khyber Pass, a much more frequented path than the route they had taken. Bhagat Ram did his best to keep checkpoints and possible official inspections to a minimum. They were in the lower reaches of the Hindu Kush mountains in late January, and it was quite cold. Bose bore up well with the strain of the trip, though he was not in the best physical condition to undertake such a journey after his imprisonment and then house confinement in Calcutta. On the main road, they were able to secure a ride in an open truck to Jalalabad, one of the chief towns on the route to Kabul. They stayed the night in a hotel and then made their way to Adda Sharif where Bhagat Ram had contacts. They took a tonga and afterwards another truck. They had been nervous about a checkpoint at Budkhak, but at 4 a.m. the officials were asleep and they passed through unnoted. Their truck took them through the Lataband Pass and the weather was bitter cold. But on the 27th, they reached Kabul.[163]

Kabul, capital of Afghanistan, a commercial and administrative center, had long been a center for what some British officials in the nineteenth century had called 'the great game'. This meant the play of diplomats, soldiers, and spies. It had been an early Mughal capital. The British assault in 1842 on the city, built in a long narrow gorge wedged between mountains on either side and protected by a surrounding wall, was repelled with the loss of almost the entire garrison. The British retaliated for this humiliation and burned part of the city. They attacked it again in 1879. Now it remained the center of a small, independent, and autocratic country. The frontier region spanning both sides of the border in India and Afghanistan was inhabited by Pathans, never easy to control or manage by either government. Kabul housed diplomatic missions of many nations, several of them then at war, and others who viewed each other warily as, for example, the Russians and the British.

Ten days had passed since Bose had left Calcutta. He was scheduled for a court appearance on January 27, but rather than have the police come and search his house and give out word of his disappearance, he had arranged for Aurobindo Bose to read a prepared announcement to the effect that he was gone to unknown parts and may have religiously retreated from the world. Playing the game of cover-up and bluff as well as they could, family members scurried off in search of him and messages were sent asking if he had been seen.

It has been suggested by some writers that Bose's plans or whereabouts later in Kabul were known to the authorities and that they left him alone because they were happy to see him go. However, the Home Department file dealing with his disappearance and the subsequent Bengal Governor's

Report for the following few months show internal confusion and lack of any concrete information. The initial and most important file contains a report by J.V.B. Janvrin, deputy commissioner of police, Special Branch, Calcutta, which reads in part,

> The news of Subhas Bose's disappearance was received by the 'Hindustan Standard' between 2 a.m. and 3 a.m. in the morning (27/1/41). . . . This morning an inspector of this branch went to make inquiries into the circumstances of his disappearance. The family members informed him that for the past 10 or 12 days Subhas Bose has been practising 'Yog'. A curtain was fixed up dividing his room into two portions. . . . His nephew Aurobindo would put the food in front of the curtain. . . . On the 25th morning milk and fruit was brought as usual but when on the following day it was found not to have been consumed Aurobindo looked behind the curtain . . . and found that he had disappeared. They say he took no warm clothing . . . or shoes with him and they believe that he has renounced the world and turned 'sanyasi'. He did this once before at the age of 16. . . . His mother is said to have taken no food since last night and was weeping. . . . She has been enquiring indirectly from the Special Branch whether we can help her to locate her son.
>
> The above explanation of Subhas Bose's disappearance is plausible but there are grave reasons to doubt whether it is the true explanation. A representative of the Associated Press tells me that he last saw Bose about 12 days ago . . . to his mind the whole story sounds most fantastic.[164]

The officer went on to summarize additional information, including an intercepted letter of Aurobindo Bose of some days earlier in which he told a confederate that something special would happen around the 27th. Then the trip of Lal Shankar Lal to Japan was mentioned with the comment that it was certainly for the purpose of obtaining foreign aid 'for subversive activities in India.'[165]

Through the following weeks, communications were exchanged between the Home Department in Delhi and the Special Branch office in Calcutta, sorting out the rumors about Bose's whereabouts. Some said that he was in religious retreat. Other stories indicated that he had traveled to Japan or Russia. One other report was that he had left Calcutta for Hong Kong on a boat called Thaisung on January 17. Officials in Delhi were unhappy with the sloppy work done in Calcutta and one Delhi officer noted on February 13,

> When Bose was unconditionally released (with the idea of putting him back again when his health permitted) it was decided not to guard his residence with police, but to keep a watch on it by agents from within. How he arranged to escape and where he now is, is still a mystery. [*The government*] . . . wanted to prevent Bose from doing harm within India or abroad. Bose

hoodwinked the police and the governor was by no means proud of the performance.[166]

From the mutual criticisms of Delhi and Calcutta intelligence officials, it seems clear that Bose had fooled them. The emotional Aurobindo Bose by his cryptic references in a letter almost gave them forewarning. The intercepted letter meant little to the police, however, until after the fact. For the moment, Bose was out of their jurisdiction, ordered to be arrested, and have his property seized in February and March 1941 for failing to appear in court when under warrant.

As the police were trying to solve the riddle of his flight from Calcutta, Bose was facing his own dilemmas in Kabul. The memoirs of Bose's confidants in the escape differ as to his expected ultimate destination. Bhagat Ram thought all along that Bose was aiming for Moscow and this fitted with his Kirti Party's outlook. Asoke Bose thought he was headed for Moscow, while Sisir Bose wrote in his detailed account about twenty-five years after the events,

> My brother [*Asoke*] had remarked that uncle appeared to be blazing the path of India's old-time revolutionaries and was perhaps going to Russia. I agreed with him generally but added that I had no doubt in my mind that his ultimate destination for the present was Germany.[167]

Bose had been trying to make contacts with foreign governments for almost a decade and had spoken to officials of the Italian, German, Japanese, and other nations. Through R. Palme Dutt and Indian communists he had made every effort to contact Soviet officials. There is no published evidence that he was given any positive feedback by the Soviets. They were probably wary of him and not at war with Great Britain. They had no reason to be particularly unfriendly—indeed Indian communists had helped Bose to reach Kabul—but they also were not especially encouraging to him.

Once in Kabul, Rahmat Khan and his deaf-mute uncle Ziauddin found a *sarai*. They insisted upon a separate room. Locking their few belongings in the room, they went to reconnoiter the local scene. From January 28 they tried to make contacts with officials of the Soviet government. Although Bhagat Ram succeeded in talking to one official briefly in Persian, they made no headway in their efforts to have earnest discussions with the Soviets. Then they had to admit failure. Now other possibilities had to be considered.

On February 2, they located the German legation and Bose, claiming a visa question, entered. He talked with a minister of the legation and a message was sent to Berlin asking for instructions as to what to do with this potential hot property. For reasons of safety, Bose was told to make further contacts through a representative of Siemens who had an office elsewhere in Kabul on the bank of the Kabul River near to the customs facilities. Bose was instructed to contact Herr Thomas on February 5 for word.

In the meantime, Bhagat Ram and Subhas Bose were approached in their *sarai* by an Afghan who claimed to be a policeman. He said they were acting suspiciously. They bribed him temporarily with small amounts of money, but were extremely anxious. He kept returning and finally they had to give him Bose's watch, a gift from his father, with which he was loathe to part. Fearing imminent arrest, they began searching for alternative accommodations. This is when Bhagat Ram decided to look for one Uttam Chand Malhotra, a relation of a family in his home village, who had set up a business in Kabul. Bhagat Ram found the shop, introduced himself, and threw himself—and Bose—into the arms of Uttam Chand. He knew that Uttam Chand had participated in the Civil Disobedience Movement, and he hoped he was still a fervent nationalist and willing to help Bose. Uttam Chand had read of Bose's disappearance in the newspapers. After brief negotiations, he agreed to give whatever help he could to Bose, including the use of a room in his own house. There were small hurdles to clear, but shortly Bose was moved to Uttam Chand's house. The latter feared that a neighbor who suddenly moved away suspected something, and then one of his friends began acting strangely. He had to take an older, nationalist friend, Haji Abdul Sobhan, into his confidence.[168]

Their briefly sagging spirits leaped when Herr Thomas informed them that a positive response had been received from Berlin. But he said that they still had to await further instructions. Days passed. They worried again and Bose and Bhagat Ram began making plans for Bose to cross into Soviet territory without an invitation. Thomas told Bhagat Ram in mid-February that Germany, Italy, and Japan had jointly asked the Soviet Union to grant Bose a transit visa for a journey through its territory on into Europe.

Fears grew about the safety of Uttam Chand's house. Bose was moved out. Then he developed a serious case of dysentery. Medicine was procured for him and then, regaining their confidence in the security of Uttam Chand's flat, they moved Bose back in where he could get better medical attention. Now Uttam Chand's wife had to be taken into confidence. She helped nurse Bose. Still, they awaited word from the Germans and the Italians with whom they had also made contact.

Bose was writing as he waited and completed a long article, 'Forward Bloc—Its Justification,' which he hoped to have delivered back to Calcutta. In it he recounted the conflicts in Indian politics from 1938 to his departure from India. He said that the only hope for Indian freedom was the left and the left had deteriorated except for the Forward Bloc. It had saved Indian nationalism from stagnation, helped create 'a new revolutionary mentality among the people,' sharpened common understanding of the differences between left and right, and pushed the Congress a little way towards confrontation with the Raj.[169] The article was a political self-justification and contained nothing new.

With the help of the Germans, Bose made contact with the Italians and had a meeting with Signor Alberto Quaroni, the Italian minister in Kabul. In Quaroni's report of his discussions with Bose, he said that Bose wanted to establish in Europe a 'Government of Free India'. With the catalytic aid of outside troops, Bose hoped to break Indians from their fear of the British and start an upheaval in India which would lead to the rapid destruction of the Raj.[170]

In late February, the Italians agreed to prepare a false passport for him and he was summoned to the Italian legation for photographs. Ziauddin was to become 'Orlando Mazzotta'. The passport was ready. The German officials still waited for final confirmation and travel plans including transit through Soviet territory. On March 15, final word came through that all was 'go'. Bose's luggage was to be picked up the following day and he was to leave Kabul on the morning of March 18. Bose was shortly packed and gave final messages and instructions to Bhagat Ram. A Bengali letter was given to the latter to deliver to Sarat Bose and the article on the Forward Bloc and another one in English were ready. Bhagat Ram and Bose spent the last night in the home of an Italian named Crishnini. The next morning Bose was picked up from this residence. He was to be taken by car and rail to Moscow. From there he was to travel on to Berlin. Bhagat Ram was to continue to serve as a link between Kabul and Calcutta. The day after Bose left for Moscow and Berlin, Bhagat Ram departed for Calcutta with the messages and article for Sarat Bose.[171]

XII

Subhas Bose had stepped into the unknown. Sarat Bose remained in his familiar milieu, but he was worried about the fate of his beloved brother. With this additional burden of anxiety, Sarat Bose had to go on with his usual pattern of life and political work as best as he could. The German blitzkrieg of 1940 which had swept through the western reaches of Europe and into Paris had a powerful impact in India and some thought the same would happen to Great Britain. Though an enemy of the Raj, Sarat Bose, according to his private secretary, had more confidence in their resiliency and did not glory in their defeats as did some Indian nationalists. His brother might have gone over to the Axis powers, but he could not wholeheartedly root for the defeat of Great Britain. He had had a significant part of his legal education there and imbibed the ideals of the law, justice, and civil liberty.[172]

The Congress was still committed to Gandhi's individual satyagraha and was slowly filling the jails with its members. Gandhi had to face charges of his own nationalist supporters that this campaign was ineffective and supported with ever less enthusiasm. He also had to answer, along with his colleagues, for Congress resignations from the ministries in many provinces, which had led to a weakening of the Congress and an opportunity for other political parties to build their strength while the Congress sat on the sidelines or worked at Gandhi's constructive program.[173] While Gandhi and his closest associates adhered to their program, the left in the Congress, mainly CSP members, pressed for mass civil disobedience and a real challenge to British rule. Gandhi resisted, for he said it was not the time for such a move which would surely bring communal trouble. Communal unity, he insisted, was necessary before a mass action could be undertaken.[174] When some said that India was facing a crisis from external forces or from conflicting internal ones, Gandhi called for the British to withdraw and to let India work out its own destiny. The British had no intention of doing this. The CSP members pushed ahead with calls for mass organizing as well as underground preparations for some kind of action.[175] They were following in Subhas Bose's footsteps. Meanwhile, V.D. Savarkar and other leaders of the Hindu Mahasabha gave stronger support to the British war effort and they called for military training for Indians which would allow them to defend their motherland.[176]

Many Indians with attachments to the Raj of various kinds rallied to the support of the British Empire. The Muslim League took an intermediate position. Jinnah and the Council of the League offered conditional assistance. Fazlul Huq, premier of Bengal, and Sikandar Hyat Khan, premier of the Punjab, however, agreed to join the National Defence Council established by the British and did so without the League's sanction. This immediately drew Jinnah's fire and after some time the Punjab leader resigned. Huq was more resistant and the quarrel continued through 1941, with Huq unhappy that he was ordered about by the president of the Muslim League.[177]

Since war still seemed far away for many in Bengal in 1941, business went on as usual. Sarat Bose attended to his legal practice. Although he had been suspended from the Congress and the Bengal Congress in the Bengal Legislative Assembly was split, Sarat Bose remained at the head of a bloc of about twenty-five Congressmen and the leader of the entire opposition in the Assembly. The year 1941 was marked by numerous issues in the Assembly which were shaped by communal passions and by a bloody communal riot in Dacca, Bengal's second city. Sarat did his best to speak for his own community and for the wider interests of Bengal and India. He had long had the respect of most Bengal Muslims and his peace-making skills were tested again by the bitter controversies which went on.

The Dacca riots started in mid-March—the first since 1930—and went on sporadically until June. Government analysts said afterwards that the Hindus in this city of about 214,000 had started the attacks, but that in the end, Muslims had destroyed a great deal of Hindu-owned property and the Hindus suffered more. The riots spread to more than eighty villages in the surrounding countryside. Peace committees and special armed police were not very effective in bringing the clashes under control.[178] The riots were discussed in the Bengal Assembly with leaders of the different parties calling for a halt to the violence.

The Assembly had been in the midst of the annual budget session, but with one difference. Nalini Sarker, previously the finance minister, was for the time being, joining opposition critics in condemning the work of the new finance minister, H.S. Suhrawardy. Sarat Bose charged that, as usual, the government had no plan for nation-building, and no plan to invigorate Bengal through its planned expenditures.. Indeed, these efforts were curtailed by increased spending for administration and the police. New taxes were planned and the sales tax bill to follow was regressive and harmful to the poor. Not only did he argue that the poor rather than the rich would suffer, but that communal patronage, especially for educational institutions, had also been built into the budget. Although not Tagore's leading admirer, he was aghast that funds for Visva-Bharati had been cut and kept sniping at the ministry on this point through the year.[179] Suhrawardy answered Sarat Bose sharply saying that the latter did not understand the budget figures, but referred him to Education Minister Huq for his criticism of educational expenditures.

About two weeks later, on April 2, before the end of the spring Assembly session, Sarat Bose moved an adjournment motion because of government orders issued against the Bengali newspaper *Dainik Basumati*. He said that it was a fundamental issue of civil liberties and an abuse of the government's wartime powers which was completely unnecessary. All opposition groups rallied to his side on this motion but it lost nonetheless.[180]

A few days before this, on March 31, Bhagat Ram Talwar reached Calcutta from Kabul and came to Sarat Bose's house. He made contact with Sisir Bose to whom he handed over the messages and articles from Subhas Bose. Before the day was out, he told the whole story of the journey, the hardships, the difficulties in Kabul, and the eventual departure of Subhas Bose for Berlin on March 18, to Sarat Bose. During his few days in Calcutta, he asked for a Bengali to come for training to the frontier area and through Satya Ranjan Bakshi, the Bengal Volunteers supplied Santimoy Ganguli for this mission. Bhagat Ram met Bakshi, was given some funds for his return, and shortly was off for NWFP and then Kabul again.[181] Bhagat Ram, Ganguli, a number of other Kirti Party men, and Frontier Congressmen became messengers passing across the border areas into Afghanistan. As the war progressed, the Germans asked them to help cause disruption in the semi-organized border region to distract the British.[182]

The Russo-German Pact in 1939 had been a body blow to anti-fascists in many countries who had rationalized the agreement as Stalin's effort to protect 'socialism in one country' and give the Soviets time to prepare for war. Since Soviet records are not easily available, it is hard to answer this question. Any reader of *Mein Kampf* would surely know that the Soviet Union and all Slavic peoples were on Hitler's hit list. The military historian B.H. Liddell Hart has written, 'Early on Sunday morning, June 22, the German flood poured across the frontier. . . .'[183] Almost overnight new alignments had to be constructed. The Soviets were now on the same side as Great Britain and the British Empire and as other Allied powers opposing the fascist fanaticism of Hitler and the German war machine.

Those most affected were the Indian communists, but even socialists like the CSP, and Nehru and the Boses had to rethink their commitments. The CPI had been declared illegal in the 1930s and some had been arrested in 1940 for opposing the 'Imperialist War' between the Allies and Nazi Germany. With the invasion of their second motherland, the Indian communists, under pressure from R. Palme Dutt and the Comintern, gradually shifted to a new line and by 1942 they were enrolled, somewhat ambiguously, with the Raj fighting a 'Peoples' War' against fascism. The CPI was legalized, communists released from jails, and members found those activities for the war effort which were most in tune with their own concerns. For example, they became involved in 'grow more food' campaigns. Similarly, M.N. Roy and the Radical Democratic Party, formerly the League of Radical Congressmen, who had split with the Congress on the war issue even earlier, now supported the war effort.[184]

For Bhagat Ram Talwar and his comrades in the Kirti Party, there were practical decisions to be made. They were in frequent contact with the Germans in Kabul and had to find out whether they could continue to press the Germans for aid against the British while the Germans were also at war with the Soviet Union. They became more and more suspicious of German intentions, but tried for the time being to get Subhas Bose's messages from German representatives in Kabul and have them sent on to Sarat Bose and the Forward Bloc in Calcutta. However, as Bhagat Ram said he told the Germans, '. . . this new situation has made our work very difficult.'[185] He tried to keep on working with the Forward Bloc and the Bengal Volunteers, but was cautioned against this by CPI leaders.

Bhagat Ram and those working closely with him were one channel by which messages were sent by Subhas Bose from Berlin to Calcutta. In 1941, another path for the delivery of messages from Subhas Bose in Berlin to Sarat Bose and other political colleagues in Calcutta was worked out. Subhas Bose gave his message to the Japanese embassy in Berlin, they forwarded it to Tokyo, and then it was cabled to the Japanese consulate in Calcutta. As Asoke Bose has explained.

> The Consul-General of Japan used to meet father in secret at our country house at Rishra to convey uncle's messages to father and to carry father's messages in reply for onward transmission. Though the Consul-General used to be driven in father's car to Rishra by Sisir after being picked up from predetermined points, it was apparent that father's movement used to be closely shadowed by the Police, specially after uncle's disappearance from Calcutta.[186]

Although the Boses and their closest associates like Satya Ranjan Bakshi and some of the BV members tried to conceal these meetings, the Intelligence Branch was well informed about them. From a number of different sources of information, they certainly knew by now where Subhas Bose was and what he was up to. They could have arrested Sarat Bose at any time. But since Great Britain and British India were not at war with the Japanese, they chose to wait. The contacts went on through the middle and second half of 1941.[187]

The invasion of the Soviet Union undoubtedly troubled Sarat Bose in Calcutta as it did Subhas Bose in Berlin. However, like the CSP and many other Congressmen, they were determined to continue to oppose the Raj while India was unfree, even though their sympathies were with the Soviet Union against Germany. For his part, Sarat Bose continued to work in the Legislative Assembly and at Bengal party politics, intensely concerned with the ever-growing communalism in Bengal. Whatever the course of the war and the difficulties of his brother in Germany, he could do little about these. He could, however, work at rapprochement between parties and communities in his home province.

The Dacca riots were one manifestation of communal unrest, but the conflict was expressed in more restrained fashion in the debate over many bills and issues in the Bengal Legislative Assembly. As leader of the opposition, Sarat Bose had to sum up for his party and for the entire opposition when possible, but he also tried to find out whether there was some *via media,* some way to reach a compromise with the Coalition Ministry. Amendments to the Calcutta Municipal Act were raised again during this year, but more important for Bengal's long-term development were the Floud Commission Report and the Secondary Education Bill. The first recommended abolition of the Permanent Settlement of 1793 and thus touched every rent-receiver and tenant in the province. The second concerned changes in secondary education which potentially could touch every child attending school. The shaping of the next generation, the problem of religious and moral education at this level, and the whole structure of the educational establishment in Bengal were involved with this bill.

The Krishak Praja Party, at the head of which Fazlul Huq rode to power in 1937, was committed to abolition of the Permanent Settlement. The ministry appointed a commission to investigate the whole issue of land-holding, a vital one, in Bengal. The report issued in 1940, together with several volumes of evidence, called for the abolition of the 1793 Settlement, the compensation of the zamindars for their rights by the Government of Bengal, and the future payment of rents by tenant-cultivators directly to the state without intermediaries. In 1941, the Bengal Assembly did not move for these far-reaching changes, but simply brought the report in for discussion.[188]

Sarat Bose spoke on the report, but went beyond it to give his vision of a future Bengal, shaped by lessons learned from the Soviet Russian experiment with a planned economy and collective, state-owned enterprise. He did agree that long-term bonds should be issued as compensation to the zamindars in exchange for giving up their rights. Then he discussed what he saw as successes in socialism in the Soviet Union saying, in part,

> I would suggest . . . regarding the position of the State *vis-à-vis* the peasants, the experiment which has been conducted with so much success in Soviet Russia ought to be the basis on which we in Bengal should move. What is really wanted . . . is planned economy in this province . . . which will comprise not only agriculture and agriculturalists but also industries, finance and currency, internal and foreign trade, inland waterways, communications, exploration and survey of the province, labour, position of women, housing construction, public health services, social insurance, public education, sports and athletics, literature, music and art.[189]

Anticipating that he would be charged with advocating communism, he tried to undercut his critics by suggesting that all the world religions and Plato's *Republic* were 'frankly communistic in their ideology.' Therefore, he was not breaking with the great cultural ideals, but bringing them to the present for the future benefit of mankind. Quoting Harold Laski's pamphlet on 'Communism' enthusiastically, he said to his supporters and to the backers of the Coalition Ministry,

> . . . I ask them to hearken to the call for social justice, to the call for an equality greater than man has ever known before and lay the foundations here and now for the material and spiritual liberation of mankind.[190]

Instead of influencing his colleagues in the direction of idealistic socialism—towards which he himself was moving closer by his reading of Laski and others—Sarat Bose drew the fire of Revenue Minister Sir Bijoy Prasad Singh Roy. The minister, who had put the Land Revenue Commission Report on the table for discussion, said, 'It is not the first time that we have heard of Socialism and Communism, but certainly earning a big income in the High Court is neither Socialism nor Communism. They do not go together.'[191] Arguments ensued over whether the minister had been unparliamentary and abusive to Sarat Bose and the day's session ended, as others did that year, in tumult and then adjournment.

The Bengal Assembly did not take any immediate action on the landholding question, but they were intensely involved with the Secondary Education Bill. It was reported back from a select committee in 1941, was repeatedly challenged by the opposition, and was discussed extensively in August and September, until the body was prorogued by Governor Herbert on September 18. Many points were at issue. Among them was the removal of control of secondary education from the auspices of Calcutta University—which caste Hindus predominantly controlled—to a new body, one which would have a specified communal membership and be under the control of the government. The whole debate was colored by communal passions, with the Coalition Ministry trying to wrest control of secondary education from the Hindu establishment. Both sides felt the righteousness of their cause. The opposition put forth a motion on September 2, asking that the bill be referred back to the select committee with a host of recommended changes which would guarantee the independence of the new board from communal and government control, and protect vested, or as they put it,'academic' interests.[192]

The motion for referral back to the select committee failed and the discussion continued through September. In trying to work out a formula that would gain some agreement from the opposition, talks were even held between party leaders outside the house. In his major speech on the bill,

Sarat Bose said,

> ... the time has come for us to consider, not whether we should cast our wistful eyes towards Delhi or Whitehall, not whether we should cast our wistful eyes towards Arabia, Kashan, Isfahan or Teheran but whether we should cast our eyes towards our own districts, our own homes, our own villages and our own people, whether Hindus, Muslims, Sikhs or Christians. A few days ago, I said at a conference ... that before discussions were started we should make up our mind ... was it our idea and ideal to train up our sons and daughters as good Bengalis and good Indians or was it our idea and ideal to train up our sons and daughters as mere Hindus or mere Muslims or mere Christians? The response that I had was encouraging; but, unfortunately I found eventually that in certain important matters ... those who represented the Government ... had come forward with their minds made up, not with their minds open to the reception of new ideas.[193]

He regretted, he said, that when the discussants returned to the Assembly, 'communal demands' were put even higher than before. He appealed to Fazlul Huq, also the education minister, to have an open mind and said, in part,

> We hold no brief for the University of Calcutta. We do not complain and we shall not complain, if the Secondary Education Board takes upon itself the control of the Matriculation Examination. . . . What we want is that examination should be conducted by an independent statutory body not liable to be influenced by this community or that, not liable to be influenced either by Writers' Building or by College Square.
>
> I appeal to friends . . . to approach this Bill from a purely nationalist standpoint. A new order is coming upon us, whether we will it or not. The new order calls for a synthesis of the different cultures which exist in this land. . . . Do not do anything which will destroy that synthesis of cultures which is the result of the last few centuries. Do not do anything which will make our children and our children's children consider that they are Hindus and against Muslims or that they are Muslims and against Hindus. Do not forget that Bengal is our common land for common purposes. . . . Let Hindus and Muslims today co-mingle and unite in one determined march for the creation of a new order—the new order which will be heralded by the independence of India.[194]

When Fazlul Huq replied, he said that the time had come for Muslims to have their due and their role in the educational structure of Bengal. He insisted that in so far as they were in charge they would protect the rights of the minority or Hindu community. The debate on this bill went on and was not settled when the session was prorogued on September 18. The matter was to be brought up again at the next session. Other political matters intervened, though, and the debate was not resumed.

Almost at the same time that the deadlock over the Secondary

Education Bill stalled the Bengal Assembly, Fazlul Huq was involved in another and even more important conflict shaping Bengal's and his political future. As noted above, he had wholeheartedly supported the war effort and joined the viceroy's Defence Council. Since this was done without Jinnah's approval and varied from Muslim League policy, Jinnah insisted that Huq and Sikandar Hyat Khan resign. Eventually they did, but Huq was furious and so he not only dropped out of the Defence Council, but also relinquished his position in the Working Committee of the Muslim League. When he did so, he sent a blast at Jinnah in the form of a long letter to Liaquat Ali Khan, secretary of the Muslim League, on September 8, 1941, which said in part,

> I maintain that acceptance of membership of Defence Council in no way involves breach of League's principle or policy. . . . Having regard to my provincial war activities my membership of Defence Council pales into insignificance: I consider it absurd that I should be called upon to non-cooperate with Government of India at centre. . . . President's indiscreet and hasty announcement creating feeling in Muslim minds that we have accepted membership of Council from personal interests or to oblige high officials has produced most baneful consequences. . . . I protest emphatically against manner in which Bengal and Punjab Muslim interests are being imperilled by Muslim leaders of 'Minority Provinces'. . . . They neither realise responsibilities of Muslim Premiers of these provinces nor care for repercussions on politics of Bengal and Punjab Muslims of their decisions for Muslim India as a whole. They should not meddle too much with politics of majority provinces. At present I feel that Bengal does not count much in counsels of political leaders outside province, though we constitute more than one third of total Muslim population of India. . . . As mark of protest against arbitrary use of powers vested in President I resign from membership of Working Committee and Council of All India Muslim League.[195]

With Huq's resignation from the League Working Committee, conflict burst forth with some Muslim Leaguers holding demonstrations against Huq and Huq retaliating by backing a no-confidence motion against one of his own ministers, H.S. Suhrawardy.

Huq said he was defending the Bengal Muslims against a dictator from outside who was not working in their best interests. Huq was and remained primarily a Bengali Muslim leader. He no doubt believed his charges against extra-Bengal control. However, he was an ever changeable person, never satisfied with any alliance and always seeking something better. Based on his many changes of direction, it was hard to take him at his word and to rely in the early morning light on an agreement made in the shadowy night before. Although everyone knew this, Huq was also the most popular mass leader of Bengal Muslims in this period, particularly in East Bengal.[196] Therefore, an alliance with Huq always had attractions. For this reason, Sarat Bose had been carrying on private, but scarcely secret, negotiations with Huq since 1937. These talks became more serious in the fall of 1941 as Huq was breaking with the League and Sarat Bose, suspended by the Congress, was no longer bound by the strictures of his national organization.

As these negotiations for a new political alliance and possible new ministry for Bengal went on, word was given in the Council of State in Delhi on November 10 by Mr Conran Smith, the home secretary, that the government now had information that Subhas Bose 'had gone over to the enemy' and was in Berlin or Rome. Mr Smith said that he did not know how Subhas Bose had reached Europe. Writers in the Indian press and Indian politicians had their doubts, but the *Statesman,* organ of the Europeans in Calcutta, leaped in to classify him as a Nazi,

> Mr Bose's views are those of the Nazis, and he makes no secret of it. . . . Mr Bose gives reasons [*in his book*] why Communism will not be adopted in India, and indicates clearly his preference for Fascism . . . what he really looks for is a synthesis of Communism and Fascism. . . . If therefore Mr Subhas Bose is with the Nazis—and the German radio claimed to know his whereabouts as early as last January—he is where he belongs. . . . Proceedings . . . on a charge against him were, we believe, pending at the time and he was under police surveillance. How came it that he was allowed to disappear?[197]

The *Statesman* had never been a friend of Bose and just as they lumped all protesters against the Raj together as terrorists, so they quickly concluded that Bose was a Nazi because he was on the opposite side from the Raj in the war.

Though shaped through the war by the information selected by the British and fed to them, many Indians hesitated to see Bose as an enemy. For example, the imprisoned Jawaharlal Nehru wrote in his diary on November 11:

> Today's papers contained the Govt. announcement that Subhas was either in Berlin or Rome. . . . One of the head warders asked us if this was true and added that it was like Vibhishan leaving his brother Ravana to join Ramachandra! The British Govt., with all its *atyachar* [*atrocities*] in India was like Ravana, he said. Probably this represents a fairly widespread public reaction.[198]

Nehru did not spell out his own response at this time.

In late November, Sarat Bose's negotiations with Fazlul Huq finally came to fruition as the old ministry was falling. The new grouping of MLAs gathered at Huq's house, Sarat Bose wrote out the new agreement, and Huq stood forth as leader of the new Progressive Coalition Party in the Bengal Assembly. On December 3, Huq announced,

> It is with humility . . . that I accept the leadership of the Progressive Coalition Party, which has been kindly offered to me by the leaders of the various sections in the House. The formation of this party, bringing together as it does the diverse elements in India's national life, is an event unprecedented in the history of India, and should . . . be an augury not only for the cessation of communal strife, but also for the carrying out of a programme for the good of all sections of the people in this country. . . . The present Progressive Coalition Party is composed of members of the Muslim League, the Krishak Praja, the· Congress, the Hindu Maha Sabha, the Nationalists, Indian Christians, Anglo-Indians, Labour members, Scheduled Castes and other elements of the legislature. It is my firm belief that it is this party alone that can bring relief to all communities . . . the coalition party of 1937 has obviously ceased to exist. I was therefore justified in accepting the leadership of the Progressive Coalition Party in the confident hope that it will usher in a new era of peace and prosperity.[199]

On the Hindu side there was rejoicing that what they saw as a communalist Muslim League ministry had fallen. Hindus and Muslims were now to share power with leaders such as Sarat Bose, expected to become ministers in Huq's new government.

The solid Muslim Leaguers like Nazimuddin, Ispahani, and Suhrawardy felt that they had been betrayed by the unscrupulous Fazlul Huq. They announced that Huq, rather than furthering the interests of Bengal's Muslims as he said, had sold them down the river to the Hindu Mahasabha and the dissident Congress.[200] Fazlul Huq was expelled from the Muslim League and shortly was subjected to a ferocious campaign of charges and insults by its members and leaders. Huq tried to answer that the League itself had allied with the Boses in the Calcutta Corporation in 1940 and the national organization had tried to make agreements with the Congress from 1936 on, but had failed. Where they had not succeeded, he had. This argument made sense, but carried no weight with the leadership of the League, which no longer dominated the ministry in one of the largest Muslim-majority provinces of India. M.A.H. Ispahani wrote to Jinnah on November 29, just as the new party was formed,

> Fazlul Huq has cheated all and has gained his object . . . . We woke up this morning to be faced with a *fait accompli*. . . . Huq asked for time, not to bring back his men to the fold of the Coalition but to fix up with Wardha. The mandate reached Calcutta last night and so out came the conspiracy that has been hatched for many months. . . . He has sold Muslim interests to the Hindus. . . . Now the war is on. Huq has gained a tactical advantage. However, our cause is just and Allah will help us.[201]

There was some delay in forming the new ministry because Governor

Herbert did not want Huq at the helm if he could help it. He would have preferred the stolid Nazimuddin, now the leader of the Muslim League group. However, Huq demonstrated that he had the backing of a majority in the Bengal Assembly and the governor had to allow him to form a new ministry.[202]

On December 7, 1941, the Japanese struck Pearl Harbor. They also attacked the British Empire and within a day the United States and Great Britain declared war on Japan. The Japanese navy and army assaulted the British in Malaya and so the possibility of the war reaching India was now much greater and another powerful enemy had to be faced. The Government of India knew of Sarat Bose's 'secret' meetings with the Japanese consul in Calcutta, but they allowed them to go on. Just as the new ministry was to be announced—it was said that Sarat Bose wanted to be the home minister—the Government of India moved.

On the morning of December 11, Deputy Police Commissioner Janvrin appeared at Woodburn Park. Mrs Bose became flushed. Her husband had told her what to expect. Sarat Bose was asked to come down. Orders for his arrest had been issued by the Government of India because his Japanese contacts were considered 'a very definite and real danger' to the security of India.[203] Richard Tottenham of the Home Department in Delhi noted that the government had considered arresting Sarat Bose the previous August, but waited. Now, however, the situation was critical. Britain, and thus India, was now at war with Japan and, '. . . it goes without saying . . . that it would be impossible to contemplate having Sarat Chandra Bose as a Minister. . . .'[204]

Sarat Bose was taken to the Presidency Jail, but Huq went ahead and completed his cabinet without him. Santosh Basu and Pramatha Nath Banerjee of his group were taken into the ministry. However, a Hindu leader of greater stature was needed to replace Sarat Bose. The only formidable one available and willing was the Hindu Mahasabha leader Shyama Prasad Mookerjee. This, though, weakened the new ministry gravely because the Muslims, who generally respected Sarat Bose, saw Mookerjee as an enemy of their community. The long-term hopes for Hindu-Muslim amity were dealt a hard knock at the onset of the new government.[205]

During the first few weeks of the new ministry, while Sarat Bose was in a Calcutta jail, ministers including Huq went to consult him, and the Bengal Assembly voted that all steps should be taken to bring about his immediate release.[206] At the end of the month, the Government of India decided to move him to distant Madras. Shortly thereafter the Viceroy Lord Linlithgow wrote to the secretary of state for India, Mr Amery,

It is obvious that it was well to have got Sarat Bose away from here, for from what I gather the restriction on his interviews were of the lightest, and in fact one individual went so far as to suggest that it was almost the case that Cabinet meetings were held in his quarters in the jail! . . . though I realise the difficulties of local officials in debiting interviews with the Chief Minister . . . against Sarat Bose's quota, I see myself no reason why he should not have been subject to precisely the same degree of restriction as the ordinary prisoner of his class, while his contacts with the Japanese were an additional reason for exercising the greatest care in his case.[207]

Two members of Sarat Bose's group were allowed to become ministers because they were not believed to be a security risk. However, other members of the Forward Bloc and BV and those in the Bose family believed to have been involved with Subhas Bose's work and escape, were interrogated and, in some cases, imprisoned. While Britain and India were at war with Germany and Japan and Subhas Bose was cooperating with the other side, Sarat Bose was to be held. Both were out of the field of Indian politics for the time being, though Subhas Bose tried to shape Indian developments from outside and Sarat Bose had attempted to shift the course of Bengal politics from the dead end of communal enmity.

When Subhas Bose left India to try to find allies outside to help him fight the Raj, he hoped that ministries might be formed in some provinces, particularly border or coastal ones, with members favorable to his views. Now dissident Congressmen from the Bose faction were ministers in Bengal and later some joined the ministry in Orissa. Hare Krishna Mahatab has suggested that this was part of his plan to bring about the downfall of the Raj.[208]

The break with the National Congress, nevertheless, did weaken the ability of the Boses to influence Congress policy. And, similarly, Huq's split with the Muslim League prevented him from henceforward having a voice in their policies. So dissidents from both important national organizations had come together to try to break out of the previous mold. This effort was fatally harmed by the imprisonment of Sarat Bose, which, in turn, was largely due to Subhas Bose's escape and activities abroad. It remained to be seen whether the activities of Subhas Bose and his brother helped the left in India and the cause of Hindu-Muslim alliance. And also unclear were what the reverberations would be of the temporary pact Subhas Bose had made with the devil, Nazism.

CHAPTER TEN

Axis Collaborator? Subhas Bose in Europe, 1941–43

. . . the value of this upstart is not clear.

Count Ciano[1]

'Chandra Bose to Berlin, received by Hitler—Once more, he has made the plunge. At one time to the right, at another to the left. Moscow, Berlin, Tokyo. . . . These Bengalis, violent, impulsive, never a politics of reason, they obey the somersaults of their passions, victims of their own vulnerability to jealousy, vanity, stung to the quick by fleshwounds.'

Romain Rolland[2]

The resolute never relinquish their goal.

Bhartrihari, #52[3]

I

Subhas Bose, now Orlando Mazzotta according to his Italian passport, traveled by car and train to Moscow and then by plane to Berlin where he arrived by the first week of April 1941, about two-and-a-half months after he had left Calcutta.[4] In the midst of the greatest war mankind had ever seen, he had to make his way, however haltingly, towards his goal of Indian liberation. The challenge was more formidable than in the 1930s since the world around him had changed. The Germans might be at war with Great Britain and the British Empire, but Hitler was quite ambivalent about whether he wanted war or peace with Britain even in 1941. A reliable informant told Ernst von Weizsäcker, state secretary of the German Foreign Office, late in 1941, 'England was still Hitler's love. His picture of the future was that some time Germany would join with England against the USA. This fantastic idea often recurred to Hitler.'[5] Even as he had the Luftwaffe bomb London mercilessly, Hitler had an open hand ready to grasp that of Britain if she would agree to a 'deal'.

During the First World War, a small number of Indian nationalists working abroad in Europe, the Americas, and Asia had searched for assistance outside India. At that time there were a number of groups, often rivaling each other rather than cooperating, and there was no general agreement among these revolutionaries abroad on either ends or means. They were isolated from the mainstream of Indian nationalism at home.[6] Of those involved in these plots, a few, like M.N. Roy, had eventually returned to India and joined the Congress and a few others remained outside for long years awaiting another opportunity to help nationalist activity. Of the latter, only Rash Behari Bose, who remained in Japan from the First to the Second World War, was in a position to play an important role at this time. In 1938, he had reached out to Subhas Bose, but the British had intercepted his letter and turned it aside. In 1941 he was in touch with top Japanese authorities hoping that they might be ready to ally with Indian nationalists in toppling the British Raj.[7]

By the time that Subhas Bose reached Berlin in April 1941, Operation Barbarossa—the German attack on the Soviet Union—was already in the works. As the preparations for this opening of a new front in the war were underway, officials of the Third Reich were still reaching out to Britain in hopes that a *modus vivendi* could be arranged allowing fellow 'Aryans' to divide up the world before Barbarossa began. But the Germans learned that the British had no 'serious intention' of making such a bargain at this time.[8] Nonetheless, while the war in Russia began, Hitler abandoned plans for a cross-channel invasion and still held up the British Empire as a model he wished to emulate. He said in his *Secret Conversations* in early August 1941 to a captive audience:

> The basic reason for English pride is India. Four hundred years ago the English didn't have this pride. The vast spaces over which they spread their rule obliged them to govern millions of people—and they kept these multitudes in order by granting a few men unlimited power. . . . What India was for England, the territories of Russia will be for us. If only I could make the German people understand what this space means for our future.[9]

Hitler was obsessed by power and jealous of his rival Anglo-Saxons, the only 'racial group' or nationality he thought of as equals. India otherwise meant little to him. He put Indians way down on his racial scale and believed they deserved to be ruled by others.

From his first days in Berlin, Bose began to deal with what Milan Hauner has labeled the 'often confused and pluralistic character of Nazi foreign policy'.[10] The byzantine world of Nazi and German power politics was ruthless. The blatantly immoral Nazi leaders around Hitler were willing to use almost any means for their own advancement.[11] As they pushed and shoved to gain pre-eminence, they also created new bureaus, agencies, and institutions, which overlapped with already existing ones.

In the eight years since Hitler had come to power, he had gradually edged out the old-style diplomats and foreign service officers—often of aristocratic background—and put in his party men.[12] Long before Joachim von Ribbentrop became foreign minister in place of Neurath in 1938, he had set up an alternative structure for dealing with foreign affairs staffed by his own party hacks to undercut the professionals from the Wilhelmstrasse whom he and Hitler hated and mistrusted. From 1938, the ability of the non-Nazi foreign service men to influence German policies dwindled even more. One of Ribbentrop's rivals for control of foreign policy, Goebbels, who called him 'Ribbensnob,' said of him, 'He bought his name, he married his money, and he swindled his way into office.'[13] Like his master, before whom he fawned, Ribbentrop was given to raving speeches, blank stares, and the inability to listen.[14] As the conquests of the Reich vastly increased the territory of German administration, and as more and more nations declared war on Germany, the sphere of activity for her diplomats, particularly for the old foreign service men, dwindled.

Some of them had great antipathy to Hitler. For example, Ulrich von Hassell, reached out to fellow German nationalists in the military in hopes that some might ally with him in overthrowing Hitler and saving Germany.[15] However, as Weizsäcker and others have explained, as Hitler moved from victory to victory in the first half of the war, the opposition could make little headway, no matter how destructive they believed Hitler would be to Germany and Europe in the long run. Many Germans, in and out of the Nazi Party, wanted revenge against their enemies of the First World War and the peace treaty of Versailles that had been forced upon them. Hitler promised revival, conquest, greatness and seemed to be delivering an uncanny series of triumphs for Germany from 1938 to mid-1941.

When Subhas Bose, now dressed in Western clothes for the duration of his stay in Europe, arrived in Berlin in early April 1941, he was met by officials of the Foreign Office and lodged temporarily in Hotel Esplanade. For the first few months, it was necessary for Bose to see what was possible. The German government also had to figure out what it wanted to do with Bose. Other leaders of anti-imperialist movements such as the Mufti of Jerusalem and Rashid Ali of Iraq came to Berlin and in each case, the appropriate ministries and, ultimately, Hitler, had to make decisions as to their usefulness for German purposes.[16]

While in Kabul and just after arrival in Berlin, Bose prepared a lengthy memorandum to the German government laying out the ways in which he hoped the Axis powers would cooperate with Indian nationalists.[17] He presented himself as an appropriate spokesman for the whole nationalist enterprise although he and the Germans knew that Bose had been on the outs with Gandhi and Nehru during his last year-and-a-half in India.[18] Bose never said that he was *the* leader of Indian nationalism or the most important, but he did maintain that he had some kind of sanction to speak for Indian nationalists since he was outside the 'prison' that was British India acting in a quasi-diplomatic role. He probably believed that if he made gains for Indian independence by his actions while outside the country, then these would be accepted by the Congress, the party of which he was still a member and from which he had never broken.

Bose wrote, in part,

> The British Empire constitutes the greatest obstacle not only in the path of India's freedom but also in the path of human progress.
>
> Since the attitude of the Indian people is intensely hostile to the British in the present war, it is possible for them to materially assist in bringing about the overthrow of Great Britain. India's cooperation could be secured if the Indian people are assured that an Axis victory will mean for them a free India.[19]

He went on to propose that a 'Free Indian Government' should be set up in Berlin, recognized by the Germans, and financially backed by a loan which the new government would use to carry out its operations. A major objective throughout his stay in Europe was to get the German government to issue a declaration for a free India. Among the activities of the free Indian government were to be propaganda and the organization of a military force of 50,000 which Bose said would be sufficient to drive the diminished British garrison out of India and liberate her.[20] Bose elaborated a program for Axis-aided Indians to carry out in Europe, in Afghanistan, and then within India itself.

Dr Woermann, head of the Political Section in Berlin, listened coolly to Bose's proposals since he and his superiors wanted to be convinced that there was something for Nazi Germany in all this. Hitler had made it clear to his minions that he was not interested in recognizing governments-in-exile for territories far from the Reich simply for the sake of their populations. If it would help his armies as they rolled across the frontier of a previously-unconquered territory, then he would do it to help him reach *his* objectives. As scholars Arvinda Katpitia and Milan Hauner have shown, Bose was rather naively asking the Germans for what he wanted, but not effectively persuading them that it would be in the Reich's interest. Woermann wrote a critical memorandum about his meeting with Bose, skeptical that Bose would be of great value.

Later in April, at Hotel Imperial in Vienna, Bose met Ribbentrop and they cagily felt each other out through a long exchange of views. Bose wanted German help and expressed some agreement with Axis goals, particularly their destruction of the British Empire, but he also wanted Ribbentrop to soften Nazi racism. Ribbentrop may not have been used to confronting criticism of Nazi ideology as directly as Bose offered it and he backed away from their racist scheme as applied to Asians. But he pressed Bose about the latter's facile assumptions that the Indian army and Indian people in general were seething with hatred towards the British and on the brink of revolt if only a helping hand were reached out to them from outside. It was an appropriate questioning of Bose's basic assumptions.

Ribbentrop did promise Bose assistance, but explained the Hitler viewpoint on recognizing governments-in-exile. He said that he would look into this further and dangled the carrot of recognition before Bose. Bose sent an additional memorandum to Woermann in early May, congratulating the Germans on their victories and stating, *inter alia*, that he hoped the *status quo* would be maintained between Germany and the Soviet Union.

In the late spring, the German Foreign Office was moving to create a new structure to deal with Indian affairs and link to Bose. Rather than attach a new India section to the Political Department, they constructed the Sonderreferat Indien, Special Bureau for India, which was attached to the Information Department of the Foreign Office. Wilhelm Keppler, a Nazi and under-secretary of state of the Foreign Office was put in charge. Keppler had direct access to the foreign minister. Although Keppler remained atop, the actual work was put into the abler, more subtle, and anti-Nazi hands of Adam von Trott zu Solz. Several officers were considered for the post, but it was felt that Trott could get along with Bose and Trott had some knowledge of India. Immediately beneath Trott was Alexander Werth, an old and close friend who had spent a few years in prison under the Nazis, but had emerged almost unscathed and, like Trott, was able to move into the Foreign Office in 1940.[21] Other personnel in this grouping included F.J. Furtwaengler, A.F. Richter, H.T. Leipoldt, Prof Dr Alsdorf, Mrs Kruse, Dr Kretschmer, Baron von Zitzewitz, Baron von Lewinski, Mr Assmann and Mr Trump.[22]

Adam von Trott zu Solz was an aristocrat from an ancient landed family of Hesse. He was trained in international law, and received a Rhodes scholarship to Oxford in the 1930s, where he made many contacts. He then lived in China for almost a year and traveled widely before the war and even during the war itself. A strong German nationalist, a friend wrote of him that, '. . . the real business of his life (was) the future of Germany.'[23] During

his travels he had established connections at high levels in the public life
of Britain and the United States and traveled to Britain on a 'peace
mission' in June 1939 and then to the United States in late 1939, after the
war had broken out.[24] With the failure of these missions, Trott decided to
join the German Foreign Office to see whether he could help save his
country from within the establishment. He used his position as a cover for
continuing efforts to reach out to military officers and others who were
opposed to the direction that Nazism was taking Germany. His work in the
Information Department enabled him to travel to Switzerland, Turkey,
Scandinavia, and throughout Nazi-occupied Europe, making contacts.
His mission, which he saw as the salvaging of the great traditions of
humanistic Germany and Europe, was one for which he risked his life.

Thus Trott became the key link for Bose to the German Foreign Office,
though Bose also met with Ribbentrop, Keppler, and Woermann from
time to time. One of the tragedies of Bose's sojourn in Europe was that he
and Trott never became close, and never really trusted each other. Trott
wrote to his wife on August 8, 1941, 'He (Bose) is highly gifted, but in spite
of that on a human plane we remain very distant. We have to begin afresh
each time.'[25] And a week later, he wrote that, 'For a worthwhile relationship his fundamental attitudes are too negative. . . .'[26] To the best of my
knowledge, Bose did not know the true mission and work of Trott, though
his deputy, A.C.N. Nambiar, did grow close to Trott and probably knew.
Trott did his best to help Bose with his work of liberating India, even
deriding the mission of Sir Stafford Cripps to India in 1942, though Cripps
was a personal friend of Trott's and much admired by him. However,
feeling that Bose did not understand the Nazi tyranny and how it was
destroying what was best in the German tradition, Trott withheld his
deeper sympathy and intimate friendship from Bose. Had Trott taken a
chance, he might have found Bose close to him in outlook since they were
both idealistic nationalists, interested in Hegelian philosophy, leaned to
socialism, and had small, but important parts of their education in Britain.
There was, though, a failure by each to come closer to the other. Trott's
young and intelligent wife, Clarita von Trott, said to me, 'We loved
Nambiar,' but she reiterated the lack of closeness with Bose.[27]

There is at least one other person who played a role in all this: Emilie
Schenkl. Bose's close relationship with her which grew during his years
in Europe through weekly correspondence, and then with renewed contact
in 1937, has been described earlier. After Bose reached Berlin, he asked
German officials to contact her in Vienna and ask her to come to Berlin.
She duly arrived in April and lived with Bose throughout his European
period, first in hotels, then in a house provided by the Germans in Berlin.

Most of the German Foreign Office group—Trott, Alexander Werth, Freda Kretschmer—appear to have disliked her intensely. They believed that she and Bose were not married and that she was using her liaison with Bose to live an especially comfortable life during the hard times of war.[28] For her part, Emilie Schenkl did not like Trott whom she accused of aristocratic snobbery.[29] Whatever the personal sensitivities involved, there also was a strong class bias at work. The Foreign Office officials were highly educated and had aristocratic and upper-middle-class backgrounds. They looked down on the less educated lower or lower-middle-class secretary from Vienna whom they saw living and eating much better than they were in the midst of the war. Dr Kretschmer, particularly, who claims that she was assigned by the Foreign Office to watch Fraulein Schenkl and ensure that she kept clear of politics, developed a loathing for Bose's 'personal companion,' as she is called in many Foreign Office files, and claims that the relationship had a very harmful effect on Bose. This is not supported by the other evidence.[30]

We have already seen how several accounts of Bose in Germany give one or another date for a marriage ceremony, but not a single one is written by anyone who says that he or she witnessed a marriage ceremony and no person whom I have interviewed from the Berlin period says that he or she witnessed such a formal linking.[31] But the relationship begun in the 1930s continued and deepened with the pregnancy of Emilie Schenkl in 1942, and the birth of Anita Bose in Vienna on November 29, 1942. Bose acknowledged his family. But the woman he chose, though she contributed to his own work and life, helped alienate the very anti-Nazi Foreign Office officials to whom he might have come closer.

While Bose was starting to chart out the work that was possible for him to do in Europe in the spring of 1941, he began to summon and recruit Indian students and other Indian residents of Nazi-dominated Europe, some of whom were immediately at hand. M.R. Vyas, N.G. Swami, and Abid Hasan all became devoted workers for the cause of Indian freedom as sought by Bose.[32]

Swami, from Madras, had been in Germany since 1932 pursuing technical training and was active in Indian student associations in Europe. He had met Bose in the mid-1930s, was one of the first to meet him now in Berlin, and then followed him to East Asia in 1943. Vyas, of Gujarati background and raised in Kenya, had come to Europe to study at the London School of Economics in 1937 and then gone to Germany for language work just before the war began. He had also encountered Bose on an earlier visit to Europe and joined him in April 1941. Hasan, a Muslim from Hyderabad, studied engineering at a Berlin technical college, and was asked by Swami to come and meet an Italian gentleman in April 1941. Although he had heard that Bose had disappeared from Calcutta, he was overwhelmed to meet him in Berlin. A man of courage, shrewd intelligence, and dedication, Hasan decided to work on the military side of Bose's operation in Europe and then served as his private secretary.

Among the older men readily at hand, N.G. Ganpuley from Poona, born in 1895, had traveled between Germany and India since the early 1920s and represented a number of German engineering firms, giving him considerable experience in the economic field. Habibur Rahman, a Delhi Muslim, born in 1901, had also had long experience in Germany and been employed writing for the German government. He was transferred to Bose's operation in Berlin.[33] From his earlier years in Europe, Bose also knew other Indians in Europe. As soon as Emilie Schenkl came to Berlin, Bose asked her, 'Where is Nambiar?' A.C.N. Nambiar was passing the war-time quietly in Vichy France. It took Bose almost ten months to find Nambiar and to coax him to join his operation in Germany.[34] Nambiar was about Bose's age, an experienced journalist, who Bose thought would be able to stand up to the fascists in any argument. Nambiar eventually succumbed to Bose's request to come and work with him.

During April, Bose made other contacts with Germans which were to be of value to him. G. Wirsing began to tutor Bose in German so that he could operate more freely and confidently in a German diplomatic and military milieu. Bose was a good linguist and improved his German considerably during the next year-and-a-half.[35] Walter Harbich, a determined and perceptive military officer, later helped to train Indians for military service in Europe and took to Bose immediately.[36] Later Bose came into touch again with Lothar Frank, whom he had met in the mid-1930s. Frank, a socialist, was under supervision by the police, but came occasionally from Hamburg and met Bose. Frank, who listened to the BBC and got news from other foreign sources, tried to keep Bose informed as to the real course of the war as against the official German version.[37]

Bose had contacts with the Japanese embassy headed by Ambassador Oshima which saw to the transmission of his messages to his brother in Calcutta via Tokyo.[38] Bose also befriended the Japanese military attaché Yamamoto. It is not unlikely that these messages were intercepted and decoded by the Americans, since their intelligence operation had cracked the Japanese diplomatic cipher and the project called 'Magic' made these intercepts available to the British.[39] He made the rounds of the powers associated by the Tripartite Alliance, signed on September 27, 1940. It is not clear whether Bose knew just how hollow the alliances were between the Germans and the Italians, and the Germans and the Japanese.[40] Since

Bose was a relatively empty-handed Indian abroad, he was ready and willing to seek out and listen to any offers of support from one or another of these the Axis powers. Johanna Meskill has accurately summed up the relationship between Germany and Japan:

> Germany and Japan each found the existence and policies of the other convenient . . . but. . . . nothing united Germany and Japan. . . . Germany and Japan, moreover, were caught in such delusions about each other's political and military goals and practised such secrecy and deception concerning their own objectives that even on those few occasions when their interests genuinely converged they were unable to coordinate their policies . . . the allies aimed at different and often incompatible ends, often deceiving each other and themselves into the bargain.[41]

The mutual mistrust between Germany and Japan did not help Bose.

Just around this time, Mussolini was put into a rage by German meddling in the Balkans and said on June 10 to his foreign minister (and son-in-law) Count Ciano:

> They (*i.e., the Germans*) are dirty dogs. . . . I have been thoroughly disgusted with the Germans since the time List made an armistice with Greece without our knowledge . . . robbing us of the fruits of victory. Personally, I've had my fill of Hitler and the way he acts. These conferences called by the ringing of a bell are not to my liking; a bell is rung when people call their servants. And besides, what kind of conferences are these? For five hours I am forced to listen to a monologue which is quite fruitless and boring.[42]

Hitler, for his part, though he is said to have had a certain attachment to Mussolini, saw more clearly each day that the Italians were a useless, indeed a dangerous, military ally for him. With the same mistrust that characterized his relations with other 'allies', Hitler did not tell the Italians of his plans, nor did they tell him of theirs. But Germany was a considerable military power, while the Italian military machine was a fraud.[43] But Bose hoped to get assistance from Mussolini in obtaining the declaration of a free India and other items he sought from the Germans. So he went to Rome accompanied by Emilie Schenkl, near the end of May. The Germans were not overjoyed at Bose's excursion, but they did not prevent him from going.

On June 6, he met Ciano, who wrote in his diary,

> I receive Bose, head of the Indian insurgent movement. He would like the Axis to make a declaration on the independence of India, but in Berlin his proposals have been received with a great deal of reserve. Nor must we be compromised, especially because the value of this upstart is not clear. Past experience has given rather modest results.[44]

This assessment seems harsher than what Bose might have expected. There was, however, another factor. Bose had a rival Indian contender for the favors of the Italians in this period: this was Muhammad Iqbal Shedai.

An Indian Muslim from Sialkot in the Punjab, Shedai, born in either 1892 or 1898, had left India just after the First World War. He traveled to Europe where he was engaged in political intrigue against the Raj in a minor way. Expelled from France in the late 1930s, he went to Switzerland and in October 1940 to Rome. There he made contact with some Indian residents and the Italian Foreign Office. With the assistance of the latter, he began to broadcast back to India over what was called Radio Himalaya and also made contact with Indian prisoners-of-war captured by the Italians in North Africa. Thus he was little known outside a small circle of Indian and European contacts.[45] But he did seem to have a good connection to the Italian government and did not want to be a subordinate of Bose in Berlin. They each wanted to control a possible combined propaganda operation in Europe. Also, there were significant political differences between the two which gradually emerged. Shedai came to support the Pakistan movement which was anathema to Bose. The former looked at India as closely connected to the Middle East and the Islamic world, whereas for Bose it was a world unto itself. As accusations began to be flung about, Shedai warned the Germans in private communications that Bose was recruiting a nest of communists to Berlin.[46]

Although for the most part the Italian forces in North Africa were beaten badly by the British, the Italians did succeed in capturing a few thousand Indian army troops among the total Allied forces they dealt with.[47] In the Second World War, the British desperately needed manpower and supplies from their imperial possessions and Indian forces were rapidly built up and employed in the fray, first in North Africa, later on the European continent, as well as in Southeast Asia. During this period of rapid mobilization, the Indian army grew from 189,000 in 1939 to 2,500,000 by 1945.[48] Since Bose maintained in his proposals to German and Italian officials that the Indian army was seething with discontent and very anti-British, he had to offer some proof of this by meeting with these prisoners and trying to bring them over to the other side. Shedai had met some of the prisoners. Trott and Werth, on behalf of the Germans, were negotiating with the Italians about the possible use of these prisoners to fight the British. This was an issue which had to be worked out between the two governments, their respective armies, and the Indian groups headed by Bose and Shedai. The intriguing of Shedai and the inability of Bose and Shedai to come to some rapprochement undoubtedly harmed the Indian cause in Europe. But Bose, after the Congress wars of past decades, was not easily sidetracked or halted. However, a new international development while he was in Rome forced him to rethink his entire program outside India. This was the German invasion of the Soviet Union beginning on June 22, 1941.

Privately he was distraught and one formal response was a long letter to Dr Woermann, written from Rome on July 5. Bose wrote, in part,

> I met Count Ciano after his return from Venice, as desired by him. The talk was not encouraging for me and soon after that, the war in the East broke out. The prospect for the realisation of my plans looked gloomy in the altered circumstances and I was thinking that an early return to Berlin would not be of much use, till the situation in the East was clarified. I was therefore happy to receive your letter. . . . The public reaction in my country to the new situation in the East is unfavourable towards your Government. However, I am following the situation as closely as I can and I shall discuss the whole matter with you as soon as I arrive.[49]

Encouraged by Woermann to return to Berlin and take up his work there, Bose proposed to leave Rome within a few days, stop in Vienna, and then come on to Berlin.

Bose and Emilie Schenkl returned to the Hotel Excelsior in Berlin, and Bose met with his German instructor, Wirsing. The latter wrote later that Bose sat 'deeply sunken in a lotus position in front of a world map.' Still reeling from the almost physical blow he had suffered from the German invasion of the Soviet Union, Bose spoke bitterly against Hitler to Wirsing and implied that he might be better off in East Asia.[50]

Although many Germans were now preoccupied with the expanding war against the Soviet Union, Bose continued to meet with his Foreign Office contacts, arguing for a declaration on India, and planning for a Free India Center for propaganda work and the Indian Legion for military activity. Whatever thoughts entered his head about working elsewhere, he still wanted the declaration from the Germans, along with the Italians and Japanese, if possible. He met with Keppler and Woermann. The latter reported on July 17:

> Bose first spoke in detail concerning the repercussions of the German-Russian war on public opinion in India. The Soviet Union had been popular in India, especially among the intelligentsia . . . because in India they believed that the Soviet Union was an anti-imperialist power and thus the natural ally of India against England. . . . In the German-Russian war the feelings of the Indian people were very decidedly on the Russian side, because the Indian people were sure that Germany was the aggressor and thus also an imperialist power dangerous to India. . . . Bose's statements indicated that, away from Berlin, he is strongly influenced by the Soviet thesis even in the question of the origin of the . . . conflict. . . . I told Bose that we adhered unchanged to the intention of a proclamation in favor of a free India; naturally a favorable moment had to be chosen for this.
>
> At this point Mr Bose became very excited and asked that the Foreign Minister be told that this proclamation should be issued as quickly as possible.[51]

The declaration was at the center of Bose's concerns. However, for their own reasons, the Germans were elusive and would not give it to him. Bose, through the German Foreign Office, continued to make contact with Bhagat Ram Talwar, now known as Rahmat Khan, who reported to the German embassy in Kabul. Bhagat Ram met with Forward Bloc agents, including Santimoy Ganguli, a young Bengali, who made it successfully to the frontier and back. Bose tried to give instructions and gather information about Indian politics and his own family through these exchanges. These communications did go on, but as Milan Hauner has shown, Bhagat Ram appears to have been working for several governments at once and so the British knew about his activity.[52]

Some time after his July return to Berlin, Subhas Bose, together with Emilie Schenkl, moved into a large and comfortable house at Sophienstrasse 7 in Charlottenburg. The former Kempner-Villa was procured by the Foreign Office and furnished, Werth has written, by himself. Given a quasi-diplomatic status, Bose was allotted special food and wine, along with a car, a special gasoline ration, and driver, since Bose himself did not drive. They had a small staff consisting of a cook, manservant, part-time gardener, a chauffeur, and for a while a maidservant. Through his stay in Europe, Bose gradually learned to drink in moderation, eat meat, and become a fairly heavy smoker. He told Nambiar he wanted to adapt more to European ways. Nambiar encouraged him to try more of the culinary treats of Europe and said that anyone who did not eat a good goulash, simply did not know what he was missing. In the 1930s in Vienna, Bose had told the woman who cooked his meals: 'I am a Hindu, I don't eat veal or beef.' Now he ate beef.[53]

Bose usually worked late into the night, dictating to Emilie Schenkl, and then reading and writing to 4.00 or 5.00 a.m. He rose about 11.00 a.m., ate, and, after the Free India had been established, went there for an afternoon of meetings and other work. Sometimes Emilie Schenkl went with him. She encouraged him to go in the morning to set a good example to the others. At 6.00 or 7.00 p.m., he would return home. Often some of the Indians in Berlin would visit him, occasionally one of the Foreign Office staff. Another visitor whom Bose was happy to see was Ghulam Ali Siddiqui, former foreign minister of Afghanistan.[54] From time to time there would be dinner parties.

Among the frequent visitors to the house was Dr A. Q. Faroqi, a South Indian Muslim, trained in engineering and medicine, and resident in Europe on and off for two decades.[55] He served as Bose's personal physician. Faroqi gave him glucose injections which were supposed to give him energy and enable him to deal with the stresses of his wartime situation. Along with his late nights of work, Bose meditated in private, as he had been doing since he was a teenager. He also engaged in playful activity with Emilie Schenkl, chasing her from room to room around the second floor of the house. These breaks were necessary for him to cope with the setbacks he had to encounter as he tried to carry out his mission in Europe.[56] Dr J.K. Banerji, one of his recruits to Berlin, said, 'When the bombs are falling, all kinds of things happen.' Bose, he explained, loosened up in wartime and some of his earlier inhibitions fell away.[57]

Through the second half of 1941, preparations for the establishment of a propaganda center, to be called the Free India Center (*Zentrale Freies Indien*), went forward. Hugh Toye, a former British intelligence officer, who has written an extensive manuscript on the war period called *Subhas Pasha* and a shorter published book, says that Bose's small group was called 'Stab Mazzotta' and this was expanded to become the Center. Still stalled on the issue of the declaration for a free India, Bose went off to Badgastein to sulk for a while. Again, the Germans did not make a specific declaration or give the date when it would be issued. The Foreign Ministry sent Trott to Badgastein to woo Bose back and after a long talk, Bose agreed to return even without his declaration.[58]

Things were going slowly, perhaps badly. Masking his unhappiness with the German and Italian (and Japanese) reticence to give him his declaration, he continued to coax Indians to Berlin. Some of those on the left of the political spectrum or who had strong feelings for one or the other of the defeated or threatened powers hesitated. Among these was Nambiar, number one on Bose's wanted list. Nambiar was in Foix, southern France, near the Spanish border. Remembering his earlier run-ins with the Nazis and seeing how the Germans treated the French, he hesitated to come to Berlin. He met Bose in Paris in August, shared a Dubonnet with him, listened to his arguments, then returned to Foix to think it over. Bose, never one to give up easily, persisted in his efforts and, finally, by the end of the year, overcame Nambiar's reservations. In January 1942, accompanied by the pro-French and also hesitant Girija Mookerjee, Nambiar finally came to Berlin to work with Bose.[59] Girija Mookerjee, a Bengali born in East Bengal in 1905, had studied in Europe in the 1930s and worked as a teacher and journalist. With Gandhi's close associate, C.F. Andrews, he had written *The Rise and Growth of the Indian National Congress*. Bose also applied his persuasive powers to Dr J.K. Banerji, whom he cajoled from Vichy France to Berlin in the same period. He was also a Bengali, born in Lucknow in 1907, and had been associated with communist organizations in India and Britain in the 1930s. During this decade, he studied in Paris, obtained a doctorate from the Sorbonne, did journalistic and political work, and traveled widely. Dr Banerji was more to the left than most of the Indians in Berlin and most adept at Marxist dialectics. He hoped, for his part, to have Bose add more radical revolutionary items to his program, even at the risk of alienating some of his followers. Although Bose listened to Banerji, the former did not want to split his group. He adhered to his all-class line and restrained Banerji's more radical workers and peasants program. With the arrival of men like Banerji and Nambiar in Berlin, more theoretical and lively discussions were held among the Indian group. Although Dr Banerji had his political differences with Bose and was less reverential towards him than some of the younger men were, he still appreciated that Bose listened to others courteously and genuinely wanted to hear them formulate their views.[60] Bose wanted India to have a strong central government after independence, but this did not make him a Hitler or a Mussolini or a Ribbentrop. He was not a quisling—i.e., someone who betrayed his own country—and not a fascist in the European mold of this period.[61] Bose despised Nazi racism and brutality, but he was so set on his one goal that he screened out fascist brutality more thoroughly than some of the other Indians in Berlin.

The Free India Center was formally instituted on November 2, 1941 and its headquarters were in the Lichtensteinallee. From here, by early the next year, radio scripts were prepared in more than half a dozen Indian languages and broadcast to India by a powerful German transmitter which was located at Huizen in Holland. Other materials, monthlies in German, French, and English, and a number of books on nationalist topics were prepared. *Azad Hind,* a German and English monthly, appeared from early 1942 and contained articles by Bose and many others on the staff of the Center. After some dispute, Ribbentrop had agreed that prior German censorship would not be applied to Azad Hind Radio. Broadcasts were made in English and Hindustani plus Bengali, Persian, Tamil, Telugu, Gujarati, and Pushtu. About 230 minutes of broadcasts were sent out daily from early in 1942.[62]

On November 10, 1941 the Government of India announced in the Central Legislative Assembly, to which Subhas Bose had been elected during his last imprisonment, that he had gone over to the enemy. Many Indians asked for proof, while the *Statesman,* an old enemy, chortled happily in an editorial:

> Mr Bose's views are those of the Nazis, and he makes no secret of it . . . take the trouble to read his book. . . . If therefore Mr Subhas Bose is with the Nazis—and the German radio claimed to know his whereabouts as early as last January—he is where he belongs. He is honester than those who now put up a smoke-screen of disbelief.[63]

While Bose remained Mazzotta in Berlin and still hesitated to come out publicly and announce his whereabouts and views—Goebbels said he was waiting for the most appropriate moment—most people in India and Britain now had no doubt where he had gone after disappearing from Calcutta in January.[64] Although still shielding himself partially behind the screen of his Mazzotta identity, Bose continued his usual hectic pace of work, mainly in Berlin after the early fall lull and at the Badgastein retreat. As he gathered recruits, he began to help them choose the specific area in which they would work. Hasan and Swami, two of the earliest, preferred the military side and their first assignments were to help persuade Indian prisoners to join the Axis side, work with Bose, and also to assist in gathering student recruits. But most of the students and more mature Indian recruits from among those already in Europe when war broke out, preferred the civilian side, the work of the Free India Center. Dr Werth has published a full list of the personnel and their functions and a few of these are:

(1) Dr M.R. Vyas: spoke in Gujarati and collected and edited all the news material daily.
(2) Mr P.B. Sharma: spoke in English and also wrote talks on daily events.
(3) Mr Promode Sengupta: assisted other staff in collecting material and writing talks.
(4) Dr J.K. Banerji: worked as editor of news and wrote talks on daily subjects.
(5) Mr A.M. Sultan: the main speaker of Azad Muslim Radio.
(6) Dr Kalyan Bose: spoke in Bengali and translated from English to Bengali.
(7) Dr Girija K. Mookerjee: spoke in English for Azad Hind Radio, coordinated broadcasts of National Congress Radio, and wrote talks for both.

Since the programs had to be made attractive to Indian listeners, Indian music broadcast by the BBC was re-broadcast together with the news in the various Indian languages and the timings were arranged so that they would be available in India from 11.00 a.m. to 3.00 p.m. daily. The first service was called 'Azad Hind Radio,' but with the Cripps Mission in 1942, a second service was called 'National Congress Radio,' expressing a militant nationalist point of view, and later Azad Muslim Radio was launched to appeal to nationalist Muslims.[65]

Also during the second half of 1941, Shedai made two visits to Berlin to negotiate with German Foreign Office representatives and to meet with Bose. Although the Germans would have preferred a combined operation,

Shedai and Bose were becoming ever more hostile.[66] One of Bose's recruits on the military side has written that Bose was 'not a man to make a patch up.'[67] Among the issues discussed at these conferences was the formation of the Indian Legion. It was finally agreed between the Italian and German governments that the Germans would get the Indian prisoners and they were transported in batches through 1942 to Camp Annaburg, near Dresden. On December 19, 1941, the Wehrmacht approved the training of those among the prisoners who agreed to join Bose's military force, the Indian Legion.

Bose had been eager for a military wing of the Indian national movement since his own days in the Officers' Training Corps of Calcutta University during the First World War. Bose said, 'Throughout my life it was my ambition to equip an army that will capture freedom from the enemy.'[68] In presenting his case to Nambiar and other Indians in Europe at this time, Bose stressed that the British would never leave India unless they were driven out by force. What was needed was a catalytic force from outside combined with a massive rebellion within India. He was trying to prepare the catalytic force, regardless of how far he was from India and how small the contingent. After discussion of the various possibilities, it was decided that the Germans would direct the entire training programs and the Indians would be a contingent, a special kind of unit, within the German army. All men were started at the lowest rank and the Germans were to decide who was fit to be an officer on the basis of merit.

During 1942 two training camps were established. An elite special unit (Sonderkommando 'B') under Captain Walter Harbich was to be trained at Regenwurm near Meseritz, district Frankfurt/Oder. About thirty of the more impressive of the prisoners and some volunteers from the Free India Center joined this program. Eventually it numbered about ninety trainees. Harbich, a lawyer by training, had fought as a young man in the First World War, and was careful and selective in choosing his men. In contrast to the Indian army, Bose insisted that men of different religious communities be mixed, and Harbich has written of this experiment,

> In the beginning, Indian volunteers were divided in platoons according to their religion. . . . Bose wanted a division into sections so that every platoon had a Hindu, a Sikh and a Muslim section. After a brief acclimatization to this arrangement His Excellency Bose desired a complete dissolution of the units based on religion so that the ideal which he had in mind was realised and the Indians were united in the smallest tactical unit, the section, regardless of their religious profession. Contrary to the original doubts the result was surprisingly good.[69]

The men, of course, had facilities for their private religious worship, but in the military field they were joined together. In addition to ordinary weapons and riding training, they also had special preparation in intelligence services, radio transmission, and sabotage.[70] Training in mountain warfare and parachuting was given to some. Harbich was particularly skillful at building a positive spirit in his group and he felt that, given good leadership, after his course of training, they could fight with anyone.[71] The soldiers of this unit were attached to the High Command of the German Defense Forces and wore the Germany type uniform and 'on the left sleeve of the tunic was stitched a silken emblem in the Indian national colours with the picture of the springing tiger.'[72]

The second and larger training program for the Indian Legion was begun at Frankenberg and later moved to Koenigsbruck in Saxony when the first camp proved too small. Major (later Colonel) Krappe was the commander at Frankenberg, with Captain A. Seifriz as his ADC responsible for political matters. There were a number of German officer-trainers, and German translators familiar with Hindustani.[73] Here a much larger force, about 2,500–3,000, was trained, and some more intractable problems were confronted.

Even before the prisoners were brought to Germany, Werth, Trott, Bose, and others had visited them in Italy. Encouraged by these visits, the details were worked out to bring them to the Annaburg Camp. There Hasan and Swami began to visit them and started the recruitment process. Most of the evidence, even from the critical Hugh Toye, suggests that the recruitment was voluntary and out of 15,000 to 17,000 prisoners, only about 2,500 volunteered. The rest remained prisoners of war. On the whole, this was disappointing to Bose, who expected a much larger and more eager number of volunteers, who were being given, in his terms, the opportunity to move from a mercenary army to a nationalist one. Why did so few come over?

Abid Hasan has left a vivid memoir in which he tells of his efforts to win over prisoners to the Legion and the barriers he encountered:

> Let us suppose there were some people so loyal to the British that they would never join. There were people like that. . . . A few were hesitating to join because they had taken the oath very seriously. . . . They didn't want to break the oath they had taken over the Gita, the Koran or the Gurugranth. . . . A major part of them were worried about their families. . . . Another was that they had opposed and fought against the Germans. To join hands with the enemy—went against the thinking of a soldier.[74]

The recruiters also had to contend with senior NCOs among the prisoners who resolutely opposed the shift to the German side. They branded the Indian recruiting agents and those who did agree to join the Legion as German stooges and they also heckled mercilessly at the recruiting meetings.[75] Of the first batch in the camp, only about ten per cent volunteered. This greatly grieved Hasan, but Bose told him that it was better to have a solid ten per cent than a larger number of less committed soldiers.[76]

Agehananda Bharati, in the earlier incarnation of Leopold Fischer, was a translator and member of the signal unit. The recruiting speech of Bose and his lieutenants was, he wrote, years later, very simple:

> . . . you have fought on the wrong side, the British are our enemies, this is the chance to use your skills to fight them and to make India free. Hitler is your friend, a friend of the Aryans, and you will march to India as your motherland's liberators, maybe via the Caucasus and the Khyber Pass, maybe by some other route.[77]

Shedai in his correspondence with the German and Italian Foreign ministries claimed that his rival, Bose, was not capable of speaking to ordinary soldiers and therefore could not recruit and lead an Indian Legion. In one letter, he wrote, in part:

> He himself is quite unfit (for) any such work. Firstly he is not from the province of these soldiers. He does not understand them. Their mentality is quite different from that of his. Some men who are working with the Foreign Office are not revolutionaries and do not know how to deal with revolutionary problems. Mr Mazzotta, too, belongs to the same category. Secondly Mr Mazzotta belongs to a class which has nothing in common with the soldiers. He cannot understand their needs because he is not one of them.[78]

Was Bose a poor speaker incapable of reaching and understanding the mentality of the ordinary Indian soldiers? Speaking directly to this point, Captain Wilhelm Lutz, one of the German officers involved, said that Bose was not a heavily emotional speaker like Churchill, Hitler, or Goebbels, but that he had his own kind of charisma. In a quiet voice, Bose clearly explained his political message in a way that the ordinary soldiers could understand and answered their questions. He had the powerful conviction of the correctness of his political idea and was able to address simple men. He did not, like some commanders, sit and drink with these men, but he did move them.[79] Captain Seifriz, another witness, added that Bose did not have the common touch of Rommel, but still he did create a feeling for Indian freedom and its importance among the soldiers.[80] What all these men were describing was Bose reaching out to ordinary soldiers, not their officers. Later, he had to deal with captured officers, many of a higher class in Indian society, and the results were also complex. However, some of them did come closer to him than the men depicted here and became passionately attached to him.

Hasan has described the choices available to Bose for the training of the Legion. In consultation with his staff, he decided that the best procedure would be to have German trainers and officers. All the men entering the

Legion would be considered as fresh recruits. Promotion, then, would be based on merit. Indians were to be trained or re-trained according to German standards and they were to be considered part of the German army. Hasan argues that this was necessary, so that if they were captured they would be treated as prisoners of war. They wore German uniforms with swastika and eagle.[81] Eventually they were to be the army of an independent Indian government, the Azad Hind Fauj. Therefore, they had to take the oath that German soldiers took, adapted to their special situation. It went as follows:

> I swear by God this holy oath, that I will obey the leader of the German State and People Adolf Hitler, as commander of the German Armed Forces, in the fight for the freedom of India, in which fight the leader is Subhas Chandra Bose, and that as a brave soldier, I am willing to lay down my life for this oath.[82]

As long as it was believed that the Germans led by Hitler were winning and that Hitler was on the side of Indian freedom, such an oath held some weight for them. But their training by German officers and relationship to their officers was complicated by the fact that they were of different nationalities.

The most inflexible of the German officers could not cope with the cultural complexities of the situation and some had to be relieved of their duties. Some adjustments had to be made not only for Western-Indian cultural and linguistic difficulties, but also for the mixing of Indians from different communities. German Indologists and linguists were brought in to help, but even they could not work out some of the practical problems. The Germans and the more sophisticated Indians like Hasan and Swami, had to operate pragmatically and solve problems, such as the role of religion and of the different communities, as they went.[83]

Hasan has described in detail how one small, but sticky problem was solved: different animal-slaughtering customs of Sikhs and Muslims which kept them from eating the same food. When men of one community were given larger pieces and those of the other smaller ones, those getting the smaller ones were angered and demanded the larger ones, even if the animals were killed in a different manner. Eventually all slaughtering of the sheep was left to the Germans and the soldiers ate, trained, and worked together.[84] The holidays of each were celebrated and those of the other communities were to be guests on such days.

Hasan has also recounted how a common form of greeting was eventually agreed to:

> I set about noting how each one greeted the other. We had the Garhwalis, Dogras, Rajputs, Sikhs, Muslims. . . . The Muslims were ruled out by their

'Salaam alekum' and the Sikhs by their 'Sat Sri Akal'... Some people who were supposed to be educated said 'Namaskar', but it was not a common greeting. Then I found that the Rajputs mainly greeted each other with 'Jai Ramjiki'. [*This*] ... is the common man's language. So that began to appeal to me. ... Then I thought, why not 'Jai Hindustan ki' ... [*then*] why not 'Hind'? ... 'Jai Hind'. Ah! that appealed to me.[85]

He tested this out with the soldiers, with more educated colleagues in Berlin, and with Bose, and finally it was agreed to and used. Similarly, a flag, the Congress tricolor with a springing tiger on it, became the flag, and an adaptation of Tagore's song as the anthem '*Jana Gana Mana*.'[86]

Another small, but immediate, issue for the civilians in Berlin and the soldiers in training was how to address Subhas Bose. Vyas has given his view of how a particular term was adopted:

Should we say Subhas Babu? or 'Rashtrapatiji'. . . or 'Pradhanji?' etc. It went on for a few days, till one of our [*soldier*] boys came forward with 'Hamare Neta'. We improved upon it: 'Netaji'. This may sound strange today, because since then 'Netaji' has come to be irrevocably equated with Subhas Chandra Bose.

It must be mentioned here, that Subhas Bose strongly disapproved of it. He began to yield only when he saw that our military group . . . firmly went on calling him 'Netaji'.[87]

Werth has also mentioned the adoption of 'Netaji' and observed, accurately, that it '. . . combined a sense of both affection and honour. . .'[88] It was not meant to echo 'Fuehrer' or 'Duce', but to give Subhas Bose a special Indian form of reference and this term has been universally adopted by Indians everywhere in speaking about him.

Though some of the problems were solved by the kind of imagination and ingenuity described above, some remained throughout the life of the Legion. Eventually when officers were chosen, the Germans decided that they had to balance promotions between members of different communities to help preserve communal harmony.[89] Also there were continuing tensions between Indians and Germans.[90] Though these day-to-day problems were dealt with as reasonably as could be expected given the unusual context of this force, the major questions remained: where, when, and against whom were they to fight?

Bose worked as hard as he could to see that the Germans understood that these troops were to fight only against the British, preferably close to India. But the determination of where they might fight also depended on the general course of the war over which Bose had no control at all. As 1941 was nearing its end, however, the worldwide situation changed dramatically again with the Japanese strike at Pearl Harbor and against the British and Dutch Empires in Asia. Within days, the British and their Empire were at war with Imperial Japan, and the United States was in the conflict at war with the Germans and Italians as well as the Japanese. These events had their ramifications for both Boses, one in Berlin and one in Calcutta. Subhas Bose began to look to the East for new possibilities of action and Sarat Bose, who had been receiving messages from him through the Japanese, was arrested.

By the time the Japanese moved, Bose had begun work in all the spheres possible for him in Europe. With the Japanese conquests in Southeast Asia in late 1941 and early 1942, he thought even more seriously about possibilities elsewhere. When he first arrived in Europe, only the Germans and Italians were at war with the British Empire. Now the Germans were fighting the Soviet Union as well and this conflict had upset him greatly. Besides his own sympathies for the Soviets, he knew that the German invasion had moved many of his former colleagues on the Indian left closer to their rulers' view that Nazi Germany was *the* enemy. Then, Hitler had promised a quick war in the East, but by the end of 1941 as the first Russian winter closed in around the German army, it was clear that Hitler's facile boast would not hold up.

On January 26 in Berlin, a big celebration of Indian Independence Day was held in the Hotel Kaiserhof. The Indian community in Berlin, now mostly working with Bose, and the newly arrived A.C.N. Nambiar and Girija Mookerjee, were joined by German businessmen, journalists, government officials and top military officers, as well as diplomats from other countries.[91] Bose was emerging from behind the shadowy screen of 'Mazzotta' and a few weeks later he took an even larger step into the public arena.

Although it was widely known that he was in Berlin, Bose had decided not to speak or write in his own name before the end of February 1942. With the fall of Singapore to the Japanese on February 15, and the rapid advance of the Japanese throughout Southeast Asia, Bose decided, in consultation with his German hosts, to speak out. He issued a statement to the press, which he also read over Azad Hind Radio. In part, he said,

> For about a year I have waited in silence and patience for the march of events and now that the hour has struck, I come forward to speak.
>
> The fall of Singapore means the collapse of the British Empire, and the end of the iniquitous regime which it has symbolised and the dawn of a new era in Indian history.... British Imperialism has in modern history been the most diabolic enemy of freedom and the most formidable obstacle to progress . . . the enemies of British Imperialism are to-day our natural friends.
>
> The outside world hears from time to time voices coming from India, claiming to speak either in the name of the Indian National Congress or of

the Indian people. But these are voices coming through the channels of British propaganda and nobody should make the mistake of regarding them as representative of Free India . . . the British oppressors have endeavoured to create divisions among the Indian people . . . we find in India those who openly support British Imperialism. There are others who, whether intentionally or unintentionally, help the British cause. . . [by] talk of cooperation with China, Russia and other Allies of England. There is, however, the vast majority of the Indian people who will have no compromise with British Imperialism but will fight on till full independence is achieved. . . . During this struggle . . . we shall heartily cooperate with all those who will help in overthrowing the common enemy. . . . The hour of India's salvation is at hand.[92]

Bose made clear his view that there was a clear-cut choice: the side of the British, or the side of Indian liberation. He had chosen his side and allied with the Axis powers. He did not speak out for their goals and conquests or use the terms of their ideology. He used his own terms, and emphasized the Indian struggle in the context of a changing world situation. He did not openly criticize the internal politics or policies of the Third Reich or of Imperial Japan, whatever he may have thought of them. He had what he thought was his specific task: to free India. As he made his calculations in Berlin in February 1942, his gaze was drawn ever more to Southeast Asia and the advances of the Japanese, for he knew that important developments for Indian nationalism were taking place there.[93]

II

For Indian nationalists 'Japan' evoked a powerful response. It was the one significant Asian country which had resisted foreign, especially Western, encroachment. More than this, in the Russo-Japanese War, it had proved at least the equal of one of the biggest Western nations. As nationalism stirred throughout Asia, nationalists looking for positive examples and assistance began—from the later nineteenth century—turning to Japan. Sun Yat-sen spent several years in Japan and then went back to China to help overturn the Manchu Dynasty and to usher in the Republican era. Vietnamese nationalists, foremost among them, Phan Boi Chau, also went to Japan, and brought with him Vietnamese students for education and preparation in resisting the French.[94] The most prominent Indian nationalist who went to Japan in this earlier period, around the First World War, has already been mentioned: Rash Behari Bose. Like some other Asian nationalists, Rash Behari Bose came to Japan pursued by the agents and diplomats of the power ruling this country. He turned to Toyama Mitsuru, leader of the Black Dragon Society and friend of foreign revolutionaries. Through him, he met Okawa Shumei, another ultra-nationalist and student of Indian culture, and Soma Aizo, a prominent restaurateur. These three helped him in various ways, shielding him from the British, and then providing long-term aid, which he gained by marrying Soma Aizo's daughter and settling in Tokyo.[95] Bose worked in Tokyo and did some political agitating, organizing an Asian political conference in 1926, an Indian Friendship Association in 1936, and a branch of an overseas Indian organization, the Indian Independence League, in 1937. He wrote for the Black Dragon Society's publication and edited his own journal, but he was far from India, relatively out of touch, and for the most part, a forgotten old man. However, he did have connections to the political and military elite through Toyama.

There were complicated attitudes about the relationship of Japan to these other Asian countries. Was Japan to be the 'big brother' and dominate such fledgling movements, or selflessly sponsor them so that they might grow to full, autonomous power back in their home countries? If Japan aimed to build itself in the image of European imperialists, then its aims were suspect to other Asian nationalists.

One of those critical of the aims, motives, and actions of the Japanese was Rabindranath Tagore, who visited Japan in 1916. Tagore wrote, in a comparison of Europe, India, and Japan:

> The deep foundation on which the greatness of Europe has been built up is a spiritual one; it has not risen due merely to its technical efficiency in production, but due to its high ethical ideal. . . . The attitude of devotion that admits a religious possibility in man and proceeds to realize it, is . . . an attitude that transcends worldly necessities and national self-interest. . . . As regards this attitude, Europe has more in common with India than with Japan. The palace of Japanese civilization is one-storied . . . the god most highly revered is national self-interest. This is why the Japanese have been so strongly influenced by the power-worshipping philosophers of modern Germany. . . . Today Japan boasts of her lack of religion: she presumes to be free from the demands of the Infinite and thinks to win her victory solely in this finite world.[96]

Most of the Japanese writers who responded to Tagore's critical views mentioned that he was 'the poet of a defeated country'.[97] So from the days of the First World War, there was a set of attitudes shaped on the part of both the Japanese and the Indians. Indians saw Japan's power and exemplary role, but were suspicious of her ambitions. The Japanese welcomed the awakening of those other Asian nationalists from whom they thought they would derive benefits, but saw the other Asians as 'defeated' peoples, who were not fierce enough to keep out the Westerners.

In the period of Rash Behari Bose's residence in Japan, roughly 1915 to 1945, his newly adopted nation became a world power. Through the twentieth century, Japanese intellectuals began formulating theories linking Japan to all of Asia, because Buddhism had spread from the mainland. One of Rash Behari Bose's hosts, Okawa Shumei wrote *The Establishment of the Greater East Asia Order* and explained that Japan had absorbed teachings from India and China and that '. . . the day would come when Japan would bear the great mission and responsibility for Asia.'[98] The theories about Japan's mission in Asia gradually became the policies of the Japanese government. The foreign minister, Matsuoka Yosuke, proclaimed the Greater East Asia Co-Prosperity Sphere on August 1, 1940, just around the time of the signing of the Tripartite Pact with Germany and Italy.[99] The boundaries of the Greater East Asia sphere were vague, but included certain 'Southern areas such as the Netherlands Indies and French Indo-China.'[100] Once the Japanese civilian and military ruling elites decided that they would move towards war if they could not gain their objectives in Southeast Asia by peaceful means, they added areas to the sphere. As articulated in 1941, the sphere included all of Southeast Asia up to the Burmese frontier with India, and all of the Pacific islands north of Australia and stretching eastward to Hawaii.[101] When the Japanese navy, army, and air force moved into action on December 7, 1941, they attacked in the southern region—against Dutch and British possessions—and against the United States at Pearl Harbor.

Just as the final decision for war was being made, General Tojo and the inner circle of Japanese decision-makers listed additional measures. To bring about British capitulation, they wanted to sever Britain from vital parts of her empire, including Australia and India. They would intensify their attacks on British shipping, grant independence to Burma once it had been 'liberated' from the British Empire, and take 'measures' that would encourage India to rise against the British. These steps, if successful, might also show the United States that its resistance to Japanese demands in the Pacific and East Asia was fruitless.[102] In some of his speeches Foreign Minister Matsuoka had included India in the Co-Prosperity Sphere, but usually an India independent of Britain was seen as necessarily coordinated with the defeat of Britain elsewhere.

In the second half of 1941, the Japanese were taking steps to prepare for war. These included improving her intelligence on the southern regions— all of Southeast Asia and India—and sending out agents of military intelligence to contact potentially friendly elements in the population of these regions. Although India was not clearly within the Co-Prosperity Sphere, there was a significant Indian minority in other countries in Southeast Asia amongst whom there was a potentiality for anti-British sentiment. The Japanese reached out to the Indian community, first in Thailand, but aimed to come in touch with the Indians in Malaya and Burma as well. They also knew that the Indian army was a central element in the defense of British possessions east of India, particularly Malaya and Singapore.

The Indian community in Southeast Asia numbered more than one-and-a-half million, perhaps as much as two million. Many of these were laborers on rubber plantations in Malaya, but there was also a strong trading population in Burma, Thailand, and Malaya. They were a relatively small group in Thailand and though in much larger numbers in Malaya, still only around ten per cent of the population. In Burma, however, they numbered around one million, and there was some resentment against them by the Burmese, particularly as Burmese nationalism developed from the 1920s.[103]

By the fall of 1941, the military arms of the Japanese government had stretched to Thailand and Burma, sending intelligence agents to contact Indian nationalists in Thailand and Burmese nationalists in Burma. The Japanese had captured, then given training, to the young and energetic Burmese nationalist Aung San, and through him trained a cadre of other Burmese nationalists. As long as these Burmese nationalists felt that the Japanese were helping them to liberate their country from all foreign oppressors, the relationship held. To make contact with Indians in Thailand, the Japanese selected Major Fujiwara Iwaichi, a young, highly intelligent, but relatively inexperienced officer, for this assignment. It was a momentous choice.[104]

Born in 1908 into a farming family, Fujiwara had graduated from the Japanese Military Academy in 1931. He performed well in an infantry regiment and was selected for the staff college. After passing its course, he was appointed to the Intelligence Section of the General Staff, specializing in publicity and propaganda. His promotion to major after ten years' service was a mark of distinction as was the appointment to this sensitive assignment in Thailand after only brief training in political operations and Indian affairs.[105] Working with a staff of about a dozen men, under the chief of Japanese intelligence in Bangkok, Colonel Tamura, Fujiwara reached the Thai capital in October 1941, and began to make contacts with the more politically aware elements in the Indian community. A good deal of his enormous energy became focused on the Indian part of his assignment. Fujiwara helped the Indians to organize for practical nationalist work of a kind, and became, in his own unique way, a blend of Indian nationalist and Japanese patriot. He not only saw his work as his duty, but as a special mission to be carried out with all the acumen and fervor he had.

There were two main groupings of Indians in Bangkok: the Indian Independence League(IIL), composed primarily of Sikhs and linked to the Ghadr Party of earlier nationalist fame; and the Thai-Bharat Cultural Lodge, an eclectic cultural organization with members from all the major Indian communities. Fujiwara found the greatest response to his work from two Sikhs of the IIL, the young Pritam Singh, and the elderly Amar Singh, who had spent years in Indian prisons for political activity. Pritam Singh had already thought of reaching out to the Indian troops in Malaya, but until the coming of war to the region this was not practicable.[106] With the Japanese strikes of December 7 and 8, 1941 in the Pacific and across Thai territory into Malaya, however, a new world of possibilities for political action was created.

Together with Pritam Singh and members of the IIL, Fujiwara and the F. Kikan staff organized to contact Indian troops aiding the British defense of Malaya and Singapore. The Japanese advance through Malaya was comparable to the German blitzkrieg in Europe. As the Imperial Army advanced, dozens, then hundreds, then thousands of Indian army prisoners were taken by them. Many Indian troops were almost in shock at the woeful defensive planning and lack of resistance shown by the British. Fujiwara, his staff, and his Indian civilian allies began to press a propaganda offensive onto their captive audience. Among the early and responsive listeners was Captain Mohan Singh, who first met Fujiwara about December 15, and listened carefully.[107]

Until the Japanese invasion of Malaya, Captain Mohan Singh appeared to be relatively apolitical. But now Fujiwara got a strong response from the Punjabi Sikh captain, an officer in the 1/14 Punjab Regiment of the Indian army. Mohan Singh was concerned about Japanese sincerity, about the support of the Congress Party in India for such a collaboration with the Japanese, and about the readiness of other Indian officers and soldiers to join the effort.[108] Impressed by Fujiwara and the way that the first prisoners were treated by the Japanese, Mohan Singh agreed to go ahead with the project to try to organize an Indian National Army. He hoped that the Japanese would agree that it was eventually to be dealt with as an allied army, but Fujiwara could not assure him on this point. Fujiwara promised to do his best in working out the details of the cooperative effort of Indians and Japanese in opposing the British Raj.

The Japanese offensive pressed forward and by the end of January they were besieging the supposedly impregnable island fortress of Singapore. The Japanese had raced down the Malayan peninsula, pushing the disorganized British and Indian troops ahead of them, capturing some of them as they went, and in early February, they were approaching

Singapore from the land side. The expensive and powerful artillery placed to defend the island pointed out to sea. The guns were anchored in concrete and useless. The defenders, moreover, were poorly organized and within a fortnight, even though they outnumbered the Japanese attackers, they capitulated. It was one of the worst defeats in British history. Amongst the 90,000 or so troops snared by the Japanese, many were Indians.[109]

As the Japanese advanced, one of Hitler's confidants, General Gause, said to him, 'It was a relief for us to learn of Japan's entry into the war.' Hitler answered, 'Yes, a relief, an immense relief. But it was also a turning-point in history. It means the loss of a whole continent, and one must regret it, for it's the white race which is the loser.'[110] And Goebbels wrote in his diary, 'The Fuehrer profoundly regrets the heavy losses sustained by the white race in East Asia, but that isn't our fault.'[111] However, in their hundred-day conquest of most of Southeast Asia, the Japanese did not need the help or approval of Nazi racists.[112] What worried the Japanese, however, was that they found the Indian troops much more loyal to their British officers and to the tasks of the Indian army in defending the British Empire than Indian nationalists had led them to expect.[113]

On February 17, 1942, the Japanese gathered about 45,000 of the Indian prisoners they had taken on the Farrer Park racecourse. First, Fujiwara addressed them on behalf of the Japanese, with the aid of a translator. Then Pritam Singh and Mohan Singh, Indian civilian and military spokesmen, spoke to convince the prisoners that the Japanese sincerely wanted to help the Indian independence movement.[114] Mohan Singh wrote of the responses:

> I . . . asked the soldiers to raise hands if any one from amongst them would like to volunteer to join this force and fight for the liberation of his country. There was a spontaneous response from all the soldiers. Along with the raising of hands, thousands of turbans and caps were hurled up in the air . . . soldiers jumped to their feet . . . with prolonged shouts of 'Inqilab Zindabad' (Long Live Revolution).[115]

Many of the officers, however, were indifferent for many reasons: loyalty to the Raj and to the Indian army, doubts about the Japanese, doubts about Pritam Singh and Mohan Singh, et al.. But a significant number of soldiers and some officers joined the Indian National Army at this juncture.

Fujiwara realized that though he found Mohan Singh to be 'a born revolutionary leader and a man of action' and possessor of many other impressive qualities, he was still a young and politically inexperienced Indian captain. There were many Indian officers senior to him and there were resentments that Fujiwara, and thus the Japanese, had picked him for a major role. Even at this early stage of the Japanese-Indian relationship,

Fujiwara heard repeatedly about a Bose in Berlin. Although Bose had not 'come out' officially in Berlin, word of his work in Berlin seems to have been spreading and an idealized image of him was passing into the minds of Southeast Asian Indians. In his post-war memoir, Fujiwara wrote of this period,

> After expressing his admiration for Chandra Bose . . . Capt. Mohan opined that Indians living in Asia would rise if a revolutionary such as Bose could be persuaded to come to Asia to lead the movement . . . . all the Indians whom I had come across had a great admiration for Bose, amounting almost to a religious devotion. . . . I reported to the Army General Staff the Indians' interest in Chandra Bose. At this time, the German armies were sweeping across the Near East and the German government was reluctant to release Bose from Berlin to go to Asia. At the same time, the Japanese government took a cold and shortsighted attitude towards the problem of nationalist movements in Asia including India.[116]

Fujiwara was forced to dampen Mohan Singh's eagerness to bring Subhas Bose to the scene and encouraged the Indians to develop their own movement in Southeast Asia.

On the civilian side, the primary organization was the Indian Independence League, and branches were to be developed throughout Asia. The military operation was the Indian National Army. Using the unexpected visit of senior Japanese army officials to press his views, Fujiwara urged them to expand the operation beyond a mere propaganda and espionage scheme—which is what many Japanese wanted—into a substantial revolutionary army and bring Chandra Bose, as he called him, to East Asia.[117]

Shortly after the Farrer Park rally, the Japanese decided that it would be useful to have a general conference of the Indian movement in Tokyo. The conference was called in the name of Rash Behari Bose, but, obviously, had Japanese backing and approval. It was to take place in the second week of March 1942 at the Sanno Hotel. The Indian Independence League, the Thai-Bharat Cultural Lodge, and the INA chose delegates to join those of the Indians resident in Japan. Civilians from Thailand and Malaya were: N. Raghavan, K.A.N. Ayer, S.C. Goho, K.P.K. Menon, Pritam Singh, and Swami Satyananda Puri. The INA sent Mohan Singh, N.S. Gill, and Mohammed Akram. The delegates, divided into two parties, together with members of F. Kikan and the influential Japanese officer, Colonel Iwakuro, left Bangkok for Tokyo on March 10.[118]

Calamity struck even before the conference opened. The plane carrying Swami Satyananda Puri, Pritam Singh, Mohammed Akram, and the F. Kikan members crashed in a violent storm off the Japanese coast. All were killed. The conference, chaired by Rash Behari Bose, went on, but the

Southeast Asian delegates suspected that he was a willing tool of the Japanese and insisted that a five-member Council of Action be established by a larger meeting to be held in Southeast Asia about two months hence. The representatives from Southeast Asia wondered why Japan residents A. M. Sahay and Raja Mahendra Pratap, the first a devoted Congressman, the second an elderly, eccentric revolutionary, were not present.[119]

Fujiwara had had high hopes for the progress of the movement, but was disappointed when the Japanese internal document was entitled 'Indian Strategem Plan'. He was able to make some changes in it, but at the same time, his assignment was changed and he was no longer the liaison officer between the Indians and the Japanese army. The leadership of a new and expanded operation to be called 'Iwakuro Kikan' was given to Colonel Iwakuro. He was a more senior officer than Fujiwara and involved in army politics. Iwakuro was more concerned with the propaganda and espionage activities of the INA and shared the doubts of most high-ranking Japanese officers that this force could ever be of much military value. These officers wondered about troops who surrendered and also soldiers who would switch sides.[120] As the conference met, Japanese forces were racing ahead towards the complete conquest of Burma, and General Tojo said, in part, in his message to the Tokyo Conference,

> The Japanese Empire is determined to go ahead with its mission of destruction of the Anglo-Saxon Power and will not rest until that mission is fulfilled. I want to state frankly that the Japanese Government cannot remain indifferent to the fact that Britain is going to make India the base of its East defence. . .[121]

These words did not make it clear who would run the India that the Japanese might conquer. It hardly needs saying how differently the Germans and the Japanese, allies in name, viewed the possible collapse of the British Empire.

The Indian delegates returned to Southeast Asia and to the construction of the Indian Independence League throughout the region, the building of the INA, and the organization of the Iwakuro Kikan. The latter set up an espionage training center on Penang Island and several teams were prepared and, on Japanese initiative, sent into India. Their missions were almost a complete failure.[122] As this work went on, a much larger gathering of Indians came together at Bangkok on June 15, 1942 to formally merge the diverse Indian organizations in East and Southeast Asia into the Indian Independence League. It sanctioned the development of the INA under Mohan Singh as GOC. Further, it specified that the Council of Action would be its executive body. Rash Behari Bose became president and the two civilian members were N. Raghavan and K.P.K. Menon, the two military ones Major Mohan Singh and Lt.Col. G.O. Gilani. This executive had charge over the IIL and all its branches and the INA.[123]

The conference went on to pass a series of resolutions asking for clarification of the relationship between the Indian movement and the Japanese. It asked that all Indian soldiers in areas of Japanese occupation be placed under Indian control, that the Indian National Army be accorded the status of an allied army on equal footing with the Japanese army, and that the former be used only to fight the British for Indian independence. Further, it requested that,

> . . . the Imperial government of Japan will exercise its influence with other Powers and induce them to recognize the national independence and absolute sovereignty of India. . . . Japan may be pleased to arrange with the authorities in the territories now freed from domination of the Anglo-Saxons . . . to hand over properties owned by Indians . . . to the Council of Action . . . in trust for their rightful owners. . . . Indians residing in the territories occupied by. . . Japan shall not be considered enemy nations . . . the Japanese government use its good offices to enable Subhas Chandra Bose to come to East Asia.[124]

The extensive and detailed resolutions of the Bangkok Conference showed the interests, concerns, and suspicions of the Indian movement. They made understandable requests, but the response of the Japanese to them was problematical.

The conferees had invited Subhas Bose to their meeting and he had sent them greetings which said, in part,

> I am delighted to have your message inviting me to your Conference . . . it is not possible to join you in person. . . . I must content myself with sending you . . . my most cordial greetings. . . all nationalists, whether in India or outside, must play their part . . . the Tripartite powers are our best friends and allies. . . . But the emancipation of India must be the work primarily of Indians themselves. We who are the vanguard of the National Army have the sacred mission of leading the national struggle to a successful conclusion.[125]

They responded by reiterating to the Japanese what Mohan Singh had asked of Fujiwara months earlier: bring us a real political leader from India to take charge, or help to bring us the one leader outside India, free of British control, who will also sympathize with the use of military means to destroy the Raj. Amidst the internal disagreements of the Indian movement, its convenors looked for a savior, a leader who could speak for them and face up to the Japanese. They cast Subhas Bose in this image.

In the following few months, as a crisis came to a head in India itself, Mohan Singh received Japanese sanction to raise one large division of Indian troops from the volunteers. On September 1, 1942, the First

Division of the INA, numbering 16,300 men, came into existence. There were many problems. The Japanese had only grudgingly given permission for one division though Mohan Singh envisioned a much larger force. They were given inadequate weapons by the Japanese, who, in any case, were beginning to be hard pressed. Even more serious were the scarcely hidden conflicts within the leadership of the first INA.[126] Three excellent scholars of the INA and its relationship to the Japanese—Hugh Toye, Joyce Lebra, and K.K. Ghosh—have written about these conflicts in detail.

One fundamental problem for the INA was that some of the officers who joined did so to avoid Japanese prison camps or to protect the lives of their men and of Indians in Southeast Asia. Some wanted to form an internal opposition which would shift back to the British side at any moment and destroy the INA. Among the latter was Lt. Col. N.S. Gill, a very popular officer, who worked closely with Mohan Singh. Two others, both King's Commissioned Officers (KCOs), were Major M.S. Dhillon and Lt. Col. J.R. Bhonsle.[127] With such men placed near the top, and with many others who harbored suspicions of the Japanese, the whole structure was a rickety affair.

Although Mohan Singh went ahead with the organization and training of the army during 1942, he continued to stew over the Japanese refusal to sanction more than one division or to clarify the combat role of this division. In the fall, he accepted a Japanese request to send a small group from the INA to Burma, to be used for intelligence work in conjunction with the Japanese occupation forces. N.S. Gill and M.S. Dhillon were members of it. Dhillon took the first opportunity to cross to the other side. Gill hesitated, returned to Singapore, and became increasingly critical of the Japanese and the uses they were making of the INA. A short time later, Gill was arrested by the Japanese.[128]

Two other crises were developing in 1942. In the Council of Action, the civilians, particularly N. Raghavan, felt that Mohan Singh had gathered too much power. The soldiers of the INA were asked to take an oath affirming Singh's leadership and Mohan Singh had sent INA personnel to Burma on his own authority.

At the same time, both Mohan Singh, other Indian military officers of the INA, and most of the civilians felt that the Japanese meant to use the INA for their own narrow objectives and had no commitment—as Fujiwara did—to helping Indian nationalists reach their goals. There were numerous incidents of Japanese arrogance, e.g., Japanese officers telling Indians that they should be happy to be Japanese puppets, obedient subordinates in the Co-Prosperity Sphere. Doubts about the Japanese crystalized in their lack of response to the Bangkok Resolutions passed by the June 1942

Conference of Indians in East and Southeast Asia. Iwakuro was vague and evasive. Fujiwara was asked to intervene, but could not or did not give more help.

In December 1942, an ultimatum was given to Iwakuro by the Council of Action. When no adequate response was forthcoming, Mohan Singh and two others resigned. Gill was arrested by the Japanese for espionage and this further contributed to the alienation of the INA from the Japanese. Fujiwara was forced to side with Iwakuro. Rash Behari Bose then dismissed Mohan Singh as GOC of the INA and the latter was arrested by the Japanese. Preparing for this eventuality, Mohan Singh had drawn up an order dissolving the INA which was issued to it.[129] The INA and the IIL were in disarray by the end of 1942.

1942 was also a year in which the course of the Second World War shifted. Hitler's troops were blocked in the USSR and were now facing their first Russian winter. The Japanese, after the amazing conquests of the first hundred days of their offensive, had been badly beaten in naval engagements at the Coral Sea and Midway. The enormous economic and military might of the United States was beginning to come into play. General Arisue, head of Japanese intelligence in the latter part of the war, who had been Japanese military attaché in several European capitals in the 1930s, when asked why the Japanese underestimated the American soldiers said. 'I watched American soldiers in Europe then and thought they were only good for screwing French girls.'[130] To their dismay, the Japanese learned that Americans, and their allies, could fight well and that the American economy could turn out planes, ships, and weapons in much greater numbers than the Japanese.

Now the Japanese were much more favorable to the movement of Bose from Europe to their part of the world, but details, including German agreement, had to be worked out. In the same year, as well, vital developments took place in India while Sarat Bose languished, imprisoned, in southern India.

III

After consultations at the highest level of the Government of India, Sarat Bose was shifted from Bengal to South India. Viceroy Linlithgow called him 'dangerous and insincere (sic).'[131] On December 26, 1941, he was shifted to a jail in the city of Madras from where contacts with his brother through diplomats would be impossible and communications to ministers of the Bengal Government would be extremely difficult. In January 1942 he was moved to Central Jail, Trichinopoly, Madras. Next, in the spring of 1942, he was shifted to Mercara, Coorg. Finally, in late March 1943, he was transferred to Coonoor in the Nilgiris, also in the Madras Presidency, where he spent the final two-and-a-half years of his extended term as what he light-heartedly called a 'vagabond' and a 'loafer . . . living on the money of the taxpayer and on the generosity of kind friends.'[132]

This second term of imprisonment was much harder than the first. First, it was wartime and his beloved brother had set out on an inexorably complicated mission working with foreign powers, while the Japanese advance through Southeast Asia left them within striking and bombing range of Calcutta. Second, his wife, her father, and his mother were not in good health. Third, there were severe financial problems for his large family when he was not a wage-earner. Fourth, his own health was not good, and he had diabetes together with a low-grade fever through much of his term of imprisonment. None of the jails, whether in the plains or the hills of South India, agreed with him very well, and he and his allies were unsuccessful in getting him shifted either to Bengal or to some place in northern India.[133]

After a stop in Madras city, he was taken to Trichinopoly (now Tiruchirapalli), in the plains 250 miles west of Madras proper. This 'city of the three-headed demon'—an important cultural center—was hot and unpleasant, but here at least the water was good and his diabetes was under control. With the shift to the more inaccessible Mercara in Coorg, about seventy-five miles west of Mysore, the sugar content in his urine rose to eight per cent and his slight fever continued. In Mercara he was held in an isolated bungalow surrounded by barbed wire, with guards outside and inside the compound. The civil surgeon of Coorg, Major Traynor, was also Bose's jail superintendent. It was difficult to get proper food, and he often had to cook for himself or make do with limited, untrained help. 'I keep to my bed most of the time,' he wrote to Ajit Dey in April 1942, 'and read as much or as little as I am able to.'[134] He had little company, though he was joined by Lalshankar Lal, a close associate of his brother. The next month, he wrote to Ajit Dey,

> Of course, one hardly feels comfortable when he has fever on. But there is no help for it. Life cannot be a bed of roses always. Without some suffering, one cannot really appreciate the joys of life. Both joy and suffering come from the same source.[135]

What was this 'source'? For Sarat Bose, it was the divine Mother, the guide and shaper of life, to whom he prayed and to whom he asked his closest relations to pray. He even sent Ajit Dey's wife, accompanied by his wife Biva, to the ashram at Dakhineswar to seek divine help.

He, as well as the ministers and chief minister of Bengal, friends in high places, and relations, all asked the Government of India to transfer him to his own house in Giddapahar, where he had been held during a part of his first arrest term. But while one Bose was loose, the Government of India would keep the other as far away as the borders of India would allow. Questions were raised, motions were put in the Central Legislative Assembly and the Bengal Assembly, but to no avail.

The man he called his 'guruji', Sir N.N. Sircar, undoubtedly tried as well. He wrote to his former junior about the appalling lack of properly organized relief as Europeans and Indians streamed towards India from Singapore, Malaya, and Burma. Sarat commented, 'With the fall of Rangoon, people in Calcutta may become more panicky. I am hoping against hope that adequate steps are being taken to dispel panic and to meet any emergency that may arise.'[136] This was about as close to a political comment as he was allowed in his censored correspondence. He was probably allowed to see some newspapers and magazines, but his comments on the course of the war and on the work of Subhas, in so far as he knew much about it, are not available. He could do general reading and this was mainly literature in Bengali and English, plus English translations from French and Russian, some religious texts including the *Bhagavad Gita* and some tantric texts, and books on public affairs. During this imprisonment he read the works of Bankim Chandra Chatterjee, Sarat Chandra Chatterji, and some fiction and non-fiction by Romain Rolland. He made his way through Joseph Schumpeter's difficult *Capitalism, Socialism, and Democracy* and read a number of works on modern China including Lin Yutang's *My Country and My People*, Edgar Snow's *Red Star over China*, and Gerald J. Yorke's *China Changes*. The latter book was marked heavily in red, presumably by Sarat Bose, particularly those passages about peasant support for the communist army, Chinese confidence in eventually beating the Japanese, and sketches of the main communist leaders.[137]

Sarat Bose was not a writer, but he was a great reader. His letters are filled with requests for books, and that Kiron Sankar Roy, friend and sometimes political ally, sometimes opponent, be asked to provide books because of his fine taste in literature. Reading about contemporary China was an important element of his wartime education. War was raging in East Asia and the relationship of India and China was a concern. Most politically conscious Indians seemed sympathetic to China in her war against invading Japan. During the first half of 1942, Chiang Kai-shek visited India and met Congress leaders. He offered support to their cause. Sarat Bose's extensive wartime reading on China gave him increased awareness of another powerful force that had to be reckoned with: the Communists led by Mao Tse-tung.

To the best of his ability—through the mails and through a very few visits—he tried to keep in touch with all the developments in his family and amongst his wide range of friends and associates. In February 1942, Santosh Basu and the nawab of Dacca, ministers in the Bengal government, traveled to Trichinopoly to see him. Although Sarat Bose was happy to have visitors, he was also annoyed that Santosh Basu was much more concerned with advise about Calcutta affairs than in inquiring into the difficulties of Sarat's imprisonment.[138] Some weeks later, Biva, Asoke, and Gita came to visit him and he was delighted.[139] But, for the most part, it was a lonely and unpleasant existence. He had no idea when it would end.

Just after the family visit, Sarat Bose wrote to Ajit Dey, 'I can well realise that the situation in Bengal is becoming more and more serious every day. Heaven only knows what is in store for our unhappy province!'[140] Was he prescient?

IV

Because of the surprising, even shocking advance of the Japanese military machine through Burma, the British wartime national cabinet with many pressures upon it, decided to send a special mission to India. Headed by a minister of Labour Party background with sympathies for Indian independence, Sir Stafford Cripps, it arrived in spring 1942. It has been argued by some that the Cripps Mission marks a turning point for Britain's relation to India.[141] Faced with a formidable Japanese force on the eastern frontier and with urging from non-Conservative ministers, liberal politicians in India, and the Americans, Churchill agreed to send Cripps to India to try to negotiate an agreement with the major Indian parties. In particular, all of these pressure groups wanted the British leaders to bring Gandhi and the Congress to an agreement so that the forces of Indian nationalism would rally to the Allied side in the war.

The prize held out to the Congress was dominion status after the war—implying full independence—with the power to shape an Indian constitution. During the war, the Congress would enter the viceroy's executive and be given considerable, but far from unlimited, responsibility. Moore has summarized some further provisions of the offer which was designed to bring the Muslim League and the princely states on board as well:

> Provinces dissenting from the constitution might achieve their freedom separately. The need for such a settlement was indicated by Cripps's discussions with the Muslim leaders in December 1939, and the August 1940 offer had assured the Muslims that they would not be coerced into a Hindu-dominated dominion. The right of the princes to stand out of the post-war Union of India was a further break with the no-freedom-without-unity

policy.[142]

Cripps'.negotiations were likely doomed from the start. Prime Minister Churchill had excluded India from the Atlantic Charter, convinced that it needed another generation of British tutelage; he had only begrudgingly sent Cripps on his mission. Viceroy Linlithgow proved to be a staunch ally of Churchill, informing the prime minister secretly when he felt that Cripps was going beyond his brief. Cripps blamed the Congress leaders for his failure. The plan offered that, in the present, the viceroy and the military would remain in charge; in the future the Muslim League and the princes were to be given leave to divide the subcontinent into a multiplicity of states. A few Congressmen, particularly the South Indian leader Rajagopalachari, argued that Muslim sub-nationalism had to be allowed but delimited as strictly as possible. Rajaji wanted to accept the Cripps offer, but he was overridden and temporarily left the Congress.[143]

Subhas Bose, broadcasting from Berlin, commented on the Cripps Mission and its aftermath in May 1942,

> Sisters and brothers . . . a few weeks ago I reminded you again of the deceit and hypocrisy underlying the policy of the British Government which culminated in the journey of Sir Stafford Cripps to India. Sir Stafford, on the one hand, offered independence in the future, and on the other, demanded the immediate cooperation of India in Britain's war effort. . . . The contemptible offer was . . . rejected. This was a matter for joy and pride to Indians in all parts of the world. . . . India has but one enemy . . . British Imperialism. . . . I can tell you with all seriousness that these three Powers [*Japan, Germany, Italy*] want to see India free and independent and mistress of her own destiny. They are determined to defeat and destroy the enemy of India.[144]

While Bose feared a Congress compromise with the British, the leaders of the Hindu Mahasabha, including V.D. Savarkar and S.P. Mookerjee, were focused on the problem of what they called 'the indivisibility of the Motherland'.[145] The British were beginning to hear the tune of Pakistan which Mr Jinnah kept playing. From his distant listening post, Bose was concerned with *how* the Indians would drive the British out, since he did not believe they would ever leave of their own volition. He wanted the unity of India retained as did the Congress majority.

Besides his brother and the public structure of the Forward Bloc, Subhas Bose left behind in Bengal and India, mostly in the former, a semi-underground group linking several family members, his closest associate Satya Ranjan Bakshi, and the small revolutionary party, the BV. It has been noted how the BV arose out of the 1928 Calcutta Congress and how they remained devoted to Bose through the 1930s. With the war's outbreak and then Bose's escape, the group remained ready to carry out his orders. When

Bose in Berlin communicated either through Bhagat Ram in Kabul, or through Japanese channels to Sarat Bose in Calcutta, instructions were passed on to the BV through Bakshi. From Berlin, later from Southeast Asia, Bose was preparing a revolt within India to link up to his armed entry from without. He wanted the BV team to serve in the front lines of this operation. They were to gather information about the strength and resources of the enemy and to help strike against them when the time came. Santimoy Ganguli made several trips to the frontier and across transmitting messages until he was arrested in November 1942.[146] As Sarat Bose and later Satya Ranjan Bakshi and others were arrested and removed from the scene, others including Sisir Bose, Bakshi's brother, Sudhir Ranjan Bakshi, and remaining BV men moved in to take their place.[147] These soldiers in Bose's underground army probably did succeed in sending him some useful information, but most, including Sisir Bose and Sudhir, were arrested in 1944, and there never was an uprising of the kind that Bose wanted, coordinated with his army's attack on India. The BV men tried to send operatives across the frontier to Burma in 1943 and 1944, and Bose, with Japanese assistance, tried to send small groups of men equipped with wireless into India. Most of these groups were caught, some imprisoned, a few executed. The BV men recounted meetings with a mysterious T.K. Rao in 1943 and 1944 who came to Calcutta with a letter from Bose. Information was fed to him and he tried to send it on to Bose until the circuit was disrupted by close police surveillance and then arrests in 1944.

Though Bose identified with the Congress and linked his unique efforts in Europe and later in Asia with it, the more anti-fascist of the Congressites decried his work. For example, soon after the departure of Cripps, Jawaharlal Nehru said to the press in Gauhati on April 24:

> Hitler and Japan must go to hell. I shall fight them to the end and this is my policy. I shall also fight Mr Subhas Bose and his party along with Japan if he comes to India. Mr Bose acted very wrongly though in good faith. Hitler and Japan represent the reactionary forces and their victory means the victory of the reactionary forces in the world.
>
> If a Japanese army invades Assam the attitude of the people should be one of 'no surrender and no submission.' The people should put obstacles and difficulties in the way of the aggressor. The Japanese gave independence to none and nobody gives it to others. God helps those who help themselves and we shall get independence when we will.[148]

In a press conference a few days earlier, Nehru noted that Bose had parted company from 'us', meaning presumably the Congress leadership, some years earlier. He said, in part,

> I do not . . . doubt the *bona fides* of Mr Bose. I think he has come to a certain

conclusion which I think is wrong, but nevertheless a conclusion which he thinks is for the good of India. We parted company with him many years ago. Since then we have drifted further apart and today we are very far from each other. It is not good enough for me, because of my past friendship and because I do not challenge his motives, to say anything against him. But I do realise that the way he has chosen is utterly wrong, a way which I not only cannot accept but must oppose, if it takes shape. Because any force that may come from outside will really come as a dummy force under Japanese control. It is a bad thing psychologically for the Indian masses to think in terms of being liberated by an outside agency.[149]

Nehru had become a steadfast anti-fascist in the 1930s and he remained one during the war. He opposed British rule but would not welcome the help of any foreign power in the liberation of India. He was willing to ask President Roosevelt of the United States to use his good offices to pressure the British to make concessions to Indian nationalists, but to Nehru the fascists, German, Italian, and Japanese, were barbarians from whom one could not ask or expect anything positive and human. Bose and he differed on the means to their common goal.

After Cripps returned home, the British affirmed their constitutional position and moved to gather more special powers. The Cripps offer had been put on the table and signified that there was likely to be movement on the constitutional issue after the war, but for the time being, nothing was to be done, while Churchill and Linlithgow were at the helm. On the Indian side, there was unhappiness and unrest which grew as spring turned to summer. Bose's Forward Bloc was declared illegal on June 22.[150] Bose's broadcasts, in so far as they were heard, seemed to have limited impact. He was on the other side of the globe and had no say in the acceptance or rejection of the Cripps offer.

But Subhas Bose had left another legacy to his Congress colleagues: the call for a mass struggle against the Raj. With the debacle of the Cripps Mission, and little British interest in conciliating nationalist India to the war effort, Gandhi moved on the offensive. Forward Bloc leader R.S. Ruikar wrote at the time, 'Mahatma Gandhi and the Congress Working Committee are now following the footsteps of Subhas Chandra Bose and the All-India Forward Bloc.'[151] Gandhi was making his own way towards a mass movement against the Raj in wartime. He never wanted to admit that he was now taking up Bose's line. Gandhi's strategy was always his own, shaped to the time and circumstances.

An Indian journalist also brought up Bose's name in another way. He said of the public feelings in his province,

It is more anti-British than pro-Japanese. There is a vague notion that we have had enough of this rule, and almost anything would be better than the existing state of things. People are happy when Subhas Babu says on the radio that there are no differences between him and you and when he says you are now out to fight for liberty at any cost.[152]

Gandhi used this remark to launch into a discussion of his differences from Bose. He said, in part,

... he is wrong. ... 'Liberty at any cost' has a vastly different connotation for me from what it has for him. 'At any cost' does not exist in my dictionary. It does not for instance include bringing in foreigners in order to help us win our liberty. I have no doubt that it means exchanging one form of slavery for another possibly much worse ... the Allies ... must face the opposition of those who cannot tolerate their rule and are prepared to die to get rid of it. ... I have made up my mind that it would be a good thing if a million people were shot in a brave and non-violent rebellion against British rule. It may be that it may take us years before we can evolve order out of chaos. ... I do not feel flattered when Subhas Babu says I am right. I am not right in the sense he means. For there he is attributing pro-Japanese feeling to me. If I were to discover that by some strange miscalculation I had not realised the fact that I was helping the entry of the Japanese in this country, I should not hesitate to retrace my steps. As regards the Japanese, I am certain that we should lay down our lives in order to resist them as we would to resist the British.[153]

Gandhi in the weeks before his movement was to commence laboring to spell out what he did and did not want and how he differed from Bose. He also had to persuade the devoted anti-fascist Nehru that he would not be aiding the Japanese if he actively and non-violently resisted British rule during wartime. Gandhi did not want foreign assistance—as Bose thought was necessary—and he did not want violent means used against the personnel of the Raj. But, he said that it was better to give up India to anarchy rather than the 'ordered anarchy' of the Raj and called for Indians to 'do or die'. Many wondered if he was not implying the use of any means to reach the goal.

Through his usual means of stubborn persuasion, Gandhi finally convinced a majority of the Working Committee and then the AICC meeting in Bombay in early August 1942, to confront the British. In contrast to the individual and limited satyagraha of 1940, this was to be a mass, if somewhat disorganized, movement against the Raj. Gandhi and the high command (including Nehru, Patel, Azad, et al.) were not prepared for the Raj's response. The Government of India moved swiftly to arrest the top leadership of the Congress. Some leaders—mainly the Congress Socialists who had dissolved their separate organization—were ready as the government moved and went underground. Their top leader was Jayaprakash Narayan who had been corresponding with Subhas Bose about the possibility of a mass movement in late 1940, just before Bose left India. The top echelon of the CSP helped to organize many of those who undertook acts of sabotage—mainly against property such as railway lines—in the following weeks. They were both socialists and nationalists without significant loyalty to any extra-India power. They had failed to support Bose in the 1939 Tripuri dispute, but now they carried out a Bose-like strategy against the Raj, with the sanction, they believed, of Gandhi. This proved to be the most disruptive movement against the Raj since the Civil Disobedience Movement of 1930–31.[154]

To this day, there are questions about the degree of organization and centralization involved and the extent and kinds of violence employed. To the British, who acted swiftly and repressively throughout, the movement was believed to be well-organized and spiritually guided by Gandhi and practically led by the CSP leaders. Their intelligence officers came up with an ABC guide to dislocation and instructions to freedom fighters purportedly authored by J.P. Narayan. Lohia was thought to be another key operative in the underground. Officials maintained that Congress, particularly Gandhi, deserved responsibility for pushing India towards anarchy and lighting the fuse of this explosion. Considerable property damage was carried out by the rebels and they even took brief control of some local areas including the Contai and Tamluk subdivisions of Midnapore district, Bengal, where the nationalist movement had long been well-organized and formidably backed by the Mahisya peasantry. They declared the 'Midnapore Republic' which was destroyed by a natural calamity and fierce government opposition. Most of the thousands killed were nationalists.[155] The Government of India blamed the Congress for precipitating the revolt; the nationalists blamed the British for their refusal to make significant concessions and to promptly 'Quit India'.

Some of those on the nationalist side found themselves in an uncomfortable position. These included the Indian communists (CPI) and the Bengal Progressive Coalition cabinet members. In the first phase of the war, the CPI actively opposed Indian participation in an 'imperialist war'. They stood with other nationalists. However, with the German invasion of the Soviet Union in 1941, they shifted ground. 'Socialism in one country' was threatened and it was the duty of all communists to join the resistance to fascist aggression. 'Imperialist War' became 'Peoples' War' and the Comintern line was to support the Allied powers. The Comintern position was communicated to them and by the end of 1941, Indian communists, with reservations, fell into line. Aligning with the Soviets was necessary, for as a British communist wrote, 'The Soviet Union is not a foreign power for the workers and the common people.'[156] Other Indian nationalists were on the other side of the barricades. The communists did try to build their own party, do welfare work, and help the war effort so that ordinary Indians benefited. Gandhi and the Congress did not forget where the communists stood in 1942 when they were herded off to prison. The CPI maliciously attacked Subhas Bose throughout the war as a quisling, as a tool of the fascists, when he was probably one of the few residents of Berlin who decried the German invasion of the USSR.

The members of the Bengal Progressive Coalition, because they were linked with the governing structure of a nation officially at war and were, among other things, responsible for law and order during this period, were in a ticklish situation. Whatever sympathies the Bose group of the Congress had for the rebels, one of their leaders, Santosh Basu, was minister responsible for the coordination of civil defense (in addition to Public Health and local Self-Government). Fazlul Huq, chief and home minister, was closely associated with the Raj's war effort. The eagle eyes of Governor Herbert and his senior officials were focused on the cabinet because the Japanese had reached the outer gates of Bengal with their conquest of Burma. In May 1942, the Japanese bombed the Calcutta area and there were some casualties. The cabinet was linked, perforce, to the repressive measures taken by the Raj in answer to the 'Quit India' movement. When these acts of control and reprisal took a harsh turn in Midnapore, Finance Minister Shyama Prasad Mookerjee, the most important Hindu member of the cabinet, resigned in protest in November for this among other acts. He said that the cabinet's powers were limited and that Governor Herbert was interfering with the work of the responsible Indian officials.[157]

The Progressive Coalition government was hampered from its inception by the arrest of Sarat Bose. No other Hindu leader of Bengal commanded the same respect in the Assembly, and the substitution of Shyama Prasad Mookerjee was an inadequate measure. The cabinet was besieged on all sides: by Jinnah and the Muslim Leaguers inside and outside the Bengal Assembly and Council; by more radical nationalists who felt that true patriots should not be associated with the Raj in this way; and by Governor Herbert who did not want this cabinet in office at all. He preferred either an all-parties or a Muslim League government headed by Nazimuddin. The Progressive Coalition did struggle along for about sixteen months. Its members frequently attended meetings calling for communal harmony .and it did pass the Bengal Rural Education (Amendment) Bill. Without a steady hand, such as Sarat Bose might have provided, however, the mercurial Fazlul Huq was always looking for a new coalition, a better grouping which he might head, and even though he had been thrown out of the Muslim League and was viciously maligned by them, he sought to get back in their good graces. In March 1943, Governor Herbert asked Huq to submit a resignation letter which he would use if the opportunity arose to form an all-parties government. Huq complied and Herbert surprised him by accepting the resignation and bringing down the Progressive Coalition. Even Linlithgow was chagrined at the method used to unseat Huq, the most popular Muslim politician in the province.[158]

V

As the Cripps Mission and the August movement unfolded, Subhas Bose could only watch from a distance, praising the revolt, but unhappy that it came too early. By the time of the Japanese attacks in the Pacific and Southeast Asia, Bose had '. . . built up . . . something between an official mission, a provisional government and not so fully recognised association of a group of exiles from India.'[159] Through his efforts and determination and the cooperation of the staff of the Sonderreferat Indien in the German Foreign Office, he had moved slowly toward some of his goals in Europe in spite of Hitler's refusal to grant him the declaration for Free India which he desperately wanted. When the Japanese struck, and then advanced towards India, he knew that his effort must shift to Southeast Asia. He gave his first broadcast in his own name and told Nambiar just after Singapore fell, 'I shall be leaving Europe and going to East Asia. It is just a question of time.'[160]

However, there were obstacles. The Japanese had the amenable Rash Behari Bose; did they want the younger, more stubborn, and independent Bose? After urging by Indians in Japan and Southeast Asia, the Japanese did agree to accept him after discussing the matter at a joint meeting of the Army, Navy, and Foreign Ministries on April 17.[161] The Germans, by this time, were agreeable to his move closer to his homeland to help the Axis forces confront the British. It took the better part of a year to put together a practicable transportation operation around several theaters of war, and then several months to carry and deliver Bose to East Asia. He was stuck in Europe for 1942.

The BBC announced on March 25, 1942 that he died in an air crash in East Asia. Bose was briefly and deeply disturbed by this because of the impact he thought it would have on his family, particularly his mother. Then he learned that Gandhi had sent a condolence message to his mother. Later in the day the German News Agency (DNB) and the Japanese contradicted the news. Bose was relieved, but the incident demonstrated how powerful was the continuing presence of his family with him, though they were thousands of miles away.[162] It also set up a pattern in his life, especially as it was conceived in the Indian folk imagination, of disappearance and subsequent reappearance, departure and arrival.

A few weeks after this incident, Bose received the noted Italian journalist Luigi Barzini at his home. Lunch was served and Bose was interviewed. Barzini published his artful portrait of Bose in *Popolo d'Italia* on April 19, and it read, in part,

> He lives in a solitary villa made of red brick, surrounded by a garden . . . we experienced a sense of intimacy, distance from the world. . . . Bose . . . wanted. . . to talk about (the) problems of India. European food, European service, a waiter in white gloves. . . .
>
> He is young, tall . . . with a kind of smiling expression, high forehead, finely drawn mouth, altogether a feeling of superior intelligence, (a) certain ingenuity, a grace of exaggerated adolescence. You could almost take him for a European were it not for the bronze color of the skin. . . . He has something of Buddha in his regular and open face, but a Buddha vivacious and dynamic, though peaceful in his speech and gestures. . . . The composure and control of himself . . . constitute . . . a sign of asiatic nobility. . . He speaks. . . clearly in perfect English . . . and writes. . . . with a literary grace. . . . He was a faithful and active follower of Gandhi, and still speaks with devotion and admiration of Mahatma but he has become in certain respects his antagonist.[163]

It was almost natural that Bose should meet a visiting Italian journalist and stir him to thoughts of an ancient nobility. Bose had found a response in Italy that he hardly ever received from the cooler Germans. In May 1942, Bose again traveled over the Alps to Italy in search of support from Mussolini.

Bose first met Count Ciano, who again, was skeptical, and discouraged Bose by telling him that proposals for a free India declaration had been put off indefinitely. The following day, May 5, however, Ciano noted in his diary,

> I go with Bose to the Duce. A long conference without any new developments, except the fact that Mussolini allowed himself to be persuaded by the arguments produced by Bose to obtain a tripartite declaration in favour of Indian independence. He has telegraphed the Germans proposing—contrary to the Salzburg decisions—proceeding at once with the declaration. I feel that Hitler will not agree to it very willingly.[164]

With one of the three powers in hand—agreeing to the declaration he wanted—he avidly pursued the other two. Bose demonstrated that in some one-to-one situations with important foreign leaders, he could be persuasive in pushing his case. But this was Italy. A month later he said to an Italian journalist in Berlin, 'I feel at home in Italy, there is a cultural atmosphere close to our own, perhaps it is in the Italian culture.'[165] After his one wartime meeting with Mussolini, Bose wrote to Ribbentrop requesting travel facilities to the East and pressing for the declaration.

Within a few days of that letter, Bose had his first and only meeting with Adolf Hitler. There is some disagreement about where and on which day it took place, but it was either May 27 or 29.[166] Accompanied by Ribbentrop and Keppler, Bose greeted Hitler as 'an old revolutionary' from whom he could gain advise. Given this opening, Hitler lectured Bose on the world situation, the great distance from German advances to the Indian frontier, and his unwillingness to make any moves or issue any proclamations that could not have practical effect.

Then, according to the minutes prepared by P.O. Schmidt, Hitler's chief interpreter, the Führer continued,

> India was endlessly far from Germany. The only possibilities of communication with India was by land or air. . . . In any case, the path would be only over the corpse of Russia.
>
> He considered Japan's astonishingly rapid advance to be the historical event of the world of the last half year, by means of which, her armies had practically advanced to the borders of India. Japan's aim was not known to him. He did not know whether the Japanese considered it more important first to relieve their flanks from being threatened by Chiang Kai-shek or to seek to turn to Australia or India. The defeat of their power in East Asia would possibly lead to the collapse of the British Empire. Such a collapse would naturally mean a great relief for Germany and would spare her a lot of blood.[167]

Although it probably did not surprise Bose, Hitler's lack of knowledge of Japanese objectives demonstrates how loosely the Axis were allied.

Hitler went on to tell Bose that he would facilitate his trip to East Asia. The Führer advised against an air route and said that he would place a submarine 'at his disposal' for the sea journey which would be much safer. Bose was surely gratified to learn that the next stage of his journey was in the works. Turning to other items on his agenda, Bose asked Hitler about the declaration for a free India that he wanted and also about what he considered to be passages offensive to Indians in *Mein Kampf*. Hitler did not answer either point very directly. He talked of Indian objectives in a general way and German economic support for India after the war. He did not address the question of the declaration straight on, but Bose understood that Hitler was still unwilling to issue it. The burden of Bose and his goals was being shifted to the Japanese. On the offending references to Indians in his book, Hitler waffled by saying that he was trying to discourage passive resistance in Germany. On these two matters, Bose made no progress.[168]

According to several sources, German and Indian, Bose was shaken by the lack of communication and support evident in this audience with Hitler. After enduring the dangers of his escape from India, after working industriously for a year and waiting for his chance to put his case to Hitler directly, Bose learned that little was to be forthcoming from the Germans. His only gratification was that there were very positive developments— from his point of view—going on in Southeast Asia, and Hitler would help him to go there.[169] Of course, with all the discouragements that he had received from the Nazi elite in nearly a decade of reaching out to them, Bose should not have been surprised. That he should have had some hopes vis-à-vis these barbarians only evinces his naiveté and the shortcomings of the aphorism, 'The enemy of my enemy is my friend.'

Although draft versions of the declaration for a free India continued to circulate amongst the Germans, Italians, and Japanese which mentioned 'India for the Indians', the wickedness of British imperialism, and general backing for the independence of India, none was jointly signed and issued while Bose was in Europe.[170] Nevertheless, Bose put on a good face when he held a press conference on June 12, 1942. He said, in part, in his opening statement,

> I regard myself as a servant of the Indian nation and my present task is to lead the fight for India's independence. But as soon as India is free, it will be the duty of the Indian people to decide what form of Government they desire and who should guide the future Indian state. I certainly have my own ideas regarding post war reconstruction in Free India, but it will be for Free India to decide upon them. . . . My own experience has now convinced me that by the logic of history, the Tripartite Powers have become our natural friends and allies. Every blow struck at the British Empire is a help to India in her fight for freedom. . . . I am convinced that during the course of this war, India will be free. The freedom of India will mean the expulsion of Anglo-American Imperialism from Asia and it will afford a powerful stimulus to freedom movements all over the world.[171]

In many wartime statements, Bose disclaimed that he sought to be the dictator of India. Some critics have tossed him into the fascist camp. When he spoke of the shape of a free India, he did suggest that he thought that India would need a strong central government, perhaps an authoritarian one, to get started on the road to modernization, industrialization, and reconstruction. But he knew that the Indian people would choose their leader or leaders. In the same press conference, when asked of his own future plans, he said, '. . . the plans of a revolutionary must always be adapted to the circumstances of the moment and to the needs of the situation in which he is interested.'[172] Though he was referring specifically to his travel plans, he generally thought that one had to adapt to the changing environment. Also noteworthy is his self-image as 'a revolutionary'. Because of the presence of the Raj, he would not label himself in this way in India. Outside India, he linked himself to a tradition of violent resistance stretching back to the earliest days of British conquest. In this Bose history of the Raj, Gandhian mass, non-violent resistance was one strategy which had raised the consciousness of many, but not ended the Raj. For that, an Indian army coming from without coordinated with an uprising within was necessary.

His departure for East Asia was not fixed. Indeed, Hauner has documented that the Japanese changed their minds several times about whether they wanted him in their sphere. So through 1942, Bose continued to develop the Free India Center, and visited his recruits in the Indian Legion to encourage them and to inspect their progress.[173] One of the recruits, Gurbachan Singh Mangat, has maintained that there were endless difficulties and betrayals within the Legion.[174] By December the force had grown to four battalions but it was unclear where, if anywhere, they would be used.

One of the earliest members of the Free India Center, M.R. Vyas, has recorded that by mid-1942, its work was going smoothly. One controversy which did arise, according to Girija Mookerjee, was whether the civilians working at the Center should take an oath like the one the soldiers took, pledging their allegiance to Bose himself. There were, he says, some heated disagreements, until Bose stepped in and said there should be no oath-taking. Mookerjee gives this as one piece of his portrayal of Bose as a believer in liberal values and socialism, not a dictator in the present or a dictator-to-be.[175]

Bose was willing to accept a summons from 'the Indian people' in the independence period as all of his wartime actions make clear. He had definite ideas of the shape he thought a free India should take. These had been articulated in his Congress presidential speeches, especially the Haripura one, and in articles for the *Forward Bloc* and other articles he wrote from about 1938 on. He repeated these views during the war. In free India, he expected that there would be a strong national army, a devoted and capable administrative cadre, and,

> There will be a strong Central Government. Without such a Government, order and public security cannot be safeguarded. Behind this Government will stand a well-organised, disciplined all-India party, which will be the chief instrument for maintaining national unity.
>
> The state will guarantee complete religious and cultural freedom for individuals and groups and there will be no state religion. In the matter of political and economic rights there will be perfect equality. . . . When the new regime is stabilised and the state machinery begins to function smoothly,

power will be decentralized and the provincial governments will be given more responsibility.[176]

In light of the problems of India, this surely sounded like utopia. Like many others on the Indian left, Bose thought that, 'The Mohammedan (or Muslim) problem in India today is an artificial creation of the British similar to the Ulster-problem in Ireland and the Jewish problem in Palestine. It will disappear when British rule is swept away.'[177] Surely, this was wishful thinking. None of these sub-nationalisms, or powerful ethnic movements, of the Ulster Protestants, of the Jews, or that of the Indian Muslims, 'disappeared' with the demise of British rule.

As Bose spoke frequently on the radio using German facilities, Goebbels, the Nazis' propaganda expert who liked to keep a finger in every propaganda pie (and loved to irritate Ribbentrop) wrote in his diary,

> Bose's propaganda, conducted from Berlin, is extremely embarrassing to the English. It is being heard more widely than I at first thought possible. All the better that we have not yet revealed where he is staying![178]

The British disputed that Bose was having much impact and they certainly had no doubts about where he was. In so far as the British allowed news of Bose to filter into India, they tried to have him described as a 'quisling' who had forsaken his country. Bose is also said to have written about the Indians as Aryans in an article for Goebbels' *Angriff* and to have made some anti-Jewish statements.[179] The actual article that Bose is said to have written has not been located and the comments in *The Jewish Chronicle* of that time are quite hostile to Bose. What Bose is reported to have said about the Aryans is not inaccurate and only passionate Indian nationalist remarks are quoted directly. The other remarks are summarized and these views are not in keeping with Bose's sympathies for Jewish friends in Europe in the 1930s.

On September 11, 1942, Bose traveled to Hamburg to open a new Indo-German Society.[180] This kind of activity was of a piece with his 1930s work in many European countries of establishing cultural links between each of them and India. Many of these societies—in Germany, Czechoslovakia, France, etc.—survived the war and have continued as bridges between India and the West.

In the. fall of 1942, however, Bose undertook other intra-European travel more closely related to his number one goal: reaching East Asia. Although Hitler had cautioned him about the dangers of traveling to the East by air, Bose made arrangements with the Italians who had completed one non-stop journey to Asia. Bose said his farewells to the brass of the German Foreign Office including Ribbentrop, Keppler, and Trott, and left for Rome on October 14. But the flight was delayed, rescheduled, and canceled. Bose lingered in Rome for a month, hoping against hope that it would go. At the end of the second week of November, all Italian efforts to make such flights were put off for several months. Bose talked to diplomats and cultural figures like Professor Tucci in Rome during his wait.[181] The indefinite cancelation hit him hard. Vyas says he went into decline.[182]

After visiting Czechoslovakia, France, and Belgium, Bose reached Vienna about mid-November. His chosen companion in life, Emilie Schenkl, was more than eight months pregnant. She had left Berlin, partly because the couple did not want her to be openly seen in this condition, and also because she wanted to give birth near her family, in her native city. Bose returned to Berlin about November 15, and Emilie Schenkl gave birth to Anita Bose on November 29.

Early in 1943, Woermann discussed Bose's journey with Ambassador Oshima and plans for a long, complicated sea voyage and a rendezvous between a German and a Japanese submarine somewhere near the tip of Africa were worked out.[183] Alexander Werth mentions that,

> Shortly before Bose's departure the Japanese Naval Command raised objections because of an internal Japanese regulation not permitting civilians to travel on a warship in war-time. When Adam von Trott received this message by cable from the German Ambassador in Tokyo, he sent the following reply: 'Subhas Chandra Bose is by no means a private person but Commander-in-Chief of the Indian Liberation Army.' Thus the bureaucratic interference was overcome.[184]

Bose and the Germans did not want to openly reveal his plans. A big Independence Day celebration was held—as in 1942—with more than 600 in attendance. Some said later that Bose mentioned that he would be going to the front to observe troops in action. Programs for Azad Hind Radio were pre-recorded. Only Nambiar and presumably Emilie Schenkl and some Foreign Office officials knew of the travel program. In late January, Bose had a scare when he had a bad reaction to one of Dr Faroqi's glucose injections, but he recovered.[185]

Emilie Schenkl came to Berlin about January 20 to say goodbye. Bose left a Bengali letter with her addressed to his brother Sarat Bose.[186] It is not clear whether Subhas Bose had much of an opportunity to see his newborn daughter. Personally this was a wrenching break, but duty beckoned. Nambiar was left in charge of the Indian operation in Germany.

At first Bose thought he might be able to take two or three aides, but, in the end, he was allowed only one companion in the submarine. He chose Abid Hasan who had worked on the military side, but had all the skills necessary to act as private secretary and assistant. Hasan was not told of the voyage in advance. When he was told he was to leave for an unknown destination, he thought that he might be going to Greece and started to study Greek. When the train arrived at Kiel and he saw Keppler, Werth, and Nambiar there to say farewell to Bose, he realized that another destination was planned.[187] Hasan wrote, 'I was quite fascinated by the romance of having to travel by the submarine. But the moment I entered the submarine, all romance of it went away.'[188]

At dawn, February 8, 1943, Bose and Hasan climbed into German submarine U-180, captained by Commander Werner Musenberg. The boat had four officers and fifty-one sailors, was a bigger sub of the 9D type, and had a special E motor to enable it to go faster. It could travel at eighteen knots on the surface and seven-and-a-half knots under water. It departed the following day for its long journey through dangerous waters, around the British Isles, and south through the Atlantic.[189] Not only were the waters infested with enemy ships and some patrolled by enemy planes, but the U-boat sent the usual radio messages which were likely decoded by the British. Ronald Lewin, an expert on Allied intelligence in the war, wrote,

> ... his [*Bose's*] trip was not so secret as was assumed. Special messages were transmitted to him by radio to keep him abreast of the nationalist situation. Intercepted and deciphered, these told the Allies not only about his presence aboard but also a great deal about the Free India Movement and its membership.[190]

Though it is very likely that the British knew of Bose's trip from the Japanese diplomatic messages which were deciphered by the Americans and passed on to them, and from their own cracking of the German cipher, the British either could not or did not choose to intercept the submarine. Did they think that Bose was not a big enough fish to be worth the effort? Or did they not have the appropriate air and sea forces to do so?

They were not closely pursued or attacked and on one occasion, on April 18, 1943, U-180 sank the British merchant ship *Corbis*. Everything was done in close quarters and, according to Hasan, everything stank of diesel oil. When they were served large greasy pieces of beef, even these had this unpleasant odor. The Indians struggled manfully to adapt. Hasan searched around and found a bag of rice and some lentils. He prepared *dal-bhat* for Bose and himself and they survived on it during the German part of the trip.[191] Bose worked hard during these two-and-a-half months, preparing changes for a new edition of *The Indian Struggle,* and making as detailed plans as possible for his new agenda in East and Southeast Asia.

On April 24, they made their connection with the Japanese submarine I-29 in the Indian Ocean, east of Madagascar, at approximately 25 degrees South Latitude and 60 degrees East Longitude. The seas were rough and the transfer took some time to carry out. Finally, passing on his final farewells and thanks to his German hosts of the past two years, Bose now became a guest of the Imperial Japanese Navy.[192]

It was now April 1943. When he made his initial choice to go to Europe, Germany and Italy were at war with the British Empire and Japan was not. As determined as he might be himself, and he was a believer in the enormous power of the human will, he had to face changed circumstances which offered fewer opportunities than earlier. Had he been in Southeast Asia in early 1942 as the Japanese were on the offensive, then he might have persuaded them to push on into India when the British defenses were weakened. But he was in Germany. A whole year had passed during which the Japanese had not made any move towards India and were beginning to feel the weight of American muscle against them. Just as Bose was getting set to journey to the East, the Germans suffered their greatest defeat at Stalingrad. The momentum of the war was shifting against the loosely connected Axis powers. Now Bose was going closer to the Indian troops and Indian community who could give him the manpower and material backing he had been seeking for a political-military venture into India from outside.

CHAPTER ELEVEN

An Indian Samurai: Subhas Bose in Asia, 1943–45

You wash evil from the world in a flood of warriors' blood.
Gita Govinda

the pulse of the people throbs in my blood
and calls me to those barren fields
filled by vultures
where millions of my brothers die.
Samar Sen, 'Scorched Earth'[2]

The Way of the Samurai is found in death. When it comes to either/ or, there is only the quick choice of death. . . . Be determined and advance. To say that dying without reaching one's aim is to die a dog's death is the frivolous way of sophisticates. When pressed with the choice of life or death, it is not necessary to gain one's aim.

We all want to live. And in large part we make our logic according to what we like. But not having attained our aim and continuing to live is cowardice. This is a thin dangerous line. To die without gaining one's aim is a dog's death and fanaticism. But there is no shame in this. . . . If by setting one's heart right every morning and evening, one is able to live as though his body were already dead, he gains freedom in the Way.
Yamamoto Tsunetomo, *Hagakure, the Book of the Samurai*[3]

I

Once Bose and Hasan climbed out of their small rubber dinghy and into the large Japanese submarine I–29, bigger than the German submarine, and commanded by Captain Izu, not only could they enjoy the increased space, but,

> . . . we did feel that we had come back to an Asian nation . . . it was something akin to a home-coming. Immediately we had that feeling. . . . We could be

less formal, although we had to be more formal. . . of course, the food was . . . entirely to our liking.[4]

Bose had spent a good deal of his travel months preparing for this encounter, his first with the Japanese. He discussed many possibilities with Hasan and even had role-playing sessions with his secretary taking the part of Prime Minister Tojo. There had been many disappointments in Europe. The years there were almost like a huge detour, with little movement directly towards his goal. But he was now back in Asia, he felt some kinship with the Japanese for cultural and political reasons, and he wanted to approach them more successfully than he had the Germans.

On May 6 at Saban Island naval base, Bose was met by Captain Yamamoto, the former military attaché from Berlin, and by Senda, an important member of the Iwakuro Kikan. They traveled on by plane, making several stops before reaching Tokyo around mid-May, where they stayed in the Imperial Hotel, designed by Frank Lloyd Wright, with Bose using the name Matsuda.[5] Bose's plan was to meet a range of military officers, and learn the ropes in a new territory, before climbing the main peak. Although some said that General Tojo was reticent to meet Bose, Hasan has insisted that it was not the case.[6] Bose wanted to prepare the ground carefully before approaching Tojo with his largest requests. Yamamoto was his only acquaintance. As Hasan put it, Bose '. . . wanted a sort of interrogation of himself to take place. . . .'[7] That is, he wanted to be questioned by groups or individuals in the Japanese elite so that they might come to know, understand, even appreciate him and his mission. He wanted to create a 'Subhas lobby' which would help him carry through his work in Asia. According to some of the officers he met, such as General Arisue, he made a powerful impression. General Sugiyama, army chief of staff, found Bose direct and far from humble. This was unlike the behavior of the Japanese. Both the Japanese and Bose had to learn to live with each other. Bose met with Sugiyama, Foreign Minister Shigemitsu, Navy Minister Yonai, and section chiefs of the relevant ministries.[8]

Bose had undoubtedly come to see that Tojo was not a dictator in the Hitler or Mussolini mold and the Japanese ruling group was very different from the German or Italian. The ruling military group had the power of decision and they had chosen Tojo for the top post; they could also bring him down if he was not successful.[9] So Bose's courtship of a range of officers and officials besides Tojo, even if in partial preparation for the most momentous meeting, made good sense.

Rash Behari Bose had returned from Southeast Asia, and he and Bose, to the relief of the Japanese, seemed to hit it off excellently. The elder Bose knew that the time had come to pass the torch of the Indian revolutionary struggle for freedom to a younger, more vigorous, and more renowned leader. He had urged the Japanese to bring Subhas Bose from Europe. The older man was in failing health—tuberculosis—and had pushed as far as he could. Subhas Bose was also happy to meet the famed Toyama of the Black Dragon Society during his first weeks in Japan.[10] During the period when he was meeting Japanese officials from mid-May to mid-June, Bose toured Japanese schools, hospitals, and factories, as Yamamoto tried to give him a wider view of the Japanese effort.

Finally on June 10, 1943, Bose had his first meeting with Tojo. The prime minister, a reserved man of rather narrowly military and nationalistic outlook, was impressed. The passionate nature, confidence, and very presence of the Indian made a surprisingly positive impact on Tojo. He became a firm supporter of Bose. Bose pressed Tojo on support for Indian independence. Tojo said he unreservedly backed it. Bose wanted a military push across the border from Burma into India. On this point Tojo hedged. It was a military matter which involved many different factors. The seed was planted, but Tojo likely knew that the Allies had been sending their Chindit raiders into Burma since February and had been moving against Japanese positions in the Arakan. In the Pacific, the Japanese for the first time were beginning to lose land battles and the Allied counter-offensive called Cartwheel was on the drawing board. Bose attended a session of the Diet on June 16 at which Tojo said, 'We firmly resolve that Japan will do everything possible to help Indian independence.'[11]

A few days later Bose held a press conference attended by sixty journalists. In his opening statement, Bose said, in part,

> Indians view the present World War as a struggle between two ideologies. It is a struggle between those who want the *status quo* to continue and those who are determined to tear that old rag into pieces. . . . Our sincere support is for the New Order. . . . If the Axis Powers win . . . India will regain her lost freedom. . . . We should . . . get our freedom only by shedding our own blood. . . . Since the enemy fights with his sword we too should fight with the sword. . . . Only if a large number of Indians undergo this baptism of fire can they win the race and get the reward of freedom.[12]

As he had begun to do in broadcasts from Europe, Bose made explicit his connection to a revolutionary and violent stand in Indian nationalism which he said had been there since at least the nineteenth century. Gandhi's way was valuable, but had proved insufficient. Picking up such teachings as the *Bhagavad Gita*, read as Aurobindo had read it, Bose called for the shedding of warriors' blood in a righteous cause. Although Gandhi is reported to have said on the eve of the Quit India movement, 'Do or die,' there was still some distance between Gandhi's non-violent resistance, even the sabotage of the Congress Socialists, and Bose's armed struggle for freedom. Another element of Bose's viewpoint here is that Indians *earn* their freedom by death and martyrdom.

At the same press conference, Bose made the first of several comments he was to make in the following months about China. He identified with the Nanking government of Wang Ching-wei and called upon Chiang Kai-shek to come to terms with the Japanese rather than '. . . serving as a tool of the Anglo-Americans. . . .'[13] Bose said that the Japanese had now put forward a new pro-Asian policy which all Asians, including the besieged Chinese, should back. This Chinese puppet regime of a frustrated patriot rested on the weight of Japanese arms.[14] Was Bose naive enough to put much store in Japanese policy announcements after their brutal actions in China for a decade and more? Bose made many pronouncements in his speeches and broadcasts foreseeing an Axis victory and, in this case, calling upon the Chinese to make what would have been a humiliating peace with the Japanese. It is hard to know whether to take these statements at face value, as some analysts have, or to see parts of them as propaganda messages which he felt he should make to second his allies.[15] Bose had enough sophistication and knowledge of the world to see the shortcomings of the Japanese, as he had of the Germans, but he usually avoided criticizing his allies or commenting on what he called their 'internal affairs'. Was he simply being a 'good soldier' in the Japanese cause, so that the latter would give him his offensive into India?

After his news conference, Bose began broadcasting almost daily from Radio NHK Tokyo, and his broadcasts continued through the remainder of the war. Several themes have already been noted: the need for an armed struggle to win Indian freedom and the cooperation of the Japanese to do so. He was also concerned, as he had been from the late 1930s onward, about his Congress colleagues. He seemed to think that any deal, any treaty, anything short of driving the British out by force of arms would be tainted. Therefore, any conference of Indian leaders and the British was not seen as a danger. Without his presence in India, he feared a sell-out. The British, on the other hand, were worried about Bose and the INA movement. They did their best to follow a 'policy of silence' demanding that the media ignore the INA and Bose, but confidentially, they wrote, '. . . every Indian (is) a potential fifth columnist.'[16]

In deference to Bose's preferences, Colonel Yamamoto replaced Colonel Iwakuro as head of the Kikan and it was renamed Hikari Kikan. With his oldest Japanese acquaintance on the team, Bose flew off to Singapore.[17] From the press and radio coverage and his speeches, the

Indian soldiers and community in Southeast Asia knew that he had arrived in Japan and a few knew that he would shortly descend on them. He was met at the airport in Singapore by all those Indian military officers who had kept the INA alive from December 1942 onwards and refused Mohan Singh's dissolution order. As one of these officers said, the INA was not the creature of Mohan Singh, but of the IIL and the entire Indian nationalist movement in Southeast Asia. Therefore, Mohan Singh had no power to dissolve it.[18] Bose was met with chants of 'Subhas Chandra Bose *Zindabad'*. Colonel Prem Sahgal, who had attended some of his political meetings in India, had looked forward to this auspicious event marking the advent of new leadership. Some, said Sahgal, '. . . felt that almost a God had come there *ı* . . here was the man who had come in answer to their prayers. They [*the large crowd of Indians*] had trust in him that he would be able to lead them on the right path, the path to Indian independence.'[19] Sahgal became his military secretary.

Two days later at a public meeting at the Cathay Theater, Rash Behari Bose presented Subhas Bose to the cheering throng. The elder Bose said, in part,

> Friends and comrades-at-arms! . . . I have brought you this present. Subhas Chandra Bose . . . symbolizes all that is best, noblest, the most daring, and the most dynamic in the youth of India. . . . In your presence today, I resign my office as President of the Indian Independence League in East Asia. From now on, Subhas Chandra Bose is your President, your leader in the fight for India's independence, and I am confident that . . . you will march on to battle and to victory.[20]

Thus the torch was passed. There is no indication if there was any meeting to elect Subhas Bose to the presidency, but the IIL had requested him to come from Germany more than a year earlier, so there can be no doubt that he was the man many wanted. With this speech, Rash Behari Bose stepped back to the position of an elder adviser and Subhas Bose moved into the center of all Indian affairs for the INA and IIL for the remainder of the war.

In his own speech, Subhas Bose announced his intention to organize a Provisional Government of Free India 'to mobilize all of our forces effectively. . . to lead the Indian Revolution . . . to prepare the Indian people, inside and outside India, for an armed struggle which will be the culmination of all our national efforts since 1883.'[21] To gain Indian freedom, her fighters would have '. . . to face hunger, thirst, privation, forced marches— and death.'[22] Speaking to gatherings of Indian troops and officers during the following days, Bose gave them the slogan, '*Chalo Delhi*! To Delhi— To Delhi!' Tojo, in Southeast Asia for other purposes, was invited to attend a special review of the INA and he and Bose pledged to work together for their common goals. Bose renamed the INA the 'Azad Hind Fauj' and said to the civilians in Southeast Asia that their slogan should be 'Total Mobilization for a Total War'. Bose promised, 'Give me the total mobilization of Indian manpower and material resources in East Asia, and I promise you a second front—a real second front in India's war of independence.'[23]

Once the marching passed and the great rallies were over, Bose and his colleagues had to set themselves to the real work of organizing a small fighting force which could stand side-by-side with the Japanese at the battle front. And they had to shape the provisional government and collect resources for it to carry on. In the midst of the turmoil of war, at a time when the major patron was beginning to suffer major setbacks in the Pacific, these were no small or easy tasks. Although Bose always talked of victory and the relentless march forward, he tried to get accurate information about the progress of the war, not only from his allies, but also from his enemies and independent sources. He did place a great weight on moral or political motivations in the war ahead, and tried to get the fullest measure of human and material support he could, and though the results were sometimes gratifying, they were often a great disappointment.

The structures he created and the procedures he followed indicate the shape he wished an independent India to take. One of his innovations in the INA, and eventually in the provisional government, had to do with the role of women. For two decades he had wanted to make Indian women full partners in the struggle for independence and encouraged many women to work with the Congress. Now Bose had the idea of a women's regiment trained to fight alongside Indian men. This proved to be a difficult task, but he persevered in his intention and found some remarkable women who were willing to come forward. In Singapore, he had recommended to him a young Indian doctor, Lakshmi Swaminathan (also written Swaminadhan). Born in 1914 in Madras, she had been a private medical practitioner in Singapore before the war, and had been active in the women's section of the IIL. At his invitation, she met him for a lengthy discussion on July 12. She recounted years later,

> He frankly told me that it was his ambition and dream to form a regiment of women who would be willing to take up arms and fight just as the men. . . he asked me straight, 'Would you volunteer yourself for such a fighting unit,' and I said, 'Yes.' Then he said, 'Do you think that you can get a hundred other women from Malaya to do it?' I said, 'Hundred is no number, I think we should try and get at least five thousand women and if it is gone about in a proper manner, I think we will be able to do it.'[24]

In this choice, Bose was most fortunate: she was intelligent,

determined, a fiery speaker, and beautiful as well. The regiment was to be
called after the Rani of Jhansi, a heroine of 1857, and a link to a 'glorious
tradition' of Indian heroines.[25] Bose also believed that seeing Indian
women fighting at their side, the men would fight even more fiercely. The
Japanese were asked to vacate a training base for the women and thought
that surely Bose was joking. He was not. It took some doing, but the women
finally got their training facility where they were trained by male members
of the Azad Hind Fauj. They eventually numbered about 1,000, of whom
the less suited to fight were assigned to nursing and support duties. The
most able became NCOs. They were all later sent to the Burma front. When
Bose formed his provisional government a few months later, he appointed
Lakshmi Swaminathan to be minister for women's affairs.

Several of the outstanding recruits of the Rani of Jhansi Regiment, who
went on to exceptional careers of service after the war, mentioned that
Bose acted 'fatherly' towards them, and was immensely concerned for
their welfare. The man who could not watch his own daughter grow up
because of the circumstances of war told the Ranis that he was their
'mother and father'.[26] He wrote to one girl of sixteen, 'If you want to live,
live for others.' She applied this lesson to her life and became one of the
most noted secondary school principals in her country.[27] To another girl of
sixteen, who later became the organizer of the girl guides of her country,
he wrote, 'I hope the confidence I've placed in you will take you far.'[28]
Whether it was Bose's confidence or simply their own abilities that took
them far, I cannot say. But the powerful impact of Bose on these unusual
women—witnessed decades later—is unmistakable.

The recruitment of Lakshmi Swaminathan also illustrates a vital point
about Bose's wartime leadership. He was able to find some able,
occasionally exceptional people, who became entirely devoted to him.
Captain Lakshmi, as she came to be called, described the impact of this first
interview,

> When I came out of that meeting, I would say that I was completely awe-
> struck because I could have never imagined such a man who had such a big
> vision and yet who in himself was very simple, who made himself very
> clear, who was not at all arrogant or trying to force his opinion on others. He
> all the time in a very level-headed, persuasive and rational manner, step by
> step, was trying to explain why he was doing certain things and what his
> reasons were and what he believed would be the outcome. His utter, absolute
> sincerity struck me most and I felt that this man would never take a wrong
> step and that one could trust him completely and have the utmost confidence
> in him.[29]

Bose found a core of devoted recruits and a large number of others willing
to cooperate as he rebuilt the INA and set the civilian side in order. These

most devoted ones were ready to walk into fire for the course of action he set. Some did die in the effort. Some, like Lakshmi Swaminathan and Prem Sahgal, came through alive.

Of course, there were others who did not help, some who worked with Bose for narrow and personal ends, some who opposed him, and some who were looking for the opportunity to go over to the other side as Colonel Dhillon had. Bose hoped for hundreds of thousands of devoted national workers and a flow of money into the movement's coffers. He got some thousands of good workers and some contributions from rich and poor among the Indian community. With his boundless energy and passion for the cause, he was able to get some very able volunteers passionately attached to him.

Bose became the supreme commander of the INA, but did not take a military rank. He gave up the civilian dress he had worn in Europe and usually wore military-style clothing. After the crisis of late 1942, the number in the INA had fallen to about 12,000. Another 10,000 or so were recruited from amongst the prisoners by what the British called 'the demagogic oratory of S.C. Bose,' and during 1943 to 1945 about 18,000 Indian civilians in Southeast Asia were recruited. Although different figures have been given for the total, most seem to be in the 40,000 range. Bose wanted three divisions and at least 50,000 men. The Japanese sanctioned the first division. Without heavy artillery or air power, and confined mainly to small arms, these men were prepared for guerrilla warfare. Senior officers of the INA were active in recruiting and training the civilians who helped to man the other two divisions which were eventually sanctioned. There were training centers in Malaya and Burma. The forces of the INA were given spiritual, or more accurately, political training. British intelligence believed that this political emphasis was given to the detriment of ordinary military training. The British also said that there were not sufficient officers of quality to staff the army.[30]

The Japanese, particularly Field Marshal Count Terauchi, commander of the Southern Expeditionary Forces, viewed them as a propaganda unit to be attached to the real fighting forces. This, of course, infuriated Bose and he spent a good deal of his energy arguing with the Japanese for an important combat role for the INA. They would, he declared, lead the way in the reconquest of India from its foreign occupiers. In his talks with the Japanese, with Colonel Mohan Singh, whom he visited, and with other experienced military and civilian Indians, Bose displayed great optimism that, once Indian national forces commanded by their Netaji entered India, there would be a great rising against the British. Many of his listeners were dubious about this. Bose had read many books on warfare and had many discussions with military leaders. He continued to overestimate the weight of the morale or political factor in warfare. The Japanese also believed that 'spirit' was an important variable. But they knew that planes and artillery and supplies also counted.

Bose had underestimated the difficulties in raising the money needed to finance the INA and the provisional government. He did get contributions from the Indian community, often more enthusiastically from the poorer and middle class sections than from the rich. One of his closest colleagues, an experienced journalist, later wrote that,

> Rich Indians in East Asia . . . were not easily moved by Netaji's appeals . . . he was determined not to lose his temper or patience with them but he did not waver for a moment in his decision to reduce them to utter poverty, if necessary, in getting their money for India's war of liberation. . . . He was frankly disappointed at the initial indifference of the moneyed Indians to his passionate appeals for funds. His disappointment was considerably offset by his gratification at the sight of the tremendous enthusiasm of the comparatively poor Indians . . . he uttered mild threats. . . . Much against his will he translated some of the threats into action.[31]

A wealthy Mr Habib of Rangoon gave his entire fortune to the cause, but he was the exception. Bose was forced to take loans from the Japanese. Free India was to repay them. And pressure was exerted on the wealthy Indians of Southeast Asia to encourage them to contribute more than token amounts. Some, according to M. Sivaram, used all kinds of tricks to avoid paying.[32]

On July 5, at the Singapore airport, Bose first met Ba Maw of Burma. A former premier and fervent Burmese nationalist, Ba Maw agreed to head the administration of Burma under the Japanese. His cause and Bose's were linked, for both wanted Japanese aid in destroying British imperial rule, but each also wanted independence for his country and not subservience to a new foreign ruler. In addition, if the INA, in league with the Japanese army, was to plunge into India, the springboard had to be Burma. There had been a large and flourishing Indian community in pre-war Burma but it was often disliked by the Burmese who felt that Indian businessmen and professionals were holding positions which should be filled by Burmese.

The Japanese conquest of Burma in cooperation with some Burmese nationalists followed the British debacle in Malaya and Singapore in the first half of 1942. Aung San and Ba Maw and other Burmese nationalists had reached out to the Japanese as Bose had to the Germans and other enemies of the British Empire. The Japanese, particularly Colonel Keiji

Suzuki, who played the Fujiwara role in the Burmese drama, helped create the Burmese Independence Army. This force went out of control during and immediately after the Japanese conquest and was disbanded. In its place the Japanese later set up a civil administration, which Ba Maw agreed to head, and the Burma Defence Army.[33]

Ba Maw and many other Burmese nationalists began their cooperation with the Japanese holding great expectations. But Ba Maw described the fate of the Burmese and other Asian peoples under Japanese occupation:

> As for the Japanese militarists, few people were mentally so race-bound ... and in consequence so totally incapable either of understanding others, or of making themselves understood by others. ... For them there was only one way to do a thing, the Japanese way ... only one destiny ... to become so many Manchukuos or Koreas tied forever to Japan. These racial impositions. .. made any real understanding between the Japanese militarists and the peoples of our region virtually impossible.[34]

Before becoming aware of the hard realities of the Japanese drive to use and humiliate other Asians, Ba Maw had headed the 'Trust Japan' program.[35] As a concession to Burmese nationalist objections to their harsh rule, the Japanese agreed to grant 'independence' to Burma on August 1, 1943. A Burmese constitution and native structure was elaborated, but the Japanese army remained, and relations between the Japanese occupiers and the Burmese were often harsh and unpleasant. Ba Maw became head, or *Adipadi*, of this new government, which contained authoritarian elements, but was established in the name of the people. He invited Subhas Bose, who he said agreed with him that an authoritarian government was a necessity in a time of transition, to the independence ceremonies.[36] To the ethnically diverse and often divided Burmese population, Dr Ba Maw provided the slogan, 'One Blood! One Voice! One Command!' A sincere nationalist, he was, no doubt, eager to rule, but lacked solid support throughout the society and had to argue constantly with the top officers of the occupation army.

Ba Maw has described his impressions of his Indian guest at the ceremonial moment,

> We next met in Rangoon when Burma declared her independence. . . he came and witnessed. ... He ... heard us declare war on Britain and America. I saw the dream again in his eyes which I had seen before, but it was now a little sad and wistful, and so was his smile ... seeing Burma as the first colony to win its independence out of the war, he must have been thinking of the long, bloody journey still ahead of him and his forces before India too would be free.[37]

Ignoring the ravaging of the Indian minority in Burma by the advancing Japanese and hostile Burmese, Bose broadcast a message congratulating

India's neighbor on her achievement, in which he said,

The independence of Burma in this momentous crisis in world history has a twofold significance for us. It shows . . . what a nation can achieve if it knows how to seize an opportunity which history has offered. Secondly, just as the conquest of India supplied the British with a jumping-off ground for their attack on Burma in the nineteenth century, similarly the emancipation of Burma has supplied the Indian independence movement in East Asia with a springboard for its attack on Britain's army of occupation in India during the twentieth century.[38]

Although Ba Maw saw the evils of the very Japanese occupation with which he cooperated, he also saw its positive impact: it had destroyed the legitimacy and mystique of British rule. Bose, too, was not oblivious to the ruthlessness of the Japanese military spirit rampant in East and Southeast Asia. He had written about their attack on China in the 1930s and he could see at first hand how they treated the Chinese and other Asian peoples in Southeast Asia.

He returned to Singapore with renewed determination to establish the provisional government of free India and to try to encourage the Japanese to carry out an invasion of India as soon as possible. He had built up a good relationship with Ba Maw in a short time and knew he needed Burmese cooperation as well in his efforts. This one-to-one relationship helped soften, but did not and could not eliminate Burmese hostility to the Indian minority.

As he worked in Singapore to expand and train the second INA and prepare for the provisional government, Bose surely knew that the course of the war was changing. In Singapore, as in Berlin, he listened to Allied radio news and so could adjust Japanese and German versions of events accordingly. His supporter, Mussolini, had fallen from power; the Germans had occupied much of Italy; and the new Italian government had declared war on the Germans. At the same time the Germans were retreating in the Soviet Union, and British and American planes were bombing Germany unceasingly. The Japanese, too, were being pushed back from their most advanced island bases in New Guinea and the Solomons. The Americans were beginning their tactics of island-hopping, outflanking Japanese positions as the Japanese had employed mobile tactics in Southeast Asia, hooking around British forces and forcing them back in Malaya and Burma in 1942. [39] The Allies had recently named a supreme commander for Southeast Asia, Lord Louis Mountbatten.

However, Bose pushed ahead for a provisional government. A Japanese liaison conference on October 9 in Tokyo backed the establishment of this government which 'would be recognized by Japan in

order to strengthen the propaganda offensive in its India policy.'[40] Bose
speeded up his schedule and the Provisional Government of Azad Hind (or
Free India Provisional Government, FIPG) was announced on October 21.
It was based at Singapore and consisted, in the first instance, of five
ministers, eight representatives of the INA, and eight civilian advisers
representing the Indians of Southeast and East Asia. Bose was head of
state, prime minister and minister for war and foreign affairs. The four
other ministers were Captain Lakshmi Swaminathan (women's organizations), S.A. Ayer (publicity and propaganda), Lt. Col. A.C. Chatterji
(finance), and A.M. Sahay (secretary with ministerial rank).[41] On October
23, the Japanese government announced its recognition, followed by that
of Germany, Italy, Croatia, Manchukuo, Nanking, the Philippines,
Thailand, and Burma. Eamon de Valera sent personal congratulations to
Bose. The following day, the Azad Hind Government declared war on
Britain and the United States. To a cheering crowd of 50,000 Indians in
Singapore, Bose said it would be a war to the finish and the end result
would be the freedom of India. He asked for sacrifices and the throng rose
and shouted, '*Netaji Ki Jai! Inqilab Zindabad! Chalo Delhi!*'[42]

While he was in Singapore, Bose frequently visited the Ramakrishna
Mission in Norris Road and spent hours in the shrine room meditating.
While bombs were beginning to fall on Berlin, he practised his spiritual
exercises late at night in his own home, but in Japanese-occupied
Singapore he was able to make a connection to the congenial monks of the
Ramakrishna order who spread the teachings of Sri Ramakrishna and
Swami Vivekananda which had so moved Bose in his youth and were still
meaningful to him. It was a haven from the surrounding storm of war and
a place where he could make contact for himself with things eternal.[43]

Bose left for Tokyo to meet Japanese leaders once again and was also
invited as a special observer to the gathering called the Greater East Asia
Conference, to be held on November 5 and 6, 1943.[44] Bose requested
additional military and financial help from the Japanese to increase the
strength of the INA. On November 1, Tojo agreed in a meeting with Bose
to hand over administration of Indian evacuee property in Burma to the
provisional government, and to consider Bose's request for Indian control
of Indian territories under Japanese occupation.[45]

Bose was especially keen to have some Indian territory over which the
provisional government might claim sovereignty. Since the Japanese had
stopped east of the Chindwin River in Burma and not entered India on that
front, the only Indian territories they held were the Andaman and Nicobar
Islands in the Indian Ocean. The Japanese navy was unwilling to transfer
administration of these strategic islands to Bose's forces, but a face-saving

agreement was worked out so that the provisional government was given a 'jurisdiction', while actual control remained throughout with the Japanese military.[46] Bose eventually made a visit to Port Blair in the Andamans in December and a ceremonial transfer took place. Renaming them the *Shahid* (Martyr) and *Swaraj* (Self-rule) Islands, Bose raised the Indian national flag and appointed Lieutenant-Colonel Loganadhan, a medical officer, as chief commissioner. Bose continued to lobby for complete transfer, but did not succeed.[47]

On November 5 and 6, Bose, along with representatives of Burma, Manchukuo, China, Thailand, and the Philippines, met in the conference room of the Diet. Tojo led the Japanese delegation. Ba Maw, in an emotional speech, said, in part,

> For years in Burma I dreamed my Asiatic dreams. . . . Today . . . I hear Asia's voice calling again, but this time not in a dream. . . . I have listened with the greatest emotion to all the speeches. . . . I seem to hear in them the same voice of Asia gathering her children together. It is the call of our Asiatic blood. . . . Asia as a homeland did not exist a few years ago. Asia was not one then, but many, as many as the enemies which kept her divided. . . . We have once more discovered that we are Asiatics. . . . Let us therefore march ahead . . . into a new world where East Asiatics will be forever free. . . .[48]

Ba Maw also spoke on the Indian struggle for independence, backing Bose's efforts. Bose, in turn, gave a passionate speech, which he repeated the next day to a huge throng in the Hibiya Park. Bose declared,

> This is not a conference for dividing the spoils among the conquerors. . . . This is an assembly of liberated nations, an assembly that is out to create a new order in this part of the world on the basis of the sacred principles of justice, national sovereignty, reciprocity in international relations, and mutual aid and assistance. . . . This is not the first time that the world has turned to the East for light and guidance. . . . But we have to pay the price of our liberty. . . . The Indian people have yet to fight and win their freedom . . . we have no illusions about the magnitude of the task. . . . I do not know how many members of our national army will survive the coming war, but that is of no consequence to us . . . what is of consequence is that India shall be free. . . .[49]

Both Ba Maw and Bose knew that the Japanese were hard bargainers and could be ruthless conquerors. But they also saw that the Japanese were destroying European empires in Asia. As true nationalists, they did not want *any* new ruler, Asian or otherwise. They would live with Japanese assistance for the present and continue to work for complete national independence in their different circumstances. The conference ended with the enunciation of a Joint Declaration about mutual respect for each other's independence and cooperation.[50] After the conference, Bose went off on a brief tour of some of the so-called 'liberated' nations, including Japanese-occupied China and the Philippines, before returning to his work in Singapore.

II

While Subhas Bose was busily at work revamping the INA and establishing the provisional government of Azad Hind, he was, as usual, also vitally concerned with what was going on in India itself. Although most Congress leaders were imprisoned, a new government had taken office in Bengal, and a great tragedy was unfolding in the summer and fall of 1943: the Bengal Famine. This greatest famine of twentieth-century South Asia probably cost about three-and-a-half million Bengalis their lives. It has been extensively studied by government commissions and recently in a number of excellent works which treat it thoroughly.

The Bengal Famine has often been called a 'man-made' one.[51] Greenough has argued that many Bengali peasants had been getting an increasingly poorer diet since the end of the nineteenth century. There were large numbers of landless workers in Bengal and Bengal had become a rice-importing area, after a long period as a rice exporter. The war exacerbated the problem of importing rice from outside, for Burma had been a major exporter, but from 1942 sent only Indian refugees and defeated British and Indian troops. In preparation for a possible invasion, the government began a boat-denial policy, later a rice-denial policy. Although intended to deprive Japanese invaders of transport and food, it interrupted the usual flow of foodstuffs in the Bengal countryside. A severe cyclone hit some of the districts bordering on the Bay of Bengal, particularly Midnapore, and further hindered the flow.

Starting in late 1942, cultivators began holding back grain supplies and prices began to rise. The Government of Bengal intervened in the market process, trying price controls, threats against hoarding, and then allowing the market process free rein. The government was also determined to see that Calcutta, center of the Raj in eastern India, did not experience a significant shortfall. Some traders were allowed to buy up what they could in the countryside to help see that Calcutta did not starve. These traders were not closely supervised and seem to have played a negative role.

Chief Minister Fazlul Huq issued some warnings in late 1942, but he and the Progressive Coalition were out of office before the full force of the famine hit in summer and fall 1943. The Muslim League-dominated coalition headed by Khwaja Nazimuddin took office in April 1943, though Governor Herbert had promised an all-parties national coalition.[52] H.S. Suhrawardy had become minister for civil supplies and some criticism for the inept handling of the deteriorating situation has been laid at his door. However, though there have been direct charges that he allowed certain Muslim speculators to flourish, this has not been convincingly proved. It does appear that there was ineffectual handling of the grave situation at every level of government from the impassive and reactionary viceroy, Lord Linlithgow, who refused to visit Bengal as the famine struck, to the dunderheaded governor, Sir John Herbert, to ICS officers like L.G. Pinnell, who meant well, but were out of their depth.

Many, including Greenough, have argued that there was *not* a serious shortfall in grain production, but that of the factors mentioned above, particularly the breakdown of the grain-marketing system and the failure of the usual distribution system were most responsible. Relief efforts were also inadequate and neighboring provinces refused to rush to Bengal's aid. The new viceroy, Lord Wavell, assumed office in mid-October 1943, and immediately visited Bengal and did his best to improve the situation and prevent a recurrence the following year.[53]

Both Boses watched the famine from afar. Sarat Bose, in Coonoor, wrote to Ajit Dey, on September 7, 1943:

> I was glad to learn that Sudhi was devoting his time and energy to the relief of starving humanity. From the accounts I get . . . it appears that the condition for the middle and poorer classes is simply appalling and the relief that is being given is nowhere near what is necessary. I shudder to think of the condition of the people in the mofussil. . . . Distress of the present magnitude did not overtake our province during the last 50 years and more. Blessed are they that mourn and work for the poor and the distressed! But how few they are! I do not find any signs of life-giving activity on the part of people who were closely associated with me in Assembly work. I am grievously disappointed.[54]

If Sarat Bose was concerned about inadequate relief efforts and an insufficient civic spirit among his colleagues, Subhas Bose, across the battle lines in Southeast Asia, made an offer of grain supplies. He said just at the time of the creation of the provisional government on October 21,

> There can be no doubt that these famine conditions have been largely due to the policy of ruthless exploitation of India's food and other resources for Britain's war purposes over a period of nearly four years. You are aware that, on behalf of our League, I made a free and unconditional offer of one hundred thousand tons of rice for our starving countrymen at home as a first instalment. Not only was this offer not accepted by the British authorities in India, but we were given only abuse in return.[55]

Burma itself was in a good deal of economic chaos as it was disrupted by the Japanese occupiers whose first concern was to take care of themselves.[56] Whether Bose could, in fact, have supplied any grain to

Bengal was not tested.

Sarat Bose, incarcerated at Coonoor throughout 1943, kept up his lobbying efforts, personally and through friends and relations, to improve his living conditions, but to little avail. He continued his heavy reading of Bengali and English-language works, reading a good deal about China, about world politics, the Indian situation, and re-reading whatever he could of his favorite authors including the great authors of the English literary tradition and a personal favorite, George Bernard Shaw. In June 1943, he wrote to his daughter Gita, 'I have been an admirer of Bernard Shaw since my student days in England. In freshness, vivacity and sarcasm he is miles ahead of his contemporaries.'[57] The regular letters to Gita during this imprisonment reveal another facet of Sarat Bose: the teacher. Since Gita was studying English literature, close to his heart and his own subject when he was a student, these letters contain many comments on literature and suggestions to her about what to read and also about how learning only begins in the classroom, but continues as a lifelong project of self-education.

Some of his correspondents suggested that he write a book. He wrote to Gita,

> Yes, Barada Babu suggested that I should start writing a book. I replied that I felt that I had not the intellectual equipment necessary to become an author. And I have the same feeling still. Words flow from me when I am on my feet and get warmed up, but not in cold blood. . . . At times I have thought of writing 'my reminiscences, legal and political'; but not having kept any notes of events as they happened and not having the opportunity at the present moment of verifying the accuracy of my recollection, I felt it would be unwise to make the attempt now. Whether I shall make the attempt in future, when circumstances and opportunities are more favourable, is more than I can say today.[58]

In later letters, he asked family members to gather papers for him and kept a sketchy diary on current events and passing thoughts. But he never wrote the work of reminiscences which might have been a treasure to posterity.

For reasons that are not clear, he sat down the same summer, in July, and wrote a lengthy letter to Lord Linlithgow on the general Indian situation and expressed his antipathy to any foreigners dominating India. He said, in part,

> . . . if British Imperialism has so far blighted India's hopes . . . for freedom, imperialism of the Nazi, Fascist and 'Rising Sun' brands would, to my mind, prove much worse. . . . I am prepared to do whatever in me lies to prevent my country from coming under the latter's domination . . . whenever a foreign army landed on Indian soil . . . it almost invariably became an army of occupation; and we definitely do not want a repetition of the same

experience. We shall continue to fight for India's independence. . . .[59]
This letter had no impact on the view that the Government of India had of
Sarat Bose: he was a dangerous and dishonest politician, capable of
treason, and as long as his brother was with the enemy, Sarat Bose would
be carefully confined.

At the end of the year, Sarat Bose and the entire Bose family had to bear
with renewed sorrow when his mother Prabhabati died at the age of sixty-
six. As his mother was near the end, Sarat Bose requested permission to see
her, but this was refused. He was also refused leave to participate in the
ceremonial rites. He did write to Ajit Dey,

> I wish I had the spiritual strength that my revered mother had. She had in her
> lifetime—
>
> 'To suffer woes which Hope thinks infinite;
> To forgive wrongs darker than death or night;
> To defy Power, which seems omnipotent;
> To love and bear'
>
> And she did it till the end. . . . The only request she ever made to the
> authorities was to permit me to come to her bedside . . . even that was turned
> down. . . . I read Sisir's, Dada's and your and Gita's letters with tears; and
> the tears relieved the oppression on my mind. . . . I am trying to bear as
> calmly as is humanly possible. It is not possible for me to live the life that
> the Gita inculcates upon us. I have my worldly attachments, my weaknesses,
> my limitations; and they cling to me with all their force. But I shall always
> resist . . . being overpowered by them. . . .[60]

It is not clear when Subhas Bose learned of his mother's death. Lieutenant-
General Isoda, who replaced Colonel Yamamoto as head of the Hikari
Kikan in 1944, has recounted that a news report came of Mrs Bose's death.
'I went to give my condolences to Bose. Bose said that he was his mother's
favorite, with tears in his eyes. It was the first and last time that I ever saw
Bose being kind of a sissy.'[61] The two Bose brothers—like their siblings—
were powerfully attached to their mother. They had now lost both their
parents and Subhas Bose had been in exile at the time of the death of each
parent. Like Sarat in his South Indian prison, Subhas Bose simply had to
go on. And momentous events were afoot.

III

As the monsoon broke in 1942, advancing Japanese forces had reached the
Chindwin River in west Central Burma, near the Indian frontier. Here they
halted as the depleted and demoralized British and Indian troops and
Indian refugees from Burma dragged themselves across the mountains
into Manipur and Assam. The Japanese had greatly extended their lines of
supply and transport. They, too, had to pause and regroup. The British

feared an imminent attack on India against weak defenses. They did not know how far Japanese ambitions extended. The British were fortunate in their appointment of William Slim as a general of the retreating British forces in Burma, later as commander of the 14th Army, and then of all British forces in Burma. An astute and resourceful commander, he orchestrated the British recovery, preparation for, and later reconquest of Burma. Slim, in the lucid account he wrote later of these events, said that the British were confused when retreating as to what their objectives should be; they were not unsure once they had recuperated sufficiently to see that the recapture of their empire and the destruction of Japanese forces was their aim.

The Japanese, however, were less certain of what their next objective should be—after reaching the Chindwin River—for they had greatly expanded their empire and were certain to be challenged by the British, Americans, and forces of the British Empire. They were still engulfed in a debilitating war in China which they could not end. There were proposals, even in 1942, for a push into India, but these were postponed indefinitely.[62] These delays gave the British time to gather resources— human and material—and decide what they needed to do to defeat the Japanese in Burma. The early Japanese victories in Malaya, Singapore, and Burma, a good deal of which involved jungle warfare, had given the Japanese an aura of invincibility. This had consequences for both sides: the Japanese were overconfident; the British and the Allies had to train and fight to defeat the Japanese, dissolving as they did so the halo of superiority, particularly in the jungle.

In early 1943, the British, along with Indian troops, tried first to take some small steps forward in the Arakan area of Burma, but they were beaten back by the Japanese. Later in the same year, the British realized that the Japanese were preparing for an offensive in the same area. Japanese proposals had been discussed, rejected, postponed, and changed. As 1943 progressed, there were both military and political considerations affecting their decision about an Indo-Burma offensive. The Southern Army was commanded by General Terauchi, the Burma Army created in 1943 by General Kawabe, and the 15th Army, which was to be the main offensive force for the contemplated move, by General Mutaguchi. Also in 1943, Colonel Katakura, later called the 'Tiger of Burma', became staff officer to the 15th Army and Major Fujiwara, creator of the INA, its intelligence officer. Intense discussions went on for months about the possible attack across the frontier into India and what its goals would be. Terauchi and Katakura were skeptical throughout, as were a number of important officers, both in Southeast Asia and at home. Mutaguchi too, at first, was a doubter, but then became a true believer, arguing that all problems of supplies, communications, and air power inferiority could be overcome. The demands of Subhas Bose were added to the Japanese need for an important victory on the mainland of Asia at a time when they were beginning to lose in the Pacific Islands.[63] After the many debates and delays, Tojo finally gave approval from his bath for the campaign in December 1943.[64]

Meanwhile, after his trip to Japan, then to China, and other parts of Southeast Asia, Bose returned to Singapore in late 1943. The training of the INA was proceeding apace and Bose continued to argue with the Japanese for a prominent role for his forces in any move across the Indian frontier. As in Germany, Bose made every effort to build a unified Indian identity which would eclipse any local or community ones. He wanted his men and women to be Indians first. They were to work together, eat together, talk together (using Hindustani, to be written in Roman script), and fight together.[65] Both the Japanese and the British had their doubts about these troops. The Japanese said that low standards were employed and they did not expect much of turncoats in any case. The British noted that the INA had limited supplies and only light weapons. They also thought that there were too few good officers and that the INA was weak in basic military skills which had been neglected in order to impart political indoctrination.[66]

Yet a further problem for Bose and his men was their relationship—in and out of battle—with the Japanese at all levels of linkage between the much larger, tested, and confident Japanese forces and the smaller, untested INA. S.A. Ayer, an experienced journalist and one of those given a number of responsible positions by Bose in these years, has described the 'Manchurians' (or the arrogant, racist Japanese officers). Ayer wrote later,

> ... men of this type proved the ruin of Japan. They made enemies for Japan; they antagonised all thinking men of other nationalities, especially Indians. To them nothing else mattered except the Japanese Empire, its survival and expansion. They were so narrow-minded that they literally foamed at the mouth at the very mention of reciprocity between the INA and the Japanese army as war-time allies. . . . East Asia was studded with 'little' Japanese of this type.[67]

To such Japanese, Indians were inferiors and the conquest of India was to be carried out by the Japanese for the greater glory of Imperial Japan. When Bose or his officers talked of equality between allied armies, of priority for Indian troops in any invasion of India, and for rule by the provisional government of any territory of India recaptured from the British Empire, they were frequently rebuffed. So there was a struggle with the Japanese, who most of the Indians did not trust and who many of his subordinates said Bose did not trust, whatever he said in some of his speeches and broadcasts.

At the end of 1943 and the first days of 1944, Bose moved his headquarters, that of the INA, and, in effect, the locus of the provisional government, to Rangoon, Burma. Here, not only did Bose have to deal with his mortal enemy, the British, and his insensitive ally, the Japanese, but also with the Burmese, many of whom had long-term resentments against the Indian settlers in Burma. Bose knew this and expressed on many occasions his thankfulness to his wartime 'host' and tried to make his fellow Indians sensitive to the problem.[68]

A crucial conundrum for the INA—never solved—was that of adequate supplies. As Bose and the INA learned, the Japanese saw themselves as the main fighters. Therefore, weapons, transport, and food for others were secondary. Since the Japanese were overextended and starting to lose supplies, weapons, and air and shipping capacity heavily in other sectors of the war, they were loathe to 'waste' any on the INA. In public, Bose said sweet words about his ally and how the Japanese had 'changed' from the nasty aggressor of the 1930s in China. In private, Bose argued for more weapons, transport, air cover, and food from the Japanese. Since the Japanese were only stingily forthcoming, Bose tried to make other arrangements.

The key operative in this procurement effort was Zora Singh, a Punjabi, who was born in India in 1911, but had been raised in Rangoon. He was put in charge of supplies for the army and the civilians who had moved with Bose to Burma at the beginning of 1944. Some supplies were sent from Singapore, but medicine was very short. This could not be purchased with Japanese currency, but had to be obtained for gold (collected from the Indian community) on the black market. He tried to get this medicine to the frontline INA troops. Later on he traded liquor to the Japanese for engine oil which they had in their godowns, but would not give to the INA.[69] Although Mr Singh was resourceful at his job of supplier the deficiencies were so great that the shortage of supplies of every kind was a major hurdle never cleared by the INA.

Bose did not like his financial dependence on the Japanese. Over their objections, he created the National Bank of Azad Hind on April 5, 1944, which was to print Indian currency and finance the war effort. He tried to repay some of his loans from the Germans and Japanese as he went. Insisting that the Indians were not clients of the Japanese, but a temporarily weak co-equal government and army, Bose promised that all these IOUs would be honored by free India.[70]

In preparation for the occupation of parts of liberated India, Bose also saw to the training of a cadre of administrative and service personnel, the Azad Hind Dal. Headed by General A.C. Chatterji, a medical officer who was appointed chief administrator of the Liberated Territories, these men were prepared to follow closely behind as the INA and Japanese drove the British out and terminated the Raj.[71] The Dal also included a large number of laborers and personnel to operate wireless sets and infiltrate into enemy territory.

Once the Japanese were determined to make the push, they began mobilizing their forces and also had to look more practically at the geographical setting which has been pithily described by Slim:

> Along the Indo-Burmese border, in a shallow curve, sweeps the wide belt of jungle-clad, precipitous hills, rail-less, roadless, and, for six months of the year during the monsoon rains, almost trackless. Sparsely populated by wild tribes, disease infested, and even unmapped in places.... It could fairly be described as some of the world's worst country, breeding the world's worst diseases, and having for half the year at least the world's worst climate.... To supply, move, and fight great armies in or through the mass of jumbled hills had for so long been regarded as impossible that no serious defence measures had ever been taken on India's eastern frontier. Nor had any effective communications either for trade or war been built. Such roads, railways, and navigable rivers as there were stopped abruptly each side of the mountain barrier, a couple of hundred miles apart.[72]

The Japanese, proud and cocky, who had advanced almost with ease to the Chindwin River in 1942, were now prepared to cross this jungly, hilly terrain with their forces. Their main objective was the capture of Imphal, the largest center in eastern Assam, set on a plain, and the smaller town of Kohima to the north. The road from the railhead at Dimapur, in the west, to Kohima and then down to Imphal was the only British supply route *by road* in the area.

Slim considered several alternative strategies, but finally decided to withdraw two divisions which occupied the west bank of the Chindwin. He wanted the strongest possible defensible position and chose Imphal. If he could draw the main Japanese forces into the Imphal plain, their supply routes would be stretched across the nearly impassable frontier territory, whereas his would be more compact. Slim also knew that he was likely to have air superiority this time. His troops also outnumbered the Japanese attackers and had been prepared carefully in fighting skills, health precautions, and morale over the year-and-a-half since the last major confrontation with the Japanese.

The Japanese were risk-takers: they carried an absolute minimum of supplies, believing that they would overrun the British and Indian troops as they had done in 1942 and capture the enemy's supplies. If they failed to do this, then they would be caught in an almost hopeless position to the west of the hill and jungle wall. The Japanese were slow to mobilize and were not ready to push against Imphal and Kohima until the beginning of March 1944. The monsoon was only a little more than two months away.

Of all the Japanese planners of this operation, Bose made the most positive connection to General Mutaguchi. Both believed that the operation was bound to be a success and the Japanese general who had favored a plan by which the Japanese would drive further and further into India found a kindred spirit. Bose is reported to have said to Mutaguchi, 'If the Japanese Army succeeds in the Imphal invasion and pushes the INA forward in the Assam plain, the Indian people as well as officers and men in the British-Indian Army will respond to the INA. This will spread all over India, especially in my home state of Bengal.'[73] Though both Bose and Mutaguchi were eager for the battle to begin, there were serious differences between Bose and the Japanese generals responsible for this campaign over the role of the INA. As mentioned before, the Japanese were dubious that the INA could hold their own. And, after all, the INA division numbered about 8,000 out of a Japanese-INA force of about 95,000. They were attacking positions held by about 1,55,000 British-led forces, which included Britishers, West Africans, and Indians.[74]

The Japanese saw a limited propaganda role for the INA and also envisioned defensive or guerrilla roles for Bose's army if they were to fight. Bose wanted the INA to have a vital function, including a sector of the front in which they were the attacking spearhead. Bose seems to have been temporarily pacified by assurances that good use would be made of the INA, though privately the Japanese throughout doubted that he had much military understanding.[75]

When Shah Nawaz, commanding the Nehru Regiment, one of the guerrilla regiments which constituted the first division of the INA, reported to Mutaguchi for his orders, he was told that his regiment was to hold a defensive position of the Haka-Falam section in the Chin Hills and protect Japanese supply lines. This assignment, far from the key Japanese thrust forward, was a blow to INA morale and to whatever trust they had in their ally. His troops were given no field supplies by the Japanese and a few months into the campaign were reduced to eating dry-field rice grown by the Nagas along with jungle grass.[76] In April, this regiment was ordered to help in the assault on Kohima which was already faltering and by the time they arrived, the Japanese were already retreating. Near Kohima, on Indian soil, Shah Nawaz's men raised the Indian tricolor.

Troops of the INA had entered India, but only for a brief stay.[77]

In February 1944, the British forces made another move in the Arakan and this time the Japanese could not dislodge them. Neither side was fooled into thinking that this was to be the central battleground. In early March, crossing the almost impenetrable barrier between the Chindwin and the Imphal plains, the Japanese began their main thrusts at Kohima and Imphal. Both sides fought fiercely, but the Japanese could not dislodge the defenders though they nearly did so at Kohima. Slim's field commanders ordered their men to hold these positions and the Allied troops were resupplied by air. Although the Japanese had some attacking fighters in the early stages of the campaign, they were outnumbered and beaten badly. The Allies gained control of the air which allowed them to resupply their troops and strafe the Japanese (and INA) forces almost at will. The longer the Allied troops held out at Imphal and Kohima, the more difficult the position became for the besieging forces. The Japanese had very limited reinforcements. Knowing that the monsoon was coming and that supplies of all kinds were running low, Mutaguchi called for the ultimate effort, but this time the British and their allies were well prepared, had the shorter supply lines, and fought with ever more buoyant morale against an enemy they had once thought unbeatable. Slim wondered why the Japanese, especially at Kohima, held so rigidly to a preconceived plan and did not adapt better to difficult circumstances. Dimapur, both sides knew, was the key transport junction, but the Japanese, to Slim's delight, never made an effort to go around Kohima to the more crucial and less defended Dimapur. At one point, Mutaguchi ordered such a strike, but General Kawabe countermanded the order.[78] Slim, for his part, thanked the Japanese commander at Kohima, General Sato, for being too bull-headed to attack Dimapur.

The Japanese were forced to give up the sieges at Kohima and Imphal. It was the beginning of the end for them in Burma and ultimately in Southeast Asia. Their remaining air forces had been sent to the Pacific, a more important theater of the war for them, and one where they were under heavy pressure from the Americans. In Burma in 1942, the British were disorganized, unprepared, lacking air support, and unable to defend the native population or themselves. In 1944, the Japanese, now the occupiers of Burma, fell back from one defensive position to another, fighting fiercely as always, almost never surrendering, but now being beaten and beaten badly. Before the campaign started, Slim had paid great attention to the morale factor and addressed small groups of his men informally, explaining that *they* were fighting for freedom against a foe aiming to deprive them of it. Slim compared himself to a stump speaker on the political trail as he did this work, but it paid off in results. It was, in the end, one of the worst defeats of the war for the Japanese and many officers including Kawabe and Katakura were recalled. But the replacement of Kawabe by Kimura could not help.

In writing of the INA, Slim refused them this title and condescendingly referred to them as 'Jiffs' (Japanese-influenced forces) of whom he thought little. He was somewhat concerned when they were employed in 'attempts to confuse and suborn our Indian troops.'[79] This effort, Slim said, was 'unavailing' because the Indian troops fighting with the British had a long period of indoctrination in their imperial mission in league with the British. They were kept from knowledge of the nationalist rationale of the INA by the British 'policy of silence' which blacked out information about it in India. Bose knew that the British were engaged in anti-INA propaganda, such as noting that a few puppet Indians were cooperating with the Japanese, as well as blacking out the rest of the picture. Given wartime censorship in India and the fact that many of his supporters were in jail, he could do little about this.

Across the border in Burma, Bose had worked assiduously to raise the morale of his men for the coming fray as Slim had in his way on the other side. Although Slim and some subsequent writers have mocked the INA, the evidence of British intelligence reports, Japanese military reports, and memoirs of participants on the INA side demonstrate that before they were completely demoralized by the total British dominance in this campaign, the INA men fought courageously. But, as noted, in numbers and supplies and weapons, they were dwarfs among giants. They fought bravely in particular actions as the Japanese were retreating, but since their numbers were so relatively small, whatever their patriotic fervor, they made little dent on the military conduct of the campaign.[80] For example, in a long and detailed account of the INA prepared by the Intelligence Department of the Government of India, it is noted,

> A measure of courage cannot be denied to the leaders of INA front-line units in Burma in 1945 when . . . they faced up to British equipment, tanks, guns, and aircraft with rifles and bullock-carts and empty stomachs.[81]

Along with the superior forces with which the British-led army hit the Japanese and INA, the unhealthiness of the area and then the monsoon helped to deliver the knockout blows. Those under Slim had been carefully prepared with the latest medical knowledge and prophylactics to fight malaria. Slim also arranged that the seriously wounded and ill would be treated near the front by expert doctors and then flown back to hospitals. Shah Nawaz recounts that about seventy per cent of his men were stricken ill; medicines, already in short supply, ran out, and many of his men died in the jungle. The rate of such illness and death on the British side fell appreciably from 1942 rates. The contrast between the forces under Slim and those under Kawabe in this regard could not have been starker. Japanese and INA troops had braved the Indo-Burma frontier and made it into India. A great majority died in the fighting around Imphal and Kohima or retreating through the Indo-Burma area.

The most important causes of the Japanese-INA defeat have been enumerated. However, in his bitterness at what he saw as paltry help from the Japanese, added to a first assignment away from the primary target, Shah Nawaz has heaped most of the blame on the Japanese. He wrote after the war,

> . . . with a clear conscience I can say that the Japanese did not give full aid and assistance to the Azad Hind Fauj during their assault on Imphal . . . they let us down badly and had it not been for their betrayal of the I.N.A. the history of the Imphal campaign might have been a different one . . . the Japanese did not trust the I.N.A. They had found out through their Liaison officers that the I.N.A. would not accept Japanese domination in any way, and that they would fight the Japanese in case they attempted to replace the British. . . . They were too confident of themselves and thought that they would be able to capture Imphal without assistance and without much difficulty.[82]

Shah Nawaz was one of the officers who was late in joining the INA and always had a deep mistrust of the Japanese. He was not being completely fair to the Japanese who also died in large numbers, had limited supplies and medicine, and suffered from lack of air cover.[83] The Japanese did give the INA even less supplies, food, and medicine than they gave to their troops. Looking at the broad picture of this campaign, a somewhat different distribution of the same amount of supplies would not have changed the outcome. The Japanese were worried that men who had changed sides once might change sides again. Some INA officers did desert and in a few cases gave important intelligence to the British. Despairing over this betrayal, Bose ordered that any further deserters who were caught were to be summarily shot. As the retreat went on, more and more men, in a completely hopeless position, did surrender. Even some Japanese began to surrender and General Sato, in a famous act of insubordination, refused an order to die in place and ordered his men to retreat rather than die to a man.[84] It was a rout and no change in one small element would have made any difference. Slim and his army savored the sweetness of revenge.

After the monsoon hit, the Japanese finally decided that they had to retreat from the Imphal plain and the neighborhood of Kohima. Bose resisted the order to retreat and said he wanted his men to stay and fight to the last. Shah Nawaz explained,

> Netaji was supremely confident of our victory. He said, 'Even if the Axis
> powers lay down their arms, we must continue our struggle. There is no end
> to our struggle until the last British quits the shores of our country.' He was
> of the opinion that the British should not be allowed to advance or break
> through our front, even if all the I.N.A. soldiers were killed. What he wanted
> most was that the I.N.A. 'shaheeds' should leave behind such a legend and
> tradition of heroism that future generations of Indians would be proud of
> them.[85]

In the end, Bose accepted the order for retreat, but wanted his men to
contir'ie fighting the enemy as well as they could while so doing. This
doggedness changed little. The superior forces and strategy of Slim led
gradually through the second half of 1944 and the first half of 1945 to his
main objective: destruction of the Japanese army and, incidentally, of the
INA in Burma. The retreat of the Japanese and the INA was drawn out for
the better part of a year down through Central Burma to southern Burma
and then through Thailand back to Malaya and Singapore, but there was
little doubt of the outcome.

During the first few months of the retreat, Bose spoke on the lessons to
be learned from it,

> We started the operations too late. The monsoon was disadvantageous to
> us. . . . In the Kaladan Sector, we routed the enemy and advanced. In Tiddim
> we advanced, in Palel and Kohima also we advanced. In the Haka Sector we
> held them. And all this in spite of the numerical superiority that the enemy
> had, plus equipment and rations. . . . We have received our baptism of
> fire. . . . Our troops have gained much confidence. We have learnt that the
> Indian troops with the enemy are willing to come over. . . . We have also
> learnt our defects. Transport and supply were defective. . . . We had no Front
> Line Propaganda.[86]

As some of his listeners noted, Bose spoke as if the campaign was soon to
begin again, and that his forces had just lost one battle. But the military war
was lost and he gradually had to come to terms with this. This in itself was
a shock and left him in anguish. The defeat here and others in the Pacific
led shortly to the fall of Prime Minister Tojo. This was a second shock. At
the end of October 1944, Bose made his third and final trip to Japan to see
what new arrangements could be made as the Japanese were being forced
back toward their home islands.

In a post-war report of the Government of Japan on the alliance with
the INA, the author compares the treason of Aung San, who turned his
forces against the Japanese in the spring of 1945, with the INA: 'When we
compare this with the INA led by Bose which fought to the last even after
the Imphal operations and regardless of the very adverse turn of events,

how can we help loving the INA with all our heart?'[87] At the same time that the Japanese appreciated the firmness with which most of Bose's forces continued to fight, they were endlessly exasperated with him. A number of Japanese officers, even those like Fujiwara, who were devoted to the Indian cause, saw Bose as a military incompetent as well as an unrealistic and stubborn man who saw only his own needs and problems and could not see the larger picture of the war as the Japanese had to. In the same review of the Japanese-INA connection, regarding Bose's last visit to Japan, it is noted,

> Though proper replies were given to Bose's various requests and demands, it required tremendous negotiating powers to convince Bose about anything. In his demands regarding the relations of the two armies there were a number of points which were unreasonable and especially under the circumstances they could never be accepted completely.[88]

Elsewhere the author says bluntly,

> It was quite unreasonable for Bose to have given his judgement on strategy and military affairs and operations of the past since he had no knowledge of such things. The fact that he behaved in a conceited way in matters he knew nothing about may be because of his own self-confidence. Especially since he was the political and military head of the government and . . . since there were no outstanding persons around him . . . this tendency might have gone a little too far. . . .[89]

What was Bose asking for at this late date? He had become frustrated with the Hikari Kikan as an intermediary between his provisional government and the Japanese government. He wanted to work through a full-fledged ambassador and terminate the Kikan. Of course, he wanted supplies, air support, more weapons, ammunition, et al. Since the Japanese felt that their own home islands were now in danger, they could not spare much for Bose. But they also had a hard time convincing him of this. He believed that the Japanese cow could still be milked.

There was bargaining back and forth. Bose finally agreed that the third INA division would help defend Malaya. In exchange, the Japanese would send an ambassador. But they insisted that they had no more arms to supply and even asked that some be returned.[90] Bose began to look around for other options. He saw that the Indians must become more self-sufficient in Southeast Asia and less dependent on the Japanese. From the late 1930s on, Bose had sent feelers out to the Soviets with little response. With his present allies beginning to sink, he looked around for another life raft, a power not too friendly with the British. The Japanese and the Soviets were not yet at war, but his hosts did not like Bose's efforts in this regard. The Japanese later noted,

During his stay in Tokyo he constantly sought an interview with the Russian
Ambassador to Japan. With the consent of the military authorities he fixed
up a meeting also. But it could not take place and so he sent a letter to the
Russian Ambassador. But it was returned. Though the matter ended there,
it had a meaning in the context of his past intentions and his actions from
then onwards.[91]

He asked Anand Sahay to try to contact the Soviet ambassador, Jacob
Malik, when his own efforts during this visit failed. In his speeches
throughout the remainder of the war, he began to differentiate between the
Anglo-Americans and the Soviets. He said in 1945, some months after his
Japan trip,

> It is clear by·now that the war aims of the Soviet Union are quite different
> from those of the Anglo-Americans, although they had (a) common enemy
> in Germany . . . at the San Francisco Conference . . . Molotov refused to
> submit to the Anglo-American demands. . . . Molotov went so far as to
> challenge the credentials of the puppets of Britain and America who came
> to represent India and the Philippines. . . . The differences . . . are only a
> precursor of a much wider and deeper conflict between the Soviet(s) and the
> Anglo-Americans which the future has in store for the world.[92]

There is no evidence that the Soviets gave Bose any positive response
through these months, though the opening of Soviet archives on such
matters might prove something different.

During his few weeks in Japan, Bose met the top Japanese military
officials and the new prime minister, General Koiso. He went to see the
dying Rash Behari Bose, the dismissed prime minister Tojo, and also
visited a group of Indian teenagers, his cadets, getting Japanese military
training. It was a changed and depressing Japan, now being heavily
bombed by the Americans, who wanted to soften up the home islands as
they recaptured the Philippines. Bose returned via Shanghai to Burma near
the end of 1944.[93]

Although the Japanese had to lift their siege of Imphal and Kohima in
June 1944, the war in Burma raged on for nearly another year. The
Japanese were forced by the intense pressure from superior forces to retreat
stage by stage, first to the Chindwin, then to the Irrawaddy, then finally
back to Lower Burma. Detachments of the INA continued to fight with
them in this defensive war.[94]

When Bose returned to Rangoon, a War Council to direct INA operations
was chosen and included General Bhonsle, General Chatterji, General
M.Z. Kiani, Col. Aziz Ahmad, Col. Ehsan Qadir, Col. Habibur Rahman,
Col. Gulzara Singh, Sri Parmanand, Sri Raghavan, Col. I.J. Kiani, Col.
Shah Nawaz Khan, and Bose. Recruiting efforts were redoubled, the No.
2 Division was ordered to Burma, and the No. 3 Division was raised in

Malaya. By this push, the INA reached about 50,000. Bose also broadcast on the radio nearly every day exhorting Indians in Southeast Asia and those who could hear him in India to support the campaign.[95]

Carrying out the agreement reached in Tokyo, Bose appointed General Chatterji his foreign minister and was ready to receive the newly appointed Japanese ambassador, Hachiya, in his small ship of state. Hachiya endured a difficult journey to Rangoon and then was faced with a new dilemma. Bose sent word that without an appointment letter from the emperor, he would not receive him. Hachiya had rushed away from a previous post without such a letter. So he sat and waited while Bose insisted upon the proper formalities.[96]

Given the war situation, a good deal of confusion could be expected. Sivaram, one of Bose's most critical wartime associates, has given a description of the movement at that moment:

> Morale in Burma was at a low ebb. . . . The Japanese had given the Provisional Government of Azad Hind a free hand in dealing with the Indian population . . . some of . . . Bose's associates, to whom authority in any form was a novelty, exploited this privilege in their own way, adding to the distress of the common people. There were nearly 4,000 Indian civilians working for the independence movement in Rangoon . . . but few people knew precisely what they were doing and to whom they were responsible. The organization was chaotic. . . . . I was not surprised . . . by the spate of intrigue and opportunism. . . . Bose was apparently trying to stem the rot . . . through a vigorous propaganda drive . . . the persistent call for the next offensive, a series of public meetings, loyalty demonstrations and . . . parades. It seemed unreal but, perhaps there was no alternative.[97]

Though Bose undoubtedly knew that the military situation was very poor for the Japanese and his forces, he was unwilling to give ground. Indeed, he thought increased energy was required by his men and women. A big celebration was held for his birthday on January 23 in Rangoon and considerable collections of gold, jewelery, and cloth were made to support the work.[98]

A Japanese military police sergeant, Takeo Kitano, who both protected and watched Bose in Rangoon on behalf of the Japanese army, has described Bose's establishment there. He lived in a simple, two-storied house, close to Lake Victoria and the university. Upstairs Bose had his living quarters and a conference room. On the ground floor there were additional meeting rooms, parlor, and kitchen. Nearby were buildings housing the offices of the provisional government and the INA headquarters. Although Bose was quite friendly with Senda and Kanizuka of the Hikari Kikan and they came to see him frequently, no Japanese were permitted upstairs. The Indians who did meet on the second floor, often spoke in Hindustani. Once the Japanese sergeant had to go upstairs to carry out an errand and he chanced upon a high-quality shortwave receiver. Bose's adjutant carefully listened to broadcasts from India and other places to get a more realistic picture of the war situation. The sergeant said that he did not report on the radio set, but noticed that after the Imphal debacle, Bose knew he could count less on the Japanese.[99]

One matter about which witnesses from this period differ is whether Bose should appropriately be called a democrat or a dictator, and extrapolating, did Bose envision a democratic or authoritarian future for India. The most critical of the East Asian Indians, A.M. Nair, who had liked Rash Behari Bose, called Bose a fascist.[100] However, many other Indian participants have given a different picture. For example, S.A. Ayer wrote,

> ...he was a democrat at heart and a dictator in effect...he was conscientious and fastidious in his democratic ways, and yet I know in my heart of hearts that he had his own way every time. .... He did high-powered thinking, planning and working out of the minutest details...occasionally sounding his 'inner cabinet' on broad policy and details...he would take his own time to look at his plans and details from every possible angle...he would come to the Cabinet meeting or meeting of his Military High Command fully prepared to explain, patiently...the why and the wherefore of his main idea, listen attentively to the differing viewpoints of his colleagues, answer every one of the objections.... He was a stickler for democratic procedure...once the decision was officially taken by the Cabinet, then he would use his discretion to speak in the name of the Government....[101]

Ayer says that some colleagues differed from Bose such as in bracketing the Americans with the British as enemies. But, 'in all essential matters he carried his Government and INA associates with him.... For all practical purposes he was a dictator on supreme occasions.'[102]

On the wider implications of what kind of government Bose would like in a free India, he did say on numerous occasions that in the transitional period, it would need a strong government. But, his military secretary and one of his INA commanders, P.K. Sahgal, has argued that,

> He made it clear...that it was for the people of free India to decide freely the form of government they wanted to have. There was no question of imposing the will of say Subhas Chandra Bose himself or the groups of people who would come with him . . . from private conversations and discussions with him, one could gather that his idea was more for a presidential form of government than a parliamentary form of government. There again, his idea for a presidential form of government was not a dictatorship but an elected government.[103]

Sahgal and the other devoted men and women close to Bose during the war have objected to the label of fascist or dictator. They felt that he made every effort to persuade them to do what he wanted and to take their views into consideration. Nair, the hostile critic of Bose and long-time resident of Japan, says that Bose had the Japanese arrest one of his most severe critics, K.P. Kesava Menon.[104] Even if we accept Nair's version, it does not prove that Bose was a fascist, for he may have believed that Menon was endangering the solidarity of the movement. Bose was the unquestioned leader of the movement for many Indians in Southeast Asia. He had been summoned to the region by the IIL. Sivaram, another critic and friend of Nair, has mentioned that Bose saw himself as a 'man of destiny'.[105] This, too, may have been true, but this linked into the desire of the Indian community and INA men who called for Bose to rush to East Asia and take charge in 1942. He was a controversial figure in India, but a man of political standing in the nationalist movement, and, furthermore, had escaped British control and was available. For his part, Bose would not refuse any call to leadership from a constituency of the people of India.

There was one matter which did set Bose off into occasional hostile words about what he saw as the present legitimate leadership of India, the Congress of Gandhi, Nehru, Patel, et al. Sivaram has written, '. . . Bose . . . seemed obsessed with the idea that any political move by Mahatma Gandhi would be the prelude to a compromise with Britain.'[106] Since Bose thought that the British would never leave unless driven out, any negotiations into which the Congress entered were likely to lead to a sell-out. It had also been several years since he had any direct contact with these Congress leaders and he was very summary and rigid in his judgments of them. This was the plight of the exile—to fall more and more out of touch with his native land, however much he might hear and read of it. Some of his broadcasts were addressed to Gandhi, with whom he pleaded not to make any compromise with the British which would damage the essential interests of the Indian people. One such compromise might be on the issue of Pakistan. Bose did view the efforts of Rajagopalachari as passing beyond the line of rapprochement to complete sellout and Bose begged Gandhi not to take Rajaji's stance in his own talks with Jinnah in 1944. Later—in 1945—Bose addressed similar pleas to Gandhi at the time of the Simla Conference called by Lord Wavell. He rejoiced when the conference failed. Bose simply could not imagine a negotiated settlement of which he would approve.

In February, Bose insisted, over the objections of Indian and Japanese officers, on going to the front in Central Burma. He wanted to exhort his men to give their all from just behind the very lines of battle. The INA detachments fought near Mandalay, on the banks of the Irrawaddy, across which the Allied forces forced numerous crossings, and at Mt. Popa. Bose remained near the front most of February and March and into April.

In March, Slim completely outwitted the Japanese commander, Kimura, sending a division around the Japanese lines to attack the crucial junction and supply base at Meiktila. The Japanese withdrew some of their forces from the north to try to hold Meiktila, and fought bravely, but it was lost to them before the end of the month. This month also marked another blow to the Japanese in Burma: Aung San, encouraged by the British, turned his Burma National Army against his former allies, the Japanese. The BNA harassed the Japanese severely throughout their remaining months in Burma, but it was implicitly agreed between the BNA and the INA that they would not fight each other.[107] There were INA men who surrendered, some who deserted, and some who fought to the death, with inadequate equipment. Slim says the INA had little stomach for the fight against these odds. Several of their commanders who fought on, Shah Nawaz Khan, Sahgal, and Dhillon—these three later tried for treason together—all say most of their men strove valiantly and that many died during the long retreat and battles of the second half of 1944 and the first half of 1945.[108] Shah Nawaz Khan and his men, overwhelmed by the odds, finally surrendered in May, not wishing to die a futile death.[109]

During the retreat, Bose, with his bodyguards and military advisers, came under fire several times. He seems to have taken quite extraordinary chances on several occasions in exposing himself to enemy attack. Did he *want* to die, or did he think himself invulnerable? Interspersed with his pep talks to his troops and consultations on the course of the battles, Bose relaxed by reading a fat book on the Irish struggle against British rule. Major Takahashi, of the Hikari Kikan, was accompanying Bose, and reports what Bose said to the INA commander at Pyinmana, south of Meiktila,

> Looking at the hills, Bose said, 'The book on Irish independence says that, at the beginning of the campaign . . . all the patriots were killed. . . .But after some decades, people appeared who followed the line of those patriots and finally won independence. Now we face (such a) situation. And I am prepared to die in my last fight with my soldiers of the first division against the British-Indian army.' He called divisional commander Kiani and said clearly, 'I will die here.'[110]

Takahashi and Kiani argued with him. Then Takahashi telegraphed the Hikari Kikan headquarters in Rangoon and had them send Bose a telegram urging him to withdraw to Rangoon. Takahashi said if Bose was to offer his life, then he too would have to offer his. Finally, Bose agreed that he should not die uselessly in a local skirmish against vastly superior forces and deprive the movement of its leader.[111] Several of his followers in the movement noted his risk-taking. For example, Shah Nawaz Khan wrote, 'He was absolutely fearless and did not seem to care for his life, or comfort. He seemed to lead a charmed life for I have personally seen him miss death by inches several times. . . .'[112] Ayer wrote that, '. . . he was made for martyrdom. . . .'[113] It did seem in these weeks at the front in Burma that Bose was ready to become one of the shaheeds he demanded and that he thought India needed. Whether he thought that he lived a charmed life and that the British could not easily kill him, I cannot tell. But he did seem ready to die.

In April, Bose was in Rangoon and the Japanese told him that they were withdrawing and that he must too. He was loathe to leave Burma, the country bordering on India, from which his forces had made their way into India and planted the tricolor. Again there were arguments, cajoling, and begging. Finally, he agreed to withdraw with his forces, including the Rani of Jhansi regiment, to Bangkok, and then Malaya, as the British pressed hard on their heels.

IV

While Bose was retreating with his troops in Burma, the establishment he had left behind in Europe, though shrinking and now even less important, continued to function. For more than two years, under the leadership of A.C.N. Nambiar, whom he had left in charge, it continued to wobble along without Bose. From afar, he continued to send communications by radio, cable, letter, and even telephone. When he set up the provisional government of Azad Hind in October 1943, Nambiar was made 'resident minister in Europe' with a seat in the cabinet. But as Girija Mookerjee pointed out, '. . . we realised more and more strongly that our work had become superfluous.'[114]

Subhas Bose had exited from Germany just before the heaviest Allied bombing set Berlin and other targets ablaze almost every night. Emilie Schenkl returned to Vienna, her home, after seeing Bose off in February 1943 and remained there raising her infant daughter, and getting a few letters from Bose. The Free India Center group was moved to Hilversum in Holland in October 1943 as the bombing of Berlin increased and work there became more difficult. The large transmitter at Huizen developed by the Philips Company, and used for their broadcasts, was nearby. The Center members lived together in the Hotel Heidepark until the Allied invasion at Normandy forced another move to Helmstedt in Germany.[115] In Holland they had been occasionally harassed by Dutch resistance activity, but broadcasts continued almost uninterrupted as did the publicatipn program of the Center. But it would be hard to argue that their work had much impact.

The Indian Legion also continued its training and the more elite group begun under Walter Harbich was melded in with the main body of the Legion. Bose had been promised that his force would only be used against the British and when it was clear that he was gone, the soldiers grew restless. Then they were moved to Belgium and then to the southwestern coast of France to help with the defenses against the expected Allied invasion. Unsure as to how they would be used, or unhappy at the interruption of their peaceable life in training camp, some of the soldiers proved hard to control. Their control was shifted to the Waffen SS. In 1944 they were moved again back into Germany and were subject to raids of the French Maquisards en route. A few were killed in these skirmishes. As the Allied tide swept across Europe, reconquering it from the Germans, the Legion gradually disintegrated and most were eventually captured by the Allies. They certainly did not fulfill the hopes that Bose had for them and they were never thrown into a major campaign against the British as were their counterparts in Southeast Asia.[116]

Amongst all of the Indian establishments built up by Bose in Europe, probably only Nambiar knew of the secret work of Trott. Suddenly on July 20, 1944, the news was flashed of the attempted assassination of the Führer. During this period, Trott used to meet occasionally with a beautiful young woman of Russian extraction who was part of Berlin's flashy international society. She, Marie Vassiltchikov, wrote in her diary a few days before the culmination of years of plotting,

> Adam Trott and I dined . . . together . . . we discussed the coming events which, he told me, are now imminent. . . . I continue to find that too much time is being lost perfecting the details, whereas to me only one thing is really important now—the physical elimination of the man. What happens to Germany once he is dead can be seen to later . . . for Adam it is essential that some kind of Germany be given a chance to survive. This evening we had a bitter quarrel about this. . .[117]

The plot failed. Hitler was wounded only slightly and the attempted seizure of control of the military and of communications in Berlin and elsewhere was shortly repressed. Trott knew that he was so deeply implicated, that he was bound to be arrested. He had been trying desperately for years to interest Allied representatives in Switzerland and Scandinavia in the efforts of 'good' Germans to overthrow the Nazis and get some expression of support from the former for the underground plotting. But the Allies were bent on unconditional surrender and Churchill did not allow any encouragement to them. Trott was to be a top official of the Foreign Office if the Nazis were overthrown. With the debacle of the underground scheme, some were executed summarily.

Trott was not arrested immediately, but he did not try to escape to Switzerland because he feared for his family. On July 25, he was arrested, and some weeks later, tried before the so-called 'People's Court,' presided over by the notorious judge Ronald Freisler. He screamed viciously at the defendants as they tried to make their statements. Nambiar went to a top SS official, Kaltenbruner, who had been rounding up the conspirators. It was quickly made clear to Nambiar that if he continued in his efforts to help Trott, then he too would be arrested. But he tried and those close to Trott appreciated his efforts. The main conspirators, including Trott, '. . . are not simply hanged, but are slowly strangulated with piano wire on butchers' hooks. . .' wrote Trott's young Russian friend in her diary.[118] Hitler had a film made of the executions and watched it over and over again. Clarita von Trott was arrested and then released; she and her young children survived the war. Alexander Werth, though next in line below Trott in the Sonderreferat Indien, and probably informed of the plot, was not arrested or directly implicated. He also survived. Trott, with his compatriots, died a martyr's death for the sake of his beloved Germany. What Bose knew of the fate of his main contact in the German Foreign Office is unknown.

After the Free India Center had been moved from Berlin, a bomb hit the building and all the records were destroyed. Nambiar had moved into the villa that Bose and Emilie Schenkl had inhabited for about a year-and-a-half, but had left there when a bomb also destroyed that building. As the Third Reich wound down, the Free India Center ended with its last broadcast on April 6, 1945. A few weeks later, on May 7, with Hitler and some of his close associates dead, the Third Reich surrendered and the war in Europe was ended. As they were captured here or there in Europe, some of those who had worked with Bose were interrogated, some held in camps, and all eventually released.

V

Throughout the Japanese invasion of India in early 1944, the fierce battle on the Indo-Burma frontier, and the eventual Allied victory, life went on in India, shaped by the war's course, but for the most part, not directly involved. Listening to the discussions of 1944 and 1945 in Indian political circles as they debated the future of their country, it is almost as if the war were 1,000 miles away instead of at the eastern end of Assam and just across the Burmese frontier. The war was left to the British and their allies. Most Indians, unless their family members were fighting, seemed to feel little involvement. Even an occasional Japanese bombing raid on Calcutta, as on December 5, 1943, or on the Orissa coast, did not awaken most Indians to an interest in the war. As 1944 proceeded, and the Japanese began to be pushed back in Burma and in the Pacific and there was no longer an air threat to India, the war faded even more from their concerns.

For Bengal and Bengalis, though they lived in a frontline province, the major worry was the food and clothing situation after the calamitous famine of 1943. Then, of course, there was the tangled course of Bengal politics. The new ministry headed by Khwaja Nazimuddin, which took office in the spring of 1943, included Tulsi Goswami as finance minister and Barada P. Pain as minister for communication and works. It contained four other Hindus, three of them from the Scheduled Caste group in the assembly, and five other Muslims from the Muslim League. Though there were six Hindus in the ministerial coalition, none had any significant following though it was striking that the Scheduled Caste group did join a League-dominated ministry. Messrs Goswami and Pain had once been associated with the Bose group and the Congress, and Sarat Bose was chagrined to find them in this new ministry replacing the Huq ministry of 1941–43 which he had largely fashioned just before his imprisonment.

Through 1944 one issue that was debated bitterly and at length in the Bengal Assembly was the Secondary Education Bill put forth by the government. Squabbling over this matter, often in acrimonious communal terms, had gone on for years and was renewed again as members debated how the board controlling secondary education was to be chosen. The ministry pushed for increased Muslim membership, chosen by separate electorates, and a larger Muslim role in the direction of education. They saw education as linked to the advancement of their community. The smaller, but extremely vocal, Hindu contingent insisted that the ministry wished to communalize education.[119] Outside the Assembly, Shyama Prasad Mookerjee organized meetings and demonstrations against the bill.

From his prison cell, Sarat Bose, in a letter of July 5, 1944 to the new governor, Lord Casey, an able and intelligent Australian, gave his version of what had been happening in Bengal during his absence, including the introduction of this bill. In part, he wrote,

> My activities in connection with the downfall of the previous Ministry and the formation of the Fazlul Huq Ministry of December 1941 found me within prison bars very soon. But I do not regret it. The fact that I had succeeded in extinguishing the communal flame in Bengal was sufficient consolation to me, even though I had burnt my own fingers in making the attempt. . . . I have followed closely all that had happened and is happening in my province since the 11th December 1941. The rights and liberties of the

people have been trodden under foot, they and their natural leaders have been distrusted, policies were thoughtlessly adopted in 1942–43 by the then Governor and the permanent departments behind the backs of the then Ministers and in utter disregard of their disastrous consequences . . . the communal monster has again reared its head. And, to fill the cup of agony to the brim, a bill known as the Secondary Education Bill has been introduced into the Assembly, the effect of which has been to convert the different parties in the Assembly into so many warring groups.

I have always been of opinion . . . that the rights and interests of the people could be . . . promoted only if the Hindu and Muslim members of the legislature combined to free themselves from the malignant influence of the agents of British Imperialism. . . . I have also been consistently of the opinion that secondary education . . . should be planned and directed entirely on non-communal lines and solely in the interests of educational uplift.[120]

Sarat Bose then condemned his old friends Barada Pain and Tulsi Goswami, for he said he was 'staggered' to find that they supported such a narrow and communal bill. Casey certainly did not accept Sarat Bose's views, but, for his own reasons, was unhappy with the inefficiency and corruption of the ministry and of the whole administrative structure of Bengal. He appointed the Rowlands Commission to assess the administration.

While Sarat Bose chafed at his imprisonment and Subhas Bose was at work in other spheres, the war seemed to be winding down. Political India began to face the future. With the Congress largely absent from 1942 to 1945, the Muslim League thrived. The Pakistan movement made significant headway, though no one seemed to know, or at least agree upon, what it meant. Jinnah knew that the Muslim League had to demonstrate much greater support for 'Pakistan', whatever it meant, than had been evident in the 1937 elections for the provincial legislatures. He was particularly concerned for the Muslim majority areas and had pressed for the fall of the second Huq cabinet, now accomplished. That was a negative step forward towards his goal. Now what was necessary was positive support for 'Pakistan' in the Assembly, in the Muslim League outside the legislature, and among the more politically conscious of the Muslim community.[121]

In 1943, H.S. Suhrawardy, blocked in his efforts to be chief minister, successfully supported Abul Hashim, a Bengali Muslim from Burdwan district, in his move to become general secretary of the League organization in Bengal. Under Hashim's guidance, Huq was hounded at political meetings and his support in Bengal Muslim politics undercut. Hashim began to build up the League organization in every district and as this structure was fashioned, some of the KPP men shifted to the League. Students and intellectuals worked for the League in increasing numbers.

For the first time in Bengal, the Muslim League had a deeper and wider base.[122]

The Lahore or 'Pakistan' Resolution of 1940 demanded that Muslim majority areas in the northwest and eastern parts of India should constitute 'Independent States', autonomous and sovereign. For Jinnah there was to be one Hindustan and one Pakistan; for Hashim, it was not so simple. His version, presented in a widely circulated pamphlet, 'Let Us Go to War,' (1945) stated, in part:

> Free India was never one country. Free Indians were never one nation. . . . Liberated India must necessarily be . . . a subcontinent having complete independence for every nation inhabiting it. . . . Muslim India to a man will resist all attempts of the Congress to establish dictatorship in India of any coterie, group or organisation. Pakistan means freedom for all, Muslims and Hindus alike. And the Muslims of India are determined to achieve it, if necessary through a bloodbath. . . Muslims of India are opposed to every kind of domination and exploitation—British or Indian. In Pakistan there will be just and equitable distribution of the rights and privileges of the state amongst all its citizens irrespective of caste, colour and creed. And it is not the contemplation of the Muslims to reserve any advantage for themselves except their right to govern their own society according to the laws of the *Shariat*.[123]

For Hashim, who considered himself a Bengali and a Muslim, India was multi-national and Bengal was one of the constituent nations. It happened that in the Bengal nation Muslims were a majority. But he did not want to create an exclusivist Muslim nation in Bengal. He wanted a socialist nation that for the moment would be joined to the Muslim nation in the northwest of India. In this Bengal nation, all Bengalis would be welcome and the Muslims would be governed by the *Shariat* as the Hindus would be governed in social and religious matters by their own laws. He tried to remind League leaders, even as he was building League support, that the Pakistan Resolution read 'Independent States'.[124] The Congress had reorganized in the early 1920s on the basis of linguistic regions, but insisted that these linguistic regions were not separate nations. They were parts of one, multi-linguistic, multi-cultural nation. Hashim was saying that each of these linguistic or cultural regions was a nation and that some of the nations would be Muslim-majority nations. He did not define nationality on the basis of religion as many in the League were doing in the 1940s. So we are left with the curious fact that the man most responsible for erecting the League organization had a different concept of nationality from the Muslim League.[125]

At a meeting in Calcutta during 1945, concerned with giving some cultural meaning to 'Pakistan', a recent convert to the Muslim League,

Abul Mansur Ahmad, writer and journalist, said that 'Pakistan' surely meant 'cultural autonomy'. He thought that religion and culture were different. By culture he seemed to mean Bengali culture and literature, which he said was to some extent similar for Hindus and Muslims in Bengal, and to some extent dissimilar. He tried to demarcate what the culture of East Pakistan should be. It was to be Bengali culture freed from Hindu linguistic and religious shackles. It was to be Muslim, but distinctive from the culture of the West Pakistanis. So it was to be Bengali and Muslim, but divergent from the culture of other Bengalis and other Muslims.[126]

These regional views, especially that of Hashim, come quite close to the wartime views of the Communist Party of India as put forth by one of its top ideologues, G.D. Adhikari.[127] Adapting Stalin's views on the nationality question to India, and praising the harmony of autonomous nationalities in the USSR, Adhikari put forth the view that there was a 'rational kernel' to the Pakistan demand. India was, he said, composed of many nations and they should have autonomy, once the foreign ruler left, up to and including the possibility of sovereignty. He said that the '. . . peoples of the Muslim nationalities [had] their just right to autonomy in free India.'[128] Even more bluntly, he argued that,

> Our solution concedes to the 'constituent units' of the zones specified in this [*Pakistan*] resolution—namely to Sind, N.W.F.P., Punjab and Eastern districts of Bengal, the right of self-determination to the point of secession. . . . The National Congress must recognise the right of these Muslim nationalities as of the other nationalities of which India is composed. . . . . Muslim peoples and their leaders are not bent upon separation. Grant them the right of equality and you create the basis for national unity today, and for the greater and more glorious unity of India tomorrow.[129]

By siding with the League, or appearing to, the CPI certainly helped to legitimize their claims as did C. Rajagopalachari on the Congress side, and the proposals of the Cripps Mission on the government-side. These attempts, however facile, well-meaning, or politically calculated, helped swell the support for Pakistan during the war.

The Boses, though they were devoted to communal cooperation, were steadfastly against the division of India. But like almost all the Congress leadership, they were off the playing field, at least for the duration of the war. The one organization that firmly rejected any truck with 'Pakistan' for the moment and could operate openly was the Hindu Mahasabha. For example, M.D. Biswas, writing to the Mahasabha president from the Bengal Provincial Hindu Mahasabha office on October 6, 1944, stated:

... no Hindu worth the name will support the vivisection of India. I may also assure you with all the emphasis at my command that not a single patriotic Hindu of Bengal will ever flinch from fighting the move of vivisection to the last drop of his blood.[130]

Because of Rajagopalachari's proposal to accept the autonomy of dissenting regions, the Mahasabha was concerned that the Congress might accept some kind of partition. Hindus, they said, must stand together in the hour of need.

Lord Wavell, in contrast to his predecessor, was concerned that the political deadlock in India be broken, and saw to Gandhi's release in 1944. The wartime rump Congress passed a resolution opposing Japan's advance into Assam, and then ignored the war situation. When Gandhi was free again and could engage in political dialogue, he arranged for a series of meetings with Jinnah in September 1944, which dragged on without progress from the 9th to the 27th. Jinnah insisted that the League be accepted as the bargaining agent for all Indian Muslims. Gandhi would not concede the point.

At the end of March 1945, the Nazimuddin ministry suffered a defeat in the Assembly when the agricultural budget was voted down, 106 to ninety-seven. The speaker, Syed Nausher Ali, a KPP veteran and no friend of the League, said the ministry could no longer function and adjourned the House *sine die*. Although Casey thought that the speaker had assumed a prerogative that he did not have, the governor decided that it was an opportune moment to issue a proclamation under section 93 of the Government of India Act of 1935, and take over the administration of the province. At the same time that support for the Muslim League was growing outside the Assembly, inside it was weakening. Now governor's rule was the order of the day.[131]

Wavell, after extensive consultations in London in early 1945, called a conference of Indian political leaders in Simla.[132] Top Congress leaders were released from prison and met during June in Bombay to prepare for this summit.[133] In Simla, Wavell proposed that the Viceroy's executive be reformed with nominees of each organization participating. The Congress agreed and put forth its slate which included two Muslims, one of them Congress President Maulana Azad. Jinnah refused to agree to the reconstitution of the viceroy's executive unless he was given the right to nominate all Muslim members. Neither the Congress nor Wavell would agree to this and the conference ended in failure. Jinnah proclaimed that he had avoided a clever 'snare'.[134]

Following the Simla Summit, Maulana Azad went to Calcutta and met with prominent Congress leaders. However, the two most prominent ones,

Subhas and Sarat Bose, were not available. Sarat Bose, was still imprisoned and found 'A life of inactivity irksome . . .'[135] Since he could read the newspapers, he was at least informed about the outlines of Indian political developments, though he, like other Indians, was kept in the dark about Subhas Bose and the Indian National Army.

Sarat Bose was, of course, concerned that there be some solution to the communal problem. He lamented that Gandhi, Nehru, Azad, and Patel had not agreed to coalition ministries in 1937. He wrote in his prison diary in mid–1944:

> Gandhiji's acceptance of Rajaji's formula is nothing short of a tragedy in India's political life. He, who not long ago declared vivisection of India to be a sin, has now blessed it! . . . I cannot help feeling that Gandhiji has been making blunder after blunder since 1937, acting on the advice of Jawaharlal and Maulana. If he had agreed to the formation of coalition ministries in 1937, Jinnah and his followers would have been satisfied and Hindu-Muslim differences would have been narrowed down. But that was not to be as Gandhiji preferred to lie low along with Jawaharlal and Maulana—the former a muddle-headed theorist, the latter Jawaharlal's ditto man. . . . They had all made up their minds in favour of pure Congress Ministries. Jawaharlal was thinking all the time that I was supporting a Congress-Coalition Ministry because of Bengal's peculiar position. He never appreciated that it would have the effect of liquidating Muslim suspicion of an opposition to the Congress.[136]

In his dialogue with himself, Sarat Bose said that he wanted the Congress either to refuse to form any ministries and '. . . create a deadlock and make the working of the 1935 Constitution impossible', or to form coalition ministries to allay the Muslim fears. 'But neither the one nor the other was accepted. There was a dead wall between me and my colleagues.'[137]

It was not altogether clear how Sarat Bose wanted to proceed at this juncture—if he had been free to advocate a line in Indian politics in 1944–45—but he did write,

> Truck or compromise with the 'Communalist' (as the word is understood in our country) will force us into deeper and deeper waters. We do not want 'Communalists', either Hindu or Muslim. No quarters to them. They only cloud the real issue and make Indian independence more difficult of attainment.[138]

At the same time, he wrote, 'even now . . . a composite or Coalition Government is an unavoidable necessity in this country and will be so for some time to come.'[139] How could such a coalition be constructed except with the 'communalist' Muslim League participating? They had to be dealt with in a situation in which the communal gap, as Sarat Bose noted, had widened because of Congress failures in 1937 and subsequently. Jinnah had also hardened his line and even Sarat Bose, a more trusted Hindu leader of the Congress than most, would have been hard put to reach a workaBle agreement with the Muslim League. When the Boses were at liberty to make alliances, they made them with the Krishak Praja Party or with the Muslim League as the situation allowed and the occasion demanded. If Sarat Bose had been a free man, suitably informed, at this juncture he would have been talking to the Muslim League as Gandhi had already, fruitlessly, been trying to do.[140]

From afar Sarat Bose also had to cope with other kinds of problems. Both his wife Biva and his daughter Gita encountered life-threatening health problems, but overcame them. He wanted his sons to get on with their careers and was particularly concerned with Amiya, his second son, after his return from Britain. Then there was the question of the marriage of his next eligible daughter, Gita. The search for a suitable bridegroom went on through 1944 and early 1945, and Sarat Bose advised from afar. He wrote to Gita in May 1945,

> Day after tomorrow Amalendra [*Biswas*] will be coming to Woodburn Park to meet you. Please take your own time to think about the matter and after you have done so, communicate your views to your mother without reserve. I need hardly tell you that your views will be the deciding factor. Our experience of the world and our judgement of men and things can guide you; but they will not dictate to you.[141]

Gita did choose to accept the proposal and the engagement ceremony was held in the late spring of 1945, with Sarat Bose still imprisoned.

As he brooded about this important moment in a favorite daughter's life, Sarat Bose dozed off, dreamt of it. He referred to his faith in the Divine Mother. A few months earlier he had written in connection with another dream,

> Sometimes my dreams set me thinking and wondering what they could have meant. After a time I feel comforted. Since the creation of the world, the Divine Mother has been proclaiming to her children through her chosen and anointed ones, 'Have faith in Me'. But we, the mortal children of the Immortal One, fail to hearken to Her Message and hence, all our griefs and woes. How I wish I could for once catch a glimpse of the Divine purpose behind the joys, the struggles and the sorrows of life![142]

Another matter which troubled Sarat Bose was the second imprisonment of his third son, Sisir Bose, who was arrested in October 1944. Sarat Bose wrote to Ajit Dey after he learned of the arrest,

> Knowing Sisir as I do, it is impossible for me to believe that he has infringed the law in any way, either knowingly or unknowingly. Nor can I believe that any 'prejudicial' documents were found in my house. . . . I feel sorry for Sisir. In 1942 he suffered for no fault of his. After two years he is passing through the same experience . . . it will eventually be found that he has done

no wrong. The crime of being my son is there, of course. And, he has to suffer for that![143]

Sarat Bose was not unaware of Sisir's role in Subhas Bose's escape in 1941 and must also have known, at least in outline, of his later contacts with the BV and with agents smuggled into India. This pose of innocence seems to have been offered as a smokescreen to the government censors. It did not work. Sisir was held incommunicado for some time and moved to the Lahore Fort for serious interrogation. After some months, word was sent to his family that he was in good health. They remained anxious. Aurobindo and Dwijen Bose were also imprisoned during the war, as were almost all of those active in the Bose-BV network.

In connection with an appeal—one of many—to move Sarat Bose back to Bengal, a member of the Intelligence Bureau, Home Department, Government of India, wrote in early 1944,

> . . . Bose and the Japanese, for their offensive and to hamper ours and our defense, are relying on revolutionary help from this country and particularly from Bengal. Constant appeals are being made for this help and these will continue. However, Bose is not relying on appeals alone; he is also sending agents who are better equipped and better selected than any despatched before. Some of these have been captured but some are still at large and the search for them is going on.[144]

The argument continued that Sarat Bose would be considered as the head of the secret network of agents and revolutionaries if he was returned to Bengal. So he had to remain in Coonoor.

The Intelligence Branch was accurate in its assessment. Bose and the Japanese continued to send in parties of agents during 1944. Some surrendered voluntarily, some were captured, some few carried on for a considerable time undetected. Although the training at Penang was probably better in 1943 and 1944 than in 1942, the operations were beset with difficulties. One of those involved in the training was Mahmood Khan Durrani, a fanatical and clever anti-Hindu Muslim officer, who worked his way into the confidence of the Japanese responsible for the training school. Durrani has told his story in *The Sixth Column,* of how he convinced the Japanese that it would be invaluable to send a party of Muslim agents to the Northwest Frontier area to create unrest. Secretly Durrani instructed this group of Muslim trainees that they were to surrender immediately to the British authorities upon landing in India and do their best to help the Raj. For long, perhaps suspicious, the Japanese put off sending the Muslim party. Finally, in early 1944, the group left in a Japanese submarine and eventually landed on the coast near Karachi. They surrendered forthwith and did their best to help the Allies. One Japanese officer committed suicide over this matter and Durrani was arrested and tortured with Bose's approval. Although threatened with execution again and again, Durrani survived the war and lived to win a British medal.[145]

Almost all of the 1942 and 1943 parties sent into India were soon captured and most of the agents tried and executed. Some of the operations directed more closely by Bose also ended in fiascos, but not all. One group including Dr Pabitra Mohan Roy, T. Mukerjee, Mahinder Singh, and Americk Singh, traveled from Penang to the Andaman Islands in April 1944, and landed at night at Konarak in Orissa, near the great sun temple. They moved on to Calcutta and contacted local Bose men, including Haridas Mitra, eldest son-in-law of Suresh Chandra Bose, and Jyotish Chandra Bose. Roy and Americk Singh set up a transmitter in Behala, Calcutta, and began sending out messages. Mahinder Singh moved to the Punjab where he carried out his part of the mission. T. Mukerjee disappeared and was suspected by the remaining three of having betrayed them. The operation continued for about a year when Roy, Americk Singh, Haridas Mitra, and Jyotish Bose were captured. Mukerjee turned King's witness at the trial of his former associates and information was also supplied to the investigators by members of the Durrani group. The four accused were tried and sentenced to death. During a transfer at Sealdah Station, Americk Singh, handcuffed, saw a momentary opening and made a dash for freedom through the streets of Calcutta. He was not caught. For more than a year, with the help of Bose associates whom he contacted, he hid out and later returned to Malaya. Americk Singh's older brother, Gurchan Singh, a policeman in pre-war Malaya, led an underground movement against the Japanese during the war and was called 'Singa, the Lion of Malaya'. Americk Singh, too, was a *singa* for the side which he chose.[146]

Haridas Mitra, through the intervention of Gandhi and Patel, eventually had his sentence commuted and later was released. Another contact man, Gopal Sen, committed suicide to avoid capture on July 22, 1944. Others from the BV network, including Sisir Bose, were captured, and held as long as the war was on. Though not a complete failure, the underground missions organized by the Japanese and by Bose with their help had very limited successes and many failures. On his side of the battlefield in 1945, Subhas Bose had to cope with the even larger failure of the Japanese invasion of India and its consequences for the INA, the Azad Hind movement, and himself.

VI

As the Japanese and their Indian allies, the INA, retreated from north to south in Burma through the second half of 1944 and the first half of 1945, they still fought fiercely. But without air cover and supplies and with ammunition running low, even as determined a fighting force as the Japanese began to fall apart. For the INA, recently organized, insufficiently trained and equipped, it was even worse. Though most Japanese were thoroughly imbued with the credo that they must fight to the death and did so, some surrendered. A much larger percentage of the INA deserted and surrendered as the chase went on.[147]

Slim wanted his forces to enter Rangoon before an amphibious assault on the city began. He pushed hard on his troops. With every mile, every hill, every village, they recalled their ignominious retreat of 1942.

After another argument with his own officers and the Japanese, Bose was finally convinced that he should not allow himself to be killed or captured in Rangoon, and left on April 24. He told those whom he left behind as well as those evacuating with him,

> If I had my own way, I would have preferred to stay with you in adversity and share with you the sorrows of temporary defeat. But on the advice of my ministers and high-ranking officers, I have to leave Burma in order to continue the struggle for emancipation. Knowing my countrymen in East Asia and inside India, I can assure you that they can continue the fight under any circumstances and that all your suffering and sacrifices will not be in vain.[148]

Bose spoke of 'temporary defeat' and of the battles to come. But, in contrast to the Japanese, Bose felt that even INA defeats might contribute to eventual political triumph. He told Nambiar before he left Europe that the unsettling, convulsive effects of the war with Indian participation might help in undermining the British Empire even if the Axis did not win.

The retreat from Rangoon was to take Bose through Moulmein and on to Bangkok. The party included members of Bose's military and civilian staff, Ambassador Hachiya, and some Japanese personnel from the Hikari Kikan. Then there was the question of the remaining women from the Rani of Jhansi regiment. Some had been sent home as early as the middle of 1944 when the Imphal campaign was going badly. Some, including Captain Lakshmi Swaminathan, remained in Burma through the Allied victory. But several hundred had to be sent back to Malaya and Singapore at about this moment. They were scheduled to leave by train, but then the trains were full. They were stranded. Bose was angry and insistent: he would not leave without them. In the end, Bose and his party retreated with the Ranis. It was an arduous and dangerous trip. Allied fighters controlled the air and the Allied forces were pressing ahead rapidly behind them.

Initially at least, they had lorries to take them, but when several of these ceased to function, they had to walk. Bose, the solicitous father throughout, trekked along with them. All the walkers developed blisters including the commander-in-chief in his high, tight boots. At the Waw River there was a terrible traffic snarl of retreating men, women, and vehicles and the Ranis had to wade across through neck-deep water. They plunged in; they got across. As they walked along the road, they were strafed. Bose again exposed himself, refusing to take cover. He told one of the young women, 'Don't worry, the Britishers will never take me, dead or alive.'[149] After reaching Moulmein, the party rested briefly and then were put aboard trains for Bangkok. Bose gave a final talk to the group of Ranis before they left, telling them that they had set a fine example and braved all dangers like seasoned soldiers. During the retreat several had been killed. The rest returned from Bangkok to their families.[150] Bose made a powerful impression upon them that has lasted with many of them through their whole lives.

Bose, his party, and the group of Ranis did not reach Bangkok until the second week of May. By then another stage had been reached in the great conflagration. Hitler had committed suicide and Germany had surrendered on May 8. Okinawa was also under assault and the home islands of Japan were under bomber attack. In a broadcast a few weeks later from Singapore, Bose looked back and ahead as he commented on the German defeat:

> The courage, tenacity and fortitude with which the armed forces of Germany fought till the moment of Herr Hitler's death must have evoked the admiration of the whole world.... It was the foreign policy of Germany, vis-à-vis Soviet Russia and other countries, that was fundamentally responsible for the military disaster.... One of the blunders ... was its total disregard of Bismarck's advice ... never to fight on two fronts ... the collapse of Germany will be the signal for the outbreak of an acute conflict between the Soviets and the Anglo-Americans. ... In post-war Europe there is only one ... power that has a plan which is worth a trial, and that power is the Soviet Union.... I cannot help reiterating on behalf of the Indian people and myself our heartfelt gratitude to the German people and nation for the sympathy and support that they gave us in our struggle for freedom.[151]

Still on the side of the Axis, but looking back to the Germans' half-hearted help of 1941 to 1943, Bose conveniently forgot the difficult, frustrating months he had spent in Germany. He did express his admiration for the Soviets' 'heroism, tenacity and sacrifice' as he looked ahead to a new historical period in which he hoped for assistance from them. Nowhere did he express any sympathy for the millions of victims of Nazi aggression and brutality. He was, Nambiar said, 'a one-idea man', and that idea was Indian freedom.

Although he talked of other battles, a new offensive, the next round of struggle, Bose understood by June 1945 that the Japanese could offer him no further help. Behind the scenes, Foreign Minister Togo and several advisers close to the Japanese emperor were trying to conclude the war with a surrender that protected the imperial institution. The Japanese, too, were seductively reaching out to the Russians, unaware that the latter had already committed themselves to enter the war against Japan a few months after the war in Europe was terminated.[152]

As the Japanese were finally driven from Burma and the Allies prepared for the invasion of Singapore and Malaya at the western end of the Japanese sphere, the Americans were pressing towards Japan's home islands from the south and the east. Bose, during these last months of war, had his eyes on the fate of Japan, on his hopes for Soviet aid, but also on the renewed negotiations in India. As with the Cripps Mission of 1942, he was dead set against any bargaining with the Raj, for he was certain it would lead to disaster. He believed that Viceroy Wavell had an ulterior motive behind his offer to reconstitute his executive council. Bose commented on June 19 from Singapore,

> The real motive underlying the British offer is somehow to get, with the approval of the Indian nationalists and the full connivance of the Congress, half a million troops with necessary material to fight Britain's imperialist war in the Far East. . . . In a fit of pessimism and defeatism some Congressmen are forgetting their life-long principles and are now reconsidering the offer which they rejected in 1942.[153]

He believed that in exchange for places in the government, Congressmen were giving up their quest for complete independence, which he said neither Cripps nor Wavell had offered. So one of his small joys of these depressing months of withdrawal and hardship was the failure of the Simla Conference.[154] 'Netaji Week' was celebrated from July 4 to 11.[155] The Japanese understood the disastrous 'trend of the Burma campaign and urged Bose to withdraw his troops and headquarters to Saigon. He was slow to accept their suggestion but continued to solidify contacts in Vietnam and Shanghai.[156]

With the dropping of the atomic bombs on Hiroshima (August 6) and Nagasaki (August 9) and the Japanese offer to surrender if the status of the emperor remained unchanged (August 10), Bose finally had to face up to the end of the war and of his tie to Japan. August 10 also marked the entry of the USSR into the Pacific War on the side of the Allies. Some amongst the Japanese military had believed that they would have an advantage in the battle for the home islands against an invading foe and that Japanese 'spirit' could not be defeated, but saner heads finally prevailed. The latter did not want the ultimate sacrifice: the destruction of the Japanese people and nation. Even 'unconditional surrender', with a small proviso concerning the imperial structure was preferable. For the Japanese the choice to surrender was finally made.[157]

But Bose was the head of a separate 'government', however weak, and was ready to move in a new direction. On August 16, Bose sent a message to the Japanese,

> Along with the trusted persons of my cabinet I would like to go to the Soviet Union. If it is necessary I shall enter the Soviet Union alone. In that case I request the Japanese Government to allow any of my cabinet members to take charge.[158]

Bose had been trying to make contact with the Soviet Union since the late 1930s and although he passed through Moscow on his way to Berlin in 1941, there has been no evidence made public so far that he ever received any positive encouragement from them. On his last visit to Tokyo, Ambassador Malik refused to see him or receive a message from him. However, seeing no other choices, he was willing to take his chances. The Japanese were unhappy with his efforts to reach out to the Soviets when the two nations were still observing their neutrality pact. Now, after August 10, 1945, the Japanese and the Soviets were at war. One important Japanese source indicates that the Japanese agreed to help Bose reach Manchuria and there make contact with the advancing Soviet army.[159]

Bose took the remainder of the funds at his disposal and distributed them to his military and civilian personnel. He had also tried to see that all the women of the Rani of Jhansi regiment had been safely returned to their homes.[160] About a month before the final moment in Singapore, he had a tribute erected to the INA which read,

> The future generations of Indians who will be born, not as slaves but as free men, because of your colossal sacrifice, will bless your names and proudly proclaim to the world that you, their forebears, fought and suffered reverses in the battles in Manipur, Assam and Burma, but through temporary failure you paved the way to ultimate success and glory.[161]

Bose was still in Malaya when he learned of the atomic bomb attacks on Hiroshima and Nagasaki and then the Japanese surrender offers of August 10 and final capitulation on August 14. He hurriedly made his plans. Some top military personnel were left behind in Singapore including Major-General Kiani, Major-General Alagappan, and the civilian A.N. Sarkar. Bose had similarly left key personnel behind in Rangoon to care for Indian affairs when he left.

On August 16, Bose flew to Bangkok. Then, arranging that a number of his top staff people should join him, he flew to Saigon on August 17. Here a gathering of several of those closest to him through the last two years of the war took place. These included Colonel Habibur Rahman, Colonel Pritam Singh, Colonel Gulzara Singh, Major Abid Hasan, Debnath

Das, and S.A. Ayer, and some other civilians. Also present was T. Negishi, Bose's long-time Japanese translator.[162] Bose hoped to take all in the named group and a few more with him as he took another step into the unknown. A few other top INA and Azad Hind government personnel were shortly to arrive, including Major-General A.C. Chatterji.

But in Saigon plans had to be changed, for Bose learned that no special plane was available for his party. He also came to know that Lieutenant General Shidei, a Japanese expert on the Soviets, was to fly to Dairen, Manchuria, where he was to take command of the Kwantung Army and work out the surrender there. Bose was at first told that there was only one place available on this plane which was to leave the same day for Taipei and then Dairen. General Isoda of the Hikari Kikan negotiated with the top officers of the Southern Army staff and finally secured one more place. Bose had to accept the two seats on this plane or stay in Saigon. He decided to take them, insisting that the rest of his party be sent on as soon as possible. He selected Colonel Habibur Rahman to accompany him. He told Mr Negishi that he would become a Russian prisoner. He wanted to put himself in their hands for, he said, 'They are the only ones who will resist the British. My fate is with them.'[163]

Others of Bose's party were quite unhappy, but the Japanese were in charge and decided who was to go. Then there was a problem about the luggage because the plane, a twin-engined heavy bomber of the 97-2 (Sally) type, was already overloaded. They could not take all of Bose's luggage. He discarded a good deal of it. Then two heavy suitcases said to be filled with gold and jewelry were brought to the plane. Although the crew protested, after Bose's insistence, they were loaded on.

On the plane were: Bose, Shidei, Rahman. Also: Lt. Col. Tadeo Sakai, a staff officer of the Burma Army; Lt. Col. Shiro Nonogaki, an air staff officer; Major Taro Kono, an air staff officer, who was sitting behind the pilot and assisting him; Major Ihaho Takahashi, a staff officer; Capt. Keikichi Arai, an air force engineer; chief pilot Major Takizawa; co-pilot W/O Ayoagi; navigator Sergeant Okishta; radio-operator NCO Tominaga. The crew was in the front of the aircraft and the passengers were wedged in behind, some, like Bose, with cushions, because there were no proper seats on this aircraft. The plane finally took off between 5.00 and 5.30 p.m. on August 17. Since they were so late in starting, the pilot decided to land for the night at Tourane, Vietnam, spend the night there, and start early the next morning. Tourane later became famous as the huge American base of Da Nang and is now an international air center on the coast of the People's Republic of Vietnam.

Bose already knew Shidei and was introduced to some of the other

Japanese officers, all of whom had heard of him. Bose and the others spent the night at a hotel serving as an army hostel in Tourane. While they were resting, the pilot and Major Kono, who had noticed the difficulty in taking off at Saigon due to overloading, did their best to lighten the cargo. Major Kono said later that they took off about 600 kilos of machine guns, ammunition, and excess luggage.

The take-off from Tourane at about 5 a.m. was normal and they flew at about 12,000 feet. It was quite cold in the plane, but the weather was favorable and they flew to Taipei (Japanese: Taihoku). Major Kono has testified that they received information during the flight that the Russians had occupied Port Arthur, so it was essential for them to hurry on and reach Dairen before the Russians reached there too. The flight took six to seven hours and the landing was smooth. They stopped for lunch and Rahman changed into warmer clothes during the break. Bose, he said, laughed off the need for more appropriate clothing, but he handed him a sweater anyway.[164] Colonel Sakai gave his coat to Colonel Nonogaki who felt cold.[165]

At Taipei, Major Kono, the pilot, and ground personnel checked the engines and noticed some problem with the left one. There was some unusual vibration, but they did not know the source or what to do about it. Major Takizawa adjusted the engine and they hoped the problem was solved. Major Kono was also unhappy because, even 600 kilos lighter than in Saigon, he still thought they were overloaded with the number of passengers they had on board.[166] Colonel Nonogaki noticed the engine check and observed that Major Kono had discovered some problems. The former also heard Bose ask if they would again be flying as high as earlier. When the answer was positive, he put on the woollen sweater that Rahman had handed him.[167] There was a tent set up near the air strip and they ate lunch there. They had been told that they would leave by 2.00 p.m.

The crew and passengers took their places as before and they were ready to go at about 2.30. As on previous take-offs, the heavy aircraft needed the full 1,500 meters of the airstrip to negotiate this one. Just as they left the ground—barely thirty meters up and near the edge of the airfield—there was a loud noise. Part or all of the left engine including the propeller had fallen off. The pilot could not control the aircraft. As the ground peered up at him faster and faster, he tried to switch off the engine. Major Kono seated behind him also tried, but failed. With an enormous crash they hit the ground and the airplane broke into two large parts. Within seconds there was a fire raging. Major Kono released a lock on the canopy, opened it, and slid out. As he was getting out, some gasoline splashed on him and he caught on fire. Once on the ground, he rolled around and Colonel

Nonogaki helped him.[168]

When the crash took place, Rahman, seated near Bose, was momentarily knocked unconscious. This is what he told S.A. Ayer, a few weeks later, about what happened next:

> When I recovered consciousness . . . I realised that all the luggage had crashed on top of me and a fire had started in front of me. So exit by the rear was blocked by the packages and exit by the front was possible only through the fire. Netaji was injured in the head but he had struggled to his feet and was about to move in my direction to get away from the fire and to get out of the plane through the rear. But this was out of the question. . . . Then he tried to make his way through the nose of the plane which was already smashed and burning. With both his hands he fought his way through the fire. . . . When the plane crashed, Netaji got a splash of petrol all over his cotton khaki and it caught fire when he struggled through the nose of the plane. So he stood with his clothes burning and himself making desperate efforts to unbuckle the belts of his bushcoat and round his waist.
>
> I dashed up to him and tried to help him remove the belts. My hands were burnt in the process. As I was fumbling with his belts I looked up and my heart nearly stopped when I saw his face, battered by iron and burnt by fire. A few minutes later he collapsed and lay on the ground of the Taihoku aerodrome.[169]

Major Kono, who was lying on the ground a short distance from the plane, and saw Bose on fire, described him as a 'living Fudomyoo', a Japanese Buddhist temple guardian who is usually represented with 'fierce visage . . . hair aflame, face contorted and weapons in hand'.[170] According to the accounts of all the survivors, Bose was very badly burnt. The pilot and General Shidei were killed on impact.

Ground personnel immediately called for vehicles to take the injured to the nearest hospital. Major Kono, though burnt on his hands and face, did not pass out. He watched and waited ten minutes or so before a car and an open truck were brought out to the edge of the field where the crash had taken place. The injured, including Bose and Rahman and the surviving Japanese officers, were taken to Nanmon Army Hospital. Ground personnel at the airfield had already called the hospital shortly before 3 p.m. and notified Dr Taneyoshi Yoshimi, the surgeon in charge of the hospital, to prepare to receive the injured.[171]

Dr Yoshimi, who had never heard of Bose, was told that he was 'Chandra Bose' and that Rahman was the only other Indian. Upon arrival the doctor noticed that Bose was naked except for the blanket wrapped around him. He had third degree burns all over his body, but they were worst on his chest. His body '. . . had taken on a greyish colour like ash. Even his heart had burns. His face was swollen. . . . His eyes were also swollen. He could see, but had difficulty in opening them. He was in his sense when he was brought in. . . . He was in high fever. . . . The condition of his heart was also weak.'[172] Dr Yoshimi doubted that he would live.

Bose and Rahman were quickly taken to the treatment room and the doctor started to work on Bose, the much more critically injured man. Dr Yoshimi was assisted by Dr Tsuruta. A disinfectant, Rivamol, was put over his body and then a white ointment was applied and he was bandaged over most of his body. Dr Yoshimi gave Bose four injections of Vita-camphor and two of Digitamine for his weakened heart. These were given about every thirty minutes. Since his body had lost fluids quickly upon being burnt, he was also given Ringer solution intravenously. A third doctor, Dr Ishii, gave him a blood transfusion. An orderly, Kazuo Mitsui, an army private, was in the room, and several nurses were also assisting. Bose still had a clear head which Dr Yoshimi found remarkable for one with such severe injuries. He was thirsty and asked for 'meju' which the Japanese interpreted as their word for water. The orderly brought him water.[173] Must he have been asking for his *mej-da*?

Mr Nakamura, an interpreter, also attended Bose for some time, and Rahman was kept in the same room. Some of the Japanese officers who were also hospitalized were not sure whether they were kept in the same large room with a divider, or in another. There are a few small discrepancies in the versions of some of the injured men as to who was in which room. But everyone who was conscious learned that Bose was the most seriously injured and likely to die. What, if anything, did he say in these last hours? Private Mitsui says that Bose did talk briefly to Nakamura in English, but he himself only heard Bose ask for water. Rahman told Ayer that Bose told him shortly before he sank away into unconsciousness,

> Habib, my end is coming very soon. I have fought all my life for my country's freedom. I am dying for my country's freedom. Go and tell my countrymen to continue the fight for India's freedom. India will be free, and before long.[174]

Mitsui also believes that Bose said something about India's independence before he died. Even if Bose did not say these precise words to Rahman, dramatically, just before he died, Rahman, who was one of his intimates, surely knew that India's freedom was his life's passion and his final concerns would likely be with this cause.

Bose's condition worsened as the evening darkened. His heart grew weaker. Finally, between 9.00 and 10.00 p.m., Bose succumbed to his terrible burns. Dr Yoshimi filled out a death certificate and put the cause of death of 'Chandra Bose' as 'burns of third degree'. He says that this certificate, filled out in Japanese, was filed with the municipal office. This certificate has not been located and Japanese records for that period of Taiwanese history seem to have been destroyed.[175] No photographs were taken of Bose at the end or just after his death. Some Japanese said this was not their custom. Then, too, Bose had been completely bandaged except for eye slits.[176]

Private Mitsui remembers that Dr Yoshimi told the staff to try to preserve the body and 'homoline' was injected. Cotton batting was used to close the body openings and the body was wrapped in a white kimono. The next day an army officer came for the body. Rahman had hoped to have the body removed to Singapore or Tokyo, but practical difficulties intervened. The coffin could not be shipped, even to Japan, at this moment when Japan was still carrying out the surrender terms and the American occupation had not yet officially begun. So the body was taken to the main Taipei crematorium and cremated. Rahman told Ayer that the cremation took place on August 20 and that the ashes were kept in an urn in the shrine attached to the hospital.[177]

VII

Subhas Bose was dead. But the public was slow to learn of his death and some among them even slower to accept. The tremendous weight of evidence, I believe, supports his death following the crash of the Japanese military plane. General Shidei, a most important Japanese officer, was killed. His death is accepted. Only about Bose do some harbor doubts. After all, there had been a dramatic disappearance in 1941, the story of his death in a crash in 1942, and then his risk-taking before Allied bombs in the retreat from Burma. In light of these events, some thought he could not die. His wife, his daughter (with whom some of my interviews in Japan were carried out), many of his relations, almost all the INA officers, and all the personnel with whom he worked have accepted his death, some later than others.

Why was the news of his death slow to come out? One reason is surely the chaos of the moment in world history when the Pacific War was being wound up. Second, for some reason, the Japanese commander in Taiwan wanted to keep the information secret and so only some top military personnel were informed immediately. But the lag was really quite short. By August 20, only one full day after Bose's death late in the evening of August 18, a Japanese officer informed S.A. Ayer in Vietnam of his death, and other Japanese military personnel in Southeast Asia and Japan began to let out word. On August 23, the Japanese news agency flashed the details of Bose's death and so it was widely known in India and elsewhere by the following day.[178]

Sarat Bose, still imprisoned in Coonoor, learned of his brother's death on August 25. Sarat Bose wrote in his diary,

> Today's *Indian Express* and *Hindu* brought the heart-rending news of Subhas's death as the result of an aeroplane crash. Divine Mother, how many sacrifices have we to offer at your altar! Terrible Mother, your blows are too hard to bear! Your last blow was the heaviest and cruellest of all. What divine purpose you are serving thereby you alone know. Inscrutable are your ways!
>
> Four or five nights back dreamt that Subhas had come to see me. He was standing on the verandah of this bungalow and appeared to have become very tall in stature. I jumped up to see his face. Almost immediately thereafter, he disappeared.[179]

The agony continued for him and he wrote to his daughter Gita on August 30:

> The last six days have been days of great pain and agony for me. . . . How shall I console you all, how shall I console myself?. . . He is gone to his rest and never more shall we see his forehead furrowed with thoughts for his country or catch the light in his magnificent eyes or hear his great accents. But I hope the memory of his intellectual attainments, his limitless capacity for suffering and sacrifice and his saintly character will continue to beam on us and beacon to us from afar and give us the comfort and strength we need at this dark hour of our lives.
>
> Since the 25th instant I have been reading all that the papers have been publishing about his life and his death. It gave me some little comfort to find that some of his colleagues who had insulted him by their malevolence in recent years had some good words to say about him after his death.[180]

In these immediate responses of Sarat Bose there seems not the slightest hesitation in believing that Subhas died from the burns suffered in the crash. He may or may not have had doubts—quite a few did—but at first it seems quite clear that he did not. In Bombay, August 25 was observed as 'Subhas Day' out of respect for his memory.[181]

It took Rahman some time to recover from his burns. On September 5, 1945, Rahman and Colonel Sakai were to travel to Tokyo along with Bose's ashes. Lieutenant Tatsuo Hayashida, a staff officer from Taiwan Military Headquarters, was ordered to take the one-and-a-half foot square wooden-box containing the ashes with a white cloth covering it and accompany them to Japan. Hayashida dressed in civilian clothes for this duty, and carried the box in the Japanese way, with a cloth around his neck to which the box was attached. He was told that they were the ashes of a very important person and he took scrupulous care of them throughout. The party flew to Ganosu Airport in Kyushu. Rahman and Sakai flew on to Tokyo. Hayashida then called Western Army Headquarters. He was told to stay overnight and then take the train to Tokyo the following day. For the last part of the journey, he was joined by Corporal Watanabe and two privates. They arrived in Tokyo on September 7, 7.00 p.m. They were met by a truck sent by Eastern Army Headquarters. Hayashida delivered the box to the headquarters of the chief of staff where the duty officer, Major Kinoshita, took charge of them. Proud that he had been selected for this mission, and that he had completed it as ordered, Hayashida left.[182]

The following morning, the new duty officer, Lieutenant Colonel Takakura, called Ramamurti, president of the Indian Independence League, Tokyo, and asked him to come and collect the ashes. They were handed over to Ramamurti and Colonel Rahman at the entrance to army head-quarters. First they were taken to Ramamurti's house. Then, a few days later, they were moved to a Buddhist temple, the Renkoji temple, in the Suginamiku quarter of Tokyo in which Ramamurti lived. There a Buddhist priest, Mr Mochizuki, conducted a ceremony around September 18. About one hundred persons, mostly Indian, but including Colonel Takakura, representing Imperial General Headquarters, attended. The ashes, in a small shrine area of the temple, have remained there and are there today.[183]

There were a number of interested parties that made inquiries into Subhas Bose's death shortly afterwards. The Government of India sent out two groups of intelligence officers headed by Finney and Davies to seek to locate Bose if he was alive and arrest him. Members of those parties testified before the Shah Nawaz Commission that they went to Saigon and Taipei and,

> The conclusion of the police officers was that Netaji had died as a result of air crash, and they reported to the Government of India accordingly . . . the report was definite that Netaji was dead, and thereafter the Government of India withdrew the warrant of arrest against Netaji Subhas Chandra Bose. The Bangkok party [*one of the two groups*] seized a telegraphic message conveying the information that the plane carrying Netaji had crashed at Taipeh, on the 18th August, and that Netaji had expired on the same day.[184]

In another parallel inquiry made at about the same time for the office of the supreme commander, Southeast Asia, or Lord Mountbatten's office, Colonel John Figgess, a top British Intelligence man investigated from the Japanese end and wrote a report. I have not been able to obtain a copy of his report, but Colonel, now Sir John Figgess, wrote to me in 1979:

> There is no doubt in my own mind that Bose died in the crash of a Japanese military airplane that took him to Taipei. I do not have access to a copy of my report of 8.10.1945 . . . but I am certain that I put forward the same conclusion then . . . all my information was gathered from Japanese army sources and in particular from Major Habibur Rahman, Bose's aide, who was with him in the airplane and who was himself quite badly burned.[185]

There are thus three almost contemporaneous reports made just after Bose's death which confirmed it for the Governments of India, Britain, and the United States. They probably exist in some restricted corner of the archives of these governments. They have not been made public or made available to researchers.

Why were these governments so interested in Bose's presumed death and why did they want certitude? Bose would have been potentially a very important figure if he had survived and been able to return to India. The Government of India was also considering what legal action it might take against him and other personnel of the Indian National Army and the Azad Hind Government. Then, too, most Congress leaders had been released, but Sarat Bose was still languishing in Coonoor. If Subhas Bose was dead, then the Government of India was more willing that Sarat Bose be released. There is some uncertainty expressed in Government of India documents in late August and September 1945.[186]

The Government of India was pretty much convinced of Bose's death in the crash by early September and began to move on Sarat Bose's release. One remaining barrier was that Lord Casey, governor of Bengal, did not agree to it. Casey had some suspicion that Subhas Bose might not be dead and wanted to wait for all inquiries to be completed. He also thought it would be wise to hold Sarat Bose until after the winter elections were held. But Casey was overruled and the Government of India, whose prisoner Sarat Bose was, decided to release him.[187] There had been numerous calls for Bose's release, one jointly by a large group of Bengal politicians on September 6. Finally, on September 14, 1945, after nearly four years of unpleasant imprisonment, Sarat Bose was released. He was given an ovation from friends, family, and supporters when he arrived at Howrah Station on September 17.[188]

His health had deteriorated through these years of confinement and he had written to Ajit Dey the previous year, 'I have run my race. The few years that remain to me I shall limp through somehow.'[189] He had also learned during his last month of imprisonment of the death of his mentor, Sir N.N. Sircar. On top of this came the crushing blow of Subhas' death. But Sarat Bose was a steady and involved man. He still had heavy familial and national responsibilities to meet. Wounded in body and spirit, he intended to do just that. Just after returning to Calcutta, he called for Congress unity and for maximum Muslim participation in and with the Congress. Whatever the differences of 1939 to 1941, he saw political unity in facing the Raj as essential at this historical moment. For this he planned to work.[190]

VIII

Alongside the actual presence and activity of Sarat Bose in India just after the war, there was a specter. This was the story of Subhas Bose's wartime work and the efforts of the Indian National Army. During the war, the Government of India had effectively carried out the 'policy of silence' and blacked out Bose, his army, and provisional government of Free India. Although Bose sent radio messages to India frequently, few were able to hear him and understand what he was up to. Now, with the end of the war, and the release of political prisoners, the open functioning of the Congress once more, and the freer flow of information, the tales of the war period, once only whispered by a handful, were broadcast everywhere. The British officials and the Government of India contributed to the maximum publicity now given to Bose's work, to the way in which they dealt with the INA prisoners, and particularly their decision to put some of them on public trial in New Delhi. Had Bose lived, he could not have arranged for better promotional efforts.

Bose could now be seen as one of the agents of the Asian resurgence which flourished as a direct and indirect result of Japanese aggression in Southeast Asia. He could be put in the company of nationalist leaders who worked with and against the Japanese, but always in favor of the nationalism of their people. Bose was linked to Aung San, Ba Maw, Sukarno, Ho Chi Minh, Mao Tse-tung, and 'thousands of others who wanted a new day for Asia, free of foreign imperialism. Some were puppets of the Japanese, but others were true and devoted nationalists who saw a way to end European imperialism by joining, temporarily, with the Japanese. The shifting of Aung San from one side to the other shows how rocky the nationalist road was.

Although the Japanese had only begrudgingly helped Asian nationalists, some of them truly admired Bose. General Arisue, one of the directors of Japanese Intelligence, described Bose as the embodiment of a samurai. In particular, Arisue mentioned that his seemingly soft exterior covered a strong heart, a powerful spirit inside, and extolled Bose's insistence on keeping his promises.[191] Another Japanese of those days, an expert in the history of Japanese culture, mentioned the warrior ethic to which Bose adhered: worldly gain was unimportant, physical courage, and devotion to the cause at hand were all-important. A few Japanese military men of the war period said that Bose more fully incarnated the samurai spirit than any of their own leaders.[192] So it is no wonder that even with all of his difficulties in dealing with the Japanese, Bose did find a resonance for his way of going at things. This was because, in his own way, he was an Indian samurai.

CHAPTER TWELVE

'Extremists have the upper hand':[1]
To Partition, 1945-47

S.C. Bose may be dead but much that he did lives still.
Government of India, confidential file, 1945[2]

*Here was Islam, his own country, more than a Faith, more than a
battle-cry. . . he seemed to own the land as much as anyone owned
it. What did it matter if a few flabby Hindus had preceded him there,
and a few chilly English succeeded?*
E.M. Forster, *A Passage to India*[3]

We are doing very well. We expect to exterminate every Muslim.
A Hindu Sub-Inspector of Police to *Daily Express*
Correspondent Sydney Smith, in Ludhiana, August 1947[4]

*. . .one must understand the evil spirit of 1946, to understand why the
partition was accepted in 1947.*
The Indian Annual Register[5]

I

Sarat Bose was free at last, but his health had deteriorated seriously during
almost four years in unpleasant and unwanted imprisonment. Fearing the
machinations of the Boses, officials of the Raj had been unwilling to put
him on a looser rein in his own house near Darjeeling as they had in the
1930s. The consequence was that Sarat Bose remained in poor health for
the rest of his life. He again began to do his legal work in order to support
his family, but his main focus was to help secure independence with unity
for India. Subhas Bose was gone and Sarat was more than ever before in
a crucial position as a leading Indian nationalist of Bengal.

Even while imprisoned, Sarat Bose paid close attention to political
matters and seemed set on working with the mainstream of the Congress

when he emerged from prison. He had been leading a dissident group of Congressmen inside and outside the Bengal Legislative Assembly when he was arrested in 1941. A lot of water had flowed down the Ganges into the Hooghly and on out to sea since then. On June 20, 1945, he wrote in his diary:

> The proposals [*of Lord Wavell at Simla*] *as they stand* now ought to be rejected by the Congress. . . . Sardar Patel has struck the right note. . . . Will Sardar be able to prevent the Congress from degenerating into a communal organization of 'Caste Hindus'? Locked up as I am, I can do nothing, though the situation is most serious.[6]

And again on June 30, he wrote,

> Reading the newspapers carefully every day, I find that the only man among Congresssmen who is talking practical politics is Sardar Patel. Jawaharlal is as usual talking in the air—internationalism and all the rest of it! If I had been free, I would have discussed with Sardar the ways and means of setting the country on its feet. I cannot think of any one else who can do it now except, possibly, Ami. If he goes to Bombay in the near future, he can meet Sardar. . .[7]

These passages indicate his admiration for Patel, his criticism of Nehru—with whom relations had become and remained strained—and his estimation of his son Amiya Nath Bose's talents. The latter became a kind of political secretary for his father.

Once freed, Sarat Bose reached out to the Congress as its high command stretched out its arms to embrace him again. Sarat Bose was a supporter but not a member of the Forward Bloc, the small grouping within the nationalist fold which Subhas Bose had founded in 1939. Within a month or so after his release, Sarat Bose had joined the Congress and Bengal Election Boards and was strenuously working with Sardar Patel on organizing the Congress election efforts, first for the Central Legislative Assembly, and later for the Bengal Legislative Assembly. He roved as far as the Punjab to assist with fundraising and to advise on the choice of candidates. He was in close touch with Patel and Maulana Azad about these matters and they were all especially concerned that the Congress make a decent showing in some Muslim constituencies.[8] Sarat Bose met several times with Fazlul Huq, his erstwhile coalition partner. The Congress tried to help nationalist Muslims in the fight for the Muslim seats, but to small avail. While Sarat Bose had been in prison, there had been a big shift to the Muslim League in Bengal and he gradually came to see that to deal with the Muslims in Bengal politics, he now had to talk to the Muslim League rather than to Huq and the Krishak Praja Party.

The decision for elections to the provincial and all-India legislative assemblies had come in the wake of the debacle at Simla. Lord Wavell,

often and unfairly abused for his actions as viceroy, had been trying to
unblock the log jam of Indian politics since 1944. Prime Minister Churchill
had been a formidable barrier. Nevertheless, Wavell had persuaded the
Conservative secretary of state, Leopold Amery, to join him in pressing
Churchill to allow new initiatives in India. The Gandhi–Jinnah meetings
in 1944 had been encouraged by the viceroy and the Simla Conference in
June was his show.[9] This latter effort, set afloat by Wavell was wrecked,
in his view, on the shoals of an unbending stand taken by Jinnah for the
Muslim League. Wavell wrote to Amery on July 11, 1945:

> Jinnah said at once that it was impossible for him to co-operate unless (a)
> all Muslim members were drawn from the Muslim League, and (b)
> Governor-General's veto was reinforced by special safeguard, e.g., that no
> decision objected to by Muslims should be taken in Council except by clear
> two-thirds majority or something of that kind. These conditions were
> fundamental and he could do no more unless I accepted them.[10]

Wavell told Jinnah that he could not accept his conditions, and that the
conference was over. After this collapse and the summer elections in
Britain which put the Labour Party in power, the new government moved
for elections in India.[11]

II

At the same time that Sarat Bose was reentering his legal work and political
activity and rejoining his family, he had another important matter with
which to deal. This was the Indian National Army, the Azad Hind
movement in Southeast Asia, and the legacy of Subhas Bose. During the
war there were times when Sarat Bose was not even sure on what continent
Subhas Bose was active. However, with the end of the war and of the
blackout of news about the the INA, Sarat Bose quickly learned about the
movement and met with INA and Azad Hind government personnel. He
identified the movement with the Congress and mainstream Indian
nationalism as an effort to secure India's freedom. As the British were
bringing some of the INA officers to trial, he joined the large Indian chorus
which shouted that no retribution must be taken against these patriots.[12]

From the work of his brother and the INA, Sarat Bose extracted certain
values which he put forward in the following months and years as the 'INA
spirit'. He hoped this would be instilled in all Indians. This spirit, he said,

> ... which recognises no distinction between Hindu and Muslim, between
> one community and another, between one class and another, between one
> caste and another, between one creed and another, has lighted the path for
> us all.[13]

He tried to use this lesson of communal harmony which he found in the
INA to combat the senseless communal violence which erupted in the

years after the war. Sarat Bose found other values as well in the INA including unity, strength, and discipline. He began to call in this post-war period for the training of volunteers to combat communalism. They were to have military-inspired discipline, but be devotees of non-violence. In this he was at one with Gandhi.

Sarat Bose worked with the INA Relief Committee in which Sardar Patel was active, and encouraged INA personnel to take an active role in Indian politics. But he decided against any separate INA political movement and against tying himself to the Forward Bloc or any combination of the two. By his reckoning, he had been a Congressman since 1905—forty years of his life—and he identified the Congress with the quest for Indian freedom. He remained with the Congress as it pressed for British withdrawal from India.

Besides Sarat Bose, every Indian nationalist, indeed, every political actor, Indian or British, had to come to terms with the INA in the fall and winter of 1945–46.[14] Among Indian nationalists, Mahatma Gandhi and Jawaharlal Nehru, who had been extremely critical of Subhas Bose from 1939 to 1945, found it easier to deal with him in death than in life. The INA movement made a powerful impression on the Indian public in the months after its capitulation. Gandhi and Nehru brought it and Subhas Bose back into the mainstream of Indian nationalism. They were also able to yoke the powerful emotions of support for the INA to the Congress bullock cart.

When Gandhi first learned of Subhas Bose's death, he wrote, 'Subhas Bose has died well. He was undoubtedly a patriot though misguided.'[15] Later Gandhi thought that Bose was still alive until he talked with Habibur Rahman and allowed Bose to rest in peace.[16] Gandhi gave one of his fullest evaluations of Bose and the INA in an article of February 15, 1946, 'How to Canalize Hatred,' where he wrote,

> The hypnotism of the Indian National Army has cast its spell on us. Netaji's name is one to conjure with. His patriotism is second to none. His bravery shines through all his actions. He aimed high but failed. Who has not failed? Ours is to aim high and to aim well. . . . My praise and admiration can go no further. For I knew that his action was doomed to failure, and that I would have said so even if he had brought his I.N.A. victorious to India, because the masses would not have come into their own in this manner. The lesson that Netaji and his army brings to us is one of self-sacrifice, unity irrespective of class and community, and discipline. If our adoration will be wise and discriminating, we will rigidly copy this trinity of virtues, but we will as rigidly abjure violence . . . I . . . welcome the declaration made by Capt. Shah Nawaz that, to be worthy of Netaji, on having come to Indian soil, he will act as a humble soldier of non-violence in Congress ranks.[17]

Gandhi skillfully selected what he wanted: communal and class unity, self-sacrifice, and discipline. He also said that Shah Nawaz had declared that Bose's last wishes were for the INA to return to India, retain their discipline and patriotism, but act non-violently and help the Congress. This suited Gandhi perfectly. Gandhi had assimilated the INA troops into his non-violent army. He had given due recognition to Bose, but discarded his use of violent means.

As the British Raj moved to put some leading officers of the INA on trial for treason against the King-Emperor and other charges, Indian nationalists closed ranks to defend them. The first and main trial was conducted by a military court in the Red Fort in Delhi. The Raj made it easier for all Indians to identify with the defendants by choosing to try together a Muslim, Captain Shah Nawaz Khan, a Hindu, Captain P.K. Sahgal, and a Sikh, Lieutenant G.S. Dhillon. Distinguished lawyers and noted nationalists with legal credentials rushed to join the defense team. Even Jawaharlal Nehru, who had said in 1943 that he would personally go to the front and fight Bose and the Japanese if they invaded India, donned robes which he had not worn for decades and met several times with the defendants. As the trial went forward, Nehru spoke about the INA in the course of a speech demanding the release of Jayaprakash Narayan. He said, in part,

> The I.N.A. trial has created a mass upheaval. Wherever I went, even in the remotest villages, there have been anxious enquiries about the I.N.A. men. There are profuse sympathies for these brave men, and all, irrespective of caste, colour and creed, have liberally contributed to their defence. . . . The deeds of the I.N.A. patriots should have been tried and judged at the bar of public opinion. The verdict will be overwhelmingly in favour of the I.N.A. men. The continuance of the trial is sheer madness undermining the position of the British in this country. The trial has taken us many steps forward on our path to freedom. Never before in Indian history had such unified sentiments been manifested by various divergent sections of the population . . . . This is not the only and solitary contribution of the I.N.A. trial, but there is also another formidable one and it is that it has broken the impenetrable barriers that separated earlier the Government-controlled Indian Army and public opinion. . . . The trial has brought the two closer. It is transparently clear that the Government army also shares the feelings and aspirations of the country.[18]

Nehru went on to extol the patriotism of the INA soldiers. Nehru in his remarks also touched in his remarks on one of the crucial issues involved in the INA trial and its impact: the problem of the loyalty of the Indian army to the Raj. The British rulers had decided to try the INA officers to show that disloyalty to one's oath to the King-Emperor would be punished. They expected that Indian troops and the Indian public would see the point. What they did not foresee was the powerful political impact that the story of the INA would have on a nation primed for independence after the war. After all, this war, like the First World War, had been fought by the British and their allies in the name of democracy and self-determination.

The British, of course, viewed the INA movement as a traitorous one. Usually sober soldiers drenched it with invectives: fascists, quislings, Japanese tools, treacherous and faithless renegades or rebels, cowards, etc. With suitable pomp, they brought the three officers before a military tribunal, expecting that the right side, their side, would control the show. What followed was a surprise to Viceroy Wavell, Commander-in-Chief Auchinleck, and down the line of the British military establishment. An example of British military thinking is the view of General O'Connor writing to Auchinleck during the trial:

> You, I know, have in addition politics to consider, I have really only the Army to consider. And I just can't be influenced by logical arguments about de Gaulle and the Maquis! Everyone knew the INA were traitors; nobody ever considered them anything else, least of all the men themselves.... Now they . . . say they were patriots.
>
> If there is sympathy for them in the Army, which I still doubt, then it is because we have allowed these arguments to be used without any sort of reply. . . . How can we expect to keep loyalty if we don't condemn disloyalty?[19]

They had not counted on the fact that Subhas Bose was a widely known and recognized patriot who could not easily be labeled a Japanese tool. Indeed, he had not been one, as even the British knew. Furthermore, there were many shades of opportunists in the INA; there were also quite a few devoted patriots and they had a formidable lawyer, Bhulabhai Desai, to put forth their case. He was considerably to the right of the Boses in the Congress spectrum, but he mounted a keen defense backed by legal and political precedents and parallels from British, American, French, Latin American, and Asian traditions.

The kernel of Desai's defense was that,

> . . . modern international law has now recognised the right of subject races which are not for the time being or at the moment independent, to be so organised, and if they are organised and fight an organised war through an organised army, the individual members of that army are unanswerable before any municipal court for what was done in prosecution of that war. . . you do reach a stage where the organisation, call it rebel if you like, call it insurgent; insurgents or rebels may reach a stage of organisation for the purpose of liberating themselves when what they do after declaring war is subject to the laws of war . . . in view of the fact that a state of war existed

between the Provisional Government of Azad Hind and the British, any act done in prosecution of that war has not the consequences which the Crown claims . . . in the case of a private individual.[20]

Desai pressed his case that the Government of Azad Hind was a recognized belligerent opposing Britain and the British Raj and that the former's army was operating under the Indian National Army Act. He claimed that the British had turned over the Indian prisoners in Malaya and Singapore to the Japanese and that these Indians could then take an oath to a new Indian government which superseded their oath to the King-Emperor. He differentiated Indian subjects of the King from British subjects and said that Bose's government claimed and received the loyalty of Indians resident in Southeast Asia. Among the precedents for insurgents becoming a recognized belligerent power, Desai cited the former American colonies in North America and included a recitation of virtually all of the Declaration of Independence in his final speech along with a host of legal citations.

The prosecution counsel, Sir Naushirwan Engineer, denied that the Government of Azad Hind was a separate entity, and said that it was simply a Japanese ploy to help the Japanese conquer India. He said that the three defendants were subject to Indian army and British Indian domestic law, and not international law. However, even the prosecutor admitted that,

> There is a good deal of evidence to the effect that what the accused did was done by them not with any mercenary motive, but out of what the accused *bona fide* consider to be patriotic motives and impelled by a sense, whether wise or misguided, of doing service to India. This, while not affording any defence to the accused in law, may legitimately be taken into consideration on the question of punishment. . .[21]

The trial held centerstage for almost two months. Then the defense and prosecution summed up, the judge-advocate instructed the judging officers, and the verdict was given. On cue, the defendants were found guilty and sentenced to cashiering and transportation for life. Now, though, Auchinleck had to pay some attention to the roaring support and demonstrations for the accused in the public arena.

Auchinleck reflected on the matter and then made his decision, taking military and political considerations into account. If he had the three officers transported for life, the uproar would continue. His conclusions read in part,

> As regards confirmation of the sentence for 'waging war', I hold that it is our object to dispose of this most difficult problem of how to deal with the so-called 'I.N.A.' in such a way as to leave the least amount of bitterness and racial feeling in the minds of the peoples of India and Britain . . . and at the same time to establish in law that those who joined the 'I.N.A.' committed

a crime against the State. . . . It is of no use trying to judge these unfortunate people by the standards which we apply to British officers and men captured by the enemy . . . a great number of them . . . believed that Subhas Chandra Bose, was a genuine patriot. . . . Bose acquired a tremendous influence over them . . . the accused might have acted in good faith, forsaking their original allegiance. It is quite obvious that this is the general opinion held in India, not only by the public, but . . . by quite a considerable part of the Indian Army as well.[22]

Since he said that he did not want to make them martyrs and have the 'political campaign of bitterness and racial antipathy' continue, he decided to commute the sentences of all three to 'one of cashiering and forfeiture of pay and allowances'.[23] With this, Shah Nawaz, Sahgal, and Dhillon were released. They have been lionized ever since as the three heroes of the INA and the Red Fort trial.

Although it appeared with this sensible decision by Auchinleck that the British Raj had learned a lesson the hard way, it was not learned well enough. Another trial was started on February 10, 1946, again in the Red Fort. This time Captain Abdul Rashid of the INA was before the bar. Public demonstrations against this trial began in many Indian cities. In Calcutta, huge student meetings were held on February 12, 13, and 14, and military forces had to be called out to contain them. Several students were killed. One demonstrator-cum-historian has maintained that governmental control was on the edge of collapse and that it was a true revolutionary moment. Although the Congress backed away from the students' rallies, while the Communist Party of India encouraged them, the severe repression by the Raj succeeded.[24] Gautam Chattopadhyay, in chronicling this brief upheaval, has pointed out that all communities and political parties joined the INA demonstrations. They deflected negative communal emotions and transmuted them into powerful anti-imperialist ones. Both kinds of sentiments were there as these and other events of 1945 to 1947 amply demonstrate.

During the first INA trial, the Calcutta students at their big meeting on November 21, 1945 called for Sarat Bose to come out and lead them. Gautam Chattopadhyay has written,

> Students expected that some top Congress leaders would surely come and take up the leadership of the demonstration. They expected, at least, Sarat Bose to come. But none came—neither Sarat Bose nor Kiran Sankar Roy. They both sent letters through couriers, calling on the students to 'disperse' and not to be 'misled into adventurist actions, instigated by the Communists.'[25]

Some have reported that Sarat Bose was badly advised throughout this period by his newly-installed political secretary, his son Amiya, but it is surely more than this. Sarat Bose was not a mass leader willing to stand at the head of confrontational demonstrations. Subhas Bose had been one, but never Sarat Bose. He was a fine speaker, but he shied away from this kind of leadership role and sought rather the legislative chamber and the negotiating session. Amiya Nath Bose was not a popular man, and this probably harmed Sarat Bose in these years. But also, Sarat Bose was not cut out for the new role of mass leader that offered itself to him.[26] Although he called for 'revolution' in a speech to the Calcutta Corporation on October 4, 1945, what he meant was that '... all public utility services, such as electricity, gas, tramways and transport . . . should be fully and thoroughly municipalised.'[27] Presumably this would be carried through by municipal and provincial elected bodies. This might mean a significant change in the delivery of these services, but it was not what Lenin or Mao or Ho Chi Minh had in mind when they called for revolution. Some family members and associates called for Sarat Bose to form a new party uniting the INA, Forward Bloc, Socialists of the August 1942 movement, and other leftists into a radical party.[28] But he was not prepared to do this. He did not want to split the Congress.

The rallies and the impact of the INA on the Indian army, navy, and air force were one factor influencing the British to quit India. General Tuker, GOC of the Eastern Command covering the region up to Delhi, has noted that, 'During 1946 there were serious cases of mutiny in the Royal Indian Navy, less serious in the Royal Air Force and Royal Indian Air Force and minor troubles in the Indian Army.'[29] The most serious of these was the Royal Indian Navy mutiny in Bombay, February 1946, which was shortly put down by determined repression and with calming words by Sardar Patel and Nehru instructing the young men to halt their uprising. Like Sarat Bose, these other top Congress leaders pulled away from actions which might have spread into widespread and violent unrest.[30]

Sarat Bose had his differences with Nehru. These were usually muted, but the strain remained, and occasionally burst forth into the public press. One of these areas of difference had to do with international affairs, particularly assessments of China. In an interview in *Blitz* in September 1945, Sarat Bose, presumably quoted accurately, called Chiang Kai-shek 'the Arch-Fascist tyrant of China,' and continued,

> I accuse Chiang Kai-Shek, the 'great humanitarian', of indulging in numerous bloodbaths in China, with the sanctification of foreign powers and the financial help of foreign capitalists.
>
> I accuse Chiang Kai-Shek, 'one of the Big Four' for pursuing a pro-Japanese policy from 1931 to '36, in defiance of the large and growing volume of public opinion in his own country.[31]

Based on his extensive wartime reading about China which reshaped his views, Sarat Bose went on to praise Mao Tse-tung and the Chinese Communists. He said,

> It was said . . . that our internationalists never gave us the real and true picture of China during the days of our struggle and never mentioned one word about the great man and his heroic band of workers. . .[32]

It was one thing to hold these views and discuss them privately, but this widely-read interview, addressed to the 'internationalists' of the Congress, surely meaning Jawaharlal Nehru, did not go unanswered. Nehru wrote to Sardar Patel,

> . . .You would have noticed in the press a totally unnecessary controversy between Sarat Bose and me. I am afraid Sarat has for some reason or other got a grievance against me. . . . He is . . . dead set against Chiang Kai-shek, which seems to me bad and harmful and likely to create unnecessary trouble all round. None of us admires all that Chiang Kai-shek has done. But it does seem to me wrong for us to attack him in this way. He happens to be the head of the Chinese State and so far as India is concerned his attitude has always been very friendly. For my part I have kept up friendly relations not only with Chiang Kai-shek and the Chinese Government but with many of his critics in China. I do not want this controversy with Sarat, but to remain silent became impossible for me.[33]

In his statement to the press on September 29, 1945, Nehru suggested that Sarat Bose was not very well informed after his years in prison, that he did not speak for the Congress, and that it was no business of the Congress to criticize the heads of friendly states. Nehru said it was not for Indians in responsible positions to discuss China's internal problems. He reiterated his thanks for the warm hand which Chiang had extended to Congress nationalists during the war. It was ridiculous, Panditji said, to call the Chinese leader a fascist.[34] It was certainly not within Nehru's scope to admit that some other Congressmen might know more about an aspect of international affairs than he did. Sarat Bose may have been intemperate, but he had a more accurate view of what was happening and what was to come in China than did Nehru. When the Chinese Communists came to power in 1949, Sarat Bose immediately sent off a congratulatory telegram to Mao Tse-tung. Mao thanked Sarat Bose for his greetings to the People's Republic and called for broad friendship between India and China.[35]

While Sarat Bose was full of praise for the Chinese Communists who, he said, were true nationalists, he did not have the same positive view of Indian communists. In fact, he saw Indian communists in the CPI and M.N. Roy's Radical Democratic Party as enemies of Indian nationalism for their collaborationism with the Raj during the Second World War. In a speech to students in Patna on February 1, 1946, Sarat Bose said,

The Communist Party and the Radical Party are all branches of British organisations. When the Congress went to jail, the Communist Party found the field open, entered it and raised the false slogan of 'People's War' to mislead their countrymen . . . these parties which thrive on British patronage can never serve the interests of the Indian people which are diametrically opposed to British interests. I have no hesitation in proclaiming these parties as enemies of India's freedom. . . . Unlike the communists in India who are agents of British Imperialism, Mao has said that the first objective of the Chinese Communists . . . was to make China free and independent.[36]

Sarat Bose and Nehru were in accord that the Indian communists had let down Indian nationalism during the war and should be banished from the Congress. It was Mahatma Gandhi who took the lead in purging the communists from the Congress in 1945 after considering their wartime role. Socialists Sarat Bose and Jawaharlal Nehru were prepared to go along with Gandhi and Patel in this.[37] Nehru said that the Communist Party of India, by its own policies, was gradually isolating itself from the Indian masses.[38]

Another point of agreement between Nehru and Sarat Bose was that Indian troops should not be used to put down independence movements in Vietnam and Indonesia, a Congress concern in these years.[39] Indian troops, as part of the Southeast Asia command headed by Mountbatten at the end of the war, were used to help Western imperialists reoccupy Vietnam and Indonesia. General Auchinleck saw the political repercussions of such utilization of Indian troops and insisted that they be withdrawn.[40] This issue illustrates Nehru's insight that the INA trials had brought the army and the society closer together and helped to politicize the army. He was subsequently concerned that this politicization not go too far and he came around to agree with the British military establishment that the INA personnel should not be brought back into the army.

III

One of Sarat Bose's tasks in the election campaigns of 1945 and 1946 was to deal with the communal parties including the Hindu Mahasabha. He had to cross swords with a personal friend who could be a formidable political foe or an ally: Shyama Prasad Mookerjee. The initial campaign was for the Central Legislative Assembly and Sarat Bose decided to stand for one of the six non-Muhammadan seats in Bengal. He was not sure of the relative strength of the Congress and Mahasabha and at first he offered Shyama Prasad Mookerjee one of the six seats, then offered two to the Hindu Mahasabha if it did not oppose the Congress. At this point, both the Mahasabha and the Congress stood for Indian freedom with unity. Though a communally-oriented party, the Mahasabha, or at least its leader, had joined the Huq cabinet in place of Sarat Bose in 1941. But the Mahasabha did not accept this offer and there was an open contest between the two parties in these Hindu constituencies.[41]

Both parties said they were determined to oppose Pakistan. This is how Sarat Bose put the Congress position:

> The Congress is most definitely against Pakistan and the partition of India ... the Congress alone...will be able to defeat Mr M.A. Jinnah's claim for Pakistan and partition of India. The Mahasabha may shout against both... but when it comes to action I am certain it will be nowhere.... Which are the organisations that are today fighting Mr Jinnah's Muslim League candidates over the Muslim seats in the Central Assembly?... all the six Muslim seats in the Central Assembly are being contested—four by Nationalist Muslims and two by Congress Muslims. . . . All that the Mahasabha seems to be doing today is to create disruption among the Hindus. It has not the strength to fight Mr Jinnah and never had.[42]

The results of the December election must have brought Sarat Bose some joy and a lot of tears. The Congress did sweep the six non-Muhammadan seats and even won the landholders' seat. Sarat Bose beat the Mahasabha candidate standing against him in Calcutta by 7,290 to eighty-eight. Nagendra Nath Mukhopadhyay won over Shyama Prasad Mookerjee in the Calcutta Suburbs seat by 10,216 to 346.[43]

What Sarat Bose called 'the debacle' came in the Muslim constituencies.[44] The Muslim League swept all six and beat the nationalist Muslim candidates as badly as the Congress had humiliated the Hindu Mahasabha. This was strong evidence of the popular backing that the Muslim League had achieved during the latter years of the war. The polarization of Hindus and Muslims had grown and a popular Muslim party of any weight independent of the League no longer existed. The Congress tried to help in the central and then provincial legislative elections, but the Muslim League was now *the* power among the Muslim voters of Bengal. Fazlul Huq won a seat in the provincial assembly, but the Krishak Praja Party was almost non-existent otherwise. Huq, seeing the writing on the wall, once again applied to join the Muslim League.[45] The elections for the Bengal Legislative Assembly also demonstrated the polarization: the Muslim League won 113 out of 121 total Muslim seats; the Congress won a great majority of the non-Muslim seats.[46] One prominent Congress leader of that period, S.M. Ghosh, maintained that the League's success was due to the power of its *goondas* rather than to the popularity of its program.[47] However, the League captured 2,036,775 out of 2,434,100 Muslim votes for the Bengal legislature and it is hard to believe that the *goonda* factor was so large. The shift of prominent Krishak Praja Party leaders and the student community to the League and the determined canvasing by Suhrawardy and Abul Hashim were much more important factors.[48]

The Muslim League had fought the election on the basis of its Pakistan platform and protection of Muslim interests and rights. Hashim, general secretary of the League and a kind of Islamic socialist, had put forth his views in 'Let Us Go to War'. In his memoirs he mentions that he had help from communist ideologues, particularly a young man named Nikhil Chakravartti, in drawing up the program.[49] Because of the socialist elements, Nazimuddin suspected Hashim of being a communist wolf in Islamic sheep's clothing. Hashim, the key man in bringing Suhrawardy and the League to victory in Bengal in 1945 and 1946, wrote of the latter:

> Mr Suhrawardy had no affinity with my ideology. On one occasion he said, 'Hashim, I don't appreciate your insistence on ideology. Ideology had never been of any use to me in public life.' On another occasion he said, 'Hashim, you are fortunate. You believe in some ideology but I believe in none.' Exigencies of power politics was the guiding principle of Mr Suhrawardy's political decisions.[50]

Such was the man who became the new chief minister of Bengal in 1946, according to his second-in-command, who defends Suhrawardy vehemently against many charges in his memoirs. Suhrawardy had impressive intellectual and political credentials: he had graduated with honors from Oxford and been called to the bar from Gray's Inn; he had been deputy mayor of Calcutta under C.R. Das and associated with the Swarajists; he had writing, debating, and administrative abilities. But he was too eager for power, used communalism for this end when necessary, and was drawn by no high ideals.[51]

With his election to the Central Legislative Assembly, Sarat Bose had to arrange to spend part of the following year in New Delhi. But before he left for Delhi and the Assembly session, there was a happy family matter to conclude. The betrothal of his and Biva's daughter, Gita, to Amalendu Biswas had been arranged while Sarat Bose was still imprisoned. He was delighted that his release in September allowed him to be present at the wedding in December. Numerous Congress notables including Sardar Patel, Sarojini Naidu, and Jawaharlal Nehru attended. It was the first time that Jawaharlal Nehru stayed at Woodburn Park since the controversy at Tripuri in 1939. Gandhi saw Gita and gave her and her family his best wishes, but declined to attend the wedding. He had developed a rule to attend only weddings of those from different castes and communities.[52] Since Sarat Bose's older brother Satish had no daughters, he gave the bride away. Gita was twenty-three and had had the higher education denied to her older sister Meera, who had been married at seventeen, a more usual marriage for high-caste Bengali girls.[53] Under pressure from Subhas, Sarat Bose had changed his ideas about women and higher education.

By the middle of January, Sarat Bose left for New Delhi to take up his duties there as leader of the Congress Party in the Central Assembly. This was a step up from his leadership of the Congress and the opposition in the Bengal Legislative Assembly from 1937 to 1941. This position enabled him to use his political and negotiating skills as well as his speaking talent in the service of his party and his country. Bhulabhai Desai, who had ably led the Congress in the Central Assembly in prior years and defended the INA officers, was in deteriorating health. He died on May 6, 1946. Sarat Bose was a worthy replacement for him.

Although the Central Assembly did not have vital business to legislate in the waning days of the British Raj and the more significant focus was outside this arena, the debates gave Sarat Bose an opportunity to present his vision of free India. This vision was implicitly and explicitly contained in his speeches on a variety of issues which he confronted between late January and early April. On the domestic side, he attacked 'police raj': the failure to release all political prisoners and remaining INA men, and the use of the intelligence branch to spy on Indian leaders. One feature of Sarat Bose's vision was that of basic constitutional freedoms for all citizens, impossible under foreign rule. The budget debate gave him a chance to criticize excess spending for the police and the military. In reference to the latter, he said that India could no longer afford to pay for an army of occupation at extravagant prices. A second aspect of his view of a future India was one in which the nation's resources were used to meet the basic needs of the people rather than for law and order charges.

On January 30, 1946 he made an interesting speech on the issue of food. First, he described how the British government at home had provided subsidized basic foods for the population during the war. Then he linked this action to the inaction in India, suggesting,

> In spite of the fact that food subsidy has played a most important role in the production of more food in England and in stabilising the prices there, no approach even to this question has been made by the Government of India. It is well known that large sections of the population are not able to buy even the ration of rice that is allowed. There is no reason why the Government of India should not follow the same policy as England and buy at least the foodgrains—rice, wheat and millets—at remunerative prices from the growers and sell them at reduced prices to the consumers . . . if money can be found to finance the war, surely money can be found to finance the feeding of the people.[54]

At the conclusion of his speech, he put forward a list of concrete proposals for permanent government intervention in the feeding of the Indian populace, for increased use of 'science and technology to grow and produce more food', and for determined efforts by Indian representatives abroad to see that India got her share from the 'world pool of foodstuffs'. He pointed out that the Government of Great Britain made sure that its people ate well, but the Government of India failed to work as doggedly for its people. Until there was a national government, he said, the resolve would not be there. On the issues of the sterling balances and other budget issues, he argued for a free and socialist India as the only solution, or the only beginning of a solution, to India's difficult problems.[55]

IV

In mid-1946 Sarat Bose made a brief visit to Burma. His primary object was to help civilians who had helped the INA and whom the British had decided to put on trial.[56] He had made an earlier trip to see his brother Subhas in Mandalay Jail in April 1925. Now Sarat Bose was greeted warmly by Aung San, who had met Subhas Bose frequently during the war. Aung San mentioned the common cause of the Boses and himself of opposing British imperialism and promised Sarat Bose his cooperation. In fact, Aung San helped in the dismissal of the cases against the Indian civilians.

For his part, Sarat Bose thanked Aung San and also spoke of their common cause of ending British rule. He said that he was glad to learn of the wartime cooperation of Indian and Burmese patriots. In the course of his remarks, he made a Biblical reference, typical for him, unusual for Indian nationalists:

> I feel confident that Indians and Burmese are fully determined to work for, to suffer for and if necessary to die for their freedom. Their blood has been spilled in their struggle for freedom. In the Bible, it is said that the blood of the martyr is the seed of the church. With a slight alteration, I may say that the blood of the martyr is the seed of freedom. The united determination of both countries cannot be resisted by the British government. . . . Let us march together, stage by stage, to the goal of freedom.[57]

Then he went on to talk of the immediate need for freedom and its aftermath:

> We must get, first of all, our freedom, our independence. The only 'ism' that we must have is Nationalism, strong and ardent Nationalism. When we are free, our endeavour should be to build up socialist States in India and Burma. We must also have an Asiatic Federation. In China, Sun Yat Sen talked about it. . . . In India Deshbandhu C.R. Das talked about it. Of course, the time is not yet ripe for an Asiatic Federation, but we must keep it in view.[58]

In closing, he asked Indians in Burma, particularly the Indian business community, to fully identify with Burmese aspirations. He was trying to approach the touchy problem of Burmese antipathies to the Indians in Burma which Subhas Bose had also been concerned with during the war.

V

While Sarat Bose was busy in New Delhi and later visiting Burma, a new Bengal ministry formed and then set to work in Calcutta. An internal struggle had been going on for several years within the Muslim League between Suhrawardy and his backers, against Nazimuddin and his supporters. Jinnah and Liaquat Ali Khan favored Nazimuddin, but could not intervene to direct Bengal affairs. Suhrawardy gained control of the Muslim League parliamentary board in Bengal and had a dominant role in naming the new cabinet. It does not appear that there were serious discussions at this point about a coalition involving the League and the Congress. Suhrawardy named a Muslim League cabinet with only three Hindus in it, two of them Scheduled Caste men, and none an important leader of Bengali Hindus.[59] During February 1946, Bengal had a new governor as well. He was Sir Frederick Burrows, a Laborite from the railwaymen's union. Burrows came out to replace Lord Casey, a firmer and more experienced administrator, at a crucial time of conflict and change in Bengal.

A month or so after Burrows arrived, a more important trio of British leaders, the Cabinet Mission including Sir Stafford Cripps, Lord Pentinck-Lawrence, and Lord Alexander, called the 'three wise men' or 'magi', reached India to try to sort out the question of India's constitutional advance to self-government. In line with the Labour goverment's desire to transfer power to Indian hands, they had to determine when, how, and to which hands power was to be transferred. They saw themselves as friends of India, as conciliators embodying 'the British passion for compromise'.[60]

One salient feature of the Mission and subsequent political and constitutional discussions from the Bengal point of view is that during all these talks in 1946 and then again in 1947, no Bengali leader was an insider or important figure in them. Although Sarat Bose was shortly added to the Congress Working Committee, there was no Bengali among the leading spokesmen of either the Congress or the Muslim League.

From his position outside the negotiations, Sarat Bose issued a number of statements to the press in March and April 1946. He insisted that India wanted complete independence and doubted that dominion status would give this. On the possible division of provinces, he said, '. . . if any proposals are made in future for the dissection of the Punjab or of Bengal they will be strenuously resisted. There is absolutely no case for dissection. . .'[61] In the Central Assembly and outside he made the case against Pakistan. But he did see the Congress line first put forth by Rajagopalachari and then Gandhi that if the right of secession or self-determination was to be given to provinces, then the Hindu population of Bengal and Punjab had to be given a chance to register their views.[62] What Sarat Bose spoke in favor of was a large measure of provincial autonomy within independent India and mutual tolerance between communities in the 'INA spirit'.[63]

The complicated negotiations of the Cabinet Mission with Muslim League and Congress leaders cannot be explored at length here. The thrust of the repeated statements both in the UK and by the Cabinet Mission in India was that they desired an orderly transfer of power to a united, federated India. The Cabinet Mission (and the viceroy), with the British Cabinet behind them, may have been trying to bridge the unbridgeable. One writer on these events, H.V. Hodson, has noted, 'It was a clash of Pakistan-plus against Unity-minus.'[64] The Muslim League wanted, or argued for a large, six-province Pakistan, but might accept a minimal federal government to which Pakistan and Hindustan would delegate a few of their powers. The Congress wanted a strong central government which would delegate some of its powers to the provinces.

The Mission listened to position statements from many leaders, several of which indicated the many different meanings of and rationales for Pakistan. From a Pakistan supporter from a Muslim minority area, they learned of the hostage theory: Muslims left in India would be protected when there was a sovereign Pakistan because Hindus remaining in Pakistan would be fellow hostages. The practical British spokesmen, at that point, found Pakistan in any version politically unacceptable (because the Congress and all other groups aside from the Muslim League were against it) and an administrative nightmare.

When Jinnah, for the League, rejected a small Pakistan (five provinces, but with Bengal and Punjab partitioned) and said, 'Pakistan without Calcutta would be like asking a man to live without his heart,' the Cabinet Mission was led to issue its own award: the famous three-tier plan.[65] Under the plan, there were three levels: the provinces; the groups of provinces: (a) Madras, Bombay, UP, Bihar, CP, and Orissa; (b) Punjab, NWFP, Sind, and Baluchistan; (c) Bengal and Assam; and, finally, the Union. These three groups of provinces were to draw up constitutions and to participate in the union constitution-making process. Within the groups there was to be majority voting until the constitution-making process was complete.

The Mission plan made clear its antipathy to 'Pakistan'. Moore has given a lucid summary of the anti-Pakistan features of the plan and of the implications which the Congress and Muslim League read into it:

> The name Pakistan and the concept of 'sovereignty' were suppressed, parity was withdrawn, the Muslim provinces were split into two groups . . . the creation of 'groups' became dependent on the wish of the provinces . . . the Union was accorded power to raise revenue, any appearance of compulsory grouping was avoided by referring to the provinces being convened in constitution-making 'sections', and no provision for secession from the Union was made. . . . The period finally proposed as the interval before the constitution could be revised was ten years. Yet Jinnah and the League were, in due course, to accept the statement in order to work for Pakistan within its boundaries. On the other hand Congress were never to accept the temporary suspension of provincial autonomy pending the making of group constitutions by sections.[66]

The League agreed to grouping in sections which was compulsory and provinces or parts thereof could not opt out before the constitution-making process by the section. To the Congress, this grouping in sections was not compulsory and so Assam and perhaps other provinces could opt out of their sections immediately upon their meeting.[67] Although the Congress formally agreed to the final Cabinet Mission plan, Nehru cast serious doubt on the Congress commitment by asserting in July 1946 that once the constituent assembly met, it could do what it liked. This implied to Jinnah and the League that the Congress had agreed to the plan simply as a step towards Hindu-majority rule which would follow the British transfer of power to an Indian constitution-making body.

To many, the whole Cabinet Mission plan was a logical, but unworkable scheme. Prime Minister Attlee wrote to the Mission, on May 8, 1946, 'The conception of a centre with very limited powers, which is nevertheless responsible for minorities, seems to us open to criticism.'[68] A staff member of the Mission wrote to his superior at the India Office:

> The Mission are firmly opposed to real Pakistan in the sense of separate sovereignty. . . . As far as I know, a three tier system is quite an innovation in constitutional science and it is going to be infernally complicated. But it seems the only way out of the difficulty and therefore we can only hope that they will agree to get down to an attempt to work it out.[69]

The Congress and the Muslim League accepted this 'infernally complicated' plan. But as R.J. Moore has persuasively argued, it was only 'the illusion of an agreement'.[70] The Congress and the Muslim League had conflicting interpretations of the agreement which generated bitterness, particularly on the League side. Besides the long-range three-tier plan, there was an immediate effort by Viceroy Wavell to form an Interim

Government with Congress and Muslim League participation. At first only the League agreed to this. Wavell, seemingly belying his word that he would take in ministers of whichever party or parties accepted the proposal, refused to form the Interim Government without the Congress. By early August, Jinnah had a double grievance: the disagreement on the meaning of grouping and Nehru's statement about an all-powerful constituent assembly; and what he saw as the viceroy's duplicity on the question of forming the Interim Government. The drift seemed to be going against 'Pakistan'. Jinnah decided to move in a different direction.

For the first time in its history, the Muslim League adopted a resolution calling for 'direct action'. What the League meant by 'direct action' was ambiguous and when Jinnah was asked whether the action was to be violent or non-violent, he said, 'I am not going to discuss ethics.'[71] The League then announced that August 16, 1946, would be 'Direct Action Day'. The Suhrawardy ministry moved to make that day a public holiday, although the Hindus strenuously objected. Former chief minister Nazimuddin announced on August 11:

> Our plans have not yet been finalized. There are one hundred ways in which we can create difficulties, especially when we are not restricted to non-violence. The Muslim population of Bengal know very well what 'direct action' would mean, and so we do not need to bother to give them any lead.[72]

An even more inflammatory statement was published in a pamphlet under the name of S.N. Usman, mayor of Calcutta and secretary of the Calcutta Muslim League, which read in part,

> The call to the revolt comes to us from the Quaid-e-Azam. This is the policy for the nation of heroes. . . . The day for an open fight which is the greatest desire of the Muslim nation has arrived. . . . By fighting you will go to heaven in this holy war. . . . Let us all cry our victory to Pakistan, victory to the Muslim Nation and victory to the army which has declared jehad.[73]

Although there had been tensions and demonstrations in Calcutta over the years, there had not been a serious communal riot since 1926. The demonstrations in the civil disobedience period and then during the 1942 Quit India movement and the 1945–46 massive rallies for the INA had not pitted one community against the other. Indeed, Hindus, Sikhs, and Muslims had joined to support the INA.

Now things were different. The Muslims, though less than thirty per cent of the Calcutta population, but fifty-four per cent in Bengal as a whole and in control of the ministry, wanted to show that they controlled Calcutta and Bengal. Richard Lambert, who carefully investigated this period a few years later and had access to police and government files, has suggested that Suhrawardy planned to have a large demonstration with 'occasional outbreaks of violence which would be quickly controlled by the police.'[74]

However, with all communities arming—some buying wartime American weapons on the black market—and extremist political organizations and *goondas* preparing for a showdown, such events could not be controlled. Furthermore, under the Suhrawardy regime, up-country Muslims had been brought in to increase the Muslim percentage in the police. The law-and-order forces, including the police and even the army, could not be counted on to be non-communal. On the Hindu side, the Hindu Mahasabha circulated handbills asking the Hindus to break the Muslim League-declared *hartal*.[75] Kiron S. Roy, the Congress leader in the Bengal Assembly, also told the Hindus not to observe the *hartal*. A leader of the small Sikh community of Calcutta said that if there was rioting, the Sikhs would support the Congress and 'give the Muslims a good thrashing'.[76]

What followed was not wanted by anyone. Muslims returning from the huge meeting in central Calcutta began to attack Hindu shops. The violence escalated on August 16 into the worst communal riot in the history of Calcutta. The police were at hand on the main streets, but they often appeared passive in the face of brutal attacks by one side on the other. The army was ready, but Governor Burrows toured the streets and decided they were not needed. What neither the police nor later the army could deal with were cowardly murders and attacks in the small lanes and by-ways of the city. The police and later the army might sweep through a main thoroughfare and break up a conflict, leaving an apparently peaceful scene. A few moments later dead bodies would be thrown from side streets out into the main streets. The rioting lasted for four days, but isolated incidents continued for months.[77] As Lambert puts it, 'Every section of the city became a battleground or a fortress.'[78] No area and no section of the population was spared. The fire brigades had to deal with many more Hindu properties than Muslim and the hospitals admitted more Hindu than Muslim casualties. Both sides suffered grievously, but the Hindus may have had the worst of it.[79] The carnage could not be estimated accurately. By most accounts at least 5,000 people died, likely many more, during those four days. The wounded were at least five times the number killed. In north Calcutta, Tuker noted, '. . . many were horribly mutilated'.[80]

The army and local defense organizations which were quickly formed helped to bring the rioting under control. Political leaders from the two major communities including Sarat Bose walked the streets. Sarat Bose met the governor four times within a few days and Bose also telephoned the viceroy to insist that military patrols be continued even after the fourth day of rioting.[81] The leaders called for an end to the shameful work of hatred and death which had shaken the ground of Calcutta and broken the remaining trust between communities.

Sarat Bose was grieved but also angry about the conduct of the ministry and of the British governor. In a statement of August 20, 1946, he said, in part,

> . . . the Governor has completely failed in the discharge of his special responsibilities to maintain law and order in the city. Whether it is due to utter incompetency or to surrendering himself completely into the hands of the Bengal Ministry, it is difficult for me to say . . . the Governor has proved himself unfit . . . the Governor should be recalled and the present Ministry should be dismissed. . . . The Governor's tours, conducted by the Ministry which has been responsible for the present state of things have little or no use. What has been done is to show the Governor large numbers of Muslim dead bodies. But he has been given no idea of the mass massacre of Hindus. . . . What has happened in Calcutta will be very useful to British imperialists and reactionaries in carrying on their propaganda that India is not fit to govern itself.[82]

Sarat Bose called for the resignation of the Muslim League ministry and the formation of an all-party government. Neither the Congress nor the Muslim League national leadership would have supported this. Sarat Bose thought that Hindus and Muslims together had to run Bengal. But many Congressmen and the Hindu Mahasabha were determined to blame the Muslims. Once the situation was calmer, the Congress Party in the Legislative Assembly brought a no-confidence motion in against the Suhrawardy government. The chief minister was given a good share of the blame from many quarters. For example, Subimal Dutt, a Bengali ICS officer then, thought Suhrawardy 'unscrupulous' and has testified that the government only presented a facade of impartiality. Sir Arthur Dash, a very senior British ICS officer, labeled Suhrawardy a 'truculent communalist', and thought he justly deserved some responsibility for the terrible riot.[83] General Tuker said that Suhrawardy was 'more critical than helpful' during the riots.[84] Though he was at police headquarters just after serious rioting had begun, he seems to have simply watched the proceedings and not attempted to stop what he had helped to start. Many participants in the events of that time whom I have interviewed have seen in the Great Calcutta Killing a watershed. After this, many Hindus would never agree to live under a Muslim League government, in free Pakistan, or in united, independent Bengal, or in a free federated India.[85] As the Muslim majority in the Bengal Assembly beat back the Congress no-confidence motion against the ministry, much of the Hindu community grew more alienated from the Muslims, and communal identification became one's primary identity.[86] Sarat Bose stayed true to his faith that cooperation between communities was the only path which could save Bengal and India.

It was within this context of increasing bitterness and alienation that Lord Wavell went forward with his plans to install the Interim Government. Only the Congress was agreeable to join in August. It had gotten Wavell to drop an earlier requirement that there be parity between the Congress and the League in the cabinet. The Congress nominated a slate of ministers which included Sarat Bose.

At first, the viceroy objected to Sarat Bose because of the INA and Japanese connections. The Congress was insistent. Finally, the viceroy gave way and Sarat Bose was included in the list announced on August 24, 1946, which also included Jawaharlal Nehru, Sardar Patel, Rajendra Prasad, C. Rajagopalachari, Asaf Ali, John Mathai, Baldev Singh, Shafaat Ahmed Khan, Jagjivan Ram, Syed Ali Zaheer, and Coverji Hormusji Bhabha. They replaced the previous members of the Viceroy's Executive Council and took office on September 2. Sarat Bose was named minister for works, mines, and power.[87] The viceroy still wanted a government including the Muslim League and left the door open to them if they changed their minds.

Sarat Bose was a minister for just about six weeks, but he took his job seriously. He started to look at future planning for mines and power and their development in a free, and hopefully, socialist India. He told family members that he was aghast at the widespread corruption in the Government of India, and was moving to combat this stigma, when he was asked for his resignation in mid-October.[88] This was to allow Muslim League members to join the Interim Government. Some Congressmen had to leave and he dutifully submitted his resignation. S.M. Ghosh, a leader of the Bengal Congress, said years later that Sarat Bose made a mistake in so readily giving up his post.[89] But Sarat Bose remained a member of the Working Committee of the Congress and was elected to the Constituent Assembly.

The problem for Sarat Bose and other concerned Indian leaders in the fall of 1946 was not what positions they did or did not hold, but the spreading communal violence. From Calcutta in August, the focus of the dreadful carnage moved to Noakhali District in East Bengal. What General Tuker and later analysts have insisted is that a carefully planned attack by a Muslim force on the small Hindu minority was systematically carried out.[90] In the rural areas where one community often greatly outnumbered the other, when there was violence it became a pogrom.[91] The Hindus were nearly defenseless. Leaders of Hindu resistance were killed, some were forcibly converted to Islam, including some Hindu women whose marriages and lives were broken.

Coming on the heels of the Muslim League's 'Direct Action Day' which had resulted in thousands of deaths, this new strike in a Muslim area

brought charges from Hindu leaders, particularly Shyama Prasad
Mookerjee of the Hindu Mahasabha, that there was a concerted plot to
destroy the Hindus of Bengal. Congress leaders made strong
condemnation of the events in Noakhali which some believed were a 'trial
run in the creation of Pakistan'.[92] Gandhi wrote in *Harijan* that 'the battle
of India was being fought in East Bengal.'[93] These events and the
Mahasabha and Congress responses to them sharpened the communal
antipathies of Bengali Hindus, many of whom felt that they had been losing
ground since the unfair Communal Award of 1932. Amidst the rising
violence, it was difficult for a tolerant, reasonable voice like that of Sarat
Bose to make itself heard. As the voice of Sarat Bose became harder to
hear, that of Shyama Prasad Mookerjee's became sharper and louder. The
latter was even a Congress nominee to the Constituent Assembly.

In late November and early December, Sarat Bose made a tour of
Noakhali and Tippera to see the results of the devastation there and to talk
to survivors. As in the case of Calcutta, he blamed the local and regional
officials of the Bengal government and demanded the removal of those
who were not determined to put down violence. But he was pessimistic that
government action alone could or would solve such problems. He called
for the formation of volunteer organizations to resist communal conflict:

> I have also advocated the formation of volunteer corps in each and every
> district of Bengal and . . . I took steps to form volunteer corps in some
> districts. . . . Such volunteer corps should be drawn from all communities
> and sections of the people and they should be above communal and party
> considerations. . . . Our volunteer corps should be inspired by the ideal and
> the spirit of the I.N.A. . . .[94]

He went on to praise Gandhi for working for communal harmony in his
own way. However, he severely criticized the Bengal Congress for its
inaction and for its '. . . policy of keeping out tried and active workers'.[95]
He meant that those in charge of the Congress organization did not want
the Forward Bloc and the Bengal Volunteers to move back in and take
control of the organization. Jyotish Joarder, a leader of the BV, claimed
that they had 12,000 volunteers in East Bengal by early 1947 promoting
communal reconciliation.[96] But the Forward Bloc itself had split into
Marxist and non-Marxist sections which severely weakened it.[97]

Sarat Bose and the Forward Bloc continued the effort to have a political
orientation that overarched communal identifications. Sarat Bose was
unhappy that 'peaceful and sober elements among the Muslims' failed to
control other Muslims who were attacking Hindus.[98] But this did not lead
him into stereotyping all Muslims. He said, 'I shall admit that the
disturbances which began from the 16th August have made a large number

of Hindus think in communal terms. But I believe it is only a passing phase.'[99] Although he did not think 'in communal terms', he was too sanguine about many of his fellow Hindus. He was also too ingenuous in thinking that preaching socialism and freedom to the masses of Bengalis would turn back the rushing tide of communalism.

From Noakhali, the communal spark set off new violence in Bihar. This time the majority Hindus slaughtered the minority Muslims. The Bihari Hindus believed that they were avenging their fellow Hindus in East Bengal. Then the torch was passed on to UP and the Punjab. With so many areas aflame it became difficult for even the army to quell the violence.[100]

While violence was spreading at the grassroots, deadlock became the password of the Interim Government once the Muslim League joined. The Congress had been forced to give the League at least one important portfolio and Liaquat Ali Khan became finance minister. From this post, he made the operation of the Interim Government a nightmare for the Congress. Nehru and Patel began to ask themselves if life without the League might be easier. If they were to try to lead a federal government with reduced powers, would they be able to govern at all in combination with the Muslim League?

The long-range and short-term policies of the Attlee government and the viceroy were stalled. The Constituent Assembly met, but the Muslim League did not attend. The League and Congress members of the Interim Government were increasingly at loggerheads. Wavell's latest proposal, prepared and communicated secretly to London, was the so-called 'scuttle' scheme for phased British withdrawal from India without an agreement between the main parties. This was totally unacceptable to the British Cabinet.

In a new effort, Indian party leaders were invited to London so that they might meet the India Committee of the Cabinet face-to-face. At first the Congress declined to attend. But finally Nehru agreed and he went along with Baldev Singh for the Sikhs, Jinnah and Liaquat Ali Khan for the Muslim League. No progress to speak of was made.[101] The British government issued a statement on December 6, 1946, giving their interpretation of grouping:

> The Cabinet Mission have throughout maintained the view that the decisions of the Sections should, in the absence of agreement to the contrary, be taken by simple majority vote of the representatives in the Sections. This view has been accepted by the Muslim League, but the Congress have put forward a different view. They have asserted that the true meaning of the Statement . . . is that the Provinces have a right to decide both as to grouping and as to their own constitution. . . . On the matter immediately in dispute

His Majesty's Government urge the Congress to accept the view of the Cabinet Mission. . .[102]

The Congress would not give in and the stalemate continued. The Cabinet was unhappy at the failure of their previous approaches and began to search for a new approach and a new viceroy.

VI

The British Cabinet was not alone in its unhappiness with the situation at the end of December 1946. Sarat Bose changed the direction of his political efforts. He felt the need to break with the Congress and explain why it was not helping to bring freedom with unity for India and Bengal. At a meeting of the AICC on January 6, a motion was passed to ratify the Working Committee's acceptance of the British government view of the procedure to be followed in the sections in the Constituent Assembly. This seemed to disregard provincial autonomy and give a simple majority control in the sections.[103] To Sarat Bose, this was the last straw. He resigned from the Congress Working Committee. He said in his statements of January 6, 1947:

> I was opposed to the acceptance of the Cabinet Mission's proposals and in fact, the decision of mine was the only voice in the Congress Working Committee raised against their acceptance. . . . I have served on the Working Committee in spite of serious differences with my colleagues since May last. . . . The resolution drafted by the Working Committee stultifies the Congress, makes the Constituent Assembly a subservient body, irreparably destroys the integrity of India and actually compels provinces to accept grouping against their will and to surrender provincial autonomy while giving them misleading assurances that no compulsion or interference is involved and that provincial autonomy will remain intact.[104]

He insisted that the Congress must resist the December 6 British government interpretation of grouping and feared that statement would lead Jinnah and the Muslim League to continue to boycott the Constituent Assembly. He went on, 'Mr Jinnah wants to have his "Pakistan" by merely sitting quiet.'[105]

Sarat Bose had been in ill health before his resignation, but the trend of events and the fear of Congress concessions was troubling him as well. No one seemed concerned with the need for provincial autonomy that he felt to be vital. Through all these negotiations, Sarat Bose, though a first-rank Congressman, leader of the Congress in the Central Assembly, and even, for a while, a central government minister, had felt excluded. He was not alone in this feeling. Even Gandhi, super-president of the Congress, was not as close to developments as he once was. Gandhi kept calling for communal harmony, but with little impact on the course of events and even on Congress policy.[106] Sarat Bose, for his part, surely saw that no Bengali voice was among the inner circle of Congressmen. Though Nehru and Patel were as devoted to the Congress ideals as Sarat Bose and Gandhi, they were also the top ministers in a government stalled in its working. As pragmatic politicians, this disturbed them greatly. Patel, in exasperation at one point, asked the League ministers to resign if they could not work with the rest of the Interim Government team.

On January 30, Sarat Bose announced the formation of the Azad Hind Party at a meeting of INA personnel and others in Calcutta. It listed many noble objectives including the complete independence of India, the establishment 'in this country of a Union of Socialist Republics', a common language for India, equality of the sexes, 'sovereignty and freedom of development . . . guaranteed to all the cultural and linguistic groups of India', religious freedom, etc.[107] Although some personnel from the INA and from the BV and Forward Bloc continued to work closely with Sarat Bose through this difficult time, the number was relatively small. He did not have a significant political base. The troops were, as they had long been, with the Congress, and Sarat Bose was now seeking to work separately from the main Congress organization.

VII

Through the months of no progress in late 1946, the Attlee government was groping for a new line. They decided the present viceroy, a military man, about whom many politicians at home had doubts, had run his course. They finally set a terminal date for British withdrawal for June 1948 and selected a new viceroy, Lord Mountbatten. After much discussion, they issued their policy statement of February 20, 1947, which read in part:

> His Majesty's Government desire to hand over their responsibility to authorities established by a constitution approved by all parties in India in accordance with the Cabinet Mission's plan, but unfortunately there is at present no clear prospect that such a constitution and such authorities will emerge. The present state of uncertainty is fraught with danger and cannot be indefinitely prolonged. His Majesty's Government wish to make it clear that it is their definite intention to take the necessary steps to effect the transference of power into responsible Indian hands by a date not later than June 1948.[108]

The political deadlock, the frightening communal riots, the growing ineffectiveness, indeed, communal corruption, of the police, fears about the future of British and Commonwealth economic and defense interests in the region, brought the Attlee government to this route to the transfer of power.

The statement made it explicit that whether there was to be one or more new sovereign governments to be worked out by Mountbatten in consultation with Indian political leaders and through public opinion in India expressed in a variety of possible ways, such as plebiscites or votes of legislative assemblies.

In response, the Hindu Mahasabha started a new campaign in February 1947 led by Shyama Prasad Mookerjee. Mookerjee was the son of the eminent educationist Sir Ashutosh Mookerjee, had had his own education at Calcutta University and then been called to the bar at Lincoln's Inn. He did not practise as a lawyer, but became vice-chancellor of Calcutta University in 1934. By that time, he had entered the Bengal Legislative Council first as a Congressman, and later as an independent. In the late 1930s, he came under the influence of V.D. Savarkar and by 1939, Mookerjee became acting president of the Hindu Mahasabha. In 1941 he took Sarat Bose's place as the leading Hindu in Fazlul Huq's Progressive Coalition Ministry. An excellent debater and forthright speaker, he saw India as a Hindu nation and political community. The Congress view of diversity, of many communities sharing the stage, was not his. He was more narrowly focused on the fate of his people, the Hindus.[109]

While welcoming the February 20 announcement, Mookerjee warned:

> We shall demand with one voice that the transfer of power must be made to a strong Central Government in respect of the whole of British India. Hindus will resist with their life blood any scheme of the perpetuation of slavery which will be inevitable if Bengal, as she is constituted and administered today, is allowed to become a separate independent unit cut off from the rest of India. Nothing can justify the transfer of nearly 35 millions of persons belonging to one community to the perpetual domination of an artificial majority which refuses to identify itself with the rising aspirations of the entire people.[110]

Although the Mahasabha was still against Pakistan, or 'vivisection' of the fatherland, and for a strong central government, they now wanted the division of Bengal into a Hindu-majority West Bengal and a Muslim-majority East Bengal. Bengal Hindus would have at least one part of Bengal they could control, either in a federated India or if part of Bengal was detached to make a Bengali wing of Pakistan. Through the early months of 1947, the Hindu Mahasabha carried on a strong, vocal campaign for a Bengali Hindu homeland, matching Jinnah's cry of 'Islam in danger!' with one of 'sacred Hindustan and Hindus in danger!' Mookerjee put it this way in a statement of March 19:

> Partition of Bengal alone will offer a peaceful solution of the grave communal problem confronting the province. This will give the two major communities in Bengal full freedom to develop their own culture and tradition in the areas where they are in predominant numbers; both are sure

to recognize soon that it will be to their mutual interest to guarantee full protection to the respective minorities in the two (proposed) provinces.[111] S.P. Mookerjee soon won the majority of the Bengal Congress and Bengal Hindu representatives in the central and provincial legislative assemblies to his side. While continually condemning the wickedness of the idea of Pakistan, the Mahasabha and Congress allies were using a parallel argument calling for the partition of Bengal (and the Punjab) whether there was an overall partition of India or not. They were virtually admitting the two-nation theory of Jinnah. There is a connecting line from the views of Rajagopalachari during the war, to Mookerjee and the Congress in 1947: if Pakistan is to be conceded, then the arrangement must be such that the largest number of non-Muslims be given the opportunity to remain in India. S.M. Ghosh, a top Congress leader from East Bengal, maintained that S.P. Mookerjee was saying privately: let us divide now and let the British leave. Later we will take over the whole territory.[112] Mookerjee also believed that the division of Bengal would provide a double-hostage arrangement. This would give the Hindus of West Bengal and India leverage to protect their brethren in East Bengal and Pakistan.

The Congress Working Committee passed a resolution in early March recommending division of the Punjab and Bengal. Although not yet fully armed with any alternative except to preserve the unity of India, Sarat Bose said on March 15:

> By accepting religion as the sole basis of the distribution of provinces, the Congress has cut itself away from its natural moorings and has almost undone the work it has been doing for the last 60 years. The resolution . . . is the result of a defeatist mentality. A sort of fear complex seems to have worked havoc in the minds of many of us . . . . Even if the provinces were to be so divided, Hindus and Muslims will still have to live side by side in them and the risk of communal conflicts will remain. Supposing we divide Bengal and the Punjab on the basis of religion, what about the Muslims in Western Bengal and the Hindus in Eastern Bengal or about the Muslims in Eastern Punjab and the Hindus and Sikhs in Western Punjab?. . . The resolution of the Congress . . . pushed to its logical conclusion would mean the creation of such religious states or pockets and the result would be that the risk of armed communal conflicts . . . would increase hundredfold . . . it will mean pushing her [*India*] back into the medieval ages. . . . An over-hasty surgical cure will involve us in confusion and disaster.[113]

Sarat Bose may well have been right about the 'defeatist mentality' and 'fear complex' but his was a minority voice.

VIII

Mountbatten arrived in New Delhi on March 22 to assume his duties as the last viceroy and governor-general. He was related to the royal family, not only of Britain, but to all the former ruling dynasties of pre-First World War Europe, and had commanded Allied forces in Southeast Asia during the latter part of the Second World War. He was well acquainted with India and, though coming from a military background like Wavell, was a more worldly, charming, and assertive personality. His political sentiments were in tune with the Labour Party even though his genes were aristocratic. He came out to India to do a job: transfer power to the most appropriate party or parties by a specific date. Many including the retiring viceroy told him that the task was impossible. Mountbatten was shrewd, practical, confident. He was forty-seven years old and had taken on tough assignments before. He had had setbacks, but never failed. Not only was he determined to succeed, but he brought out- a press officer, Alan Campbell-Johnson, to tell the world how brilliantly the Raj's last viceroy was succeeding. Mountbatten displayed great administrative skills, diplomacy, and an authoritarian streak, all of which he needed to cope with the horrific political mess which he faced.[114]

He plunged into a series of meetings with the most important political leaders, concentrating at first on Gandhi and Jinnah, and then Nehru. Gradually, he (and his wife Edwina) moved closer to Nehru and a special rapport developed which helped Mountbatten in working out the eventual partition plan.[115] Although Mountbatten met briefly with Nazimuddin, Suhrawardy, and Kiron Sankar Roy, the foremost leaders of Bengal, these three and also Sarat Bose, were hardly consulted as the negotiations went forward. Mountbatten wanted to hear many views, but, in the end, wanted to deal with those who could 'deliver the goods' for the Indian National Congress and the All-India Muslim League. A Congress–League accord was foremost in his mind. When other proposals (such as for Bengal) were put before him, he said, 'If you can't get support, don't waste my time.'[116] Mountbatten excluded Sarat Bose because he had some residual bitterness against the Boses for the sin of the INA. The viceroy said, 'I hated Subhas; he brought together the dregs of Indians in his army.'[117]

Mountbatten later said that he drove Jinnah 'crazy' with the view that if India had to be divided, then Bengal and the Punjab would have to be divided as part of such a settlement.[118] But Jinnah also infuriated Mountbatten, for the viceroy would have preferred handing over power to only one new government. Mountbatten wrote in his April 17 report, 'I regard Jinnah as a psychopathic case; in fact until I had met him I would not have thought it possible that a man with such a complete lack of administrative knowledge or sense of responsibility could achieve or hold down so powerful a position.'[119] He also began to meet the other leaders, but Jinnah's insistence that 'Pakistan' was the only solution led Mountbatten to the tentative conclusion, only a month or so into his tenure, that there would have to be a division. By late April the matter had virtually been decided. As he circulated a plan for partition, Mountbatten explained, for London's ears and eyes only, that it was not what he personally wanted:

> The more I look at the problem in India the more I realise that all this partition business is sheer madness and is going to reduce the economic efficiency of the whole country immeasurably. No one would ever induce me to agree to it were it not for this fantastic communal madness that has seized everybody and leaves no other course open.[120]

The Unionist government in the Punjab fell in March and then as the governor dickered with Muslim League leaders about forming a League government there, first demonstrations and then rioting began. Sporadic violence again started up in Calcutta in March and April. There was nothing yet to match the 'Great Calcutta Killing' of August 1946, but the incidents were widespread and disturbing. Master Tara Singh, the Akali leader, said at Lahore on March 12, 'Punjab is drifting towards a Civil War.' Insisting that the fault lay with Muslim League aggression, he said that the Sikhs would not be intimidated and he would not join in an appeal for peace. The League, he maintained, should halt its violence first.[121] With such intransigence as shown by Jinnah, the Hindu Mahasabha, and the Sikhs, more conciliatory suggestions such as those made by Gandhi, Sarat Bose, and even Mountbatten, made little progress.

Mountbatten listened to proposals in April 1947 from Suhrawardy, Kiron Sankar Roy, and Bengal governor Burrows for an independent Bengal. Burrows wanted to ensure that Calcutta remained as a premier port of India and he suggested that some kind of international arrangement be made for it. This did not suit Mountbatten who thought it would be a serious blow to his developing plan for partition. The viceroy summoned Burrows to New Delhi and told him that an internationalized Calcutta did not fit into his scheme. He told Burrows that he had to take an all-India view and merely provincial concerns such as the economic complications of the jute trade were secondary. Burrows had to accept this and drop his scheme.[122] Suhrawardy met Mountbatten on April 26, and said that Bengal would remain united. He indicated that Jinnah was willing to accept an independent, united Bengal.[123] Mountbatten listened, but said that Suhrawardy and any other proposers of such plans must demonstrate that their proposal had wide backing, or it would have to be dropped.

In his original scheme for division, which Moore has called 'Plan Balkan,' Mountbatten thought that a united Bengal was a live possibility and he sketched out the voting procedure by which this might be achieved:

> Whereas it was my original intention to have one straight vote taken on a single day by all the Bengal members of the Constituent Assembly on the issue of 'partition or unity' and that only if unity were decided upon would a further vote be taken on whether they wished to be independent or go to Pakistan or Hindustan; my new proposal is that there should be provision for a preliminary vote in Bengal (and therefore of course also in the Punjab) by all the Provincial members of the Constituent Assembly to decide whether on the assumption that the Province remains unified, they want to be independent or to join Pakistan or Hindustan. A week or a fortnight later another vote will be taken to decide whether they want partition or not, in the light of this.[124]

Later in the same report, he said, 'I have no doubt myself that unity is necessary for Bengal; for if the Province is divided, eastern Bengal even with Sylhet will be an uneconomic entity which is bound gradually to fail, and cannot receive any help from the rest of Pakistan.'[125] Up to the end of April and into early May, the door was still open for the possibility of united Bengal to enter. Each for their own reasons, Mountbatten, Suhrawardy, and Sarat Bose thought positively about it.

Suhrawardy had been under fire since the Calcutta riots, not only from Hindus, but from Muslims. Jinnah was said not to trust him and Liaquat Ali Khan to dislike him intensely.[126] But he had good reason to want a united Bengal: he was a West Bengal man, based in Calcutta, with some trade union backing. Where would he be in a 'Pakistan' composed of a west-wing and an east-wing formed out of predominantly rural East Bengal districts? An ambitious man, his main chance was a united Bengal including Calcutta. But such a scheme needed the firm backing of Jinnah for the League, and the Hindu community of Bengal. Only Kiron Sankar Roy, another East Bengal man, and Sarat Bose were willing to work with him on this. A waggish contemporary said of the plan for United Bengal: 'This plan has two authors—one has no past, Shaheed Suhrawardy, the other has no future, Sarat Chandra Bose. Their commodity has, therefore, no market.'[127] As discussions of United Bengal went forward, there were frequent and malicious attacks on Sarat Bose and the other protagonist, including threats of physical violence.

Suhrawardy returned from his meeting with Mountbatten and held a press conference in Calcutta on April 27, 1947. He appealed to the Hindus of Bengal and said,

> Undivided Bengal would be a great country, the richest and the most prosperous in India, capable of giving to its people a high standard of living,

where a great people will be able to rise to the fullest height of their stature, a land that will be truly plentiful ... is it not possible to evolve a system of government by all of us sitting together which will satisfy all sections of the people and we would revive the glory and splendour that was Bengal? I would go very, very far indeed to meet the wishes of the Hindus of Bengal, if they would only accept the principle of a sovereign, undivided Bengal..... I can assure them the future is not going to be like the present.[128]

Press questioners passed over this bit of hyperbole, and tried to pin Suhrawardy down on what relationship such a sovereign Bengal would have to Pakistan of which he previously had been a supporter. What promises had he and Mr Jinnah exchanged? He was asked: if Hindus and Muslims can live together in one Bengal, then why can't they remain in one, united India? His answers were evasive.[129] As the discussions went forward, Suhrawardy and others met with Gandhi. Although British officials felt that Suhrawardy had moderated his views since the catastrophe of the previous August, Gandhi found Suhrawardy quite an irresponsible person, and this did not help.[130]

Shyama Prasad Mookerjee argued with both Suhrawardy and Sarat Bose, who was associated with the proposal. Mookerjee said, 'Suhrawardy's picture of the paradise to come is hardly comparable to the hell that now exists in Bengal.'[131] Mookerjee and many other Hindus felt that Suhrawardy's plan was only a ruse to try to bring all of Bengal into Pakistan as part of a deal with Jinnah. Mathur has argued, correctly, that there was no evidence of widespread support from any quarter for Suhrawardy's plan.[132]

Sarat Bose was also meeting with Abul Hashim, secretary of the Muslim League. The pace of their talks did not match with that of Mountbatten's steps to find a solution to the all-India questions involved in the transfer of power. During the first half of May, while the Bose-Hashim talks were going on—with others including Jinnah, Suhrawardy, and Gandhi, as well as many provincial politicians being consulted— Mountbatten took Nehru away with him to Simla for a few days to show him the draft of 'Plan Balkan' which had been sent to London.[133]

Angered and confused at this plan, Nehru wrote, it was sure to bring 'fragmentation and conflict and disorder.'[134] With the help of V.P. Menon, constitutional adviser and pipeline to the Congress, Mountbatten had the plan redrafted into 'Plan Partition', a much more satisfactory proposal from the Congress high command's point of view. In Plan Balkan, Bengal and the Punjab would have had the independence option and this implied that other areas, such as the NWFP and some of the larger princely states might have had it as well. In Plan Partition, several areas, including provinces and parts of two provinces would be given the opportunity to opt out of the union of India and form 'Pakistan'. The new plan had the backing of Nehru and Patel and thus the All-India Congress. It meant the death knell of United Bengal unless extraordinary and powerful backing for this alternative was to come from the main Hindu and Muslim leaders of Bengal and then be accepted by the all India organizations.

While Mountbatten took the new plan off to London, Sarat Bose and Abul Hashim, who had been talking privately since the fall of 1946, finally formulated a proposal for a free state of Bengal.[135] When a draft was submitted to the press on May 22, Sarat Bose mentioned that he had been in ill health for six months and this had hampered his effort to press forward on this matter. The proposal stated that Bengal was to be a free state and would decide for itself its relations to the rest of India; there would be joint electorates; a new coalition ministry would be formed in Bengal with an equal number of Hindus and Muslims and, for the time being, there would be equality in the services; and it specified the formation of a constituent assembly of thirty members (sixteen Muslims; fourteen non-Muslims). There were a few more details about voting for the legislative assembly to ensure that both major communities expressed their preferences. The following day, Sarat Bose further indicated that the signers wanted Bengal to be a completely free, socialist republic and said that socialism must be preached to combat communalism.[136]

The presenters of this proposal—including some Congress and Muslim League leaders besides Sarat Bose and Abul Hashim—realized that powerful support was needed if it was to float and they immediately reached out to Gandhi, to Jinnah, and to the Congress high command. At first Gandhi offered encouragement and wrote to Sarat Bose on May 24:

> I have your note. There is nothing in the draft stipulating that nothing will be done by mere majority. Every act of Government must carry with it the cooperation of at least two-thirds of the Hindu members in the Executive and the Legislature. There should be an admission that Bengal has common culture and common mother tongue—Bengali. Make sure that the Central Muslim League approved of the proposal notwithstanding reports to the contrary. If your presence is necessary in Delhi I shall telephone or telegraph. I propose to discuss the draft with the Working Committee.[137]

There was also some encouragement from Jinnah, but the coalition of Congress and Hindu Mahasabha members in Bengal was against it and it met a stone wall in the person of Sardar Patel. The latter wrote to Sarat Bose the same day the plan was announced, trying to get Bose to join the Congress-Mahasabha team:

> I'm sorry to find that you have isolated yourself so completely from all-India politics and even in provincial politics you have not kept in touch with

us. In these critical times, we cannot afford to be standoffish and must pool our resources and take a united stand. Vital matters which will leave their mark on generations to come have to be settled, and in such settlement it behooves all of us to contribute our best to the combined strength of the Congress.[138]

Sarat Bose tried to convert Patel to his view of Indian and Bengal unity. On May 27, he wrote to Patel:

Today the position is that communal frenzy is not the monopoly of the Muslim Leaguers; it has also overtaken large sections of Hindus, both Congressites and Mahasabhaites. The Congress stand had been taken advantage of ... to inflame communal passions further. It has also brought back the Hindu Mahasabha to life ... I consider it most unfortunate that the Congress Working Committee conceded Pakistan and supported partition. It is true that I have not been able to address public meetings yet for reasons of health; but having been in close touch with public opinion in West and East Bengal, I can say that it is not a fact that Bengali Hindus unanimously demand partition. As far as East Bengal is concerned, there is not the slightest doubt that the overwhelming majority of Hindus there are opposed to partition. As regards West Bengal, the agitation for partition has gained ground because ... communal passions have been roused among the Hindus on account of the happenings since August last. The demand for partition is more or less confined to the middle classes. When the full implications of partition are realised and when people here find that all they will get for Western Bengal province will be roughly one-third of the area of Bengal and only about half of the total Hindu population in Bengal, the agitation for partition will surely lose support. I entirely agree with you that we should take a united stand; but I shall say at the same time that the united stand should be for a united Bengal and a united India. Future generations will, I am afraid, condemn us for conceding division of India and supporting partition of Bengal and the Punjab.[139]

If one uses the evidence of the Congress files, which contain numerous letters from East Bengal Hindus calling for partition, then Patel was right and Sarat Bose was indeed isolated.[140] But Sarat Bose was also right: the middle classes in West Bengal were the main propagators of the partition idea and the Mahasabha was calling the tune. And he was correct in suggesting that the partition would not solve the communal problem. But Sarat Bose's ideas did not gain wide currency or backing. He held no public meetings and is said to have been blacked out of the Congress press. He worked only on the top political level with a few Congress and League leaders, though the Bengal Volunteers and Forward Bloc did constitute a small and firm base for him.

A few other voices, with little support in the major communities, were raised against the division of Bengal. J.N. Mandal, Scheduled Caste leader and law member of the Interim Government (nominated by the Muslim League) said that the communal trouble would not be resolved by partition. 'It was,' he said, 'not in the interests of the Hindus to divide, and the Scheduled Castes were definitely opposed to the idea.' He insisted that the Hindus of East Bengal would lose all their property and be forced to migrate, so they should reconsider their support for partition.[141] But Mandal had little backing among the Scheduled Castes in Bengal, most of whose Assembly members were Congressmen.

The *Statesman*, a European voice amidst a chorus of Indian nationalists and Muslim Leaguers, also decried the likely division of Bengal in an editorial entitled 'Twilight of Bengal,' on April 24, commenting, in part,

> Extremists have the upper hand. . . . Politically-minded Hindus, though they could probably even now get seats in the Cabinet for the asking, have become so embittered that nothing less than the division of the province will content them. During ten weeks or so, the movement for repartition of Bengal has grown from a cloud no bigger than a man's hand into a storm which blows over all the province and outside its borders, though the centre remains Calcutta. Fostered initially by the Hindu Mahasabha, which has not lost its influence with its seats in the Legislatures, it received strong impetus from the . . . Congress Working Committee's resolution of March 8 on partition of the Punjab. It has now been taken over by the Provincial Congress Committee, which demands regional ministries . . . . What is needed . . . is . . . enlightened collaboration between leaders of all communities to restore peace. . . . Bengal which once led the struggle for liberty and made its own union the token thereof, is plunging backwards, forging its own fetters of mutual suspicion and misery. Too few recognize the tragedy—to the extent . . . of doing anything practical to arrest it.[142]

Sarat Bose and Hashim continued in their efforts into June but the veto by Nehru and Patel was crucial as was the pro-partition coalition forged by Shyama Prasad Mookerjee. Gandhi, Jinnah, and Mountbatten—for their different reasons—moved toward and then backed away from the United Bengal plan. A widely-noted survey of Hindu public opinion by the *Amrita Bazar Patrika* in early May found that an overwhelming majority, ninety-seven per cent, supported partition. Their findings were presented in an article, 'Homeland for Bengali Hindus.'[143]

IX

Mountbatten returned from London at the end of May. He did present Nehru and the Congress leadership with one last opportunity to preserve the unity of Bengal. Nehru said that the Congress was only willing to have Bengal remain united if it stayed within the Indian Union. Since the Muslim League would not find this acceptable, Bengal, given the likely vote of its legislative assembly, would be divided.[144]

The viceroy pressed ahead to gain acceptance for Plan Partition as approved in London and he achieved this by the time of the public broadcast to the nation on its future on June 3, 1947. Jinnah would get his Pakistan, but it would almost certainly be the moth-eaten, truncated one he despised, for the Hindus of West Bengal and the Hindus and Sikhs of East Punjab would certainly vote to remain in India. The Legislative Assemblies of the two provinces were not to be allowed to vote for an independent Bengal or independent Punjab option. The choices were the present Constituent Assembly (India) or the new one (Pakistan). Mountbatten, following Nehru on this, said, 'I could not allow the Balkanization of India.'[145] When Mountbatten, following a suggestion of Suhrawardy, asked Patel if Calcutta could remain under joint control for six months after partition, Patel replied to the messenger, V.P. Menon, 'Not even for six hours.'[146]

The June 3 statement by His Majesty's Government on Indian policy said that the British desire had been to transfer power in accord 'with the wishes of the Indian people themselves.'[147] Since an accord for a united India had not been forthcoming, the British put forth Plan Partition. The rules for voting procedures in the Bengal and the Punjab Legislative Assemblies were:

> The Provincial Legislative Assemblies of Bengal and the Punjab (excluding the European members) will therefore each be asked to meet in two parts one representing the Muslim majority districts and the other the rest of the Province. . . . The members of the two parts of each Legislative Assembly sitting separately will be empowered to vote whether or not the Province should be partitioned. If a simple majority of either party decided in favour of partition, division will take place and arrangements will be made accordingly.[148]

Following the presentation of this plan and its acceptance, as already worked out by Mountbatten, each of the major leaders for the Congress, Muslim League, and the Sikhs, spoke on All-India Radio recommending the plan. Jinnah was most evasive. Nehru, eloquent as usual on such occasions, said, in part:

> It is with no joy in my heart that I commend these proposals to you, though I have no doubt in my mind that this is the right course. For generations we have dreamt and struggled for a free and independent united India. The proposals to allow certain parts to secede, if they so will, is painful for any of us to contemplate. Nevertheless, I am convinced that our present decision is the right one. . . . The united India that we have laboured for was not one of compulsion and coercion, but a free and willing association of a free people. It may be that in this way we shall reach that united India sooner than

> otherwise and that she will have a stronger and more secure
> foundation. . . . I have no doubt that we are ushering in a period of greatness
> for India.[149]

Nehru and Patel had been firm that there had to be only two dominions
issuing forth from the womb of British India. They carried the Congress,
the Hindu community, and then the viceroy and his government with them
on this point.

Sarat Bose made one last try. He wrote to the leaders of the Muslim
League and Congress, requesting that they instruct their representatives in
the Legislative Assemblies to vote against partition. Of course, since the
Muslim League wanted all of Bengal and the Punjab, they would vote
against partition and for the whole province joining the new constituent
assembly, i.e., Pakistan. The Bengal Hindu members were the crucial
voters. Sarat Bose requested that they be given freedom to vote as they
wished, i.e., not be dictated to by a party decision. The Congress high
command was against this and further, it probably did not make any
difference. These members were going to vote for partition because that is
what they wanted.

At the same time there were rumors of bribery: that the Muslim League
was paying for Hindu legislators to vote against partition. Sarat Bose's
effort was tainted by these rumors. Even Gandhi believed them. He wrote
to Sarat Bose on June 8:

> I have now discussed the scheme roughly with Pandit Nehru and then
> Sardar. Both of them are dead against the proposal and they are of opinion
> that it is merely a trick for dividing Hindus and Scheduled Caste leaders.
> With them it is not merely a suspicion but almost a conviction. They also feel
> that money is being lavishly expended in order to secure Scheduled Caste
> votes. If such is the case, you should give up the struggle at least at present.
> For the unity purchased by corrupt practices would be worse than a frank
> partition, it being a recognition of the established division of hearts and the
> unfortunate experiences of the Hindus. I also see that there is no prospect of
> transfer of power outside the two parts of India.[150]

Gandhi's letter and a reference to corrupt practices in his evening prayer
address brought a furious telegram followed by a letter from Sarat Bose,
who demanded an open inquiry instead of snide gossip. 'If information
false, punish informants, if information true, punish bribe-givers and
bribe-takers.'[151] Gandhi was not prepared to conduct an inquiry and he
simply tried to calm Sarat Babu and have him, however unwillingly,
accept that most Hindus and the Congress had agreed to partition.

Sarat Bose may have run out of practical avenues, but his faith
remained. He wrote to Gandhi on June 14:

I can say definitely and emphatically that there was nothing in the nature of trickery . . . the feeling or suspicion that money is being expended to secure Scheduled Caste votes is entirely baseless.

My faith remains unshaken and I propose to work in my own humble way for the unity of Bengal. Even after the raging and tearing campaign that has been carried on in favour of partition, I have not the slightest doubt that if a referendum were taken, the Hindus of Bengal by a large majority would vote against partition. The voice of Bengal has been stifled for the moment but I have every hope that it will assert itself.[152]

In addition to his pleas to party leaders, Sarat Bose also issued several statements to the press on the Mountbatten Plan on June 5 and 8, 1947. He believed that dominion status offered less than complete independence and he was firmly against accepting it. He said, in part:

HMG's India Plan has dealt a staggering blow to the cause of Indian unity and independence—a blow from which we may not be able to recover for many years . . . instead of accelerating our pace towards the goal of freedom, it makes its attainment more difficult. What has surprised me most is that those who were until recently most vehement in demanding that India should remain one and undivided should have so readily supported division of India and even partition of provinces.[153]

He continued to maintain that if Bengal Hindus could freely vote, they would reject partition. However,

Bengal's voice has to be stifled and she has to continue to be a pawn in the all-India game . . . if Bengal is rent in twain, the two Provinces of Bengal will be exploited more and more by exploiters, white and brown. The Bengali Hindu and the Bengali Muslim will become quill-drivers of those exploiters.[154]

He returned to his vision of a free, socialist republic run by a coalition of the two communities, since this was *his* vision.

X

The June 3 plan included the 'necessity for speed'.[155] And Mountbatten meant to adhere to this. August 15, 1947 was fixed as the date for the transfer of power and the Bengal and Punjab Legislative Assemblies were to vote on June 20 on the partition issue. In Bengal, the members met jointly and then in West Bengal and East Bengal groups. At the joint session ninety voted to join the existing Constituent Assembly (i.e., stay with India), while 126 voted to join the new constituent assembly (i.e., join Pakistan). The vote was almost wholly along communal lines with these exceptions: J.C. Gupta, a Congress leader was out of the country and did not vote; Fazlul Huq deliberately absented himself from the meeting and did not vote; Maulana Shamsul Huda, a Muslim member from

Mymensingh, and Rup Narayan Roy, a Scheduled Caste member from Dinajpur, did not vote; four Scheduled Caste members from East Bengal voted with the Muslims; and two well-known communists, Jyoti Basu, the present chief minister of West Bengal, and Ratanlal Brahmin, a labor leader from Darjeeling, did not vote.[156]

Then the members divided into two groups. The maharajah of Burdwan presided over the meeting of members from the non-Muslim majority areas. They voted for partition fifty-eight to twenty-one. On this vote Jyoti Basu and Ratanlal Brahmin joined the other Hindu members and voted for partition. In the meeting of members from the Muslim majority areas, presided over by Nurul Amin, the delegates voted against partition by 106 to thirty-five. Again four Scheduled Caste members voted with the Muslim majority and Fazlul Huq did not appear. Thus the Congress-Mahasabha alliance successfully maneuvered to keep West Bengal as a Hindu-majority province within a divided India. The Hindu Bengalis had voted to split Bengal and remain part of a larger political entity, India. A united Bengal separate from Pakistan was not a choice. Even Sarat Bose's own brother, Satish Bose, who took his seat in the Assembly, and Kiron Sankar Roy voted for partition. In later years, Shyama Prasad Mookerjee used to brag, 'Congress partitioned India and I partitioned Bengal.'[157]

The responses were as might be expected. West Bengal and Calcutta Hindus were joyful, East Bengal Hindus were apprehensive, East Bengal Muslims were pleased, and West Bengal and Calcutta Muslims were unhappy. Some said that the Muslims of Calcutta would fight before they gave up the city, but forces of many kinds were arrayed against this possibility.[158]

Leaders as well as ordinary people had to make choices about their future places of residence. Suhrawardy contested the leadership of the Muslim League for East Bengal and was beaten by Nazimuddin. Suhrawardy rushed back to the West Bengal group and decided to remain, for the time being, in Calcutta. Abul Hashim, as well, decided not to shift from his ancestral home in Burdwan, and stayed in West Bengal and in the Assembly.

On the Hindu side, Kiron Sankar Roy was elected leader of the East Bengal Congress Assembly Party, but later decided to shift to Calcutta. S.M. Ghosh, from Mymensingh, tried to have the Congress continue as an organization covering all of Bengal regardless of the new international frontier that was shortly to be erected.[159] The Hindu Mahasabha, which had skillfully orchestrated the demand for partition of Bengal, now passed a resolution that declared, '... there will never be peace unless the separated areas are brought back into the Indian Union and made its integral parts.'

They said that the proposed allocation of territories was unjust to the non-Muslim groups and demanded additional compensation for them. Furthermore, they wanted Indian citizenship for East Bengal Hindus and nationalist Muslims. It was their belief that it was just a matter of time before East Bengal would be brought back into the Indian Union.[160] They decried the 'vivisection' of the country which they had contributed to so mightily, and attacked the Congress for agreeing to it, though they admitted that the June 3 plan probably had to be accepted.

On the practical side, there was the work of constructing two separate governments for Bengal. P.C. Ghosh was elected head of the Congress group and thus was to be the chief minister of the West Bengal province of the Indian Union from August 15. Jinnah interfered with the immediate formation of regional ministries for the two parts of Bengal as originally proposed by Mountbatten, but ministers without portfolio for West Bengal were sworn in and sat in cabinet meetings and had a veto over the application of measures affecting West Bengal. Mountbatten and the Congress were very annoyed with Jinnah over the road-blocks he placed in front of several practical moves and this led to similar restrictions on the formation of a Pakistan cabinet at the center.[161] Mountbatten formed a partition council at the center and parallel partition committees in Bengal and the Punjab. In addition, the most important work was undertaken by Lord Radcliffe as head of the two boundary commissions.[162]

As the division of the spoils went forward, some were exhilarated by the daunting prospects of dual new nationhood. Not Gandhi, who said to Mountbatten in June, that the latter had ruined his life's work.[163] Mountbatten, who had affection and respect for Gandhi, tried to calm him. When Gandhi was asked by Nirmal Kumar Bose in early August why he had not continued to struggle against the partition, Gandhi said,

> With whom was I going to carry on the fight? Don't you realize that, as a result of one year of communal riots, the people of India have all become communal? They can see nothing beyond the communal question. They are tired and frightened. The Congress has only represented this feeling of the whole nation. How can I then oppose it?[164]

Sarat Bose, who had rejoined the Congress mainstream in 1945 upon leaving prison, announced on August 1 that he had resigned from the Congress and formed the Socialist Republican Party. In his press statement, he said:

> The Indian struggle has entered on a new phase. The sufferings and sacrifices of the people during the last twenty years raised hopes in their minds that independence of India free from British influence and control was within their grasp. The acceptance of the June 3 Plan . . . has, for the time being, dashed those hopes . . . we have to-day a dismembered India and,

instead of independence, Dominion Status under British influence and patronage. . . . Why then have we failed? We have failed because of weakness and vacillation on the part of our leaders, we have failed because of anxiety on their part to accept compromises even on matters fundamental, we have failed because of their failure at all critical moments to give a bold correct lead to the country.[165]

He asked for members of all communities to forsake communalism and '. . . to undertake the work of reunifying the country on a socialist basis . . . "All power to the Indian people" shall be our battle cry, as it was the battle cry of Netaji.'[166]

On August 15, 1947, Sarat Bose sat in silence in his garden at Woodburn Park. Gandhi and he were among the few not celebrating on that day. Nehru announced that India had met her 'tryst with destiny' and Mountbatten wrote, 'The 15th August has certainly turned out to be the most remarkable and inspiring day of my life.'[167] All sides were indignant once the boundary awards were published and Mountbatten took this as a good rather than as a negative sign.[168]

XI

Had Sarat Bose and his colleagues failed just at the moment they seemed to be winning their greatest victory, the termination of British rule in India? Were there other choices, other paths that should have been taken?

Sarat Bose's view was somewhat different from that of the other all-India leaders of the Congress and the Muslim League. He was a Bengali as well as an Indian; in Bengal the two communities were more even in their distribution than in the all-India picture. He could not, even with partition, give up the ideal of one Bengal. It seemed to him that simply by making an international boundary, the problems of the relations of the two communities would not be resolved. Hindus were likely to remain in large numbers in East Bengal and Muslims in large numbers were likely to remain in West Bengal. So the dilemmas had been internationalized, made more complex, not dissolved.

He had remained consistent with what he took to be the Congress creed of one India composed of many communities and religious groupings. He felt the other leaders on the Hindu side had let him down. Gandhi went farthest along the no-division route with him, but even the Mahatma gave in to the communal fever that infected everyone.

August 15, 1947, however, did not mean the end, but a new beginning. As he put it, a new phase of the Indian struggle was now starting. Weary and ill in body, he drew mental and emotional sustenance from the work and determination of his departed brother. Sarat Bose determined to go on and follow his conscience in what he thought of as semi-free India and divided Bengal.

CHAPTER THIRTEEN

Divided Bengal and Independent India: Hard Realities and Soft Myths

If I tell the people Netaji is dead, they will kill me.
Pradip Sen, an ordinary Bengali, 1964

And who am I to jeer at life-giving illusions? Is there any better way to pass these last days than in dreaming of a saviour with a sword who will scatter the enemy hosts and forgive us the errors that have been committed by others in our name and grant us a second chance to build our earthly paradise.
J.M. Coetzee, *Waiting for the Barbarians*[1]

This dawn that's marked and wounded. . .
It's not the dawn we expected
It's not the dawn we were looking for. . .
It's all changed, our leaders' struggling zeal;
celebration is the order of the day, mourning forbidden.
Yet anguish of the heart, unfulfilled desire,
nothing is cured by this false dawn. . .
This is not the moment of our freedom.
Keep moving, keep moving!
We have not arrived!
Faiz Ahmed Faiz, 'Freedom's Dawn'[2]

I

With partition came communal riots, even massacres, throughout the late summer and fall of 1947. For the moment, Calcutta and the rest of Bengal were largely spared. Lord Mountbatten had sent most of his 55,000-strong boundary force to the Punjab. With no more troops at his disposal as August 15 neared, Mountbatten asked Gandhi to go to Calcutta. Gandhi's calming presence was severely tested in this period and the Mahatma, teamed with Suhrawardy (for his influence over the Muslim community), had to resort to a fast-unto-death to stop serious rioting. The incidents were halted, many weapons were turned in to the authorities, and Gandhi's 'miracle of Calcutta' is remembered as a moral victory for the Gandhian way.[3]

Calcutta and West Bengal, though spared extensive bloodshed, were beset by a host of problems, as was the new nation of India. Sarat Bose's prophecy that West Bengal would be only a fraction of united Bengal was relatively accurate, but the new state had several more districts than he had suggested. West Bengal was now one of the smallest states of the Indian Union, but densely populated. Where once Bengal had had clout in all-India matters, now it had little.[4]

The first chief minister of West Bengal was P.C. Ghosh, a devoted Gandhian, who had frequently been a member of the Congress Working Committee. The Bengal Congress remained riven by factionalism and there was considerable dissatisfaction with Ghosh. He had hardly warmed the chief minister's seat before he was displaced by Dr B.C. Roy in January 1948. Although not a Gandhian in quite the same way that Ghosh was—the one hundred per cent khadi-type—Dr Roy had long been a physician for, and confidant of Gandhi, and had gained the trust of Nehru and Patel. Once an ally of the Boses, Dr Roy and the Boses had drifted apart. He had cooperated with Sarat Bose in running the 1936–37 elections, but they had never been close again and Dr Roy's participation in political developments from the late 1930s to independence had been intermittent.

Dr Roy had the firm backing of the Hooghly group in the Congress led by Atulya Ghosh, with the support of P.C. Sen. West Bengal men like Ghosh now had more weight in the Congress and East Bengal men like S.M. Ghosh, head of the so-called Jugantar group, had less. Dr Roy concentrated on the serious administrative, economic, and social problems of West Bengal and turned over the management of Congress Party matters to Atulya Ghosh. Dr Roy also brought Nalini Ranjan Sarker back from Congress banishment and made him his deputy chief minister and finance minister. Sarker, like Dr Roy, was a confidant of Gandhi, but Sarker was also a prominent businessman, close to the Birla family. With the inclusion of Sarker, Dr Roy's ministry was immediately labeled a capitalist team by the Indian left. Not only was there a push away from the socialist agenda at the center, but in left-leaning West Bengal as well.[5]

The flood of refugees coming across the border from East Bengal, now Pakistan, led Dr Roy and his Congress colleagues at the center to strengthen the Congress cabinet in West Bengal and the Indian representation in Dacca. Kiron Sankar Roy, an East Bengali and a prominent Congressman for many years, had tried to work in East Bengal, but he was shortly persuaded by Dr Roy to join the West Bengal ministry as home minister. Santosh Basu, once a close associate of Sarat Bose, was asked to become deputy high commissioner for India in Dacca to deal with problems at that end.[6] Meanwhile, Shyama Prasad Mookerjee joined Nehru's cabinet at the center though he was not a Congressman. Nehru and Patel wanted someone from Bengal in their government. With Sarat Bose out of the Congress and in the opposition, the choice fell on S.P. Mookerjee, though this did not please the outgoing viceroy or the incoming prime minister of India.[7]

While many former colleagues now faced the onerous duties of office in the new nation of India, Sarat Bose, who had cut his ties with the Congress, was one of a growing number of vocal and active opposition members. Most of the Congress Socialist Party, including J.P. Narayan and R.M. Lohia, were outside and formed the Socialist Party. There were also several small leftist parties in West Bengal: the Revolutionary Socialist Party (RSP), the Revolutionary Communist Party of India (RCPI), the Bolshevik Party of India, and, by this time, two Forward Bloc parties, the Marxist Forward Bloc and the Subhasist Forward Bloc. They were later to be joined by other dissidents as some individuals and groups became frustrated and disillusioned with the fruits of independence.[8]

Though the communists from the CPI had been banished from the Congress in 1945 by Gandhi and the high command, the more moderate wing within the CPI remained favorably inclined to Nehru and thus to the Congress government at the time of independence. However, this honeymoon was very brief. The left faction led by B.T. Ranadive challenged P.C. Joshi and the Moderates and won control of the CPI. Following international pressures to move leftwards, the CPI shifted by the end of 1947 and early in 1948 to a violent, revolutionary line. Emboldened by the revolt in Telengana, Ranadive said, 'Telengana today means Communists and Communists mean Telengana.'[9] With the shift of the party to this left, or violent, line for attacking the Congress government, many communists had to go underground as the West Bengal government banned the party. Among those who went into hiding were Renu Chakravartti (Dr Roy's niece), her husband, Nikhil Chakravartti, and Jyoti Basu.[10]

There were many able and articulate people in the opposition, socialist and communist, functioning openly or secretly, using a variety of means, but they were unable to make any dent in the widespread Congress hold on the country. Yet the opposition was important to challenge the Congress to work purposefully towards the dreams Indians held while India was a subject nation.

II

Mobilizing what energies he had remaining—and he certainly hoped to go on for many years—Sarat Bose continued his legal work, but more importantly, in the period after independence, he became a sharp, critical voice expressing his views on regional, national, and international issues. He saw the need for a unified left to bring about an egalitarian, socialist India.

One of his first concerns was how the diminished Bengal, now West Bengal, might bring more of the Bengali-speaking population in India—presently in Bihar—back to the fold. He spoke forcefully for the rejoining of the Manbhum and Singhbhum districts and the Santhal Parganas with West Bengal, in the week after partition and during the months and years following. On one occasion, he wrote,

> The demand for the redistribution of boundaries on the linguistic basis is not a craze, nor a separatist tendency as Pandit Nehru would have us believe. It is a demand voiced long ago and reiterated since then with frequency, during the last four decades.[11]

He believed that the Congress high command, listening to its Bihari member, Rajendra Prasad, was stalling on this legitimate request. The coming of independence had forced every Indian to reconsider his or her identity. Sarat Bose, as a man of consistency and constancy, remained a Bengali who wanted the maximum number of Bengali-speakers in one political community. He would have been happiest to have East Bengal back with West Bengal. This hope seemed forever dead. But gaining back some districts which he thought had a majority of Bengali-speakers was not far-fetched.

The other Bengal issue with which he was concerned was, of course, the question of the flow of refugees across the border, particularly Hindus from East Bengal to Calcutta. Sarat Bose wrote in his newspaper, *The Nation,* on September 3, 1948, that the grave economic situation and the rising Muslim communalism in East Bengal was the impetus behind 'The Exodus'.[12] He had hoped that since the two Bengals still were one in his mind, a more positive relationship would be worked out.

Before India and Pakistan had been free from the Raj for thirteen months, two of the principal players in the game, each considered the father of his respective nation, was dead. Gandhi was assassinated in January 1948; Jinnah died of natural causes in September 1948. Sarat Bose had kind words for each, though they had not given him what he wanted of them: firm backing for a united and independent Bengal. Of Gandhi, he said,

> The Father of the nation is no more with us, and we who are orphaned seem
> to be moving in a sort of vacuum, paralysed by an overpowering sense of
> despair and frustration. . . . But the immortal spirit of Gandhiji is there to
> give us light and inspiration. . .[13]

And, somewhat later:

> . . . Gandhiji was against partition. I requested him again and again to assert
> himself and resist partition. . . . I clearly visualised that two things would
> happen immediately partition was effected. One was that the North-West
> Frontier Province would pass into the hands of the League. The next was that
> Kashmir would be swallowed up by Pakistan. Gandhiji was against partition
> but he did not agree with me that the two results I had mentioned to him
> would flow from it and he gave me his reasons for disagreeing with me.
> Towards the end of May, 1947, I came to Delhi and had discussions with
> Gandhiji and also with Mr Jinnah. I have not the slightest doubt myself that
> if the Congress leaders had displayed a certain amount of statesmanship, the
> partition of Bengal could have been prevented.[14]

Sarat Bose was also generous in his praise of Jinnah, whom he usually
opposed:

> By the death of Quaid-e-Azam . . . Jinnah the Muslim world has lost one of
> its greatest statesmen and Pakistan its life-giver, philosopher and guide. No
> one within living memory has done more to raise the stature of the Muslims
> of India than he . . . I have had my differences with him and sometimes they
> were very serious, I shall not refer to them now . . . in June 1947, he agreed,
> in his conversations with me in New Delhi, to Bengal remaining united and
> becoming independent with a Constituent Assembly of her own to decide
> to which union she would accede.[15]

During the first year of independence, Sarat Bose had made occasional
speeches and issued a few press statements. He held public meetings,
particularly about the issue of linguistic redistribution and realignment of
state boundaries, and some of these drew a thousand and more to them, but
these methods of communication did not reach many. To make a greater
impact, he decided that he had to start a newspaper. He had long been
unhappy with the Indian press, for he felt that first they ignored opposition
voices to the partition and then to the new Congress government. He talked
to many people. Some friends promised funds but did not deliver. To meet
the cost of the equipment, Sarat Bose took a bank loan and ran a deficit. On
September 1, 1948, after months of planning, *The Nation* was born. J.N.
Ghosh suspended his high court practice and became managing director of
the newspaper. Sarat Bose kept up his practice since the income was
essential, but he came from the high court to the paper's office to write
editorials. As Ghosh was distracted by the financial woes while trying to
do the editorial work, Sarat Bose told him that this would not do. Bose said

as he turned to write an editorial, 'If you want to do great things in life, you must learn to concentrate on the task at hand.' Once the paper got rolling, its circulation was about 15,000 to 20,000, and they could not print enough copies to meet the demand. The paper gained in popularity and became the first-class paper that Sarat Bose desired, but the financial problems remained. Nevertheless, it gave him a platform from which to present his views on a range of issues.[16]

In his prolegomena on September 1, 1948, Sarat Bose wrote:

> What does 'The Nation' stand for? It stands for the Complete Independence of India . . . free from British or any other foreign influence and control. . . . It believes that land in a free and liberated India must belong to the actual tillers of the soil and will work for the abolition of all intermediate interests . . . all our basic and key industries should belong to the community and be run and managed by the State. . . . It believes in complete equality of the sexes. . . . It will demand of the State that religious freedom, secular education and civil liberties should be guaranteed to all.[17]

He enlisted his late brother's name to talk of a synthesis of nationalism and socialism which he sought. He identified his concerns with those of the common man arguing that the state in 'the New India' should be their servant, not their master.

The theme of labor versus capital, the workers versus management, was one which Sarat had been hammering out before he established his paper. In his presidential address to the All-India Sugar Factory Workers' Conference a few months earlier, he had described how the new India, governed by the Congress Party, looked to him:

> It is indeed the same old story of bureaucratic administration run by I.C.S. officials . . . [*with*] the continuation of all the evils associated with the old regime—namely, corruption, jobbery, red-tapism, profiteering and black-marketing. . . . The principle of nationalization of basic and key industries which the Congress accepted seventeen years ago has been relegated to the background. . . . Pandit Nehru and his government . . . deliberately play into the hands of capitalists and betray the cause of labour.[18]

He thought that from the first day in office the Congress had forsaken the trust placed in it by India's workers and peasants, and that Congress Raj was really Birla Raj. He pointed to the gap between Nehru's socialist professions and the actualities of capitalist India.

On international issues as well, Sarat Bose had had differences from Nehru and those he referred to as 'fashionable internationalists'.[19] Before independence, Bose had pushed for breaking with the Commonwealth and he spoke of this again. The Commonwealth tie, he thought, sucked India into a de facto relationship with the 'Anglo-American' powers and prevented true independence and true neutrality in international affairs.[20]

Picking up a perspective which he thought had been started in India by C.R. Das, Bose presented the case for a united states of South Asia, or a united nations of Asia. He was much bolder than the Indian government or Nehru in arguing for Indian support for the Democratic Republic of Vietnam, a free Indonesia, and then recognition of the People's Republic of China. When Bose wanted to send direct assistance to the Vietnamese government of Ho Chi Minh, Nehru demurred that he did not want to antagonize the French.[21]

III

Early in September 1948, the Boses suffered another personal blow when Satish Bose, the oldest of Sarat's brothers died. He was a warm-hearted man who was missed by all. His death also left vacant his South Calcutta seat—once Sarat Bose's seat—in the West Bengal Legislative Assembly.

Late in 1948, Sarat Bose decided to take his wife and several of his children with him on a journey to Europe. He had not been to Europe since his student days in 1914, and wanted his family to see something of it. He also had another purpose. This was not explained to his daughters, Roma, then about twenty, and Chitra, then eighteen, who were traveling with their parents and their brother Sisir. When the family reached Prague, Sisir Bose said to his sisters, 'Father is calling you.' Sarat Bose said to them, 'We are going to meet someone in Vienna.' Roma asked, 'Rangakakababu?' (Subhas Bose) 'No,' Sarat Bose replied, 'not him, but his wife and daughter. They were married late in 1941. I have come to see them. It is the purpose of my visit.'[22]

On February 8, 1943, just before he left Germany for Southeast Asia, Subhas Bose had written a Bengali letter addressed to Sarat Bose which he gave to Emilie Schenkl. In it he said that she was his wife and Anita was his daughter and that if anything happened to him, Sarat Bose was to take care of them. After the war, Emilie Schenkl had resumed her work with the post office in Vienna and raised her daughter as best she could. She had written to Sarat Bose a few times and sent him photocopies of Subhas' 1943 letter, but he did not receive the first letters. Finally he did receive one and wrote to her in 1948 that he was coming to see her.[23]

The Bose family group arrived late at the Vienna airport. They finally met Emilie Schenkl at the city terminal. Roma found her '. . . very fair . . . [*with*] pink cheeks and sharp features. She was very good looking but short.'[24] Sarat and Biva went straight up to her and she said to Sarat Bose, 'I have been waiting for this day.' She produced the original of Subhas Bose's letter, which she handed to Sarat Bose, thinking to herself, 'It is he [*i.e., Subhas*] only advanced in years.' Then Emilie Schenkl and Sarat

Bose broke down and he embraced her. She said to him, 'Call me Mimi,' and he said to her, 'Call me "Mej-da".' She stayed with them at their hotel late into the night talking.[25]

The next morning she returned with Anita. They all concurred that there was a striking family resemblance. Seven-year-old Anita spoke little English, but she loved to spend time with her new-found relations. Sarat Bose spent ten days in Vienna and tried to persuade Emilie Schenkl to come back to Calcutta, but she refused. She was a European woman who then and always has liked her privacy.[26] But contact was now made and she and Anita were taken into the family circle. Emilie Schenkl and Sarat Bose had been tempted to believe that Subhas was not dead, but as time passed they gave up such hopes.[27] Nevertheless, she and Anita were now Boses.

While in Europe, the Sarat Bose party also visited Italy, Czechoslovakia, France, the United Kingdom, and Ireland.[28] Sisir Bose has further described his father's trip,

> ... the European sojourn ... fulfilled a desire that he had nursed for a long time to see something of the historical places of Europe and its culture. . . . Wherever he went he sought out Indian students. . . . He was particularly interested in meeting former members of the Free India Centre and the Indian Legion. . . . In Zurich he went up in a glider aircraft . . . and discussed possibilities of introducing glider training for young men and women in India . . . in Paris the General Assembly of the United Nations was meeting there. Father was very interested to hear Vyshinsky. . .[29]

In London, Sarat Bose addressed a meeting at the Conway Hall, presided over by Fenner Brockway, a friend of Indian freedom. They searched for the Hampstead house in which Sarat Bose had lived as a student, but it had been destroyed in the war.

The Bose party visited Dublin, strengthening the ties that Subhas Bose had forged in the 1930s on his visit. They met President Sean O'Kelly, Eamon de Valera, and Madame Maud Gonne McBride. Sarat Bose recalled to the latter that he had met her all too briefly in Paris during 1914 when she was already a famous Irish patriot. To the president, after their meeting, Sarat Bose wrote, congratulating him on 'the national recognition of the republic'. What the Indian leader surely had in mind was an Indian republic similarly detached from the Commonwealth and from any kind of allegiance to the Crown. While the rest of the party returned via Paris and Cairo to India, Sisir Bose remained in England for his studies.[30]

IV

In January 1949, Sarat Bose returned to India: to the high court bar, to *The Nation,* and to his chosen task of forging a united left. He chaired a meeting of leftist groups including his Socialist Republican Party, the Forward Bloc, and the Peasants' and Workers' Party of Maharashtra, in Bombay early in April. He urged the delegates to form a coordinating council to facilitate left unity.[31] Myron Weiner has summarized the fruits of their labor,

> . . . a Provisional Left Coordination Committee was appointed and resolutions were passed demanding that India declare itself a sovereign republic . . . that a new Constituent Assembly be elected on the basis of adult franchise, and that the country be administered on socialistic lines. Other resolutions called for land to the tiller . . . nationalization of key industries; organization of industries on socialistic lines; establishment of linguistic provinces; civil liberties; free education . . . the right to food and shelter; and abolition of blackmarketeering, profiteering, corruption, and nepotism.[32]

This was the line Sarat Bose had been advocating in *The Nation* and what some of the other small leftist parties desired. The problem for the left was not that they did not have large areas of agreement. Rather, it was that they had to learn—if this was possible—to cooperate and give up some of their party 'sovereignty' in order to make a viable left alternative.

Hardly had the meeting adjourned and Sarat Bose returned to Calcutta, when he suffered a heart attack. After consultation with physicians including his brother Sunil, Sarat Bose was strongly advised to go to a clinic in a healthy mountain climate, like that of Switzerland, for a curative rest. On May 16, he left again for Europe and headed for the Val-Mont, Clinique Medicale, Glion, Switzerland.

Before he left for Europe, the Government of West Bengal had announced the bye-election for the South Calcutta (General) constituency, which Sarat Bose and then his late brother had held. Seizing the opportunity to confront the Congress in an electoral contest, Sarat Bose declared his candidacy, even though he would not be able to fight the campaign in person. While the Socialist Party, the Revolutionary Socialist Party, the Bolshevik Party, the Revolutionary Communist Party, the Socialist Unity Center, the Forward Bloc (Subhasist and Marxist), and Bose's own Socialist Republican Party, all worked for him on the ground, all that Bose could do was to send his election manifesto to the voters from Glion.[33]

In a long list of rhetorical questions, he asked why he could not be tolerated by members of the Congress high command. Through these questions, he pointed out his differences with the Congress since the end of 1946. Then he turned to a more direct expository form of attack and said, in part,

The state machinery is being run by a handful of Capitalists. . . . The Press has been gagged, civil liberties of the people have been ruthlessly suppressed. . . . Inflation has not been checked, prices of the necessaries of life have been soaring higher and higher. . . . Several departments of the Government of West Bengal have become cesspools of nepotism, favouritism and corruption. . . . The province has been ruled by the 'lawless law' known as the West Bengal Security Act, which I have previously described as the 'concentrated essence of repressive legislations in British times'; and yet, not a single Congress legislator has demanded its repeal . . . it did not take me a minute to decide that I should contest the seat . . . . The very existence of West Bengal is at stake . . . . Friends, I look forward to the 12th June in the hope that you will reiterate your confidence in me by your votes.[34]

On June 14, the result was announced: Congress candidate Suresh Das polled 5,750 votes; Sarat Bose polled 19,300 votes.[35]

Dr Roy said graciously, 'I congratulate Shri Sarat Bose on his success and welcome him back to parliamentary life after he had been out of it for nearly two years or more.'[36] However, the Congress felt strongly negative reverberations from this defeat, as Saroj Chakrabarty has pointed out,

This defeat shook the very foundation of the Ministry and the Congress organisation in this province which almost went underground for months thereafter. . . . A storm was raging in the Congress circle in Delhi over the defeat of the Congress candidate . . . on July 16th an emergency session of the Congress Working Committee discussed for 2 1/2 hours the administrative and political problems of West Bengal.[37]

In an immediate and emotional response, Nehru said that Dr Roy should resign. The prime minister took the vote as a general condemnation of Dr Roy's ministry with which he had had some differences over center-state relations. Dr Roy objected to this reading of the results, though he did point out in a letter to the Working Committee some of the reasons why the voters felt aggrieved with the consequences of partition.[38]

On July 28, the Congress Working Committee passed a resolution recommending a general election in West Bengal within six months, reshuffling of the ministry, and reconstruction of the provincial Congress executive committee.[39] When this resolution was approved, Dr Roy was in Europe for a rest and Nalini Sarker was acting chief minister. After Dr Roy returned, he presented the West Bengal position as he understood it and wanted it, and the Working Committee backed away from its suggestions. S.M. Ghosh continued to lead an important group in the Bengal Congress executive, but Dr Roy and Atulya Ghosh remained in charge of the state and party.[40]

From his clinic in Switzerland, Sarat Bose had achieved one of his goals: he had shaken up the Congress and stimulated· them to consider, at the very least, why there was such a drop in their popularity in Calcutta as to allow him a resounding victory. After his three-year isolation by his Congress colleagues, he must have had some small measure of delight in this solid backing by the voters of South Calcutta.

Shortly after his heart attack, Sarat Bose wrote to his son Sisir, 'Please do not get anxious for me. I have many more years to live and work.'[41] But he knew a period of rest and recuperation was necessary. After a few weeks in Glion, on May 29, he wrote to Sisir in England that he would be permitted to take long walks, but must avoid climbing. Emilie Schenkl and Anita came to Switzerland to see him.·The former then wrote to Sisir Bose that he was just like Subhas: he would not go slowly just because the doctors told him to.[42]

On July 9, 1949, Sarat Bose flew to London to see a heart specialist. The London cardiologist gave him a positive report.[43] Then he returned to Switzerland and flew from Geneva, arriving in Bombay on July 23. He began a round of political meetings, opening the Karnataka Youth Conference on July 27, attending meetings in Poona and Bombay. Spurred on by his election victory, his main objective was that the steps towards the formation of the United Socialist Organization (USO), a true socialist alternative to the Congress, should go forward. He wrote to Sisir Bose that the Maharashtrian group was solidly behind him and that there were great displays of enthusiasm at the public and private meetings. Socialist unity, he hoped, would be achieved whether or not Jayaprakash's group (i.e., the Socialist Party) joined them. Even with this tiring round of meetings, he wrote to Sisir Bose, 'I am none the worse for the tour.'[44]

Sarat Bose and his wife returned to Calcutta from Bombay. On August 6, he held a press conference dealing primarily with regional and national issues. The status of basic freedoms in India was one focus:

> All the repressive legislations of the past are still there. In addition, we have Security Acts in every province; and one has only to read one of the Security Acts to be convinced that they are a complete negation of civil liberties.
>
> The Constitution as drafted is even worse than the Government of India Act, 1935. . . . The wide powers that are being conferred on the Provincial Authorities and the Central Authorities are bound to convert our so-called democratic state into a totalitarian state.[45]

He moved on to condemn Congress one-party rule, widespread corruption, and the failure to deal seriously with the question of linguistic provinces. He listed the program of a consolidated left and said that he expected a united socialist party would eventually evolve, but not overnight. In response to questions about the Communist Party of India, he said that

Indian communists had been suspect since the last war, and until 'suspicions' were removed, he doubted they could be admitted to a united socialist party.[46]

As he was beginning to settle into his routine in Calcutta, he was struck down again. Sisir Bose has described this period:

> . . . I learnt from mother's letters he was overworking himself. If anybody sought to warn him about the possible consequences of such reckless action he would say: 'I am a racing horse. I shall die galloping!' When mother cautioned him and asked him to go slow he would say: 'I cannot rest now, let Subhas return and then I shall retire.' (*'Subhas ele amar chhuti'*). He again suffered a major heart attack on 20th August 1949 while addressing a public meeting and thereafter he could not return to a fully active life.[47]

There was no Subhas to give him a vacation. But given his public mission of criticizing the government for its follies and shaping a viable political opposition, he did not intend to withdraw quietly from the field. He continued to write editorials for *The Nation* and invited delegates to a United Socialist Conference in Calcutta.

The conference had to be delayed due to his weakened state of health. From his bed, he wrote editorials about nepotism and corruption in Calcutta University and the necessity of recognizing Communist China immediately. His criticisms were to the point and he frequently noted the shortcomings of Prime Minister Nehru. Although Nehru and he had long cooperated and differed over two decades, Nehru was the special target of Bose's scorn in the post-independence period. The same age as Sarat Bose, the dashing colleague and rival of his younger brother for the support of the Indian left, Nehru had survived all the twists and turns of the nationalist period and ended up at the top. Sarat Bose must have thought that Nehru did not deserve the position and the accolades he received, for there is hardly a hint of praise amidst an avalanche of criticism.

On the international side, Bose was unhappy that Nehru believed that he was *the* expert on India's role and place in the world. Nehru, Bose believed, was gradually leading India into the capitalist camp, favoring the West and her Commonwealth partners at the expense of the Soviet Union, Communist China, and other new nations in Asia. For example, Sarat Bose wrote on October 16, 1949, in an editorial,

> Our Prime Minister has thrown off the mask of neutrality which he has been wearing since the 15th August 1947. He has succumbed to America's deft diplomacy. . . . Our Prime Minister has tried to raise a dust-storm by his platitudinous speech . . . he has practically acquiesced in British, French and Dutch Imperialism, and has not dared to raise his voice against the menace to freedom, or the threat to justice, or aggression in South Asian countries.[48]

Bose noted examples throughout Southeast Asia arguing that freedom movements in Indonesia, Vietnam, Malaya, and Hong Kong needed India's support. He exchanged telegrams with Mao Tse-tung on the occasion of the communist triumph, and tracing the British conquest of Hong Kong, said it was time for the British to depart and turn Hong Kong back to China, the new China.[49] Would the development of Indian-Chinese relations and the course of the Vietnam War been any different if Sarat Bose's approach had been followed rather than the cautious line of Nehru?

At the end of October, the long-delayed United Socialist Conference convened in Netaji Bhavan, Calcutta, and Sarat Bose presented his presidential address to the 200 representatives of the many leftist groups whom he had invited. It was his pre-partition idea that socialism was the only cure for communal fever and the division of the country, and he now diagnosed the Indian body politic as suffering from right-wing blunder-itis. First, he described the alliance he saw between the national bourgeoisie and semi-feudal elements in league with British imperialism. These had brought setbacks to basic freedoms and the movement towards a more egalitarian society, as corruption, nepotism, and profiteering flourished in the new India.

Then, he turned to his positive vision. He laid out the socialist program which Subhas Bose had come to in the late 1930s, adapted to a free India. Sarat Bose listed a lengthy number of objectives including nationalization of key industries, and especially those controlled by foreigners, basic freedoms, exit from the Commonwealth, free education for all, equality of the sexes, et al. A critical concern was how this multiplicity of small parties would work to form one powerful alternative to the Congress. He said, in part,

> I need hardly say that if I had considered it possible to bring about the immediate dissolution of all the existing Socialist, leftist and progressive parties and to form a United Socialist Party overnight, I would have recommended that step . . . there are some practical difficulties that way . . . beginning with a flash and ending in smoke has never appealed to me in my political career of nearly three decades. . . . I am recommending at this stage the formation of the United Socialist Congress with the firm hope that through common endeavour the existing . . . parties will gradually dissolve themselves and a United Socialist Party will evolve out of the United Socialist Congress.[50]

The gathering passed resolutions and formed a Provisional General Council with Sarat Bose as president. Sub-committees began work, and the Council sponsored some demonstrations. Following Bose's suggestion, Netaji's birthdate, January 23, 1950, was celebrated with mass rallies and meetings as 'Anti-Commonwealth Day' [51]

Sarat Bose's active participation in the Council's work was hampered by his health. In mid-November he was able to do drafting lying in bed, and by mid-December, he was working in his study for a few hours every morning. Then on December 23, 1949, he went to the bar library. He wrote to Sisir Bose in England, 'I liked the diversion. I expect to attend court regularly from the beginning of next year, but I shall not take much work.'[52]

His infirm body prevented him from attending the West Bengal Legislative Assembly, but not from attacking the actions of the government in power. During the second half of 1949 and the opening of 1950, one focus—long a paramount concern—was with the new constitution of India. As a barrister, a civil libertarian, and an Indian patriot, he wanted a constitution providing, *inter alia,* for basic freedoms and the sharing of power between the states and the center. On August 15, 1949, he wrote,

> On the anvil of a dull and docile Constituent Assembly . . . they are hammering out a Draft Constitution, which is the longest in size, the biggest in volume but the poorest in democratic quality . . . our legislators are denying the Indian masses their fundamental rights. . . . The various Security measures . . . are a challenge to the fundamental concept of civil liberties. Suppression of public opinion, restrictions on the right of association and assembly . . . gagging the Press, detentions without trial—these are some of the furies which the Governments have let loose . . . all in the name of 'law and order'—the law and order of the capitalist order![53]

The constitution was completed and Sarat Bose scrutinized the document in the context of Indian constitutional development under the Raj and since August 15, 1947. The constitution, he thought, had fundamental flaws. He wrote a critique, 'A Constitution of Myths and Denials,' which was published in the *Indian Law Review* in January 1950.[54]

What were his main objections? He felt that the executive (potentially, at least, the president) and the central government were much too strong, the states too weak. 'The centripetal tendency in the Indian Constitution militates against the spirit of federalism . . . reducing autonomy of the States to a mockery.'[55] He wrote that the constitution '(gives) . . . enormous powers to the executive to suppress the liberty of the press.' Rather than eliminating repressive acts passed since 1947, 'All the Press and Security Acts remain in full force and effect and power is given to the Indian Parliament to increase and multiply them.'[56] He noted that if an emergency was declared—a mere supposition in 1950—all basic rights would be suspended. Under preventive detention, he argued, those held would be denied due process of law. 'The constitution,' he concluded, 'is an undeclared war upon opposition, present and future.'[57] Why had such a constitution been produced? Sarat Bose insisted that the extreme centralization of power and the suppression of basic freedoms was due to the power-hungry desires of the ruling party, and, in turn, the class behind them, the capitalists, who were to be given free rein in the new India.

As Sarat Bose remained weakened, but recuperating, in February 1950, new communal riots broke out in East Bengal and a renewed flood of Hindu refugees rushed towards Calcutta. The fires of communal violence spread to Calcutta. Dr Roy was in constant contact with Prime Minister Nehru to coordinate Indian responses.[58] From his sick-bed, Sarat Bose wrote to Nurul Amin, premier of East Bengal, encouraging him to protect the Hindu minority. In a statement issued to the press on February 11, Bose could not help but recall his predictions that partition would not solve the problem of Hindu-Muslim relations:

> That the result of the partition of the country will be no solution of the communal problem but will mean its continuance in another form has been my prognosis since the idea of dismembering the country was first mooted by the then leaders of the Congress and the Hindu Mahasabha. . . . I never made any distinction at any time of my life between Hindu and Muslim in undivided Bengal or in divided Bengal. . . . The States are two, but the people in each are one and indivisible. . . . Both the communities are integral to each other; whether here or across the border, they are each other's bone of bone and flesh of flesh.[59]

He ended with a plaintive, heartfelt plea, '. . . to abjure the cult of violence, to restore sobriety and sanity and re-establish communal peace and harmony.'[60]

The day before Sarat Bose wrote this statement, his brother Sudhir died, just on the eve of the marriage of Sarat's daughter, Roma. Within a few years, Sarat had lost Subhas, Satish, and Sudhir. The wedding went on, but Bose relations could not attend and celebrate. Roma came to see her father every day.[61]

On February 20, Sarat Bose wrote an editorial for *The Nation* appealing for communal peace and suggesting, '. . . that East Bengal as a distinct and separate State should join the Indian Union. . .'[62] A Bengali to the end, he was trying to work some way out of the trap of communal warfare.

A half hour later, in the presence of his son Amiya and J.N. Ghosh, Sarat Bose died at the age of sixty-one. The long years of imprisonment, which worsened his diabetes and general health, probably too much hearty eating, and the unwillingness to give up his legal and political work for a more complete rest, contributed to his death. Dr Roy came the next morning to pay a silent tribute; some time later Jawaharlal Nehru came to see Biva. In the same year Sardar Patel and Sri Aurobindo died as well. The titans of modern India's freedom struggle were passing from the stage, one by one.

V

With the death of Sarat Bose, the political tandem of Subhas and Sarat Bose was gone from the Indian political stage. But legacies, myths, and historical assessments remained living on into the present and toward the future. In a practical way, the United Socialist Organization floundered without Sarat Bose. He had been working effectively to get the multiplicity of leftist parties and personalities to seriously consider working together. Within a year, however, the organization was dead and the cherished offspring of his last years, *The Nation,* was halted.[63]

The most powerful mythology having to do with the Boses dealt with the life and life-after-life of Subhas Bose. That Subhas Bose had a wife and child was not widely known. After Sarat Bose's death, his widow Biva published the Bengali letter which Subhas Bose had written on February 8, 1943, explaining his relationship to Emilie Schenkl and Anita Bose. Although the Bose family accepted them into their fold, some Indians refused to believe that Subhas Bose had a wife or fathered a child. One of his closest associates, Satya Ranjan Bakshi, continued to insist through his lifetime that Bose had no wife or child. Bose was seen as a man so pure and so committed to work for his country's freedom, that he could not marry while the British Raj still existed. Basanti Devi, the widow of C.R. Das, told me in the mid-1960s that Subhas Bose had *never* said that he would not marry. This pledge was projected upon him by his followers for their own reasons. Since Emilie Schenkl has never visited India and has never made any public statement about her marriage, and, furthermore, since there are confusions about the marriage date which have not been adequately resolved, doubts remain in the minds of some. However, I have no doubt that Subhas Bose had a long-term relationship to Emilie Schenkl and they lived together during the Second World War. Anita was born in November 1942; Subhas Bose claimed Emilie and Anita as his wife and daughter in a letter to Sarat Bose; Sarat Bose went to Europe and took them lovingly into the Bose family. Anita Bose, now Anita Pfaff, has visited India a number of times, and is widely accepted as Subhas Bose's daughter. So some of the stories should be put to rest.[64]

A more powerful myth or legend is that Bose never died and may be alive even today (though in 1990 he would be ninety-three years old). The initial confusion about the plane crash and how the Japanese released news of it, the cremation, and lack of documentary evidence in Taiwan, have already been related. In the period just after his death, some famous voices—and some obscure ones—suggested that he was alive: Gandhi quickly said that he doubted the crash story (but then recanted after meeting Habibur Rahman); Lakshmi Swaminathan (now Sahgal) said on April 22, 1946, 'Sj. S.C. Bose is probably alive and it is more likely that he is in China, rather than in Russia. . .'[65] During the same period, immediately after the war, 'sightings' began. In April 1946, Mr K.S.M. Swami of Aradhanam claimed that he had met Bose in a third-class compartment of the Bombay Express one Thursday.[66]

The stories of Bose's reappearances in India, or the likelihood that he was in Russia or China, have continued to circulate orally and in the press ever since. Resulting from pressures put upon it, the Government of India has held two official inquiries, the Shah Nawaz Committee in 1956, and the Khosla Commission which reported its findings in 1974.

The Shah Nawaz Committee, or Netaji Inquiry Committee, consisted of Shah Nawaz Khan, MP, a former INA colonel and one of those tried in the Red Fort in 1945; Suresh Bose, an elder brother of Subhas Bose; and S.N. Maitra, ICS, nominee of the Government of West Bengal. This group collected information from April to July 1956 in India, Japan, Thailand, and Vietnam, but never visited Taiwan. Though this committee worked in a somewhat informal manner, it did interview the survivors of the plane crash and Dr Yoshimi, who treated Bose during his last hours. In the stories gathered by the committee some eleven years after the crash, there are a number of discrepancies in details, but the main thrust of the evidence is clear. Rahman came from Pakistan to testify before the committee and he and several of the Japanese survivors had scars from burns received in the crash.

Though Suresh Bose signed an initial list of findings of the committee, he refused to sign the final report, and, insisting later that his brother was alive, wrote his own *Dissentient Report* which he published in 1956. He claimed that the Shah Nawaz Committee did shoddy and dishonest work, deprived him of materials to do his own report, and was directed from the start to find that Subhas Bose had died in the plane crash. Its role, he wrote, was to gather evidence supporting this hypothesis and to ignore other evidence. He indicated that the direction for this line came from the top, i.e., from Prime Minister Nehru. He suggested that a conspiracy existed including the other two committee members and Dr B.C. Roy, to try to induce him by unsubtle means to sign the majority report.[67]

He resisted these pressures, he wrote, because his more open-minded approach had led him to the conclusion that there had been no plane crash, that Bose, Rahman, and the Japanese had all plotted the false crash story to help Bose escape, and that Subhas Bose was somewhere in the world, alive, in 1956. Out of the 181-page repetitious document that constitutes Suresh Bose's report one main principle for dealing with the evidence emerges: if two or more stories by witnesses have any discrepancies between them, then the whole testimony of the witnesses involved is thereby discredited and assumed to be totally false. Using this principle, Bose is able to dismiss eye-witness testimony of all the crash victims and medical personnel and find that there was no crash and that his brother lives. There also appears to be one other half-stated assumption: Subhas Bose could not die before India achieved her freedom. Therefore, he did not die in a plane crash said to have taken place on August 18, 1945.[68] In the course of this report, Suresh Bose says that many others did not believe as of 1956 that Subhas Bose was dead. He gives names of family members and other Indians. Some of these, like Gandhi, changed their minds; others remained in the Suresh Bose camp.

After the findings of the Shah Nawaz Committee were published, the rumors about Subhas Bose's continued existence did not diminish, but, rather, in the early 1960s, increased. The tale of the Shaulmari sadhu and the propaganda of the Subhasbadi Janata constitute the most elaborate and widespread story about Subhas Bose, and may properly be called a myth. The key figure in this movement was Major Satya Gupta, a former political associate of Subhas Bose, who visited the Shaulmari Ashram in North Bengal in 1961 and 1962 and then announced that its chief sadhu was none other than Subhas Bose. During 1962, Gupta formed the Subhasbadi Janata, an organization whose stated aim was to spread the truth that the sadhu was Netaji. Uttamchand Malhotra, with whom Bose had stayed in Kabul in 1941 during 'the great escape' from Calcutta to Berlin, joined the group and became one of the most vociferous in insisting that the sadhu was Bose. One Haripada Bose, a purged member of the ashram (for insisting that the sadhu was Bose) also joined the shadowy circle around Uttamchand and Satya Gupta. The group issued pamphlets, held public meetings, and published numerous different weekly papers in English and Bengali from 1962 through the mid-1960s. Among these papers were *Dak, Mahabharat, Shaulmari* (in English and Bengali), *Jagrithi, Jai Hind, Jugbani,* and *Bishan.*[69] It appears that they would publish a weekly under one name for some months and then switch the name from one week to the next, perhaps to keep up public interest and to give the illusion that there was more than one publication discussing the latest doings of Netaji. When I met Major Gupta in the 1960s and attended a small exhibition his group was holding, he told me that 'Netaji passed my way,' suggesting that he had seen him recently.

Spurred by the propaganda of the Subhasbadi Janata, numerous inquiries were made into the identity of the sadhu. Surendrà Mohan Ghosh, an elderly and respected Congress leader who had known Bose well, visited the ashram and decided forthwith that the sadhu was not Bose.[70] Though many visited the ashram, some receiving darshan from the sadhu, some having it refused, the sadhu steadfastly maintained that he was not Netaji. The ashram officials protested that Satya Gupta, Uttamchand, and their group were exploiting the ashram. The principals are now dead and the Subhasbadi Janata defunct. But the story of the sadhu was believed by many in the mid-1960s who waited breathlessly for him to reveal his true identity at a moment of national crisis.

The story of Subhas Bose as a sadhu (1948–59) and then the Shaulmari sadhu from 1959 to the mid-1960s can be culled from the publications of the Subhasbadi Janata. According to their life of Netaji, he returned to India in 1948, and as he had been a sadhu in his youth, so he became one again. After attending Gandhi's cremation, he went around India three times on foot.[71] Around 1952 he was in Benares and then he was at Etawah where he organized student and youth groups. After this he stayed with Sri B.P. Joshi at Anand Bhavan in Almorah.[72] In the years 1956 to 1959, he lived like a yogi at a Bareilly Shiva temple and gave out medicines and cured the local people.[73] During this period he often stayed in caves, would not give darshan, and used a variety of pseudonyms including Col. Joginder Singh of the INA and Hanuman Gir. He miraculously cured a tuberculosis patient and visited other places including Naxalbari in 1957 and Etawah in 1958. He is said to have sent a letter to Suresh Bose and then come to see his brother in Calcutta in 1959, but Suresh Bose did not recognize him. In that year he established the Shaulmari Ashram, calling himself Srimat Saradanandaji. He was in this guise when Major Satya Gupta came to the ashram, recognized him, and founded the Subhasbadi Janata. They were to spread the message that India's Netaji was alive, had never married or had a child, and was carrying out a great mission, not only for India, but for the world.

At a time of Indian and world crisis, the 'Great Monk of India' was doing *tapasya* to save mankind as a continuation of his original mission to save India. Transformed by his sadhana, the sadhu would raise India from her present degradation to a future glory. He would bring about a Divine Age on earth.[74] The great yogi was in the process of working out a religious synthesis which would fulfill the work of Ramakrishna, Vivekananda, and Sri Aurobindo. He would bring Vedanta Consciousness to earth. Part of the work of the sadhu was to train a cadre to carry his message to the world.

As 'Viswapita' (world father), he made those around him conscious of their inner divinity by his very presence. Besides 'Viswapita', he was also referred to as 'warrior saint'.[75]

Why do not India and the world recognize that the sadhu, Netaji, has brought a great message that will save mankind? The Subhasbadi literature maintains that there is a gigantic conspiracy of all the 'anti–Netaji elements of the World' preventing the true identification of him. These included Prime Minister Nehru, the Congress Party, Shah Nawaz and his committee, the Indian left including certain members of the Forward Bloc (Hemanta Basu and Lila Roy), the Indian press, foreign powers including the United States, and even some Bose family members.[76]

Other stories were spread that Netaji was in Russia or China. In 1963 to 1965, rallies were announced at which Netaji was supposed to appear and identify himself. Meetings were held, one on the Calcutta maidan on July 12, 1963, another at Kalyani in 1965, but Netaji did not appear. The sadhu was said to have attended Nehru's funeral and an issue of *Dak*, one of the Subhasbadi papers, with a photograph of a monk with shaved head (resembling a plump, elderly Netaji) at this event, was widely circulated in Calcutta in 1964.

The ashram and the sadhu issued denials.[77] The Janata responded that the sadhu had become a cosmic force, 'a yogiraj with divine power'. The official ashram position was put forth by Dr Gope Gurbax, who the Subhasbadi group claimed later recanted, admitting that the sadhu was Netaji.[78]

In time the non-appearance of Netaji led to the dissolution of the Subhasbadi Janata. The sadhu was believed to have died in 1977. The activity of the group, however, encouraged the spread of Netaji-is-alive stories through West Bengal. I was told some of these stories by ordinary people in the mid-1960s and in 1977. Riding in the second-class compartment in a train from Bolpur to Calcutta in April 1964, I heard some Bengalis hold an elaborate discussion of the woes of India and Bengal and conclude that only Subhas Bose could save them and that the Government of India feared to look into the question of the Shaulmari sadhu.[79]

The conspiratorial and savior elements are present in other tales about Netaji since 1945. One former associate of Bose in Germany during the war told me in the late 1970s that Habibur Rahman hinted to him that the crash story was concocted. This man, a respected professional in his field, said that Bose went on to either China or Russia, most likely the latter, and was held by the Russians in a concentration camp. The imprisonment of Netaji in the Soviet Union, he argued, allowed the Russians to hold a whip hand over Nehru. Since Bose would be a threat to Nehru's rule if he returned, Nehru 'paid' the Russians by taking their side at every turn. This course of Indian foreign policy culminated in the Indo-Soviet Friendship Treaty completed by Nehru's daughter, Mrs Indira Gandhi, who continued this secret arrangement. All my arguments about why India cooperated in various ways with the Soviet Union were dismissed as insufficient. This gentleman, as some other Bose admirers, insisted that if Bose had returned at any time during Nehru's tenure, or even today, he would be made prime minister.[80]

Some believe that Bose is a Chinese military officer. A photograph was circulated in the mid-1960s showing a Chinese military parade and one of the heads was circled and the magazine proclaimed that this was indeed Subhas Bose marching in peking. But why would this lover of Bengal and India remain a Chinese military official? No logical questions or answers were adequate—or relevant?—to the purveyors of these and the other stories.

Around 1970, the Government of India set up a second inquiry commission to investigate the 'disappearance' of Bose. It consisted of only one man: G.D. Khosla, retired chief justice of the Punjab High Court. Though he began work in 1970, other duties prevented him from finishing his report until 1974 when the Government of India released his 'Report of the One-Man Commission of Inquiry into the Disappearance of Netaji Subhas Chandra Bose.' Though working many years after the events of 1945, Justice Khosla brought intelligence and legal acumen to his task. Not only does he skillfully put together the positive evidence for what did happen, but he also critically examines all of the alternative stories, showing their illogicality and fancifulness. Justice Khosla suggests that the motives of many of the story-purveyors are less than altruistic. Some, he says, have clearly been driven by political goals or simply wanted to call attention to themselves. His patience in listening to some tales is surely remarkable. What could he, or anyone, have thought as he listened to the testimony of P.M. Karapurkar, agent of the Central Bank of India at Sholapur, who '... claimed that he receives direct messages from Bose by tuning his body like a radio receiving apparatus?'[81]

A section of the Khosla Report is devoted to the activities of Professor Samar Guha, formerly a member of parliament. In March 1978, Guha issued his new book, *Netaji: Dead or Alive?* He was pictured in the leading dailies presenting a copy to Mr Sanjiva Reddy, then president of India, and provoked a promise from the president that new efforts would be made to get foreign governments, including the Soviet Union, to help the curious 'unravel the mystery of Netaji's death'.[82] 'Mr Reddy ... said that the Soviet Union had been cooperative and he would coax the Soviet authorities to "send Netaji back if he is there" '[83] The book itself is a concoction of misinformation and misquotation.[84] When I visited Japan and interviewed many of the same people quoted by Guha, I read out passages from his book to them. Invariably, they said he had put down the opposite of what they told him.

On January 23, 1979, Guha perpetrated a new hoax. He issued a photograph to the press which he said was of Subhas Bose at the present time. Bose family members noticed that parts of two old photographs, the body of Sarat Bose from one, the head of Subhas Bose from another, had been pasted together to make a 'new' photograph. It was, one Bose quipped, a joining of the two Boses before the present writer could finish his book. At the same time, Guha issued a statement asserting that Nehru had known that Subhas Bose was in a Soviet prison. He was sued; he backed down; fortunately for him, he was acquitted.

Another small, related matter often mentioned in connection with the death of Bose is the fate of the 'treasure'. Bose did take with him one or two trunks said to contain gold and jewelry on the fatal flight. Justice Khosla mentions that he decided not to investigate this aspect of the story. Some valuables were scattered around the crash site and were said to have been retrieved and taken on to Tokyo. Then the story gets even more confused.[85] Speculation has gone on for decades about 'Netaji's treasure' and a novel has even been produced centering around its fate, entitled *The Bengali Inheritance*, by Owen Sela.[86] Although some of those who have wondered about the crash and several tale creators have elaborated on the 'mystery' of the valuables, there is no hard evidence that any significant amount survived.

VI

What is one to make of these tales? Some are surely calculated to draw attention to the creator, while others seem to have arisen more spontaneously as an expression of cultural needs. West Bengal (and East Bengal, now Bangladesh) have had their share of tragedies and suffering from the Bengal Famine to the Great Calcutta Killing to the intermittent riots and flows of refugees across the border. West Bengal was once part of proud, united Bengal that 'thought today what India will think tomorrow'. Bengalis were in the vanguard not only of Indian cultural achievements but of her freedom movement. But, the nationalist leadership of the Bengalis was displaced by Gandhi and for a variety of reasons, including the shift of the capital to New Delhi, Bengal and Bengalis became less important.

After partition, West Bengal was a small, less important state in India, while East Bengal was the most populous, but less powerful wing of Pakistan. Difficulties continued. Many politically active Bengalis in West Bengal lived under the Congress Raj, but were discontented. Even Dr Roy, who was holding the fort for the Congress from 1948 to his death in 1962, had serious disagreements with the central government. In this context, old grievances and present ones produced a variety of 'symptoms'. Among these was the continuing attachment to a hero, the last Congress president from Bengal, who had, according to the story, gone on to become a great warrior and then 'disappeared'. If there were no hero among the present pantheon of leaders, perhaps the last 'big one' might return and bring Bengal and the whole Indian nation to greatness.[87] This was the hope.[88]

To remember and 'use' Subhas Bose for present purposes, it was necessary to simplify and amplify aspects of his life into familiar cultural molds. Ascetic and mystical traits were stressed by some and he could be presented as a sadhu, as a holy man, but this might be linked to benevolent purposes in the secular world as well. One Indian model to which Bose was assimilated was that of the saintly king as delineated in the *Arthasastra* or the *Ramayana*.[89] Numerous biographers and the Subhasbadi Janata have stressed the sadhu element more than the kingly element and depicted him as a warrior sadhu or nationalist karmayogin. Rather than a dichotomy between an ascetic seeking power and a saint imbued with goodness, we have been given a political activist seeking both power and goodness. Or, rather, reaching for power in order to do good.

Another, related, model into which Bose has been fitted both before and after 1945 is that of an Indian hero. This pattern involves both specific qualities and a developmental life course. J.A.B. Hans van Buitenen has suggested that among the characteristics of an Indian hero are perseverance, presence of mind (*buddhi*) by which the hero takes advantage of his adversary's mistakes, and relinquishment.[90] Bose certainly saw himself as struggling (for decades) with a great evil and he certainly did sustain his efforts to overcome this adversary to his last breath. Many believe that he sought nothing, except to be remembered as one who sacrificed in this quest. There are wildly different opinions as to how successful he was in fighting British imperialism and how wise he was in his choice of means to reach the goal of Indian freedom. But, a strong case has been made for his life of struggle, sacrifice, and devotion to the cause. What some Indians have done since 1945, particularly in West Bengal, is to bring back this hero, symbolically, to the fray to continue the fight in which the odds are great and the cause is worthy.

A final question, dealt with partially above, is: why Subhas Bose? Why is he the hero who is desired, resurrected, not allowed to rest in peace? Not

only was he the last Congress president from Bengal, but he 'stood up'—
he argued with Gandhi and the Congress high command. He had his own
perspective: push, push, push, and, if necessary, use any means. This view
had great appeal to many Indians not enamored of the Gandhian way. In
the war and then as this period was described in the Indian press after the
war, Bose was shown as the man who said, 'Give me your blood and I will
give you freedom.' For those to whom martial values are meaningful,
Subhas Bose was *the* hero. He left India craftily, contacted foreign powers,
helped raise funds and an army of Indians. He said that it was necessary to
have martyrs in order to have freedom. Indians had to prove that they were
worthy of freedom. He offered his own life. He braved bombs and bullets
rather recklessly. He died a martyr's death, retreating so that he could fight
for freedom another day. The appeal to many regional groups and
communities in India is plain. Bose had his appeal in Punjab and
Maharashtra as well as Bengal before he died. The memories and the tales,
simplified but strong, live on.

Conclusions

A detached historical assessment of the Boses made by a foreigner—albeit one who has spent a good deal of time worrying about them—must, perforce, differ from the glorifying tales of Bose devotees and from the judgments of Indian nationalists.

There are, nonetheless, many ways in which they are and should be remembered. First, as brothers. Subhas and Sarat Bose were a most remarkable pair. They became specially devoted to each other at a relatively early age. Sarat Bose said to one of his daughters once, 'If I have Subhas on one side and all of you (i.e., his immediate family) on the other, he will be heavier.'[1] The love and tenderness he had for Subhas did not preclude a little joking. They sat in adjoining rooms. If someone looking for Subhas mistakenly came to the door of Sarat's room, he said, 'Not in this room. Go to that room. The Prince of Vagabonds sits there.'[2] Subhas needed and accepted the love and assistance of his brother. He could never have done what he did without his whole family, and particularly Sarat and Biva.

Sarat, the older, deferred to his younger, more charismatic brother in most political matters, though it is likely that there were differences that were suppressed. They are hard to discover. The military theme runs much more strongly through the life of Subhas Bose than through that of Sarat Bose. In the end, Sarat identified himself with his brother's actions, but he did not join the Forward Bloc and call for India's liberation by violent means. He may have agreed with Subhas that at some point violence becomes necessary, and Sarat Bose defended violent revolutionaries in court and with financial aid. But even when he spoke of the INA after the war, he, like Gandhi, praised it and subtracted the violence. Sarat Bose saw what the internal consequences of violence might be for India even in the name of a noble cause.

Though one could never for a second doubt that they were both Indian patriots, there was also a powerful regional identification. They were Bengalis and this element was always there, though during the war when someone wanted a favor from Bose because he or she was a fellow Bengali, Bose insisted that Indian-ness came first. But the Bengali element was important because it gave Subhas and Sarat Bose a different perspective on the Indian struggle and on relations between the major communities in India. Since they came from a province with about equal numbers of Muslims and Hindus—with Muslims having an edge in numbers—they could never conceive of Hindu dominance. They were both personally religious and were capable of understanding the faith of those of different religions. In public life, however, they thought that men from all communities must work together. The idea of an India divided on the basis of religion was foreign to them and each resisted the idea to the end. On the last day of his life, Sarat Bose wanted to bring East Bengal back into India; he wanted a large group of his brother Bengalis back in the fold. Their perspective on Bengal and India set them apart from those from other regions, but also from Bengalis like Shyama Prasad Mookerjee.

They joined actively in the Congress mainstream in the early 1920s under C.R. Das, not Gandhi. Though there were numerous controversies through the years, they did work with Gandhi and his team. Gandhi, for his reasons, never explicitly stated, agreed to put forth Bose for Congress president at the end of 1937. But when Bose decided to run for a second term, he precipitated the acrimonious disputes which led to his suspension from Congress leadership positions. But Subhas and Sarat Bose, consequently, separated from the Congress mainstream from 1939 to 1945, though they still considered themselves Congressmen. They continued to adhere, more fiercely than most, to the Congress credo that it was an organization of and for all Indians, regardless of community. They could never agree that India be divided on the basis of religion and thought it went against not only their own outlook, but this very Congress credo.

After the death of Subhas Bose, Sarat Bose rejoined the Congress mainstream, which also, at the same time, incorporated the actions of the INA as part of their patriotic past. Gandhi and Nehru, for the Congress, but also Indians throughout the land, legitimized the INA. But this legitimization also brought its complications. It seemed to sanctify violent actions in a good cause. This was, indeed, the view of Subhas Bose, though never of Gandhi. Gandhi tried to sort out what was acceptable and what was unacceptable in the INA, but many Indians agreed that violence in a noble cause was the way of Bose and backed by the *Bhagavad Gita,* the Kshatriya model, and other Indian religious and political traditions. In independent India, this legitimation of violence in what the political actors see as a good cause has brought a variety of bloody deeds by many groups in the society. We cannot know how Subhas Bose would have spoken and acted with respect to the use of violence in an independent India. Sarat Bose saw how violent actions between Indians from 1945 to 1950 were bringing ruin to his dreams of a new day for his country. He opposed this violence resolutely.

Both Boses had a similar vision of a free India, but there were some differences in emphasis. Both wanted a socialist society, egalitarian and industrialized. Although they mentioned the evils of caste and untouchability, this was not a main focus. They wanted all socialists to cooperate in building a unified left that would bring this socialist vision to life. Gradually each had become disillusioned with Congress promises of socialism and Sarat Bose, who lived a few years into the independence era, was particularly vehement about this. They were both skeptical of communist cooperation and at different times each questioned the patriotism of the communists whose extra-Indian ties, commitment to world communism and to the Soviet Union's objectives, might come before Indian ones. Like Gandhi and Nehru in their different ways, they said, in effect, 'Demonstrate your overriding commitment that is as powerful as mine.' Even cooperation with other socialists was difficult, but the commitment of Jayaprakash Narayan or R.M. Lohia to India was never in doubt, however difficult it was for them to work together.

Subhas Bose's talk of a synthesis between fascism and communism leading to a new ideology for India confused and irritated other leftists. Then he actually went and sat across the table from Hitler and other Nazis. Did this make him a fascist? A Nazi collaborator? An enemy of the left in India and worldwide? Subhas Bose was a pragmatic Indian nationalist, not a socialist ideologue. He was searching desperately for the means to free India from the British Raj. He never believed that the British would leave peacefully. Therefore, he allied with countries like Germany and the Japan in order to fight the British. Throughout these war years, 1941 to 1945, he never claimed to be representing the Congress, but stepped forward as a leading nationalist. He resisted German or Japanese attempts to 'use' him. He certainly would never agree to be anyone's puppet. But he would take temporary support from any power in order to free India. He borrowed money in the name of India that he tried to pay back. To most German and Japanese officials, he was someone to be 'used'. So there was a tug-of-war going on between Bose and his 'allies'. He thought of his work and his operations in Germany and Southeast Asia as independent, Indian nationalist efforts. The way in which the Indian public and most Indian political organizations rallied to the support of the INA in 1945 makes clear that few Indians believed that he was a pawn of the Axis powers, however much they may have disliked his choice of allies.

Both Boses feared a Congress compromise with British imperialism. Subhas Bose got into the bad books of his Congress colleagues in the late 1930s by suggesting that they were ready to accept less than independence and make a 'deal' with the British over the federal aspects of the 1935 Government of India Act. During the war, as each new set of negotiations started, Subhas Bose broadcast frantically from abroad against compromise. Any kind of negotiations with the wily British, Labour or Conservative, seemed dangerous to him and so he was as hostile to the Cripps Mission as to the Simla Conference of 1945.

Sarat Bose participated in the developments at the end of the empire and the first few years of the dawn of independence. He, too, disliked the idea of dominion status almost as much as he did the partition. But, dominion status and Commonwealth membership, however bad, could be terminated rather easily. Partition was another matter. Once India was divided on the basis of religion, it would be very difficult to put it together again. But the Congress high command agreed to both the partition and dominion status in the Commonwealth as part of the Mountbatten package. Sarat Bose was now an outsider with his resignation at the end of 1946 from the Working Committee, and later from the Congress itself. After August 15, 1947, down to the last days of his life and the propagation of the program of the United Socialist Organization, he pushed for an exit from the Commonwealth and from any hint of 'Anglo-American' influence over Indian policies.

Of the two Boses, Sarat Bose was the one who stressed to a greater extent the need for protection of basic freedoms in independent India. Many years before, Surendranath Banerjea had said, 'We have been fed on the strong food of English constitutional freedom.'[3] Like Banerjea, Sarat Bose had been trained in England and imbibed their lessons about the fundamental rights of all citizens. Through his life as lawyer and nationalist, and then in free India, he continued to demand of the government in power that it live up to its promises of basic freedoms and protections for all. He was dubious about the Raj, for he spent almost seven years of his life imprisoned without charges. He despised the security acts and the special powers that the central and provincial governments assumed under the Raj. So it was no surprise that he was even more unhappy with the shortcomings that he saw in free India. He had hoped for the end to security acts, special powers, emergency powers, and limitations on basic rights. Just before his death, he completed his damning critique of the new Indian constitution, 'A Constitution of Myths and Denials.'

The Boses were members of the relatively small, urban elite class growing up in British India. Though the father of Janaki Nath Bose was a poor villager, Janaki Nath Bose was able, by powers of mind and determination, to climb out of this limited world into the elite favored under the Raj. His rise enabled his sons and daughters to have many opportunities, the sons for professions, the daughters for marriage. Of the offsprings, Sarat Bose was a favorite, displaying intellectual gifts, drive, commitment, and following his father into the legal profession. With the generation of the sons going to Calcutta for their higher education, Janaki Nath Bose established a base in Calcutta. The Boses made contact with others in the Indian elite and many of those who at one time or another were political opponents of Sarat and Subhas Bose, were throughout personal friends, or at least as long as that was possible. For example, Shyama Prasad Mookerjee and Kiron Sankar Roy were family friends, but in 1946 and 1947, the former was a bitter enemy of Sarat Bose.

The Boses did not have the experience of the village that even their father had. Though they grew up in a small city, Cuttack, and visited the ancestral village, Kodalia, still, they were Calcutta men. They were educated in Calcutta, came to manhood, and professional, political, and public prominence there. They were not cut off from village India, but their political efforts touched mainly the urban middle classes, educated young men, and trade unionists. Subhas Bose identified throughout his life with the young, with the future creators of a freer, hopefully better, India. Sarat Bose privately helped young men, as his father had, and often addressed youth groups. Both of them often used the populist language of socialism, declaring that they were working for the masses, the workers and peasants, although since they and the Congress high command stressed that the Congress was an all-class movement, they tried not to drive away business and landed interests summarily. The speeches of both Boses often contained condemnations of capitalist exploitation, but they leaned to the pragmatic stance of Jawaharlal Nehru through the nationalist period. After independence, Sarat Bose took a harsher line and Nehru's softness on capitalist interests was a prime target.

They deserve to be grouped with nationalists of many Asian and African countries who devoted themselves to the cause of their country's freedom from foreign rule with passion and idealism. Although Subhas Bose worked on the Axis side during the Second World War, so did some other nationalists like Aung San and Ba Maw of Burma. With the world at war, nationalists of subject nations chose the side they thought might best help their cause. Some, including myself, might believe that Subhas Bose was shortsighted in working with the Germans, but he thought that the

British would never leave unless they were driven out and he had to make the only practical alliance offered to him with an enemy of the British Empire. During the war, there were British, Indian communists and other Indian nationalists who thought he was a pawn of the fascists. He was incorporated back into the pantheon of Indian nationalist heroes after the war and his death.

Of all the foreign nationalists, both the Boses had a special feeling for the Irish. Both visited Ireland, both talked of the lessons which India had to learn from the bravery of Irish patriots and the determination with which the Irish worked for complete independence from the British Empire. Realizing that they faced a common enemy, and appreciating the warm-hearted support they received from de Valera and other Irish leaders, the Boses were equally sympathetic in turn.

The Boses now live in the historical imagination of their countrymen. Bound by love and a common cause, they struggled against imperialism with great perseverance and courage. They had their successes and failures as they worked for what they thought was the central political concern of India in the first half of the twentieth century: complete independence from the British Raj. They should be remembered for the zest and devotion they gave to their country as they tried to fulfill their own and India's destiny.

Notes

CHAPTER ONE

1. Prof Ramanujan made this remark in a personal conversation and I have formalized it slightly here.

2. The Bengali of the family name might be more closely approximated by the English 'Bashu' or 'Basu', but the more Anglicized Bose was the form the family used in English and that usage is adopted here. There is little written on Sarat Bose, but several valuable recent publications are: *Sarat Bose Commemoration Volume*, ed., Nirmal Chandra Bhattacharyya, Calcutta: Sarat Bose Academy, 1982; Sisir K. Bose, *Remembering My Father: A Centenary Offering*, Calcutta: Netaji Research Bureau, 1988; Nirad C. Chaudhuri, *Thy Hand, Great Anarch! India 1921–1952*, London: Chatto and Windus, 1987, Book VI.

3. On the parents and family of Subhas and Sarat Bose, see Subhas Bose, 'Brief Life Sketch of Janaki Nath Bose' (in Bengali), printed as an appendix to his *Bharat pathik*, Calcutta: Netaji Research Bureau, 1965; but the appendix is omitted in the English version of Subhas Chandra Bose, *An Indian Pilgrim*, Bombay: Asia Publishing House, 1965. The first three chapters of the autobiography itself give a good deal of family background. Also see Dinabandhu Kulabhusan Ghatak, *Kayastha–karika*, I, Calcutta: n.p., 1886, which gives elaborate accounts of Kayastha families. On the family of Prabhabati Dutt, see Loke Nath Ghose, *The Modern History of the Indian Chiefs, Rajas, Zamindars, & c.*, Part II, Calcutta: n.p., 1881. Additional information was obtained from interviews with Sailesh Bose, Bombay, December 30, 1964, and Dacca, May 28, 1972; Amiya Nath Bose, Calcutta, January 21, 1976; Asoke Nath Bose, Calcutta, February 17, 1979; Aurobindo Bose, Calcutta, August 25, 1976; Dwijen Bose, Calcutta, August 22, 1977; Sisir K. Bose, Calcutta, May 9, 1972, July 5, 1973, January 12, 1976; Gita (Bose) Biswas,

Calcutta, January 17, 1976; Shila (Bose) Sen Gupta, New Delhi, November 29, 1978; Aruna Som, Calcutta, February 28, 1979; Ajit Dey, Calcutta, August 20, 1972; Nirad C. Chaudhuri, Oxford, November 26, 1971; Anil Ganguli, Calcutta, August 24, 1977. Two valuable accounts of changes in this period are by Pradip Sinha, *Nineteenth Century Bengal: Aspects of Social History*, Calcutta: KLM, 1965, and *Calcutta in Urban History*, Calcutta: KLM, 1978.

4.   On Bengal under the Raj, see the relevant census volumes: Government of India, *Census of India*, 1872, 1881, 1891, 1901, 1911, Calcutta: Government of India Press. Also, L.S.S. O'Malley, *History of Bengal, Bihar and Orissa under British Rule*, Calcutta: Bengal Secretariat Book Depot, 1925; C.E. Buckland, *Bengal under the Lieutenant-Governors*, 2 vols., 2nd ed., Calcutta: S.K. Lahiri, 1902; Rajat Kanta Ray, *Social Conflict and Political Unrest in Bengal 1875–1927*, Delhi: Oxford U. Press, 1984. Recent population figures for Bangladesh are from *Far Eastern Economic Review*, *Asia Yearbook 1989*, Hong Kong: Review Publishing, 1989; and for West Bengal from *Statistical Outline of India 1986–87*, Bombay: Tata Services Limited, 1986. Figures for the United Kingdom and Minnesota are from *World Almanac and Book of Facts*, New York: Scripps Howard, 1989.

5.   On the Kayasthas, the most penetrating study is Ronald B. Inden, *Marriage and Rank in Bengali Culture: A History of Caste and Clan in Middle Period Bengal*, Berkeley: U. of California Press, 1976. A Bengali work of a previous generation is Nagendranath Vasu, *Banger jatiya itihasa* [History of Bengal Jatis], Kayastha volume, Calcutta: N. Vasu at Visvakosa Press (1340), 1933. An older study which ranks castes and describes sects is J.N. Bhattacharya, *Hindu Castes and Sects*, Calcutta: Editions Indian, 1973 reprint [first published in 1896].

6.   Interview with Sailesh Bose.

7.   Interview with Sailesh Bose, and Sinha, *Nineteenth Century Bengal, passim*.

8.   Subhas Bose, 'Janaki Nath Bose'.

9.   Interviews with Sailesh Bose and Dwijen Bose.

10. On Cuttack, see W.W. Hunter, *A Statistical Account of Bengal*, Vol.XVIII, London: Trubner & Co., 1875 [reprinted, Delhi: D.K. Publishing House, 1973] and Government of India, *Imperial Gazetteer of India*, Provincial Series, *Bengal*, Vol. II, Calcutta: Superintendent of Government Press, 1909, 245–64.

11. Hunter, *Statistical Account*, XVIII, 6, 20.

12. *Imperial Gazetteer, Bengal*, II, 253.

13. Interview with Anil Ganguli; interview with Mohammed Ayoob, New York, November 24, 1975; Subhas Bose, *Indian Pilgrim*, 28; Sinha, *Calcutta*, 251–52.

14. Interviews with Aruna Som and Anil Ganguli.

15. Interviews with Shila Sen Gupta and Anil Ganguli. On the use of 'Sahib,' see William Crooke ed., *Hobson–Jobson*, Delhi: Munshiram Manoharlal, 1968, 781 [reprint of 1903 edition].

16. Interviews with Anil Ganguli and Sailesh Bose. I have examined what remained of the libraries of Janaki Nath Bose, Sarat Bose, and Subhas Bose, kept in Netaji Bhavan, 38/2 Elgin Road, Calcutta, and listed and classified the books into the 'Bose Library List'. I found copies of books by Milton, Cowper, Arnold, and Kipling with Janaki Nath Bose's name written on them. Anil Ganguli told of the love that his father and Janaki Nath Bose had for Shakespeare. Several of Sarat Bose's English literature books are there as well and his children have all testified to his love of English literature.

17. Subhas Bose, 'Janaki Nath Bose'.

18. Bengal Legislative Council, *Proceedings* [hereafter, *PBLC*], XLIV, Calcutta, 1912. I have drawn on part of an investigation by Sugata Bose, detailed in his personal letter to me of May 30, 1988.

19. *PBLC*, XLIV, January 17, 1912, 14.

20. *PBLC*, XLIV, January 17, 1912, 15.

21. This is evident from the *PBLC* and from the writings and speeches of the first generation of Indian nationalists. On them, see Leonard A. Gordon, *Bengal: The Nationalist Movement 1876–1940*, New York: Columbia U. Press, 1974, Chapter One.

22. *PBLC*, XLIV, March 6, 1912, 48.

23. *PBLC*, XLIV, 14–15, 48–49, 94, 121–22, 130, 147, 194, 217–18, 224.

24. Bose, *Indian Pilgrim*, 2–3; interviews with Aruna Som and Shila Sen Gupta. Janaki Nath Bose kept a notebook in which he noted the birth date and birth time for each of his children, and it is preserved in Netaji Bhavan.

25. Bose, *Indian Pilgrim*, 3; interviews with Dwijen Bose, Shila Sen Gupta, and Sisir K. Bose. On the suggestion that Sarat Bose's mother provided his discipline, see P.B. Mukharji, 'Sarat Chandra Bose the Lawyer,' originally published by Netaji Research Bureau, and reprinted in *Sarat Bose Commemoration Volume*, 18.

26. Interviews with Aurobindo Bose, Shila Sen Gupta, and Aruna Som.

27. Subhas Bose, 'Janaki Nath Bose' and his *Indian Pilgrim*, 32–34;

Sarat Chandra Bose, *I Warned My Countrymen*, Calcutta: Netaji Research Bureau, 1968, 92–93, where Sarat Bose notes his admiration for Sri Ramakrishna and Swami Vivekananda.

28. Lucille K. Forer, *The Birth Order Factor*, New York: Pocket Books, 1977, 193.

29. Alfred Adler, *The Individual Psychology of Alfred Adler*, eds., Heinz L. Ansbacher and Rowena R. Ansbacher, New York: Harper and Row, 1967, 376–82; and Forer, *Birth Order*, 231.

30. See Marvin Davis, *Rank and Rivalry: The Politics of Inequality in Rural West Bengal*, New York: Cambridge U. Press, 1983, 114ff; also interview with Aurobindo Bose.

31. Interview with Sisir K. Bose. Ranajit Ghosh, 'Sarat Chandra Bose,' in Ermine Brown ed., *Eminent Indians*, Calcutta: Shanti Mitra, 1946, 18, suggests that Sarat Bose had many similarities to his father. I had written my own account about this before I read Ghosh's essay. It is one of the few useful sketches of Sarat Bose's life written while he was still alive.

32. Interview with Sisir K. Bose. Bose, *I Warned My Countrymen*, 92–3.

33. Interview with Sailesh Bose.

34. Interview with Sailesh Bose.

35. Henry Cotton, *Calcutta Old and New*, Calcutta: W. Newman, 1907, 242.

36. The mere mention of Calcutta to a Westerner in the past generation brings a shudder and a tear, but the idea of Calcutta as a hell-hole began in the eighteenth and nineteenth centuries and was helped along by Rudyard Kipling, 'The City of Dreadful Night,' in *Selected Prose and Poetry of Rudyard Kipling*, Garden City, New York: Garden City Publishing, 1937, 187–251. The best account of Calcutta in the nineteenth century is Sinha, *Calcutta*, 17ff. Though it is quite superficial, Geoffrey Moorhouse, *Calcutta*, London: Weidenfeld and Nicolson, 1971, is useful as an overview. I have recently written to the editors of *The New York Times*, about the unfair stereotype of Calcutta which they continually use to show how bad things are getting in New York, letter published January 7, 1989.

37. Rhoads Murphey, 'The City in the Swamp: Aspects of the Site and Early Growth of Calcutta,' *Geographical Journal*, 1960, 130, 241–56.

38. O.H.K. Spate, *India and Pakistan: A General and Regional Geography*, London: Methuen, 1954, 543.

39. Spate, *India and Pakistan*, 544.

40. For a modern view which shows some of the pride, see Sudhindranath Datta, 'Calcutta,' in *The World of Twilight*, Calcutta:

Oxford U. Press, 1970, 77–93.

41. Sinha, *Calcutta*, 243–45.

42. Sinha, *Calcutta*, 244–45.

43. Quoted in Moorhouse, *Calcutta*, 177.

44. Government of Bengal, Education Department, *Presidency College Register*, ed., Surendrachandra Majumdar, Calcutta: Bengal Secretariat Book Depot, 1927; includes entries for Sarat, 165, Satish, 312, Subhas, 313, Sudhir, 314, Sunil, 314, Suresh, 314.

45. Subhas Bose, 'Janaki Nath Bose,' mentions the freedom his father allowed his sons in their choice of profession.

46. Sarat Bose mentions those early sympathies in a speech given much later, January 13, 1946, printed in his *I Warned My Countrymen*, 92.

47. This is based on an examination of the library in Netaji Bhavan and of his correspondence with his family, particularly during his two long periods of imprisonment.

48. Ghosh, in Brown, *Eminent Indians*, 19.

49. Interviews with Ajit Dey and Sisir K. Bose.

50. Interviews with Sisir K. Bose, Gita Biswas, and Nirad C. Chaudhuri.

51. Interview with Amiya Nath Bose. An interesting and detailed record of his life in London, his feelings, new experiences, and ties to home, is found in his frequent letters home (in Bengali) to his wife Biva. These letters are in the Netaji Research Bureau and cover August 1912 to July 1914.

52. See Romesh Chunder Dutt, *Three Years in Europe 1868 to 1871, with an Account of Subsequent Visits to Europe in 1886 and 1893*, Calcutta: S.K. Lahiri, 1896, 2; on Gandhi's London period, see Mohandas K. Gandhi, *An Autobiography, The Story of My Experiments with Truth*, Boston: Beacon Press, 1957, 39–41, the chapter entitled 'The Outcaste,' explains the taboo on crossing the Black Waters. Also see the superb study by James D. Hunt, *Gandhi in London*, New Delhi: Promilla and Co., 1978.

53. Secretary of State for India, Committee on Indian Students in the United Kingdom, *Report*, 1907, and Secretary of State for India, Committee on Indian Students in the United Kingdom, *Report*, 1921, London: His Majesty's Stationery Office, for the India Office, 1922. I am thankful to Gautam Chattopadhyay for this valuable reference.

54. Committee on Indian Students, *Report*, Appendix IV, 1921, 74.

55. Important sources for the institution which he joined, its traditions, procedures, and demands, are: W.C. Richardson, *A History of the Inns of Court*, Baton Rouge: Claitor's Publishing Division, 1975;

and Ronald Roxburgh ed., *The Black Books: The Records of the Honorable Society of Lincoln's Inn, 1845–1914*, Vol. V, London: Lincoln's Inn, 1968. I have also examined other records of Lincoln's Inn and the Council on Legal Education, particularly the examinations given and the requirements for students in these years. A useful brief history is Sir Gerald Hurst, *A Short History of Lincoln's Inn*, London: Constable, 1946.

56. Some precise data, at least on one of the inns of court, the Middle Temple, is provided by Bernard S. Cohn's unpublished study of Indian students attending, 1860–1940. Cohn found that 13 Indians were admitted in the 1860s, 11 of them Bengalis; in the 1870s, 18 of 41 were Bengalis; in the 1880s, 30 of 127 were from Bengal. By the 1880s an increasing number of Indians from other regions were admitted to all the inns of court. On the legal profession in India and Bengal, see Samuel Schmitthenner, 'The Development of the Legal Profession in India' (seminar paper for South Asia 700, University of Chicago, 1965). On the requirements, see Report of the Council of Legal Education, November 8, 1909, quoted in Roxburgh, *The Black Books*, V, 377–79.

57. Sarat Bose, letters to Biva, January 2, 1913 and June 26, 1913.

58. Sarat Bose, letter to Biva, February 12, 1914.

59. Sarat Bose, letter to Biva, May 29, 1913.

60. Sarat Bose, letter to Biva, July 24, 1913.

61. Sarat Bose, letter to Biva, August 14, 1913.

62. Sarat Bose, letter to Biva, August 15, 1913. Rabindranath Tagore also wrote praising Western women; see Krishna Kripalani, *Rabindranath Tagore*, New York: Grove Press, 1962, 86ff.

63. Sarat Bose, letters to Biva, March 14 and August 7, 1913.

64. Sarat Bose, letters to Biva, May 29, July 13, July 24, September 17, 1913, and April 16, 1914.

65. Sarat Bose, letter to Biva, July 13, 1913.

66. Sarat Bose, letter to Biva, July 13, 1913.

67. Sarat Bose, letters to Biva, February 27, March 14, December 19, 1913.

68. Sarat Bose, letter to Biva, January 30, 1914.

69. Sarat Bose, letter to Biva, April 3, 1913.

70. Sarat Bose, letter to Biva, December 19, 1913.

71. Extracted from the records for that year of the Council of Legal Education, and *Calendar 1913–1914* and *Calendar 1914–15*, London, 1913 and 1914.

72. Sarat Bose, letter to Biva, December 19, 1913. Records of the

Council on Legal Education, *Calendars*, for 1913–14 and for 1914–15.

73. Sarat Bose, letter to Biva, March 10, 1914; and brief, unpublished notes on Mr Khaitan and Mr Pandit from C.C. Chowdhuri, Calcutta, 1979.
74. Sarat Bose, letter to Biva, June 5, 1914.
75. Sarat Bose, letter to Biva, May 22, 1913.
76. Sarat Bose, letters to Biva, October 13, 1912, July 31 and September 17, 1913, and June 25, 1914. On Maud Gonne, see the section on her in F.X. Martin ed., *Leaders and Men of the Easter Rising: Dublin, 1916*, London: Methuen and Co., 1967, 228–30.
77. This is based on Sarat Bose's many statements through his career in speeches and private correspondence about the legal traditions which he believed and defended. For example, see his speech to the Bengal Legislative Assembly, *Proceedings, 1937* [hereafter *PBLA*], Second Session, LI, No. 2, 60–61; and his article, 'A Constitution of Myths and Denials,' *Indian Law Review*, 1950, reprinted in his *I Warned My Countrymen*, 335–44.
78. Sarat Bose's copy of Bagehot's work is in the library of the Netaji Research Bureau.
79. There are many works of Shaw and Wells in his library and he mentions in several of his jail letters, 1932–35 and 1941–45, how much he was devoted to these writers. More specific details will be presented in later chapters.
80. Interview with Ajit Dey; Mukharji, 'Sarat Bose the Lawyer,' in *Sarat Bose Commemoration Volume*, 19; Ghosh, in *Eminent Indians*, 19–20.
81. Mukharji, 'Sarat Bose the Lawyer,' in *Sarat Bose Commemoration Volume*, 19–20.
82. Interview with Sisir K. Bose.
83. Interview with Gita Biswas. See the early letters of Subhas Bose to Sarat Bose in which Subhas expresses joy at receiving letters from his 'Mej–da', Bose, *Indian Pilgrim*, 116, 132ff. Most of the several dozen Bose relations with whom I have talked have mentioned the close, even remarkable tie between the brothers.

CHAPTER TWO

1. I have drawn 'Good Boy and Mischief-Maker' from Subhas Bose's own words, paraphrased slightly. In a letter to his close friend

Hemanta Kumar Sarkar, November 11, 1915, Subhas Bose wrote, teasingly, to his confidant, 'I was sorry to receive your letter as you have showed me up as a mischievous person. You know very well that I have always been a "good boy"—am I capable of any naughtiness? So, what is the meaning of this accusation of yours? Can one who has always been a "good boy" be up to any mischief at any time? So, I cannot be a "naughty boy" and any mischief on my part is impossible.' This letter is included in Subhas Chandra Bose, *An Indian Pilgrim*, Bombay: Asia Publishing House, 1965. In several other of his writings, as will be evident below, Bose was concerned with taking to task those who were just good boys and thought that their deeds would not be sufficient to lead India to freedom and greatness. This statement will be placed in context in the chapter, below.

2.   Henry David Thoreau, *A Week on the Concord and Merrimack Rivers*, New York: Thomas Y. Crowell, 1961, 161.

3.   In some of his early letters to Hemanta Sarkar, Bose related himself to Indian traditions of pilgrimage. See Bose, *Indian Pilgrim*, 157–58, 175. Exactly what he meant by 'pilgrim' is not altogether clear. But the idea of the wandering pilgrim, perhaps with a mission, in quest of God and fulfillment, may be connected to what he was driving at. Through his life, he made statements like the following which he is reported to have made while speaking at Comilla in 1931, 'As for himself he had forsaken the beaten path of life and had taken a plunge into the unknown. His was a life of adventures in quest of this ideal. He would never give up this thorny path of life till India was free.' Quoted in *Amrita Bazar Patrika*, May 12, 1931. For Bose, the idea of the quest of the pilgrim seems related to his own formulation of his ideals and sense of mission which relates the religious and the political.

4.   Commentators on and theorists of the pilgrimage include, Victor Turner, *Dramas, Fields and Metaphors*, Ithaca: Cornell U. Press, 1974, 166ff; Diana Eck, *Banares, City of Light*, New York: Alfred Knopf, 1982, 34ff.

5.   Bose, *Indian Pilgrim*, 157.

6.   Bose, *Indian Pilgrim*, 2, 24.

7.   Lucille K. Forer, *The Birth Order Factor*, XV, New York: Pocket Books 1977, comments on what she calls later middles, 54–55, 103, 105, 169.

8.   Forer, *Birth Order*, 54ff.

9.   Bose, *Indian Pilgrim*, 113–31, contains many letters that Subhas

Bose wrote to his mother, 1912–13, in which he tried to explain his growing religious and social consciousness to her. Also, interview with Sailesh Bose.

10. Bose, *Indian Pilgrim*, 19–25; Subodh Chandra Ganguli, *Early Life of Netaji*, Calcutta: Calcutta Book House, 1955?, 6–12.

11. Bose, *Indian Pilgrim*, 23; Ganguli, *Early Life*, 8.

12. This search is recorded in Bose, *Indian Pilgrim*, both in the contemporary letters, 113ff, and in the autobiographical account written years later, mostly in late 1937, 29ff.

13. Bose, *Indian Pilgrim*, 27–28, 59, 120–27; the mother in him is also mentioned by one of his closest and lifelong friends, Dilip Kumar Roy, *The Subhas I Knew*, Bombay: Nalanda Publications, 1946, 34. It was also mentioned to me by his brother Sailesh Bose, interview, Bombay, December 30, 1964.

This quality of motherliness, of caring tenderly for others, has often been ascribed to Gandhi, but not to the militant Subhas Bose, but I think it is a quality which they shared. Some analysts of Gandhi have argued that he wanted to be a mother, but it is also possible that this tender quality of caring may be part of a man's personality in India and may indicate that in the West we have long had too rigid a definition of what is male and paternal and what is female and maternal.

14. Bose, *Indian Pilgrim*, 27, where he mentions his resolve and progress. Ganguli, *Early Life*, 15–16, mentions his competitiveness. It appears obvious from his test results that he studied hard at certain times in his life and was an excellent test-taker.

15. Bose, *Indian Pilgrim*, 40.

16. Bose, *Indian Pilgrim*, 23ff. According to Dr Sisir K. Bose, his father, Sarat Bose, and his uncle, Subhas Bose, used to kid each other about their respective cultural proclivities, one more inclined to the Western, the other to the Bengali and Indian, though they both contained different syntheses of the West and India within themselves. Interviews with Sisir K. Bose, 1964, and conversations on many occasions since.

17. See M. [Mahendra Nath Gupta] ed., *The Gospel of Sri Ramakrishna*, trans. Swami Nikhilananda, 4th ed., Mylapore, Madras: The Ramakrishna Mission, 1964, 64–113, 385–90, 522–29; Christopher Isherwood, *Ramakrishna and His Disciples*, New York: Simon and Schuster, 1965, 13ff.

18. Swami Vivekananda, 'Lectures from Colombo to Almora,' in *The Complete Works of Swami Vivekananda*, III, 9th ed., Calcutta: The

Ramakrishna Mission, 1964, 131, 159–61, 188–89, 272–73, 277, 325–27; also see Bhupendranath Datta, *Swami Vivekananda Patriot–Prophet*, Calcutta: Nababharat, 1954, *passim*. Mr Datta, the younger brother of Vivekananda, long involved in left-wing politics, wanted to demonstrate the political relevance of his older brother's message, but many others saw the connection without his help.

19. Bose, *Indian Pilgrim*, 137, letter of January 8, 1913.

20. Bose, *Indian Pilgrim*, 126–27.

21. On Bankim Chandra Chatterjee, see Rachel Rebecca Van Meter, 'Bankimchandra and the Bengali Renaissance,' unpublished Ph.D. dissertation, U. of Pennsylvania, 1964; T.W. Clark, 'The Role of Bankimchandra in the Development of Nationalism,' in *Historians of India, Pakistan and Ceylon*, ed., C.H. Philips, London: Oxford U. Press, 1962, 429–40. Bose, *Indian Pilgrim*, 35ff; the many letters to Hemanta Sarkar, collected in the same book, 138–78, mention various activities of the two of them and the group which they joined, but these were not political.

22. Bose, *Indian Pilgrim*, 34–35.

23. Bose, *Indian Pilgrim*, 34–36.

24. Bose, *Indian Pilgrim*, 34–36; also see 63, 140.

25. Bose, *Indian Pilgrim*, 45. Care has to be taken in comparing letters written at the time, some of which are collected in the second part of the *Indian Pilgrim* and others of which only appear in Hemanta Kumar Sarkar, *Subhaser songe baro bochor* [Twelve Years with Subhas], Calcutta: Sarkar & Co., 1946?, with Bose's autobiography written many years later. In the letters his antipathy for some family members is expressed much more powerfully than in the later document.

26. Bose, *Indian Pilgrim*, 44ff; Ganguli, *Early Life*, 41; Sarkar, *Subhaser songe*, *passim*.

27. Bose, *Indian Pilgrim*, 32ff, describes the awakening process.

28. Sarat Bose is reported to have had an extraordinary memory in addition to his other powers of mind, but his test results, by Indian standards, do not seem to match his talents. Subhas, on the other hand, performed beyond expectations on almost every important occasion. The difference does not seem to have been one of desire, but rather some psychological one of relative anxiety or confidence, with the younger brother outperforming both of his eldest brothers, as well as almost every other student taking the examination in question.

29. Roy, *The Subhas I knew*, 10ff.
30. Bose, *Indian Pilgrim*, 45.
31. Bose, *Indian Pilgrim*, 67ff. What he read and studied will be evident also from the account of the meetings of the Philosophical Society at Scottish Churches College.
32. See Subhas Bose's letter to Sarat Bose several years later when the former was trying to explain to his brother why he was resigning from the ICS, April 6, 1921. Here he described the small, but significant difference in his youthful experience. Parts of the letter are quoted below in dealing with the 1921 decision.
33. On the first generation of Congress leaders, see Leonard A. Gordon, *Bengal: The Nationalist Movement 1876–1940*, New York: Columbia U. Press, 1974; Chapters One and Two; John R. McLane, *Indian Nationalism and the Early Congress*, Princeton: Princeton U. Press, 1977; S.R. Mehrotra, *The Emergence of the Indian National Congress*, Delhi: Vikas, 1971; Stanley A. Wolpert, *Tilak and Gokhale: Revolution and Reform in the Making of Modern India*, Berkeley: U. of California Press, 1962.
34. On Tilak, see Wolpert, *Tilak and Gokhale*, and Richard I. Cashman, *The Myth of the Lokamanya: Tilak and Mass Politics in Maharashtra*, Berkeley: U. of California Press, 1975; source material on the early violent acts against the British in Maharashtra is collected in Government of Bombay, *Source Material for a History of the Freedom Movement in India 1885–1920*, Vol. II (Collected from Bombay Government Records), Bombay: Government Central Press, 1958.
35. This paragraph and several subsequent ones on Aurobindo Ghose are a summary of Gordon, 'Aurobindo Ghose: Secrets of the Self and Revolution,' Chapter Four of *Bengal*.
36. The finest work on the Swadeshi period is Sumit Sarkar, *The Swadeshi Movement in Bengal 1903–1908*, New Delhi: People's Publishing House, 1973.
37. Gordon, *Bengal*, 123–30.
38. Aurobindo Ghose, *The Doctrine of Passive Resistance*, 2nd ed., Pondicherry: Sri Aurobindo Ashram, 1952, 29–30, 66–68.
39. Ghose, *Passive Resistance*, 29.
40. Gordon, *Bengal*, 130–34.
41. On the revolutionaries and their suppression, see Government of India, Sedition Committee, 1918, *Report*, Calcutta: Superintendent Government Press, 1918; James Campbell Ker, *Political Trouble in India 1907–1917*, Delhi: Oriental Publishers, 1973 [reprint of

1917], Government of India, Home Department report prepared for internal circulation, as also, H.W. Hale, *Political Trouble in India 1917–1937*, Allahabad: Chugh Publications, 1974. All of these reports give summaries of great masses of Home Department reports on individual incidents and regions. Some shortcomings of these reports, particularly the Sedition Committee *Report*, are pointed out in Gordon, *Bengal*, 142ff. There are also, of course, many memoirs by former revolutionaries and numerous secondary works in Bengali. A valuable general work is Suprakas Ray, *Bharater baiplabik sangramer itihas* [History of the Indian Revolutionary Struggle], Calcutta: Indian Book Stall, 1955. David M. Laushey, *Bengal Terrorism and the Marxist Left*, Calcutta: Firma KLM, 1975, has a more extensive bibliography and an overview of the period.

42. Bose, *Indian Pilgrim*, 53–56.
43. He later became quite critical of Sri Aurobindo and his retreat from politics. This caused heartache for his devoted friend Dilip Roy who was a disciple of Sri Aurobindo and who tried to explain Aurobindo's point of view to Subhas Bose. See Roy, *Subhas I Knew*, 90–100; Subhas Chandra Bose, *Correspondence, 1924–1932*, Calcutta: Netaji Research Bureau, 1967, 87, 89, 97, 104–5, 413. Although he has on occasion overstressed the religious and mystical side of Subhas Bose, Dilip Roy is the one writer who has tried to detail the private, religious life of Bose from college days to 1940, in *Subhas I Knew* and in his *Netaji—The Man, Reminiscences*, Bombay: Bharatiya Vidya Bhavan, 1966.
44. Bose, *Indian Pilgrim*, 58–59.
45. Many of Tagore's essays on these themes are collected in Rabindranath Tagore, *Rabindra racanabali* [Collected Works of Rabindra], Vols. XII and XIII, Calcutta: Government of West Bengal, 1961. *Gora* was published around 1910 and later translated into English, *Gora*, London: Macmillan, 1961; on Bose's tour of Bengal, see *Indian Pilgrim*, 44ff; Ganguli, *Early Life*, 42–46.
46. For the letters which express their feelings and describe the relationship, see Bose, *Indian Pilgrim*, and Sarkar, *Subhaser songe*. Such friendships between young men of this age are common in many cultures. For example, see Paul Fussell, *The Great War and Modern Memory*, New York: Oxford U. Press, 1977, 272, on such relationships in British public schools, and R.F. Delderfield, *To Serve Them All My Days*, New York: Pocket Books, 1973, where these relationships are called "ninging" and described, 329ff. They are common in India, as well, but are not frequently described. A famous

portrayal of such a relationship between boys of fourteen is in Thomas Mann's story 'Tonio Krüger,' in *Stories of Three Decades*, New York: Alfred A. Knopf, 1936, 84–132. There the relationship is asymmetrical, with Tonio the lover courting his friend's love and attention.

47. The most passionate passage in this letter of Subhas Bose to Hemanta Sarkar, in Sarkar, *Subhaser songe,* 25–27, is difficult to translate, but an effort to put it into English by Bharati Mukherjee is as follows:

'Never in your life have you wronged me—you can't. Would you believe my word? I have sinned so much. I have caused your heart so much pain that you have been driven toward suicide. "[*I*] have no right to ask forgiveness." If at all you seek forgiveness, I have always forgiven you before you ask for it. Even if you could not ask, I would do it—even if you could not lift your face and ask for love, I would offer a thousandfold the love of my tiny heart at your feet, the feet "of the Lord of all my days". Even if you cannot ask, can't I give? Am I giving you love because you want it or am I giving you love for love's sake? That's why even if you don't ask me today, even if you can't, reading your heart, reading the want in your heart, I shall give a thousandfold. [*After all*] I am forever yours—you are forever mine—don't forget this, that you are my Lord, my eternal Lord, until now my heart laments that I am not [*deemed*] worthy of worshipping that Lord. Don't you know that you have always been my Krishna? No matter what the people of the world say of you—you are my Lord forever. To the devotee, Krishna is the incarnation of love. Today you are the eternal incarnation of love to me. I have nothing to do with right and wrong—I don't understand sin and virtue.

'From where would you call and where would you have [*me*] sit? Have I abandoned your heart even for a moment that you will [*have to*] call again? If I had left, then of course you would have had to call. But, even for a moment, I haven't been able to give up the craving for that throne—I cannot. None can rout me from there—if they drive me away, I shall not move even an inch, [*for*] I am unshakably installed there. From lifetime to lifetime I have been living there—why should I let go of this property of mine now?

'There is no need to ask him to sit on the throne of the heart, because he has been sitting there forever, [*he*] has never moved, so why are you suffering? Open your eyes and see, he's still there.'

Bharati Mukherjee writes of the problem of translating this letter that,

'Subhas as letter-writer seems to have some stylistic peculiarities. For instance, he moves inexplicably from *tor* (possessive of *tui*) to *tomar*, and from a colloquial diction to a slightly more formal diction within a paragraph. He also slides from the direct and engaging you—I format of the first two paragraphs—to a more impersonal third-person format in the final paragraph. His punctuation is imprecise. . .' (personal letter, June 12, 1984).

48. In writing of this period, including some time earlier and some time later—Subhas Bose mentioned powerful sexual drives which were felt by him. He seems to have adopted the 'Ramakrishna solution': transform the women around you into forms of the Mother Goddess. See Bose, *Indian Pilgrim*, 48–52; he also tried to persuade Basanti Devi, some years later, that she was the mother of all of India's sons, in Bose, *Correspondence, 1924–32*, 52–54, 137–38, letters of 1925 and 1926.

49. The letters to Hemanta are in Sarkar, *Subhaser songe, passim*, and some in Bose, *Indian Pilgrim*, 138–78. I do not know the details of marriage offers to the Bose family for Subhas, but he certainly declined them. As he came close to the Dharmavir family in England and then in India, he always treated their daughters as his younger sisters rather than as eligible young women. This seems to have been his usual way of dealing with young women. See Dharmavir Papers, Nehru Memorial Library. I will discuss his relationship to this family below.

50. Bose, *Indian Pilgrim*, 60.

51. Bose, *Indian Pilgrim*, 60ff.

52. Bose, *Indian Pilgrim*, 139, letter of June 19, 1914.

53. Bose, *Indian Pilgrim*, 140.

54. I will deal with several of his other rebellions below, but I believe that the family and his relationship to his parents is the place to begin. For studies of rebellion against the acceptance of authority, see Theodore Adorno ed., *The Authoritarian Personality*, New York: Harper and Row, 1950, 52–53, and *passim*; Phyllis Greenacre, *The Quest for the Father*, New York: International Universities Press, 1963, 13–15, 90ff; Robert D. Hess, 'The Socialization of Attitudes toward Political Authority: Some Cross–National Comparisons,' *International Social Science Journal*, XV, No. 4, 1963, 542–59. I have suggested on several occasions that the pattern of his rebellions and acceptance of authorities indicated ambivalence on his part. When I have said this in India, Indian listeners have often disliked this kind of suggestion and probing. For example, see my essay

'Themes in a Political Biography of Subhas and Sarat Chandra Bose,' in Sisir K. Bose ed., *Netaji and India's Freedom*, Calcutta: Netaji Bhavan, 1975, 1–26, and the response by Prof Gautam Chattopadhyay, 27.

55. Bose, *Indian Pilgrim*, 60–63, 138ff; Ganguli, *Early Life*, 36ff, 47–9; Sarkar, *Subhaser songe*, 47.

56. Some information is found in *The Presidency College Magazine*, Vols. I–III, covering 1914 to 1916; also see Bhola Nath Roy, *Oaten Incident 1916: A Chapter in the Life of Netaji Subhas Bose*, Calcutta: S.C. Sarkar, 1975, 17ff; Bose, *Indian Pilgrim*, 45–71.

57. Roy, *Subhas I Knew*, 21–22.

58. See Roy's two books, *Subhas I Knew* and *Netaji*. My remarks are also based on conversations with Mr Roy in Calcutta and at his ashram in Poona, where I stayed briefly in 1965.

59. Roy, *Netaji*, 10; also Roy, *Subhas I Knew*, 21–28.

60. Roy, *Netaji*, 10.

61. Roy, *Subhas I Knew*, 56–57, 61, 65, 67.

62. Bose, *Indian Pilgrim*, 148, letter of September 16, 1915.

63. An older but valuable account of Darjeeling is by Arthur J. Dash, *Darjeeling, Bengal District Gazetteers*, History, Alipore, Bengal: Bengal Government Press, 1947, Chapter II.

64. *Imperial Gazetteer of India*, Provincial Series, Vol. II, Bengal, Calcutta: Superintendent of Government Printing, 1909, 193.

65. Bose, *Indian Pilgrim*, 154.

66. Bose, *Indian Pilgrim*, 152–53, letter to Hemanta of October 19, 1915.

67. Bose, *Indian Pilgrim*, 155, letter to Hemanta of November 7, 1915.

68. *Presidency College Magazine*, III, No. 1, September 1916, 22–25.

69. Government of India, Department of Education, *A. Proceedings*, November 1916, Nos. 4–6. The file is concerned with the transfer of Mr H.R. James from his post as principal of Presidency College, but contains other material on events at the college during this tumultuous time.

70. Roy, *Oaten Incident*, 21.

71. Bose, *Indian Pilgrim*, 71.

72. Subhas Chandra Bose, *The Mission of Life*, Calcutta: Thacker, Spink, 1953, 165. This remark was made in the course of an address to a conference of students in 1929. Roy, *Oaten Incident*, 36ff, gives a detailed account. Some of the story from the official side is also given in Government of India, Department of Education, *A. Proceedings*, November 1916, Nos. 4–6. An account of this incident and

of Presidency College at the time is given by Irene A. Gilbert, 'Autonomy and Consensus under the Raj: Presidency (Calcutta); Muir (Allahabad); M.A.–O (Aligarh),' in Susanne Hoeber Rudolph and Lloyd I. Rudolph eds., *Education and Politics in India*, Delhi: Oxford U. Press, 1972. More details are given in Government of India, J&P/1861/1916, India Office Library, London, and in Government of India, Department of Education, June 1916, Nos. 122–127.

73. Bose, *Indian Pilgrim*, 163, letter of February 29, 1916.

74. Subhas Bose, letter to Sarat Bose, April 23, 1921, in Subhas Chandra Bose, *Netaji Collected Works*, ed., Sisir K. Bose, Vol. I, Calcutta: Netaji Research Bureau, 1980, 233.

75. Bose, *Indian Pilgrim*, 70–71.

76. Bose, *Indian Pilgrim*, 79; Ganguli, *Early Life*, 63–71; Sailesh Bose, 'My Brother Subhash,' *Sunday Standard Magazine*, January 18, 1981.

77. Government of India, Department of Education, June 1916, Nos. 122–27.

78. Government of India, Department of Education, June 1916, Nos. 122–27.

79. Rabindranath Tagore, 'Indian Students and Western Teachers,' *Modern Review*, Calcutta, April 1916.

80 Sailesh Bose, 'My Brother Subhash'.

81. Bose, *Indian Pilgrim*, 72.

82. Bose, *Indian Pilgrim*, 75.

83. Bose, *Indian Pilgrim*, 77.

84. Sailesh Bose, 'My Brother Subhash'.

85. Interview with Nirmal Kumar Bose, Calcutta, February 11, 1964; K.P. Chattopadhyay, 'Subhas at Cambridge,' Netaji Supplement, *The Loka–Sevak*, January 23, 1954 (translated from Bengali); Asoke Nath Bose, *My Uncle Netaji*, Calcutta: ESEM Publications, 1977, 2–3; Bose, *Indian Pilgrim*, 72–78.

86. Bose, *Indian Pilgrim*, 78–9.

87. Bose, *Indian Pilgrim*, 79; although Subhas had been harshly condemned for his role in the Oaten affair, he had a good record in his studies and was acceptable in college activities prior to his rustication. He had attended the Protestant European School in Cuttack. Furthermore, his family, particularly his father and his brother Sarat had good connections to Sir Ashutosh Mookerjee and other important men in the Indian establishment in Calcutta, so this helped him to regain a place in a fine college after his years of banishment.

88. Bose, *Indian Pilgrim*, 80–84.

89. *Scottish Churches College Magazine*, VIII, No. 5, March 1918, 218–19. The back volumes of this magazine are to be found in the library of the college and contain a full record of his efforts for the Philosophical Society.

90. *Scottish Churches College Magazine*, VIII, No. 5, March 1918, 219.

91. *Scottish Churches College Magazine*, IX, No. 2, September 1918, 59–60.

92. *Scottish Churches College Magazine*, IX, No. 2, September 1918, 60.

93. Bose, *Indian Pilgrim*, 104–110, should be compared with the college formulation summarized in *Scottish Churches College Magazine*, IX, No. 2, September 1918, 59–60.

94. Bose, *Indian Pilgrim*, 80–82. Jawaharlal Nehru refers to his interest in *The Selected Works of Jawaharlal Nehru*, Vol. I, New Delhi: Orient Longman, 1972, 105ff. On the general question of the 'martial races', see Nirad C. Chaudhuri, 'The "Martial Races" of India,' *The Modern Review*, Calcutta, Part I, XLVIII, No. 1, July 1930; Part II, XLVIII, No. 3, September 1930; Part III, XLIX, No. 1, January 1931; Part IV, XLIX, No. 2, February 1931. There are also a few comments in Gordon, *Bengal*, 134–35.

95. The 'reporter' was Subhas Bose and the article is in *Scottish Churches College Magazine*, VIII, No. 3, November 1917, 52–56. The pages in *Indian Pilgrim*, 80–82, are his version of the same experience described twenty years later.

96. Bose, *Indian Pilgrim*, 81–82.

97. *Scottish Churches College Magazine*, IX, No. 5, March 1919, 230–31.

98. Bose, *Indian Pilgrim*, 83–84.

99. Bose, *Indian Pilgrim*, 168, letter of August 26, 1919.

100. Roy, *Netaji*, 26; comments on the journey and British experience are in Bose, *Indian Pilgrim*, 85–103.

101. Government of India L/J & P/6238/20, ICS. Open Competition Result, India Office Library, London.

102. Roy, *Netaji*, 26; also Roy, *Subhas I Knew*, 47ff.

103. Bose, *Indian Pilgrim*, 92–193.

104. The books are in the library of the Netaji Research Bureau, Calcutta. I have compiled a detailed list and classification of the books of Janaki Nath Bose, Sarat Bose, and Subhas Bose that remain there, 'Sarat–Subhas–Janaki Nath Library Breakdown,' of which a copy is retained in the library itself.

105. See Bose, *Indian Pilgrim*, 85–103, 169–187; and Roy, *Subhas I*

Knew, 47–75.

106. Bose, *Indian Pilgrim*, 170, letter of November 12, 1919.

107. Bose, *Indian Pilgrim*, 90; see the comments on Mr Bates in his letter of September 9, 1920, in Bose, *Netaji's Collected Works*, I, 207. He also grew close to the Dharmavir family and Mrs Dharmavir was a European. He also mentioned the help given to him by Mr Reddaway, the censor of Fitzwilliam Hall.

108. Roy, *Netaji*, 30.

109. See Joseph R. Levenson, *Liang Ch'i–Ch'ao and the Mind of Modern China*, Cambridge, Massachusetts: Harvard U. Press, 1959, *passim*.

110. Roy, *Netaji*, 29.

111. Bose, *Indian Pilgrim*, 91.

112. Bose, *Indian Pilgrim*, 89, 170, 174–5; two other Indian contemporaries make mention of Bose at this time: M.C. Chagla, *Roses in December*, Bombay: Bharatiya Vidya Bhavan, 1974, 41–2; and B.R. Sen, *Towards a Newer World*, Dublin: Tycooly, 1982, 15.

113. Secretary of State for India, Committee on Indian Students in the United Kingdom, *Report*, 1921–22, 41–2.

114. Government of India, L/J&P/6238/20. Of the maximum score of 6000, P. Ramalingam finished first with 2716, A.F. Bateman second with 2695, A.N. Shah third with 2377, and S.C. Bose fourth with 2284. Bose received 360 marks in English Composition, 255 in Sanskrit, 105 in Geography, 173 in English History, 125 in General Modern History, 344 in Logic and Psychology, 304 in Moral and Metaphysical Philosophy, 229 in Political Economy and Economic History, 248 in Political Science and 130 in English Law. The maximum score in English Composition was 500 marks and Ramalingam and Bose tied with 360 for the first place.

115. Bose discusses his decision in *Indian Pilgrim*, 93–103, and contemporary letters are gathered in Bose, *Netaji Collected Works*, I, 206–36. His friends of the time have also described his crucial decision: Roy, *Netaji*, 45ff; and K.P. Chattopadhyay, 'Subhas at Cambridge'. Chagla, *Roses*, claims that Bose discussed his decision with Jinnah who advised him to stay in the ICS, 42.

116. Subhas Bose, letter to Sarat Bose, September 22, 1920, in Bose, *Netaji Collected Works*, I, 206–209.

117. Bose, *Netaji Collected Works*, I, 208–9.

118. Bose, *Indian Pilgrim*, 172–73.

119. Bose, *Netaji Collected Works*, I, 223–27, letter to Sarat Bose, April 6, 1921.

120. Bose, *Netaji Collected Works*, I, 224, letter to Sarat Bose, April 6,

1921.

121. The original of this letter is in Government of India, L/J&P/6238/20.

122. Some of the details of the British attempt to dissuade him from his resignation are in the same file, Government of India, L/J&P/6238/20.

123. Subhas made explicit his idea of each family offering a sacrifice for the national cause in his letter to Sarat of April 6, 1921. In the letters he wrote to Sarat at the time, he again and again invoked the example of Aurobindo Ghose. Although he wanted his father's consent to his course of action, Subhas wrote to Sarat that it was his, Sarat's, agreement that was essential to him. In his letter of February 23, 1921, he wrote to Sarat,

'I realize that it will require more strength of mind on your part to consent to my proposal than has been required of me in formulating this proposal. But I am fully confident that you possess the requisite strength of mind. I am sure that if you are convinced of the soundness of my proposal you will not allow any other consideration to withhold your consent.

'Aurobindo Ghose is to me my spiritual guru. To him and to his mission I have dedicated my life and soul. My decision is final and unchangeable, but my destiny is at present in your hands.

'Can I not expect your blessings in return and will you not wish me Godspeed in my new and adventurous career?'

Both of these letters are collected in Bose, *Netaji Collected Works*, I, 219–227. On the side of his choice, Subhas invoked the heroes and cause of Indian nationalism in Bengal, the notion of sacrifice for the Motherland, and even played on Sarat's 'strength of mind' to persuade. It is not clear what choice Sarat and their father had if they had not agreed to Subhas' resignation. From hints in his letters—Sarat's if they survive are not presently available—it appears that he thought Sarat would come down on his side and later it seems that his mother did as well. Sarat's agreement is mentioned by Khitish Chattopadhyay, 'Subhas at Cambridge'. In the end, his family became reconciled to his choice and his mission.

124. Subhas Bose's letters to Das are in Bose, *Netaji Collected Works*, I, 210–17, and he mentions Das' reply in a letter to Sarat Bose of April 23, 1921, in the same volume, 235.

125. Letter to Sarat Bose, April 23, 1921, in Bose, *Netaji Collected Works*, I, 235; also see Asoke Bose, *My Uncle*, 5.

126. These are the books that remain of his Cambridge days in the library of the Netaji Research Bureau and are marked, Subhas C. Bose,

Cambridge. He also mentioned in his description of his Cambridge days how much he liked being able to walk into a bookshop and charge books on his account, Bose, *Indian Pilgrim*, 88.

127. K.P. Chattopadhyay, 'Subhas at Cambridge'.

128. See Dilip Roy's account in *Netaji*, 36ff, 157–64; as mentioned above, the Dharmavir Correspondence is in the Nehru Memorial Library. I also checked some points about this relationship with the late Dr Santosh Sen, who married into the Dharmavir family and also knew Subhas Bose well in Vienna in the 1930s. Dr Sen died in 1979.

129. Roy, *Netaji*, 157.

130. Roy, *Netaji*, 159.

131. Roy, *Netaji*, 161–62.

132. I am not sure whether Subhas Bose visited Ireland during this period, but his later visit in the 1930s will be described below. There will be many references to Ireland later and to the special connection that the Boses felt for that troubled country, to their identification with another land that had suffered badly, they thought, under British imperialism.

133. Bose, *Indian Pilgrim*, 179.

134. Bose, *Netaji Collected Works*, I, 232–33, letter of April 23, 1921.

135. Roy, *Netaji*, 165.

136. Roy, *Subhas I Knew*, 173, 191.

137. Roy, *Netaji*, 165.

138. Subhas Bose letter to Mrs Dharmavir, May 7, 1921, in Dharmavir Papers.

139. Subhas Bose letter to Mrs Dharmavir, May 7, 1921, in Dharmavir Papers.

140. Bose, letter to Mrs Dharmavir, May 7, 1921, in Dharmavir Papers.

141. Bose, letter to Mrs Dharmavir, May 7, 1921, in Dharmavir Papers.

142. Roy, *Netaji*, 214.

CHAPTER THREE

1. Kazi Nazrul Islam, *The Rebel and Other Poems*, trans. Basudha Chakravarty, New Delhi: Sahitya Akademi, 1974, 30–31.

2. The works on Gandhi are legion. Some of the better ones are: B.R. Nanda, *Mahatma Gandhi*, London: Allen & Unwin, 1958; Judith M. Brown, *Gandhi's Rise to Power: Indian Politics 1915–1922*, Cambridge: Cambridge U. Press, 1974, and her *Gandhi and Civil Disobedience: The Mahatma in Indian Politics 1928–34*, Cam-

bridge: Cambridge U. Press, 1977; R. Kumar ed., *Essays on Gandhian Politics: The Rowlatt Satyagraha of 1919,* London: Oxford U. Press, 1971; Erik H. Erikson, *Gandhi's Truth: On the Origins of Militant Nonviolence,* New York: Norton, 1969; Penderel Moon, *Gandhi and Modern India,* London: The English Universities Press, 1968. All of these works have valuable analyses and some shortcomings. The above volumes all touch on the crucial period of 1915 to 1922 when Gandhi came to the fore, except for Judith Brown's second volume. Students of Gandhi also have invaluable source material in *The Collected Works of Mahatma Gandhi,* New Delhi: Government of India, Publications Division, 1958 to the present, now comprising about ninety volumes. Another useful reference work is D.G. Tendulkar, *Mahatma: Life of Mohandas Karamchand Gandhi,* 8 vols, revised ed., New Delhi: Government of India, Publications Division, 1960.

3.   Subhas Chandra Bose, *The Indian Struggle 1920–1942,* Bombay: Asia Publishing House, 1964, 54–55.

4.   Bose, *Indian Struggle,* 55; Bose had met Das earlier after the Oaten affair and had corresponded with him from England. See Bose, *Indian Pilgrim,* 101–102, 179–86.

5.   On Chittaranjan Das, see Gordon, *Bengal,* 164–70; Prithwas Chandra Ray, *The Life and Times of C.R. Das,* Calcutta: Oxford U. Press, 1927; Hemendranath Das Gupta, *Deshbandhu Chittaranjan Das,* Delhi: Government of India, Publications Division, 1960; Dilip Kumar Chatterjee, *C.R. Das and Indian National Movement,* Calcutta: Post-Graduate Book Mart, 1965; J.H. Broomfield, *Elite Conflict in a Plural Society: Twentieth–Century Bengal,* Berkeley: U. of California Press, 1968.

6.   M.R. Jayakar, *The Story of My Life,* Vol. I, New York: Asia Publishing House, 1958, 344–46; B.R. Nanda, *The Nehrus, Motilal and Jawaharlal,* New York: John Day, 1963, 181ff; Das Gupta, *Deshbandhu,* 50ff.

7.   Nanda, *Nehrus,* 181ff; on the decline of the Extremist group, Gordon, *Bengal,* 158–60; on Das in this period, see Das Gupta, *Deshbandhu,* 27–39.

8.   Ray, *Bharater baiplabik sangramer itihas,* 166–218.

9.   Das Gupta, *Deshbandhu,* 30.

10.   C.R. Das, *India for Indians,* 3rd ed., Madras: S. Ganesh, 1921, 13–14.

11.   Das' speech is in Rajen Sen and B.K. Sen eds., *Deshbandhu Chitta Ranjan,* Calcutta: n.p., 1926, 9–10. Extracts from the same speech

are given in Das Gupta, *Deshbandhu*, 141–47.

12. Rabindranath Bhattacharyya ed., *Tagore Birth Centenary 1861–1961*, Supplement Issue, *The Calcutta Municipal Gazette*, LXXV, No. 21, 156–57; there are comments on this point in many of Tagore's political essays of the period which are collected in *Rabindra racanabali*, XII, 673–1099 and XIII, 1–438.

13. Sen and Sen, *Deshbandhu*, 12–63, where he picks up on all of these themes.

14. According to the 1931 census, high-caste Hindus formed 6.1 per cent of the population of Bengal but 28.9 per cent of the Calcutta population. Government of India, *Census of India 1931*, Calcutta: Government of India, V, Part 2, 1932, 225–32.

15. See Gordon, *Bengal*, Chapter One; on Bankim Chandra, see T.W. Clark, 'The Role of Bankimchandra in the Development of Nationalism,' in C.H. Philips ed., *Historians of India, Pakistan and Ceylon*, London: Oxford U. Press, 1962, 429–40, and Rachel R. Van Meter, 'Bankimchandra's View of the Role of Bengal in Indian Civilization,' in David Kopf ed., *Bengal Regional Identity*, East Lansing: Michigan State U. Press, 1969, 61–70.

16. Amalendu De, *Roots of Separatism in Nineteenth Century Bengal*, Calcutta: Ratna Prakashan, 1974, 3ff; Gordon, *Bengal*, 8–9. A recent and penetrating study of the Muslims in the late nineteenth century is Rafiuddin Ahmed, *The Bengal Muslims 1871–1906: A Quest for Identity*, Delhi: Oxford U. Press, 1981.

17. For numbers, see H. Beverley ed., Government of India, *Report on the Census of Bengal*, Calcutta: Government of India, 1872, and J.A. Bourdillon ed., *Report on the Census of Bengal*, I, Calcutta: 1881; Mustafa Nurul Islam, *Bengali Muslim Public Opinion as Reflected in the Bengali Press 1901–1930*, Dacca: Bangla Academy, 1973, 218ff; Kenneth McPherson, *The Muslim Microcosm: Calcutta, 1918 to 1935*, Wiesbaden: Franz Steiner Verlag, 1974, 9ff; M.K.A. Siddiqui, 'Caste among the Muslims of Calcutta,' in Surajit Sinha ed., *Cultural Profile of Calcutta*, Calcutta: The Indian Anthropological Society, 1972, 34, 44, 47; W.C. Smith, *Modern Islam in India*, New York: Russell and Russell, 1972; P. Hardy, *The Muslims of British India*, Cambridge: Cambridge U. Press, 1972, 116ff; Sufia Ahmed, *Muslim Community in Bengal 1884–1912*, Dacca: Oxford U. Press, 1974, 28ff; R. Ahmed, *Bengal Muslims*; interview with Abu Sayyid Ayyub, Calcutta, November 24, 1972; for a discussion of non-identification with Bengal on the part of a Muslim who spent a good part of his life there, see Gordon, *Bengal*, 60ff, analysis of

Ameer Ali.

18. Interview with Buddhadeva Bose, Calcutta, July 9, 1973.

19. Anisuzzaman, 'Cultural Trends in Bangladesh: A Redefinition of Identity,' Seminar paper, Nuffield College, Oxford, February 17, 1975; also Anisuzzaman, 'The'World of the Bengali Muslim Writer in the Nineteenth Century (1870–1920),' Seminar paper, U. of Sussex, May 9, 1975.

20. Z.H. Zaidi, 'The Political Motive in the Partition of Bengal,' *Journal of the Pakistan Historical Society*, April 1964; Pardaman Singh, 'Lord Minto and the Partition Agitation,' in *Bengal Past and Present*, Calcutta, July–December 1966, 141ff; Richard Paul Cronin, *British Policy and Administration in Bengal: Partition and the New Province of Eastern Bengal and Assam,* Calcutta: Firma KLM, 1977, Chapter I, Sumit Sarkar, *Swadeshi Movement*, Chapter One; John R. McLane, 'The 1905 Partition of Bengal and the New Communalism,' in Alexander Lipski ed., *Bengal East and West*, East Lansing: Michigan State U. Press, 1969.

21. Mary, Countess of Minto, *India Minto and Morley 1905–1910*, London: Macmillan, 1934, 109ff, gives Minto's view; other views of the reforms are given in Gordon, *Bengal*, 94–6. Under the 1909 reforms, the Legislative Council of the Lieutenant-Governorship of Bengal had twenty-six elected members and four of these seats were reserved for' members of the Muslim community, the first such reservation in the Council. The number was small, but it was a first step and was the result of vigorous lobbying by Muslim League leaders. *Parliamentary Papers*, Vòl. 67, No. 5, 1910; also see Broomfield, *Elite Conflict*, 35–38.

22. Aga Khan, *The Memoirs of Aga Khan, World Enough and Time*, London: Cassell, 1954, 76ff.

23. C.H. Philips, H.L. Singh, B.N. Pandey eds., *The Evolution of India and Pakistan 1858 to 1947*, London: Oxford U. Press, 171–73, 192.

24. Gordon, *Bengal*, 159; on Huq, see *Times of India, Indian Year–book and Who's Who 1947*, Bombay: 1947, 1109; J.H. Broomfield, 'The Forgotten Majority: The Bengal Muslims and September 1918,' in D.A. Low ed., *Soundings in Modern South Asian History*, London: Weidenfeld & Niçolson, 1968, 204–7; A.S.M. Abdur Rab, *A.K. Fazlul Huq*, Lahore: Ferozsons, 1966?; Robert Reid, *Years of Change in Bengal and Assam*, London: Ernest Benn, 1966, 120–22.

25. Philips et al., *Evolution*, 264–69.

26. Edward Hallett Carr, *The Bolshevik Revolution 1917–1923*, III, Baltimore: Penguin Books, 1966, 232–71; Hans Kohn, 'The

Russian Revolution and the Orient', in his *A History of Nationalism in the East*, New York: Harcourt Brace, 1929; Bose, *Indian Struggle*, 99; the Indian nationalist paper of Das' party, *Forward*, had a regular column on Irish developments; A.J.P. Taylor, *English History 1914–1945*, London: Oxford U. Press, 1965, 153–61.

27. Edwin Montagu, *An Indian Diary*, London: Heinemann, 1930, 91.

28. Montagu, *Indian Diary*, 58.

29. Report on Indian Constitutional Reforms, 1918, Cd. 9109, the proposals for changes are outlined, 147ff.

30. See Sedition Committee, 1918, *Report*, Calcutta: Government Printing, 1918, where the extent of the different revolutionary groups is overemphasized and the conflict between the groups is ignored. Thus the threat from the groups is overblown.

31. See Jayakar, *Story*, I, 219ff; Gandhi, *Collected Works*, XV, 516ff; Tendulkar, *Mahatma*, I, 234ff. The Congress report on the Amritsar massacre and its causes is printed in Gandhi, *Collected Works*, XVII, 114–291. Jayakar, *Story*, I, 504ff, describes the process of collecting the materials for it. Gandhi, Das, and Motilal Nehru served on the Congress investigation committee and brought away from this experience an emotional bond which endured through all of their disagreements of the following years. For testimony on this see Jawaharlal Nehru, *Toward Freedom*, Boston: Beacon Press, 1968, 109. An analysis of British responses to the massacre is presented in Helen Fein, *Imperial Crime and Punishment: The Massacre at Jallianwala Bagh and British Judgment, 1919–1920*, Honolulu: U. Press of Hawaii, 1977.

32. *The Statesman: An Anthology*, compiled by Niranjan Majumdar, Calcutta: The Statesman, 1975, 346–47.

33. Gandhi's associate, G.D. Birla, a leading Indian businessman, who was in communication with high government officials, continually pointed out to them that they had better deal with Gandhi or be faced with leftists and revolutionaries with whom they could not deal at all. See G.D. Birla, *In the Shadow of the Mahatma*, Bombay: Orient Longman, 1953, *passim*. On the revolutionaries as threats, real and imaginary, see Gopal Haldar, 'Revolutionary Terrorism,' in his *Studies in the Bengal Renaissance*, ed., Atulchandra Gupta, Jadavpur, Calcutta: National Council of Education, 1958, 224–57; and previously cited works: Laushey, *Bengal Terrorism*; Hale, *Political Trouble*; Ray, *Bharater baiplabik sangramer itihas*. References will be given below to files dealing with specific incidents of revolutionary activity.

34. On the reorganization of the Congress in this period under Gandhi's hand, see Gopal Krishna, 'The Development of the Indian National Congress as a Mass Organization, 1918–1923,' *The Journal of Asian Studies*, XXV, No. 3, May 1966, 413–30.

35. The report is in Gandhi, *Collected Works*, XVII, 114–291; it has been included in Gandhi's collected works because he played the key role in its compilation, as Jayakar, *Story*, I, 504ff, has pointed out.

36. This streak is analyzed by Dennis Dalton, 'Gandhi: Ideology and Authority,' *Modern Asian Studies*, Nos. 3 and 4, 1969, 377–93; I have suggested elsewhere that this streak is related to Indian traditions of the Indian raja and Indian kingship, Leonard A. Gordon, 'Erik Erikson's Truth and Mahatma Gandhi's India,' *Journal of Social History*, Vol. 4, No. 4, Summer 1971, 431. Some classical sources relevant to this point are: G. Bühler, ed., 'The King,' in his *The Laws of Manu*, Delhi: Motilal Banarsidass, 1964 reprint, 215–52; *Kautilya's Arthasastra*, ed., R. Samasastry, Mysore: Mysore Printing and Publishing House, 1960, *passim*. On Gandhi's uncrowned rulership of the Congress, see Rajendra Prasad, *Autobiography*, Bombay: Asia Publishing House, 1957, *passim*; Nirmal Kumar Bose, *Studies in Gandhism*, 3rd ed., Calcutta: Merit, 1962, 177ff; Michael Brecher, *Nehru, A Political Biography*, London: Oxford U. Press, 1959, Chapters VI–X; P.D. Kaushik, *The Congress Ideology and Programme 1920–47*, New Delhi: Allied, 1964.

37. Krishna, 'Congress,' 413ff; Birla made it clear that Gandhi could always depend on him for funds, *Shadow*, 38.

38. A succinct selection of Gandhi's views is presented in Nirmal Kumar Bose ed., *Selections from Gandhi*, 2nd ed., Ahmedabad: Navajivan, 1957.

39. The idea of trusteeship has always been a target for Marxist and leftist critics of Gandhi. See M.N. Roy, *India in Transition*, Geneva?, 1922; R. Palme Dutt, *India Today*, London: Victor Gollancz, 1940, 307ff; Barrington Moore Jr., *Social Origins of Dictatorship and Democracy*, Boston: Beacon Press, 1966, 370ff.

40. *Statesman: Anthology*, 336.

41. The progressive steps in a satyagraha campaign are presented in Joan V. Bondurant, *Conquest of Violence: The Gandhian Philosophy of Conflict*, Princeton: Princeton U. Press, 1958, 38–41.

42. See Gordon, *Bengal*, Chapters Six to Nine. On Maharashtrian Brahmin antipathy to Gandhi, see J.A. Curran Jr., *Militant Hinduism*

in Indian Politics, New York: International Secretariat, Institute of Pacific Relations, 1951; Dhanajay Keer, *Savarkar and His Times*, Bombay: Popular Prakashan, 1950; Balshastri Hardas, *Armed Struggle for Freedom*, Poona: KAL Prakashan, 1958; Stanley Wolpert, *Nine Hours to Rama*, New York: Bantam Books, 1963; John Frederick Muehl, *Interview with India*, New York: John Day Co., 1950, 152–213; Larry Collins and Dominique Lapierre, *Freedom at Midnight*, New York: Simon and Schuster, 1975, Chapters 16–20.

43. B.D. Shukla, *A History of the Indian Liberal Party*, Allahabad: Indian Press, 1960, 198–206; Jayakar, *Story*, I, 209ff; Surendranath Banerjea, *A Nation in Making*, Calcutta: Oxford U. Press, 281ff [1963 reprint of 1925 ed.,].

44. Gordon, *Bengal*, Chapters Six and Seven; some assessments of Das are given at the end of Chapter Seven. Also see *Statesman: Anthology*, 372–73; Maulana Abul Kalam Azad, *India Wins Freedom*, Bombay: Orient Longman, 1959, 18–21.

45. Krishna, 'Congress,' 423; Nripendra Chandra Banerji, *At the Crossroads (1885–1946)*, Calcutta: Jijnasa, 1950, 161-62 [1974 reprint].

46. Jayakar, *Story*, I, 344–46.

47. See Bose's letters to Das and references to Das, in Bose, *Netaji Collected Works*, III, 210ff.

48. Interviews with Sisir K. Bose, Aurobindo Bose, Gita (Biswas) Bose.

49. This can be seen in the Bose family itself where the eldest daughter did not go on for higher education, but the younger three did, with the youngest getting a post-graduate degree. On the growth of education, see Aparna Basu, *The Growth of Education and Political Development in India 1898–1920*, Delhi: Oxford U. Press, 1974, especially Chapter 5.

50. Interview with Aurobindo Bose.

51. In one letter to Sarat Bose, Subhas Bose wrote, 'If the *ghataks* (matchmakers) come to trouble you again, you can ask them straight away to take a right about turn and march off.' Letter of September 22, 1920, in Bose, *Netaji Collected Works*, I, 209. The details in this paragraph were given to me by Basanti Devi (Mrs C.R. Das) whom I talked with on October 31, 1964.

52. P.B. Mukharji, 'Sarat Chandra Bose the Lawyer,' in *Sarat Bose Commemoration Volume*, 19–20.

53. Interviews with Sisir K. Bose, Gita (Biswas) Bose, Meera (Roy) Bose, Sailesh Bose, Lila (Mitra) Bose.

54. Some anthropologists have suggested that Indians have a great talent

for compartmentalization, e.g., A.K. Ramanujan, 'Is There an Indian Way of Thinking?' unpublished manuscript; Milton Singer, *When a Great Tradition Modernizes*, New York: Praeger, 1972, 320–25. Sarat Bose's library contains many works of Russell, Trotsky, and Shaw. Several of the volumes are heavily marked, I believe, by him. His children have testified to his strong and conventional religious beliefs and practices.

55. Interview with Gita (Biswas) Bose who mentioned to me that her father was a good rider and loved the mountains. Subhas Bose's devotion to the mountains has been mentioned above.

56. On the impact of Nazrul Islam, see Buddhadeva Bose, *An Acre of Green Grass*, Calcutta: Orient Longman, 1948, 36–9; Kazi Abdul Wadud, *Creative Bengal*, Calcutta: Thacker Spink, 1949, 123–34; interview with Bishnu Dey, Calcutta, July 6, 1973.

57. Quoted in Basudha Chakravarty, *Kazi Nazrul Islam*, New Delhi: National Book Trust, 1968, 9–10.

58. Asoke Nath Bose, *My Uncle Netaji*, 8; interview with Dilip Kumar Roy, Poona, January 1965; Bose, *Indian Struggle*, 55ff. References to the different kinds of work Subhas Bose was doing through these years can be found in Bose, *Correspondence, 1924–32*, 121ff, and in *Amrita Bazar Patrika*, May 25, 1923.

59. Upendra Nath Banerjee, 'Subhas,' *Masik Basumati*, Magh 1352, January 1945.

60. On the opposition of two formidable Bengalis to the boycott of the schools, see Probodh Chandra Sinha, *Sir Asutosh Mookherjee*, Calcutta: The Book Co., 1928, 263ff; R.K. Prabhu and Ravindra Kelekar eds., *Truth Called Them Differently (Tagore–Gandhi Controversy)*, Ahmedabad: Navajivan Publishing House, 1961, 18–23; Das, *India for Indians*, 14ff.

61. P.C. Bamford, *Histories of the Non–Co-Operation and Khilafat Movements*, Delhi: Government of India Press, 1925, 101–108 [reprinted, Delhi: Deep Publications 1974].

62. See Gandhi's comments and disappointment about this, Mahatma Gandhi, *Swaraj in One Year: Speeches in Bengal*, Madras: S. Ganesh and Co., 1921, 49–50; Bamford, *Histories*, 104.

63. Subhas Chandra Bose, unpublished Prison Notebook #3, Netaji Research Bureau.

64. See for example, Government of Bengal, Political Department, 1922, File No. 195, Serial 1–8, Annual Report on the Press in Bengal for the Year 1921, which says that *Banglar Katha* was shaping

students' minds.

65. On the Non–Cooperation Movement, see Bamford, *Histories*; Nehru, *Toward Freedom*, 65–79; Mahatma Gandhi, *Young India 1919–1922*, New York: B.W. Huebsch, Inc., 1923, 134ff; H.N. Mitra, *The Indian Annual Register*, II, Calcutta: The Annual Register Press, 1921, 236–59; Brown, *Gandhi's Rise*, 250ff; Rajat Ray, 'Masses in Politics, Non–Cooperation Movement in Bengal 1920–22,' *Indian Economic and Social History Review*, XI, No. 4, December 1974, 343–410.

66. Nehru, *Toward Freedom*, 65–79, 109–110.

67. Haldar, 'Revolutionary Terrorism,' 249; Narendra Nath Das, *History of Midnapur*, Calcutta: Midnapur Samskriti Parishad, 1962, 55ff; Ray, *Itihas*, 392–94; interview with Surendra Mohan Ghose, New Delhi, September 27, 1964; Mr Ghose was then a member of the Jugantar Party.

68. Bamford, *Histories*, 136–63; Gail Minault, *The Khilafat Movement: Religious Symbolism and Political Mobilization in India*, New York: Columbia U. Press, 1982; M.K. Gandhi, *Communal Unity*, Ahmedabad: Navajivan Publishing House, 1949, 3–40.

69. Gandhi, *Swaraj in One Year*, 54–59.

70. Bamford, *Histories*, 100ff.

71. Bamford, *Histories*, 42–43.

72. Interview with Basanti Devi, 1964; Broomfield, *Elite Conflict*, 219ff. Das later commented bitterly on his having sent his whole family to prison, only to have Gandhi call off the movement, Jayakar, *Story*, I, 509; Bose, *Indian Struggle*, 65; Das Gupta, *Deshbandhu*, 68–69.

73. Banerjee, 'Subhas'.

74. Banerjee, 'Subhas'.

75. Das, *India for Indians*, 64.

76. Bose, *Indian Struggle*, 65.

77. Janaki Nath Bose, letter to Sarat Bose, December 12, 1921, Netaji Research Bureau.

78. Subhas Chandra Bose, *The Mission of Life*, Calcutta: Thacker Spink, 1953, 107.

79. Bose, *Mission of Life*, 107–8.

80. See the lengthy account of his 1924–27 imprisonment in the following chapter.

81. Quoted in Jayakar, *Story*, I, 509.

82. B. Pattabhi Sitaramayya, *History of the Indian National Congress*,

Vol. I (1885–1935), Bombay: Padma Publications, 1946 223–29 [reprint of 1935 ed.].

83. Gandhi, *Collected Works*, XXII, 118.
84. *Statesman* leader of September 28, 1921, in *Statesman: Anthology*, 355.
85. Bamford, *Histories*, 69–70.
86. Bamford, *Histories*, 70–71.
87. Bose, *Indian Struggle*, 73ff; Nehru, *Toward Freedom*, 80ff.
88. See D.A. Low, 'The Government of India and the First Non–Co–operation Movement,' in Kumar, *Essays on Gandhian Politics*, 298ff, where the shrewd calculations of the Government of India are detailed; Bamford, *Histories*, 75.
89. Bose, *Indian Struggle*, 69–70.
90. Government of Bengal, Reports on the Native Press, 1922 (covering 1921).
91. An excellent account of their relations is Nepal Majumdar, *Rabindranath o subhaschandra* [Rabindranath and Subhaschandra], Calcutta: Saraswati Library, 1968, 1–3, which mentions these first meetings.
92. See Stephen N. Hay, *Asian Ideas of East and West: Tagore and His Critics in Japan, China, and India,* Cambridge: Harvard U. Press, 1970, 49ff; Krishna Kripalani, *Rabindranath Tagore*, New York: Grove Press, 1962, 213ff; Rabindranath Tagore, *Nationalism*, New York: Macmillan, 1917, *passim*.
93. Prabhu and Kelekar, *Truth Called*, 64–65.
94. See the essays collected in Prabhu and Kelekar, *Truth Called*, *passim*; and Gordon, *Bengal*, 184–88.
95. Prabhu and Kelekar, *Truth Called*, 76ff.
96. See Krishna, 'Congress,' 426; Birla, *Shadow, passim*.
97. Useful studies of the trade union movement are Sukomal Sen,*Working Class of India: History of Emergence and Movement 1830–1970,* Calcutta: K.P. Bagchi, 1977; Shiva Chandra Jha, *The Indian Trade Union Movement*, Calcutta: Firma K.L. Mukhopadhyay; Sukbhir Choudhary,*Peasants' and Workers' Movement in India 1905–1929,* New Delhi: People's Publishing House, 1971.
98. Rajat Ray, 'Masses in Politics, Non–Cooperation Movement in Bengal 1920–22,' *Indian Economic and Social History Review*, XI, No. 4, December 1974, 393ff (article 343–410).
99. Jayakar, *Story*, I, 607–13.

CHAPTER FOUR

1. Kazi Nazrul Islam, quoted in Basudha Chakravarty, *Kazi Nazrul Islam*, 12.

2. *Banglar Katha*, January 26, 1923, extracts in Government of Bengal, Home Department files, West Bengal State Archives, Writers' Building, Calcutta.

3. Hemendranath Das Gupta, *Subhas Chandra*, Calcutta: Jyoti Prokasalaya, 1946, 53.

4. Das Gupta, *Subhas Chandra*, 55.

5. See Gordon, *Bengal*, Chapter Seven; the press of these years, particularly 1923 to 1925, is filled with the charges and counter–charges of the Pro-Changers and No-Changers. There are numerous articles in *Forward* and in the *Amrita Bazar Patrika* presenting one side or another. Some examples will be given below.

6. Nehru, *Toward Freedom*, 262; R.C. Majumdar, *History of the Freedom Movement in India*, III, Calcutta: Firma K.L. Mukhopadhyay, 1963, 263ff.

7. The speech is included in an appendix to Das Gupta, *Deshbandhu*, 157–207.

8. Bose, *Indian Struggle*, 78ff; Das' first important statement on the Swarajist line is 'C.R. Das on Civil Disobedience Enquiry Committee,' in Mitra, *Indian Annual Register*, I, 1923, 180–81.

9. Gordon, *Bengal*, 191–93; Das Gupta, *Deshbandhu*, 88ff, describes Das' tours of different parts of India in building support for the Swarajists. Some of these details come from articles in *Times of India, Who's Who in India*, Bombay, 1925–1947, an annual publication which provided biographical data on many of these individuals. I also consulted Satya Ranjan Bakshi in Calcutta, 1964.

10. Bose, *Indian Struggle*, 85–88; the prospectus for *Forward* mentioned these names; Subhas Bose wrote in the *Indian Struggle*, 85, that he edited *Banglar Katha*. From the correspondence of Subhas and Sarat Bose when Subhas was imprisoned, 1924–27, it is manifest just how deeply involved Sarat had become in nationalist work and particularly with *Forward*. See Bose, *Correspondence, 1924–32, passim*. Erik H. Erikson, *Gandhi's Truth*, 102, 109, 132, 158, 164, 369, 401, notes that sons who come to politics, sometimes radical politics, may, in turn, recruit their fathers and other family members to their cause, and go beyond their fathers.

11. Government of Bengal, Home Department, 'Revolutionary Press Propaganda in Bengal,' File No. 257/25.

12. Government of Bengal, Reports of the Native Press, No. 7 of 1923, February 17, 1923, 142.

13. *Forward*, October 20, 1925.

14. This is clear from the many extracts from *Atma Sakti* in the Government of Bengal, Reports of the Native Press for these years. For example, see article March 14, 1923, on the meaning of swaraj, in Reports of the Native Press, Government of Bengal, No. 12 of 1923; article of January 31, 1923, Reports of the Native Press, No. 6 of 1923.

15. An invaluable source for this history is the multi-volume, *Documents of the History of the Communist Party of India*, ed., G. Adhikari et al., New Delhi: People's Publishing House, 1971 to the present, of which Volumes I, II, III, Parts A,B, C, and VII, and VIII have appeared. The first two volumes covering 1917–22 and 1923–25 cover the period under scrutiny in this chapter and contain lengthy extracts from the writings of M.N. Roy and other communist writers of this period. The history of the communist and socialist movements in India is given in the introductions to the *Documents* series mentioned above and in Gene D. Overstreet and Marshall Windmiller, *Communism in India*, Berkeley: U. of California Press, 1959; David N. Druhe, *Soviet Russia and Indian Communism*, New York: Bookman, 1959; Kaushik, *Congress Ideology*, where the influence of socialist ideas is shown; Thomas A. Rusch, 'Role of the Congress Socialist Party in the Indian National Congress,' unpublished Ph.D. dissertation, U. of Chicago, 1955; L.P. Sinha, *The Left Wing in India*, Muzaffarpur: New Publishers, 1965; John Patrick Haithcox, *Communism and Nationalism in India: M.N. Roy and Comintern Policy 1920–1939*, Princeton: Princeton U. Press, 1971; and in numerous official sources of the Government of India, particularly, Sir Cecil Kaye, *Communism in India (1919–1924)*, a secret Home Department report, Calcutta: Editions Indian, 1971 [reprinted]. Also of value is Satyabrata Rai Chowdhuri, *Leftist Movements in India 1917–47*, Calcutta: Minerva, 1977, which, like Sinha, *Left Wing*, tries to take an overview of the spectrum of leftist groups and organizations. There are also numerous memoirs of participants of varying usefulness. One of the most charming and insightful of these is Philip Spratt, *Blowing Up India*, Calcutta: Prachi Prakashan, 1955. Many of the above books touch on the life of M.N. Roy and there is a lengthy biography by V. B. Karnik, *M.N. Roy: Political Biography*, Bombay: Nav Jagriti Samaj, 1978.

16. Their marked copy of Russell's book is in the library of the Netaji

Research Bureau, along with many other books on European politics
published during the inter-war years. Jawaharlal Nehru and his
father traveled to the Soviet Union in 1927. See Jawaharlal Nehru,
Soviet Russia, Allahabad: Lala Ram Mohan Lal, 1928. Rabindranath Tagore visited in September and October 1930; see his
Letters from Russia, Calcutta: Visva-Bharati, 1960, which consists
of contemporary letters and some reflections.

17.   Government of Bengal, Reports of the Native Press, No. 12 of 1923,
      article of March 14, 1923.
18.   See the last letter in Hemanta Kumar Sarkar, *Subhaser songe,* 151,
      written to him by Subhas Bose, October 5, 1924, in which Subhas is
      responding to Hemanta's sharp attack on him for taking an official
      position and a princely salary.
19.   Government of Bengal, Reports of the Native Press, No. 6 of 1923,
      article of January 31, 1923.
20.   As noted earlier, Ray, *Itihas*, is a reliable general history of the revo-
      lutionaries. In Buddhadeva Bhattacharyya ed., *Freedom Struggle
      and Anushilan Samiti*, Calcutta: Anushilan Samity, 1979, 197,
      226–42, there are some comments on Subhas Bose and the revolu-
      tionaries which I believe are accurate. I have also relied on many
      interviews with Surendra Mohan Ghose, Delhi, 1964 & 1972, for
      information which I have tried to check against other sources and
      other interviews. The theme of Laushey, *Bengal Terrorism*, is the
      conversion process.
21.   Interview with Chinmohan Sehanabis, Calcutta, 1978; Hale, *Politi-
      cal Trouble*, 15, also mentions Breen. Subhas and Sarat Bose had an
      interest in Ireland and read books about Ireland while imprisoned.
      Some of their comments about Ireland and the connection they saw
      and felt will be mentioned below.
22.   A hint of the kind of surveillance underway can be gathered from
      Government of India, Home Department, Political File No. 61 of
      1924, 'Note of the Connection between the Revolutionists and the
      Swarajya Party in Bengal,' but the actual police and Intelligence
      Branch data was much more detailed and extensive and often
      incorrect. Also see Hale, *Political Trouble, passim*, which is yet
      another step removed from the actual raw data.
23.   The peasant organizations as they developed in Bengal were strong
      in some districts, but even these were not closely tied to the
      Congress. Local studies—politics at the grassroots—is presently a
      burgeoning field in Indian historiography. An overview (rather than
      a local study) is given by Binay Bhushan Chaudhuri, 'Agrarian

Movements in Bengal and Bihar: 1919–39,' in *Peasant Struggles in India*, ed., A.R. Desai, Bombay: Oxford U. Press, 1979, 337–74.

24. Moni Ghosh, *Our Struggle*, Calcutta: Das Gupta, 1959?, 8–12.

25. An article mentioning Bose's early labor interest is in *Amrita Bazar Patrika*, May 3, 1923, and again, August 23, 1923. Bose's views on labor organizing will be explored more fully below in Chapter Five.

26. There are endless press articles dealing with these quarrels. For example, see Bose's defense in his letter of June 4, 1923, to the *Amrita Bazar Patrika,* published June 6, 1923.

27. *Amrita Bazar Patrika*, June 6, 1923.

28. See *Amrita Bazar Patrika*, May 25, August 18, and December 19, 1923.

29. The names of the members of the BPCC were collected from *Forward*, September–October 1924. With the help of Profs Ralph W. Nicholas, Ronald B. Inden, and Moni Nag, I tried to calculate percentages of Hindus and Muslims, and then high-and-low-caste Hindus. The Muslim percentage was thirteen per cent in this period and lower in earlier times. The complete list of names and calculations are in my original Ph.D. thesis, 'Bengal and the Indian National Movement,' Harvard U., 1969. On the Bengal Pact, see Mitra, *Indian Annual Register*, I, 1924, 665–68; Azad, *India Wins Freedom*, 20–21; Chaudhri Muhammad Ali, *The Emergence of Pakistan*, New York: Columbia U. Press, 1967, 21.

30. Sen and Sen eds., *Deshbandhu*, 265–68.

31. Mitra, *IAR*, I, 1924, 671.

32. Das Gupta, *Subhas Chandra*, 66.

33. Das Gupta, *Subhas Chandra*, 67.

34. Mitra, *IAR*, I, 1924, 629.

35. On electoral politics in Bengal, see Gordon, *Bengal*, 201ff; Broomfield, *Elite Conflict*, 244ff; Gautam Chattopadhyay, *Bengal Electoral Politics and Freedom Struggle 1862–1947*, New Delhi: Indian Council of Historical Research, 1984, 69ff; Rajat Ray, *Urban Roots of Indian Nationalism: Pressure Groups and Conflicts of Interest in Calcutta City Politics, 1875–1939*, New Delhi: Vikas, 1979, 108ff.

36. The figures are given in Government of Bengal, *Report on the Working of the Reformed Constitution in Bengal, 1921–27*, Calcutta: Bengal Secretariat Book Depot, 1929, 130–31; this report was also issued as Indian Statutory Commission, *Memorandum submitted by the Government of Bengal to the Indian Statutory Commission*, Vol. VIII, London: His Majesty's Stationery Office, 1930.

37   See Gordon, *Bengal*, 201ff; Banerjea, *Nation in Making*, 152–53. 325–40.

38.   Broomfield, *Elite Conflict*, 240–42.

39.   Government of Bengal, *Report on 1921–27*, 143.

40.   The governor, the Earl of Lytton, in his memoirs, *Pundits and Elephants*, London: P. Davies, 1942, 34ff, blames all his woes and troubles on the nationalists and Das, of whom he gives a vicious account, an example of a small man trying to belittle a much bigger one. Also see Government of Bengal, *Report on 1921–27* and the Bengal Legislative Council *Proceedings* [hereafter *PBLC*], 1924–25. More details and an effort to sort out votes on important issues and to demonstrate the support of Muslim members for the Swarajists during 1924 and 1925 can be found in Gordon, 'Bengal and the Indian National Movement,' in the chapter on the Swarajists and in the appendix. Also see Gordon, *Bengal*, 207–16, and Broomfield, *Elite Conflict*, 169ff, who takes a much different view of Das and the Swarajists.

41.   *PBLC*, XIV, No. 5, 1924, 164–84; Government of Bengal, *Report on 1921–27*, 170–71.

42.   Bose, *Indian Struggle*, 98–9; Nanda, *Nehrus*, 207–70.

43.   The approach which sees only the conflicts and pushes the inevitability of the partition back to the earlier twentieth century or even the nineteenth century seems much too historicist and needlessly deterministic. I have argued against this approach in 'Divided Bengal: Problems of Nationalism and Identity in the 1947 Partition,' *The Journal of Commonwealth and Comparative Politics*, XVI, No. 2, July 1978, 136–38, and used arguments presented by Isaiah Berlin, 'Historical Inevitability,' *Four Essays on Liberty*, London: Oxford U. Press, 1969, to aid me in my view. Also see Gordon, *Bengal*, 208–14, for more details.

44.   Das Gupta, *Subhas Chandra*, 68–9.

45.   See Bose's letter to Hemanta Sarkar, *Subhas songe*, 151.

46.   *Calcutta Municipal Gazette*, No. 6, June 20, 1925 [hereafter *CMG*].

47.   See Bose's speech in *CMG*, September 27, 1930, 873.

48.   Das Gupta, *Deshbandhu*, 97–9.

49.   Binoy Jiban Ghosh, 'Netaji's Great Citadel in Freedom's Fight: Calcutta Corporation,' *Loka–Sevak*, Netaji Supplement, January 23, 1954.

50.   See the many references to Bose's work and ideas in *CMG*, I, 1924–25.

51.   Das Gupta, *Subhas Chandra*, 71–2.

52. Sarat Bose was known as Bose-sahib, while Subhas Bose was called Subhas-babu, which was an indication of the younger brother being more informal and more Bengali in his relationships. Dilip Roy has many descriptions of his informality among his friends and his stiffness vis-à-vis the British, Roy, *Subhas, passim.*

53. *CMG*, II, 1925–26, No. 17, September 5, 1925.

54. See the tribute to Bose in the opening issue of the *CMG*, I, No. 1, November 15, 1924.

55. *Amrita Bazar Patrika*, July 17, 1924.

56. *Amrita Bazar Patrika*, July 17, 1924.

57. Gandhi, *Collected Works*, Vol. XXIV, 479.

58. *Forward*, September 14, 1924.

59. Bose, *Indian Struggle*, 128.

60. *CMG*, I, 1924–25, No. 7, speech of October 29, 1924.

61. Lytton, *Pundits and Elephants*, 60–70.

62. Government of Bengal, Political Department, 840/32, Serial No. 1–7.

63. Government of Bengal, Political Department, 257/25.

64. Government of India, Home Department, Political File No. 61 of 1924, 'Note of the Connection between the Revolutionists and the Swarajya Party in Bengal,' and Hale, *Political Trouble*, 8.

65. See *PBLC*, XVII, No. 2, 1, 1925, and *PBLC*, 1925, 19th session, 422–35.

66. Bose, *Indian Struggle*, 105–110.

67. Bose, *Correspondence*, 5–20; then the letters resume from Mandalay, 20ff; Bose, *Indian Struggle*, 128–41.

68. Jogesh Chandra Chatterji, *In Search of Freedom*, Calcutta: Firma KLM, 1967, 264–69.

69. Chatterji, *In Search,* 267.

70. Bose, *Indian Struggle*, 129.

71. Bose, *Indian Struggle*, 130.

72. Charles F. Keyes, *The Golden Peninsula: Culture and Adaptation in Mainland Southeast Asia*, New York: Macmillan, 1977, 264–69; these remarks are based on Keyes, on a visit to Mandalay in June 1979, and on L.F. Rushbrook Williams, *A Handbook for Travellers in India, Pakistan, Burma and Ceylon*, 19th ed., London: John Murray, 1962, 546–49.

73. Keyes, *Golden Peninsula*, 269.

74. Bose, *Correspondence*, 28.

75. Bose, *Indian Struggle*, 131.

76. Some of the fruits of this prison writing are well-known, including

several books of Jawaharlal Nehru, B.G. Tilak, M.N. Roy, and others. During 1931 to 1936, M.N. Roy secretly smuggled letters in and out. Many of the revolutionaries carried on political recruitment, teaching, and contacts with the outside during their imprisonments. Jogesh Chatterji, briefly a prison-mate of Bose, has many comments in Chatterji, *In Search, passim*.

77. Most of the details in this paragraph and about Bose's imprisonment have been gleaned from Bose, *Correspondence*, 3–363, and Bose, *Indian Struggle*, 128–41. Some additional information comes from Subhas Bose's Prison Notebooks, numbered 1–8, kept in the Netaji Research Bureau. I also talked with Surendra Mohan Ghose in New Delhi, 1964 & 1972, about Bose in Mandalay. Mr Ghose was one of his fellow prisoners.

78. Bose, *Correspondence*, 29ff.

79. Bose, *Correspondence*, 63.

80. Bose, *Correspondence*, 63.

81. Bose, *Correspondence*, 64.

82. Bose, *Indian Struggle*, 131.

83. This observation is based on a visit to Mandalay in June 1979.

84. Bose, *Correspondence*, 83–84.

85. Bose, *Correspondence*, 83–84; Bose, *Indian Struggle*, 131. He was of course in Burma during the Second World War, but was concerned with the war effort and hardly had time for reflection during this tumultuous time.

86. This Buddha is in the possession of Dr and Mrs Sisir K. Bose.

87. Some of these details come from Bose, *Correspondence, passim*; I also talked with Surendra Mohan Ghose who claimed that he helped guide Bose in his studies of Indian religion, but I think it is appropriate to call them 'classmates'.

88. Bose, *Correspondence*, 39.

89. Bose, *Correspondence*, 84, letter of September 11, 1925.

90. Bose, *Correspondence*, 296.

91. See Gordon, *Bengal*, 81, 110, 112–14, 128–9, 132–3, 156, 178, 227.

92. Bose, *Correspondence*, 127.

93. Bose, *Correspondence*, 128.

94. Bose, Notebooks, 1–8.

95. Bose, *Correspondence*, 127–8.

96. The idea for doing this was spread by Sri Ramakrishna who Bose took as one of his guides in life from an early age. See Bose, *Pilgrim*, 34ff, especially 48–9. One can see the way young women have been turned into sisters in the Dharmavir Papers. His wife mentioned to

me that he was peculiarly timid upon meeting young women. She
recalled an incident in Berlin when an unknown girl came into their
garden and Bose became quite flustered.'

97. Bose, *Correspondence*, 145, 164, 297.
98. Bose, *Correspondence*, 145.
99. Bose, *Correspondence*, 3ff.
100. Bose, *Correspondence*, 187.
101. Bose, *Correspondence*, 187.
102. Bose, *Correspondence*, 284–85.
103. Bose, *Correspondence*, 184ff. Although the attorneys for the *States-man* tried to get the governments in question to release evidence and also tried to have the Government of Bengal bring Subhas Bose to Calcutta for questioning in court, there seems to have been no practical chance of the government cooperating in light of the way in which he was held without any charges ever having been made public, made in court, or even revealed to him.
104. Lytton, *Pundits,* 54–56.
105. *PBLC*, XIV, No. 5, 1924, 238.
106. For the continual questioning by the Swarajists about the condition of the prisoners, see *PBLC*, 1924–25, *passim*. Of course, the nationalist press in Calcutta, led by *Forward* also pressed for accurate information and used whatever information they could obtain to criticize the government's treatment of the prisoners. On the Council, *PBLC*, 19th session, 1925, 32–40, 195–215.
107. *PBLC*, XVII, No. 4, 1925, 234–37.
108. Gordon, *Bengal*, 210–11; see *PBLC*, 1925–27.
109. Bose, *Correspondence*, 196.
110. Bose, *Correspondence, passim*.
111. Bose, *Correspondence*, 49.
112. Bose, *Correspondence*, 302.
113. Bose, *Indian Struggle*, 107–110; Das Gupta, *Deshbandhu*, 118.
114. 'Mr C.R. Das' Manifesto,' quoted in Mitra, *IAR*, I, 1925, 87.
115. Broomfield, *Elite Conflict*, 264; 'The European View,' quoted in Mitra, *IAR*, I, 1925, 88–89.
116. Gordon, *Bengal*, 216–22; Haldar, 'Revolutionary Terrorism,' 249–51.
117. Das Gupta, *Deshbandhu,* 125–37.
118. Das Gupta, *Deshbandhu*, 138.
119. Gordon, *Bengal*, 219ff; I have argued for the skill and successes of Das while trying to see the fragility of his work. The governor of Bengal, Lytton, denigrated Das' work as being wholly negative.

Broomfield, *Elite Conflict*, 240ff, highlights his shortcomings and gives him scant credit for any political accomplishments.

120. *CMG*, II, No. 7, June 27, 1925.
121. *Statesman: Anthology*, 372–73.
122. Bose, *Indian Struggle*, 110ff; Bose, *Correspondence*, 45ff.
123. Bose, *Correspondence*, 52–54.
124. Bose, *Correspondence*, 55, 85–6, 136, 179–80, 285–88, 366–69.
125. Bose, *Correspondence*, 66.
126. Bose, *Correspondence*, 66–67.
127. Bose, *Correspondence*, 68.
128. Bose, *Mission of Life*, 113–14.
129. Bose, *Mission of Life*, 114–15.
130. Bose, *Mission of Life*, 115–18.
131. Bose, *Mission of Life*, 118–19.
132. Bose, *Mission of Life*, 120.
133. Bose, Prison Notebooks, especially 3, 5, 6, 7, 8.
134. Bose, Prison Notebook, 3 (translated from Bengali).
135. Bose, Prison Notebook, 3 (translated from Bengali).
136. Bose, *Mission of Life*, 122.
137. Many of the writings and speeches in *Mission of Life*, 125ff, are specifically addressed to students and youths.
138. Bose, Prison Notebook, 3 (translated from Bengali).
139. Bose, Prison Notebook, 3 (translated from Bengali); in Sarat Bose's copy of Tennyson's poems, in the Library of the Netaji Research Bureau, this last line is marked, and he often quoted it.
140. Bose, Prison Notebook, 3 (translated from Bengali).
141. Bose, Prison Notebooks, 1, 3; Bose, *Correspondence*, 88, 97.
142. Bose, *Mission of Life*, 123–24.
143. Bose, *Correspondence*, 55, 85–6, 136, 179–80, 285–88, 366–69.
144. Bose, *Indian Struggle*, 137–38; Government of India, Home Department, 47/26; Bose, Prison Notebook, 8; Bose, *Correspondence*, 116ff.
145. Bose, *Correspondence*, 116.
146. Bose, *Correspondence*, 263.
147. Bose, *Correspondence*, 116, 263.
148. Bose, *Correspondence*, 121; Bose, *Indian Struggle*, 137–38.
149. Bose, *Correspondence*, 121.
150. On Gandhi's use of old techniques in new ways, see Joan V. Bondurant, *The Conquest of Violence: The Gandhian Philosophy of Conflict,* rev.ed., Berkeley: U. of California press 1965; and Lloyd I. Rudolph and Susanne Hoeber Rudolph, *The Modernity of Tradition*:

Political Development in India, Chicago: U. of Chicago Press, 1967, 186; Bose wrote a lot about Gandhi, and Bose employed fasting himself in a political context on a number of occasions, but never said that he was following Gandhi's method, technique or model.

151. Bose, *Correspondence*, 58.

152. On Sen Gupta, see Padmini Sengupta, *Deshapriya Jatindra Mohan Sengupta*, Delhi: Publications Division, Government of India, 1968; article by A.C. Banerjee on Sen Gupta in *Dictionary of National Biography*, ed., S.P. Sen, IV, Calcutta: Institute of Historical Studies, 1974, 126–27 [hereafter referred to as Sen, *DNB*].

153. Das Gupta, *Subhas Chandra*, 90; Bose, *Indian Struggle*, 123; Sengupta, *Deshapriya*, 74–76.

154. Das Gupta, *Subhas Chandra*, 93; Mitra, *IAR*, I, 1926, 94–96.

155. Sengupta, *Deshapriya*, 62ff.

156. Bose, *Correspondence*, 65, 102, 113, 241–43.

157. *CMG*, II, No. 18, September 12, 1925, and No. 19, September 19, 1925.

158. *CMG*, IV, No. 16, 1926, 685.

159. *CMG*, IV, No. 16, 683–87.

160. *CMG*, V, No. 16, March 12, 1927, 775.

161. *CMG*, V, No. 16, March 12, 1927, 779.

162. This is based on my earlier portrayal of Sarat Bose's education; on an analysis of his remaining books in the library of the Netaji Research Bureau; on a reading of his speeches in the *PBLC*, 1937–39; on *Sarat Bose Commemoration Volume* and on Sisir Kumar Bose ed., *The Voice of Sarat Bose*, Calcutta: Netaji Bhavan, 1979, and the Collected Works 1945–50 of Sarat Chandra Bose, *I Warned My Countrymen*, Calcutta: Netaji Research Bureau, 1968.

163. *CMG*, I, No. 21, April 18, 1925, 914.

164. The remarks quoted from the *Statesman* assessment above are typical. For remarks in a similar vein, written in the 1950s, see Hugh Toye, *Subhash Chandra Bose: The Springing Tiger*, Bombay: Jaico Publishing House, 1978 [reprint of 1959], 24, 181, 185, where Toye refers again and again to Subhas Bose's 'racial complex' and 'racial hatred'.

165. On the riots, see Government of India, Home Department, 1926, Political.File No., 11/XXV/26, Confidential File on the Calcutta Riots of April 1926 and File No., 11/VII/1926; Richard D. Lambert, 'Hindu–Muslim Riots,' Ph.D. dissertation in sociology, U. of Pennsylvania, 1951, 93–100; McPherson, *Muslim Microcosm*, 90ff, Broomfield, *Elite Conflict*, 276–78; Suranjan Das, Department of

History, Calcutta U., has presented several papers on these riots and is preparing a Ph.D. thesis on communal riots in Calcutta during the twentieth century.

166. Home Department, 11/XXV/26 and 11/VII/1926.
167. Home Department, 11/XXV/26 and 10/16/1931; on the conflicts between revolutionary nationalists over the few arms available or stolen, see Sedition Committee, *Report*, 66–67, and Government of India, Home Department, 1917, Nos. 299–301. The theme of disarming interpreted or felt as emasculation is one which runs through all the literature of the Indian revolutionary movement from the late nineteenth century to independence.
168. Lambert, 'Hindu–Muslim Riots,' *passim.*
169. Bose, *Correspondence*, 210–11.
170. *CMG*, IV, No. 6, June 26, 1926, 221.
171. Bose, *Correspondence*, 227, letter of August 26, 1926; McPherson, *Muslim Microcosm*, 93ff.
172. On the fate of the Swarajists and the upcoming Bengal elections, see Bose, *Correspondence*, 213ff, and Bose, *Indian Struggle*, 115–20.
173. Bose, *Correspondence*, 213ff.
174. Bose, *Indian Struggle*, 139.
175. Bose, *Correspondence*, 262.
176. Bose, *Correspondence*, 246–47.
177. Bose, *Correspondence*, 252ff.
178. Bose, *Indian Struggle*, 139.
179. Bose, *Correspondence*, 27.
180. Bose, *Correspondence*, 293.
181. Bose, *Correspondence*, 290ff; for the Government of India side, see Home Department, File No. 1/1927; also Bose describes this period in *Indian Struggle*, 139–41.
182. Bose, *Correspondence*, 327–29.
183. Government of India, Home Department, Political File No. 104/1927.
184. Bose, *Correspondence*, 339.
185. Bose, *Correspondence*, 340.
186. Bose, *Correspondence*, 341–42.
187. Bose, *Indian Struggle*, 140.
188. Bose, *Indian Struggle*, 141.
189. Bose, *Correspondence*, 363ff.
190. Bose, *Correspondence*, 299.
191. Bose, *Correspondence*, 374.
192. Bose, *Correspondence*, 373.

193. Bose, *Correspondence*, 376–77.
194. Bose, *Correspondence*, 385–86.
195. Bose, *Correspondence*, 375.
196. Bose, *Correspondence*, 94.
197. Chatterji, *In Search*, 268.
198. Bose, *Correspondence*, 303.

CHAPTER FIVE

1. Bose, *Correspondence, 1924–32*, 401–2.
2. Bose's own account of the period is in Bose, *Indian Struggle*, 121ff; I have argued that the gap was not unbridgeable in 'Divided Bengal,' 142ff; others have argued that the divide was almost too wide to be spanned, e.g., Broomfield, *Elite Conflict*, 280.
3. See the many works on the history of communism in India, cited above, Chapter Four, note 15. Especially valuable is Adhikari, *Documents*, III C, 1928; on the Nehrus' trip abroad, see Nanda, *Nehrus*, 252–53; Nehru, *Soviet Russia;* Michael Brecher, *Nehru, A Political Biography*, London: Oxford U. Press, 1959, Chapter V; B.N. Pandey, *Nehru*, London: Macmillan, 1976, 116ff; Sarvepalli Gopal, *Jawaharlal Nehru: A Biography*, I, Cambridge, Mass.: Harvard U. Press, 1976, Chapter 8.
4. Tagore lectured widely abroad. See Krishna Kripalani, *Rabindranath Tagore*, New York: Grove Press, 1962; Rabindranath Tagore, *The Religion of Man*, Boston: Beacon Press, 1961 [reprint of 1931 ed.], and *Lectures and Addresses*, London: Macmillan, 1962, are some of his collected lectures given abroad in the period when he was regarded as a wise man from the East.
5. Nehru and Bose, soon to be regarded as among the most important younger leaders of the Indian national movement, particularly its left-wing, certainly had their eyes on these developments and these actions culminated in their collaborative effort to establish the first planning committee for India in 1938.
6. Bose, *Indian Struggle*, 121ff; the most important source is Bengal Legislative Council *Proceedings* [hereafter *PBLC*] 1926–29, which again and again shows the increased mistrust between Hindus and Muslims during these years. Nonetheless, I still do not believe that the gap was unbridgeable for they were able to cooperate and even form a ministry together in 1941.
7. On the 'Responsivists' see Majumdar, *Freedom Movement*, III,

255ff; Bose, *Indian Struggle*, 123; also see Chattopadhyay, *Electoral Politics*, Chapter Six.

8. Government of Bengal, *Report on 1921–27*, 143ff.
9. *PBLC*, XXIV, January 17, 1927, 43.
10. *PBLC*, XXIV, 44.
11. *PBLC*, XXIV, 44–5.
12. *PBLC*, 1924–29, *passim*; there are many studies of the reforming process and endless government documents. An older work is R. Coupland, *The Constitutional Problem in India: The Indian Problem, 1833-1935*, Part I, London: Oxford U. Press, 1944; a recent study is R.J. Moore, *The Crisis of Indian Unity 1917–1940*, London: Oxford U. Press, 1974; most of Moore's study deals with 1928 to 1933. Among the important government documents is the two-volume Joint Committee on Indian Constitutional Reform, *Report*, 2 vols., London: His Majesty's Stationery Office, 1934.
13. *PBLC*, XXV, March 12, 1927, 96.
14. *PBLC*, XXV, 98.
15. *PBLC*, XXV, 471.
16. *PBLC*, XXVII, 230.
17. *PBLC*, XXV, 425.
18. *PBLC*, XXV, 338.
19. *PBLC*, XXV, 334.
20. *PBLC*, XXV, 341.
21. *Amrita Bazar Patrika*, August 24, 1927.
22. Bose, *Indian Struggle*, 169.
23. A.N. Moberly presented his findings at a meeting on August 28, 1929, and these are printed in his 'Review of the Political Situation,' Government of Bengal, Political Department, Calcutta, 1929.
24. *PBLC*, XXVI, August 25, 1927, 235–36.
25. *PBLC*, XXV, February 23, 1927, and XXVI, August 25, 1927, 248-–52.
26. *PBLC*, XXVI, August 25, 1927. 258–61.
27. *PBLC*, XXVII, December 14, 1927, 145.
28. *PBLC*, XXVII, 147.
29. Interviews with Dr Sisir K. Bose, 1972–73; several of the sons of Sarat Bose still lived in this house when I first came to Calcutta and I often visited it.
30. Interviews with Dr Sisir K. Bose, Asoke Nath Bose, Gita (Biswas) Bose, Meera (Roy) Bose, Shila (Sengupta) Bose, Aurobindo Bose, Roma (Roy) Bose, and several other Bose family members.
31. Interview with Dr Sisir K. Bose.

32. Interviews with Gita, Roma, and Meera Bose.
33. Interviews with Gita, Roma, Meera, Shila, Asoke, Sisir, and Aurobindo Bose.
34. Interview with Sisir K. Bose.
35. Interview with Gita Bose.
36. Interview with Gita, Roma, and Meera Bose.
37. From the autograph book of Gita Bose.
38. Interview with Aurobindo Bose.
39. Interviews with Sisir and Aurobindo Bose.
40. Interview with Aurobindo Bose.
41. Das Gupta, *Subhas Chandra*, 95–6.
42. There are more details in Gordon, *Bengal*, 242ff, and the footnotes have references to more biographical sources about Dr B.C. Roy and Nalini R. Sarker.
43. See, for example, *Amrita Bazar Patrika* of November 13, 1927, and the editorials of the days following, for an attack on Bose for being too friendly to the Muslims.
44. J. H. Broomfield, who has written a book of value, *Elite Conflict*, on modern Bengal, consistently lumps all the high-caste Hindus or bhadralok together and rarely differentiates, for example, between the Boses and the Hindu Mahasabha leader, Shyama Prasad Mookherjee. Broomfield's most inaccurate pages are in his final chapter, VII, 'Reapers of the Whirlwind,' covering 1927 to 1947. I will try to demonstrate the accuracy of my view in the pages which follow when I show the efforts of the Boses to work with Muslim leaders on many occasions.
45. *Amrita Bazar Patrika*, November 13, 1927.
46. *Amrita Bazar Patrika*, November 13, 1927.
47. *Amrita Bazar Patrika*, November 1927, *passim*.
48. Bose, *Indian Struggle*, 145–46; Sitaramayya, *Congress*, I, 329.
49. *Forward*, December 29, 1927.
50. On Saklatvala's tour and the spread of leftist ideas in 1927, see Adhikari, *Documents*, III B, 1927. *Forward* was the organ of the Boses and the BPCC with both Subhas and Sarat Bose involved in its running.
51. *Amrita Bazar Patrika*, April 4, 1928, has the full text of Sen Gupta's statement.
52. *Amrita Bazar Patrika*, April 4, 1928.
53. The speech is reproduced in *Amrita Bazar Patrika*, May 3, 1928; Bose himself mentioned the significance of this speech in *Indian Struggle*, 152, where he said that it embodied themes he had been

mulling over while he was imprisoned in Burma.

54. *Amrita Bazar Patrika*, May 3, 1928.
55. *Amrita Bazar Patrika*, May 3, 1928.
56. *Amrita Bazar Patrika*, May 3, 1928.
57. *Amrita Bazar Patrika*, May 3, 1928.
58. *Amrita Bazar Patrika*, May 3, 1928.
59. *Amrita Bazar Patrika*, May 3, 1928.
60. *Amrita Bazar Patrika*, May 3, 1928.
61. *Amrita Bazar Patrika*, May 3, 1928.
62. *Amrita Bazar Patrika*, May 3, 1928.
63. *Amrita Bazar Patrika*, May 3, 1928.
64. *Amrita Bazar Patrika*, May 3, 1928.
65. *Amrita Bazar Patrika*, May 3, 1928.
66. This is a main theme of Gordon, *Bengal*, and the conclusions have references to parallels in Maharashtra.
67. *Amrita Bazar Patrika*, April 14, 1928, editorial entitled, 'Revolutionary Outlook'.
68. On the trade union movement and organizers, see Sukomal Sen, *Working Class of India*, Calcutta: K.P. Bagchi, 1977; V.B. Karnik, *Indian Trade Unions*, 2nd ed., Bombay: Manaktalas, 1966; Report of the Royal Commission on Labour in India. Command Paper 3883, 1931; Eduard M. Lavalle, 'Confrontation within a Confrontation: Subhas C. Bose and the 1928 Strike,' in *Bengal in the Nineteenth and Twentieth Centuries*, ed., John R. McLane, Michigan State U. Press, Fall 1975, 169–70; Adhikari, *Documents*, IIIA, B, C, 1978, 1979, 1982.
69. Adhikari, *Documents*, IIIB, 254–64.
70. Adhikari, *Documents*, IIIC, presents a detailed record of the events of 1928.
71. Adhikari, *Documents*, IIIC, 135–41, 332–40.
72. *Amrita Bazar Patrika*, April 17, 1928.
73. *Amrita Bazar Patrika*, April 17, 1928.
74. *Amrita Bazar Patrika*, April 21, 1928.
75. Moni Ghosh, *Our Struggle*, 18–40; Sen, *Working Class*, 210, 271, 275; Lavalle, 'Confrontation'.
76. Lavalle, 'Confrontation'.
77. Ghosh, *Our Struggle*, 17ff; Lavalle, 'Confrontation,' 172ff.
78. *Times of India*, September 15, 1928, quoted in Lavalle, 'Confrontation,' 181.
79. Lavalle, 'Confrontation,' 180–90; see Bose's statements and the articles in *Liberty*, July 7 and 9, 1929, on how the company, in his

opinion, was using Homi.
80. Lavalle, 'Confrontation,' 180–90; Ghosh, *Our Struggle*, 90–95, for a letter on this matter written in 1935 by Bose.
81. Lavalle, 'Confrontation,' 187–90.
82. Bose, *Indian Struggle*, 145ff; Sen, *Working Class*, 303ff.
83. See *PBLC*, XXX, No. 2, 30th session, August 13–18, 20–25, 27, 28, 30, 31, and September, 1, 3, 4, 1928.
84. The literature on the Permanent Settlement and its consequences is vast. Among the useful sources are: Tapan Raychaudhuri, 'Permanent Settlement in Operation: Bakarganj District, East Bengal,' in Robert Eric Frykenberg ed., *Land Control and Social Structure in Indian History*, Madison: U. of Wisconsin Press, 1969, 163–74; K.B. Saha, *Economics of Rural Bengal*, Calcutta: Chuckervertty, Chatterjee, 1930, Chapter IV; M. Azizul Huque, *The Man behind the Plough*, Calcutta: The Book Company, 1939, Chapters VI–IX, XI–XVIII; Ratnalekha Ray, *Change in Bengal Agrarian Society c.1760–1850*, Delhi: Manohar, 1979, *passim*, who has a somewhat different view of the impact of the Permanent Settlement than the older sources; Narendra Krishna Sinha ed., *The History of Bengal (1757–1905)*, Chapters by N.K. Saha and Benoy K. Chowdhury, Calcutta: U. of Calcutta, 1967; Government of Bengal, Land Revenue Commission, 1940, *Report*; M.N. Gupta, *Land System of Bengal*, Calcutta: U. of Calcutta, 1940, Chapters VIII–XII.
85. Since the beginning of the Indian membership in the Bengal Legislative Council, there were landholder representatives and they spoke for large holders rather than small holders. See Chattopadhyay, *Bengal Legislature*, 106ff.
86. *PBLC*, XXX, No. 2, 47–50, 431–32.
87. *PBLC*, XXX, No. 2, 606, August 25, 1928.
88. A record of the votes is in *PBLC*, XXX, No. 2, and this comment is based on a complete reading of the proceedings.
89. *PBLC*, XXX, No. 2, 557–61.
90. *PBLC*, XXX, No. 2, 561.
91. *PBLC*, XXX, No. 2, 561.
92. *PBLC*, XXX, No. 2, 139–40, August 15, 1928.
93. *PBLC*, XXX, No. 2, 564.
94. *PBLC*, XXX, No. 2, 610–11, August 25, 1928.
95. *PBLC*, XXX, No. 2, 154.
96. *PBLC*, XXX, No. 2, 660.
97. *PBLC*, XXX, No. 2, 674; and No.2, 685–86.
98. See Bazlur Rohman Khan, 'Some Aspects of Society and Politics in

Bengal 1927 to 1936,' Ph.D. dissertation, U. of London, 1979, 60–76; Shila Sen, *Muslim Politics in Bengal 1937–1947*, New Delhi: Impex, 1976, 58ff; Humaira Momen, *Muslim Politics in Bengal*, Dacca: Sunny House, 1972, 35ff; Abul Mansur Ahmad, *Amar dekha rajnitir panchasa bachar* [Fifty Years of Politics as I Saw It], 3rd ed., Dacca: Nauroj, 1975, 165ff.

99. Momen, *Muslim Politics*, 35ff; Khan, 'Aspects of Society,' 60–76; Ahmad, *Amar dekha*, 174–95.

100. Majumdar, *Freedom Movement*, III, 307ff; Khalid B. Sayeed, *Pakistan, The Formative Phase 1857–1948*, London: Oxford U. Press, 1968, 64ff.

101. Many materials are gathered in File No. 2 of 1928, Nehru Report, Communal Electorates, All–Parties Conference, AICC Papers, Nehru Library, New Delhi; *Report*, All Parties Conference, 1928.

102. *Forward*, February 4, 1928, in Government of Bengal, Reports on Newspapers and Periodicals, January to June 1928.

103. *Banglar Katha*, February 22, 1928, in Government of Bengal, Press Reports, 1928.

104. *PBLC*, XXIX, 71, July 9, 1928.

105. *PBLC*, XXIX, 105–6, July 9, 1928.

106. *PBLC*, XXIX, 171–72, July 10, 1928.

107. *PBLC*, XXIX, 182, July 10, 1928, gives the vote on the motion of cooperation with the Simon Commission; a few Muslim members of Council voted with the Swarajists and against cooperation.

108. *PBLC*, XXX, No. 1, 94, August 1, 1928.

109. *PBLC*, XXX, No. 1, 97–98, August 1, 1928.

110. *PBLC*, XXX, No. 1, 109–13.

111. Quoted by J.N. Moitra, in *PBLC*, XXIX, 96.

112. Nehru Committee All Parties Conference, *Report*, 89.

113. File 2 of 1928, Nehru Report, AICC Papers.

114. File 2 of 1928, Nehru Report, AICC Papers.

115. See the excellent article on the Nehru Report and its fate by Mushirul Hasan, 'Communalism in Indian Politics: A Study of the Nehru Report,' *The Indian Historical Review*, IV, No. 2, January 1978, 379–404.

116. Hasan, 'Communalism,' 392–97.

117. Sayeed, *Pakistan*, 70.

118. Mitra, *Indian Annual Register*, II, 1928, 130–31.

119. Hasan, 'Communalism,' 397ff; Sayeed, *Pakistan*, 75ff.

120. Hasan, 'Communalism,' 397ff.

121. Jawaharlal Nehru and Subhas Bose were among those who believed

and hoped that the communal question would go away.

122. Nirad C. Chaudhuri, *The Continent of Circe*, London: Chatto and Windus, 1965, 103–4. On some of the other meetings, some secret, taking place at this time in Calcutta, see Adhikari, *Documents*, IIIC, 1928, 740–65; Balshastri Hardas, *Armed Struggle for Freedom*, Poona: KAL Prakashan, 1958, 332; Bhattacharyya, *Freedom Struggle*, 230–48.

123. Notices in *Banglar Katha*, 15–20 Agrahayana 1335 B.Y.

124. Government of Bengal, Press Reports, 1928, 414–19.

125. *PBLC*, XXXIII, 170, August 7, 1929. It was just after this period that Rabindranath Tagore, also concerned with the physical well-being and development of Indian youth, brought a jujitsu instructor to India at his own expense. He hoped eventually that the Swarajists in the Corporation would find a way to fund this training for the youths of Calcutta. However, he did not succeed. See Nepal Majumdar, *Rabindranath o subhaschandra*, 18–24.

126. *The Modern Review*, Part I, XLVIII, No. 1, July 1930; Part II, XLVIII, No. 3, September 1930; Part III, XLIX, No. 1, January 1931; Part IV, XLIX, No. 2, February 1931.

127. Das Gupta, *Subhas Chandra*, 98–100; Bose, *Indian Struggle*, 157.

128. Mitra, *IAR*, II, 1928, 367.

129. Subhas Bose, Address to Rashtra Bhasa Sammelan, December 1928.

130. Bose, *My Uncle Netaji*, 40.

131. Bijoy Ratna Mazumdar, 'Youth Movement,' in Biswanath De, *Subhas smriti* [Remembering Subhas], Calcutta: Sahityam, 1975, 193–96. Youth movements played a vital part in nationalist movements in other parts of the Third World, particularly in China. On the importance of the youth movement in China in the 1910s and 1920s, see Maurice Meisner, *Mao's China*, New York: The Free Press, 1979, 14–19, where the significance of the New Youth Movement and the May 4th Movement are spelled out.

132. Quoted in Geraldine Forbes, 'The Women Revolutionaries of Bengal,' *The Oracle*, II, No. 2, April 1980, 7.

133. In the *Amrita Bazar Patrika*, April 22, 1931, it is stated that Bose came out of Mandalay Jail with the idea of bringing women more fully into the movement. On the women's groups, see Forbes, 'Women Revolutionaries'; Khan, 'Some Aspects of Society,' *passim*; Laushey, *Bengal Terrorism*, 98ff; Bhola Chatterji, *Aspects of Bengal Politics in the Early Nineteen Thirties*, Calcutta: World Press, 1969.

134. Interview in Calcutta, September 2, 1976. S.C. Sengupta, *India Wrests Freedom, passim.*
135. N.K. Gangapadhyaya memoirs, told to the author by S.M. Ghose, Delhi, October 10, 1972.
136. Ray, *Itihas*, 444ff.

CHAPTER SIX

1. Quoted in John W. Wheeler–Bennett, *John Anderson: Viscount Waverly*, London: Macmillan, 1962, 126.
2. Mahatma Gandhi, *Collected Works*, Vol. XLI, Ahmedabad: Publications Division, Government of India, 1970, 319.
3. Gandhi, from *Navajivan*, reprinted in *Young India*, 5–9–29, in *Collected Works*, Vol. XLI, 276.
4. Subhas Chandra Bose, *Selected Speeches*, Delhi: Publications Division, Government of India, 1962, 49.
5. Bose, *Selected Speeches*, 50.
6. Circular Letter No. 15, March 17, 1929, from BPCC, in AICC Papers, File No. P–6/1929, Part 2, Nehru Memorial Library.
7. Circular Letter No. 15, AICC Papers, File No. P–6, 1929, Part 2.
8. Interview with Surendra Mohan Ghose, Delhi, September 20, 1964.
9. *Liberty*, August 20, 1929.
10. Sabitriprasanna Chattopadhyay, 'Subhas the Music Lover,' in *Subhas smriti* [Remembering Subhas], Calcutta: Sahityam, 1970, 210–14.
11. Chattopadhyay, 'Music Lover,' 210.
12. Chattopadhyay, 'Music Lover,' 211.
13. Chattopadhyay, 'Music Lover,' 212.
14. Chattopadhyay, 'Music Lover,' 213.
15. Chattopadhyay, 'Music Lover,' 213–14.
16. Chattopadhyay, 'Music Lover,' 214.
17. See Chapter V, section on the Bengal Tenancy Act Amendment 1928, and Partha Chatterjee, 'Agrarian Relations and Politics in Bengal: Some Considerations on the Making of the Tenancy Act Amendment 1928,' Occasional Paper No. 30, Centre for Studies in Social Sciences, Calcutta, n.d., 31ff; also Gautam Chattopadhyay, *Bengal Electoral Politics and Freedom Struggle 1862–1947*, Delhi: Indian Council of Historical Research, 1984, 106–112.
18. See Chapter V, section on the preparation of the Nehru Report. Bose said in 1928 that he gave much thought to the matter and found that only joint electorates were compatible with nationalism. He held

consistently to this position throughout his life. For example, see Bose, *Indian Struggle*, 214–15.

19. *Liberty* presented Bose's views on this conflict frequently, e.g., September 22 when the BPCC held Sachin Sen Day and when Bose spoke praising him. Also see, Chatterjee, 'Agrarian Relations,' 19–24; Buddhadeva Bhattacharyya et al., *Satyagrahas in Bengal 1921–39*, Calcutta: Minerva Books, 1977, 128–58.

20. The main source for his work in the Corporation is the *Calcutta Municipal Gazette* [hereafter *CMG*], Vols. IX–XV, which covers 1928 to 1932.

21. *CMG*, X, 13, July 1929, Special Supplement; also articles in issues of June 15, July 20.

22. *CMG*, X, 116–118a (in July 13, 1929 Special Supplement).

23. *CMG*, July 20, 1929, 430. Succeeding volumes of *CMG*, *passim*, mention the work of Dey.

24. Quoted in *CMG*, July 6, 1929.

25. Bengal Legislative Council *Proceedings* [hereafter *PBLC*], XXXI, No. 2, 35–100.

26. This is evident in *PBLC*, XXXII, July 1929, and XXXIII, August 1929.

27. *PBLC*, XXXIII, August 6, 1929, 87–138.

28. *PBLC*, XXXIII, August 9, 1929, 285–311.

29. *PBLC*, XXXIII, August 9, 1929, 299.

30. *PBLC*, XXXIII, 300.

31. *PBLC*, XXXIII, 301.

32. See Subhas Chandra Bose, *The Indian Struggle 1920–1942*, Calcutta: Asia Publishing House, 1964, 168–69; Chattopadhyay, *Bengal Electoral Politics*, 118–20; also *Liberty*, 1929, *passim*. The issue came up many times in the Congress and a decision on the matter was taken at the Lahore Congress in December 1929.

33. *Liberty*, July 11, 1929.

34. Subhas Chandra Bose, *Correspondence, 1924–1932*, Calcutta: Netaji Research Bureau, 1967, 401–2, letter of 16.6.29.

35. See 'Note on the Golmuri Tinplate Workers' Strike,' September 1929, AICC File No. G–71/1929, in *Selected Works of Jawaharlal Nehru*, Vol. 4, New Delhi: Orient Longman, 1973, 59–65. *Liberty*, during 1929, ran numerous articles about this strike.

36. *Liberty*, July 17, August 3, August 4, 1929.

37. *Liberty*, July 17, August 3, August 4, August 17, August 23, August 29, September 4, September 7, et al., 1929. On all of these dates, as well as many others, there are accounts of his speeches to labor

meetings.

38. *Liberty*, August 17, 1929.

39. The standard work on the background and accomplishments of the economic nationalists is Bipan Chandra, *The Rise and Growth of Economic Nationalism in India*, New Delhi: People's Publishing House, 1966. On Romesh Chunder Dutt, see Gordon, *Bengal*, 39–60. Bose, like every nationalist of his time, must have been acquainted with Dutt's *Economic History of India under British Rule*, a very widely-read two-volume work, which gives a clear statement of the theory of the drain.

40. *Liberty*, August 17, 1929.

41. Subhas Chandra Bose, *Boycott of British Goods*, Calcutta: Sree Adwait Press, 1929 (?).

42. Bose, *Boycott*, 24.

43. Bose, *Boycott*, 24–25.

44. Bose, *Boycott*, Section II, 3.

45. Bose, *Boycott*, Section II, 26.

46. Bose, *Boycott*, Section II, 25–26.

47. Viceroy to Secretary of State, Telegram P. No. 257–S., January 19, 1929, in Subodh Roy, ed., *Communism in India: Unpublished Documents 1925–1934*, Calcutta: Ganasahitya Prakash, 1972, 109.

48. There are numerous other documents on the case in Roy, *Communism*, 31ff. Also see, *Selected Works of Jawaharlal Nehru*, Vol. 3, New Delhi: Orient Longman, 1972, 331–58; Overstreet and Windmiller, *Communism in India*, 76ff; Philip Spratt, *Blowing Up India*, Calcutta: Prachi Prakashan, 1955, 47–59; Bose, *Indian Struggle*, 165.

49. Government of India, Home Department, Political File No. 179/29, in National Archives of India, New Delhi.

50. Nehru, *Selected Works*, Vol. 3, 331ff.

51. *Liberty*, October 25, 1929.

52. Moberly Report, Government of Bengal, Political Department, August 28, 1929.

53. Government of India, Home Department, Political File No. 179/29.

54. Government of India, Home Department, Political File No. 223/ 1929 and 257/VII, 1930.

55. On Subhas Bose and Jatin Das, see *Liberty*, September 14, October 28, 1929; Bose, *Indian Struggle*, 160–63; *CMG*, X, September 21, 1929, has details on Das' life.

56. Ajoy Ghosh, 'Bhagat Singh and His Comrades,' in his *Articles and Speeches*, Moscow: Publishing House for Oriental Literature, 1962,

16–18.

57. *Liberty*, July 7, 1929.
58. Balshastri Hardas, *Armed Struggle for Freedom*, Poona: KAL Prakashan, 1958, 332–33. There are no footnotes or bibliography in this book, but many of the details may be accurate.
59. *CMG*, X, September 21, 1929, 893.
60. Gandhi, *Collected Works*, Vol. XLII, Ahmedabad: Publications Division, Government of India, 1970, 6–7, comment of 17/10/29.
61. *Liberty*, October 19, 1929.
62. *Liberty*, October 19, 1929.
63. *Liberty*, October 19, 1929.
64. *Liberty*, October 19, 1929.
65. *Liberty*, October 19, 1929.
66. *Liberty*, October 19, 1929.
67. All these details of his tour and return to Calcutta are from *Liberty*, October 19–29, 1929.
68. Bose, *Correspondence*, 402–3, letter of 26/10/29.
69. *Liberty*, October 29, 1929.
70. The best source for the details of this controversy are the AICC Files including P6/1929, Parts I and II; G–2, 1929; G–120/ 1930, Parts I and II; G–120/1931, Parts I–IV; P–15/1931; each side had its newspaper; *Liberty* for the Bose side, *Advance*, started in early 1930 for the Sen Gupta side, and these record every step of the argument. Also see, Das Gupta, *Subhas Chandra*, 111ff; Padmini Sengupta, *Deshapriya Jatindra Mohan Sengupta*, New Delhi: Publications Division, Government of India, 1968, 106ff. I also discussed this split with Satya Ranjan Bakshi, Calcutta, 1965; Surendra Mohan Ghosh, Delhi, 1964 and 1972; and Nirad C. Chaudhuri, Delhi, 1964 and 1965.
71. The disgust and concern of Gandhi and Nehru is recorded in their many comments on the split in their works of this period, Gandhi, *Collected Works*, Vols. XLII–XLVII, 1929–31, *passim*; and Nehru, *Selected Works*, Vols. 3–5, 1929–31, *passim*. Although both Nehru and Gandhi tried to maintain satisfactory relations with both sides, it seems that the sympathies of Gandhi were more with Sen Gupta as the Mahatma's many letters to Satish Das Gupta show, while Nehru leaned to the Bose side and was especially angry with the Sen Gupta side for abusing Subhas Bose after the latter resigned as BPCC president in 1931. See Nehru, *Collected Works*, Vol. 5, New Delhi: Orient Longman, 1973, 256.
72. Sengupta, *Deshapriya*, 62ff; Das Gupta, *Subhas*, 90.

73. Das Gupta, *Subhas*, 90–96; Mitra,*The Indian Annual Register*, I, 1926, 94–96, and I, 1928, 398–400; interview with Satya Ranjan Bakshi conducted by Prof Edward C. Dimock, Calcutta, September 28, 1966. A running account of the connection of the revolutionary groups and the Bengal Congress from the government angle is found in Government of India, Home Department, Political File No. 4/21/32, The Congress–Terrorist Alliance.

74. From a surface reading of the records of the Bengal Legislative Council and the Calcutta Corporation (*PBLC*, 1927–30; *CMG*, IX–XV), it is difficult to tell that the Boses and Sen Gupta were at odds. But the controversy boils to the surface in the *CMG* account of the August 1930 struggle for the mayoral chair. See *CMG*, Supplement to issue of August 23, 1930.

75. AICC File No. P–6/1929, Part II.

76. AICC File No. G–120/1930, letter of November 11, 1929.

77. AICC Files G–117, 119, 120, 122/1929.

78. Das Gupta, *Subhas*, 113–15; AICC File No. G–120/1929.

79. AICC Files G–117, 119, 120, 122/1929, contain a record of the endless wrangling.

80. Das Gupta, *Subhas*, 111–12; interview with Nirad C. Chaudhuri, Delhi, 1964.

81. Quoted in R.C. Majumdar, *History of the Freedom Movement in India*, Vol. III, Calcutta: Firma K.L. Mukhopadhyay, 1963, 322.

82. Majumdar, *History*, III, 323.

83. Bose, *Indian Struggle*, 171–72; Majumdar, *History*, III, 322–24.

84. The details can be found in *Liberty*, November 3, 5, 8, 20, 1929.

85. Bose, *Correspondence*, 403.

86. The complicated relationship of Bose and the younger Nehru will be touched on again, particularly in the late 1930s when Bose gets most angry at Nehru and felt most keenly the lack of support from Nehru in his controversy with the Gandhian high command. Bose's private view of Nehru can be found mostly in his correspondence, and in the recorded comments of his friends and close associates, e.g., Dilip Kumar Roy, *Netaji—The Man Reminiscences*, Bombay: Bharatiya Vidya Bhavan, 1966, 112–14.

87. Bose, *Correspondence*, 404.

88. Bose, *Correspondence*, 404–5.

89. Bose, *Correspondence*, 405–6.

90. Bose letter dated Lahore, 27/12/29, in AICC File No. G–120/1929.

91. The father-son imagery is often used by the participants in these political-cum-personal relationships, so Bose says Motilal Nehru is

just like a father to him and Gandhi says Jawaharlal Nehru and Subhas Bose are like sons to him. These terms were used by the participants to indicate closeness and tenderness, but as modern psychology has demonstrated, the relations of children and parents are often fraught with ambivalences and I believe that these are there in the relationships between Bose and Motilal Nehru and Gandhi. For psychological descriptions of the complexity and ambiguity of parent-child and authority conflicts, see Greenacre, *The Quest for the Father, passim*; D. Hess, 'The Socialization of Attitudes toward Political Authority: Some Cross–National Comparisons,' 542–59; Adorno, et al., *The Authoritarian Personality*, 52–3, *passim*.

92. Mahatma Gandhi, *Collected Works*, Vol. XLII, 342–43.
93. Government of India, Home Department, Political File No. 4/21/32.
94. Bose, *Selected Speeches*, 60.
95. Gandhi, *Collected Works*, LXII, 352, 356.
96. Bose, *Indian Struggle*, 168–69; Chattopadhyay, *Bengal Electoral Politics*, 118–20.
97. A.M. Zaidi and S.G. Zaidi, eds., *The Encyclopedia of the Indian National Congress*, Vol.9, New Delhi: S. Chand, 1980, 631; Das Gupta, *Subhas*, 119–23; *Liberty*, January 3, 7, 28, 1930. Bose and Iyengar and a few others formed the Congress Democratic Party in response to what they thought was the lack of democracy in the Congress, but this organization never amounted to anything and mention of it shortly died away. See *Liberty*, January 7, 1930, which mentioned that Bose was excluded 'on the ground of incompatibility of temperament' and claimed that Gandhi's list for Working Committee members was pushed through. Sen Gupta said that the formation of the Congress Democratic Party had 'broken his heart', quoted in *Liberty*, January 3, 1930. By the end of January 1930, all mention of it was gone.
98. Bose, *Indian Struggle*, 174–75.
99. I have suggested that this pattern began with Bose's relationship to his own father and continued vis–a–vis other important authorities, the British and the Congress particularly, through his life. Bose coped well with these rejections and they did not prevent him from continuing to work with Gandhi and the Congress leadership.
100. Bose, *Indian Struggle*, 166–67; Sen, *Working Class of India*, 301–8, 345.
101. *Liberty*, December 6, 1929.
102. Sen, *Working Class*, 301–8; V.B. Karnik, *Indian Trade Unions: A Survey*, 2nd ed., Bombay: Manaktalas, 1966, 65–66; Nehru, *Works*,

Vol. 4, 56.

103. Government of India, Home Department, Political File Nos. 223/ 1929; also 257/VII/1930.

104. *CMG*, XI, January 11, 1930, and January 25, 1930.

105. *CMG*, XI, January 25, 1930.

106. Government of India, Home Department, Political File No. 257/VII/ 1930.

107. Government of India, Home Department, Political File No. 257/VII/ 1930.

108. Bose, *Correspondence*, 406, letter of 23/1/30.

109. *Liberty*, January 10, 1930.

110. There is hardly a speech that Bose made between 1929 and the end of 1931 in which he does not mention Ireland. See *Liberty* for the period, e.g., July 16, 1929, in a speech to the Barisal District Political Conference, and January 1, 1930, to the Lahore Congress.

111. Gandhi, *CollectedWorks*, XLII, 438, from *Young India*, 30/1/30.

112. Zaidi and Zaidi, *Encyclopedia of Congress*, Vol. 10, 23.

113. Gandhi, *Collected Works*, XLIII, 132–34, from *Young India*, 27/3/ 30.

114. Gandhi, *Collected Works*, XLIII, 32, from *Navajivan*, 9/3/30.

115. Das Gupta, *Subhas*, 126.

116. Das Gupta, *Subhas*, 123–30; Subhas Bose, unpublished Prison Notebook, No. 2, January–February 1930, in Netaji Research Bureau, Calcutta, translated by Leonard A. Gordon and Keshub Sarkar.

117. Bose, Prison Notebook, No. 2.

118. Bose, Prison Notebook, No. 2, entry for 14/2/30.

119. Sengupta, *Deshapriya*, 95ff; Government of India, Home Department, Political File No. 256/II/1930.

120. See Brown, *Gandhi and Civil Disobedience*, 99ff; Dennis Dalton, 'The Dandi Drama,' in *Rule, Protest, Identity*, eds., Peter Robb and David Taylor, London: Curzon Press, 1978, 133–34.

121. *CMG*, XI, 1930, April 12, 1930.

122. AICC File No. G–86/1930; Tanika Sarkar, 'The First Phase of Civil Disobedience in Bengal, 1930–1,' *Indian Historical Review*, IV, No. 1, 75–95; Hitesranjan Sanyal, 'Congress Movements in the Villages of Eastern Midnapore, 1921–1930,' *Colloques Internationaux du CNRS*, No. 582—Asie du Sud, 169–78.

123. Sanyal, 'Congress Movements,' 175–76; Government of India, Home Department, Political File No. 5/1931, 'Law and Order in Midnapur,' report of Non–Official Enquiry Committee.

124. Government of India, Home Department, Political File No. 4/21/

1932.
125. *Liberty*, November 12, 1930.
126. Brown, *Gandhi*, 124; Sumit Sarkar, 'The Logic of Gandhian Nationalism: Civil Disobedience and the Gandhi–Irwin Pact (1930–1931),' *Indian Historical Review*, III, No.1, 114–46.
127. *CMG*, XI, 854–55, March 22, 1930.
128. For example, see *Liberty*, July 30, 31, August 2, 1930.
129. *CMG*, XI, Supplement to May 3, 1930.
130. *CMG*, XI, Supplement to May 3, 1930.
131. *CMG*, XI, Supplement to May 3, 1930.
132. *CMG*, XI, Supplement to May 3, 1930.
133. *CMG*, XI, Supplement to May 3, 1930.
134. *CMG*, XI, Supplement to May 3, 1930.
135. *CMG*, XI, 1011.
136. *CMG*, XII, May 13, May 25, June 7, June 14, 1930.
137. *CMG*, XII, June 7, 1930.
138. Ray, *Bharater baiplabik sangramer itihas* [History of the Revolutionary Struggle in India], 470–90, 496; Gopal Haldar, 'Revolutionary Terrorism,' *Studies in the Bengal Renaissance*, ed., Atulchandra Gupta, Jadavpur, Calcutta: National Council of Education, 1958, 255; Bose, *Indian Struggle*, 188–89; Nisith Ranjan Ray et al., eds., 'Chittagong Uprising,' in their *Challenge, A Saga of India's Struggle for Freedom*, Part I, New Delhi: People's Publishing House, 1984; H.W. Hale, *Political Trouble in India 1917–1937*, Secret Home Department Report [reprinted Allahabad: Chugh Publications, 1974], 17–24.
139. Hale, *Political Trouble*, 23–24.
140. Government of India, P&J 7542/45, India Office, London.
141. Majumdar, *Statesman: An Anthology*, Calcutta: The Statesman Ltd., 1975, 410–11.
142. Gandhi, *Collected Works*, XLII, 381, from *Hindi Navajivan*, 9/1/30.
143. For examples of the use of the *Gita*, see Gordon, *Bengal*, 118–20, 140–43, 146; a much more literal and common interpretation of the *Gita* is that put forth by Aurobindo Ghose (Sri Aurobindo) in *Essays on the Gita*, Pondicherry: Sri Aurobindo Ashram, 1959.
144. *CMG*, XI, April 26, 1930.
145. *CMG*, XI, April 26, 1930, 1065–68(c).
146. *CMG*, XI, May 3, 1930, 1118–19.
147. AICC File No. G–159, Dacca Inquiry Committee Report; Government of Bengal, Political Department, Report of the Dacca Enquiry Committee, 1930; on the general subject of communal riots in the

pre-independence period, see Richard D. Lambert, 'Hindu–Muslim Riots,' unpublished Ph.D. dissertation in sociology, U. of Pennsylvania, 1951.

148. S.C. Sen Gupta, *India Wrests Freedom*, Calcutta: Sahitya Samsad, 1982, 96–109; Sen Gupta gives a detailed account of Bose's ties to the BV and of the assassination campaign of the BV in the period 1929–33.

149. Hale, *Political Trouble*, 24.

150. Gandhi, 'The Black Regime,' *Collected Works*, XLIII, 296, from *Young India*, 24/4/30.

151. Brown, *Gandhi*, 153ff and Sumit Sarkar, 'Logic of Gandhian Nationalism,' offer different interpretations of why the Gandhi–Irwin talks began in February 1931, but neither gives much importance to the role of the revolutionaries' campaign in this period. But it is evident that both parties to these talks were quite unhappy about the acts of revolutionary terrorism and wanted a face-saving formula for both sides which would halt the Civil Disobedience Movement and move the parties towards a settlement. Gandhi, as has been indicated, not only wanted to end the violence or repression of the Government of India, but that of the revolutionaries as well. Part of the final terms of the bargain were that civil disobedience prisoners would be released but not those tried or suspected of revolutionary involvements.

152. Bose, Prison Notebook, No. 4, translated by Leonard A. Gordon and Keshub Sarkar.

153. Bose, Prison Notebook, No. 4.

154. *Liberty*, July 3, 1930.

155. *Liberty*, July 30, 1930, letter sent to *Advance*.

156. *CMG*, Supplement to issue of August 23, 1930.

157. *CMG*, September 27, 1930.

158. *CMG*, September 27, 1930.

159. *CMG*, September 27, 1930, 873.

160. Francesco Nitti, *Bolshevism, Fascism and Democracy*, London: Unwin, 1927, 72. A copy with Subhas Bose's name in it and marked Alipore Jail, 1930, is in the Bose family library, Netaji Bhavan, Calcutta.

161. Ivanoe Bonomi, *From Socialism to Fascism: A Study of Contemporary Italy*, London: Martin Hopkinson, 1924, 135–45. A copy with Subhas Bose's name in it and marked Alipore Jail, 1930, is in the Bose family library, Netaji Bhavan, Calcutta. These two books on Italian fascism and European politics were surely read by Bose in

prison in 1930. He may have read other works too, but no other ones are marked 'Alipore Jail, 1930'.

162. See *Liberty*, 1930, *passim*, and *CMG*, XII and XIII.
163. *CMG*, November 8, 1930.
164. *CMG*, October 25, 1930, XII, 989–90.
165. Das Gupta, *Subhas*, 130.
166. Article, 'What Calcutta Needs,' *CMG*, 6th anniversary number, November 22, 1930. On Sarker's career and his link to G.D. Birla, a Gandhi favorite, see Gordon, *Bengal*, 252–53.
167. See Government of India, P&J/174/II/35 and P&J/7542/45, India Office London. A recent account of Indian nationalists and the Corporation is Rajat Ray, *Urban Roots of Indian Nationalism: Pressure Groups and Conflict of Interests in Calcutta City Politics, 1875–1939*, New Delhi: Vikas, 1979, 109 ff. Ray deals with this period, but there is scarcely a hint that the nationalists did anything positive and the author is only able to see political infighting.
168. *CMG*, November 1 and 29, 1930, give accounts of the two parties.
169. *CMG*, December 20, 1930, Christmas Number.
170. *CMG*, December 20, 1930, Christmas Number, 308–9.
171. *Liberty*, December 2 and 3, 1930.
172. *Liberty*, November 25, and December 2, 1930, gives accounts of Bose's meetings with Indian merchants and his concerns for meeting foreign competition. Bose was still friendly with Nalini Sarker in this period and Sarker was a rising star in Indian business circles. See the article on Sarker in *The Times of India, Indian Yearbook and Who's Who*, Bombay: 1947, 1206–7. Gandhi's idea of trusteeship is, of course, well-known. See Nirmal Kumar Bose ed., *Selections from Gandhi*, Ahmedabad: Navajivan, 1957, 168, 210, 275ff. Sumit Sarkar tries to establish the importance of Gandhi's business connections in 'Logic of Gandhian Nationalism,' 125ff.
173. *Liberty*, December 9, 1930.
174. Das Gupta, *Subhas*, 115; on youth and student organizations in Bengal, see, Government of India, Home Department, Political File No. 212/30, Youth Organizations in Bengal; Bhola Chatterji, *Aspects of Bengal Politics in the Early Nineteen Thirties*, Calcutta: World Press, 1969, 12, 33; Bazlur Rohman Khan, 'Some Aspects of Society and Politics in Bengal 1927 to 1936,' Ph.D. dissertation, University of London, 1979, Chapter III, 'Students and Politics'; Bose's angry reply to Biren Das Gupta's attack on him in the context of the student movement is recounted in *Liberty*, December 11, 1929.

175. Bose, *Indian Struggle*, 193; this is reflected in the tone and content of Gandhi's communications to Bose as against his messages to a 'true' Gandhian, Satish Das Gupta and others with whom Gandhi felt in tune; see Gandhi, *Works*, Vols. XLI–XLIX, in this period. Bose continues to play an important role because he is president of the BPCC, but he is not among those in the top inner circle of the Congress high command.
176. Sen Gupta, *Indian Wrests Freedom*, 106–111.
177. *Liberty*, December 11, 1930.
178. *Liberty*, December 11, 1930.
179. *Liberty*, January 19 and 20, 1931; *CMG*, XIII, January 24, 1931.
180. *CMG*, XIII, January 31, February 14, February 21, 1931.
181. *CMG*, XIII, January 31, 1931.
182. *CMG*, XIII, January 31, 1931.
183. *CMG*, XIII, January 31, 1931.
184. Gandhi, *Works*, XLV, 131.
185. Majumdar, *Freedom Movement*, III, 376.
186. Quoted in Majumdar, *Freedom Movement*, III, 377.
187. Both versions are to be found in Gandhi, *Works*, XLV, 196 for Irwin's, 200 for Gandhi's.
188. Gandhi, *Works*, XLV, 301–302; Bose, *Indian Struggle*, .198ff; *Liberty*, March 9–29, 1931, gives Bose's views of the question upon coming out of prison.
189. Gandhi, *Works*, XLV, 200.
190. Durga Das, *India from Curzon to Nehru and After*, New York: John Day, 1970, 147; Majumdar, *Freedom Movement*, III, 384; Brown, *Gandhi*, 200; Das Gupta, *Subhas*, 133.
191. Gandhi, *Works*, XLV, 360.
192. Bose, *Selected Speeches*, 63; *Liberty*, March 28 and 29, 1931.
193. *Liberty*, March 28, 1931.
194. Bose, *Selected Speeches*, 62–63.
195. Brown, *Gandhi*, 201; Zaidi and Zaidi, *Encyclopedia of Congress*, X, 79–81.
196. Gandhi, *Works*, XLVI, 357–59.
197. Zaidi and Zaidi, *Encyclopedia of Congress*, X, 86–7, 96.
198. Zaidi and Zaidi, *Encyclopedia of Congress*, X, 98–100.
199. Zaidi and Zaidi, *Encyclopedia of Congress*, X, 111ff, 181–83; Brown, *Gandhi*, 203–4; Bose *Indian Struggle*, 207; Gopal, *Jawaharlal Nehru*, Vol. One, 152–53.
200. Zaidi and Zaidi, *Encyclopedia of Congress*, X, 30–32. Roy's role is also reflected in his growing and amicable correspondence with

Jawaharlal Nehru which is to be found in the AICC Files P–6/1929, Part II, and other files concerning Bengal Congress affairs.

201. *Liberty*, April 10, 1931.
202. Government of India, Home Department, Political File No. 143/ 1931.
203. *Statesman: An Anthology*, 416–17, extract from April 11, 1931.
204. The details are boring and repetitious and many can be found in AICC Files G–120/1931, Parts I, II, and III. *Liberty*, May 19, 1931, has an account of one of his speeches in which he reiterated his offer to resign as BPCC president.
205. *CMG*, XIII, April 18, 1931.
206. *Liberty*, April 17 and 23, 1931.
207. *Liberty*, April 20, 1931.
208. *Liberty*, April 20, 1931.
209. *Liberty*, May 16, 1931. In most of Bose's speeches there is a religious sub-text, i.e., there are direct and indirect references to Hindu religious concepts relevant, in his view, to political activism.
210. *Liberty*, May 16, November 17, 1931.
211. Zaidi and Zaidi, *Encyclopedia of Congress*, X, 187.
212. AICC File No. G–120/1931, Part I.
213. Datta Gupta, *Comintern*, 182–83.
214. *Liberty*, July 6, 9, 11, 1931; Sen, *Working Class*, 309ff; Karnik, *Indian Trade Unions*, 70–1; Bose, *Indian Struggle*, 233.
215. Sen, *Working Class*, 317ff; Karnik, *Indian Trade Unions*, 71ff.
216. *Liberty*, July 11, 1931.
217. *Liberty*, July 11, 1931.
218. Bose, *Selected Speeches*, 69.
219. See, for example, Jyoti Basu, 'Looking Back: Netaji and Indian Communists,' in *The Oracle*, Vol. I, No. 1, Calcutta, January 1979, 47–51; Hiren Mukerjee, *Bow of Burning Gold: A Study of Subhas Chandra Bose,* New Delhi: People's Publishing House, 1977.
220. *CMG*, XIV, August 22, 1931, 576 (d–e).
221. *Liberty*, October 29, 1931.
222. In a speech reported in *Liberty*, November 5, 1931, Bose mentioned his study of Irish history and its significance for Indian nationalists. In other speeches, reported in *Liberty*, April 5, May 4, October 29, he also made extensive use of Irish parallels.
223. *Liberty*, October 29, 1931. Bose felt that repression should be resisted, but that it often rebounded to the favor of the nationalists. The same point, in an Irish context, is made by Dan Breen, *My Fight for Irish Freedom*, Dublin: Anvil Books, 1964 [reprint of 1924],

124, where he suggests that British repression brought the IRA the support of the Irish people. Breen's book was one work on the Irish freedom struggle which was familiar to Indian nationalists. Interview with Chinmohan Sehanavis, Calcutta, January 1984.

224. *Liberty*, September 18, 1931; AICC File No. G–120/1931, Part I.

225. *Liberty*, September 18, 1931.

226. AICC File No. G–120/1931, Part I, which contains Aney's Report of September 25, 1931.

227. Nehru, *Works*, Vol. 5, 256.

228. Government of India, Home Department, Political File No. 4/49/32 and 13/32/32.

229. Bose, *Indian Struggle*, 234–35.

230. Sengupta, *Deshapriya*, 151ff; Gandhi, *Works*, XLVIII, 338, in which Gandhi mentions a consultation with Sen Gupta in London, in his speech to the Federal Structure Committee meeting at the Round Table Conference.

231. Gandhi, *Works*, XLVIII, 338–39.

232. Gandhi, *Works*, XLVIII, 341.

233. *Liberty*, December 17, 1931. Bose had made this point on several occasions in the previous few years. For example, in a speech to the Howrah District Political Conference, September 28, 1929, he said that a few bombs would not bring the revolution that India needed. He said the age of terrorism had passed and that India needed a mass movement leading to freedom and socialism. He called for mass organizing to bring this about (*Liberty*, September 29, 1929).

234. Gandhi, *Works*, XLVIII, 512.

235. Gandhi, *Works*, XLVIII, 453.

236. *Liberty*, January 3, 1932.

237. Gandhi, *Works*, XLIX, 544.

238. Brown, *Gandhi*, 282ff; Sanyal, 'Congress Movements,' 177; Bose, *Indian Struggle*, 244; AICC File No. 4/1932 describes efforts in Tamluk.

239. *Liberty*, February 6, 1932.

240. Government of India, P&J 7542/45, India Office Records.

241. Sarat Bose letter to Asoke Bose, February 10, 1932.

242. P.B. Mukharji, 'Sarat Chandra Bose the Lawyer,' in *Sarat Bose Commemoration Volume*, Calcutta: Sarat Bose Academy, 1982, 18ff. [This article is a reprint of a speech given at and published by the Netaji Research Bureau]. In his excellent article on Calcutta, the late Sudhin Datta mentioned about the professional men of Calcutta that 'they were loyal to their professions.' 'Calcutta,' reprinted in

Sudhindranath Datta, *The World of Twilight, Essays and Poems*, Calcutta: Oxford U. Press, 1970, 82.

CHAPTER SEVEN

1. W.H. Auden, *Collected Poems*, ed., Edward Mendelson, New York: Random House, 1976, 198. Poem dated February 1939.
2. Asoke Nath Bose, *My Uncle Netaji*, Calcutta: ESEM Publications, 1977, 63. Letter of October 27, 1932.
3. Sarat Bose, weekly letters to Asoke Nath Bose, from February 10, 1932 on. Many details in this chapter about both brothers are drawn from these letters and also from Dr Bose's very valuable and carefully done memoir of his uncle and father which draws upon these letters to his father and many others.
4. Satish Bose, letter to Asoke Nath Bose, February 10, 1932. Interview with Ajit Dey, Calcutta, August 20, 1977. He was Sarat's brother-in-law and very close to him.
5. The details of Sarat Bose's many appeals through lengthy letters to the Government of India, Government of Bengal, Governor of Bengal, are to be found in Government of India, Home Department, Political File No. 31/101/32.
6. Asoke Bose, *My Uncle*, 69; interview with Aurobindo Bose, Calcutta, August 25, 1976.
7. Satish Bose, letter to Asoke Bose, February 10, 1932.
8. These worries are expressed in his letters to the government in Government of India, Home Department, Political File No. 31/101/32, and indirectly in Sarat Bose's letters to Asoke in which he often asks Asoke not to worry.
9. Sarat Bose, letters to Asoke Bose, 1932 to 1935, *passim*. Several government files also mention the diabetes, including Government of India, Home Department, Political File No. 31/101/32, which gives details of the decision to transfer him from Jubbulpore to house detention in Kurseong, and gives his health problems as one of the reasons.
10. Details are given in Government of India, Home Department, Political File No. 44/8 of 1933.
11. These details have been gathered through a systematic examination of the Bose library in Netaji Bhavan.
12. Library list and interview with Dwijen Bose, Calcutta, August 22, 1977.

13. Government of India, Home Department, Political File No. 31/ 101/32.

14. Government of India, Home Department, Political File No. 31/101/ 32.

15. Government of India, Home Department, Political File No. 31/101/ 32.

16. Government of India, Home Department, Political File No. 31/101/ 32.

17. Government of India, Home Department, Political File No. 31/101/ 32.

18. Government of India, Home Department, Political File No. 31/101/ 32.

19. Government of India, Home Department, Political File No. 31/101/ 32.

20. Government of India, Home Department, Political File No. 31/101/ 32.

21. Government of India, Home Department, Political File No. 31/101/ 32.

22. Government of India, Home Department, Political File No. 31/101/ 32. The Government of Bengal believed on the basis of the reports of its agents that Sarat was much more intimately in touch with the absconders in the Chittagong Armoury Case, had shielded the relatives of one of them in his own house, and was in touch with other revolutionaries in Calcutta. There are also suggestions in this file and elsewhere that Subhas and Sarat Bose had some connection to the attempts on the life of Sir Charles Tegart, police chief of Calcutta.

23. Government of India, Home Department, Political File No. 31/101/ 32.

24. The first few letters to Santosh Basu are in Subhas Chandra Bose, *Correspondence, 1924–1932*, Calcutta: Netaji Research Bureau, 1967, 407–10, 414–15, and the remainder are in the unpublished collection in the Netaji Research Bureau, Calcutta, and will be published in the succeeding volumes of his collected works.

25. Subhas Bose letters to Dilip Roy, in *Correspondence*, 412–13, and see the two versions by Dilip Roy, which include other letters, *The Subhas I Knew*, Bombay: Nalanda Pubs., 1946, and *Netaji—The Man, Reminiscences*, Bombay: Bharatiya Vidya Bhavan, 1966, 90ff. It appears that Subhas made some of his valuable contacts in Europe through Dilip, who had spent time in Europe as a student and young man. Also see Dilip Kumar Roy, *Among the Great*, Jaico

Books: 1950? Dilip recounts his growing relationship with Romain Rolland. Mrs Hedy Fülop-Müller, another friend of Dilip, whom he called 'Nilima,' also became a special friend of Subhas.

26. See A.B. Purani, *The Life of Sri Aurobindo (1872–1926)*, 2nd ed., Pondicherry: Sri Aurobindo Ashram, 1960; Dilip Roy, *Among the Great*, 199ff.

27. Bose, *Correspondence*, 412–13, letter of 10/9/32.

28. Bose, *Correspondence*, 413.

29. Government of India, Home Department, Political File No. 31/101/ 32; Government of India, Public and Judicial/174/Part I, India Office Library and Records, London; Bose, *My Uncle*, 68ff. Also see Subhas Bose, statement to the Free Press, issued February 25, 1933, prior to his sailing for Europe.

30. Bose, *My Uncle*, 68–9.

31. Bose, *My Uncle*, 69ff.

32. Bose, statement issued to the Free Press, February 25, 1933.

33. Subhas Bose letter to Dilip Roy, March 5, 1933.

34. Bose to Dilip Roy, March 5, 1933.

35. Bose's full statement of the role of Indians abroad is 'Indians Abroad,' in Subhas C. Bose, *Through Congress Eyes*, Allahabad: Kitabistan, 1938?, 76–93. Also see Bose, *My Uncle*, 69ff, and Subhas Bose, unpublished correspondence, 1933–1941, in Netaji Research Bureau, Calcutta.

36. Government of India, Home Department, Political File No. 31/101/ 32.

37. Government of India, Home Department, Political File No. 31/101/ 32.

38. Government of India, Home Department, Political File No. 31/101/ 32.

39. Sarat Bose, unpublished Prison Notebook, 1933–34 and 1942, in Netaji Research Bureau.

40. Sarat Bose, Prison Notebook. For support of this view of Gandhi, see E. Stanley Jones, *The Christ of the Indian Road*, London: Hodder and Stoughton, 1925, 86ff.

41. Sarat Bose, Prison Notebook, entry for August 19, 1933.

42. See Sanyal, 'Congress Movements in the Villages of Eastern Midnapore, 1921–1930,' 169–78, and Brown, *Gandhi and Civil Disobedience*, 263ff; Sumit Sarkar, *Modern India 1885–1947*, Delhi: Macmillan India, 1983, 320–25, gives a convenient summary.

43. See Brown, *Gandhi*, 243ff; many details of the London maneuvering are given in R.J. Moore, *The Crisis of Indian Unity 1917–1940*,

Oxford: Clarendon Press, 1974, 208ff.

44. Moore, *Crisis*, 250ff.

45. Moore, *Crisis*, 263; also of value are Government of India, Private Office Papers L/PO/49, Communal Decision, and Anderson Collection, MSS. Eur.F.207, India Office Library and Records; Files 3, 4, 5, 7; and Zetland Collection, MSS. Eur. D., 609, India Office Library and Records, File 60, and his memoirs, The Memoirs of Lawrence, Second Marquess of Zetland, *'Essayez'*, London: John Murray, 1956, 117ff.

46. Zetland, *'Essayez'*, 121.

47. Ram Gopal, *Indian Muslims, A Political History (1858–1947)*, Bombay: Asia Publishing House, 1959, 241ff; Mitra, *The Indian Annual Register*, 1931, 1932, gives reports of meetings of nationalist Muslims advocating joint electorates in 1931 and 1932. They often also wanted at least fifty per cent of the seats in the new legislature. Some examples of nationalist Muslims are Abul Hayat of Burdwan, Ashraffudin Choudhury of Comilla, Rezaul Karim, Syed Badruddoza of Murshidabad; and communists like Muzaffar Ahmed and Abdullah Rasul; also Krishak Praja Party members close to the Congress and in some cases having joint membership in both parties were Abul Mansur Ahmad, Nausher Ali, Shamsuddin Ahmed, Humayun Kabir, Jehangir Kabir. Discussions with Abul Mansur Ahmed in Dacca, May 31, 1972, and with Jehangir Kabir, Calcutta, July 20, 1973. Also see Kenneth McPherson, *The Muslim Microcosm: Calcutta, 1918 to 1935*, Wiesbaden: Franz Steiner Verlag, 1974, 107ff, which gives a detailed account.

48. McPherson, *Muslim Microcosm*, 107ff; interviews with Abul Mansur Ahmad, Dacca, May, June 1972; Shila Sen, *Muslim Politics in Bengal 1937–1947*, New Delhi: Impex India, 1976, 61ff.

49. File No. G24 (i), 1936, AICC Papers, Nehru Memorial Library, New Delhi, Communal Award, General Correspondence by Pandit Jawaharlal Nehru; *Bengal Anti-Communal Award Movement: A Report*, Calcutta: 1939; John Gallagher, 'Congress in Decline: Bengal 1930 to 1939,' in John Gallagher; Gordon Johnson and Anil Seal, *Locality Province and Nation: Essays on Indian Politics 1870–1940*, Cambridge: Cambridge U. Press, 1973, 297–300; Zetland Collection, India Office Library, File on the Communal Award, especially the numerous pamphlets by B.C. Chatterjee and the clippings from the Hindu press of the period; B.N. Dutta Roy, ed., *Sir N.N. Sircar's Speeches and Pamphlets*, Calcutta: The Book Company, 1934.

50. Brown, *Gandhi*, 313ff.

51. Dutta Roy, *Sircar's Speeches*, 3–4. AICC File No. G24 (i), 1936.

52. These discussions went on through the 1930s and B.C. Chatterjee and A.H. Ghaznavi were among the frequent discussants. See Zetland Collection, India Office Library, File on the Communal Award, B.P. Singh Roy Papers, Nehru Memorial Library, letters to Sir John Anderson, refers to such talks.

53. Quoted in Donald Eugene Smith, *India as a Secular State*, Princeton: Princeton U. Press, 1963, 458–9; *Hindutva* was first published in 1923.

54. Quoted in Smith, *Secular State*, 458.

55. There is no adequate biography of Shyama Prasad Mookerjee; one by a disciple is Balraj Madhok, *Dr. Syama Prasad Mookerjee*, New Delhi: Deepak Prakashan, 1954; some of Mookerjee's statements are collected in his *Awake Hindustan!*, Calcutta: n.d., 1944; *PBLC*, 1937 to 1947, contain many of his speeches; some of his letters are to be found in Akhil Bharat Hindu Mahasabha Papers, Nehru Memorial Library, New Delhi.

56. For example, see the speech by N.C. Chatterjee to the Barisal Hindu Conference, September 9, 1944; and other pamphlets of the Hindu Mahasabha in the organization's files in the collection of the Nehru Memorial Library.

57. *Bengal Anti-Communal Award Movement*, 31–2.

58. Dr B.C. Roy ran this election campaign for the Congress in Bengal; see his papers, Nehru Memorial Library, file on the 'Revival of the Swaraj Party,' November 1933–May 1934, and file, 1934, as general secretary of the Congress Parliamentary Board; 'Nationalist' in this context had Hindu communalist overtones. Also see Bose, *My Uncle*, 100–1.

59. Subhas Bose to Satyen Mitra, 18/10/34; also see Subhas Chandra Bose, 'The White Paper and the Communal Award,' in *The Indian Struggle*, Bombay: Asia Publishing House, 1964, 276ff.

60. Bose, *My Uncle*, 73ff.

61. Julius Braunthal, *The Tragedy of Austria*, London: Gollancz, 46.

62. Stefan Zweig, *The World of Yesterday*, Lincoln: U. of Nebraska Press, 1964, 281.

63. On Patel, see the detailed biography by Gordhanbhai Patel, *Vithalbhai Patel*, 2 vols., Bombay: U. of Bombay, 1950, on Patel's Irish visit, Book Two, 1209ff. Bose's letters to Mrs Woods begin on 7/12/33 and continue through the 1930s.

64. Reprinted in Bose, *Indian Struggle*, 357.

65. Nathalal D. Parikh, 'Reminiscences,' in P.D. Saggi ed., *Life and Work of Netaji Subhas Chandra Bose*, Bombay: Overseas Publishing House, n.d., 38.

66. The speech he wrote and wanted to deliver in London is printed in Bose, *Indian Struggle*, 358–79. Government of India, Home Department, Political File No. 35/11/33 describes the proscription of Bose's speech to be given in London.

67. On the bluff, see Government of India, Public and Judicial/174/Part I/1935, India Office Records, London, which describes it and gives a detailed account of Bose's stay in Europe through 1934. The story is picked up in 1935 in P&J/174/Part II/1935, and continued through 1937.

68. Bose, *Indian Struggle*, 358.

69. Bose, *Indian Struggle*, 367–68.

70. Bose, *Indian Struggle*, 377–79.

71. See, P&J/174/Part I/1935.

72. Bose, *My Uncle*, 84; Parikh, 'Reminiscences,' 38.

73. Bose, *My Uncle*, 99; Patel, *Patel*, Book Two, 1250–73.

74. The extensive collection of letters written by Subhas Bose to Mrs Vetter is in the Netaji Research Bureau, Calcutta, and will be published in his collected works. When I visited Mrs Vetter in Vienna on April 30, 1965, she proudly showed me her copy of the *Indian Struggle* inscribed, 'Dedicated to Dr. and Mrs. Vetter to whose company I owe some of the happiest moments of my life in Europe between 1933 and 1935; this book commenced and completed in Vienna is presented in grateful appreciation of their friendship, 16/2/35, Vienna.'

75. His letters about a proposed book on Vienna were written to Santosh Basu, then mayor of Calcutta, May 11, 1933 and June 10, 1933. Further letters on European municipalities to Basu were written on July 1, 1933 and August 7, 1933. A brief article on Vienna, Prague, Warsaw and Berlin, written on November 25, 1933, is in the collection of the Netaji Research Bureau. Some of Bose's articles written in the 1930s are collected in Bose, *Through Congress Eyes*.

76. Details gathered from Bose, *My Uncle*, 71ff, and Bose's letters to Mrs Vetter, 1933 to 1938.

77. See Miloslav Krása, *Looking towards India: A Study in East–West Contacts*, Prague: Orbis, 1969, 102; Bose, *My Uncle*, 93–4; Bose to Mrs Vetter, 10/7/33.

78. Bose to Mrs Vetter, 22/7/33.

79. Bose, *My Uncle*, 83–88; Lothar Frank's account of Bose in Europe

in the 1930s is a valuable source and analysis of his views and is found in 'India's Ambassador Abroad 1933–1936,' in Sisir K. Bose and Alexander Werth eds., *A Beacon across Asia*, Delhi: Orient Longman, 1973, 46–68. I also gained some further information about Bose by discussing these matters with Mr Frank in Wiesbaden, October 5, 1978.

80. There are many comments on Bose's views in Bose, *My Uncle*, 83ff and in Bose's letters to friends in Europe in this period, e.g., Bose to Amiya Chakravarty, 11/3/36; several of Bose's letters and statements on Germany and India will be mentioned and quoted below.

81. Adolf Hitler, *Mein Kampf*, Boston: Houghton Mifflin, 1943, 657.

82. Hitler, *Kampf*, 658.

83. Details are found in the German Foreign Office Records, Archives, Bonn, Auswärtiges Amt., Politisches Abteilung III, Politische Beziehungen Indiens zu Deutschland, Band 3, January–December 1933. The letters of the British Ambassador are dated 8/3/33 and 18/3/33.

84. Many protests were made by Indians in Europe including Bose, but the German Foreign Office maintained that there was no animus against India and no concerted campaign to blacken the name of India, however much Hitler thought that India deserved to be ruled by the British. Auswärtiges Amt., Politisches Abteilung III, Beziehungen Indiens zu Deutschland, Band 3. Bose's statement, 'Germany and India,' dated March 1936, sums up his views in this period. This statement was issued to the press in Geneva. Bose's communications to the German Foreign Office are also contained in the above-mentioned German Foreign Office file and there are reports by officials on each of his visits, e.g., March 28, 1934; Frank, 'Ambassador,' in Bose and Werth, *Beacon*, 49–55.

85. Frank, 'Ambassador,' in Bose and Werth, *Beacon*, 52.

86. See Bose's proposal to the German government, April 5, 1934, in Auswärtiges Amt., Politisches Abteilung III, Politische Beziehungen Indiens zu Deutschland, Band 3; Tarak Nath Das, an Indian nationalist long resident abroad, insisted that the treatment of Nambiar was an unusual incident and that Indians could still thrive in Germany, in Tarak Nath Das, 'Position of Indian Students in National Socialist Germany,' *Modern Review*, August 1933, 184–85. Another generally positive view of Nazi Germany, is G.S. Khair, 'German Education under National Socialism,' *Modern Review*, January 1935, 38–43.

87. See Bose's comments on Gandhi's visit to Mussolini in Bose, *Indian*

Struggle, 231; Bose, *My Uncle*, 87ff, which has many details; Frank, 'Ambassador,' in Bose and Werth, *Beacon*, 58–60; Amiyanath Sarkar, 'The Oriental Students' Congress and the Third Convention of the Indian Students in Europe, Rome, 1933,' *Modern Review*, March 1934, 276–80. Bose letter to Mrs Vetter, 12/1/34, is a lengthy account of Bose's view of the meetings in Rome.

88.   Denis Mack Smith, *Mussolini, A Biography*, New York: Vintage Books, 1983, 111, 125, 171.

89.   Krishna Kripalani, *Rabindranath Tagore: A Biography*, New York: Grove Press, 1962, 327.

90.   Gandhi, *Collected Works*, Vol. XLVIII, 429–30, letter of December 20, 1931.

91.   Tarak Nath Das, 'New Italy and Greater India,' *Modern Review*, June 1931, 644–45; also see Tarak Nath Das, 'The New Greater Italy and Signor Mussolini,' in *Modern Review*, June 1926, 643–51; another Indian with a very positive view of Mussolini was P.N. Roy, e.g., 'Eleven Years of Fascism,' *Modern Review*, January 1934, 35–43, and 'India and Italy—A Plea for Cultural Co–operation,' *Modern Review*, November 1933, 505–9.

92.   Bose to Mrs Vetter, 12/1/34.

93.   Bose to Mrs Vetter, 12/1/34.

94.   Frank, 'Ambassador,' in Bose and Werth, *Beacon*, 60. Bose's comment about the big boss is in a letter quoted in Bose, *My Uncle*, 91.

95.   Bose, *My Uncle*, 87ff, mentions most of the visits. Frank, 'Ambassador,' in Bose and Werth, *Beacon*, 58–60. Bose's positive attitude towards Mussolini is also found in his letters to Mrs Vetter, e.g., 12/1/34. Bose was also in touch with Maggiore Rapicavoli, of the Italian government, and there are some of Bose's letters to him in the collection of the Netaji Research Bureau. Although several excellent scholars have written on Bose's relations to the Axis powers none has, to my knowledge, made a careful search of the Italian records which may reveal other aspects of Bose's relations to the Italian government of Mussolini between 1933 and 1943.

96.   Smith, *Mussolini*, 111, 171.

97.   Bose, *Indian Struggle*, 430–31.

98.   Bose, *Through Congress Eyes*, 77.

99.   Bose, *Through Congress Eyes*, 90.

100. Bose, *Through Congress Eyes*, 90–1.

101. There are many comments in Bose's letters to Mrs Vetter through this period; also see Bose, *My Uncle*, 73ff; comments here and there

in Bose, *Through Congress Eyes, passim*; in the *Modern Review* in the 1930s there are almost monthly reports on the activities of Bose in Europe and on meetings of Indian students and the various binational cultural organizations established at this time. One specific plan for commercial cooperation between India and Austria worked out by Bose will be mentioned below.

102. Bose, *Through Congress Eyes*, 154–58.
103. Krása, *Looking towards India*, 102; 'Czechoslovak India Society,' *Modern Review*, October 1934, 470.
104. Bose to Mrs Vetter, 6/2/34.
105. Bose, *Through Congress Eyes*, 159–63.
106. Bose to Mrs Vetter, 21/5/34.
107. Frank, in Bose and Werth, *Beacon*, 53–55; Bose, *My Uncle*, 92–3; many communications by Dr Thierfelder to the German Foreign Office are contained in Auswärtiges Amt., Politisches Abteilung III, Beziehungen Indiens zu Deutschland.
108. Bose letter to Dyckhoff, an official of the German Foreign Office, April 5, 1934, in Auswärtiges Amt., Politisches Abteilung III, Beziehung Indiens zu Deutschland.
109. Bose was sensitive to racism throughout his life, from his early days in India, to his student days in England, through his nationalist years as a mature man. When protesting the applications of the Nazi racist laws, he does mention the general extent of their coverage. He did not feel it was his part, as a visitor in Germany and Europe, to fight Nazi racism against the Jews, though he was well aware of it and discussed it with European friends, as Mrs Kurti, mentioned below. On Gandhi in South Africa, see Robert A. Huttenback, *Gandhi in South Africa*, Ithaca: Cornell U. Press, 1971; James D. Hunt, *Gandhi in London*, New Delhi: Promilla, 1978, Chapter Two, 40–57; Mohandas K. Gandhi, *An Autobiography, The Story of My Experiments with Truth*, Parts II, III, IV, Boston: Beacon Press, 1957.
110. This relationship is chronicled in Kitty Kurti, *Subhas Chandra Bose As I Knew Him*, Calcutta: Firma K.L. Mukhopadhyay, 1966. I have also discussed these meetings with Mrs Kurti at her home in West Hartford, Connecticut, August 30, 1980.
111. Kurti, *Bose*, 11.
112. Kurti, *Bose*, 39.
113. Kurti, *Bose*, 53.
114. Kurti, *Bose*, 48.
115. Kurti, *Bose*, 49.
116. Interview with Mrs Vetter in Vienna, 4/30/65.

117. Interview with Mrs Vetter in Vienna, 4/30/54. Bose's many letters to Santosh Basu on municipal issues are mentioned in footnote 75 above.
118. This was the view of Mrs Kurti, interview, August 30, 1980, and of other friends in Europe. It is also the view of his nephew Asoke; see Bose, *My Uncle*, 73ff, *passim*.
119. Bose to Mrs Vetter, 9/12/33.
120. See Otto Faltis, 'India and Austria,' *Modern Review*, February 1936, 205–7.
121. Subhas Chandra Bose, 'The Austrian Riddle,' *Modern Review*, April 1934, 461–68. For other views of this period, see Andrew Whiteside, 'Austria,' in Hans Rogger and Eugen Weber eds., *The European Right: A Historical Profile*, Berkeley: U. of California Press, 1966, 308–63; Zweig, *World of Yesterday*, Chapters XII–XVI; Braunthal, *Tragedy of Austria*, 43ff; Gordon Brook-Shepherd, *Dollfuss*, London: Macmillan, 1961.
122. Bose, 'Austrian Riddle,' 466.
123. Bose, 'Austrian Riddle,' 463–67.
124. Bose, 'Austrian Riddle,' 467.
125. Details given to me by Emilie Schenkl, in Vienna, October 14, 1978. I have also found of value the interview conducted by B.R. Nanda (interviewer), with Madame Emilie Schenkl (interviewee), November 11, 1971, Oral History Transcript, Nehru Memorial Museum and Library.
126. Emilie Schenkl, interview, October 14, 1978. Asoke Bose mentions that his uncle was studying German, in Bose, *My Uncle*, 75. He also took up studying German again from 1941 on and learned it sufficiently well to give a brief speech in German. I am not sure how well he learned to read.
127. Bose, *My Uncle*, 98.
128. Bose, *Indian Struggle*, 178, 200, 202, 297–98.
129. Bose, *Indian Struggle*, 60–1.
130. Bose, *Indian Struggle*, 114–15.
131. Bose, *Indian Struggle*, 67–71, 141, 312–16.
132. In interviews with important members of the Communist Party of India, they have frequently expressed this view. Among those who mentioned this were Somnath Lahiri, Calcutta, January 27, 1976, and P.C. Joshi, New Delhi, February 6, 1965. But many other Indian intellectuals of the period who were non-communist also found fascism repugnant, e.g., Buddhadeva Bose, interview, Calcutta, July 9, 1973. Also the antipathy of Nehru to fascism is often

mentioned in his writings. See the following footnote.

133. Brecher, *Nehru*, 9, 188, 210, 221, 258, 262; Bipan Chandra, 'Jawaharlal Nehru and the Capitalist Class, 1936,' in his *Nationalism and Colonialism in Modern India*, Delhi: Orient Longman, 1979, 172, 176–77, 211–12. In Nehru's own writings, see 'Fascism and Empire,' a 1937 spèech in his *Eighteen Months in India 1936–1937*, Allahabad: Kitabistan, 1938; 'India and the World,' 1936 article in his collection, *India and the World*, London: Allen and Unwin, 1936; *Selected Works of Jawaharlal Nehru*, Vol. Seven, Delhi: Orient Longman, 1975, 567–71. There are, of course, numerous other mentions of fascism in Nehru's extensive works, but no extended examination.

134. Fascism is dealt with in R. Palme Dutt, *World Politics 1918–1936*, New York: International Publishers, 1936. This was a book that Bose asked Nehru to lend him when the former was held under house detention in 1936. M.N. Roy's most thorough work on the subject is his *Fascism: Its Philosophy, Professions and Practice*, Calcutta: D.M. Library, 1938? It is likely that Roy started this book during his long imprisonment in the 1930s and then·completed it after *his* release. Fascism in Europe and in India was a frequent theme in the writings of Roy, who even decided in the 1940s that Bose, Nehru, and Gandhi represented fascistic trends in India. See M.N. Roy, *I.N.A. and the August Revolution*, Calcutta: Renaissance Publishers, 1946; *The Problem of Freedom*, Calcutta: Renaissance Publishers, 1946?; M.N. Roy and G.D. Parikh, *Alphabet of Fascist Economics*, Calcutta: Renaissance Publishers, 1944? Many other treatments of fascism are to be found in Roy's extensive writings.

135. Roy, *Fascism*, 2ff.

136. For example, see his remarks to Mrs Kurti, in Kurti, *Bose*, 11; and his rather detached view of the Italian invasion of Abyssinia, in which he speculates on a war between Britain and Italy, Subhas Chandra Bose, 'The Secret of Abyssinia and Its Lesson,' *Modern Review*, November 1935, 571–77.

137. Bose to Rabindranath Tagore, August 3, 1934, copy in Netaji Research Bureau, Calcutta.

138. Majumdar, *Rabindranath o subhaschandra*, Calcutta: Saraswati Library, 61–2.

139. Majumdar, *Rabindranath*, 62–3.

140. Bose to Mrs Vetter, 24/9/34.

141. Bose, *My Uncle*, 105–6.

142. Bose to Mrs Vetter, 7/12/34. In Sarat Bose's letters to Asoke Bose

during 1934 there are several comments on the deteriorating health of Janaki Nath Bose.

143. Interview with Gauri Nath Sastri, Calcutta, May 18, 1979.
144. Interview with Shila (Sengupta) Bose, New Delhi, November 29, 1978.
145. Details from Gauri Nath Sastri, Calcutta, May 18, 1979.
146. Interview with Aurobindo Bose, Calcutta, August 25, 1976.
147. Details from Sarat Bose's letters to Asoke Bose, 1933–35.
148. Sarat Bose to Asoke Bose, May 7, 1934.
149. Sarat Bose, letters to Asoke Bose, 1935, and Bose, *My Uncle*, 102–3.
150. Sir N.N. Sircar letter to Sir John Anderson, April 13, 1935 in Anderson Collection, India Office Library, London, MSS. Eur.F.207.
151. Sircar to Anderson, April 13, 1935.
152. John W. Wheeler–Bennett, *John Anderson: Viscount Waverly*, VII, London: Macmillan, 1962, mentions this, but many former ICS officers also described him in this way and said he was 'the best brain they ever saw'. Others also had some resentment at the way he used his critical skills. The generally glowing reports were by Leonard Pinnell, ICS, Woking, July 22, 1969; R.L. Walker, ICS, East Grinstead, 17/8/71; Sir R.H. Hutchings, ICS, Lymington, 13/9/71; R.N. Gilchrist, ICS, Aberdeen, 2/8/69.
153. Sir John Anderson to the Marquess of Zetland, August 31, 1935, in Anderson Collection, India Office Library.
154. Sarat Bose to Asoke Bose, August 2, 1935.
155. Bose, *My Uncle*, 106–7; Bose letters to Mrs Vetter, 7/12/34, 8/1/35.
156. Bose, *My Uncle*, 107–110. During this visit to Rome, Bose was taken in by an overzealous policeman who demanded to see his papers. Bose was wearing his Indian dress and attracted attention and did not have his papers on him when he was questioned by the police. Bose, *My Uncle*, 107–8.
157. See the brief note in the *Modern Review*, March 1935, 390.
158. Quoted in the *Modern Review*, March 1935, 390.
159. See Government of India, P&J/174/II/35, India Office Library, and Government of India, Home Department, Political File No. 22/29/35.
160. Bose, *My Uncle*, 109.
161. Sobhanlal Datta Gupta, *Comintern, India and the Colonial Question, 1920–37*, Calcutta: K.P. Bagchi, 1980, 208ff.
162. See the report in the *Modern Review*, May 1935, 607–8; and Bose letter to Mrs Vetter, 25/3/35.
163. Bose described his visit in 'What Romain Rolland Thinks,' in

Through Congress Eyes, 140–53.

164. The book with Dilip Roy's inscription, dated 20/5/25, is in the library of the Netaji Research Bureau, Calcutta.

165. Rolland's letter, dated February 22, 1935, is printed on a separate page, just before the preface, to the 1948 edition of *The Indian Struggle 1920–1934*, Calcutta: Thacker, Spink, 1948.

166. 'Bose–Rolland Interview,' reprinted in Bose, *Indian Struggle*, 1964 edition, 389. All references to the *Indian Struggle* are to this edition, unless otherwise noted.

167. See Romain Rolland, *Inde*. Journal (1915–1943), Paris: Editions Albin Michel, 1960, 477–80.

168. This correspondence is collected in *Romain Rolland and Gandhi Correspondence*, New Delhi: Publications Division, Government of India, 1976.

169. Bose, *My Uncle*, 115.

170. Mentioned to me by Dr Sisir Bose, January 15,1976.

171. Bose, *My Uncle*, 115.

172. Bose to Mrs Vetter, 1/10/35.

173. Brecher, *Nehru*, 203–11.

174. Bose to Nehru, 4/10/35, from Hofgastein.

175. Some of the letters from Bose to Nehru are dated 4/10/35, 4/3/36, 13/3/36. Some Nehru letters to Bose are dated 26/3/36 and 30/3/36 and are in Nehru's *Selected Works*, Vol. 7, 407–8.

176. Bose, *Indian Struggle*, 169–70, 173–75, 201.

177. Bose, *Indian Struggle*, 264.

178. Bose, *Indian Struggle*, 264n.

179. Nehru was much more dignified and restrained in his criticism of Bose than Bose was in talking of Nehru. The long-pent-up anger only exploded some years later; but see Nehru, *Selected Works*, Vol. 6, 332.

180. Bose to Amiya Chakravarty, 23/12/35.

181. Robert Briffault, *Breakdown: The Collapse of Traditional Civilization* , 2nd ed., New York: Coward McCann, 1935, 48ff.

182. Briffault, *Breakdown*, 155–89.

183. Briffault, *Breakdown*, 190–203.

184. Briffault, *Breakdown*, 280–81.

185. Briffault, *Breakdown*, 274ff.

186. Bose, 'Abyssinia,' 572ff.

187. Bose, 'Abyssinia,' 574.

188. Denis Mack Smith, *Mussolini's Roman Empire*, New York: Penguin Books, 1977, 59ff.

189. Bose, 'Abyssinia,' 571.

190. Bose, 'Abyssinia,' 577.

191. See for example, Kurti, *Bose*, 11; Bose to Amiya Chakravarty, 11/3/36; also see his detached comments on European rivalries and the possibility of war in Bose, 'Abyssinia,' 571–77, and 'Europe: To-day and To-morrow,' in Bose, *Through Congress Eyes*, 214–39. Of course, many of his wartime comments illustrate this. They will be quoted and commented upon in due course.

192. See his many letters to Santosh Basu, then mayor of Calcutta, mentioned above in footnote 75 and his brief article on European cities dated November 25, 1933.

193. Bose to Saklatvala, 15/11/35, from Vienna, answering his letter of August 15; 1935.

194. Bose to Saklatvala, 15/11/35.

195. J.L. Keenan, 'Note on Labour in Jamshedpur,' in *Modern Review*, December 1935, 704–8.

196. Subhas C. Bose, 'Labour in Jamshedpur—The other side of the picture,' in *Through Congress Eyes*, 94–118.

197. Bose to Santosh Basu, 3/1/36.

198. Bose to Santosh Basu, 3/1/36.

199. Bose to Amiya Chakravarty, 23/12/35, from Vienna.

200. Bose to Mrs Vetter, 29/11/35. Enclosed with his letter was a statement about his problem in German to be used by Dr Vetter in attempting to help him.

201. Bose to Mrs Vetter, 30/1/36.

202. Bose speech to Indian Students' Association of Berlin, February 4, 1936, in Netaji Research Bureau.

203. Bose to Amiya Chakravarty, 11/3/36.

204. Parikh has given a detailed account of his visit in his valuable 'Reminiscences' and Bose describes his trip in his letter to Mrs Vetter, 30/1/36.

205. Parikh, 'Reminiscences,' 40.

206. Parikh, 'Reminiscences,' 40; Asoke Bose, *My Uncle*, 107, mentions another incident in which Bose had trouble because of his unusual dress, this time in Italy.

207. Bose to Mrs Woods, 7/12/33; Bose to Mrs Woods, December 21, 1935; Bose, *My Uncle*, 126.

208. *Amrita Bazar Patrika*, February 20, 1936.

209. Bose to Mrs Woods, 7/12/33.

210. *Sunday Independent*, Dublin, 2/2/36.

211. *Irish Press*, 4/2/36.

212. *Irish Independent*, 4/2/36.
213. Amiya Chakravarty, 'Subhaschandra,' in *Subhas smriti*, ed., Biswanth De, 1st ed., Calcutta: Sahityam, 1970, 265.
214. A collection of pamphlets given to Subhas Bose by the Sinn Fein Standing Committee was given to me by Emilie Schenkl. The expression 'Freak State,' is in the first sentence of 'The Sinn Fein Outlook,' by J.J. O'Kelly. There is a listing of his talks with opposition leaders in *Amrita Bazar*, 20/2/36, and Bose also mentions these talks in an interview with United Press in Lausanne, 30/3/36. Copy of the interview in Netaji Research Bureau.
215. See the many pamphlets by J.J. O'Kelly, 'The Sinn Fein Outlook,' 'The Republic of Ireland Vindicated,' 'The Robbery of Ireland and the Remedy', and many others, copies given to Bose during his visit to Ireland to acquaint him with their point of view. An overview by a leading historian is F.S.L. Lyons, *Ireland Since the Famine*, London: Weidenfeld and Nicolson, 1971, 506ff.
216. Bose to United Press, 30/3/36.
217. Bose to United Press, 30/3/36.
218. *Irish Press*, 4/2/36.
219. Robert Kee, *Ireland*, Boston: Little Brown, 1982,156.
220. On de Valera, see Lyons, *Ireland*, 376ff, and Calton Younger, 'Eamon deValera,' in *A State of Disunion*, London: Fontana, 1972, 221–329.
221. *Irish Press*, 12/2/36: 'Mr S.C. Bose, the Indian Nationalist leader, had a surprise yesterday when in his Dublin Hotel he met Lieut-Col. J.H. Smith, District Government Office, Burma, who had been governor of the prison at Mandalay, Burma, when Mr Bose was a prisoner there for over two years.

Lieut-Col. Smith, who is a native of Boyle and is on holiday, was passing through to the west of Ireland from the six counties. The two men had a talk and exchanged views on their last meeting in different circumstances.'
222. Bose to Mrs Woods, 5/3/36.
223. Bose to Mrs Woods, 30/3/36.
224. Bose to Mrs Woods, 5/3/36.
225. Bose to Mrs Vetter, 30/1/36; Bose, *My Uncle*, 126–7.
226. Bose speech, 17/3/36, to French Section of League against Imperialism, copy in Netaji Research Bureau.
227. Bose speech, 17/3/36, in Paris
228. Bose spent a good deal of time with Nehru and not only the Paris Speech, but his Haripura Congress presidential address of 1938

expresses the same views. Compare Bose's views with those of Nehru at about this time as analyzed by Chandra, 'Nehru and the Capitalist Class,' 172ff. His enthusiastic reading of the popular Marxism of Briffault has also been described above.

229. Bose to Nehru, March 4, 1936.

230. Bose to Nehru, 13/3/36.

231. Nehru to Bose, 26/3/36, in *Selected Works*, Vol. 7, 407.

232. Bose to Rolland, 25/3/36.

233. Asoke Bose also sees this departure as the end of an important period in his life, Bose, *My Uncle*, 130.

234. Chakravarty, 'Subhaschandra,' 265–55.

235. See P&J/174/II/35. From his correspondence with the government in early 1936, Bose undoubtedly expected to be arrested.

236. Bose, *My Uncle*, 132; Nehru, *Selected Works*, Vol. 7, 407–9.

237. Sarat Bose's activities beginning from his release in mid–1935 will be dealt with in the next chapter.

CHAPTER EIGHT

1. Rabindranath Tagore, 'Deshanayak' [Leader of the Country], *Kalantar*, Calcutta: Visva-Bharati, 1962, 371. Tagore addressed this essay to Subhas Bose in 1939 after he had endured the difficulties of the Congress crisis.

2. Bose, *My Uncle Netaji*, Calcutta: Esem, 1977, 120. Sarat Bose letters to Asoke Bose, 1935, *passim*.

3. Sarat Bose letter to Asoke Bose, September 27, 1935.

4. See AICC Papers, File No. G–24 (i) of 1936, on Bengal politics and the Communal Award. Also Government of India, Home Department, Political File No. 24/17/36.

5. *Calcutta Municipal Gazette*, XXII, May 25, 1935 [hereafter, *CMG*].

6. *CMG*, XXII, May 25, 1935.

7. Periodic reports appeared in *CMG*, XXIII, December 21, 1935; January 18, 1936; January 25, 1936; February 15, 22, 29, 1936; March 14, 28, 1936; April 4, 11, 1936.

8. *CMG*, XXIII, December 14, 1935.

9. Abul Mansur Ahmed, *Amar dekha rajnitir panchas bachhar* [50 Years of Politics As I Saw Them], 3rd ed., Dacca: Nawroze Kitabistan, 1975, 160–61.

10. *CMG*, XXIV, October 17, 1936; XXVI, November 25, 1937.

11. Government of India, Home Department, Political File No. 43/37/

36.
12. Government of India, Home Department, Political File No. 43/37/ 36.
13. Interview with Leonard Pinnell, Woking, July 22, 1969, and comments in Government of India, Home, Political File No. 43/37/36.
14. On the trade union movement in this period, see Chamanlal Revri, *The Indian Trade Union Movement: An Outline History 1880-1947*, New Delhi: Orient Longman, 1972, 185ff; Sen, *Working Class*, 329ff. Sumit Sarkar's excellent general text on the period emphasizes popular movements, *Modern India 1885-1947*, Delhi: Macmillan, 1983, 334ff.
15. The most detailed and astute study of the CSP is Rusch, 'Role of the Congress Socialist Party in the Indian National Congress, 1931–1942.' Also see Jaya Prakash Narayan, *Towards Struggle*, Bombay: Padma, 1946; Minoo Masani, *Bliss Was It in That Dawn . . .*, Delhi: Arnold–Heinemann, 1977; Surendranath Dwivedy, *Quest for Socialism*, New Delhi: Radiant, 1984; L.P. Sinha, *The Left Wing in India*, Muzaffarpur: New Publishers, 1965, Chapters 6–9.
16. Quoted in Datta Gupta, *Comintern, India and the Colonial Question*, 215.
17. On the Communists in this period, see Overstreet and Windmiller, *Communism in India*, Chapters 7, 8. Also, Masani, *Bliss*, 120ff; Narayan, *Struggle*, 165ff; Rusch, 'CSP,' 342ff.
18. Sen, *Working Class*, 354ff; V.B. Karnik, *Indian Trade Unions*, 2nd ed., Bombay: Manaktalas, 1966, 108ff.
19. Binay Bhushan Chaudhuri, 'Agrarian Movements in Bihar and Bengal, 1919–1939,' in B.R. Nanda ed., *Socialism in India*, Delhi: Vikas, 1972; M.A. Rasul, *A History of the All India Kisan Sabha*, Calcutta: National Book Agency, 1974, Chapter 1; N.G. Ranga, *Fight for Freedom*, Delhi: S. Chand, 1968, 191ff.
20. Rusch, 'CSP,' 226; also this view on the part of the Boses has been explicated in Chapters Five, Six, Seven, above.
21. There are many details in Government of India P&J/174/Part II/ 1935 India Office Library, London. See Nehru's article, 'Subhas Day,' in his *Selected Works*, Vol.7, 414–15.
22. Bose, *My Uncle*, 132–33; Sarat-Bose letters to Asoke Bose, June 3, June 18, August 13, 1936. Also Government of India, Home Department 44/95/36 and 24/40/36.
23. These letters are in the possession of Dr Sisir Bose who has read extracts aloud to me.
24. AICC Papers, File No. P–5, 1937, P–6, 1936; A.M. and S.G. Zaidi

eds., *The Encyclopedia of the Indian National Congress*, Vol. 11, 1936–38, New Delhi: S. Chand, 1980, 161ff and *passim*; Reginald Coupland, *The Constitutional Problem in India: Indian Politics, 1936–1942*, Part II, London: Oxford U. Press, 1944. 16ff; Nehru, *Works*, Vol. 8, Part Two.

25. See Zaidi and Zaidi, *Congress*, Vol. 11, 36ff; AICC Papers, File No. G24 (i), 1936. There are many additional details in Leonard A. Gordon, 'Divided Bengal: Problems of Nationalism and Identity in the 1947 Partition,' *Journal of Commonwealth and Comparative Politics*, London, XVI, No. 2, July 1978, 143ff.

26. The letters are in AICC Papers, File No. G24(i), 1936.

27. AICC Papers, File No. G24(i), 1936.

28. AICC Papers, File No. G24(i), 1936.

29. Letter of October 9, 1936, in AICC Papers, File G24 (i), 1936.

30. On Jinnah and Bengal politics in this period, see M.A.H. Ispahani, *Qaid-e-Azam Jinnah As I Knew Him*, 2nd ed., Karachi: Forward Publications, 1967, 14ff; *M.A. Jinnah–Ispahani Correspondence 1936–1948*, ed., Z.H. Zaidi, Karachi: Forward Publications, 1976, 75ff; Humaria Momen, *Muslim Politics in Bengal: A Study of Krishak Praja Party and the Elections of 1937*, Dacca: Sunny House, 1972, 35ff; Shila Sen, *Muslim Politics in Bengal 1937–1947*, New Delhi: Impex India, 1976, 73ff; Humayun Kabir, *Muslim Politics 1906–47 and Other Essays*, Calcutta: Firma K.L. Mukhopadhyay, 1969, 21–22; Abul Mansur Ahmed, *Politics*, 125ff; and interview with Abul Mansur Ahmed, Dacca, May 31, 1972.

31. Interview with Abul Mansur Ahmed, May 31, 1972; interview with Jehangir Kabir, Calcutta, July 20, 1973. This description is also based on interviews with several British ICS officers of this period: Leonard Pinnell, 1969; M.O. Carter, Bristol, August 23, 1971; Sir R.H. Hutchings, Lymington, September 13, 1971; Sir Arthur Dash, Ashford, Kent, April 21, 1972. There are a number of books about Huq in Bengali and English, among them: A.S.M. Abdur Rab, *A.K. Fazlul Haq*, Lahore: Ferozsons, 1966? There is endless evidence on Huq's mercurial changes in Bengal Governors' Reports, 1937–43, India Office Library L/P&J/5, and Bengal Legislative Assembly Proceedings [hereafter *PBLA*], 1937–43.

32. Sen, *Muslim Politics*, 80; Momen, *Muslim Politics*, 53.

33. Unpublished letter of Sarat Bose, from Simla, October 21, 1936, Netaji Research Bureau.

34. Zaidi and Zaidi, *Congress*, Vol. 11, 225, 191.

35. Zaidi and Zaidi, *Congress*, Vol. 11, 135–36.

36. Zaidi and Zaidi, *Congress*, Vol. 11, 138.
37. India Office Library 1/PO/57; Mitra, *The Indian Annual Register*, I, January–June 1937, Calcutta, 168 (e–m); R.L. Gilchrist ed., *Report of the Reforms Office, Bengal 1932–1937*, Calcutta: Government of Bengal, Home Department, 1938.
38. Momen, *Muslim Politics*, 62ff; Sen, *Muslim Politics*, 85–87.
39. Sir John Anderson letter to the secretary of state for India, Lord Zetland, March 25, 1937, in Anderson Collection, MSS.Eur.F.207, Box 6, India Office Library.
40. Unpublished letter of February 3, 1937, Netaji Research Bureau.
41. Unpublished letter of February 3, 1937.
42. Unpublished letter to Anil, August 8, 1937. In a letter to his friend Kitty Kurti from Darjeeling, July 25, 1936, Bose wrote, 'At the present moment I am studying Freud's book on Dreams and also applying his theory to the interpretation of my own dreams.' Printed in the Appendix to Kitty Kurti, *Subhas Chandra Bose As I Knew Him*, Calcutta: Firma K.L. Mukhopadhyay, 1966, 61.
43. Government of India, Home Department, Political File No. 44/26/36.
44. Government of India, P&J/174/II/35.
45. Sir John Anderson to the viceroy, Lord Linlithgow, February 8, 1937, in L/PO/57, India Office Library, Government of India. K.G.M. Faroqui was a Muslim zamindar and politician from East Bengal.
46. Anderson to Linlithgow, February 8, 1937, L/PO/57.
47. This is a subject about which leaders of the period have expressed strong opinions and each blamed the other, but particularly noted the short-sightedness of the central Congress leadership. Interviews with Abul Mansur Ahmed, Dacca, May 31, 1972; Sasankar Sanyal, New Delhi, August 6, 1973; Jehangir Kabir, Calcutta, July 20, 1973. It is not clear just how early in 1937 the Boses decided it would be better for Bengal to have a coalition government with Huq. Certainly at mid-year, they saw how badly—from their point of view—trends were moving and begged the central Congress leadership to allow them to move towards a coalition with Huq. Also see Chattopadhyay, *Bengal Electoral Politics and Freedom Struggle,* 145–47. Chattopadhyay quotes a number of leaders who lamented the failure to form a KPP-coalition, but, amazingly, a few pages later, he seems to take the side of the Congress leaders who prevented such a coalition, 157–58.
48. Mitra, *IAR*, I, 1937, 192–93; Chattopadhyay, *Bengal Electoral*

Politics, 147; Coupland, *Constitutional Problem*, II, 27. B.P. Singh Roy Papers, Nehru Museum, contain some references to the coalition.

49.   On Sarker, see *The Times of India, Indian Yearbook and Who's Who*, Bombay, 1947, 1206–7; G.D. Birla, *In the Shadow of the Mahatma*, Bombay: Orient Longman, 1953, *passim*. See the friendly reference to Sarker in Gandhi's December 1938 letter, quoted below.

50.   Chattopadhyay, *Bengal Electoral Politics*, 149–50; Sen, *Muslim Politics*, 119–20.

51.   Roy, *Netaji*, 132–33.

52.   *CMG*, April 10, 1937.

53.   *CMG*, April 10, 1937.

54.   *CMG*, April 10, 1937.

55.   Jawaharlal Nehru to Subhas Bose, April 16, 1937, Nehru Memorial Library.

56.   The steps towards erecting Mahajati Sadan are chronicled in *CMG*, June 18, July 2, July 30, August 6, 1938. Tagore laid the foundation stone on August 19, 1939, and spoke briefly as did Subhas Bose. Bose's speech is in Subhas Bose, *Crossroads*, 2nd ed., Calcutta: Netaji Research Bureau, 1981, 202–3. Tagore's is 'Mahajati–Sadan,' in *Kalantar*, 377–79.

57.   Subhas Bose to Mrs Vetter, May 27, 1937, unpublished letter, Netaji Research Bureau.

58.   Subhas Bose letter to Dr and Mrs Dharmavir, March 22, 1938, Dharmavir Collection, Nehru Memorial Library.

59.   Subhas Bose to Mrs Vetter, May 27, 1937, unpublished letter, Netaji Research Bureau.

60.   Subhas Bose letter to Anil (?), August 8, 1937, unpublished letter, Netaji Research Bureau.

61.   Subhas Bose to Anil (?), August 8, 1937.

62.   Subhas Bose letter to Khitish Chattopadhyay, August 9, 1937, unpublished letter in possession of Gautam Chattopadhyay.

63.   Subhas Bose, 'Japan's Role in the Far East,' reprinted in his book, *Through Congress Eyes*, Allahabad: Kitabistan, 1938?, 212–13.

64.   Bose, 'Japan's Role,' 213.

65.   Bose, 'Europe: Today and Tomorrow,' in *Through Congress Eyes*, 239.

66.   Subhas Bose to Santosh Basu, August 17, 1937, from Dalhousie, unpublished letter, Netaji Research Bureau.

67.   *CMG*, August 14, 1937.

68.   The connection between Subhas Bose and Das has often been noted,

particularly since Das favored Subhas Bose and treated him almost like a son. But Sarat Bose was also recruited to politics in the Das period as were the Hindu and Congress political leaders and some Muslims as well who were to predominate in Bengal politics from the 1920s into the 1960s. Many were beholden to Das. Besides Sarat Bose, B.C. Roy, Tulsi Goswami, Kiran Sankar Roy, H.S. Suhrawardy, Nalini Sarker, others too learned parliamentary and political skills from Das. J.M. Sen Gupta also was a Das man and he led the Congress group in the Bengal Legislative Council, as has been noted above, in the later 1920s, and Sarat Bose was the leader in the Bengal Assembly from 1937 to 1941, though a split in the Congress weakened his role from 1939 to 1941.

69. The phrase about 'words flow(ing)' comes from an unpublished letter to his daughter Gita (Biswas) Bose, August 26, 1943. In his library, part of which is still retained in Netaji Bhavan, there are a number of collections of speeches and books on parliamentary procedure, which he studied.

70. More details will be given below on this matter. Sarat Bose is said to have written to the press that Sarker was 'a government man,' but I have been unable to find the letter to the press in the 1930s that I have heard Sarat Bose wrote then.

71. *PBLA*, LI, Part I, August 5, 1937, 235–37.

72. *PBLA*, LI, Part I, August 5, 1937, 252–53.

73. Chattopadhyay, *Bengal Electoral Politics*, 146–49. There were questions by the Congress members of the ministers about political prisoners at almost every opportunity in the Assembly. *PBLA*, 1937–41, *passim*.

74. *PBLA*, LI, Part 2, August 9, 1937, 9, 16.

75. *PBLA*, LI, Part 2, August 9, 1937, 60–1.

76. *PBLA*, LI, Part 2, August 9, 1937, 66–7.

77. *CMG*, August 14, August 21, September 11, 1937; Coupland, *Constitutional Problem*, II, 32.

78. Coupland, *Constitutional Problem*, II, 32.

79. *PBLA*, LI, No. 4, September 8, 1937, 1162–63.

80. *PBLA*, LI, No. 4, September 8, 1937, 1163.

81. *PBLA*, LI, No. 4, September 8, 1937, 1165.

82. *PBLA*, LI, No. 4, September 8, 1937, 1330.

83. Chatterjee, *Bengal 1920–1947*, 172. I read Chatterjee's after I had been through the debates and shaped my own views. Also see, Chattopadhyay, *Bengal Electoral Politics*, 150–51. Sarat Bose also had to defend the stand of the Bengal Congress Legislative party to

Jawaharlal Nehru.

84. *PBLA*, LI, No. 4, September 30, 1937, 2292–93.
85. *PBLA*, LI, No. 4, September 30, 1937, 2294.
86. *PBLA*, LI, No. 4, September 30, 1937, 2294–95.
87. *PBLA*, LI, No. 4, September 30, 1937, 2310–11.
88. Jawaharlal Nehru to Subhas Bose, October 20, 1937, in *Works*, Vol.8, 187–88.
89. Nehru, *Works*, Vol.8, 185n.
90. See the exchanges between Subhas Bose and Tagore on this matter in Majumdar, *Rabindranath o subhaschandra*, 1968, 58–84.
91. *CMG*, October 30, 1937.
92. Bose, *My Uncle*, 159–60. Interviews with Amiya Nath Bose, Calcutta, January 21, 1976; Aurobindo Bose, August 25, 1976; Gita (Biswas) Bose, January 17, 1976; Lila (Mitra) Bose, February 15, 1979; Meera (Roy) Bose, August 9, 1977; Ranajit Bose, January 22, 1987; Roma (Roy) Bose, August 10, 1977; Sisir K. Bose, May 9, 1972, July 5, 1973, January 12, 1976, and on many other occasions.
93. The hiring of Mr Chaudhuri and his role in the household is based on some of the above interviews with Bose family members and on the many talks I have had with Mr Chaudhuri in India and Oxford over the past twenty-three years, including November 26, 1971, when he particularly talked about Sarat Bose. He became known outside a relatively small circle after the publication of *The Autobiography of an Unknown Indian*, New York: Macmillan, 1951. There is also a marriage connection which was formed by the marriage of Mr Chaudhuri's favorite niece, Krishna, to Dr Sisir Bose, the third son of Sarat Bose. Some family members not in the immediate family of Sarat Bose have expressed some hostility to Mr Chaudhuri, who has delighted in creating controversies as he has grown older. It is difficult for me to write of him in a detached way since he has been both a teacher and a friend to me, but also someone with whom I have argued upon occasion. He has said that in the second volume of his autobiography, he would write about Sarat Bose. This long-awaited volume is now available
94. Interview with Sisir K. Bose, January 12, 1976.
95. Bose, *My Uncle*, 140–41.
96. *CMG*, October 30, 1937. There are numerous references in Gandhi's *Works*, to these negotiations, including Vol. LXVI, 286, 296, 329–31, 405, 412.
97. Gandhi, *Works*, Vol. LXVI, 284.
98. Subhas Bose to Mrs Dharmavir, December 6, 1937, Dharmavir

Collection, Nehru Memorial Library.

99. *CMG*, November 13, 1937.
100. *CMG*, October 9, 1937.
101. Subhas Bose to Maggiore Rapicavoli, December 31, 1937 and November 25, 1937.
102. Bose, *My Uncle*, 147.
103. The original manuscript with the outline of the whole plan including the unwritten chapters is in the Netaji Research Bureau.
104. Subhas Chandra Bose, *An Indian Pilgrim*, Bombay: Asia Publishing House, 1965, 4, 24, 30, 32, 41, 43, 48–9.
105. Bose, *Pilgrim*, 44.
106. Bose, *Pilgrim*, 104–110.
107. Interview with Emilie Schenkl, Vienna, October 14, 1978. She also told Mr B.R. Nanda about the important changes in 1937, when he interviewed her in Vienna, November 11, 1971, on behalf of the Oral History Project of the Nehru Memorial Library. She asked Mr Nanda not to include her answer about this in his transcript.
108. Bose, *Pilgrim*, 49n.
109. Subhas Bose, letter to Mrs Dharmavir, March 22, 1938; letter of Subhas Bose to Asoke Bose, July 8, 1938, in Bose, *My Uncle*, 161–2.
110. *Illustrated Weekly of India*, August 20, 1972.
111. A.C.N. Nambiar to Leonard Gordon, November 23, 1978.
112. Sisir K. Bose has mentioned this to me on several occasions. Das Gupta, *Subhas Chandra*, mentions, that when he arrived from Europe in Karachi, 'He was curiously asked by someone whether or not he was thinking of entering into matrimony to which his reply was—"I have no time to think of that."' (155).
113. Bose, *My Uncle*, 150. The story of the British fakery has been extracted from P&J/174/II/1935, India Office Library, Government of India file.
114. *CMG*, January 15, 1938.
115. Bose was quoted in *CMG*, January 15, 1938.
116. *CMG*, January 15, 1938.
117. Government of India, P.O. File L/PO/57, report of January 12, 1938.
118. Subhas Chandra Bose, *The Indian Struggle 1920–1942*, Bombay: Asia Publishing House, 1964, 393–94. R. Palme Dutt, however, remained critical of Bose as is revealed in his interview with B.R. Nanda, October 12, 1971, Oral History Interview, Nehru Memorial Library.
119. Lord Zetland's report is in Government of India, L/PO/57, India Office Library.

120. *CMG*, January 22, 1938. Other details are in Government of India, L/PO/57.
121. *CMG*, January 22, 1938.
122. Article of January 11, 1938, in Government of India, L/PO/57.
123. Gandhi, *Works*, Vol. LXVI, 346.
124. The letter on Bose's proposed secret visit to Mussolini is dated December 31, 1937.
125. Bose, *My Uncle*, 152.
126. Bose, *My Uncle*, 153–58.
127. Zaidi and Zaidi, *Congress*, Vol. 11, 341.
128. Zaidi and Zaidi, *Congress*, Vol. 11, 316–53.
129. Zaidi and Zaidi, *Congress*, Vol. 11, 346. Also, Bose, *My Uncle*, 154.
130. Bernard S. Cohn, 'Representing Authority in Victorian India,' in *The Invention of Tradition* eds., Eric Hobsbawm and Terence Ranger, Cambridge: Cambridge U. Press, 1984, 165–210, discusses how the British created their imperial traditions in British India. The Congress sessions were opportunities for the Indians to reinvent their own traditions.
131. Zaidi and Zaidi, *Congress*, Vol. 11, 399.
132. Zaidi and Zaidi, *Congress*, Vol. 11, 407–10.
133. Zaidi and Zaidi, *Congress*, Vol. 11, 408–9.
134. Zaidi and Zaidi, *Congress*, Vol. 11, 418.
135. Zaidi and Zaidi, *Congress*, Vol. 11, 420.
136. Zaidi and Zaidi, *Congress*, Vol. 11, 428.
137. Masani, *Bliss*, 117–19; Rusch, 'CSP,' 372; Narayan, *Struggle*, 136. Also, Oral History Interview of Dr Hare Krishna Mahatab, January 26, 1979, by Dr Hari Dev Sharma, 102–21, 130–85.
138. B.R. Tomlinson, *The Indian National Congress and the Raj, 1929–1942: The Penultimate Phase*, London: Macmillan, 1976, 50ff, *passim*, gives no weight to ideological differences, but, in the usual Cambridge school approach, sees simply a struggle for power and pre-eminence. The participants and many other analysts have given weight to ideology and to differing views of the world between Indian participants. These different views can be linked to a struggle for power and control.
139. Gandhi, *Works*, Vol. LXVI, 382.
140. A number of followers of M.N. Roy have mentioned this to Prof Dennis Dalton and myself. One prominent Congress leader from Bengal, who had been in the Jugantar group with Roy and was an intimate to Congress power struggles, described to me how Sardar Patel put Roy in his place. Interview with Surendra Mohan Ghosh,

New Delhi, July 30, 1964.

141. Rusch, 'CSP,' 342ff; Masani's pamphlet entitled 'Communist Plot against the CSP', was published in 1938. Masani's later account is in *Bliss*, 113–54. Narayan who long held out against purging the communists from the CSP gives his version in *Struggle*, 165ff. There is also an account in Overstreet and Windmiller, *Communism*, 161ff.

142. In the course of his presidential year, Bose toured extensively in Bengal and also visited Bombay, Assam, and some other provinces. I learned of the closeness of Somnath Lahiri and Gopal Haldar to Bose during interviews in Calcutta on January 27, 1976 and May 17, 1972, respectively. Documents relating to M.N. Roy's group of radical Congressmen and Bose are in the M.N. Roy Papers. These were formerly in his home in Dehradun and are now in the Nehru Memorial Library. Roy had files related to Bose entitled, 'Tripuri Congress,' and 'Subhas Bose and Forward Bloc'. From the early 1930s on, Bose always had a small band of supporters referred to as the BV which has been described above. Some details about this group and Bose are in S.C. Sen Gupta, *India Wrests Freedom*, Calcutta: Sahitya Samsad, 1982, *passim*. Bombay and the Punjab were provinces in which Bose was popular during his life and is remembered fondly two generations later.

143. Bose's address to them is in Bose, *Crossroads*, 65–70.

144. Nehru, *Works*, Vol. 9, 397, letter to Bose, June 21, 1939.

145. See the account in Sarvepalli Gopal, *Jawaharlal Nehru: A Biography*, Vol. One, 1889–1947, Cambridge, Mass.: Harvard U. Press, 1976, 245–48.

146. These details come from the Interview of H.V. Kamath (interviewer), Dr Hari Dev Sharma (interviewer), May 7, 1969, Nehru Memorial Library. I also discussed these matters with Mr Kamath in Delhi, January 10, 1976.

147. See Subhas Bose, *Crossroads*, 65ff and Bose's praise of Kemal Ataturk for moving towards planning, *CMG*; for Gandhi's antipathy to planning, see Gandhi, *Works*, Vol. LXVIII, 258.

148. Rusch, 'Congress Socialists,' 299ff.

149. See Rusch, 'CSP,' 241–44; Nehru, *Selected Works*, Vol. 9, 309–11; Bose, *Crossroads*, 124.

150. Mitra, *IAR*, II, 1938, 278–79; M.K. Gandhi, 'That Unfortunate Walk Out,' *Harijan*, Vol. VI, October 15, 1938; Subhas Bose, letter to Jawaharlal Nehru, October 19, 1938.

151. Gandhi, *Works*, Vol. LXVII, 137, letter of June 25, 1938.

152. N.B. Khare, *My Political Memoirs or Autobiography*, Nagpur: J.R. Joshi, 1959?, 19.

153. Coupland, *The Constitutional Problem in India*, Part II, 108. Khare, in *My Political Memoirs, passim*, rants and raves about Gandhi's 'Hitlerian' methods.

154. Khare, *My Political Memoirs*, 48–9.

155. Zaidi and Zaidi, *Encyclopedia of Congress*, Vol. 11, 487–89.

156. Zaidi and Zaidi, *Encyclopedia of Congress*, Vol. 11, 499.

157. Zaidi and Zaidi, *Encyclopedia of Congress*, Vol. 11, 500.

158. See Mitra, *IAR*, II, 1938, 260, 279, AICC Papers, File No. G–60, 1938–39, Resolutions of W.C. Prasad account of Bengal–Bihar controversy.

159. Nirad C. Chaudhuri, 'Subhas Chandra Bose,' *The Illustrated Weekly of India*, LXXVI, No. 38, September 18, 1955, 1-8.

160. Chandra letter in AICC papers, File No. P–5 (i), 1937, BPCC. He also wrote to Subhas Bose urging him to devote more energies to the mass contact program of the Congress which he said was a flop. He asked Subhas to come to Vikrampur where he would greet him and try to give him an idea of the magnitude of the problem of reaching rural Bengal.

161. Sarat Bose letter to Jawaharlal Nehru, August 14, 1937, in AICC papers, File No. P–5, 1937, Bengal PCC matters.

162. Interviews with Abul Mansur Ahmed, Dacca, 1972, 1976; Malcolm Carter, Bristol, August 29, 1971; R. Hutchings, Lymington, September 13, 1971; Leonard Pinnell, Woking, July 22, 1989. Sen, *Muslim Politics in Bengal*.

163. Chattopadhyay, *Bengal Electoral Politics,* 149–50; Abul Mansur Ahmed, *CMG*, XXVIII, June 23, 1938.

164. *PBLA*, LIII, No. 2, August 9, 1938, 70.

165. Robert Reid, *Years of Change in Bengal and Assam*, London: Ernest Benn, 1966, 131–32.

166. *PBLA*, LIII, No. 2, August 9, 1938, 73.

167. *PBLA*, LIII, No. 2, August 8, 1938, 33–36.

168. *PBLA*, LIII, No. 2, August 10, 1938, 99.

169. *PBLA*, LIII, No. 2, August 10, 1938, 99.

170. *PBLA*, LIII, No. 2, August 10, 1938, 100.

171. *PBLA*, LIII, No. 2, August 10, 1938, 100–1.

172. *PBLA*, LIII, No. 2, August 10, 1938, 101–2.

173. *PBLA*, LIII, No. 2, August 10, 1938, 118.

174. The entire debate and the crucial votes are in *PBLA*, LIII, No. 2, August 8–10, 1938, 3–124. Also see Chattopadhyay, *Bengal Leg-*

islature, 151–55.

175. See Shamsuddin Ahmed's resignation speech and Huq's reply, *PBLA*, LIV, No. 1, February 17, 1939.
176. Gandhi's letter can be found in Gandhi, *Collected Works*, Vol. LXVIII, 218.
177. A copy from the original letter by Subhas Bose is in the possession of Nirad C. Chaudhuri, who was at the time private secretary to Sarat Bose. Bose's letter is dated December 21, 1938.
178. *CMG,* XXVIII, June 25, 1938.
179. Quoted in *CMG*, XXVIII, July 2, 1938.
180. *CMG*, XXVIII, July 2, 9, 16, 23, 1938.
181. Chaudhuri, 'Bose,' *Illustrated Weekly*, 18.
182. See *CMG*, XXVII, December 11, 1937; XXIX, February 4, 1939.
183. Bose, *Crossroads*, 127, letter to Nehru of March 28, 1939.
184. Bipan Chandra has discussed Gandhi's method of determining the 'readiness' of the masses for a large-scale movement in his article, 'Masses and Leaders,' *Mainstream*, XXIV, No. 17, December 28, 1985, 17–22.
185. The text of Urchs' report on the interview has been reprinted from German records by Milan Hauner in the appendix to his excellent and exhaustive work, *India in Axis Strategy: Germany, Japan, and Indian Nationalists in the Second World War*, Stuttgart: Klett–Cotta, 1981, 644–53.
186. Reprinted in Bose, *Crossroads*, Appendix 1, 412–13.
187. Nehru, *Works*, Vol. 9, 238.
188. See the Tagore–Noguchi exchanges in *The Modern Review*, Vol. 64, October 1938, 486-89; November 1938, 636.
189. For example, see the report of the second All–India Progressive Writers' Association conference held in Calcutta, December 1938, reprinted in Sudhi Pradhan, ed., *Marxist Cultural Movement in India: Chronicles and Documents (1936–1947)*, 2nd ed., Calcutta: Pustak Bipani, 1985, 101–4.
190. Nehru, *Works*, Vol. 9, 131–32. Also see D.P. Mishra, *Living an Era*, Delhi: Vikas, 1975, 258–59.
191. For example, see Nehru, *Works*, Vol. 9, 517n.; Bose, *Crossroads*, 85–6.
192. Gandhi, *Works*, Vol. LXVIII, 72, Letter to Manibehn Patel, October 28, 1938.
193. See references of Tagore's efforts in Gandhi, *Works*, Vol. LXVIII, 144, 161.
194. Gandhi, *Works*, Vol. LXVIII, 227, Gandhi letter to Nehru from

Wardha, December 21, 1938.

195. The text of the telegrams and then statement issued by Patel are in Bose, *Crossroads*, 88–90.

196. Bose, *Crossroads*, 91, statement of January 25, 1938.

197. Mitra, *IAR*, I, 1939, 45–6.

CHAPTER NINE

1. Mahatma Gandhi, *Collected Works*, Vol. LXXIII, 264, letter to Subhas Bose; December 29, 1940. This was Gandhi's last known letter to Subhas Bose and will be referred to later in this chapter.

2. Gandhi, *Works*, Vol. LXVIII, 359–60, Statement to the Press, January 31, 1939.

3. Prof Mukherjee mentioned this telegram to me in an interview in Delhi, December 9, 1972.

4. Gandhi, *Works*, Vol. LXXI, 94, from 'The Charkha,' *Harijan*, January 13, 1940.

5. For the regional distribution of votes, see Mitra, *Indian Annual Register*, I, 1939, 45–6. It is as follows:

	Sitaramayya	Bose
Burma	6	8
Utkal (Orissa)	99	44
Tamilnadu	102	110
Gujarat	100	5
Punjab	86	182
Vidharbha	21	11
Bengal	79	404
Kerala	18	80
Andhra	181	28
United Provinces	185	269
Delhi	5	10
Bihar	197	70
Maharashtra	86	77
Assam	22	34
Bombay	14	12
Sind	21	13
Nagpur	17	12
Ajmer	6	20
Karnatak	41	106
Mahakoshal	68	67
NWFP	23	18
Total	1375	1580

6. Gandhi, *Works*, Vol. LXVIII, 359–60. Originally published in *Harijan*, February 4, 1939.

7. *Statesman*, February 4, 1939.

8. Interview with J.B. Kripalani, New Delhi, September 10, 1976.

9. M.N. Roy letter of February 1, 1939, in file, 'Bose and Forward Block,' M.N. Roy Papers.

10. Rusch, 'CSP,' 378. He bases his statements on interviews with M.R. Masani, Sardar Sardul Singh Caveeshar, and Ellen Roy, conducted in the early 1950s.

11. Nehru, *Works*, Vol. 9, 495, article published in the *National Herald*.

12. Nehru, *Works*, Vol. 9, 495–6.

13. See *Calcutta Municipal Gazeetee* [hereafter referred to as *CMG*] March 11, 1939. Bose later wrote an unusual essay about his prolonged fever, 'My Strange Illness,' *Crossroads*, 134–44. This was originally published in the *Modern Review*, April 1939.

14. Gandhi wrote to Nehru on February 3, 1939; 'After the election and the manner in which it was fought, I feel that I shall serve the country by absenting myself from the Congress at the forthcoming session.' Gandhi, *Works*, Vol. LXVIII, 368. Gandhi's statement on Rajkot is in *Works*, Vol. LXVIII, 346–48.

15. Mitra, *IAR*, I, 1939, 332.

16. Rusch, 'CSP,' 353, 404, 413; Narayan, *Struggle*, 136–43, 177; Jogesh Chandra Chatterji, *In Search of Freedom*, Calcutta: Firma K.L. Mukhopadhyay, 1967, 415ff. Interviews with Niharendu Dutt-Mazumdar, Calcutta, July 28, 1973 and Tridib Chaudhuri, New Delhi, August 17, 1973.

17. Interview with Dutt-Mazumdar, July 28, 1973. Somnath Lahiri, an important Bengal communist, agreed with the main factual points about the CPI shift to oppose the resolution in an interview, Calcutta, January 27, 1976. Nehru had written an article entitled, 'Have We the Strength?' suggesting that Indian nationalists were not ready for a renewed mass movement. Lahiri wrote in the *Hindusthan Standard*, 'We Have the Strength.'

18. Mitra, *IAR*, I, 1939, 51, 335.

19. Rusch, 'CSP', 379–91.

20. Interview with Somnath Lahiri, January 27, 1976. Mr Lahiri says that Rajaji's speech made a strong impression on the delegates.

21. Mitra, *IAR*, I, 1939, 335.

22. Mitra, *IAR*, I, 1939, 335.

23. Mitra, *IAR*, I, 1939, 51.

24. Rusch, 'CSP', 380–81.

25. Editorial of March 12, 1939, in *The Statesman: An Anthology*, 461.
26. Bose, *My Uncle*, 172–73.
27. Bose, *Crossroads*, 142–43.
28. Bose, *Crossroads*, 143.
29. Sarat Bose's letter is in *Sarat Chandra Bose, Commemoration Volume*, 243–47.
30. Bose, *Crossroads*, 154, from letter of March 31, 1939.
31. Bose, *Crossroads*, 112. The brother, father, and son imagery between the three: Gandhi as the father, Nehru and Bose as the sons, one favored and loved, the other rebellious and out of favor, will be mentioned and quoted from time to time.
32. There are references here and there in Nehru's letters to Bose and in the former's correspondence with others. For example, see Jawaharlal Nehru, *A Bunch of Old Letters*, Bombay: Asia Publishing House, 1958. Letter by Nehru to Bose, February 4, 1939, 317–21, and Patel's frank letter to Nehru, February 8, 1939, 322. Also see Nehru, *Works*, Vol. 9, 103, 128–29, 131–32. Nirad C. Chaudhuri, Sarat Bose's private secretary at the time, told me Sarat Bose said that Subhas should not have picked up and pursued the federation issue and made his aspersion about the Old Guard since he could not prove it. Interview, November 26, 1971, and July 2, 1977, Oxford.
33. Nehru, *Bunch*, 356–57, letter of April 3, 1939.
34. Nehru, *Bunch*, 350–63, letter of April 3, 1939.
35. Nehru, *Works*, Vol. 9, 553–54, letter of April 17, 1939.
36. Bose, *Crossroads*, 115, 130. Letter of March 28, 1939. In its original hand-written form, this letter was almost thirty pages. The entire correspondence between the Boses, Gandhi, and Nehru is in Bose, *Crossroads*, Nehru, *Works*, Vol. 9 and *Bunch*, and *Sarat Bose Commemoration Volume*. Additional related letters are in Gandhi, *Works*, Vol. LXVIII, and Nehru, *Works*, Vol. 9.
37. Bose, *Crossroads*, 127.
38. Bose, *Crossroads*, 117.
39. For Nehru's side, see his letter of April 3, 1939, in his *Works*, Vol. 9, 537, 542. When Nehru went to Europe in 1938, he almost immediately traveled to Barcelona to better understand and support the republican cause. See his many articles and comments in *Works*, Vol. 9, 17ff.
40. Gandhi, *Works*, Vol. LXIX, 186.
41. Gandhi, *Works*, Vol. LXIX, 131, letter of April 11, 1939.
42. Bose, *Crossroads*, 144, letter of April 11, 1939.
43. Gandhi, *Works*, Vol. LXVIII, 'Internal Decay,' written January 23,

1939, and published in *Harijan*, January 28, 1939.

44. Interview with J.B. Kripalani, New Delhi, September 10, 1976.
45. Mitra, *IAR*, I, 1939, 53.
46. See M.N. Roy file, 'Subhas Bose and Forward Bloc.'
47. Interview with Tridib Chaudhuri, August 17, 1973. Also see Jogesh Chatterji's account of his confused and confusing moves in this period, *In Search*, 524–25.
48. Interview with Prof Mukherjee, December 9, 1972.
49. *Forward*, April 8, 1939.
50. Nehru, *Works*, Vol. 9, 561, letter to Maulana Azad, April 20, 1939.
51. Mitra, *IAR*, I, 1939, 346.
52. Nehru, *Works*, Vol. 9, 562–64. Also see the account in Mitra, *IAR*, I, 1939, 346–47.
53. Interview with Gita (Biswas) Bose, Calcutta, January 17, 1976. She said that she felt unhappy but could not show it while she served him his tea. After this he did not stay with the Boses again. But after her father's death, he came to visit her mother which they all appreciated.
54. Gandhi, *Works*, Vol. LXIX, 209–10, May 5, 1939.
55. Gandhi, *Works*, Vol. LXIX, 211.
56. Mitra, *IAR*, I, 1939, 30.
57. Mitra, *IAR*, I, 1939, 32(g). Also see Bose, *The Indian Struggle*, 337–38, and 'Forward Bloc—Its Justification,' 395–414, the latter article written after he left India in 1941.
58. See S.P. Sen, ed., *Dictionary of National Biography*, Vol. IV, Calcutta: Institute of Historical Studies, 1974, 7–8. N.G. Ranga, *Fight for Freedom*, Delhi: S. Chand, 1968, 219–40. On the Left Consolidation Committee, see Rusch, 'CSP', 398–401; Overstreet and Windmiller, *Communism*, 171, 175, 180. Bose mentions the disintegration of the Left Consolidation Committee in *Crossroads*, 331–32, in a speech of June 18, 1940.
59. Bose, *My Uncle*, 181ff. Mitra, *IAR*, II, 1939, 2, 11.
60. Bose, *Indian Struggle*, 338–40 and *Crossroads*, 216–26, which gives a blow-by-blow account of his national tour.
61. Bose, *Crossroads*, 230.
62. Bose, *Crossroads*, 229.
63. Mitra, *IAR*, II, 1939, 27.
64. Mitra, *IAR*, II, 1939, 5.
65. Mitra, *IAR*, II, 1939, 13.
66. Mitra, *IAR*, II, 1939, 14.
67. Mr Ganguli's testimony comes from an extensive interview con-

ducted in Calcutta, August 24, 1977.

68. *CMG*, March 4, 1939.

69. There were articles about opposition to the bill in almost every issue of the *CMG* during 1939 and in much of the Hindu-controlled press as well.

70. Mitra, *IAR*, I, 1939, 151, 154–55.

71. Quoted in Mitra, *IAR*, I, 1939, 161. The original debate is in Bengal Legislative Assembly *Proceedings* [hereafter *PBLA*], LIV, Part 2, 14–67, 101ff.

72. Mitra, *IAR*, I, 1939, 161.

73. *CMG*, May 20, 1939. Sarat Bose's letter was dated May 12.

74. Mitra, *IAR*, I, 1929, 165, 172–75; II, 109, 125.

75. Quoted in the *CMG*, May 27, 1939. Strong criticism of Singh Roy and Sarker was also printed in the *Amrita Bazar Patrika* and the *Servant of India*.

76. Mitra, *IAR*, II, 1939, 123–4.

77. See *PBLA*, LIV, Part 1, 159–77, February 17, 1939.

78. There are many letters exchanged between Huq and Nehru in the Jawaharlal Nehru Papers, Nehru Memorial Library, New Delhi. Many of these are published in Nehru, *Works*, Vol. 10, 461–72. They are dated October 30 to December 26, 1939.

79. K.K. Aziz, ed., *Muslims under Congress Rule 1937–1939: A Documentary Record,* 2 vols. (Vol. I includes the Pirpur Report), Islamabad: National Commission on Historical and Cultural Research, 1978.

80. *PBLA*, LIV, No. 10, June 27, 1939, 179.

81. *PBLA*, LIV, No. 10, 184–85.

82. A summary of the argument and quotations from Nazimuddin and Sarat Bose is in Mitra, *IAR*, II, 1939, 109–113.

83. *CMG*, articles almost weekly through 1939, e.g., August 5 and 12, 1939.

84. *PBLA*, LIV, No.1, February 25, 1939, 304. *CMG*, February 25, 1939, gives another and different tribute by Sarat Bose to Lord Brabourne.

85. Interview with Malcolm O. Carter, ICS, Bristol, August 23, 1971; R.L. Walker, ICS, East Grinstead, August 17, 1971; Leonard Pinnell, ICS, Woking, July 22, 1969. I also met Sir John Herbert's son, Robin Herbert, Esq., London, July 31, 1969, and he promised to provide documentation for his father's governorship, but he and his offer of help disappeared.

86. Zaidi and Zaidi, *Congress*, Vol. 12, 246–7.

87. Bose, *Crossroads*, 200, dated August 19, 1939.

88. Rusch, 'CSP', 325–29.

89. Mitra, *IAR*, II, 1939, 224–5.

90. Many of the relevant documents are in *Working Committee and Bengal Congress*, published by the BPCC, Calcutta, 1940. This is a Bose-group version. Also see Mitra, *IAR*, II, 1939, 224–25, 271–75. Many documents are to be found in AICC Papers P–5, 1939–40; BPCC, P–5 (Part I), 1939–40, and other parts of the P–5 file for those years, Nehru Memorial Library.

91. *Working Committee and Bengal Congress*, 20.

92. Rabindranath Tagore, *'Deshanayak'*, original in *Kalantar* [End of an Era], Calcutta: Visva-Bharati, 1962, 371–76. This essay is translated in Shri Ram Sharma, ed., *Netaji, His Life and Work*, Agra: Shiva Lal Agarwala, 1948, V–VII. I have used the original and the translation of Sharma to make my own English version.

93. Tagore's telegram to Gandhi is in Gandhi, *Works*, Vol. LXXI, 50, footnote 2. Gandhi explained to Tagore that the Working Committee was unable to do so.

94. Gandhi, *Works*, Vol. LXXI, 94, from 'The Charkha,' *Harijan*, January 13, 1940.

95. Gandhi, *Works*, Vol. LXXI, 113–14, letter to C.F. Andrews, January 15, 1940.

96. Nehru, *Works*, Vol. 10, 345–46, letter of March 2, 1940.

97. Mitra, *IAR*, II, 1939, 21.

98. Mitra, *IAR*, II, 1939, 22.

99. Mitra, *IAR*, II, 1939, 23, statement of September 8.

100. Mitra, *IAR*, II, 1939, 23. Sir P.C. Roy, Sir Manmathanath Mukherjee and other Bengal leaders signed a joint statement.

101. Mitra, *IAR*, II, 24 announced in a speech to the two houses of the Central Legislature, September 11, 1939.

102. Mitra, *IAR*, II, 1939, 32.

103. Mitra, *IAR*, II, 1939, 40–5. On the CSP responses to the war, see Rusch, 'The War Issue and the Demise of the CSP,' in his 'CSP,' 416ff.

104. Bose, *Crossroads*, 264–65, Presidential Address to the All-India Students' Conference, Delhi, January 1940.

105. Bose, *Crossroads*, 267.

106. *M.A. Jinnah-Ispahani Correspondence, 1936–1948*, ed., Z.H. Zaidi, Karachi: Forward Publications Trust, 1976, 130–33. Ispahani wrote to Jinnah on December 12, 1939, 'I did not expect such a command from you, because you have all along kept politics on a very high and

strong pedestal. The order was bereft of your fighting spirit.'

107. *PBLA*, LV, No. 3, December 13, 1939, 59–60.

108. Ispahani to Jinnah, December 16, 1939, in *M.A. Jinnah–Ispahani Correspondence,* 135. Ispahani and his supporters also insisted that Sarker had to be censured if he did not go with his colleagues in the majority. He and Siddiqi won on this point.

109. *PBLA*, LV, No. 3, December 13, 1939, 71.

110. *PBLA*, LV, No. 3, December 13, 1939, 80.

111. *PBLA*, LV, No. 3, 84. The Irishman is Roger Casement whose famous speech from the dock at his trial for treason, Sarat Bose is in part paraphrasing here.

112. See Sarker's speech, *PBLA*, LV, No. 3, 222–29, December 18, 1939.

113. Quoted in Mitra, *IAR*, II, 1939, 123–24.

114. *PBLA*, LV, No. 3, 393, response to Sarker's resignation speech on December 20, 1939.

115. Bose, *Crossroads*, 272ff.

116. This is a main theme of my earlier book, *Bengal: The Nationalist Movement 1876–1940*, New York: Columbia U. Press, 1974.

117. Bose, *Crossroads*, 287–88.

118. Mitra, *IAR*, I, 1940, 80. This was, I believe, the last time that Gandhi and Bose met. They continued, however, to exchange letters. Gandhi throughout maintained that his differences with Bose were not personal, but political and that he remained friendly to Bose. A lost son, but a son nonetheless.

119. Bose, *Crossroads*, 322ff.

120. Bose, *Indian Struggle*, 343–44. He said that Jinnah was focused on his Pakistan, and Savarkar on military training for Hindus, and neither could see the larger picture of working assiduously in the war context for India's freedom.

121. Bose, *Crossroads*, 295–97.

122. Bose, *Crossroads*, 308–10. Also see *Jinnah–Ispahani Correspondence*, 141.

123. Bose, *Crossroads*, 310–11.

124. C.H. Philips, H.L. Singh, B.N. Pandey, eds., *The Evolution of India and Pakistan 1858 to 1947 Select Documents*, London: Oxford U. Press, 1962, 354–55.

125. Mitra, *IAR*, I, 1940, 54ff, gives a chronicle of events and statements from March 24 on, including many protests against the League's Lahore Resolution.

126. Interviews with Abul Mansur Ahmed and Jehangir Kabir.

127. Bose, *Crossroads*, 344.

128. Bhagat Ram Talwar in his, *The Talwars of Pathan Land and Subhas Chandra's Great Escape*, New Delhi: People's Publishing House, 1976, 56–62, says that Bose was planning to escape from India and the arrest and subsequent imprisonment long delayed this move.

129. For government exchanges on Bose's arrest—between Calcutta, Delhi, and London—see L/P&J/394/1939, India Office Library. The entire file deals with many developments between 1939 and 1942.

130. *PBLA*, LVI, No. 1, February 16, 1940, 138.

131. *PBLA*, LVI, No. 5, April 9, 1940, 510, where the government order is quoted in the course of the debate on it.

132. *PBLA*, LVI, No. 5, 512–13.

133. *PBLA*, LVI, No. 5, 514–15.

134. *PBLA*, LVII, No. 1, July 18, 1940, 279–80.

135. *PBLA*, LVII, No. 1, July 18, 1940, 281.

136. *PBLA*, LVII, No. 1, 279ff; No. 2, 86, 179–80.

137. *PBLA*, LVII, No. 5, August 28, 1940, 283ff, on the Secondary Education Bill; LVII, No. 6, September 10, 1940, 405–14, for the speech on the Calcutta Municipal Bill.

138. Mitra, *IAR*, II, 1940, 38. On the developments through this period relating to Sarat Bose's expulsion and the responses, see 33–54.

139. Zaidi and Zaidi, *Congress*, Vol. 12, 342, 551ff.

140. Bose, *Indian Struggle*, 345.

141. Bose, *Indian Struggle*, 345.

142. Bose, *My Uncle*, 182–83; interview with Amiya Bose, Calcutta, January 21, 1976.

143. Interview with Dwijen Bose, Calcutta, August 22, 1977.

144. Bose, *My Uncle*, 183; interview with Dwijen Bose.

145. Bhagat Ram Talwar, *Talwars*, New Delhi: People's Publishing House, 1976, 56–59.

146. Bose, *Crossroads*, 372–73, letter of October 30, 1940 to the Superintendent of the Presidency Jail.

147. Bose, *Crossroads*, 380–81.

148. The most important sources used for the following version are written or oral accounts by participants including: Talwar, *Talwars*; Bose, *My Uncle*, 197ff; Uttam Chand, *When Bose Was Ziauddin*, Delhi: Rajkamal, 1946?; Sisir K. Bose, *The Great Escape*, Calcutta: Netaji Research Bureau, 1975; interviews with Amiya Bose, Dwijen Bose, and Aurobindo Bose, cited above.

149. Talwar, *Talwars*, 58–59. This was one Ram Kishan.

150. Talwar, *Talwars*, 60ff.

151. Most of these letters are now collected in Bose, *Crossroads*, 398ff.

152. Bose, *Crossroads*, 399.

153. Bose, *Crossroads*, 399.

154. Bose, *Crossroads*, 399–400.

155. Bose, *Crossroads*, 405–6.

156. Bose, *Crossroads*, 420–24. Although the letter is unsigned and undated, Dr Sisir Bose showed the letter to Jayaprakash Narayan many years later and he verified that he had written it at this time.

157. These and many other details in the first part of the escape come from Bose, *Great Escape*, 18ff.

158. Bose, *My Uncle*, 199. This was also mentioned by Dwijen Bose.

159. Bose, *My Uncle*, 192–93. Asoke Bose says that this was quite unlike his uncle's usual behavior, but elements of the irrational seemed to be increasing in Subhas Bose's account of 'My Strange Illness,' mentioned above. There were undoubtedly many other family members and associates much more addicted to such consultations and 'assistance' who encouraged him to seek this kind of advice.

160. Details from Bose, *Great Escape*, 26ff, and interviews with Aurobindo Bose and Dwijen Bose.

161. Details in Bose, *My Uncle*, 197ff.

162. Talwar, *Talwars*, 65.

163. All these details are from Talwar, *Talwars*, 66ff.

164. Government of India, Home Department, Political File No. 135/41, National Archives of India, New Delhi. The suggestions about British knowledge about Bose's escape and whereabouts have been by Hugh Toye in a 1985 Granada Television film concerning Bose and the Indian National Army and by Milan Hauner in *India in Axis Strategy*, 242.

165. Home Department, 135/41.

166. Home Department, 135/41.

167. Bose, *Great Escape*, 38. Asoke Bose's view is stated in *My Uncle*, 208. Bhagat Ram Talwar adheres to Moscow as the goal through the preparatory planning phase, the trip to Kabul, and during early days in Kabul. Then he vividly recounts their inability to make serious contacts with Russian officials. See Talwar, *Talwars*, 57ff.

168. Talwar, *Talwars*, 96ff. Also see Uttam Chand, *When Bose Was Ziauddin*, Delhi: Rajkamal, 1946?, 11ff.

169. The article is contained in Bose, *Indian Struggle*, 395–414.

170. Quaroni's report is reprinted in Bose, *Indian Struggle*, 415–18.

171. Talwar, *Talwars*, 117–121.

172. On the impact of the German blitzkrieg, see, for example, Coupland,

Constitutional Problem, 238–39. Nirad C. Chaudhuri's impressions of Sarat Bose's views at this time come from several discussions with him in Oxford, 1971, 1972, 1978.

173. Coupland, *Constitutional Problem*, II, 247ff. Mitra, *IAR*, I, II, 327, 100.
174. Coupland, *Constitutional Problem*, II, 247ff.
175. Mitra, *IAR*, II, 1941, 31.
176. Mitra, *IAR*, I, 1941, 38, 44, 74.
177. See Sen, *Muslim Politics*, 126ff, and *Jinnah–Ispahani Correspondence*, 141ff.
178. See the Government of India Report on the Dacca Riots, the McNair Committee Report, Home, Political, File No. 5/7/42, in the National Archives of India. Also Government of Bengal, Bengal Governors' Reports, No. 5, March 20, 1941.
179. *PBLA*, LIX, No. 2, 256–62, March 3, 1941, and 460–64, March 6, 1941.
180. *PBLA*, LIX, No. 5, 219–23, 246, April 2, 1941.
181. Talwar, *Talwars*, 126ff. Interview with Santimoy Ganguli, September 2, 1976.
182. There are numerous details in Talwar, *Talwars*, 141ff. Milan Hauner has challenged the veracity of Bhagat Ram and suggested that he was working for three and perhaps even four governments simultaneously and supplying information for all of them and extracting payments from all. See Hauner, *India in Axis Strategy*, 335ff.
183. B.H. Liddell Hart, *History of the Second World War*, I, New York: Capricorn Books, 1972, 159.
184. See Overstreet and Windmiller, *Communism*, 191ff.
185. Talwar, *Talwars*, 142, and 142ff on the whole dilemma created by the new war alignment.
186. Bose, *My Uncle*, 216–17.
187. On the information concerning and later arrest of Sarat Bose because of these contacts, see Government of India, Home Department, Political File No. 94/26/41/ entitled, 'Detention under Rule 26 of the Defence of India Rules of Sarat Chandra Bose.'
188. See Chatterjee, *Bengal 1920–1947*, 168. Also Chattopadhyay, *Bengal Electoral Politics*, 162ff.
189. *PBLA*, LX, No. 1, 115, July 29, 1941.
190. *PBLA*, LX, No. 1, 112–13, July 29, 1941.
191. *PBLA*, LX, No. 1, July 29, 1941, 115.
192. *PBLA*, No. 4, 54ff; Harendra Nath Chaudhuri put forth the motion for referral which listed some eleven changes they wanted in the bill.

193. *PBLA*, LX, No. 4, 154–55, September 4, 1941.

194. *PBLA*, LX, No. 4, 157–58, September 4, 1941.

195. Huq's letter is reprinted in Sen, *Muslim Politics*, 264–67. The Muslim League point of view is expressed by M.A.H. Ispahani in his letters to Jinnah in this period in *Jinnah–Ispahani Correspondence*, 141–231.

196. This characterization of Huq is based on interviews with many participants in the events of that period, including Abul Hashem, Dacca, May 30, 1972, and Abul Mansur Ahmed, Dacca, May 31, 1972. Mr Ahmed told me a joke, widely circulated at that time: Fazlul Huq could never sleep at night unless he had made his 'century', i.e., told one hundred lies that day. Late one night, he was found by his servant pacing up and down. The servant thought to himself, 'He has not made his century today. He probably has told only 99 lies and can't go to sleep.' So he asked, 'Mr. Huq, have you arranged for the new job you promised me?' Huq said, 'Of course.' Then he went in and fell asleep right away. Many ICS officers of the period with whom I have spoken also described Huq in this way, but at the same time praised his fine speaking abilities.

197. Editorial of November 19, 1941, reprinted in *Statesman: Anthology*, 474.

198. Nehru, *Works*, Vol. 11, 735.

199. Huq's full statement is in Mitra, *IAR*, II, 1941, 147–48.

200. See Suhrawardy's and Jinnah's statements in Mitra, *IAR*, II, 1941, 147–50.

201. Ispahani letter in *Jinnah–Ispahani Correspondence*, 212–15.

202. For Governor Herbert's views, see Bengal Governors' Reports L/P & J/5/148, India Office Library, especially his reports for the first and second half of December. On December 5, Herbert wrote, 'A Government virtually controlled by Sarat Bose would be disastrous.'

203. Government of India, Home Department, Political File No. 94/26/41, National Archives, New Delhi, and Government of India, Public and Judicial 7542/45, India Office Library.

204. Government of India, Home Department, Political File No. 94/26/41.

205. I have been writing and saying this for years, e.g., in my article, 'Themes in a Political Biography of Subhas and Sarat Chandra Bose,' in Sisir K. Bose, ed., *Netaji and India's Freedom*, Calcutta: Netaji Research Bureau, 1975, 21. I see that Shila Sen has made the same point in her *Muslim Politics*, 162–63.

206. The assembly motion and discussions are in *PBLA*, LXI, December 12, 1941.
207. Government of India, P&J/7542/1945. Extract from Private and Personal letter from Lord Linlithgow to Mr Amery, December 30, 1941.
208. See interview with Dr Harekrishna Mahatab (interviewee) recorded by Dr Hari Dev Sharma (interviewer), January 26, 1979, Nehru Memorial Museum and Library, Oral History Interview, 140ff.

CHAPTER TEN

1. Malcolm Muggeridge, ed., *Ciano's Diary 1939–1943*, London: William Heinemann, 1947, 355.
2. Romain Rolland, *Inde. Journal (1915–1943)*, Paris: Éditions Albin Michel, 1960, 513–14.
3. Barbara Stoler Miller trans., *Bhartrihari: Poems*, New York: Columbia U. Press, 1967.
4. Milan Hauner, *India in Axis Strategy: Germany, Japan, and Indian Nationalists in the Second World War*, Stuttgart: Klett–Cotta, 1981, 242–43. Hauner's massive and detailed work on Axis, particularly German views of India from 1939 to 1942, is the most valuable single work on the context of Bose's activities in Europe during these years. Also, Sisir K. Bose and Alexander Werth, *A Beacon Across Asia*, New Delhi: Orient Longman, 1973, 116. Dr Werth was a German Foreign Office official who dealt with Bose from 1941 to 1943.
5. *Memoirs of Ernst von Weizsäcker*, London: Victor Gollancz, 1951, 258.
6. The best work on the First World War period is Arun Coomer Bose, *Indian Revolutionaries Abroad, 1905–1922: In the Background of International Developments*, Patna: Bharati Bhawan, 1971, *passim*. Some of the Government of India materials on this activity are mentioned in Chapter Two, footnote 43, above.
7. On Rash Behari Bose, see Uma Mukherjee, *Two Great Indian Revolutionaries: Rash Behari Bose and Jyotindra Nath Mukherjee*, Calcutta: Firma KLM, 1966; Radhanath Rath and Sabitri Prasanna Chatterjee, eds., *Rash Behari Basu His Struggle for India's Independence*, Calcutta: Biplabi Mahanayak Rash Behari Basu Smarak Samity, 1963; A.M. Nair, *An Indian Freedom Fighter in Japan*, Bombay: Orient Longman, 1982. Mr Nair, whom I met in Tokyo in

1979, lived most of his life in Japan and was close to Rash Behari Bose throughout. See 52ff, where Mr Nair is severely critical of every other Indian except Rash Behari Bose, a problem with such memoirs.

8.	*Memoirs of Ernst von Weizsäcker*, 251–52.

9.	Hitler, *Secret Conversations* (1941–1944), New York: Farrar, Straus and Young, 1953, 20. Entry for August 8–11, 1941. Hitler repeatedly made statements of this kind about the need for *Lebensraum* and the Soviet Union serving this purpose and being equivalent to Britain's empire in India.

10.	Hauner, *India in Axis Strategy*, 34.

11.	On this maze of plotters, see Joachim C. Fest, *The Face of the Third Reich: Portraits of the Nazi Leadership*, New York: Ace Books, 1970; Joachim C. Fest, *Hitler*, New York: Vintage Books, 1975; Karl Dietrich Bracher, *The German Dictatorship: The Origins, Structure and Effects of National Socialism*, New York: Praeger, 1970; Alan Bullock, *Hitler: A Study in Tyranny*, rev. ed., New York: Harper Torchbook, 1964.

12.	On the German Foreign Office, see Christoph M. Kimmich, ed., *German Foreign Policy 1918–1945*, Wilmington, Delaware: Scholarly Resources, 1981; Paul Seabury, *The Wilhelmstrasse: A Study of German Diplomats under the Nazi Regime*, Berkeley: U. of California Press, 1954; *The von Hassell Diaries 1938–1944*, London: Hamish Hamilton, 1948. The works of Hauner and Weizsäcker noted above also contain a picture of this world.

13.	Quoted in Fest, *Face of the Third Reich*, 265.

14.	Fest, *Face of the Third Reich*, 259–75. Weizsäcker, his immediate deputy, has given a chilling description of Ribbentrop at work, *Memoirs*, 118ff, and of his own inability to even learn what was going on and planned by Hitler and his closest cohorts.

15.	The most thorough work on the anti-Nazi activity is Peter Hoffman, *The History of the German Resistance 1933–1945*, Cambridge: MIT Press, 1977. Also see, Rudolf Lill and Heinrich Oberreuter, eds., *20, Juli: Portraits des Widerstands*, Düsseldorf: Econ Verlag, 1984. Ulrich von Hassell has left a fascinating record in *The Von Hassell Diaries*. An important resistance worker, Adam von Trott zu Solz, was Bose's key contact in the German Foreign Office and Trott and Bose will be discussed below. On Trott, see Christopher Sykes, *Troubled Loyalty: A Biography of Adam von Trott zu Solz*, London: Collins, 1968. Trott's widow, Clarita von Trott zu Solz has written an unpublished biography, *Adam von Trott zu Solz*, for his friends.

This has been translated into English by Elke Langbehn and will be used below.

16. See Lukasz Hirszowicz, *The Third Reich and the Arab East*, London: Routledge and Kegan Paul, 1966.

17. Detailed descriptions and analyses of this period and the Bose-German interchanges are presented in Hauner, *India in Axis Strategy*, 245ff and Arvinda Katpitia, *Subhas Chandra Boses Verhandlungen über eine Unabhängigkeitserklärung für Indien 1941–1943*, Ph.D. dissertation, Johannes Gutenberg–Universität zu Mainz, 1972, 78ff. Bose's memorandum of April 9, 1941 is presented in Subhas Chandra Bose, *The Indian Struggle, 1920–1942*, Bombay: Asia Publishing House, 1964, 419–30.

18. The German side is presented in German Foreign Ministry, Bureau of the Secretary of State India, Serial No. 195, Vol. I. These records are in the German Foreign Office Archives in Bonn and also on microfilm in the National Archives of the U.S. in Washington, D.C. Bose's first important meeting was with Dr Woermann, Director of the Political Department and later he met with Foreign Minister von Ribbentrop.

19. Bose, *Indian Struggle*, 419.

20. Bose, *Indian Struggle*, 419–30.

21. See Hauner, *India in Axis Strategy*, 358ff. Clarita von Trott, *Trott*, 137ff. Lukasz Hirszowicz, *The Third Reich and the Arab East*, 204ff. Bose and Werth, *Beacon across Asia*, 116ff.

22. Bose and Werth, *Beacon across Asia*, 122–26.

23. Clarita von Trott, *Trott*, 27.

24. Clarita von Trott, *Trott*, 115ff. Also see Christabel Bielenberg, *Christabel*, New York: Penguin Books, 1989, 140ff, on Trott in this period. This memoir by the wife of a close friend has recently been republished and made into a television series thereby drawing attention to the work of Trott and his allies.

25. Clarita von Trott, *Trott*, 139.

26. Clarita von Trott, *Trott*, 139, letter of August 16, 1941.

27. Interview with Clarita von Trott, Berlin, August 18, 1984. Her views and those of her husband are also expressed in her unpublished biography cited above, *Trott, passim.*

28. Interview with Dr Freda (Kretschmer) Mookerji, Bonn, October 19, 1978. Interview with Clarita von Trott. Unpublished manuscript of Alexander Werth, dated November 1957, in the possession of Clarita von Trott. Werth prepared this manuscript as a favor to Dr von Trott as she was writing her biography of her husband. Dr von

Trott explained to me that Dr Werth was nastiest about Emilie Schenkl speaking in person, slightly less nasty in the unpublished manuscript and not nasty at all in the book he published with the nephew of Subhas Bose, Dr Sisir Bose, *Beacon across Asia*. It is interesting that the German snobbery against Emilie Schenkl is shared by the Bengali writer, Nirad C. Chaudhuri, a relation by marriage of the Bose family. See his *Thy Hand, Great Anarch! India 1921–1952*, London: Chatto and Windus, 1987, 797.

29. Interview with Emilie Schenkl, Vienna, October 14, 1978.

30. Dr J.K. Banerji, another person present in Berlin, who saw a good deal of Bose, disagrees with Dr Kretschmer and says that Bose never let personal matters disturb his single-minded efforts to work for India's liberation. Interview with Dr Banerji, New York, November 9, 1978.

31. For example, see Girija K. Mookerjee, *Europe at War (1938–1946): Impressions of War, Netaji and Europe*, Meerut: Meenakshi Prakashan, 1968, 242; N.G. Ganpuley, *Netaji in Germany: A Little–known Chapter*, Bombay: Bharatiya Vidya Bhavan, 1959, 139; Nathalal D. Parikh, 'Reminiscences,' in P.D. Saggi, ed., *Life and Work of Netaji Subhas Chandra Bose*, Bombay: Overseas Publishing House, n.d., 50. Werth, unpublished manuscript referred to above, says they were not married. The variations are almost endless. Every Indian whom I have interviewed who was in Berlin during the war had a different version. If Bose wanted to confuse people about his marriage, he succeeded. Emilie Schenkl's version has been given in Chapter Eight.

32. See M.R. Vyas, *Passage through a Turbulent Era*, Bombay: Indo-Foreign Publications, 1982. Abid Hasan Safrani, 'A Soldier Remembers,' *The Oracle*, Calcutta, January 1984, 24–65, and January 1985, 17–29. British information about many of these Indians whom Bose gathered in Berlin during the war is contained in India Office Records, Public and Judicial L/WS/1/1363, 'Notes on Suspect Civilian Indians on the Continent of Europe,' July 1944. Also see Ganpuley, *Netaji in Germany*, and Mookerjee, *Europe at War (1938–1946)*. Interviews with others of these recruits will be cited below.

33. Details from I.O.R., P&J L/WS/1/1363, 'Notes on Suspect Civilian Indians. . .'

34. Interview with A.C.N. Nambiar, Zurich, July 5, 1975. Mr Nambiar and I corresponded for some years and some of his letters will be cited below. Mr B.R. Nanda, then Director of the Nehru Memorial

Library, conducted an excellent interview with Mr Nambiar, Oral History Interview, Shri A.C.N. Nambiar (interviewee) recorded by Shri B.R. Nanda (interviewer), November 18, 1972, Nehru Memorial Museum and Library, Oral History Interview. Mr Nambiar also supplied a manuscript to Dr Clarita von Trott for her research, dated 20.4.1963.

35. See G. Wirsing, 'Bekanntschaft mit Indien,' (preface) in his *Indien —Asiens gefahrliche Jahre*, Düsseldorf, 1968. Emilie Schenkl has also noted that he became much more capable in German as his time in Germany passed.

36. Walter Harbich, 'A Report on the Training and Organisation of the Free India Army in Europe,' in *Netaji in Germany*, Calcutta: Netaji Research Bureau, 1970. Also interview with Walter Harbich, Munich, October 12, 1978.

37. Interview with Lothar Frank, Wiesbaden, October 5, 1978. Mr Frank was greatly responsible for the two European chapters in Bose and Werth, *Beacon across Asia*. A certain Frau von Harbou is mentioned as a friend of Indians in Germany during the 1930s and early 1940s. See Hugh Toye, *Subhas Pasha*, unpublished manuscript, 30.

38. On Oshima, see Carl Boyd, *The Extraordinary Envoy: General Hiroshi Oshima and Diplomacy in the Third Reich, 1934–1939*, Washington: U. Press of America, 1980. Although the detailed account ends in 1939, one chapter deals with the later period.

39. On 'Magic,' see Ronald Lewin, *The American Magic*, 10, New York: Penguin Books, 1982. He mentions the Americans reading Oshima's messages from Berlin, and also suggests that the Americans and, in turn, the British, knew of Bose's trip to the East in February 1943. I will return to this matter at the end of the present chapter.

40. On these alliances, see Hauner, *India in Axis Strategy, passim*; Johanna Menzel Meskill, *Hitler and Japan: The Hollow Alliance*, New York: Atherton Press, 1966. There is an extensive literature on this subject most of which is listed in Hauner's bibliography.

41. Meskill, *Hitler and Japan*, 3–4.

42. Malcolm Muggeridge ed., *Ciano's Diary (1939–1943)*, London: William Heinemann, 1947, 356. As the war turns against the Germans and the Italians, the comments of Mussolini and Ciano become ever more bitter. In the end both paid with their lives for their folly of allying with Hitler and bringing great destruction to their country.

43. Denis Mack Smith, *Mussolini's Roman Empire*, New York: Penguin Books, 1977, 169ff.

44. *Ciano's Diary*, 354–55.

45. I am told there is an Urdu literature on Shedai, who returned to Pakistan after independence. In English there are very limited sources including I.O.R., P&J/L/WS/1/1363 and references in Hauner, *India in Axis Strategy*, 366ff. Johannes H. Voigt also mentions him in his important work, *Indien im Zweiten Weltkrieg*, Stuttgart: Deutsche Verlags–Anstalt, 1978, 104–5; and also see Vyas, *Turbulent Era*, 288–89.

46. G.F.O.; Informations–und Kulturpolitische Abteilung. Geheim: Indien. 4748H/E and 4757H/E and 4758/E. These documents which contain many communications about Shedai and Bose cover primarily 1941–42.

47. On the campaign in North Africa, see B.H. Liddell Hart, *History of the Second World War*, Vol. I, New York: Capricorn, 1972, 109ff.

48. On the history and traditions of the Indian Army, see Philip Mason, *A Matter of Honour*, New York: Holt, Rinehart and Winston, 1974. Mason mentions that in addition to this enormous growth of the army, '. . .a force of eight million men were employed for special tasks required by the defence services, five million in war industries and an extra million to meet the strain on the railways.' 495.

49. G.F.O., Serial 195, #139183, letter of Bose to Woermann of July 5, 1941, signed O. Mazzotta.

50. Wirsing, *Indien*, 8–9.

51. *Documents on German Foreign Policy 1918–1945*, Washington: Series D. Vol. XIII, United States Government Printing Office, 1962. No. 120, 165–66.

52. G.F.O., Serial 195, #139191–96, 139216, and many other messages included in this file on the Kabul–Berlin and Kabul–Rome exchanges. Also see Hauner, *India in Axis Strategy*, 334ff. And Talwar, *Talwars* 141ff.

53. Interview with Emilie Schenkl, Vienna, April 30, 1965.

54. Vyas, *Turbulent Era*, 285, 314, 392; interview with Emilie Schenkl, October 14, 1978; Hauner, *India in Axis Strategy*, 161ff, *passim*, describes the activities of Ghulam Siddiqui Khan, in Berlin, and his brother-in-law, King Amanullah, who stayed in Rome.

55. There is a note on Faroqi in I.O.R., P&J/L/WS/1/1363, 'Notes on Suspect Civilian Indians. . .' Mrs Bose and others have told me that occasionally Subhas Bose had a bad reaction to the glucose injections that Faroqi gave him.

56. Interview with Emilie Schenkl, Vienna, October 14, 1978.
57. Interview with Dr J.K. Banerji, New York, December 27, 1975. Interview with Emilie Schenkl in Vienna, April 30, 1965, confirmed that Bose acquired such new habits in wartime and called him 'a chain smoker' by 1942. Vyas also mentions these changes in his *Turbulent Era*, 312.
58. G.F.O., Serial 195, #139222, letter of Bose to Dr Woermann, dated 25.9.41. in which he thanks the Germans for their help and tells of Trott's visit.
59. The tale is spun out in Mr B.R. Nanda's interview with Mr Nambiar and I also heard many of the same details in my interview with him in 1975. Nambiar was and remained more anti-Nazi than Bose and closer to Jawaharlal Nehru in his outlook.
60. Interview with Dr J.K. Banerji, December 27, 1975 and November 9, 1978. Dr Banerji is also listed in the I.O.R. file, 'Notes on Suspect Civilian Indians. . .' Also see Vyas, *Turbulent Era*, 310.
61. For example, Chaudhuri, *Thy Hand*, 504. Mr Chaudhuri wrote more sensible things about Subhas Bose thirty years ago than in some pages of his recent volume.
62. Vyas, *Turbulent Era*, 344–45.
63. Article of November 19, 1941, *Statesman: Anthology*.
64. Louis P. Lochner ed., *The Goebbels Diaries*, New York: Award Books, 1971, 125–26.
65. See Werth (with Lothar Frank's aid) section in Bose and Werth, *Beacon across Asia*, 130–33.
66. G.F.O., Serial 4757H, #E233861, and Serial 4758H, #E234014.
67. Gurbachan Singh Mangat, *The Tiger Strikes: An Unwritten Chapter of Netaji's Life History*, Ludhiana: Gagan Publishers, 1986, 72.
68. Subhas Chandra Bose, *Selected Speeches*, 146, from a speech to the Indian Legion, June 1942.
69. Harbich, in Werth and Harbich, *Netaji in Germany*, 53.
70. Werth, in Werth and Harbich, *Netaji in Germany*, 32.
71. Interview with Walter Harbich, Munich, October 12, 1978. Hugh Toye, a critical analyst, has also pointed out their superior training in his *Subhas Pasha*, 264–68.
72. Harbich, in Werth and Harbich, *Netaji in Germany*, 51. The oath and some other aspects of their sub-culture will be mentioned below.
73. Some of the details come from an interview with Captain W. Lutz, Stuttgart, October 8, 1978 and Captain A. Seifriz, Stuttgart, October 9, 1978. Also from Toye, *Subhas Pasha*, 268ff, and Werth, in Werth and Harbich, *Netaji in Germany*. There is a valuable, but occasion-

ally careless article by Agehananda Bharati, 'Bose and the German INA,' in *New Quest*, No. 26, March–April 1981, 73–85, and an invaluable memoir recorded as an interview, Abid Hasan Safrani, 'A Soldier Remembers,' *The Oracle*, Vol. VI, No. 1, Calcutta, January 1984, 24–65, and continued in *The Oracle*, Vol. VII, No. 1, January 1985, 17–29.

74. Safrani, 'Soldier Remembers,' Part I, 29.

75. Mangat, *Tiger Strikes*, 74ff. Safrani, 'Soldier Remembers,' Part I, 29–30, where he describes Bose's efforts to speak over the hooting of the hostile elements.

76. Safrani, 'Soldier Remembers,' Part I, 32; on the recruiting, also see Werth, in Werth and Bose, *Beacon across Asia*, 134; Toye, *Subhas Pasha*, 268ff, and Bharati, 'Bose and the German INA,' 75ff.

77. Bharati, 'Bose and the German INA,' 75.

78. G.F.O. Serial 4757H, E233877–883, Shedai letter to Counsellor, German Embassy, Rome. 21.9.41.

79. Interview with Wilhelm Lutz, Stuttgart, October 8, 1978.

80. Interview with A. Seifriz, Stuttgart, October 9, 1978.

81. Safrani, 'Soldier Remembers,' Part I, 47.

82. Quoted in Toye, *Subhas Pasha*, 272.

83. Interview with A. Siefriz, October 9, 1978; Bharati, 'Bose and the German INA,' 78ff; Safrani, 'Soldier Remembers,' Part I, 32ff.

84. Safrani, 'Soldier Remembers,' Part I, 37–39.

85. Safrani, 'Soldier Remembers,' Part I, 42–43. Also see Vyas, *Turbulent Era*, 324.

86. Safrani, 'Soldier Remembers,' Part I, 43ff; Werth, in Werth and Bose, *Beacon across Asia*, 129. Also see Vyas, *Turbulent Era*, 325.

87. Vyas, *Turbulent Era*, 324.

88. Werth, in Werth and Bose, *Beacon across Asia*, 129.

89. Interview with Wilhelm Lutz, October 8, 1978.

90. Mangat, *Tiger Strikes*, 194ff.

91. Mookerjee, *Europe at War*, 196.

92. Printed in *Azad Hind*, No. 2, 1942, with German translation. Bose wrote some articles for this magazine signing himself 'O.M.'. From the spring of 1942, many statements of his are published under his own name.

93. For a detailed picture, see Hauner, *India in Axis Strategy*, 423ff.

94. On Asian nationalists in Japan, see David Marr, *Vietnamese Anti-Colonialism 1885–1925*, Berkeley: U. of California Press, 1971, 105ff. He draws upon Marius Jansen, *The Japanese and Sun Yat-sen*, Cambridge: Harvard U. Press, 1954.

95. Joyce C. Lebra, *Jungle Alliance: Japan and the Indian National Army*, Singapore: Asia Pacific Press, 1971, 48–49. There are many references to Toyama and his role in Japanese politics in Richard Storry, *The Double Patriots: A Study of Japanese Nationalism*, Westport: Greewood Press, 1976, 12ff.

96. Rabindranath Tagore, *A Visit to Japan*, New York: East West Institute, 1961, 98–99. See, for the context of and responses to Tagore's visit, Stephen N. Hay, *Asian Ideas of East and West: Tagore and His Critics in Japan, China, and India*, Cambridge: Harvard U. Press, 1970, Chapters Two and Three.

97. Hay, *Asian Ideas*, 73ff.

98. Quoted from selection in Joyce C. Lebra, ed., *Japan's Greater East Asia Co-Prosperity Sphere in World War II: Selected Readings and Documents*, Kuala Lumpur: Oxford U. Press, 1975, 40.

99. It is printed in Lebra, *Japan's East Asia Sphere*, 71–72.

100. Lebra, *Japan's East Asia Sphere*, 72.

101. On the vague specifications of the Greater East Asia Sphere, see Lebra, *Japan's East Asia Sphere*, 57ff; Robert J.C. Butow, *Tojo and the Coming of the War*, Stanford: Stanford U. Press, 1961, 161–62; Willard H. Elsbree, *Japan's Role in Southeast Asian Nationalist Movements 1940 to 1945*, New York: Russell and Russell, 1953, 15ff.

102. Butow, *Tojo*, 328–29.

103. On the Indians in Southeast Asia, see I.J. Bahadur Singh, ed., *Indians in Southeast Asia*, New Delhi: Sterling, 1982; Sinnappah Arasaratnam, *Indians in Malaysia and Singapore*, rev. ed. Kuala Lumpur: Oxford U. Press, 1979; John F. Cady, *A History of Modern Burma*, Ithaca: Cornell U. Press, 1958, 82ff, *passim*; G.P. Ramachandra, 'The Indian Independence Movement in Malaya 1942–45,' unpublished M.A. thesis, U. of Malaya, October 1970.

104. On Fujiwara, see Lebra, *Jungle Alliance*, 1ff; Toye, *Subhas Pasha*, 40; Fujiwara Iwaichi, *F. Kikan: Japanese Army Intelligence Operations in Southeast Asia during World War II*, Hong Kong: Heinemann Asia, 1983; K.K. Ghosh, *The Indian National Army: Second Front of the Indian Independence Movement*, Meerut: Meenakshi Prakashan, 1969, 17ff. Interview with Lt. General Fujiwara, Tokyo, August 6, 1979.

105. Details from Toye, *Subhas Pasha*, 40. None of the other writers on the Indian National Army gives an account of Fujiwara's career and background. I have occasionally found Toye's information questionable, but finding no other, I have used it here.

106. The story is told very well in Lebra, *Jungle Alliance*, 3ff.

107. There are numerous accounts of the Japanese conquest and the work of Fujiwara at this time. See Lebra, *Jungle Alliance*, 16ff; Toye, *Subhas Pasha*, 43ff; T.R. Sareen, *Japan and the Indian National Army*, Delhi: Agam Prakashan, 1986, 29ff; Mohan Singh, *Soldiers' Contribution to Indian Independence*, New Delhi: Army Educational Stores, 1974, 55ff; K.K. Ghosh, *Indian National Army*, 13ff; Fujiwara, *F. Kikan*, 50ff; S. Woodburn Kirby, *The War against Japan: The Loss of Singapore*, Vol. I, London: Her Majesty's Stationery Office, 1957, 97ff.

108. For a skillful account of these interchanges, see Lebra, *Jungle Alliance*, 18ff.

109. The story is told in numerous books on the war including Peter Calvocoressi and Guy Wint, *Total War: Causes and Courses of the Second World War*, New York: Penguin, 1979, 713ff. A lengthy and dramatic account is by Noel Barber, *Sinister Twilight: The Fall of Singapore*, Glasgow: Fontana/Collins, 1970.

110. Hitler's *Secret Conversations,* New York: Farrar, Strauss and Young, 1953, 149.

111. *The Goebbels Diaries*, ed., Louis P. Lochner, New York: Award Books, 1971, 72.

112. For example, see Fujiwara's arguments used in persuading Mohan Singh to cooperate, cited in Lebra, *Jungle Alliance*, 20.

113. G.F.O. Serial 4758H, Telegram from German Ambassador Ott, Tokyo, to Berlin, January 16, 1942.

114. See Lebra, *Jungle Alliance*, 37–38; Mohan Singh, *Soldiers' Contribution*, 108–9.

115. Mohan Singh, *Soldiers' Contribution*, 108–9.

116. Fujiwara, *F. Kikan*, 89.

117. Lebra, *Jungle Alliance*, 26ff.

118. Lebra, *Jungle Alliance*, 39ff; Ghosh, *Indian National Army*, 44ff; Mohan Singh, *Soldiers' Contribution*, 114ff.

119. Lebra, *Jungle Alliance*, 45–8.

120. Lebra, *Jungle Alliance*, 65ff; Ghosh, *Indian National Army*, 51ff.

121. Quoted in Ghosh, *Indian National Army*, 51.

122. Lebra, *Jungle Alliance*, 71–4.

123. Ghosh, *Indian National Army*, 55–6.

124. Resolutions quoted in Lebra, *Jungle Alliance*, 78.

125. Bose's message and other conference documents are printed in Sopan, ed., *Netaji Subhas Chandra Bose: His Life and Work*, Bombay: Azad Bhandar, 1946, 140–41ff.

126. See Ghosh, *Indian National Army*, 37ff.

127. These details are drawn from the incisive analysis of Ghosh, *Indian National Army*, 62ff.

128. The story of the crisis and Gill's role is more complicated as explained by Ghosh, *Indian National Army*, 63–64, 93ff, and those interested in the machinations within the INA should consult his work.

129. Ghosh, *Indian National Army*, 93ff, gives a detailed account.

130. Interview with General Seizo Arisue, Tokyo, August 9, 1979.

131. Government of India, P&J/7542/45. An extensive file with many details on his imprisonment is in Government of India, Home Department File No. 94/26/41–Pol (I), Detention under Rule 26 of the Defence of India Rules of Sarat Chandra Bose.

132. Letter to Ajit Dey, March 14, 1942.

133. This summary and much of what follows about his prison life are based on letters to his family, especially to his son Asoke Nath Bose and his brother-in-law, Ajit Dey, written 1942 to 1945.

134. Letter to Ajit Dey, April 30, 1942.

135. Letter to Ajit Dey, May 24, 1942.

136. Letter to Ajit Dey, March 14, 1942.

137. These comments are based on an examination of some of Sarat Bose's books in the library of Netaji Bhavan.

138. Letter to Ajit Dey, March 14, 1942. There is also a mention of the visit in Mitra, *IAR*, I, 1942, 43. A virtual transcript of the interview is in Government of India, Home Department 94/26/41. Among other things, the two ministers were concerned that the communal attitudes of Shyama Prasad Mookerji was weakening the ministry in the absence of Sarat Bose.

139. Letter to Ajit Dey, April 8, 1942. There are many details of the visit in Government of India, Home Department 94/26/41. After the visit, Mrs Bose issued a statement to the press about the poor conditions in which she found her husband and the shabby way she felt he was being treated to the detriment of his health. See Mitra, *IAR*, I, 1942, 69.

140. Letter to Ajit Dey, April 8, 1942.

141. The most stimulating work on the higher politics involved is R.J. Moore, *Churchill, Cripps, and India 1939–1945*, Oxford: Clarendon Press, 1979. Extensive documents are contained in Nicholas Mansergh, ed., *The Transfer of Power 1942–7: The Cripps Mission January–April 1942*, Vol. I, London: Her Majesty's Stationery Office, 1970.

142. Moore, *Churchill, Cripps, and India*, 75.
143. Moore, *Churchill, Cripps, and India*, 88. Mitra, *IAR*, I, 1942, 84.
144. Bose's broadcast is reprinted in George Orwell, ed., *Talking to India*, London: George Allen and Unwin, 1943, 157–58.
145. See Savarkar's statement in Mitra, *IAR*, I, 1942, 68.
146. See his account, Santimoy Ganguli, 'Netaji and B.V.,' *The Oracle*, Vol. I, No. 4, Calcutta, October 1979, 28–32.
147. See the account by Santimoy Ganguli, Sudhir Ranjan Bakshi, Dhiren Saha Roy, Ratul Roy Chowdhury, and Sisir K. Bose, 'Netaji's Underground in India during World War II,' *The Oracle*, Vol. I, No. 2, Calcutta, April 1979, 7–14.
148. *Selected Works of Jawaharlal Nehru*, Vol. 12, New Delhi: Orient Longman, 1979, 262–63.
149. *Selected Works of Nehru*, Vol. 12, 225–26. Answer to questions in a press conference, April 12, 1942.
150. Mitra, *IAR*, I, 1942, 94.
151. Quoted in the secret report of T. Wickenden, ICS, on the 1942 movement, completed in November 1943, and reprinted and edited by P.N. Chopra, *Quit India Movement: British Secret Report*, Faridabad: Thomson Press, 1976, 70.
152. Quoted in *Harijan*, August 2, 1942. Reprint of the journal, IX, 1941–42, New York: Garland Publishing, 1973, 257.
153. Gandhi's remarks printed in *Harijan*, August 2, 1942.
154. There is a large literature on the 1942 movement including the Wickenden Report, cited above, and P.N. Chopra, ed., *Quit India Movement: British Secret Documents*, New Delhi: Interprint, 1986, which contains many individual Home Department extracts. Nicholas Mansergh, 'Quit India', in *The Transfer of Power 1942–7*, Vol. II, London: Her Majesty's Stationery Office, 1971, also contains numerous documents. Also of value are: Govind Sahai, *'42 Rebellion*, Delhi: Rajkamal, 1947; Francis G. Hutchins, *Spontaneous Revolution*, Delhi: Manohar, 1971; A. Moin Zaidi, *The Way Out to Freedom*, New Delhi: Orientalia, 1973; Arun Bhuyan, *The Quit India Movement*, New Delhi: Manas, 1975. Sumit Sarkar, *Modern India*, 388–405, gives a succinct summary.
155. Satish Samanta, et al., 'August Revolution and Two Years National Government in Midnapur,' Calcutta: People's Publishing House?, 1946. The Government of India, Home Department, Political, File No. 3/87/43, gives details of acts of rebellion, small and large, in almost every district of Bengal. Sahai, *'42 Rebellion*, 275ff, gives details on this district, and Sarkar, *Modern India*, 400–1, gives a

summary.

156. Quoted in Overstreet and Windmiller, *Communism in India*, 192. Details are given of the CPI shift in this work, 191ff.

157. See Government of India, Home Department, Political, File No. 33/45/42, S.P. Mookerjee Resignation.

158. John Glendevon, *The Viceroy at Bay: Lord Linlithgow in India 1936–1943*, London: Collins, 1971. Fazlul Huq bitterly denounced Herbert in his *Bengal Today*, Calcutta: n.p., 1944.

159. Bose and Werth, *Beacon across Asia*, 127.

160. Nanda interview with Nambiar, 54.

161. This is mentioned in Joyce Lebra, 'Bose's Influence on the Formulation of Japanese Policy toward India and the INA,' in Sisir K. Bose, ed., *Netaji and India's Freedom*, Calcutta: Netaji Research Bureau, 1975, 319.

162. See the vivid account in Vyas, *Turbulent Era*, 365–67.

163. Luigi Barzini, 'With Chandra Bose in His Home,' *Popolo d'Italia*, April 19, 1942.

164. *Ciano's Diary*, 465.

165. 'Subhas Chandra Bose Speaks to *Popolo d'Italia* ', June 18, 1942.

166. See Hauner, *India in Axis Strategy*, 485, and Appendix, Document 7, which is the official G.F.O. version of the interview, 672–77. There is an English translation in Bose, *Netaji and India's Freedom*, 310–15.

167. From translation in Bose, *Netaji and India's Freedom*, 312–13. The German is in Hauner, *India in Axis Strategy*, 674–75.

168. See Hitler's evasive words in Bose, *Netaji and India's Freedom*, 314–15, and Hauner, *India in Axis Strategy*, 676–77.

169. On the Hitler interview, see Bose and Werth, *Beacon across Asia*, 138–40; Hauner, *India in Axis Strategy*, 485–87.

170. Hauner, *India in Axis Strategy*, Documents 5 and 6, gives German and Japanese versions discussed during the first half of 1942, 668–71. He discusses Hitler's unwillingness to give Bose the declaration he wanted, 487ff.

171. This statement is printed in Hauner, *India in Axis Strategy*, Document 8, 678–80.

172. From document in Hauner, *India in Axis Strategy*, 678.

173. For example, Ganpuley, *Netaji in Germany*, 60ff, gives a detailed account of the training, as does Toye, *Subhas Pasha*, 265ff.

174. Mangat, *Tiger Strikes*, 116ff.

175. Mookerjee, *Europe at War*, 225ff. Stories of dictatorial ambitions on the part of Subhas Bose apparently reached his mother, who, on

her death bed, is said to have denied that he was a would-be-king. See Roy, *Netaji—The Man*, 153n.

176. Subhas Chandra Bose, 'Free India and Her Problems,' published in *Azad Hind*, Berlin, 1942, and reprinted in Bose, *Indian Struggle*, 454–55.

177. Bose, *Indian Struggle*, 455–56.

178. *Goebbels Diaries*, 166, entry for March 26, 1942.

179. 'India's Anti–Jewish Quisling,' *The Jewish Chronicle*, August 21, 1942.

180. Vyas, *Turbulent Era*, 419.

181. Details, almost day-by-day are in G.F.O., Bureau of Secretary of State, India, Serial No. 195, Vol. III, 139955–140026.

182. Vyas, *Turbulent Era*, 421.

183. G.F.O. Bureau of the Sec. of State, India, Serial No. 195. Vol. III, has messages concerning the arrangements.

184. Bose and Werth, *Beacon across Asia*, 143.

185. Vyas, *Turbulent Era*, 430–32.

186. Interview with Emilie Schenkl, October 14, 1978.

187. Safrani, 'Soldier Remembers,' Part I, 48ff. Werth also mentions that Hasan was not told for security reasons, Bose and Werth, *Beacon across Asia*, 144.

188. Safrani, 'Soldier Remembers,' Part I, 52.

189. Details on the ship from Bose and Werth, *Beacon across Asia*, 144, and from an interview with Prof J. Rohwer, Institute for World History, Stuttgart, October 10, 1978. Prof Rohwer is the leading authority on German U-boats in the Second World War and checked his records on this submarine and this voyage during the course of this discussion.

190. Lewin, *American Magic*, 216.

191. Safrani, 'Soldier Remembers,' Part I, 54–5.

192. Most of the details of the voyage come from Safrani, 'Soldier Remembers,' Part I, 48ff, and a few from the interview with Rohwer.

CHAPTER ELEVEN

1. Jayadeva's *Gita Govinda*, trans. Barbara Stoler Miller, New York: Columbia U. Press. 1977, 70.

2. *The Complete Poems of Samar Sen*, Calcutta: Writers Workshop, 1970, 6.

3. Yamamoto Tsunetomo, *Hagakure, The Book of the Samurai*, New

York: Avon Books, 1979, 17.

4. Safrani, 'Soldier Remembers,' Part 2, 22.

5. *History of the Showa Emperor,* Vol. 8, Tokyo: Yomiuri Shimbun-sha, 1969, 420. This is a documentary history based on interviews with participants in the events prepared by a Japanese newspaper. It concerns the period of the Showa Emperor and use is made here of Vol. 8; Vol. 9(1969); Vol. 10(1970). Translations from the Japanese have been made by Akiko Matsunobu. These volumes are referred to subsequently simply as *Showa*, 8, 9, or 10, with the page number.

6. For example, see Lebra, *Jungle Alliance*, 115–16, where she gives all kinds of reasons why Tojo did not want to meet Bose. There may be some truth in all this, but Hasan's version now has to be taken into account.

7. Safrani, 'Soldier Remembers,' Part 1, 62.

8. See the detailed account in Lebra, *Jungle Alliance*, 114ff.

9. Robert J.C. Butow, *Tojo and the Coming of the War*, Stanford: Stanford U. Press, 1961, 423.

10. There are a number of accounts of Bose's first visit to Japan, e.g., Lebra, *Jungle Alliance*, 114ff; *Showa*, Vol. 8, 420ff, and Safrani, 'Soldier Remembers,' Part I, 61ff.

11. Quoted in Lebra, *Jungle Alliance*, 116. The above details about Bose's meetings with Japanese leaders are drawn from Lebra's account and from *Showa*, Vol. 8, 421, where Yamamoto is quoted at length.

12. Bose, *Selected Speeches*, 160–61. This speech had gone through translation and retranslation, but is offered here in English.

13. Bose, *Selected Speeches*, 162.

14. John K. Fairbank, Edwin O. Reischauer, Albert M. Craig, *East Asia Tradition and Transformation*, Boston: Houghton Mifflin, 1973, 800ff.

15. Christopher Thorne, *The Issue of War,* New York: Oxford U. Press, 1985, 6, 23, 30, 67, 80, 87, et al., makes Bose a simple-minded pro-Japanese spokesman and seems to have no comprehension of Indian nationalism at all.

16. See I.O.L. P&J/L/WS/1/1711, on the INA.

17. Some of the details are from Lebra, *Jungle Alliance*, 117–18.

18. See Col. Prem Kumar Sahgal (interviewee), recorded by Shri S.L. Manchanda (interviewer), 15.7.77, Nehru Memorial Museum and Library, Oral History Interview, 18ff.

19. Sahgal interview, Nehru Memorial Library, 29.

20. M. Sivaram, *The Road to Delhi*, Tokyo: Charles Tuttle, 1967,

122–23.
21. Sivaram, *Road to Delhi*, 123–24.
22. Sivaram, *Road to Delhi*, 124.
23. Quotations and slogans from Sivaram, *Road to Delhi*, 127–28.
24. Quoted from Dr (Mrs) Lakshmi Sahgal (interviewee), recorded by Shri S.L. Manchanda (interviewer), April 15, 1977, Nehru Memorial Museum and Library, Oral History Interview, 11.
25. See Bose's speeches to the women recruits, in Bose, *Selected Speeches*, 189–92, 208.
26. Interview with Mrs Bhupalan, Kuala Lumpur, Malaysia, July 10, 1979.
27. Interview with Mrs Bhupalan.
28. Interview with Datin Janaki Athinappan, Kuala Lumpur, Malaysia, July 6, 1979.
29. Lakshmi Sahgal interview, Nehru Museum, 16–17.
30. On the details from the British point of view, see I.O.L., L/WS/2/45, a long and detailed guide to the INA. From a more detached, though Indian point of view, see Ghosh, *Indian National Army*, 148ff.
31. S.A. Ayer, *Unto Him a Witness: The Story of Netaji Subhas Chandra Bose in East Asia*, Bombay: Thacker and Co., 1951, 245.
32. Sivaram, *Road to Delhi*, 173. Also see the details in Ghosh, *Indian National Army*, 157-60.
33. On the Japanese role and Burma in this period, see John F. Cady, *A History of Modern Burma*, Ithaca: Cornell U. Press, 1958, 427ff; Ba Maw, *Breakthrough in Burma: Memoirs of a Revolution, 1939-1946*, New Haven: Yale U. Press, 1968, 22ff; Joyce C Lebra, *Japanese-Trained Armies in Southeast Asia*, Hong Kong: Heinemann Educational Books, 1977, Chapter 3; Field Marshal The Viscount Slim, *Defeat into Victory*, London: Corgi, 1971, 14ff.
34. Ba Maw, *Breakthrough,* 185.
35. Cady, *History of Burma*, 446.
36. Ba Maw, *Breakthrough,* 95. Also see Cady, *History of Burma,* 456ff.
37. Ba Maw, *Breakthrough*, 351–52.
38. Quoted in Ba Maw, *Breakthrough*, 329-30.
39. Slim explains how the Japanese advanced in Burma in *Defeat into Victory*, 23ff. Slim studied Japanese methods very carefully to use what he could for the future and to see what weaknesses he could find. He learned a lot and he was well prepared for the campaigns of 1943 and 1944. Many details on the war are drawn from Robert Goralski, *World War II Almanac: 1931-1945*, New York: Perigee

Books, 1981, and Peter Young and Richard Natkiel, *Atlas of the Second World War*, New York: Paragon Books, 1979.

40. Lebra, *Jungle Alliance*, 129.

41. Ghosh, *Indian National Army*, 155, and note 98, contains a complete list of members, representatives of the army, and civilian advisers.

42. See the vivid account of these events in Lebra, *Jungle Alliance*, 129–30.

43. Interview with Swami Siddhartananda and Swami Sthidananda, Singapore, July 13, 1979. Several of his subordinates in the INA have mentioned that he visited the Ramakrishna Mission.

44. Ghosh, *Indian National Army*, 161ff.

45. Ghosh, *Indian National Army*, 162–64: Lebra, *Jungle Alliance*, 132–35.

46. Lebra, *Jungle Alliance*, 133–35.

47. Lebra, *Jungle Alliance*, 134–35. N. Iqbal Singh, *The Andaman Story*, New Delhi: Vikas, 1978, 237ff, gives a picture of the brutalities of the Japanese occupation. He says that Bose, in his naivete regarding the ways of Nippon, ignored them.

48. Quoted in John Toland, *The Rising Sun*, New York: Bantam, 1971, 519–20. Also see the account in Ba Maw's *Breakthrough*, 336–47.

49. Quoted in Ba Maw, *Breakthrough*, 345–46.

50. The declaration is presented in Ba Maw, *Breakthrough*, 347.

51. See the discussion of this point in one of the best works on the famine, Paul R. Greenough, *Prosperity and Misery in Modern Bengal: The Famine of 1943–44*, New York: Oxford U. Press, 1982, 85ff. Greenough mentions that the *Statesman* and other papers of the time started describing it as 'Man-made' from its inception. Also see Government of India, Famine Inquiry Commission, *Final Report*, and *Report on Bengal*, Delhi : Government Press, 1945. Sir John Woodhead, one of Bengal's most able and experienced ICS officers headed the Commission.

52. Some details of the ministerial shifts are in Sen, *Muslim Politics*, 172ff.

53. See Wavell, *The Viceroy's Journal*, ed., Penderel Moon, London: Oxford U. Press, 1973, 15ff.

54. Letter to Ajit Dey, September 7, 1943. What would Sarat Bose have said had his letters not been censored? One cannot tell, but this passage does seem to embody his true feelings.

55. Bose, *Selected Speeches*, 206.

56. See Cady, *History of Burma*, 458ff.

57. Letter of June 13, 1943 to Gita (Bose) Biswas, printed in *Sarat Bose*

Commemoration Volume, 101.

58. Sarat Bose letter to Gita (Bose) Biswas, August 26, 1943.
59. Letter to Lord Linlithgow, July 17/24, 1943, from Coonoor, in I.O.L., P&J/7542/45.
60. Letter to Ajit Dey, from Coonoor, January 4, 1944.
61. Quoted in *Showa*, 9, 365.
62. See Lebra, *Jungle Alliance*, 149ff, where many different Japanese plans and proposals are described.
63. All of the complexities of the Japanese pros and cons of the offensive and the positions of each officer are described in Lebra, *Jungle Alliance*, 149ff. Also of value is a Japanese document entitled 'Subhas Chandra Bose and Japan,' translated and printed in Sisir K. Bose, ed., *Netaji and India's Freedom*, Calcutta: Netaji Research Bureau, 1976. This document is dated 1956 and seems to be the same one mentioned by Ghosh, *Indian National Army*, 168, n. 10. Ghosh says that General Kawabe told him that he prepared the document for the Government of Japan after the war. It seems to utilize the testimony of many of the actors in this complex drama, particularly the Japanese ones.
64. Lebra, *Jungle Alliance*, 171–73.
65. On these efforts, see Ayer, *Witness*, 7, 229; Shah Nawaz Khan, *My Memories of I.N.A. and Its Netaji*, Delhi: Rajkamal Publications, 1946, 14.
66. For the Japanese view, see 'Bose and Japan,' 340ff. The British view is presented in Government of India, L/WS/2/45.
67. Ayer, *Witness*, 187.
68. See Sivaram, *Road to Delhi*, 188; Government of India, L/WS/2/45; and Ba Maw, *Breakthrough*, 352ff.
69. Interview with Zora Singh, Rangoon, June 27, 1979. His work is also mentioned by one of the INA's top officers, Shah Nawaz Khan, *My Memories of I.N.A.*, 123.
70. Ayer, *Witness*, 9, 195.
71. A.C. Chatterji, *India's Struggle for Freedom*, Calcutta: Chuckervertty, Chatterjee, 1947, 161–2.
72. Slim, *Defeat into Victory*, 150–51. Also see O.H.K. Spate, *India and Pakistan*, 551ff, and Lebra, *Jungle Alliance*, 153–55.
73. Quoted in Lebra, *Jungle Alliance*, 175–76.
74. The best calculations about the opposed forces have been made by Ghosh, *Indian National Army*, 182.
75. For example, see Fujiwara, *F. Kikan*, XXIV; 'Subhas Bose and Japan,' 383ff.

76. Lebra, *Jungle Alliance*, 177.
77. Shah Nawaz Khan, *My Memories of I.N.A.*, 100: Also Ayer, *Witness*, 8.
78. Slim, *Defeat into Victory*, 270ff. Slim savored this error by one of his opposing number and told his air forces not to try to kill Major-General Sato, the besieging commander at Kohima, for he thought Sato one of the most helpful generals on his side. Also Lebra, *Jungle Alliance*, 182.
79. Slim, *Defeat into Victory*, 265.
80. See Slim, *Defeat into Victory*, 265, 288–89, 348, 359, 364, 366, 385, 411, 413, 421. Comments on the courage of the INA soldiers in battle are in Government of India, L/WS/2/45, and the Japanese report, 'Subhas Bose and Japan,' 379. The idea has entered the recent work of Nirad Chaudhuri that the INA never even fought. See Chaudhuri, *Thy Hand, Great Anarch!*, 781ff. He does not cite any relevant government materials or memoirs. If this volume is a memoir based on first-hand knowledge, what is Mr Chaudhuri's personal, first-hand source about the Indo-Burma campaign of 1944 and 1945? What he has written is contradicted by a great variety of sources, intelligence reports, memoirs, et. al..
81. I.O.R., L/WS/2/45.
82. Shah Nawaz Khan, *My Memories of I.N.A.*, 126.
83. According to a documentary film on the campaign made by Granada television in the mid-1970s, 53,000 of 83,000 Japanese troops in the Imphal-Kohima offensive died of disease. Many others, of course, died in battle. This figure is in keeping with those offered by Slim and historians of the campaign.
84. On the Sato affair, see Alvin D. Coox, 'Maverick General of Imperial Japan,' in *Army*, Vol. 15, No. 12, Washington, D.C., July 1965, 68-74. Also see the description of Sato's action and Mutaguchi's response, in Lebra, *Jungle Alliance*, 189.
85. Shah Nawaz Khan, *My Memories of I.N.A.*, 143.
86. Bose, *Selected Speeches*, 219–20, August 13, 1944.
87. 'Subhas Bose and Japan,' 411.
88. 'Subhas Bose and Japan,' 401.
89. 'Subhas Bose and Japan,' 409. This report is studded with similar remarks on Bose's lack of military knowledge, his unrealism, and his stubbornness.
90. Ghosh, *Indian National Army*, 193–94.
91. 'Subhas Bose and Japan,' 404.
92. Bose, *Selected Speeches*, 228. Delivered at Bangkok, May 21, 1945.

93. Sivaram, *Road to Delhi*, 230; *Showa*, 9, 343. On the Indian cadets, see Moti Lal Bhargava, *Indian National Army–Tokyo Cadets*, New Delhi: Reliance, 1986.

94. See Shah Nawaz Khan, *My Memories of I.N.A.*, 151ff; Slim, *Defeat into Victory*, 304ff. There are excellent maps and a brief account of these battles in Young and Natkiel, *Atlas*, 180ff.

95. Shah Nawaz Khan, *My Memories of I.N.A.*, 130–1; Ghosh, *Indian National Army*, 192–96.

96. Chatterji, *India's Struggle*, 251–52; *Showa*, 9, 348.

97. Sivaram, *Road to Delhi*, 220–21.

98. Ayer, *Witness*, 12–13; *Showa*, 9, 351.

99. *Showa*, 9, 358–61.

100. Nair, *An Indian Freedom Fighter in Japan*, 250.

101. Ayer, *Witness*, 250–51.

102. Ayer, *Witness*, 253.

103. Sahgal interview, Nehru Memorial Library, 37–38.

104. Nair, *Indian Freedom Fighter*, 249–51.

105. Sivaram, *Road to Delhi*, 119.

106. Sivaram, *Road to Delhi*, 210.

107. Slim, *Defeat into Victory*, 409ff, where he gives a detailed account of his discussions with Aung San. Shah Nawaz Khan, *My Memories of I.N.A.*, 174, 187; Chatterji, *India's Struggle for Freedom*, 256; Ba Maw, *Breakthrough*, 383ff, where he gives his version of some of the Burmese complexities.

108. Shah Nawaz Khan, *My Memories of I.N.A.*, 128ff. Sahgal interview in Nehru Memorial Library, 52ff. G.S. Dhillon, 'The Nehru Holds the Irrawaddy,' *The Oracle*, October 1983, Vol. V, No.4, 1–30, and January 1984, Vol. VI, No.1, 66-99. Slim, *Defeat into Victory*, 364–65, 385.

109. Shah Nawaz Khan, *My Memories of I.N.A.*, 191ff.

110. *Showa*, 9, 356–57.

111. *Showa*, 9, 357–58.

112. Shah Nawaz Khan, *My Memories of I.N.A.*, X.

113. Ayer, *Witness*, 264.

114. Mookerjee, *Europe at War*, 257.

115. Werth and Harbich, *Netaji in Germany*, 23–25.

116. On the end of the Indian Legion, see Hauner, *India in Axis Strategy*, 587–90; Ganpuley, *Netaji in Germany*, 151ff; Toye, *Subhas Pasha*, 483ff; Mangat, *Tiger Strikes*, 134ff.

117. Marie Vassiltchikov, *Berlin Diaries 1940-1945*, New York: Alfred Knopf, 1987, 186.

118. Vassiltchikov, *Berlin Diaries*, 222. For other accounts of these events, see Werth and Harbich, *Netaji in Germany*, 13; Vyas, *Turbulent Era*, 472–78; Hoffman, *German Resistance*, 315ff; Clarita von Trott, *Trott*, 122ff; A.C.N. Nambiar, unpublished manuscript, 'über Trott,' 20.4. 1963, written for Clarita von Trott, and in her possession.

119. See *PBLA*, LXVII, No. 5, May 10, 1944, and on through May 98ff.

120. Sarat Bose letter to Casey reprinted in Sarat Bose, *Commemoration Volume*, 327–28. The letter also contains harshly worded attacks on British officials and the European community in Bengal which can only have served to have alienated Lord Casey. A year later, he vigorously opposed the release of Sarat Bose and was overruled by the Government of India.

121. There are references to some of the literature on the growth of the Pakistan movement in Leonard A. Gordon, 'Divided Bengal: Problems of Nationalism and Identity in the 1947 Partition,' *The Journal of Commonwealth & Comparative Politics*,' XVI, No. 2, July 1978, *passim*. A recent work of great value is Ayesha Jalal, *The Sole Spokesman: Jinnah, the Muslim League and the Demand for Pakistan*, Cambridge: Cambridge U. Press, 1985. Jalal mentions the question of what it all means, 107. For Bengal, Sen, *Muslim Politics*, is still an essential work, especially 160ff.

122. Interviews with Abul Hashim and Abul Mansur Ahmad, Dacca, June 1972; Sen, *Muslim Politics*, 182ff; Peter Hardy, *The Muslims of British India*, Cambridge: Cambridge U. Press, 1972, 235ff; Begum Shaista Ikramullah, *From Purdah to Parliament*, London: Cresset Press, 1963, 99ff.

123. Abul Hashim, *In Retrospection*, Dacca: Mowla Brothers, 1975, 176.

124. Later, in 1946, Jinnah insisted that this phrase be changed as follows: '...shall be grouped together to constitute independent states which shall be one national homeland in which the constituent units are autonomous and sovereign.' See the note on this matter in Gordon, 'Divided Bengal,' n. 70.

125. Hashim, *Retrospection*, 134ff.

126. Anisuzzaman, 'Cultural Trends in Bangladesh: A Redefinition of Identity,' Seminar paper, Nuffield College, Oxford, February 17, 1975, 6–7, where Abul Mansur's views are analyzed. Also see Abul Mansur Ahmad's collected essays, *End of a Betrayal and Restoration of Lahore Resolution*, Dacca: Khoshroz Kitab Mahal, 1975, *passim*. Also, interview with Abul Mansur Ahmad, Dacca, June 1972.

127. G.D. Adhikari, 'Pakistan and National Unity,' 3rd rev. ed., Bombay: People's Publishing House, 1944.

128. Adhikari, 'Pakistan,' 29.

129. Adhikari, 'Pakistan,' 47–48.

130. Hindu Mahasabha Papers, Nehru Memorial Library, 1940–45, Working Committee file.

131. See Mitra, *Indian Annual Register*, I, 1945, 54–55. Jalal, *Spokesman*, 108; Sen, *Bengal Politics*, 191ff; Chattopadhyay, *Bengal Electoral Politics*, 195–96; Lord Casey, *Personal Experience, 1939–1946*, London: Constable, 1962, 216–37. Casey's published book is based on a much more extensive diary now housed in the India Office Library, Photo Eur. 48, 4 vols. Casey mentions that Fazlul Huq and H.S. Suhrawardy approached him about forming a new ministry in 1945, but he thought it was best that Bengal go to the expected elections under Section 93.

132. Johannes H. Voigt, *India in the Second World War*, New Delhi: Arnold-Heinemann, 1987, 254ff. Voigt's work was originally published in German in 1978. Wavell, *The Viceroy's Journal*, 118ff. Mansergh, *The Transfer of Power*, V, September 1, 1944–July 28, 1945, *passim*. Both Wavell's journal and Mansergh's collection of documents record the endless frustrations and rebuffs which Wavell had in trying to get Churchill to move forward on the Indian question. Wavell has been abused in some quarters for his silence and obtuseness, but at least he tried to begin discussions, the exchange of proposals, and start negotiations after the deadening years of the Linlithgow viceroyalty and against the wishes of his own, reactionary prime minister.

133. Mitra, *IAR*, I, 1945, 68–74.

134. Mitra, *IAR*, I, 1945, 74ff; II, 3–4. Voigt, *India*, 261.

135. Letter to Ajit Dey, May 10, 1944.

136. Sarat Bose prison diary, 'Stray Thoughts,' in *Commemoration Volume*, 181.

137. Bose, 'Stray Thoughts,' *Commemoration Volume*, 182.

138. Bose, 'Stray Thoughts,' *Commemoration Volume*, 182.

139. Bose, 'Stray Thoughts,' *Commemoration Volume*, 183.

140. Fazlul Huq and some other nationalist Muslims met in Delhi in May 1944 and then met again in September, but they could not resist the incoming tide of the League. See Mitra, *IAR*, I, 1944, 47 and II, 15.

141. Sarat Bose letter to Gita (Bose) Biswas, May 3, 1945.

142. Sarat Bose to Gita (Bose) Biswas, June 29, 1944.

143. Sarat Bose to Ajit Dey, October 20, 1944. The letter also contains

details of what has to be done to rearrange the household with the arrest of Sisir.

144. Government of India, Home Department, Political File No. 44/1/ 44–Poll(I), reprinted in Bose, *Commemoration Volume*, 161.

145. The story is told in laborious and self-serving detail in Mahmood Khan Durrani, *The Sixth Column*, London: Cassell, 1955. Durrani, in contrast to Muslims in the INA, describes Bose as violently anti-Muslim. In fact, all Sikhs and Hindus in the INA are described as fanatically anti-Muslim. Also see Moti Lal Bhargava and Americk Singh Gill, *Indian National Army—Secret Service*, New Delhi: Reliance Publishing House, 1988, 16–17, 108.

146. Americk Singh's story which was presented orally at the Netaji Research Bureau, January 1979, has been put in writing in Bhargava and Singh Gill, *Indian National Army*, 94ff. Gurchan Singh recorded his story in *Singa, The Lion of Malaya*, Kuala Lumpur: Printcraft, n.d.

147. For a first-hand account of how the Japanese, even at the end, fought and died almost recklessly, see John Masters, *The Road Past Mandalay*, New York: Harper & Brothers, 1961, 305ff. The figures for those killed in this phase of the war for Burma indicate the disparity: about 5,000 Allied troops as against more than 100,000 Japanese and INA.

148. Bose, *Speeches*, 226.

149. Interview with Datin Janaki Athinappan, Kuala Lumpur, July 6, 1979. Part of her diary of those days is reproduced in Shah Nawaz Khan, *My Memories of I.N.A.*, 204ff. Ayer, *Witness*, 13ff, presents a detailed account of the retreat from Rangoon to Bangkok.

150. Ayer, *Witness*, 37ff.

151. Bose, *Speeches*, 230–31, 'The German Defeat,' broadcast from Singapore, May 25, 1945.

152. On the Japanese and their surrender, see Robert J.C. Butow, *Japan's Decision to Surrender*, Stanford: Stanford U. Press, 1954. My comments are based on this superb study.

153. Bose, *Selected Speeches*, 233–34.

154. See Chatterji, *India's Struggle*, 271ff. Bose, *Speeches*, 232–37.

155. Chatterji, *India's Struggle*, 283.

156. 'Subhas Bose and Japan,' 414–15.

157. Butow, *Japan's Decision to Surrender*, 189ff.

158. 'Subhas Bose and Japan,' 415.

159. 'Subhas Bose and Japan,' 415. The details in this paragraph and following are based on this and a number of printed sources as well

as my own interviews. The most important of these printed sources are: Ayer, *Witness*, 48ff; Chatterji, *India's Struggle*, 284ff; *Netaji Inquiry Committee Report*, Government of India, 1956; Government of India, *Report of the One-Man Commission of Inquiry into the Disappearance of Netaji Subhas Chandra Bose*, New Delhi: Government of India, 1974; Harin Shah, *Verdict from Formosa, Gallant End of Netaji Subhas Chandra Bose*, Delhi: Atma Ram, 1956; Tatsua Hayashida, *Netaji Subhas Chandra Bose*, Bombay: Allied, 1970. The interviews will be referred to individually. There are, of course, some writers who do not accept the death of Bose and their works have also been consulted. See, for example, Suresh Chandra Bose, *Dissentient Report*, 2nd ed., Kodalia: S.C. Bose, 1961, Samar Guha, *Netaji Dead or Alive?* New Delhi: S. Chand, 1978. No one can settle the question of Bose's death in the 1945 Taipei plane crash definitively, but the weight of evidence seems quite clear to me. Those who want to dispute this heavy weight of evidence and fantasize about his return will do so regardless of any account that I or anyone else produces. Their claims are usually based on emotion, not reason, and so any reasoning will not suffice. There is some confusion, but this was, after all, the week the war ended with the most catastrophic defeat in Japanese history. There had to be confusion.

160. Ayer, *Witness*, 56ff, describes some of these last actions.
161. Copied from a reproduction of the Singapore monument outside Netaji Bhavan, Calcutta.
162. Ayer, *Witness*, 62ff. Interview with T. Negishi, Tokyo, August 3, 1979. Khosla Commission Report.
163. Interview with T. Negishi, August 3, 1979. Also see the version in *Netaji Inquiry*, 14, where he is also quoted and other sources are mentioned.
164. See Rahman's account as told to Ayer not long after the event, in Ayer, *Witness*, 111–14. Also *Netaji Inquiry*, 17, which also interviewed Rahman in addition to the surviving Japanese officers.
165. Interview with Colonel Sakai, Tokyo, August 6, 1979.
166. Interview with Major Kono, August 4, 1979. Also see *Netaji Inquiry*, 17–18, for more details.
167. Interview with Colonel Nonogaki, Tokyo, July 25, 1979.
168. Interview with Major Kono, August 4, 1979.
169. Quoted in Ayer, *Witness*, 112–13. This also fits with the accounts in *Netaji Inquiry*, 19ff, and *Report of One-Man Commission*, 23ff, and my interviews with Major Kono, Colonel Sakai, and Colonel

Nonogaki.
170. *Showa*, 10, 30. The description comes from the entry under 'Myoo' in *The Kodansha Encyclopedia of Japan*, Vol. 5, Tokyo: Kodansha, 1983, 291: '*Myoo* were originally non-Buddhist Hindu deities who were adopted into the pantheon of esoteric Buddhism. They are considered to be incarnations of the cosmic Buddha who proselytize and save obdurate nonbelievers with the power of sacred words.
 Most of them are represented with fierce visages: hair aflame, face contorted, and weapons in hand, they trample evil figures. The deities have been especially popular in Japan, chiefly since the introduction of esoteric Buddhist traditions in the ninth century, and numerous artistic representations are extant. . .The most popular of the *myoo* is Fudo; the temple of Shinshoji (Naritasan) in Chiba Prefecture is the center of the Fudo cult.' The article is by Tsuchida Tomoaki.
171. The following details are from the interview with Dr Yoshimi, Takajo Machi, Kyushu Island, Japan, August 1, 1979.Also see *Netaji Inquiry*, 27–30; T.R. Sareen, ed., *Select Documents on Indian National Army*, Delhi: Agam Prakashan, 1988, 241–44, which reprints a 1946 interview with Dr Yoshimi.
172. *Netaji Inquiry*, quotation from Dr Yoshimi, 28.
173. Details from interview with Dr Yoshimi, August 1, 1979, and from *Netaji Inquiry*, 28–30. Also interview with Private Kazuo Mitsui, the orderly, Hakata, Japan, July 30, 1979. Mr Mitsui was also interviewed by the Shah Nawaz Commission.
174. Ayer, *Witness*, 114, quoting Rahman in September 1945, telling him of Bose's death.
175. There are different versions of the exact time of death. See *Netaji Inquiry*, 30, for a discussion of this. Also interview with Dr Yoshimi, August 1, 1979, and with Private Mitsui, who suggests 10 p.m., July 30, 1979. I went to the municipal office in Taipei, July 18, 1979, and talked to those then in charge. They insisted that the Japanese records no longer exist. Harin Shah was more successful, years earlier, in uncovering some details. See his *Verdict from Formosa*, *passim*.
176. For a discussion of the photography question and some other objections to the evidence, see the closely reasoned presentation in *Report of the One-Man Commission* (Khosla Commission), 28ff.
177. Ayer, *Witness*, 114. Also see Harin Shah, *Verdict from Formosa*, 106–113. I also visited what I believed to be the crematorium on July 18, 1979, but there are no records of that period.

178. Ayer, *Witness*, 79. Also see *Netaji Inquiry*, 30ff, which goes into this matter thoroughly. Mitra, *IAR*, I, 1945, 11, notes that the Japanese news agency spread the information on August 23. Chatterji, *India's Struggle*, 287, heard the news in Hanoi, but did not believe it.

179. Sarat Bose diary for 1945 in Netaji Research Bureau, entry for August 25, 1945.

180. Sarat Bose letter to Gita (Bose) Biswas, August 30, 1945.

181. Mitra, *IAR*, II, 1945, 11.

182. Details from interview with Lieutenant Tatsuo Hayshida, Hakata, Japan, July 30, 1979. Also interview with Colonel Tadao Sakai, Tokyo, August 6, 1979. See Ayer, *Witness*, 107ff.

183. Most of these details are from *Netaji Inquiry*, 45ff. Also see Ayer, *Witness*, XV. I visited the temple and shrine with General Fujiwara in 1979. Although Japanese officers including General Fujiwara long urged the Government of India to accept these ashes and take them back to India, the Government of India has not done so. They probably fear the outbursts of those few who say that Bose did not die and therefore there can be no ashes.

184. *Netaji Inquiry*, 33–34.

185. Sir John Figgess, letter to Leonard Gordon, September 20, 1979. He also wrote in the same letter, 'If there is any mystery surrounding his demise, it has been created and deliberately maintained, I believe, by certain interested parties in India.'

186. See Mansergh, *Transfer of Power*, VI, documents 57, 81, 109, 154, et al.. Some critics have pointed to the late date in this very set of documents when the Government of India finally accepted that Bose was dead. But, it was in the interest of the Government of India to be cautious and to make their own investigation. Once they were convinced that Bose was out of the way, they moved to deal with INA personnel. However, discussions about what to do with INA prisoners after the war had been going on for some time, even as the war raged. Also see Wavell, *Journal*, 164, where he suggests 'most careful enquiries' into the story of Bose's death before the government accept it.

187. See I.O.R, Government of India P&J/7542/45, Sarat Bose. Also Casey, Personal Diary, Vol.4, entry for September 10, 1945.

188. Mitra, *IAR*, II, 1945, 15-16.

189. Sarat Bose letter to Ajit Dey, December 14, 1944.

190. Mitra, *IAR*, II, 1945, 16.

191. Interview with General Seizo Arisue, Tokyo, August 4, 1979.

192. Based on discussions with many Japanese military officers of World
War II during July and August 1979 in Japan and also with philosophy professor Hajime Nakamura. There are, of course, numerous
works on the samurai in Japanese history and culture, for example,
H. Paul Varley, *Samurai*, New York: Delacorte Press, 1970. Bose's
willingness to confront death day-after-day also puts him with the
samurai.

CHAPTER TWELVE

1. *The Statesman*, April 24, 1947.
2. I.O.R, Government of India, L/WS/2/45, file on INA.
3. *A Passage to India*, New York: Harcourt Brace, 1952 [first published 1924], 19,23.
4. Quoted in Sir Francis Tuker, *While Memory Serves*, London: Cassell, 1950, 447.
5. *The Indian Annual Register*, I, 1946, 67.
6. Sarat Bose Diary for 1945 in Netaji Research Bureau.
7. Sarat Bose Diary 1945, June 30 entry.
8. See entries in Sarat Bose Diary 1945, October-December 1945,
where he had scheduled numerous meetings with Patel and others on
election matters. There are also numerous references in Durga Das,
ed., *Sardar Patel's Correspondence 1945–50*, II, Ahmedabad: Navajivan Publishing House, 1972, Chapters I, II, VI, X.
9. See the endless documentation in Nicholas Mansergh, ed., *The
Transfer of Power 1942–7*, Vol. V, London: Her Majesty's Stationery Office, 1974, *passim*.
10. Mansergh, *Transfer*, V, 1225.
11. The main work on the British approach, besides documents in the
Mansergh volumes, is R.J. Moore, *Escape from Empire: The Attlee
Government and the Indian Problem*, Oxford: Clarendon Press,
1983. Also valuable is Partha Sarathi Gupta, 'Imperial Strategy and
the Transfer of Power,' in Amit Kumar Gupta, ed., *Myth and
Reality: The Struggle for Freedom in India, 1945–47*, New Delhi:
Manohar, 1987, 7ff.
12. For Sarat Bose's view of the INA, see Sarat Chandra Bose, *I Warned
My Countrymen*, Calcutta: Netaji Research Bureau, 1968, 79, 92,
106, 126, 133, 148ff, 159, 175, 230, 235.
13. Bose, *I Warned My Countrymen*, 159.
14. The best account of the impact of the INA on the Indian political

scene is the final chapter, 'The I.N.A. in Indian Politics (1945–47),' in K.K. Ghosh, *The Indian National Army*, Meerut: Meenakshi Prakashan, 1969, 198ff.

15. *The Collected Works of Mahatma Gandhi*, Vol. LXXXI, 161, letter to Amrit Kaur, August 24, 1945.

16. See Gandhi's statements in *Collected Works*, Vol. LXXXII, 334, 391; Vol. LXXXIII, 339; Vol. LXXXIV, 186, article of May 22, 1946, where he records his view, that Bose really was dead (after meeting with Rahman).

17. *Collected Works*, Vol. LXXXIII, 135.

18. *Selected Works of Nehru*, Vol. 14, 279–80, report on speech of December 24, 1945.

19. Letter quoted in John Connell, *Auchinleck*, November 24, 1945, London: Cassell, 1959, 805.

20. Extracts from Desai's summation address in *Two Historic Trials in Red Fort*, ed., Moti Ram, New Delhi: Roxy Press, n.d., 154, 157.

21. *Two Historic Trials*, 265.

22. Connell, *Auchinleck*, 807–808.

23. Connell, *Auchinleck*, 808–809.

24. See Gautam Chattopadhyay, 'The Almost Revolution, A Case Study of India in February 1946,' in *Essays in Honour of Prof. S.C. Sarkar*, New Delhi: People's Publishing House, 1976, 427–50. Gautam Chattopadhyay has also written about these events in a somewhat different form in 'Bengal Students in Revolt against the Raj, 1945-46,' in Gupta, *Myth and Reality*, 152–71.

25. Chattopadhyay, 'Bengal Students in Revolt,' 155.

26. Interview with Aurobindo Bose, August 25, 1976. Gautam Chattopadhyay and other CPI men have told me that Sarat Bose's popularity with the students of Bengal plummeted in one moment on that November 1945 day and never rose high again. Also interview with Madhusudan Chakravarty, journalist, May 23, 1979, Calcutta, who said the same thing.

27. Bose, *I Warned My Countrymen*, 38.

28. Interview with Amiya Nath Bose, Calcutta, January 21, 1976; interview with Aurobindo Bose, Calcutta, August 25, 1976. The latter told me that representatives of all these groups met in Bombay in 1946, but no independent party or grouping was formed.

29. Tuker, *While Memory Serves*, 80.

30. See the excellent article on the mass movement dimension of politics at this time, Sucheta Mahajan, 'British Policy, Nationalist Strategy and Popular National Upsurge, 1945–46,' in Gupta, *Myth*

and Reality, 54–98.

31. Bose, *I Warned My Countrymen*, 25–26. The quotation marks in this interview from *Blitz* are very confusing and I have tried to regularize them in my extract here.

32. Bose, *I Warned My Countrymen*, 27.

33. Nehru, *Selected Works*, Vol. 14, 448.

34. Nehru, 'Rejoinder to Sarat Chandra Bose,' in *Selected Works*, Vol. 14, 446–47.

35. Bose, *I Warned My Countrymen*, 298.

36. Bose, *I Warned My Countrymen*, 107–108.

37. See Mitra, *IAR*, II, 1945, 112–22. Also see Nehru, *Selected Works*, Vol. 14, 259, 523–48.

38. See Nehru, *Selected Works*, Vol. 14, 544–45. In contrast to Gandhi and Patel, Nehru lamented that the communists were isolating themselves from the masses.

39. For example, see Nehru, *Selected Works*, Vol. 14, 455, where he insists that no Indian troops be used in Indonesia.

40. See Connell, *Auchinleck*, 823–25.

41. There are details in Bose, *I Warned My Countrymen*, 68–73.

42. From Sarat Bose letter to Shyama Prasad Mookerjee, November 12, 1945, in Bose, *I Warned My Countrymen*, 72.

43. *Return Showing the Results of Elections to the Central Legislative Assembly and the Provincial Legislatures in 1945–46*, New Delhi: Government of India Press, 1948, 13–15.

44. Sarat Bose letter to Sardar Patel, December 29, 1945, in *Patel's Correspondence*, Vol. 2, 384–85.

45. See *Jinnah-Ispahani Correspondence*, 467ff.

46. Mitra, *IAR*, I, 1946, 230–31, reports that the Congress won 86 seats, the Muslim League 113, the Hindu Mahasabha 1, the Scheduled Caste Federation 1, the Communist Party 3, Europeans 25, non-League Muslims 9, and Independents 12, for a total of 250 seats in the Bengal Legislative Assembly.

47. Interview with S.M. Ghosh, New Delhi, June 23, 1972.

48. Sen, *Muslim Politics*, 194–99. Also see Hashim, *In Retrospection*, 95ff.

49. Hashim, *In Retrospection*, 79. The strong leftist leanings of the family were continued by Hashim's son, the noted writer of East Pakistan, later Bangladesh, Badruddin Umar.

50. Hashim, *In Retrospection*, 45–6. Hashim goes on to describe Nazimuddin: 'Khwaja Nazimuddin was a perfect gentleman but very unfortunately he did not carry a head over his shoulder and a heart

within his breast.'

51. P.S. Mathur supplies many of these details in his article, 'Fall of Nazimuddin,' *Hindusthan Standard*, October 17, 1971, copy in manuscript supplied by the author. Mathur's description fits with that of many other contemporaries, British and Indian, of Suhrawardy.

52. See Gandhi's letter to Sarat Bose from Sodepur, December 3, 1945, in Gandhi, *Works*, Vol. LXXXII, 160–61.

53. These details are from an interview with Gita (Biswas) Bose, Calcutta, January 17, 1976.

54. Bose, *I Warned My Countrymen*, 101.

55. Bose, *I Warned My Countrymen*, 94–147, *passim*.

56. Details on this trip come from the account by Dina Nath, 'Burma—A Goodwill Visit,' in *Commemoration Volume*, 49–52.

57. *Commemoration Volume*, 57.

58. *Commemoration Volume*, 58.

59. On the cabinet see Sen, *Muslim Politics*, 210ff; also Hashim, *In Retrospection*, 107ff.

60. Mansergh, *The Transfer of Power*, VII, 263. This volume contains hundreds of pages of documents on the Mission. Moore gives an able account in *Escape from Empire*, 82ff.

61. Bose, *I Warned My Countrymen*, 154, from statement of April 21, 1946, issued in Calcutta.

62. Bose, *I Warned My Countrymen*, 133, statement to the press, March 21, 1946, New Delhi.

63. Bose, *I Warned My Countrymen*, 132–34.

64. H.V. Hodson, *The Great Divide: Britain-India-Pakistan*, London: Hutchinson, 1969, 145.

65. Jinnah's statement is in Mansergh, *Transfer of Power*, VII, 124.

66. Moore, *Escape from Empire*, 107–108.

67. At one point Gandhi consulted Sarat Bose as a legal expert on the meaning of grouping and Bose agreed with the Congress line that the grouping was not compulsory. See Gandhi, *Collected Works*, LXXXIV, 365n.

68. In Mansergh, *Transfer of Power*, VII, 458.

69. Sir W. Croft to Sir D. Montheath, Permanent Under-Secretary of State for India, May 3, 1946, in Mansergh, *Transfer of Power*, VII, 187.

70. Moore, *Escape from Empire*, 141.

71. Quoted in Richard D. Lambert, 'Hindu-Muslim Riots,' Ph.D. Dissertation in Sociology, University of Pennsylvania, 1951, 166.

Liaquat Ali Khan said that the League could not eliminate any method.

72. *Hindusthan Standard*, August 12, 1946, quoted in Lambert, 'Hindu-Muslim Riots,' 169.

73. Quoted in Lambert, 'Hindu-Muslim Riots,' 169–70.

74. Lambert, 'Hindu-Muslim Riots,' 171. Hashim insists that the Muslim League planned and expected no violence, *In Retrospection*, 113ff. His comments seem rather ingenuous, if truthful.

75. Lambert, 'Hindu-Muslim Riots,' 171.

76. Tuker, *While Memory Serves*, 155–56.

77. Lambert, 'Hindu-Muslim Riots,' 172ff; Tuker, *While Memory Serves*, 156ff. Also see Mitra, *IAR*, II, 1946, 182–94. Suranjan Das has recently published an article which contains some sharp, though abbreviated comments on the riot, 'Towards an Understanding of Communal Violence in Twentieth Century Bengal,' *Economic and Political Weekly*, August 27, 1988, 1804–8.

78. Lambert, 'Hindu-Muslim Riots,' 173.

79. Lambert, 'Hindu-Muslim Riots,' 173. Each side claimed that it was relatively innocent and had the worst of it. From the Muslim side, see Hashim, *In Retrospection*, 113ff, where he says that the Muslims suffered much more. Lambert's figures contradict this assertion.

80. Tuker, *While Memory Serves*, 163.

81. Mitra, *IAR,* II, 1946, 185.

82. Bose, *I Warned My Countrymen*, 155–57.

83. Interview with Subimal Dutt, Calcutta, August 25, 1976. Interview with Sir Arthur Dash, Ashford, Kent, April 21, 1972.

84. Tuker, *While Memory Serves*, 164.

85. Some of the interviewees were: B.K. Acharya, ICS; M.O. Carter, ICS; R.C. Dutt, ICS; Ajoy K. Ghosh, ICS; Sir P.J. Griffiths, ICS; J.L. Llewellyn, ICS; Peter N. McWilliam, ICS; L.G. Pinnell, ICS; Annada Sankar Ray, ICS; and A.W. Mahmood, who was in the Education Service. The political leaders included: Abul Mansur Ahmad, Santosh Kumar Basu, Tridib Chaudhuri, P.C. Ghosh, Surendra Mohan Ghosh, Samar Guha, Gopal Haldar, Abul Hashim, Jehangir Kabir, Hiren Mukherjee, Sasankar Sanyal, and P.C. Sen.

86. I wrote this sentence for my 1978 article, 'Divided Bengal,' and Suranjan Das, using fancier terminology, calls the same process 'psychological crystallisation' in his recent article, 'Communal Violence in...Bengal,' 1806.

87. Mitra, *IAR,* II, 1946, 19. On the controversy about including Sarat Bose, see Wavell, *Memoirs*, 295–96; Moore, *Escape from Empire*,

127–29; Mansergh, *Transfer of Power*, VII, 521, 523, 553, 560; Gandhi, *Collected Works*, LXXXIV, 344n.

88. Letter from Dr Sisir Bose, December 8, 1988. Further documentary work should be done on Sarat Bose's period as a minister.

89. Interview with S.M. Ghosh, New Delhi, July 4, 1972. Mr Ghosh said further that Nehru did not like Sarat Bose and neither did Acharya Kripalani, but they begrudgingly accepted him into the cabinet. When the first opportunity came to get rid of him, they leaped at the chance.

90. Tuker, Wh*ile Memory Serves*, 170–79. Lambert, 'Hindu-Muslim Riots,' 181–85.

91. Lambert, 'Hindu-Muslim Riots,' 162.

92. Lambert, 'Hindu-Muslim Riots,' 184, paraphrasing Kripalani.

93. Quoted in Lambert, 'Hindu-Muslim Riots,' November 24, 1946, 184.

94. Bose, *I Warned My Countrymen*, 164, statement of December 4, 1946, after returning from his tour.

95. Bose, *I Warned My Countrymen*, 167.

96. Interview with Jyotish Joarder, Calcutta, September 2, 1976.

97. Interview with Joarder, September 2, 1976. Also interviews with Aurobindo Bose, Calcutta, June 12, 1979, and H.V. Kamath, New Delhi, January 10, 1976.

98. Bose, *I Warned My Countrymen*, 161.

99. Bose, *I Warned My Countrymen*, 165.

100. See Tuker, *While Memory Serves*, 180ff; Lambert, 'Hindu-Muslim Riots,' 185ff.

101. Moore, *Escape from Empire*, 176–78.

102. Mansergh, *Transfer of Power*, IX, 295–96, statement of December 6, 1946.

103. Mitra, *IAR,* I, 1947, 26.

104. Bose, *I Warned My Countrymen*, 173–74.

105. Bose, *I Warned My Countrymen*, 173–74.

106. For Gandhi's relationship to crucial developments at this time, see Nirmal Kumar Bose, *Studies in Gandhism*, 3rd ed., Calcutta: Merit Publishers, 1962, 250ff. The most detailed study of Gandhi at this time is Pyarelal, *Mahatma Gandhi—The Last Phase*, 2 vols., Ahmedabad: Navajivan, 1956.

107. See the program as laid out in Bose, *I Warned My Countrymen*, 178–80.

108. Mansergh, *Transfer of Power*, IX, 774.

109. Many of the details here come from the very partisan sketch of

Mookerjee by Balraj Madhok in S.P. Sen, ed., *Dictionary of National Biography*, Vol. III, Calcutta: Institute of Historical Studies, 1974, 171–74. The last few sentences of this paragraph are my opinion and not that of Madhok, who stretches the truth past the breaking point in some details of this article.

110. Quoted in Mitra, *IAR*, I, 1947, 38.
111. Quoted in Mitra, *IAR*, I, 1947, 48.
112. Interview with S.M. Ghosh, New Delhi, June 26, 1972.
113. See Bose, 'On the Division of India,' in *I Warned My Countrymen*, 181–82; part is quoted in Mitra, *IAR*, I, 1947, 46. The statement is dated March 15, 1947.
114. This description of Mountbatten is based on my own interview with him, London, July 1, 1975, and some of the enormous literature which he had created to firmly establish his role in history: Philip Ziegler, *Mountbatten*, New York: Knopf, 1985; Alan Campbell-Johnson, *Mission with Mountbatten*, London: Robert Hale, 1951; Larry Collins and Dominique Lapierre, *Freedom at Midnight*, New York: Simon and Schuster, 1975. His weekly personal reports are in the India Office Library and Records, L/PO/433. Mountbatten's Personal Reports, April-August 1947. He also narrated his own life story in a multi-part television series. Though concerned to do the job well, he also wanted his role in history fully and positively portrayed.
115. See Mountbatten's note on his close friendship to Nehru in his report of May 15. Nehru also developed an intimate friendship with Lady Mountbatten which Ziegler has described with tact in *Mountbatten*, 472–76.
116. Interview with Lord Mountbatten, London, July 1, 1975.
117. Interview with Mountbatten, July 1, 1975.
118. Mountbatten's vivid account of his talks with Jinnah is in his reports of April 9 and 17, 1947.
119. Mountbatten's report of April 17, 1947, I.O.L.
120. Mountbatten's personal report of May 1, 1947.
121. Quoted in Mitra, *IAR*, I, 1947, 45.
122. See Mountbatten's account in his personal report of May 1, 1947.
123. Hodson, *Great Divide*, 245-47, 274-77.
124. Mountbatten, personal report of May 1, 1947.
125. Mountbatten, personal report of May 1, 1947. In my July 1, 1975 conversation with Mountbatten, he mentioned that he knew then that he was creating two Pakistans, not one, though he did not like the idea of even one. And he told Rajagopalachari in 1947 that he did not

think that the union of the two wings of Pakistan would last twenty-five years. When Bangladesh was formed in 1971, Mountbatten said that Rajagopalachari remembered the Viceroy's 1947 remarks and commented on it.

126. A partisan, but interesting inside account is provided by P.S. Mathur, then deputy press officer in the Bengal Government, in his article, 'Sovereign·Bengal,' August 2 and 3, 1971, *Hindusthan Standard*, Calcutta. I have used a typed copy provided for me by Mr Mathur and also drawn on an interview with him, July 26, 1973, Calcutta.

127. Mathur in·'Sovereign Bengal,' 58, quoting Altaf Hussain.

128. Quoted in Mathur, 'Sovereign Bengal,' 59.

129. Details of the press conference from Mathur, 'Sovereign Bengal,' 59-61.

130. See Gandhi's comments in Pyarelal, *Gandhi—the Last Phase*, Vol. II, 182. For example, see Mountbatten's view of Suhrawardy and how he was gradually becoming more statesman-like, in Mountbatten's personal report, May 15, 1947.

131. Quoted in Mathur, 'Sovereign Bengal,' 61.

132. Mathur, 'Sovereign Bengal,' 58–63.

133. There are a number of accounts of this incident, for example, Collins and Lapierre, *Freedom at Midnight*, 159ff. Also see Moore, *Escape from Empire*, 259ff.

134. Quoted in Collins and Lapierre, *Freedom at Midnight*, 161.

135. See Hashim's account, *In Retrospection*, 134ff. Some relevant documents are in Bose, *I Warned My Countrymen*, 183ff. Also see Pyarelal, *Gandhi—The Last Phase*, Vol. II, 176–90.

136. See Bose, *I Warned My Countrymen*, 188–90.

137. Gandhi's letter reprinted in Bose, *I Warned My Countrymen*, 190. It was written from Patna.

138. *Patel's Correspondence 1945-50*, IV, 44.

139. Bose's entire letter is in *Patel's Correspondence 1945-50*, IV, 45–46.

140. See AICC Files, Bengal Partition Papers, CL–14C, CL–21, Nehru Memorial Library.

141. *Statesman*, April 22, 1947.

142. *Statesman*, April 24, 1947.

143. Interview with Tushar Kanti Ghosh, editor of the *Amrita Bazar Patrika*, Calcutta, June 12, 1979. This survey is also noted in Bengal Governors' Reports, 1947. India Office Library, L/P & J/5/154, Burrows to Mountbatten, May 11, 1947.

144. Moore, *Escape from Empire*, 285–86.
145. Interview with Mountbatten, July 1, 1957.
146. Mountbatten's personal report, June 5, 1947.
147. The statement is printed in full in Mansergh, *Transfer of Power*, XI, 89–94.
148. Mansergh, *Transfer of Power*, XI, 90.
149. Speech in Mansergh, *Transfer of Power*, XI, 95–96.
150. Gandhi's letter is printed in Pyarelal, *Gandhi—The Last Phase*, Vol. II, 187—88.
151. Telegram in Pyarelal, *Gandhi—The Last Phase*, Vol. II, 188.
152. Sarat Bose's letter reprinted in Pyarelal, *Gandhi—The Last Phase*, Vol. II, 188.
153. Bose, *I Warned My Countrymen*, 195.
154. Bose, *I Warned My Countrymen*, 198–99.
155. Mansergh, *The Transfer of Power*, XI, 93.
156. See Mitra, *IAR*, I, 1947, 5, 12; Hashim, *In Retrospection*, 162; *PBLA*, June 20, 1947.
157. This statement is quoted in Balraj Madhok's article on Mookerjee in *Dictionary of National Biography*, III, 173.
158. Bengal Governors' Reports for the second half of June, July, and early August give an idea of the responses to the votes and the sentiments of the different communities.
159. Interview with S.M. Ghosh, New Delhi, June 26, 1972.
160. See Mitra, *IAR*, I, 1947, 74. Also Bengal Governors' Reports for first half of June, July, and second half of July.
161. See Mountbatten's personal reports of June 12, June 27, July 4, and July 11.
162. See Government of India, Legislative Department, Reforms, *Report of the Bengal Boundary Commission: Partition Proceedings*, Vol. VI, Bengal, August 17, 1947, contains the very different reports and pleadings of the Muslim and non-Muslim members. A similar report was prepared by Lord Radcliffe on the Punjab. Also see Hodson, *Great Divide*, 332ff.
163. Mountbatten's personal report of June 12, 1947.
164. Nirmal Kumar Bose, *Lectures on Gandhism*, Ahmedabad: Navajivan, 1971, 111.
165. Bose, *I Warned My Countrymen*, 201.
166. Bose, *I Warned My Countrymen*, 203–204.
167. Mountbatten, personal report of August 16, 1947.
168. Mountbatten, personal report of August 16, 1947.

Chapter THIRTEEN

1. *Waiting for the Barbarians*, New York: Penguin Books, 1982, 143.
2. In *The Penguin Book of Modern Urdu Poetry*, trans. Mahmood Jamal, Middlesex, England: Penguin Books, 1986, 31.
3. See Mountbatten's account of his recruitment of Gandhi, in Larry Collins and Dominique Lapierre, *Mountbatten and Independent India: 16 August 1947–18 June 1948*, New Delhi: Tarang Paperbacks, 1985, 37ff. Dennis Dalton has written an excellent account of Gandhi during this period, 'Gandhi during Partition: A Case Study in the Nature of Satyagraha,' in C.H. Philips and Mary Doreen Wainwright, eds., *The Partition of India: Policies and Perspectives 1935–1947*, London: Allen and Unwin, 1970, 222–244.
4. For an excellent, though now somewhat dated, account of West Bengal, see Marcus F. Franda, 'Political Development in West Bengal,' in his *Political Development and Political Decay in Bengal*, Calcutta: Firma K.L. Mukhopadhyay, 1971, 1ff. This essay was first published in Myron Weiner, ed., *State Politics in India*, Princeton: Princeton U. Press, 1968, 247–320. A recent and valuable collection of essays is Rakhahari Chatterji, ed., *Politics in West Bengal*, Calcutta: The World Press, 1985.
5. On the push away from socialism at the center, see Sarvepalli Gopal, *Jawaharlal Nehru: A Biography*, Vol. Two, 1947–1956, Delhi: Oxford U. Press, 1979, 34. Sarker has entered the story many times before during the 1920s and 1930s when he was finance minister in Fazlul Huq's first cabinet from 1937 to 1939.
6. A valuable account of all of these developments from inside the Dr B.C. Roy team is Saroj Chakrabarty, *My Years with Dr B.C. Roy*, Calcutta: Sree Saraswati Press, 1982, 7ff. There are also valuable documents and accounts in Pulinbihari Sen, et al., eds., *Towards a Prosperous India: Speeches and Writings of Bidhan Chandra Roy*, Calcutta: Sri Gouranga Press, 1964.
7. Chakrabarty, *My Years with Dr. B.C. Roy*, 79–80.
8. For a detailed account of opposition politics in this period, see the excellent study by Myron Weiner, *Party Politics in India*, Princeton: Princeton U. Press, 1957. On the leftist parties, 25ff.
9. Quoted in Overstreet and Windmiller, *Communism in India*, 272, where they give a detailed account of this shift, 252ff.
10. See Chakrabarty, *My Years with Dr. B.C. Roy*, 69; Overstreet and Windmiller, *Communism in India*, 277.

11. Bose, *I Warned My Countrymen*, 244.
12. Editorial in *The Nation*, September 3, 1948. The paper began just a few days earlier as will be explained below.
13. Bose, *I Warned My Countrymen*, 219.
14. Bose, *I Warned My Countrymen*, 231–32. Sarat Bose said these words in a speech at the opening ceremony of the Hindi daily *Netaji*, at New Delhi, April 13, 1948.
15. From a statement issued by Sarat Bose, September 12, 1948, and reprinted in Bose, *I Warned My Countrymen*, 254.
16. Many of these details come from an interview with J.N. Ghosh, Calcutta, January 19, 1976.
17. This first editorial is reprinted in Bose, *I Warned My Countrymen*, 237–39.
18. This speech is reprinted in Bose, *I Warned My Countrymen*, 219–30, and the quotations come from 221 and 227.
19. Bose, *I Warned My Countrymen*, 233.
20. Bose, *I Warned My Countrymen*, 261–64
21. Bose, *I Warned My Countrymen*, 215–18, 261–64, 298–303. Also see Parimal Kumar Das, *India and the Vietnam War*, New Delhi: Young Asia Publications, 1972, 20ff; for the Nehru perspective, see Gopal, *Nehru*, Vol. Two, 43ff.
22. These details and many of the following ones come from an interview with Roma (Bose) Roy, Calcutta, August 10, 1977.
23. Interviews with Emilie Schenkl, April 29, 1965 and October 14, 1978. The Netaji Research Bureau has reproduced copies of Subhas Bose's 1943 letter to his brother. Sisir Kumar Bose has also written about this visit in his recent, *Remembering My Father: A Centenary Offering, Sarat Chandra Bose 1889-1989*, Calcutta: Netaji Research Bureau, 1988, 163.
24. Interview with Roma (Bose) Roy, August 10, 1977.
25. Details from interview with Roma (Bose) Roy, August 10, 1977.
26. Interview with Roma (Bose) Roy, August 10, 1977. This is also based on my talks with Emilie Schenkl and my impression about her devotion to her privacy. Asoke Bose also discusses the possibility of Emilie Schenkl and Anita living in India which was his father's wish, in *My Uncle Netaji*, 220–21.
27. Interview with Roma (Bose) Roy, August 10, 1977, and with Emilie Schenkl, April 29, 1965. The latter was dubious about the air crash story, but said that she was gradually convinced that he was dead. Sarat Bose, according to his daughter, believed the first story of the crash, then doubted it, then came to believe before his death that

Subhas was dead. 'If he is alive,' Sarat Bose is reported to have said, 'he would have sent me news.'

28. Details are from Sisir Bose, *Remembering My Father,* 158, 163–64.

29. Bose, *Remembering My Father,* 158, 163.

30. Details from Sisir Bose, *Remembering My Father,* 163–64. Sarat Bose wrote to President Sean O'Kelly on December 23, 1948, thanking him for the cordial reception he received, recalling the proclamation of the Irish Republic as long ago as 1916, and promising to send him *The Nation.* A hand-written copy of this letter is in the Netaji Research Bureau.

31. Weiner, *Party Politics,* 139ff.

32. Weiner, *Party Politics,* 140.

33. See Chakrabarty, *My Years with Dr. B.C. Roy,* 41ff; Weiner, *Party Politics,* 141; Bose, *Remembering My Father,* 172; and Bose, *I Warned My Countrymen,* 276ff.

34. Bose, *I Warned My Countrymen,* 278–81.

35. Chakrabarty, *My Years with Dr. B.C. Roy,* 41.

36. Quoted in Chakrabarty, *My Years with Dr. B.C. Roy,* 42.

37. Chakrabarty, *My Years with Dr. B.C. Roy,* 41–2, 46.

38. Chakrabarty, *My Years with Dr. B.C. Roy,* 42–48.

39. Chakrabarty, *My Years with Dr. B.C. Roy,* 50,

40. Chakrabarty, *My Years with Dr. B.C. Roy,* 51ff. S.M. Ghosh mentioned to me, in an interview in New Delhi, June 26, 1972, that he wanted to continue one Congress organization for all of Bengal, even with partition, but eventually this had to be abandoned.

41. Sarat Bose letter to Sisir Bose, May 6, 1949.

42. Emilie Schenkl to Sisir Bose, August 3, 1949.

43. Bose, *Remembering My Father,* 172.

44. Letter to Sisir Bose, July 31, 1949.

45. Bose, *I Warned My Countrymen,* 282.

46. Bose, *I Warned My Countrymen,* 283–91.

47. Bose, *Remembering My Father,* 174.

48. Bose, *I Warned My Countrymen,* 304–305.

49. Bose, *I Warned My Countrymen,* 301–303.

50. Bose, *I Warned My Countrymen,* 313. Weiner, *Party Politics,* 141ff, has placed this whole process in context and given a good idea of 'the practical difficulties'.

51. Weiner, *Party Politics,* 147.

52. This quotation is from Sarat Bose letter to Sisir Bose, December 23, 1949, and the information in this paragraph also draws on letters of November 14 and December 17 of Sarat Bose to Sisir Bose.

53. Bose, *I Warned My Countrymen*, 294.
54. Bose, *I Warned My Countrymen*, 333ff, has a reprint of the article.
55. Bose, *I Warned My Countrymen*, 342.
56. Bose, *I Warned My Countrymen*, 340.
57. Bose, *I Warned My Countrymen*, 343.
58. Chakrabarty, *My Years with Dr. B.C. Roy*, 70ff.
59. Sarat Bose, press statement of February 11, 1950, reprinted in Bose, *I Warned My Countrymen*, 350.
60. Bose, *I Warned My Countrymen*, 350.
61. Interview with Roma (Bose) Roy, August 10, 1977.
62. Bose, *I Warned My Countrymen*, 351.
63. On the end of the United Socialist Organization, see Weiner, *Party Politics*, 147-63. On the fate of *The Nation*, interview with J.N. Ghosh, Calcutta, January 19, 1976.
64. In a letter to the *Indian Observer*, January 31, 1964, K. Pratihar, Midnapore, writes, 'It has been proved incontrovertibly that the father of Miss Anita is one Colonel Brigette. Sri Sarat Bose. . . once wrote a very strong letter to Sri Nehru for fabricating this dirty lie against Netaji. . . Shri Dwijen Bose, a nephew of Netaji, had asserted on oath in the Court of the Chief Presidency Magistrate, Calcutta, that Netaji never married.'
65. *Amrita Bazar Patrika*, April 24, 1946.
66. *Amrita Bazar Patrika*, April 25, 1946.
67. Bose, *Dissentient Report*, 98–101, 179.
68. Bose, *Dissentient Report*, 125ff.
69. With the help of a Bengali friend, Pradip Sen, I collected copies of many issues of these papers from 1963 to 1965 and a few from earlier years. These are used in reconstructing the Subhasbadi Janata version of Subhas Bose's life since 1945 presented below.
70. Interview with S.M. Ghosh, New Delhi, June 21, 1972. Ghosh was much more involved in this affair than I have suggested here. He had known Satya Gupta for a long time and had been sorting out stories about Bose for years. He claimed that he had an arrangement with Nehru to inform him immediately if he believed that the sadhu was, indeed, Bose.
71. *Mahabharat*, No. 6.
72. *Mahabharat*, No. 3.
73. The idea of Bose having curative powers appears in a number of instances. For example, there is the story reported by the *Amrita Bazar Patrika*, May 5, 1946, about one Dr Bidhu Bhushan Roy of Cuttack, a former INA doctor, who told of five dysentery patients

dying in spite of the best medical aid. They craved Netaji's touch, he said, and when he gave it, they got a new lease of life. 'Referring to the epic story of Netaji and INA's burning faith in his super-human powers Major Roy said, while in charge of a block hospital in Rangoon and later in forward Field Hospitals in Prome and Mague, he was simply surprised how dying soldier patients from Imphal Front used to be saved [by] the magic touch of Netaji, who was regarded like a god-head.'

74. *Shaulmari,* No. 1; *Mahabharat,* No. 2; 'Netaji is Coming,' pamphlet published by the Subhasbadi Janata, 1966?

75. 'Netaji is Coming,' *passim.*

76. 'Netaji is Coming,' 28,33; *Mahabharat,* Nos. 7, 11, 13; *Shaulmari,* No. 1.

77. 'Two Documents,' published by Shaulmari Ashram, 1965?

78. *Mahabharat,* No. 8.

79. I was with my friend David McCutchion and suggested to him at the time that he had this staged for my benefit, but he had not.

80. This particular version of the Russian imprisonment story was told to me by Dr R. Madan, interview in New Delhi, September 5, 1977. A more elaborate version is that put forth by Satyanarayan Sinha in his book, *Netaji Mystery,* Calcutta: Prakash Chandra Saha, 1965, and in a series of articles in the *Hindusthan Standard,* January 26, February 14 and 21, and March 28, 1965. Sinha says that Bose was held in Yakutsk Prison in Siberia.

81. Khosla Commission, *Report,* 106.

82. *Times of India,* March 9, 1978.

83. *Times of India,* March 9, 1978.

84. Samar Guha, *Netaji: Dead or Alive?* Delhi: S. Chand, 1978. For example, Colonel Nonogaki, Tokyo, July 25, 1979; Dr Yoshimi, Kyushu, August 1, 1979; and, Major Kono, Tokyo, August 4, 1979, are among those to whom I read out passages from this book and had them directly contradicted. Guha also has the geography of the airfield at Taiwan wrong. More accurate versions of interviews with the relevant witnesses detailing the last days and hours of Bose's life are presented in the reports of the Shah Nawaz and Khosla Commissions.

85. Khosla Commission, *Report,* 122.

86. Published by Pantheon Books, New York, 1975.

87. There have been a variety of myths of return in many cultures. A famous one was the myth of Frederick Barbarossa, which is spelled out in Chapter I, 'The Kyffhauser Legend,' inPeter Munz, *Frederick*

Barbarossa: A Study in Medieval Politics, Ithaca: Cornell U. Press, 1969. There is an Islamic myth about the twelfth imam, as well.

88. In the early 1960s, Marcus Franda conducted a study of attitudes of employed and unemployed young men in the Calcutta area. Of about hundred, around thirty percent named Subhas Bose as the greatest Indian, living or dead. From his interview material with these young men, Franda suggested to me that those choosing Bose tended to be the more religious ones. They often mentioned Bose's self-sacrifice for the country as especially appealing. All of these young men were too young to have had any personal contact with Bose. Personal communication from Marcus Franda.

89. R. Shamasastry, ed. and trans., *Kautilya's Arthasastra*, 6th ed., Mysore: Mysore Publishing House, 1960, 10–12. There are numerous versions of the *Ramayana* in every Indian language, e.g., Makhan Lal Sen, trans., *The Ramayana: A Modernized Version in English Prose*, Calcutta: Firma KLM, 1976. Through the Ram Lila performances, this epic is very alive today. See N. Hein, 'The Ram Lila,' in Milton Singer, ed., *Traditional India: Structure and Change*, Philadelphia: American Folklore Society, 1959, 279–304.

90. J.A.B. van Buitenen, 'The Indian Hero as a Vidyadhara,' in *Traditional India: Structure and Change*, ed., Milton Singer, Philadelphia: American Folklore Society, 1959, 99–105.

CONCLUSIONS

1. Interview with Roma (Bose) Roy, August 10, 1977.
2. Interview with Chapala Kanta Bhattacharya, Calcutta, May 19, 1979.
3. From Surendranath Banerjea's 1895 presidential address to the Congress, in Stephen Hay, ed., *Sources of Indian Tradition*, Vol. Two, 2nd ed., New York: Columbia U. Press, 1988, 101.

Selective Bibliography

The bibliography is arranged under the following main headings:

I. Primary Sources
   A. Manuscript Collections
   B. Official Records and Reports
   C. Newspapers and Periodicals
   D. Interviews
   E. Other works

II. Secondary Works
   A. Books, Articles, Unpublished Theses and Papers
   B. Reference Works

I. Primary Sources

A. Manuscript Collections

All-India Congress Committee Files, 1927-47. Jawaharlal Nehru Memorial Library, New Delhi.

All-India Hindu Mahasabha Files, 1935-47. Jawaharlal Nehru Memorial Library, New Delhi.

All-India Muslim League Files. Karachi University Library (xerox copy), Karachi.

Anderson Papers (Sir John). India Office Library, London.

Bose, Subhas and Sarat Chandra, Papers. Netaji Research Bureau, Calcutta.

Casey, Sir Richard, Collection. India Office Library, London.

Dharmavir Papers, Jawaharlal Nehru Memorial Library, New Delhi.

Hasan, Syed Shamsul, Collection, Karachi. With the permission of Khalid Shamsul Hasan.

Oral History Transcripts. Jawaharlal Nehru Memorial Library, New Delhi.

Roy, M.N., Papers. Indian Renaissance Institute, Dehradun, and Jawaharlal Nehru Memorial Library, New Delhi.

Singh Roy, Sir B.P., Collection. Jawaharlal Nehru Memorial Library, New Delhi.

Zetland Collection. India Office Library, London.

B. Official Records and Reports

Governments of India and of Bengal:

Bamford, P.C., *Histories of the Non-Co-Operation and Khilafat Movements*, Delhi: Government of India Press, 1925 [reprinted, Delhi: Deep Publications, 1974].

Government of Bengal, Appointments Department, Reforms. *Report on the Working of the Reformed Constitution in Bengal 1921–27.* Calcutta, 1929.

Government of Bengal, Bengal Legislative Assembly. *Proceedings.* Calcutta, 1937-47.

Government of Bengal, Bengal Legislative Council. *Proceedings.* Calcutta, 1912-47.

Government of Bengal. *Governor's Fortnightly Reports,* 1936-47.

Government of Bengal, Home Department. *Report of the Reforms Office, Bengal 1932-1937.* R.N. Gilchrist, ed., Calcutta, 1938.

Government of India, Home Department. *Political Proceedings and Files,* 1907-45.

Government of India. *Census of India.* Volumes for Bengal and for Calcutta, 1872, 1881, 1901, 1911, 1921, 1931, 1951.

Government of India, Famine Inquiry Commission. *Final Report* and *Report on Bengal.* Delhi: Government of India Press, 1945.

Government of India, Home Department, Political. *India and Communism.* Simla, 1933.

Government of India, Judicial and Public. *Proceedings,* 1919-45.

Government of India, Legislative Department, (Reforms). *Report of the Bengal Boundary Commission: Partition Proceedings,* Vol. VI. Bengal, August 17, 1947.

Government of India. *Netaji Inquiry Committee Report.* Government of India, 1956.

Government of India. *Report of the One-Man Commission of Inquiry into the Disappearance of Netaji Subhas Chandra Bose.* New Delhi: Government of India, 1974.

Government of India, Sedition Committee. *Report.* Calcutta, 1918.

Hale, H.W., *Political Trouble in India 1917-37,* Government of India, Intelligence Bureau, Home Department [reprinted, Allahabad: Chugh Publications, 1974].

Kaye, Sir Cecil, *Communism in India 1919-1924,* Government of India, Intelligence Bureau, 1925 [reprinted, Calcutta: Editions Indian, 1971].

Ker, James Campbell, *Political Trouble in India 1907-1917,* Calcutta: Government Printing, 1917 [reprinted, Delhi: Oriental Publishers, 1973].

Mansergh, Nicholas, ed., *The Transfer of Power 1942-7,* 12 vols., London: Her Majesty's Stationery Office, 1970-83.

Petrie, Sir David, *Communism in India 1924-1927,* Government of India, Intelligence Bureau, 1927 [reprinted, Calcutta: Editions Indian, 1972].

Secretary of State for India, Committee on Indian Students in the United Kingdom. *Report, 1907 and 1921.* London, 1922.

Williamson, Sir Horace, *Communism in India,* Government of India, Intelligence Bureau, 1933 [reprinted, Calcutta: Editions Indian, 1976].

German government records:

German Foreign Office records, 1933-45. Foreign Office Archives, Bonn.

Japanese government records:

Japanese Foreign Ministry records, 1941-45. Foreign Ministry Archives, Tokyo. Diaries of Japanese Military Officers in Second World War. War Archives, Tokyo.

C. Newspapers and Periodicals

Amrita Bazar Patrika, Calcutta.
Azad Hind, Berlin.
Bombay Chronicle, Bombay.
Calcutta Municipal Gazette, Calcutta.
Forward, Calcutta.
Hindusthan Standard, Calcutta.
Independent India, Delhi.
Liberty, Calcutta.
The Modern Review, Calcutta.
The Nation, Calcutta.
The Oracle, Calcutta.

Presidency College Magazine, Calcutta.
Scottish Churches College Magazine, Calcutta.
The Statesman, Calcutta.
The Times, London.

D. Interviews

Ahmad, Abul Mansur, political worker and writer. Dacca, May 31, 1972, August 15, 1977.
Ali, Aruna Asaf, political worker. Delhi, January 5, 1976.
Arisue, General Seizo, in charge of Japanese military intelligence, 1943-45. Tokyo, August 4, 1979.
Athinahappan, Puan Sri Datin Janaki, Rani of Jhansi Regiment, INA. Kuala Lumpur, July 6, 1979.
Ayyub, Abu Sayyid, writer and editor. Calcutta, November 24, 1972.
Bakshi, Satya Ranjan, political worker. Calcutta, July 17 and November 14, 1964, September 28, 1966.
Banerji, J.K., political worker and writer. London and New York, October 3, 1963, August 1, 1965, December 29, 1965, January 29, 1966, December 27, 1975, November 9, 1978.
Basu, Jyoti, communist political leader. Calcutta, July 15, 1973.
Basu, Santosh Kumar, political worker. Calcutta, November 28, 1972.
Basu, Sudangshu, journalist. Calcutta, August 24, 1977.
Bhattacharya, Chapala Kanta, journalist. Calcutta, May 19, 1979.
Bhupalan, Mrs, Rani of Jhansi Regiment, INA. Kuala Lumpur, July 10, 1979.
Biswas, Gita (Bose), daughter of Sarat Bose. Calcutta, January 17, 1976.
Bose, Amiya Nath, son of Sarat Bose. Calcutta, January 21, 1976 and Rangoon, June 28, 1979.
Bose, Aurobindo, son of Suresh Bose. Calcutta, August 25, 1976.
Bose, Dwijen, son of Satish Bose. Calcutta, August 22, 1977.
Bose, Ranajit, son of Suresh Bose. Calcutta, January 22, 1987.
Bose, Sailesh, brother of Subhas and Sarat Bose. Bombay, December 30, 1964 and Dacca, May 28, 1972.
Bose, Sisir K., son of Sarat Bose. Calcutta, May 9 and 18, 1972, July 5, 1973, January 12 and 15, 1976.
Carter, Malcolm O., ICS. Bristol, England, August 23, 1971.
Chakravarty, Madhusudan, journalist. Calcutta, May 23, 1979.
Chattopadhyay, Gautam, scholar and political activist in CPI. Calcutta, December 21, 1978, February 5, 1979.
Chaudhuri, Nirad C., former private secretary to Sarat Bose and relation

by marriage of the Boses. Delhi, May 17, 1964, Oxford, September 4, 1971, November 26, 1971, July 2, 1977, September 13, 1978.

Chaudhuri, Tridib Kumar, political worker. New Delhi, August 17, 1973.

Chawla, Narain Singh, Indian Independence League worker. Bangkok, July 2, 1979.

Chidambaran, Mrs M.K., Rani of Jhansi Regiment, INA. Singapore, July 13, 1979.

Chunder, Praṭap Chandra, son of Nirmal C. Chunder, political worker. Calcutta, July 31, 1973.

Das, Mrs C.R. (Basanti Devi), political worker and friend of Subhas Bose. Calcutta, 1965.

Dash, Sir Arthur, ICS. Ashford, Kent, England, April 21, 1972.

Dey, Ajit, brother-in-law of Sarat Bose. Calcutta, August 20, 1977.

Dhillon, Col. G.S., INA. Calcutta, January 25, 1976.

Dutt, Rabindra Chandra, ICS in pre-partition period. New Delhi, August 8, 1973.

Dutt, Rajani Palme, general secretary of Communist Party of Great Britain. London, November 5, 1965.

Dutt, Subimal, ICS in pre-partition period. Calcutta, August 25, 1976.

Dutt-Mazumdar, Niharendu, political worker. Calcutta, July 28, 1973.

Dwivedy, S.N., political worker. New Delhi, August 17, 1976.

Frank, Lothar, friend of Subhas Bose in Germany. Wiesbaden, October 5, 1979.

Fujiwara, General Iwaichi, officer in charge of F-Kikan, liaison between Japanese Army and INA. Tokyo, August 6, 1979.

Gandhinathan, M., Indian Independence League worker. Kuala Lumpur, July 8, 1979.

Ganguli, Anil, Bose neighbor in Cuttack and junior of Sarat Bose at the Calcutta bar. Calcutta, August 24, 1977.

Ganguli, Charu Chandra, Bose neighbor in Cuttack and retired judge. Calcutta, July 15, 1973.

Ganguli, Santimoy, member of Bengal Volunteers. Calcutta, September 1, 1976.

Ghose, Surendra Mohan, ex-revolutionary and Congress leader. New Delhi, September 20 and 27, 1964, June 8, 16, 21, 26, July 4 and 23, and October 10, 1972, August 14, 1973.

Ghosh, Ajoy Kumar, ICS in pre-partition period. New Delhi, August 12, 1973.

Ghosh, Tushar Kanti, publisher, *Amrita Bazar Patrika*. Calcutta, June 12, 1979.

Griffiths, Sir P.J., ICS and European member of Bengal Legislative

Council. London, August 21, 1969.

Guha, Arun Chandra, political worker. New Delhi, August 9, 1973.

Guha, Samar, political worker. New Delhi, August 9, 1973.

Gupta, Indrajit, political worker for CPI. Calcutta, August 29, 1976.

Haldar, Gopal, writer and CPI activist. Calcutta, May 7, 1965, May 17, November 25, 1972, January 19, 1985.

Harbich, Walter, trainer of Indian Legion. Munich, October 12, 1979.

Hasan, Abid (Safrani), Indian Legion and INA. Calcutta, January 22 and 26, 1979.

Hashim, Abul, Muslim leader in Bengal. Dacca, May 30, 1972.

Hayashida, Tatsuo, carried Bose's ashes from Taiwan to Tokyo. Hakata, Japan, July 30, 1979.

Himatsingka, P.D., businessman and political worker. Calcutta, August 2, 1973.

Hutchings, Sir R.H., ICS. Lymington, England, September 13, 1971.

Joarder, Jyotish, leader of Bengal Volunteers. Calcutta, September 2, 1976.

Joshi, P.C., leader of CPI. New Delhi, February 6, 1965.

Kabir, Jehangir, Muslim political worker in Bengal. Calcutta, July 20, 1973.

Kabir, Shanti, widow of political worker Humayun Kabir. New Delhi, August 7, 1973.

Kamath, H.V., political worker. New Delhi, January 10, 1976.

Katakura, General Tadashi, Japanese officer in Burma campaign. Tokyo, August 2, 1979.

Khaitan, B.P., solicitor, businessman, political worker. Calcutta, July 23, 1973.

Khan, Anjoli, Bose family friend and relation of Debendra Lall Khan of Narajole, important Bose supporter. Calcutta, July 30, 1977.

Kono, Major Taro, Japanese military officer in Taiwan crash. Tokyo, August 4, 1979.

Kripalani, J.B., secretary of Congress during Subhas Bose's presidency and long-time Congressman. New Delhi, September 10, 1976.

Kundo, Sudhir, Sarat Bose masseur. Calcutta, May 19, 1979.

Lahiri, Somnath, political worker for CPI. Calcutta, January 27 and August 27, 1976.

Larkin, Alfred S., ICS. Eastbourne, England, August 18, 1972.

Llewellyn, J.L., ICS. London, February 2, 1972.

Lutz, Captain Wilhelm, trainer of Indian Legion in Germany. Stuttgart, October 8, 1978.

Madan, Dr R., Indian Legion. Delhi, September 2, 1977.

Mahmood, A.W., Muslim educator in Bengal. Calcutta, July 23, 1973.

Mahtani, S.T., Indian businessman who worked with Azad Hind government. Bangkok, July 1, 1979.

Mitra, Lila (Bose), daughter of Sunil Bose. Calcutta, February 15, 1979.

Mitra, N.C., Bose family solicitor. Calcutta, September 1, 1976.

Mitra, Pratima, niece of Sarat and Subhas Bose. Calcutta, June 6, 1979.

Mitsui, Kazuo, orderly at Bose's deathbed. Hakata, Japan, July 30, 1979.

Mookerjee, Freda, German Foreign Office in India Section. Bad Godesberg, West Germany, October 19, 1979.

Mookerjee, Girija, Free India Centre. New Delhi, January 23, 1965.

Mookerjee, I.P., younger colleague of Sarat Bose at the Calcutta bar. Calcutta, December 2, 1972.

Moon, Sir Penderel, ICS and scholar. Oxford, August 9, 1969.

Mountbatten, Earl, of Burma. London, July 1, 1975.

Mukherjee, Ajoy K., political leader in Bengal. Calcutta, July 19, 1973.

Mukherjee, Hirendranath, political worker for CPI. New Delhi, December 9, 1972.

Mukherjee, Vivekananda, journalist. Calcutta, August 2, 1973.

Nair, A.M., Indian nationalist in Japan. Tokyo, August 8, 1979.

Nambiar, A.C.N., Free India Centre. Zurich, July 5, 1975.

Nath, Dina, civilian worker for INA. Rangoon, June 28, 1979.

Negishi, T., Japanese translator for Subhas Bose in Southeast Asia. Tokyo, August 3, 1979.

Nonogaki, Colonel, Japanese military officer in Taiwan crash. July 25, 1979.

Pinnell, Leonard, ICS. Woking, July 22, 1969.

Puthucheary, J.J., Indian Independence League worker. Kuala Lumpur, July 9, 1979.

Rasul, Abdullah, political worker for CPI. Calcutta, July 30, 1973.

Ray, Annada Sankar, former ICS officer and writer. Calcutta, November 30, 1972.

Ray, Niharanjan, ex-revolutionary and scholar. New York, February 1, 1968.

Roxburgh, Sir T. J., ICS. London, July 18, 1969.

Roy, Meera (Bose), daughter of Sarat Bose. Calcutta, August 9, 1977.

Roy, Roma (Bose), daughter of Sarat Bose. Calcutta, August 10, 1977.

Sahgal, Colonel Lakshmi, leader of Rani of Jhansi Regiment, INA. January 23, 1979.

Sahgal, Colonel Prem, military secretary to Subhas Bose, INA. January 23, 1979.

Sakai, Colonel Tadao, Japanese military officer in Taiwan crash. Tokyo,

August 6, 1979.

Schenkl, Emilie, wife of Subhas Bose. Vienna, April 29, 1965, October 14, 1978.

Seifriz, Adalbert, trainer of Indian Legion. Stuttgart, October 9, 1979.

Sen, P.C., Congress political worker. Calcutta, August 2, 1973.

Sen, Santosh K., doctor and Subhas Bose's friend. New Delhi, January 8 and 28, 1976.

Sengupta, Shila (Bose), niece of Subhas and Sarat Bose. New Delhi, November 29, 1978.

Sharma, Balakrishna, Free India Centre. Vienna, October 16, 1978.

Siddhartananda, Swami, Ramakrishna Mission. Singapore, July 13, 1979.

Singh, Americk, spy for INA infiltrated into India. Kuala Lumpur, July 6, 1979.

Singh, Joginder, press officer for Provisional Government of Azad Hind. Singapore, July 12, 1979.

Singh, Mehervan, accountant for Provisional Government of Azad Hind. Singapore, July 11, 1979.

Singh, Colonel Mohan, organizer of first INA, outside Ludhiana, Punjab, March 7, 1979.

Singh Nirulla, Iswar, Indian Independence League worker. Bangkok, July 2, 1979.

Singh, Zora, civilian worker for INA. Rangoon, June 27, 1979.

Som, Aruna (Mitra), niece of Subhas and Sarat Bose. Calcutta, February 1979.

Soni, Dr R.L., Indian doctor for northern Burma under Japanese occupation. Mandalay, June 25, 1979.

Spies, Professor Otto, cultural adviser for Indian Legion. Bonn, October 4, 1979.

Stephens, Ian, journalist. Cambridge, September 17, 1971.

Thein, U. Myint, contemporary of Subhas Bose at Cambridge. Rangoon, June 28, 1979.

Trott zu Solz, Clarita von, widow of Adam von Trott zu Solz, key German Foreign Office official dealing with Subhas Bose. Berlin, August 5, 1984.

Vetter, Mrs Naomi, friend of Subhas Bose. Vienna, April 30, 1965.

Walker, R.L., ICS. East Grinstead, England, August 17, 1971.

Wilkinson, H.R., ICS. Hadlow Down, England, August 25, 1972.

Yamaguchi, Major Gento, member of F-Kikan. Kyoto, July 30, 1979.

Yoshimi, Dr Taneyoshi, doctor who treated Subhas Bose in Taiwan, August 1945. Takajo Machi, Kyushu Island, Japan, August 1979.

E. Other Works

Adhikari, G.D., 'Pakistan and National Unity,' 3rd ed., Bombay: People's Publishing House, 1944.

Adhikari, G.D., ed., *Documents of the History of the Communist Party of India*, Vol. One, 1917-1922; Vol. Two, 1923-1925; Vol. III, A, 1926, B, 1927, C, 1928, New Delhi: People's Publishing House, 1971-82.

Ahmad, Abul Mansur, *Amar dekha rajnitir panchasa bachar* [Fifty Years of Politics as I Saw It], 3rd ed., Dacca: Nauroj, 1975.

Ayer, S.A. *Unto Him a Witness*, Bombay: Thacker, 1951.

Azad, Maulana Abul Kalem, *India Wins Freedom*, Bombay: Orient Longman, 1959.

Aziz, K.K., ed., *Muslims under Congress Rule 1937-1939: A Documentary Record,* 2 vols., Islamabad: National Commission on Historical and Cultural Research, 1978.

Ba Maw, *Breakthrough in Burma*, New Haven: Yale U. Press, 1968.

Banerjea, Surendranath, *A Nation in Making*, Bombay: Oxford U. Press, 1963 [reprint of 1925 edition].

Banerji, Nripendra Chandra, *At the Crossroads (1885-1946)*, Calcutta: Jijnasa, [1974 reprint].

Bengal Anti-Communal Award Movement. A Report. Calcutta: n.p., 1939.

Bengal Provincial Congress Committee. *Working Committee and Bengal Congress*. Calcutta: BPCC, 1940.

Bhargava, Moti Lal and Americk Singh Gill, *Indian National Army—Secret Service*, New Delhi: Reliance Publishing, 1988.

Birla, G.D., *In the Shadow of the Mahatma*, Bombay: Orient Longman, 1953.

Bose, Asoke Nath, *My Uncle Netaji*, Calcutta: Esem, 1977.

Bose, Nirmal, *My Days with Gandhi*, Calcutta: A. Chatterjee, 1953.

Bose, Pradip, *Growing Up in India*, Calcutta: Minerva, 1972.

Bose, Sarat Chandra, *I Warned My Countrymen*, Calcutta: Netaji Research Bureau, 1968.

Bose, Sisir K., *Remembering My Father: A Centenary Offering*, Calcutta: Netaji Research Bureau, 1988.

Bose, Sisir K., *The Great Escape*, Calcutta: Netaji Research Bureau, 1975.

Bose, Sisir K., ed., *The Voice of Sarat Chandra Bose*, Calcutta: Netaji Bhavan, 1979.

Bose, Subhas Chandra, 'The Austrian Riddle,' *The Modern Review*, Calcutta, April 1934, 461-68.

Bose, Subhas Chandra, 'The Secret of Abyssinia and Its Lesson,' *The*

Modern Review, Calcutta, November 1935, 571-77.

Bose, Subhas Chandra, *An Indian Pilgrim: An Unfinished Autobiography and Collected Letters 1897-1921*, Calcutta: Asia Publishing House, 1965.

Bose, Subhas Chandra, *Boycott of British Goods*, Calcutta: Sree Adwait Press, 1929?

Bose, Subhas Chandra, *Correspondence, 1924-1932*, Calcutta: Netaji Research Bureau, 1967.

Bose, Subhas Chandra, *Crossroads*, 2nd ed., Calcutta: Netaji Research Bureau, 1981.

Bose, Subhas Chandra, *Impressions in Life*, Lahore: ?, 1947.

Bose, Subhas Chandra, *Netaji Collected Works*, 6 vols, Calcutta: Netaji Research Bureau, 1980-87.

Bose, Subhas Chandra, *Selected Speeches of Subhas Chandra Bose*, Delhi: Government of India, Publications Division, 1962.

Bose, Subhas Chandra, *The Indian Struggle 1920-1942*, Calcutta: Asia Publishing House, 1964.

Bose, Subhas Chandra, *The Mission of Life*, Calcutta: Thacker Spink, 1953.

Bose, Subhas Chandra, *Through Congress Eyes*, Allahabad: Kitabistan, 1938?

Briffault, Robert, *Breakdown: The Collapse of Traditional Civilization*, 2nd ed., New York: Coward McCann, 1935.

Campbell-Johnson, Alan, *Mission with Mountbatten*, London: Robert Hale, 1951.

Casey, Lord, *Personal Experience 1939-1946*, London: Constable, 1962.

Chagla, M.C., *Roses in December*, Bombay: Bharatiya Vidya Bhavan, 1973.

Chakrabarty, Saroj, *My Years with Dr B.C. Roy*, Calcutta: Sree Saraswati Press, 1982.

Chand, Uttam, *When Bose Was Ziauddin*, Delhi: Rajkamal, 1946?

Chatterji, A.C., *India's Struggle for Freedom*, Calcutta: Chuckervertty, Chatterjee, 1947.

Chatterji, Jogesh Chandra, *In Search of Freedom*, Calcutta: Firma K.L. Mukhopadhyay, 1967.

Chattopadhyay, K.P., 'Subhas at Cambridge,' *The Loka-Sevak*, Netaji Supplement, January 23, 1954.

Chaudhuri, Nirad C., *Thy Hand, Great Anarch!* London: Chatto and Windus, 1987.

Das, Chittaranjan, *Songs of the Sea*, in Aurobindo Ghose, *Collected Poems and Plays*, Vol. II, Pondicherry: Sri Aurobindo Ashram, 1942.

Das, Chittaranjan, *The Way to Swaraj*, Madras: Tamil-Nadu Swarajya Party, 1923.

Das, Chittaranjan, *India for Indians*, Madras: S. Ganesh, 1921.

Das, Durga, ed., *Sardar Patel's Correspondence 1945-50*, 5 vols, Ahmedabad: Navajivan, 1972.

Das, Durga, *India from Curzon to Nehru and After*, New York: John Day, 1970.

Datta, Sudhindranath, *The World of Twilight*, Calcutta: Oxford U. Press, 1970.

De, Biswanath, ed., *Subhas smriti* [Remembering Subhas], Calcutta: Sahityam, 1975.

Durrani, Mahmood Khan, *The Sixth Column*, London: Cassell, 1955.

Dutt, Rajani Palme, *World Politics 1918-1936*, New York: International Publishers, 1936.

Dutt, Rajani Palme, *India Today*, London: Victor Gollancz, 1940.

Dutt, Romesh Chunder, *Three Years in Europe 1868 to 1871, With an Account of Subsequent Visits to Europe in 1886 and 1893*, Calcutta: S.K. Lahiri, 1896.

Dutta Roy, B.N., ed., *Sir N.N. Sircar's Speeches and Pamphlets*, Calcutta: The Book Company, 1934.

Fujiwara Iwaichi, *F. Kikan*, Hong Kong: Heinemann Asia, 1983.

Gandhi, Mohandas K., *The Collected Works of Mahatma Gandhi*, 88 vols., Delhi: Government of India, Publications Division, 1958-1983.

Gandhi, Mohandas K., *An Autobiography: The Story of My Experiments with Truth*, Boston: Beacon Press, 1959.

Ganguli, Subodh Chandra, *Early Life of Netaji*, Calcutta: Calcutta Book House, 1955?

Ganpuley, N.G., *Netaji in Germany*, Bombay: Bharatiya Vidya Bhavan, 1959.

Ghose, Aurobindo, *The Doctrine of Passive Resistance*, 2nd ed., Pondicherry: Sri Aurobindo Ashram, 1952.

Ghosh, Ajoy, *Articles and Speeches*, Moscow: Publishing House for Oriental Literature, 1962.

Ghosh, Moni, *Our Struggle*, Calcutta: Das Gupta, 1957?

Ghosh, Sudhir, *Gandhi's Emissary*, London: Cresset Press, 1967.

Harbich, Walter and Alexander Werth, *Netaji in Germany*, Calcutta: Netaji Research Bureau, 1970.

Hashim, Abul, *In Retrospection*, Dacca: Mowla Brothers, 1974.

Hassell, U. von, *Diaries 1938-1944*, London: Hamish Hamilton, 1948.

History of the Showa Emperor [In Japanese], Vols. 8-10, Tokyo: Yomiuri Shimbun-sha, 1969 and 1970.

Hitler, Adolph, *Mein Kampf*, Boston: Houghton Mifflin, 1943.
Hitler, Adolph, *Secret Conversations*, New York: Farrar, Strauss and Young, 1953.
Huq, Fazlul, *Bengal Today*, Calcutta: n.p., 1944.
Islam, Kazi Nasrul, *The Rebel and Other Poems*, trans. Basudha Chakravarty, New Delhi: Sahitya Akademi, 1974.
Ispahani, M.A.H., *Qaid-e-Azam Jinnah as I Knew Him*, rev. ed., Karachi: Forward Publishing, 1967.
Jayakar, M.R., *The Story of My Life*, Vol. I, New York: Asia Publishing House, 1958.
Khan, Shah Nawaz, *My Memories of I.N.A. and Its Netaji*, Delhi: Rajkamal Publications, 1946.
Khare, N.B., *My Political Memoirs or Autobiography*, Nagpur: S.R. Joshi, 1959.
Kipling, Rudyard, *Selected Prose and Poetry of Rudyard Kipling*, Garden City, New York: Garden City Publishing, 1937.
Kurti, Kitty, *Subhas Chandra Bose As I Knew Him*, Calcutta: Firma K.L. Mukhopadhyay, 1966.
Lebra, Joyce, ed., *Japan's Greater East Asia Co-Prosperity Sphere in World War II: Selected Readings and Documents*, Kuala Lumpur: Oxford U. Press, 1975.
Lochner, Louis, ed., *The Goebbels Diaries*, New York: Award Books, 1971.
Lohia, Rammanohar, *Guilty Men of India's Partition*, Allahabad: Kitabistan, 1960.
Lytton, Earl of, *Pundits and Elephants*, London: P. Davies, 1942.
Majumdar, Niranjan, ed., *The Statesman: An Anthology*, Calcutta: The Statesman, 1975.
Masani, Minoo, *Bliss Was It In That Dawn. . .*, New Delhi: Arnold-Heinemann, 1977.
Masters, John, *The Road Past Mandalay*, New York: Harper, 1961.
Montagu, Edwin, *An Indian Diary*, London: Heinemann, 1930.
Mookerjee, Girija K., *Europe at War (1938-1946)*, Meerut: Meenakshi Prakashan, 1968.
Mookerjee, Shyama Prasad, *Awake Hindustan!* Calcutta: n.p., 1944?
Muggeridge, Malcolm, ed., *Ciano's Diary 1939-1943*, London: William-Heinemann, 1947.
Nair, A.M., *An Indian Freedom Fighter in Japan*, Bombay: Orient Longman, 1982.
Narayan, Jayaprakash, *Towards Struggle*, Bombay: Padma, 1946.
Nehru, Jawaharlal, *Soviet Russia*, Allahabad: Lala Ram Mohan Lal, 1928.

Nehru, Jawaharlal, *A Bunch of Old Letters*, New Delhi: Asia Publishing House, 1958.

Nehru, Jawaharlal, *Toward Freedom*, Boston: Beacon Press, 1958.

Nehru, Jawaharlal, *Selected Works*, 15 vols., New Delhi: Orient Longman, 1972-82.

Nehru, Jawaharlal, *Selected Works*, 2 vols, second series, New Delhi: Oxford U. Press, 1984.

Pandey, B.N., ed., *The Indian Nationalist Movement 1885-1947: Select Documents*, London: Macmillan, 1979.

Philips, C.H., H.L. Singh, and B.N. Pandey, eds., *The Evolution of India and Pakistan 1858-1947*, London: Oxford U. Press, 1962.

Prabhu, R.K., and Ravindra Kelekar, eds., *Truth Called Them Differently (Tagore-Gandhi Controversy)*, Ahmedabad: Navajivan, 1961.

Prasad, Rajendra, *Autobiography*, New Delhi: Asia Publishing, 1957.

Ranga, N.G., *Fight for Freedom*, Delhi: S. Chand, 1968.

Reid, Sir Robert, *Years of Change in Bengal and Assam*, London: Benn, 1966.

Rolland, Romain, *Inde. Journal (1915-1943)*, Paris: Éditions Albin Michel, 1960.

Ronaldshay, Earl of [The Marquess of Zetland], '*Essayez*', London: John Murray, 1956.

Roy, Bidhan Chandra, *Towards a Prosperous India: Speeches and Writings*, Calcutta: Assembly House, 1964.

Roy, Dilip Kumar, *The Subhash I Knew*, Bombay: Nalanda, 1946.

Roy, Dilip Kumar, *Netaji—The Man, Reminiscences*, Bombay: Bharatiya Vidya Bhavan, 1966.

Roy, M.N., *India in Transition*, Geneva: n.p., 1922.

Roy, M.N., *Fascism*, Calcutta: D.M. Library, 1938?

Roy, M.N., *M.N. Roy's Memoirs*, Bombay: Allied, 1964.

Safrani, Abid Hasan, 'A Soldier Remembers,' *The Oracle*, Calcutta, Vol. VI, No. I, Jan. 1984, 24-65; Vol. VII, No. 1, Jan. 1985, 17-29.

Sarat Chandra Bose Commemoration Volume, Calcutta: Sarat Bose Academy, 1982.

Sareen, T.R., ed., *Select Documents on Indian National Army*, Delhi: Agam Prakashan, 1988.

Sarkar, Hemanta Kumar, *Subhaser songe baro bochor* [Twelve Years with Subhas], Calcutta: Sarkar and Co., 1946?

Sen, Samar, *The Complete Poems of Samar Sen*, Calcutta: Writers Workshop, 1970.

Singh, Gurchan, *Singa, The Lion of Malaya*, Kuala Lumpur: Printcraft, n.d.

Singh Mangat, Gurbachan, *The Tiger Strikes*, Ludhiana: Gagan Publishers, 1986.

Singh, Mohan, *Soldiers' Contribution to Indian Independence*, New Delhi: Army Educational Stores, 1974.

Sivaram, M., *The Road to Delhi*, Tokyo: Charles Tuttle, 1967.

Slim, Viscount, *Defeat into Victory*, London: Corgi, 1971.

Sopan, ed., *Netaji Subhash Chandra Bose*, Bombay: Azad Bhandar, 1946.

Spratt, Philip, *Blowing Up India*, Calcutta: Prachi Prakashan, 1955.

Tagore, Rabindranath, *Gora*, London: Macmillan, 1961.

Tagore, Rabindranath, 'Indian Students and Western Teachers,' *Modern Review*, April 1916.

Tagore, Rabindranath, *Kalantar*, Calcutta: Visva-Bharati, 1962.

Tagore, Rabindranath, *Lectures and Addresses*, London: Macmillan, 1962.

Tagore, Rabindranath, *Letters from Russia*, Calcutta: Visva-Bharati, 1960.

Tagore, Rabindranath, *Rabindra racanabali* [Collected Works of Rabindra], 14 vols, Calcutta: West Bengal Government, 1961.

Talwar, Bhagat Ram, *The Talwars of Pathan Land and Subhas Chandra's Great Escape*, New Delhi: People's Publishing House, 1976.

Trott zu Solz, Clarita von, *Adam von Trott zu Solz*, unpublished manuscript.

Tuker, Sir Francis, *While Memory Serves*, London: Cassell, 1950.

Vassiltchikov, Marie, *Berlin Diaries 1940-1945*, New York: Alfred Knopf, 1987.

Vyas, M.R., *Passage through a Turbulent Era*, Bombay: Indo-Foreign Publications, 1982.

Wavell, Lord, *The Viceroy's Journal*, ed., Penderel Moon, London: Oxford U. Press, 1973.

Weizsäcker, Ernst von, *Memoirs*, London: Victor Gollancz, 1951.

Zaidi and Zaidi, eds., *The Encyclopedia of the Indian National Congress*, Vols. 9-12, Delhi: S. Chand, 1980.

Zaidi, Z.H., ed., *M.A. Jinnah-Ispahani Correspondence 1936-1948*, Karachi: Forward Publications, 1976.

Zweig, Stefan, *The World Of Yesterday*, Lincoln: U. of Nebraska Press, 1964.

II. Secondary Works

A. Books, Articles, Unpublished Theses and Papers

Adler, Alfred, *The Individual Psychology of Alfred Adler*, ed., Heinz L.

Ansbacher and Rowena R. Ansbacher, New York: Harper and Row, 1967.

Adorno, Theodore, ed., *The Authoritarian Personality*, New York: Harper and Row, 1950.

Ahmed, Rafiuddin, *The Bengal Muslims 1871-1906*, Delhi: Oxford U. Press, 1981.

Ahmed, Sufia, *Muslim Community in Bengal 1884-1912*, Dacca: Oxford U. Press, 1974.

Allen, Louis, *The End of the War in Asia*, Brooklyn: Beekman, 1979.

Amin, Shahid, 'Gandhi as Mahatma: Gorakhpur District, Eastern UP, 1921-22.' *Subaltern Studies III*. Ed., Ranajit Guha, Delhi: Oxford U. Press, 1984.

Anisuzzaman, 'Cultural Trends in Bangladesh: A Redefinition of Identity,' Seminar Paper, Nuffield College, Oxford: February 17, 1975.

Anisuzzaman, 'The World of the Bengali Muslim Writer in the Nineteenth Century (1870-1920),' Seminar Paper, University of Sussex, May 9, 1975.

Basu, Aparna, *The Growth of Education and Political Development in India 1898-1920*, Delhi: Oxford U. Press, 1974.

Berlin, Isaiah, *Four Essays on Liberty*, London: Oxford U. Press, 1969.

Bhattacharya, J.N., *Hindu Castes and Sects*, Calcutta: Editions Indian, 1973 [reprint of 1896 edition].

Bhattacharyya, Buddhadeva, et al., *Satyagrahas in Bengal 1921-39*, Calcutta: Minerva Books, 1977.

Bhattacharyya, Buddhadeva, ed., *Freedom Struggle and Anushilan Samiti*, Calcutta: Anushilan Samity, 1979.

Bhuyan, Arun, *The Quit India Movement*, New Delhi: Manas, 1975.

Bondurant, Joan V, *The Conquest of Violence*, Princeton: Princeton U. Press, 1958.

Bose, Arun Coomer, *Indian Revolutionaries Abroad, 1905-1922*, Patna: Bharati Bhawan, 1971.

Bose, Buddhadeva, *An Acre of Green Grass*, Calcutta: Orient Longman, 1948.

Bose, Mihir, *The Lost Hero*, London: Quartet Books, 1982.

Bose, Nirmal Kumar, *Studies in Gandhism*, 3rd ed., Calcutta: Merit, 1962.

Bose, Sisir K. and Alexander Werth, eds., *A Beacon across Asia*, Delhi: Orient Longman, 1973.

Bose, Sisir K., *Netaji and India's Freedom*, Calcutta: Netaji Bhavan, 1975.

Bose, Sugata, *Agrarian Bengal*, Cambridge: Cambridge U. Press, 1986.

Bose, Suresh Chandra. *Dissentient Report*, 2nd ed., Kodalia: S.C. Bose, 1961.

Brass, Paul R., *Language, Religion and Politics in North India*, Delhi: Vikas, 1975.

Brecher, Michael, *Nehru, A Political Biography*, London: Oxford U. Press, 1959.

Broomfield, J.H., *Elite Conflict in a Plural Society*, Berkeley: U. of California Press, 1968.

Brown, Ermine, ed., *Eminent Indians*, Calcutta: Shanti Mitra, 1946.

Brown, Judith M., *Gandhi and Civil Disobedience*, Cambridge: Cambridge U. Press, 1977.

Brown, Judith M., *Gandhi's Rise to Power*, Cambridge: Cambridge U. Press, 1974.

Buckland, C.E., *Bengal under the Lieutenant-Governors*, 2vols., 2nd ed., Calcutta: S.K. Lahiri, 1902.

Butow, Robert J.C., *Japan's Decision to Surrender*, Stanford: Stanford U. Press, 1954.

Butow, Robert J.C., *Tojo and the Coming of the War*, Stanford: Stanford U. Press, 1961.

Cady, John F., *A History of Modern Burma*, Ithaca: Cornell U. Press, 1958.

Calvocoressi, Peter and Guy Wint, *Total War*, New York: Penguin Books, 1979.

Carr, E.H., *The Bolshevik Revolution 1917-1923*, III, V, Baltimore: Penguin Books, 1966.

Cashman, Richard I, *The Myth of the Lokamanya: Tilak and Mass Politics in Maharashtra*, Berkeley: U. of California Press, 1975.

Chandra, Bipan, *Nationalism and Colonialism in Modern India*, Delhi: Orient Longman, 1979.

Chandra, Bipan, *The Rise and Growth of Economic Nationalism in India*, New Delhi: People's Publishing House, 1966.

Chatterjee, Dilip Kumar, *C.R. Das and Indian National Movement*, Calcutta: Post-Graduate Book Mart, 1965.

Chatterjee, Partha, *Bengal 1920-1947: The Land Question*, Calcutta: K.P. Bagchi, 1984.

Chatterji, Bhola, *Aspects of Bengal Politics in the Early Nineteen Thirties*, Calcutta: World Press, 1969.

Chatterji, Rakhahari, ed., *Politics in West Bengal*, Calcutta: The World Press, 1985.

Chattopadhyay, Gautam, 'The Almost Revolution, A Case Study of India in February 1946,' in *Essays in Honour of Prof. S.C. Sarkar*, New Delhi: People's Publishing House, 1976.

Chattopadhyay, Gautam, *Bengal Electoral Politics and Freedom Struggle 1862-1947*, New Delhi: Indian Council of Historical Research,

1984.

Chaudhuri, Nirad C., *The Continent of Circe*, London: Chatto and Windus, 1965.

Chopra, P.N., ed., *Quit India Movement: British Secret Report*, Faridabad: Thomson Press, 1976.

Choudhary, Sukbhir, *Peasants' and Workers' Movement in India 1905-1929*, New Delhi: People's Publishing House, 1971.

Cohn, Bernard S., 'Representing Authority in Victorian India,' in Eric Hobsbawm and Terence Ranger, eds., *The Invention of Tradition*, Cambridge: Cambridge U. Press, 1984.

Collins, Larry and Dominique Lapierre, *Freedom at Midnight*, New York: Simon and Schuster, 1975.

Connell, John, *Auchinleck*, London: Cassell, 1959.

Cotton, Henry, *Calcutta Old and New*, Calcutta: W. Newman, 1907.

Coupland, Reginald, *The Constitutional Problem in India*, Parts I,II, and III, London: Oxford U. Press, 1944.

Cronin, Richard P., *British Policy and Administration in Bengal*, Calcutta: Firma KLM, 1977.

Das Gupta, Hemendranath, *Deshbandhu Chittaranjan Das*, Delhi: Government of India, Publications Division, 1960.

Das Gupta, Hemendranath, *Subhas Chandra*, Calcutta: Jyoti Prokasalaya, 1946.

Das, Narendra Nath, *History of Midnapur*, Calcutta: Midnapur Samskriti Parishad, 1962.

Das, Parimal Kumar, *India and the Vietnam War*, New Delhi: Young Asia Publications, 1972.

Datta Gupta, Sobhanlal, *Comintern, India and the Colonial Question, 1920-37*, Calcutta: K.P. Bagchi, 1980.

Davis, Marvin, *Rank and Rivalry: The Politics of Inequality in Rural West Bengal*, New York: Cambridge U. Press, 1983.

De, Amalendu, *Roots of Separatism in Nineteenth Century Bengal*, Calcutta: Ratna Prakashan, 1974.

Desai, A.R., ed., *Peasant Struggles in India*, Bombay: Oxford U. Press, 1979.

Druhe, David N., *Soviet Russia and Indian Communism*, New York: Bokman, 1959.

Dwivedy, Surendranath, *The Quest for Socialism*, New Delhi: Radiant, 1984.

Eck, Diana, *Banares, City of Light*, New York: Alfred Knopf, 1982.

Elsbree, Willard H., *Japan's Role in Southeast Asian Nationalist Movements 1940 to 1945*, New York: Russell and Russell, 1953.

Erikson, Erik H., *Gandhi's Truth*, New York: Norton, 1969.

Fest, Joachim C., *Hitler*, New York: Vintage Books, 1975.

Fest, Joachim C., *The Face of the Third Reich*, New York: Ace Books, 1970.

Forer, Lucille K., *The Birth Order Factor*, New York: Pocket Books, 1977.

Franda, Marcus F., 'Political Development in West Bengal,' in Myron Weiner, ed., *State Politics in India*, Princeton: Princeton U. Press, 1968.

Fuchs, Stephen, *Rebellious Prophets*, Bombay: Asia Publishing House, 1965.

Gallagher, John, 'Congress in Decline; Bengal 1930 to 1939,' in John Gallagher, Gordon Johnson, Anil Seal eds; *Locality Province and Nation: Essays on Indian Politics 1870-1940*, Cambridge: Cambridge U. Press, 1973.

Ghose, Loke Nath, *The Modern History of the Indian Chiefs, Rajas, Zamindars, & c*, Part II, Calcutta: n.p., 1881.

Ghosh, K.K., *The Indian National Army*, Meerut: Meenakshi Prakashan, 1969.

Ghurye, G.S., *Gods and Men*, Bombay: Popular Book Depot, 1962.

Glendevon, John, *The Viceroy at Bay: Lord Linlithgow in India 1936-1943*, London: Collins, 1971.

Gopal, Ram, *Indian Muslims, A Political History (1858-1947)*, Bombay: Asia Publishing House, 1959.

Gopal, Sarvepalli, *Jawaharlal Nehru: A Biography*, Vol. I., Cambridge: Harvard U. Press, 1976, Vol. II., Delhi: Oxford U. Press, 1979.

Gordon, Leonard A., *Bengal: The Nationalist Movement 1876-1940*, New York: Columbia U. Press, 1974.

Greenough, Paul R., *Prosperity and Misery in Modern Bengal: The Famine of 1943-44*, New York: Oxford U. Press, 1982.

Guha, Samar, *Netaji Dead or Alive?*, New Delhi: S. Chand, 1978.

Gupta, Amit Kumar, ed., *Myth and Reality: The Struggle for Freedom in India, 1945-47*, New Delhi: Manohar, 1976.

Gupta, Atulchandra, ed., *Studies in the Bengal Renaissance*, Jadavpur, Calcutta: National Council of Education, 1958.

Gupta, Partha Sarathi, *Imperialism and the British Labour Movement, 1914-1964*, London: Macmillan, 1975.

Haithcox, John P., *Communism and Nationalism in India: M.N. Roy and Comintern Policy 1920-1939*, Princeton: Princeton U. Press, 1971.

Hardas, Balshastri, *Armed Struggle for Freedom*, Poona: KAL Prakashan, 1958.

Hardy, P., *The Muslims of British India*, Cambridge: Cambridge U. Press, 1972.

Hart, B.H. Liddell, *History of the Second World War*, 2 vols., New York: Capricorn, 1972.

Hasan, Mushirul, 'Communalism in Indian Politics: A Study of the Nehru Report,' *The Indian Historical Review*, IV, No. 2, January 1978, 379-404.

Hauner, Milan, *India in Axis Strategy: Germany, Japan, and Indian Nationalists in the Second World War*, Stuttgart: Klett-Cotta, 1981.

Hay, Stephen N., *Asian Ideas of East and West*, Cambridge: Harvard U. Press, 1970.

Hayashida, Tatsua, *Netaji Subhas Chandra Bose*, Bombay: Allied, 1970.

Hirszowicz, Lukasz, *The Third Reich and the Arab East*, London: Routledge and Kegan Paul, 1966.

Hodson, H.V., *The Great Divide: Britain-India-Pakistan*, London: Hutchinson, 1969.

Hoffman, Peter, *The History of the German Resistance 1933-1945*, Cambridge: MIT Press, 1977.

Hunter, W.W., *A Statistical Account of Bengal*, V, XVIII, Delhi: D.K. Publishing House, 1973 [originally published, London: Trubner, 1875].

Hurst, Gerald, *A Short History of Lincoln's Inn*, London: Constable, 1946.

Hutchins, Francis G., *Spontaneous Revolution*, Delhi: Manohar, 1971.

Ienaga, Saburo, *The Pacific War*, New York: Pantheon, 1978.

Inden, Ronald B., *Marriage and Rank in Bengali Culture: A History of Caste and Clan in Middle Period Bengal*, Berkeley: U. of California Press, 1976.

Isherwood, Christopher, *Ramakrishna and His Disciples*, New York: Simon and Schuster, 1965.

Islam, Mustafa Nurul, *Bengali Muslim Public Opinion as Reflecting the Bengali Press 1901-1930*, Dacca: Bangla Academy, 1973.

Jalal, Ayesha, *The Sole Spokesman: Jinnah, the Muslim League and the Demand for Pakistan*, Cambridge: Cambridge U. Press, 1985.

Jog, N.G., *In Freedom's Quest*, Bombay: Orient Longman, 1969.

Kabir, Humayun, *Muslim Politics 1906-47*, Calcutta: Firma K.L. Mukhopadhyay, 1969.

Karnik, V.B., *Indian Trade Unions*, 2nd ed., Bombay: Manaktalas, 1966.

Katpitia, Arvinda, *Subhas Chandra Bose's Verhandlungen über eine Unabhängigkeitserklärung für Indien 1941-1943*, Ph.D. dissertation, Johannes Gutenberg-Universität zu Mainz, 1972.

Kaushik, P.D., *The Congress Ideology and Program 1920-47*, New Delhi:

Allied, 1964.

Keer, Dhanajay, *Savarkar and His Times*, Bombay: Popular Prakashan, 1950.

Keyes, Charles F., *The Golden Peninsula*, New York: Macmillan, 1977.

Khan, Bazlur Rohman, 'Some Aspects of Society and Politics in Bengal 1927 to 1936,' unpublished Ph.D. thesis, University of London, 1979.

Kirby, S. Woodburn, *The War against Japan: The Loss of Singapore*, I, London: Her Majesty's Stationery Office, 1957.

Kohn, Hans, *A History of Nationalism in the East*, New York: Harcourt, Brace, 1929.

Krasa, Miloslav, *Looking towards India: A Study in East-West Contact*, Prague: Orbis, 1969.

Kripalani, Krishna, *Rabindranath Tagore*, New York: Grove Press, 1962.

Krishna, Gopal, 'The Development of the Indian National Congress as a Mass Organization, 1918-1923,' *The Journal of Asian Studies*, XXV, No. 3, May 1966, 413-30.

Kumar, Ravinder, ed., *Essays on Gandhian Politics*, London: Oxford U. Press, 1971.

Lambert, Richard D., 'Hindi-Muslim Riots,' unpublished Ph.D. thesis, University of Pennsylvania, 1951.

Laushey, David, *Bengal Terrorism and the Marxist Left*, Calcutta: Firma KLM, 1975.

Lavalle, Eduard M., 'Confrontation within a Confrontation: Subhas C. Bose and the 1928 Strike,' in *Bengal in the Nineteenth and Twentieth Centuries*, ed., John R. McLane, East Lansing: Michigan State U. Press, 1975.

Lebra, Joyce C., *Japanese-Trained Armies in Southeast Asia*, Hong Kong: Heinemann Educational Books, 1977.

Lebra, Joyce C., *Jungle Alliance: Japan and the Indian National Army*, Singapore: Asia Pacific Press, 1971.

Levenson, Joseph R., *Liang Ch'i-Ch'ao and the Mind of Modern China*, Cambridge: Harvard U. Press, 1959.

Lewin, Ronald, *The American Magic*, New York: Penguin Books, 1982.

Low, D.A., ed., *Congress and the Raj*, London: Arnold-Heinemann, 1977.

Low, D.A., ed., *Soundings in Modern South Asian History*, London: Weidenfeld and Nicolson, 1968.

Lyons, F.S.L., *Ireland since the Famine*, London: Weidenfeld and Nicolson, 1971.

Madhok, Balraj, *Dr. Syama Prasad Mookerjee*, New Delhi: Deepak Prakashan, 1954.

Majumdar, Nepal, *Rabindranath o subhaschandra* [Rabindranath and Subhaschandra], Calcutta: Saraswati Library, 1968.

Majumdar, R.C., *History of the Freedom Movement in India*, Vol. III, Calcutta: Firma K.L. Mukhopadhyay, 1963.

Markovits, Claude, *Indian Business and Nationalist Politics 1931-1939*, Cambridge: Cambridge U. Press, 1985.

Mason, Philip, *A Matter of Honour*, New York: Holt, Rinehart and Winston, 1974.

McLane, John R., *Indian Nationalism and the Early Congress*, Princeton: Princeton U. Press, 1977.

McPherson, Kenneth, *The Muslim Microcosm: Calcutta 1918-1935*, Wiesbaden: Franz Steiner Verlag, 1974.

Mehrotra, S.R., *The Emergence of the Indian National Congress*, Delhi: Vikas, 1971.

Menon, V.P., *The Transfer of Power in India*, Bombay: Orient Longman, 1957.

Meskill, Johanna Menzel, *Hitler and Japan: The Hollow Alliance*, New York: Atherton Press, 1966.

Minault, Gail, *The Khilafat Movement*, New York: Columbia U. Press, 1982.

Momen, Humaira, *Muslim Politics in Bengal*, Dacca: Sunny House, 1972.

Moon, Penderel, *Divide and Quit*, London: Chatto and Windus, 1962.

Moon, Penderel, *Gandhi and Modern India*, London: The English Universities Press, 1968.

Moore, Barrington, Jr., *The Social Origins of Dictatorship and Democracy*, Boston: Beacon Press, 1966.

Moore, R.J., *Churchill, Cripps, and India 1939-1945*, Oxford: Clarendon Press, 1979.

Moore, R.J., *The Crisis of Indian Unity 1917-1940*, London: Oxford U. Press, 1974.

Moore, R.J., *Escape from Empire: The Attlee Government and the Indian Problem*, Oxford: Clarendon Press, 1983.

Moorhouse, Geoffrey, *Calcutta*, London: Weidenfeld and Nicolson, 1971.

Muehl, John Frederick, *Interview with India*, New York: John Day, 1950.

Mukherjee, Uma, *Two Great Indian Revolutionaries*, Calcutta: Firma KLM, 1966.

Murphey, Rhoads, 'The City in the Swamp; Aspects of the Site and Early Growth of Calcutta,' *Geographical Journal*, 1960, 130, 241–56.

Nanda, B.R., *Mahatma Gandhi*, London: Allen and Unwin, 1958.

Nanda, B.R., *The Nehrus: Motilal and Jawaharlal*, New York: John Day, 1963.

Nanda, B.R., ed., *Socialism in India*, Delhi: Vikas, 1972.

O'Malley, L.S.S., *History of Bengal, Bihar and Orissa under British Rule*, Calcutta: Bengal Secretariat Book Depot, 1925.

Overstreet, Gene D. and Marshall Windmiller, *Communism in India*, Berkeley: U. of California Press, 1959.

Pandey, B.N., *Nehru*, London: Macmillan, 1976.

Philips, C.H. and Mary Doreen Wainwright, eds., *The Partition of India: Policies and Perspectives 1935-1947*, London: Allen and Unwin, 1970.

Pyarelal, *Mahatma Gandhi—The Last Phase*, 2 vols, Ahmedabad: Navajivan, 1956.

Rab, A.S.M. Abdur, *A.K. Fazlul Huq*, Lahore: Ferozsons, 1966?

Rai Chowdhuri, Satyabrata, *Leftist Movements in India 1917-47*, Calcutta: Minerva, 1977.

Ram, Moti, ed., *Two Historic Trials in Red Fort*, New Delhi: Roxy Press, n.d.

Ramachandra, G.P., 'The Indian Independence Movement in Malaya 1942-45,' unpublished M.A. thesis, University of Malaya, 1970.

Ramanujan, A.K., 'Is There an Indian Way of Thinking?,' unpublished manuscript.

Rasul, M.A., *A History of All-India Kisan Sabha*, Calcutta: National Book Agency, 1974.

Rath, Radhanath and S.P. Chatterjee, eds., *Rash Behari Basu His Struggle for India's Independence*, Calcutta: Biplabi Mahanayak Rash Behari Basu Smarak Samity, 1963.

Ray, Nisith Ranjan, et al., eds., *Challenge*, New Delhi: People's Publishing House, 1984.

Ray, Prithwas Chandra, *The Life and Times of C.R. Das*, Calcutta: Oxford U. Press, 1927.

Ray, Rajat Kanta, *Social Conflict and Political Unrest in Bengal 1875-1927,* Delhi: Oxford U. Press, 1984.

Ray, Rajat, *Urban Roots of Indian Nationalism*, New Delhi: Vikas, 1979.

Ray, Suprakas, *Bharater baiplabik sangramer itihas* [History of the Indian Revolutionary Struggle], Calcutta: Indian Book Stall, 1955.

Revri, Chamanlal, *The Indian Trade Union Movement*, New Delhi: Orient Longman, 1972.

Richardson, W.C., *A History of the Inns of Court*, Baton Rouge: Claitor's Publishing Division, 1975.

Robb, Peter and David Taylor, eds., *Rule, Protest, Identity*, London: Curzon Press, 1978.

Roy, Bhola Nath, *Oaten Incident 1916*, Calcutta: S.C. Sarkar, 1975.

Rudolph, Lloyd I. and Susanne Hoeber Rudolph, eds., *The Modernity of Tradition,* Chicago: U. of Chicago Press, 1967.

Rudolph, Susanne Hoeber and Lloyd I. Rudolph, eds., *Education and Politics in India,* Delhi: Oxford U. Press, 1972.

Rusch, Thomas A., 'Role of the Congress Socialist Party in the Indian National Congress,' unpublished Ph.D. dissertation, University of Chicago, 1955.

Saggi, P.D., ed., *Life and Work of Netaji Subhas Chandra Bose*, Bombay: Overseas Publishing House, n.d.

Sanyal, Hitesranjan, 'Congress Movements in the Villages of Eastern Midnapore, 1921-1930,' *Colloques Internationaux du C.N.R.S.,* No. 582—Asie du Sud, 169-78.

Sareen, T.R., *Japan and the Indian National Army,* Delhi: Agam Prakashan, 1986.

Sarkar, Sumit, *Modern India 1885-1947*, Delhi: Macmillan, 1983.

Sarkar, Sumit, 'The Logic of Gandhian Nationalism: Civil Disobedience and the Gandhi-Irwin Pact (1930-1931),' *Indian Historical Review*, III. No. i, 114-46.

Sarkar, Sumit, *The Swadeshi Movement in Bengal 1903-1908*, New Delhi: People's Publishing House, 1973.

Sarkar, Tanika, 'The First Phase of Civil Disobedience in Bengal, 1930-1,' *Indian Historical Review*, IV, No. 1, 75-95.

Sayeed, Khalid B., *Pakistan, The Formative Phase 1857-1948*, London: Oxford U. Press, 1968.

Sen Gupta, Subodh Chandra, *India Wrests Freedom*, Calcutta: Sahitya Samsad, 1982.

Sen, Shila, *Muslim Politics in Bengal 1937-1947*, New Delhi: Impex, 1976.

Sen, Sukomal, *Working Class of India*, Calcutta: K.P. Bagchi, 1977.

Sengupta, Padmini, *Deshapriya Jatindra Mohan Sengupta*, Delhi: Government of India, Publications Division, 1968.

Shah, Harin, *Verdict from Formosa, Gallant End of Netaji Subhas Chandra Bose*, Delhi: Atma Ram, 1956.

Sharma, Shri Ram, ed., *Netaji, His Life and Work,* Agra: Shiva Lal Agarwala, 1948.

Shukla, B.D., *A History of the Indian Liberal Party*, Allahabad: Indian Press, 1960.

Singer, Milton, ed., *Traditional India: Structure and Change*, Philadelphia: American Folklore Society, 1959.

Singer, Milton, *When a Great Tradition Modernizes*, New York: Praeger, 1972.

Singh, Anita Inder, *The Origins of the Partition of India 1936-1947*, Delhi: Oxford U. Press, 1987.

Singh, N. Iqbal, *The Andaman Story*, New Delhi: Vikas, 1978.

Sinha, L.P., *The Left Wing in India*, Muzaffarpur: New Publishers, 1965.

Sinha, Pradip, *Nineteenth Century Bengal: Aspects of Social History*, Calcutta: KLM, 1965.

Sinha, Pradip, *Calcutta in Urban History*, Calcutta: KLM, 1978.

Sinha, Probodh Chandra, *Sir Asutosh Mookherjee*, Calcutta: The Book Co., 1928.

Sinha, Surajit, ed., *Cultural Profile of Calcutta*, Calcutta: The Indian Anthropological Society, 1972.

Sitaramayya, B. Pattabhi, *History of the Indian National Congress*, 2 vols, Bombay: Padma, 1946.

Smith, Denis Mack, *Mussolini, A Biography*, New York: Vintage Books, 1983.

Smith, Denis Mack, *Mussolini's Roman Empire*, New York: Penguin Books, 1977.

Smith, Donald E., *India as a Secular State*, Princeton: Princeton U. Press, 1963.

Spate, O.H.K., *India and Pakistan, A general and Regional Geography*, London: Methuen, 1954.

Sykes, Christopher, *Troubled Loyalty: A Biography of Adam von Trott zu Solz*, London: Collins, 1968.

Taylor, A.J.P., *English History 1914-1945*, London: Oxford U. Press, 1965.

Tendulkar, D.G., *Mahatma*, 8 vols, New Delhi: Government of India, Publications Divison, 1960.

Toland, John, *The Rising Sun*, New York: Bantam, 1971.

Tomlinson, B.R., *The Indian National Congress and the Raj, 1929-1942*, London: Macmillan, 1976.

Toye, Hugh, *Subhas Chandra Bose*, Bombay: Jaico, 1978.

Toye, Hugh, *Subhas Pasha*, unpublished manuscript.

Turner, Victor, *Dramas, Fields, and Metaphors*, Ithaca: Cornell U. Press, 1974.

Voigt, Johannes, *Indien im Zweiten Weltkrieg*, Stuttgart: Deutsche Verlags-Anstalt, 1978. [now in English, *India in the Second World War*, New Delhi: Arnold-Heinemann, 1987].

Wadud, Kazi Abdul, *Creative Bengal*, Calcutta: Thacker Spink, 1949.

Weiner, Myron, *Party Politics in India*, Princeton: Princeton U. Press, 1957.

Wheeler-Bennett, John W., *John Anderson: Viscount Waverly*, London:

Macmillan, 1962.

Wolpert, Stanley A., *Tilak and Gokhale*: *Revolution and Reform in the Making of Modern India*, Berkeley: U. of California Press, 1962.

Younger, Calton, *A State of Disunion*, London: Fontana, 1972.

Zaidi, Z.H., 'The Political Motive in the Partition of Bengal,' *Journal of the Pakistan Historical Society*, April, 1964.

Ziegler, Philip, *Mountbatten*, New York: Knopf, 1985.

B. Reference Works

Ghose, Kali Charan, *The Footprints on the Road to Indian Independence*, Calcutta: Sahitya Samsad, 1975.

Goralski, Robert, *World War II Almanac: 1931-1945,* New York: G.P. Putnam, 1981.

Mitra, H.N., ed., *The Indian Annual Register: 1919-1924*, Calcutta: The Annual Register Press, published annually.

Mitra, Nripendera Nath, ed., *The Indian Annual Register: 1925-1947*, Calcutta: The Annual Register Press, published annually (also called *The Indian Quarterly Register)*.

Sen, S.P., ed., *Dictionary of National Biography*, 4 vols, Calcutta: Institute of Historical Studies, 1972-1974.

Times of India, Indian Yearbook and Who's Who, Bombay: Times of India Press, published annually.

Williams, Neville, *Chronology of the Modern World*: *1763 to the present time*, New York: David McKay, 1967.

Yule, Henry and A.C. Burnell, *Hobson-Jobson*, ed., William Crooke, Delhi: Munshiram Manoharlal, 1968 [reprint of 1903 edition].

Index